VISUAL QUICKSTART GUIDE

ADOBE
FLASH CS3
PROFESSIONAL

FOR WINDOWS AND MACINTOSH

Katherine Ulrich

 Peachpit Press

Visual QuickStart Guide
Adobe Flash CS3 Professional for Windows and Macintosh
Katherine Ulrich

Peachpit Press
1249 Eighth Street
Berkeley, CA 94710
510/524-2178
510/524-2221 (fax)

Find us on the Web at: www.peachpit.com
To report errors, please send a note to errata@peachpit.com
Peachpit Press is a division of Pearson Education

Copyright © 2008 by Katherine Ulrich

Project Editor: Wendy Sharp
Production Editor: Connie Jeung-Mills
Contributor: Andreas Heim
Copyeditor: Jacqueline Aaron
Tech Editor: Mark R. Jonkman
Compositor: WolfsonDesign
Indexer: FireCrystal Communications
Cover design: Peachpit Press

ISBN-13: 978-0-321-50291-9
ISBN-10: 0-321-50291-4

9 8 7 6 5 4

Printed and bound in the United States of America

Dedication

To Perry Whittle, whose support, both moral and technical, helps me keep it all in perspective, and who downplays my failings and promotes my successes shamelessly.

Thank You

Special thanks to the editor of this edition, Wendy Sharp, Senior Acquisitions Editor, for her helpful editorial direction, words of encouragement, and perseverance throughout the process of creating this book. A huge thank you to Andreas Heim, Director of Technology, Smashing Ideas, for writing Chapter 13 and devising basic interactivity tasks that let even brand-new Flash users start putting ActionScript 3.0 to work. Thanks to Mark R. Jonkman for reading the manuscript with an eye for technical clarity and errors and for offering tips and advice along the way. A round of applause to copy editor Jacqueline Kan Aaron, it's been wonderful having her eagle eye watching my back for errors of spelling, grammar, logic, and style. Kudos to Production Editor Connie Jeung-Mills and compositor Owen Wolfson for making these pages clean and clear. Thanks also to Emily Glossbrenner for expert indexing on a tight timeline and to Michael J. Ulrich for help in testing import of Adobe Illustrator artwork. And much appreciation to Becky Morgan for pitching in to help see the book through its final stages.

A tip of the hat to those whose various forms of assistance in past editions still echo in this one: Brad Bechtel, Lisa Brazieal, Erika Burback, Jeremy Clark, Cliff Colby, Pat Christenson, Peter Alan Davy, Jane DeKoven, Jonathan Duran, Lupe Edgar, Victor Gavenda, Suki Gear, Becky Morgan, Erica Norton, Christi Payne, Janice Pearce, Nancy Reinhardt, Sharon Selden, Kathy Simpson, James Talbot, Tiffany Taylor, Bentley Wolfe, and Lisa Young.

And finally, heartfelt thanks to Marjorie Baer, for her supportive friendship and for bringing me to this project in the first place.

Contents at a Glance

TABLE OF CONTENTS

TABLE OF CONTENTS

INTRODUCTION

Vectors on the Web! That was the early promise and excitement of Flash, back when the Internet was expanding exponentially and suddenly everybody wanted a Web presence, filled with color and motion. Flash gave Web designers an efficient way to send artwork and animation over the limited-bandwidth connections that most viewers had. Plus it offered a full set of natural-style drawing tools for creating graphic content and animating it. Another Flash advantage was its easy scripting for adding interactivity.

Ultimately, Flash's efficiency at feeding graphics through the Internet's bandwidth constrictions attracted Web-content developers seeking to create complex interactive and data-driven sites, developers who were more knowledgeable about coding and scripting. The ActionScript scripting language became available to fill their needs. As high-bandwidth connections became more common, Flash developers pushed to add longer, more-complicated animation. Flash added the ability to display video. With each new generation of Flash, the product's capabilities have grown. Adobe Flash CS3 Professional addresses the needs not only of designers who want to create beautiful, low-bandwidth artwork and animation, but also of developers who want to create robust multimedia Internet applications.

About Flash

Flash began life as FutureSplash Animator, a nifty little program for creating and animating vector art. In 1997, Macromedia acquired FutureSplash Animator, changed the name to Flash, and promoted the program as a tool for creating graphic content for the World Wide Web. In 2005 Adobe acquired Macromedia and took up the Flash baton.

The early Flash excelled as an application for Web-site design, providing everything needed to create visually interesting (as opposed to text-only) Web sites: tools for creating graphic elements, for animating those elements, for creating interface elements and interactivity, and for writing the HTML necessary to display all those elements in a Web page via a browser. Flash CS3 continues to provide those tools, but also includes more-sophisticated graphics tools, specialized import features for working with Adobe Photoshop and Adobe Illustrator artwork, tools for importing and displaying video, user-interface and data-handling components, and ActionScript 3.0 for scripting complex interactivity. Flash has become a toolkit for creating what have come to be called Rich Internet Applications (RIAs). An RIA might be anything from an online store to a corporate training module to a video-clip-display site to a snazzy promotional piece describing this year's hottest new car, complete with customizable virtual test-drives.

Vectors vs. Bitmaps

The data that creates vector graphics and the data that creates bitmapped graphics are similar, in that they're mathematical instructions to the computer about how to create images onscreen. Bitmaps, however, are often lengthier and result in a less versatile graphic; vector graphics are compact and scalable. Bitmap instructions break a whole graphic into dots and describe each one; vector instructions describe the graphic mathematically as a series of lines and arcs (**Figure i.1**). Picture a 1-inch black horizontal line on a field of white. For a bitmap, the instructions would go something like this: make a white dot, make a white dot, make a black dot, make a black dot, make a black dot, repeating until there are enough black dots to make a 1-inch line. Then the white-dot instructions start again and continue to fill the rest of the screen with white dots. The vector instructions would be a formula for a straight line, plus the coordinates that define the line's position onscreen.

Figure i.1 For a computer to draw a bitmapped graphic, it must receive a set of instructions for each dot (each bit of data) that makes up the image. Instructions for a vector graphic describe the lines and curves that make up the image mathematically. The bitmapped line (left) appears much rougher than the vector line (right). You can't enlarge the bitmapped line without losing quality. But you can make the vector line as big as you like; it retains its solid appearance.

What Makes Flash a Special Web-Design Tool?

Flash's early claim to fame was its ability to deliver vector images over the Web. What's the advantage of using vector graphics? Vectors keep file sizes down, which keeps download times shorter. And vectors are scalable: this means you can maintain control of what a Web site looks like when your viewer resizes the browser window, for example, making the whole thing stay in proportion as the window grows or shrinks.

Another advantage that Flash provides is the use of progressive downloading and streaming. These delivery techniques allow some elements of a Web site to display immediately upon download while more information continues to arrive over the Internet. Both the use of vector images and the use of progressive download or streaming enhance the viewer's experience.

Other facets of Flash's appeal include its ability to create original artwork with both Bézier and natural-style drawing tools; its ability to handle imported artwork, sound, and video; and its ability to assist designers and developers in creating animation and interactivity. Over time, Flash's tools for creating interactivity have become more robust. Flash CS3 contains a full-fledged object-oriented scripting language, in two versions: ActionScript 2.0 and 3.0. Both are compliant with the ECMA-262 specification, which is also the foundation for JavaScript, so they should feel familiar to anyone who already knows JavaScript.

How Flash Animates

Flash uses standard animation techniques to create the illusion of movement. You create a series of still images, each slightly different from the next. By displaying the images rapidly, one after another, you simulate continuous movement. Flash's animation tools help you create, organize, and synchronize the animation of multiple graphic elements, sounds, and video clips.

Flash File Formats

Flash provides both an authoring environment for creating content and a playback system for making that content viewable on a local computer or in a Web browser. You create artwork, animation, and interactivity in Flash-format files. These files have the extension .fla and are often referred to as *FLAs*. To make that content viewable on the Web, you convert the FLA files to Flash Player format; Flash Player files have the extension .swf. Another name for the playable format is *SWF* (pronounced *swif*).

How Flash Delivers

Flash's publishing feature creates the necessary HTML code to display your Flash content in a Web browser. You can also choose alternate methods of delivering Flash content—as animated GIF images, for example, or as a QuickTime movie. Flash creates those alternate files during the publishing process.

Flash CS3: What's New?

Adobe has worked hard to integrate products from the Adobe and Macromedia lines, resulting in changes and improvements to the Flash user interface that make it more consistent with other Adobe programs. As part of the Adobe Creative Suite, Flash can more easily incorporate content from such programs as Photoshop and Illustrator. In addition, this release of Flash includes some new graphics tools, tools for reusing animation, and the latest version of ActionScript (3.0). Let's look at the highlights.

Interface Improvements

Docking for all. Users on the Windows platform have always been able to dock panels; now Macintosh users can also take advantage of docking to optimize screen usage. Undocked panels become transparent as you drag them, helping you to position them precisely on screen.

Panel icons. To clear space on your desktop, you can collapse a docked panel (or panel group) to a small icon (**Figure i.2**). A single click opens the icon to a full-size panel. You set preferences to have the panel return to icon form automatically when you click outside it, or to stay open until you click a special close button.

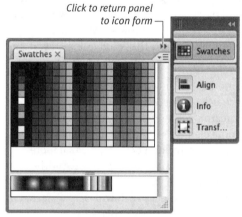

Figure i.2 In Flash CS3, you can reduce docked panels (and panel groups) to a small icon (top). Clicking the icon opens the full panel (bottom). Preference settings let you determine whether the panel returns to icon form as soon as you click outside the panel, or if you must explicitly close the panel by clicking the double arrows.

About Flash Player

In Flash's early days, the need to use a player to view Flash content was considered a drawback to creating Web content with Flash. Designers feared that users would be reluctant to spend time downloading another helper application for their browsers. But Flash has become the de facto standard for delivering Web rich-media content—especially interactive vector art and animation—and Flash Player is now widely distributed. Adobe estimates that roughly 96 percent of machines that are being used to access the Internet already have Flash Player version 6 or later installed, and that more than 80 percent of viewers in the United States, Canada, the United Kingdom, Germany, France, and Japan have already adopted Flash Player 9.

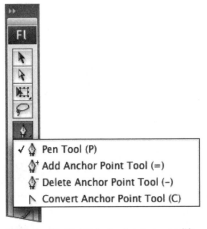

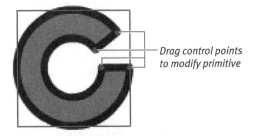

Figure i.3 Flash's Bézier tools let you modify paths by adding, removing, and converting points. (The pen tool retains its old ability to modify the points on a path as well.)

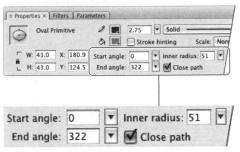

Drag control points to modify primitive

Enter new values for primitive properties

Figure i.4 The properties that define primitive shapes, such as this oval-primitive, remain editable even after you create the shape. You can modify these properties by entering values in the Property inspector and by manipulating control points on the primitive itself.

Design Enhancements

Bézier-tool revisions. The pen tool in Flash CS3 works more like the pen tool in Illustrator. Changes to the pen tool's behind-the-scenes mathematics mean it creates paths more accurately, using fewer points. Flash now provides specific Bézier tools for modifying existing paths (**Figure i.3**).

Primitive shapes. Flash CS3 introduces two new shape-drawing tools: oval-primitive and rectangle-primitive (**Figure i.4**). While you could always modify some properties of rectangles and ovals after you created the shape (such as dimensions, or stroke weight and color), primitives make more properties accessible for editing. You can, for example, change the degree of roundness of a rectangle-primitive's corners through the Property inspector or by dragging control points on the rectangle-primitive itself.

Bounding boxes reveal object types. You can identify what type of object you've selected (a drawing object, primitive-shape, symbol, group, or other) by the color of its bounding box. You assign bounding-box colors through Preferences settings.

9-slice visibility. Previously, 9-slice scaling was visible only in symbol-editing mode, or in Flash Player. In Flash CS3, you can preview 9-slice scaling for movie-clip symbols within the authoring environment.

Reusable filters. You can copy and paste filters and filter settings from one object to another.

FLASH CS3: WHAT'S NEW?

Photoshop and Illustrator import.

Flash CS3 provides special import tools for working with Photoshop and Illustrator content. The PSD and AI importers let you choose how to import individual layers from Photoshop and Illustrator files, preserving layer structure and editability of vector elements or converting layers and/or elements to bitmaps (**Figure i.5**).

Animation Enhancements

Reusable motion tweens. You can quickly re-create motion-tween animations using various objects. You copy the changes that make up a motion-tween for a selected object using the Copy Motion command, then apply the same changes and motion-tween property to a different object using the Paste Motion command.

Motion tweens translated to script. Similar to the Copy Motion command, the new Copy Motion As ActionScript 3.0 command lets you copy an existing motion tween and apply it to a different object. This command, however, translates the Timeline animation to code, which you can paste into the ActionScript editor. The script then targets an object instance on the Stage.

ActionScript 3.0 and More

Flash CS3 includes the latest version of ActionScript 3.0, as well as the earlier ActionScript 2.0. A new QuickTime-export feature lets you deliver Flash content (both Timeline animation and ActionScript-generated animation) to end users as a QuickTime MOV file. Flash's publishing templates now create a small JavaScript file that activates content to make it immediately available to viewers using Microsoft Internet Explorer.

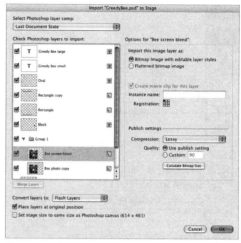

Figure i.5 Using the PSD Importer, you decide how to deal with each layer of a Photoshop file. The import settings let you balance image quality with editability when you work with Photoshop files. The AI Importer works similarly for Illustrator files.

How to Use This Book

Like all Visual QuickStart Guides, this book seeks to take you out of the passive reading mode and help you get started working in the program. The tasks in the book teach you to use Flash's features. The book is suitable for beginners who are just starting to use Flash and for intermediate-level Flash designers. The initial chapters cover the basics of creating graphic elements by using Flash's unique set of drawing tools. Next, you learn how to turn graphic elements into animations. After that, you learn to create basic user-interface elements, such as rollover buttons. To make your content interactive, you'll work with the Actions panel to create ActionScript for basic interactivity. You'll also learn about importing and working with various non-Flash content: artwork from other applications, sounds, and video. Finally, you'll learn to use Flash's Publish feature to create HTML for putting your Flash creations on the Web.

What You Should Already Know

In order to get you started quickly, this book makes a few assumptions:

◆ Adobe Flash CS3 is already installed on your computer.

◆ You're familiar with the workings of your operating system.

◆ You can carry out basic tasks, such as opening, closing, and saving documents; opening, closing, resizing, collapsing, and expanding document windows and dialogs; using hierarchical menus, pop-up menus, radio buttons, and check boxes; and carrying out standard application commands such as copy, cut, paste, delete, and undo.

Cross-Platform Issues

The Flash authoring environment has a very similar interface on the Macintosh and Windows platforms. Still, differences exist where the user interfaces of the platforms diverge. When these differences are substantial, this book describes the procedures for both platforms. Illustrations of dialog boxes come from both platforms, but generally, there is no special indication as to which platform is shown. If a given feature differs greatly between platforms, the variations are illustrated. If a feature is available only on one platform, that is noted in the text.

Originally, Macintosh computers required Macintosh keyboards, and some key names were unique to that keyboard: for example, Return (instead of Enter) and Delete (instead of Backspace). This book generally uses Enter and Delete for these two key names.

Keyboard Shortcuts

Most of Flash's menu-based commands have a keyboard equivalent. That equivalent appears in the menu next to the command name. When this book first introduces a command, it also describes the keyboard shortcut. In subsequent mentions of the command, however, the keyboard shortcut usually is omitted. You'll find a complete list of these commands on Peachpit Press's companion Web site for this book, **http://www.peachpit.com/title/0321502914**

Contextual Menus

Both the Macintosh and Windows platforms offer contextual menus. To access one of these contextual menus, Control-click (Mac) or right-click (Windows) an element in the Flash movie. You'll see a menu of commands that are appropriate for working with that element. For the most part, these commands duplicate commands in the main menu; therefore, this book doesn't generally note them as alternatives for the commands described in the book. The book does point out when using the contextual menu is particularly handy or when a contextual menu contains a command that is unavailable in the main menu bar.

Artwork and Scripts

The Flash graphics in this book are easy to draw. In most cases the examples are based on simple geometric shapes, which means you can spend your time seeing the Flash features in action instead of re-creating fancy artwork. To make it even easier for you to follow along, Flash files containing the graphic elements that you need for each task are available on Peachpit Press's companion Web site for this book, **http://www.peachpit.com/ title/0321502914**. In Chapter 13, you'll learn to create scripts for basic interactivity. Flash files containing the completed scripts for these tasks are also available on the companion Web site.

THE FLASH AUTHORING TOOL

Before you get started creating projects in Adobe Flash CS3 Professional, it's helpful to take a look around the authoring environment and begin to recognize and manipulate its components. When you open Flash for the first time, you'll see the Flash Welcome screen. This screen acts as a gateway to many documents and operations in Flash. When you open a Flash document, you enter the Flash authoring environment. Each Flash document consists of four basic items: the Timeline, a record of every frame, layer, and scene in your movie; the Edit bar, which displays identifying text and menus for choosing symbols and scenes to work on; the Stage, the actual area in which your movie displays; and the Pasteboard, extra work space that surrounds the Stage. The Stage and Pasteboard are present when you edit a document. You can choose to hide the Timeline or the Edit bar or both, and you can open any combination of other panels and tools that you need to work with your Flash content.

What does the Flash authoring environment look like? And how do you access tools and different views? This chapter presents a quick tour: subsequent chapters explain in more detail what's what as you get into using each element.

Working with Flash Documents

Most of the basic document operations in Flash—opening, closing, and saving files—are straightforward to experienced computer users. Creating new documents may be a little different than in other programs, because Flash creates a variety of document types. Flash's Welcome screen assists you in opening and creating these various Flash documents.

To set launch preferences:

1. From the Flash application menu (Mac) or Edit menu (Windows), choose Preferences.

   The Preferences dialog appears. The General category is selected by default.

2. From the On Launch menu, choose one of the following (**Figure 1.1**):

   ▲ No Document. Flash's menu bar and panels appear at launch, but no document opens.

   ▲ New Document. Flash opens a new document at launch.

   ▲ Last Documents Open. Flash opens the documents that were open when you ended the previous work session.

   ▲ Welcome Screen. (The default setting.) Flash displays the Welcome screen at launch and anytime you have closed all the documents during a work session.

3. Click OK.

✔ Tip

■ To change launch preferences to the New Document option quickly, click the Don't Show Again button in the lower-left corner of the Welcome screen. A dialog appears to remind you that you must change the launch settings in the General tab of the Preferences dialog to see the Welcome screen again.

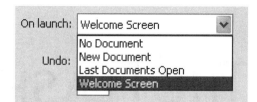

Figure 1.1 The On Launch options in the General category of the Preferences dialog tell Flash what type of document(s), if any, to open on when you launch Flash.

About Preferences

To see, or not to see, the Welcome screen is just one of many preference settings in Flash. To choose new settings, you open the Preferences dialog. From the Flash menu (Mac) or Edit menu (Windows), choose Preferences, and select a category from the list in the left-hand pane. Choose settings for that category in the main window. Preferences fall into nine categories: General, ActionScript, Auto Format, Clipboard, Drawing, Text, Warnings, PSD File Importer, and AI File Importer. You'll learn about specific Preferences settings as they relate to specific tasks throughout this book.

Touring the Welcome Screen

Flash's default setting opens the Welcome screen when you launch. The Welcome screen contains active links that let you open documents quickly. You can open a new document, a document that you worked on recently, or a template document. You can link to Flash tutorials or to the Adobe Exchange site, where you can download third-party extensions such as new components, Timeline Effects, and Behaviors as they become available (**Figure 1.2**).

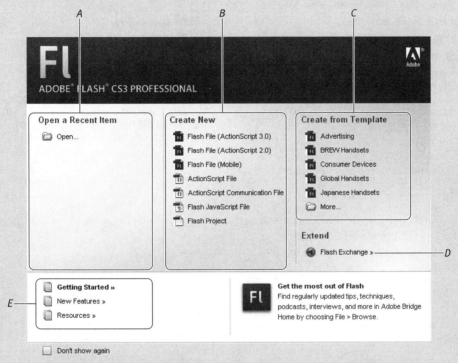

Figure 1.2 The Welcome screen presents common operations you might want to carry out at the beginning of a work session: opening a document you worked on recently (A), creating a new Flash document (B), or creating documents from templates (C). There are also links for browsing the Adobe Exchange site, to find third-party extensions (D). For new users, there are links to the tutorials that come with Flash as well as other training resources (E).

To create a new Flash document:

◆ From the Welcome screen, in the Create New section, click the Flash File (ActionScript 3.0) link.

Flash opens a new blank document.

or

1. Choose File > New, or press ⌘-N (Mac) or Ctrl-N (Windows).

Flash opens the New Document dialog (**Figure 1.3**). This dialog has two views: General and Templates. General is selected by default.

2. In the General view, select Flash File (ActionScript 3.0).

3. Click OK.

Flash opens a new blank document.

✔ Tip

■ To switch views in the New Document dialog, click the appropriate button (Mac) or tab (Windows) at the top of the dialog.

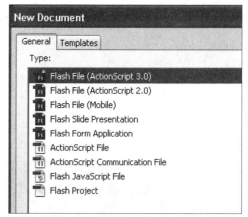

Figure 1.3 To create a new document in Flash, choose File > New. The New Document dialog opens, with the General view and Flash File (ActionScript 3.0) selected by default. Click OK to create a new document.

Which Flash File Type to Create?

The Create New section of the Welcome screen lists seven types of files; which one is right for you? In this book, we'll work exclusively with Flash files, but you still have two choices: ActionScript 3.0 or ActionScript 2.0. For many of the graphics, text, and animation tasks you'll do, either choice is fine. The difference becomes important when you start scripting. (You'll learn about scripting in Chapter 13.) The scripting options and features available to you depend on which version of ActionScript you use. This book deals with ActionScript 3.0. When an exercise asks you to create a new file, unless instructed otherwise, choose Flash File (ActionScript 3.0). If you decide to use a different version of ActionScript later, you can change the file type to ActionScript 2.0 (or 1.0) in the Publish Settings dialog. (You'll learn about publishing in Flash in Chapter 17.)

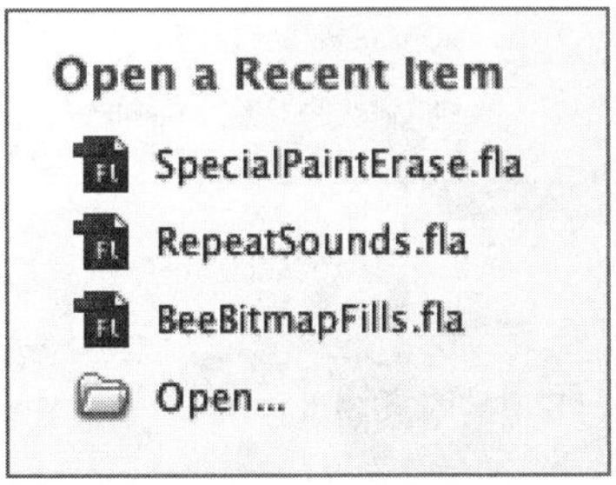

Figure 1.4 The Open a Recent Item section of the Welcome screen allows you to view links to the last nine documents you worked on. Clicking a filename opens the document.

Figure 1.5 Viewing multiple open documents as tabs in a single window is the default setting for Flash CS3. Click an inactive title tab to bring that document to the front. To close the active document, click the close button in the tab.

To open an existing document:

◆ From the Welcome screen, in the Open a Recent Item section, click the name of a recent file (**Figure 1.4**). Flash opens that file directly.

or

1. From the Welcome screen, in the Open a Recent Item section, click the Open link.

   or

   Choose File > Open.

   The Open dialog appears.

2. Navigate to the file you want to open.

3. Select the file.

4. Click Open.

✔ Tips

■ In Flash's default environment, multiple open documents appear as tabs at the top of the application window. Tabs for inactive documents are a darker grey. Click a tab to bring that document to the front (**Figure 1.5**). To view documents in separate windows, choose Tile or Cascade from the Window menu. On the Mac you can also set a preference for viewing documents as tabs or separate windows. From the Flash menu, choose Preferences; in the General category, deselect the Open Documents in Tabs check box; and click OK.

continues on next page

WORKING WITH FLASH DOCUMENTS

- You can change the order of the tabs for open documents by dragging a tab to a new position (**Figure 1.6**).

- When you've been working with a document, adding and deleting graphic materials, sounds, video, and so on, the file size builds up because data about the deleted items remains in the file. Choosing File > Save and Compact reduces the file size. When you begin editing the file, it again bulks up quickly. You may wish to compact the file only at the end of the authoring process or when file size is crucial—for example, if you need to email the file to a colleague.

Figure 1.6 To change the tab position for open documents, click the name area of a tab and drag to the right (or left). The current document stays selected, but the tab position changes (bottom).

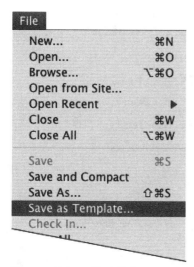

Figure 1.7 To turn a Flash file into a template that can be the basis of future documents, chose File > Save as Template.

Figure 1.8 The Save as Template command lets you save Flash documents for reuse. You can create your own template categories and provide a brief description of the template file you're saving in the Save as Template dialog.

✔ Tip

- Once you've completed the template, close the document. You may think that after saving the document as a template you're working in a copy made from the template, but you're not. You're still working in the master template document until you close it.

Working with Template Documents

If you work repeatedly with one type of Flash document—for example, you create banner ads of a specific size with a consistent background or elements—you can save that basic document as a template.

To create a template document:

1. Open the document that you want to turn into a template.

2. Choose File > Save as Template (**Figure 1.7**).

   The Save as Template dialog appears, showing a preview of your document (**Figure 1.8**).

3. In the Name field, type a name for the template.

4. To specify a category, do either of the following:

   ▲ To select an existing category, from the Category pop-up menu, choose the desired category.

   ▲ To create a new category, in the Category field, type a name.

5. In the Description field, type a brief summary or reminder of what the template is for.

   Although you can enter as much text as you like in this field, once you click Save, Flash limits the description that accompanies the actual template to the first 255 characters. Still, it's a good idea to give some indication of the intended uses for the template or what its special features are.

6. Click Save.

   Flash saves the file as a master template document in a folder named Templates within the Configuration folder (see "The Mystery of the Configuration Folder," later in this chapter).

To open a new document from a template document:

1. From the Welcome screen, in the Create from Template section, click the name of a specific template or click the folder named More (**Figure 1.9**).

   The New from Template dialog appears.

   or

   Choose File > New.

   The New Document/New from Template dialog appears (**Figure 1.10**). The New Document and New from Template dialogs are identical except for their names. Both display two views: General and Templates. The dialog's name changes to reflect the active view. When you click a template folder in the Welcome screen, the Templates view is selected by default in the dialog.

2. From the Category list, choose the appropriate category.

3. From the Templates list, choose the template you want to use.

   The dialog previews the selected template's first frame and provides a brief description of the template, if one is available.

4. Click OK.

   Flash opens a new document with all the contents of the template.

✔ Tips

- When you choose File > New, Flash displays the document-creation dialog based on the type of file you created previously. The New Document dialog appears if the last file you created was a document. The New from Template dialog appears if the last file was a template.

Create from Template

- Advertising
- BREW Handsets
- Consumer Devices
- Global Handsets
- Japanese Handsets
- More...

Figure 1.9 Choose a template link in the Welcome screen to access the New from Template dialog.

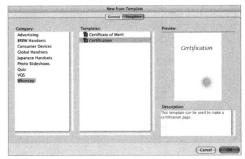

Figure 1.10 The Templates view of the New from Template (or New Document) dialog displays a preview and a description (when available) for the item selected in the Category and Templates lists.

- On the Mac, when the New from Template dialog opens, the name of the last template you used is highlighted in the Templates list. The preview window, however, shows the first template in the list. If you click OK now, Flash opens the previewed template, not the one that appears to be selected. If you want to use that highlighted template, click its name and wait till it appears in the preview window before clicking OK.

The Mystery of the Configuration Folder

The operating systems that run Flash CS3 can be configured for multiple users, storing each user's files and special settings separately. To handle customized settings, Flash uses three Configuration folders: The Application-Level Configuration folder governs settings for everyone who uses Flash on the computer; you must have administrative privileges to make changes to this folder. The All-User-Level Configuration folder contains master files for all users; the User-Level Configuration folder contains the files that each user has customized while working with Flash on this computer.

When you create a template document, for example, Flash stores it in a Templates folder inside your User-Level Configuration folder. The templates that come with Flash are stored in the Application-Level Configuration folder.

To add, delete, or rename items in a Configuration folder manually, you must have the required access privileges and navigate the hierarchy of nested folders on your hard drive to open the folder.

The folder that will most concern individual Flash users is the User-Level Configuration folder. The first part of its folder hierarchy is slightly different in each operating system:

Windows XP/2000 or Vista: `BootDrive\Documents and Settings\userName\Local Settings\Application Data\`

Mac OS X: `HardDriveName:Users:userName:Library:Application Support:`

From there on, the hierarchy of folders is always the same. For those using the English version of Flash, it's `Adobe\Flash CS3\en\Configuration`. Users of localized versions will see their language code instead of `en` in the folder hierarchy.

About the Flash Authoring Environment

When you open Flash, you enter Flash's authoring environment. As in most applications, the menu bar is always present at the top of the screen, but you can control other parts of the environment, opening and closing documents and panels, and positioning them where you prefer. In Flash, this customizable screen real estate is called the *workspace*.

Touring the Workspace

Flash's default workspace docks commonly used panels at edge of the screen (**Figure 1.11**). You can customize the workspace by opening, closing, resizing, and repositioning panels. (You'll learn to manipulate panels later in this chapter). You can save any arrangement of panels as a custom workspace for reuse. Flash also remembers which panels are opened, which are grouped, or docked, how large each should be, and so on, from one work session to the next.

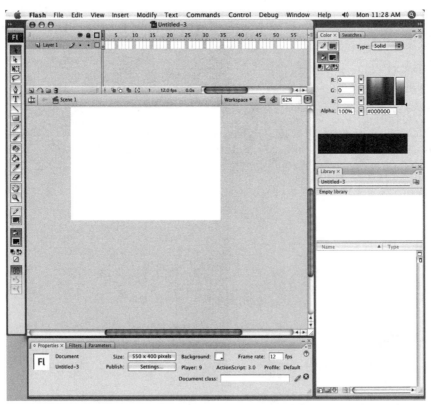

Figure 1.11 Flash's default workspace docks the Tools panel on the left, in a single column; the Property inspector on the bottom; and the Color, Swatches, and Library panels on the right.

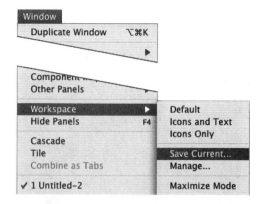

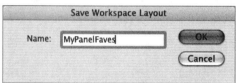

Figure 1.12 Choose Window > Workspace > Save Current (top) to access the Save Workspace Layout dialog (bottom). Enter a name for your current desktop configuration and click OK.

Figure 1.13
The Workspace pop-up menu in the Edit bar gives you quick access to workspace-management commands and saved workspaces.

To save a custom workspace:

1. Configure panels the way you like them using the techniques you'll learn later in this chapter.

2. Choose Window > Workspace > Save Current.

   The Save Workspace Layout dialog appears (**Figure 1.12**).

3. In the Name field, enter a title for this workspace.

4. Click OK.

   Flash saves that configuration and adds it to the Workspace menu.

To restore the default workspace:

◆ Choose Window > Workspace > Default.

   Flash places the Tools panel on the left and the Property inspector on the bottom, and creates a dock on the right side of the screen for the Library panel as well as a tabbed panel-group containing the Color and Swatches panels.

✔ Tips

■ You can also save and choose workspaces from the Workspace pop-up menu in a document's Edit bar (**Figure 1.13**).

■ To restore a custom workspace, choose the custom name from the Window > Workspace menu or from the Workspace pop-up menu in the Edit bar.

Touring a Document

A Flash document consists of the Timeline, which holds the frames, layers, and scenes that make up your movie; the Stage, which holds the movie's graphic content; the Edit bar, which displays information about what you're currently editing and provides access to other scenes and elements; and the Pasteboard, which extends beyond the Stage on all sides (**Figure 1.14**). In addition, in the authoring environment you have access to panels that provide tools for working with Flash content (see "Using Panels," later in this chapter).

Touring the Timeline

The Timeline visually represents every element of a movie, and is the framework for building projects. You'll use it extensively when you create animations (see Chapter 8).

Figure 1.15 identifies the major Timeline elements. You can dock the Timeline to any side of a Flash window, float it as a separate window, collapse it, or hide it completely to create more room for working with elements on the Stage.

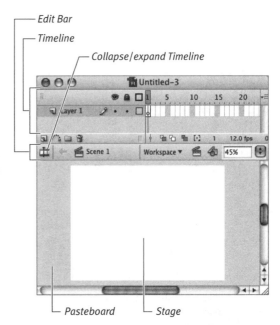

Edit Bar
Timeline
Collapse/expand Timeline
Pasteboard
Stage

Figure 1.14 A Flash document consists of the Timeline, the Stage, the Edit bar, and the Pasteboard.

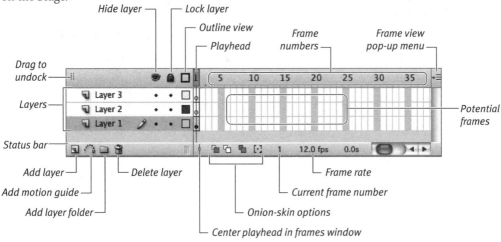

Hide layer — Lock layer
Outline view
Frame numbers
Frame view pop-up menu
Playhead
Drag to undock
Layers
Potential frames
Status bar
Add layer
Add motion guide
Delete layer
Frame rate
Current frame number
Add layer folder
Onion-skin options
Center playhead in frames window

Figure 1.15 The Timeline is the complete record of your movie. It represents all the scenes, frames, and layers that make up the movie. Frames appear in chronological order. Clicking any frame in the Timeline takes you directly to that frame and displays its contents on the Stage.

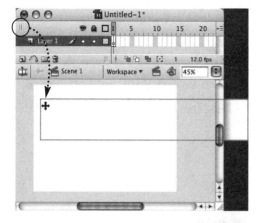

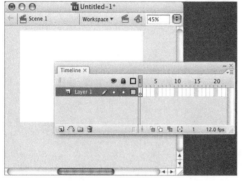

Figure 1.16 Drag the Timeline by the *gripper*—the textured portion of the title bar (top)—and then release the mouse button. The Timeline floats in its own window (bottom).

— *Hide Timeline button*

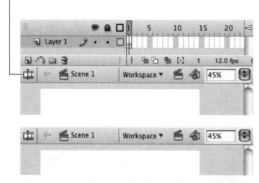

Figure 1.17 The Hide Timeline button appears in the Edit bar when the Timeline window is open. Click the button when the Timeline is visible (top) to hide it; when the Timeline is hidden (bottom), click the button to show the Timeline.

To undock the Timeline window:

1. Position the pointer over the *gripper* (the textured area) on the left side of the bar at the top of the Timeline.

   The pointer changes to the move icon.

2. Click and drag away from the document window (**Figure 1.16**).

   A gray outline represents the Timeline's new position.

3. Release the mouse button.

✔ Tips

■ To redock the Timeline, reverse the procedure. Drag the Timeline preview to the top of the document window or to any other edge. When you drag the Timeline to the right or left edge of the Stage, the Timeline docks vertically.

■ In Flash CS3, once the Timeline is undocked, to reposition it on the desktop you must drag the floating window by its title bar. Dragging the floating Timeline by the gripper won't move the floating window; release the gripper and the window pops back to where it started. You can, however, drag the Timeline's gripper to the edge of your screen to redock the Timeline.

■ On the Mac, if the Timeline is docked to the bottom or one side of the document window, double-click the gripper to redock the Timeline at the top of the window.

■ To collapse the Timeline window, click the Hide Timeline button on the left side of the Edit bar (**Figure 1.17**). To view the hidden Timeline, click the button again.

About Document Properties

The Document Properties dialog lets you define the Stage (its dimensions, the color of the background on which your artwork appears, and the units of measure for rulers and grids) and set a frame rate for playing your movie. Frames are the lifeblood of your animation, and the frame rate is the heart that keeps that blood flowing at a certain speed. Flash's default setting is 12 frames per second (fps)—a reasonable setting for animations viewed over the Web. (By comparison, the standard frame rate for film movies is double that speed.) You'll learn more about how frame rates affect animation in Chapter 8.

In Flash CS3, the Document Properties dialog also has features for creating metadata for SWF files. Metadata allows search engines to find your creations by title and/or keywords when you publish them to the Web. You can also use the Document Properties tab of the Property inspector to set some document properties. You'll learn more about using the Property inspector later in this chapter.

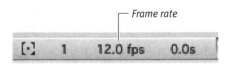

Frame rate

Figure 1.18 Double-clicking the frame-rate display in the Status bar is a quick way to access the Document Properties dialog.

The Mystery of SWF Metadata

The Document Properties dialog contains fields for Title and Description text. When you publish your document (see Chapter 17), the text in these fields gets turned into metadata attached to the SWF file. Search engines use this metadata to help potential users find your creation. Even though versions of Flash before 8 did not create SWF metadata, when you publish from Flash CS3 to an earlier version, Flash CS3 still creates the metadata for that SWF file. Note that the title and keywords in the Description field don't become part of the metadata of the HTML file you publish; you must create metadata for the HTML file yourself.

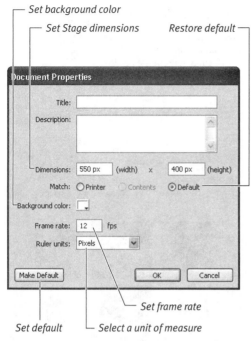

Set background color

Set Stage dimensions   Restore default

Set default   Select a unit of measure

Set frame rate

Figure 1.19 The Document Properties dialog is where you set all the parameters for viewing the Stage. Selecting a unit of measure for the rulers resets the unit measurement for all the Stage's parameters. Clicking the color control pops up the current set of colors and lets you choose one for the background. Clicking the Make Default button sets the parameters for all new documents you create.

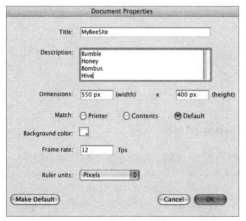

Figure 1.20 By entering a title in the Title field and descriptive keywords in the Description field, you add metadata to your published movie (SWF file), making the metadata available to search engines for searching.

To open the Document Properties dialog:

Do either of the following:

◆ Choose Modify > Document; or press ⌘-J (Mac) or Ctrl-J (Windows).

◆ In the Timeline's Status bar, double-click the frame-rate display (**Figure 1.18**). The Document Properties dialog appears (**Figure 1.19**).

✔ Tip

■ The Document Properties tab of the Property inspector also contains a shortcut to the Document Properties dialog. Just click the Size button. You'll learn more about the Property inspector later in this chapter.

To create SWF metadata:

1. Open the Document Properties dialog.

2. In the Title field, enter a title for your document.

3. In the Description field, enter descriptive words, or *keywords* (**Figure 1.20**).

   When you publish your movie, the SWF file will contain metadata from the Title and Description fields. To learn about publishing movies, see Chapter 17.

ABOUT DOCUMENT PROPERTIES

To set the size of the Stage:

1. Open the Document Properties dialog, and do one of the following:

   ▲ To set the Stage's dimensions, type values for width and height in the appropriate fields of the Dimensions section (**Figure 1.21**). Flash automatically assigns the units of measure currently selected in Ruler Units.

   ▲ To create a Stage big enough to cover all the elements in your movie, in the Match section of the Document Properties dialog, select the Contents radio button (**Figure 1.22**). Flash calculates the minimum Stage size required to cover all the elements in the movie and enters those measurements in the width and height fields of the Dimensions section.

   ▲ To set the Stage size to the maximum print area currently available, in the Match section of the Document Properties dialog, select the Printer radio button (**Figure 1.23**). Flash gets the paper size from the Page Setup dialog, subtracts the current margins, and puts the resulting measurements in the width and height fields of the Dimensions section.

2. Click OK.

Figure 1.21 To assign new proportions to your Stage, type a width and height in the Dimensions section of the Document Properties dialog.

Figure 1.22 To make your Stage just big enough to enclose the elements in your movie, select the Contents radio button in the Match section of the Document Properties dialog (top). Flash creates a Stage that's just big enough to show all the objects you've created and placed at the time you select the radio button (bottom). (If you've placed an object on the Pasteboard, Flash sizes the Stage to include that object.)

About the Pasteboard

Flash CS3's Pasteboard grows to accommodate your need for extra space. As you drag items from the Stage to the Pasteboard area, Flash enlarges the Pasteboard to hold them. If you move a large graphic element onto the Pasteboard, and some of it lies outside the area of the open document window, you can see the scroll bar move back toward the center of its range. There is now more Pasteboard area that's hidden from view. Use the scroll bars to view your graphic element and the enlarged Pasteboard. (You'll learn about creating graphic elements in Chapter 2 and repositioning them in Chapter 4.)

Figure 1.23 When you choose the Printer radio button in the Match section of the Document Properties dialog, Flash creates a Stage that will fit within the margins currently set for Page Setup.

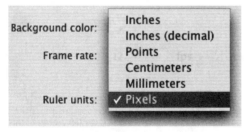

Figure 1.24 To set the units of measure for your Flash document, choose the type of units from the Ruler Units menu in the Document Properties dialog.

✔ Tips

- If you've entered new dimensions, either manually or by selecting Printer or Contents for matching, you can return to the default Stage dimensions by clicking the Default radio button.

- To set the units of measure for your document, in the Document Properties dialog, from the Ruler Units menu, choose the units of measure you prefer (**Figure 1.24**). You can work in inches, decimal inches, points, centimeters, millimeters, and pixels. Flash uses these units to calculate all measured items on the Stage: rulers, grid spacing, and dimensions.

- If you want a banner that's 1 inch tall and 5 inches wide, but you don't know what that size is in pixels (the standard unit of measure used for working on the Web), Document Properties can figure it out for you. First, set Ruler Units to inches. Type 1 in the height field and 5 in the width field. Then, return to Ruler Units and choose pixels. Flash does the math and sets the Stage dimensions. (Note that Flash uses screen pixels in its calculations. This means an inch in your movie may differ from an inch in the real world, depending on the resolution of the monitor on which the Flash movie is viewed.)

ABOUT DOCUMENT PROPERTIES

To set the background color:

1. Open the Document Properties dialog.

2. Click the Background Color control.

   The pointer changes to an eyedropper, and a set of swatches appears (**Figure 1.25**).

3. To select a background color, do either of the following:

   ▲ Click a swatch with the eyedropper.

   ▲ Click the hexadecimal-color field (to activate it), type a value, and press Enter.

   The selected color appears in the Background Color control.

4. Click OK.

   The Stage now appears in the color you selected.

✔ Tip

■ The Document Properties tab of the Property inspector also contains a Background Color control for selecting the movie's background color. You'll learn more about the Property inspector later in this chapter; you'll learn about using color controls in Chapter 2.

To set the frame rate:

1. Open the Document Properties dialog.

2. In the Frame Rate field, type the number of frames you want Flash to display in 1 second (**Figure 1.26**).

3. Click OK.

   The frame-rate setting appears in the Status bar of the current document.

To save your settings as the default:

◆ In the Document Properties dialog, click the Make Default button (**Figure 1.27**).

   The current settings in the Document Properties dialog become the defaults.

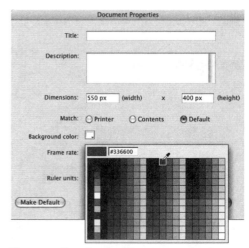

Figure 1.25 To assign your Stage a new color, choose one from the Background Color control in the Document Properties dialog.

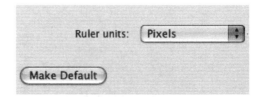

Figure 1.26 Typing a frame rate for your movie in the Frame Rate field of the Document Properties dialog sets Flash to display that number of frames in 1 second.

Figure 1.27 To save the current document-property settings as the defaults for all new documents, click the Make Default button in the lower-left corner of the Document Properties dialog.

Touring the Edit Bar

Another feature of the Flash document window is the Edit bar. Its default position is below the Timeline, when the Timeline is docked to the top edge of the Stage. You can also position the Edit bar above the top-docked Timeline. When the Timeline is floating, or docked to the bottom or side of the Stage, the Edit bar remains linked to the top of the Stage. You can even make the Edit bar disappear.

The Edit bar lets you know what mode you're working in (editing your document, or editing a drawing-object, group, or symbol within the movie). The Edit bar's pop-up menus give you the power to switch scenes, to choose a symbol to edit and immediately switch to symbol-editing mode, and to change the magnification for viewing the Stage. You can also choose a new workspace or manage workspace sets (see the sidebar "Touring the Workspace," earlier in this chapter). When you're editing a drawing-object, group, or symbol, the Edit bar identifies the element you're editing (**Figure 1.28**). To learn about editing drawing-objects and groups, see Chapter 5; for symbols, see Chapter 7; for scenes, see Chapter 11.

To reposition the Edit bar, ⌘-Shift double-click (Mac) or Alt-Shift double-click (Windows) any blank area within the Edit bar. If the Edit bar was initially below the Timeline, the procedure sends it above the Timeline. If the Edit bar started out in the high position, the procedure puts it on the bottom. To hide the Edit bar, choose Window > Toolbars > Edit Bar or click the Hide Edit Bar button at the far left side of the Edit bar. If you hide the Edit bar, however, you may find it more difficult to know when you're editing drawing-objects, groups, or symbols within your document and when you're working on the Stage in the main document.

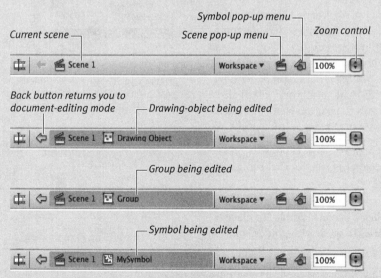

Figure 1.28 The Edit bar is located above the Stage. You can use it to access symbols and scenes and to change magnification. When you're editing a drawing-object, group, or symbol, the Edit bar identifies the item you're editing. Clicking the Back button takes you up the hierarchy of items you are editing, eventually returning you to document-editing mode.

ABOUT DOCUMENT PROPERTIES

Using Rulers, Grids, and Guides

Flash offers rulers, grids, and guides to help you place graphic elements on the Stage. You turn on these visual aids from the View menu (**Figure 1.29**). Choose the feature you want to use; a checkmark indicates that the feature is currently on. None of the visual aids appear in your final movie.

To show/hide grids, guides, and rulers:

From the View menu, choose any of the following (or use a keyboard shortcut):

◆ Choose Rulers, or press Option-Shift-⌘-R (Mac) or Ctrl-Alt-Shift-R (Windows).

Ruler bars appear on the left side and top of the Stage (**Figure 1.30**). You can set ruler units in the Document Properties dialog.

◆ Choose Grid > Show Grid, or press ⌘-apostrophe (') (Mac) or Ctrl-apostrophe (') (Windows).

When Show Grid is active, Flash superimposes crisscrossing vertical and horizontal lines on the Stage (**Figure 1.31**). The grid acts as a guide for drawing and positioning elements, the way that graph paper functions in the nondigital world. Flash also uses the grid to position elements when you activate the Snap to Grid feature.

◆ Choose Guides > Show Guides, or press ⌘-semicolon (;) (Mac) or Ctrl-semicolon (;) (Windows).

When Show Guides is active, any guides you've placed become visible. To place guides, see "To work with guides," later in this section.

◆ You can quickly access all of the snapping, guide, ruler, and document options at any time by right clicking in an empty part of the stage or in the Pasteboard and choosing the appropriate submenu.

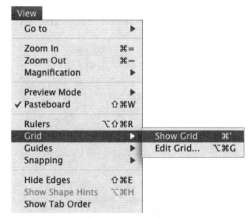

Figure 1.29 Flash offers three visual drawing aids: rulers, grids, and guides. To show or hide these features during authoring, use the View menu. Here, for example, is the command for showing grids.

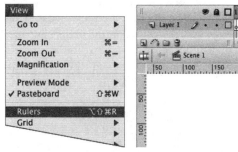

Figure 1.30 Choosing View > Rulers (left) makes rulers visible on the Stage (right).

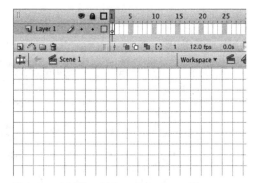

Figure 1.31 Visible grid lines help you position elements on the Stage during authoring.

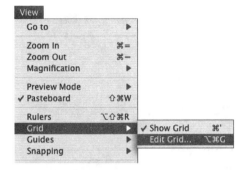

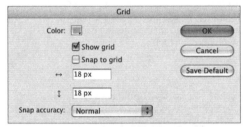

Figure 1.32 Choosing View > Grid > Edit Grid opens the Grid dialog, where you can change grid parameters.

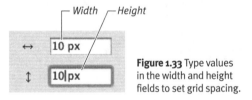

Figure 1.33 Type values in the width and height fields to set grid spacing.

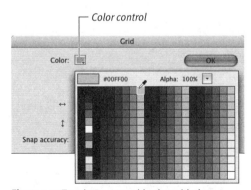

Figure 1.34 To select a new grid color, with the eyedropper pointer, click anywhere in the pop-up set of swatches. The swatch set displays the currently selected color set.

To set grid parameters:

1. Choose View > Grid > Edit Grid, or press Option-⌘-G (Mac) or Ctrl-Alt-G (Windows).

   The Grid dialog appears (**Figure 1.32**).

2. To set grid spacing, do the following:
   ▲ Type a value in the width field.
   ▲ Type a value in the height field (**Figure 1.33**).

3. To select a grid color, do the following:
   ▲ Click the Color control.

   The pointer changes to an eyedropper, and a set of swatches appears.

   ▲ Click a color in the swatch set (**Figure 1.34**).

   The new color appears in the Color control in the Grid dialog.

4. To control how close an item must get to the grid before Flash snaps the item to the grid, from the Snap Accuracy menu, choose a tolerance setting.

5. Click OK.

✔ Tips

■ Grids need not consist of perfect squares.

■ You can create new default settings for the grids in all new documents. After entering the desired settings in the Grid dialog, click the Save Default button, and then click OK.

To work with guides:

1. With rulers visible, position the pointer over the vertical or horizontal ruler bar.

   If you're using a tool other than the selection tool, the pointer changes to the selection arrow.

2. Click and drag the pointer onto the Stage.

   As you click, a small directional arrow appears next to the pointer, indicating which direction to drag (**Figure 1.35**).

3. Release the mouse button.

   Flash places a vertical or horizontal line on the Stage.

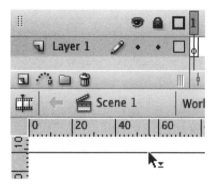

Figure 1.35 As you drag a guideline from the ruler bar, a direction indicator appears next to the selection tool.

✔ Tips

- To move a guide, position the selection tool over the guide. A direction arrow appears next to the pointer, indicating that the guide can be dragged (**Figure 1.36**). Drag the guide to a new location, and release the mouse button. To remove a guide, drag it completely out of the open document window.

- To avoid repositioning guides accidentally, choose View > Guides > Lock Guides, or press Option-⌘-semicolon (;) (Mac) or Ctrl-Alt-semicolon (;) (Windows). The directional arrow no longer appears next to the selection tool when you place it over a guideline. To unlock the guides, choose View > Guides > Lock Guides or press the keyboard shortcut again.

- If you've placed numerous guides in your document, dragging them from the Stage may get tedious. To remove them all at once, choose View > Guides > Clear Guides, or access the Guides dialog and click the Clear All button.

- To set parameters for guides, open the Guide dialog by choosing View > Guides > Edit Guides or pressing Option-Shift-⌘-G (Mac) or Ctrl-Alt-Shift-G (Windows).

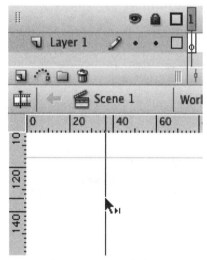

Figure 1.36 You can position individual vertical and horizontal guides anywhere you want on the Stage.

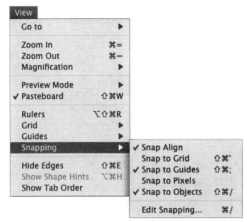

Figure 1.37 Choose View > Snapping to open a menu with Flash's snapping options. Select an unchecked item to activate it; select a checked item to deselect and deactivate it.

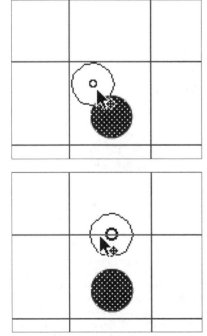

Figure 1.38 As you drag elements, the *snap ring,* a small circle, appears near the tip of the pointer (top). The snap ring grows larger when it moves over an item that you've chosen to snap to, such as a grid, a guide, or the edge or center of another element.

Working with Snapping

Flash's five snapping features help you align elements on the Stage. Snap to Grid helps you position the edge or center of an element to sit directly on top of a user-defined grid. Snap to Guide does the same thing with elements and guidelines. Snap to Objects helps you position one element in relation to another. Snap to Pixels helps you move elements in whole-pixel steps; at magnifications of 400 percent or greater it displays a 1-pixel-by-1-pixel grid. Snap Align helps you align elements once you've dragged them within a user-definable distance from one another or from the edge of the Stage.

To turn snapping options on and off:

1. Choose View > Snapping.

    The menu items with check marks are currently active (**Figure 1.37**). Select an unchecked item to activate it; select a checked item to deactivate it.

2. To activate/deactivate a snapping option, from the Snapping submenu, choose any of the following:

    ▲ *To snap elements to a grid,* choose Snap to Grid, or press Shift-⌘-apostrophe (') (Mac) or Ctrl-Shift-apostrophe (') (Windows).

    With Snap to Grid active, as you drag an element, a circle called the snap ring appears near the tip of the selection tool. As the element comes close to a grid line, Flash highlights potential snap points by enlarging the snap ring (**Figure 1.38**).

    ▲ *To snap elements to guides,* choose Snap to Guides, or press Shift-⌘-semicolon (;) (Mac) or Ctrl-Shift-semicolon (;) (Windows).

    continues on next page

▲ *To snap elements to elements,* choose Snap to Objects, or press Shift-⌘-/ (Mac) or Ctrl-Shift-/ (Windows).

▲ *To snap elements to pixels,* choose Snap to Pixels.

Flash creates a grid whose squares measure 1 pixel by 1 pixel. To see the grid, you must set the Stage's magnification to at least 400 percent (**Figure 1.39**). You'll learn more about magnified views in "Viewing at Various Magnifications," later in this chapter.

▲ *To view alignment guides while positioning elements,* choose Snap Align.

With Snap Align active, as you drag elements on the Stage, Flash displays an alignment guide (a dotted line) whenever the element's edge or center gets close to being in alignment with the edge or center of another element, or when the element gets within a user-specified distance of another element's edge, its center, or the edge of the Stage (**Figure 1.40**).

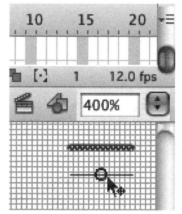

Figure 1.39 With Flash's Snap to Pixels feature enabled, a 1-pixel grid becomes visible at magnifications of 400 percent or greater. You can use this mode for precise positioning of graphic elements.

✔ Tips

■ You can also turn off snapping for grids and guides from within the dialogs where you set their parameters. Choose View > Grid > Edit Grid (or View > Guides > Edit Guides); in the dialog that appears, deselect the Snap to Grids (or Snap to Guides) check box.

■ When you are using many of the drawing tools, a magnet button appears in the lower portion of the tool panel (the options section). Click the button to activate/deactivate the Snap to Objects option.

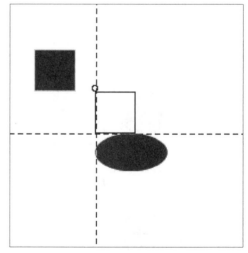

Figure 1.40 Flash's Snap Align feature displays a dotted alignment guide whenever the element you're dragging meets certain conditions. For example, you can set Snap Align to display a dotted line when the edge of the object you're dragging aligns with the edge of another object, or when the dragged object's edge gets to a certain distance from the edge of the Stage.

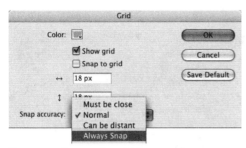

Figure 1.41 Choose a Snap Accuracy setting to determine how close an element must be to the grid before Flash snaps the element to the grid line. Choosing Always Snap forces the edge or center of an element to lie directly on a grid line.

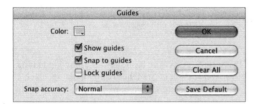

Figure 1.42 In the Guides dialog, you can set how close items must be before they will snap to the guides. You can also choose a guide color, set the visibility of guides, and set their status as locked or unlocked.

- The snap ring appears roughly in the place where the selection tool connects with the element you're dragging. Flash can snap an element only by its center point or a point on its perimeter, however. If you have trouble seeing the snap ring, try grabbing the element nearer to its center, an edge, or a corner.

- Although the Snap to Pixels feature uses a 1-pixel grid, the graphic elements you move don't snap to the grid's coordinates unless you set the element's x and y position to a whole number in the Info panel or Properties tab of the Property inspector. (You'll learn to set coordinates for graphic elements in Chapter 4.)

To set parameters for snapping to the grid:

1. Choose View > Grid > Edit Grid or press Option-⌘-G (Mac) or Ctrl-Alt-G (Windows).

2. In the Grid dialog, choose a parameter from the Snap Accuracy pop-up menu (**Figure 1.41**).

3. Click OK.

To set parameters for snapping to guides:

1. Choose View > Guides > Edit Guides or press Option-Shift-⌘-G (Mac) or Ctrl-Alt-Shift-G (Windows).

2. In the Guides dialog, choose a setting from the Snap Accuracy pop-up menu (**Figure 1.42**).

3. Click OK.

To set snap-align options:

1. Choose View > Snapping > Edit Snapping. The Edit Snapping dialog opens. If the Snap Align settings aren't visible in the dialog, click the Advanced/Basic button (**Figure 1.43**).

2. To adjust the way Snap Align interacts with elements and the Stage, do any of the following.

   ▲ To have alignment guides appear when a dragged object reaches a specified distance from the edge of the Stage, enter a value in the Stage Border field.

   ▲ To have alignment guides appear when the top or bottom edge of a dragged object reaches a specified distance from the top or bottom edge of another object, in the Object Spacing section, enter a value in the Vertical field.

   ▲ To have alignment guides appear when the side of a dragged object reaches a specified distance from either side of another object, in the Object Spacing section, enter a value in the Horizontal field.

   ▲ To have guides appear when the center of a dragged object aligns horizontally and/or vertically with the center of another object, in the Center Alignment section, select the Horizontal and/or Vertical check boxes.

Click to hide Advanced options

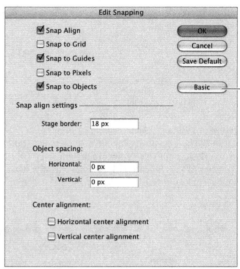

Figure 1.43 You set the tolerance for Snap Align in the Advanced section of the Edit Snapping dialog. Flash's default settings are shown here.

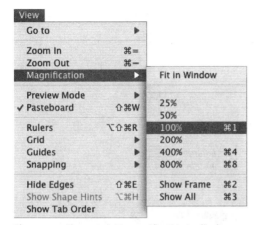

Figure 1.44 Choose 100% magnification to display graphics at the size they will be in the final movie.

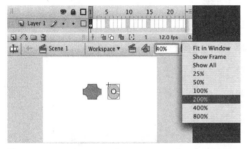

Figure 1.45 Enter a percentage greater than 100 in the Zoom Control field to magnify elements on the Stage. The pop-up menu to the right of the field offers several common magnification levels.

Viewing at Various Magnifications

Flash offers several ways to adjust the magnification of elements on the Stage.

To view elements at actual size:

◆ Choose View > Magnification > 100% (**Figure 1.44**), or press ⌘-1 (Mac) or Ctrl-1 (Windows).

or

◆ In the Zoom Control field, at the right side of the Stage's Edit bar, type 100%. Press Enter.

At 100%, Flash displays elements as close as possible to the size they will be in the final movie. (Some monitors and video cards may display elements at a slightly different size than the system on which you created the element.)

To zoom in or out on the Stage:

1. In the Zoom Control field, type the desired percentage of magnification (**Figure 1.45**).

2. Press Enter.

✔ Tip

■ Click the scroll button next to the Zoom Control field to open a menu that duplicates the choices in the View > Magnification submenu. Choose a percentage from this menu to change magnification immediately. This menu also lets you choose Fit in Window (to display the full Stage area in the current window, without scroll bars), Show Frame (to display the full Stage area in the current window, with scroll bars), and Show All (to scale the Stage so that all elements on the Stage and in the Pasteboard appear in the current window).

To reduce or enlarge specific areas:

1. In the Tools panel, select the zoom tool (or press M or Z on the keyboard).

   The pointer changes to a magnifying glass.

2. To enlarge an area or element, click and drag to create a selection rectangle that encompasses the area or element.

   Flash fills the window with your selection (**Figure 1.46**). This technique works whether the zoom tool is set to Enlarge or Reduce mode.

To zoom in or out:

1. With the zoom tool active, in the lower portion of the Tools panel, select one of the tool's modifiers:

   ▲ Enlarge (the magnifying-glass icon with the plus sign)

   ▲ Reduce (the magnifying-glass icon with the minus sign)

2. On the Stage, click the area or element you want to enlarge or reduce.

   Flash places the spot you clicked at the center of the viewing window and changes the percentage of magnification specified in the Zoom Control field. With the zoom tool set to Enlarge, Flash doubles the percentage; with the zoom tool set to Reduce, Flash halves the percentage.

✔ Tip

■ With the zoom tool selected, to switch temporarily from Enlarge to Reduce, and vice versa, hold down the Option key (Mac) or Alt key (Windows).

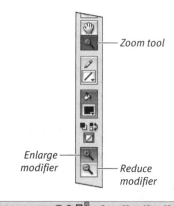

Zoom tool

Enlarge modifier — Reduce modifier

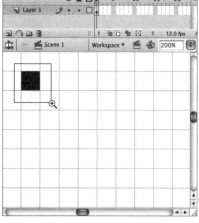

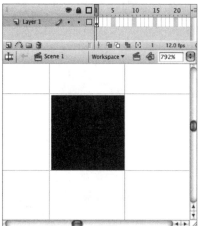

Figure 1.46 Use the zoom tool (top) to draw a selection rectangle around an element (middle). Flash enlarges your selection to fill the open window (bottom).

VIEWING AT VARIOUS MAGNIFICATIONS

Using Panels

Flash organizes drawing and authoring tools as *panels* inside windows. As we've seen earlier in this chapter, panels can be open on the desktop for quick access as you work. Some panels contain tools for creating or modifying graphic elements. Others help you organize and navigate your Flash document. You can open panel windows that float, positioning them anywhere in the workspace; you can *group* multiple panels in one window or *stack* multiple panel windows vertically; and you can *dock* panels to the edge of the workspace. You'll learn to work with specific panels in later chapters of this book. For now, you'll learn general features of panels and how to manage them in the workspace. No matter what form a panel window takes, you use the same basic techniques to manipulate it.

Touring a Panel Window

Open panels appear as tabs inside a window. The window may contain just one panel tab or several. Panel windows have the following parts (**Figure 1.47**): the title bar (the gray area underlying the panel tabs at the top of the window), one or more panel tabs, a minimize/maximize-window button, and a close-window button. (When panel windows are stacked vertically, these last two items appear only in the topmost window and work to control the entire stack.) Each panel in the window contains a close-panel button and a panel menu.

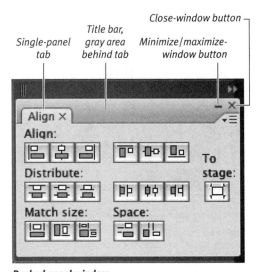

Single-panel tab · Title bar, gray area behind tab · Close-window button · Minimize/maximize-window button

Docked panel window

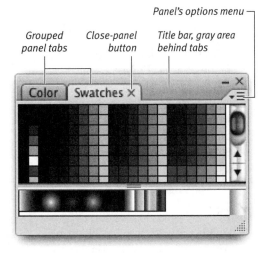

Grouped panel tabs · Close-panel button · Title bar, gray area behind tabs · Panel's options menu

Floating panel window

Figure 1.47 Common panel-interface elements help you to configure panel windows to save space. Buttons that relate to an entire panel window reside on the window's title bar; buttons that relate to a specific panel reside in the tab bearing the panel's name.

To open (or close) panel windows via menu:

◆ From the Window menu, select the desired panel—for example, Color (**Figure 1.48**). One of the following actions takes place:

▲ If the selected panel is closed, a window containing that panel opens. The window may appear inside a dock or floating on the desktop, depending on the selected workspace and any modifications you've made to it.

▲ If the selected panel's window is collapsed, it expands.

▲ If the selected panel is obscured behind other tabs or floating panel windows, the selected panel moves to the front.

▲ If the selected panel is the only tab— or the front tab—in a window that is already open, expanded, and in front, the window (including all its tabs) closes.

To close panel windows by clicking:

◆ Click the close button at the right side of the title bar (**Figure 1.49**).

The panel window closes. If the window contains grouped panels, clicking the window's close button closes all of the tabs within the window. If the window contains stacked panels, only the top window has a close button; clicking it closes the entire stack.

✔ Tips

■ Another way to close an open panel window is to Ctrl-click (Mac) or right-click (Windows) the title bar, and choose Close Group(s) from the contextual menu.

■ To hide all the open panels (including the Tools panel, the Property inspector, and any open Library panels), press F4. Press F4 again to show the panels.

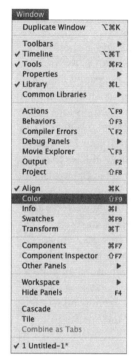

Figure 1.48 The Window menu contains a list of the panels in Flash.

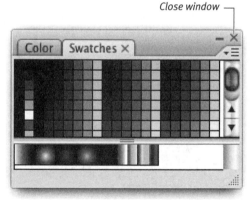

Figure 1.49 Clicking the close button in a panel window's title bar closes the window.

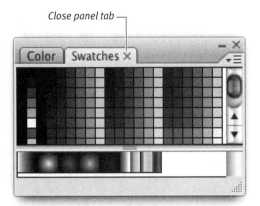

Close panel tab

Figure 1.50 Clicking the close button on a panel tab closes just that panel; other panels in the stack or group remain open in the window.

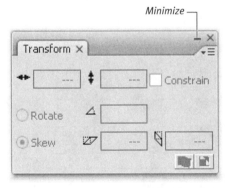

Minimize

Maximize

Figure 1.51 A full-size panel window displays a minimize button, a short, horizontal line; clicking it collapses the window to its title bar. In the collapsed state, a panel window displays the maximize button, a small rectangle; clicking it expands the window.

To close individual panels within a group or stack:

◆ Click the close button to the right of the name in the panel tab (**Figure 1.50**).

Flash closes that panel, so that it's no longer visible in the group or stack.

✔ Tip

■ When you close a grouped or stacked panel individually, it still belongs to its group or stack. The next time you choose that panel from the Window menu, the panel opens inside a window containing its stack or group.

To collapse or expand a panel window:

◆ Click the minimize (or maximize) button (**Figure 1.51**).

The window toggles between its collapsed and expanded states.

✔ Tips

■ When you click the minimize button for stacked panel windows, Flash minimizes all the windows in the stack. You wind up with a stack of title bars.

■ Another way to minimize or maximize an open panel window is to Ctrl-click (Mac) or right-click (Windows) the panel's title bar, and choose Minimize Group(s)/Restore Group(s) from the contextual menu.

■ You can also single click in the title bar area of a panel group or double click the tab of a panel and it will toggle the group between minimized/maximized states.

USING PANELS

To reposition panel windows:

◆ Click the panel's title bar, and drag the window to a new location (**Figure 1.52**). The panel window becomes transparent as you drag, allowing you to position it among other items on the desktop.

✔ Tip

■ Docking, grouping, and stacking panels is just a matter of repositioning them in specific ways (see "Combining and Docking Panels," later in this section).

To resize a floating panel window:

Do any of the following:

◆ To resize a panel window vertically and/or horizontally, click and drag the resize box at the bottom-right corner of the window (**Figure 1.53**).

◆ To resize a panel window vertically, position the pointer over the top or bottom edge of the panel. When the pointer changes to a double-headed arrow, drag up or down to lengthen or shorten the panel.

◆ To resize a window panel horizontally, position the pointer over the left or right edge of the panel. When the pointer changes to a double-headed arrow, drag the edge left or right to narrow or widen the panel.

✔ Tip

■ Some panels can't be resized. If a panel window has no resize box, then its panel has a fixed size. If a panel window contains a group with both sizable and fixed-size panels, the resize box appears only when a sizable panel is active.

Figure 1.52 Drag a panel window by its title bar to reposition it in the workspace. The panel becomes transparent as you drag it.

Pointer ready to resize horizontally

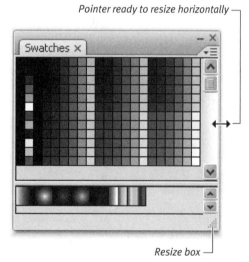

Resize box

Figure 1.53 Resizable panel windows have a textured resize box in the lower-right corner; drag the resize box as you would to change the dimensions of any document window. You can also resize the window in one direction by positioning the pointer over one side of the window, when the double-arrow pointer appears, drag that side.

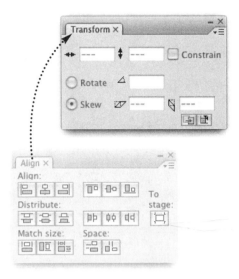

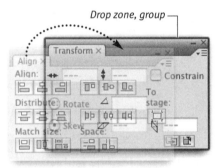

Drop zone, group

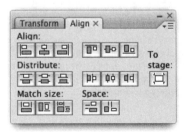

Figure 1.54 When you drag a panel over the title bar of another panel window (top), the perimeter of the target window highlights (middle). Releasing the panel into this drop zone creates a group of tabbed panels in the target window (bottom).

Combining and Docking Panels

To use desktop space efficiently, you can combine panels into groups (multiple panel tabs within one window) and stacks (multiple panel windows linked vertically). You can dock single panels, groups, and stacks to any edge of your screen. To save more space, you can view docked panels as icons, accessing the full panels individually as you need them (see the sidebar "Saving Space with Panel Icons," later in this chapter).

To group panels as tabs in one window:

1. With two or more panels open on the desktop, click the name on one panel tab. Flash highlights the tab in gray.

2. Drag that panel over another open panel window, the target panel window.

   The panel being dragged becomes transparent (**Figure 1.54**). As the pointer touches various parts of the target panel, Flash highlights *drop zones* in blue, indicating how the panels will combine.

3. Position the pointer over the target panel's title bar.

   Flash highlights the perimeter and title bar of the target panel in blue, indicating the drop zone for creating a group of tabbed panels.

4. Release the mouse button.

   The panel you dragged now appears as a tab in the target panel window.

To stack single-panel windows vertically:

1. With two or more single-panel windows open on the desktop, click one panel's tab.

   The tab highlights in gray.

2. To stack the first panel above the second, with the mouse button still down, drag the tab until the position of the mouse pointer aligns with the top edge of the target panel window.

   or

   To stack the first panel below the second, position the pointer along the bottom edge of the target panel window.

   Flash highlights the target window's drop zone for stacking with a blue line (**Figure 1.55**).

3. Release the mouse button.

   The first panel now appears stacked above or below the target window.

✔ Tip

■ You can also stack windows containing panel groups. Instead of dragging an individual panel tab, drag the title bar of the group's panel window. When you drag a title bar, however, you have fewer drop-zone options. The drop zone at the top of the target window will not activate. Similarly, if you drag a title bar to an existing stack, the drop zone above the top window in the stack will not activate.

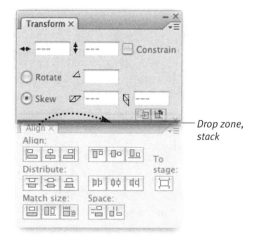

Drop zone, stack

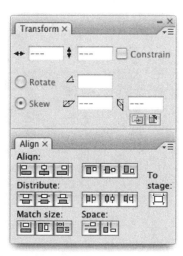

Figure 1.55 To create a panel stack, drag one panel to the top or bottom edge of another. Releasing the dragged panel over the drop zone at the bottom edge of the target panel window (top) stacks the panels with the target window on top (bottom).

USING PANELS

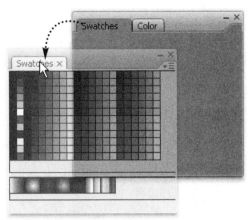

Figure 1.56 Dragging a panel by its tab lets you remove that panel from a group.

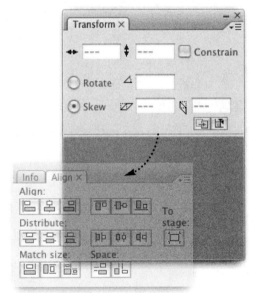

Figure 1.57 To remove a panel window from a stack, just drag it. You can drag a single panel by its tab; for grouped panels, drag the window by its title bar.

To separate grouped panels:

1. To remove one panel from a group, click the name on the panel's tab.

On the Mac, Flash highlights the tab in gray.

2. Drag the tab away from the panel window.

The panel being dragged becomes transparent, and its spot in the original window turns gray (**Figure 1.56**).

3. Release the mouse button.

The panel's tab appears in a separate window.

To separate stacked panel windows:

◆ To separate a single-panel window from its stack, click the name on the panel tab and drag away from the stack.

or

1. To separate a panel group other than one in the top window, from its stack click the title bar of the group's window and drag away from the stack.

The window being dragged becomes transparent, and its location in the original stack turns gray (**Figure 1.57**).

2. Release the mouse button.

Flash creates a floating window for the dragged panel or group.

✔ Tip

■ When you drag a panel tab out of a stack to create a separate window, that tab can be located anywhere in the stack. When you drag a title bar, however, there are limitations. If you drag the title bar of the top window in a stack, you move the stack as a unit. The only way to unstack a group window when it lies at the top of a stack is to dismantle the whole thing, dragging each of the lower windows away until the top window stands alone.

USING PANELS

To create a "new" dock:

1. Click the title bar of any floating panel window.

   The window may contain a single panel tab, a group of panel tabs, or a stack of panel windows.

2. Drag the title bar to the right, left, bottom, or top edge of the desktop.

   A gray rectangle edged with a blue line appears (**Figure 1.58**). The rectangle is the border of the dock, and the blue line is the dock's drop zone. When a dock is empty, it stays hidden, waiting in the wings until you drag a panel to it.

3. Release the mouse button.

   Flash adds the panel window to the dock.

✔ Tip

■ You can resize most docks. Position the pointer over the edge of the dock closest to the Stage. When the pointer changes to a double-headed arrow, drag in or out to make the dock narrower or wider. Some docked panels, such as the Tools panel, are not resizable. If the pointer doesn't change when you position it on the edge of a docked panel, you can't change the dock dimensions for that panel.

Drop zone, dock

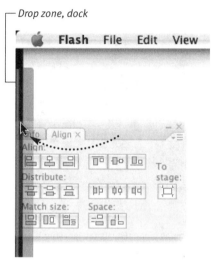

Figure 1.58 Dragging a panel window to the edge of your desktop activates a dock. When the blue drop-zone highlight appears (top), release the mouse button and Flash adds the panel window to the dock (bottom).

Tools and Help: Not Like Other Panels

The *Tools panel* contains Flash's drawing tools. Unlike other panels, the Tools panel can't be fully collapsed or resized, nor can it be grouped with other panels. You can make the Tools panel one column or two; you can dock the panel to the left or right edge of the screen, but not the top or bottom. You'll learn about working with the Tools panel and its tools in Chapter 2. The *Help panel* works like most Flash panels, but you won't find it in the Window menu with the other panels. To access the Help panel, choose Help > Flash Help (or press F1).

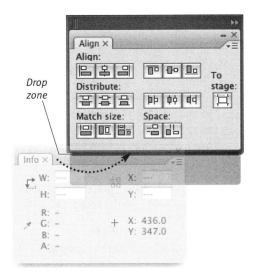

Drop zone

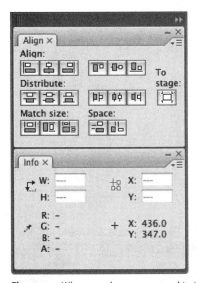

Figure 1.59 When you drag a new panel to the top or bottom edge of an already docked panel window, the drop zone highlights in blue. Release the mouse button when the drop zone appears in the location you want (top); Flash adds the panel window to the dock (bottom).

To add panels to an existing dock:

1. Click the title bar of a floating panel window.

   The window may contain a single panel tab, a group of panel tabs, or a stack of panel windows.

2. Drag the title bar to an existing dock.

   The window being dragged becomes transparent. As the pointer touches various areas of the dock, drop zones highlight in blue.

3. To add a new panel window inside the dock, do the following:

   ▲ To add the new panel window above a currently docked one, position the pointer along the top edge of the docked panel window; to add the new panel window below the docked one, position the pointer along the bottom edge of the docked panel window (**Figure 1.59**).

   ▲ Release the mouse button.

   Flash creates a separate window for the panel within the dock.

   or

   To create a new panel group in the dock (or to add to an existing group), do the following:

   ▲ Position the pointer over the title bar of a docked panel window; the drop zone highlights the perimeter of that window.

   ▲ Release the mouse button.

   Flash adds the panel's tab to the target window within the dock (**Figure 1.60**).

USING PANELS

✔ Tips

- You can drag a panel stack into a dock, but the panel windows lose their connection. You can only drag them out of the dock as individuals.

- You can create double docks. When you drag a panel window to the edge of an existing dock, you can activate a drop zone along the left or right edge of the dock. Releasing a dragged panel window when one of these drop zones appears creates another layer of dock (**Figure 1.61**).

To remove panels from a dock:

1. To remove an item from the dock, do one of the following:

   ▲ To remove a single-panel window, click the name on the panel tab and drag away from the dock.

   ▲ To remove a panel group, click the title bar of the group's window and drag away from the dock.

   Drag the items away from the dock until their place in the dock turns gray.

2. Release the mouse button.

   Flash creates a floating panel window.

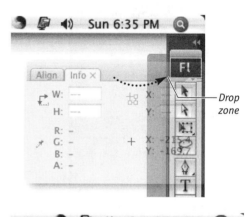

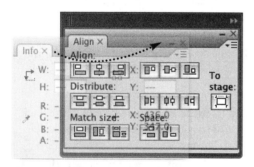

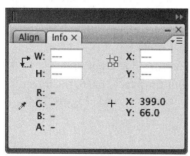

Figure 1.60 Dragging a panel window over the title bar of a window in the dock highlights the drop zone for creating a group (top). Release the mouse button to add the panel tab to the window.

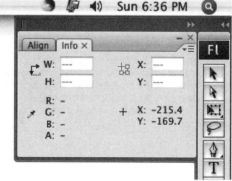

Figure 1.61 Double-docking can be useful. Drag a panel window to either side of an existing dock till the drop zone appears (top), then release the mouse button to add another layer of dock (bottom).

USING PANELS

Saving Space with Panel Icons

To create the most room on your desktop, you can collapse panel windows in docks on the left and/or right side of the workspace to small icons. (Panels in docks at the top or bottom of the workspace cannot collapse to icons, although you can minimize them to their title bars.) To switch between icon and full-panel view, click the double triangle at the top of the dock (**Figure 1.62**). With the dock in icon view, click an icon to open its panel window to full size; if the window contains grouped panels, the icon reflects that and the complete group opens.

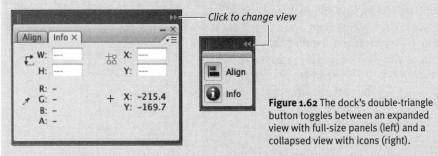

Click to change view

Figure 1.62 The dock's double-triangle button toggles between an expanded view with full-size panels (left) and a collapsed view with icons (right).

There are two styles for collapsing a full panel window to its icon. By default, Flash automatically collapses the panel window when you're done using it; clicking anywhere outside the open window closes it to icon form. To prevent Flash from closing the windows automatically, you must change preference settings. To do this quickly, Ctrl-click (Mac) or right-click (Windows) any icon in the dock, then deselect Auto-Collapse Icon Panels in the contextual menu that appears. Flash works behind the scenes to change that setting in the General section of the Preferences dialog. (To access the dialog yourself, choose Show Interface Preferences from the same contextual menu or choose Flash (Mac) or Edit (Windows) > Preferences.) When auto-collapse is inactive, to close an open panel window you must click the double triangles in the window's upper-right corner (**Figure 1.63**).

Panel windows in icon form lack close buttons. To remove an icon panel from the workspace, you must first expand the panel window to full size, then click its close button. You can also drag the icon from the dock; the panel window expands and you can click its close button.

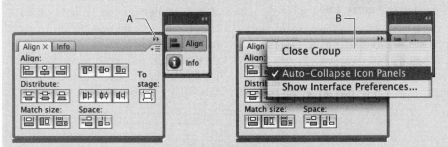

Figure 1.63 With the dock in icon mode and autocollapse inactive, you close an open panel window by clicking its double triangles (A). To change the autocollapse setting quickly, Ctrl-click (Mac) or right-click (Windows) an icon in the dock to access the contextual menu (B).

About the Property Inspector

By default, Flash CS3 creates a tabbed-panel group known as the Property inspector. This panel group has three tabs: the Properties tab displays information about the properties and attributes of tools and graphic elements (such as color, style, and font for the text tool); the Parameters tab displays information about components (you'll learn about one type of component, a button, in Chapter 12). The Filters tab lets you add special effects to text and certain symbols (to learn about symbols, see Chapter 7). You can use any of the techniques in the preceding exercises to change the grouping of the Property inspector's panels. For now, leave them in the default arrangement, even though you'll work mostly with just the Properties tab in this book.

The Properties tab of the Property inspector is context-sensitive, changing to reflect the tool or element you have selected. You'll learn about specific versions and tabs of the Property inspector in later chapters. For now, just learn the general rules of operation.

To access the Properties tab of the Property inspector:

◆ Choose Window > Properties > Properties, or press ⌘-F3 (Mac) or Ctrl-F3 (Windows) (**Figure 1.64**).

Flash opens the Property inspector with the Properties tab active. The panel displays information about whatever item you have selected in the Flash document (see "The Power of the Property Inspector").

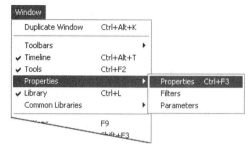

Figure 1.64 To access the Properties tab of the Property inspector, choose Window > Properties; from the submenu, select the tab you want to be active in the panel.

✔ Tip

■ Depending on the tool or element you select, the Properties tab displays different amounts of information. The Line Tool, for example, has fewer properties than does the Text Tool. You can resize the Property inspector vertically to save space when viewing a tab with fewer properties. If you switch tools, you may need to resize the Property inspector to view all the information you need.

The Power of the Property Inspector

Think of the Property inspector as being a context-sensitive superpanel—a panel that changes to reflect whatever item you have selected. The Properties tab of the panel displays information about the active Flash document or a selected tool, graphic element (a merge shape, drawing-object, primitive shape, grouped shape, symbol, text field, bitmap, or video clip), or frame. The Parameters tab displays information about a selected component. The Filters tab displays information about special effects applied to text, a movie clip, or a button.

The Properties tab of the Property inspector is also the place for choosing many tools' settings and for changing the attributes of selected elements.

Select the line tool, for example, and the Properties tab of the Property inspector becomes the Line Tool Properties tab (**Figure 1.65**). In this incarnation, the Properties tab presents all the line tool's attributes for you to set: color, thickness, and style. Select a merge-shape line on the Stage, however, and the Properties tab becomes the Shape Properties tab. When the selected shape is a line, the Shape Properties tab displays attributes similar to those shown in the Line Tool Properties tab; change the settings in the Properties tab, and Flash changes the selected line to match.

Figure 1.65 The Property inspector displays information about selected items and allows you to modify them. The Line Tool Properties tab of the Property inspector, for example, lets you set the color, thickness, and style for lines that the line tool creates.

Click a blank area of the Stage, and you'll see the Document Properties tab of the Property inspector, which gives you access to various document settings. Select a symbol instance on the Stage, and the Properties tab reveals the instance's heritage (which master symbol it came from), as well as its height, width, and Stage position. Change those settings in the Properties tab, and Flash makes those changes in the selected symbol instance.

In many modes, the Property inspector requires you to enter a value in a field to change a parameter. You can always type a new value. When modifying selected items, usually you must press Enter to apply the new value to selected items.

A small triangle to the right of an entry field indicates the presence of a pop-up slider for entering values quickly. Often, a slider previews new values interactively. The following methods work for most sliders:

◆ Click and drag. Click the small triangle, and hold down the mouse button; you can start dragging the slider's lever right away. Release the mouse button. Flash enters the current slider value in the field and—in most cases—applies that value to selected elements automatically.

◆ Click and click. Click the small triangle, and release the mouse button right away; the slider pops up and stays open. You can drag the slider's lever or click various locations on the slider to choose a new value. Flash enters the value in the field. To apply the value to selected items, you must click somewhere off the slider.

CREATING SIMPLE GRAPHICS

About Strokes and Fills

What do *stroke* and *fill* mean? A stroke is an outline, and a fill is a solid area of color. Think of a coloring book, with black lines creating the pictures: those lines are strokes. When you fill in the areas outlined by strokes—say, with crayon—that colorful area is the fill. In a coloring book, you start with an outline and create the fill inside it. In Flash, you can also work the other way around—start with a solid shape and then create the outline as a separate element.

Flash's rectangle, oval, rectangle-primitive, oval-primitive, and polystar tools can create an element that's just a stroke or just a fill; they can also create the stroke and fill elements simultaneously. The line tool, as you might guess, creates only strokes. The pen tool creates both strokes and fills.

The concept of fills and strokes is a bit trickier to grasp in relation to the brush tool. This tool creates fills. These fills may look like lines or brushstrokes, but they are shapes you can outline with a stroke. Flash has special tools for adding, editing, and removing strokes and fills: the ink bottle, the paint bucket, and the faucet eraser. See Chapter 4 for more details.

This chapter teaches you to use Adobe Flash CS3 Professional's drawing tools to create basic shapes from lines and areas of color—in Flash terminology, *strokes* and *fills*. Flash offers natural drawing tools that imitate the feel of working on paper with a pencil or brush; geometric-shape tools that create predefined shapes; and a pen tool that lets you draw with precision, using Bézier curves.

These tools let you create three types of shapes. Tools set to Merge Drawing mode create raw shapes—shapes that interact with other raw shapes on the same layer (you'll learn about shape interactions in Chapter 5). Tools set to Object Drawing mode create editable shapes that don't interact with other shapes. Flash CS3 introduces a new type of shape, the *primitive*-shape. Two new tools, the rectangle- and oval-primitive tools, create non-interactive shapes with a set of defining parameters. You can edit a primitive's parameters (changing the roundness of a rectangle's corners, for example), but you can't freely edit a primitive's outline (turning an oval into a free-form blob, for example).

Once you create a shape, you can edit it (see Chapter 4). You can also import graphics from other programs (see Chapter 14).

Touring the Tools

The Tools panel holds all the tools you need to create and modify graphic elements (**Figure 2.1**). Flash CS3 gives you tools for creating graphic elements, for scrolling the Stage and zooming in and out, and for setting colors for the elements you create.

You click a tool to select it for use. If the selected tool has options, the appropriate buttons and/or menus for choosing options and settings appear at the bottom of the Tools panel.

✔ Tip

■ By default the Tools panel appears in single-column mode. Figure 2.1 shows the panel in space-saving two-column mode. Click the double-triangle icon in the panel window's title bar to switch modes (**Figure 2.2**).

— Toggle between views

Figure 2.2 To change between a single- and double-column Tools panel, click the double triangles in the panel's upper-left corner.

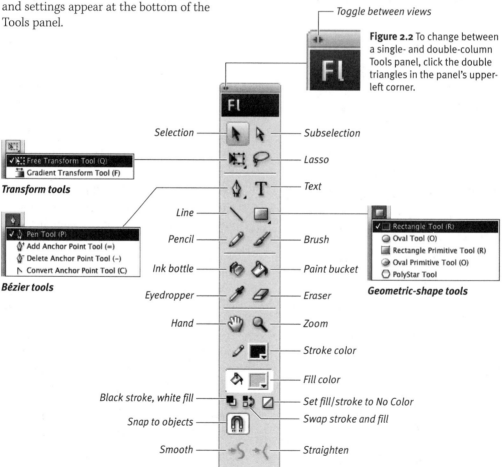

Selection — Subselection
Free Transform Tool (Q)
Gradient Transform Tool (F)
Transform tools
Lasso
Text
Pen Tool (P)
Add Anchor Point Tool (=)
Delete Anchor Point Tool (–)
Convert Anchor Point Tool (C)
Bézier tools
Line
Pencil — Brush
Ink bottle — Paint bucket
Eyedropper — Eraser
Hand — Zoom
Stroke color
Fill color
Black stroke, white fill — Set fill/stroke to No Color
Snap to objects — Swap stroke and fill
Smooth — Straighten

Rectangle Tool (R)
Oval Tool (O)
Rectangle Primitive Tool (R)
Oval Primitive Tool (O)
PolyStar Tool
Geometric-shape tools

Figure 2.1 The Tools panel contains tools for drawing, editing, and manipulating graphic elements in Flash. Click the current transform-tool icon to view the free-transform and gradient-transform tools; click the current Bézier-tool icon to view the pen and path-editing tools; click the current geometric-shape–tool icon to choose the rectangle, oval, rectangle-primitive, oval-primitive, or polystar tool.

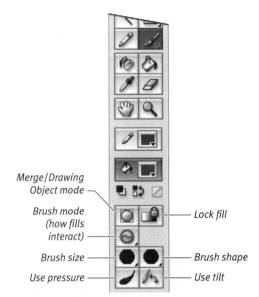

Merge/Drawing
Object mode

Brush mode
(how fills
interact)

Brush size ——————— Brush shape

Use pressure ——————— Use tilt

Lock fill

Figure 2.3 When you select a tool, its modifiers appear at the bottom of the Tools panel. Here the settings for using the brush appear. Click a button to toggle settings such as Merge mode; select a setting from a menu, such as Brush mode.

To access tools and options:

1. With the Tools panel open, click a tool—for example, the brush tool.

The relevant modifiers for the selected tool appear at the bottom of the panel.

2. Click a button or select an option to modify the way the selected tool works (**Figure 2.3**).

✔ Tips

■ Flash's default setting makes tool tips active (when the pointer hovers over a tool, an identifying label appears). You can change the tool tip setting in the Preferences dialog: Select the General category, select (or deselect) the Show Tooltips check box, and click OK to close the dialog. (For details on opening the Preferences dialog, see Chapter 1.)

■ In addition to displaying tool names, tool tips show keyboard shortcuts. As you get more familiar with the tools, activating them from the keyboard will speed your operations.

■ To close the open Tools panel (or open it when it's closed), Choose Window > Tools.

■ The single-column Tools panel is very narrow, making it a good candidate for double-docking. Drag another panel window to the edge of the Tools panel to double-dock the two (for more details on docking, see Chapter 1).

TOURING THE TOOLS

Creating Solid Colors and Gradients

Although you can define fill and stroke colors from most color controls (see the sidebar "The Mystery of Color Controls"), the Color panel gives you the widest variety of options for defining fill and stroke colors. You can choose colors visually, by clicking a graphic representation of a *color space*—all the available colors in a given color-definition system; or you can choose colors numerically, by entering specific values for color components. You can also set a color's transparency in the Color panel. To define new gradients, you must use the Color panel.

Before you define a color or gradient, you must choose whether the color or gradient applies to fills or strokes by activating the Fill Color control or the Stroke Color control. As you define new colors, Flash updates all the related color controls. If you define a new fill color, for example, that color becomes the current setting for all the tools that use fills.

To assign solid-color attributes in the Color panel:

1. Access the Color panel (if it's not open, choose Window > Color).

2. From the Type menu, choose Solid.

3. To choose a color space, from the panel's options menu, choose one of the following:

   ▲ To define colors as mixtures of red, green, and blue, choose RGB.

   ▲ To define colors by percentage of hue, saturation, and brightness, choose HSB (**Figure 2.4**).

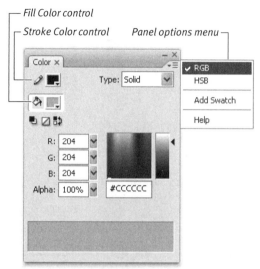

Fill Color control

Stroke Color control *Panel options menu*

Figure 2.4 The Color panel lets you choose a color from the color-space window or enter values directly to define a color in the RGB or HSB color space. Choose the desired color space from the panel's options menu.

What Are Hex Colors?

The term *hex color* is short for *hexadecimal color*, which is a fancy way of saying "a color defined by a number written in base 16." Hexadecimal coding is the language of bits and bytes that computers speak.

Hex coding is the way to specify color in HTML. In Flash, entering a single hex code for your color may be easier than entering three different values for red, green, and blue (RGB).

If you remember studying bases in high-school math, you'll recall that the decimal system is base 10, represented by the numbers 0 through 9. In hex color, to get the extra six digits, you continue coding with letters A through F.

CREATING SOLID COLORS AND GRADIENTS

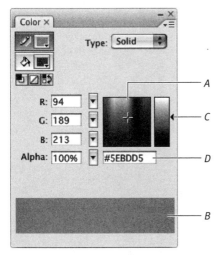

Figure 2.5 The Color panel displays a color-space window (A), a preview window for the new color (B), a luminosity/lightness slider (C), and a text field for entering the precise hex value of a color (D). Click in the color-space window to choose a new color visually.

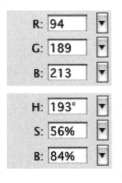

Figure 2.6 Enter RGB values to specify the amount of red, green, and blue that make up the color. Enter HSB values to specify the color by hue, saturation, and brightness. The new color appears in the selected color control.

4. To determine where Flash applies the new color, do one of the following:

   ▲ To set a new stroke color, choose the Stroke Color control by clicking the pencil icon.

   ▲ To set a new fill color, choose the Fill Color control by clicking the paint-bucket icon.

To define a new color visually in the Color panel:

1. With the Color panel open, choose a color space.

2. Position the pointer over the desired hue in the color-space window.

3. Click.

   Flash places a crosshair cursor in the window where you clicked and selects the color within the crosshairs (**Figure 2.5**).

✔ Tip

■ If you have trouble clicking exactly the right color, click and drag around within the color-space window. A preview of the new color appears above the old color in the preview window. When the color you want appears, release the mouse button. Flash enters the values for that color in the appropriate fields.

To define a new color numerically in the Color panel:

1. With the Color panel open, choose a color space.

2. To define a new color, do one of the following:

   ▲ For RGB colors, enter values from 0 to 255 for red, green, and blue in the R, G, and B fields (**Figure 2.6**).

   ▲ For HSB, enter values for hue, saturation, and brightness in the H, S, and B fields.

To define a color's transparency:

1. With the Color panel open, define a color.

2. Enter a value in the Alpha field
(**Figure 2.7**).

   A value of 100 (100 percent) results in a completely solid color; a value of 0 results in a completely transparent color.

To create a linear gradient:

1. Open the Color panel.

2. From the Color panel's Type menu, choose Linear (**Figure 2.8**).

   The tools and options for defining gradients appear (**Figure 2.9**). The default gradient starts with two pointers, black on the left and white on the right.

3. For Overflow, leave the default setting, Extend (on the Mac the Overflow menu setting is labeled Extend; in Windows, the menu is iconic and the Extend setting appears as a black-to-white gradient).

   Overflow determines how gradient colors fill a shape when you resize the gradient to be narrower than the shape it fills (to learn about resizing gradients, see Chapter 4).

4. To add a new color to the gradient, do the following:

   ▲ Position the mouse pointer on or below the gradient-definition bar.

   Flash adds a plus sign to the pointer, indicating that you can add a new gradient pointer in this area.

   ▲ Click anywhere along the gradient-definition bar.

   Flash adds a new gradient pointer.

5. To change the color of a gradient pointer, click it to select it, and define a new color using any of the methods described in the preceding section.

Figure 2.7 Enter an Alpha value of less than 100 percent to define a transparent color.

Figure 2.8 Choose Linear from the Type menu to access the tools for defining linear gradients.

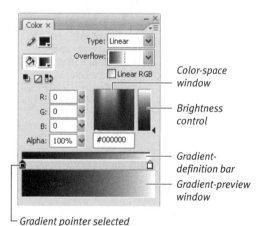

Color-space window

Brightness control

Gradient-definition bar

Gradient-preview window

Gradient pointer selected

Figure 2.9 When you choose Linear or Radial as the Type, the Color panel displays the gradient-preview window, gradient-definition bar, and a color-space window.

Gradient starts with white and blends first to gray and then to black

Move pointers in to increase width of outside bands

Click to add pointers

Figure 2.10 Choose a color for each gradient pointer. The colors and positions of the pointers on the bar define a gradient's color transitions. Place pointers closer together to make the transition between colors more abrupt; place them farther apart to spread the transition out over more space.

or

Double-click the gradient pointer to open a pop-up swatch set, and do one of the following:

▲ Click a swatch to copy the swatch color.

▲ Click an item on the desktop to copy its color.

▲ Enter a new value in the Hex field.

▲ Click the Color Picker button in the upper-right corner of the pop-up swatch set to access the System Color Picker for assigning new colors.

6. To remove a color from the gradient, drag its pointer downward, away from the gradient-definition bar. The pointer disappears as you drag. The gradient preview changes to blend the colors in the remaining gradient pointers.

7. Repeat steps 4 through 6 to create the colors you want in your gradient.

You can add up to 13 pointers (for a total of 15 colors) to a gradient.

8. Drag the pointers to position them on the gradient-definition bar (**Figure 2.10**).

As you modify the gradient, your changes appear in all the Color controls for strokes or fills, depending on whether you assigned the gradient to strokes or fills.

About Using the System Color Pickers

You can create colors in one of the System Color Pickers. These color pickers let you specify colors with a method that may be more to your liking than the RGB/HSB offered by the Color panel. The Windows System Color Picker lets you specify colors according to Hue, Saturation, and Luminosity values. The Macintosh OS offers five different System Color Pickers, including one with CMYK sliders. To access the System Color Picker(s), Option–double-click (Mac) or Alt–double-click (Windows) the Fill Color or Stroke Color control in the Color panel, Tools panel, or Properties tab of the Property inspector. You can also access the System Color Picker(s) by clicking the color control once, to open the swatch set, then clicking the Color Picker button in the upper-right corner.

To create a radial gradient:

1. Open the Color panel.

2. From the Type menu, choose Radial.

   The tools for defining circular gradients appear. The gradient-definition bar looks the same as it does for linear gradients, but the preview shows your gradient as a set of concentric circles (**Figure 2.11**). The leftmost pointer defines the inner ring; the rightmost pointer defines the outer ring.

3. Follow steps 3–8 of the previous task, "To create a linear gradient," to define the color transitions in the radial gradient.

✔ Tips

- To modify an existing gradient, choose it in the Swatches panel. Flash switches the Color panel to gradient mode and displays the selected gradient. Now you can make any changes you need.

- Gradients can have transparency. You simply use a transparent color in one or more gradient pointers (see "To define a color's transparency," earlier in this chapter). If a gradient has transparency, a grid shows up in the gradient pointer, in the Fill Color or Stroke Color control, and in the transparent part of the gradient in the preview window (**Figure 2.12**).

- Each pointer in a gradient can have a different alpha setting. To create fade effects, try creating a gradient that blends from a fully opaque color to a transparent one.

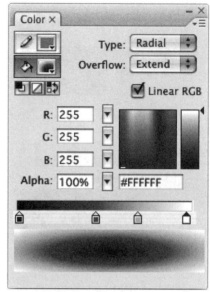

Figure 2.11 Choose Radial from the Type menu to create a circular gradient. The preview window translates the horizontal gradient-definition bar into the appropriate circular color transitions.

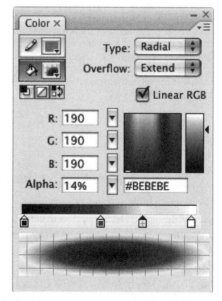

Figure 2.12 When transparent colors make up part of a gradient, grid lines appear in the gradient pointer, the Fill Color or Stroke Color control, and the gradient-preview window.

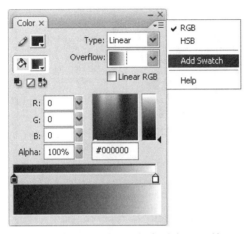

Figure 2.13 The options menu in the Color panel has a command for adding the current color to the Swatches panel.

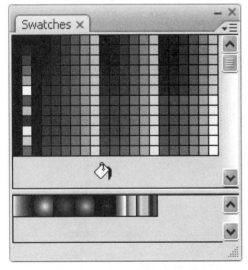

Figure 2.14 Positioning the pointer over a blank spot in the Swatches panel changes the pointer to a paint bucket. Click to add whatever color is currently specified in the Color panel. Solid color swatches are added to the upper half of the Swatches panel; gradient swatches, to the lower half.

Working with Swatches

You can save a new color or gradient for the duration of your work session by adding the color currently displayed in the Color panel to the Swatches panel. The Fill Color and Stroke Color controls found in the Tools panel, in the Properties tab of the Property inspector, and in the Color panel also give you quick access to the current set of swatches..

To add a color or gradient to the Swatches panel:

1. Create a new color or gradient using any of the techniques outlined in the preceding sections.

2. In the Color panel, do either of the following:

   ▲ From the options menu, choose Add Swatch (**Figure 2.13**).

   ▲ Position the pointer over the blank area of the Swatches panel; when the paint-bucket pointer appears, click.

   Flash adds the new solid color or gradient to the appropriate section of the Swatches panel (**Figure 2.14**).

✔ Tips

■ You can add new colors to the Swatches panel even if it's closed. But if you want to get feedback when you add a swatch, open the Swatches panel. Resize the panel window so that a bit of space appears below the existing swatches.

■ To remove a swatch from the Swatches panel, select a swatch, and from the panel's options menu, choose Delete Swatch.

■ If the swatches in the Swatches panel are too small for you, resize the panel. The swatches grow bigger as the window widens.

WORKING WITH SWATCHES

Creating Color Sets

Flash stores a default set of colors and gradients in the system color file, but it stores the colors and gradients used in each document with that document. Flash lets you define what colors and gradients make up the default set. In addition, you can create and save other color sets and load them into the Swatches panel. This practice makes it easy to maintain a consistent color palette when you're creating several documents for use in a single movie or on a single Web site.

To define a new set of colors:

1. Define the colors and gradients for your color set (see "Creating Solid Colors and Gradients," earlier in this chapter).

   You don't need to define them all at once, but after you have a set you want to save, go to step 2.

2. Access the Swatches panel.

3. From the panel's options menu, choose Save Colors (**Figure 2.15**).

   The Export Color Swatch dialog appears (**Figure 2.16**).

4. Navigate to the folder where you want to store your color set.

5. Enter a name for the color set in the Save As (Mac) or File Name (Windows) field.

6. From the Format (Mac) or Save As Type (Windows) pop-up menu, choose one of two formats:

   ▲ To save colors and gradients in Flash's proprietary Flash Color Set (CLR) format, choose Flash Color Set.

   ▲ To save the colors in Color Table (ACT) format, choose Color Table.

   The ACT format saves only colors (not gradients) but lets you share color sets with other programs, such as Adobe Fireworks.

7. Click Save.

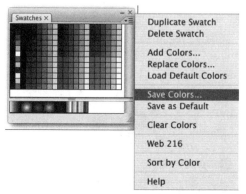

Figure 2.15 The options menu in the Swatches panel offers commands for working with color sets.

Figure 2.16 To save a set of colors for reuse, in the Export Color Swatch dialog, choose Flash Color Set from the Format menu (Mac, top) or Save As Type menu (Windows, bottom).

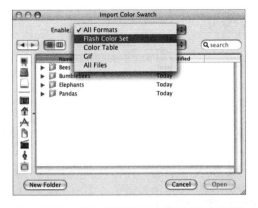

Figure 2.17 To reload a saved set of colors, in the Import Color Swatch dialog, choose Flash Color Set from the Enable menu (Mac, top) or Files of Type menu (Windows, bottom).

✔ Tip

■ The options menu in the Swatches panel also offers some handy shortcuts for dealing with color sets. To reload the default color set, choose Load Default Colors. To remove all color swatches from the current panel window, choose Clear Colors. To load the standard Web-safe colors, choose Web 216. To arrange colors by hue, choose Sort by Color. (Note that you can't undo the color sorting. Be sure to save your current set of colors if there's any chance that you'll want to restore the unsorted order.)

To load a set of colors:

1. From the options menu in the Swatches panel, choose either of the following:

   ▲ To add to the color set currently displayed in the Swatches panel, choose Add Colors.

   ▲ To replace the entire set currently displayed in the Swatches panel, choose Replace Colors.

   The Import Color Swatch dialog appears (**Figure 2.17**).

2. To determine what types of files to display, from the Enable pop-up menu (Mac) or Files of Type (Windows) pop-up menu, choose one of the following:

   ▲ All Formats, which displays CLR, ACT, and GIF files

   ▲ Flash Color Set, which displays only CLR files

   ▲ Color Table, which displays only ACT files

   ▲ GIF, which displays only GIF files

   ▲ All Files, which displays files of any format

   Note that the Color Table and GIF formats are for color import only; these formats don't handle gradients. Flash Color Set handles both colors and gradients.

3. Navigate to the file you want to import.

4. Click Open.

Setting Fill Attributes

Flash offers five fill types: none, solid, linear gradient, radial gradient, and bitmap. You can create new fill colors and gradients in the Color panel (see "Creating Solid Colors and Gradients," earlier in this chapter). To assign colors or gradients to selected tools or graphic elements, you can use the Color panel; the Tools panel; or any fill-related Property inspectors, such as the one that accompanies the rectangle tool.

To assign fill colors from the Tools panel:

1. In the Tools panel, click directly on the color chip in the Fill Color control (the one identified by a paint-bucket icon).

   The Fill Color control highlights, the pointer changes to an eyedropper, and a set of swatches pops up (**Figure 2.18**).

2. To assign a new fill color or gradient, do one of the following:

   ▲ To assign a gradient, select one of the linear or radial gradient swatches.

   ▲ To select a solid color, click a solid swatch or an item on the Stage; the color directly below the tip of the eyedropper becomes the assigned fill color.

   ▲ To define a new fill color, enter hex values in the field above the swatches.

   ▲ To define transparency for the current fill color, enter a percentage less than 100 in the Alpha field and press Enter. Note, gradient fills do not have the transparency option in this control as transparency is a part of the gradient definition.

   The new color appears in all Fill Color controls (in the Tools panel, the Properties tab of the Property inspector, and the Color panel) and will be used by any of the tools that create fills.

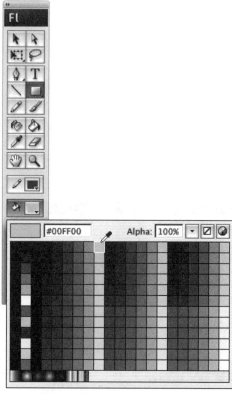

Figure 2.18 To set the fill color from the Tools panel, click the color chip in the Fill Color control. A set of swatches opens and you can choose the new fill color.

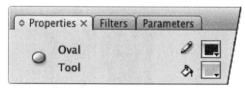

Figure 2.19 When nothing is selected on the Stage and you select a tool that creates fills, such as the oval tool, the Properties tab of the Property inspector displays a Fill Color control.

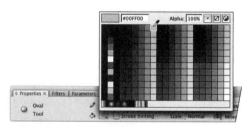

Figure 2.20 The color controls on the Property inspector work just like those in the Tools and Color panels. Click the color chip to access a set of color swatches.

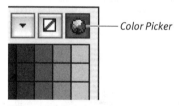

Color Picker

Figure 2.21 Click the Color Picker button to access the system's color picker(s) for defining a color that's not in the current swatch set.

To assign fill colors from the Properties tab of the Property inspector:

1. Access the Properties tab of the Property inspector.

2. In the Tools panel, select one of the tools that creates fills.

   The rectangle, oval, rectangle-primitive, oval-primitive, polystar, brush, and paint-bucket tools all create fills. When one of these tools is selected, the Properties tab of the Property inspector displays a Fill Color control (**Figure 2.19**).

3. In the Properties tab of the Property inspector, click directly on the color chip in the Fill Color control (the one identified by a paint-bucket icon).

   The current set of swatches appears (**Figure 2.20**).

4. To assign a new fill color, follow the instructions in step 2 of the preceding task.

✔ Tip

■ To access a System Color Picker for assigning fill colors, click the color chip in one of the Fill Color controls and then click the Color Picker button from the pop-up swatch window (**Figure 2.21**).

The Mystery of Color Controls

You'll find color controls—a color chip with an open-menu triangle in the lower right corner—throughout Flash. To operate a color control, click the color chip; a panel of color swatches pops up, and the pointer changes to an eyedropper. To assign a new color, position the pointer over a swatch and click the color you want; enter a new value in the Hex Color field; enter a transparency value in the Alpha field; choose No Color; or click the Color Picker button to access the System Color Picker(s). With many color controls you can also position the eyedropper pointer over an element on the Stage or desktop and click to select that color.

You can use any Stroke Color or Fill Color control to assign color attributes. The specs for the color you select appear in the Color panel, and all the other color controls update to match.

SETTING FILL ATTRIBUTES

Setting Stroke Attributes

A line has three main attributes: color, thickness (also known as *weight* or, in Flash, *stroke height*), and style. You set all three in the Properties tab of the Property inspector for any tool that creates strokes. The Properties tab of the Property inspector also lets you control the way the ends of lines (*caps*) look and the way lines connect (*joins*).

To set stroke properties:

1. With the Properties tab of the Property inspector open, in the Tools panel, choose a tool that creates strokes (the pen, line, rectangle, oval, rectangle-primitive, oval-primitive, polystar, pencil, and ink-bottle tools all create strokes).

   The Properties tab of the Property inspector for the selected tool appears, displaying the current settings for strokes.

2. To select a stroke color, do the following:

   ▲ In the Properties tab of the Property inspector (or in the Tools panel), click the Stroke Color control.

   The pointer changes to an eyedropper, and a set of swatches appears (**Figure 2.22**).

   ▲ Click the swatch with the desired color.

3. To set the stroke's weight, in the stroke-height field, enter a number between 0.25 and 200, or drag the slider next to the field (**Figure 2.23**).

4. To set the stroke's style, select a style from the stroke-style pop-up menu (**Figure 2.24**).

   There are seven styles to choose from: hairline, solid, dashed, dotted, ragged, stippled, and hatched.

   A graphic representation of your selected style appears in the stroke-style menu.

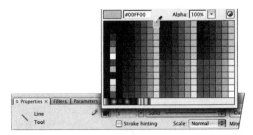

Figure 2.22 Clicking the Stroke Color control in the Properties tab of the Property inspector opens a set of color swatches and provides an eyedropper pointer for selecting a new color.

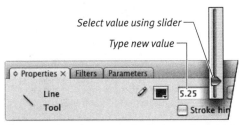

Select value using slider

Type new value

Figure 2.23 Entering a new value in the stroke-height field sets the weight, or thickness, for strokes created by tools that draw strokes.

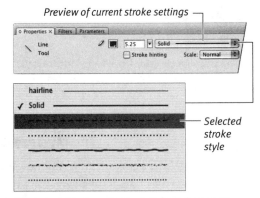

Preview of current stroke settings

Selected stroke style

Figure 2.24 Choose a stroke style from the pop-up menu in the Properties tab of the Property inspector.

None

Round

Square

Figure 2.25 Set a Cap style in the Properties tab of the Property inspector to control the look of the ends of lines. The None option keeps the line's original length and makes the end flat; Round extends and rounds the line's end; and Square extends and squares off the end.

Miter

Round

Bevel

Figure 2.26 Set a join style in the Properties tab of the Property inspector to control the way lines connect. Miter makes a clean pointed corner, Round makes a rounded corner, and Bevel slices a flat piece off the corner. The Cap and Join options are available only when the stroke properties are set to Solid or Hairline.

5. To set the way a solid or hairline stroke ends, from the Cap pop-up menu, choose a cap style.

▲ *None* ends the stroke exactly where you stop drawing it.

▲ *Round* extends the stroke by half the current stroke height, creating a rounded end.

▲ *Square* extends the stroke by half the current stroke height, creating a square end (**Figure 2.25**).

6. To set the way solid or hairline strokes meet, click the Join pop-up menu.

▲ *Miter* creates a sharp corner.

▲ *Round* creates a slightly curved corner.

▲ *Bevel* creates a slightly flattened corner (**Figure 2.26**).

✔ Tips

■ The Tools panel displays three buttons for setting basic stroke (and fill) colors quickly. Clicking the overlapping black and white squares sets the Stroke Color control to black (and the Fill Color control to white). Clicking the small squares with an arrow next to them makes the current stroke and fill colors change places. Clicking the square with the red line through it sets the currently selected color control (fill or stroke) to No Color.

■ In Flash, the hairline setting is considered a stroke style, not a stroke height. (Use the stroke-style pop-up menu to get the hairline setting.) Hairlines in a symbol don't change thickness when you resize the symbol. Other lines in a symbol grow thicker or thinner as you scale the symbol up or down. (To learn about symbols, see Chapter 7.)

continues on next page

SETTING STROKE ATTRIBUTES

- To constrain the way strokes scale in your published movie, with a stroke (or stroke-creating tool) selected, choose a setting from the Scale menu in the Properties tab of the Property inspector. In the default (Normal) mode, a 1-pixel stroke becomes a 2-pixel stroke if your final movie gets enlarged to 200 percent. To prevent a selected stroke from scaling at all, choose None. To allow the stroke to scale in one direction only, choose Horizontal or Vertical.

- Click the Stroke Hinting check box in the Properties tab of the Property inspector to ensure crisp lines in your final output. Without hinting, lines sometimes appear slightly blurry on some monitors.

- You can modify Flash's stroke styles. You might, for example, want larger dots in the dotted line or bigger spaces in the dashed line. Select a stroke-creating tool; in the Properties tab of the Property inspector, select the stroke style you want to modify, and then click the Custom button. The Stroke Style dialog appears, in which you can assign new settings. Click OK to close the dialog and confirm the settings. Those settings continue in force for that style until you change them or end the work session.

- You can also set stroke color from any Stroke Color control (in the Properties inspector, the Tools panel, or the Color panel). Click the Stroke Color control, and select a color as described in "Setting Fill Attributes," earlier in this chapter.

- You can set the Join property for rectangles created with the rectangle-primitive tool, but you'll only see the joins on sharp corners (those with a corner radius setting of 0).

Merge Drawing vs. Object Drawing vs. Primitive-Shapes

Flash CS3 creates three types of graphic objects: *merge-shapes* (also called raw shapes), *drawing objects,* and *primitive-shapes*. You can use most of the drawing tools to create merge-shapes or drawing objects simply by selecting the appropriate drawing mode. To create primitives, you must select either the rectangle-primitive or oval-primitive tool.

In **Merge Drawing** mode, the strokes and fills you create are raw shapes and are ready for editing directly on the Stage; raw shapes on a single layer interact with one another, dividing and replacing strokes and fills that overlap or intersect (you'll learn more about how shapes interact in Chapter 5).

continues on next page

Merge Drawing vs. Object Drawing vs. Primitive-Shapes *continued*

In **Object Drawing** mode, the strokes and fills you create are still directly editable on the Stage, but they don't interact with other shapes on the same layer. Shapes created in Object Drawing mode act somewhat as if they were isolated on a separate layer or protected using the Group command (you'll learn more about working with grouped shapes in Chapter 5 and about shapes on separate layers in Chapter 6). But shapes created in Object Drawing mode can be modified directly on the Stage (see Chapter 4), whereas grouped objects generally can't.

Primitive-shapes—those created with the rectangle-primitive and oval-primitive tools—do not interact with other shapes on the same layer. Behind the scenes, Flash creates these shapes in Object Drawing mode but locks and constrains them so that they always exhibit certain defining characteristics. Those characteristics are editable and appear as properties in the Property inspector when you select a primitive tool in the Tools panel or a primitive-shape on the Stage. You can edit these properties of a primitive anytime, but you can't freely edit a primitive the way you can edit a shape created in Merge/Object Drawing mode. For example, you can change the inner radius setting for on oval-primitive to transform a solid oval to a donut shape, but you can't edit an oval-primitive's outline to give it pointy ends and transform it into a football shape.

Flash's default mode for drawing tools is Merge Drawing. To turn on Object Drawing mode, select a tool that creates strokes and/or fills, and then click the Object Drawing button in the Tools panel (**Figure 2.27**). Once you activate Object Drawing mode for any tool, all tools that create strokes and fills are set to Object Drawing mode. To return to Merge Drawing mode, you must click the Object Drawing button again to deselect Object Drawing mode (or press J on the keyboard to toggle between Merge Drawing and Object Drawing). Whichever Merge/Object Drawing setting is active when you end a work session will be active the next time you open Flash. The Merge/Object Drawing mode button is absent from the Tools panel when you choose one of the primitive tools (**Figure 2.28**).

For many tasks, you'll see no difference between working with the three types of shapes; in some tasks, however, the difference is crucial. For the exercises in this book, unless otherwise noted, you can create shapes using either drawing mode or using the primitive-shape tools.

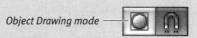

Object Drawing mode

Figure 2.27 You can set the drawing tools to create shapes that don't interact with other shapes on the same layer. Select Object Drawing mode in the Tools panel.

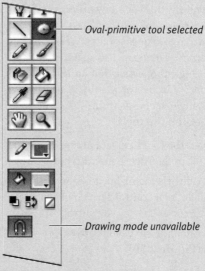

Oval-primitive tool selected

Drawing mode unavailable

Figure 2.28 The drawing-mode button does not appear in the Tools panel when you select the oval-primitive or rectangle-primitive tool.

Making Geometric Shapes

Flash provides separate tools for drawing ovals, rectangles, and polygons or stars. The tools work similarly; all can draw a shape as an outline (just a stroke) or as a solid object (a fill). You can also create a geometric shape with a fill and a stroke simultaneously. There are special properties that define rectangles and ovals that you can set as precise values in the Property inspector.

To create geometric outlines:

1. To select a geometric-shape tool, do the following:

   ▲ In the Tools panel, click the active geometric-shape tool.

   ▲ From the submenu that appears, choose a tool—for example, the oval tool (**Figure 2.29**).

2. In the Property inspector, enter values and choose settings for the properties you wish to control.

   When creating an outline shape, you may want to select new properties for the stroke's color, height, and style (see "Setting Stroke Attributes," earlier in this chapter). There are also specific oval and rectangle properties that appear in the Property inspector when you select the rectangle, rectangle-primitive, oval, and oval-primitive tools.

3. To set the tool to create an outline with no fill, in the Tools panel, do the following:

   ▲ Click the paint-bucket icon of the Fill Color control; Flash highlights Fill Color as the active control.

   ▲ Click the No Color button (**Figure 2.30**).

4. Move the pointer over the Stage.

   The pointer turns into a crosshair.

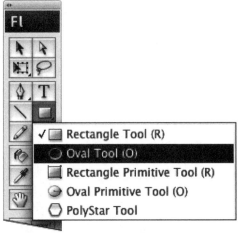

Figure 2.29 The Tools panel combines all the geometric-shape tools under a pop-up submenu. To view them all, click the geometric-shape tool that's visible, then click a tool to select it and close the submenu.

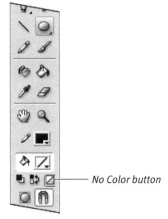

Figure 2.30 When the Fill Color control is selected in the Tools panel, selecting the No Color button allows whatever tool you select to create a shape with no fill.

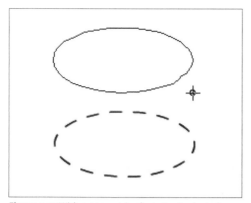

Figure 2.31 With a geometric-shape tool selected, click the Stage and drag to create an outline preview of a shape (top). Release the mouse button, and Flash creates a shape using the current settings for fills and strokes. In this case, the oval tool is set to black stroke color, no fill, dashed stroke style, and a stroke height of 1 point (bottom).

5. Click and drag to create the geometric shape (**Figure 2.31**).

Flash previews the shape as you drag.

6. Release the mouse button.

Flash draws an outline.

✔ Tips

- To draw a perfect circle (or square), hold down the Shift key while you draw with the rectangle, oval, rectangle-primitive, or oval-primitive tool.

- To make ovals (or rectangles) grow outward from the center point as you draw, position the pointer where you want the center of the shape to be; hold down the Option key (Mac) or Alt key (Windows) as you drag. Shapes drawn with the polystar tool always grow from the center.

What Makes a Primitive Different?

The properties for geometric shapes are the same whether you're creating a merge-shape/drawing-object or a primitive. In fact, behind the scenes, Flash uses a master template that specifies all the properties that define ovals and rectangles. The regular oval tool and the oval-primitive tool both create ovals from the same master template. Once you've drawn a merge-shape or drawing-object oval, however, the oval's connection to the master template is severed. The "oval shape" becomes a path that you can modify using the selection and subselection tools. An oval-primitive always retains a connection to its master template. You have access to some of the master-template properties via the Property inspector and the primitive's control points. The Property inspector reveals a bit of how the master-template connection (and disconnection) works. When you select the oval tool, for example, the Property inspector displays exactly the same properties and controls as when you select the oval-primitive tool. When you select an oval-primitive on the Stage, the Property inspector displays all of the shape's oval properties and controls; changing the controls that specifically define the shape as an oval (such as Start Angle, End Angle, and Inner Radius) modifies the shape interactively, but only within the parameters of the oval master-template. You can change the oval-primitive's inner radius, for example, but you can't freely transform an oval-primitive into an amoeba shape. When you select a merge-shape or drawing-object oval on the Stage, the Property inspector displays some of the shape's properties and controls (such as Stroke Color and Fill Color), but none of the controls that specifically define the shape as an oval. You can modify the merge-shape oval's path to create an amoeba shape, for example, but you can't interactively adjust the inner radius of a merge-shape oval. You can convert primitive-shapes into drawing-object or merge-shapes. You'll learn about modifying shapes in Chapter 4.

To create geometric fills:

1. To select a geometric-shape tool follow steps 1 and 2 in the preceding exercise. For this task, for example, select the rectangle tool.

2. To set the tool to create just a fill with no outline, in the Tools panel, do the following:

   ▲ Click the pencil icon of the Stroke Color control; Flash highlights Stroke Color as the active control.

   ▲ Click the No Color button (**Figure 2.32**).

3. Follow steps 4 through 6 in the preceding exercise.

   Flash draws a geometric fill, using the currently selected fill color (**Figure 2.33**).

✔ Tip

■ You can create polygons and star shapes with the polystar tool (choose it from the geometric-shape tool's submenu in the Tools panel). To set the number of sides in the polygon and to switch from polygons to stars, select the polystar tool and click the Options button in the Polystar Tool Properties tab of the Property inspector. The Tool Settings dialog appears. Enter values for the number of sides and how sharp the star points are, then click OK.

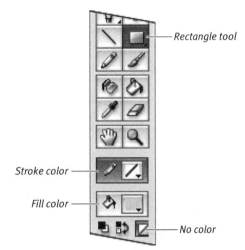

Rectangle tool

Stroke color

Fill color

No color

Figure 2.32 To create a geometric shape that's just a fill (no outlining stroke), in the Tools panel, select the Stroke Color control and click the No Color button.

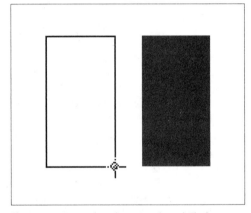

Figure 2.33 As you drag the rectangle tool, Flash creates an outline preview of a rectangle (left). To complete the fill shape, release the mouse button (right).

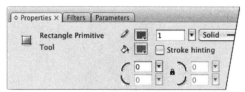

Figure 2.34 When you select the rectangle or rectangle-primitive tool, the Property inspector displays special properties for defining a rectangle. The properties are the same for both tools.

— Constrain corner radius

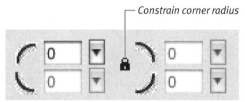

Figure 2.35 By default, the rectangle and rectangle-primitive tools create shapes whose corners all have the same radius. When the closed-lock icon appears, there is just one field for entering values and the settings are constrained.

Figure 2.36 When you select the oval or oval-primitive tool, the Property inspector displays special properties for defining an oval. The properties are the same for both tools.

— Drag slider to reposition control point

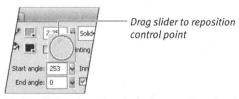

Figure 2.37 Entering values in the Start Angle and End Angle fields creates partial ovals like those often used in pie charts. Click the triangle to the right of the field to open a circular slider for entering values.

To set rectangle properties:

1. In the Tools panel, select the rectangle or rectangle-primitive tool.

   The Property inspector displays the tab for the selected tool (**Figure 2.34**).

2. To create a rectangle with four identical corners, set the Constrain Corner Radius button to the locked state (**Figure 2.35**).

   Clicking the lock icon toggles between the unconstrained (open-lock icon) and constrained (closed-lock icon) states.

3. To create a rectangle with rounded corners, in the Rectangle Corner Radius field enter a positive number.

   or

   To create a rectangle with indented corners, in the Rectangle Corner Radius field enter a negative number.

To set oval properties:

1. In the Tools panel, select the oval (or oval-primitive) tool.

   The Property inspector displays the tab for the selected tool (**Figure 2.36**). The properties are the same for both tools.

2. To create variations on the oval shape, in the Oval (Primitive) Tool tab of the Property inspector, do any of the following:

   ▲ To create pie-wedge shapes, in the Start Angle and/or End Angle field, enter a number from 0 to 360 (**Figure 2.37**).

   continues on next page

MAKING GEOMETRIC SHAPES

▲ To create open arcs, deselect the Close Path check box. When you create pie-wedge shapes, this setting creates an open path. Flash removes the shape's fill (if one is present) and deletes the straight line segments from the wedge shape (**Figure 2.38**).

▲ To create ovals with hollow centers, in the Inner Radius field, enter a number from 0 to 99.

Flash draws a hollow oval inside the first (**Figure 2.39**). The inner-radius setting corresponds to the percentage of the outer oval's "fill" that gets removed by the inside oval. (The outer oval may have a fill of No Color, in which case the inner oval just appears as an outline.)

✔ Tip

■ You can change an oval-primitive's start- or end-angle settings interactively. Select the shape on the Stage. In the Property inspector, click the triangle to the right of the Start Angle or End Angle field, and a circular slider appears. Click anywhere on the slider or drag the control point to change the setting; the shape on the Stage changes interactively. Press enter or click away from the slider to confirm the new value.

Shape with closed path

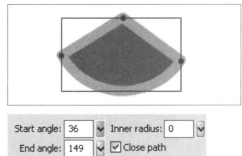

Shape with open path

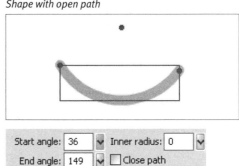

Figure 2.38 Deselecting the Close Path check box lets you create arcs out of pie-wedge oval shapes. If the shape has an inner-radius setting greater than o, in its open-path form, it appears as two arcs.

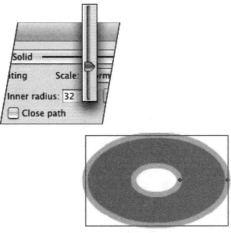

Figure 2.39 Entering a number greater than 0 in the Inner Radius field creates an oval with a hollow center.

The Mystery of Oval Angles

The Oval (Primitive) Tool tab of the Property inspector offers controls for start angle and end angle; the angle settings let you create pie-wedge shapes but can be a bit difficult to interpret at first. Imagine drawing a circle on the face of an analog clock. The start angle is the point where you put your pencil down to begin drawing; the end angle is the point where you lift the pencil and stop drawing. (When Flash creates oval-primitives on the Stage, it turns the start and end angles into control points that you can drag to modify the beginning and ending of the oval's outline.) The values you enter into the Start Angle and End Angle fields correlate to degrees of a circle. The value 0 corresponds to 3 o'clock, 90 to 6 o'clock, 180 to 9 o'clock, and so on; Flash draws clockwise when creating oval-primitives. When the start and end angle have the same value, both control points sit on the same spot, and the circle is complete. When the values differ, there's a gap in the circle. When you set the oval-primitive to be a closed path, Flash finishes the shape by drawing straight-line segments to the center of the oval, creating a pie-wedge. If the oval has an inner-radius value greater than 0, the segments connect with the inner oval, creating a C shape or a partial C shape (**Figure 2.40**). To get a feel for how this works, create an oval-primitive on Stage, then select it, and experiment with the various options in the Property inspector. Use the interactive start- and end-angle controls to see the relationship of angles to the clock face example above. Experiment with the inner radius and close-path settings as well.

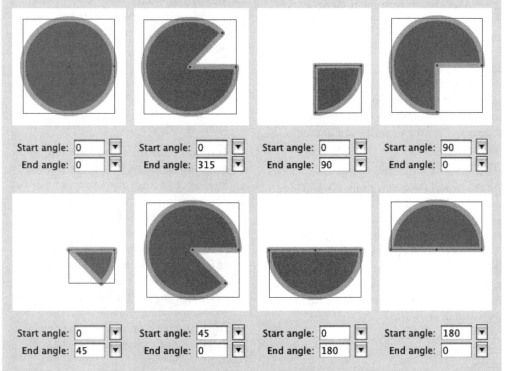

Figure 2.40 By changing the Start Angle and End Angle values in the Oval (Primitive) Tool tab of the Property inspector, you set the oval or oval-primitive tool to create partial circles and pie wedges.

Creating Free-form Shapes

Flash offers three tools for creating free-form shapes: the pencil, pen, and brush. The pencil and pen tools create stroke outlines, and the brush tool creates fills without strokes. The pencil and pen tools create only outlines, even if you draw a closed shape. Once you've created a shape, you can always modify it— say, to fill an empty outline or add an outline to a plain fill shape.

The pencil tool lets you draw lines (strokes) naturally, as you would with a real-world pencil, but using the mouse or a graphics tablet and pen. Flash hides information about the anchor points and curves of a stroke drawn with the pencil. With the pen tool, you place anchor points and adjust Bézier curves to create strokes. You can use the pen tool not only to create Bézier curves initially, but also to modify them once they are on the Stage. In addition there are three anchor-point tools for modifying Bézier curves on the Stage—the add-anchor-point tool, the delete-anchor-point tool, and the convert-anchor-point tool. In this chapter, you'll use the pen tool to create free-form shapes; in Chapter 4, you'll learn to use the pen tool and the anchor-point tools to modify shapes.

For the tasks below, make sure the grid is visible (see Chapter 1) and set drawing preferences as follows: choose Flash > Preferences (Mac) or Edit > Preferences (Windows) to open the Preferences dialog; choose Drawing from the Category list, and select the Show Pen Preview and Show Solid Points check boxes; leave the other items at their default settings.

About Drawing Assistance

Flash's pencil tool offers two assisted line-drawing modes: Straighten and Smooth. For total freedom in drawing, the pencil's Ink mode leaves shapes exactly as you create them.

Straighten mode refines any blips and tremors in a rough hand-drawn line into straight-line segments and regular arcs. This mode also carries out what Flash calls *shape recognition*. Flash evaluates each rough shape you draw, and if the shape comes close enough to Flash's definition of an oval or a rectangle, Flash turns your rough approximation into a shape neat enough to please your high-school geometry teacher.

Smooth mode transforms your rough drawing into one composed of smooth, curved line segments. Note that Smooth mode doesn't recognize shapes; it simply smoothes out the curves you draw. Smoothing reduces the number of points in a shape, resulting in smaller files and thus improving the performance of your final, published work.

Tolerance settings are all-important, especially for Straighten mode. You can set Flash to change almost anything ovoid into a circle and anything slightly more oblong into a rectangle. You set the degree of drawing assistance in the Preferences dialog. Choose Flash > Preferences (Mac) or Edit > Preferences (Windows); in the Preferences dialog that opens, choose Drawing from the Category list, and then choose tolerance levels from the Connect Lines, Smooth Curves, Recognize Lines, and Recognize Shapes menus. Click OK to close the dialog.

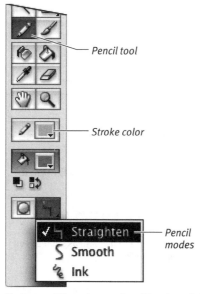

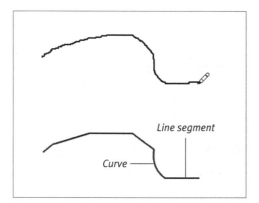

Figure 2.41 When the pencil tool is selected, the Tools panel displays a pop-up menu of pencil modes.

Figure 2.42 With the pencil in Straighten mode, when you draw a squiggle, Flash previews it for you. When you release the mouse button, Flash applies straightening, turning your rough squiggle (top) into a set of straight-line segments and smooth curves (bottom).

Figure 2.43 Select the pen tool to create paths.

To draw free-form strokes with the pencil tool:

1. In the Tools panel, select the pencil tool, or press Y.

2. From the Pencil Mode menu (**Figure 2.41**), choose one of the following assistance modes:

   Straighten resolves minor variations into straight-line segments.

   Smooth resolves minor variations into smooth curves.

   Ink provides very little assistance, leaving minor variations.

3. Move the pointer over the Stage.

   The pointer changes to a pencil icon.

4. Click, and draw a squiggle.

   Flash previews your rough line.

5. Release the mouse button.

   Flash recasts the line you've drawn according to the assistance mode you chose in step 2, creating a set of straight-line segments and regular curves (**Figure 2.42**).

✔ Tip

- You can apply smoothing and straightening (even shape recognition) after you've drawn an outline or shape by selecting it on the Stage and then clicking the Straighten or Smooth modifier of the Selection tool (you'll learn more about making and modifying selections in Chapter 4).

To draw free-form strokes with the pen tool:

1. In the Tools panel, select the pen tool; or press P, =, -, or C (**Figure 2.43**).

2. Set the stroke attributes for your path.

continues on next page

3. Move the pointer over the Stage.

The pen tool appears with a small *x* next to it (**Figure 2.44**). The *x* indicates that you're ready to place the first point of a path.

4. Click where you want your line segment to begin.

The pointer changes to a solid arrowhead; a small hollow circle indicates the location of the anchor point on the Stage.

5. Reposition the pen tool where you want your line segment to end.

Flash extends a preview of the line segment from the first point to the tip of the pen as you move around the Stage.

6. Click.

Flash completes the line segment using the selected stroke attributes. The anchor points appear as solid squares (**Figure 2.45**).

7. To add a straight segment to your line, click the Stage where you want the segment to end, and release the mouse button (**Figure 2.46**).

8. To add a curve segment, click the Stage where you want the curve segment to end, and then drag the pointer.

Flash places a preview point on the Stage, the pointer changes to a solid arrowhead, and Bézier handles (sometimes referred to as tangent handles) appear (**Figure 2.47**).

Figure 2.44 The *x* next to the pen tool indicates that you're about to start a new path. Click to place the first anchor point.

First point previewed   *Preview line segment*

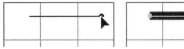

Click to place second point   *Completed line segment*

Figure 2.45 Flash previews points as you place them (top), and it adds a stroke to the path as soon as you complete a segment (bottom).

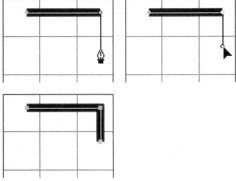

Figure 2.46 Continue clicking to add segments to your free-form shape. A quick click (top) adds a straight line segment (bottom).

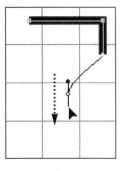

Figure 2.47 Click and drag to create a curve point; as you drag, the point's Bézier handles activate. The bulge of the curve grows away from the direction of your drag. For example, to make the curve bulge upward, drag downward.

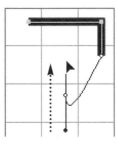

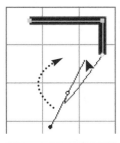

Figure 2.48 To make the curve bulge downward, drag upward. Dragging the handles out further deepens the curve.

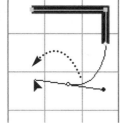

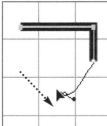

Figure 2.49 Move the handles clockwise or counter-clockwise around the point to modify the curve shape (top). Drag the handles in or out to make the curve deeper or shallower (bottom).

Figure 2.50 When you finish positioning handles for a segment and release the mouse button, Flash adds a stroke to the segment.

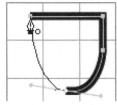

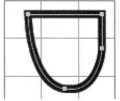

Figure 2.51 To create a closed shape, position the pointer over the first anchor point you placed. When you see the hollow-circle icon, click that first point (left). Flash adds the finishing segment, creating a closed path (right).

9. Drag the pointer in the opposite direction from which you want your curve to bulge.

The Bézier handles extend from the anchor point, growing in opposite directions as you drag. Flash previews the curve you're drawing (**Figure 2.48**).

10. Still keeping the mouse button down, drag the pointer to reposition the Bézier handle.

Dragging the handle clockwise or counter-clockwise around its anchor point controls the direction of the bulge; dragging the handle farther from the anchor point deepens the curve (**Figure 2.49**).

11. When the curve preview looks the way you want, release the mouse button.

Flash completes your curve segment with a stroke (**Figure 2.50**).

12. To create an open path, ⌘-click (Mac) or Ctrl-click (Windows) the Stage.

or

To create a closed shape, do the following:

▲ Position the pointer over your first anchor point.

▲ Flash previews the closing segment of your shape. A small hollow circle appears next to the pen tool (**Figure 2.51**).

▲ Click the first anchor point.

▲ Flash closes the shape, adding a stroke to the path.

Once the path is complete, the pen tool pointer displays a small *x*, indicating that the tool is ready to place the first anchor point of a new path.

✔ Tips

- There are other ways to end open paths. Choose Edit > Deselect All, or press ⌘-Shift-A (Mac) or Ctrl-Shift-A (Windows). In the Tools panel, click a different tool. You can also double-click the last point you placed. To use this technique you must be drawing a path that ends with a straight-line segment that doesn't involve Bézier handles.

- In previous versions, Flash would automatically fill a shape drawn with the pen tool, using the current fill color. In Flash CS3, you must use the paint-bucket tool to add a fill to a closed shape drawn with the pen.

- The pen tool can add to a line created earlier (**Figure 2.52**). To extend outward from the original line, position the pointer over the end of the line (the *terminal anchor point*). A modifier—a small slash—appears next to the pen icon. Click the terminal anchor point and the pen links to that point as if you'd just placed it; continue adding segments as you learned to do in the previous exercises. You can also join to an existing line during the process of creating a new line. Click to place the anchor points of the new line, but don't double-click to end the line. Instead, position the pointer over one of the terminal anchor points of the line you want to join. A modifier appears next to the pen icon; if you link to a merge-shape segment, the modifier is a small hollow circle; if you link to a drawing-object, the modifier is a chain-link icon. Click the existing terminal anchor point, and Flash joins the two lines.

Extend Line

Join Line

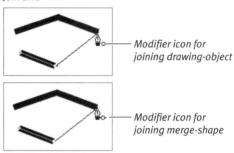

Modifier icon for joining drawing-object

Modifier icon for joining merge-shape

Figure 2.52 You can use the pen tool to add to existing line segments. Position the pointer over the end point of the existing line and click (top), then continue clicking to place more points. Or, place new points first, then position the pointer over the end point of the line you want to join (bottom). When the modifier icon appears, click to join the lines.

About Path Math in Flash

A *path*—a series of points and connecting lines—is the skeleton of your graphic-object. With most Flash tools, the math that goes into creating a path takes place behind the scenes. You draw a complete line or a shape; Flash places points (without showing them), connects them, and adds a stroke. With the pen tool, you place the defining points—called *anchor points*—and adjust the curve segments that connect them, using controllers called *Bézier handles* or *tangent handles*. When you've finished placing points with the pen tool, Flash fleshes out the path by applying a stroke to it.

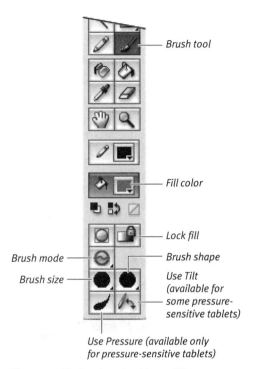

Brush tool

Fill color

Lock fill

Brush mode —— *Brush shape*

Brush size —— *Use Tilt (available for some pressure-sensitive tablets)*

Use Pressure (available only for pressure-sensitive tablets)

Figure 2.53 The brush tool and its modifiers.

Figure 2.54 The Brush Mode options give you control over how fills created with the brush tool interact with other shapes on the same layer. Choosing Paint Normal lets you paint merge-shape fills that act like any other fills when they overlap other shapes.

To create free-form solid fills with the brush tool:

1. In the Tools panel, select the brush tool or press B (**Figure 2.53**).

2. To optimize the brush for a particular painting task, in the lower portion of the Tools panel, select any of the following:

   ▲ From the Brush Size pop-up menu, choose a size for the brush tip.

   ▲ From the Brush Shape pop-up menu, choose a shape for the brush tip.

   ▲ From the Brush Mode pop-up menu, choose a painting mode; for this exercise, choose Paint Normal (**Figure 2.54**). The painting modes let you control how brushstroke fills act when you use the brush tool to paint over other shapes.

   Overlapping shapes interact in different ways depending on whether they are merge-shapes, drawing-objects, or primitives. (You'll learn about how overlapping shapes interact in Chapter 5.)

   ▲ To paint brushstroke fills that vary in thickness, choose Use Pressure. This option appears only when a graphics tablet is connected to your computer.

3. Select or define a solid fill color using any of the techniques outlined earlier in this chapter.

4. Move the pointer over the Stage.

   The pointer changes to reflect the current brush size and shape.

   continues on next page

5. Click and draw on the Stage.

Flash previews your brushwork in the currently selected fill (**Figure 2.55**).

6. When you complete your shape, release the mouse button.

Flash creates the final shape, smoothing it according to settings in the Property inspector (see the sidebar "The Mystery of Brush Smoothness Settings," later in this chapter).

✔ Tip

■ You can change the size of your brushstroke by changing the magnification at which you view the Stage. To create a fat stroke without changing your brush-tip settings, set the Stage view to a small percentage. To switch to a thin stroke, zoom out to a higher percentage (**Figure 2.56**). Be sure to check your work in 100% view.

Figure 2.55 Drawing with the brush creates a preview of your shape (left); Flash recasts the shape as a vector graphic with the currently selected fill color and smoothing settings (right).

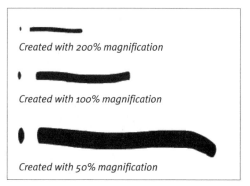

Created with 200% magnification

Created with 100% magnification

Created with 50% magnification

Figure 2.56 Flash created these three brushstrokes with exactly the same brush size—only the magnification level of the Stage was changed for each stroke.

About the Brush Tool

Flash's brush tool offers a way to create free-flowing swashes of color. These shapes are actually free-form fills drawn without a stroke. The brush tool lets you simulate artwork you'd create in the real world with a paintbrush or marking pen. A variety of brush sizes and tip shapes helps you create a painterly look in your drawings.

If you have a pressure-sensitive drawing tablet, the brush can interact with it to create lines of varying thickness, imitating the thick and thin lines of real-world brushwork. The more pressure you apply, the thicker the brushstroke (**Figure 2.57**).

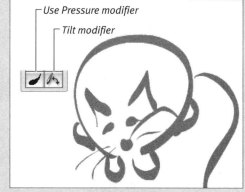

Figure 2.57 Selecting the brush tool's Use Pressure modifier activates the pressure-sensitive capabilities of a connected pressure-sensitive pen and graphics tablet. To produce lively lines of varying thickness, apply more or less pressure as you draw. Flash created all the lines in this cat with a single brush size and shape.

Figure 2.58 Deselect the Lock Fill modifier to paint with an unlocked gradient.

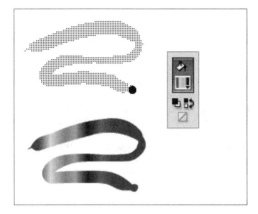

Figure 2.59 A brushstroke shape painted with an unlocked linear-gradient fill (top) and one painted with radial-gradient fill (bottom).

To paint with gradients:

1. Follow steps 1 and 2 in the preceding task.

2. Using one of the methods described earlier in this chapter, select (or define) a linear or radial gradient fill.

3. To lock or unlock the gradient, in the Tools panel, do either of the following:

   ▲ To paint shapes that contain the full gradient-spectrum, deselect Lock Fill (**Figure 2.58**).

   ▲ To paint shapes that reveal just a portion of the gradient (as if the shape were a window onto a gradient that filled the whole Stage area), select Lock Fill.

4. Paint with the brush as described in steps 4–6 in the preceding task.

   Flash can't preview the shape you paint with a gradient fill. The preview shape has a black-and-white pattern.

   Flash redraws the painted shape, using the current lock-fill and fill-color settings (see the sidebar "The Mystery of Gradients and Flash's Drawing Models," later in this chapter).

   For unlocked fills, the full gradient is visible in the shape (**Figure 2.59**).

   continues on next page

For locked fills, just a portion of the gradient is visible in the shape (**Figure 2.60**).

✔ Tips

■ Try painting a variety of brushstrokes in both drawing modes; use locked and unlocked gradients; use different areas of the Stage; and make the shapes different lengths. Notice the way each shape displays the gradient.

■ If the first gradient you paint in a work session has a locked fill, Flash puts the center of the underlying locked gradient along the left edge of the Stage. That means half the gradient lies on the Pasteboard, not on the Stage. To choose a different location for the center of a locked gradient, first use the brush tool to paint an unlocked gradient that's centered the way you want. When you switch to painting with Lock Fill active, the underlying locked gradient aligns with the last unlocked gradient you painted. You can then delete the unneeded unlocked gradient, use the paint-bucket tool to change it to a locked gradient (see Chapter 4).

■ After you've created a shape with a gradient fill, you can adjust the location of the center of the gradient by using the gradient-transform tool (see Chapter 4).

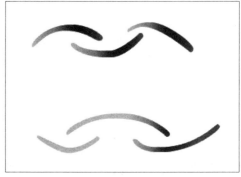

Figure 2.60 With the brush tool's Lock Fill modifier deselected, each brushstroke fill you paint contains the full range of the current gradient (top); with Lock Fill selected, each brushstroke fill appears to reveal a section of a gradient that runs the width of the Stage and the Pasteboard (bottom).

The Mystery of Gradients and Flash's Drawing Models

When you use the brush tool to paint a shape with a gradient fill and the Lock Fill modifier is deselected, it makes no difference if you're painting in Merge Drawing mode or Object Drawing mode. Flash centers the gradient in the shape's bounding box (an invisible rectangle that's just the right size to enclose the shape); the full gradient is visible in the shape.

When you paint the same kind of shape and Lock Fill is selected, however, shapes created in the two drawing modes behave differently.

For locked fills, Flash creates a virtual gradient that underlies the Stage and Pasteboard. (By default, Flash aligns the center of the locked gradient with the left edge of the Stage.) Each shape you create with a locked fill reveals just the portion of the gradient that corresponds to that area of the Stage. If you paint multiple merge-shapes with a locked gradient, the same virtual gradient underlies each shape; you can use the gradient-transform tool to shift the gradient within all the shapes. Multiple drawing-objects each have their own personal virtual gradient. These virtual gradients are all centered in the same way, so initially it looks as though there's one underlying gradient, as with merge-shapes. But the gradient-transform tool shifts the gradient in each drawing-object separately.

The Mystery of Brush Smoothness Settings

Flash gives you control over how your brushstrokes translate into vector shapes. To access this control, in the Properties tab of the Property inspector for the brush tool, enter a value in the Smoothing field. The stroke-smoothness setting determines how closely Flash re-creates each movement of the brush as a separate vector segment; the setting ranges from 0 to 100, and the default is 50. The lower the setting, the more faithfully Flash reproduces the shapes you draw. (It does this by using more vectors, which has an impact on the size and animation performance of your final file.) With a higher setting, Flash re-creates your flourishes more roughly, using fewer vectors.

To see the difference clearly, select the brush tool, assign a smoothing value of 1, and draw a curved line on the Stage. Now change the smoothing setting to 30. Draw a second curved line. Using the subselection tool (you'll learn about using this tool in Chapter 4), select each shape. The line drawn with smoothing set to 1 displays many more points—that is, it contains many more vector segments.

Adding Strokes and Fills

As you've learned earlier in this chapter, you can use the line, pencil, pen, and geometric-shape tools to create outline shapes—strokes without fills. To create fill shapes that have no stroke outline, you use the brush, pen, and geometric-shape tools. At any point you can add the missing element to such shapes. The ink-bottle tool adds strokes that outline plain fill shapes; the paint-bucket tool adds fills inside plain outline shapes. (You can also use these tools to modify strokes and fills; see Chapter 4.)

To add strokes to fills:

1. On the Stage, draw a fill that has no stroke, or work with an existing unstroked shape.

   For a merge-shape, make sure the fill is deselected; for a drawing-object, the fill can be selected or deselected.

2. In the Tools panel, select the ink-bottle tool or press S (**Figure 2.61**).

3. In the Ink Bottle Tool Properties tab of the Property inspector, set the desired stroke attributes (see "Setting Stroke Attributes," earlier in this chapter).

4. Position the pointer over a fill shape that has no stroke.

   The pointer appears as a little ink bottle, spilling ink.

Ink bottle ——

Figure 2.61 The ink-bottle tool applies all the stroke attributes currently set in the (Ink Bottle Tool) Properties tab of the Property inspector.

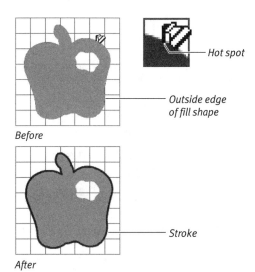

Before

Hot spot

Outside edge
of fill shape

After

Stroke

Figure 2.62 As you move the ink bottle over a filled shape, the hot spot appears as a white dot at the end of the ink drip that's spilling out of the bottle. To add a stroke around the outside edge of your fill shape, position the hot spot along that edge (top) and then click. Flash adds a stroke with the current attributes set in the (Ink Bottle Tool) Properties tab of the Property inspector (bottom).

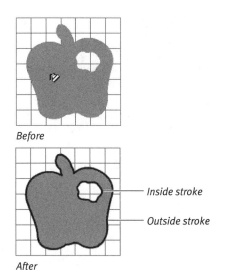

Before

Inside stroke

Outside stroke

After

Figure 2.63 Position the ink bottle's hot spot in the middle of your fill shape (top), and then click. Flash uses the current stroke attributes to add a stroke around the outside and inside of your shape (bottom).

5. With the ink bottle's hot spot, click a fill shape in one of the following ways:

▲ To add a stroke around the outside of your shape, click near the outside edge of the shape (**Figure 2.62**).

▲ To add a stroke around the inside of a shape that has a hole cut out of it, click near the inside edge of the shape.

▲ To outline both the outside of a shape and the hole inside the shape, click in the middle of the shape (**Figure 2.63**).

Flash adds strokes to the outside edge, inside edge, or both, using the Properties tab of the Property inspector's current settings for color, thickness, and style.

✔ Tips

■ Flash lets you use gradients for strokes. In step 3 of the preceding task, in the Properties tab of the Property inspector, choose a linear or radial gradient from the Stroke Color control's pop-up swatch set. Why might you want a gradient stroke? For an oval shape, adding a thick stroke with a radial gradient can help create the illusion of 3D depth or make the shape appear to glow.

■ Another way to "add" missing strokes to drawing-objects and primitive-shapes is to modify them using the Property inspector. First select the drawing-object or primitive on the Stage. Then change the stroke properties, including color, in the Property inspector. You can use this technique to add strokes to multiple drawing-objects and/or primitives (the technique doesn't work for merge-shapes, however). You'll learn more about modifying graphic objects in Chapter 4.

ADDING STROKES AND FILLS

To fill an outline shape with solid color:

1. On the Stage, draw an outline stroke that has no fill, or work with an existing outline shape.

The outline can be selected or deselected.

2. In the Tools panel, select the paint-bucket tool, or press K (**Figure 2.64**).

3. From the Gap Size menu in the Tools panel, choose the amount of assistance you want (**Figure 2.65**).

If you draw your shapes precisely, medium or small gap closure serves you best; you don't want Flash to fill areas that aren't meant to be shapes. If your drawings are rougher, choose Close Large Gaps. This setting enables Flash to recognize less-complete shapes.

4. From any Fill Color control, select a solid fill color.

5. Place the paint bucket's hot spot (the tip of the drip of paint) inside the outline shape (**Figure 2.66**).

6. Click.

The shape fills with the currently selected fill color (**Figure 2.67**).

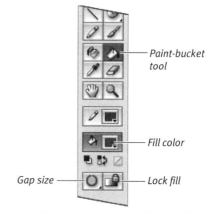

Paint-bucket tool

Fill color

Gap size — Lock fill

Figure 2.64 The paint-bucket tool and its modifiers.

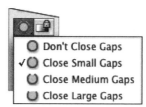

Don't Close Gaps
✓ Close Small Gaps
Close Medium Gaps
Close Large Gaps

Figure 2.65 The Gap Size menu controls Flash's capability to fill shapes that aren't fully closed.

Figure 2.66 The hot spot on the paint-bucket tool is the little drip at the end of the spilling paint. The hot spot changes to white when you move the paint bucket over a darker color.

Figure 2.67 Clicking inside an outline shape with the paint bucket (top) fills the shape with the currently selected fill color (bottom).

ADDING STROKES AND FILLS

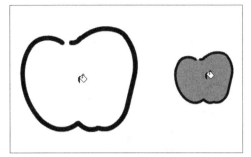

Figure 2.68 The paint bucket can't fill this apple shape with the setting of Close Large Gaps and a magnification of 100 percent (left). But in a 50 percent view, the paint bucket with the same large-gap closure setting recognizes this shape as complete and fills it.

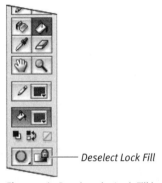

— Deselect Lock Fill

Figure 2.69 Deselect the Lock Fill button to fill a shape with an unlocked gradient.

✔ Tips

■ You may be unaware that your shape has any gaps. If nothing happens when you click inside a shape with the paint bucket, try changing the Gap Size setting in step 3.

■ Gap-closure settings are relative to the amount of magnification you're using to view the Stage. If the paint bucket's largest gap-closure setting fails at your current magnification, try again after reducing magnification (**Figure 2.68**).

■ Another way to "add" missing fills to drawing-objects and primitives is to modify them using any Fill Color control. First select the outline drawing-object or primitive on the Stage. Then choose a color from the Fill Color control in the Tools, Color, or Property inspector panel. You can use this technique to add fills to multiple drawing-objects and/or primitives (the technique doesn't work for outline merge-shapes, however). You'll learn more about modifying graphic objects in Chapter 4.

To fill outline shapes with unlocked gradients:

1. In the Tools panel, select the paint-bucket tool.

2. In the Color panel, define a new gradient (see "Creating Solid Colors and Gradients," earlier in this chapter),

   or

   From any Fill Color control, select an existing linear or radial gradient (see "Setting Fill Attributes," earlier in this chapter).

3. In the Tools panel, make sure that Lock Fill is deselected (**Figure 2.69**).

continues on next page

ADDING STROKES AND FILLS

4. Follow steps 5 and 6 in the preceding task.

Each outline shape you click fills with the gradient currently displayed in the Fill Color control. If you chose a linear gradient in step 2, Flash centers the unlocked gradient within the outline shape (**Figure 2.70**). If you chose a radial gradient, the location you click with the paint bucket's hot spot determines where the center of the unlocked gradient appears (**Figure 2.71**).

To fill outline shapes with locked gradients:

1. Follow steps 1 and 2 in the preceding task.

2. In the Tools panel, select the Lock Fill button.

3. Follow steps 5 and 6 in "To fill an outline shape with solid color," earlier in this section.

Each outline shape you click fills with a portion of the gradient currently set in the Fill Color control (see the sidebar "The Mystery of Gradients and Flash's Drawing Models," earlier in this chapter).

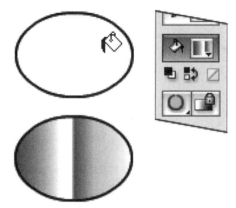

Figure 2.70 You can use the paint-bucket tool to apply a linear-gradient fill. An unlocked gradient is centered within the outline shape's bounding box.

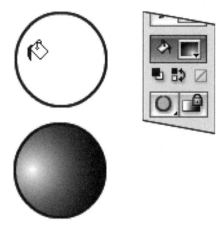

Figure 2.71 The paint-bucket tool can also apply a radial-gradient fill. Click where you want to locate the center of the gradient.

Gradients Add Overhead

Gradients can enhance the look of your graphics, but gradients increase file sizes and thereby slow the loading of published movies. Each area of gradient fill requires an extra 50 bytes of data that a solid fill doesn't need.

In addition, gradients take processor power. If you use too many, you may see slower frame rates, which translates to slower animations, in your finished movie.

WORKING WITH TEXT

Adobe Flash CS3 Professional's text tool doesn't just create graphic-objects in the shape of letters, it also creates text fields filled with live text; in the authoring environment, the contents of a text field are fully editable. As you create text elements, you must decide how they will be used in the published movie and assign them a type property. If you want the end user to interact with a text field (for example, to enter personal information), set the text field's type property to *input*. If you want to update the text at runtime (for example, using ActionScript to download and display new basketball scores to a sports site), set the type property to *dynamic*. If the text will just sit there looking pretty, set the type property to *static*.

Flash CS3 uses a text-rendering engine called Flash Type, which makes fonts more legible, especially at small sizes. This legibility shows up in the authoring environment, as you create your movies, but it also comes into play for your end users if you publish your files for Adobe Flash Player 8 or later (see Chapter 17).

In this chapter you'll learn about using static text. The manipulation of input and dynamic text fields requires a more advanced level of ActionScripting than this book can cover; if you need to know more, check out *Adobe Flash CS3 Professional; Visual QuickPro Guide* (Peachpit Press).

Using the Text Tool

The text tool creates blocks of editable text. You can set the text to read horizontally or vertically. You can also apply a variety of text attributes to text—including text and paragraph styles.

To create a single line of text for use as a graphic element:

1. In the Tools panel, select the text tool or press T (**Figure 3.1**).

   For this task, use the current settings for font and paragraph styles. You learn to change these settings in upcoming tasks.

2. Move the pointer over the Stage.

   The pointer turns into a crosshair with a letter *T* in the bottom-right corner (**Figure 3.2**).

3. Click the Stage at the spot where you want your text to start.

   Flash creates a resizable bounding box with a blinking insertion point, ready for you to enter text (**Figure 3.3**).

   Each corner of the box has a draggable resize handle; the round handle in the upper-right corner indicates that word wrap hasn't been set on this text field.

4. Start typing your text.

   The bounding box grows to accommodate whatever you type (**Figure 3.4**).

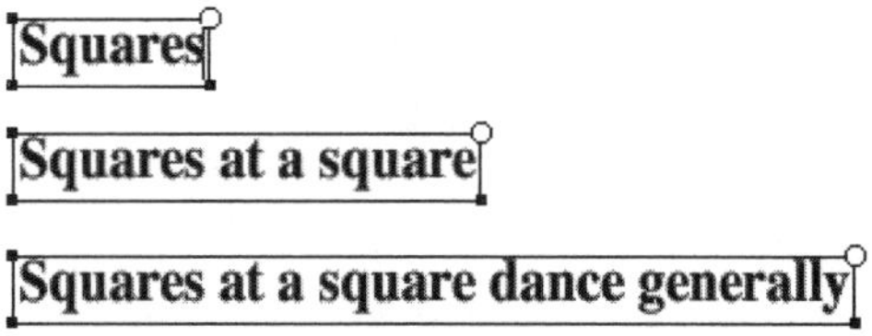

5. When you finish typing, click elsewhere on the Stage (or change tools) to deselect the text.

   Flash hides the bounding box, leaving just the text visible. When you click this text with the selection tool, Flash selects the text field so that you can reposition it, resize it, or change the text's attributes directly.

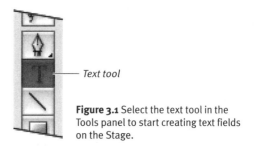

Figure 3.1 Select the text tool in the Tools panel to start creating text fields on the Stage.

Figure 3.2 The text-tool pointer.

Figure 3.3 Click the Stage with the text tool to create a text field. The round resize handle indicates that the text field does not have word wrap turned on.

Squares

Squares at a square

Squares at a square dance generally

Figure 3.4 As you type, the text field grows horizontally to accommodate your text. The text won't wrap.

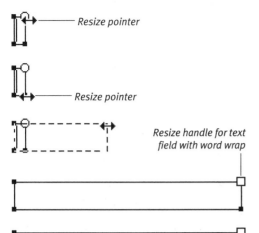

Resize pointer

Resize pointer

Resize handle for text field with word wrap

Squares at a square

Squares at a square dance

Squares at a square dance generally dance with squares|

Figure 3.5 Click and drag any resize handle of a text field's bounding box to create a text field with a specific width. The top-right handle changes to a square, indicating that the text you enter will wrap to fit the column width of the text field. The text field continues to grow in length—but not width—as you enter more text.

To create a text field with set width and word wrap:

1. With the text tool selected in the Tools panel, click the Stage at the spot where you want your text to start.

2. Move the pointer over any of the resize handles.

   The pointer changes to a double-headed arrow.

3. Click and drag one of the handles until the text field's bounding box is as wide as you want it (**Figure 3.5**).

   The resize handle in the upper-right corner changes to a square, indicating that word wrap is set for this text field.

4. Release the mouse button.

   The blinking insertion point appears in the text field.

5. Enter your text.

   Flash wraps the text horizontally to fit inside the column that the text field's bounding box defines. The box automatically grows longer (not wider) to accommodate your text.

✔ Tips

- To reposition a text field with the text tool active, position the pointer along the edge of the bounding box. The pointer changes to the selection arrow. Now you can drag the text field to a new location.

- To restore a text field to its original state (in which text doesn't wrap), double-click the square handle in the upper-right corner of the field's bounding box. It changes back to a circle, which indicates the text field will grow horizontally.

USING THE TEXT TOOL

Setting Text Attributes

You can set the attributes of your text in the context-sensitive Properties tab of the Property inspector. When you choose the text tool in the Tools panel, the Properties tab is labeled Text Tool; this tab provides options for setting font, size, style, spacing between letters, line spacing, and color; for controlling *tracking* (the amount of space between letters and words in a chunk of selected text); for defining text as superscript or subscript; and for creating live links between text and URLs. When you select an existing text field, the label for the Properties tab disappears, but the tab displays all the text-attribute options listed above and adds options for setting attributes of the text field itself, such as size and location on the Stage. When you need to distinguish one tab from the other, this book will refer to them as the Text Tool Properties tab and the Text Properties tab; when referring to either or both tabs, this book will call it the Text (Tool) Properties tab.

You can set attributes in advance so that as you type, the text tool applies them automatically, or you can apply attributes to existing text. The text tool always uses whatever settings currently appear in the Text (Tool) Properties tab (**Figure 3.6**).

For the following tasks, keep the Properties tab of the Property inspector open (choose Window > Properties > Properties if it's not already open).

✔ Tip

- In addition to setting text attributes in the Text (Tool) Properties tab, you can set the font, size, style, paragraph alignment, and tracking from the Text menu. You can use the Text menu to change the properties of selected text or to load text properties into the text tool.

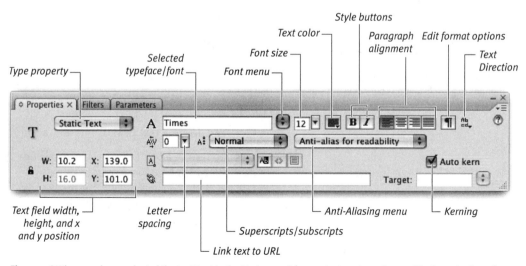

Figure 3.6 When you have selected the text tool in the Tools panel (or you have selected a text block on the Stage), the Properties tab of the Property inspector displays the type attributes to be created by the text tool (or applied to the current text selection).

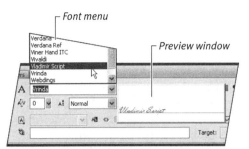

Font menu

Preview window

Figure 3.7 As you move the pointer through the font list in the Text (Tool) Properties tab of the Property inspector, you see a preview of each installed font.

Vertical Text

Using Flash's static text fields, you can create a single vertical text column, or create text that flows from column to column. You can set the columns to read left to right (as in English) or vice versa (as in Japanese text). With the text tool active, you can set the text-flow direction in the Properties tab of the Property inspector by choosing one of the vertical modes from the Change Orientation of Text menu (**Figure 3.8**). You work with vertical text fields just as you do with horizontal ones, resizing to set word wrap; in vertical text, the wrap forces words to the next column, not the next line. As you enter text, Flash places one character below another until the text reaches the bottom edge of the text field's bounding box, then text jumps to the next column. You can force text to flow to the next column by adding a paragraph return.

Figure 3.8 When you have selected the text tool or a text field, the Properties tab of the Property inspector displays a text-direction menu, with options for setting the direction in which your text flows.

To select text to apply character attributes:

♦ Do either of the following:

▲ With the text tool active, drag over existing text to highlight just a portion of text.

▲ With the selection tool active, click a text field to select all the text within it.

✔ Tips

■ You can select multiple text fields with the selection tool and modify them at the same time. (You'll learn more about selections in Chapter 4.)

■ The contact-sensitivity settings in the General category of the Preferences dialog also apply to selecting text fields with a selection outline. (You'll learn more about making such selections in Chapter 4.)

To choose an installed font:

1. Select the text you want to modify.

2. In the Text Properties tab of the Property inspector, click the scroll arrow to the right of the Font field.

   A scrolling list of your installed fonts appears, together with a font-preview window (**Figure 3.7**).

3. Move the pointer over a font name.

   Flash highlights the font name and displays its preview.

4. Click to select the currently highlighted font and close the scrolling list.

   The selected font name appears in the Font field. Flash changes the selected text to the new font.

✔ Tips

■ You can also enter a font by typing its name in the Font field in the Text (Tool) Properties tab. The field isn't case-sensitive, but you must type accurately. If you make a mistake in typing the name of an installed font, Flash assumes that it's dealing with a missing font and substitutes the system default font.

■ Another way to select a font is to choose it from the Text > Font menu.

■ You can allow end users to copy text from static text fields. During authoring, select the text that you want users to be able to copy. In the Text Properties tab of the Property inspector, click the Selectable Text button (the button labeled with the letters *Ab*, just below the pop-up menu for creating superscripts and subscripts).

The Mystery of Device Fonts

When you assign an installed font to a static text field, usually you want the text to look exactly the same during playback as it does during authoring. Yet you have no way of knowing if the font that you assigned is installed on the end user's system. In order to re-create your static text field font accurately during playback, Flash saves information about the outlines of the letter forms with the published (SWF) file (you'll learn more about publishing files in Chapter 17). During playback, Flash Player uses those outlines to draw the letters correctly. Saving outline information increases the size of your SWF file. Device fonts allow you to eliminate that information. You can apply device fonts two ways: Select one from a font menu, or choose Use Device Fonts from the Anti-Aliasing menu in the Text (Tool) Properties tab of the Property inspector.

By choosing a device font from one of the font menus, you retain some control over the look of the text the end user sees, but you give up the use of a specific font. Three device fonts appear in the font menu in the Text (Tool) Properties tab and the Text > Font menu: _sans, _serif, and _typewriter. During movie playback of static text for which you chose a specific device font, the end user's system supplies a font that has the same type style. For static text set as _serif, the end user's system supplies a font with *serifs*, those little hooks and tails you see at the ends of some letters' strokes in fonts such as Times Roman. For _sans (short for *sans serif*, or "without serifs"), the end user's system supplies a plainer font, one without hooks and tails; Helvetica and Arial are good examples. For _typewriter, the end user's system supplies a *monospaced* font (one in which each letter form takes up the same amount of space, like the letters on a typewriter); Courier is one example.

Choosing a specific font for your static text and then choosing Use Device Fonts from the Anti-Aliasing menu in the Text (Tool) Properties tab of the Property inspector gives the end user's system the greatest liberty in choosing a substitute font. The system looks for the closest match from its installed fonts, but there's no guarantee that it will substitute a font with the same style as the font you originally specified.

Although the use of Device Fonts helps keep your SWF files slim, the results are often unattractive. If you want to try this option, be sure to test your published movie on a variety of systems to get an idea of what your users might actually wind up seeing. The savings in file size may not be worth the loss of quality.

Figure 3.9 Drag the font-size slider to change the point size of selected text interactively on the Stage.

The Mystery of Anti-aliasing

Anti-aliasing is a method of *rendering* (drawing lines and curves) that softens edges. For text, this means making the letter forms appear slightly blurry. Anti-aliasing text at large point sizes makes it easier to read, but at smaller sizes, text may appear fuzzy and indistinct. In early versions of Flash, applying anti-aliasing to text in small sizes made that text difficult to read. Flash Type (the font-rendering engine found in Flash versions 8 and later) lets you apply anti-aliasing to small font sizes and still have readable text, provided the text isn't animated.

To set the font size:

1. Select the text you want to modify.

2. In the Text Properties tab of the Property inspector, double-click (or click and drag) in the Font Size field to highlight the current value.

3. Enter the desired point size.

4. Press Enter.

   or

1. Click the triangle to the right of the Font Size field.

   A slider pops open (**Figure 3.9**).

2. Drag the slider's lever to choose a value between 8 and 96 points.

   Flash previews the changes on the Stage as you drag the slider lever.

3. Click outside the slider to confirm the new font size.

✔ Tips

■ For even quicker changes, click and drag the slider triangle. When you release the slider's lever, Flash automatically confirms the new font size.

■ To enter font sizes outside the slider's range, you must type the value in the Font Size field.

■ You can also select a font size from the Text > Size menu.

To set the font-rendering method:

1. Select the text field you want to modify.

2. In the Text tab of the Property inspector, from the Anti-Aliasing menu (**Figure 3.10**), choose one of the following:

   Use device fonts. Choose this setting when smaller file sizes are more important than being able to re-create the precise font outlines on the end user's system (see "The Mystery of Device Fonts").

   Bitmap text (no anti-alias). Choose this setting when you want your text to have hard edges instead of softened (*anti-aliased*) edges. Fonts are embedded in your published movie, without anti-aliasing. (Bitmap text can greatly increase your SWF file size.)

   Anti-alias for animation. Choose this setting for animated text fields or when you plan to publish your movie to Flash Player 7 or earlier. Flash embeds font outlines for these text fields but ignores some information about aligning and kerning to help speed playback. Flash Type doesn't do the rendering.

   Anti-alias for readability. (This is the default setting for publishing to Flash Player 8 and later; see Chapter 17.) Choose this setting for text fields that you don't plan to animate. The Flash Type font-rendering engine draws text with this setting on the Stage as you create your FLA file. When you publish, Flash embeds the fonts in the SWF file. The Flash Type engine renders this text for playback.

   Custom anti-alias Choosing this setting gives you access to the Custom Anti-Aliasing dialog, where you can determine how soft and blurry the anti-aliased letter forms are. The dialog's Sharpness and Thickness settings control the transitional blurred area between each letter and the background against which it appears.

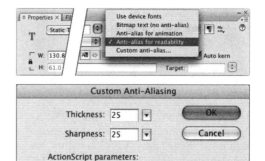

Figure 3.10 To control the degree of anti-aliasing, in the Text (Tool) Properties tab of the Property inspector, select an option from the Anti-Aliasing menu (top). The Custom Anti-Aliasing option gives you access to a dialog for setting more precise anti-aliasing controls (bottom).

✔ Tip

■ Even when you choose an option that evokes Flash Type anti-aliasing, certain situations cause Flash to turn off anti-aliasing. When you skew, flip, or distort a text field, Flash Type doesn't anti-alias that text. Flash Type doesn't work on fonts larger than 255 points. (Note that when you zoom in on a text field during authoring, you may effectively be asking to see fonts at a size larger than 255 points, even though the text field is set to a smaller point size.) In the published movie for Flash Player 8 or later (the SWF), anti-aliasing is applied; but when you view the magnified text on the Stage, you won't see anti-aliasing.

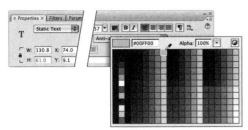

Figure 3.11 You can choose a color for text created with the text tool from the color control in the Text (Tool) Properties tab of the Property inspector.

Figure 3.12 Access bold and italic styles by clicking the Bold (left) and Italic (right) buttons in the Text (Tool) Properties tab of the Property inspector.

To choose a text color:

1. Select the text you want to modify.

2. In the Text Properties tab, click the Text (Fill) Color control (note that text in Flash is a type of fill).

   The standard color-control swatch set appears (**Figure 3.11**).

3. Select a color.

   Because Flash considers text to be a fill, you can change the text color by using any of the methods described for setting fill attributes in Chapter 2.

✔ Tip

■ Flash changes all the settings in the Text (Tool) Properties tab to match the attributes of selected text, which means that by selecting text, you load the text tool with that text's attributes. Keep blocks of text with formatting you use often on the Pasteboard, and click one to re-create its settings for the text tool quickly.

To choose a style:

1. Select the text you want to modify.

2. In the Text Properties tab of the Property inspector, do one of the following:

   ▲ To create boldface text, click the Bold button (**Figure 3.12**).

   ▲ To create italic text, click the Italic button.

   ▲ To create text that is both boldface and italic, click the Bold and Italic buttons.

✔ Tip

■ You can toggle boldface style by pressing Shift-⌘-B (Mac) or Ctrl-Shift-B (Windows). (Take special note of that Shift key if you're used to using another application for creating text: it's not part of the usual command.) To toggle italic, press Shift-⌘-I (Mac) or Ctrl-Shift-I (Windows).

To apply tracking (letterspacing):

1. Within a text field in a Flash document, select the text to track.

2. In the Text Properties tab's Letter Spacing field, enter the desired point size.

   A negative value reduces the space between the letters; a positive value increases it (**Figure 3.13**).

3. Press Enter.

   or

1. In the Text Properties tab's Letter Spacing field, click the triangle to the right of the field.

   A slider pops open.

2. Drag the slider's lever to a value between –60 and 60.

   Flash previews the changes interactively on the Stage as you drag.

3. Release the slider to confirm the new spacing.

✔ Tips

- To increase tracking of selected text, choose Text > Letter Spacing > Increase *or* press Option-⌘–right arrow (Mac) or Ctrl-Alt–right arrow (Windows). To decrease tracking, choose Text > Letter Spacing > Decrease, or use the keyboard commands with the left arrow. Add the Shift key to the keyboard shortcuts to double the amount of increase or decrease.

- You can also track interactively by using the keyboard shortcuts. The space between letters continues to expand or contract as long as you hold down the key combination.

- To reset the font's original letterspacing, choose Text > Letter Spacing > Reset *or* press Option-⌘–up arrow (Mac) or Ctrl-Alt–up arrow (Windows).

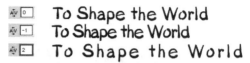

Figure 3.13 Enter a negative letter-spacing value to bring characters closer together. Enter a positive value to space characters out. Enter 0 to use a font's built-in tracking value.

What Is Kerning?

Whereas *tracking* affects the space between characters and words in an entire line or paragraph of text, *kerning* affects the space between a pair of letters. Because of the way fonts are constructed, with each letter being a separate element, some pairs of letters look oddly spaced when you type them. The space between a capital *T* and a lowercase *o*, for example, may seem too large because of the white space below the crossbar of the *T*. To make the characters look better, you can reduce the space between them, or *kern in* the pair. Some letters may seem to be too close together—say, a *t* and an *i*. You can *kern out* the pair so that it looks better.

Font designers often build into their fonts special information about how to space troublesome pairs of letters. Flash takes advantage of that embedded kerning information when you select the Auto Kern check box in the Text (Tool) Properties tab of the Property inspector. It's a good idea to turn on kerning to make your type look its best.

You can kern manually in Flash instead of using the embedded kerning or in addition to it. Select the character pair that you want to kern, then use Flash's Letter Spacing feature to bring the letters closer together or move them farther apart.

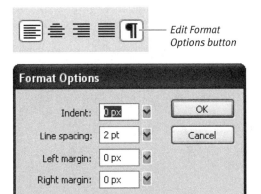

Edit Format Options button

Figure 3.14 In the Text (Tool) Properties tab of the Property inspector, click the Edit Format Options button (top) to access a dialog for setting text attributes such as alignment, indents, margins, and space between lines of text (bottom).

Setting Paragraph Attributes

Flash allows you to work with paragraph formatting much as you would in a word processor. The Text (Tool) Properties tab of the Property inspector lets you set left and right margins, a first-line indent, line spacing, and alignment (flush left, flush right, centered, or justified) (**Figure 3.14**). You can set paragraph attributes in advance so that as you type, the text tool applies them automatically. And you can apply paragraph attributes to existing text. The text tool uses whatever settings currently appear in the Text (Tool) Properties tab of the Property inspector.

The following tasks show you how to modify existing text; keep the Properties tab of the Property inspector open. (Choose Window > Properties > Properties if it's not already open.)

To select paragraphs to modify:

◆ Do one of the following:

▲ With the text tool, click within the paragraph you want to modify.

▲ With the text tool, click and drag to select multiple paragraphs within one text field.

▲ With the selection tool, click a text field to select all the paragraphs within the field.

To set paragraph alignment:

1. Select the paragraphs you want to modify.

2. In the Text Properties tab of the Property inspector, do one of the following (**Figure 3.15**):

   ▲ To align horizontal text on the left (vertical text on the top), click the first alignment button.

   ▲ To center horizontal or vertical text, click the second alignment button.

   ▲ To align horizontal text on the right (vertical text on the bottom), click the third alignment button.

   ▲ To justify text (force all lines except the last line of a paragraph to fill the full column width), click the fourth alignment button.

✔ Tip

■ To select all the paragraphs within a text field, click with the text tool anywhere inside the text field, then choose Edit > Select All. Flash highlights the entire text field.

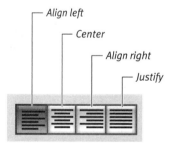
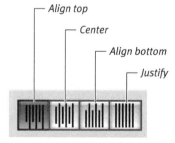

Figure 3.15 The paragraph-alignment buttons let you format the text of a paragraph in four ways. A graphic representation of the selected paragraph-alignment style appears on each button in the Text (Tool) Properties tab of the Property inspector. The images on the buttons reflect whether the text field is set for horizontal (left) or vertical (right) text flow.

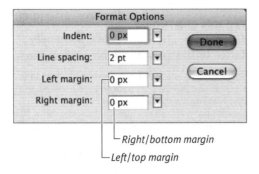

Right/bottom margin

Left/top margin

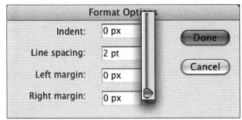

Figure 3.16 You can enter a value for right and left margins (horizontal text) or top and bottom margins (vertical text) directly in the appropriate field of the Format Options dialog (top) or use the slider to select a value (bottom).

To set margins:

1. In the Text (Tool) Properties tab of the Property inspector, click the Edit Format Options button (the one with the paragraph symbol).

   The Format Options dialog appears.

2. In the Left Margin or Right Margin field, enter the desired margin size.

   The units of measure used for the margin are the ones set in the Document Properties dialog (see Chapter 1).

3. Click Done (**Figure 3.16**).

   Flash uses the values that you enter to create margins from the left and right sides of the text field's bounding box. Your audience won't see the margins unless you're creating text that they can edit, in which case you can make the border of the text field visible.

✔ Tips

- For easy entry of new values, click the triangle to the right of the Margin field. A slider pops open. Drag the slider's lever to choose a value between 0 and 72 pixels.

- Flash incorporates the current margin settings into text fields as you create them. With margins set to the default (0 pixels), clicking the text tool on the Stage creates a small bounding box, just large enough for the blinking insertion point. If you get a longer box than you expect when you click the Stage with the text tool, check your margin settings in the Text (Tool) Properties tab of the Property inspector and adjust them as needed.

- Flash creates margins as large as 720 pixels. To get values above the slider's 72-pixel limit, enter the value directly in the Left Margin or Right Margin field.

To set a first-line indent:

◆ In the Format Options dialog, in the Indent field, use the value-entry techniques described in the preceding task to enter a value for indenting the first line of text in a paragraph.

Flash calculates the indent from the left margin; when the left margin is set to 0, Flash measures the indent from the left edge of the text field's bounding box.

To set line spacing:

◆ In the Format Options dialog, in the Line Spacing field, use the value-entry techniques described earlier in this chapter to enter a value for the amount of space you want between lines of text.

If your text contains various point sizes, Flash bases the spacing between two lines on the larger font (**Figure 3.17**).

✔ Tips

■ *Points* are the most common unit of measure for working with type. Regardless of the units you've set in the Document Properties dialog, Flash always enters the line-spacing value with the abbreviation *pt* (for *points*).

■ If you're using a font that creates larger line spacing than you like, enter a negative number for line spacing. Acceptable values for the line-spacing field are –36 points to 720 points.

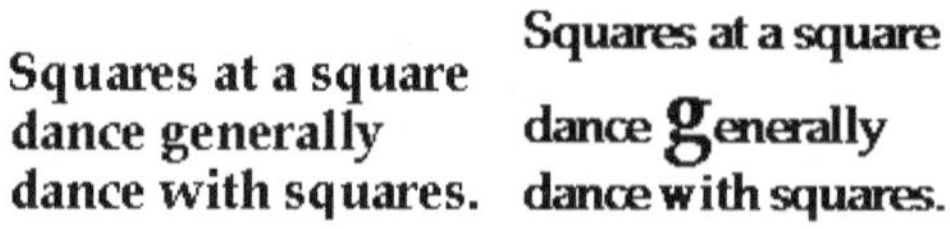

Squares at a square
dance generally
dance with squares.

Squares at a square
dance generally
dance with squares.

Figure 3.17 The line spacing for the text block on the left is set to 0 points. The space you see between lines is the space specified as part of the font. Because the text is all one size, the spacing above and below the middle line of text is the same. In the text block on the right—with the same 0-point line spacing—one letter is a larger point size. Flash increases the space between lines to make room for the larger text

MODIFYING SIMPLE GRAPHICS

4

One way to modify graphics in Adobe Flash CS3 Professional is to select one or more shapes and edit them by changing their attributes (such as color, size, and location) in the Properties tab of the Property inspector or in other appropriate panels.

You can also modify the path that creates the shape of an element. Some operations—such as straightening lines, adjusting Bézier curves, and assigning new attributes—require that the element be selected. Others, such as reshaping a line segment or curve with the selection tool, require the element to be deselected. A few operations let you edit the element whether it's selected or not—using the paint-bucket tool to change a fill color, for example.

This chapter covers using the selection tools, lasso tools, and subselection tools to select and modify the elements you learned to make in Chapter 2. You also learn about using the Properties tab of the Property inspector and other panels to modify elements' attributes.

Setting Selection Preferences

There are two basic ways to make selections in Flash: one is to click an element directly, and the other is to enclose all or part of an element with a selection outline. You can set preferences to gain more control over these two methods. For the click method, you choose whether you must Shift-click to select multiple items or whether you can merely click additional items to add to a selection. For the selection-outline method, you decide if the outline must fully enclose a graphic-object to select it or if enclosing any part of a graphic-object selects the whole thing.

To set selection methods for the selection tools:

1. From the Flash menu (Mac) or the Edit menu (Windows), choose Preferences.

The Preferences dialog appears.

2. From the Category list, choose General (**Figure 4.1**).

3. In the Selection section, choose either of the following check boxes:

Shift Select. In Shift Select mode (Flash's default setting), you must Shift-click to add items to the current selection. With Shift Select turned off, each new item you click with the selection tool is added to the current selection.

Figure 4.1 Select General in the Category list of the Preferences dialog to choose a selection method.

Contact-Sensitive Selection and Lasso Tools. With Contact-Sensitive Selection on (the default), when a selection outline touches a graphic-object or text field (see Chapter 3), a grouped shape (see Chapter 5), or a symbol instance (see Chapter 7), Flash selects the whole thing. When Contact-Sensitive Selection is off, the selection outline must fully enclose the item to select it. This setting has no effect on merge-shapes; a selection outline always defines the precise area of the merge-shape that is selected (see the next section, "Making Selections").

4. Click OK.

Choose Your Own Highlights

Whenever you select a graphic element on the Stage, Flash highlights it. By default, Flash CS3 uses a different color to highlight each type of graphic-object (drawing-objects, primitives, groups, symbols, and all other elements).

In certain situations the selection highlight may be difficult to see. If you're using a background color that's similar to a highlight color, for example, the selection highlight may blend in. You can change these highlight colors in the Preferences dialog. From the Flash menu (Mac) or Edit menu (Windows), choose Preferences; in the Category list, choose General. To use the layer-outlines color as the selection-highlight color for all graphic-objects on a layer, select the Use Layer Color radio button (you'll learn about layers and their outline view in Chapter 6). To use separate colors for each type of graphic-object, select the radio button next to the list of objects (Drawing Objects, Drawing Primitives, Groups, Symbols, and Other Elements). To choose a new color, click the color control for the type of graphic-object whose highlight you want to change. Then choose a color from the set of swatches that pops up (**Figure 4.2**).

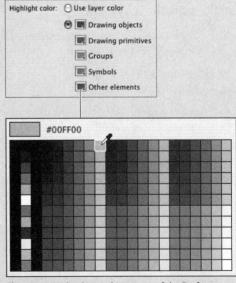

Figure 4.2 In the General category of the Preferences dialog, you can choose new colors for highlighting selection elements. Click the color control next to the type of graphic-object to choose its new selection-highlight color.

Making Selections

Merge-shapes, drawing-objects, and primitives all behave slightly differently when being selected. What you think of as a single shape may contain several segments. The rectangle tool creates a square whose stroke is actually four separate line segments. Clicking one side of a merge-shape square's stroke selects just that segment. To fully select the square's stroke, you must select each segment (you could use Shift-click to add the remaining sides to the initial selection). If you create the square as a drawing-object or a rectangle-primitive, Flash treats the four stroke segments as a unit. Clicking the stroke on any side of a drawing-object square or rectangle-primitive selects the entire stroke.

Flash highlights selected areas of merge-shapes with a pattern of tiny dots. Make sure all the parts of the merge-shape stroke or fill you intend to select display this pattern.

To make selections by clicking:

1. In the Tools panel, choose the selection tool, or press V on the keyboard.

2. To select elements created as merge-shapes, do one of the following,

   ▲ To select a merge-shape fill, position the pointer over the fill and click.

   The selection icon appears next to the selection pointer when it is over the fill. Flash highlights the selected fill with a dot pattern (**Figure 4.3**).

   ▲ To select a merge-shape stroke, position the pointer over a line segment and click.

   Flash appends a little arc or a little right-angle icon to the selection tool (**Figure 4.4**).

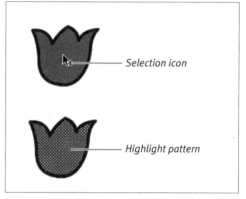

Figure 4.3 When the pointer sits above a filled area, it changes into the selection arrow (the cross icon appears next to the pointer, indicating that the tool is ready to move or select an item). Click a fill to select it. A dot pattern in a contrasting color highlights the selected fill.

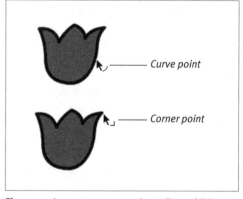

Figure 4.4 As you prepare to select a line, additions to the pointer icon indicate what kind of point lies beneath the pointer.

Double-Click Tricks

Double-clicking any segment in a series of connected merge-shape strokes selects all the segments. Double-clicking the fill of a merge-shape that has a fill and a stroke selects the fill and the stroke together.

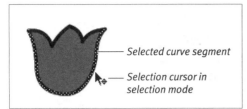

Selected curve segment

Selection cursor in selection mode

Figure 4.5 When you click a merge-shape line, Flash selects and highlights just one segment.

Figure 4.6 When you position the selection tool over an unselected drawing-object (left), the pointer displays the same icons as for merge-shapes (move/select cross for fills, curve-point arc or corner-point angle for strokes). Click anywhere on the drawing-object, and Flash selects the entire drawing-object, highlighting its bounding box (right).

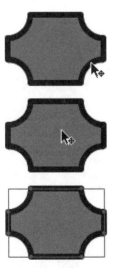

Figure 4.7 Whether you position the selection pointer over the stroke (top) or fill (middle) of a primitive-shape, the selection icon appears by the pointer. Clicking anywhere on the shape selects the whole thing (bottom).

These icons indicate that the tool is over a point in a line segment and show what type of point it is: a curve point or a corner point. (For more information about points, see the sidebar "About Curve and Corner Points," later in this chapter). Flash highlights just the segment you clicked with a dot pattern (**Figure 4.5**).

3. To select elements created as drawing-objects, position the pointer over any portion of the shape and click.

 The arc or angle icon appears next to the selection pointer as described above for merge-shape fills and strokes. Flash selects the entire shape and highlights it by displaying the bounding box—a rectangle that encloses the shape (**Figure 4.6**).

4. To select elements created as primitives, position the pointer over any portion of the shape and click.

 The selection icon appears next to the selection pointer whether it's over a fill or a stroke. Flash selects the entire shape and highlights its bounding box (**Figure 4.7**).

continues on next page

5. To add elements to a selection, do one of the following,

▲ With Shift Select (Flash's default selection style) active, hold down the Shift key as you click each item you want to include (**Figure 4.8**).

▲ If you turned off the Shift Select option in the General category of the Preferences dialog, click each item you want to include. Flash highlights each new item and adds it to the selection.

✔ Tips

■ To switch to the selection tool temporarily while using another tool, press ⌘ (Mac) or Ctrl (Windows). The selection tool remains in effect as long as you hold down the modifier key.

■ To select everything that's currently on the Stage, choose Edit > Select All, or press ⌘-A (Mac) or Ctrl-A (Windows).

■ The bounding box for a round or irregular drawing-object or primitive-shape is easy to see because the box sits outside the shape like a frame, and the bounding box for a rectangle-primitive has control points that make it more visible; but the bounding box for a drawing-object rectangle sits right on the edge of the rectangle. Therefore, depending on the color of your drawing-object rectangle, the highlighted bounding box can be difficult to see. If you have trouble seeing the highlight on selected drawing-object rectangles, choose a contrasting highlight color in the General category of the Preferences dialog (see the sidebar "Choose Your Own Highlights," earlier in this chapter).

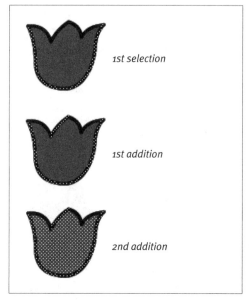

1st selection

1st addition

2nd addition

Figure 4.8 With Flash's default Preferences setting for selections, Shift-click unhighlighted line segments or fill areas to add them to a selection.

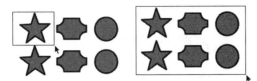

Figure 4.9 Clicking and dragging with the selection tool creates a selection rectangle (left). Be sure to start from a point that allows you to enclose all the elements you want to select within the rectangle (right). Release the mouse button, and Flash selects those elements.

Drag selection rectangle

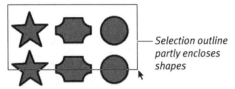

Selection outline partly encloses shapes

Selected shapes

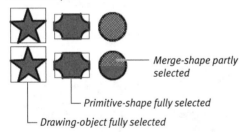

Merge-shape partly selected

Primitive-shape fully selected

Drawing-object fully selected

Figure 4.10 When Flash's default contact-sensitive selection mode is active, a selection includes any drawing-objects or primitives that are touched or partially enclosed by the selection rectangle. Only the parts of merge-shapes that fall within the selection rectangle are selected. (Here the star shapes are drawing-objects, the indented rectangles are primitives, and the circles are merge-shapes.)

To use a contact-sensitive selection rectangle:

1. Make sure the selection preferences are set for contact sensitivity (see "Setting Selection Preferences," earlier in this chapter).

2. In the Tools panel, select the selection tool.

3. Click and drag to pull out a selection rectangle (**Figure 4.9**).

   This rectangle isn't a graphic element; it just defines the boundaries of your selection.

4. Continue dragging until the rectangle encloses all the merge-shapes you want to select and at least some part of each drawing-object.

5. Release the mouse button.

   Merge-shapes. Flash highlights any portions of fill or stroke that fall inside the selection rectangle; portions of merge-shape fills or strokes that lie outside the rectangle remain unselected (**Figure 4.10**).

   Drawing-objects and primitive-shapes. If the selection rectangle touches any part of a drawing-object or primitive, Flash selects the entire thing, highlighting its bounding box.

To use a non–contact-sensitive selection rectangle:

1. Make sure contact sensitivity is turned off (see "Setting Selection Preferences," earlier in this chapter).

2. Follow steps 2 through 4 in the preceding exercise, but this time, fully enclose the drawing-objects you want to select.

   Merge-shapes. Flash highlights any portions of fill or stroke that fall inside the selection rectangle; portions of merge-shape fills or strokes that lie outside the rectangle remain unselected (**Figure 4.11**).

   Drawing-objects and primitives. Flash selects only those drawing-objects or primitive-shapes that are completely enclosed within the selection rectangle. If the selection rectangle touches or includes just a part of a drawing-object or primitive-shape, Flash leaves the entire object deselected.

✔ Tips

- If the lines or shapes you want to select are located close to other lines, you may have difficulty selecting just what you want with a rectangle. The lasso tool can create an irregular selection outline. In the Tools panel, select the lasso tool, or press L. Click and draw a free-form line around the elements you want to select (**Figure 4.12**). Close the selection outline by bringing the lasso pointer back over the spot where you began the selection outline. Release the mouse button. Flash highlights whatever falls inside the shape you drew with the lasso.

- The lasso's Polygon mode lets you define a selection area with a series of connected straight-line segments. With the lasso tool selected, click the Polygon mode button in the Tools panel. Now you can click your way around the elements you want to select (**Figure 4.13**). Double-click to end the selection outline.

Drag selection rectangle

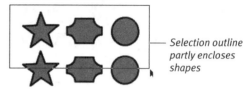

Selection outline partly encloses shapes

Selected shapes

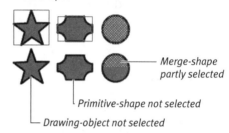

Merge-shape partly selected

Primitive-shape not selected

Drawing-object not selected

Figure 4.11 When contact-sensitivity is inactive, a selection includes just those parts of merge-shapes that fall within the selection rectangle. For drawing-objects or primitives to be selected, they must be fully enclosed by the selection rectangle. (Here again the star shapes are drawing-objects, the indented rectangles are primitives, and the circles are merge-shapes.)

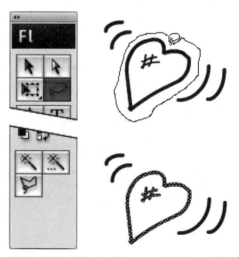

Figure 4.12 The lasso tool lets you select elements that are oddly shaped or too near other elements to allow use of the selection rectangle. Any merge-shapes inside the selection outline become highlighted and selected when you release the mouse button. Whether or not you must fully enclose drawing-objects and primitives in a lasso selection outline to select them depends on the contact-sensitivity setting in the Preferences dialog.

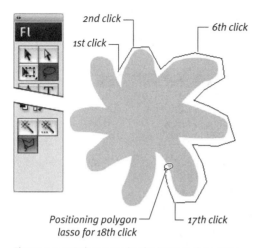

Figure 4.13 In Polygon mode, the lasso tool creates a series of connected line segments to outline whatever element you want to select. Double-clicking finishes the shape by drawing a line from the point where you double-clicked to the starting point.

To deselect individual items:

1. In the Tools panel, select the selection tool.

2. Hold down the Shift key.

3. Click any highlighted drawing-objects, primitives, or merge-shape strokes or fills you want to remove from the current selection.

   Flash deselects the items you clicked (**Figure 4.14**). No matter which method you used to select items, you must Shift-click with the selection tool to remove items from a selection.

✔ Tips

■ To deselect everything, choose Edit > Deselect All, or press Shift-⌘-A (Mac) or Ctrl-Shift-A (Windows).

■ To deselect all elements quickly, click the selection tool in an empty area of the Stage or Pasteboard.

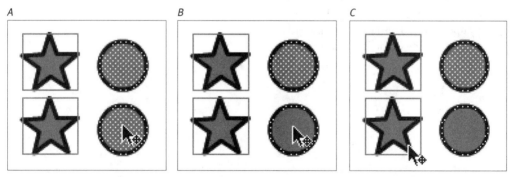

Figure 4.14 With the selection tool selected, position the pointer over the element you want to remove from the selection (A). Shift-click the item to deselect it (B). Repeat the process to deselect another item (C). (In this image, the stars are drawing-objects, and the circles are merge-shapes.)

MAKING SELECTIONS

Using the Clipboard

Flash supports the standard cut, copy, and paste operations familiar to most computer users. Flash also provides special pasting operations for graphic elements; you can paste items in the center of the Stage or in their original location.

To perform basic editing operations:

1. Select the elements you want to delete, cut, or copy.

2. From the Edit menu (**Figure 4.15**), choose one of the following:

   ▲ To delete the selection, choose Clear, or press the Delete key.

   ▲ To cut the selection, choose Cut, or press ⌘-X (Mac) or Ctrl-X (Windows).

   ▲ To copy the selection, choose Copy, or press ⌘-C (Mac) or Ctrl-C (Windows).

   After you cut or copy an item, it resides on the Clipboard until your next cut or copy operation. To retrieve the Clipboard's contents use one of the Paste commands.

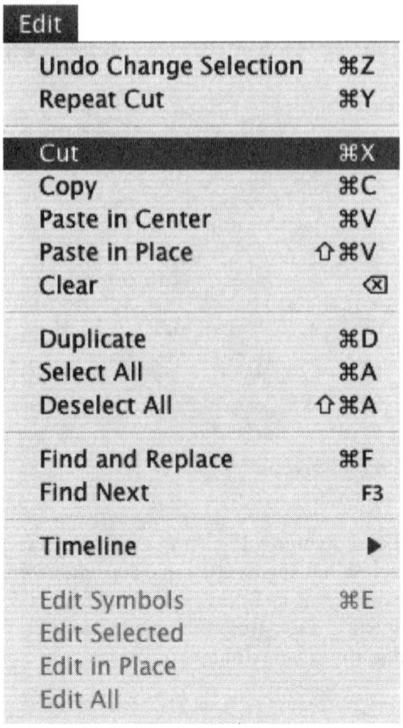

Edit	
Undo Change Selection	⌘Z
Repeat Cut	⌘Y
Cut	⌘X
Copy	⌘C
Paste in Center	⌘V
Paste in Place	⇧⌘V
Clear	⌫
Duplicate	⌘D
Select All	⌘A
Deselect All	⇧⌘A
Find and Replace	⌘F
Find Next	F3
Timeline	▶
Edit Symbols	⌘E
Edit Selected	
Edit in Place	
Edit All	

Figure 4.15 The Edit menu offers all the basic cut, copy, and paste commands for working with graphic elements.

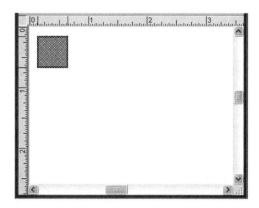

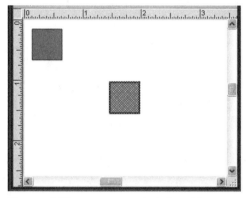

Figure 4.16 When you copy a selected graphic element (top) and choose Edit > Paste in Center, Flash pastes a copy of the element from the Clipboard to the center of the current view (bottom).

To paste the Clipboard's contents in the center of the window:

◆ Choose Edit > Paste in Center, or press ⌘-V (Mac) or Ctrl-V (Windows).

Flash pastes the Clipboard's contents in the center of the current view (**Figure 4.16**).

To paste the Clipboard contents in their original location:

◆ Choose Edit > Paste in Place, or press Shift-⌘-V (Mac) or Ctrl-Shift-V (Windows).

Flash pastes the Clipboard contents to their original location on the Stage. The value of this command becomes more apparent when you work with layers and animation; it can be crucial to have elements appear in precisely the same spot but on a different layer or frame.

✔ Tips

■ The Duplicate command is another way to make copies. Select the elements you want to copy. Choose Edit > Duplicate, or press ⌘-D (Mac) or Ctrl-D (Windows). Flash creates a copy of the selected items. The duplicate appears on the Stage, offset from the original item. The duplicate is selected, to prevent a merge-shape duplicate from interacting with the original. (For more information on interaction between elements, see Chapter 5.) The Duplicate command doesn't change the contents of the Clipboard.

■ Using the selection tool, Option-click (Mac) or Alt- or Ctrl-click (Windows) and drag any single element to create a copy. Be sure to keep the modifier key down until the copy appears.

■ You can drag to duplicate multiple items: first select them, then use the selection tool or lasso tool, Option-click (Mac) or Alt- or Ctrl-click (Windows) and drag the selection to create a copy.

Resizing Graphic Elements

Flash gives you several ways to resize, or *scale*, graphic elements. You can scale selected elements interactively on the Stage. You can also set specific scale percentages or dimensions for your element in the Transform panel, the Properties tab of the Property inspector, and the Info panel.

To resize a graphic element interactively:

1. In the Tools panel, select the free-transform tool (**Figure 4.17**).

2. On the Stage, click the element you want to resize.

   Flash selects and highlights the element and places transformation handles on all four sides and at the corners of the element's bounding box.

3. In the Tools panel, choose the Scale modifier.

4. Position the pointer over a handle.

   The pointer changes to a double-headed arrow, indicating the direction in which the element will grow or shrink as you pull or push on the handles.

5. To resize the graphic element, do one of the following:

   ▲ To change the graphic element's width, click and drag one of the side handles.

   ▲ To change the element's height, click and drag the top or bottom handle.

   ▲ To change the size of the element proportionally, click and drag one of the corner handles.

   Dragging toward the center of the element reduces it; dragging away enlarges it (**Figure 4.18**).

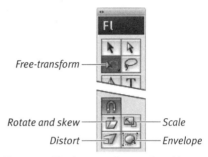

Figure 4.17 The free-transform tool enables you to select and scale elements interactively.

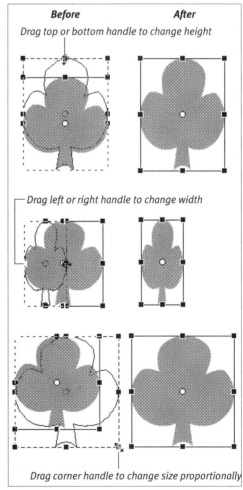

Figure 4.18 Activating the free-transform tool's Scale modifier places a set of handles around a selected element. Click and drag the handles to change the size of the element.

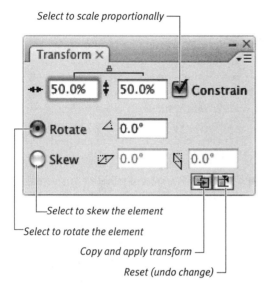

Select to scale proportionally

Select to skew the element

Select to rotate the element

Copy and apply transform

Reset (undo change)

Figure 4.19 Enter new values in the Transform panel's Width and Height fields to resize an element. With the Constrain check box selected, as you enter the value in one field, Flash automatically updates the other field. The Transform panel also lets you enter values for rotating and skewing selected elements.

✔ Tip

■ In the default scaling mode, the selection scales graphic elements from the control point opposite the one you're dragging. To scale relative to the center of a selection, hold down the Option key (Mac) or Alt key (Windows) as you drag. For symbols (see Chapter 7), it's the reverse: the default mode scales the symbol from its transformation point (which is the center by default), and pressing the Option key (Mac) or Alt key (Windows) lets you scale from the opposite control point.

To resize an element via the Transform panel:

1. With the Transform panel open, on the Stage, select the element you want to resize.

   A value of 100% appears in the Width and Height fields of the Transform panel.

2. To resize the element, do either of the following:

   ▲ To resize proportionally, select the Constrain check box next to the Width and Height fields, and enter a new value in either field (**Figure 4.19**). As you enter the value in one field, Flash automatically updates the other field.

   or

   ▲ To allow the aspect ratio to change, in the Transform panel, deselect the Constrain check box; enter new percentages in the Width field and Height field.

   A value less than 100% shrinks the element; a value greater than 100% enlarges the element.

3. Press Enter.

   Flash resizes the element.

✔ Tips

■ The Transform panel resizes a merge-shape on an absolute scale as long as the shape remains selected. Once you deselect the shape, the current size becomes the shape's new 100%. You can also make changes on a relative scale for merge-shapes. With the merge-shape selected, enter a new value in the Width and Height fields of the Transform panel, then deselect the shape. Select the shape again (the Width and Height fields now show a value of 100%). Enter a percentage for the second transformation.

■ The Transform panel always resizes drawing-objects, primitives, text fields, groups, and symbols on an absolute scale (applying the percentage you enter into the panel to the element's original size).

■ To scale several elements at the same time, select all the elements and then use any of the scaling methods described earlier in this section. When you use the Transform panel, the bounding box that contains the elements scales relative to its center point, and the entire selection grows or shrinks to fit the new box. When you use the free-transform tool, the bounding box scales from the corner opposite to the one you're dragging.

■ If you select several items and scale them using the Transform panel, Flash resizes them on a relative scale. After you enter new width and height values and confirm them (by pressing Enter) Flash resizes the elements and resets the values in the Width and Height fields to 100%.

■ To undo a Transform panel's transformation quickly, click the Reset button in the bottom-right corner of the Transform panel or press Shift-⌘-Z (Mac) or Ctrl-Shift-Z (Windows). For merge-shapes, you must not have deselected the element; for drawing-objects, primitives, text fields (see Chapter 3), groups (see Chapter 5), and symbols (see Chapter 7), you can select the object and click Reset in the Transform panel at any time to restore the item to 100% size.

■ To transform a copy of the element, click the Copy and Apply Transform button in the Transform panel. This feature can be tricky if you use it with merge-shapes, because Flash doesn't offset the copy it makes. You must be sure to move the copy yourself before deselecting it.

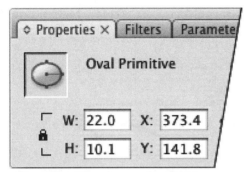

Figure 4.20 The (Shape) Properties tab of the Property inspector displays the width and height of the bounding box of a selected element. Enter new values to resize the element. In Constrain mode Flash preserves the ratio of width to height. Check the lock icon to enter independent width and height values.

Registration/Transformation Point icon

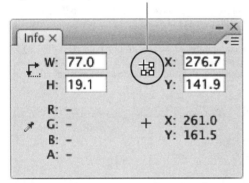

Figure 4.21 You can enter precise dimensions for an element's width and height in the Info panel. The Registration/Transformation Point icon shows whether changes will be relative to the top-left corner of the element's bounding box or to the transformation point. To apply the values you entered in the panel to the selected graphic element, press Enter or click the Stage.

To resize an element via the Property inspector:

1. With the Property inspector open, in the workspace, select the element you want to resize.

   The Width and Height fields of the (Shape) Properties tab of the Property inspector display the measurements of the selected shape's bounding box.

2. To resize the element, do either of the following:

   ▲ To resize proportionally, set the lock icon (to the left of the Width and Height fields) to Constrain mode (a closed-lock icon). Now enter a new value in either field (**Figure 4.20**). As you enter the value in one field, Flash automatically updates the other.

   or

   ▲ To allow the aspect ratio to change, in the Property inspector, set the lock icon to Unconstrained mode (an open-lock icon); enter new percentages in the Width field and Height field.

3. Press Enter.

   Flash resizes the element.

✔ Tip

■ The Info panel lets you resize a selected element relative to its *registration point* (the top-left corner of its bounding box) or *transformation point*. Click the Registration/Transformation Point icon to toggle between modes (**Figure 4.21**). A crosshair in the upper-left corner of the icon means the values are relative to the registration point; a circle in the icon's lower-right corner means the values are relative to the transformation point. Values in the Property inspector are always relative to the registration point. (For more details, see the sidebar "How Flash Tracks Elements," later in this chapter.)

RESIZING GRAPHIC ELEMENTS

Positioning Graphic Elements

If you aren't happy with the position of an element, you can always move it. You can position elements visually by dragging them around on the Stage with the selection tool. You can also position a selection numerically by specifying a precise Stage location in *x*- and *y*-coordinates. You can enter the *x*- and *y*-coordinates in either the (Shape) Property inspector or the Info panel.

To reposition an element via the Property inspector:

1. With the Properties tab of the Property inspector open, on the Stage, select an element on the Stage.

   The coordinates for the element's current position of the element's registration point appear in the *x* and *y* fields in the Properties tab, and a label—for example, Oval Primitive—appears, identifying the type of element selected (**Figure 4.22**).

2. To position the element, do one or both of the following:

   ▲ Enter a new *x*-coordinate for the element's position along the horizontal axis.

   ▲ Enter a new *y*-coordinate for the element's position along the vertical axis.

3. Press Enter to confirm the last coordinate value you entered.

   Whenever you tab to or click another field, or press Enter, Flash confirms your change, and the element moves to its new position (**Figure 4.23**).

✔ Tip

■ By default, the transformation point corresponds to a point at the center of a shape's bounding box. You can change that. With the free-transform tool, drag the hollow circle that represents the transformation point to a new location.

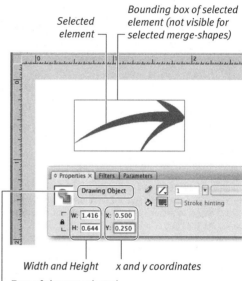

Selected element *Bounding box of selected element (not visible for selected merge-shapes)*

Width and Height   *x and y coordinates*
Type of element selected

Figure 4.22 With an element selected on the Stage, the Properties tab of the Property inspector reveals attributes of a selected element, including the *x*- and *y*-coordinates of the registration point. This drawing-object is located ½ inch to the right along the horizontal axis and ¼ inch down the vertical axis.

Enter values for x- and y-coordinates

Figure 4.23 Changing the *x*- and *y*-coordinates in the Properties tab of the Property inspector changes the location of a selected element. This arrow is now located 1 inch to the right along the horizontal axis and ¾ inch down the vertical axis.

How Flash Tracks Elements

To keep track of an element's size and position on the Stage, Flash encloses each element in a *bounding box*—an invisible rectangle just big enough to hold the element. Flash then treats the Stage as a giant graph, with the top-left corner of the Stage as the center of the *x*- and *y*-axis (**Figure 4.24**). The units of measure for the graph are those currently selected in the Document Properties dialog (to learn more about document properties, see Chapter 1). The Property inspector and the Info panel display information about the size of the element (the width and height of the bounding box) and the position of the element (the *x*- and *y*-coordinates for one important point in the element).

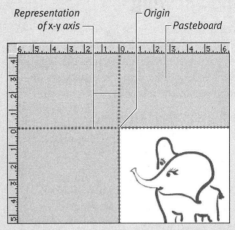

Figure 4.24 The dotted line here represents the *x-y* axis of the Stage. The origin—the o point both horizontally and vertically—is the top-left corner of the Stage.

By entering new values for Height and Width in the Properties tab of the Property inspector or the Info panel, you can change an element's size.

By entering new *x*- and *y*-coordinates in those panels, you can change an element's position on the Stage. (For more information about resizing elements, see "Resizing Graphic Elements," earlier in this chapter.)

Depending on which panel you use to enter values for an element, you can use either of two points to position an element: the *registration point* or the *transformation point*. For merge-shapes, drawing-objects, and primitives, the registration point is always located at the top-left corner of an element's bounding box. For symbols, you determine the location of registration point, which stays the same for all instances of the symbol. For shapes, text fields, and groups, Flash places the transformation point at the center of the bounding box; for symbols, you get to place the transformation point wherever you like; you can position the transformation point differently for individual symbol instances (see Chapter 7).

The Property inspector always tracks elements by the registration point. The Info panel allows you to track elements by either point. You choose the point by clicking the Registration/Transformation icon to toggle between the two tracking styles. When a crosshair appears in the top-left corner of the icon, the Info panel settings position and size elements by the registration point. When a circle appears in the bottom-right corner of the icon, the Info panel settings position and size elements by the transformation point.

When you use ActionScript to dynamically move symbols at runtime, Flash always uses the registration point to position them.

Flipping, Rotating, and Skewing

Flash lets you flip, rotate, and skew selected elements. You can either manipulate elements freely with the free-transform tool's Rotate and Skew modifier or use a variety of commands to do the job with more precision.

To flip a graphic element:

1. Select the element you want to flip.

2. Choose Modify > Transform.

3. From the submenu (**Figure 4.25**), choose either of the following:

   ▲ To reorient the element so that it spins 180 degrees around its horizontal central axis like a Rolodex file, choose Flip Vertical.

   ▲ To reorient the element so that it spins 180 degrees around its vertical central axis like a weathervane, choose Flip Horizontal.

   Figure 4.26 shows the results of the two types of flipping.

✔ Tip

■ You can flip and scale elements simultaneously by using the free-transform tool's Scale modifier. With the selected element in Scale mode, drag one handle all the way across the bounding box and past the handle on the other side. To flip a selected element vertically and horizontally, for example, drag the handle in the bottom-right corner diagonally upward, past the handle in the top-left corner (**Figure 4.27**). The flipped element starts small and grows as you continue to drag away from the element's top-left corner. Flash previews the flipped element; release the mouse button when the element is the size you want.

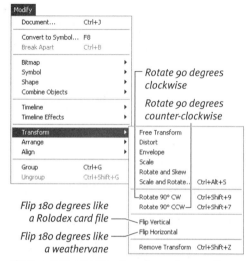

Rotate 90 degrees clockwise

Rotate 90 degrees counter-clockwise

Flip 180 degrees like a Rolodex card file

Flip 180 degrees like a weathervane

Figure 4.25 The Modify > Transform submenu offers commands for flipping graphic elements vertically and horizontally. It also provides commands for rotating an element in 90-degree increments, both clockwise and counterclockwise.

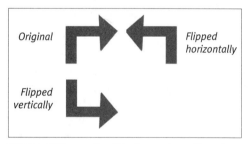

Original

Flipped horizontally

Flipped vertically

Figure 4.26 The results of flipping an element by using the Flip commands in the Modify > Transform submenu.

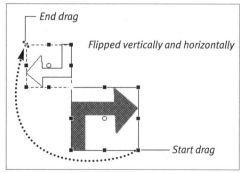

End drag

Flipped vertically and horizontally

Start drag

Figure 4.27 The free-transform tool's Scale modifier can flip and scale an element simultaneously. Here, the Scale modifier is flipping the element both vertically and horizontally.

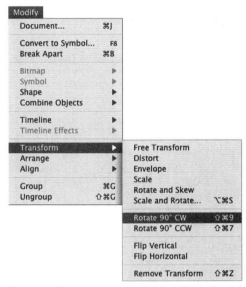

Figure 4.28 To rotate a selected element in 90-degree increments, use the Modify > Transform menu. Repeat the command to rotate the element 180, 270, or 360 degrees.

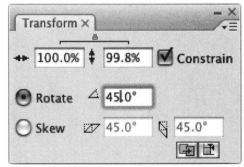

Figure 4.29 The Transform panel lets you rotate graphic elements in precise increments. Select the Rotate radio button and enter a value for the degrees of rotation. Positive values rotate the element clockwise; negative values rotate it counterclockwise.

To rotate an element in 90-degree increments:

1. Select the element you want to rotate.

2. Choose Modify > Transform (**Figure 4.28**).

3. From the submenu, choose either of the following:

   ▲ To rotate the element clockwise 90 degrees, choose Rotate 90° CW.

   ▲ To rotate the element counterclockwise 90 degrees, choose Rotate 90° CCW.

✔ Tips

■ To rotate an element around one of its corners instead of its transformation point, press Option (Mac) or Alt (Windows) while dragging.

■ To constrain rotation by 45-degree increments, hold down the Shift key while rotating.

To rotate an element by a user-specified amount:

1. Access the Transform panel (**Figure 4.29**). If the panel isn't open, choose Window > Transform.

2. Click the Rotate radio button.

3. To specify the direction and amount of rotation, do either of the following:

   ▲ To rotate the element counterclockwise, enter a negative value (–1 to –360) in the Rotate field.

   ▲ To rotate the element clockwise, enter a positive value (1 to 360).

4. Press Enter.

✔ Tips

■ When you work with drawing-objects and primitive-shapes, you can undo changes in width, height, rotation, and skewing at any time, even after you've deselected the item and made other changes. To restore the original Width, Height, Rotate, and Skew settings, select the item and click the Transform panel's Reset button (**Figure 4.30**).

■ For merge-shapes, the Reset button works as long as the shape remains selected. Once you deselect the element, however, you must use the Undo command or the History panel to restore the shape to its original form (to learn more about Undo and the History panel, see Chapter 7).

To skew an element by a user-specified amount:

1. With the Transform panel open, select the element you want to skew.

2. In the Transform panel, click the Skew radio button.

3. Enter the desired skew values in the horizontal and vertical fields (**Figure 4.31**).

4. To complete the transformation, press Enter.

✔ Tip

■ To skew a copy of the selected element, in the Transform panel, click the Copy and Apply Transform button.

 — Reset

Figure 4.30 To undo the changes you've made in the Transform panel, click the Reset button. This technique works whether you made the changes via the Transform panel or interactively with the free-transform tool.

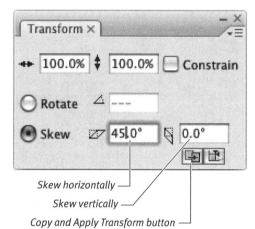

Skew horizontally

Skew vertically

Copy and Apply Transform button

Figure 4.31 Use the Transform panel to skew selected elements. You can set separate values for horizontal and vertical skewing.

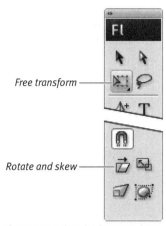

Free transform

Rotate and skew

Figure 4.32 Select the free-transform tool's Rotate and Skew modifier to access handles for rotating or skewing a selected element interactively.

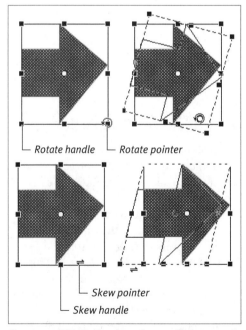

Rotate handle   *Rotate pointer*

Skew pointer

Skew handle

Figure 4.33 With the free-transform tool's Rotate and Skew modifier selected, you can drag one of the corner handles of a selected element's bounding box to rotate that element (top). Drag one of the side handles to skew the element (bottom).

To rotate or skew an element interactively:

1. Select an element to rotate or skew.

2. In the Tools panel, select the free-transform tool; then click the Rotate and Skew modifier (**Figure 4.32**).

   Solid square handles appear on all four sides and at the corners of the element's bounding box.

3. To modify the selected element, do either of the following:

   ▲ To rotate the element, position the pointer over one of the corner handles.

   The pointer changes to a circular arrow. Click and drag to rotate the element. Flash spins the element around its transformation point (**Figure 4.33**).

   ▲ To skew the element, position the pointer over one of the side handles of the element's bounding box.

   The pointer changes to a two-way arrowhead. Click and drag the side handle to skew the element.

4. Release the mouse button.

   Flash redraws the modified element.

✔ Tip

■ When you select an object with the free-transform tool and move the pointer over a corner handle, the icon changes to the double-headed arrow for scaling. Move the pointer slightly away from the corner handle, and the icon changes to the rotation arrow. Click and drag to rotate the object. Position the pointer along the edge of the bounding box between handles, and the icon changes to the two-way arrows. Click and drag in the direction you wish to skew the object.

FLIPPING, ROTATING, AND SKEWING

Distorting Graphic Elements

The free-transform tool's Distort modifier lets you distort some graphic elements by changing the shape of the bounding box. You can reposition one or more corners of the box individually; you can manipulate paired corner handles simultaneously to turn the rectangular box into a trapezoid; and you can stretch, shrink, and/or skew the box by moving the side handles of the bounding box. The selected element(s) stretch or shrink to fit the new bounding box. The Distort modifier works only on merge-shapes and single, selected drawing-objects; Distort doesn't work on primitive-shapes, text fields (see Chapter 3), groups (see Chapter 5), symbols (see Chapter 7), or selections containing multiple drawing-objects.

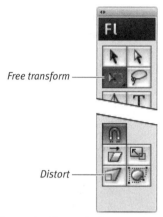

Free transform

Distort

Figure 4.34 Choose the free-transform tool's Distort modifier to reposition the corner points of the bounding box containing your selection independently.

To distort an element freely:

1. Using the free-transform tool, select the element you want to distort.

   A bounding box with transformational handles appears.

2. In the Tools panel, select the Distort modifier (**Figure 4.34**).

   Note that the center point of your selection disappears, indicating that you are in Distort mode.

3. Position the pointer over one of the transformational handles.

   The pointer changes to a hollow arrowhead.

Distorted Perspective

As beginning art students discover, it's not difficult to add depth to objects made up of rectangular shapes. You adjust the appropriate edges to align with imaginary parallel lines that converge at a distant point on the horizon—the *vanishing point*. Doing so creates the illusion that the objects recede into the distance. Adding perspective to nonrectangular shapes takes a bit more experience and the ability to imagine the way that those shapes should look. The Distort modifier of Flash's free-transform tool helps you because it encloses your selected shape—circle, oval, or squiggle—within a rectangular bounding box. All you need to do is adjust that box as you would a rectangular shape.

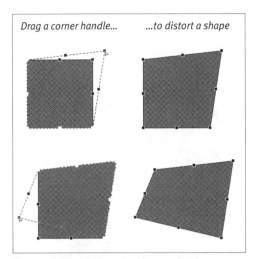

Drag a corner handle...   ...to distort a shape

Figure 4.35 Use the free-transform tool's Distort modifier to redefine the shape of an element's bounding box. You can drag each corner handle separately.

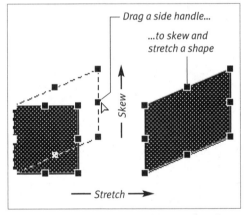

Drag a side handle...

...to skew and stretch a shape

— Skew —

— Stretch —

Figure 4.36 When the Distort modifier is selected, dragging the side handles of a selected element's bounding box skews the element. To enlarge (or shrink) the element at the same time, move the side handle away from (or in toward) the center of the original shape.

4. To change the shape of the bounding box, do one of the following:

▲ To relocate one corner of the element's bounding box, position the pointer over one of the corner handles; then click and drag the handle to the desired location. You can position each corner handle independently (**Figure 4.35**).

▲ To skew the element, position the pointer over one of the side handles; then drag the handle to the desired position. The element skews toward the direction you drag.

▲ To stretch the element as you skew it, move the selected side handle away from the element's center (**Figure 4.36**).

▲ To shrink the element as you skew it, move the selected side handle toward the element's center.

5. Release the mouse button.

Flash redraws the selection to fill the new bounding-box shape.

✔ Tips

■ When you select multiple drawing-objects, the free-transform tool's Distort modifier is inactive. To distort multiple drawing-objects simultaneously, you must combine them into a single drawing-object (see "Converting Shape Types," later in this chapter).

■ If your selection mixes one or more merge-shapes with a single drawing-object, the Distort modifier of the free-transform tool is available, and you can distort the merge-shapes and that one drawing-object.

To distort a graphic element symmetrically:

1. Follow steps 1 and 2 of the preceding task to prepare an element for distorting.

2. To taper the element, do either of the following:

   ▲ To make the top of the bounding box narrower than the bottom, Shift-click and drag the top-right corner handle toward the top-left corner handle, or vice versa (**Figure 4.37**).

   ▲ To make the top of the bounding box wider than the bottom, Shift-click and drag the top-right corner handle away from the top-left corner handle, or vice versa.

   As you drag, the two corner handles move in tandem, coming together if you drag in or moving apart if you drag out.

3. Release the mouse button.

   Flash redraws the bounding box and its contents. If you dragged in, the box appears to taper toward the top. If you dragged out, the box appears to taper toward the bottom. You can follow these procedures for the sides or bottom of the bounding box to taper the box in any direction.

✔ Tips

■ To access the free-transform tool's hollow-arrowhead pointer temporarily without selecting the Distort modifier, press ⌘ (Mac) or Ctrl (Windows). Then you can drag or Shift-drag to distort selected elements.

■ If you make a mistake while distorting a graphic, and you choose Edit > Undo so you can fix it, your graphic will be selected with the free-transform tool but the Distort modifier won't be active. You must reselect the Distort modifier in the Tools panel to continue your distortion.

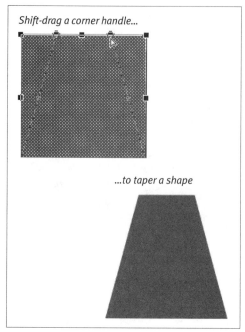

Shift-drag a corner handle...

...to taper a shape

Figure 4.37 Using the Distort modifier of the free-transform tool, Shift-click and drag a corner handle to taper selected elements.

■ Although you can use the free-transform tool on text fields, groups, and symbols, the Distort modifier doesn't work on these items. If your selection includes merge-shapes and one or more text fields, groups, or symbols, the free-transform tool's Distort modifier is available, but the distortion affects only the merge-shapes.

■ You can use the free-transform tool to distort multiple merge-shapes simultaneously. Select the merge-shapes you want to modify. Then, using the Distort modifier of the free-transform tool, redefine the shape of the bounding box that surrounds the shapes. The shapes change as a unit.

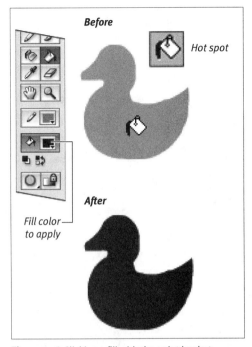

Figure 4.38 Clicking a fill with the paint bucket applies whatever color is selected in the Fill Color control. Use this technique to change existing fills.

Modifying Fills and Strokes

Flash provides two methods for modifying existing fills and strokes: you can apply new attributes with a tool (the paint-bucket tool for fills, the ink-bottle tool for strokes), or you can select the fill or stroke on the Stage and choose new attributes in an appropriate panel. For fills or strokes that contain a gradient, you can also modify the way the gradient fits in the shape by using the gradient-transform tool.

To change fill color with the paint-bucket tool:

1. In the Tools panel, select the paint-bucket tool, or press K.

2. Select new fill attributes (see Chapter 2).

3. Click the paint bucket's hot spot (the tip of the drip of paint) somewhere inside the fill you want to change.

   The fill can be selected or deselected. The fill changes to the new color (**Figure 4.38**).

✔ Tips

■ When you select multiple merge-shapes, clicking one shape with the paint bucket changes all selected merge-shape fills. The ink-bottle tool works the same way on merge-shape strokes (see "To change stroke color with the ink-bottle tool," later in this section). When you select multiple drawing-objects or primitive-shapes, however, these tools can't modify all of the fills or strokes in the selection; you must click each fill and stroke individually, or use a panel to make the changes (see the sidebar "Use Panels to Change Selected Fills and Strokes," below).

■ To pick up the color of a stroke or fill and use it for both strokes and fills, Shift-click with the eyedropper tool. Flash loads the selected color into the Fill Color and Stroke Color controls in the Tools panel, the Color panel, and the Properties tab of the Property inspectors relevant to the selected color.

MODIFYING FILLS AND STROKES

Use Panels to Change Selected Fills and Strokes

You can modify the fill and stroke attributes of a selected graphic element by changing the settings in any appropriate panel. For example, draw an oval with a red fill and a solid, 1-point, blue stroke; then select the whole shape (note that if you create the oval as a drawing-object or primitive-shape, Flash automatically selects it). Now access the Properties tab of the Property inspector; it displays the attributes of the selected shape (or drawing-object or primitive). Select green from the Fill Color control; the oval fill changes to green. Increase the stroke height or choose a new stroke style; the oval stroke changes to match.

You can choose new colors for selected fills and strokes from any appropriate panel—Color, Swatches, Tools, or Property inspector.

When a selected merge-shape has a stroke or fill set to No Color, however, the only way to change that setting is to add a fill or stroke by using the paint-bucket or ink-bottle tool (see Chapter 2).

When your selected shape is a drawing-object or primitive-shape, changing the fill or stroke attributes in a panel adds the missing element (**Figure 4.39**).

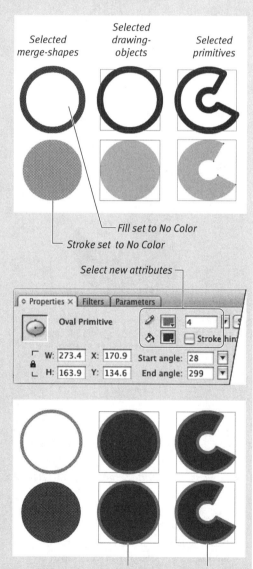

Figure 4.39 Changing the attributes of a drawing-object or primitive-shape whose fill or stroke was originally set to No Color causes Flash to add the missing element, whereas doing the same thing for a selected merge-shape has no effect.

MODIFYING FILLS AND STROKES

For merge-shapes, drawing-objects, primitives

With nothing selected, click stroke or fill

With fill and stroke selected, click stroke or fill

For merge-shapes only

With just fill selected, click stroke

With part of stroke selected, click selection

Warning: Clicking a selected fill with unselected stroke does nothing

Figure 4.40 You don't have to select a stroke to change its attributes; just click the stroke or the unselected fill with the ink bottle. Warning: If the fill is selected, you must click the stroke itself; you can't click the selected fill to change an unselected stroke.

To change stroke color with the ink-bottle tool:

1. In the Tools panel, select the ink-bottle tool, or press S.

2. Select new stroke attributes (see Chapter 2).

3. Click the ink bottle's hot spot (the tip of the drip of paint) in one of the following ways:

▲ Click directly on the stroke.

▲ If a shape has both stroke and fill, and both are deselected, click the fill.

▲ If a shape has both stroke and fill, and both are selected, click the fill.

▲ If a shape has both stroke and fill, and only the fill is selected, click the stroke.

The stroke takes on its new attributes (**Figure 4.40**).

✔ Tip

■ To save time, you can copy the fill and stroke attributes of one element and apply them to another. In the Tools panel, select the eyedropper tool, or press I. The pointer changes to an eyedropper. To copy a fill color or gradient, position the eyedropper over a fill and click. To copy all of a stroke's attributes, position the eyedropper over the stroke and click. Flash switches tools; the paint bucket appears for fills, the ink bottle for strokes. The attributes of the clicked item appear in all related panels; when you click a fill, for example, the fill type and fill color appear in the Tools panel, the Color panel, and the Properties tab of the Property inspector. You can then use the loaded paint-bucket or ink-bottle tool to apply the attributes to a different graphic element.

MODIFYING FILLS AND STROKES

To change a gradient fill's center point:

1. In the Tools panel, from the transform-tools submenu, select the gradient-transform tool (**Figure 4.41**).

2. Position the pointer over the graphic element whose gradient you want to modify; the gradient can be located in a fill or in a stroke.

   The pointer changes to the gradient-transform pointer.

3. Click.

   Handles for manipulating the gradient appear (**Figure 4.42**). You can rotate the gradient or change its size and/or center point.

4. Position the pointer over the gradient's center-point handle, the circle icon.

   The move icon appears.

5. Drag the center-point handle to reposition the center point of the gradient (**Figure 4.43**).

✔ Tip

- When you create a graphic element containing a locked gradient, by default Flash positions the gradient so that its center aligns with the left-hand side of the Stage. With the Stage set to larger viewing magnifications, when you select such an element with the gradient-transform tool, all of the gradient-transform handles may be outside the viewing area of your computer screen. It can seem as if the gradient-transform tool doesn't work. If you click a gradient with the gradient-transform tool and nothing seems to happen, try choosing a new magnification level. Viewing the Stage at 50% usually allows you to see all the gradient-transform handles for a selected gradient.

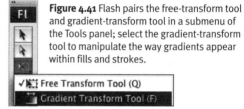

Figure 4.41 Flash pairs the free-transform tool and gradient-transform tool in a submenu of the Tools panel; select the gradient-transform tool to manipulate the way gradients appear within fills and strokes.

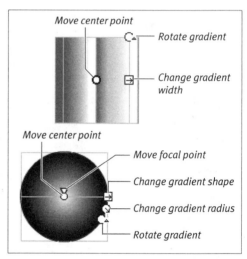

Figure 4.42 Handles for transforming gradients appear when you click a gradient with the gradient-transform pointer.

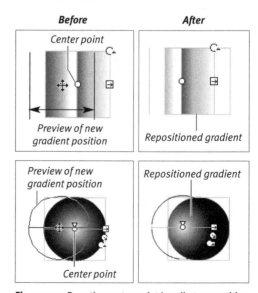

Figure 4.43 Drag the center-point handle to reposition the center of the gradient within your shape.

MODIFYING FILLS AND STROKES

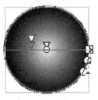

Preview of new focal point position   *Repositioned focal point*

Figure 4.44 This gradient blends from white (in the leftmost gradient pointer) to black (in the rightmost). This arrangement puts white at the center of a radial gradient, giving the illusion of highlighting on a three-dimensional object. By moving the focal point, you can mimic changes in the way light hits the object.

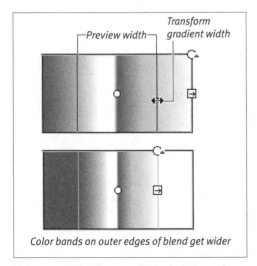

Color bands on outer edges of blend get wider

Figure 4.45 With a linear gradient selected, use the gradient-transform tool to drag the square handle inward and create a narrower rectangle for a gradient.

To change a radial gradient's focal point:

1. Follow steps 1 through 3 in the preceding task.

2. Position the gradient-transform pointer over the focal-point handle, the triangle.

   The pointer changes to a triangle.

3. Click and drag the focal-point handle to a new location (**Figure 4.44**).

   The focal point, where you have the most concentrated amount of the gradient's central color, shifts to the new location.

To resize a gradient in a fill or stroke:

1. With the gradient-transform tool selected in the Tools panel, click the graphic element that contains the gradient you want to modify.

2. To change the way the gradient fits inside the fill or stroke, do one of the following:

   ▲ To change the width of a linear gradient, drag the square handle (**Figure 4.45**).

   The pointer changes to a double-headed arrow. Dragging toward the center of your shape squeezes the transition into a narrower space; dragging away from the center of your shape spreads the transition over a wider space.

continues on next page

MODIFYING FILLS AND STROKES

▲ To change the shape of a radial gradient, drag the square handle (**Figure 4.46**).

The pointer changes to a double-headed arrow. Dragging toward the center of your shape creates a narrower oval space for the transition; dragging away from the center of your shape creates a wider oval space.

▲ To change the radius of a radial gradient, drag the circular handle next to the square handle (**Figure 4.47**).

The pointer changes to an arrow within a circle. Dragging toward the center of your shape squeezes the transition into a smaller circular space; dragging away from the center of your shape spreads the transition over a larger circular space.

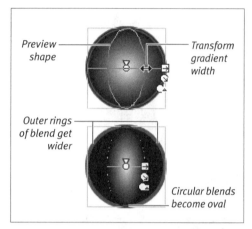

Figure 4.46 With a radial gradient selected, use the gradient-transform tool to drag the square handle inward to create a narrower oval for a gradient.

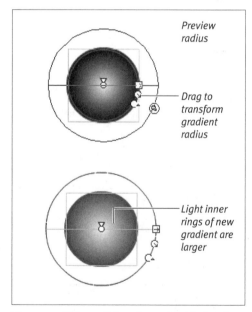

Figure 4.47 With a radial gradient selected, drag the first round handle outward to create a larger radius.

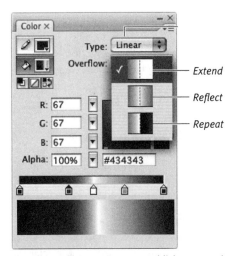

Figure 4.48 When you're set to publish your movie to Flash Player 8 or later (see Chapter 17), the Color panel's Overflow menu is active. You can choose how Flash fills out a gradient that you have made narrower than the shape it sits in.

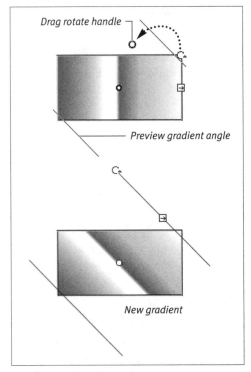

Figure 4.49 As you drag the gradient's rotate handle with the gradient-transform tool, you spin the gradient around its center point.

To control overflow:

1. Follow the steps in the preceding task to create a gradient that is narrower than the shape it sits in.

2. In the Color panel, from the Overflow menu (**Figure 4.48**), choose one of the following:

   ▲ To extend the colors in the leftmost and rightmost gradient pointers, choose Extend (the first menu item).

   ▲ To repeat the gradient, but with the colors in reverse order, choose Reflect (the second menu item).

   ▲ To repeat the gradient with colors in the original order, choose Repeat.

   Note that to view the Overflow menu, your Publish Settings must be set to publish for Flash Player 8 or above (see Chapter 17).

To rotate a gradient fill:

1. With the gradient-transform tool selected in the Tools panel, click the fill or stroke containing the gradient you want to modify.

2. To rotate the gradient, do either of the following:

   ▲ To rotate a linear gradient, drag the round handle (**Figure 4.49**).

   ▲ To rotate a radial gradient, drag the round handle farthest from the square handle.

   The pointer changes to a circular arrow. You can rotate the gradient clockwise or counterclockwise.

✔ Tip

■ Click and drag with the paint-bucket tool to rotate the gradient as you apply it. To constrain the gradient angle to vertical, horizontal, or 45-degree angles, hold down the Shift key as you drag.

MODIFYING FILLS AND STROKES

Modifying Shapes: Natural Drawing Tools

All the strokes and fills you create in Flash can be edited after you've drawn them. You can edit merge-shapes and drawing-objects in Flash's natural-drawing style, using the selection tool to change the path that defines the shape, or you can work directly with the path's anchor points and Bézier curves by using the subselection, pen, and anchor-point tools (see "Modifying Shapes: Bézier Curves," later in this chapter). You can modify primitive-shapes by manipulating their control points with the selection or subselection tools, or you can change their properties in the Property inspector.

When you use the selection tool, the merge-shape or drawing-object you want to modify must be deselected. If the element is selected, the selection tool moves the element as a unit. Always note what kind of icon the selection pointer is displaying as it hovers over the path you want to modify.

For the following tasks, make sure the item you want to modify is deselected. These tasks all deal with modifying strokes, but the same techniques work for modifying fills by reshaping their paths (see the sidebar "The Mystery of Fill Paths," later in this chapter).

About Curve and Corner Points

Flash's selection and subselection tools let you modify an element's curves and lines. The subselection tool lets you do so by moving the curve and corner points that define the element's path and by rearranging the curves' Bézier handles. When you drag a selection rectangle to enclose a path with the subselection tool, Flash reveals any curve points' Bézier handles. (Corner points have no handles.)

When you use the selection tool, Flash hides all that technical stuff. You simply pull on a line to reshape it. Still, the selection tool has its own hidden version of curve and corner points, which are evident only in the changing icons that accompany the tool as it interacts with an unselected line or curve (**Figure 4.50**).

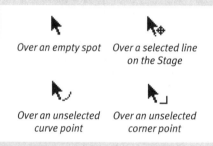

Over an empty spot *Over a selected line on the Stage*

Over an unselected curve point *Over an unselected corner point*

Figure 4.50 The small icons appearing with the selection pointer indicate what lies beneath the pointer.

For the selection tool, corner points appear at the end of an unselected segment or at the point where two segments join to form a sharp angle. All those other in-between points—even those in the middle of a completely flat line segment—are curve points. When you tug on a curve point with the selection tool, you pull out a range of points in a tiny arc. When you tug on a corner point with the selection tool, you pull out a single point.

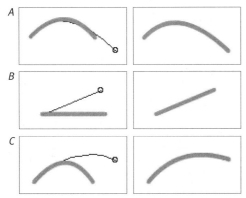

Figure 4.51 Drag away from the existing curve or line segment to lengthen it (A). Reposition the end point to change the direction of the line or curve segment (B, C).

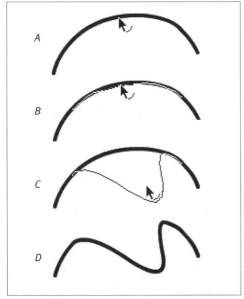

Figure 4.52 Click the middle of a curve (A). Flash activates the curve segment (B). Drag the curve to a new position (C). When you release the mouse button, Flash redraws the curve (D).

To activate the end of a segment with the selection tool:

1. Position the pointer over the end point of a deselected line segment.

   The corner-point modifier appears.

2. Click the end point.

   The end of the segment becomes active.

3. Reposition the end point in any of the following ways:

   ▲ Drag away from the existing line or curve to lengthen the segment.

   ▲ Drag toward the existing line or curve to shorten the segment.

   ▲ Drag at an angle to the original line to pivot a straight-line segment to a new position or reshape the end of a curve segment.

   As you drag, the end of the line changes to a small circle, showing that the line is active for modifications; Flash previews the modified segment as you drag (**Figure 4.51**).

4. Release the mouse button.

   Flash redraws the line segment.

To reshape a curve with the selection tool:

1. Position the selection tool's pointer over the middle of an unselected curve segment.

   The curve-point modifier appears.

2. Click and drag the curve to reshape it (**Figure 4.52**).

   Flash previews the curve you're drawing.

3. Release the mouse button.

   Flash redraws the curve.

MODIFYING SHAPES: NATURAL DRAWING TOOLS

To turn a straight-line segment into a curve segment with the selection tool:

1. Position the selection tool's pointer over the middle of an unselected line segment.

   The curve-point modifier appears.

2. Click and drag the line to reshape it (**Figure 4.53**).

   Flash previews the curve that you're drawing.

3. Release the mouse button.

   Flash redraws the line, giving it the curve you defined.

To create a new corner point with the selection tool:

1. Position the selection tool's pointer over the middle of an unselected line or curve segment.

   The curve-point modifier appears.

2. Option-click (Mac) or Ctrl-click (Windows).

   After a brief pause, the selection tool's modifier changes to the corner-point modifier, and a circle appears where the pointer intersects the line. You're now activating a corner point.

3. Drag to modify the line or curve segment and add a new corner point (**Figure 4.54**).

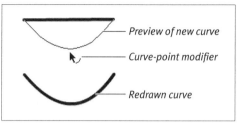

Preview of new curve

Curve-point modifier

Redrawn curve

Figure 4.53 Although this line doesn't look curved (top), Flash considers all its middle points to be curve points. Drag one of those points to create a line that looks like a curve (bottom).

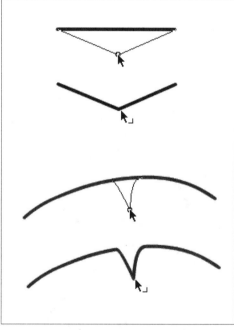

Figure 4.54 Option-click (Mac) or Ctrl-click (Windows) to create a new corner point for editing your line. Dragging a corner point from a straight-line segment creates a sharp V (top). Dragging a corner point from a curve creates a V with curving sides that comes to a sharp point (bottom).

Figure 4.55 Use the subselection tool to modify the path of a line segment.

Modifying Shapes: Bézier Tools

The subselection tool lets you see and manipulate the anchor points of a path. You can reposition anchor points to change the path and you can manipulate a point's Bézier handles to modify the slope and depth of the curve. You can add and delete points and convert existing curve points to corner points, or vice versa, with the three anchor-point tools or the pen tool. Flash has two styles for displaying anchor points: hollow (the default) and solid. To pick a style, from the Flash menu (Mac) or the Edit menu (Windows), choose Preferences. In the dialog that appears, from the Category list, choose Drawing. In the Pen Tool section, select/deselect the Show Solid Points radio button; click OK.

The tasks in this book assume that Show Solid Points is active.

To view a path and anchor points:

1. In the Tools panel, choose the subselection tool, or press A (**Figure 4.55**).

   The pointer changes to a hollow arrow.

2. On the Stage, click the line or curve you want to modify.

   Flash selects and highlights the path and anchor points. To manipulate a particular point, you must select it directly.

✔ Tip

- When the subselection tool is selected in the Tools panel, the Select All command— ⌘-A (Mac) or Ctrl-A (Windows)—highlights the path and anchor points for all the graphic elements on the Stage and Pasteboard.

The Mystery of Fill Paths

Although a fill shape without a stroke has no outline, it does have a path that defines its shape. The selection, pen, and subselection tools all work to reshape fill paths just as they do to reshape strokes, as outlined in the tasks in this chapter (**Figure 4.56**).

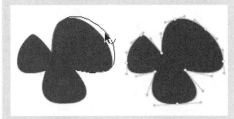

Figure 4.56 When you position the pointer over the edge of a fill shape, the selection tool displays either the curve-point or corner-point modifier. Clicking the edge of the fill activates a portion of the path outlining the shape (left). Selecting the edge of a fill shape with the subselection tool highlights the full path and its anchor points. You can reposition anchor points and Bézier handles to modify the fill shapes (right).

To select an anchor point:

1. In the Tools panel, select the subselection tool.

2. Move the subselection pointer over the path you want to modify.

   A small solid square appears next to the hollow-arrow when the pointer is above a curve or line segment; a small hollow square appears next to the hollow-arrow icon when the pointer is directly above an anchor point (**Figure 4.57**).

3. Click an anchor point.

   Flash highlights the selected point and displays its Bézier handles.

✔ Tip

- You can select multiple points on a path directly with the subselection tool. Draw a selection rectangle that includes the points you want to select. Flash highlights the entire path and selects any points that fall within the rectangle.

To move a corner point:

1. Use the subselection tool to highlight the path and anchor points of the element you want to modify.

2. Position the pointer over a corner point.

3. Click and drag the desired corner point to a new location.

   Flash redraws the path (**Figure 4.58**).

✔ Tip

- Corner points are often easy to identify without highlighting the path. You can click and drag such points directly without first highlighting the path. If you don't click right on the point, however, you'll move the whole path, not just the intended point.

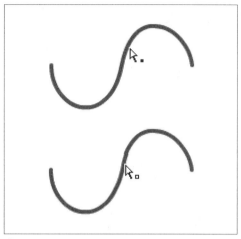

Figure 4.57 A solid square appears next to the subselection tool when it's ready to select the entire path (top). When a hollow square appears (bottom), the tool is ready to select and manipulate a single anchor point.

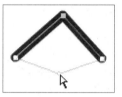 

Figure 4.58 Using the subselection tool, drag a corner point to reposition it.

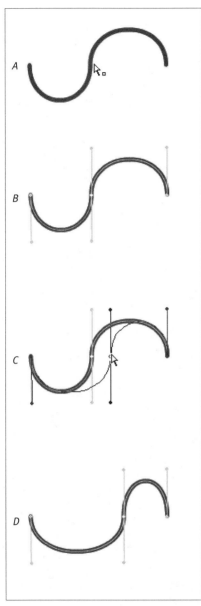

Figure 4.59 When you select an anchor point (A), Flash highlights the entire path (B). You can drag the anchor point to modify the path (C). The path and anchor points remain highlighted when you're done (D).

To move a curve point:

1. Use the subselection tool to highlight the path and anchor points of the element.

2. Position the pointer over a curve point. The anchor-point modifier appears.

3. Click and drag the point to a new location (**Figure 4.59**).

Flash previews the new curve as you drag.

After you move a curve point, the path remains selected, and the Bézier control handles become active so that you can further manipulate the curve.

To reshape a curve with the Bézier handles:

1. With the subselection tool, click the curve you want to modify.

2. Click one of the anchor points that define the curve you want to modify. Bézier handles appear.

3. Click and drag one of the Bézier handles. The pointer changes to a solid arrowhead as you drag.

4. To modify the curve, do one or more of the following:

▲ To make the curve more pronounced, position the Bézier handle farther from the curve in the direction in which the curve bulges.

▲ To make the curve flatter, position the Bézier handle closer to the curve.

▲ To make the curve bulge in the opposite direction, move the Bézier handle past the existing curve, in the opposite direction from the current bulge.

continues on next page

MODIFYING SHAPES: BÉZIER TOOLS

▲ To make the curve deeper, position the Bézier handle farther from the anchor point.

▲ To make the curve shallower, position the Bézier handle closer to the anchor point.

Flash previews the new curve as you manipulate the Bézier handle (**Figure 4.60**).

✔ Tips

■ A curve point that connects two curve segments has two Bézier handles. By default, the handles act in concert as you move them, modifying the curves on either side of the anchor point. You can choose to adjust just one handle (one curve) at a time. Using the subselection tool, Option (Mac) or Alt (Windows) drag the handle. Or, with the anchor point selected and the Bézier handles active, in the Tools panel, select the convert–anchor-point tool. Use the caret pointer to drag a handle independently.

■ To select an anchor point and activate its Bézier handles quickly, use the subselection tool to draw a selection rectangle around the curve you want to modify. Even if the path wasn't highlighted, Flash selects the curves and the anchor points that fall within the selection and activates their handles.

■ You can move selected anchor points with the arrow keys. To move in larger increments, press the Shift–arrow key.

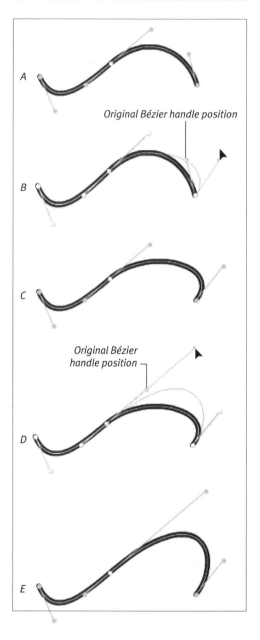

Figure 4.60 When you select anchor points, their Bézier handles appear (A). Leaning a Bézier handle away from a curve (B) makes that curve segment more pronounced (C). Leaning the handle toward the curve flattens that part of the curve. Dragging the Bézier handle away from its anchor point (D) makes the curve deeper (E); dragging the handle toward the anchor point makes the curve shallower.

The Mysterious Modes of the Pen Tool

In Flash CS3, there are three new Bézier tools: add anchor point, delete anchor point, and convert anchor point. In previous versions of Flash, the pen tool did all the work of converting, deleting, and adding anchor points. The pen tool still retains the ability to perform many of those functions. As you position the pen pointer over the Stage and existing paths, various modifiers appear next to the pen icon, indicating the tool's current function (**Figure 4.61**).

Create initial anchor point. A small x indicates the pen is ready to place the first point in a path. Click any empty spot on the Stage to start your path.

Create sequential points. The pen tool has no modifier when you are in the middle of placing a series of anchor points. Clicking the Stage adds points and segments to the path you are creating.

Add anchor point. A plus sign appears when you position the pointer over a selected path, between anchor points. In this mode, clicking the path with the pen tool adds new points to the path. Clicking between two corner points adds a new corner point; clicking between two curve points (or between a curve and a corner point) adds a curve point.

Convert curve point to corner point. A caret appears when you position the pen pointer over a curve point in a selected path. Click the curve point and it changes to a corner point.

Delete corner point. A minus sign appears when you position the pen pointer over a corner point in a selected path. Click the corner point and Flash removes it.

Extend path. A slash appears when you position the pen pointer over a terminal anchor point (the first or last point in an open path). Clicking the point links the pen tool to that path; now clicking on the Stage creates a new point that extends the existing path.

Close path. A circle appears when you position the pen pointer over the initial anchor point of the path you are currently creating. (The circle modifier also appears if you are using the pen tool to create a merge-shape path and you position the pointer over a terminal anchor point in a different merge-shape path.)

Join drawing-object path. A chain-link icon appears when you are creating a new path, and you position the pen pointer over one of the terminal anchor points in an existing drawing-object path.

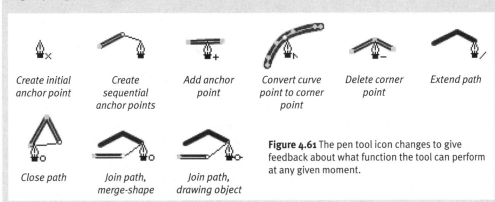

| Create initial anchor point | Create sequential anchor points | Add anchor point | Convert curve point to corner point | Delete corner point | Extend path |

| Close path | Join path, merge-shape | Join path, drawing object |

Figure 4.61 The pen tool icon changes to give feedback about what function the tool can perform at any given moment.

To convert a corner point to a curve point:

1. Use the subselection tool to highlight the path and anchor points of the path you want to modify.

2. In the Tools panel, click the current Bézier tool and from the submenu that opens, choose Convert Anchor Point Tool (**Figure 4.62**).

   The pointer changes to an upward-pointing caret.

3. Position the caret pointer over a corner point.

4. To activate Bézier handles, click the point, then drag away.

   Flash converts the corner point to a curve point that has Bézier handles (**Figure 4.63**). As you drag, the handles extend and move, modifying the curve.

✔ Tip

■ You can also use the subselection tool to convert a corner point to a curve point. Position the hollow-arrow pointer over a selected corner point, then Option-drag (Mac) or Alt-drag (Windows) away from the point to pull out the Bézier handles.

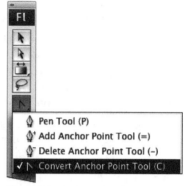

Figure 4.62 Flash CS3 has four tools for modifying the anchor points and Bézier curves of a path. Click the current Bézier tool in the Tools panel to access a submenu showing all four.

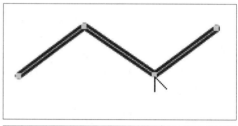

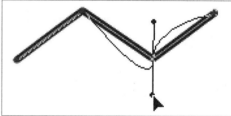

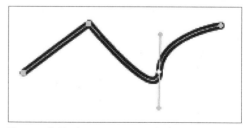

Figure 4.63 To change a corner point into a curve point (one with Bézier handles) using the convert–anchor-point tool, click (top) and drag a corner point. You pull Bézier handles out of the point instead of relocating the point (middle). When you release the mouse button, Flash redraws the curve (bottom).

Figure 4.64 Clicking a curve point with the convert–anchor-point tool (left) reduces the point to a corner point (right). Flash redraws the path accordingly.

Figure 4.65 Click an anchor point with the delete–anchor-point tool to remove the point. Flash redraws the path accordingly.

✔ Tips

- To access the delete–anchor-point tool temporarily while using the add–anchor-point tool, hold down the Option key (Mac) or Alt key (Windows).

- While you can also delete anchor points by selecting them with the subselection tool and pressing Backspace or Delete, the results may surprise you. If the selected anchor point connects two segments, pressing Delete removes the anchor point and reshapes the path. If the anchor point lies at the intersection of three or more segments, however, Flash removes not only the anchor point, but also all the line and curve segments that directly attach to the point. You may wind up removing more than you bargained for.

To convert a curve point to a corner point:

1. Using the subselection tool, select the path you want to modify.

2. In the Tools panel, from the Bézier-tools submenu, select the convert–anchor-point tool.

3. Position the caret pointer over a curve point.

4. Click the curve point.

   Flash converts the curve point to a corner point, removing the Bézier handles and flattening the curved path (**Figure 4.64**).

✔ Tip

- When using the pen tool, you can access the convert–anchor-point tool temporarily by holding down the Option (Mac) or Alt (Windows) key.

To delete an anchor point:

1. Using the subselection tool, select the path you want to modify.

2. In the Tools panel, click the current Bézier tool, and from the submenu that opens, choose the delete–anchor-point tool.

   The pointer changes to a pen icon with a remove-point modifier (a minus sign).

3. Position the pointer over an anchor point and click.

   Flash removes the anchor point and reshapes the path to connect the remaining points (**Figure 4.65**).

MODIFYING SHAPES: BÉZIER TOOLS

To add a point within a path:

1. Use the subselection tool to select the path you want to modify.

2. In the Tools panel, from the Bézier-tool menu, select the add–anchor-point tool.

   The pointer changes to a pen with a plus-sign modifier.

3. Position the pointer over the path and do any of the following:

   ▲ Click between two corner points to create a new corner point.

   ▲ Click between two curve points to create a new curve point.

   ▲ Click between a corner point and a curve point to create a new curve point.

   Flash adds a new point (**Figure 4.66**).

✔ Tip

■ To access the add–anchor-point tool temporarily while using the delete–anchor-point tool, hold down the Option key (Mac) or Alt key (Windows).

To extend a path:

1. In the Tools panel, from the Bézier-tool submenu, select the pen tool.

2. Position the pointer over the anchor point at either end of the path (a *terminal anchor point*).

   The continue-path modifier—a small slash—appears next to the pen icon.

3. Click the terminal anchor point.

   The pen links to that point as if you'd just placed it.

4. Click to add points as you learned to do in Chapter 2.

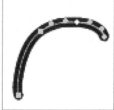

Figure 4.66 When you position the pen tool between existing anchor points, a small plus sign appears next to the pointer (left). With the plus-sign modifier active, click the path to add a new point (right).

✔ Tips

■ To switch between the Bézier and subselection tools quickly, use the keyboard shortcuts: press A for the subselection tool, P for the pen tool, = (equal sign) for the add–anchor-point tool, - (minus sign) for the delete–anchor-point tool, and C for the convert–anchor-point tool.

■ You can extend a path you are creating by linking to an existing path, but the path and the pen tool must be in the same drawing mode. Use the pen tool to place the anchor points of your path. When you're ready to link, position the pointer over a terminal anchor point in the path you want to join. One of two modifiers appears next to the pen icon: when the pen is in merge-shape mode and you link to a merge-shape path, the close-path modifier (a hollow circle) appears; when the pen is in drawing-object mode and you link to a drawing-object path, the join-paths modifier (a chain-link icon) appears. Click the existing terminal anchor point, and Flash joins the merge-shape path or the two drawing-object paths.

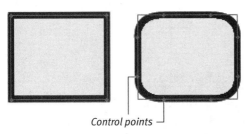

Control points

Figure 4.67 The rectangle-primitive has two control points for the corner radius of each corner. When the corner radius is set to 0, the corner is a sharp 90-degree angle, and the control points sit directly on top of one another.

Modifying Primitive-Shape Paths

Flash's rectangle- and oval-primitive tools create shapes whose paths are defined, and constrained, by a set of properties specific to that shape. You cannot change the outline of a primitive-shape freely the way you can change the outline of a merge-shape or drawing-object (for example, you can't add or move points on the path describing an oval-primitive to make a curvy amoeba shape). You can change the specific properties that define the primitive by dragging control points in the shape itself or by setting new values for those properties in the Property inspector.

To change a rectangle-primitive's properties interactively:

1. Using the selection or subselection tool, on the Stage, select the rectangle-primitive you want to modify.

   The shape's bounding box highlights, and control points appear (**Figure 4.67**). Each corner has two control points. For sharp corners with a corner-radius setting of 0, the points sit directly on top of one another; for rounded corners, a control point appears at either end of the arc that defines the corner. The two points work in concert; dragging one moves the other.

2. Position the pointer over one of the control points.

   The pointer changes to a small solid arrow.

   continues on next page

3. To modify the shape, do one of the following:

▲ To increase the radius (make the corner more rounded), drag the point inward.

▲ To decrease the radius (make the corner less rounded), drag the point outward.

You can drag diagonally toward (or away from) the center of a shape, or you can drag vertically or horizontally toward (or away from) the center of the edge containing the control point (**Figure 4.68**).

✔ Tip

■ By default, Flash constrains the corner-radius settings so that all four corners of a rectangle-primitive have the same degree of roundness. To create corners with various degrees of roundness, select the rectangle-primitive, access the Rectangle Primitive Properties tab of the Property inspector, and click the Constrain Corner Radius button to change to the unlocked state (the open-lock icon). You can then drag the control points for each corner independently, creating a variety of shapes (**Figure 4.69**).

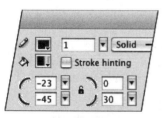

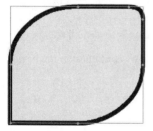

Figure 4.69 With the Constrain Corner Radius button set to its unlocked state, you can enter values for each corner separately to create a variety of shapes.

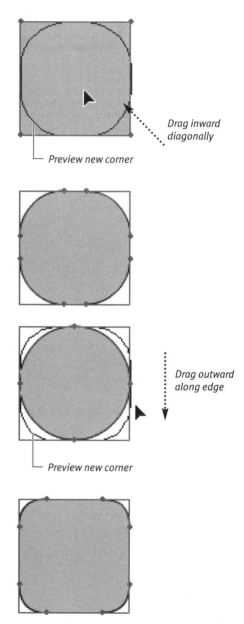

Drag inward diagonally

Preview new corner

Drag outward along edge

Preview new corner

Figure 4.68 As the corner radius increases, two control points appear at the end of the arc defining the corner. Drag inward to round the corner more, outward to round it less.

Figure 4.70 Dragging the control points of an indented corner (one with a corner radius value less than 0) changes the size of the indent. If you drag all the way back to a sharp corner, however, the control points revert to creating rounded corners as you drag. To get another indented corner, you must enter a negative value in the Property inspector.

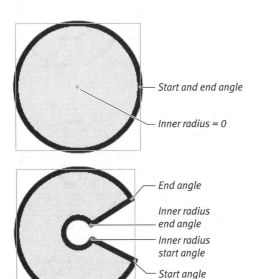

Start and end angle

Inner radius = 0

End angle

Inner radius end angle

Inner radius start angle

Start angle

Figure 4.71 An oval-primitive has control points that control the start angle and end angle for the outer and inner oval shapes.

To change a rectangle-primitive's properties precisely:

1. With the rectangle-primitive selected on the Stage, access the Rectangle Primitive Properties tab of the Property inspector.

2. To modify the shape, in the Rectangle Corner Radius fields, do one of the following:

   ▲ To create rounded corners, enter positive values.

   ▲ To create indented corners, enter negative values.

   For more details about setting the values of the various properties for rectangle-primitives, see Chapter 2.

✔ Tip

■ You can't change a square or rounded corner to an indented corner by dragging the control points; you must set a negative value in the Property inspector. Once the rectangle-primitive has an indented corner, however, you can drag its control points to adjust the size of the indent (**Figure 4.70**).

To change an oval-primitive's properties interactively:

1. Using the selection or subselection tool, on the Stage, select the oval-primitive you want to modify.

   The shape's bounding box highlights, and control points appear. Oval-primitives have four control points: one pair for the start and end angle of the outer oval and another pair for the start and end angle of the inner oval (**Figure 4.71**). When the start angle and end angle of an oval have the same value, the control points lie directly on top of one another.

continues on next page

MODIFYING PRIMITIVE-SHAPE PATHS

2. Position the pointer over a control point. The pointer changes to a solid arrow.

3. To modify the shape, do any of the following:

▲ To change the start angle, drag the control point clockwise or counter-clockwise around the perimeter of the oval (**Figure 4.72**).

▲ To change the end angle, drag the control point clockwise or counter-clockwise around the perimeter of the oval.

▲ To increase the inner radius (to create a larger space inside the oval), drag outward (**Figure 4.73**).

▲ To decrease the inner radius (to create a smaller space inside the oval), drag inward.

To change an oval-primitive's properties precisely:

1. With the oval-primitive selected on the Stage, access the Oval Primitive Properties tab of the Property inspector.

2. In the Start Angle, End Angle, or Inner Radius fields, enter new values.

For more details about setting the values of the various properties for oval-primitives, see Chapter 2.

✔ Tip

■ Although you can't alter the paths of primitives to create fanciful free-form shapes, you can use a primitive as the starting point from which to create a shape whose paths can be modified freely. After you set the primitive's properties, convert the shape to a merge-shape or drawing-object (see "Converting Shape Types," later in this chapter). Then modify the merge-shape or drawing-object using any of the techniques discussed earlier in this chapter.

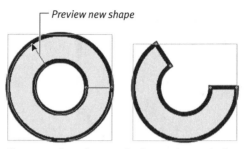

Preview new shape

Figure 4.72 Drag the control points on the outer edge of an oval-primitive clockwise (or counterclockwise) to change the start and end angle of the shape.

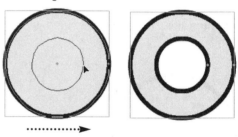

Preview larger inner radius

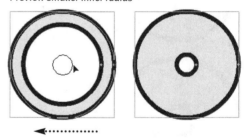

Preview smaller inner radius

Figure 4.73 Drag the control points on the inner edge of an oval-primitive to resize the radius of the inner oval: Drag toward the center of the shape to close down the opening in the middle of the shape; drag away from the center to open up a bigger space.

Modifying Shapes with the Eraser Tool

Flash's eraser tool lets you modify merge-shapes and drawing-objects by deleting parts of fills and strokes. (The eraser tool doesn't work on primitive-shapes, except in its Faucet mode.) To use the eraser tool, click and scrub on the Stage, as you'd rub an eraser over a piece of paper.

The eraser tool has five modes; you select one from the Eraser Mode menu in the Tools panel. The eraser modes govern how the tool interacts with fills and strokes. For simple shapes on a single layer, Erase Normal is a good setting; it enables the eraser tool to remove any line or fill you drag over. The other eraser modes limit what the tool affects and the tool affects only fills; in Erase Lines, the tool affects only strokes; in Erase Selected Fills, the tool erases only from fills that have been selected; and in Erase Inside, the tool affects only the fill in which you begin an erasure. These modes become important when you work with complex graphics that have multiple elements (see Chapter 5).

Another eraser option is the Faucet modifier. The faucet speeds removal of strokes and fills for any type of shape. Clicking a deselected stroke with the eraser in Faucet mode deletes all the segments that make up that stroke. In a selection containing multiple merge-shape strokes and/or fills, clicking any of the selected items with the faucet deletes the entire selection. In a selection containing multiple drawing-objects or primitive-shapes, however, the faucet deletes the individual fills or strokes you click, one at a time. (Undoing changes for primitives is a bit unreliable.)

In addition, the Faucet mode overrides the complex eraser-mode settings. For example, with the eraser set to Erase Lines, you can't scrub to erase a fill; but without changing the Erase Lines setting, you can choose the Faucet mode and then click a fill to erase it.

The eraser tool's quickest trick is to clear the decks completely. Double-click the eraser tool in the Tools panel to delete the entire contents of the Stage.

Converting Shape Types

Flash offers a variety of shape types: fills, strokes, merge-shapes, drawing-objects, primitives, and text. It's possible to convert some types of shapes into others. For example, you can convert strokes to fills; you can convert merge-shapes to drawing-objects and vice versa; you can convert primitive-shapes to merge-shapes and drawing-objects; and you can convert text, a special type of fill, to a regular merge-shape fill. You cannot, however, convert merge-shapes or drawing-objects to primitive-shapes.

Figure 4.74 To transform strokes into fills, choose Modify > Shape > Convert Lines to Fills.

To convert a stroke to a fill:

1. Select a stroke on the Stage.

2. Choose Modify > Shape > Convert Lines to Fills (**Figure 4.74**).

   Flash converts the stroke to a fill shape that looks exactly like the stroke. You can now edit the path of the "stroke's" outline as though you were working with a fill created with the brush tool (**Figure 4.75**).

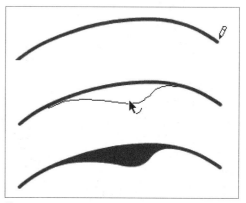

Figure 4.75 You can convert a stroke, such as this line drawn with the pencil tool (top), to a fill. The fill's outline then has its own editable path (middle and bottom).

The Mystery of Text Fills

Flash considers text to be a type of fill, but the letterforms don't act like fill shapes you sketch with the drawing tools. The letter shapes are unified as text within a container that acts as a single graphic-object. Flash lets you *break apart* text—that is, divide one text block containing multiple editable characters into multiple text blocks, each containing one editable character. This feature lets you scale, reposition, or distort individual letters. The ability to place letters in separate text fields also comes in handy for animating text. (You learn more about animation techniques in Chapters 8–11.) These single-letter text fields are still graphic-objects, however. To convert text fills to true merge-shape fills, you must break them apart twice: once to get them into separate text fields, then a second time to convert each letter to a merge-shape. This technique is useful when you have a small amount of text that you can't (or don't want to) supply to every end user, but you need to ensure the text looks exactly the same in the finished product. as it did during the authoring phase.

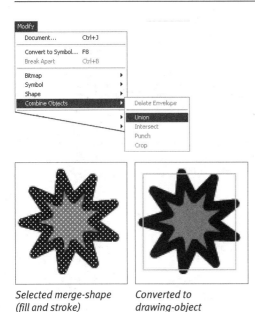

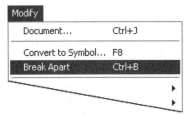

Selected merge-shape (fill and stroke)   *Converted to drawing-object*

Figure 4.76 Choose Modify > Combine Objects > Union to convert the shape selected on the Stage into a drawing-object.

Figure 4.77 Choose Modify > Break Apart to convert a drawing-object or primitive-shape to a merge-shape.

To convert a merge-shape or a primitive to a drawing-object:

1. Select a merge-shape or primitive on the Stage.

2. Choose Modify > Combine Objects > Union.

   Flash converts the selected shape to a drawing-object; it remains selected (**Figure 4.76**).

✔ Tip

- The Modify > Combine Shapes commands (Union, Intersect, Punch, and Chop) work on multiple, selected drawing-objects and primitives; the last three commands work on overlapping drawing-objects or primitives. In effect, these commands convert the drawing-objects or primitives to merge-shapes (so that they interact) and then convert the resulting shape(s) back into a drawing-object. Note that primitives lose their status as primitives once you combine them. You'll learn more about combining shapes in Chapter 5.

To convert a drawing-object or a primitive to a merge-shape:

1. Select a drawing-object or primitive-shape on the Stage.

2. Choose Modify > Break Apart, or press ⌘-B (Mac) or Ctrl-B (Windows) (**Figure 4.77**).

   Flash converts the selected drawing-object or primitive-shape to a merge-shape; it remains selected.

CONVERTING SHAPE TYPES

To divide a text block into single-letter text fields:

1. Select a text block on the Stage.

2. Choose Modify > Break Apart (**Figure 4.78**).

   Flash places each letter in its own text field and selects all the text fields. Each text field is just wide enough to hold one letter. Each letter is fully editable on its own, although the group is no longer linked.

To transform letters into merge-shapes:

1. Follow the steps in the preceding task to place letters in individual text fields.

2. Choose Modify > Break Apart.

   This second Break Apart command transforms the editable letters into raw shapes on the Stage (**Figure 4.79**). You can edit them as you would any other fill, but you can no longer change their text attributes with the text tool.

Figure 4.78 Choose Modify > Break Apart to place each letter of a text block in its own text field.

Figure 4.79 Applying the Break Apart command once transforms selected text (top) into single-letter text fields (middle); applying the command again creates merge-shapes out of the individual letters (bottom).

COMPLEX GRAPHICS ON A SINGLE LAYER

In Chapters 2 and 4, you learned to make and modify simple individual shapes from strokes (lines) and fills by using Adobe Flash CS3 Professional's drawing tools. In your movies, you'll want to use many shapes together, and you'll need to combine strokes and fills in complex ways. You might combine several shapes, such as ovals and rectangles, to create a robot character, for example. To work effectively with complex graphics, you must understand how multiple graphic elements—merge-shapes, drawing objects, and primitive-shapes—interact when they're on the same layer or on different layers. In this chapter, you learn how to work with multiple graphic elements on one layer in a Flash document. (To learn more about the concept of layers, see Chapter 6.)

Two of Flash's drawing tools—the brush tool and the eraser—offer special modes for use with multiple fills and strokes on a single layer. In this chapter, unless you're specifically requested to do otherwise, leave both tools at their default settings of Paint Normal (for the brush tool) and Erase Normal (for the eraser).

When Merge-Shapes Interact

You can think of each frame in a Flash movie as being a stack of transparent acetate sheets. In Flash terms, each sheet is a layer. Graphics on different layers have a depth relationship: items on higher layers block your view of items on lower layers, just as a drawing on the top sheet of acetate would obscure drawings on lower sheets.

Imagine that you have two layers in your movie. If you draw a little yellow square on the bottom layer and then switch to the top layer and draw a big red square directly over the yellow one, the little square remains intact, but you can't see it. The square on the top layer is in the way.

On a single layer in Flash, however, merge-shapes interact with one another, almost as though you were painting with wet finger paint. Here's a quick rundown of how lines (strokes) and shapes (fills) created in Merge Drawing mode interact within a single layer.

When Merge-Shape Lines Intersect

Intersecting merge-shape lines drawn on the same layer affect one another. Draw one line in Merge Drawing mode, and then draw a second line that intersects the first. The second line cuts—or, in Flash terminology, *segments*—the first. Segmentation happens whether the lines are the same color or different colors, but it's easiest to see with contrasting colors (**Figure 5.1**).

You might expect that the second line you drew would wind up on top of the first, but sometimes that's not the case. Start with a red line, and then draw a blue line across it; the blue line jumps *behind* the red one when you release the mouse button. Flash creates a stacking order for merge-shape lines based on the hex-color value of the line's stroke-color setting. The higher the hex value of the stroke color, the higher the line sits in a stack of merge-shape lines drawn in one layer. A merge-shape line whose stroke color is set to a hex value of 663399 always winds up on top of one whose stroke color is set to 333399.

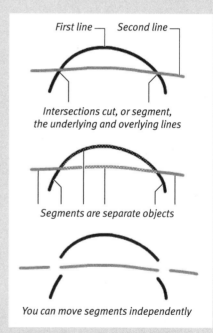

First line ⌐ Second line ⌐

Intersections cut, or segment, the underlying and overlying lines

Segments are separate objects

You can move segments independently

Figure 5.1 When you draw one line across another in Merge Drawing mode, every intersection creates a separate segment.

When Merge-Shape Lines and Fills Intersect

A fill that has no stroke still has a path (the invisible outline that describes the fill shape). When you work in Merge Drawing mode, fill paths can cut the strokes of other shapes. When you place merge-shape lines over merge-shape fills, you can wind up with lots of little segments. Try drawing lines (strokes) with the pencil tool and arcs (fills) with the brush tool; set the tools to Merge Drawing mode. If you paint a fill that intersects a stroke, the fill remains one solid object, but the stroke gets segmented (**Figure 5.2**). If you draw a stroke that intersects a fill, the stroke cuts the fill, and the path of the fill cuts the stroke (**Figure 5.3**).

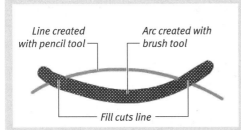

Figure 5.2 When a merge-shape fill overlays a merge-shape stroke, the fill segments the stroke. As the selection highlighting shows, the fill remains one solid object.

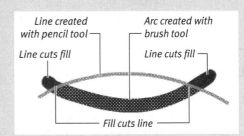

Figure 5.3 When a merge-shape line overlays a merge-shape fill, the line's path cuts the fill, and the fill's path cuts the line.

When Merge-Shape Fills Intersect

When intersecting fills created in Merge Drawing mode are the same color, the newer fill adds to the merge-shape (**Figure 5.4**).

When fills of different colors interact, the newer fill replaces the older one where the two overlap (**Figure 5.5**).

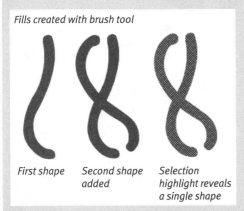

Figure 5.4 When you draw overlapping fills in the same color in Merge Drawing mode, Flash puts the two shapes together to create a single merge-shape.

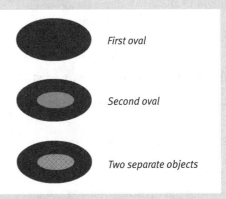

Figure 5.5 When one merge-shape fill overlaps another of a different color, the fills don't meld but remain separate. The second oval here replaces the first where they overlap.

Working with Groups

A *group* is a type of virtual container that holds graphic elements. Groups serve several functions. They prevent selected merge-shapes from interacting. They also lock down the attributes of shapes and preserve spatial relationships among graphic elements. Although you can also group drawing-objects and primitive-shapes, for the tasks in this section you want to see the interaction with merge-shapes; make sure the Object Drawing button in the Tools panel is deselected.

To create a group:

1. Select one or more items on the Stage using any of the methods discussed in Chapter 4 (**Figure 5.6**).

2. Choose Modify > Group, or press ⌘-G (Mac) or Ctrl-G (Windows).

   Flash groups the items, placing them within a bounding box (**Figure 5.7**). The visible bounding box lets you know that the group is selected. When the group isn't selected, the bounding box is hidden.

✔ Tip

■ If you choose Modify > Group when nothing is selected, you immediately enter group-editing mode: anything you draw on the Stage is part of a new group.

To return objects to ungrouped status:

1. Select the group that you want to return to ungrouped status.

2. Choose Modify > Ungroup, or press Shift-⌘-G (Mac) or Ctrl-Shift-G (Windows).

   Flash removes the bounding box and selects all the items.

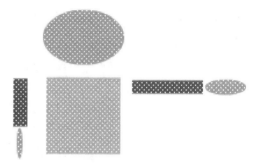

Figure 5.6 The first step in grouping is selecting the shapes you want to use in the group.

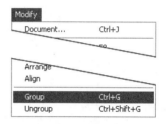

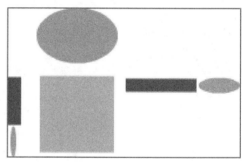

Figure 5.7 The Modify > Group command unites multiple selected shapes within a single bounding box.

✔ Tips

- The command for breaking apart symbols (Modify > Break Apart or ⌘-B (Mac) or Ctrl-B (Windows)) also works to ungroup groups. However, it can produce unexpected results on groups containing a mix of shape types. When a merge-shape is part of a group, the Break Apart command converts all the shapes to merge-shapes, even if they were drawing-objects or primitives originally. Break apart a group that contains no merge-shapes, and the group members revert to their original types. To retain the original status of all elements in a mixed group, use the Modify > Ungroup command.

- Interactions between strokes and fills occur not only when you draw a shape but also when you place a copy of a shape or move a shape. Be careful when placing copies of merge-shape fills and strokes on a single layer; you can inadvertently add to or delete part of an underlying merge-shape. If you ungroup a grouped shape that overlaps merge-shapes on a single layer, the shapes will segment one another.

Preventing Interactions

Shapes created in Merge Drawing mode act as if their paint is still wet. Here are some ways to "dry" the paint and prevent interactions.

Drawing-objects. In Drawing Object mode, the drawing tools create merge-shapes, but Flash isolates them inside a container. Fills and strokes inside the drawing-object container don't interact with fills and strokes outside the container, but you can modify the path and the fill and stroke attributes of a drawing-object directly on the Stage (see Chapter 4). You can also open a drawing-object container to work with its merge-shape contents directly.

Primitive-shapes. The rectangle- and oval-primitive tools create drawing-objects with specific properties that define the shape. Flash places those drawing-objects inside a more restrictive, primitive container. Primitive fills and strokes don't interact with fills and strokes outside the container. You can modify the fill and stroke attributes of a primitive directly, using the paint-bucket and ink-bottle tools. You can modify the defining properties of the shape (such as the corner radius for rectangle-primitives) using the selection tool and the primitive's control points, but you can't freely modify the shape's outline. You can open a primitive's container, to modify the drawing-object inside, but doing so converts the shape to a drawing-object permanently.

Groups. When you group selected fills and strokes, they stop interacting with other fills and strokes. Grouped items also stop being directly editable. To modify any attributes of the shapes in a group, you must enter a special editing mode.

Symbols. Fills and strokes inside symbols don't interact with fills and strokes of other graphic elements. Symbols also require editing in a special mode (see Chapter 7).

Layers. Placing merge-shapes on separate layers prevents them from interacting (see Chapter 6).

To prevent interaction between merge-shapes on one layer:

1. In the Tools panel, choose the oval tool in Merge Drawing mode.

2. Set the stroke color to No Color and the fill color to red.

3. On the Stage, draw a fairly large oval (**Figure 5.8**).

4. In the Tools panel, switch to the selection tool, and select the oval you just drew.

5. To make the oval a grouped element, Choose Modify > Group (**Figure 5.9**).

6. Back in the Tools panel, choose the oval tool and a different fill color.

7. On the Stage, draw a smaller oval in the middle of your first oval (**Figure 5.10**).

   When you finish drawing the new oval, it immediately disappears behind the grouped oval (**Figure 5.11**). That's because grouped objects always stack on top of ungrouped objects (see the sidebar "Understanding Stacking Order," later in this chapter).

8. Switch to the selection tool, and reposition the large oval so that you can see the small one (**Figure 5.12**).

9. Deselect the large oval, and select the small oval (**Figure 5.13**).

10. To make the small oval a grouped element, Choose Modify > Group.

    Flash puts the small oval in a bounding box and brings it to the top of the stack (**Figure 5.14**). Flash always places the most recently created group on the top of the stack. Now you can reposition the two ovals however you like, and they won't interact.

Figure 5.8 The oval before grouping.

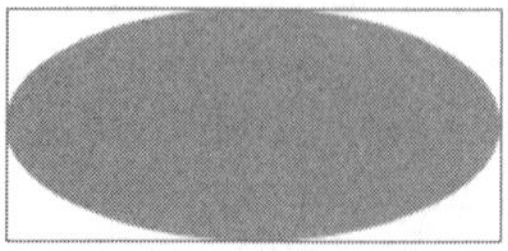

Figure 5.9 The oval after grouping.

Figure 5.10 Draw a second oval on top of the grouped oval.

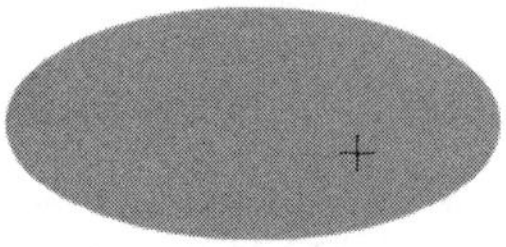

Figure 5.11 The ungrouped oval stacks beneath the grouped oval.

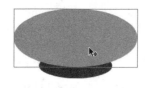

Figure 5.12 Drag the grouped oval to make the ungrouped oval visible.

Figure 5.13 Select the small oval.

Figure 5.14 After grouping, the small oval—the most recently created group—pops to the top of the stack.

Document-editing mode

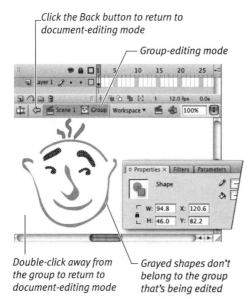

Click the Back button to return to document-editing mode

Group-editing mode

Double-click away from the group to return to document-editing mode

Grayed shapes don't belong to the group that's being edited

Figure 5.15 The eyes and eyebrows are a selected group (top). In group-editing mode (bottom), the selected shapes are ready to edit; the other items on the Stage are grayed out to indicate that you can't edit them.

Editing Groups

Although you can transform a group as a whole (scale, rotate, and skew it), you can't directly edit the individual shapes within the group the way you can edit an ungrouped shape. To edit the shapes within a group, use the Edit Selected command.

To edit the contents of a group:

1. In the Tools panel, choose the selection tool.

2. On the Stage, select the group you want to edit.

3. Choose Edit > Edit Selected.

   Flash enters group-editing mode (**Figure 5.15**). The Edit bar just above the Stage changes to indicate that you're in group-editing mode. The bounding box for the selected group disappears, and Flash dims all the items on the Stage that aren't part of the selected group. These dimmed items aren't editable; they merely provide context for editing the selected group.

4. Make changes to the contents of the group.

5. To return to document-editing mode, do one of the following:

   ▲ Choose Edit > Edit All.

   ▲ Double-click an empty area of the Stage or the Pasteboard.

   ▲ Click the current scene name in the Edit bar.

   ▲ Click the Back button in the Edit bar.

✔ Tips

- To enter group-editing mode quickly, double-click a grouped item on the Stage with the selection tool.

- When the Properties tab of the Property inspector is open, you can see—and change—the height, width, and *x*- and *y*-coordinates of the bounding box of a selected group (**Figure 5.16**).

- When you're editing a group nested within another group, clicking the Back button moves you up one level in the nesting hierarchy.

- You can also enter group-editing mode for a selected item by choosing Edit > Edit in Place. When you edit groups, there is no difference between this command and Edit > Edit Selected. There is a difference when you use these commands to edit symbols. (You'll learn about symbols in Chapter 7.)

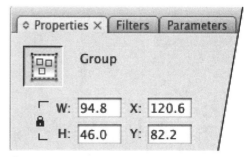

Figure 5.16 The Property inspector displays the height, width, and *x*- and *y*-coordinates for the bounding box of a group you've selected on the Stage. Enter new values to change any of those parameters.

Editing Inside the Drawing-Object Container

As you learned in Chapter 4, you can modify drawing-objects directly as they sit on the Stage (in essence reaching through the drawing-object container). But you can also work directly with the merge-shapes inside the container. To do so, you must open the container and work in drawing-object–editing mode. There is no menu command for entering this edit mode, but double-clicking a drawing-object on the Stage opens that object's container so you can edit the contents. (Note that double-clicking a primitive-shape brings up a dialog that lets you convert the primitive to a drawing-object and open its container for editing the contents.)

In drawing-object–editing mode—as in group-editing mode—selected shapes appear in full color, and other shapes appear dimmed. In drawing-object–editing mode, you can modify or delete the original merge-shapes or add new shapes. Note that the contents of a drawing-object must be merge-shapes. You can create new drawing-objects or primitives while you work in drawing-object–editing mode, but when you return to document-editing mode, Flash converts your original drawing-object to its constituent merge shapes, adds the new drawing-object(s) or primitive(s), selects all these items, and turns them into a group.

To return to document-editing mode, you use the same techniques as when editing a group (for example, click the Back button in the Edit bar).

EDITING GROUPS

Controlling Stacking Order

Within a single layer, text fields, grouped objects, drawing-objects, and primitives stack as if they were sitting on sublayers above any ungrouped merge-shapes. Stacking order exists even if objects don't literally lie on top of one another. If you have a group on one side of the Stage and a drawing-object on the other, you can't see which one stacks higher than the other; but if you drag the objects so they overlap, the order becomes apparent. (Symbols, which you'll learn about in Chapter 7, are another type of graphic-object that stacks on top of ungrouped merge-shapes.)

Understanding Stacking Order

Merge-shapes on a single layer always stay on the same layer, segmenting one another whenever they inhabit the same space on the Stage. All graphic-objects (drawing-objects, primitives, text fields, groups, and symbols) stack on top of one another. By default, Flash stacks each new graphic-object that you create on top of the preceding one; the last graphic-object created winds up on top of all the others (**Figure 5.17**). A higher-level graphic-object obscures any graphic-object that lies directly beneath it.

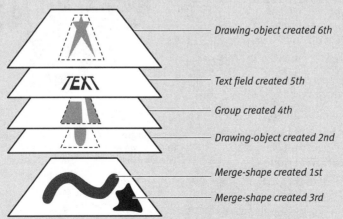

Drawing-object created 6th

Text field created 5th

Group created 4th

Drawing-object created 2nd

Merge-shape created 1st

Merge-shape created 3rd

Figure 5.17 This schematic shows Flash's default stacking order for graphic-objects. The most recently created graphic-object is on top. Merge-shapes are always on the bottom.

You can change the stacking order of graphic-objects via the Modify > Arrange menu. You can move objects up or down in the stacking order one level at a time, or you can send an object to the top or bottom of the stack of sublayers.

To change position in a stack by one level:

1. On the Stage, create at least three graphic-objects.

Use any combination of grouped shapes, drawing-objects, primitives, or text fields.

2. Select one of the graphic-objects.

3. From the Modify > Arrange menu, choose either of the following:

▲ To move the selected item up one level, choose Bring Forward, or press ⌘–up arrow (Mac) or Ctrl–up arrow (Windows).

▲ To move the selected item down one level, choose Send Backward, or press ⌘–down arrow (Mac) or Ctrl–down arrow (Windows).

Flash moves the selected item up (or down) one sublayer in the stacking order (**Figure 5.18**).

To move an element to the top or bottom of the stack:

1. On the Stage, select one of the graphic-objects you created in the previous task.

2. From the Modify > Arrange menu, choose either of the following:

▲ To bring the item to the top of the stack, choose Bring to Front, or press Option-Shift–up arrow (Mac) or Ctrl-Shift–up arrow (Windows).

▲ To move the item to the bottom of the stack, choose Send to Back, or press Option-Shift–down arrow (Mac) or Ctrl-Shift–down arrow (Windows).

Flash places the selected item at the top (or bottom) of the heap.

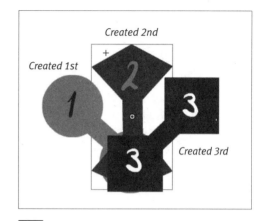

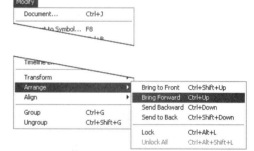

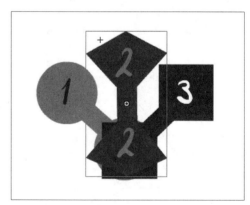

Figure 5.18 Each dumbbell-like shape here is a separate group (top). Choose Modify > Arrange > Bring Forward (middle) to move a selected group up one level in the stacking order (bottom).

CONTROLLING STACKING ORDER

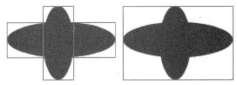

Figure 5.19 Applying the Modify > Combine Objects > Union command to drawing-object or primitive-shape fills of the same color (left) melds the fills and creates a single drawing-object (right).

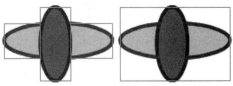

Figure 5.20 Applying the Modify > Combine Objects > Union command to drawing-objects (or primitive-shapes) of different colors (left) causes the selected fills and strokes to replace and segment one another as merge-shapes would. The resulting shapes unite in a single drawing-object (right).

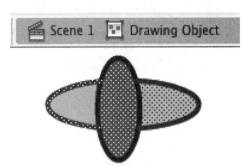

Figure 5.21 Try double-clicking the new drawing-object after you've applied Union to drawing-objects (or primitives) of different colors. In drawing-object–editing mode, you can see how the shapes segment one another. Each chunk of stroke and fill is a separate shape.

Combining Drawing-Objects and Primitives

Drawing-objects and primitive-shapes don't interact with one another or with merge-shapes, even when they overlap. You can force them to interact by using the Modify > Combine Objects commands. Flash converts combined primitives to drawing-objects.

To unite multiple drawing-objects or primitives:

1. Use the drawing tools in Object Drawing mode, or the rectangle- or oval-primitive tools, to create overlapping shapes:

   ▲ Make two or more overlapping fills with the same colors.

   ▲ Make two or more overlapping shapes with fills and strokes; use different colors for the fills and strokes in each shape.

2. Select the overlapping fills that are the same color.

3. Choose Modify > Combine Objects > Union. The two fills become a single drawing-object shape (**Figure 5.19**).

4. Select the overlapping shapes of different colors.

5. Repeat step 3.

   The fills and strokes of the shapes segment one another, but you wind up with a single drawing-object containing all those segmented shapes (**Figure 5.20**).

✔ Tips

■ You can also use the Modify > Combine Objects > Union command to combine a mix of merge-shapes, drawing-objects, and primitives into a single drawing-object.

■ To access and edit merge-shapes inside a drawing-object, double-click it (**Figure 5.21**).

To use one drawing-object to remove part of another:

1. Use the drawing tools in Object Drawing mode, or the rectangle- or oval-primitive tools, to create two or more overlapping shapes with a variety of fills and strokes.

2. From the Modify > Combine Objects menu, choose one of the following:

   Intersect retains fills and strokes only where all the selected shapes overlap, and deletes all other fills and strokes. The resulting shape(s) take stroke and fill attributes from the topmost shape.

   Punch uses the topmost shape like a cookie cutter to *remove* any shapes directly below it. (Imagine the shape left in the cookie dough after you've cut out a cookie; that's what Punch creates.) The resulting shape(s) retain their original attributes.

   Crop uses the topmost shape like a cookie cutter to *select* a new shape from any shapes that lie below it. (Imagine the cookie cutter again, but this time you wind up with the cookie itself.) The resulting shape(s) retain their original attributes (**Figure 5.22**).

✔ Tips

- When you select merge-shapes, the Modify > Combine Objects menu only offers the Union command. You can use this command instead of grouping merge-shapes. The Union command preserves the spatial relationships between shapes but gives you the ability to change fills and strokes directly on the Stage as described in Chapter 4.

- If you choose Modify > Combine Objects > Intersect and all your shapes disappear, it means there was no place where they all intersected. That result may seem self-evident, but if you've selected many shapes or your shapes are complex, it may be difficult to see.

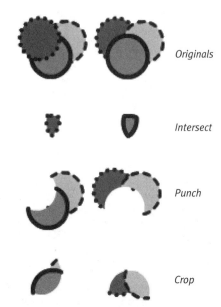

Originals

Intersect

Punch

Crop

Figure 5.22 The last three commands in the Modify > Combine Objects menu have different results depending on which object lies on top of the stack. Intersect creates a new shape from the intersection of all selected shapes, using the top shape's attributes. With Punch, the top shape takes a bite out of the others and removes it; the remaining shapes keep their original attributes. With Crop, the top shape takes the same bite but this time removes everything else; the resulting shapes keep their original attributes.

GRAPHICS ON MULTIPLE LAYERS

In Adobe Flash CS3 Professional, you create an illusion of three-dimensional depth by overlapping graphic elements. As you learned in Chapter 5, you can create this overlapping effect on one layer by stacking drawing-objects, primitive-shapes, groups, and symbols. The more elements the layer contains, however, the more difficult it becomes to manipulate and keep track of their stacking order. Layers help you to bring that task under control.

You can think of a Flash document as being like a stack of filmstrips: a sheaf of long, clear acetate strips divided into frames. Each filmstrip is analogous to a Flash layer. Shapes painted on the top filmstrip obscure shapes on lower strips; where the top filmstrip is blank, elements from the lower strips show through.

When you place items on separate layers, it's easy to control and rearrange the way the items stack up. You can make shapes appear to be closer to the viewer by putting them on a higher layer. Additionally, raw shapes on different layers don't interact, so you don't need to worry about grouping merge-shapes or having one merge-shape inadvertently delete another. You can hide and show layers and label them to make it easier to work with multiple layers and elements in a Flash document.

Touring the Timeline's Layer Features

Flash graphically represents each layer as one horizontal section of the Timeline and provides controls for viewing and manipulating these graphic representations. Several handy features help you work with graphics on layers, such as viewing the items on layers as outlines and assigning different colors to those outlines so you can easily see which items are on which layers. You can lock layers so you don't edit their contents accidentally, and you can hide layers to make it easier to work with individual graphics in a welter of other graphics. You can create special guide layers for help in positioning elements, masks for hiding and revealing layer contents selectively, and guides for animating motion along a path. (You learn more about motion paths in Chapter 9.)

Complex movies contain dozens of layers. Viewing and navigating such hefty Timelines can get tedious and confusing. Flash lets you create layer folders to organize the layers in a movie. You can keep all the layers related to one character or element together in one folder, for example. Flash considers a folder to be another type of layer, and the methods for adding and deleting layer folders are similar to those for adding and deleting layers. Layer folders don't by themselves hold graphic content, however, and folders have neither frames nor keyframes in the Timeline. (Keyframes are special frames in which you place your graphic elements; you'll learn about them in Chapter 8.)

Figure 6.1 offers a road map to the important layer features in the Timeline.

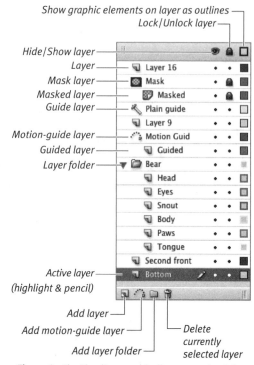

Figure 6.1 The Timeline graphically represents all the layers in a Flash movie. Layer folders let you organize layers in a complex movie. You can do much of the work of creating and manipulating layers and folders by clicking buttons in the Timeline.

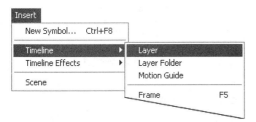

Figure 6.2 Choose Insert > Timeline > Layer to add a new layer to the Timeline.

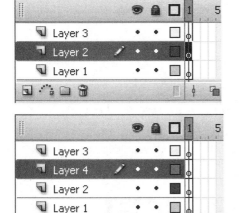

Figure 6.3 Select the layer that you want to wind up beneath the new layer (top); Flash inserts a new layer directly above the selected layer and gives the new layer a default name (bottom).

Creating and Deleting Layers and Folders

While creating the ingredients of a particular scene in your movie, you can add new layers and layer folders as you need them.

To add a layer or a folder:

1. In the Timeline, select a layer or a folder.

   Flash always adds the new layer or folder directly above the one you selected, so be sure to select the layer or folder that should wind up directly beneath the new one. To add a layer or folder beneath the current bottom layer, create the layer first, then click and drag it to reposition it at the bottom of the stack.

2. To add a layer, do either of the following:

   ▲ Choose Insert > Timeline > Layer (**Figure 6.2**).

   ▲ In the Timeline's Status bar, click the Insert Layer button (the folded-page icon).

   Flash adds a new layer and gives it a default name—for example, *Layer 4* (**Figure 6.3**).

   continues on next page

3. To add a folder, do either of the following:

▲ Choose Insert > Timeline > Layer Folder.

▲ In the Timeline's Status bar, click the Insert Layer Folder button (the folder icon).

Flash adds a new layer folder and gives it a default name—for example, *Folder 1* or *Folder 2* (**Figure 6.4**).

Flash bases the number in default names on the number of layers or folders already created in the active scene of the movie, not on the number of layers and folders that currently exist or their current position. Flash tracks layer and folder numbers separately; the first folder you insert among numerous layers gets the name *Folder 1.*

To delete a layer or a folder:

1. In the Timeline, select the layer or folder you want to delete.

2. Click the Delete Layer button (the Trash icon) (**Figure 6.5**).

Flash removes that layer (and all its frames) or that folder (and all the layers it contains) from the Timeline.

✔ Tip

■ The contextual menu for layers offers some choices that otherwise are available only via buttons in the Timeline—for example, the Delete Layer and Delete Folder commands (**Figure 6.6**). To access this menu, Control-click a layer on the Mac or right-click it in Windows.

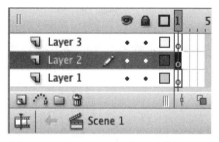

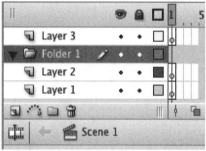

Figure 6.4 Select the layer that should be below the new folder (top). Flash creates a new folder above the layer you selected (bottom). Flash names new folders based on the number of folders that have been created in the current scene of the movie.

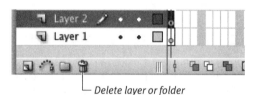

— *Delete layer or folder*

Figure 6.5 Click the Delete Layer button to delete a selected layer or folder.

Figure 6.6 The contextual menu for layers gives you easy access to layer commands, including some that you can otherwise access only via buttons—for example, Delete Layer. To access the contextual menu for layers, Control-click (Mac) or right-click (Windows) the icon of the layer you want to work with.

Layer selected for deletion

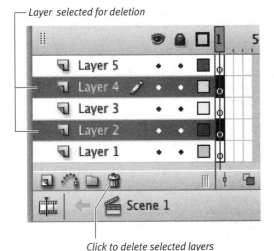

Click to delete selected layers

After deletion

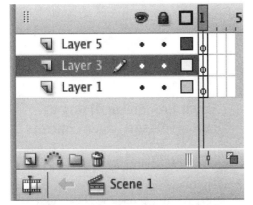

Figure 6.7 To delete noncontiguous layers, ⌘-click (Mac) or Ctrl-click (Windows) the layers you want to add to your selection; then click the Delete Layer button.

To delete multiple layers and/or folders:

1. In the Timeline, select the first layer or folder you want to remove.

2. ⌘-click (Mac) or Ctrl-click (Windows) every layer or folder you want to remove.

   This method of selection allows you to choose multiple layers that aren't contiguous (**Figure 6.7**).

3. Click the Delete Layer button (the Trash icon).

   Flash removes the selected layers (and their frames) from the Timeline.

   If your selection includes folders containing layers, a dialog appears, warning that deleting the layer folder will also delete all the layers it contains.

4. To delete the folder and its layers, click Yes.

   or

   To cancel the delete operation, click No.

✔ Tips

■ To select a range of layers, click the lowest layer you want to delete, then Shift-click the highest layer you want to delete. Flash selects the clicked layers and all the layers in between.

■ You can drag selected layers to the Delete Layer button (the Trash icon) to delete them in one step.

■ You can't delete all the layers in the Timeline. If you select all the layers and folders and click the Delete Layer button, Flash keeps the bottom layer and deletes the rest. Even if the bottom layer is nested in a folder, Flash keeps it and promotes it to regular layer status.

■ You can also Control-click (Mac) or right-click (Windows) selected layers or folders to bring up the context menu, which contains commands for deleting layers and folders.

Controlling Layers and Folders

Layer properties are the settings that define the look and function of a layer. Layer folders are a type of layer in Flash. You can name layers and folders. You can hide or show the contents of layers and folders, lock them to prevent editing their contents, and view them in outline form. Flash generally gives you two ways to control the properties of a selected layer or folder: set the property in the Layer Properties dialog, or set the property via button controls in the Timeline.

To work with the Layer Properties dialog:

1. In the Timeline, select the layer whose properties you want to define or change.

2. Choose Modify > Timeline > Layer Properties.

    The Layer Properties dialog appears (**Figure 6.8**).

3. To name the layer, enter text in the Name field.

4. To define the layer type, select one of the following radio buttons.

    ▲ Normal (the default layer type)

    ▲ Guide (aids in positioning elements; not part of published movie)

    ▲ Guided (used with motion guide to animate along a path)

    ▲ Mask (hides and reveals elements on linked layers)

    ▲ Masked (contains elements to be masked)

    ▲ Folder (used to organize layers)

5. To hide the contents of a layer (or layer folder), deselect the Show check box.

    To show the contents, select the box.

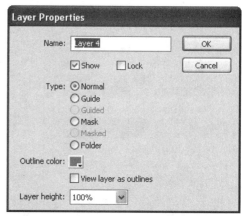

Figure 6.8 You can define a layer's type and other features in the Layer Properties dialog. Most of these properties can also be set directly in the Timeline. The only properties that can't be set in the Timeline are Layer Height, Outline Color, and Type: Guide (which makes the layer act as a set of guide lines for positioning elements).

Layer Properties Dialog vs. Timeline-Based Layer Controls

If you just want to set layer visibility, lock layer contents, or view layer elements as outlines, it makes no difference whether you call up the Layer Properties dialog to do so or click the various layer-property controls in the Timeline. Selecting a property in the dialog offers no more permanence than setting that property in the Timeline.

The Layer Properties dialog does offer functions that lack button equivalents: creating plain guide layers, changing the height of a layer in Timeline view, choosing an outline color, and changing an existing layer from one type to another.

The Timeline offers the capability to create motion guides, whereas the Layer Properties dialog doesn't.

CONTROLLING LAYERS AND FOLDERS

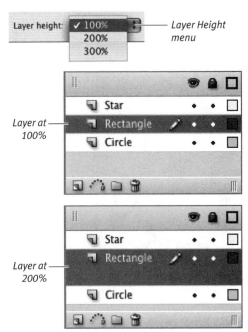

Layer height: ✓ 100% —— *Layer Height menu*
200%
300%

Layer at 100%

Star
Rectangle
Circle

Layer at 200%

Star
Rectangle
Circle

Figure 6.9 Flash offers two enlarged layer views. The larger layers in the Timeline are especially useful for working with sounds. To increase the height of a selected layer, choose a larger percentage from the Layer Height menu in the Layer Properties dialog.

■ Double-clicking a layer's folded-page icon or folder icon in the Timeline opens the Layer Properties dialog for that layer or folder.

■ When you select the "View layer as outlines" check box for a layer folder, Flash displays the contents of all the layers contained in the folder as outlines. Although you can specify an outline color for a layer folder, the color has no effect on what you see on the Stage. When you turn on outline view for the folder, each layer within the folder displays its contents in the outline color for that layer.

6. To prevent changes in the contents of a layer or folder, select the Lock check box. To permit changes, deselect the box.

7. To view the contents of a layer as outlines, select the "View layer as outlines" check box.

   To view the contents as solid graphic elements, deselect the box.

8. To choose a color for the outlines on this layer, use the Outline Color control (see Chapter 2, "Creating Solid Colors and Gradients").

   You can change this property only via the Layer Properties dialog.

9. To change the height at which layers or folders display in the Timeline, choose a percentage from the Layer Height pop-up menu (**Figure 6.9**).

   You can change this property only via the Layer Properties dialog.

10. Click OK.

    Flash applies all the selected settings to the current layer.

✔ Tips

■ To change the size of the graphic representation of all the layers in the Timeline, choose a size from the Frame View pop-up menu located in the top-right corner of the Timeline. The Preview and Preview in Context options display thumbnails of the contents of each frame in the layers.

■ To have Flash highlight all the selected graphic elements on one layer with the same color, open the Preferences dialog— from the Flash menu (Mac) or Edit menu (Windows), choose Preferences—then choose the General category and click the Use Layer Color button in the Color Highlight section.

CONTROLLING LAYERS AND FOLDERS

Setting Layer Properties via the Timeline

The Timeline represents each layer or layer folder as a horizontal field containing a name and three buttons for controlling the way the layer's or folder's contents look on the Stage. You can hide a layer or folder (making all the elements on that layer or within that folder temporarily invisible), lock a layer or folder (making the contents visible but uneditable), and view as outlines the items on the layer or within the folder. These controls are helpful when you're editing numerous items on several layers.

To rename a layer or folder:

1. In the Timeline, double-click the layer or folder name.

   Flash activates the name's text-entry field.

2. Type a new name.

3. Press Enter, or click anywhere outside the name field.

To hide/show the contents of a layer or folder:

◆ In the Timeline for the layer or folder that you want to hide or show, click the icon in the Eye column (**Figure 6.10**).

   The layer or folder toggles between the hidden and visible state. A red *X* in the column indicates that the layer or folder is hidden; its contents no longer appear on the Stage. A bullet indicates that the layer is visible. The hidden setting has no effect on the final movie. When you publish a movie (see Chapter 17), Flash includes all the contents of hidden layers and folders.

Toggles visibility of the layer's contents

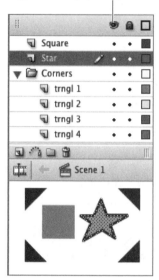

Layer contents hidden

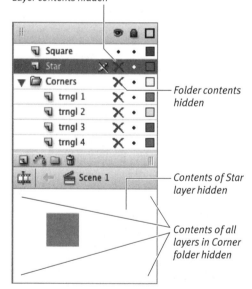

Folder contents hidden

Contents of Star layer hidden

Contents of all layers in Corner folder hidden

Figure 6.10 The column below the eye icon controls the visibility of layers. Each of these six elements (top) is on a separate layer. The four triangles at the corners are located in the Corners folder. Hiding the Star layer makes the star disappear from the Stage; hiding the Corners folder makes the four triangles disappear as well (bottom).

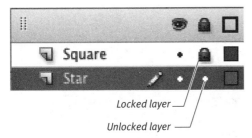

Locked layer ⎯

Unlocked layer ⎯

Figure 6.11 The padlock icon indicates that a layer is locked. The contents of a locked layer appear on the Stage, but you can't edit them.

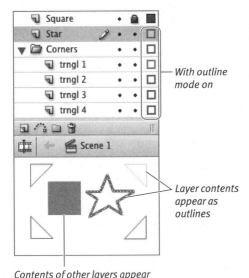

With outline mode on

Layer contents appear as outlines

Contents of other layers appear as solids

Figure 6.12 A hollow square in the Outline column indicates that graphic elements on that layer appear as outlines. Setting a folder to outline mode automatically changes all the layers within it to outline mode.

To lock/unlock a layer or folder:

◆ In the Timeline for the layer or folder that you want to lock or unlock, click the icon in the Lock column (**Figure 6.11**). The layer or folder toggles between the locked and unlocked state. A padlock icon in the column indicates that the layer or folder is locked; its contents appear on the Stage, but you can't edit them. A bullet indicates that the layer or folder is unlocked; its contents are editable. Locking a layer or folder has no effect on the final movie.

To view the contents of a layer or folder as outlines or solids:

◆ In the Timeline for the layer or folder that you want to view as outlines or solids, click the icon in the Outline column (the one topped by a square icon) (**Figure 6.12**). The layer or folder toggles between outline mode and solid mode. When the square in the column is just a color outline, the contents of the layer or folder appear on the Stage as outlines. When the square in the column is solid color, the layer or folder contents appear in their complete form. For regular layers, the color of the outline square indicates what color Flash uses to create the outlines for the contents of that layer. (For layer folders, the color of the square has no meaning; the square just shows which mode the folder is in.) Placing a layer or folder in outline mode doesn't affect the final movie.

✔ Tip

■ Setting a folder to outline mode makes all the layers within the folder display their contents as outlines. Click the outline square of individual layers within the folder to see that layer's content as solid shapes.

Organizing with Layers and Folders

You can organize layers by rearranging their position in the Timeline and by placing them within folders. Layers and folders make it easy to change the stacking order of numerous elements at the same time. You can, for example, bring all the elements on one layer to the top of the stack by dragging that layer to the top of the list in the Timeline. Doing so brings those elements to the front of the Stage (overlapping any items on other layers) in every frame of the movie. Repositioning a folder in the Timeline changes the stacking order of all the layers within that folder. When you place layers in a folder, you have the ability to hide or show those layers within the Timeline by collapsing or expanding the folder.

To reorder layers or folders:

1. In a document with several layers, in the Timeline, position the mouse pointer over the layer icon or folder icon of the layer or folder you want to move.

   The folder can be open or closed (see "To hide/show layers inside folders in the Timeline," later in this section).

2. Click and drag the layer.

   Flash previews the layer's new location with a thick gray bar.

3. Position the preview bar in the layer order you want (**Figure 6.13**).

4. Release the mouse button.

   Flash moves the layer or folder to the new location and selects it in the Timeline. The contents of single layers are selected on the Stage; the contents of the layers inside a repositioned folder are not selected.

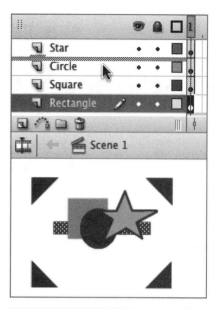

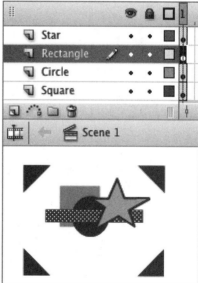

Figure 6.13 The gray line (top) represents the new location for the layer you're dragging (here it's the Rectangle layer). Release the mouse button to drop the layer into its new position. Flash selects the layer and its contents (bottom). The rectangle shape moves from the bottom of the heap, below the square, to just under the star.

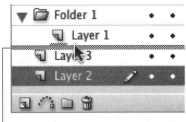

Layer goes inside folder

Layer goes outside folder

Figure 6.14 When you position layers below an open folder, you need to let Flash know whether you want the layers to wind up inside or outside the folder. The bump on top of the preview bar for the layer indicates where the layer will go. Dragging to the left aligns the bump with the folder icon, placing the layer outside the folder; dragging to the right aligns the bump with the layer icon, placing the layer inside the folder.

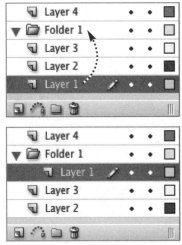

Figure 6.15 When you drag a layer over a folder layer, the preview bar disappears (top). Release the mouse button to drop the layer into that folder. Flash selects the layer and its contents (bottom).

✔ Tip

■ Positioning layers beneath an open folder is a bit tricky; you must choose to put the layer inside the folder or outside. With the layer in position beneath the last layer in the open folder, watch the preview bar; a gray bump on the top of the preview bar shows where the layer will go. To put the layer outside the open folder, drag to the left until the gray bump lines up beneath the folder icon (**Figure 6.14**). To put the layer inside the folder, drag to the right until the bump lines up beneath the layer icon of the last layer inside the folder.

To move existing layers into folders:

1. In a document with several layers and folders, in the Timeline, position the mouse pointer over the layer you want to place in a folder.

2. Click and drag the layer over the folder layer where you want to place it.

   As you drag, Flash previews the layer's new location with a thick gray bar; when you position the pointer directly over a folder, the preview bar disappears (**Figure 6.15**).

3. Release the mouse button.

   Flash moves the layer into the folder (making the moved layer the first layer in the folder), indents the layer name in the Timeline, selects the layer in the Timeline, and selects the layer's contents on the Stage.

✔ Tip

■ If you don't want the dragged layer to be at the top of the stack of layers in the folder, don't release the mouse button over the folder layer. Instead, position the preview bar between two layers inside the folder. Flash places the dragged layer in that folder location when you release the mouse button.

To hide/show layers inside folders in the Timeline:

◆ In the Timeline, click the triangle to the left of the folder icon (**Figure 6.16**). The folder layer toggles between the open and closed state. When the triangle points to the right, the closed-folder icon appears, and the Timeline hides all the layers contained in that folder. When the triangle points downward, the open-folder icon appears, and the Timeline displays all the layers contained in the folder.

✔ Tip

■ You can open or close all the folders in a movie at the same time via the contextual menu. Access the menu by Control-clicking (Mac) or right-clicking (Windows) any Timeline layer. Then, choose Expand All Folders or Collapse All Folders (**Figure 6.17**).

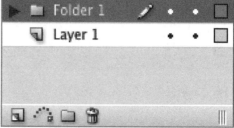

Figure 6.16 Clicking the triangle to the left of the folder icon toggles between open (top) and closed (bottom) folder views.

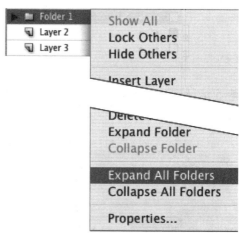

Figure 6.17 To open or close all folders at the same time, Control-click (Mac) or right-click (Windows) any layer to access the contextual menu for layers. Then choose Expand All Folders or Collapse All Folders.

ORGANIZING WITH LAYERS AND FOLDERS

Active layer

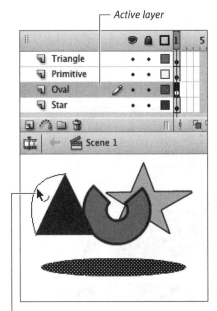

Use selection tool to modify shape on inactive layer

No change in active layer

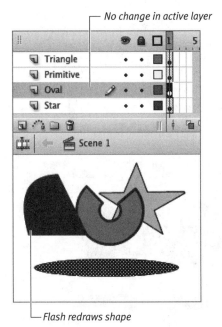

Flash redraws shape

Figure 6.18 Oval is the active layer, but you can still edit merge-shapes or drawing-objects on inactive layers. Modifying a shape's outline with the selection tool doesn't activate the shape's layer.

Working with Graphics on Different Layers

Unless you lock shapes, or lock or hide layers, the merge-shapes and drawing-objects on all layers are available for editing using the selection, paint-bucket, and ink-bottle tools; primitives are available for editing using the paint-bucket and ink-bottle tools. You can add shapes only on the active layer (the one that's currently selected).

To activate a layer:

◆ To select the layer where you want to add a graphic-object, do either of the following:

▲ In the Timeline, click the layer name.

The area containing the layer name highlights in blue, and a pencil icon appears to the right of the layer name. Flash selects all the graphic-objects on that layer.

▲ On the Stage, click a graphic-object.

Flash selects that graphic-object, highlights the layer name in gray, and puts the pencil icon to the right of the layer name.

To edit merge-shape and drawing-object outlines on inactive layers:

1. In a document with merge-shapes or drawing-objects on two or more layers, using the selection tool, position the pointer over a shape on an inactive layer (one without the pencil icon).

   The curve or corner-point icon appears.

2. Drag the outline of the shape on the inactive layer.

3. Release the mouse button.

   Flash redraws the shape (**Figure 6.18**). The layer that was active originally remains active.

✔ Tips

■ Unlike with merge-shapes and drawing objects, using the selection tool to modify the outline of a primitive on an inactive layer makes that layer active. You can start the modification—for example, using the selection tool to reposition the control points for a rectangle-primitive's corner radius—while the primitive is deselected; once you finish the modification, however, Flash selects the primitive on the Stage, and that layer becomes the active layer in the Timeline.

■ The Bézier tools work to modify shapes only on active layers.

To edit fills across layers:

1. In a document with shapes on two or more layers, select the paint-bucket tool from the Tools panel.

2. From the Color panel, choose a new fill color.

3. Position the paint bucket over a shape on an inactive layer and click.

   Flash fills the shape with the new color, but the layer remains inactive (**Figure 6.19**).

✔ Tips

■ When you're working with merge-shapes, get into the habit of creating each one on a separate layer. That way, if you need to tweak the stacking order, you can. It won't hurt to have drawing-objects or primitives on separate layers too; more layers don't increase the file size of your final movie.

■ Remember that any fill shapes that are selected on the active layer when you choose a new fill color will change to that color. To preserve the color of shapes on the active layer, deselect them before performing step 2.

— Active layer

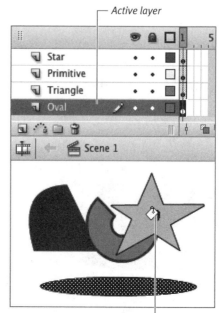

Use paint bucket to modify — fill on inactive layer

— No change in active layer

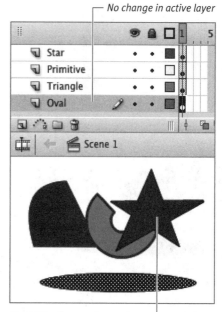

Flash fills shape with new color —

Figure 6.19 Using the paint-bucket tool to change a fill color on an inactive layer doesn't activate that layer.

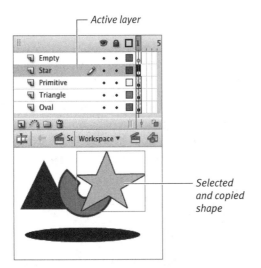

Active layer

Selected and copied shape

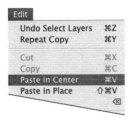

Select new active layer

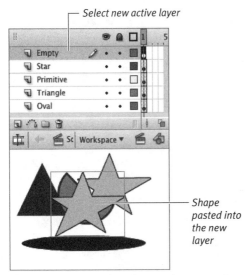

Shape pasted into the new layer

Figure 6.20 Copying a shape from one layer to another involves selecting the shape (top), copying it, selecting the target layer, and then pasting the copy there. The Paste in Center command (middle) positions the pasted shape in the center of the window (bottom).

Cutting and Pasting Between Layers

Flash lets you create and place graphics only on the active layer of a document. But you can copy, cut, or delete elements from any visible, unlocked layer. You can select items on several layers, cut them, and then paste them all into a single layer. Or you can cut items individually from one layer, and redistribute them to separate layers.

To paste across layers:

1. Create or open a document that contains several layers.

2. Place at least one element on all but one layer.

   To make the elements easier to work with, create them as drawing-objects or primitives, or group each merge-shape. Leave one layer empty.

3. On the Stage, select a shape.

   Flash highlights the layer in the Timeline in gray.

4. Choose Edit > Copy.

5. In the Timeline, select the empty layer.

6. Choose Edit > Paste in Center.

   Flash pastes the copy of the shape in the empty layer, in the middle of the window (**Figure 6.20**). Now you can move the shape to a new position, if you wish.

To use the Paste in Place command across layers:

1. In a document that has several layers containing shapes and one layer that has no shapes, select one shape.

   In the Timeline, the layer containing the selected shape becomes the active layer.

2. Using the techniques you learned in Chapter 4, add other shapes to your selection.

   In the Timeline, the layer containing the most recent addition to the selection becomes the active layer.

3. Choose Edit > Cut.

   Flash removes the selected shapes (**Figure 6.21**).

4. In the Timeline, select the empty layer.

5. Choose Edit > Paste in Place (**Figure 6.22**). Flash pastes all the shapes back into their original locations on the Stage but on a different layer (**Figure 6.23**). Try hiding the empty layer temporarily; you should no longer see those shapes.

Two Ways to Paste

Flash offers two pasting modes: Paste in Center and Paste in Place. Paste in Center puts elements in the center of the open Flash window. (Note that the center of the window may not necessarily be the center of the Stage; if you want to paste to the center of the Stage, you must center the Stage in the open window.) Paste in Place puts an element at the same x- and y-coordinates it had when you cut or copied it. Paste in Place is useful for preserving the precise relationships of all elements in a scene as you move items from one layer to another.

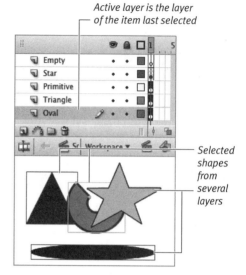

Active layer is the layer of the item last selected

Selected shapes from several layers

After cutting the shapes

Figure 6.21 The first step in consolidating items from several layers on a single new layer involves selecting all the items and cutting them. Later, you'll paste them into the new active layer.

CUTTING AND PASTING BETWEEN LAYERS

Figure 6.22 Choose Edit > Paste in Place to paste items back into their original positions.

Shapes after pasting in place

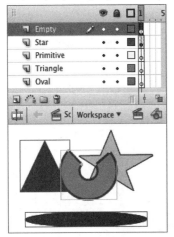

Click to hide the layer

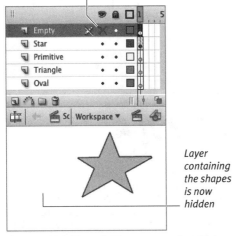

Layer containing the shapes is now hidden

Figure 6.23 The Paste in Place command positions the pasted items in the new layer. Each shape occupies the same coordinates it had on its former layer, but now all the shapes are together on the new layer. Hide the new layer to make sure you moved the elements from their old layers.

✔ Tips

■ Selecting an element on the Stage causes Flash to select that element's layer in the Timeline. As you move elements between layers, it helps to know that selections work the other way around, too. When you select a layer in the Timeline, Flash selects all the elements for that layer on the Stage.

■ The highlight color of the active layer in the Timeline changes depending on whether the Timeline or the Stage has focus. Blue highlighting means the Timeline has focus (for example, you just clicked the layer in the Timeline). Gray highlighting means the Stage has focus (for example, you just selected an item on the Stage, or you used the Paste command to paste an element onto the Stage). It's a subtle distinction, but it can help you keep track of what operation you've just completed.

■ The process of cutting elements and using the Paste in Place command is time-consuming, because you have to keep selecting new layers as you place the elements. To automate the process, use the Distribute to Layers command (see "Distributing Graphic Elements to Layers," the next section in this chapter).

Where Do Pasted Graphic Elements Go?

A Flash document can have only one layer active at a time. Any new shapes you create wind up on the currently selected, or active, layer. The same is true of placing copies of shapes or instances of symbols; if you copy and paste an element, Flash pastes the copy on the active layer. When you drag a symbol instance from the Library window, it winds up on the active layer.

CUTTING AND PASTING BETWEEN LAYERS

Distributing Graphic Elements to Layers

As you draw elements for your movie, you may not always remember to create a new layer for each one. Using the Cut and Paste in Place commands can be tedious. Flash's Distribute to Layers feature automates the process, putting each element of a selection on a separate layer. This feature comes in handy when you start creating a type of animation called *motion tweening*, in which each element being animated must be on its own layer. (You'll learn more about motion tweening in Chapter 9.)

To place selected elements on individual layers:

1. Open a new document, and, on the Stage, create several separate shapes on a single layer.

2. Choose Edit > Select All.

   Flash highlights all the shapes.

3. Choose Modify > Timeline > Distribute to Layers, or press Shift-⌘-D (Mac) or Ctrl-Shift-D (Windows) (**Figure 6.24**).

   Flash creates a layer for each shape and adds the new layers to the bottom of the Timeline. Each shape winds up in the same location on the Stage, but on a separate layer.

✔ Tips

- Distribute to Layers works with selected graphic-objects (text fields, drawing-objects, primitives, groups, and symbols) as well as with selected raw shapes. (You learn about symbols in Chapter 7.) Flash distributes each selected graphic-object to its own layer; the various elements of the graphic-object remain joined.

- When you use Distribute to Layers, any unselected elements remain on their original layer. Only the selected shapes move to new layers.

Layers set to preview in context

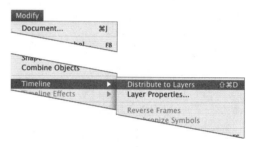

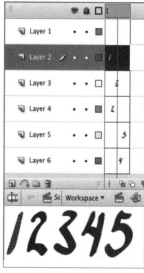

After Distribute to Layers

Figure 6.24 Selecting elements on the Stage (top) and choosing Modify > Timeline > Distribute to Layers (middle) automatically cuts each element and pastes it in place in a new layer. The new layers follow the order in which you placed the elements on the Stage originally. In this series of numbers, the numeral 1 was drawn first, so it winds up at the top of the section of new layers (bottom).

Figure 6.25 Select Guide as the layer type in the contextual menu for layers to change a normal layer to a guide layer.

Figure 6.26 Select a layer (top) and define it as a guide layer. In the Timeline, Flash identifies the guide layer with a T-square icon; compare that with the icon for the motion-guide layer (bottom).

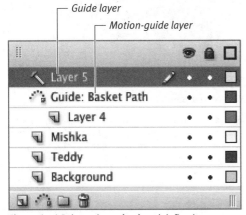

Working with Guide Layers

Flash offers two types of guide layers: guides and motion guides. Plain old guides can contain any kind of content: lines, shapes, or symbols. The contents of a regular guide layer merely serve as a point of reference to help you position items on the Stage. Flash doesn't include the graphic content of guide layers in the final exported movie.

Motion-guide layers contain a single line that directs the movement of an animated element along a path. (To learn more about creating and animating with motion guides, see Chapter 9.) Another distinction to remember is that Flash creates motion guides by adding a new layer directly to the Timeline. To create plain guides, you must redefine an existing layer as a guide layer.

To create a plain guide layer:

1. Do either of the following:
   - ▲ Create a new layer in the Timeline (for example, by clicking the Insert Layer button). Flash selects the new layer.
   - ▲ Select a layer that already exists.

2. Control-click (Mac) or right-click (Windows) the layer you want to define as a guide, and choose Guide from the contextual menu (**Figure 6.25**).

   Flash turns the selected layer into a guide layer and places a little T-square icon before the layer name (**Figure 6.26**). You can rename the layer to identify it as a guide, if you wish.

continues on next page

3. To make guide elements easier to use, choose View > Snapping, and from the submenu, choose any of the following settings:

▲ Choose Snap to Objects (**Figure 6.27**).

Flash forces items that you draw or drag to snap to lines or shapes.

▲ Choose Snap Align.

Flash displays alignment guides as you drag shapes or graphic-objects near to other shapes or graphic-objects. Now you can more easily align items to the elements on your guide layers.

✔ Tips

■ When you've placed guide elements where you need them for a certain scene, lock the guide layer so you don't move the guides accidentally as you draw on other layers.

■ The Snap to Guide feature sounds like it might help you snap to items on a guide layer, but it doesn't. The guides in this mode are the guide lines you drag out from rulers (see Chapter 1).

■ Because the graphic content of guide layers doesn't become part of your published movie, you can use guide layers as a space for making notes to yourself, adding instructions to other people who may be working on the file.

■ When positioning layers beneath a guide layer, it's easy to transform the guide layer into a motion-guide layer by accident. (Motion guides are used in certain types of animation.) As you drag a layer beneath a guide layer, watch the preview bar and the icon in the guide layer. To maintain the guide layer as a guide layer, drag to the left until the preview bar's gray bump lines up beneath the guide layer's T-square icon. To create a motion-guide layer, drag to the right; the guide icon changes to a dotted arc icon indicating a motion guide (to learn about motion guides, see Chapter 9).

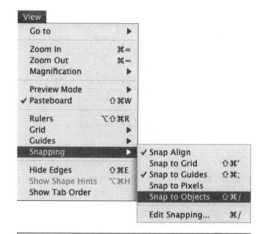

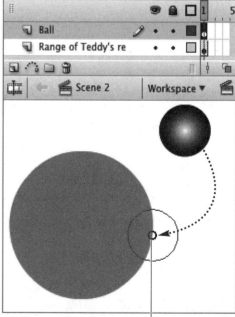

Center point snaps to other elements as you drag

Figure 6.27 Choose View > Snapping > Snap to Objects (top) to force items that you drag to snap to other lines or shapes, such as those on a guide layer (bottom).

Figure 6.28 To define a layer as a mask, choose Mask from the contextual menu for layers.

Mask layer
Masked layer

Figure 6.29 The mask-layer icon imitates the masking effect with a dark mask shape over a checkerboard pattern. Masked layers are indented and have a checkerboard pattern on the layer icon in the Timeline, indicating that the layer is masked.

■ Positioning a layer beneath a list of masked layers can be tricky. When you position a layer's preview bar after the last layer in the masked set, you have the choice of adding the layer to the masked set or placing it at the main level of the Timeline. Use the preview bar's subtle clues to place the layer where you want it. Position the layer directly beneath the last masked layer. To add the layer to the masked set, drag slightly to the right until the bump on the top of the preview bar lines up beneath the masked-layer's folded-page icon. To add the layer to the main level of the Timeline, drag slightly to the left until the bump lines up beneath the mask icon.

Working with Mask Layers

Mask layers are special layers that let you hide and show elements on underlying layers. In the final movie, shapes on the Mask layer become holes that let items on linked layers show through.

To create a mask layer:

1. Do either of the following:

   ▲ Create a new layer in the Timeline (for example, by clicking the Insert Layer button). Flash selects the new layer.

   ▲ Select a layer that already exists.

   In general, you should create (or select) a layer directly above the layer containing content you want to mask, although you can always create the mask separately and link the masked layers to it later.

2. Control-click (Mac) or right-click (Windows) the layer to access the contextual menu for layers, and choose Mask (**Figure 6.28**).

   Flash automatically defines the layer as a mask, links the layer beneath the selected layer to the mask, and locks both layers so that masking is in effect (**Figure 6.29**). You can also rename the layer to identify it as a mask, if you wish.

✔ Tips

■ To link existing layers to a mask layer quickly, drag them in the Timeline so they sit directly below the mask or one of its linked layers.

■ Once you have linked a layer to the mask, you can create additional new linked layers for that mask quickly. Select the linked (masked) layer; and then follow the steps for creating a new layer. Flash adds the new layers as masked layers directly above the selected layer.

WORKING WITH MASK LAYERS

To create the mask:

1. Create one or more layers containing graphic elements you want to reveal only through a mask.

2. Create a mask layer above your masked-content layers, and make sure that it's selected, visible, and unlocked.

   The layer should be highlighted in the Timeline, and the Eye and Lock columns should contain bullets (not *X* or padlock icons).

3. Use the drawing tools to create a fill shape on the mask layer (**Figure 6.30**).

   Flash uses only fills to create the mask and ignores any strokes on the mask layer.

✔ Tips

- It's best to limit your mask to a single merge-shape or a single graphic-object (drawing-object, primitive-shape, group, symbol, or text field with static text). If the mask layer contains multiple merge-shapes, the mask may work initially. Move one of the parts, however, and Flash stops treating that shape as part of the mask. If the mask layer contains a merge-shape and a graphic-object, Flash uses just the merge-shape to create the mask. If the mask layer contains multiple graphic-objects, Flash uses just the bottom-most one. (For more details on stacking order for graphic-objects, see Chapter 5.)

- If you want to use multiple shapes in a mask, select them and turn them into a single drawing-object: choose Modify > Combine Objects > Union.

- You can also set up mask and masked layers in the Layer Properties dialog (see "Controlling Layers and Folders," earlier in this chapter).

When you define this layer as a mask...

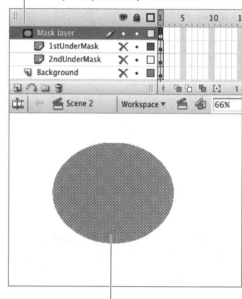

...this merge-shape fill becomes the mask

Figure 6.30 The content for the layers that the mask will reveal is just like any other content. You must use fill shapes to create "holes" in the mask; all those shapes must be on the same sublevel of the mask layer. In other words, you must either use only merge-shapes or combine all your shapes into a single drawing-object.

Figure 6.31 The Show Masking command in the contextual menu for layers locks all layers linked to the selected mask.

To see the mask's effect:

◆ Lock the mask layer and all linked layers.

or

1. Control-click (Mac) or right-click (Windows) a mask (or masked) layer.

2. From the contextual menu, choose Show Masking (**Figure 6.31**).

   Flash automatically locks the mask layer and all the layers linked to it.

   In document-editing mode, you must lock the mask layer and any masked layers beneath it to see the mask effect (**Figure 6.32**). You can see the effect without locking the layers in one of Flash's test modes (see Chapter 8).

Transparent fill helps you see what the mask will reveal

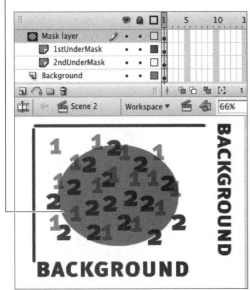

Masking not on

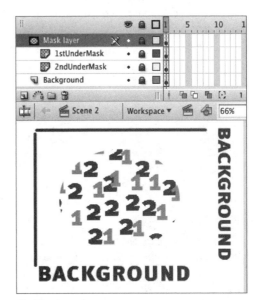

Masking turned on

Figure 6.32 After defining the mask and masked layers, you must lock them to see the mask in effect in document-editing mode.

To edit a mask:

1. In the Timeline, select the mask layer.

2. Make sure that the layer is visible and unlocked.

3. Use any of the techniques you learned in preceding chapters to create and edit fills.

✔ Tips

- To break the connection between a mask and its linked layers, redefine the layer type for the masked layer in the Layer Properties dialog.

- If you delete a mask layer, Flash redefines all the layers linked to it as normal layers.

- Keep in mind that masks use processor power. Using too many masks can slow the frame rate in your final movie. In addition, masked-off areas are published in your final movie and add to file size.

The Mystery of Masks

A mask layer is like a window envelope (the ones you get bills in). The envelope may contain whole sheaves of papers covered with numbers, but the outside presents a blank white front with only a little window that lets you see the portion of the bill showing your name and address. The mask layer is the window envelope, and the linked, or masked, layers are the papers inside.

In Flash, you create the window in the envelope by drawing and painting on a mask layer. (As you'll learn in Chapter 11, you can animate that window to create special effects.) A fill shape on the mask layer becomes a window in the final movie. That window reveals whatever lies on the linked (or masked) layers inside the envelope. Within that envelope, you can have several layers that act just like any other Flash layers.

Here's where it gets a bit tricky. Any areas of the envelope (the mask layer) that you leave blank hide the corresponding areas of all the layers inside the envelope (the masked layers). But the same blank areas of the envelope allow all *unlinked* layers outside and below the envelope to show through.

WORKING WITH SYMBOLS

In previous chapters, you learned to create and edit static graphics. Ultimately, you'll want to animate those graphics, and you're likely to want to use the same graphic over and over again. You may want an element to appear several times in one movie, or you may want to use the same element in several movies. You can save graphic elements for reuse by storing them in a library; to do that, you first turn the graphics into *symbols*.

Every Flash document has its own library; the library contains the symbols you create and other *assets*, reusable elements that you import for use in your movie (see the sidebar "Library Terminology").

In this chapter, you learn to work with libraries and to create symbols that are static graphics. In later chapters, you learn about creating animated symbols and buttons (see Chapters 11 and 12), using bitmapped graphics (see Chapter 14), adding sounds (see Chapter 15), and adding video (see Chapter 16).

Library Terminology

The general term for an item stored in a Flash library is an *asset*. More specifically, graphics created with Flash's drawing tools and stored in a library are called *symbols;* fonts stored in a library are called *font symbols;* and imported sounds, video clips, and bitmaps (which are always stored in a library) are just called *sounds, video clips,* and *bitmaps.* Flash refers to each copy of a library asset that you use in a movie as an *instance* of that asset.

Understanding the Library Panel

The Library panel offers several ways to view a library's contents and allows you to organize your symbols, sounds, video clips, and bitmaps in folders. The Library panel provides information about when an item was last modified, what type of item it is, and how many times the movie uses it. The Library panel also contains shortcut buttons and menus for working with symbols. Flash has shortcuts for creating new folders, for renaming elements, and for deleting items quickly.

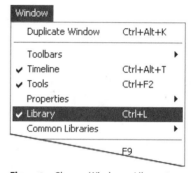

Figure 7.1 Choose Window > Library to open the Library panel of the currently active Flash document.

To open the library of the current movie:

◆ Choose Window > Library, press F11, or press ⌘-L (Mac) or Ctrl-L (Windows) (**Figure 7.1**).

The Library panel appears on the desktop (**Figure 7.2**). The Library panel contains the libraries of all the Flash documents currently open on your desktop.

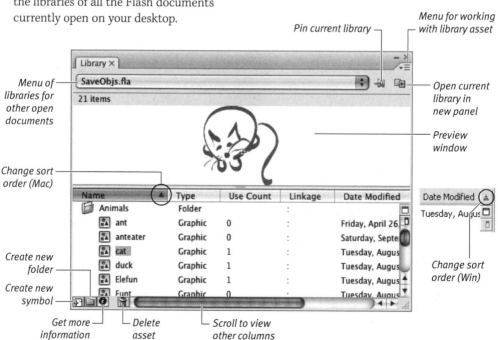

Figure 7.2 The Library panel lists the assets assigned to the current document. Items are sorted by the selected column; click the Sort Order button to reverse the sort order.

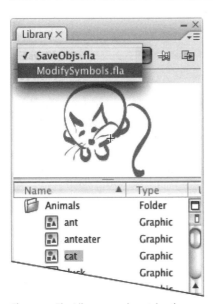

Figure 7.3 The Library panel contains the libraries of all the currently open documents. To view a different library without switching documents, choose one from the menu of open documents.

■ The variety of menus from which you can open a library of some sort can be daunting at first. Here's a short rundown. To open the Library panel for an open, active document, choose Window > Library; to view the library of an open, inactive document, choose it from the menu of open documents in the Library panel; to open the library of a closed document, choose File > Import > Open External Library; to open one of the common libraries, choose Window > Common Libraries (see the sidebar "What Are Common Libraries?").

To view the library of another open document:

1. Open two or more Flash documents.

2. With the library panel open, do either of the following:

   ▲ In the Library panel, from the menu of open documents, choose the desired inactive document (**Figure 7.3**).

   or

   ▲ Select the open document whose library you want to view.

   For documents in a tabbed window, click the document's tab; for documents in separate windows, click the desired window to make it active.

   The contents of the Library panel change to display the assets of the selected document.

✔ Tips

■ The Library panel displays the assets of just one document at a time. To view libraries for multiple documents simultaneously, open multiple Library panels. In the open Library panel, click the New Library Panel button (the double-document-arrow icon just below the options menu). Flash opens the current library in a new panel window; you have two panels showing the assets of the same document. Choose a different library in one of the panels.

To open the library of a closed Flash document:

1. Choose File > Import > Open External Library, or press Shift-⌘-O (Mac) or Ctrl-Shift-O (Windows) (**Figure 7.4**).
   The Open As Library dialog appears.

2. Navigate to the file whose library you want to open, select it, and click Open.
   The Library panel appears on the desktop, making those symbols available for use in other movies.

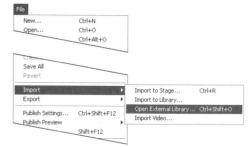

Figure 7.4 Choose File > Import > Open External Library to access symbols from the library of a closed Flash document.

What Are Common Libraries?

Flash makes a set of *common libraries* available from the Menu bar—a sort of library of libraries. Flash ships with three common libraries, but you can add your own. The libraries in the Common Libraries menu are Flash files that live in the Libraries folder of the application-level Configuration folder (see the sidebar "The Mystery of the Configuration Folder," in Chapter 1). If you have administrative privileges, you can add FLA files to that folder. If you don't have privileges, you must add a folder named Libraries to the User-Level Configuration folder. Any files you add to that Libraries folder also appear in the Common Libraries menu when you restart the application (**Figure 7.5**). Choosing an item from the Common Libraries menu opens only the library, not the file itself.

You might create a common library to keep all the symbols, sounds, video clips, and bitmaps for a work project accessible from the Menu bar. As you create or import assets, add a copy of each item to a special file with a meaningful name—for example, MyShapes. Make the file one of your common libraries. When you choose MyShapes from the Window > Common Libraries menu, Flash opens the library containing all your project's items.

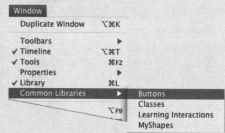

Figure 7.5 The Common Libraries menu gives you quick access to the libraries of Flash Documents located inside a Libraries folder that's available to all users.

UNDERSTANDING THE LIBRARY PANEL

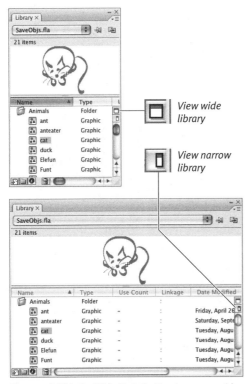

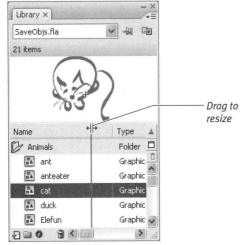

Drag to resize

Figure 7.6 Click the Wide State button to open a wide Library panel. Click the Narrow State button to open a narrow one.

Figure 7.7 Drag the divider between column headers to resize a column in the Library panel.

View wide library

View narrow library

To change Library panel width:

◆ In the open Library panel, do one of the following:

▲ To switch from narrow to wide, click the Wide State button (**Figure 7.6**).

Flash widens the panel to twice the width of the default panel size.

▲ To switch from wide to narrow, click the Narrow State button.

Flash returns the panel to the default width.

To resize library columns:

1. In the Library panel, position the pointer over a column-head divider.

The pointer changes to a double-arrow divider-moving icon.

2. Click and drag the divider (**Figure 7.7**).

✔ Tips

■ Flash tracks how many times you use a symbol instance, but the Use Count column doesn't display the latest number automatically. To change that setting, from the Library panel's options menu, choose Keep Use Counts Updated. (This setting can slow Flash.) To update use counts periodically, choose Update Use Counts Now as needed.

■ When in doubt about whether or not to make a graphic element a symbol, opt for making it a symbol. You can always break it apart into its original shapes. When you publish a movie to make it available to end users, unused symbols don't export (unless you specifically set them up to export). So unused symbols add nothing to the SWF file's size. Check it out for yourself by generating a size report when you publish your movie (see Chapter 17).

185

Understanding Library Hierarchy

Flash lets you create folders and subfolders to organize assets hierarchically within the library.

To create a library folder:

1. Open the Library panel.

2. To select a location, do either of the following:

   ▲ To add a root-level folder, select an item at the root level.

   ▲ To add a subfolder, select an item within the folder where you want to add the new subfolder. (Do not select the folder itself.)

3. To create the new folder, do either of the following:

   ▲ From the pop-up options menu in the top-right corner of the window, choose New Folder (**Figure 7.8**).

   ▲ At the bottom of the window, click the New Folder button (**Figure 7.9**).

   Flash creates a new folder, selects it, and activates the text-entry field.

4. Type a name for your folder.

5. Press Enter.

✔ Tips

■ To sort items in the Library panel, click the heading of the column you want to sort by. To sort by name, for example, click the Name column header.

■ To toggle between alphanumeric and reverse-alphanumeric sort order, click the Sort button. In Windows, the button (stacked lines that form a triangle) appears on the far-right side of the column headings; on a Mac, the button (a triangle) appears next to the heading of the currently selected column (see Figure 7.2).

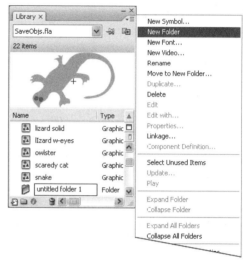

Figure 7.8 From the options menu in the Library panel, choose New Folder to create a library folder.

Figure 7.9 To create new folders and subfolders, click the New Folder button.

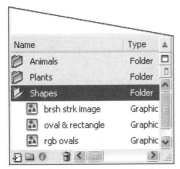

Figure 7.10 Open folders in the Library panel to display their contents.

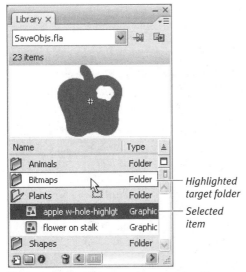

Figure 7.11 In the Library panel, you can drag items between folders. The target folder highlights when it's ready to receive the dragged item.

To work with library folders:

1. In the Library panel, select a closed folder.

2. To open a closed folder, do either of the following:
   - ▲ Double-click the folder icon.
   - ▲ From the Library panel's options menu, choose Expand Folder.

   The folder's contents appear in the Library panel (**Figure 7.10**).

3. To close an open folder, do either of the following:
   - ▲ Double-click the folder icon.
   - ▲ From the Library panel's options menu, choose Collapse Folder.

✔ Tip

- ■ To open all library folders at the same time, from the Library panel's options menu, choose Expand All Folders. To close all folders, choose Collapse All Folders.

To move items between library folders:

1. In the open Library panel, select the item you want to move.

2. Drag the selected item over the icon of the destination folder.

   Flash highlights the target folder (**Figure 7.11**).

3. Release the mouse button.

   Flash moves the item into the new folder.

✔ Tip

- ■ To move an item to a new folder quickly, from the Library panel's options menu, choose Move to New Folder. A dialog for naming the new folder appears. Type a name and press Enter. Flash creates a folder on the same level as the selected item and places that item inside.

UNDERSTANDING LIBRARY HIERARCHY

Converting Graphics to Symbols

Not all graphics in a Flash movie are symbols; you need to take special steps to define the items you create as symbols. You can convert elements you've already created into symbols or create symbols from scratch in the symbol editor. Symbols reside in the library of the document in which you create them. You can copy a symbol from one document to another or from one library to another document; the symbol then resides separately in each document's library.

The standard library of a Flash document contains all the symbols used in that document; it can also contain unused symbols.

The following task covers creating static graphic symbols. But you can also turn graphics into symbols that are animations (see Chapter 11) or buttons (see Chapter 12).

Why Use Symbols?

Flash uses vectors to hold down file size: Each vector shape is just a set of instructions—a recipe for creating the shape. This fact makes vector shapes efficient to begin with. Symbols allow you to reuse elements in a way that's more efficient than duplicating vector shapes.

A symbol is a master recipe. Imagine a busy restaurant that serves three kinds of soup—chicken noodle, cream of chicken rice, and chicken with garden vegetables—and each pot of soup has its own cook. The head chef could go over with each cook all the steps required to make chicken broth, but that would involve a lot of repetition and take a lot of time. If the restaurant has a master recipe for chicken broth, the chef can instruct all the cooks to make a pot of chicken broth and then tell each cook just those additional steps that distinguish each dish—add noodles for chicken noodle; add rice and cream for cream of chicken rice; and add potatoes, carrots, and peas for garden vegetable.

Symbols act the same way in Flash. The full recipe is in the library. Each instance on the Stage contains just the instructions that say which recipe to start with and how to modify it—for example, use the recipe for the red rectangle, but make it twice as large, change the color to blue, and rotate it 45 degrees clockwise. Because symbols can themselves contain other symbols, it really pays to break your graphic elements into their lowest-common-denominator parts, make each individual part a symbol, and then combine the parts into larger symbols or graphics.

Each instance of a symbol (each place you use the same symbol in your Flash document) is linked to one master symbol. Instead of adding a full set of instructions for each instance, Flash adds a note to repeat the instructions, possibly with certain modifications. This method of reusing elements helps keep the published file size small. In addition, if you decide you want the symbol to look different (you want a perfect circle instead of an oval in your logo, for example), you can update one master graphic element instead of making the same change over and over in your document.

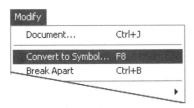

Figure 7.12 To turn a selection into a symbol, choose Modify > Convert to Symbol. In the Convert to Symbol dialog, name your symbol, define its type, and set its registration point. (Click the Advanced button to expand the box to set linkages for sharing and import/export.)

Selected merge-shape

Converted to a symbol

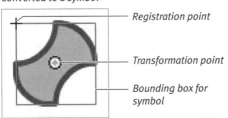

Registration point

Transformation point

Bounding box for symbol

Figure 7.13 A selected merge-shape on the Stage is highlighted with dots. When you convert that shape to a symbol, the bounding box is the only item that gets highlighted. A crosshair indicates where the symbol's registration point is. A circle indicates the symbol's transformation point.

To turn an existing graphic into a symbol:

1. On the Stage, select the graphic element(s) you want to convert to a symbol.

   Flash highlights the selected element(s).

2. Choose Modify > Convert to Symbol, or press F8 on the keyboard.

   The Convert to Symbol dialog appears (**Figure 7.12**). Flash gives the symbol a default name—for example, Symbol 16—based on the number of symbols previously created for the library.

3. If you don't want to use the default name, type a new name for your symbol.

4. Choose Graphic as the symbol type.

5. To set the symbol's registration point (see the sidebar "Registration Point vs. Transformation Point for Symbols"), click one of the squares in the registration model.

   By default, Flash registers a symbol by the upper-left corner of its bounding box. Click a different square on the registration model—another corner, the center, or the middle of a side—to make Flash register the symbol by the corresponding point on the symbol's bounding box.

6. Click OK.

   Flash adds the symbol to the library. The selected graphic element(s) on the Stage become an instance of the symbol. A crosshair appears, indicating the location of the registration point; a circle, known as the transformation point, appears at the center of the symbol (**Figure 7.13**). You can no longer edit the item directly on the Stage; you must open it in one of Flash's symbol-editing modes.

Converting Graphics to Symbols

✔ Tips

■ A graphic symbol can consist of one or more merge-shapes, drawing-objects, primitive-shapes, grouped shapes—you name it. You can even include symbols within symbols. Whatever is selected on the Stage when you choose Convert to Symbol becomes part of the symbol.

■ To convert graphic elements to a symbol quickly, select the elements on the Stage and drag the selection to the lower half of the document's Library panel. The Convert to Symbol dialog appears. Name and define your symbol as described in the preceding task.

■ The registration model is elusive. It appears only in the Convert to Symbol dialog. That means you get one chance to use the model to position the registration point at preset locations on the symbol's bounding box or at its center. However, you can always go into symbol-editing mode and reposition the graphic elements in relation to the registration point (see "Editing Master Symbols," later in this chapter).

About Symbol Types

In Flash, you must specify a symbol type for each symbol. (In early versions of Flash, this was called the symbol's behavior.) You have three choices: graphic, button, and movie clip.

Graphics are, as you might expect, graphic elements, but they can also be animated graphic elements. The feature that distinguishes one symbol type from another is the way the symbol interacts with the Timeline of the movie in which it appears. Graphic symbols operate in lock step with the Timeline of the movie. A static graphic symbol takes up one frame of the movie in which you place it (just as any graphic element would). A three-frame animated graphic symbol takes up three frames of the movie (see Chapter 11).

Buttons have their own four-frame Timeline; a button instance sits in a single frame of the main movie Timeline but displays different frames as a user's mouse interacts with the button (see Chapter 12).

Movie clips have their own multiframe Timeline that plays independently of the main movie Timeline (see Chapter 11).

Registration Point vs. Transformation Point for Symbols

The *registration point* (represented by a small crosshair) is the point that Flash uses to *register* a graphic-object—that is, to locate the object via coordinates on the Stage during authoring and playback. For drawing-objects, primitives, groups, and text fields, the registration point is always the upper-left corner of the object's bounding box. For symbols, the location of the registration point is flexible (**Figure 7.14**). When you select elements on the Stage and convert the selection to a symbol, you can put the point at any of nine preset locations (see "Converting Graphics to Symbols," earlier in this chapter). When you create a symbol from scratch in symbol-editing mode, you determine where the registration point goes by positioning elements around a crosshair icon on the Stage (see the next section, "Creating Symbols from Scratch"). The location of the registration point stays the same for all instances of the same symbol.

The *transformation point* (represented by a small circle) is the reference point Flash uses for transforming the symbol. When you rotate a symbol with the free-transform tool in Rotate and Skew mode, for example, the transformation point is the pivot around which the symbol spins. You can also use the transformation point for snapping operations. By default, Flash places the transformation point in the center of a master symbol, but you can change the transformation point's location for individual symbol instances by using the free-transform tool.

The Info panel and Properties tab of the Property inspector display coordinates that locate a selected symbol instance in space during authoring. The Properties tab of the Property inspector always displays the coordinates of a symbol's registration point. The Info panel gives you the option to view coordinates for the registration point or the transformation point. You choose which method via the Registration/Transformation Point button (for more details about using the Info panel and Properties tab of the Property inspector, see Chapter 4).

Registration model

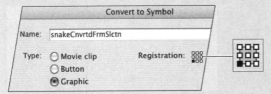

Converted symbol

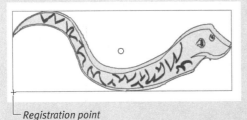

Registration point

Symbol from scratch

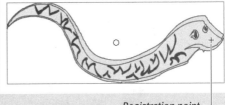

Registration point

Figure 7.14 When you convert a selection to a symbol, the registration model lets you position the registration point in the center, in any corner, or in the middle of any side of the symbol's bounding box; the location highlighted in the model becomes the registration point in the symbol. When you create a symbol from scratch, you can position the registration point freely.

Creating Symbols from Scratch

You can avoid the conversion process described in the preceding section by creating graphics directly in symbol-editing mode. This practice makes all the tools, frames, and layers of the Flash editor available, but Flash defines the element you're creating as a symbol from the start.

To create a new symbol:

1. To enter symbol-editing mode, do one of the following:
   - ▲ Choose Insert > New Symbol, or press ⌘-F8 (Mac) or Ctrl-F8 (Windows).
   - ▲ From the Library panel's options menu, choose New Symbol (**Figure 7.15**).
   - ▲ In the bottom-left corner of the Library panel, click the New Symbol button (**Figure 7.16**).

   The Create New Symbol dialog appears.

2. Type a name for your symbol.

3. Choose Graphic as the symbol type.

Figure 7.15 From the Library panel's options menu, choose New Symbol to create a symbol from scratch.

Figure 7.16 Click the Library panel's New Symbol button to create a symbol from scratch.

4. Click OK.

Flash enters symbol-editing mode. Flash displays the name of the symbol you're creating in the Edit bar, places a crosshair in the center of the Stage, and hides the Pasteboard (**Figure 7.17**). The crosshair indicates the symbol's registration point.

5. Create your graphic on the Stage of the symbol editor as you would in the regular editing environment.

continues on next page

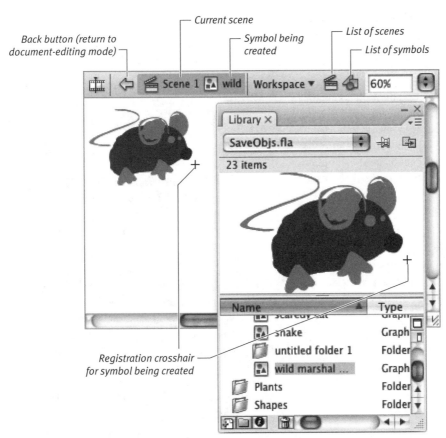

Back button (return to document-editing mode)

Current scene

Symbol being created

List of scenes

List of symbols

Registration crosshair for symbol being created

Figure 7.17 In symbol-editing mode, the name of the symbol being worked on appears in the Edit bar just above the Stage.

6. To return to document-editing mode, do one of the following:

▲ Choose Edit > Edit Document. Flash returns you to the current scene.

▲ In the Edit bar, click the Back button or the Current Scene link (**Figure 7.18**). Flash returns you to the current scene.

▲ From the Edit Scene pop-up menu in the Edit bar, choose a scene (**Figure 7.19**). Flash takes you to that scene.

✔ Tips

■ When you're creating new symbols, be sure to consider how the registration point should work with your finished symbol so you can place your graphic elements appropriately in relation to the registration crosshair. Will you want to align this symbol by its center? Then position your elements evenly around the crosshair. Will you want to align this symbol by a specific area? (You might want to register a bird figure, for example, by a point at the tip of the beak.) Then position your elements accordingly.

■ When you enter symbol-editing mode for an existing symbol, the registration crosshair may be outside the current viewing area. To bring the registration crosshair to the center of your window, choose View > Magnification > Show Frame.

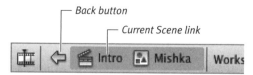

Back button
Current Scene link

Figure 7.18 Click the Back button or the Current Scene link to return to document-editing mode.

Figure 7.19 Choose a scene from the Edit bar's Edit Scene menu to return to document-editing mode.

Where Am I?

When you edit symbols in a Flash document, the current window switches to symbol-editing mode. It's easy to get confused about whether you're editing the main document or a symbol. Learn to recognize the following subtle visual cues; they're the only indication that you're in symbol-editing mode.

In symbol-editing mode, a Flash document displays the name of the scene and symbol you're editing in the Edit bar and activates the Back button. The Pasteboard disappears. Also, a small crosshair, which acts as a registration point for the symbol, appears on the Stage. If you entered symbol-editing mode via the Edit in Place command, any elements on the Stage that aren't being edited appear in a ghostly form. Apart from these changes, the Timeline, the Stage, and the tools all appear and work just as they do in document-editing mode.

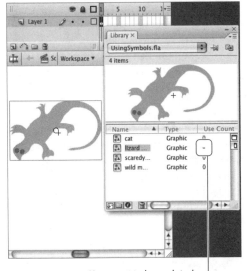

Preview location of symbol on the Stage

Use count to be updated

Figure 7.20 When you drag a symbol from the Library panel to the Stage (top), Flash places the symbol on the Stage, selects it, and updates that symbol's use count internally (bottom). When you aren't keeping use counts updated constantly, the dash in the Use Count column indicates a change. To see the actual figure, choose Update Use Counts Now from the Library panel's options menu.

Using Symbol Instances

A *symbol instance* is a pointer to the full description of the symbol. Symbols help keep file sizes small. If you converted a graphic on the Stage to a symbol, you have one symbol instance on the Stage. To use the symbol again, or if you created your symbol in symbol-editing mode, you'll need to get a copy out of the library and onto the Stage.

To place a symbol instance in your movie:

1. In the Timeline, select the layer and keyframe where you want the graphic symbol to appear.

   Flash can place symbols only in keyframes. If you select an in-between frame, Flash places the symbol in the preceding keyframe. (To learn more about keyframes, see Chapter 8.)

2. Open the library containing the symbol.

3. In the Library panel, navigate to the symbol you want; click it to select it.

   Flash highlights the chosen symbol and displays it in the preview window.

4. Position the pointer over the preview window.

5. Click and drag a copy of the symbol onto the Stage.

   Flash previews the symbol's location on the Stage with a rectangular outline as you drag (**Figure 7.20**).

6. Release the mouse button.

   Flash places the symbol on the Stage and selects it.

✔ Tip

- To place a symbol instance quickly, drag the symbol name directly from the Library panel to the Stage without using the previewed image.

Modifying Symbol Instances

You can change the appearance of individual symbol instances without changing the master symbol itself. As with any other element, you can resize and reposition an instance (for example, scale and rotate it) by using the tools in the Tools panel, Info and Transform panels, and the Properties tab of the Property inspector (see Chapter 4).

You can also change a symbol instance's color and transparency, but the method differs from the methods you've learned for assigning colors to merge-shapes, drawing-objects, and primitive-shapes. You modify the color, intensity, and transparency of a symbol instance via the Color menu in the Properties tab of the Property inspector.

To change an instance's color property:

1. On the Stage, select the symbol instance you want to modify.

2. Access the Properties tab of the Properties inspector.
   Settings for the symbol instance appear.

3. From the Color menu, choose one color property to modify.
   The properties available for you to modify are Brightness (amount of black or white in the color), Tint, Alpha (transparency), and Advanced (simultaneous changes to alpha and RGB values).

4. Enter settings for your selected color change as outlined in the tasks that follow.

5. Press enter to confirm the new settings.
   Flash applies the new settings to the symbol on the Stage.

Tips for Transforming Symbols

You can change the dimensions and orientation of symbol instances using the same techniques you use to modify graphic-objects (see Chapter 4). You can enter precise values in the Properties tab of the Property inspector or in the Transform or Info panels; you can also modify symbol instances interactively with the free-transform tool. Here are some tips for using that tool.

When you use the free-transform tool to scale a symbol instance, it scales in relation to the instance's transformation point (by default, the center of the symbol instance). Hold down the Option key (Mac) or Alt key (Windows) to scale the symbol instance relative to the bounding-box corner diagonally, opposite the corner you're dragging.

You can change the transformation point of individual symbol instances. Using the free-transform tool, click the small white circle in the middle of the symbol instance. Drag the circle to a new location.

To position a symbol instance's transformation point at the same location as the symbol's registration point, select the instance with the free-transform tool. Then double-click the transformation point.

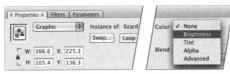

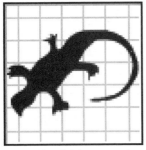

Figure 7.21 Use the Brightness settings in the Color section of the Properties tab to change the intensity of a symbol instance. Enter a high value to make the symbol instance lighter or a low value to make it darker.

−100 percent brightness setting

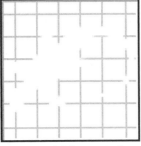

100 percent brightness setting

Figure 7.22 At its extremes, the Brightness setting lets you turn a symbol instance completely black or completely white.

Tint amount
Tint color

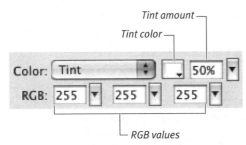

RGB values

Figure 7.23 Use the Tint settings in the Color section of the Properties tab to change the color of a symbol instance.

To change an instance's brightness:

1. In step 3 of the preceding task, from the Color menu, choose Brightness.

   A field for entering a new brightness percentage appears (**Figure 7.21**).

2. Enter a value in the Brightness field.

   A value of −100 makes the symbol black; a value of 0 leaves the symbol at its original brightness; a value of 100 makes the symbol white (**Figure 7.22**).

To change the instance's color:

1. In step 3 of the first task in this section, from the Color menu, choose Tint.

   Tint settings appear (**Figure 7.23**).

2. To choose a new color, do either of the following:

   ▲ In the Red, Green, and Blue fields, enter new RGB values.

   ▲ Click the Tint Color control, and choose a color from the pop-up swatch set.

3. Type a percentage in the Tint Amount field.

   The tint percentage indicates how much of the new color to blend with the existing colors. Applying a tint of 100 percent changes all the lines and fills in the symbol to the new color. Applying a lesser percentage mixes some of the new color with the existing colors in the symbol; it's almost like placing a transparent film of the new color over the symbol.

MODIFYING SYMBOL INSTANCES

To change the instance's transparency:

1. In step 3 of the first task in this section, from the Color menu, choose Alpha.

   A field for the Alpha percentage appears (**Figure 7.24**).

2. Enter a new value in the Alpha field.

   A value of 0 makes the symbol completely transparent; a value of 100 makes the symbol completely opaque.

✔ Tip

■ Instead of pressing Enter to confirm a value you enter in one of the fields on the Properties tab of the Property inspector, you can click elsewhere in the Properties tab or click the Stage.

Figure 7.24 Use the Alpha settings in the Color section of the Properties tab to change the transparency of a symbol instance.

The Mystery of Advanced Effect Settings

The Advanced Effect settings let you change the RGB values and alpha values for a symbol instance simultaneously. The sliders in the left-hand column control what percentage of the RGB and alpha values that make up the colors in the original symbol appear in the symbol instance. The sliders on the right add to or subtract from the red, green, blue, and alpha values of the original colors.

Imagine a symbol with three ovals. One is pure red, one is pure green, and one is pure blue. The alpha setting is 50 percent. Changing the red slider in the left-hand column (the percentage of the current red value) affects only the red oval. The green and blue ovals contain 0 percent red; doubling the value makes no visible change. Moving the right-hand slider upward adds red to everything, including the green and blue ovals. These ovals start to change color when you increase the red value. (If you move the right-hand slider downward, decreasing the red value, you'll see no difference in the green and blue ovals where there was no red to begin with.)

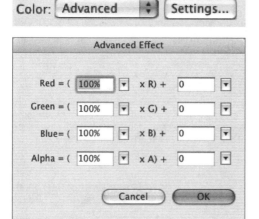

Figure 7.25 Choose Advanced from the color menu and click the Settings button in the Properties tab (top) to access the Advanced Effect dialog (bottom). Enter new values to change the color and transparency of a symbol instance.

To change the instance's tint and alpha simultaneously:

1. In step 3 of the first task in this section, from the Color menu, choose Advanced.

   A Settings button appears to the right of the menu.

2. Click the Settings button.

   The Advanced Effect dialog appears (**Figure 7.25**). This dialog contains sliders and text fields for changing red, green, blue, and alpha values.

3. Adjust the values to fine-tune the color and transparency of the symbol instance (see the sidebar, "The Mystery of Advanced Effect Settings").

4. To apply the color effect, click OK.

✔ Tip

■ To preview new color values interactively, access the slider to the right of any color-related entry field (for example, the Tint Amount field). Flash updates the symbol on the Stage as you drag the slider lever.

MODIFYING SYMBOL INSTANCES

Timeline Effects: A Dubious Source of Symbols

Flash's Timeline Effects commands (found in the Insert menu) are an attempt to help less-experienced Flash users create a few common special effects and simple animations. If you use Timeline Effects, Flash creates symbols for you (some are static symbols, such as the ones described in this chapter; others are animated symbols, which are described in Chapter 11). You should not reuse or modify timeline-effects symbols according to the methods described in this chapter; doing so risks interfering with the effect. If you double-click the finished effect symbol on the Stage, nothing happens; if you select the finished symbol and choose an editing command (such as Edit > Edit Selected), you get a warning that if you continue with the edit, you'll lose the ability to edit the effect; if you attempt to reuse the finished symbol, or reuse or edit any of the subordinate symbols that create the effect, however, you get no warning. In general, Timeline Effects are not a good option for creating animation and effects in Flash. Therefore, they are not covered in this book.

Swapping One Symbol Instance for Another

Flash lets you replace one symbol instance with another while retaining all the modifications you've made in the symbol instance. If, for example, you want to change the look of a logo in certain places in your site but not everywhere, you can create the new logo as a separate symbol and swap it in as needed. (To change the look for every instance, edit the master logo symbol directly, as you learn to do in "Editing Master Symbols," later in the chapter.) You perform symbol swapping in the Properties tab of the Property inspector (**Figure 7.26**).

To switch symbols:

1. On the Stage, select the symbol instance you want to change.

2. In the Properties tab of the Property inspector, click the Swap button.

   The Swap Symbol dialog appears, listing all the symbols in the current document's library (**Figure 7.27**). Flash highlights the name of the symbol you're modifying. In the Windows operating systems Flash also places a bullet next to the name in the Symbol list.

3. From the Symbol list, select the replacement symbol.

   In Windows, the original symbol remains bulleted; Flash highlights the new symbol and places it in the preview window.

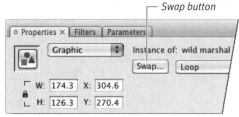

Swap button

Figure 7.26 The Swap button in the Properties tab lets you replace a selected symbol instance with an instance of a different symbol from the same document.

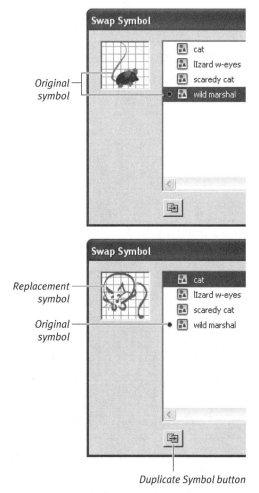

Original symbol

Replacement symbol

Original symbol

Duplicate Symbol button

Figure 7.27 Select a replacement symbol from the list in the Swap Symbol dialog, and click OK to exchange one symbol for another.

Unmodified instance of mouse

Unmodified instance of cat

Instance of mouse scaled and rotated before swapping

After swapping: scaling and rotation applied to cat

Figure 7.28 When you swap symbols, any modifications you have made for the selected instance you're swapping apply to the replacement instance.

4. Click OK.

Flash places the new symbol on the Stage, locating the new symbol where the old one was located and applying any modifications you previously made for that instance (**Figure 7.28**).

✔ Tips

■ To swap symbols quickly, double-click the new symbol in the Swap Symbol dialog. Flash replaces it and closes the dialog.

■ The Duplicate Symbol button in the Swap Symbol dialog lets you make a copy of whatever symbol is selected in the list (Figure 7.27). If you know you need to tweak the master version of the replacement symbol for this instance, but you also want to keep the current version, click the Duplicate Symbol button, name it in the dialog that appears, and click OK. Make sure you select the duplicate as the replacement in the Swap Symbol dialog, and click OK. You can edit the duplicate's master symbol later.

SWAPPING ONE SYMBOL INSTANCE FOR ANOTHER

Editing Master Symbols

After you create a symbol, you can refine and modify it in symbol-editing mode. Unlike modifications of a symbol instance, which affect just that instance on the Stage and leave the master symbol in the library unchanged, modifications made in symbol-editing mode affect the master symbol and all instances of that symbol in your movie.

You can enter symbol-editing mode in several ways.

To enter symbol-editing mode from the Stage:

1. On the Stage, select the symbol you want to edit.

2. To open the symbol editor, do one of the following:

   ▲ Choose Edit > Edit Symbols, or press ⌘-E (Mac) or Ctrl-E (Windows) (**Figure 7.29**).

   ▲ Choose Edit > Edit Selected.

   ▲ From the pop-up list of symbols in the Edit bar, choose the symbol you want to edit (**Figure 7.30**).

Flash opens the symbol editor in the current window. You can edit the symbol using any of the techniques you've learned for modifying graphics and creating and deleting content.

✔ Tip

■ The Edit in Place command lets you edit your master symbol in context on the Stage with all other items grayed out (**Figure 7.31**). To evoke the Edit in Place command, select a symbol instance and choose Edit > Edit in Place. Any changes you make affect all instances of that symbol.

Figure 7.29 Choosing Edit > Edit Symbols takes you from document-editing mode to symbol-editing mode. If you have selected a symbol on the Stage, choosing Edit > Edit Selected also takes you to symbol-editing mode.

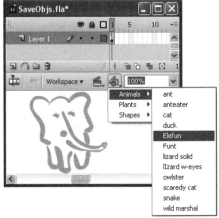

Figure 7.30 Choosing a symbol from the Edit Symbol pop-up menu in the Edit bar takes you into symbol-editing mode.

Symbol being edited

Figure 7.31 The Edit in Place command allows you to see your symbol instance in context with other items on the stage. The symbol instance appears in full color; the other elements on the Stage are grayed out. In this mode, changes made to the instance affect the master symbol and all the instances in the movie.

EDITING MASTER SYMBOLS

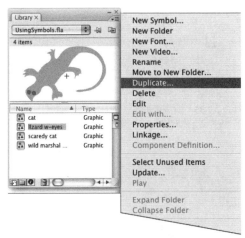

Figure 7.32 From the options menu in the Library panel, choose Duplicate to make a copy of the selected symbol.

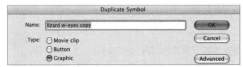

Figure 7.33 In the Duplicate Symbol dialog, you can name the new symbol (the default name is the original name plus the word *copy*) and assign its type.

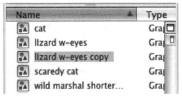

Figure 7.34 Flash puts duplicated symbols at the same library level as the original symbol.

Duplicating Master Symbols

Although you can always modify the instances of a symbol on the Stage, if you need to use one variation of a symbol over and over, you can duplicate the original master symbol and then modify the duplicate to create a new master symbol with those variations.

To create a duplicate symbol:

1. In the Library panel, select the symbol you want to duplicate.

2. From the options menu, choose Duplicate (**Figure 7.32**).

   Flash opens the Duplicate Symbol dialog, giving the duplicate symbol a default name (**Figure 7.33**).

3. If you want, type a new name for your symbol.

4. Choose the symbol type—for example, Graphic.

5. Click OK.

   Flash adds the new symbol to the library at the same level in the hierarchy as the original (**Figure 7.34**). The duplicate doesn't link to the original symbol in any way. You can change the duplicate without changing the original, and vice versa.

Deleting Master Symbols

Deleting symbols can be a little trickier than deleting shapes or groups on the Stage. Deleting one instance of a symbol from its place on the Stage is easy; use the methods for cutting or deleting graphics discussed in Chapter 4. Deleting symbols from the library isn't difficult but does require some thought, because instances of the symbol may still be in use in your movie.

To delete one symbol from the library:

1. In the Library panel, select the symbol you want to remove.

2. To delete the symbol, do either of the following:

   ▲ At the bottom of the window, click the Delete button (the trash-can icon) (**Figure 7.35**).

   ▲ From the pop-up options menu in the top-right corner of the window, choose Delete (**Figure 7.36**).

To delete a folder of symbols from the library:

1. Select the folder you want to remove.

2. Follow step 2 of the preceding task.

   Flash removes the folder and all the symbols it contains from the library.

✔ Tip

■ Always check the usage numbers before you delete library items (**Figure 7.37**). You don't want to delete a symbol that you're currently using in a movie, which is especially easy to do if you've nested symbols within symbols. Some earlier versions of Flash warned you when you tried to delete an item that was in use in a movie. Flash CS3 doesn't.

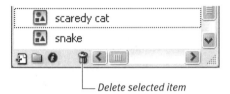

Delete selected item

Figure 7.35 Click the trash-can icon to delete a selected library item.

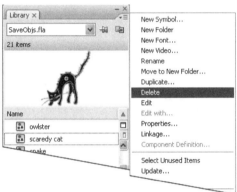

Figure 7.36 You can also choose Delete from the Library panel's options menu to remove selected symbols from the active document.

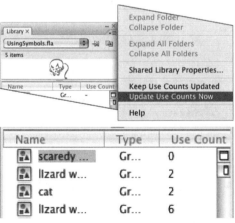

Figure 7.37 Be sure to update use counts before deleting a symbol: from the Library panel's options menu, choose Update Use Counts Now. Then check to be sure the item you want to delete has a use count of zero.

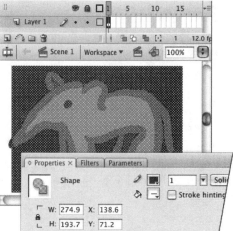

Figure 7.38 The Properties tab of the Property inspector reveals that the selected graphic is a symbol instance (top). To break the link with its master symbol, choose Modify > Break Apart. The Properties tab of the Property inspector reveals that the selection now consists of shapes; it's no longer a symbol instance (bottom).

Converting Symbol Instances to Graphics

At times, you'll want to break the link between a placed instance of a symbol and the master symbol. You may want to redraw the shape in a specific instance but not in every instance, for example. To convert a symbol back to an independent shape or set of shapes, break it apart.

To break the symbol link:

1. On the Stage, select the symbol instance whose link you want to break.

2. Choose Modify > Break Apart, or press ⌘-B (Mac) or Ctrl-B (Windows) (**Figure 7.38**).

   Flash breaks the link to the symbol in the library and selects the symbol's elements. The Properties tab of the Property inspector no longer displays information about the instance of the symbol; it displays information about the selected shapes.

   If the original symbol contained any grouped elements, they remain grouped after you break the link; ungrouped elements stay ungrouped. Any symbols that existed within the original symbol remain as instances of their respective master symbols. Now you can edit these elements as you learned to do in previous chapters.

The Mystery of Object-Level Undo

Every computer user gets familiar with the Undo command. ⌘-Z (Mac) or Ctrl-Z (Windows) becomes an automatic "oops" response to fix mistakes. Flash CS3 provides two types of undo: Document-level Undo and Object-level Undo. (Flash 8 also provides these two types of undo, but earlier versions of Flash do not.)

In Document-level Undo, Flash tracks every undoable step you take. Open the History panel (choose Window > Other Panels > History); you'll see the steps you've done listed in order. In Object-level Undo, Flash also tracks every undoable step but makes a distinction between steps that pertain to working in the main document and steps that pertain to working on master symbols.

Object-level Undo tracks the steps for each master symbol separately; each time you create a master symbol, Object-level Undo starts a separate History-panel list for that symbol. Within one work session (provided you haven't made changes in the History panel yourself), whenever you edit that master symbol, the History panel loads the steps for that symbol; any edits you make are added to the list. If you edit a different symbol, the panel loads the steps for that symbol. When you leave symbol-editing mode and return to document-editing mode, the History panel displays only the steps you've used in the main document.

Note that modifications you make to an instance of a symbol on the Stage are part of the history of the document, not of the master symbol.

To change from one type of undo to the other, choose Flash > Preferences (Mac) or Edit > Preferences (Windows). In the General category, from the Undo menu, choose the style you want. To track the history of master symbols separately, choose Object-level Undo; to track all your steps in one integrated list, choose Document-level Undo. It's best to choose your undo style at the beginning of a work session. If you switch in the middle, Flash wipes the current History panel clean.

CONVERTING SYMBOL INSTANCES TO GRAPHICS

FRAME-BY-FRAME ANIMATIONS

8

Frame-by-frame animation was the traditional form of animation used before the days of computers. Live-action movies and video are really a form of frame-by-frame animation. The camera captures motion by snapping a picture every so often. Animation simulates motion by showing drawings of elements at various stages of a movement.

Traditional animators, such as those who worked for the early Walt Disney or Warner Bros. studios from the 1930s through the 1960s, had to create hundreds of images, each one slightly different from the next, to achieve every movement of each character or element in the cartoon. To turn those drawings into animations, they captured the images on film, putting a different image in each frame of the movie.

Traditional animators painted individual characters (or parts of characters) and graphics on transparent sheets called *cels*. They stacked the cels to create the entire image for the frame. The cel technique allowed animators to save time by reusing parts of an image that stayed the same in more than one frame.

In Adobe Flash CS3 Professional, you, too, can make frame-by-frame animations by placing different content in different frames. Flash calls the frames that hold new content *keyframes*.

Using the Timeline

In the Timeline, you have five size options for viewing frames and two options for previewing thumbnails of frame contents. A Flash movie may contain hundreds of frames; the Timeline's scroll bars let you access frames not currently visible in the Timeline window. You can temporarily hide the Timeline so there's more room to view the Stage. You can also undock the Timeline so that it floats as a separate window and resize it to show more or fewer frames.

Figure 8.1 shows the Timeline for a movie with one layer and 15 defined frames.

To size the Timeline separately from the document:

1. Open a new Flash document.

   The default Timeline appears.

2. Position the pointer over the gripper (the textured area on the left side of the title bar at the top of the Timeline).

3. Click and drag away from the document window.

   A gray outline represents the Timeline window's new position.

4. With the Timeline in its new location, release the mouse button.

   The Timeline turns into a separate resizable window.

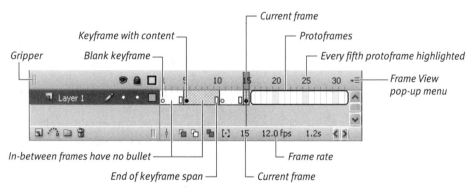

Figure 8.1 Similar to an interactive outline, the Timeline represents each frame of your movie. Click any frame, and Flash displays its contents on the Stage.

✔ Tips

■ To redock the Timeline, reverse the procedure. Click the Timeline's gripper, and drag toward the top of the document window. Position the pointer over the Edit bar above the Stage or over the document's title bar, and release the mouse button. The Timeline redocks.

■ You can dock the Timeline to any side of the document window. Drag the Timeline's gripper to the edge of the document where you want the Timeline to dock. When you release the gripper, the Timeline docks in its new position.

■ To reposition a floating Timeline window, you must drag the window by its title bar, not by the gripper.

■ You can also choose Frame View > Placement to view a submenu with choices for floating the Timeline or docking it to any side of the Flash document.

The Mystery of Timeline Display

When you create a new Flash document, the Timeline displays a single layer with hundreds of little boxes. The first box has a solid black outline and contains a hollow bullet; the rest of the boxes are gray outlines. Every fifth box is solid gray. The box with the black outline and bullet is a *keyframe;* the boxes outlined in gray are undefined placeholders, or *protoframes.*

When you define a range of frames by adding keyframes (see "Creating Keyframes," later in this chapter), the outline for the range of frames—or *keyframe span*—changes to black in the Timeline.

For a blank keyframe (one that has no content on the Stage), the Timeline displays a hollow bullet. For a keyframe that has content, the Timeline displays a solid bullet. The frames that fall between keyframes are *in-between frames.*

Any in-between frames that follow a keyframe with content display that content on the Stage. In the Timeline, the last in-between frame of a span contains a hollow rectangle. If you've set Frame View to Tinted Frames (the default), the in-between frames with content also have a tinted highlight in the Timeline.

USING THE TIMELINE

To hide/show the Timeline:

◆ In the Edit bar, click the Hide Timeline button.

The Timeline toggles between its visible and hidden mode (**Figure 8.2**). Double-clicking the scene name or any gray area of the Edit bar also toggles the Timeline between its two modes. Note that the Hide Timeline button appears on the Edit bar only when the Timeline is active and docked at the top of your document.

To close/open the Timeline:

◆ Choose Window > Timeline or press Option-⌘-T (Mac) or Ctrl-Alt-T (Windows).

Flash closes an open Timeline window. To view the Timeline again, open it from the Window menu.

To view frames in the Timeline at various sizes:

◆ In the Timeline, from the Frame View menu, choose a display option (**Figure 8.3**).

Flash resizes the frame representations in the Timeline to reflect your choice (see the sidebar "Frames of Many Sizes").

Timeline visible

Hide Timeline button

Timeline hidden

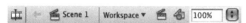

Figure 8.2 To hide the Timeline temporarily, click the Hide Timeline button; to view the hidden Timeline, click the button again.

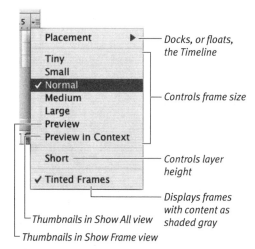

Docks, or floats, the Timeline

Controls frame size

Controls layer height

Displays frames with content as shaded gray

Thumbnails in Show All view

Thumbnails in Show Frame view

Figure 8.3 The Timeline's Frame View menu lets you control the display of frames in the Timeline.

Frames of Many Sizes

Flash's Frame View menu gives you options for setting frame size for viewing the Timeline. For documents with many layers and frames, choosing Tiny from the menu lets you squeeze the greatest number of frames into the Timeline window, but it can be hard to distinguish what you're seeing. Normal and Medium are better choices when you need to distinguish keyframes with content, from blank keyframes, from in-between frames. The Preview mode and Preview in Context mode let you see thumbnails of a frame's content within the Timeline. **Figure 8.4** shows some of the frame views available.

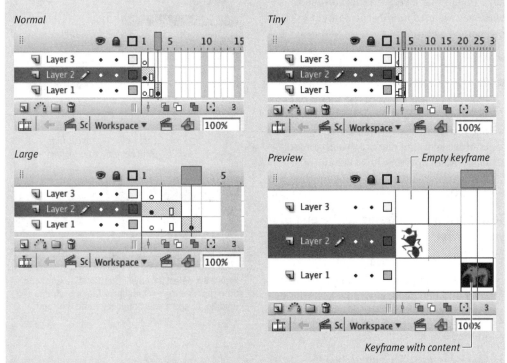

Figure 8.4 Flash can display the frames in the Timeline in a variety of sizes, from Tiny to Large. You can also preview the contents of each frame in the Timeline.

USING THE TIMELINE

Creating Keyframes

Flash offers two commands for creating keyframes. Insert > Timeline > Blank Keyframe defines a keyframe that's empty; use this command when you want to change the contents of the Stage completely. Insert > Timeline > Keyframe defines a keyframe that duplicates the content of the preceding keyframe in that layer; use this command when you want to modify the content of the preceding keyframe.

✔ Tip

■ The tasks in this section access frame-related commands from the Menu bar, but all the relevant commands for working with frames are available from the contextual frame menu as well. Control-click (Mac) or right-click (Windows) a frame in the Timeline to bring up the contextual frame menu.

To add a blank keyframe to the end of your movie:

1. Create a new Flash document.

   The new document by default has one layer and one blank keyframe at frame 1.

2. In the Timeline, click the protoframe for frame 10 to select it.

3. Choose Insert > Timeline > Blank Keyframe (**Figure 8.5**).

   Flash revises the Timeline to give you information about the frames you've defined. A hollow rectangle appears in frame 9, and a black line separates frame 9 from frame 10. This line indicates where the content for one keyframe span ends and the content for the next keyframe begins. Flash replaces the gray bars separating protoframes 2–9 with gray tick marks and removes the gray highlight that appeared in every fifth frame of the undefined frames.

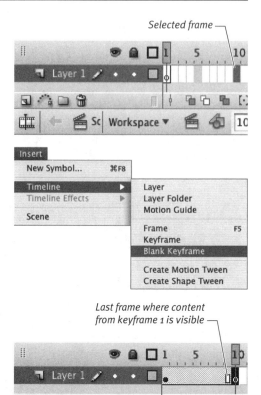

Selected frame

Last frame where content from keyframe 1 is visible

Figure 8.5 Select a frame in the Timeline (top) and then choose Insert > Timeline > Blank Keyframe (middle) to add a new blank keyframe (bottom).

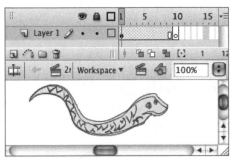

Figure 8.6 When you place content in a keyframe, Flash displays that frame in the Timeline with a solid bullet. The gray tint on the in-between frames indicates that content from the preceding keyframe appears during these frames. The hollow square indicates the end of the span of in-between frames displaying the same content. The hollow circle indicates a blank keyframe.

Figure 8.7 When you convert an in-between frame that displays content to a blank keyframe, Flash removes content from the Stage for that frame. Frames 6–9 are tinted when they display the content of frame 1 (top). When you insert a blank keyframe at frame 5 (bottom), the tint disappears, because these frames now display the content of the most recent keyframe, frame 5, which is empty.

To create a blank keyframe in the middle of your movie:

1. Follow the steps in the preceding task to create a single-layer, 10-frame movie.

2. In the Timeline, click frame 1 to select it.

3. Draw a shape on the Stage.

   Flash updates the Timeline, adding a solid bullet to frame 1 (**Figure 8.6**).

   With Tinted Frames selected in the Frame View menu (Flash's default setting), Flash shades frames 1–9 with gray. The shading indicates that keyframe 1 has content that remains visible through frame 9 in this layer. A hollow rectangle appears in frame 9, indicating the end of the span of in-between frames that displays the content of keyframe 1.

   Frame 10 still contains a hollow bullet, meaning that it has no content.

4. In the Timeline, in the area above the layers, click the number 5 or drag the playhead to position it in frame 5.

   Flash displays frame 5 on the Stage. Notice that this in-between frame continues to display the content of the preceding keyframe, frame 1.

5. Choose Insert > Timeline > Blank Keyframe.

   Flash converts the selected in-between frame to a keyframe and removes all content from the Stage (**Figure 8.7**).

To duplicate the contents of the preceding keyframe:

1. Open a new Flash document and place content in keyframe 1.

2. In the Timeline, select frame 3.

   The playhead doesn't move into the protoframe area, but frame 3 is highlighted as the current selected frame.

3. Choose Insert > Timeline > Keyframe.

   Flash creates a new keyframe, duplicates the contents of frame 1 in frame 3, and places a solid bullet in the Timeline at frame 3 and a hollow rectangle in frame 2 (**Figure 8.8**). The content of frames 1 and 3 is totally separate.

✔ Tips

- The word *insert* used in connection with keyframes is a bit misleading. Choosing Insert > Timeline > Keyframe *adds* frames only if you've selected a protoframe. If you select an existing in-between frame, Insert > Timeline > Keyframe converts that frame to a keyframe and leaves the length of the movie as it was. The Insert > Timeline > Frame command always adds frames to your movie.

- You can't add a blank keyframe between back-to-back keyframes. With keyframes in frames 5 and 6, select frame 5 and choose Insert > Timeline > Blank Keyframe. The playhead moves to frame 6, but Flash doesn't add a new blank keyframe. With frame 5 selected, you must choose Insert > Timeline > Frame. Flash creates an in-between frame at frame 6. Now select frame 5 or frame 6 and choose Insert > Timeline > Blank Keyframe; Flash converts frame 6 to a keyframe.

Current frame —

Content of the
first keyframe —

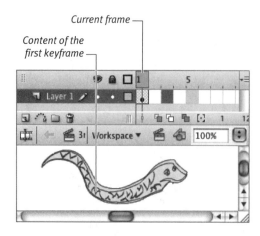

Duplicate of the first keyframe —

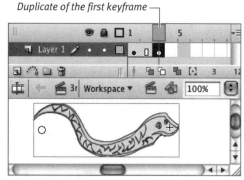

Figure 8.8 The Insert > Timeline > Keyframe command creates a keyframe that duplicates the contents of the preceding keyframe in that layer.

Keyframe Mysteries: Insert vs. Convert

In addition to the Insert > Timeline > Keyframe and Insert > Timeline > Blank Keyframe commands, Flash offers commands for converting frames to keyframes. Choose Modify > Timeline > Convert to Keyframes (or press F6) or choose Modify > Timeline > Convert to Blank Keyframes (or press F7). These conversion commands are also found in the contextual menu for frames—Control-click (Mac) or right-click (Windows) a frame in the Timeline to access the menu.

Whether you should insert or convert keyframes depends on how many frames you have selected when you issue the command and how many frames you want to create. The Insert commands create a single keyframe regardless of how many frames you have selected; the Modify commands create multiple keyframes, one for each selected frame.

With a single frame selected, the Insert > Timeline > Keyframe command and the Modify > Timeline > Convert to Keyframe command work identically. If you select one protoframe or in-between frame, both commands transform that frame to a keyframe and duplicate the content of the preceding keyframe (if any). If you select a keyframe that is followed by an in-between frame or a protoframe, both commands transform that following frame to a keyframe with the same content as the selected frame. Neither command has any effect on a selected keyframe that is followed by another keyframe.

With multiple protoframes or in-between frames selected, the Insert > Timeline > Keyframe command creates a single keyframe, usually in the same frame as the playhead (if you select frames at the end of your movie, Flash places the new keyframe in the last selected frame). The remaining selected frames become in-between frames.

With multiple protoframes or in-between frames selected, the Modify > Timeline > Convert to Keyframes command creates a keyframe in every selected frame.

The commands for blank keyframes work similarly. Insert > Timeline > Blank Keyframe creates one keyframe in the same frame as the playhead; the remaining frames become in-between frames. Modify > Timeline > Convert to Blank Keyframe creates a blank keyframe in all the selected frames.

Creating In-Between Frames

The frames that appear between keyframes are in a sense tied to the keyframe that precedes them. They display its content and allow you a space in which to create tweened animation (see Chapters 9 and 10). Flash makes the connections between these frames clear by highlighting them and placing a hollow rectangle at the end of the keyframe span.

To add in-between frames:

1. Open or create a Flash document with keyframes and content in frame 1 and frame 2.

2. In the Timeline, position the playhead in keyframe 1.

3. Choose Insert > Timeline > Frame, or press F5 (**Figure 8.9**).

    Flash adds an in-between frame (**Figure 8.10**). Your movie now contains a keyframe at frame 1, an in-between frame at frame 2, and another keyframe at frame 3.

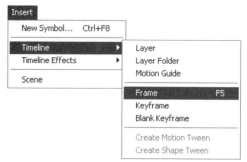

Figure 8.9 Choose Insert > Timeline > Frame to add in-between frames to the Timeline.

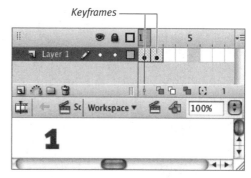

Keyframes

Timeline before evoking Insert > Timeline > Frame

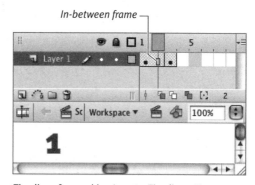

In-between frame

Timeline after evoking Insert > Timeline > Frame

Figure 8.10 The Insert > Timeline > Frame command adds an in-between frame after the frame where the playhead is located.

What Are Keyframes and In-Between Frames?

In the early days of animation, it took veritable armies of artists to create the enormous number of drawings that frame-by-frame animation requires. To keep costs down, the studios broke the work into categories based on the artistic skill required and the pay provided. The work might start with creating spec sheets for each character. Then came storyboards that outlined the action over the course of the animation. Eventually, individual artists drew and painted hundreds of cels, each slightly different, to bring the animation to life.

To make the process manageable, animators broke each movement into a series of the most crucial frames that define a movement, called *keyframes*, and frames that incorporate the incremental changes necessary to simulate the movement, called *in-between frames*.

Keyframes define a significant change to a character or graphic. Imagine a 25-frame sequence in which Bugs Bunny starts out facing the audience and then turns to his right to look at Daffy Duck. This scene requires two keyframes—Bugs in a face-on view and Bugs in profile—and 23 in-between frames.

In the early days, some artists specialized in creating keyframes. Other artists—usually lower-paid—had the job of creating the frames that fell in between the keyframes. These in-betweeners (or tweeners, for short) copied the drawings in the keyframes, making just the slight adjustments necessary to create the intended movement in the desired number of frames while retaining the continuity of the character. In Chapters 9 and 10, you learn how to turn Flash into your own personal wage slave. The program takes on the drudgery of in-betweening for certain types of animation.

In Flash, you must use keyframes to define any change in the content or image, no matter how large or small the change. Flash doesn't use the term *in-between frames;* it uses the term *frame* for any frames that aren't defined as keyframes. For clarity, the tasks in this book use the term *in-between frames* to refer to any defined frames that aren't keyframes.

CREATING IN-BETWEEN FRAMES

Selecting Frames

Flash offers two styles for selecting frames in the Timeline. The default selection style, frame-based selection, treats every frame as an individual. The span-based style treats frames as members of a *keyframe span*—the keyframe plus any in-between frames that follow it and display its content. In the span-based selection style, clicking one frame in the middle of a span selects the entire span.

Except where noted, the examples in this book use Flash's default selection style, frame-based selection.

To choose a selection style:

1. Choose Flash > Preferences (Mac) or Edit > Preferences (Windows).

   The Preferences dialog appears.

2. From the Category list, select General.

   The General settings appear in the right-hand pane of the dialog (**Figure 8.11**).

3. In the Timeline section, choose either of the following frame-selection styles:

   ▲ To manipulate keyframe spans in the Timeline, select the Span Based Selection check box (**Figure 8.12**).

   ▲ To manipulate individual frames in the Timeline, deselect the Span Based Selection check box (**Figure 8.13**).

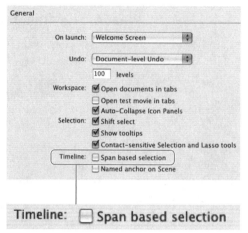

Timeline: ☐ Span based selection

Figure 8.11 Choose the way frame selection works in the Timeline from the General category of the Preferences dialog.

Timeline: ☑ Span based selection

Figure 8.12 In the General section of the Preferences dialog, select the Span Based Selection check box to work with keyframe spans as a unit in the Timeline.

Timeline: ☐ Span based selection

Figure 8.13 In the General section of the Preferences dialog, deselect the Span Based Selection check box to work with individual keyframes in the Timeline.

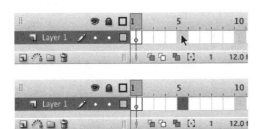

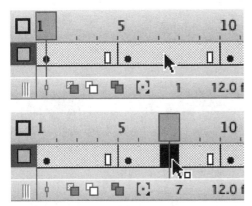

Figure 8.14 Both frame-selection styles treat protoframes identically for selection. Position the pointer over a protoframe (top) and click to select it (bottom).

Figure 8.15 In Flash's frame-based selection style, clicking a frame in the middle of a span (top) selects just that frame (bottom).

To select undefined frames:

To work with protoframes, do any of the following:

◆ To select one protoframe, click it (**Figure 8.14**).

◆ To select two protoframes and all the frames between them, Shift-click the first and last protoframes.

◆ To select noncontinguous protoframes, ⌘-click (Mac) or Ctrl-click (Windows) the protoframes.

The process of selecting frames that have not been defined works identically in Flash's two frame-selection styles.

To select defined frames individually:

In the Timeline—with preferences set to frame-based selection style—do one of the following:

◆ To select a keyframe, click it.

◆ To select the last frame in a keyframe span, click it.

◆ To select just a middle frame in a keyframe span, click that frame (**Figure 8.15**).

◆ To select an entire keyframe span, double-click any frame in the span.

◆ To add frames to your selection, Shift-click the additional frames. Flash selects all the frames between the last selected frame and the frame you Shift-click.

◆ To select a range of frames, Shift-click the first and last frame in the range; or with no frames selected, click and drag through the range of frames.

To select defined frames in span-based mode:

In the Timeline—with preferences set to span-based selection style—do one of the following:

- To select a keyframe, click it.

- To select the last frame in keyframe span, click it.

- To select one in-between frame, ⌘-click (Mac) or Ctrl-click (Windows) that frame.

- To select an entire keyframe span, click a middle frame in the keyframe span (**Figure 8.16**); or Shift-click the first or last frame in the span.

- To add other spans to your selection, Shift-click any frame in each additional span. The selection can include noncontiguous spans (**Figure 8.17**).

- To select a range of frames in the Windows operating system, Ctrl-drag through the frames.

✔ Tips

- Span-based selection style gives the first and last frames of a span a special additive selection capability. Once you've made any type of selection, clicking the first or last frame of a span adds that frame to the selection.

- In both selection styles, you can select all the frames in a layer by clicking the layer name. In the span-based selection style, you can also select all the frames in a layer by double-clicking any frame.

- In both selection styles, you can select noncontiguous frames by ⌘-clicking (Mac) or Ctrl-clicking (Windows) each frame that you want to include.

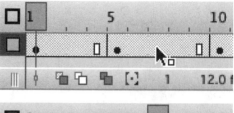

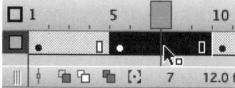

Figure 8.16 In Flash's span-based selection style, clicking a frame in the middle of a span (top) selects the whole span (bottom).

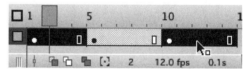

Figure 8.17 With Flash's span-based frame-selection style, you can Shift-click to select keyframe spans that aren't contiguous.

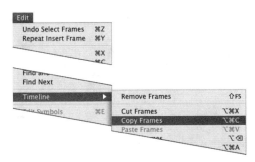

Figure 8.18 Flash's Edit menu provides special commands for copying and pasting frames in the Timeline.

Copy Keyframe 3

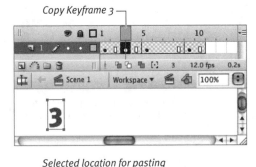

Selected location for pasting

Flash pastes copied Keyframe 3 content into Frame 4

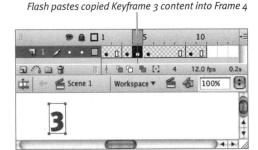

Figure 8.19 When you paste a frame with new content into an in-between frame, Flash converts the frame to a keyframe.

Manipulating Frames in One Layer

You can't copy or paste frames by using the standard Copy and Paste commands that you use for graphic elements. Flash's Edit menu provides special commands for copying and pasting frames. Flash also lets you drag selected frames to new locations in the Timeline.

For the following tasks, open a new Flash document. Create a ten-frame movie with keyframes at frames 1, 3, 5, and 9. Using the text tool, place a text field in each keyframe, and enter the number of the frame in the text field; this technique makes it easy to tell what frame winds up where as you practice.

To copy and paste a single frame:

1. In the Timeline, select keyframe 3.

2. Choose Edit > Timeline > Copy Frames, or press Option-⌘-C (Mac) or Ctrl-Alt-C (Windows) (**Figure 8.18**).

   Flash copies the selected frame to the Clipboard.

3. In the Timeline, click frame 4 to select it as the location for pasting the copied frame.

4. Choose Edit > Timeline > Paste Frames, or press Option-⌘-V (Mac) or Ctrl-Alt-V (Windows).

   Flash pastes the copied frame into frame 4 (**Figure 8.19**).

   continues on next page

5. Paste another copy into frame 5 (**Figure 8.20**).

Flash replaces the contents of keyframe 5 with the content of keyframe 3.

6. Paste another copy into protoframe 12.

Flash extends the movie to accommodate the pasted frame. Note that the playhead won't move to protoframe 12 until after you've pasted the copy to create a defined frame.

✔ Tips

■ You can copy and paste multiple frames; in step 1 of the preceding task, select a range of frames.

■ To copy and paste the content of a keyframe, you can also copy an in-between frame that displays that content. When you paste, Flash creates a new keyframe.

■ Warning: Flash always replaces the content of the selected frame with the pasted frame (or, for multiple-frame pastes, with the first pasted frame). If you're not careful, you may eat up the content of keyframes you intended to keep. To be safe, always paste frames into in-between frames or blank keyframes. You can always delete an unwanted keyframe separately.

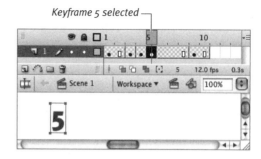

Keyframe 5 selected

Pasted content from keyframe 3

Figure 8.20 When you paste a frame with new content into a keyframe, Flash replaces the keyframe's content.

Select and drag: either selection style

Selected frames —

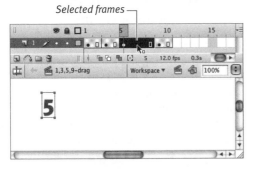

Frames ready for dragging —

Preview of new frame location —

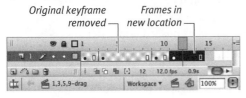

After drop: frame-based selection style

Original keyframe removed — Frames in new location —

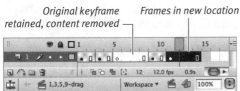

After drop: span-based selection style

Original keyframe retained, content removed — Frames in new location

Figure 8.21 The process of dragging and dropping frames in the Timeline to relocate them is the same in Flash's two frame-selection styles (top). The results, however, are quite different (bottom). The frame-based selection style removes selected keyframes from their original location, leaving only in-between frames. The span-based style retains the original keyframes but removes their content.

To move frames using drag and drop:

1. In the Timeline of your practice document, select the keyframe span that starts with keyframe 5 and ends with frame 8.

2. Position the pointer over the selected frames.

3. Click and drag the selected frames. Flash further highlights the selection with a rectangle of hatched lines. Flash uses this rectangle to preview the new location for the selected frames as you drag in the Timeline.

4. To move the selected frames to the end of your movie, drag the rectangle past the last defined frame and into the area of protoframes, and release the mouse button.

   Flash adds frames to the end of the movie; these frames display the content from frames 5–8. In frame-based selection style, Flash completely removes the content from frames 5–8 and adds those frames to the preceding span. In span-based selection style, Flash removes the content but keeps a blank keyframe at frame 5 (**Figure 8.21**).

5. To move the selected frames to the beginning of your movie, drag the selected frames to frame 1 and release the mouse button.

   The dragged frames replace the content of frames 1–4; there is no longer a keyframe at frame 5.

MANIPULATING FRAMES IN ONE LAYER

223

✔ Tips

- To drag a copy of selected frames in the Timeline, hold down Option (Mac) or Alt (Windows) as you drag.

- No matter which frame-selection style you use, pressing the ⌘ key (Mac) or Ctrl key (Windows) lets you access some of the functionality of the other style temporarily. In frame-based selection, the modifier lets you access the double-headed arrow pointer for extending keyframe spans. In span-based mode, the modifier gives you the arrow pointer for selecting individual frames.

- If you make a mistake in modifying the frames in the Timeline, you can undo your steps by choosing Edit > Undo. Flash tracks the selection and deselection of frames as part of the undo history. Operations such as dragging frames to move them or to extend spans may require repeated Undo commands, because some of the steps involved are things Flash does behind the scenes.

The Trick to Extending Keyframe Spans

In span-based selection style, the pointer becomes a double-headed arrow when it hovers over a keyframe or an end-of-span frame. You can use this pointer to drag an unselected keyframe or end-of-span frame to the right or the left to increase or decrease the length of the span.

Resizing a span in the middle of other spans gets a bit tricky. Flash won't let your expanding span eat up the content of other keyframes. Your expansion can reduce the length of a neighboring span, however. In your practice document, for example, using span-based selection, position the pointer over frame 4 (the end of keyframe 3's span); the frame must not be selected. With the double-headed arrow pointer, drag frame 4 to the right. When you get to frame 7, you can drag no farther. Release the mouse button. The span that starts at frame 3 now extends through frame 7. The content that was originally in keyframe 5 still exists, but Flash has pushed it into frame 8.

To increase the length of a span without affecting the length of neighboring spans, select the span or any frame within it; then choose Insert > Timeline > Frame or press F5. Flash adds an in-between frame to the selected span and pushes all subsequent spans to the right in the Timeline.

When you reduce the size of a span by dragging, Flash creates blank keyframe spans to cover any gaps between the end of the span you're resizing and the beginning of the neighboring span. To simply reduce the number of in-between frames, you can use the Remove Frames command (see "Removing Frames," the next section in this chapter).

Before clearing the keyframe

Selected keyframe
is frame 5 —

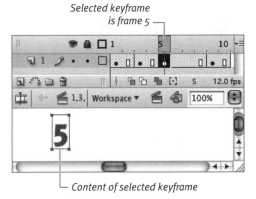

— Content of selected keyframe

After clearing the keyframe

Frame 5 becomes an
in-between keyframe —

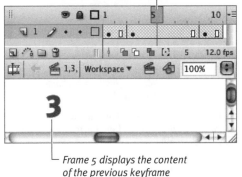

— Frame 5 displays the content
of the previous keyframe

Figure 8.22 The Modify > Timeline > Clear Keyframe command removes the contents of the selected keyframe from the Stage and converts the keyframe to an in-between frame. The Clear Keyframe command doesn't change the overall length of the movie.

Removing Frames

Flash has two commands for removing frames: Clear Keyframe and Remove Frames. Clear Keyframe removes keyframe status from a selected frame or range of frames (converting the keyframes to in-between frames) and deletes the keyframes' content from the movie. Clear Keyframe has no effect on the number of frames in the movie. Remove Frames removes frames (and their content, if they're keyframes) from the movie. Remove Frames reduces the number of frames in the movie. For the following tasks, use the same practice document you created for working with the tasks in "Manipulating Frames in One Layer," earlier in this chapter.

To remove keyframe status from a frame:

1. In the Timeline, select keyframe 5.

2. Choose Modify > Timeline > Clear Keyframe, or press Shift-F6.

Flash removes the bullet from frame 5 in the Timeline (indicating that the frame is no longer a keyframe) and removes the graphic element it contained. Frame 5 becomes an in-between frame, displaying the contents of the keyframe at frame 3 (**Figure 8.22**). The total number of frames in the movie remains the same.

To delete a single frame from a movie:

1. With your practice file in its original state (keyframes at 1, 3, 5, and 9), select frame 4 in the Timeline.

   Frame 4 is an in-between frame associated with keyframe 3.

2. Choose Edit > Timeline > Remove Frames, or press Shift-F5.

   Flash deletes what was frame 4, reducing the overall length of the movie by one frame (**Figure 8.23**). The keyframe content that was in frame 5 moves back one frame to become keyframe 4.

3. Select keyframe 3 and choose Edit > Timeline > Remove Frames again.

   Flash deletes the selected keyframe and its content, and reduces the length of the movie by one frame. The keyframe content that was just in frame 4 moves back one frame to become keyframe 3.

✔ Tip

- Flash doesn't allow you to use Clear Keyframe to remove keyframe status from the first frame of a movie, but you can delete it. If you select all the frames in one layer and choose Edit > Timeline > Remove Frames, Flash removes all the defined frames in the Timeline, leaving only protoframes. You must add back a keyframe at frame 1 to place content on that layer.

Selected in-between frame

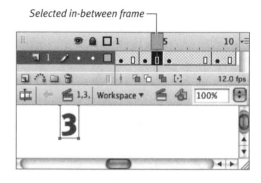

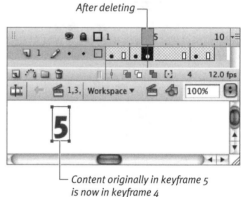

After deleting

Content originally in keyframe 5 is now in keyframe 4

Figure 8.23 The Edit > Timeline > Remove Frames command removes frames from the movie and thus reduces its length.

REMOVING FRAMES

Figure 8.24 The Edit > Timeline > Remove Frames command can delete a selected range of frames. Because an entire keyframe span (frames 3 and 4) is included in the selection (top), Flash not only reduces the number of frames but also removes the content of that keyframe span (middle). Where only part of a span was selected (originally frames 5 and 6), the span gets shorter, but the content remains the same (bottom).

To delete a range of frames:

1. Using your practice file in its original state (keyframes at 1, 3, 5, and 9), in the Timeline, select frames 3–6.

2. Choose Edit > Timeline > Remove Frames. Flash removes all the selected frames (**Figure 8.24**).

✔ Tip

■ With the frame-based selection style active, you can quickly replace the contents of one keyframe with those of another. Select an in-between frame that displays the contents you want to copy. Drag that source frame over the keyframe whose contents you want to replace. Flash replaces the contents of the target keyframe with the contents of the source keyframe.

Making a Simple Frame-by-Frame Animation

In traditional cel animation or flip-book animation, you create the illusion of movement by showing a series of images, each slightly different from the rest. When you create each of these drawings and place them in a series of keyframes, that process is called *frame-by-frame animation*. When you create only the most crucial images and allow Flash to interpolate the minor changes that take place between them, you're creating *tweened animation*. You learn more about tweening in Chapters 9 and 10.

A classic example of frame-by-frame animation is a bouncing ball. A crude animation of a bouncing ball takes just three frames.

To set up the initial keyframe:

1. Create a new Flash document, and name it something like Frame-by-Frame Bounce.

   By default, Flash creates a document with one layer and a keyframe at frame 1. Choose View > Grid > Show Grid to help with positioning graphics in this task.

2. In the Timeline, select keyframe 1.

   Use the Frame View pop-up menu to set the Timeline to Preview in Context mode. This setting makes it easy to keep track of what you do in the example.

3. In the Tools panel, select the oval tool.

4. Set the stroke color to No Color.

5. Near the top of the Stage, draw a circle (**Figure 8.25**).

   This circle will be your ball. Make it fairly large. To make the most efficient use of your graphic, convert the circle to a symbol (see Chapter 7).

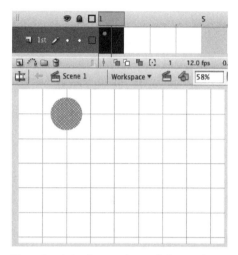

Figure 8.25 In keyframe 1, draw a circle near the top of the Stage. This circle will become a bouncing ball.

When to Use Frame-by-Frame Animation

With frame-by-frame animation, the more frames you add, the smaller you can make the differences between frames and the smoother the action is. Adding keyframes, however, also adds to your final movie's file size, which in turn affects the download time for people viewing your movie over the Web. Your goal is to strike a happy medium.

In the bouncing ball example, you could help keep file size down by making the ball a symbol so that adding another keyframe for the ball in a new position added little to the size of the file. In the real world, however, if you can use a symbol, you might prefer to use a more labor-efficient animation technique, *motion tweening*. Reserve frame-by-frame techniques for animations where shapes are constantly changing in subtle ways that you need to control precisely. Otherwise, use Flash's motion-tweening and shape-tweening tools (see Chapters 9 and 10).

MAKING A SIMPLE FRAME-BY-FRAME ANIMATION

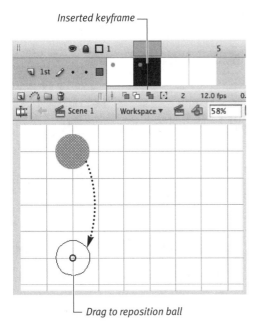

Inserted keyframe ⎯

Drag to reposition ball

Figure 8.26 Use the Insert > Timeline > Keyframe command to duplicate the ball from keyframe 1 in keyframe 2. Then drag the ball to reposition it.

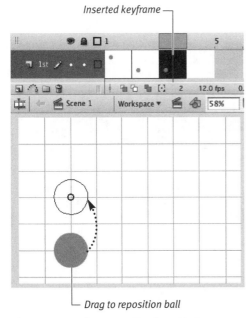

Inserted keyframe ⎯

Drag to reposition ball

Figure 8.27 Use the Insert > Timeline > Keyframe command to duplicate the ball from keyframe 2 in keyframe 3. Drag the ball to reposition it again.

To create the second keyframe:

1. In the Timeline, select frame 2.

2. Choose Insert > Timeline > Keyframe.

   Flash creates a keyframe in frame 2 that duplicates your ball from keyframe 1.

3. In keyframe 2, select the ball and reposition it at the bottom of the Stage (**Figure 8.26**).

To create the third keyframe:

1. In the Timeline, select frame 3.

2. Choose Insert > Timeline > Keyframe.

   Flash creates a keyframe in frame 3 that duplicates your ball from keyframe 2.

3. In keyframe 3, select the ball and reposition it in the middle of the Stage (**Figure 8.27**).

   That's it. Believe it or not, you have just created all the content you need to animate a bouncing ball. To see how it works, in the Timeline, click keyframes 1, 2, and 3 in turn. As Flash changes the content of the Stage at each click, you see a very crude animation.

MAKING A SIMPLE FRAME-BY-FRAME ANIMATION

Previewing the Action

Although you can click each frame to preview a movie, Flash provides more sophisticated ways to see your animation. The Controller window offers VCR-style playback buttons. The Control menu has commands for playback. You can also have Flash export the file and open it for you in Flash Player.

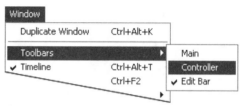

Figure 8.28 To access the Controller, choose Window > Toolbars > Controller.

To use the Controller:

1. Choose Window > Toolbars > Controller (**Figure 8.28**).

   Flash opens a window containing standard VCR-style buttons.

2. In the Controller window, click the button for the command you want to use (**Figure 8.29**).

✔ Tip

- For those who prefer not to clutter the desktop with more floating windows, the Control menu in the Menu bar duplicates the Controller's functions.

To step sequentially through frames:

1. In the Timeline, select frame 1.

2. From the Control menu (**Figure 8.30**), choose Step Forward One Frame, or press the period (.) key.

   Flash moves to the following frame.

3. Choose Control > Step Backward One Frame, or press the comma (,) key.

   Flash moves to the preceding frame.

✔ Tip

- You can *scrub* (scroll quickly back and forth) through the movie. Drag the playhead backward or forward through the frames in the Timeline. Flash displays the content of each frame as the playhead moves through it.

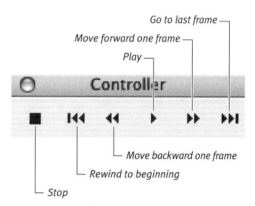

Figure 8.29 The Controller window contains VCR-style buttons for controlling playback of Flash movies.

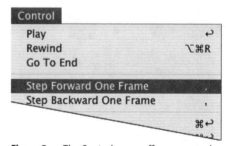

Figure 8.30 The Control menu offers commands for playing the whole Flash movie or stepping through it frame by frame.

PREVIEWING THE ACTION

Figure 8.31 Choosing Control > Loop Playback sets Flash to show your movie repeatedly when you subsequently issue a play command from the Controller, the Control menu, or the keyboard.

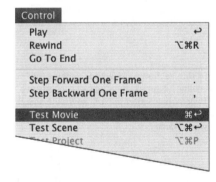

Figure 8.32 Choose Control > Test Movie to see your movie in action in Flash Player.

To play through all frames in the Flash editor:

◆ To play through the frames once, choose Control > Play, or press Enter.

Flash displays each frame in turn, starting with the current frame and running through the end of the movie. The Play command in the Control menu changes to a Stop command, which you can use to stop playback at any time.

✔ Tip

■ To play through the frames repeatedly, choose Control > Loop Playback (**Figure 8.31**). Now, whenever you issue a Play command, Flash plays the movie repeatedly until you issue a Stop command.

To play through frames in Flash Player:

◆ Choose Control > Test Movie or press ⌘-Enter (Mac) or Ctrl-Enter (**Figure 8.32**).

Flash exports your movie to a Flash Player (SWF) file and opens it in a separate window. Flash stores the SWF file at the same hierarchical level of your system as the original Flash file. The SWF file has the same name as the original, except that Flash appends the .swf extension.

PREVIEWING THE ACTION

Smoothing the Animation by Adding Keyframes

The three-frame bouncing ball you created in the preceding task is crude; it's herky-jerky and much too fast. To smooth out the movement, you need to create more snapshots that define the ball's position in the air as it moves up and down. This means adding more keyframes and repositioning the ball slightly in each one.

In the preceding task, the ball moves from the top of the stage to the bottom in one step. In the following task, you expand that first bounce movement to three steps.

To add keyframes within an existing animation:

1. In the Timeline of the three-frame bouncing ball animation, select keyframe 1.

2. Choose Insert > Timeline > Frame; then choose Insert > Timeline > Frame again.

   Flash creates new in-between frames at frames 2 and 3, and relocates the keyframes that show the ball at the bottom and middle of the Stage to frames 4 and 5 (**Figure 8.33**).

3. In the Timeline, select frames 2 and 3.

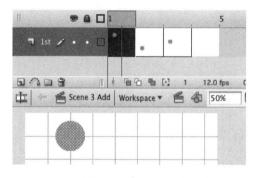

New in-between frames —

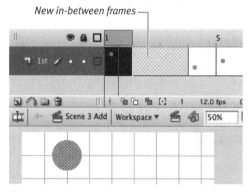

Figure 8.33 With keyframe 1 selected, invoking the Insert > Timeline > Frame command twice inserts two new in-between frames after the first keyframe and pushes the original keyframe 2 (the ball at the bottom of the Stage) to frame 4.

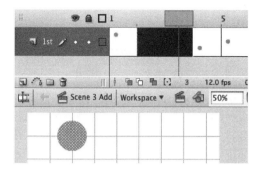

Duplicates of Keyframe 1 —

Figure 8.34 Modify > Timeline > Convert to Keyframes changes the selected in-between frames to keyframes containing the content of the preceding keyframe.

Frames previewed in context —

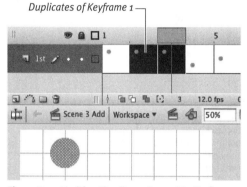

Figure 8.35 Reposition the ball in keyframes 2 and 3 to make the first bounce smoother.

4. Choose Modify > Timeline > Convert to Keyframes.

Flash converts the in-between frames to keyframes that duplicate the content of keyframe 1 (**Figure 8.34**).

5. In the Timeline, select keyframe 2, and then reposition the ball on the Stage.

You can use the grid line to help you visualize where to place the ball; position it about a third of the distance between the top and bottom of the Stage.

6. In the Timeline, select keyframe 3, and then reposition the ball on the Stage (**Figure 8.35**).

Position the ball about two-thirds of the distance between the top and bottom of the Stage.

7. Preview the animation using any of the methods described in the preceding section.

The initial bounce movement is smoother. Repeat these steps to add even more frames with incremental movement to the first half of the bounce. You can also add frames to make the second half of the bounce smoother.

SMOOTHING ANIMATION BY ADDING KEYFRAMES

Using Onion Skinning

In the preceding section, you repositioned a circle to try to create smooth incremental movement for a bouncing ball. To make this task easier, Flash's onion-skinning feature lets you see the circle in context with the circles in surrounding frames.

Onion skinning displays dimmed or outline versions of the content of surrounding frames. You determine how many of the surrounding frames Flash displays. The buttons for turning on and off the various types of onion skinning appear at the bottom of the Timeline, in the Timeline's Status bar.

To turn on onion skinning:

◆ In the Status bar of the Timeline, click the Onion Skin button.

The content of all the frames included in the onion-skin markers appears in a dimmed form (**Figure 8.36**). You can't edit the dimmed graphics—only the full-color graphics in the current frame.

To turn on outline onion skinning:

◆ In the Status bar of the Timeline, click the Onion Skin Outlines button.

The content of all the frames included in the onion-skin markers appears in outline form (**Figure 8.37**). You can't edit the outline graphics—only the solid graphics that appear in the current frame.

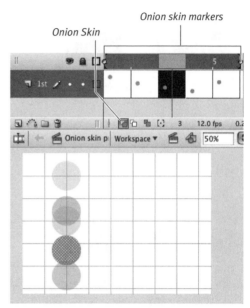

Onion skin markers

Onion Skin

Figure 8.36 In Onion Skin mode, Flash displays the content of multiple frames but dims everything that's not on the current frame. The onion-skin markers in the Timeline indicate how many frames appear.

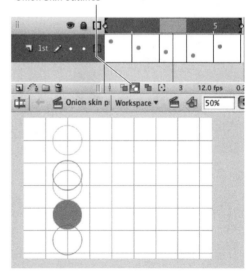

Onion Skin outlines

Figure 8.37 In Onion Skin Outlines mode, Flash displays the content of multiple frames, but it uses outlines for everything that's not in the current frame.

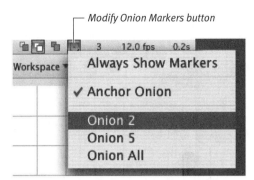

Modify Onion Markers button

Figure 8.38 The Modify Onion Markers pop-up menu gives you control over the number of frames that appear as onion skins.

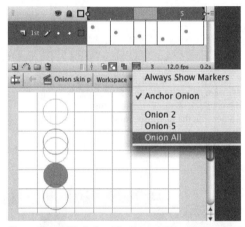

Figure 8.39 With Onion All selected from the Modify Onion Markers menu, Flash extends the markers to enclose all the frames of the Timeline.

To adjust the number of frames included in onion skinning:

1. In the Status bar of the Timeline, click the Modify Onion Markers button.

   A pop-up menu appears, containing commands for setting the way the onion-skin markers work (**Figure 8.38**).

2. To see frames on either side of the current frame, do one of the following:

   ▲ To see two frames on either side of the current frame, choose Onion 2.

   ▲ To see five frames on either side of the current frame, choose Onion 5.

   ▲ To see all the frames in the movie, choose Onion All (**Figure 8.39**).

   Flash moves the onion-skin markers around in the Timeline as you move the playhead. Flash always includes onion skins (either solid or outline) for graphics in the selected number of frames before the current frame and after it.

✔ Tips

■ Flash doesn't show the contents of locked layers in onion-skin views.

■ Drag onion-skin markers in the Timeline to include more frames or fewer frames in the onion-skin view.

■ You can prevent the onion-skin markers from moving each time you select a new frame in the Timeline. Set the markers to encompass the frames you want to see together. From the Modify Onion Markers menu, choose Anchor Onion. As long as you keep selecting frames inside the anchored range, the anchored set of frames stays in Onion Skin mode.

Editing Multiple Frames

If you decide to change the location of an animated element, you must change the element's location in every keyframe in which it appears. Repositioning the items one frame at a time is not only tedious but also dangerous. You may forget one frame, and you can easily get the animated elements out of alignment. Flash solves this problem by letting you move elements in multiple frames simultaneously. The same markers that indicate the frames to include in onion skinning indicate the frames you're allowed to edit simultaneously in Edit Multiple Frames mode.

To relocate animated graphics on the Stage:

1. Open your frame-by-frame animation of a bouncing ball.

2. In the Timeline's Status bar, choose Edit Multiple Frames (**Figure 8.40**).

Flash displays all graphics in all frames within the onion-skin markers and makes them editable.

3. From the Modify Onion Markers menu, choose Onion All.

Now you can see the ball at each stage of its bounce, and you can edit each of these stages.

4. Using the selection tool, draw a selection rectangle that includes all the visible balls on the Stage (**Figure 8.41**).

Frames available for editing ⌐   *Current frame* ⌐

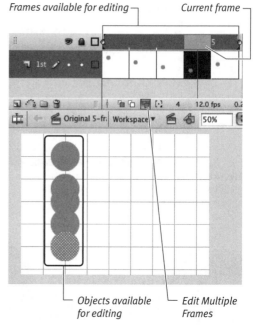

Objects available for editing   *Edit Multiple Frames*

Figure 8.40 In Edit Multiple Frames mode, Flash displays and makes editable all the graphics in the frames that the onion-skin markers indicate. This feature makes it possible to move an animated graphic to a new location in every keyframe at the same time.

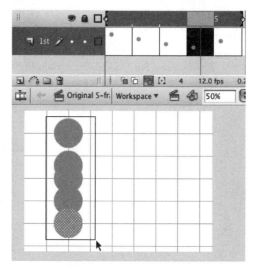

Figure 8.41 In Edit Multiple Frames mode, you can use the selection tool to select graphics in any of the frames enclosed in the onion-skin markers.

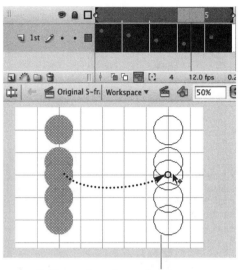

*Outline previews the new location
as you drag selected graphics*

Figure 8.42 In Edit Multiple Frames mode, you can relocate an animated graphic completely, moving it in every keyframe with one action.

*Outline-mode
toggle*

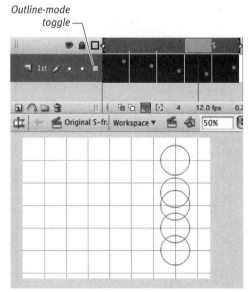

Figure 8.43 Turn on Outline mode to make it easier to work with graphics in multiple frames.

5. Drag the selection to the opposite side of the Stage (**Figure 8.42**).

With just a few steps, you've relocated the bouncing ball. (Imagine how much more work it would have been to select each keyframe separately, move the circle for that frame, select the next keyframe, line up the circles precisely in the new location, and so on.)

✔ Tip

■ When you select Edit Multiple Frames, Flash no longer displays onion skinning for keyframes; onion skinning does appear for in-between frames with tweened content. If you find it confusing to view solid graphics in multiple keyframes, turn on Outline view in the layer-properties section of the Timeline (**Figure 8.43**).

Setting the Frame Rate

In Flash, you can set only one frame rate for the entire movie. You set the frame rate in the Document Properties dialog.

To set the frame rate:

1. To access the Document Properties dialog, do either of the following:

   ▲ Choose Modify > Document, or press ⌘-J (Mac) or Ctrl-J (Windows).

   ▲ In the Timeline's Status bar, double-click the frame-rate number (**Figure 8.44**).

2. In the Document Properties dialog, enter a value in the Frame Rate field (**Figure 8.45**).

3. Click OK.

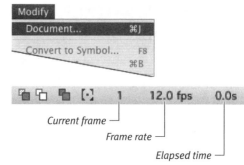

Current frame
Frame rate
Elapsed time

Figure 8.44 To call up the Document Properties dialog, choose Modify > Document (top) or double-click the frame-rate number in the Timeline's Status bar (bottom).

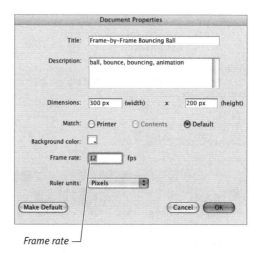

Frame rate

Figure 8.45 In the Document Properties dialog, enter a new value in the Frame Rate field. Flash's default frame rate is 12 fps.

Understanding Frame Rate

The illusion of animation relies on the human brain's ability to fill in gaps in continuity. When you see a series of images in very quick succession, your brain perceives a continuous moving image. In animation, you must display the sequence of images fast enough to convince the brain that it's looking at a single image.

Frame rate controls how fast Flash delivers the images. If the images come too fast, the movie turns into a blur. Slow delivery too much, and your viewers start perceiving each frame as a separate image; then the movement seems jerky. In addition, when you're working in Flash, you're most likely planning to deliver the movie over the Internet, and you don't always know what types of systems your viewers will be using. That means you won't necessarily be able to deliver a fast frame rate.

The standard rate for film is 24 frames per second (fps). For graphic animation that's going out over the Internet, 12 fps (Flash's default) is a good lowest-common-denominator setting. If you know your target audience uses low-bandwidth connections, consider lowering that to 10 fps; if your target uses high-bandwidth connections, try 15 fps. Today's high-bandwidth connections and Flash Player 9's capabilities, however, make still higher frame rates a possibility. If you're confident that your target audience has the capability to handle it, try for something closer to film's rate. Flash creators who like to deliver even smoother animations or whose creations contain video may want to use a frame rate of 30 fps.

Varying the Speed of Animations

Although the frame rate for a movie is constant, you can make any particular bit of animation go faster or slower by changing the number of frames it takes to complete the action. You can lengthen a portion of an animation by adding more keyframes or by adding in-between frames. In the bouncing-ball example, the ball may drop down slowly (say, over five frames) but rebound more quickly (over three frames). The smoothest frame-by-frame animation has many keyframes, each showing the ball in a slightly different position. Adding keyframes, however, increases file size. Sometimes you can get away with adding in-between frames to slow the action. In-between frames add little to the exported movie's file size.

To add in-between frames:

1. Open (or create) a five-frame bouncing-ball movie.

   Keyframe 1 shows the ball at the top of the Stage, keyframes 2 and 3 show the ball at two places in its descent, keyframe 4 shows the ball at the bottom of the Stage, and keyframe 5 shows the ball bouncing halfway back up. (For step-by-step instructions, see the tasks in "Smoothing the Animation by Adding Keyframes," earlier in this chapter.)

2. Choose File > Save As, and make a copy of the file.

   Give the file a distinguishing name, such as BounceSlower.

   continues on next page

3. In the copy's Timeline, select frame 1.

4. Control-click (Mac) or right-click (Windows) to access the contextual menu for frames.

5. Choose Insert Frame.

Flash inserts an in-between frame at frame 2 and pushes the keyframe that was there to frame 3 (**Figure 8.46**).

6. Repeat steps 3–5 for the second and third keyframes in the movie.

You wind up with keyframes in frames 1, 3, 5, 7, and 8 (**Figure 8.47**).

7. Choose Control > Test Movie.

Flash exports the movie to a SWF file and opens it in Flash Player. Play through the regular five-frame bouncing ball, and then play through the one you just created (the one named BounceSlower). You can see that the action in the movie with added in-between frames feels different from the action in the movie in which one keyframe directly follows another. The added frames slow the motion.

✔ Tip

■ Keep in mind that this example serves to illustrate a process. In most animations, you shouldn't overuse this technique. If you simply add many in-between frames, you'll slow the action too much and destroy the illusion of movement.

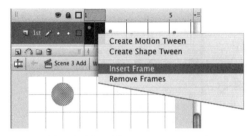
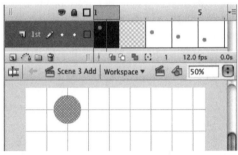

Figure 8.46 Select a frame; Ctrl-click (Mac) or right-click (Windows), and choose Insert Frame from the contextual menu (top); Flash inserts an in-between frame directly after the selected frame (bottom).

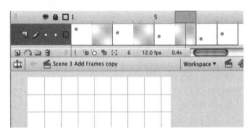

Figure 8.47 With in-between frames separating the initial keyframes, the first part of the animation moves at a slower pace than the second.

ANIMATION WITH MOTION TWEENING

Animating movement and changes to shapes by hand (frame by frame) is labor-intensive. Adobe Flash CS3 Professional reduces the number of frames you must draw when you use a process called *tweening*. In Chapter 8, you created a three-frame animation of a bouncing ball by changing the position of the ball graphic in each of the three keyframes. Then you learned how to stretch out the animation by adding in-between frames that repeated the contents of the preceding keyframe. With tweening, you create similar keyframes, but Flash breaks the keyframe changes into multiple steps and displays them in the in-between frames.

To tween a graphic, Flash creates a series of incremental changes to that graphic; these changes are simple enough that Flash can describe them mathematically. Flash performs two types of tweening: motion tweening and shape tweening. This chapter covers motion tweening; Chapter 10 covers shape tweening.

Both types of tweening follow the same basic pattern. You give Flash the beginning and end of the sequence by placing graphic elements in keyframes. Then you tell Flash to spread the change out over a certain number of steps by placing that number of frames between the keyframes. Flash creates a series of images with incremental changes that accomplish the movement in the desired number of frames.

Motion Tweening and Graphic Containers

Flash requires that graphics being used in motion tweens be inside some form of container. Some of Flash's drawing tools create containers automatically: the text tool, tools set to Object Drawing mode, and the oval- and rectangle-primitive tools all create graphics inside containers. You can also put graphic elements into containers by grouping the elements or placing them inside a symbol.

Creating a Bouncing Ball with Motion Tweening

To create a motion tween, you must place the appropriate type of content in the beginning and ending keyframe, then set the initial keyframe span's Tween property to Motion. The content for a motion tween must be a graphic-object (a drawing-object, primitive-shape, group, symbol, or text field). You set the Tween property in the Frame Properties tab of the Property inspector. You can use motion tweening to create the same bouncing ball you made in Chapter 8, but this time you tell Flash to change the ball's position.

Which Frames Contain Tweening?

As your road map of the movie, the Timeline provides visual cues about which frames contain tweens. Flash draws an arrow across a series of frames to indicate that the frames contain a tween (**Figure 9.1**). (Note that the arrow doesn't appear if you've set Frame View to Preview or Preview in Context.)

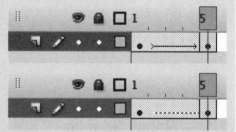

Figure 9.1 An arrow in a span of frames indicates that the frames contain a proper tween sequence (top). A dotted line indicates that the span is set to tween, but there's a problem with the tween (bottom).

Flash color-codes frames in the Timeline to distinguish motion tweens from shape tweens. With Tinted Frames active (choose it from the Frame View pop-up menu at the right end of the Timeline), Flash applies a shade of light bluish-purple (Mac) or bluish-gray (Windows) to the frames that contain a motion tween. If Tinted Frames is inactive, the frames are white (Mac) or patterned (Windows), and Flash changes the arrow that indicates the presence of a tween from black to red. Flash indicates shape tweens by tinting frames light green (if Tinted Frames is active) or by changing the tweening arrow to light green (if Tinted Frames is inactive).

Frames containing a dotted line are set to contain a tween (either Motion or Shape), but something is wrong and Flash can't complete the tween. Such tweens are called *broken* tweens.

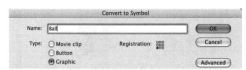

Figure 9.2 The elements of a motion tween must be in a container. A good way to create the container is to use a symbol. Flash can motion-tween any type of symbol: movie clip, button, or graphic.

Keyframes

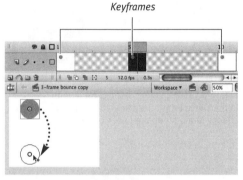

Reposition graphic-object

Graphic-object in new position

Figure 9.3 The initial keyframes for a motion tween are similar to those of a frame-by-frame animation. The difference is that you must use a graphic-object (a drawing-object, primitive-shape, symbol, group, or text field) and set the keyframe span's Tween property to Motion.

✔ Tip

■ You could create the oval for this task as a drawing-object or primitive-shape (or create it as a merge-shape and then group it) and then skip steps 5 and 6. The most efficient practice for creating graphic elements for motion tweens, however, is to use symbols.

To prepare keyframes for motion tweening:

1. Create a new Flash document, and name it something like MotionTweenBounce.

   Flash creates a document with one layer and a keyframe at frame 1.

2. In the Timeline, select keyframe 1.

3. In the Tools panel, choose the oval tool, and set the stroke to No Color.

4. Near the top of the Stage, draw a circle. This circle will be the ball.

5. Select the circle, and choose Modify > Convert to Symbol.

   The Convert to Symbol dialog appears. The symbol can be any type, but for this task, choose Graphic (**Figure 9.2**).

6. Enter a name for your symbol—for example, Ball—and click OK.

7. In the Timeline, select frame 5, and choose Insert > Timeline > Keyframe.

   Flash creates a new keyframe that duplicates the contents of the preceding keyframe.

8. Select frame 10, and choose Insert > Timeline > Keyframe.

9. Select keyframe 5, and drag the ball to the bottom of the Stage.

   You have just set up a frame-by-frame animation quite like the one you did in Chapter 8. In keyframe 1, the ball is at the top of its bounce; in keyframe 5, the ball is at the bottom of its bounce; and in keyframe 10, the ball is back up at the top (**Figure 9.3**). To complete a tweened animation, you must set the tween property for the in-between frames in each keyframe span.

To set the span's property to Motion Tween:

1. To define a motion tween for the first half of the ball's bounce, in the Timeline, select any of the frames in the first keyframe span 1, 2, 3, or 4 (**Figure 9.4**). Flash automatically selects the ball symbol. To define a motion tween, the item to be tweened must be selected.

2. In the Frame Properties tab of the Property inspector, from the Tween pop-up menu, choose Motion (**Figure 9.5**).

   The settings for motion tweens appear.

   Flash defines frames 1–4 as a motion tween, updating the Timeline to give you information about the tween (**Figure 9.6**). (See the sidebar "Which Frames Contain Tweening?" earlier in this chapter.) These in-between frames no longer display the content of the preceding keyframe; instead they display the incrementally changed content that Flash creates. This tween content is shielded so you can't select it (clicking a graphic-object on an in-between frame set to tween is just like clicking a blank area of the Stage). You can, however, drag tween content, but doing so transforms the in-between frame into a keyframe.

Figure 9.4 Select any frame in a keyframe span to set the span's Tween property.

Figure 9.5 To access the settings for motion tweens, in the Frame Properties tab of the Property inspector, choose Motion from the Tween pop-up menu.

Figure 9.6 Flash adds information to the Timeline to indicate when frames contain motion tweens. Here, a blue tint and an arrow signify a completed motion tween.

Figure 9.7 With two motion-tween sequences, you can create a bouncing ball: one sequence shows the downward motion, and the other shows the rebound.

Range of frames being displayed as onion skins

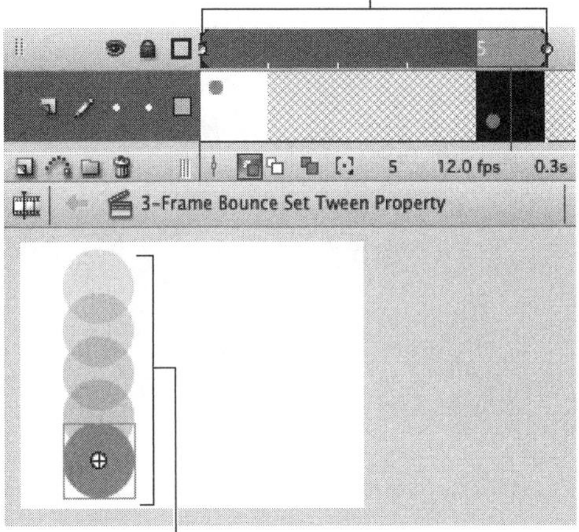

3-Frame Bounce Set Tween Property

Position of ball in the three in-between frames

Figure 9.8 Turn on onion skinning to preview the positions of a tweened object on the Stage.

3. To define the motion tween for the second half of the ball's bounce, in the Timeline, select any of the frames in the second keyframe span—5, 6, 7, 8, or 9.

4. Repeat step 2.

Flash creates the second half of the ball's bounce with another motion tween (**Figure 9.7**).

✔ Tips

■ When you choose Preview or Preview in Context from the Frame View pop-up menu (at the right end of the Timeline), the tweening arrow doesn't appear in the frames containing tweens. Nor can you see the incremental steps Flash creates for the tween. But if you turn on onion skinning, you can see all the in-between frames in position on the Stage (**Figure 9.8**).

■ Oddly enough, although you can't select a symbol on an in-between frame, you can edit it. Double-clicking a symbol on an in-between frame opens that symbol in symbol-editing mode. This trick doesn't work for drawing-objects or groups, however; you must be in a keyframe to edit those graphic-objects. If you set up your tween using primitive-shapes, double-clicking the primitive on an in-between frame brings up a dialog warning that you must convert the primitive to a drawing-object to edit it. If you click OK, you still don't enter editing mode, but Flash does convert the primitive in the span's initial keyframe to a drawing-object. And you must be careful when you double-click; if you drag the tweened graphic on an in-between frame even a tiny bit, Flash creates a new keyframe.

Adding Keyframes to Motion Tweens

After you have set up a motion tween, Flash creates new keyframes for you when you reposition a tweened graphic on an in-between frame. You can also add new keyframes by choosing Insert > Timeline > Keyframe.

To add keyframes by repositioning a tweened graphic:

1. Create a ten-frame motion tween of a bouncing ball, following the steps in the preceding task.

2. In the Timeline, select frame 3.

   On the Stage, you see the ball symbol in one of the in-between positions Flash created.

3. In the Tools panel, choose the selection tool.

4. Drag the ball to a new position—slightly to the right of its current position, for example.

   Flash inserts a new keyframe at frame 3 and splits the preceding five-frame tween into separate tweens (**Figure 9.9**). The new keyframe contains another instance of the ball symbol.

To add keyframes by command:

1. Continuing with the document from the preceding task, select frame 7 in the Timeline.

2. Choose Insert > Timeline > Keyframe.

   Flash creates a new keyframe in frame 7. A new instance of your symbol appears on the Stage in the position Flash created for it in that in-between frame. You can now reposition the symbol.

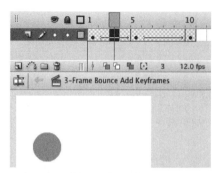

In the selected frame, the ball appears in its tweened position

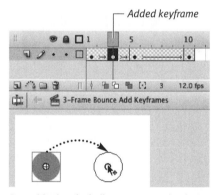

Repositioning the ball creates a new keyframe

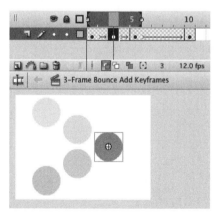

Onion-skin view of other tween positions for the ball

Figure 9.9 Repositioning the ball in an in-between frame that's part of a tween creates a new keyframe and a revision of the tweened frames.

Figure 9.10 You can change the color of a symbol, as well as its position, in a motion tween. Flash creates transitional colors for each in-between frame.

Animating Color Effects

Tweening isn't just about changing the position of an item on the Stage. When you use motion tweening to animate changes to symbol instances in keyframes, you can also tween changes in color, by changing the symbol's Color property. (This technique works only with symbols; although you can tween other types of graphic objects, you cannot animate color changes to them using motion tweening.)

To change a symbol's color over time:

1. In a new Flash document, or in a new layer of an existing document, in keyframe 1, place a symbol instance on the Stage.

2. In the Timeline, select frame 5, and choose Insert > Timeline > Keyframe.

   Flash duplicates the contents of keyframe 1 in a new keyframe.

3. With keyframe 5 as the current frame, select the symbol.

4. To change the symbol's color, in the Properties tab of the Property inspector, from the Color menu, choose new settings. (For detailed instructions on modifying symbol color, see Chapter 7.)

5. Select any of the frames in the first keyframe span (1, 2, 3, or 4).

6. In the Properties tab of the Property inspector, from the Tween pop-up menu, choose Motion.

   Flash recolors the graphic-object in three transitional steps—one for each in-between frame (**Figure 9.10**).

✔ Tip

■ You can motion-tween a change in a symbol's transparency (Alpha) to make that symbol appear to fade in or out.

Animating Graphics That Change Size

You can animate changes to the size of a graphic-object from one keyframe to the next by motion tweening the object's Horizontal Scale and/or Vertical Scale properties. To tween graphics that grow or shrink, you must select the Scale check box in the Frame Properties tab of the Property inspector. You can tween size changes for any type of graphic-object; for simplicity, the tasks that follow describe using a symbol.

To tween a growing and shrinking graphic:

1. In a new Flash document, or in a new layer of an existing document, in keyframe 1, place a symbol instance on the Stage.

   (To review the creation and use of symbols, see Chapter 7.)

2. To create a keyframe that defines the end of a growing sequence, in the Timeline, select frame 5; then choose Insert > Timeline > Keyframe.

   Flash duplicates the symbol from keyframe 1 in the new keyframe.

3. Select any of the frames in the keyframe span (1, 2, 3, or 4).

4. Set the Tween property for the span to Motion.

   To do so, in the Frame Properties tab of the Property inspector, from the Tween pop-up menu, choose Motion. The motion-tween arrow and color coding now appear in frames 2–4.

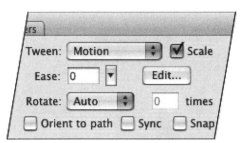

Figure 9.11 To make a graphic grow in equal steps, set the Tween property of the keyframe span to Motion, and choose the Scale property. You set the properties for a selected frame in the Frame Properties tab of the Property inspector.

Figure 9.12 To tween a shrinking graphic, make it smaller in the end keyframe of the sequence. Turn on Onion Skin mode to see the size of the graphic Flash creates for each in-between frame.

5. With the playhead in keyframe 5, select the symbol instance and make it bigger. (For detailed instructions on resizing graphics, see Chapter 4.)

6. In the Timeline, select any of the frames in the first keyframe span (1, 2, 3, or 4).

7. In the Properties tab of the Property inspector, make sure the Scale check box is selected (it is selected by default) (**Figure 9.11**).

Flash increases the size of the symbol instance in equal steps from keyframe 1 to keyframe 5.

8. To add the ending keyframe for a shrinking sequence, in the Timeline, select frame 10; then press F6.

Flash duplicates the symbol from keyframe 5 in the new keyframe.

9. Select any of the frames in the keyframe span (5, 6, 7, 8, or 9).

10. Set the Tween property for the span to Motion (see step 4).

The motion-tween arrow and color coding now appear in frames 5–9. The Scale property is already selected.

11. With the playhead in keyframe 10, select the symbol instance and make it smaller.

Flash creates a tween that shrinks your graphic in five equal steps (**Figure 9.12**).

✔ Tip

■ As long as you don't change the settings in the Frame Properties tab of the Property inspector, the Scale check box remains selected, and Flash updates the tween anytime you change the content in one of the keyframes in this series. You don't have to have the Frame Properties tab of the Property inspector open to fine-tune the size of your scaling graphic.

ANIMATING GRAPHICS THAT CHANGE SIZE

Rotating and Spinning Graphics

You can animate a spinning graphic-object by tweening its Rotation property. For motion tweens that involve spinning, creating beginning and ending keyframes isn't enough. You need to specify the direction of rotation, and the number of times to spin. You can tween rotation for any type of graphic-object; for simplicity, the tasks that follow describe using a symbol.

To rotate a graphic less than 360 degrees:

1. In a new Flash document, or on a new layer, in keyframe 1, place a symbol instance on the Stage.

   You can create a new symbol or use an existing one; use a graphic that looks different at various stages of its rotation— for example, a triangle or an arrow. (To review symbol creation, see Chapter 7.)

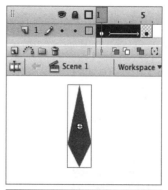

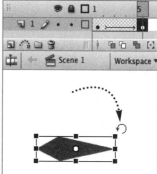

Figure 9.13 To prepare a rotational tween, in the keyframe that ends the sequence, rotate the item to its ending position.

Creating Rotation with Just Two Keyframes

You can't create tweens of rotating and spinning graphics quite as easily as you create the types of motion tweens presented in earlier tasks, because you can't describe rotation accurately with just two keyframes.

Imagine, for example, trying to rotate the pointer of a compass 180 degrees so that it turns from pointing north to pointing south. The initial keyframe contains the pointer pointing up; the ending keyframe contains the pointer pointing down. But how should the pointer move to reach that position?

Flash gives you three choices: rotate the pointer clockwise, rotate it counterclockwise, or flip it upside down. Trying to describe the pointer spinning all the way around the compass in just two keyframes would be even less informative, because the beginning and ending keyframes would be identical.

To clarify the motion, you could create a series of keyframes, rotating the pointer a few degrees in each one. That method is tedious, however. Fortunately, the Frame Properties tab of the Property inspector lets you provide extra information about tweens so that Flash can create rotational tweens with just two keyframes.

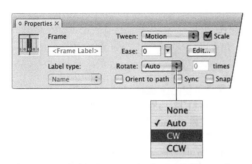

Figure 9.14 The Rotate menu in the Frame Properties tab of the Property inspector lets you tell Flash the direction in which to rotate a tweened object.

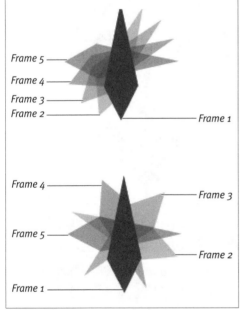

Figure 9.15 To create a tween that involves rotation, you can specify the direction of the rotation as clockwise or counterclockwise. You can also choose Auto to let Flash pick the direction that involves the smallest change, which allows Flash to create the smoothest motion. Compare the degree of change in each frame between rotating an arrow clockwise from 12 o'clock to 3 o'clock (top) versus rotating the arrow counterclockwise to reach the same position (bottom).

2. In the Timeline, select frame 5, and choose Insert > Timeline > Keyframe.

Flash duplicates the symbol from keyframe 1 in the new keyframe.

3. On the Stage, in keyframe 5, rotate the symbol instance 90 degrees clockwise (**Figure 9.13**).

(For detailed instructions on rotating elements, see Chapter 4.)

4. In the Timeline, select any of the frames in the first keyframe span (1, 2, 3, or 4).

5. In the Frame Properties tab of the Property inspector, from the Tween pop-up menu, choose Motion.

The settings for motion tweening appear in the panel.

6. From the Rotate menu (**Figure 9.14**), choose one of the following options:

▲ To rotate the graphic in the direction that requires the smallest movement, choose Auto (**Figure 9.15**).

▲ To rotate the graphic clockwise, choose CW.

▲ To rotate the graphic counterclockwise, choose CCW.

7. To rotate less then 360 degrees, in the Times field, to the right of the Rotate menu, enter 0.

Flash tweens the graphic so that it rotates around its transformation point. Each in-between frame shows the graphic rotated a little more.

To spin a graphic 360 degrees:

1. Follow steps 1 and 2 of the preceding task to create a five-frame sequence with identical keyframes in frame 1 and frame 5.

   You don't need to reposition your graphic, because the beginning frame and ending frame of a 360-degree spin should look exactly the same.

2. In the Timeline, select any of the frames in the first keyframe span (1, 2, 3, or 4).

3. Set the Tween property to Motion (see step 5 of the preceding task).

4. From the Rotate menu, choose a direction of rotation.

5. In the Times field, to the right of the Rotate menu, enter the number of rotations that you want to use (**Figure 9.16**).

   The value that you enter in the Times field determines how Flash tweens the graphic. Flash creates new positions for the graphic to rotate it completely the given number times in the span of frames. Flash tweens the graphic differently depending on the number of rotations you choose (**Figure 9.17**).

   Flash tweens the item so that it spins the number of times you indicated over the span of frames that you defined as the motion tween.

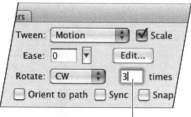

Enter the number of rotations

Figure 9.16 In the Frame Properties tab of the Property inspector, you can set the number of times a tweened item should spin.

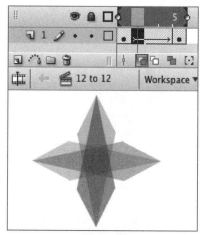

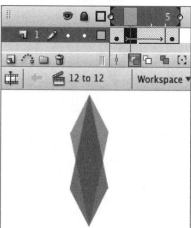

Figure 9.17 Compare a single rotation (top) with a double rotation (bottom) in the same number of frames.

Figure 9.18 The dotted line in the Timeline indicates that these 20 frames contain a motion tween, but a broken one. The final keyframe is missing.

Moving Graphics in Straight Lines

In the preceding tasks, you created a well-behaved bouncing ball—one that moves up and down. To make one that bounces around like a crazy Ping-Pong ball, add more keyframes and place the ball in various locations. The ball moves in a straight line from one position to the next, but the effect is livelier. To get frenetic bouncing, move the ball a great distance in a small number of in-between frames. To slow the action, move the ball a short distance or use a larger number of in-between frames.

To move an item from point to point:

1. In a new Flash document, or on a new layer, on the Stage, in keyframe 1, place an instance of a symbol containing a graphic of a ball.

2. In the Timeline, select frame 20, and choose Insert > Timeline > Frame.
   Flash creates 19 in-between frames.

3. In the Timeline, select any frame in the keyframe span (frames 1–20).

4. In the Frame Properties tab of the Property inspector, from the Tween pop-up menu, choose Motion.
   Flash defines frames 1–20 as a motion tween but with a dotted line in the Timeline, indicating that the tween isn't yet complete (**Figure 9.18**). You need to create keyframes that describe the ball's motion.

5. In the Timeline, position the playhead in frame 5.

continues on next page

6. On the Stage, drag the ball to a new position.

Flash creates a new keyframe in frame 5 and completes a tween for frames 1–4 (**Figure 9.19**).

7. In the Timeline, position the playhead in frame 10.

8. On the Stage, drag the ball to a new position.

Flash creates a new keyframe in frame 10 and completes a tween for frames 5–9.

9. Repeat this repositioning process for frames 15 and 20.

You now have a ball that bounces around wildly (**Figure 9.20**).

10. To add more frames, select frame 30 or frame 40, then choose Insert > Timeline > Frame.

Flash applies the motion-tween property to all the newly defined frames. Now you can add keyframes by following the procedure described earlier in this task. Just be sure you end up with a keyframe as the last frame in the series. If you have more frames than you need, you can remove them.

11. To end the tween, select the last keyframe in the series.

12. In the Frame Properties tab of the Property inspector, from the Tween menu, choose None.

If you don't change the last frame's Tween property to None, any frames that you add after that will also be set to Motion Tween, which may create unexpected results.

Completed tween segment

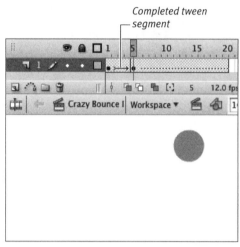

Figure 9.19 As you move the ball to new positions in different frames within the motion tween, Flash creates keyframes and completes the tween between one keyframe and the next.

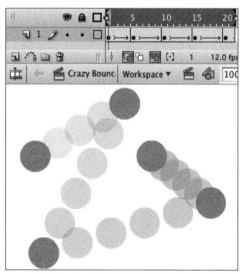

Figure 9.20 By stringing motion tweens together, you can animate a graphic-object that moves from point to point.

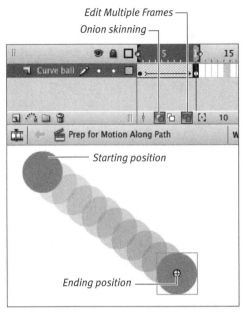

Figure 9.21 The first step in creating a tweened graphic that follows a path is defining a motion tween with the graphic in the beginning and ending positions you want to use. Here, the graphic moves from the beginning to the end in a straight line. (Onion Skin mode and Edit Multiple Frames are selected to show all the tween's components.)

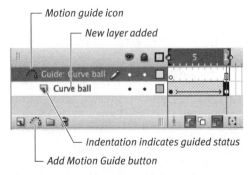

Figure 9.22 The Add Motion Guide button inserts a new layer, defined as a *motion-guide* layer, above the selected layer in the Timeline. The default name for the motion-guide layer includes the name of the layer selected when you created the motion-guide layer. The layer containing the tweened graphic is indented and linked to the motion-guide layer. Flash defines the linked layer as a *guided layer*.

Moving Graphics Along a Path

In the preceding task, you made the ball move all over the Stage in short, point-to-point hops. A ball does sometimes behave this way, but other things may require movements that are softer—trajectories that are arcs, not straight lines. You could achieve this effect by stringing together many point-to-point keyframes, but Flash offers a more efficient method: the motion guide. Motion guides describe the exact path an animated graphic-object takes.

To add a motion-guide layer:

1. Create a new Flash document containing a ten-frame motion tween.

   In the first keyframe, place the graphic-object to be tweened in the top-left corner of the Stage. In the last frame, place the graphic-object in the bottom-right corner of the Stage. Your document should resemble **Figure 9.21**.

2. Select the layer that contains the graphic-object you want to move along a path.

3. In the Timeline's Status bar, click the Add Motion Guide button.

   Flash adds the motion-guide layer directly above the layer you selected and gives it a default name of Guide, followed by the name of the layer you selected (**Figure 9.22**). The motion-guide icon appears next to the layer name. Flash also indents the layer linked to the motion-guide layer.

continues on next page

4. In the Tools panel, select a tool that creates merge-shape or drawing-object paths, such as the pencil tool.

5. In the Timeline, select the motion-guide layer.

6. Draw a line on the Stage showing the path you want the graphic-object to take (**Figure 9.23**).

Paths on a motion-guide layer create motion paths for graphic-objects on linked layers.

7. Activate View > Snapping > Snap to Objects.

For Flash to move an item along a motion path, the transformation point of the item (which appears as a small white circle within a symbol or group) must be centered on the path. Having the Snap to Objects setting active helps you position the tween graphic correctly. (To learn more about the transformation point, see Chapters 4 and 7.)

8. In keyframe 1, using the selection tool, drag the tween graphic by its transformation point to position it directly over the beginning of the motion path.

As you drag, the snapping ring enlarges slightly when it approaches any snapping elements you have set. For example, with Snap to Objects active, the ring grows larger when the point you're dragging is centered over the motion guide.

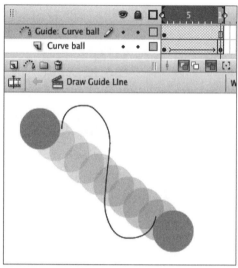

Figure 9.23 A line on a motion-guide layer acts as a path that guides the motion of a tweened graphic on a linked layer.

The Mystery of Motion Guides

A *motion guide* is a graphic you create on a special separate layer. The motion guide defines the path for a tweened graphic to follow. One motion-guide layer can control items on several layers. The motion-guide layer governs any layers linked to it. The linked layers are defined as guided layers in the Layer Properties dialog.

If you want different elements to follow different paths, create several motion-guide layers within a single Flash document. Each motion guide governs the actions of graphic-objects on its own set of linked layers.

MOVING GRAPHICS ALONG A PATH

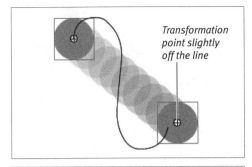

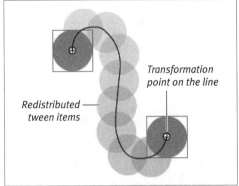

Figure 9.24 To follow the path, tweened items must have their transformation point sitting directly on the motion-guide line. (For symbols and groups the transformation point appears as a small white circle. For drawing-objects and primitives the transformation point appears only if you have moved it from its default position at the center of the object.)

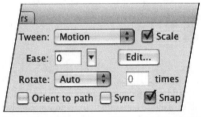

Figure 9.25 When a frame's Tween property is set to Motion, the Frame Properties tab of the Property inspector contains a Snap check box. Select Snap when the layer is linked to a motion-guide layer, and Flash automatically centers the transformation point of any graphic-object on that layer over the motion guide. Forced snapping ensures correct tweening along the motion-guide path.

9. In keyframe 10, drag the tween graphic to position its transformation point directly over the end of the motion path.

Flash redraws the in-between frames so that the graphic follows the motion path (**Figure 9.24**). Flash centers the tweened graphic over the motion path in each in-between frame. In the final movie, Flash hides the path.

✔ Tips

- After you draw the motion path, lock the motion-guide layer to prevent yourself from editing the path accidentally as you snap the graphic to the path.

- In the Frame Properties tab of the Property inspector for the keyframes containing the tweened graphics, select the Snap check box to have Flash assist you in centering keyframe graphics over the end of the guide line (**Figure 9.25**).

- You can use most of Flash's drawing tools—line, pencil, pen, oval, rectangle, polygon, polystar, and brush—to create a motion path. The tools may be set to Merge Drawing or Object Drawing mode. The paths created by the oval- and rectangle-primitive tools, however, do not work as motion guides.

- You can transform a plain guide layer in your Timeline to a motion-guide layer by repositioning the layer directly beneath the guide layer. Watch the preview bar and the icon in the guide layer; as you drag the lower layer to the right, the guide icon changes to a dotted arc icon indicating a motion guide (to learn about plain guides, see Chapter 6).

MOVING GRAPHICS ALONG A PATH

To create a second guided layer:

1. In the Flash document you created in the preceding task, select the guided layer (the one containing the circle).

2. To add a new layer, do either of the following:

   ▲ Choose Insert > Timeline > Layer.

   ▲ In the Timeline, click the Insert Layer button.

   Flash adds a new indented (guided) layer above the selected layer (**Figure 9.26**). Tweened items on this layer follow the motion guide when you position them correctly.

To add a second motion-guide layer:

1. Create a Flash document with at least one normal layer containing a motion tween and one motion-guide layer linked to a guided layer containing a motion tween.

2. In the Timeline, select the normal layer containing the motion tween.

3. Click the Add Motion Guide button.

   Flash adds a motion-guide layer above the selected layer and links the selected layer to it. Follow the steps in the preceding tasks to draw the second motion path and position the tweened item.

4. Play the movie.

   The two tweened graphics follow their own motion paths simultaneously (**Figure 9.27**).

✔ Tip

■ To convert an existing layer to a guided layer quickly, drag it below the motion-guide layer or any of its linked layers.

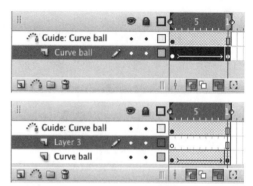

Figure 9.26 When a guided layer is selected (top), clicking the Insert Layer button creates another guided layer below the motion-guide layer (bottom).

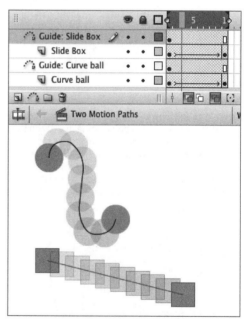

Figure 9.27 Add multiple guide layers to move graphic-objects along separate paths simultaneously.

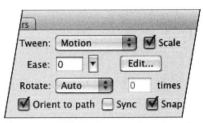

Figure 9.28 With Motion tweening selected in the Frame Properties tab of the Property inspector, select Orient to Path to make Flash rotate a tweened item to face the direction of movement.

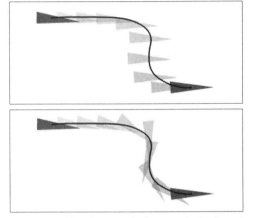

Figure 9.29 When the arrow in the tween isn't oriented to the path, the arrow stays parallel to the bottom of the Stage and moves to various points along the path (top). When the arrow in the tween is oriented to the path, the arrow rotates to align better with the path (bottom).

Orienting Graphics to a Motion Path

As a default, tweened graphics keep a fixed orientation (they don't rotate) even when they follow a motion path. To create more natural movement, you can force a tweened graphic-object to rotate to preserve its orientation to the path in each frame of a tween.

To orient a graphic-object to the path:

1. Create a ten-frame motion tween of an item that follows a motion guide, using the steps in the first task in "Moving Graphics Along a Path," earlier in this chapter.

   This time, don't use a circle; draw an arrow or a triangle or an animal.

2. Turn on onion skinning to see how the item moves along the path without orientation.

3. In the Timeline, in the layer containing the tweened graphic-object, select keyframe 1.

4. In the Frame Properties tab of the Property inspector, select the Orient to Path check box (**Figure 9.28**).

   Flash redraws the tween. In the in-between frames, Flash rotates the tweened item to align it with the path more naturally (**Figure 9.29**).

Why Orient to Path?

Imagine a waiter carrying a full tray through a crowded room, raising and lowering the tray to avoid various obstacles but always keeping the tray level to avoid spilling anything. That's how tweened animation works if you don't orient the tweened graphic-object to the motion guide. The transformation point of the tweened graphic-object snaps to a new spot on the motion guide in each frame, but the graphic-object never rotates. With a ball, that procedure may result in natural-looking motion, but with other graphic-objects, the result is often unnatural. You might want a living creature to face in the direction it's moving, rotating slightly to match the twists and turns of its path. You might want an airplane doing loops to trace the loop tightly with its nose, not stay perpendicular to the curve. Orienting the graphic-object to the motion path forces a tweened graphic-object to rotate as the motion path curves. This rotation creates the illusion that graphic-object is always facing the direction it's going along the path.

✔ Tips

■ To help the Orient to Path option create the most natural positions for your graphic-object, you may need to rotate the graphic-object in the first and/or last keyframe of a tween so that the graphic-object is facing the direction it's supposed to move in (**Figure 9.30**).

■ If, after following the preceding tip, the orientation still looks odd in spots, step through the tween one frame at a time. When you get to a frame where Flash positions the graphic-object poorly, you can fix it. In the Timeline, select the in-between frame, and choose Insert > Timeline > Keyframe. In the new keyframe that Flash creates, select the graphic-object and rotate it manually to align it with the motion guide. Flash redraws the in-between frames.

■ Turn on onion skinning as you follow the preceding tip. That way, you can see how your adjustments affect the orientation of your graphic-object in each frame of the tween.

■ Sometimes, moving the transformation point of your graphic-object helps it orient to the path in a more lifelike manner. The default transformation point of the lizard in Figure 9.30 is at the center of the graphic-object's bounding box. Because the lizard has a huge curved tail, that point isn't even inside the lizard body. Moving the transformation point to the middle of the lizard's body lets the Orient to Path setting create more lifelike movement. (Use the free-transform tool to reposition the transformation point of a graphic-object or symbol instance.)

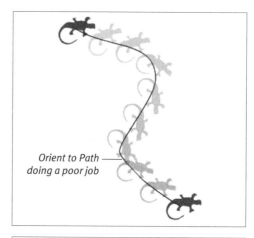

Orient to Path doing a poor job

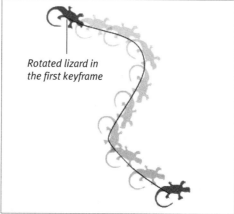

Rotated lizard in the first keyframe

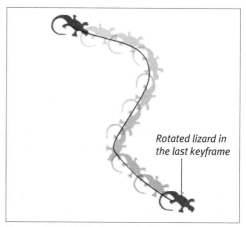

Rotated lizard in the last keyframe

Figure 9.30 Here, Flash could be doing a better job of aligning this lizard with the path (top). Rotating the lizard in the first keyframe (middle) and last keyframe (bottom) helps the Orient to Path feature do its job.

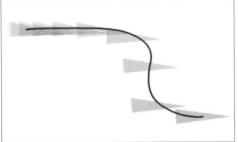

Figure 9.31 A negative Ease value (top) makes changes in the initial frames of the tween smaller and changes toward the end larger (bottom). The animation seems to start slowly and then speed up.

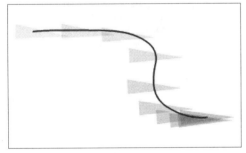

Figure 9.32 A positive Ease value (top) makes changes at the end of the animation smaller and changes in the initial frames larger (bottom). The animation seems to start quickly and then slow down.

Changing Tween Speed

In Chapter 8, you learned to make an animated item appear to move slowly or quickly by adjusting the number of in-between frames. When you create an animation with tweening, that method no longer works, because Flash distributes the motion evenly over whatever number of in-between frames you create. You can, however, make an animation slower at the beginning or end of a tween sequence by setting an Ease value.

To make the animation start slowly and accelerate (ease in):

1. Create a ten-frame motion tween of a graphic-object that follows a motion guide.

2. In the Timeline, select any of the frames in the keyframe span (frames 1–9).

3. In the Frame Properties tab of the Property inspector, enter a negative number in the Ease field (**Figure 9.31**).

4. Press Enter.
   The word *in* appears next to the field. Easing in makes the animation start slowly and speed up toward the end. The lower the Ease value, the greater the rate of acceleration.

To make the animation start quickly and decelerate (ease out):

1. Follow steps 1 and 2 of the preceding task.

2. In the Frame Properties tab of the Property inspector, enter a positive number in the Ease field.

3. Press Enter.
   The word *out* appears next to the field. Easing out makes the animation start quickly and slow toward the end (**Figure 9.32**). The higher the Ease value, the greater the rate of deceleration.

✔ Tip

- An Ease value of 0 causes Flash to display the whole animation at a constant rate (**Figure 9.33**).

To create custom easing:

1. Create a motion tween in which several properties of the tweened graphic-object change over time.

   For example, use the oval tool to draw a yellow circle and convert it to a symbol named Sun. Use the Sun symbol to create a 30-frame motion tween. In keyframe 1, place an instance of the Sun at the top of the Stage. In keyframe 30, place an instance at the bottom of the Stage; resize it to be twice as large; and use the Color setting in the Properties tab of the Property inspector to change the color to dark orange.

2. Select any frame in the keyframe span (frames 1–29).

3. To access custom easing settings, in the Frame Properties tab of the Property inspector, click the Edit button, to the right of the Ease field (**Figure 9.34**).

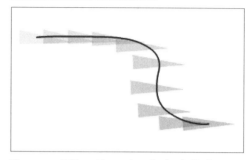

Figure 9.33 With an Ease value of 0 (top), Flash distributes the tweening changes evenly across the in-between frames (bottom). The effect is that of animation moving at a constant rate.

Figure 9.34 Keyframe spans whose Tween property is set to Motion can have custom easing applied. In the Frame Properties tab for the span, click the Edit button to access a dialog for setting custom easing.

The Custom Ease In/Ease Out dialog appears (**Figure 9.35**). The dialog shows the selected tween's changes over time on a graph; the horizontal axis represents each frame in the tween; the vertical axis represents the amount of change. When no easing values have been set, the graph begins as a straight line between a control point representing the tween's first frame (with 0 percent change) and a control point representing the tween's last frame (100 percent change). You can edit the graph to set specific easing values, frame-by-frame, for five properties of a tweened graphic-object (Position, Rotation, Scale, Color, and Filters).

4. To set easing for all five properties simultaneously, select the "Use one setting for all properties" check box.

continues on next page

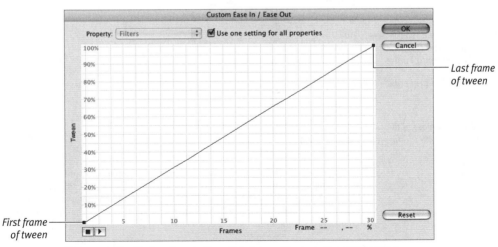

First frame of tween

Last frame of tween

Figure 9.35 The Custom Ease In/Ease Out dialog allows you to control easing precisely, frame by frame, by creating a curve that defines the rate of change in each frame. Without easing, the rate is constant, starting at 0 percent in the first frame of the tween and reaching 100 percent in the last frame of the tween.

CHANGING TWEEN SPEED

5. To modify the rate of change, click the graph's line at the frame where you want the modification to start.

Flash adds a control point with tangent-point handles; these work similarly to anchor points and Bézier handles, allowing you to adjust the graph's curve (**Figure 9.36**).

6. Drag a control point vertically to determine the amount of change that should occur by the current frame; adjust the tangent handles to fine-tune the rate of change in the frames on either side of the control point.

Dragging a control point toward the top of the graph makes the curve steeper (changes happen more quickly); dragging a control point to the bottom makes the curve flatter (changes happen more slowly). You can also manipulate the first and last control points' tangent handles to flatten or deepen the curve.

7. Repeat steps 5 and 6 as needed to speed or slow the rate of change in the desired frames of the tween.

8. Click OK.

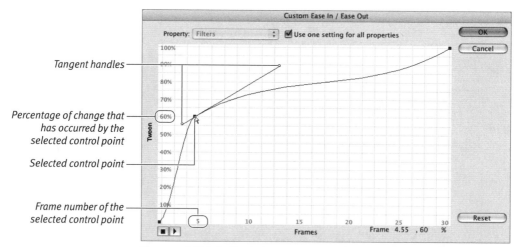

Figure 9.36 Click the line in the Custom Ease In/Ease Out dialog to add a control point. Changing a control point's vertical position makes more (or less) of a change take place by the current frame. Adjusting the tangent handles changes the slope of the curve: a steeper curve segment translates to a quicker rate of change; a flatter segment, to a slower one.

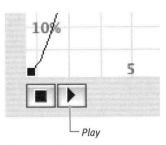

Play

Figure 9.37 To see the effects of your custom easing curve, click the Play button in the Custom Ease In/Ease Out dialog to preview the animation.

Figure 9.38 Deselecting the "Use one setting for all properties" check box activates the Property menu. Choose a property to create custom easing settings for that specific change.

✔ Tips

■ To preview your settings, click the Play button in the lower-left corner of the Custom Ease In/Ease Out dialog (**Figure 9.37**). The tween plays in the Flash document window. You may need to move the custom-easing dialog to see the document window.

■ If you have already set a regular Ease value in the Frame Properties tab of the Property inspector, the easing graph in the Custom Ease In/Ease Out dialog reflects that setting. You can use the regular Ease value as a starting place for your custom settings. But be warned: If you've set custom easing, and you enter a value in the regular Ease field, that new setting is applied to the custom-easing curve, wiping out your custom adjustments.

To ease changes for different properties separately:

1. Follow steps 1–3 of the preceding task.

2. Deselect the "Use one setting for all properties" check box.

3. From the Property menu (**Figure 9.38**), select one of the following:

    Position controls the rate at which a tweened object moves around the Stage.

    Rotation controls the rate at which a tweened object spins (using the Rotation property set in the Frame Properties tab of the Property inspector).

    Scale controls the rate at which a tweened object changes size.

    Color controls the rate at which a tweened symbol instance's Color property changes.

    Filters controls the rate at which filter effects take place.

continues on next page

CHANGING TWEEN SPEED

4. Adjust the settings by following steps 5–7 in the preceding task.

5. Repeat steps 3 and 4 of this task for each property you wish to control.

6. Click OK.

✔ Tips

■ If you add keyframes within a tween span that has custom easing, Flash attempts to keep the custom settings for those frames as much as possible (**Figure 9.39**). Flash can't just break the easing curve into smaller segments, however. At each new keyframe, 0 percent of the easing for that tween span must occur; and for the final frame of each span, 100 percent of the easing must occur. Click the Edit button in the Frame Properties tab of the Property inspector to see and further edit those settings.

■ To apply the same curve to several, but not all, of the properties, use the standard Copy and Paste commands. Set the curve for the first property, press ⌘-C (Mac) or Ctrl-C (Windows) to copy the curve, select a new property from the Property menu, then press ⌘-V (Mac) or Ctrl-V (Windows) to paste the curve.

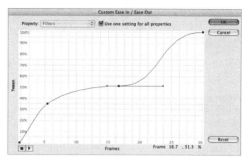

Original span's easing curve

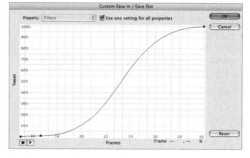

Easing curve after adding keyframe

Figure 9.39 If you add keyframes to the middle of a tween span that has custom easing, Flash tries to preserve some of the easing settings for the newly created span.

Custom Ease to Create Motion

You can use easing values to create variations on the general motion of your tween—for example, making a graphic move back and forth several times even though its tween sequence consists of just two keyframes that move the graphic in a straight line from one position to another. Imagine a 20-frame tween; in the first keyframe, the graphic sits on the left side of the Stage, and in the second, the graphic sits on the right side. Now, set custom easing values for Position in the keyframe span for this tween. Add a control point at frame 5, and position it vertically so that 50 percent of the change is made by that frame. Next, add a control point at frame 10, and position it so that 25 percent of the change has been made. The rectangle moves forward to the middle of the Stage by frame 5, moves backward between frames 5 and 10, and then moves forward again until it reaches the right side of the Stage in frame 20.

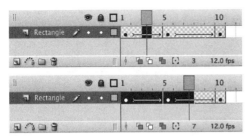

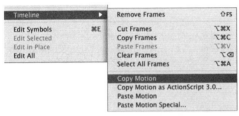

Figure 9.40 To copy information about one motion-tween, in the Timeline, select any frame in the tween's keyframe span (top). To copy information about a multiple motion-tween sequence, select the spans in the sequence (bottom). They must be contiguous, but the last span need not be fully selected.

Timeline	▶	Remove Frames	⇧F5
Edit Symbols	⌘E	Cut Frames	⌥⌘X
Edit Selected		Copy Frames	⌥⌘C
Edit in Place		Paste Frames	⌥⌘V
Edit All		Clear Frames	⌥⌦
		Select All Frames	⌥⌘A
		Copy Motion	
		Copy Motion as ActionScript 3.0...	
		Paste Motion	
		Paste Motion Special...	

Figure 9.41 The Edit > Timeline > Copy Motion command copies the properties that define a tween or tweens in a selected set of frames.

About Copy Motion

Flash's Copy Motion command copies information that defines a motion-tween sequence: changes to the tweened object's properties (such as position, rotation, scale); duration of the tween (the number of frames it takes); and other tween settings (such as Easing). The Paste Motion command lets you apply that information to a different graphic-object to change its properties in the same way, over the same number of frames, using the same Tween settings. The Paste Motion Special command lets you apply changes to the tweened object's properties selectively. The Copy Motion as ActionScript 3.0 command translates motion-tween animation to animation generated by ActionScript 3.0.

Re-creating Motion Tweens

Flash CS3 offers three new commands for reducing repetitive animation work. Copy Motion, Paste Motion, and Paste Motion Special streamline the process of animating multiple objects that go through the same "motions."

To copy motion-tween properties:

1. Using any of the techniques you've learned in this chapter, create a motion tween using a symbol on one layer.

   The motion tween can be one keyframe span or multiple spans.

2. To select the motion-tween properties, do any of the following (**Figure 9.40**):

   ▲ To select the properties for one motion tween, in the Timeline, select any frame in the keyframe span containing the desired motion.

   ▲ To select the properties for multiple motion tweens, in the Timeline, select the keyframe spans that make up the desired motions; the spans must be contiguous.

3. Choose Edit > Timeline > Copy Motion (**Figure 9.41**).

   Flash copies the changes in properties that define the motion tween for each selected (or partially selected) span: duration, x position y position, rotation and skew, x scale, y scale, color, easing, filters, and blends (to learn more about filters and blends, see Chapter 11).

To apply motion-tween properties to a different symbol:

1. To select the target symbol instance, do one of the following:

▲ On the Stage, select the symbol instance to which you want to apply the copied motion-tween properties (**Figure 9.42**).

▲ In the Timeline, select a keyframe containing the symbol instance to which you want to apply the copied motion-tween properties.

The symbol must be isolated on its own layer.

2. Choose Edit > Timeline > Paste Motion (**Figure 9.43**).

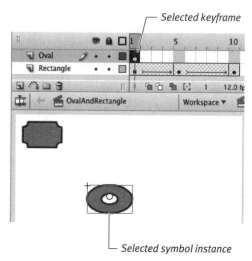

Selected keyframe

Selected symbol instance

Figure 9.42 To apply the copied motion-tween properties to a new symbol instance, select the symbol on the Stage (or select its keyframe in the Timeline).

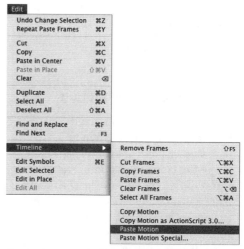

Figure 9.43 The Edit > Timeline > Paste Motion command creates a tween sequence using the copied properties. Flash inserts the keyframe span(s) before the selected frame in the Timeline and preserves that frame.

RE-CREATING MOTION TWEENS

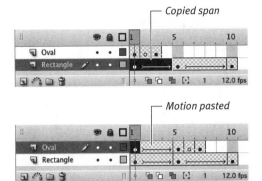

Figure 9.44 The Paste Motion command pastes the tween sequence(s) of the copied motion into the Timeline for the selected symbol. The command preserves any existing unselected frames and keyframes in the Timeline, pushing them to later frames.

Flash inserts into the Timeline the same number of keyframe spans as contained in the motion tween(s) you copied. The keyframe you selected and all subsequent frames get pushed out to later frames in the Timeline (**Figure 9.44**).

3. Play the movie.

The symbol to which you applied the copied motion-tween properties now moves and changes in the same way the original symbol did.

✔ Tip

■ The preceding tasks describe copying and pasting the motion-tween properties of a symbol, but Flash can also copy and paste the motion-tween properties of any graphic-object and apply them to another graphic-object. The graphic-object must meet the criteria for being used in a motion tween; it must be in a container, and it must be the only object on its layer. When you paste motion-tween properties, the object receiving them must have the ability to tween that property. You can copy a motion tween that slides a symbol across the Stage and apply that slide to a text field, but you can't, for example, copy a motion tween that changes a symbol's Color property and apply the color change to a drawing-object or primitive.

Pasted Motion: It's (Almost) All Relative

For the most part, Paste Motion applies its settings to graphic-objects relatively. Let's say your original graphic-object is a rectangle-primitive located in the upper-left corner of the stage, and you tween it to move diagonally to the center. If you copy that motion and apply it to an oval-primitive that is located at the center of the Stage, the oval will start out at the center, then move diagonally down and to the right, ending up near the lower-right corner of the Stage (**Figure 9.45**). If you want to exactly replicate the move from the upper-left corner to the center, you must position your target symbol in the same starting spot as your source object.

Paste Motion Special lets you select which aspects of a copied motion apply to the target object. By selecting (or deselecting) check boxes, you can have Flash apply (or skip) tweened changes to the following properties for the target object: X Position, Y Position, Horizontal Scale, Vertical Scale, Rotation and Skew, Color, Filters, and Blend. In addition, you can choose to override any scaling or rotating/skewing that has been done to the target graphic-object. If, for example, you have transformed the target object by rotating it 90 degrees clockwise, selecting the Override Target Rotation and Skew Properties tells Flash to apply the copied motion to the target object in its original state, as if you'd never rotated it (see the task "To apply copied motion-tween properties selectively").

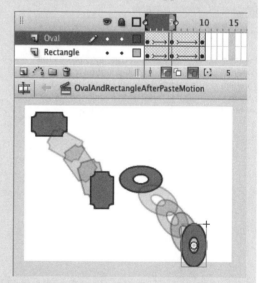

Figure 9.45 After applying the motion of the rectangle symbol to the oval symbol, Flash recreates the rectangle's diagonal downward spin for the oval. The oval moves and spins the same amount, but relative to its own start position, not to the start position of the rectangle.

Figure 9.46 Choose Edit > Timeline > Paste Motion Special to apply properties selectively.

Figure 9.47 In the Paste Motion Special dialog, select check boxes for the properties you want to apply selectively.

To apply copied motion-tween properties selectively:

1. Follow step 1 in the preceding task.

2. Choose Edit > Timeline > Paste Motion Special (**Figure 9.46**).

   The Paste Motion Special dialog appears (**Figure 9.47**).

3. To apply individual tween properties, select check boxes for any of the following:

   ▲ To re-create the horizontal motion, select X Position.

   ▲ To re-create the vertical motion, select Y Position.

   ▲ To re-create changes in size along the horizontal axis, select Horizontal Scale.

   ▲ To re-create changes in size along the vertical axis, select Vertical Scale.

   ▲ To re-create changes in rotation and skew, select Rotation and Skew.

   ▲ To apply changes to the Color property of a symbol instance, select Color. (This property is available only for symbol instances; see Chapter 7).

   ▲ To apply any filter settings, tweened changes to those settings, and states (whether enabled or disabled), select Filters. Filters can be applied only to movie-clip symbols, button symbols, and text fields.

   ▲ To apply a blend mode from an original movie-clip symbol instance to a new symbol instance, choose Blend Mode. (This property is available only for movie-clip symbols.)

   continues on next page

▲ To apply changes in scaling to a selected graphic-object relative to its original size (ignoring any scaling applied to the object on the Stage), select "Override target scale properties. Otherwise, Flash applies scaling changes relative to the object's current size on the Stage (**Figure 9.48**).

▲ To apply changes in rotation and skew relative to a selected graphic-object's original orientation (ignoring any rotation or skewing applied to the object on the Stage), select "Override target rotation and skew properties." Otherwise, Flash applies rotation and skewing changes relative to the object's current orientation on the Stage.

✔ Tip

■ You can also copy motion-tween properties in a form that can be pasted into the Actions panel or an ActionScript file. Flash translates the animation you created using graphics tools and motion tweening into animation created by ActionScript. You'll learn more about the Copy Motion as ActionScript 3.0 command in Chapter 13.

Original symbol   *Modified symbol*

Apply using scale and rotation/skew   *Override scale and rotation/skew*

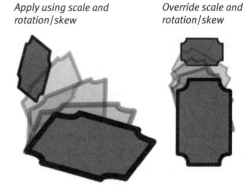

Figure 9.48 When you use the Paste Motion Special command with a graphic-object that has been modified by scaling and/or rotating and skewing, you must choose whether to tween the modified object or the object in its original form. You do that by selecting check boxes in the Paste Motion Special dialog. Here the same tween properties were applied to two instances of the modified symbol. For the symbol on the left, the "Override target scale properties" check box and the "Override target rotation and skew properties" check box were deselected; for the symbol on the right, both override options were selected.

ANIMATION WITH SHAPE TWEENING

Shape tweening in Adobe Flash CS3 Professional works much like motion tweening. You set up a keyframe span (the graphic content of the beginning and ending keyframes must be different in some way), then you set the span's Tween property to Shape. Flash redraws the graphics for each in-between frame, making the incremental changes that transform the first shape into the final one. Shape tweens can animate changes to the same types of properties as motion tweens (size, color, location, and so on), but shape tweens also animate changes to the path that defines the "shape" of your graphic content.

Flash can shape-tween more than one graphic on a layer, but the results can be unpredictable. When you have several shapes on a layer, there is no way to tell Flash which starting shape goes with which ending shape. By limiting yourself to a single shape tween on each layer, you tell Flash exactly what to change.

Because you'll be setting the Tween property throughout this chapter, keep the Properties tab of the Property inspector open. Unless otherwise indicated, you can perform the tasks in this chapter using merge-shapes, drawing-objects, or primitives.

How Do Shape Tweens and Motion Tweens Differ?

An important difference between the two tween types is that motion tweens require graphic content that is inside a container (drawing-objects, primitive-shapes, groups, symbols, and text fields all qualify), while shape tweening requires graphic content that is editable. Merge-shapes and drawing-objects fully qualify; primitives qualify, but the primitive's path can change only in the ways allowed by the primitive's defining parameters (for details about editing primitives, see Chapter 4). Shape-tweened graphics can move in straight lines, but they can't automatically follow a motion path, nor can they automatically rotate a certain number of times.

Creating a Bouncing Ball with Shape Tweening

Although shape tweens can animate changes in many properties of graphics—color, size, location—the distinguishing function of shape tweening is to transform one shape into another. You could use a shape tween to simply replicate the simple bouncing-ball animation you created in Chapters 8 and 9. A better use of shape tweening for a bouncing ball is to flatten the ball as it strikes the ground.

To define shape tweens via the Frame Properties tab of the Property inspector:

1. In a new Flash document, or in a new layer of an existing document, position the playhead in frame 1.

2. In the Tools panel, choose the oval tool. The tool can be in Merge or Object Drawing mode. Do not use the oval-primitive tool.

3. Set the stroke to No Color.

4. Near the top of the Stage, draw a circle. This circle will be the ball.

5. In the Timeline, select frame 5, and choose Insert > Timeline > Keyframe.

   Flash creates a new keyframe that duplicates the preceding keyframe.

6. Select frame 10, and choose Insert > Timeline > Keyframe (**Figure 10.1**).

7. In frame 5, select the ball, and drag it to the bottom of the Stage.

8. Use the drawing tools to reshape the oval in frame 5, flattening the bottom and elongating it a bit sideways (**Figure 10.2**).

Figure 10.1 To begin setting up the bouncing ball as a shape tween, you create keyframes 1, 5, and 10, just as in the previous chapter.

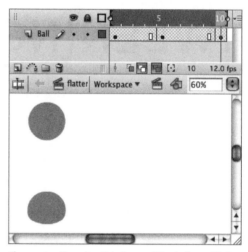

Figure 10.2 Changing the shape of the ball graphic in the keyframe representing the bottom of the bounce makes the movement appear more natural. The ball seems to respond to gravity by flattening on contact with something solid—say, the floor. (Turn on onion skinning to see the beginning and ending keyframes.)

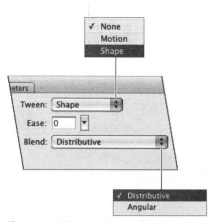

Figure 10.3 When you choose Shape from the Tween pop-up menu, the Frame Properties tab of the Property inspector displays the shape-tween settings.

Tween sequence for downward bounce

Figure 10.4 With onion skinning turned on, you can see the in-between frames Flash creates for the shape tween. This animation looks similar to the bouncing ball created with a motion tween. In this case, the change in the object's shape creates the illusion of impact.

9. To define the shape tween for the first half of the ball's bounce, in the Timeline, select any of the frames in the first keyframe span (1, 2, 3, or 4).

   Note that the ball is selected automatically. When you define a shape tween, the element to be tweened must be selected.

10. In the Frame Properties tab of the Property inspector, from the Tween pop-up menu, choose Shape.

    The settings for the shape tween appear (**Figure 10.3**).

    Flash creates a shape tween in frames 1–4 and color-codes those frames in the Timeline. With Tinted Frames active (choose it from the Frame View pop-up menu at the end of the Edit Bar), Flash applies a light green shade to the frames containing a shape tween. If Tinted Frames is inactive, the frames are white (Mac) or patterned (Windows), but Flash changes the arrow that indicates the presence of a tween from black to green.

11. From the Blend menu, choose either of the following options:

    ▲ To preserve sharp corners and straight lines as one shape transforms into another, choose Angular.

    ▲ To smooth out the in-between shapes, choose Distributive.

12. To define the shape tween for the second half of the ball's bounce, in the Timeline, select any of the frames in the second keyframe span (5, 6, 7, 8, or 9).

13. Repeat steps 10–12.

    Flash creates the second half of the ball's bounce with another shape tween (**Figure 10.4**).

CREATING A BOUNCING BALL WITH SHAPE TWEENING

✔ Tips

- Flash doesn't prevent you from defining shape tweens for frames that contain grouped shapes or symbols, but those tweens won't work. Flash does warn you by placing the broken-tween dotted line in the relevant frames in the Timeline. When you select such frames, a warning button appears in the Frame Properties tab of the Property inspector (**Figure 10.5**). When you see these warnings, go back to the Stage and reevaluate what's there. If the item you want to tween is a group or symbol, you can use motion tweening. Or, to use shape tweening, you can break the group or symbol apart (select the shape or symbol, and then choose Modify > Break Apart). If there's a symbol or group on the same layer as the editable shape you want to tween, move the extra item to its own layer (select it and choose Modify > Timeline > Distribute to Layers).

- Note that custom-easing settings aren't available for shape tweens; they're strictly for motion tweens.

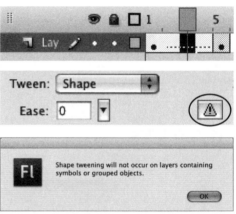

Figure 10.5 When there are groups or symbols in frames you're defining as shape tweens, Flash puts a dotted line through the frame span to indicate a broken tween (top), and a warning button appears in the Frame Properties tab of the Property inspector (middle). Click the exclamation-sign button to see the warning dialog (bottom).

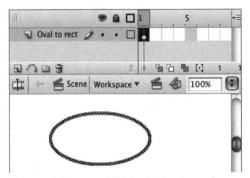

Figure 10.6 Draw an oval in the first keyframe of your shape tween.

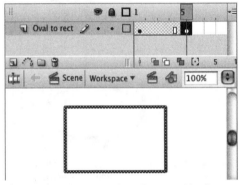

Figure 10.7 Draw a rectangle in the second keyframe of your shape tween.

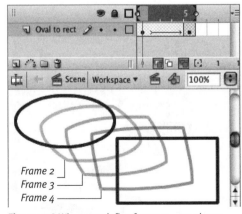

Figure 10.8 When you define frames 1–4 as shape tweens, Flash creates the three intermediate shapes that transform the oval into a rectangle. Turn on onion skinning to see the shapes for the in-between frames.

Morphing Simple Lines and Fills

Flash can transform both fill shapes and lines (strokes). In this section, you try some shape-changing tasks with both types of shapes.

To transform an oval into a rectangle:

1. In a new Flash document, or in a new layer, in frame 1, draw an outline oval on the Stage (**Figure 10.6**).

2. In the Timeline, select frame 5, and choose Insert > Timeline > Blank Keyframe.

   Flash creates a keyframe but removes all content from the Stage.

3. On the Stage, in frame 5, draw an outline rectangle (**Figure 10.7**).

   Don't worry about placing the rectangle in exactly the same location on the Stage as the oval; you'll adjust the position later.

4. In the Timeline, select any of the frames in the keyframe span (1, 2, 3, or 4).

5. In the Frame Properties tab of the Property inspector, from the Tween pop-up menu, choose Shape.

   Flash transforms the oval into the rectangle in three equal steps—one for each in-between frame (**Figure 10.8**).

   continues on next page

MORPHING SIMPLE LINES AND FILLS

6. To align the oval and rectangle, in the Timeline's Status bar, click the Onion Skin button or the Onion Skin Outlines button. Flash displays all the in-between frames.

7. In the Timeline, position the playhead in frame 1.

8. On the Stage, reposition the oval so that it aligns with the rectangle (**Figure 10.9**).

   The oval transforms into a rectangle, remaining in one spot on the Stage.

To transform a rectangle into a free-form shape:

1. In a new Flash document, or on a new layer, in frame 1, draw a rectangular fill on the Stage.

2. In the Timeline, select frame 5, and choose Insert > Timeline > Blank Keyframe.

3. On the Stage, in frame 5, use the brush tool to paint a free-form fill.

   Don't make the fill too complex—just a blob or brushstroke with gentle curves.

4. In the Timeline, select any of the frames in the keyframe span (1, 2, 3, or 4).

5. Set the Tween property to Shape (see step 5 of the preceding task).

   Flash transforms the rectangle into the free-form fill in three equal steps—one for each in-between frame (**Figure 10.10**).

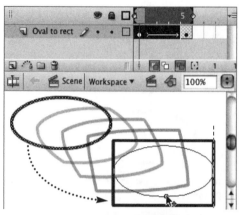

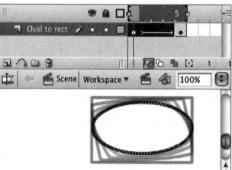

Figure 10.9 Use onion skinning to help position your keyframe shapes. Here, with frame 1 selected, you can drag the oval to center it within the rectangle (top). That makes the oval grow into a rectangle without moving anywhere else on the Stage (bottom).

Figure 10.10 Flash transforms a rectangle into a free-form brushstroke with shape tweening.

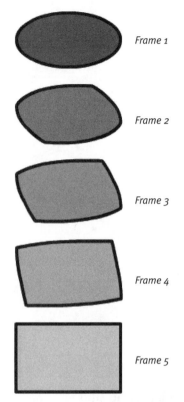

Frame 1

Frame 2

Frame 3

Frame 4

Frame 5

Figure 10.11 Here, Flash transforms a shape with a stroke in five frames. The shape tween changes not only the graphic's shape, but also its color (from dark to light).

Shape-Tweening Multiple Shapes

In motion tweening, Flash limits you to one item per tween, meaning just one item per layer. In shape tweening, however, Flash can handle more than one shape on a layer. The drawback is that you may get some strange results. The simpler and fewer the shapes you use, the more reliable your multiple-shape tweens will be. For the most predictable results, limit yourself to one shape per layer.

You may want to keep both shapes on the same layer for a fill with an outline (stroke), however. As long as the transformation isn't too complicated, Flash can handle the two together.

To shape-tween fills with strokes (outlines):

1. Follow the steps in the preceding tasks to create a shape tween of an outline oval transforming into a rectangle.

2. Fill each shape with a different color. Flash tweens the fill and the stroke together and tweens the change in color (**Figure 10.11**).

✔ Tips

■ You can tween a disappearing act: Make the stroke around a shape (or the shape, or both) get gradually lighter and lighter, until it finally disappears. Make the color of the final stroke (and/or shape) in the tween match the color of the background, or give it a fully transparent color (one with an alpha setting of 0 percent).

■ To ensure that the item in the preceding tip does fully disappear (some low-color monitors may not display tint and alpha changes accurately), select the frame following the last keyframe of the tween sequence. Choose Insert > Timeline > Keyframe to duplicate the previous keyframe; then delete your disappearing stroke (or shape). If you want both the shape and its stroke to disappear together, choose Insert > Timeline > Blank Keyframe.

When Multiple-Shape Tweens on a Single Layer Go Bad

If you're shape-tweening stationary elements, you probably can get away with having several on the same layer. But if the elements move around much, Flash can get confused about which shape goes where. Although you may intend the paths of two shapes to cross, Flash creates the most direct route between the starting shape and the ending one. **Figure 10.12** illustrates the problem.

All objects on one layer

All objects on one layer

Light circle and arrow on one layer

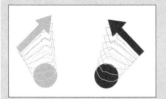

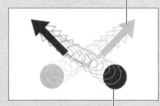

Dark circle and arrow on another layer

Figure 10.12 Tweening multiple shapes whose paths don't cross in a single layer works fine. In the left-hand image, both objects are on the same layer, and the light circle transforms into the light arrow without a hitch. In the middle image, both objects are on the same layer, but Flash transforms the light circle into the dark arrow and the dark circle into the light arrow because that's the most direct path. If you want to create diagonal paths that cross, you must put each object on its own layer, as in the right-hand image.

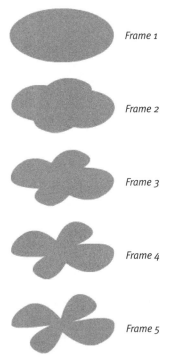

Frame 1

Frame 2

Frame 3

Frame 4

Frame 5

Figure 10.13 Flash handles the tween from an oval to a simple flower shape without requiring shape hints.

Transforming a Simple Shape into a Complex Shape

The more complex the shape you tween, the more difficult it is for Flash to create the expected result. You can help Flash tween better by using *shape hints*—markers that let you identify points on the path of the original shape that correspond to points on the path of the final shape.

To shape-tween a more complex shape:

1. In a new Flash document, or on a new layer, in frame 1, draw an oval with no stroke on the Stage.

2. In the Timeline, select frame 5, and choose Insert > Timeline > Keyframe.
   Flash duplicates the contents of keyframe 1 in keyframe 5.

3. In the Timeline, select any of the frames in the keyframe span (1, 2, 3, or 4).

4. In the Frame Properties tab of the Property inspector, from the Tween pop-up menu, choose Shape.

5. In the Timeline, position the playhead in frame 5.

6. Using the selection tool or the pen and subselection tools, drag four corner points in toward the center of the oval to create a flower shape.
   (For more detailed instructions on editing shapes, see Chapter 4.)

7. Play the movie to see the shape tween.
   Flash handles the tweening for this change well (**Figure 10.13**). It's fairly obvious which points of the oval should move in to create the petal shapes. If you modify the shape further, however, it becomes more difficult for Flash to know how to create the new shape. That's when you need to use shape hints.

To use shape hints:

1. Using the animation you created in the preceding task, in the Timeline, select frame 10, and choose Insert > Timeline > Keyframe.

   Flash duplicates the flower shape in a new keyframe.

2. In keyframe 10, edit the flower to add a stem.

   Reshape the flower's path with the selection tool or the pen and subselection tools, or add a stem with a brushstroke in the same color as the flower.

3. Define a shape tween for frames 5–9.

4. Play the movie.

   The addition of the stem to the flower makes it difficult for Flash to create a smooth tween that looks right (**Figure 10.14**).

5. To begin adding shape hints, position the playhead in keyframe 5 (the initial keyframe of this tweening sequence).

6. Choose Modify > Shape > Add Shape Hint, or press Shift-⌘-H (Mac) or Ctrl-Shift-H (Windows) (**Figure 10.15**).

   Flash places a shape hint—a small red circle labeled with a letter, starting with *a*—in the center of the object in the current frame. You need to reposition the shape hint to place it on a problem point on the shape's path.

7. With the selection tool, drag the shape hint to a problem point on the edge of the shape.

   As you drag, Flash previews the hint's position with a circle icon; the circle gets darker and thicker when it connects with the path. Don't worry about getting the shape hint in exactly the right spot; just make sure it is on the path. You can fine-tune its position later.

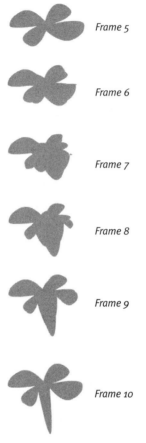

Frame 5

Frame 6

Frame 7

Frame 8

Frame 9

Frame 10

Figure 10.14 The addition of a stem to the flower overloads Flash's capability to create a smooth shape tween. Frames 7 and 8 are particularly bad.

Figure 10.15 Choose Modify > Shape > Add Shape Hint to activate markers that help Flash make connections between the original shape and the final shape of the tween.

SIMPLE SHAPE INTO A COMPLEX SHAPE

Areas of change

Figure 10.16 Start adding shape hints in the first keyframe of a tween sequence. Flash places the hints in the center of the tweened object (top). You must drag the hints into position (middle). Distribute the hints in alphabetical order along the object's path, placing them on crucial points of change (bottom). Here, the three points with hints a, b, and c define the points from which the stem of the flower will grow.

Figure 10.17 To complete the placement of shape hints, select the second keyframe of your tween sequence. Flash stacks up hints corresponding to the ones you placed in the preceding keyframe (top). You must drag them into the correct final position (bottom).

8. Repeat steps 6 and 7 until you have placed shape hints on all the problem points of your shape in keyframe 5 (**Figure 10.16**).

Each time you add a shape hint, you get another small red circle labeled with a letter. You can't place the hints at random; you must place them so they go in alphabetical order around the edge of the shape. (Flash does the best job when you place shape hints in counterclockwise order, starting in the upper-left corner of the shape, but you can also place them in clockwise order.)

9. In the Timeline, position the playhead in keyframe 10.

Flash has already added shape hints to this frame; they all stack up in the center of the shape.

10. With the selection tool, drag each shape hint to its position on the path of the new shape.

Keep them in the same order (counter-clockwise or clockwise) you chose in step 8 (**Figure 10.17**). When the end-of-tween shape hint is sitting on a path, the hint changes from red to green; if you select the initial keyframe of the span, you can see that the associated beginning-of-tween hint has turned yellow.

11. To evaluate the improvement in tweening, play the movie.

continues on next page

12. To fine-tune the shape hints' positions, select one of the tween's keyframes, and turn on Onion Skin mode.

Set the onion markers to include all the frames of the tween. Where the onion skins reveal rough spots in the tween, you may need to match the hint position better from the first keyframe to the last one (**Figure 10.18**). Repositioning the shape hints changes the in-between frames. You may need to adjust the shape hints in both keyframes. If you still can't get a smooth tween, try adding more shape hints.

✔ Tips

■ To remove a single shape hint, make the initial keyframe the current frame. Select the shape hint you want to remove, and drag it out of the document window. Or, Control-click (Mac) or right-click (Windows) the shape hint, and choose Remove Hint.

■ To remove all the hints at the same time, with the initial keyframe current, choose Modify > Shape > Remove All Hints. Or ⌘-click (Mac) or Ctrl-click (Windows) any shape hint, and choose Remove All Hints.

■ Onion skins don't always update correctly when you reposition shape hints. Clicking a blank area of the Stage forces Flash to redraw the onion skins.

■ If you can't create a smooth tween using shape hints alone, break the tween into smaller pieces by adding keyframes where the morphing gets off track. Then redraw the shapes for those frames yourself.

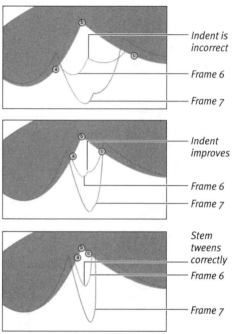

Figure 10.18 It can be difficult to match up points in the two keyframes exactly when you first place the shape hints. When you've positioned the hints in the beginning and ending keyframes of a sequence, turn on onion skinning to see where you need to adjust the placement of your hints. With the initial placement, Flash starts the stem growing with an indent at the bottom (top). Moving the points closer together improves the tween (middle). When the onion skins reveal a smooth tween, you're done (bottom).

SIMPLE SHAPE INTO A COMPLEX SHAPE

The Pitfalls of Primitive Tweens

Although you can create shape tweens using oval- or rectangle-primitives, you're likely to find the animation Flash creates with them to be a bit disappointing. When you use a primitive's control points to change the primitive's path on the Stage, there is a sense of motion as the shape redraws itself. Drag the control point for the start or end angle of an oval-primitive, and the preview radius line rotates like the minute hand of a clock. As Flash redraws the shape, there is feeling of rotation, as if you're opening and closing a folding paper fan. You might think that shape-tweening the primitive-oval would recreate that motion. But Flash doesn't animate the manipulation of control points when it tweens the shape; instead, Flash animates changes to the paths of the merge-shapes that lie at the foundation of the primitives (**Figure 10.19**). You may be able to add shape hints to achieve the look you want, or at least improve the transition. But more likely, you will need to break the primitive apart and add keyframes—or use a combination of frame-by-frame animation, motion tweens, and shape tweens—to create the feel you're going for.

Shape tween, no shape hints

Shape tween, shape hints added

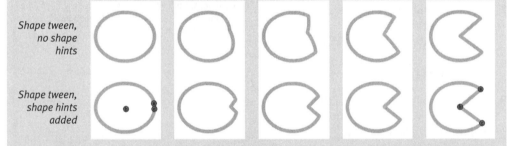

Figure 10.19 When you reposition control points to change the start and end angles of an oval-primitive, you drag the control points in an arc clockwise or counterclockwise. Flash can't animate that rotating motion in a single shape-tween; Flash can only animate the change in the path—in this case, from a full oval to an oval with a wedge removed (top). Shape hints can help Flash create a cleaner transition from the first shape to the second (bottom), but shape hints aren't enough to make Flash create the feeling of rotating and opening.

Creating Shapes That Move As They Change

You can't create shape tweens that follow a path, but you can move shapes around the Stage in straight lines. To do so, reposition the elements on the Stage from one keyframe to the next.

To shape-tween a moving graphic:

1. In a new Flash document, or on a new layer, select frame 20, and choose Insert > Timeline > Frame.

   Flash adds blank in-between frames 2 through 20.

2. In the Timeline, select any frame in the span (frames 1–20).

   Note that you must click the frame to select it; you can't just position the play-head in the frame.

3. In the Frame Properties tab of the Property inspector, from the Tween pop-up menu, choose Shape.

   Even though you have no shapes on the Stage to tween yet, Flash gives the frames the shape-tween property. In the Timeline, the frames contain a dotted line, indicating that the tween is incomplete (**Figure 10.20**). Now you can add keyframes and shapes.

4. In the Timeline, insert a blank keyframe at frames 5, 10, 15, and 20.

   Flash creates four shape-tween sequences (**Figure 10.21**). For the moment, they're broken tweens because the keyframes are empty.

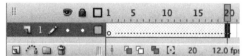

Figure 10.20 To save yourself numerous trips to the Tween pop-up menu in the Frame Properties tab of the Property inspector, you can assign the shape-tween property to a range of frames and add keyframes and shapes later. Flash defines a shape tween even though there's no content to tween yet.

Figure 10.21 When you insert keyframes into a long tween sequence, Flash breaks it into smaller tween sequences. Until you place content in the keyframes, the Timeline displays the dotted line in each span to indicate a broken tween.

Onion skinning on — ⌐ Edit Multiple
First half of the full — Frames
tween sequence

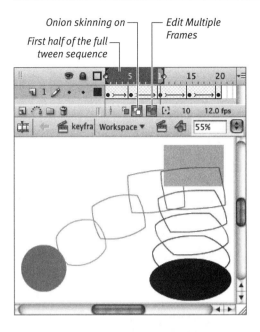

Second half of the full tween sequence —

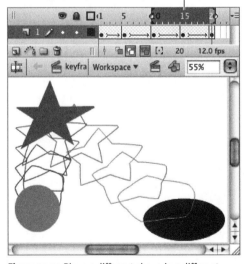

Figure 10.22 Place a different shape in a different location in each keyframe. Flash creates the intermediate steps necessary to transform the shapes and move them across the Stage. Play the movie or turn on onion skinning to examine the motion and shape changes on the in-between frames. (Here, Edit Multiple Frames is also on, making it easy to see the keyframe shapes.)

5. To complete the tween sequences, in each keyframe, draw a different shape; place each one in a different corner of the Stage.

In frame 1, for example, draw a circular fill in the bottom-left corner of the Stage. In keyframe 5, draw a rectangular fill in the top-right corner of the Stage. In keyframe 10, draw an oval in the bottom-right corner of the Stage. In keyframe 15, draw a star in the top-left corner of the Stage. And in keyframe 20, duplicate keyframe 1's circle in the bottom-left corner of the Stage. For extra variety, give each object a different color. As you add content to keyframes, Flash fills in the spans in the Timeline with tween arrows.

6. Play the movie.

You see a graphic that bounces around the Stage, morphing from one shape to the next (**Figure 10.22**).

✔ Tips

■ Although shape-tweened objects can't follow a path the way motion-tweened objects can, you can make Flash do the work of creating the separate keyframes you need to animate shape tweens that move on curved paths. First, create your shape tween. In the Timeline, select the full range of frames in the tween sequence. Choose Modify > Timeline > Convert to Keyframes. Flash converts each in-between frame (with its transitional content) into a keyframe. Now you can position each keyframe object anywhere you like. To simulate a motion guide, create a regular guide layer (see Chapter 6), and draw the path you want your morphing shape to follow. Choose View > Snapping > Snap to Objects. Reposition the shape in each keyframe. When you drag a shape close to the line on the guide layer, Flash snaps the shape to the line.

■ Alternatively, to animate a changing shape that follows a path, you can create a shape tween, save that animation as a movie-clip symbol, then create a new motion tween using that symbol and a motion guide. You'll learn about saving animation as movie-clip Symbols in Chapter 11.

MORE-COMPLEX ANIMATION TASKS

You've learned to manipulate shapes and animate them one at a time, in a single layer, but Adobe Flash CS3 Professional is capable of handling much more complicated animation tasks. To create complex animated movies, you'll need to work with multiple shapes and multiple layers. You may even want to use multiple scenes to organize long animations. In this chapter, you learn to work with multiple layers in the Timeline, stack animations on the various layers to create more-complex movement, and save animations as reusable elements for easy manipulation—either as animated graphic symbols or as movie-clip symbols. With these techniques, you can really start to bring your animations to life.

Understanding Scenes

If the Timeline is the table of contents for the "book" of your movie, scenes are the chapters. A Flash project requiring lots of animation may include hundreds of frames. You can break the animation into smaller chunks by creating scenes. When you publish a movie from a regular Flash document, the scenes play back in order unless you use the interactivity features to provide instructions for playing the scenes in a different order. (To learn more about interactivity in Flash movies, see Chapters 12 and 13.) Flash's Scene panel makes it easy to see what scenes exist in your movie, create new scenes, delete scenes, and reorganize them.

To access the Scene panel:

◆ If the Scene panel isn't open, choose Window > Other Panels > Scene.

The Scene panel appears. In a new Flash document, the Scene panel lists only the default Scene 1. When you add scenes to a movie, the Scene panel lists all the movie's scenes in order (**Figure 11.1**).

To add a scene:

Do either of the following:

◆ Choose Insert > Scene (**Figure 11.2**).

◆ In the Scene panel, click the Add Scene button.

Flash adds another scene, giving it the default name Scene 2.

Duplicate scene button —
Add scene button —
Delete scene button —

Figure 11.1 The Scene panel lists all the scenes in a movie. It also provides buttons for adding, duplicating, and deleting scenes.

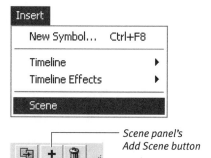

Scene panel's
Add Scene button

Figure 11.2 To add a new scene to your Flash document, choose Insert > Scene (top) or, in the Scene panel, click the Add Scene button (bottom).

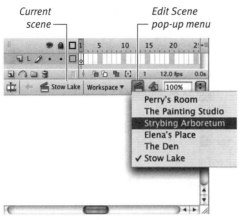

Figure 11.3 The Edit bar displays the name of the current scene. Choose a scene from the Edit Scene pop-up menu to switch scenes quickly.

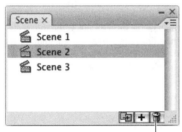

Click to delete selected scene —⌐

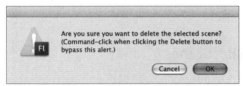

Figure 11.4 When you delete a selected scene (top), Flash asks you to confirm the deletion (bottom).

To select a scene to edit:

Do either of the following:

◆ Click the Edit Scene button in the Edit bar.

A pop-up menu of scenes appears; select a scene from the list.

◆ From the scrolling list in the Scene panel, select a scene.

Flash displays the selected scene on the Stage, puts the scene name in the current-scene box in the Edit bar, and places a check next to that scene's name in the Edit Scene pop-up menu (**Figure 11.3**).

To delete a selected scene:

1. In the Scene panel, click the Delete Scene button.

A dialog appears, asking you to confirm that you want to delete the selected scene (**Figure 11.4**).

2. Click OK.

Flash deletes the scene, removing it from the Edit Scene pop-up menu in the Edit bar as well as from the scrolling list in the Scene panel.

✔ Tip

■ If you don't want to see the warning dialog when you delete a scene, ⌘-click (Mac) or Ctrl-click (Windows) the Delete Scene button in the Scene panel.

UNDERSTANDING SCENES

To change the scene order:

◆ In the Scene panel, drag a selected scene name up or down in the list.

Flash moves the clapper icon and scene name. In Windows, a highlighted line previews the new location for the scene; on the Mac, the highlight line underscores the name of the scene that will *follow* the scene you're repositioning (**Figure 11.5**).

To rename a scene:

1. In the Scene panel, double-click the name of the scene that you want to rename.

   The Name field activates for entering text.

2. Type the new name in the Name field.

3. Press Enter.

   or

   Click outside the text-entry field.

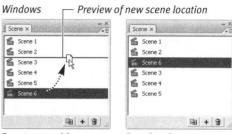

Windows — *Preview of new scene location*

Drag to reposition scene   *Reordered scenes*

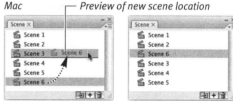

Mac — *Preview of new scene location*

Drag to reposition scene   *Reordered scenes*

Figure 11.5 Dragging a scene name in the Scene panel changes the order of scenes. In Windows, a horizontal bar previews the new location for the scene; on the Mac, the bar underlines the scene that will follow the scene you're dragging. When the scene is in the correct location, release the mouse button.

The Pitfalls of Using Scenes

Scenes in Flash are tools for organizing content during authoring; they don't exist at runtime. When you create a Flash document, each scene is like a self-contained movie, but when you publish the file, Flash links the scenes into one continuous set of frames. (Imagine a document with two scenes: Scene 1 has frames numbered 1–10, and scene two has frames numbered 1–10. The published file winds up with frames numbered 1–20.)

The fact that each scene is, in a sense, a new beginning can make it difficult to keep the continuity of actions between scenes. For movies with interactivity that requires variables, scenes may be inappropriate. In such cases, you may need to stick to a single long movie or use separate movies or separate movie clips within one movie to organize your animation.

The fact that scenes don't exist in the published movie presents other problems. For example, you must be careful to avoid using identical frame labels in multiple scenes. Otherwise, interactivities that rely on those frame labels to locate and display the appropriate frame will not work.

Click first corner

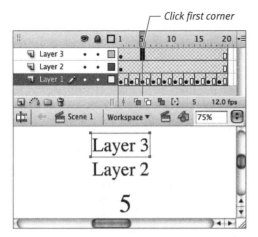

Drag to opposite corner

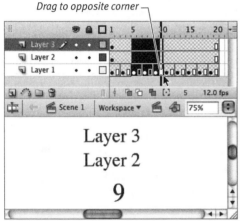

Figure 11.6 In frame-based selection mode, click and drag across frames and layers (top) to select frames in those layers (bottom).

Manipulating Frames in Multiple Layers

As your animation gets more complex, you'll need to add layers to your document. You can perform editing operations on selected frames and layers, for example, by copying, cutting, and pasting frames across multiple layers. You can also insert frames, keyframes, and blank keyframes into selected frame spans and layers.

To select and copy frames in several layers:

1. Create a Flash document that contains three layers, each with 20 frames.

   Place content in the layers to help you see what's going on as you work with the various frames and layers. Use the text tool, for example, to place the frame number in every other frame of layer 1 and to place a text block with the name of the layer in layers 2 and 3.

2. In the Timeline in layer 3, to make frame selections, do either of the following:

   ▲ In frame-based selection mode, click and drag as though you were drawing a selection rectangle from frame 5 through frame 10 in all three layers.

   ▲ In span-based selection mode, ⌘-click (Mac) or Ctrl-click (Windows), and drag to select a range of frames.

   Flash highlights the selected frames (**Figure 11.6**).

3. Choose Edit > Timeline > Copy Frames.

   Flash copies the frames and layer information to the Clipboard.

✔ Tip

■ To select a block of frames that spans several layers without dragging, in frame-based selection mode, click a frame at one of the four corners of the block. Then Shift-click the frame at the opposite corner. Flash selects all the frames in the rectangle that you've defined (**Figure 11.7**). In span-based selection style, ⌘-click (Mac) or Ctrl-click (Windows) one corner, and then Shift-⌘-click (Mac) or Ctrl-Shift-click (Windows) the opposite corner to make your selection.

To replace the content of frames with a multiple-layer selection:

1. Continuing with the document you created in the preceding task, select frames 15–20 on all three layers.

2. Choose Edit > Timeline > Paste Frames. Flash pastes the copied frames 5–10 into frames 15–20 in each of the three layers. The numbers on the Stage in layer 1 now start over with 5 at frame 15, 7 at frame 17, and 9 at frame 19.

To paste a multiple-layer selection into blank frames:

1. Continuing with the document you created in the preceding task, select frame 21 on all three layers.

2. Choose Edit > Timeline > Paste Frames. Flash pastes the copied frames 5–10 into protoframes 21–26 in each of the three layers (**Figure 11.8**). Layer 1 now displays the number 5 at frame 21, 7 at frame 23, and 9 at frame 25.

With one corner selected ⎯

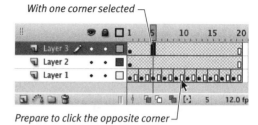

Prepare to click the opposite corner ⎤

⎡ After Shift-clicking

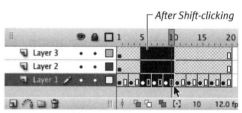

Figure 11.7 To select a block of frames without dragging, in frame-based selection mode, click one corner of the block; then Shift-click the opposite corner to define the block. In span-based selection mode, ⌘-click (Mac) or Ctrl-click (Windows) the first corner, and then Shift-⌘-click (Mac) or Ctrl-Shift-click (Windows) the opposite corner of your selection block.

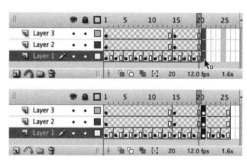

Figure 11.8 Pasting a multiple-layer, multiple-frame selection at the end of a set of defined frames (top) extends the Timeline to accommodate the new frames and layers (bottom).

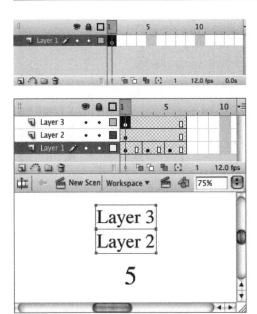

Figure 11.9 When you paste a multiple-layer, multiple-frame selection into the first frame of a new scene (top), Flash creates new layers and frames to hold the contents of the Clipboard (bottom).

To paste a multiple-layer selection into a new scene:

1. Continuing with the document you created in the preceding task, insert a new scene, following the instructions in the first section of this chapter.

   By default, the new scene has one layer and one keyframe.

2. Select keyframe 1.

3. Choose Edit > Timeline > Paste Frames.

   Flash pastes the copied selection from the first scene (frames 5–10 on layers 1–3) into the new scene. Flash adds layers 2 and 3 and creates frames 1–6 in each layer (**Figure 11.9**). Layer 1 now displays the number 5 at frame 1, 7 at frame 3, and 9 at frame 5.

MANIPULATING FRAMES IN MULTIPLE LAYERS

Animating Multiple Motion Tweens

As you learned in Chapter 9, Flash can motion-tween only one item per layer. You can tween multiple items simultaneously; you just have to put each one on a separate layer. You can use Onion Skin and Edit Multiple Frame modes to make sure all the elements line up in the right place at the right time. To get a feel for tweening multiple items, try combining three simple motion tweens to create a game of Ping-Pong. One layer contains the ball; the other layers each contain a paddle.

To set up the three graphics in separate layers:

1. Open a new Flash document, and add two new layers.

2. Rename the layers.

   Name the top layer *Ball,* the next layer *1st Paddle,* and the bottom layer *2nd Paddle.* Naming the layers helps you keep track of the elements and their locations.

3. Create the graphics as symbols (see Chapter 7).

   On the Stage, in the Ball layer, use the oval tool to create a ball; in the layer named 1st Paddle, use the rectangle tool to create a paddle; and then copy the paddle and paste the copy into the layer named 2nd Paddle. Give each shape a different color. Your file should look something like **Figure 11.10**.

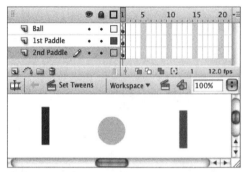

Figure 11.10 To have several graphics motion-tween simultaneously, you must place each one on a separate layer. Here, each item is on a separate layer. The descriptive layer names help you keep track of what goes where.

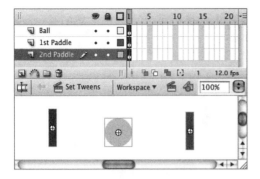

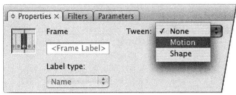

Figure 11.11 With frames selected on multiple layers (top), choosing Motion as the Tween property in the Frame Properties tab of the Property inspector (bottom) sets up motion tweens on all the layers.

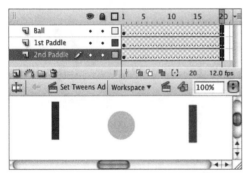

Figure 11.12 The frames on all three layers have a Tween property of Motion, but the tweens are broken, as indicated by the dotted lines. You must add keyframes and content.

To set up the tween in all layers with one command:

1. Using the document you created in the preceding task, in the Timeline, select keyframe 1 in all three layers.

2. In the Frame Properties tab of the Property inspector, from the Tween pop-up menu, choose Motion.

   Flash gives all the frames the motion-tween property (**Figure 11.11**).

3. In the Timeline, select frame 20 in all three layers.

4. Choose Insert > Timeline > Frame.

   Flash extends the motion tween through frame 20 on all three layers. A dotted line across the frames indicates an incomplete motion tween (**Figure 11.12**). Reposition the symbols and create keyframes to complete the tweens.

✔ Tip

■ Currently, all layers in this Flash document have a Tween property of Motion. If you add more frames later, they will also be set to Motion. To completely end the tweening sequences, remember to set the Tween property of the last keyframe in each layer to None.

ANIMATING MULTIPLE MOTION TWEENS

To adjust the positions of the tweened items:

1. Using the document you created in the preceding task, in the Timeline, position the playhead in frame 5.

2. On the Stage, drag the ball to the approximate location where it should connect with one of the paddles for the first hit.

   Flash makes Ball the active layer and creates a keyframe (in frame 5) for the ball in its new location (**Figure 11.13**). Flash completes the motion tween between keyframe 1 and keyframe 5 of the Ball layer and leaves the broken-tween line in all the other frames.

3. On the Stage, reposition the first paddle graphic so that the paddle connects with the ball for the first hit.

   Flash makes 1st Paddle the active layer and creates a keyframe (in frame 5) for the paddle in its new location (**Figure 11.14**).

4. In the Timeline, position the playhead in frame 10.

5. On the Stage, drag the ball to the approximate location where you want it to connect with a paddle for the second hit.

   Flash makes Ball the active layer and creates a keyframe (in frame 10) for the ball in its new location. Flash completes the motion tween between keyframe 5 and keyframe 10 of the Ball layer.

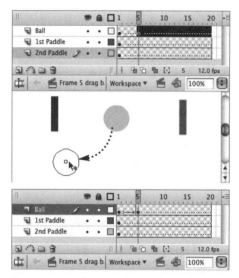

Figure 11.13 Moving a graphic in a frame that's defined as part of a motion tween causes Flash to make the layer containing the graphic the active layer (top). Flash creates a keyframe in that layer for the graphic's new position, thus completing one tween sequence (bottom).

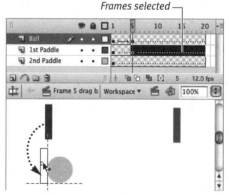

Figure 11.14 As you reposition the paddle (top), Flash appears to be selecting the wrong set of frames; but when you release the mouse button, Flash correctly tweens frames 1–4 (bottom).

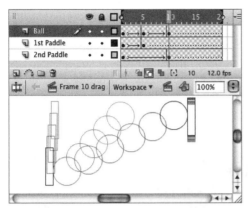

Figure 11.15 Moving an element in another frame creates another tween. Here, the paddle on the right side appears to move more slowly than the paddle on the left side, because Flash is creating a ten-frame tween for the right paddle, whereas the left paddle tweens in five frames. (Here onion skinning is turned on to make the tweened shapes visible.)

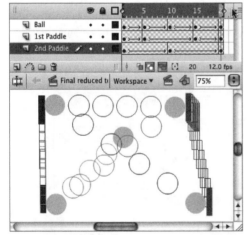

Figure 11.16 You can easily fine-tune the location of objects by selecting Onion Skin Outlines and Edit Multiple Frames. Here, the paddle on the right doesn't move in a straight line. If you want it to do so, reposition the paddle graphics in the first and final frames so that one lies directly above the other; then reposition the ball so that it comes into contact with both paddles.

6. On the Stage, reposition the second paddle so that it connects with the ball for the second hit.

   Flash makes 2nd Paddle the active layer and creates a keyframe (in frame 10) for the paddle in its new location (**Figure 11.15**).

7. Repeat steps 1–6, creating keyframes 15 and 20, to make the ball connect with each paddle one more time.

8. Play the movie to see the animation in action.

9. Select Onion Skin Outlines and Edit Multiple Frames, and then reposition objects as necessary to fine-tune the motion (**Figure 11.16**).

   Although Edit Multiple Frames doesn't show onion skins for keyframes, it does show them for tween graphics.

✔ Tips

- After you define a set of frames as tweens, any slight change you make to an object causes Flash to create a new keyframe. Even clicking and holding more than a second or two causes Flash to insert a keyframe. So that you don't change objects' positions or create new keyframes accidentally, lock or hide the layers that you're not working on.

- To position items on the Stage with greater precision than dragging allows, select an item and use the Properties tab of the Property inspector or the Info panel to set the item's x and y coordinates.

continues on next page

ANIMATING MULTIPLE MOTION TWEENS

- If you like to use Snap Align, Flash's default setting, to help you position items, you'll notice that sometimes in the preceding task, the snapping guides don't appear as you drag graphic elements in in-between frames whose Tween property is set to Motion. These guides work best when all objects involved are in keyframes. If the guides aren't appearing for you, drag items to approximate locations initially. Once Flash has created the new keyframes, you can drag your elements, and the guidelines will appear.

Tweening Text

You can use the multiple–motion tween idea to animate individual characters within a piece of text. After you create the text that you want to animate, select it and choose Modify > Break Apart. That command places each character in its own text field. Next, with each character of the text selected, choose Modify > Timeline > Distribute to Layers. Each character winds up on its own layer. Now use any of the animating techniques you learned in Chapters 8 and 9, or in earlier tasks in this chapter, to animate the individual text characters (**Figure 11.17**).

To transform the shapes of the letters, you need to use shape tweening. That means converting the letters from editable text elements to editable graphics. Select one or more text fields containing individual letters, and choose Modify > Break Apart. The letterforms look the same, but now they're raw shapes that you can modify with the drawing tools and use in shape tweens. Shape-tweening letters can get pretty complex. Remember to use shape hints (see Chapter 10) to help Flash make the transition between shapes correctly.

Broken-apart text; one character per text field

Text distributed to layers

Each letter is a separate motion tween

Figure 11.17 Using Flash's Modify > Break Apart command in conjunction with the Modify > Timeline > Distribute to Layers command, you can set up tweens quickly to animate individual text characters. Each letter in this animated text is a motion tween.

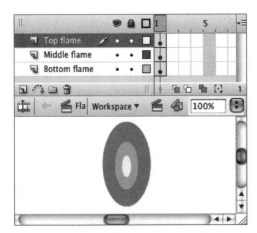

Figure 11.18 Create each part of a multiple-element shape tween on a separate layer. Name the layers to help you track what goes where.

Animating Shape Tweens in Multiple-Shape Graphics

An important thing to remember about complex shape tweens is that Flash deals most reliably with a single shape tween on a layer. In the following tasks, you create a multipart, multilayer graphic and shape-tween the whole package simultaneously.

To create shape tweens on separate layers:

1. Open a Flash document, and add two new layers.

2. Rename the layers *Top Flame, Middle Flame,* and *Bottom Flame*.

   Naming the layers helps you keep track of the objects and their locations.

3. Create the shapes.

   On the Stage, use the oval tool to create three concentric oval shapes without strokes. In the Bottom Flame layer, create a large oval; in the Middle Flame layer, create a medium oval (center it over the first oval); in the Top Flame layer, create a small oval (center it over the medium oval). Give each oval a different color. Your file should look something like **Figure 11.18**.

4. Select frame 5 in all three layers.

5. Choose Insert > Timeline > Keyframe.

   Flash creates a keyframe with the same content as keyframe 1 for each layer.

6. In the Timeline, select any of the frames in the keyframe 1 span (1, 2, 3, or 4) in all three layers.

   continues on next page

When Should One Element Span Several Layers?

Often, an element that you think of as a single entity consists of several shapes in Flash. A candle flame is a good example. To simulate the flickering of a lighted candle, you might create a flame with three shades of orange and then animate changes in the flame shape and colors.

It's natural to keep drawing each piece of the flame in one layer, especially if you're creating merge-shapes and want to see the interaction of the shapes immediately. Unfortunately, Flash has trouble tweening multiple shapes (both merge-shapes and drawing-objects) on a single layer. You're better off creating a rough version of each piece in a separate layer and then fine-tuning that version. Or, create your shapes in one layer, but then select them and choose Insert > Timeline > Distribute to Layers to place them on separate layers. That way, Flash has to tween only one shape per layer, and the result will be cleaner.

7. In the Frame Properties tab of the Property inspector, from the Tween menu, choose Shape.

Flash gives the shape-tween property to frames 1–4 on all three layers (**Figure 11.19**). To create flickering flames, you need to reshape the ovals in keyframe 5.

8. In the Timeline, position the playhead in keyframe 5.

9. On the Stage, edit the ovals to create flame shapes.

10. Play the movie to see the animation in action.

Flash handles the shape-tweening of each layer separately. For comparison, try creating the oval and flame shapes on a single layer and then shape-tweening them (**Figure 11.20**).

11. Select Onion Skin Outlines and Edit Multiple Frames; then reposition the flame objects as necessary to fine-tune the motion.

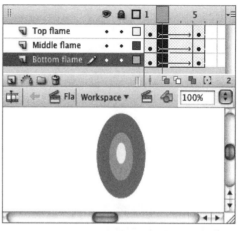

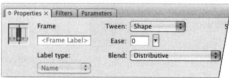

Figure 11.19 When you select multiple frames, you can set the tweening property for those frames simultaneously by choosing a property from the Tween pop-up menu in the Properties tab of the Property inspector.

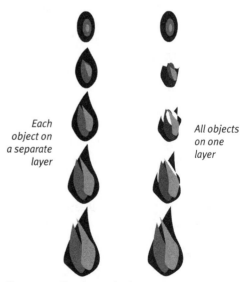

Each object on a separate layer

All objects on one layer

Figure 11.20 No matter whether you use merge-shapes or drawing objects, if you put the three flames on separate layers (left), Flash does a reasonable job of tweening even when you don't add shape hints. With all three flame shapes on a single layer (right), Flash has difficulty creating the tweens.

SHAPE TWEENING MULTIPLE-SHAPE GRAPHICS

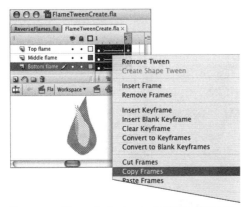

Figure 11.21 The contextual menu for frames lets you copy all selected frames with a single command.

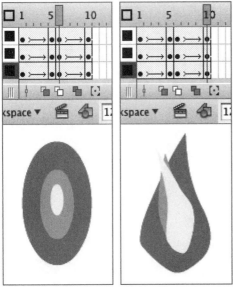

Figure 11.22 After you paste the copied selection, the second tween sequence starts with the oval flame (left) and ends with the tall, flickering flame (right).

Reversing Frames

Sometimes, you can save effort by creating just half the animation that you need and letting Flash do the rest of the work. Think of the candle flame that grows and shrinks. The shrinking phase is the reverse of the growing phase. You can make a copy of the growing-flame animation and then have Flash reverse the order of the frames.

To reverse the order of frames:

1. Open the document you created in the preceding section.

   This movie spans five frames on three layers. The first keyframe shows the flame as three concentric oval shapes; the final keyframe shows the flame in a taller, flickering configuration.

2. In the Timeline, select all five frames on all three layers.

3. In one of the selected frames, Control-click (Mac) or right-click (Windows) to access the frame-editing contextual menu; then choose Copy Frames (**Figure 11.21**).

4. In the Timeline, select frame 6 in all three layers.

5. In one of the selected frames, Control-click (Mac) or right-click (Windows) to access the frame-editing contextual menu, and choose Paste Frames.

   Your movie now contains two back-to-back animation sequences of the growing flame (**Figure 11.22**).

   continues on next page

6. In the Timeline, select frames 6–10 on all three layers.

7. Choose Modify > Timeline > Reverse Frames (**Figure 11.23**).

Flash reverses the tween in the second sequence so that the flame starts out tall and flickery, and winds up in its original oval configuration in the final keyframe (**Figure 11.24**).

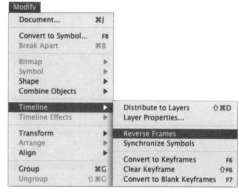

Figure 11.23 Choosing Modify > Timeline > Reverse Frames rearranges the order of selected frames. Use this command to make a selected tween run backward.

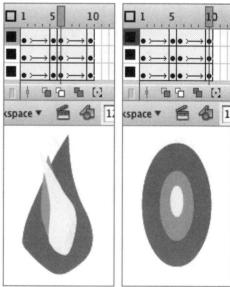

Figure 11.24 After you reverse the frames, the second tween sequence starts with the flickering flame (left) and ends with the oval flame (right).

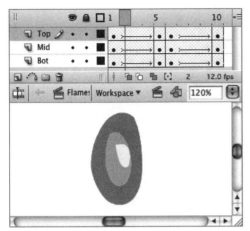

Figure 11.25 Flash's shape tween in frame 2 leaves something to be desired.

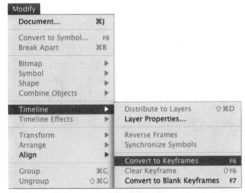

Figure 11.26 Choose Modify > Timeline > Convert to Keyframes to create a keyframe you can use to adjust your multilayer tween.

Combining Tweening with Frame-by-Frame Techniques

Especially with shape tweening, you can't always rely on Flash to create in-between frames that capture the exact movement you want. You can combine Flash's tweening with your own frame-by-frame efforts, however, letting Flash do the work whenever it can. Or, let Flash create the broad outlines of your animation, and then add keyframes to refine the movement. Flash helps with the process by letting you convert those intangible in-between frames to keyframes that you can edit and refine yourself.

In the preceding section, you created a crude version of a flickering flame. In the following tasks, you refine it.

To convert in-between frames to keyframes:

1. Open the Flash document you created in the preceding section.

2. In the Timeline, position the playhead in frame 2 by clicking the number 2 above the layers or by dragging the playhead.

   The first step in this tween isn't particularly effective: The central flame portion seems to be a bit too far to the side (**Figure 11.25**). Because frame 2 is an in-between frame, however, you can't edit it. You can try to improve the motion by adding shape hints, or you can create a new keyframe to refine the animation.

3. To convert the in-between frame to a keyframe, in the Timeline, select frame 2 in all three layers.

4. Choose Modify > Timeline > Convert to Keyframes, or press F6 (**Figure 11.26**).

continues on next page

Flash converts frame 2 from an in-between frame to a keyframe; then it creates the contents of keyframe 2 from the transitional shapes it created for the shape tween at that frame. Now you're free to edit the contents to improve the tweening action (**Figure 11.27**). If you want to create a smoother motion, expand the tween between keyframe 1 and keyframe 2.

5. To add more in-between frames, position the playhead in keyframe 1.

6. Choose Insert > Timeline > Frame, or press F5.

Flash adds new in-between frames in all layers. You can repeat the Insert > Timeline > Frame command to add as many frames as you like (**Figure 11.28**). These frames inherit the shape-tween property that you defined for keyframe 1. Now you can examine Flash's tweening for the new frames and repeat the process of converting any awkward tween frames to keyframes and editing them.

✔ Tips

■ In step 4 of the preceding task, when converting in-between frames of a shape tween to keyframes, Flash always creates the new shapes as merge-shapes (even if the shapes in the preceding keyframe are drawing-objects or primitive-shapes). This could result in unexpected consequences if your shapes are on a single layer. It's another reason to make sure your shapes are on separate layers for tweened animation.

■ Flash limits you to one color change per tween sequence. To speed the process of making several color changes, set up one long tween (either motion or shape) that goes from the initial color to the final color. Then selectively convert in-between frames to keyframes so that you can make additional color changes.

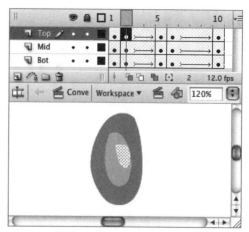

Figure 11.27 After you convert frame 2 from an in-between frame (part of a tween) to a keyframe, you can edit the flame shapes.

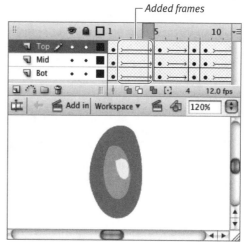

Figure 11.28 Use the Insert > Timeline > Frame command to increase the length of your new span.

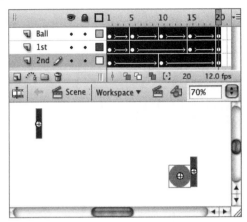

Figure 11.29 To convert an existing animation to a symbol, first select all the frames and layers that make up the animation sequence.

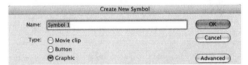

Figure 11.30 You set a new symbol's type in the Create New Symbol dialog. Movie clips operate from their own independent Timeline. Animated graphic symbols play in sync with the main movie that contains them. One frame in the main movie's Timeline displays one frame of the graphic symbol's Timeline.

Saving Animations As Graphic Symbols

In Chapter 7, you learned to save work for reuse and keep file sizes small by using symbols. Flash lets you do the same thing with entire multiple-frame, multiple-layer animation sequences. You can save such sequences either as an animated graphic symbol or as a movie-clip symbol. You can use these symbols repeatedly with a much smaller hit on file size than if you simply re-create the animation by using graphic-symbol instances within separate animations. Additionally, for complex animations, symbols help keep down the number of frames and layers that you have to deal with.

To convert an animation to a graphic symbol:

1. Open the document you created to make the Ping-Pong animation in "Animating Multiple Motion Tweens," earlier in this chapter, or create your own multiple-layer animation.

   The Ping-Pong animation is a three-layer, 20-frame animation.

2. In the Timeline, select all 20 frames in all three layers (**Figure 11.29**).

3. Choose Edit > Timeline > Copy Frames.

4. Choose Insert > New Symbol, or press ⌘-F8 (Mac) or Ctrl-F8 (Windows).

   The Create New Symbol dialog appears (**Figure 11.30**).

5. In the Create New Symbol dialog, type a name for your symbol (for example, Ping-PongAnimation).

continues on next page

6. Choose Graphic as the symbol type.

7. Click OK.

Flash creates a new symbol in the library and switches you to symbol-editing mode for that symbol.

The name of your symbol appears in the Edit bar. The default Timeline for your new symbol consists of one layer and a blank keyframe at frame 1.

8. In the symbol Timeline, select keyframe 1, and choose Edit > Timeline > Paste Frames.

Flash pastes the 20 frames and three layers that you copied from the original Ping-Pong movie into the Timeline for the Ping-PongAnimation symbol (**Figure 11.31**). If you want to make any adjustments in the animation sequence, you can do so at this point.

9. To return to document-editing mode, choose Edit > Edit Document.

Flash places a copy of the new symbol in the library of the active document.

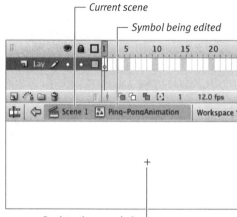

Current scene

Symbol being edited

Registration crosshair

All frames of animation pasted into Timeline

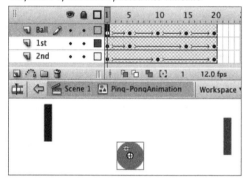

Figure 11.31 When you create a new symbol, Flash switches to symbol-editing mode, making the new symbol's Timeline available for editing (top). You must paste all the frames of your animation into the symbol's Timeline to create the animated symbol (bottom).

Symbols Reduce Layer Buildup

In general, for tweened animations, you need to place each shape on a separate layer. To animate a person, for example, create separate layers for the head, the torso, each arm, and each leg. For complex motion, you might even create separate layers for the eyes, mouth, fingers, and toes. Add some other elements to this character's environment, and you wind up dealing with many layers.

Turning an animation sequence into a symbol in effect collapses all those layers into one object. The process is a bit like grouping. On the Stage, the symbol exists on a single layer, but that layer contains all the layers of the original animation.

Animated graphic symbol

Stop and Play buttons

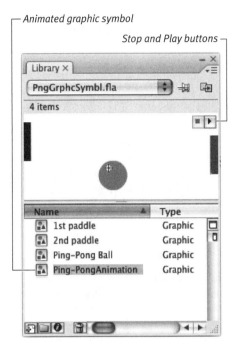

Static graphic symbol

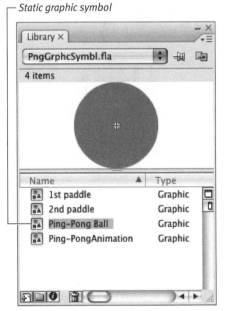

Figure 11.32 An animated graphic symbol (top) in the Library panel has Stop and Play buttons as part of its preview; otherwise, it's indistinguishable from a static graphic symbol (bottom).

✔ Tips

■ In the list of symbols in the Library panel, an animated graphic symbol looks the same as a static graphic symbol; both have the same icon, and both are listed as Graphic in the Type column. An animated graphic symbol, however, has Play and Stop buttons in the top-right corner of the preview window; a static graphic symbol doesn't (**Figure 11.32**). You can preview an animated symbol by clicking the Play button.

■ When you paste multiple frames and layers into the Timeline in symbol-editing mode, the registration crosshair may be in a strange position for the symbol as a whole. To reposition the items making up the symbol, in the Status bar, click the Edit Multiple Frames button; from the Modify Onion Markers pop-up menu, choose Onion All; finally, choose Edit > Select All to select the contents of each keyframe in each layer. Now you can position the symbol as a whole in relation to the crosshair.

How Do Animated Graphic Symbols Differ from Movie-Clip Symbols?

Flash provides for two kinds of animated symbols: graphic symbols and movie clips. The difference is a bit subtle and hard to grasp at first. An animated graphic symbol is tied to the Timeline of any movie in which you place the symbol, whereas a movie-clip symbol runs on its own independent Timeline. When the playhead stops moving in the main Timeline, an animated graphic symbol stops playing, but a movie-clip symbol continues to play.

Think of the frames of an animated graphic symbol as a tray of slides and a movie-clip symbol as a film loop. The animated graphic symbol projects its slides, one per frame, in lockstep with the frames of its hosting movie: to see the next frame of the symbol, you move to the next frame in the hosting movie. Like a tray of slides, an animated graphic symbol has no sound track. If you have sounds in a movie and you convert that movie to a graphic symbol, you lose those sounds. If you have attached ActionScript 1.0 or 2.0 to buttons, that interactivity survives the conversion to a graphic symbol (though any actions that control the Timeline affect the Timeline of the hosting movie, not the graphic symbol itself, potentially creating confusion).

Any ActionScript 3.0 that you have placed in frames on the Timeline of the converted graphic symbol will not publish; ActionScript 3.0 frame actions that are nested within symbols inside the animated graphic symbol survive the conversion but may also control a different Timeline than you expect, depending on how you set them up. Other types of interactivity do not survive the conversion. (To learn more about ActionScript 3.0 and interactivity, see Chapter 13.)

A movie-clip symbol can project all its frames one after another, over and over, in a single frame of the hosting movie. Movie clips do have a sound track and do retain their interactivity. (To learn more about sound, see Chapter 15. For interactivity, see Chapters 12 and 13.)

One more thing to know about the two symbol types is that movie clips, because they run on their own Timeline, don't appear as animations in the Flash authoring environment. You see only the first frame of the movie as a static element on the Stage. Animated graphic symbols, which use the same Timeline as the main movie, display their animation in the authoring environment.

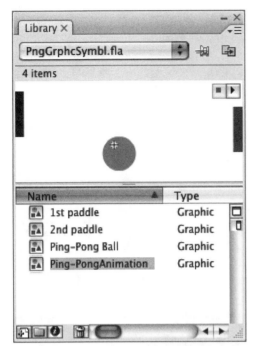

Figure 11.33 Select the graphic symbol you want to use, and then drag a copy to your Flash document to place an instance on the Stage.

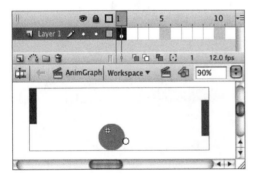

Figure 11.34 When you drag an instance of the animated graphic symbol to the Stage, you see the symbol's first frame with its graphics selected. You must add frames to allow the full animation of the symbol to play in the main movie.

Using Animated Graphic Symbols

To put an animated graphic symbol to work, you must place an instance of it in your main movie. The layer of the movie where you place the symbol must have enough frames to display the symbol. You can use instances of an animated graphic symbol just as you would any other symbol—combine it with other graphics on a layer; motion-tween it; modify its color, size, and rotation; and so on.

To place an instance of an animated graphic symbol:

1. In the movie you created in the preceding section, choose Insert > Scene to create a new scene.

   Flash displays the new scene's Timeline—a single layer with a blank keyframe in frame 1. The Stage is empty.

   Adding a new scene gives you a blank Stage to work with and makes it easy to compare the two animations: the original (created directly in the main movie Timeline) and the instance of the graphic symbol placed in the movie.

2. Access the Library panel.

   If it's not open, choose Window > Library.

3. In the Library panel for your document, select the Ping-PongAnimation symbol.

   The first frame of the animation appears in the preview window (**Figure 11.33**).

4. Drag a copy of the selected symbol to the Stage.

   Flash places the symbol in keyframe 1. At this point, you can see only the first frame of the animation (**Figure 11.34**). The animation is 20 frames long, so you need to add least 20 frames to view the symbol in its entirety.

continues on next page

5. In the Timeline, select frame 20, and choose Insert > Timeline > Frame.

Flash adds in-between frames 2–20.

6. Play the movie.

Now Flash can display each frame of the animated graphic symbol in a frame of the movie. Frame 2 of the symbol appears in frame 2 of the movie, frame 5 of the symbol appears in frame 5 of the movie, and so on (**Figure 11.35**). If you place fewer than 20 frames in the movie, Flash truncates the symbol and displays only as many frames of the symbol as there are frames in the movie.

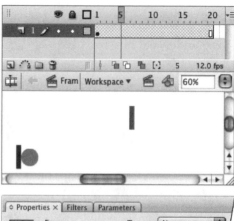

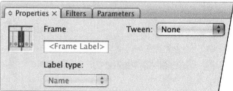

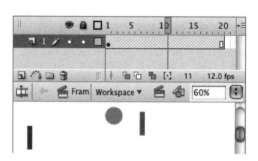

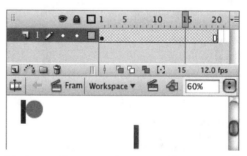

Figure 11.35 Frames 1–20 have a tweening property of None, but they still display animation. Flash displays the 20 tween frames of the graphic symbol that you placed in keyframe 1. It's as though the symbol is a tray of slides, and Flash is projecting one image per frame in the main movie. If the main movie is longer than the slide show, Flash starts the slide show over.

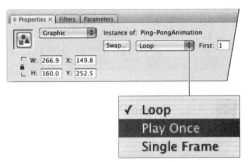

Figure 11.36 By default, animated graphic symbols move in lockstep with the Timeline of the main movie. If the symbol's animation contains fewer frames than does the layer containing the symbol instance in the main Timeline, the animated graphic symbol loops. To stop the selected symbol instance from looping, in the Properties tab of the Property inspector, from the Options for Graphics menu, choose Play Once.

✔ Tip

■ By default, Flash loops the animation of graphic symbols. If the layer containing the animated-symbol instance in the main Timeline has more frames than the symbol requires, Flash starts playing the graphic symbol over again to fill those extra frames. You can prevent such looping. Select the symbol instance on the Stage. In the Properties tab of the Property inspector, from the Options for Graphics menu, choose Play Once (**Figure 11.36**). The options settings also let you choose to start the symbol's animation with a frame other than 1. Enter the desired frame number in the First field. (You can even choose to display just one frame of the animated graphic symbol. From the Options for Graphics menu, choose Single Frame, and then enter the desired frame number in the First field. You can use this technique to pause the animation of the symbol for a certain number of frames in the main movie. At the frame where the symbol should start running, add another keyframe and another copy of the symbol and set it to loop.)

Animated Graphic Symbols Increase File Size

Although symbols are used to keep file size down, animated graphic symbols don't do as good a job at that as movie-clip symbols. For each in-between frame that displays part of an animated graphic, Flash exports roughly 12–15 bytes of data. That's true even if you're just adding extra in-between frames and looping the animated graphic. You don't need any in-between frames to display the movie-clip symbol's animation.

If you nest animated graphic symbols inside animated graphic symbols, you compound the problem because each in-between frame in the nested copy of the symbol adds its 12–15 bytes of data too. Reusing and nesting movie-clip symbols adds little extra data to your file. To test for yourself, nest an animated graphic symbol inside a copy of that symbol and place an instance of the symbol on the stage in a 20-frame keyspan. Test the movie (choose Control > Test Movie). Check the amount of data in each frame using the Bandwidth Profiler (see Chapter 17). Go back to the Flash document, change the symbols' type to Movie Clip, and test again.

Saving Animations As Movie-Clip Symbols

The procedure you use to save an animation as a movie-clip symbol is the same as for saving an animated graphic symbol, except that you define the symbol as a movie clip in the Create New Symbol dialog.

To convert an animation to a movie-clip symbol:

1. Open the document you created to make the Ping-Pong animation in "Animating Multiple Motion Tweens," earlier in this chapter.

   The Ping-Pong animation is a three-layer, 20-frame animation.

2. In the Timeline, select all 20 frames in all three layers.

3. Choose Edit > Timeline > Copy Frames (**Figure 11.37**).

4. Choose Insert > New Symbol, or press ⌘-F8 (Mac) or Ctrl-F8 (Windows).

   The Create New Symbol dialog appears.

5. In the Name field, type a name for your symbol—for example, Ping-PongClip.

   Flash remembers the symbol type you selected for the last symbol you created and selects that type for you when you choose Insert > New Symbol.

6. Select Movie Clip as the symbol type (**Figure 11.38**).

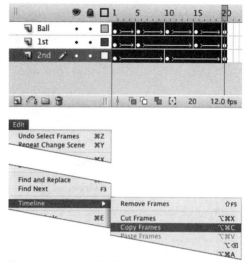

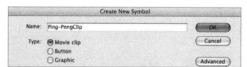

Figure 11.37 To save Timeline animation as a symbol, start by selecting all the frames (and layers) that make up the animation, then choosing the Edit > Timeline > Copy Frames command.

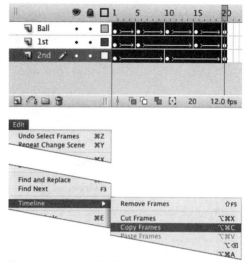

Figure 11.38 Selecting Movie Clip in the Type section of the Create New Symbol dialog defines a symbol that has an independent Timeline. The entire movie-clip symbol runs in a single frame of the main movie.

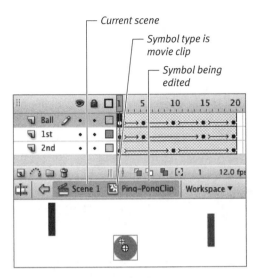

Current scene
Symbol type is movie clip
Symbol being edited

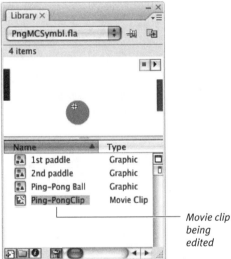

Movie clip being edited

Figure 11.39 After you name the symbol and define its type in the Create New Symbol dialog, Flash switches to symbol-editing mode. The icon that precedes the name of the symbol indicates that this symbol is a movie clip. Now you can paste the animation frames into the symbol's Timeline.

7. Click OK.

Flash creates a new symbol in the Library panel and switches you to symbol-editing mode, with that symbol selected.

The name of your symbol appears in the Edit bar. The default Timeline for your new symbol consists of one layer and a blank keyframe at frame 1.

8. In the symbol Timeline, select keyframe 1, and choose Edit > Timeline > Paste Frames.

Flash pastes all 20 frames and three layers that you copied from the original Ping-Pong animation into the Timeline for the Ping-PongClip symbol (**Figure 11.39**). If you want to make any adjustments in the animation sequence, you can do so at this point.

9. To return to document-editing mode, click the current scene name in the Edit bar.

✔ Tip

■ To make a movie clip that contains exactly the same frames as an existing animated graphic symbol (as you did in the preceding task), you can duplicate that symbol and change its type. Select the animated graphic symbol in the Library panel. From the Library panel's options menu, choose Duplicate. The Duplicate Symbol dialog appears, allowing you to rename the symbol and set its type to Movie Clip.

The Mystery of 9-Slice Scaling

One of the beauties of Flash is the way it lets you reuse elements. One of the frustrations of reusing elements is that resizing (scaling) can distort them. Imagine creating a rectangle with rounded corners; you'll resize the rectangle for various situations; it could be the graphic for an interface element, such as a button, or it could be a building block for an artistic animation. You would expect the amount of rounding in the corners to remain the same when you made the rectangle larger or smaller. In fact, the corners can change, sometimes distorting horizontally, sometimes vertically.

This distortion can occur in the Flash document, as you create your content, or at runtime when people view your movie. Runtime resizing happens if you create scripts that scale elements dynamically; it can also happen if people resize the browser window displaying your movie. You have some control over the second type of scaling when you set options for publishing a movie (see Chapter 17).

In Flash CS3, when publishing for Flash Player 9 or 8, you can also impose conditions on the way movie-clip symbols scale at runtime by invoking 9-slice scaling guides. When you acti-

vate the 9-slice guides, Flash superimposes a grid over your movie-clip symbol. The corner sections defined by the grid don't scale at all; the other sections of the grid scale up or down as required, and then the corners are pasted back on. This method allows you to keep the corners of an element uniform at all sizes.

To activate 9-slice scaling when you originally create a movie-clip symbol, open the Advanced section of the Symbol Properties dialog, and select the "Enable guides for 9-slice scaling" check box (**Figure 11.40**) To enable the guides later, select a symbol in the Library panel, choose Properties from the Library panel's options menu to open the Symbol Properties dialog, and then select the "Enable guides for 9-slice scaling" check box. (You can also enable 9-slice scaling through ActionScript.)

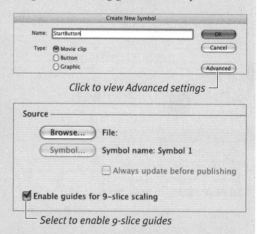

Click to view Advanced settings

Select to enable 9-slice guides

Figure 11.40 To enable 9-slice scaling for movie-clip symbols, in the Create New Symbol dialog, click the Advanced button to access the advanced settings (top). In the Source section, select the "Enable guides for 9-slice scaling" check box (bottom).

When the 9-slice guides are enabled, grid lines appear in the symbol preview window in the Library panel and also when you edit the symbol (**Figure 11.41**). In symbol-editing mode, you can drag the guide lines to define the nonscaling corner areas appropriate to the graphic content of the movie-clip symbol you're creating.

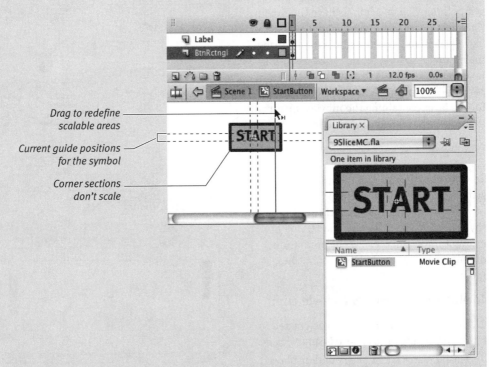

Figure 11.41 With 9-slice scaling enabled, a symbol shows its scaling guides in the Library panel. In symbol-editing mode, the guides appear on the Stage and are adjustable. Drag a guide to reposition it.

Here's another way to avoid distortion when resizing a graphic-object in the authoring environment: Create the object as a primitive-shape and scale it by changing its height and/or width in the Property inspector, Transform panel, or Info panel. When you enter new values for the primitive's height and width, Flash uses the 9-slice scaling technique to scale the objects. If you scale a primitive-shape using the free-transform tool, however, you can still get distortion.

Using Movie-Clip Symbols

You put movie-clip symbols to work by placing an instance of a symbol on the Stage in your Flash document. Unlike animated graphic symbols, movie-clip symbols have their own Timeline. A movie clip plays continuously, like a little film loop, in a single frame of the main movie. As long as the movie contains no other instructions that stop the clip from playing—a blank keyframe in the Timeline for the layer containing the movie clip, for example—the clip continues to loop.

As you work on your Flash document, you can see only the first frame of a movie clip. To view the animation of the movie-clip symbol in context with all the other elements of your movie, you must export the movie (by choosing one of the test modes, for example). You can preview the animation of the movie-clip symbol by itself in the Library panel.

To place an instance of a movie clip:

1. Continuing with the movie you created in the preceding task, choose Insert > Scene.

Flash creates a new scene and displays its Timeline: a single layer with a blank keyframe in frame 1. The Stage is empty.

2. Access the Library panel.

If it's not open, choose Window > Library.

3. Select the Ping-PongClip symbol.

The first frame of the animation appears in the preview window.

4. Drag a copy of the selected symbol to the Stage.

Flash places the symbol in keyframe 1 (**Figure 11.42**). You don't need to add any more frames to accommodate the animation, but you must export the movie to see the animation.

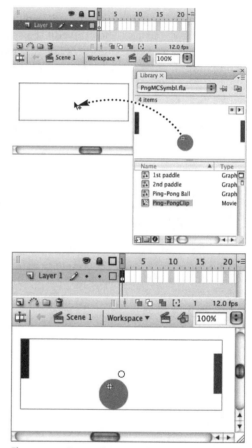

Figure 11.42 Drag an instance of your movie clip from the Library panel to the Stage (top). Flash places the instance in keyframe 1 (bottom).

Figure 11.43 Choose Control > Test Scene to preview the animation of just one scene in a movie.

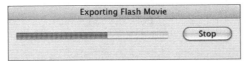

Figure 11.44 The Exporting Flash Movie dialog contains a progress bar and a button for canceling the export.

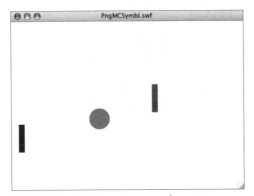

Figure 11.45 Flash Player displays your movie in a regular window. To exit the Player, close the window.

To view the movie-clip animation in context:

1. Continuing with the movie you created in the preceding task, choose Control > Test Scene (**Figure 11.43**).

   Flash exports the movie to a Flash Player format file, adding the .swf extension to the filename and using the current publishing settings for all the export options. (For more information on publishing settings, see Chapter 17.) During export, Flash displays the Exporting Flash Movie dialog, which contains a progress bar and a Stop (Mac) or Cancel (Windows) button for canceling the operation (**Figure 11.44**).

   When it finishes exporting the movie, Flash opens the SWF file in Flash Player so you can see the movie in action (**Figure 11.45**).

2. When you've seen enough of the movie in test mode, click the movie window's Close button (Mac) or Close box (Windows) to exit Flash Player.

USING MOVIE-CLIP SYMBOLS

The Mystery of Bitmap Caching

Flash's original impact on the Web was due in part to its ability to animate using vector graphics rather than bitmaps, which made Flash animations quick to download. However, when an image is complex but doesn't change much over time, especially when changes involve repositioning rather than redrawing shapes, animations may be faster and less processor-intensive when created with bitmaps rather than vectors.

An easy example to imagine is a cartoon background—say, a forest thick with trees and flowers, bushes and vines, over which you animate the creatures that move through the forest. If the background remains still, you can create a bitmap background layer that extends the length of your movie and doesn't require redrawing in each frame.

But there are drawbacks to that method. You can't create or edit the bitmap inside Flash; you must use a program such as Adobe Fireworks or Adobe Photoshop and import the image. (You must edit the image externally and re-import it each time you do.)

And what if you want the background to move from time to time? Let's say you want to create a backdrop that's much wider than the screen and then shift it to the right periodically to show a bit of the scenery that's been hidden. Nothing changes but the position of the background. If you use a bitmap image, Flash can move it pixel by pixel without too much slowdown of the movie, but you still have the inconvenience of creating the image outside Flash. If you use a vector image, Flash must recalculate all the vectors in that background for each move, bogging things down. Flash CS3 gives you the best of both worlds by turning a vector image into a bitmap at runtime.

This technique is called *bitmap caching*. To enable it, you must create your complex element as a movie-clip symbol. Select the symbol instance on the Stage. In the Properties tab of the Property inspector, for that symbol instance, select the "Use runtime bitmap caching" check box (**Figure 11.46**). At runtime, Flash captures a snapshot of the vector image by turning it into a bitmap; then Flash moves that bitmap pixel by pixel as needed, thus avoiding recalculating all those vectors.

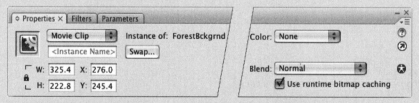

Figure 11.46 If a movie clip contains complex graphics that don't animate in complex ways, you can ask Flash to cache a bitmap of the symbols' image at runtime. Flash creates a sort of bitmap snapshot, redrawing the vector graphics only when something changes. Bitmap caching can speed processing during playback of your Flash creations. Select an instance of a movie-clip symbol on the Stage; then, in the Properties tab of the Property inspector, select "Use runtime bitmap caching."

USING MOVIE-CLIP SYMBOLS

Figure 11.47 An easy way to create a rainbow is to fill a circle with a multiple-color radial gradient and then delete the bottom half of the circle. Here, bisecting a merge-shape circle by drawing a line through it (middle) makes deletion easy; select the line and the bottom half of the circle (bottom), and press Delete.

Using Animated Masks

In Chapter 6, you learned about Flash's ability to create mask layers that hide and reveal objects on lower layers. Sometimes, the best way to create the illusion of movement is to animate a mask so that it gradually hides or reveals objects.

Imagine a line that starts at the left edge of the Stage and goes all the way to the right edge. If you create a mask that reveals the line bit by bit, you create the illusion of a line that draws itself. Reverse the process, and you have a line that gradually erases itself.

Creating rotating and shape-tweened mask graphics can give you some interesting effects. The more familiar you are with using animated masks to reveal stationary items, the better sense you'll have of when to use this technique. For practice, try animating a mask that creates a growing rainbow.

To create a stationary graphic and a moving mask that reveals it:

1. Create a Flash document that has two layers.

Name the bottom layer *Rainbow* and the top layer *Rotating Rectangle*.

2. In keyframe 1 of the Rainbow layer, on the Stage, use the drawing tools to create a rainbow graphic.

One way to create the rainbow is to use the oval tool in Merge Drawing mode to draw a perfect circle. Give the circle a radial-gradient fill that has distinct bands of color. Then erase the bottom half of the circle (**Figure 11.47**).

What's left is your rainbow shape. For safety, convert the rainbow to a symbol (select the rainbow on the Stage, choose Modify > Convert to Symbol, choose Graphic as the type, name the symbol, and click OK) so you'll have a copy of the rainbow in case you accidentally delete the original.

continues on next page

3. In the Timeline, Control-click (Mac) or right-click (Windows) the Rotating Rectangle layer.

The contextual menu for layers appears.

4. Choose Mask.

Flash converts the layer to a mask, links the Rainbow layer to the mask, and locks both layers (**Figure 11.48**).

5. In the Timeline, click the padlock icons in the Lock column of the Rainbow and Rotating Rectangle layers to unlock them.

6. On the Stage, in keyframe 1 of the Rotating Rectangle layer, use the rectangle tool to draw a rectangle just below the bottom of the rainbow (**Figure 11.49**).

The rectangle is your mask. Any items that lie directly below the rectangle on a linked layer appear; everything else is hidden.

Make the rectangle a bit larger than the rainbow so the mask can cover the whole rainbow. Using a transparent fill color lets you see the rainbow through the mask rectangle and helps you verify the mask's position. (To make the rectangle's fill color transparent, select it and then, in the Color panel, assign it a low Alpha percentage.)

✔ Tip

- You can use any of the three types of animation on a mask layer: frame-by-frame, motion tweening, or shape tweening. You can also use an animated graphic symbol or a movie-clip symbol. Advanced ActionScripters can also use ActionScript to tell one movie-clip symbol to mask another and to create transparent masks.

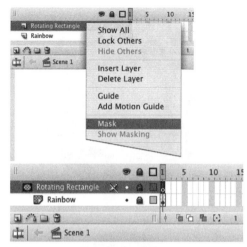

Figure 11.48 Control-click (Mac) or right-click (Windows) a layer and select Mask from the contextual menu to create a mask layer (top). Flash automatically links the layer directly below the mask layer in the Timeline and locks both layers (bottom).

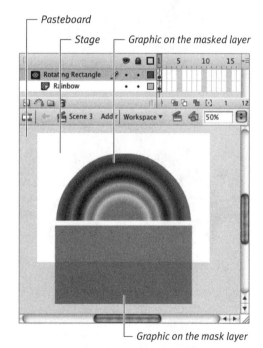

Figure 11.49 To create a mask that reveals the entire rainbow, draw a rectangle that's large enough to cover the rainbow. Positioning the rectangle below the rainbow hides the rainbow completely.

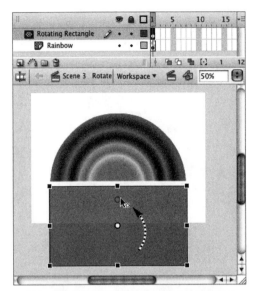

Figure 11.50 Use the free-transform tool to reposition the point around which a symbol (or grouped item) rotates. Drag to a new position the circle that indicates the transformation point. A small circle previews the new transformation-point location. With the transformation point at the center of the rectangle's top edge, the rectangle stays centered over the rainbow as you rotate the rectangle.

To prepare the mask for rotational animation:

1. Select the rectangle, and choose Modify > Convert to Symbol.

   Because you want to create rotational animation, you must use a motion tween for the mask, which means the mask graphic must be a graphic-object. You could use a drawing-object, a primitive-shape, or a grouped element, but it's a good idea to use a symbol so that you can easily reuse the mask.

   The Convert to Symbol dialog appears.

2. In the Name field, enter a name for the symbol, choose Graphic as the symbol type, and click OK.

3. Using the free-transform tool, select the rectangle on the Stage, and position the pointer over the transformation point of the object (indicated by a white circle, located in the middle of the symbol by default).

   A small white-circle modifier appears next to the arrow pointer, indicating that you can move the selected object's transformation point.

4. Drag the transformation point to the middle of the top edge of the rectangle (**Figure 11.50**).

   Now you can rotate the rectangle so that it swings up and over the rainbow but stays centered horizontally in relation to the rainbow.

USING ANIMATED MASKS

To complete the rotating-mask animation:

1. In the Timeline, in the Rainbow layer, select frame 15, and choose Insert > Timeline > Frame.

2. In the Timeline, in the Rotating Rectangle layer, select frame 15, and choose Insert > Timeline > Keyframe.

3. In keyframe 15, with the rectangle selected on the Stage, use the free-transform tool in Rotate and Skew mode to reposition the rectangle; click and drag the bottom-left corner of the rectangle and rotate it so that the rectangle covers the rainbow (**Figure 11.51**).

   The mask that covers the rainbow in authoring mode will reveal the rainbow in the final movie.

4. In the Timeline, in the Rotating Rectangle layer, select any of the frames in the keyframe 1 span (frames 1–14).

5. In the Frame Properties tab of the Property inspector, from the Tween pop-up menu, choose Motion.

6. From the Rotate pop-up menu, choose CW.

7. Enter 0 in the Times field.

   This step sets up the motion tween that rotates the rectangle 180 degrees, swinging it up and over the rainbow until it fully covers the rainbow (**Figure 11.52**).

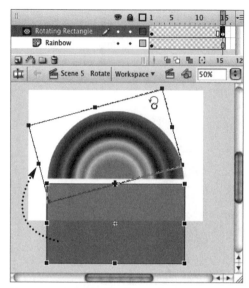

Figure 11.51 In the final keyframe of your sequence, position the mask to cover the item(s) it should reveal. Here the free-transform tool rotates the rectangle mask over the rainbow graphic.

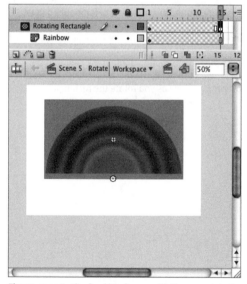

Figure 11.52 In the final keyframe with the completed motion tween for the mask object, the mask covers the rainbow completely. Giving the mask a transparent fill lets you see the objects to be revealed through it as you work. The transparency of objects on the mask layer won't appear in the final movie.

Play movie,
layers unlocked

Play movie;
layers locked

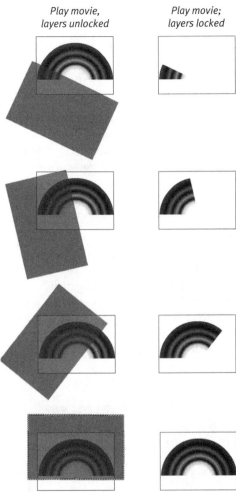

Figure 11.53 As you play the movie with the layers unlocked (left), you can see the in-between positions of the mask graphic. When you lock the layers (right), you see the masking as it will appear in the final exported movie.

To preview the animation:

◆ Choose Control > Test Movie, or Control > Test Scene.

or

◆ In the Timeline, click the padlock icon in the Lock column to lock both layers and see the masked rainbow; then play the movie to see the mask reveal the rainbow.

If the rainbow isn't fully revealed during the tween, you may need to enlarge or reposition the rectangle. Unlock both layers, and move the playhead through the movie to see where the rectangle is in each in-between frame (**Figure 11.53**).

✔ Tip

■ To make the rainbow appear to fade in gradually, tween a change in its transparency. Select frame 15 of the Rainbow layer and press F6, duplicating the rainbow-symbol instance in a new keyframe. Select keyframe 1 of the Rainbow layer; in the Properties tab of the Property inspector, from the Tween pop-up menu, choose Motion. With the rainbow symbol-instance still selected, from the Property inspector's Color menu, choose Alpha; in the Value field, enter a low percentage.

A Note About Blend Modes

Blend modes give designers control over the way graphics in different layers and sublayers interact in Flash. Blends can be used to create special graphic effects. The techniques for creating sophisticated effects with blends are beyond the scope of this *QuickStart Guide*, but here's a brief overview to give you a glimpse of the possibilities for this feature.

Anyone familiar with using blends in Adobe Fireworks or Adobe Photoshop already has an idea about what Flash's blend modes can do, because they work similarly. Blends let you force overlapping images to interact in ways that create new colors and interesting effects. Artists often use blend modes for *compositing*—overlapping multiple images so that parts of each appear in one combined image (for example, superimposing an image of a child's face on an image of a balloon to make a balloon with a face). Photographers use blend modes to enhance or correct flaws in digital photos (for example, using a blend to lighten the areas of a photo where there is too much shadow).

You apply a blend to an instance of a movie clip on the Stage. Flash calculates new colors pixel by pixel, modifying the RGB values of each pixel in the movie clip according to a formula dictated by the chosen blend mode. Whether a particular pixel changes color depends on the type of blend, the color of the pixel in the movie clip, and the color of the pixel that lies on the layer below the movie clip. The pixels on lower layers may be other movie clips, graphic elements, or the background color of the Stage. You apply blends to selected movie-clip instances through the Properties tab of the Property inspector (**Figure 11.54**).

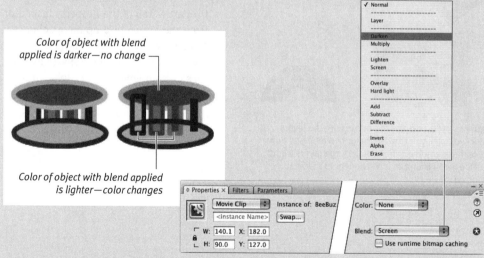

Color of object with blend applied is darker—no change

Color of object with blend applied is lighter—color changes

Figure 11.54 On the Stage, select a movie clip to which you would like to apply a blend; then choose a mode from the Blend menu (here, Darken is being chosen) in the Properties tab of the Property inspector. These two ovals are movie clips lying on a layer above the bar graphics. On the left, the ovals have a Blend property of Normal; they don't interact with the layer below. On the right, the ovals have a Blend property of Darken. Flash evaluates each pixel. Where the pixels in the object to which the blend is applied (the ovals) are lighter than the pixels in the underlying layer, Flash changes the pixels to the darker color.

Figure 11.55 To access the Filters tab of the Property inspector, choose Window > Properties > Filters.

Figure 11.56 To add a drop-shadow effect to text using filters, with a text field selected on the Stage, access the Filters tab of the Property inspector. Click the Add Filter menu and choose Drop Shadow.

Using Filters

Flash CS3 offers seven filters for creating special effects: drop shadow, blur, glow, bevel, gradient glow, gradient bevel, and adjust color. Only three types of graphic-objects—movie-clip symbols, button symbols, and text fields—can have filters applied. Start by selecting one of these objects on the Stage, then access the Filters tab of the Property inspector to choose filters and settings. One object can have multiple filters. You can copy and paste filters from one object to another and create filter presets to save filter settings and apply them to other objects. You can also animate changes to filters, to make a glowing button change colors over time, for example. The techniques for creating sophisticated filter effects are beyond the scope of this book, but the basic techniques for applying all filter types is similar.

The tasks in this section outline creating a simple drop-shadow text field as an introduction to the mechanics of applying filters in Flash.

To access the Filters panel:

◆ If the filters panel is closed, or is not foremost in the Property inspector, choose Window > Properties > Filters (**Figure 11.55**).

Flash opens or brings forward the Property inspector with the Filters tab foremost.

To add filters to an object:

1. On the Stage, select a text field, movie-clip instance, or button instance, to which you want to apply a filter.

   For this task, select a text field.

2. In the Filters tab of the Property inspector, from the Add Filter menu (the plus sign), choose a filter effect.

   For this task, choose Drop Shadow (**Figure 11.56**).

continues on next page

USING FILTERS

Flash applies the filter to the object on the Stage and adds the filter name to the list of filters applied to this object. Controls for the filter's parameters, with default values, appear on the right side of the Filters tab (**Figure 11.57**). Adjust the controls to create the effect you want.

✔ Tips

■ You can apply multiple filters to one movie-clip symbol, button symbol, or text field. The more filters you apply, however, the more processor power it demands. Avoid applying numerous filters to one object.

■ The order in which filters are applied influences how the effects look. To change the order, in the list of applied filters in the Filters tab of the Property inspector, drag one of the filter names to a new position in the list.

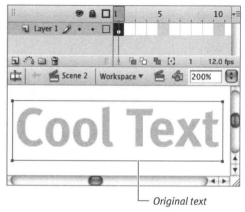

Original text

Drop Shadow filter applied

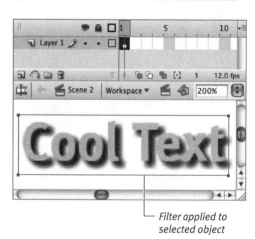

Filter applied to selected object

Figure 11.57 Choosing Drop Shadow from the Add Filter menu applies a drop-shadow filter to the selected text field.

To modify filter settings (Drop Shadow):

1. On the Stage, select a text field, button, or movie clip to which you have applied a filter.

   For this task, select the text field to which you applied the Drop Shadow filter in the preceding task.

2. In the Filters tab of the Property inspector, from the list of applied filters, select the effect you want to modify—in this case, Drop Shadow.

   The settings that define the effect appear on the right side of the Filters tab (**Figure 11.58**).

continues on next page

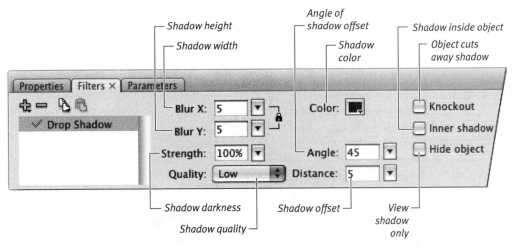

Figure 11.58 A list of filters applied to the currently selected object appears on the left side of the Filters tab. Select an item in the list to see settings for that effect on the right side of the tab. The Drop Shadow filter has ten parameters.

3. To modify the drop shadow, do any of the following:

▲ To modify the size of the shadow, enter new values in the Blur X and/or Blur Y fields. Blur X determines the width of the shadow; Blur Y determines the height. By default Flash constrains these fields so that width and height are the same value (a locked padlock icon appears with lines pointing to each field). To set different values for Blur X and Blur Y, click the Constrain button (the padlock icon) (**Figure 11.59**).

▲ To modify how dark the shadow appears, in the Strength field, enter a value between 0 and 1000 percent. Higher values translate to darker shadows (**Figure 11.60**).

▲ To modify the shadow color, click the Color control to open a set of color swatches and choose a new color (for more on using color controls, see Chapter 2).

▲ To modify how far the shadow is offset from the object, enter a value from −32 to 32 in the Distance field. Negative numbers position the shadow above the object; positive values position the shadow below the object.

▲ To modify the angle of offset, enter a value from 0 to 360 in the Angle field. Values correspond to degrees of a circle. In terms of an analog clock, 0 puts the shadow at 9 o'clock; 90 puts the shadow at 12 o'clock, 180 puts it at 3 o'clock, and so on.

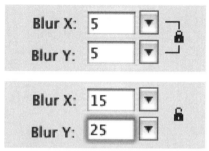

Figure 11.59 When the Constrain button (the padlock) is in its locked state (top), the values for width and height of the drop shadow are always the same. When the button is in the unlocked state (bottom), you can enter values in each field separately.

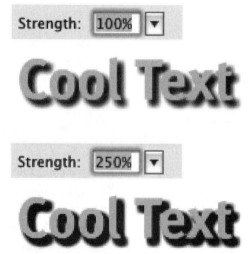

Figure 11.60 With a Color setting of black for the drop shadow, a value of 100 percent in the Strength field creates a dark gray drop shadow; at 250 percent, the shadow is almost solid black.

USING FILTERS

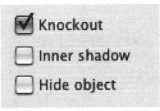

Figure 11.61 Choosing the Knockout check box creates a ghostly stencil effect with the Drop Shadow filter.

▲ To create an effect where the object appears to cut a shape out of the shadow, select the Knockout check box (**Figure 11.61**).

▲ To create an effect where the shadow appears only inside the boundaries of the object itself, select the Inner Shadow check box.

▲ To completely hide the object and see only the shadow it casts, select the Hide Object check box. This feature is helpful when you want to fine-tune the shadow without the distraction of seeing the overlying object.

▲ To set the image quality of the shadow, from the Quality pop-up menu, choose Low, Medium, or High. To assure the greatest playback speed, even on low-end machines, choose Low.

✔ Tip

■ As with most fields where you enter values, you can use a slider to change the Drop Shadow settings interactively. Click the triangle to the right of a field to activate its slider. The Angle field's slider is circular; drag the control point around the circle as if turning a dial to position the drop shadow interactively.

To remove a filter from an object:

1. On the Stage, select the object whose filter you want to remove.

2. In the Filters tab of the Property inspector, from the list of applied filters, select the filter to be removed.

3. Click the Remove Filter button (the minus sign) (**Figure 11.62**).

Flash removes the filter from the list and removes the effects related to that filter from the object on the Stage.

✔ Tips

■ If you wish to turn off a filter, but not delete it entirely, you can disable it temporarily. In the Filters tab of the Property inspector, in the list of applied filters, a green checkmark appears to the left of each filter name. Click the checkmark and it changes to a red X; Flash disables the filter and its effect is no longer visible on the Stage.

■ To disable all filters but one, Option-click (Mac) or Alt-click (Windows) the checkmark of the filter you want to keep enabled. Red X's appear beside all the other filters for that object. To enable all the filters, Option-click (Mac) or Alt-click (Windows) the lone green checkmark; Flash enables all the filters in the list.

■ To enable or disable all the items in the list of applied filters, from the Add Filter menu, choose Enable All or Disable All.

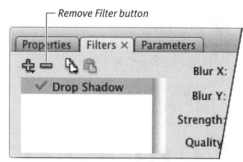

Remove Filter button

Figure 11.62 Select a filter to be removed from the list of applied filters in the Filters tab of the Property inspector. Then click the Remove Filter button.

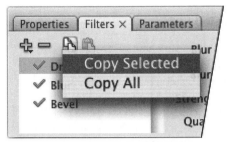

Figure 11.63 Click the double-document icon to open the Copy Filters pop-up menu. Use this feature to copy either one selected filter in the applied-filters list or all the filters in the list.

Paste Filters button

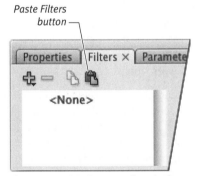

Figure 11.64 Click the Paste Filters button to apply copied filters to a movie clip, button, or text field that's selected on the Stage.

To copy filter settings from one object to another:

1. On the Stage, select the object whose filter you want to copy.

2. In the Filters tab of the Property inspector, from the list of applied filters, select a filter to be copied.

3. From the Copy Filters pop-up menu (**Figure 11.63**), choose one of the following:

   ▲ To copy just the selected filter, choose Copy Selected.

   ▲ To copy all the filters currently displayed in the applied filters list, choose Copy All.

4. On the Stage, select the object to which you want to apply the copied filter(s).

5. In the Filters tab of the Property inspector, click the Paste Filters button (**Figure 11.64**).

   Flash applies the copied filter(s) and settings to the selected object.

✔ Tips

■ You can also save filter settings as presets to create a library of commonly used filter effects. Once filters have been applied to an object and modified to your satisfaction, select the object on the Stage; in the Filters tab of the Property inspector, from the Add Filter menu, choose Presets > Save As; enter a name for the preset in the dialog that appears; and click OK. You can now apply that preset to any selected object by choosing Add Filter > Presets, and the name you chose.

■ You can share with other Flash users the preset filters you create. Filter presets are XML files that live in a folder named Filters that appears in the user-level Configuration folder (for more details on finding the Configuration folder, see Chapter 1).

USING FILTERS

Some Pitfalls of Animated Filters

You can animate changes to filters with motion tweening. Set up a motion tween using a movie-clip symbol, button symbol, or text field; apply filters to the tweened object; and use different filter settings in the initial and final keyframes of the animation sequence. Sounds simple, but it can get complex, because Flash is picky about how different the filter settings can be from start to finish. It's easiest (and safest) to tween the effects of just one filter. You might tween changes to an object's drop shadow, for example, to create the sense of a moving light source. As you add multiple filters to a tweened object, however, things get tricky, because Flash requires a certain level of consistency between the filter settings of the object in the initial and final keyframes of the sequence. The tweened object must have the same number of filters on each end of the tween, and the types of filters (and the order in which they are applied) must be the same at both ends of the tween sequence.

If you set up your tween sequence by first creating the initial keyframe with an object to which filters have been applied, selecting a later frame, then choosing Insert > Timeline > Keyframe, Flash duplicates the initial keyframe (including all the filters and filter settings for the object) in the final keyframe. You can modify those filter settings in the final keyframe of the span to create the animated change, and the tween should work safely.

If you create the beginning and ending keyframes separately, using different filters and settings for the objects in each keyframe, and assign the Motion tween property afterward, it's possible to create inconsistencies between the filters in the initial keyframe and the filters in the final keyframe of the span. Also, as you modify the tweened objects and their filters throughout the development process, it's possible to create inconsistencies between the filters in the initial keyframe and the filters in the final keyframe of a tween sequence.

Flash compares the filters and settings for the tween's initial and final keyframes. When it finds inconsistencies, Flash adds filters, adds dummy filters (adds the same type of filter as one that's missing, but sets no parameters for it), or removes filters to correct the problem. There's no warning that Flash is making these corrections, they just appear. It can be difficult to catch the fact that Flash has made changes to your document. In addition, Flash's automatic corrections may modify the animation in ways you didn't intend. If you find that your animated filter effects are not doing what you want, check the filters for the initial and ending keyframes of each tween. You may need to apply different changes to correct the problem.

BUILDING BUTTONS FOR INTERACTIVITY

After you master Flash CS3 Professional's drawing and animating tools, you can create movies that play from beginning to end. But Flash does more than make animated movies; it can create interactive environments that transform viewers into users. To move your Flash movie into the realm of interactive experience, you must add interface elements that give users control. The most common interface element is a button. Buttons have two levels of interactivity: first, responding to user input with visual feedback—for example, changing color when the pointer enters the button area; second, carrying out tasks—for example, switching to a new scene when the user clicks the button.

Flash comes with a number of predefined user-interface elements, including button symbols and button components. For these elements, built-in coding takes care of the first level of button interactivity, responding to mouse movements with visual feedback. To achieve the second level of interactivity—making buttons respond in new ways and carry out tasks—requires scripting. You'll learn some simple ways to do that in Chapter 13.

In this chapter, you learn to set up the first level of interactivity using button symbols and button components. You also learn to set up a movie-clip symbol that can act as a visually responsive button.

The Mystery of Button Symbols

In Flash, you can make a button by creating a symbol and then choosing Button as the symbol type. Buttons are actually short interactive movies—made of four frames, to be precise. When you select Button as the symbol type, Flash sets up a Timeline with four frames. You create keyframes and graphics for the first three frames to display the button in three common states: Up, Over, and Down. A keyframe in the fourth frame (never shown to the viewer) defines the active area of the button.

For the Up state, you create a graphic that looks like a static, unused button. This graphic appears whenever the pointer lies outside the active area of the button. For the Over state, create the graphic as it should look when the pointer rolls over the button. Flash automatically changes the pointer to the hand cursor for the Over state; but often, you want additional visual changes to alert the viewer that the pointer is now on a live button. For the Down state, create the graphic as it should look when someone clicks the button. For the Hit state, create a graphic that defines the boundary of the button. Any filled shape in the Hit keyframe becomes a place where mouse movements trigger the button during movie playback.

Any changes you make in the appearance of the graphic elements in the keyframes create the illusion of movement. In other Flash animation sequences, changes occur over time as the playhead moves through the frames. In button symbols, however, changes occur when the user moves the pointer over a specific area of the screen.

You can include movie clips within each keyframe of a button to create buttons that are fully animated, and you can create scripts that activate buttons to give your viewers more control of the movie.

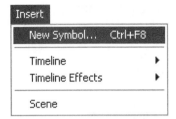

Figure 12.1 Choosing Insert > New Symbol is the first step in creating a button.

Figure 12.2 To make a button, create a new symbol and choose Button as the type in the Create New Symbol dialog. You also name the button here.

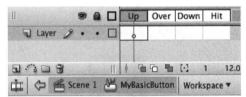

Figure 12.3 The Timeline for every button symbol contains four frames: Up, Over, Down, and Hit. Flash automatically puts a keyframe in the Up frame of a new button symbol.

Creating a Basic Button Symbol

A button is a Flash movie clip with different keyframes that represent the button in all its possible states. The button symbol has three button-state frames—Up, Over, Down—plus one frame for defining the active button area. To create the most basic button symbol, choose a simple shape and place it in the keyframe for each state; change the shape's color or add or modify internal elements for the various states. When you complete all four keyframes, your button is ready to use. Return to document-editing mode, and drag an instance of the button symbol from the Library panel to the Stage.

To create a button symbol:

1. Open a Flash document to which you want to add buttons.

2. Choose Insert > New Symbol, or press ⌘-F8 (Mac) or Ctrl-F8 (Windows) (**Figure 12.1**).

   The Create New Symbol dialog appears.

3. Type a name in the Name field (for example, MyBasicButton), choose Button in the Type section, and click OK (**Figure 12.2**).

   Flash creates a new symbol in the Library panel and returns you to the Timeline and Stage in symbol-editing mode. The Timeline for a button symbol contains the four frames that define the button: Up, Over, Down, and Hit.

   By default, the Up frame contains a keyframe (**Figure 12.3**). You must add keyframes to the Over, Down, and Hit frames and place the graphic elements in each keyframe of the button. To give users feedback about the button—so they can tell when they're on a live button and sense the difference when they click it—use a different graphic in each keyframe.

337

To create the Up state:

1. Using the file from the preceding task, in the Timeline, select the Up keyframe.

2. On the Stage, create a new graphic or place a graphic symbol (**Figure 12.4**).

   This graphic element becomes the button as it's sitting onstage in your movie, waiting for someone to click it. The crosshair in the middle of the Stage in symbol-editing mode will become the registration point for the symbol.

To create the Over state:

1. Using the file from the preceding task, in the Timeline, select the Over frame.

2. Choose Insert > Timeline > Keyframe.

   Flash duplicates the Up keyframe. Now you can make minor changes in the Up graphic to convert it to an Over graphic. Enlarge an element within the button, for example (**Figure 12.5**). Duplicating the preceding keyframe makes it easy to align all your button elements so they don't appear to jump around as they change states.

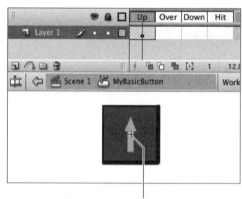

Registration crosshair marks the center of the symbol's Stage

Figure 12.4 When a button is waiting for your viewer to notice and interact with it, Flash displays the contents of the Up keyframe.

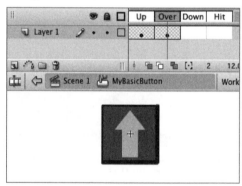

Figure 12.5 When the viewer's pointer rolls (or pauses) over the button, Flash displays the contents of the Over keyframe.

CREATING A BASIC BUTTON SYMBOL

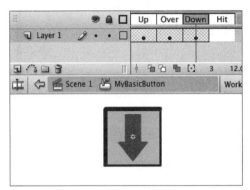

Figure 12.6 When the viewer clicks the button, Flash displays the contents of the Down keyframe.

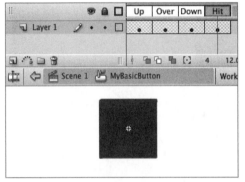

Figure 12.7 The graphic in the Hit keyframe doesn't need to be a fully detailed image of the button in any state; it just needs to be a silhouette of the button shape. Flash uses that shape to define the active button area. This Hit keyframe contains a copy of the Down keyframe that has been filled with dark gray.

✔ Tip

■ If you use a copy of the Up, Over, or Down graphic in the Hit keyframe, try enlarging that copy slightly. Using a larger image ensures that users activate the button easily as soon as they get near it. To enlarge the graphic by a small amount quickly, select the graphic. Choose Modify > Shape > Expand Fill. In the Expand Fill dialog, enter a small value (say, 2 pixels). Choose Expand, and click OK.

To create the Down state:

1. Using the file from the preceding task, in the Timeline, select the Down frame.

2. Choose Insert > Timeline > Keyframe.

    Flash duplicates the Over keyframe. Now you can make minor changes to convert the Over graphic to a Down graphic. Change the button color, for example, and reverse the shadow effect so the button looks indented (**Figure 12.6**).

    After you create graphics for the three states of your button, you need to define the active area of the button.

To create the Hit state:

1. Using the file from the preceding task, in the Timeline, select the Hit frame.

2. Choose Insert > Timeline > Keyframe.

    Flash duplicates the Down keyframe. When you use a graphic with the same shape and size for all three phases of your button, you can safely use a copy of any previous keyframe as the Hit-frame graphic.

3. If you want, use the paint-bucket and ink-bottle tools to fill the Hit-frame graphic with a single color (**Figure 12.7**). This step isn't required, but it helps remind you that this graphic isn't one that viewers of your movie will see.

4. Choose Edit > Edit Document, or click the Back button in the Edit bar.

    Flash returns you to the main Timeline. Now you can use the button symbol in your movie just as you would use any other symbol.

To place the newly created button in your movie:

◆ Continuing with the file from the preceding task, drag an instance of the button MyBasicButton from the Library panel to the Stage (**Figure 12.8**).

You can modify the instance to change its size, rotation, and color. (For more information on modifying symbol instances, see Chapter 7.)

✔ Tips

■ To create a consistent look on a Web site, you may want to use a set of buttons over and over. You can even reuse buttons in several projects with only slight changes. To save time, devote one whole document to buttons, and always create your button symbols there. Then you can copy a button from this master button file to your current Flash document and tweak the button there.

■ Always fill the graphics in the Hit keyframe with the same color—say, neon blue or another bright color that you won't use elsewhere in your movie. That way, you create a silhouette that becomes another visual cue that you're in the Hit keyframe of a button, in symbol-editing mode.

■ You can preview the Up, Over, and Down states of your button by selecting the button in the Library panel and then clicking the Play button in the preview window. Flash displays each frame in turn.

To preview button states on the Stage:

◆ Choose Control > Enable Simple Buttons (**Figure 12.9**).

Flash displays the Up, Over, and Down states as you move the pointer over the button and click. Remember, with buttons enabled, you can't select them or work with them. To turn off Enable Simple Button mode, choose Control > Enable Simple Buttons again.

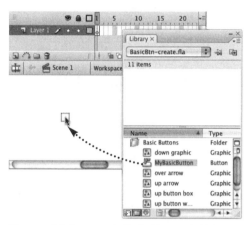

Figure 12.8 To incorporate the button symbol into your Flash movie, drag an instance from the Library panel to the Stage.

Figure 12.9 By default, in document-editing mode, button-symbol instances on the Stage display just the Up keyframe. To see the different states as the pointer interacts with a button during authoring, choose Control > Enable Simple Buttons.

CREATING A BASIC BUTTON SYMBOL

Figure 12.10 Name your button symbol and choose Button as the symbol type in the Create New Symbol dialog.

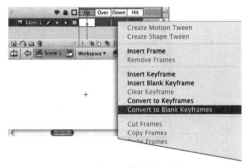

Figure 12.11 With the Over, Down, and Hit frames of a button symbol selected, Control-click (Mac) or right-click (Windows) to access the contextual menu and choose Convert to Blank Keyframes. Flash adds blank keyframes to all the selected frames.

Creating Shape-Changing Button Symbols

Button graphics can emulate real-world switches or toggles. In a game, you can disguise buttons as part of the scenery—making the blinking eye of a character a button, for example. Finding the hot spots or buttons is part of the fun. When the Up, Over, and Down keyframes of your button symbol contain graphics of different shapes and sizes, however, creating an effective graphic for the Hit keyframe can be tricky. You need to create a graphic for the Hit state that covers all of the other states.

To create Up, Over, and Down states with various graphics:

1. Open a Flash document to which you want to add buttons.

2. Choose Insert > New Symbol.
   The Create New Symbol dialog appears.

3. Enter a name in the Name field (for example, AnimatedBtn), choose Button in the Type section, and click OK (**Figure 12.10**).

   Flash creates a new symbol in the Library panel and returns you to the Timeline and Stage in symbol-editing mode. The Timeline for a button symbol contains the four frames necessary for defining the button: Up, Over, Down, and Hit.

4. In the Timeline, select the Over, Down, and Hit frames.

5. Control-click (Mac) or right-click (Windows) the selected frames and choose Convert to Blank Keyframes from the contextual menu (**Figure 12.11**).

continues on next page

CREATING SHAPE-CHANGING BUTTON SYMBOLS

Now you have a blank keyframe in every frame of your button, and you're ready to place various graphics in each keyframe.

6. With the Up keyframe selected in the Timeline, on the Stage, create a new graphic, or place an instance of the graphic symbol that you want to use for the button's Up state.

7. Repeat step 6 for the Over and Down keyframes.

For this task, use graphics that have different shapes—a circle, a star, and a double-headed arrow, for example (**Figure 12.12**).

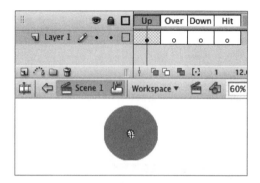

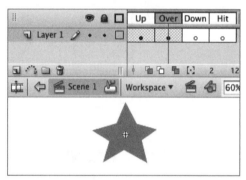

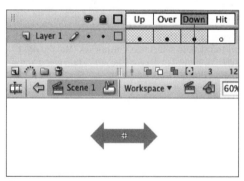

Figure 12.12 You can create fanciful buttons that change shape when a user rolls over or clicks them. In this example, the inactive button is a circle (top). When the pointer rolls over the button, the circle changes to a star (middle). When the user clicks the button, it changes to a double-headed arrow (bottom).

Onion-skin outlines

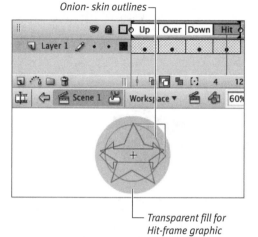

Transparent fill for Hit-frame graphic

Figure 12.13 The silhouette in the Hit keyframe needs to encompass all possible button areas in all three button modes. For example, if you duplicate only the circle as the graphic for the Hit keyframe for this button, you exclude the tips of the star. As the user moves the pointer over the tips, the button returns to its Over phase; the user can't ever click the tips to activate the button. If you duplicate only the star, the user may roll over several areas of the circle and never discover that it's a button.

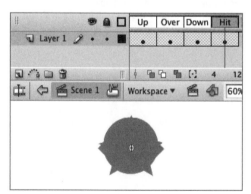

Figure 12.14 By copying the graphic in each of the button states and using the Paste in Place command to place them in the Hit keyframe, you wind up with a perfectly positioned silhouette that incorporates all the possible button areas.

To create the Hit state for graphics of various shapes:

1. Using the file you created in the preceding task, in the Timeline, select the Hit keyframe.

2. To create the graphic that defines the button's active area, do either of the following:

   ▲ Draw a simple geometric shape large enough to cover all areas of the button. Turn on onion skinning so you can see exactly what you need to cover (**Figure 12.13**).

   ▲ Use Flash's Edit > Copy and Edit > Paste in Place commands to copy the graphic elements from the first three keyframes of the button and paste them into the Hit keyframe of the button one by one. The graphics stack up in the Hit keyframe, occupying the exact area needed to cover the button in any phase of its operation (**Figure 12.14**).

3. Return to editing the document, for example, by choosing Edit > Edit Document.

   You're ready to place an instance of the button on the Stage and test it out by choosing Control > Test Movie.

✔ Tip

■ Use a transparent color (one with an alpha value less than 100 percent) for the graphic in the Hit keyframe. In Onion Skin mode the Up, Down, and Over graphics show through the Hit graphic, making it easy to see how to position or size the graphic in the Hit keyframe to cover the graphics in the other keyframes.

CREATING SHAPE-CHANGING BUTTON SYMBOLS

343

Creating Fully Animated Button Symbols

The button symbols you created in the preceding tasks are animated in the sense that they change as the user interacts with them. Flash also lets you create button symbols that are fully animated—a glowing light bulb, for example, or a little ladybug that jumps up and down, saying, "Click me!" The trick to making fully animated buttons is placing movie clips in the keyframes of your button. Because the movie clips play in their own Timeline, animated buttons remain animated even when you pause the main movie.

To animate a rollover button:

1. Open a Flash document to which you want to add buttons.

2. Choose Insert > New Symbol.
   The Create New Symbol dialog appears.

3. Name your button (for example, FullAnimBtn), choose Button in the Type section, and click OK.

4. In the Timeline, select the Over, Down, and Hit frames of the button, and choose Modify > Timeline > Convert to Blank Keyframes.
   Flash creates blank keyframes for the button's Over, Down, and Hit frames.

5. In the Timeline, select the Up keyframe, and place an instance of a movie-clip symbol on the Stage. For this example, the Up-keyframe clip contains a spinning pentagon (**Figure 12.15**).

6. In the Timeline, select the Over keyframe, and place an instance of a movie-clip symbol on the Stage.
   In this example, the Over-keyframe clip contains a pentagon that turns into a star (**Figure 12.16**).

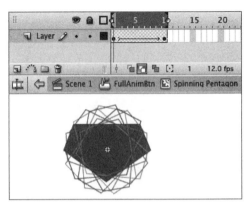

Figure 12.15 Placing an animated symbol in the Up keyframe of a button symbol makes that animation appear when the button is in the Up state. Here, onion skinning in symbol-editing mode reveals all the frames of a spinning-pentagon symbol's animation.

Figure 12.16 With an animated symbol in the Over keyframe of a button, that animation appears when the pointer rolls or rests over the button area. Here, the Preview mode of the Timeline shows the animation of a symbol that turns a pentagon shape into a star.

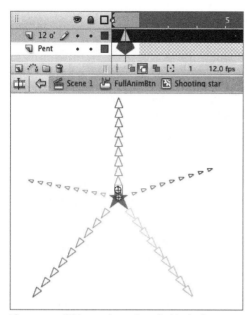

Figure 12.17 With an animated symbol in the Down keyframe of a button, the animation plays when the viewer clicks inside the button area. Here, onion skinning in symbol-editing mode reveals all the frames of a shooting-star symbol's animation.

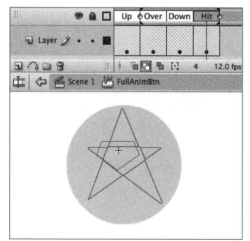

Figure 12.18 When you're creating a graphic for a Hit keyframe, use onion skinning to see the initial keyframe of the movie clip in each button frame. Here, the graphic in the Hit keyframe is a transparent fill, which also helps you position the graphic to cover the graphics in the other keyframes.

7. Repeat step 6 for the Down keyframe.

    For this example, the Down-keyframe clip contains a star that flies apart (**Figure 12.17**).

8. In the Timeline, select the Hit keyframe, and create a graphic that covers all the button areas for the three button states (Up, Over, and Down).

    A large oval works well for this purpose (**Figure 12.18**). This graphic creates an active button area that's larger than the spinning pentagon. As your viewer's pointer nears the spinning graphic during playback, the button switches to Over mode. In Over mode, the oval is big enough to encompass all points of the star, and in Down mode, the user can let the pointer drift a fair amount and still be within the confines of the button.

9. Return to document-editing mode by clicking the name of the current scene in the Edit bar.

10. Drag a copy of the FullAnimBtn symbol from the Library panel to the Stage.

✔ Tips

- You can place a movie-clip instance in the Hit keyframe of your button, but only the visible content from the clip's first frame determines the hit area.

- With buttons enabled, in document-editing mode, Flash previews the Up, Over, and Down keyframes of your button symbol but not its complete animation. For each state, you see only the initial keyframe of the movie clip. To view the fully animated button, you must export the movie and view it in Flash Player (by choosing Control > Test Movie, for example).

The Mystery of Components

Flash's components are predefined user-interface elements with built-in graphics and coding that make them easy to use. Adobe designed components to work together to give an application or a Web site a consistent look and feel. Components depend on ActionScript to carry out their intended behavior. Flash CS3 offers two types of components: those that work with ActionScript versions 1.0 and 2.0, and those that work with version 3.0.

Flash stores components in the *Components panel,* a sort of library of components. The Components panel displays different items depending on which version of ActionScript is selected in the Publish Settings dialog of the current Flash document. When you create a new Flash File (ActionScript 3.0) document, it is set to work with the 3.0 components, and those are the only components that appear in the Components panel. (To learn about Publish Settings and switching ActionScript versions for your document, see Chapter 17.)

A component is actually a sophisticated, scripted movie-clip symbol. The ActionScript 1.0 and 2.0 components are a special type of movie clip called a *compiled clip.* ActionScript 3.0's video components are also complied clips, but the 3.0 user-interface components are really just regular movie clips whose look you can easily modify. See the sidebar, "The Mystery of ActionScript 3.0 Component Skins". (It is also possible to modify the look of compiled clips, but the process is somewhat complex and beyond the scope of this book.)

Flash lets you modify certain properties of a component (for example, the label of the button component) by changing parameters in the Component Inspector panel or in the Parameters tab of the Property inspector.

Advanced Flash users can use ActionScript to make components communicate with one another and to change the components on the fly at runtime, but even someone new to scripting can use simple components to add interactivity to a project.

Advanced scripters can also create their own components and share them with other Flash users. One source for new components is the Adobe Exchange portion of the Adobe Web site. As third-party components become available, you can add them to your Components panel for easy access.

Figure 12.19 The Components panel lists all the default components that come with Flash. There are two categories of components for ActionScript 3.0: User Interface and Video. Buttons are found under User Interface. To expand or collapse the list, click the plus sign (Windows) or triangle (Mac) to the left of the title User Interface.

Using Button Components

The elements that make up the user interface (UI) of an application are the little things that let users interact with your content: menus, check boxes, scroll bars, and so on. Flash's button symbols are one type of UI element, with built-in scripting for simple behavior (displaying the common button states) and looks that you can freely define. However, Flash also offers a more complete set of UI elements in the form of components (see the sidebar "The Mystery of Components") You can modify both the behavior and the graphics of Flash components. Flash's button components have more built-in scripting to govern behavior, and they offer predefined graphics that help create a consistent look and feel for your Flash creations. To put a component to use, you place an instance of it in your Flash document.

To place an instance of the button component:

1. Open a Flash document to which you'd like to add a button component.

2. Access the following panels: Components, Component inspector, Library, and the Parameters tab of the Property inspector.

   These panels are all found under the Window menu. To access the Parameters tab, choose Window > Properties > Parameters; or, if the default Property inspector is open, click the Parameters tab.

3. If necessary, in the Components panel, expand the list of user-interface components (**Figure 12.19**).

   Click the triangle (Mac) or plus sign (Windows) to the left of the name User Interface to toggle between the expanded and collapsed views of the list.

continues on next page

4. Drag an instance of the button component to the Stage.

Flash adds the button component and a folder named Component Assets to the document's library (**Figure 12.20**).

✔ Tip

- Components work similarly to other library assets (for more about working with library assets, see Chapter 7). A confusing apparent similarity is that you can rename a component in the Library panel by double-clicking its name (Button) to activate a text field and typing a new name. It's unadvisable to do so, however. You can change the name of the master component, but on the Stage the component instance still bears the label Button. Moreover, if you bring another copy of the original button component into the same document, the two components will have the same linkage ID, which may create problems in using the components in your published movie.

Figure 12.20 A component is a special form of movie clip. When you drag a Button component from the Components panel to the Stage, the button becomes an asset (its type is Component) in the Library panel of that document.

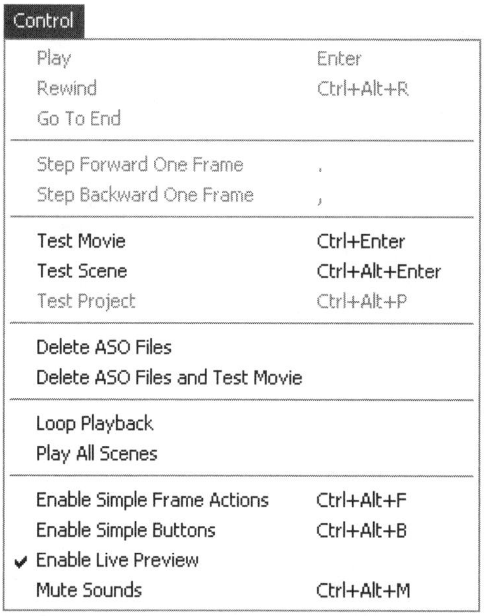

Control	
Play	Enter
Rewind	Ctrl+Alt+R
Go To End	
Step Forward One Frame	.
Step Backward One Frame	,
Test Movie	Ctrl+Enter
Test Scene	Ctrl+Alt+Enter
Test Project	Ctrl+Alt+P
Delete ASO Files	
Delete ASO Files and Test Movie	
Loop Playback	
Play All Scenes	
Enable Simple Frame Actions	Ctrl+Alt+F
Enable Simple Buttons	Ctrl+Alt+B
✔ Enable Live Preview	
Mute Sounds	Ctrl+Alt+M

Figure 12.21 Choose Control > Enable Live Preview to see the basic look of a component as you edit your Flash document.

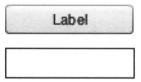

Figure 12.22 With Enable Live Preview active (Flash's default setting), you can see the component instance, with its current parameter settings, on the Stage while authoring (top). With Enable Live Preview inactive, Flash previews components with simple rectangular outlines that give no hint about what kind of element they represent (bottom).

To preview the component instance:

◆ To view a limited component preview during authoring, choose Control > Enable Live Preview (**Figure 12.21**).

The Enable Live Preview setting is active by default. If you're working with many components, this setting can slow things down; you may prefer to turn it off for a time. Whereas the Enable Simple Buttons setting lets you preview a button symbol's Up, Over, and Down states, Enable Live Preview reveals the button component in the Up state created by its current parameter settings (**Figure 12.22**). To view a fully enabled button component, you must view it in Flash Player. When Enable Live Preview is inactive, Flash previews component instances as simple rectangular outlines on the Stage.

◆ To view all the parameters and button states of a button component, choose Control > Test Movie.

USING BUTTON COMPONENTS

Modifying Button Components

The Component Inspector offers seven modifiable parameters for the button component. The tasks below work with two of them: changing the button's label and setting the button to work as a toggle. You can also use the Parameters tab of the Property inspector to change a button component's dimensions.

To modify button-component dimensions:

1. Continuing with the file you used in the preceding task, on the Stage, select the instance of Button.

2. In the Parameters tab of the Property inspector, in the W and H fields, enter new values for width and height (**Figure 12.23**).

   By default, the W and H fields are locked, so Flash preserves the component's *aspect ratio* (the ratio of width to height) when you enter new values. For this task, click the lock icon to deactivate the locked–aspect-ratio mode. Then enter the same value in both the W and H fields to create a square button.

3. Press Enter to confirm the new value(s).

   The button's dimensions change according to the value(s) you enter (**Figure 12.24**). The bounding box of the button defines the active area of the button. As you change the dimensions, Flash automatically changes the hit area for the button component to match.

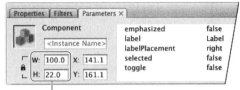

— *Enter new width and height values*

Figure 12.23 To change the dimensions of a button-component instance, access the Parameters tab of the Property inspector and enter new width and height values in the W and H fields.

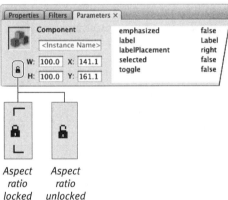

Aspect ratio locked   *Aspect ratio unlocked*

Figure 12.24 You can change the rectangular Button component to a square by entering the same value for width and height (here it's 100 pixels). You must first deactivate the component's locked–aspect-ratio mode. In the Parameters tab of the Property inspector, click the lock icon to put the width and height fields in the unlocked mode.

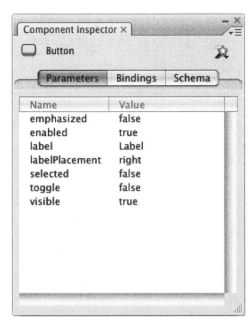

Figure 12.25 The Component inspector displays all the parameters of the button component that you can modify during authoring.

✔ **Tips**

■ There are other ways to resize the button component. You can select the component instance and resize it using the Transform panel or the free-transform tool. Alternatively, you can enter new width and height values in the Info panel or Properties tab of the Property inspector.

■ You can also rotate or skew a button component with the free-transform tool or Info panel. You should know, however, that Flash creates the button's label text using device fonts, which can't be rotated or skewed. If you rotate or skew a button component, its label text disappears at runtime.

■ You can position your button component precisely by entering values in the *x*- and *y*-coordinate fields of the Info panel or the Properties or Parameters tabs of the Property inspector.

To modify button-component labels:

1. Continuing with the file you used in the preceding task, on the Stage, select the instance of Button.

2. Access the Component inspector.

   The panel has three sections: Parameters, Bindings, and Schema.

3. If Parameters isn't active, click the Parameters button (Mac) or tab (Windows) to view the component's parameters.

   The panel displays a two-column table (**Figure 12.25**). The first column contains the parameter names; the second column contains the value for each parameter.

   continues on next page

MODIFYING BUTTON COMPONENTS

4. To modify the text that appears on your button instance, in the row for label, click the value Label.

Flash activates the text field and selects the name; enter a new name, such as testComponent (**Figure 12.26**).

5. Press Enter, or click outside the active text field.

With Flash's default settings, the new label text appears within the button-component instance (**Figure 12.27**). If you don't see the new text, choose Control > Enable Live Preview. Be fore-warned, if your text is wider than the button instance, Flash will truncate the text to make it fit within the visible button area.

✔ Tip

- You can also modify most of the button component's parameters from the Property inspector. With an instance of the button component selected on the Stage, access the Parameters tab of the Property inspector; parameter fields for the button-component instance appear in the tab.

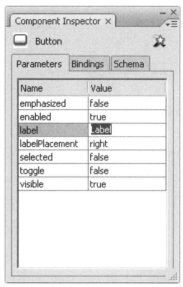

Figure 12.26 In the Component inspector click the value field in the label row to activate text entry. Type your new label text. Press Enter to confirm the new label.

Figure 12.27 With Live Preview Enabled active, Flash previews your new label text in the button-component instance on the Stage.

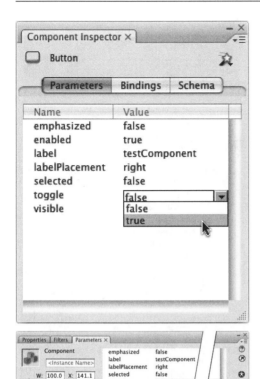

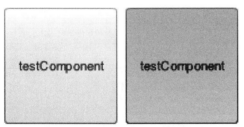

Figure 12.28 When you select the Toggle value in the Parameters section of the Component inspector (top) or in the Parameters tab of the Property inspector (bottom), you can access a menu for choosing a value of true or false.

To set the button component to act as a toggle:

1. Select an instance of a button component on the Stage.

2. In the Component inspector or in the Parameters tab of the Property inspector, set the toggle value to true (**Figure 12.28**). Click anywhere in the row labeled Toggle, to activate the value pop-up menu. Click the value field to open the menu and select true. The button now acts as a toggle, so repeated clicks turn the button on and off (**Figure 12.29**).

✔ Tips

- The Parameters tab of the Property inspector and the Parameters section of the Component inspector also contain a field for the button component's selected value (the choices are true and false). Use the selected value to set a toggle button's initial state (true sets the button to be selected initially; false sets the button to be deselected initially).

- To open the value pop-up menu quickly, double-click the value in the toggle row.

Figure 12.29 When the button-component instance has a toggle value of true, it acts as a toggle button. Here the button-component instances are viewed on the Stage with live preview enabled. The button on the left is deselected, and the one on the right is selected.

The Mystery of ActionScript 3.0 Component Skins

You can edit ActionScript 3.0's User Interface components the way you would edit any movie-clip symbol. Let's look at the Button component as an example.

When you drag an instance of the Button component to the Stage, Flash adds the master Button component and a Component Assets folder to the library of your document. Inside the assets folder is a subfolder containing the component's *skins*. For the Button component, the folder is named ButtonSkins, and it contains all the symbols that make up the Button component's states (**Figure 12.30**). You can modify these underlying symbols, as you would any symbol, to change the look of the component. To modify each skin symbol directly, double-click it in the library; Flash opens the symbol in symbol-editing mode. Alternatively, you can double-click a component instance on the Stage to gain access to all of that component's skins in symbol-editing mode. The top layer of the component symbol's Timeline is labeled assets. Keyframe 2 of the asset layer contains a symbol that itself contains all of the skins that make up the look of the component—in this case, the button states (**Figure 12.31**). Double-click any of the skins to edit it (**Figure 12.32**).

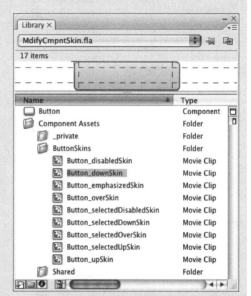

Figure 12.30 The subfolder that has the word *skin* at the end of its name holds all of the symbols that make up a component's look.

To change a button component's look yet retain a good, consistent, user-friendly button, you will probably need to modify every skin that relates to the button component. You may also need to modify other components if you plan to use them within the same application or Web site as your modified button component. The changes you make to the component's skins will affect every instance of the component in your movie.

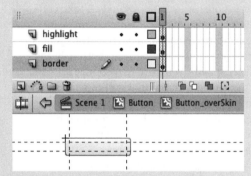

Figure 12.32 Double-click a specific skin to edit it.

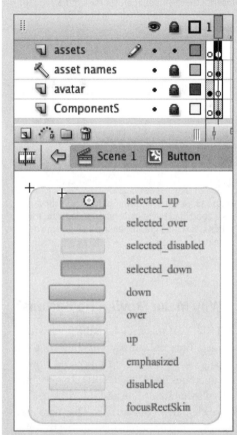

Figure 12.31 Double-clicking a component instance on the Stage opens the master component's skins for editing. The skin symbols are found in keyframe 2 of the assets layer of the master component.

Creating Movie-Clip Buttons

Flash's button symbols and button compo-nents have built-in rules about how the button displays its three states in response to the user's mouse movements. You can take con-trol of that functionality yourself and also create a button that has more than three states by making your own movie-clip button. In the following tasks, you learn to assemble artwork in the Timeline of the movie clip to create a button with four states: _up, _over, _down, and Disabled. To give the movie-clip button even the first level of interactivity, to make the movie clip respond to mouse movements by displaying different states, you must attach ActionScript. You learn to do that in Chapter 13.

To create the button states:

1. In a Flash document where you'd like to use buttons that are movie-clip symbols, choose Insert > New Symbol.

   The Create New Symbol dialog appears.

2. Type a name for your symbol, MovieClipBtn; choose Movie Clip as your symbol type; and click OK (**Figure 12.33**).

   Flash switches to symbol-editing mode. In the Timeline you see one layer, with a keyframe in frame 1.

3. Add two new layers to the Timeline, for a total of three layers.

   Each layer will hold a different type of information for your button (**Figure 12.34**). The top layer will hold ActionScript that tells the movie-clip button what to do; name this layer Actions. The second layer will hold text identifying each keyframe that represents a button state; name this layer Labels. The bottom layer will hold the graphic elements that give the button its look in each state; name this layer ButtonGraphics.

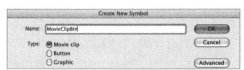

Figure 12.33 The first step in making a movie clip that acts like a button is creating a new symbol. Choose Insert > New Symbol, then set the symbol type to Movie Clip and enter a name in the Create New Symbol dialog.

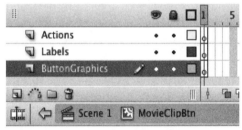

Figure 12.34 When you set up the movie-clip button, it's a good idea to create a separate layer for the actions, text, and graphic elements in the movie clip's Timeline.

Why Make Movie-Clip Buttons?

Flash's button symbols make it easy to create buttons quickly, but they limit you to just three states: Up, Over, and Down. Sometimes you'd like a button to have more states than that. The best interface designs use elements consistently. That way, users know what options are available to them and always know where to find the inter-face elements for carrying out a task. Think of a typical email form, for example. It needs a submit button. Ideally, the but-ton is always present in the same location, but it's inactive (and looks inactive) until all the required fields, such as Send To, have been completed.

When you make your own movie-clip buttons, you can create as many states as you like.

Figure 12.35 A movie-clip button needs a keyframe for each button state. Creating longer keyframe spans helps you to organize the layers visually and makes room for frame labels.

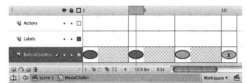

Figure 12.36 With Preview selected as your frame-viewing mode, the Timeline displays all the button-state graphics you've placed in the keyframes of the movie-clip button symbol. Use shades of gray for the graphics in the frame that represents the Disabled state. (For clarity, since this book can't show you colors, the Disabled-state graphic also contains an *X*.)

4. In the Timeline, for all three layers, insert keyframes in frames 4, 7, and 10 (**Figure 12.35**).

The layers that you added already had keyframes at frame 1. You need to add three more keyframes to accommodate all four button states: _up, _over, _down, and Disabled. Spacing out the keyframes makes them easier to deal with and lets you view the frame labels that you create in the following task.

5. In the ButtonGraphics layer, select keyframe 1; using the oval tool, draw an oval centered over the registration mark on the Stage.

This graphic represents the button's _up state. Give the oval a red fill and a black stroke. Make the stroke fairly wide to make the graphic look more buttonlike.

6. Select the oval, and choose Edit > Copy.

7. Select keyframe 4 in the ButtonGraphics layer, and choose Edit > Paste in Place.

This graphic represents the button's _over state. Change the fill color to green.

8. Repeat step 7 for keyframes 7 and 10.

In keyframe 7, change the oval fill to blue to represent the _down state. In keyframe 10, change the fill to a light gray and the stroke to a dark gray to represent the button in its Disabled state (**Figure 12.36**).

✔ Tip

■ There is no need to create a Hit-state keyframe for a movie-clip button. When you add the appropriate ActionScript (see Chapter 13), Flash uses the graphic element(s) in the frames of your movie clip that are displayed as button states to define the hit area.

To assign frame labels to button-state keyframes:

1. Continuing with the file you created in the preceding task, access the Properties tab of the Property inspector.

    If the Property inspector isn't open, choose Window > Properties > Properties.

2. In the Labels layer of the Timeline, select keyframe 1.

3. Click in the Frame Label field in the Frame Properties tab of the Property inspector to activate the field, then type the name of this button state, _up, and press Enter to confirm the name (**Figure 12.37**).

    As you type, the Label Type pop-up menu activates. Leave it at the default setting, Name. When you have finished typing the label, Flash places a red flag icon in any keyframe that has a Name label. If there's enough room in that keyframe span, Flash also displays the label text (**Figure 12.38**).

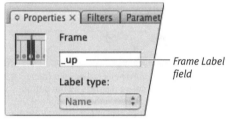

Figure 12.37 Enter the name of the button state as a label for a selected keyframe in the Frame Label field of the Property inspector.

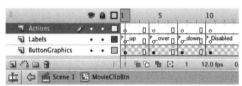

Figure 12.38 A red flag in a keyframe indicates that the frame has a label name. If there are enough in-between frames following the keyframe, Flash displays the frame label as well as the flag (here frames have been added at the end of the sequence so the Disabled label is visible). The labeled keyframes in this movie-clip symbol indicate which button state the keyframe represents.

4. Repeat steps 2 and 3 for keyframes 4, 7, and 10, entering the names _over, _down, and Disabled.

There are two reasons to assign labels to keyframes: First, the label reminds you what is in the keyframe; second, and more important, you can use ActionScript to find a frame with a particular label name and then display that frame. You'll use this technique to create the button's visual feedback in response to mouse movements (see Chapter 13).

5. Return to document-editing mode; for example, click the Back button in the Edit bar.

6. Drag an instance of the MovieClipBtn symbol to the Stage.

This movie clip is ready to be scripted to act like a button and to carry out whatever tasks you set for it with ActionScript. You'll learn to complete the button's interactivity in Chapter 13. To check out your button states, click the Play button in the symbol preview in the Library panel, or choose Control > Test Movie to play the symbol instance. Flash moves through the keyframes and displays each button state in turn.

7. Save this document for use in Chapter 13. Call it MyOwnBtn.fla.

The Mystery of Frame-Label Naming

Flash is sensitive about names. Frame-label names become part of target paths in ActionScripting; therefore, certain characters that have special meaning in scripting—slashes, equals signs, plus signs, and so on—are off-limits for labeling frames. To be safe, use only letters, numbers, and underscore characters; don't even use spaces to make word divisions in frame labels. Use capitalization and the underscore character instead.

✔ Tips

- When you use the labels _up, _down, and _over in your movie clip, ActionScript recognizes these labels as button states and you will have to do minimal scripting to get the button to work (see Chapter 13). To make a more flexible button (for example, one that responds differently to different mouse movements), use other labels. You can use MyUp, MyOver, MyDown, MyDragOut, and so on.

- Another way to add a reminder about what a keyframe does is to add a comment. To enter a frame comment, select the keyframe; in the Frame Label field in the Property inspector, type two slashes (//) followed by your comment text (**Figure 12.39**). Frame labels and frame comments are mutually exclusive: Each keyframe can have one or the other. To work around that limitation, add separate layers for comments and labels. Place keyframes in both layers, and then add comments to one layer and labels to the other, as needed.

- Instead of typing two slashes, just type the comment text. Once the Label Type pop-up menu activates, you can choose Comment. Flash adds the slashes for you.

- Because ActionScript may use frame labels to create interactivity, Flash exports frame-label text with the other movie data when you publish a Flash Player file. Keeping frame labels short helps keep files sizes small. Comments aren't exported with the final movie. You can make comments as long as you like, but remember that the next keyframe in the layer cuts off the comment text. Size your comments to fit the span containing them.

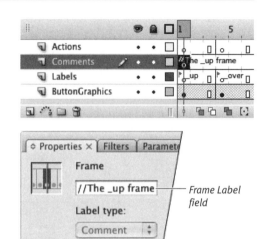

Figure 12.39 The Frame Label field in the Frame Properties tab of the Property inspector can also be used to create comments for a selected keyframe. Type two slashes in the field to begin comment text or choose Comment from the Label Type menu. Comments appear in the Timeline in the keyframe span; long comments are cut off by the next keyframe in the layer.

BASIC INTERACTIVITY

ActionScript Versions

Flash CS3 contains two flavors of ActionScript—version 2.0 (which also includes 1.0) and 3.0. ActionScript 3.0 differs significantly from the previous versions, and you cannot mix versions within one Flash creation. So which version should you use?

ActionScript (AS) 2.0 has some advantages over 3.0 for beginners who need to create only simple interactive Flash content. AS 2.0 lets you think about interactivity in a concrete way and attach scripts to buttons and other objects directly. But once you go beyond applying basic scripting concepts, things quickly become complex.

ActionScript 3.0 has its own advantages. It standardizes the procedures for scripting, making it easier to transfer knowledge from one area of scripting to another. Because AS 3.0 will be the standard going forward, this book focuses exclusively on version 3.0.

To create scripts that use AS 3.0, you must set your Flash document's publish settings to AS 3.0. (You can do that when you create the document initially or in the Publish Settings dialog. You'll learn more about publishing in Chapter 17.)

Adobe Flash CS3 Professional isn't just a tool for creating animated cartoons or blinking ad banners. You can use it to create complex, interactive Web sites for e-learning, e-commerce, and other Internet applications. Flash includes a complete scripting language, ActionScript, for developing interactivity. Scripting and the ActionScript language are complex topics, and teaching them in detail is beyond the scope of this book. However, it is possible to create scripts for a number of common tasks without much difficulty. In this chapter you will write scripts that add basic interactivity to your Flash content, using ActionScript, 3.0. To create scripts, you will enter code in meaningful segments. Some characters—such as opening and closing braces—act as a team to enclose code; both characters must be present for the script to work. To help create accurate code, you will first enter such characters as a pair, then add the code that belongs inside. You will also revise and add to scripts as you go. Other scripting help in this book comes from script figures, which show completed segments of code. For context, when a script figure illustrates specific steps in a task, the text that you enter for those steps appears in boldface; text that is already present from earlier steps appears in regular type. Full scripts are available from the companion Web site to this book (http://www.peachpit.com/title/0321502914).

Touring the Actions Panel

The Actions panel has three work areas: the Script pane, the Actions Toolbox, and the Script Navigator. To access the panel, choose Window > Actions or press Option-F9 (Mac) or F9 (Windows).

The *Script pane* is a text window where you assemble scripts. You can enter actions into the pane manually (it acts like a text editor); and you can also add actions from the Actions Toolbox or the Add pop-up menu. (To access the Add menu, click the plus sign in the toolbar above the Script pane.) You can import scripts or pieces of script from an external file, such as one created with a stand-alone text editor.

The Mystery of ActionScripting

A *script* is a series of commands, or statements, that makes Flash perform tasks at runtime—that is, when a published Flash (SWF) file runs in Flash Player for your end users to view (see Chapter 17).

Creating ActionScript basically means writing text. In Flash's default workflow you write scripts in the Script pane of the Actions Panel, and Flash stores them as part of the FLA file. You can also save scripts as separate ActionScript files (files with the extension .as), and instruct Flash to include them only when publishing. When you save scripts externally, you have the option to edit them in any external text editor.

The Actions panel's Script Assist mode helps you enter code in the Script pane. For beginners, the word *assist* sounds attractive, but the feature requires some knowledge of scripting. Script Assist lets you create code by choosing check boxes or menu items and entering text in special fields. Script Assist ensures that your ActionScript code has the correct syntax (see the sidebar "The Mystery of ActionScript Syntax," later in this chapter). To use Script Assist, however, you must already know the kind of statements you need to create an interactivity.

Previous versions of Flash tried to provide scripting assistance with Behaviors, which create the underlying code for a task you want to accomplish, such as linking to a Web site. The code created by Behaviors is incompatible with ActionScript 3.0. Hence the Behaviors panel is disabled when you choose ActionScript 3.0 as the scripting language for your document.

The best way to create interactivity in Flash is to write the necessary scripts on your own. As scary as this proposition may seem to those who have never scripted before, it is actually less work than learning how to use the tools that Flash provides to help you write code. The exercises in this book create scripts that carry out simple tasks in Flash, such as setting up buttons that start and stop playback of a movie. These techniques are inappropriate for developing an online store or a complex e-learning course. But they may be all you need to let your end users start, stop, and replay an animated cartoon; select a favorite scene to view; or link to a Web page. And with any luck, they'll whet your appetite for learning more about ActionScript.

The *Actions Toolbox* contains most of the words (actions) that make up the ActionScript language. These pieces of code appear in hierarchical lists; click one of the folder-like icons to view the contents of a category. Double-click an action to add it to the Script pane. You can also drag items from the Actions Toolbox to the Script pane. (The list of ActionScript actions also appears in the Add menu.)

The *Script Navigator* helps you locate and maneuver through the scripts in your movie. This feature is most useful when you've used a large number of frame scripts in keyframes throughout the Timeline. **Figure 13.1** shows the elements of the Actions panel.

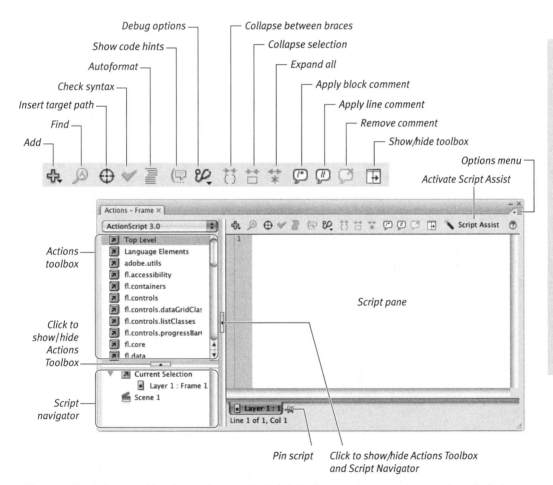

Figure 13.1 The Actions panel has three main areas: the Actions Toolbox, where you can choose actions; the Script Navigator, where Flash displays the elements in your movie that have scripts attached; and the Script pane, where Flash assembles the ActionScript.

Customizing the Actions Panel

You can modify the way the Actions panel displays to suit your taste or convenience. For example, you can resize the panel and its panes or collapse panes completely. You can customize the way scripts appear by choosing settings for font and size; highlighting script elements in different colors; and controlling the number of spaces Flash uses to indent with each tab you type. You can also turn code hints on or off.

To set preferences for the Actions panel:

1. Choose Flash > Preferences (Mac) or Edit Preferences (Windows).

   or

   From the options menu in the top-right corner of the Actions panel, choose Preferences.

   The Preferences dialog appears.

2. In the Category list, select ActionScript.

   The settings for working with statements in the Script pane of the Actions panel appear in the main window of the Preferences dialog (**Figure 13.2**).

3. To get scripting help from code hints, in the Editing section, select the Code Hints check box (**Figure 13.3**).

   Move the Delay slider to set the amount of time Flash waits before displaying the hint as you type directly in the Script pane.

Figure 13.2 In the Preferences dialog, choose the ActionScript category to access settings for customizing the way Flash displays your scripts.

Figure 13.3 To have Flash display code hints, select the Code Hints check box. To make hints appear more quickly, drag the Delay slider farther to the left.

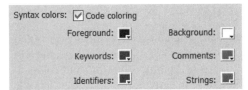

Figure 13.4 Activate syntax coloring by selecting the Code Coloring check box in the Syntax Colors section of the ActionScript category of the Preferences dialog. Change the colors to make more of a distinction between scripting "words," to get a feel for ActionScript's parts of speech.

4. To choose the font for writing scripts, in the Font section, do the following:

▲ From the pop-up menu of installed fonts, choose a font.

▲ From the pop-up menu of sizes, choose a font size.

The Actions panel can display scripts in text as small as 8 points and as large as 72 points.

5. To color-code script items, in the Syntax Colors section, select the Code Coloring check box (**Figure 13.4**).

Using the color controls to access a pop-up set of swatches, choose new colors for any of the following:

Foreground. The basic text color for your scripts.

Keywords. Words reserved for special purposes in ActionScript.

continues on next page

What Is Interactivity?

By default, a published Flash file plays through its scenes and frames sequentially. The movie opens with scene 1, plays all those frames in order, moves to scene 2, plays those frames, and so on. Sometimes that's appropriate; sometimes it's not.

Imagine an online training course where you want the same five frames of general instructions to appear before each section of the course. You can make those frames a separate scene and then duplicate the scene so it appears repeatedly between other scenes containing the training sections. But duplicating scenes increases file size, slows the performance of your published course, and makes it harder to edit later. A more efficient method is to create one scene containing the instructions and direct Flash to repeat that scene when each training section ends. Also, you may want the users taking your course to interact with the content: clicking buttons, dragging elements, or entering text to answer quiz questions, for example. And you may want the course to interact with the user, summarizing the quiz score. These are examples of interactivity in Flash.

To achieve this type of interactivity, you must create a script that directs the playback of your published Flash content, using ActionScript.

Identifiers. The names of things, such as objects, variables, and functions, that are built into ActionScript.

Background. The color against which your script displays in the Script pane.

Comments. Text that Flash ignores when it reads the script, used to make notes about what's going on in the script.

Strings. Series of characters (letters, numbers, and punctuation marks) that are enclosed within quotation marks.

6. Click OK.

Flash applies your preferences settings immediately.

✔ Tips

■ Flash's default settings for keywords and identifiers are similar shades of blue. Try setting them to wildly different colors—say, pink and orange. This technique will help you learn to recognize these different parts of ActionScript speech as they're used in the scripts you create.

■ Code hints work like tool tips within the Actions panel when Script Assist isn't active. With code hints turned on, you can make the Actions panel display certain types of scripting information in a tool-tip–type box or drop-down menu. Position the insertion point to the right of a dot (a period character) or an opening parenthesis in the Script pane, and then click the Show Code Hints button. If you enable code hints in the ActionScript Preferences, the hints appear automatically when you type a period, a colon, or an opening parenthesis in the right context.

Two Styles of Scripting

ActionScript 3.0 lets you work in two scripting styles: you can create scripts that rely on *frame actions* and scripts that rely on *custom classes*. Each style stores the ActionScript code differently. For the tasks in this book, you'll create frame-action scripts, where code is attached to keyframes and stored in the FLA file. Scripts that rely on custom classes require that you create the code in external AS files.

You create frame actions by selecting a keyframe, then opening the Actions Panel and entering the script. In the exported movie, when the playhead reaches the keyframe that contains the script, Flash carries out the script's instructions. These instructions might be to control the Timeline directly (for example, pausing playback of the movie), to set up interactivity for buttons (for example, telling Flash what to do when someone clicks a particular button), or to change the properties of objects located in that keyframe (for example, to move a symbol instance across the Stage).

Scripting with custom classes is similar to using symbols in the library. Creating or even editing classes is beyond the scope of this book. Yet by doing the tasks in earlier chapters, you have already interacted with some of Flash's built-in classes, such as Button and MovieClip. Advanced scripters can create and edit custom classes using the ActionScript editor or an external text editor.

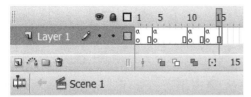

Figure 13.5 Keyframes that contain actions display the letter *a* in the Timeline.

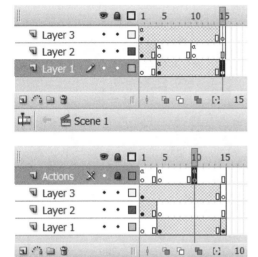

Figure 13.6 When you assign actions to many layers (top), it's harder to find them, and you may accidentally assign actions to the same frame number on different layers. Adding a separate layer for actions (bottom) makes it easy to find them all and to see whether a certain frame contains an action.

- It's useful to create separate layers for labels and sounds as well as for actions. Keeping these three types of layers together at the top of the Timeline makes it easy to find the nongraphical information they contain.

Organizing Frame Actions

A little letter *a* in the Timeline indicates a keyframe that has actions attached (**Figure 13.5**). Can you imagine scrolling through dozens—or hundreds—of layers, looking for the letter *a* when you want to edit the actions in your document? That's a recipe for eyestrain. And more than that, it's a recipe for disaster if you need (or someone else needs) to change the ActionScript later; it's difficult to remember (or guess) where the frame actions are lurking. It's a good idea to put all your frame actions in their own layer.

Restricting frame actions to their own layer also prevents you from accidentally putting actions in keyframes in two different layers for the same frame number, which can cause problems if you reorder the layers.

To create a separate layer for frame actions:

1. Open a Flash document.

2. In the Timeline, add a new layer.
   (For detailed instructions on adding layers, see Chapter 6.)

3. Rename the layer Actions.

4. Drag the layer to the top of the Timeline.
   Keeping the Actions layer near the top of the Timeline makes it easier to find actions when you need to modify or add to them (**Figure 13.6**).

✔ Tips

- To prevent yourself from adding graphic elements to the Actions layer accidentally, lock it (by clicking the bullet in the padlock column). Locking keeps you from making changes in the elements on the Stage for that layer, but it doesn't prevent you from adding actions to keyframes.

Adding Frame Actions

Some of the most basic scripting tasks involve controlling movie playback: making your movie stop and start and jump from place to place. By default, a movie begins running at playback; you can change that in the Publish Settings (see Chapter 17), but you can also do it with actions.

To make your first script in Flash, set up a multiframe document that has identifying text in each frame. Then add a `stop` action to keyframe 1, to make the movie pause on the first frame at playback. Save this file as a template for use in other scripting tasks.

To set up a document for testing frame actions:

1. Create a Flash document with two layers: Actions and Frames.

2. In the Actions layer, add in-between frames in frames 2–5; there is a keyframe in the first frame by default.

3. In the Frames layer, create keyframes in frames 2–5; there is a keyframe in the first frame by default.

4. On the Stage, for each keyframe, add text that identifies the frame number (Frame 1, Frame 2, and so on).

   Your document should look like **Figure 13.7**.

To begin scripting by adding comments:

1. Continuing with the document you created in the preceding task, in the Actions layer, select keyframe 1.

2. Access the Actions panel. (If the panel isn't open, choose Window > Actions.)

   The name Actions-Frame appears in the title bar of the Actions panel.

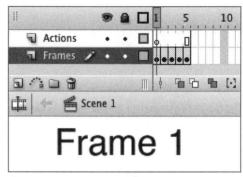

Figure 13.7 To test frame actions—actions that instruct Flash to move to a specific frame or to start and stop playback—it's useful to have a document that identifies each frame. That way, you can see the results of your scripts easily.

Figure 13.8 Open the options menu in the Actions panel to make sure that line numbering and word wrap are active (if not, select them to activate them). Visible line numbers make it easier to keep your place while scripting; word wrap makes it easier to view scripts, as it forces them to stay within the visible Script pane area.

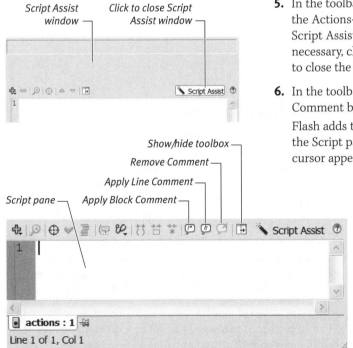

Figure 13.9 The toolbar of the Actions panel contains a number of tools for working with scripts, including Script Assist. Deselect the Script Assist button to close the Script Assist window so that you can type directly in the Script pane.

3. From the options menu, in the upper-right corner of the Actions-Frame panel, make sure Line Numbers has a check mark indicating it's active (the default setting) (**Figure 13.8**). If Line Numbers is inactive, select it.

Visible line numbers make it easier to keep your place as you script.

4. From the options menu, make sure Word Wrap has a check mark indicating it is active (the default setting). If Word Wrap is inactive, select it.

Word Wrap forces the lines of your script to break to fit within the Script pane. Such line breaks aren't meaningful in the script itself; the ActionScript syntax tells Flash where the meaningful divisions in script text occur (see the sidebar "The Mystery of ActionScript Syntax," later in this chapter).

5. In the toolbar above the Script pane of the Actions-Frame panel, make sure that Script Assist is inactive (**Figure 13.9**). If necessary, click the Script Assist button to close the Script Assist window.

6. In the toolbar, click the Apply Line Comment button.

Flash adds two slashes (//) to line 1 of the Script pane. The blinking I-beam cursor appears at the end of the line.

continues on next page

7. Type Pause the movie on frame 1 (**Figure 13.10**).

Your comment is added to the Script pane. With word wrap turned on, Flash wraps your text to fit in the Script Pane; in the real script, the comment is just one line.

Figure 13.10 The two slashes indicate the beginning of a comment. When you add a comment using the Insert Line Comment button, Flash adds slashes to the script automatically.

To set the movie to pause at playback:

1. Continuing with the document you created in the preceding task, position the cursor at the end of line 1 (your comment line), and press Enter.

Flash creates line 2 in the Script pane.

Figure 13.11 The stop(); action in line 2 sets the movie to be paused at runtime.

2. To add an action that pauses the Timeline, type stop();

The new action appears in line 2 in the Script pane; the word *stop* is highlighted in blue (**Figure 13.11**).

3. Save the document as a template for future use; name it FrameActionsMaster.

(For detailed instructions about saving documents as templates, see Chapter 1.)

4. Close the document.

About Comment Lines

The double slash is known as a *comment delimiter;* the delimiter sets the boundaries of a comment within a script. Flash ignores any text between the two slashes and the next paragraph return for the purposes of scripting. When compiling the script for playback, Flash leaves that text out of the final file, so your comments will not increase the SWF file size. It's a good idea to write notes about your script to remind yourself what you intend the script to do. Comments will also help anyone who needs to modify your script later.

For long comments, a *multiline delimiter* will exclude everything between the opening and closing delimiters from the script. Click the Apply Block Comment button in the toolbar above the Script pane to add a multiline comment to your script. A multiline comment begins with a slash followed by an asterisk (/*) and ends with an asterisk followed by a slash (*/).

When you're testing long scripts or trying different ways to achieve your scripting task, it can be useful to temporarily remove part of the script to see what happens. Comment delimiters let you do this quickly without deleting any code. If you want to block out a large section of the script temporarily, use the /* and */ delimiters.

The Mystery of ActionScript Syntax

ActionScript has its own rules, which are analogous to the rules of grammar and spelling in English. These rules, called *syntax,* govern such things as word order, capitalization, and punctuation of action statements. The following list briefly describes six crucial ActionScript punctuation marks that you'll use in writing scripts.

Dot (.). ActionScript uses *dot syntax,* meaning that periods act as links between objects and the *properties* (characteristics) and *methods* (behaviors) applied to them. In the statement

```
myClip.nextFrame();
```

the *dot* (the period) links the object (a movie-clip named `myClip`) with the method (`nextFrame`) that moves the playhead to the next frame in the Timeline. ActionScript also uses the dot in target paths (see the sidebar "The Mystery of Target Paths," later in this chapter).

Semicolon (;). A semicolon indicates the end of a statement. The semicolon isn't required—Flash interprets the end of the line of statements correctly without it—but including it is good scripting practice. The semicolon also acts as a required separator in some action statements.

Colon (:). When you first set up a variable (a container for content that changes), a colon separates the text that is the name of a variable from the text that defines what type of variable it is.

```
var myName:String;
```

A colon also separates the name of a method from its type.

Braces ({}). Braces set off ActionScript statements that belong together. For example, a set of actions that are supposed to take place after `function greeting()` must be set off by braces. Note that the action statements within braces can require their own beginning and ending braces. The opening and closing braces must pair up evenly. Pay close attention to where you're adding statements and braces within the Script pane to ensure that you group the actions as you intend.

Parentheses (()). Parentheses group the arguments that apply to a particular statement—defining the scene and frame in a `goto` action, for example. Parentheses also let you group operations, such as mathematical calculations, so that they take place in the right order.

Brackets ([ ]). Scripting frequently involves working with *arrays,* lists of similar elements. Placing a list inside brackets defines it as an array.

Programming Buttons with Frame Scripts

As you learned in the previous chapter, Flash's button symbols and button components have certain actions built in. By default, when you move the mouse into the button area, Flash jumps to the Over frame; when you click the button, Flash takes you to the Down frame. To make the button carry out a task or to refine the way a button responds to a user's mouse movements, you attach ActionScript to a keyframe and target an instance of a button symbol or button component.

To add a button to be controlled by a frame script:

1. Using the FrameActionsMaster template you created earlier in this chapter, open a new document (for details on opening new documents from templates, see Chapter 1).

2. In the Timeline, add a new layer anywhere below the Actions layer; name the new layer Buttons.

   Frame 1 of the new layer is a keyframe; frames 2–5 are in-between frames. Any items you place on this layer will be visible throughout the five-frame movie (**Figure 13.12**).

3. With the Buttons layer selected, place an instance of a button symbol on the Stage (**Figure 13.13**).

   Follow the techniques in Chapter 12 to create a new button symbol, or use one from the Common Library of buttons. (To access this library, choose Window > Common Libraries > Buttons.) Drag a button-symbol instance from the library to the Stage.

4. To name the button instance, access the Properties tab of the Property inspector and type a name in the Instance name field—for example, enterBtn (**Figure 13.14**).

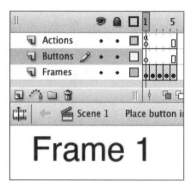

Figure 13.12 To practice with button actions, create a movie with identifying text and separate layers for buttons and actions. Add in-between frames as needed so that all the layers are the same length.

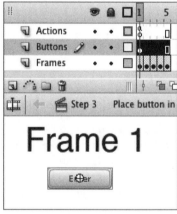

Figure 13.13 In-between frames extend the Buttons layer to the match the length of the other layers; the button symbol in keyframe 1 will be visible throughout the movie, although the identifying text from the Frames layer will change.

Instance Name field

Figure 13.14 Select the button symbol on the Stage, and enter a name in the Instance Name field in the Properties tab of the Property inspector.

Get into the habit of naming each instance of a symbol in your document. For ActionScript to be able to control a symbol, the symbol must have a unique instance name.

5. Save your file (for example, by choosing File > Save).

✔ **Tip**

■ Scripting is a complex process, often involving trial and error. As you create scripts, you may wish you could go back to a point where you know everything works. The Save As command makes that easier. Once you've set up your objects on the Stage and you're ready to add code, choose File > Save As. Each time you complete a segment of code that works the way you want, choose Save As again. Add a number, a letter, or an abbreviated description to the filename to make it easy to identify which version contains which completed work.

The Mechanics of Code Hints

How do code hints work? As you type text in the Script pane of the Actions panel, Flash tries to guess what you're about to script and help you out. Let's look at an example:

In line 1 of your script you enter the comment

`// SimpleButton startLesson;`

In subsequent lines of the script, whenever you type that instance name (`startLesson`) followed by a period (`.`), a code-hint window opens listing the actions and properties available for button symbols (**Figure 13.15**).

You can use the window's scroll bars (or the up- and down-arrow keys on your keyboard) to navigate the list of actions and properties. Select the item you want and press Enter to add it to your script. Or you can continue typing to have Flash autocomplete your code: the code-hint window narrows in on an action or property according to the letters you type. When the action or property you want is highlighted, press Enter. Flash autocompletes that piece of code in your script. You can override autocompleting by continuing to type manually in the Script pane, but autocompleting helps you avoid typos and speed the coding process.

continues on next page

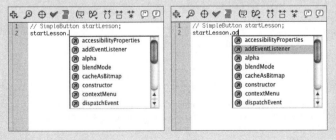

Figure 13.15 When your script contains a comment line associating an instance name with a type of object (here, line 1), a code-hint window opens whenever you type a period (.) following that instance name in the Script pane (left). As you continue typing characters, the code-hint window attempts to autocomplete your code (right).

PROGRAMMING BUTTONS WITH FRAME SCRIPTS

373

To control a button using a frame script:

1. Continuing with the file that you created in the preceding task, make sure that the Actions panel is open and that code hints are enabled in Preferences (see the section "Customizing the Actions Panel," earlier in this chapter).

2. In the Actions layer, select keyframe 1.

   The Script pane of the Actions panel displays the code you already created; line 1 displays a comment; line 2 displays the stop(); action.

The Mechanics of Code Hints *continued*

When you use code hints to automate entry of an action that requires a parameter, Flash automatically adds an open parenthesis to your script and brings up another type of code hint, a parameter hint (**Figure 13.16**). (If you override autocompleting, the parameter hint appears after you type an opening parenthesis in the Script pane.) The parameter hint, which acts something like a tool tip, displays all possible parameters for the action you just entered. Parameter hints don't autocomplete code in the Script pane, but they can help you remember which parameters you need. Sometimes the same action is available for different objects; for example, Buttons and MovieClips have addEventListener. In that case, you can use the Previous and Next arrows on the left side of the window to scroll through the parameter hints until they match the object you script. Parameter hints also help you see which category folder in the Actions Toolbox contains the code you're looking for; each parameter hint begins with the path to the category folder containing the action you entered.

If you close a code-hint window by accident, or you later want to change your selection, you can open the window by placing your cursor to the right of a period or open parenthesis and clicking the Code Hint button in the toolbar above the Script pane. You can also use the keyboard shortcut Option-spacebar (Mac) or Ctrl-spacebar (Windows).

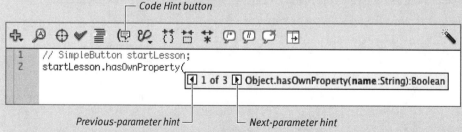

Figure 13.16 The parameter hint appears after you type an open parenthesis (or after you use code hints to automate adding an action or property that takes a parameter). If there are multiple parameter possibilities, use the Previous and Next buttons to scroll the list.

Figure 13.17 A code-hint comment needs a separate line in the Script pane. Position the cursor at the very end of line 2, press Enter, and Flash moves the cursor to line 3, where you can start entering the comment code.

Script 13.1 Defining a code-hint comment.

```
1  //Pause the movie on frame 1
2  stop();
3  // code-hint comments
4  // SimpleButton enterBtn;
```

Script 13.2 Defining the event handler.

```
3  // code-hint comments
4  // SimpleButton enterBtn;
5  // event handlers
6  function handleClick( pEvent:MouseEvent
   ):void
7  {
8  }
```

Wide Scripts—Narrow Columns

A single line of ActionScript can be quite long. You can resize the Script pane of Flash's Actions panel so that a lot of code fits on one line, but we can't resize the columns in this book. That means for longer lines of code, the text has to wrap. In the Script figures, such as Script 13.2, the line numbers make it clear where you should type a return to begin a new line. In the numbered steps of a task, we'll use a small right arrow to indicate code that runs over to a new line simply because the column is too narrow. You would enter the following code, for example, as a single line of script, pressing the Return key only after the word void.

```
function handleClick
→ ( pEvent:MouseEvent ):void
```

3. To add a code-hint comment, do the following:

▲ To start a new line, place the cursor at the end of line 2—after the stop(); action—and press Enter. Flash adds line 3 to the Script pane (**Figure 13.17**).

▲ In lines 3 and 4 type

```
// Code-hint comments
// SimpleButton enterBtn;
```

If you named the button instance something other than enterBtn, type that name instead. (**Script 13.1**).

4. To create the event-handler function, do the following:

▲ With the cursor at the end of line 4, press Enter to create a new line.

▲ In lines 5–8 type

```
// event handlers
function handleClick(
→ pEvent:MouseEvent ):void
{
}
```

After you type the colon (:), a code-hint window opens. When the code you're entering highlights, press Enter to complete the word, or keep typing to complete it manually. The code inside the parentheses, called a *parameter,* provides information about where the event comes from (pEvent) and what kind of event it is (MouseEvent); a colon separates these two pieces of information (**Script 13.2**). (To learn more about the construction of functions, see "The Mystery of Functions," later in this chapter).

continues on next page

5. To make sure the event is triggered by enterBtn:

▲ Position the pointer at the end of line 7 (after the opening brace), and press Enter to create a new line 8.

Flash indents line 8 in the Script pane to visually remind you that this code is inside the braces and is part of the function.

▲ In lines 8–10 type

```
if( pEvent.target == enterBtn )
{
}
```

After you type the opening parenthesis, a code-hint window opens; just keep typing. You have just created what's known as a *conditional statement* (see the sidebar, "The Mystery of the If Statement," later in this chapter). Flash executes the code within the braces only if the specified condition is met. In this case you are checking whether the event's target matches the button instance you want to control with your script (enterBtn) (**Script 13.3**).

6. Position the pointer at the end of line 9 (after the opening brace), press Enter to create a new line, and then in lines 10 and 11 type

```
// handle the event
nextFrame();
```

Flash uses double indents in lines 10 and 11 to visually remind you that this code is inside the braces and is part of the if statement

The nextFrame(); action will advance the playhead by one frame (**Script 13.4**).

Script 13.3 Making sure the event was triggered by enterBtn.

```
 6  function handleClick( pEvent:MouseEvent
    ):void
 7  {
 8    if( pEvent.target == enterBtn )
 9    {
10    }
11  }
```

Script 13.4 The completed event handler.

```
 1  //Pause the movie on frame 1
 2  stop();
 3  // code-hint comments
 4  // SimpleButton enterBtn;
 5  // event handlers
 6  function handleClick( pEvent:MouseEvent
    ):void
 7  {
 8    if( pEvent.target == enterBtn )
 9    {
10      // handle the event
11      nextFrame();
12    }
13  }
```

Figure 13.18 As you enter code in the script pane, the code-hint window offers possible code items you might want. When the item you want appears highlighted, press Enter, and it gets added to the Script pane.

Script 13.5 The completed frame script for controlling a button (this script becomes part of the ButtonActionsMaster template).

```
1  //Pause the movie on frame 1
2  stop();
3  // code-hint comments
4  // SimpleButton enterBtn;
5  // event handlers
6  function handleClick( pEvent:MouseEvent
   ):void
7  {
8    if( pEvent.target == enterBtn )
9    {
10     // handle the event
11     nextFrame();
12   }
13 }
14 // register events
15 enterBtn.addEventListener(
   MouseEvent.CLICK, handleClick );
```

7. To start registering the event, do the following:

Place the cursor at the end of line 13, and press Enter to create a new line, and then in lines 14 and 15 type

```
// register events
enterBtn.addEventListener();
```

After you type the period, a code-hint window opens showing a list of action statements (**Figure 13.18**). As you type more characters, the statements in the list that start with those characters highlight; after you type *ad*, the statement addEventListener highlights. Press Enter (or double-click the statement) as soon as the desired statement highlights. Flash adds addEventListener(to the script and opens another code-hint window. Ignore the second window and complete the statement by typing); .

8. To finish registering the event, do the following:

▲ In line 15, position the cursor within the parenthesis.

▲ type

MouseEvent.CLICK, handleClick

The code MouseEvent.CLICK tells Flash which of the possible button events you want your event handler to listen for (see the sidebar "The Anatomy of a MouseEvent," later in this chapter).

The code handleClick points to the event-handler function you created in the preceding steps; it must match what you typed after the keyword function in line 6.

You just programmed your first button event. The completed script should look like **Script 13.5**. It's time to see your work in action.

continues on next page

9. Select Control > Test Movie.

Flash publishes the movie and opens the SWF file in Flash Player. You see the text *Frame 1* and a button. Click the button, and the text *Frame 2* appears. Flash has moved the playhead to frame 2 in response to your clicking the button, just as you requested via ActionScript. Each click of the button moves the playhead forward one frame until the playhead reaches frame 5.

10. Save your document as a template for use throughout this chapter, and name it ButtonActionsMaster.

(For detailed instructions about saving documents as templates, see Chapter 1.)

11. Close the document.

✔ Tips

- If you don't get the expected result when you test the movie, access the Compiler Errors window (if it's not open, choose Window > Compiler Errors) and see if it shows any errors. Close the test-movie window and make sure the code you entered exactly matches Script 13.5, and then try again. Keep a particular eye out for periods, colons, semicolons, braces, and parentheses. For more details about testing your scripting work, see the section "Previewing Actions at Work," later in this chapter.

- The code-hint window doesn't stop you from typing, but it ensures that the actions you enter are spelled correctly. When the code-hint window appears, you can continue entering text by hand.

- You just created a template with a script for programming buttons. You can use this script over and over again, modifying it to meet different situations as needed.

The Anatomy of a MouseEvent

There are several ways users can interact with a button in a Flash movie. They can move the mouse into and out of the active area of a button, they can click and release inside the active area, they can click inside the active area and while still holding down the mouse button roll outside the area, and so on. The code `MouseEvent.CLICK` describes one specific button event. The `MouseEvent` part tells Flash that the event to watch for is generated by an input device (like a mouse or a graphics pen); the `CLICK` part tells Flash to notice when the user presses and then releases inside the active area of a button.

The Mystery of Event Handlers

In ActionScript as in English, the term *event* refers to something that happens, such as a user clicking a button. An *event handler* is a specific type of action statement, called a *function*, that describes what should happen in your Flash creation when a specific event occurs.

Events can be generated by humans or by the internal workings of your Flash creations. This chapter focuses on *user interactions*, events generated by people viewing and using your Flash content. (Some common user events are clicking a button, entering text, or selecting a check box.) Events not generated by users also affect the way a Flash movie runs, and you can write scripts that respond to such events. (Some common nonuser events are a movie finishing loading onto the user's computer or the playhead advancing to the next frame.)

Scripting for Interactivity

To make your Flash creation respond to a specific user interaction (event), you must create a script that does two things: *register to receive the event* created by that interaction and *handle the event*. Handling an event means creating a routine for Flash to use only after the event takes place—the *event handler*. Registering an event means writing a script that connects the object that triggers the event (for example, a button) with the event handler.

Code for handling an event takes the following format:

```
function handleEvent( event )
{
  if( event.target == eventSource )
  {
    // handle event...
  }
}
```

The event-handler function named `handleEvent` waits for an event to happen. If the event is triggered by the specified `eventSource`, the event handler will carry out its instructions. `handleEvent` represents the name you'll create for this specific situation. The `eventSource` might be a button instance, a button component, or a movie-clip instance (for more technical details, see the sidebars "The Mystery of Functions" and "The Mystery of the If Statement," later in this chapter).

Code for registering for an event takes the format

```
eventSource.addEventListener( eventName, handleEvent );
```

Here `eventSource` represents the object that will be the source of the event. `eventName` represents the event itself; the precise code depends on the source object; a `click` event, for example, can be generated by a button instance. (The code `eventName` represents actions for the objects you'll work with in this chapter and are built into ActionScript 3.0.) Finally, `handleEvent` represents the function you created for handling the event.

PROGRAMMING BUTTONS WITH FRAME SCRIPTS

The Mystery of Instance Names and Code Hints

The name of an *instance* of an object on the Stage is an identifier that may wind up as part of a script. To prevent scripting problems, make sure instance names contain no spaces or characters that have special meaning in ActionScript—for example, avoid slashes or the equals sign. To be safe, use only letters, numbers, and underscore characters. Ideally, instance names should start with a lowercase letter.

When you name instances of button symbols, movie-clip symbols, and text fields, you can give Flash extra information about the object being named. Flash uses that information to assist you—giving you *code hints* as you type in the Actions panel.

There are two ways to activate the code-hint feature for specific objects. One is to name instances with an identifying suffix. To name button instances to take advantage of code hints, use the suffix _btn; for movie clips use _mc; and for text fields use _txt.

The other way is to add a comment line that creates a connection between an *identifier* (a script element that describes the type of object) and the instance name you've created for that object on the Stage. To add a comment line that identifies the instance, in the Script pane, insert two slashes, then the identifier for the type of object, then the instance name you've created for the object. For example, the comment lines

```
// SimpleButton startLesson;
// MovieClip circle;
// TextField message;
```

identify a button instance named startLesson, a movie-clip instance named circle, and a text field named message.

The tasks in this chapter use the comment-line method, as it is the preferred convention in AS 3.0.

The Mystery of the If Statement

Often when you create Flash content, you want one thing to happen under certain conditions, and something else to happen if those conditions aren't met. Your script needs to take different paths depending on the state of affairs.

One way to accomplish this is by using the *if statement,* which takes this format:

```
if( condition )
{
   action();
}
```

continues on next page

PROGRAMMING BUTTONS WITH FRAME SCRIPTS

The Mystery of the If Statement *continued*

Here's a real-world example:

```
if( numLives == 0 )
{
  gotoAndStop( "gameOver" );
}
```

An if statement consists of the keyword if, followed by an opening parenthesis, then a condition that is either true or false, a closing parenthesis, and then a list of statements between braces. These statements only execute if the condition is true.

A condition could be a comparison. You might, for example, compare two items to see if they are equal or if the first is greater than the second. To script a comparison, you use an *operator* (a symbol or symbols) that describes the comparison. In ActionScript, the operator used to check for equality consists of two equal signs (==). ActionScript uses a single equals sign (=) to assign a value (for example, to say a rectangle's width is 1 inch), never to compare.

The most common, and important, comparison operators are as follows:

> greater than

>= greater than or equal to

< less than

<= less than or equal to

!= not equal to

When you check for a condition, you may want to run one block of code when the condition is met, and a different block of code when it's not. You could write two separate if statements or use an if-else statement.

If-else statements take the format

```
if( condition )
{
  // code
}
else
{
  // other code
}
```

Finally, it is also possible to link up multiple conditions in an if-else-if-else statement using the following format:

```
if( foodInFridge )
{
  // eat at home
}
else if( haveMoney )
{
  // go out
}
else
{
  // call a friend
}
```

The Mystery of Functions

A *function* groups a number of actions together under a single name. When the function name appears in a script, Flash executes that group of actions. The basic format looks like this:

```
function functionName():Type
{
   // function code
}
```

The code block always starts with the *keyword* function. Next comes the function's name, represented here by functionName. (You get to create your function name; make it descriptive.) Immediately following the function's name is a pair of parentheses.

Next comes a colon (:), which separates the function's name from its *type*. In this example, the code for type is represented by Type. The type defines what kind of result the function will have. To understand the purpose of type, imagine a restaurant-tip calculator; it needs to come up with numbers in the result (as opposed to letters, for example). A tip-calculator function would have Number as the type. The most common type for functions, however, is void, meaning "there is no result." Actions that control Timeline playback, for example, have void as the type.

The braces ({}) enclose code that describes what the function actually does. Flash carries out the instructions within those braces only when certain conditions are met; in our example, this is when a user clicks the calculate-tip button.

Quite often, a function needs more information to operate; parameters convey that information. The tip-calculator function needs to know the cost of the meal. When you set up a function that requires parameters, the format changes slightly:

```
function functionName( param:Type, nextParam:Type ):Type
{
   // code
}
```

When a function has multiple parameters, the parameter names still go between the parentheses after the function name, but you must separate the names with commas.

Each parameter also has a type, just as the function has one.

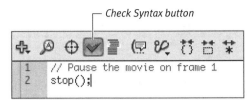

Check Syntax button

Figure 13.19 Click the Check Syntax button in the Actions panel to have Flash help you find syntax errors in your code.

Previewing Actions at Work

To see your scripts in action, you need to view the movie in Flash Player. You can do this by publishing the movie (see Chapter 17) or by using one of the test modes. *Test mode* is an abbreviated form of publishing a movie while still working in the authoring environment. To preview and test your scripts safely, follow a three-step procedure: (1) save your work; (2) check the script's syntax; and (3) test the movie.

To check the script's syntax:

1. With the document containing your script open, select the keyframe with the script you want to check, to view it in the Script pane of the Actions panel.

2. In the toolbar above the Script pane, click the Check Syntax button (the check mark icon), or press Option-T (Mac) or Ctrl-T (Windows) (**Figure 13.19**).

   Flash runs its compiler (see the sidebar "What is a Compiler?" later in this chapter) to check the selected code for errors of syntax (see the sidebar "The Mystery of ActionScript Syntax," earlier in this chapter). Flash displays a syntax-check-results dialog, with an OK button. If there are errors, Flash also opens the Compiler Errors panel.

   continues on next page

3. If the selected code contains no errors, click OK to close the syntax-check-results dialog.

or

If the selected code contains errors, click OK to close the syntax-check-results dialog, and do any of the following:

▲ Visually review the code in the Script pane and correct the errors you find.

▲ In the Compiler Errors panel, select the error and press the Go to Source button (**Figure 13.20**). Flash opens the Actions panel and highlights the line where the error occurred. Correct the error and repeat step 2.

Flash generally refuses to run scripts with errors; you need to correct them before you move on.

✔ Tips

■ Common scripting errors include missing, misplaced, or doubled commas, colons, parentheses, braces, and semicolons. Paired items, such as parentheses and braces, must have equal numbers of opening and closing elements, and they must be nested correctly (see the sidebar "The Mystery of ActionScript Syntax," earlier in this chapter).

■ A script that produces no errors doesn't necessarily do what you want it to do. The syntax check determines if your script follows the rules, but the compiler doesn't check the logic, and doesn't know what you intend the script to do.

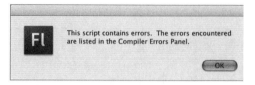

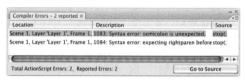

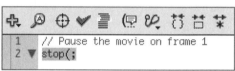

Figure 13.20 When the syntax check finds errors, a dialog informs you, and the Compiler Errors panel opens showing details about the errors in your script. Select the error in the panel and click the Go to Source button to go directly to the error in the Script pane of the Actions panel.

What Is a Compiler?

ActionScript is a computer language that lets scripters write instructions for the Flash Player to execute. Although it takes time to learn the language, humans can read it. A computer's CPU, however, works only with 0's and 1's; it can't read ActionScript directly. A *compiler* translates code written in a computer language into instructions that the processing unit can read. In the case of Flash, ActionScript is translated into compact byte-code that Flash Player understands.

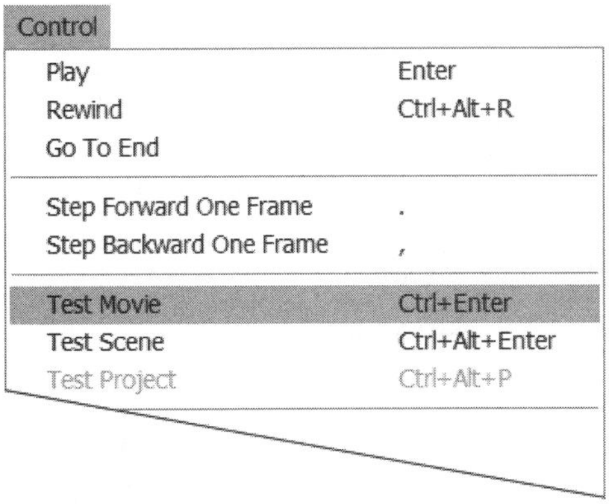

Control	
Play	Enter
Rewind	Ctrl+Alt+R
Go To End	
Step Forward One Frame	.
Step Backward One Frame	,
Test Movie	Ctrl+Enter
Test Scene	Ctrl+Alt+Enter
Test Project	Ctrl+Alt+P

Figure 13.21 To test the full animation and interactivity of ActionScript scripts, you must export your movie—for example, by choosing Control > Test Movie.

- When you choose Control > Test Scene, Flash appends the scene name and the .swf extension to the file, when it creates the Player file. This situation can make the filename exceed the number of allowable characters. If Test Movie worked fine with your file, but Test Scene brings up the warning dialog, try shortening the scene name.

- To test the interactivity of a symbol—for example, a movie clip—choose Control > Test Scene while you are working on the symbol in symbol-editing mode. Flash publishes just the symbol and the items nested within that symbol.

To test scripts:

◆ Choose Control > Test Movie or Control > Test Scene (**Figure 13.21**).

Flash exports the movie or scene to a Flash Player file, adding the .swf extension to the filename and using the current Publish settings. (For more information on Publish Settings, see Chapter 17.) During export, Flash displays the Exporting Flash Movie dialog, which contains a progress bar and a button for canceling the operation.

When it finishes exporting the movie, Flash opens the SWF file in Flash Player so you see the movie in action. The buttons and movie clips in the test window are all live, so you can see how they interact with the viewer's mouse actions. Any scripts you've created will run.

When you finish testing, exit the Player by clicking the movie window's close button (Mac) or close box (Windows). Flash returns you to the document-editing environment.

✔ Tips

- Sometimes even when a script comes through the syntax check without errors, it has errors that show up when you test the movie. Flash opens the Compiler Errors panel as soon as it encounters one of these *runtime errors*. Runtime errors may occur, for example, when you try to target an object that doesn't exist; let's say you typed enerBtn as the instance name instead of enterBtn. The script still follows the syntax rules, but fails to find the instance when it runs.

Modifying and Extending Button Scripts

When it comes to scripting, the first steps are often the most difficult; subsequent steps expand on what you've already learned. Earlier, you set up a frame script that controls a button on the Stage. In this section, that script becomes a stepping stone to creating different kinds of interactivity.

To create multiple actions in an event handler:

1. Using the ButtonActionsMaster template you created in the section "Programming Buttons with Frame Scripts," earlier in this chapter, open a new document.

   ButtonActionsMaster creates a five-frame document with identifying text for each frame, and one button instance. It also contains a **stop** action in keyframe 1, and a script that activates the button for interactivity.

2. In the Timeline, in the Actions layer, select keyframe 1.

   Flash displays the script in the Script pane of the Actions panel. If the panel is not currently visible, access it, for example, by choosing Window > Actions.

3. To have Flash print a message in the Output window, position the cursor at the end of line 11, press Enter, and in the new line 12 type

   ```
   trace( "click! new frame: " +
   → currentFrame );
   ```

   Make sure you enter this code before the closing brace (}) in line 13. Lines 12 and 13 of your code should look like **Script 13.6**.

Script 13.6 Adding the trace action to the event handler.

```
 6 function handleClick( pEvent:MouseEvent
   ):void
 7 {
 8   if( pEvent.target == enterBtn )
 9   {
10     // handle the event
11     nextFrame();
12     trace( "click! new frame: " +
       currentFrame );
13   }
14 }
```

Before clicking the button

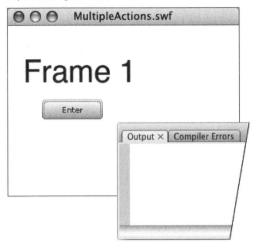

After clicking the button

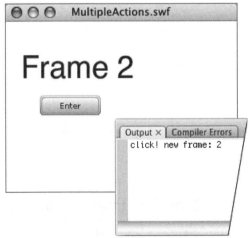

Figure 13.22 When you test a movie, the Output window displays your trace messages. For this movie, clicking the button creates a trace message.

The block of code that makes up the event handler now contains two statements. The `nextFrame` statement moves the playhead to the next frame. The `trace` statement tells Flash to print a message to the Output window. (Here, Flash builds the message out of the words inside the quotes plus the number of the frame where the playhead is currently.)

4. Save the document and give it a descriptive name, such as EventHandlerMultipleActions.

5. Check the script's syntax.

For details about trouble-shooting syntax errors, see "Previewing Actions at Work," earlier in this chapter.

6. Choose Control > Test Movie.

Your movie opens in a Flash Player window. Each time you click the button, the words *Click! new frame* appear in the Output panel, followed by the current frame number (**Figure 13.22**). If the Output window isn't visible, Flash opens it for you.

To send the playhead to a specific frame:

1. To use the script created in the previous task as a building block, create a new copy of the document EventHandlerMultipleActions by choosing File > Save As.

Give the copy a descriptive name, such as GoToFrame.

2. In the Timeline, select keyframe 1 of the Actions layer.

The script you created earlier appears in the Script pane of the Actions panel.

continues on next page

3. In the Script pane, in line 11, select the code

`nextFrame();`

and replace it with

`gotoAndStop( 5 );`

Be sure to keep the code's original indentation. Instead of moving the playhead forward one frame at a time, the `gotoAndStop` action tells the playhead to jump to the frame number specified in parentheses.

4. Preview the action.

Save the file, check the syntax (line 11 of the script should match **Script 13.7**), correct any errors, then test the movie (see "Previewing Actions at Work").

Your movie opens in a Flash Player window. When you click the button, the movie jumps to frame 5, and the message in the Output window confirms it.

To create a frame label:

1. Create a copy of the previous task's document (GoToFrame), for example by choosing File > Save As.

Give the copy a descriptive name, such as CreateFrameLabel.

2. In the Timeline, create a new layer above the Actions layer, name it Labels, and lock it.

Having the Labels layer at the top helps you organize the Timeline; you can use labels to indicate the sections of your Movie.

3. Select frame 3 of the Labels layer and insert a blank keyframe, for example by choosing Insert > Timeline > Blank Keyframe.

4. With the new blank keyframe selected, access the Property inspector; in the Frame Label field, enter `myLabel`.

Script 13.7 Sending the playhead to a frame number.

```
 6  function handleClick( pEvent:MouseEvent
    ):void
 7  {
 8    if( pEvent.target == enterBtn )
 9    {
10      // handle the event
11      gotoAndStop( 5 );
12      trace( "click! new frame: " +
        currentFrame );
13    }
14  }
```

Targeting Frame Labels

When using a `gotoAndStop` or `gotoAndPlay` action, you can enter a frame number or a frame label. There's an advantage to using frame labels. If you ever add or remove frames from the type of movie-clip button you learned to create in Chapter 12, the frame numbers for the button states may change. If they do, you must go back into the script to update the frame numbers. If you target the frame by label, you never need to update the script to accommodate changes to frame numbers.

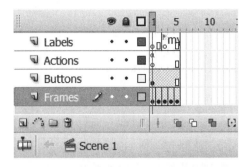

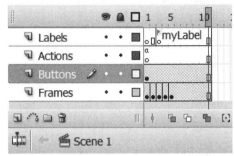

Figure 13.23 Frame labels appear truncated if the keyframe span is too short to display the full text (top). To gain the full benefit of using frame labels as visual aids, expand the span by adding in-between frames (bottom).

Script 13.8 Sending the playhead to a frame label.

```
 6  function handleClick( pEvent:MouseEvent
    ):void
 7  {
 8    if( pEvent.target == enterBtn )
 9    {
10      // handle the event
11      gotoAndStop( "myLabel" );
12      trace( "click! new frame: " +
        currentFrame );
13    }
14  }
```

✔ Tip

■ In the preceding task, you made the playhead move to a specific frame and stop playback. You can also make the playhead jump to a specific frame and resume playback from there. In step 2, replace line 11's gotoAndStop action with gotoAndPlay.

To confirm the label, press Enter, or click outside the field. In the Timeline a little red flag appears in keyframe 3 of the Labels layer. Flash displays as much of your label as there's room for in the keyframe span (**Figure 13.23**).

5. Position the playhead in frame 5, but don't select a frame.

6. Insert enough in-between frames (for example, by pressing F5) to make the span large enough to display the full label.

Frame labels help you organize your Timeline. They are most effective when you can read them in the Timeline, rather than having to check the Property inspector.

To send the playhead to a frame label:

1. Continuing with the file from the preceding task, select keyframe 1 in the Actions layer, and access the Actions panel.

Your script appears in the Script pane.

2. In the Script pane, in line 11, select the code

gotoAndStop(5);

and replace it with

gotoAndStop("myLabel");

Be sure to keep the original indentation. With the gotoAndStop action, you can have the playhead go to a frame number or to a frame label.

3. Preview the action.

Save the file, check the syntax (line 11 of your script should match **Script 13.8**), correct any errors, then test the movie (see "Previewing Actions at Work").

Your movie opens in a Flash Player window. When you click the button, the movie jumps to the frame that bears the label myLabel.

MODIFYING AND EXTENDING BUTTON SCRIPTS

389

Choosing Events

As users interact with a button, their mouse movements trigger various events. Releasing the mouse button while still over the button's active area triggers the `click` event. Rolling over and out of a button area triggers other events. To make a button react to these events, you must change your script to register for the desired event instead of `click`.

To handle an event when rolling over a button:

1. Open a new document using the ButtonActionsMaster template you created earlier in this chapter.

   Save the document using the name ButtonEvents.fla.

2. In the Actions layer, select frame 1 and access the Actions panel.

   The template's script appears in the Script pane.

3. In line 15, select the text

   `MouseEvent.CLICK`

   and replace it by typing

   `MouseEvent.ROLL_OVER`

4. Preview the action.

   Save the file, check the syntax (lines 14 and 15 of your code should match **Script 13.9**), correct any errors, then test the movie (see "Previewing Actions at Work").

   Your movie opens in a Flash Player window. Each time you roll over the button (move the pointer into the button's active area), the playhead moves one frame forward. Nothing happens when you click, other than the button showing the Down frame.

Script 13.9 Switching from a click event to a rollover event.

```
14  // register events
15  enterBtn.addEventListener(
    MouseEvent.ROLL_OVER, handleClick );
```

Script 13.10 Registering for the rollout event.

```
14  // register events
15  enterBtn.addEventListener(
    MouseEvent.ROLL_OUT, handleClick );
```

✔ Tips

- A faster way to replace the event is to delete the code `.CLICK` and retype the period to trigger the code-hint window. You could also just delete `CLICK`, position the cursor after the period, and press the Code Hint button in the toolbar above the Script pane.

- In the preceding task, the event handler is still called `handleClick`. It would be more meaningful to rename it `handleRollOver`; just make sure you change it in both lines 6 and 15.

- If you want the script to react when rolling out of the button instead of over, in line 15, select the text `MouseEvent.ROLL_OVER`, and replace it by typing `MouseEvent.ROLL_OUT` (**Script 13.10**).

Script 13.11 Adding the second event handler.

```
11      nextFrame();
12    }
13 }
14 function handleRollOver( pEvent:MouseEvent
   ):void
15 {
16   if( pEvent.target == enterBtn )
17   {
18     // handle the event
19     gotoAndStop( 2 );
20   }
21 }
22 // register events
```

To receive multiple events for a button:

1. Open a new document using the ButtonActionsMaster template you created earlier in this chapter.

   Save the document using the name ButtonMultiEvents.fla.

2. In the Timeline, in the Actions layer, select keyframe 1 and access the Actions panel.

   The template's script appears in the Script pane.

3. To define a second event handler, do the following:

   ▲ Place the cursor at the end of line 13 (after the closing brace) and press Enter to begin a new code block (the code that was originally on lines 14 and 15 moves down).

   ▲ In lines 14–21 type

   ```
   function handleRollOver(
   ⇢ pEvent:MouseEvent ):void
   {
     if( pEvent.target == enterBtn )
     {
       // handle the event
       gotoAndStop( 2 );
     }
   }
   ```

   Lines 14–21 should match **Script 13.11**.

   continues on next page

4. To register for the `rollOver` event, place the cursor at the end of line 23, press Enter to create a new line (24), and type

```
enterBtn.addEventListener(
→ MouseEvent.ROLL_OVER,
→ handleRollOver );
```

To receive multiple events from one button, you need to register for each event separately. You want the script to receive both events but react differently for each one. Defining a new event-handler function is a way to accomplish that (**Script 13.12**).

5. Preview the action.

Save the file, check the syntax (the complete script for the multi-event button should match **Script 13.13**), correct any errors, then test the movie (see "Previewing Actions at Work").

Your movie opens in a Flash Player window. Whenever you roll the pointer over the button, the playhead jumps to frame 2, and when you click the button, the playhead moves to frame 3.

Script 13.12 Pay attention to the second event (rollover).

```
22  // register events
23  enterBtn.addEventListener(
    MouseEvent.CLICK, handleClick );
24  enterBtn.addEventListener(
    MouseEvent.ROLL_OVER, handleRollOver );
```

Script 13.13 The completed multi-event script.

```
1   //Pause the movie on frame 1
2   stop();
3   // code-hint comments
4   // SimpleButton enterBtn;
5   // event handlers
6   function handleClick( pEvent:MouseEvent
    ):void
7   {
8     if( pEvent.target == enterBtn )
9     {
10      // handle the event
11      nextFrame();
12    }
13  }
14  function handleRollOver( pEvent:MouseEvent
    ):void
15  {
16    if( pEvent.target == enterBtn )
17    {
18      // handle the event
19      gotoAndStop( 2 );
20    }
21  }
22  // register events
23  enterBtn.addEventListener(
    MouseEvent.CLICK, handleClick );
24  enterBtn.addEventListener(
    MouseEvent.ROLL_OVER, handleRollOver );
```

The Mystery of Mouse Events

Button symbols and movie-clip symbols are both in a group of Flash objects called *interactive objects*. Users interacting with any of the objects via an input device such as a mouse or a graphics pen can trigger the same events—known as *mouse events*. (Button components, despite having the word *button* in the name, are actually a special type of movie clip.)

All interactive objects have a whopping 19 events built in; 9 of them are mouse events. Each of them is part of Flash and has a predefined functionality. This means you can't rename them or change how they work. The following list shows the generic name of an event—for example, click—followed in parentheses by the ActionScript constant that refers to that event—for example, (MouseEvent.CLICK).

click (MouseEvent.CLICK) occurs when a user presses and then releases the mouse button while over the active area of a button or movie clip (an interactive object).

rollOver (MouseEvent.ROLL_OVER) occurs when the user moves the pointer over the active area of the interactive object. Once a user has triggered a rollOver, the rollOver event can't be triggered again until there has been a rollOut event.

rollOut (MouseEvent.ROLL_OUT) occurs when a user has moved the pointer into the active area of an interactive object and then moves the pointer out of the active area.

mouseMove (MouseEvent.MOUSE_MOVE) occurs whenever a user moves the pointer within the active area of an interactive object.

doubleClick (MouseEvent.DOUBLE_CLICK) occurs when a user clicks twice in rapid succession over the active area of an interactive object. This event is new to ActionScript 3.0. To use this event in your scripts, the doubleClickEnabled property of the button or movie clip needs to be set to true. (You must create a line in the script with the code myBtn.doubleClickEnabled = true;.)

The first three events in the list—click, rollOver, and rollOut—are the most common ones, and should be all you need for the vast majority of your button scripting tasks. The other two, mouseMove and doubleClick, give you a glimpse at what else is possible.

Button Components

Flash contains a selection of ready-made user interface (UI) elements. They can be found in the Components panel and include items such as RadioButton and ComboBox (for drop-down menus). Scripting the click-interactivity for button components and regular button symbols is similar.

To add a button component to your movie:

1. Open a new document using the ButtonActionsMaster template you created earlier in this chapter.

   Save the document using the name ButtonComponent.fla.

2. In the Timeline, in the Buttons layer, select keyframe 1.

3. Access the Components panel and, from the User Interface category, choose Button.

   If the panel isn't visible, choose Window > Components.

4. Drag an instance of the button component onto the Stage (**Figure 13.24**).

5. Select the button-component instance on the Stage and access the Properties tab of the Property inspector.

6. In the Instance Name field, enter a name for the button-component instance—for example, myComponent (**Figure 13.25**).

   You are now ready to create a script that makes the component carry out a task.

✔ Tip

- You can modify a component's appearance by editing its skin (see Chapter 12 for details).

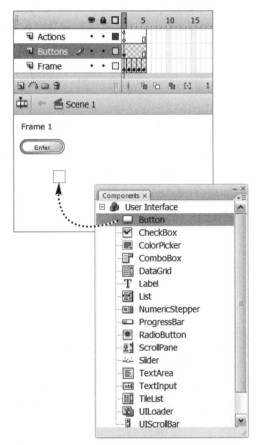

Figure 13.24 Drag an instance of the button component from the Components panel to the Stage to add it to your movie.

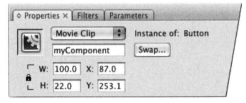

Figure 13.25 To target a component with ActionScript, you must give it an instance name. Note that the Behavior menu in the Property inspector reveals that the Button component is actually a type of movie clip.

Script 13.14 Adding the code-hint comment for the button component.

```
3   // code-hint comments
4   // SimpleButton enterBtn;
5   // Button myComponent;
6   // event handlers
```

Script 13.15 The event handler for the button component.

```
12      nextFrame();
13    }
14  }
15  function handleComponent( pEvent:MouseEvent
    ):void
16  {
17    if( pEvent.target == myComponent )
18    {
19      // handle the event
20      enterBtn.visible = false;
21    }
22  }
```

To script a button component's interactivity:

1. Continuing with the file from the preceding task, select keyframe 1 in the Actions layer and access the Actions panel.

   The template's script appears in the Script pane.

2. To enable code hints for the component instance, place the cursor at the end of line 4 and press Enter to create a new line 5, then type

   ```
   // Button myComponent;
   ```

   A button component is more complex than a regular button, and enabling full code hints for components makes scripting them easier (**Script 13.14**).

3. To create the event handler for the component, do the following:

   ▲ Place the cursor at the end of line 14 (after the closing brace) and press Enter to begin a new code block.

   ▲ In lines 15–22, type

   ```
   function handleComponent(
   → pEvent:MouseEvent ):void
   {
     if( pEvent.target ==
   → myComponent )
     {
       // handle the event
       enterBtn.visible = false;
     }
   }
   ```

   The code should match **Script 13.15**. Instead of moving the playhead to a new frame, this event handler hides the enterBtn.

continues on next page

4. With the cursor at the end of line 24 (after the semicolon), press Enter to create a new line and in line 25 type

```
myComponent.addEventListener(
→ MouseEvent.CLICK,
→ handleComponent );
```

The code should match **Script 13.16**.

5. Preview the action.

Save the file, check the syntax (the full script should match **Script 13.17**), correct any errors, then test the movie (see "Previewing Actions at Work").

Your movie opens in a Flash Player window. When you click the button component (named Label), Flash hides the button symbol (named Enter). Clicking the button symbol still advances the Timeline as you originally scripted it to do.

Script 13.16 Listening to the click event of the button component.

```
23  // register events
24  enterBtn.addEventListener(
    MouseEvent.CLICK, handleClick );
25  myComponent.addEventListener(
    MouseEvent.CLICK, handleComponent );
```

Script 13.17 Scripting a button component.

```
1  //Pause the movie on frame 1
2  stop();
3  // code-hint comments
4  // SimpleButton enterBtn;
5  // Button myComponent;
6  // event handlers
7  function handleClick( pEvent:MouseEvent
   ):void
8  {
9    if( pEvent.target == enterBtn )
10   {
11     // handle the event
12     nextFrame();
13   }
14 }
15 function handleComponent( pEvent:MouseEvent
   ):void
16 {
17   if( pEvent.target == myComponent )
18   {
19     // handle the event
20     enterBtn.visible = false;
21   }
22 }
23 // register events
24 enterBtn.addEventListener(
   MouseEvent.CLICK, handleClick );
25 myComponent.addEventListener(
   MouseEvent.CLICK, handleComponent );
```

Using One Event Handler for Multiple Events

Earlier in this chapter, you created individual event handlers for multiple events. Another way to deal with multiple events is to use one event handler with a parameter. With this technique, you create a script that examines the pEvent parameter that you've defined as part of the event-handler function to react differently for each button.

To add another button to be scripted:

1. Open a new document using the ButtonActionsMaster template you created earlier in this chapter.

   This document has one button instance—named enterBtn—on the Stage. Save the document using the name MultiEventsOneHandler.fla.

2. Select the enterBtn instance and choose Edit > Duplicate to create a new instance of the button.

   Position the duplicate so that it doesn't overlap the original button.

3. Access the Properties tab of the Property inspector, and enter prevBtn in the Instance Name field.

   Now you have two buttons on the Stage that can be scripted to use the same event handler.

To script the second button:

1. Continuing with the file from the preceding task, in the Timeline, in the Actions layer, select keyframe 1 and access the Actions panel.

   continues on next page

ONE EVENT HANDLER FOR MULTIPLE EVENTS

2. To create a code-hint comment for the second button (prevBtn), in the Action panel's Script pane, place the cursor at the end of line 4 and press Enter to create a new line 5, then type

`// SimpleButton prevBtn;`

(See **Script 13.18.**)

3. Place the cursor at the end of line 13—after the closing brace (})—and press Enter to create a new line.

Be sure to place the cursor after the correct closing brace. The brace in line 13 closes the if statement, while the brace in line 14 closes the function.

4. To update the event handler for two buttons, in lines 14–17, type

```
else if( pEvent.target == prevBtn )
{
    // handle the prevBtn event
    prevFrame();
}
```

This code extends the if statement to check for a second condition if the first condition is not met. The object of interest here is prevBtn. If prevBtn triggered the event, the script sends the playhead to the previous frame (**Script 13.19**).

5. To register for the click event of the prevBtn, place the cursor at the end of line 21, press Enter to create a new line (22), then type

`prevBtn.addEventListener(`
`→ MouseEvent.CLICK, handleClick );`

6. Preview the action.

Save the file, check the syntax (lines 3–22 should match **Script 13.20**, correct any errors), then test the movie (see "Previewing Actions at Work"). Your movie opens in a Flash Player window.

Clicking the enterBtn button advances the playhead one frame. Clicking the prevBtn sends the playhead back one frame.

Script 13.18 Adding the code-hint comment for the second button.

```
3  // code-hint comments
4  // SimpleButton enterBtn;
5  // SimpleButton prevBtn;
6  // event handlers
```

Script 13.19 The interaction for the second button.

```
12      nextFrame();
13    }
14    else if( pEvent.target == prevBtn )
15    {
16      // handle the prevBtn event
17      prevFrame();
18    }
19  }
```

Script 13.20 A single event handler for two buttons.

```
3  // code-hint comments
4  // SimpleButton enterBtn;
5  // SimpleButton prevBtn;
6  // event handlers
7  function handleClick( pEvent:MouseEvent
   ):void
8  {
9    if( pEvent.target == enterBtn )
10   {
11     // handle the event
12     nextFrame();
13   }
14   else if( pEvent.target == prevBtn )
15   {
16     // handle the prevBtn event
17     prevFrame();
18   }
19 }
20 // register events
21 enterBtn.addEventListener(
   MouseEvent.CLICK, handleClick );
22 prevBtn.addEventListener( MouseEvent.CLICK,
   handleClick );
```

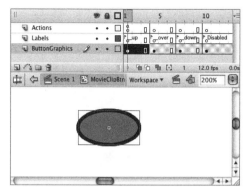

Figure 13.26 This movie-clip symbol has keyframes for four button states: the standard three (up, over, and down) plus a fourth, disabled. Each keyframe has an appropriate frame label.

Scripting Movie Clips to Act As Buttons

Flash's button symbols provide the most basic visual requirements for a button, giving you the options for different looks in the up, over, and down states. Sometimes, however, you may need additional states. In an email form, for example, the submit button should be disabled (and should look disabled) until all the required fields are filled out.

In Chapter 12 you learned how to set up a movie-clip symbol for use as a button that has a disabled state. In the following task you learn to program that symbol to work as a button.

To enable button behavior for the movie-clip button:

1. Open the file named MyOwnBtn.fla that you created in Chapter 12, in the section "Creating Movie-Clip Buttons."

   This document contains a movie-clip symbol called MoveClipBtn.

2. On the Stage, double-click the instance of the MovieClipBtn symbol to enter symbol-editing mode.

   The symbol's Timeline has three layers—Actions, Labels, and ButtonGraphics. The symbol has keyframes labeled _up, _over, _down, and Disabled, and graphics that make each state obvious (**Figure 13.26**).

3. In the symbol's Timeline, select keyframe 1 in the Actions layer.

continues on next page

4. To pause the movie-clip button, in the Script pane of the Actions panel, in line 1, type

`stop();`

By default, movie clips play at runtime. While that makes sense for animations, a button should stay in its up state until the user interacts with it.

5. With the cursor at the end of line 1, press Enter to create a new line.

6. To activate button behavior for the movie clip, in line 2, type

`buttonMode = true;`

Until you do that, the movie clip doesn't know it's supposed to act like a button, despite the special frame labels you used.

7. Save your document, check the syntax of your code (your script should match **Script 13.21**), then select Control > Test Movie.

As it rolls over the movie-clip button, the pointer changes to a hand, and the playhead goes to the movie-clip's _over frame. When you press the mouse button, the playhead goes to the _down frame— just as it does for a regular button.

8. Close the test-movie window and navigate back to the main Timeline, for example, by choosing Edit > Edit Document.

Script 13.21 The code to activate button behavior.

```
1  stop();
2  buttonMode = true;
```

SCRIPTING MOVIE CLIPS TO ACT AS BUTTONS

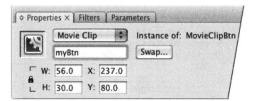

Figure 13.27 To target the movie-clip button, you must name the instance in the Property inspector's Instance Name field.

Script 13.22 A descriptive comment, pausing the Timeline, and defining the code-hint comment.

```
1  // Scripting a movie-clip button
2  stop();
3  // code-hint comments
4  // MovieClip myBtn;
```

To add a mouse event–handler that displays the disabled state:

1. Continuing with the file from the previous task, select the MovieClipBtn instance on the Stage and access the Properties tab of the Property inspector.

2. In the Instance Name field, enter a name—for example, `myBtn` (**Figure 13.27**).

3. In the Timeline of the document, create a new layer above the existing layer; name the new layer Actions.

   With multiple layers in the Timeline, it's a good idea to name them all. Give the layer containing the movie-clip button a name—for example, `MC Button`.

4. Select keyframe 1 in the Actions layer, and access the Actions panel.

5. In the Script pane, in line 1, to document your script, type // followed by a description, and press Enter to create a new line.

   Adding a comment such as `// Scripting a movie-clip button` reminds you (and informs others) of what you intend your script to do.

6. With the cursor in line 2, type `stop();` to pause the movie, then press Enter to create a new line.

7. To create a code-hint comment, in lines 3 and 4, type

   `// code-hint comments`
   `// MovieClip myBtn;`

   This comment activates code hints by telling Flash that the instance `myBtn` is a MovieClip object (**Script 13.22**).

8. With the cursor at the end of line 4, press Enter to begin a new block of code.

continues on next page

9. To define the event handler, in lines 5–13, type

```
// event handlers
function handleClick
→ ( pEvent:MouseEvent ):void
{
  if( pEvent.target == myBtn )
  {
    myBtn.enabled = false;
    myBtn.gotoAndStop( "Disabled" );
  }
}
```

Line 6 defines the event handler. Line 8 makes sure the event was triggered by the button instance you intend, myBtn. Line 10 prevents the button from receiving anymore mouse events by setting the movie-clip instance's enabled property to false. Line 11 sends the playhead to the Disabled frame of the movie-clip (without the code in line 10 the playhead would go back to the _up frame as soon as the user rolled out of the active movie-clip area) (**Script 13.23**).

10. To register for the click event, with the cursor at the end of line 13, press Enter to create a new line; in new lines 14 and 15 type

```
// register events
myBtn.addEventListener(
→ MouseEvent.CLICK, handleClick );
```

11. Save your document, check the syntax of your code (your script should match **Script 13.24**), then select Control > Test Movie.

Your movie opens in a Flash Player window. The movie-clip button displays the _over state. When you click the button, the playhead moves to the _down label. As soon as you let go of the mouse button, the playhead moves to the Disabled frame, and the movie-clip button no longer reacts to the mouse.

Script 13.23 Adding the event handler.

```
4  // MovieClip myBtn;
5  // event handlers
6  function handleClick( pEvent:MouseEvent
   ):void
7  {
8    if( pEvent.target == myBtn )
9    {
10     myBtn.enabled = false;
11     myBtn.gotoAndStop( "Disabled" );
12   }
13 }
```

Script 13.24 The completed movie-clip button script.

```
1  // Scripting a movie-clip button
2  stop();
3  // code-hint comments
4  // MovieClip myBtn;
5  // event handlers
6  function handleClick( pEvent:MouseEvent
   ):void
7  {
8    if( pEvent.target == myBtn )
9    {
10     myBtn.enabled = false;
11     myBtn.gotoAndStop( "Disabled" );
12   }
13 }
14 // register events
15 myBtn.addEventListener( MouseEvent.CLICK,
   handleClick );
```

✔ Tip

■ The procedure for scripting interactive buttons and movie-clip buttons is identical. If you start a project using buttons, and later realize you need more functionality, you don't have to start over. Replace the buttons with movie-clip buttons using the same instance names and your code will still work. You can then add movie-clip–specific scripts to display additional states, as shown in the preceding task.

Using Buttons to Control Timelines

Most Flash creations employ a mixture of interface objects: button symbols, button components, and movie clips. You can script a button (or button component) to start and stop the playback of a movie clip, or make the playhead jump to a specific frame in a movie clip. The key is to specify the correct target path.

The Mystery of Target Paths

All Flash creations have a certain amount of structural complexity. Even a simple movie like the one created with ButtonActionsMaster has a hierarchy of nested objects. (The Timeline you see when you open a Flash document in the authoring environment is actually a movie-clip object, so any objects on this main Timeline are considered nested objects.) But the structure gets really complex when you nest interactive objects inside other interactive objects—a button inside a movie clip, a movie clip inside a movie clip, a button inside a movie clip inside a movie clip, and so on.

A nested object is known as a *child object,* and the object containing that child is known as the *parent object.* As long as each parent and child has an instance name, it doesn't matter how complex the family relationship gets. You can create a script that manipulates any of the nested objects. The key is to identify the target object's place in the hierarchy of Timelines using a *target path.*

There are two types of target paths: *relative* and *absolute.* A relative target path starts with the target object and describes its relationship to other Timelines in the hierarchy—indicating, for example, that the target is me, or it's one level above me; or it's within me, one level down. An absolute target path starts with the highest-level Timeline and works its way down the hierarchy until it reaches the target object.

Just to complicate things, however, ActionScript 3.0 introduces a new type of interactive object, the sprite. A sprite is similar to a movie clip, but it has no Timeline and no frames. All of the animation and interactivity of a sprite happens because of scripting. Sprites can also be nested and have hierarchical relationships. And you use target paths to identify them. When you write target paths, you need to distinguish between sprite objects and Timeline-based objects (movie clips) by using the code `as sprite` or `as movieClip`—as shown in the examples below. (In this book, we work only with Timeline-based objects.)

continues on next page

To make a button stop movie-clip playback:

1. Open a new ActionScript 3.0 Flash document, add layers to create a three-layer document, and do the following:

   ▲ Name the top layer Actions.

   ▲ Name the second layer Buttons. In that layer, place a button-symbol instance at the upper-left corner of the Stage.

   ▲ Name the third layer MovieClips. In that layer, at the center of the Stage, place a movie-clip instance containing animation (for example, a simple motion tween of a geometric shape that rotates and shrinks).

   ▲ Save the file and name it pauseClipControl.fla.

2. To prepare the instances for scripting, do the following:

   ▲ Access the Property inspector.

   ▲ Select the button, and in the Instance Name field, enter controlBtn.

   ▲ Select the movie clip, and in the Instance Name field, enter animMc.

3. In the Actions layer, select frame 1 and access the Actions panel.

4. To comment your script and pause the main Timeline at startup, in the Script pane of the Actions panel, in lines 1 and 2, type

   ```
   // Controlling a movie clip with a
   → button
   stop();
   ```

The Mystery of Target Paths
continued

To start a relative target path, simply type the instance name of the object you want to target, such as animMc.

A relative path isn't restricted to looking at objects contained within the current Timeline. You can also go one or more levels up or down. This is where the concept of parent and child comes into play. Let's say you have a button with an instance name of controlBtn on the main Timeline where you've placed animMc. In the Timeline of animMc, you could write

```
(parent as MovieClip).controlBtn
```

This path directs ActionScript to go one level up to the parent Timeline, the one containing animMc (in this example, it's the main Timeline) and access the instance named controlBtn. (Whenever you use the code parent you must distinguish between sprites and movie clips.)

To target child objects, use dot syntax (place a period between the parent object and its child). To direct ActionScript to go down a level to access a movie-clip instance named starMc that's nested within animMc, the relative path would be animMc.starMc.

Optionally, you can start a relative target path with the code this.—for example, this.animMc.starMc is the same as animMc.starMc.

An absolute path always starts at the main Timeline, which is also known as root. The format of an absolute target path for starMC looks like this:

```
(root as MovieClip).animMc.starMc
```

(Whenever you use the code root you must distinguish between sprites and movie clips.)

Script 13.25 Commented script that pauses the Timeline, and defines code-hint comments.

```
1  // Controlling a movie clip with a button
2  stop();
3  // code-hint comments
4  // SimpleButton controlBtn;
5  // MovieClip animMc;
```

Script 13.26 Defining the event handler that checks for the event source.

```
5  // MovieClip animMc;
6  // event handler
7  function handleClick( pEvent:MouseEvent
   ):void
8  {
9    if( pEvent.target == controlBtn )
10   {
11     // handle event
12   }
13 }
```

Script 13.27 Registering the click event of controlBtn.

```
14 // register events
15 controlBtn.addEventListener(
   MouseEvent.CLICK, handleClick );
```

5. To enable code hints for the instances on the Stage, in lines 3–5 type the following code-hint comments (**Script 13.25**):

```
// code-hint comments
// SimpleButton controlBtn;
// MovieClip animMc;
```

6. To define an event handler that verifies the event source, in lines 6–13 type

```
// event handler
function handleClick(
→ pEvent:MouseEvent ):void
{
   if( pEvent.target == controlBtn )
   {
      // handle event
   }
}
```

This defines an event handler that makes sure the event is triggered by controlBtn (**Script 13.26**).

7. To register for the controlBtn's click event, in lines 14 and 15 type

```
// register events
controlBtn.addEventListener(
→ MouseEvent.CLICK, handleClick );
```

The main Timeline now receives the click event of the controlBtn, and you are ready to direct Flash to take control of the movie-clip instance animMc (**Script 13.27**).

continues on next page

USING BUTTONS TO CONTROL TIMELINES

8. Place the cursor at the end of line 11, press Enter to create a new line 12, and type

   animMc

   This is a relative target path: this script now aims from the main Timeline (where the script is located) to the animMc instance.

9. With the cursor at the end of line 12, directly after the target path, type

   .stop();

   This stop action attached to the target path tells Flash to pause playback of the movie-clip instance named animMc.

10. Preview the action.

    Save the file, check the syntax (the code should match **Script 13.28**), correct any errors, then test the movie (see "Previewing Actions at Work").

    In the Flash Player window, the animation plays in a continuous loop. When you click the button, the animation pauses.

Script 13.28 The completed script to pause a clip when a button is clicked.

```
1  // Controlling a movie clip with a button
2  stop();
3  // code-hint comments
4  // SimpleButton controlBtn;
5  // MovieClip animMc;
6  // event handler
7  function handleClick( pEvent:MouseEvent
   ):void
8  {
9    if( pEvent.target == controlBtn )
10   {
11     // handle event
12     animMc.stop();
13   }
14 }
15 // register events
16 controlBtn.addEventListener(
   MouseEvent.CLICK, handleClick );
```

The Pitfalls of Insert Target Path

The toolbar above the Script pane in the Actions panel displays an Insert Target Path button (the small crosshair icon). Click the button and Flash opens a dialog named Insert Target Path. This dialog ought to be a really helpful tool for both understanding the Timeline hierarchy and creating accurate target paths. Unfortunately, this feature didn't weather the transition to ActionScript 3.0 very well.

To make it short, the Insert Path dialog will in most cases create a broken target path. You can use it to get an understanding of the movie-clip hierarchy in your Flash creation, yet you're better off creating your target paths manually.

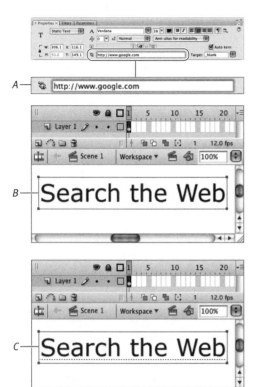

A

B

C

Figure 13.28 When you type a URL in the URL Link field of the Property inspector's Properties tab (A), the selected text field (B) turns into a live link in your published Flash movie. Text fields that are live links appear underlined in the authoring environment (C).

Figure 13.29 The Target menu specifies how Flash should open the link's URL in a browser window.

Linking to Other Web Pages

Flash gives you two ways to open new files by linking to URLs. You can select text on the Stage and turn it into a live link by entering a URL in the Link field of the Text (Tool) Properties tab of the Property inspector. You can also use ActionScript to instruct Flash Player to open a URL. Both techniques let you open the new file in a different browser window or different frame of the current window.

To create a text link to a URL:

1. On the Stage, select the text that you want to be a link.

   You can select individual letters or words using the text tool or select an entire text field using the selection tool.

2. Access the Property inspector, and enter the desired URL in the URL Link field (to the right of the chain-link icon) (**Figure 13.28**).

3. To choose a method for displaying the specified URL in the browser window, from the Target pop-up menu (**Figure 13.29**), choose one of the following:

   _blank opens the URL in a new browser window.

   _parent opens the URL in the parent of the current frame.

   _self opens the URL in same frame of the browser window as that of the content being currently viewed.

   continues on next page

_top opens the URL in the top-level frame of the current browser window.

When you open the published HTML file from you hard drive and click the link to another Web site, you may get security errors (see the sidebar "A Note About Flash Player 9's Security," in Chapter 17). For links to work properly, you need to put the published files on a Web server.

4. Choose Control > Test Movie to try out your live link text.

When you move the pointer over the text, the pointing-finger cursor appears; when you click the text, Flash opens the URL in the specified form of browser window.

To script a button that opens a Web page:

1. Open a new document using the ButtonActionsMaster template you created earlier in this chapter, and save it as LinkBtn.fla.

The Timeline has three layers—Actions, Buttons, and Frames.

2. To create the button that opens a new Web page, do the following:

▲ In the Timeline, select frame 5 of the Buttons layer, and insert a blank keyframe (for example, by choosing Insert > Timeline > Blank Keyframe).

▲ With keyframe 5 of the Buttons layer selected, drag an instance of a button symbol to the Stage, and access the Properties tab of the Property inspector.

▲ In the Instance Name field, enter an instance name, such as linkBtn.

Script 13.29 Defining an event handler that checks for the event source.

```
1   // SimpleButton linkBtn;
2   function handleLink( pEvent:MouseEvent
    ):void
3   {
4     if( pEvent.target == linkBtn )
5     {
6     }
7   }
```

Script 13.30 Registering for the click event.

```
6     }
7   }
8   linkBtn.addEventListener( MouseEvent.CLICK,
    handleLink );
```

3. In the Timeline select keyframe 5 of the Actions layer, insert a blank keyframe, and access the Actions panel.

   In previous tasks you've always created scripts in keyframe 1 that start working with objects in frame 1. One way to create a script that relates to objects in a later frame is to add a blank keyframe in the Actions layer at that frame to hold the script.

4. To create a code-hint comment, in the Script pane of the Actions panel, in line 1 type

   `// SimpleButton linkBtn;`

5. To create the event handler that checks for the event source, do the following.

   ▲ With the cursor at the end of line 1, press Enter to begin a new code block.

   ▲ In lines 2–7, type

   ```
   function handleLink(
   → pEvent:MouseEvent ):void
   {
       if( pEvent.target == linkBtn )
       {
       }
   }
   ```

   The code so far should match **Script 13.29**.

6. To register for the `click` event, with the cursor at the end of line 7 (after the closing brace), press Enter to begin line 8, and type

   ```
   linkBtn.addEventListener(
   → MouseEvent.CLICK, handleLink );
   ```

   The code should match **Script 13.30**.

continues on next page

7. To create the network request, do the following:

▲ Place the cursor at the end of line 5 (after the opening brace) and press Enter to create a new line.

▲ In line 6, type

var request:URLRequest =
→ new URLRequest("http://
→ www.google.com");

Replace the link to Google with the URL you want to link to. In ActionScript 3.0, you need to create a URLRequest object with the URL to make any kind of external connection. Here the URLRequest is then stored in a custom variable called request.

8. To create the code that tells Flash to execute the link, with the cursor at the end of line 6 (after the semicolon), press Enter to begin line 7 and type

navigateToURL(request, "_blank");

The parameter _blank is the same method for opening a browser window that you chose from a menu in step 3 of the preceding task. To use a different method, use the code _self, _parent, or _top; but be aware that you may need to create new security settings for those methods (for more details, see the sidebar "A Note About Flash Player 9's Security Settings," in Chapter 17).

9. Preview the action.

Save the file, check the syntax (the code should match **Script 13.31**), correct any errors, then test the movie (see "Previewing Actions at Work").

As you click the button in the Flash Player window, your default browser opens a new window or tab with the URL you specified.

Script 13.31 Making a button link to another Web page.

```
1  // SimpleButton linkBtn;
2  function handleLink( pEvent:MouseEvent
   ):void
3  {
4    if( pEvent.target == linkBtn )
5    {
6      var request:URLRequest = new
       URLRequest( "http://www.google.com" );
7      navigateToURL( request, "_blank" );
8    }
9  }
10 linkBtn.addEventListener( MouseEvent.CLICK,
   handleLink );
```

✔ **Tip**

■ You don't always have to create scripts in a blank keyframe. Often the Actions layer's keyframe already exists, with script for controlling another button instance. You can simply add the new script to the end of the existing script. In the preceding exercise, for example, try adding the Web-page button to keyframe 1. Create the script at the end of the script that was already in the ButtonActionsMaster document. The line numbers will be different, but the button should work just fine.

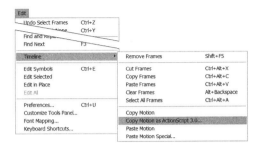

Figure 13.30 To translate Timeline animation into ActionScript, select the animation keyframes in the Timeline, then choose Edit > Timeline > Copy Motion As ActionScript 3.0.

Figure 13.31 In the Prompt dialog, specify the name of the instance to which you want to apply the copied motion code.

Transforming Timeline Animation into Code

Ever since Flash added scripting capabilities in version 4, ActionScript programmers have created motion with code. But trying to script reusable animated effects based on a graphic designer's carefully choreographed motion tweens and keyframe animations was a grueling process of trial and error.

A new command—Copy Motion As ActionScript 3.0—lets you capture the subtle nuances of keyframed motion graphics with code. You select frames of animation in the Timeline, copy them as ActionScript, then simply paste that code into your script.

To copy motion from the Timeline:

1. Open a new Flash file (ActionScript 3.0), create a new movie-clip symbol with a shape in it such as a star, and name it Star.

2. Place an instance of the Star symbol on the Stage, and animate it using the frame-by-frame and motion-tween techniques you learned in Chapters 8 and 9.

3. In the Timeline, select all the layers and frames containing the animation, and then choose Edit > Timeline > Copy Motion As ActionScript 3.0 (**Figure 13.30**).

   A dialog named Prompt appears.

4. In the Prompt dialog, enter the instance name of the movie-clip symbol (or other graphic-object) that you want to animate— for example, ovalMc (**Figure 13.31**).

   This instance doesn't have to exist yet, but it's the instance you'll animate with code.

continues on next page

5. Click OK.

Flash translates all animation created by motion tweens and frame-by-frame changes into ActionScript 3.0 code and places that code on the Clipboard, ready to paste into a script.

✔ Tip

■ This technique analyzes the animation of one graphic-object over a span of keyframes, and then applies it to another graphic-object. If your animation contains merge-shapes or multiple graphic-objects, Flash displays a warning dialog before the Prompt dialog when you choose the Copy Motion As ActionScript 3.0 command.

To paste the copied motion as ActionScript:

1. Open a new Flash file (ActionScript 3.0), and create a movie-clip symbol with a shape in it such as an oval, and name it Oval.

This is the shape you want to animate.

2. Place an instance of Oval on the stage, and give it the instance name ovalMc.

3. Create a new layer and name it Actions.

4. With frame 1 in the Actions layer selected, access the Actions panel.

5. To pause the movie at runtime, in the Script pane, in line 1, type stop();.

6. With the cursor at the end of line 1 (after the semicolon), press Enter to begin a new line.

7. With the cursor in line 2, Control-click (Mac) or right-click (Windows) and choose Paste.

Flash pastes the translation of the motion you copied. The pasted code consists of both XML and ActionScript (**Figure 13.32**).

XML begins

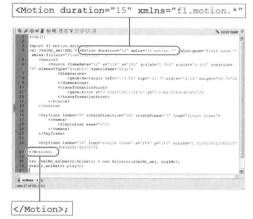

XML ends

Figure 13.32 The pasted motion code is complex, but don't let it scare you. You don't have to edit it, just use it. If you want to, you can experiment with changing the XML code or, eventually, with modifying the ActionScript code.

8. Test the movie.

In the Flash Player window, the `ovalMc` instance goes through the same motions that you created for the Star symbol in the preceding task, even though there's only one single keyframe in this FLA.

✔ Tips

- If, after pasting the script created by the Copy Motion As ActionScript 3.0 command, you discover you entered the wrong instance name in the Prompt dialog, you don't have to go back and do the whole copying procedure again. In the toolbar above the Script pane, click the Find button (the magnifying-glass icon). A standard search-and-replace dialog opens. Simply replace the incorrect instance name with the correct one in the pasted script.

- The script created by the Copy Motion As ActionScript 3.0 command can look quite complicated to a novice scripter, but don't be intimidated. If you prefer not to get involved in complex scripting just yet, there's nothing you need to do to the script. If you want to change the ActionScript-generated animation, you can always change the original Timeline animation and repeat the copy motion–paste process. For this reason, it's always a good idea to set up a system for collaboration between graphic designer and scripter. Hold on to your original Flash documents with Timeline animation until you know the project is complete.

- The script created by the Copy Motion As ActionScript 3.0 command—or more precisely, the XML part of it—is a detailed description of each keyframe of your animation. If you feel adventurous, you can modify the XML and test the results.

TRANSFORMING TIMELINE ANIMATION INTO CODE

Using Buttons to Control Graphic-Objects

Earlier in this chapter, you learned how to target a movie clip and pause it. Now that you can access a movie clip, there are a number of other things you can do to manipulate it by changing its properties. In this section you will learn how to move a clip, change its transparency, and even animate it with script. (The same techniques can be applied to buttons and text fields.)

To prepare the file for multiple controls:

1. Open the file (pauseClipControl.fla) that you created in the section "Using Buttons to Control Timelines," earlier in this chapter.

2. Save a new copy, and name it ControlGraphicObjectsStart.fla.

3. In the Timeline, in the Buttons layer, select keyframe 1 and add two more button instances to the Stage.

4. Give the new buttons the instance names moveBtn and transparentBtn.

   Select each instance on the Stage and enter the instance name in the Name field of the Properties tab of the Property inspector.

5. In the Actions layer, select keyframe 1 and access the Actions panel.

   The script you created earlier appears in the Script pane.

6. To create code-hint comments for the new buttons, place the cursor at the end of line 5, press enter and in lines 6 and 7 type

   // SimpleButton moveBtn;

   // SimpleButton transparentBtn;

   This enables code hints for the two new buttons (**Script 13.32**).

Script 13.32 Adding the code-hint comment for the buttons.

```
5  // MovieClipAnimMc;
6  // SimpleButton moveBtn;
7  // SimpleButton transparentBtn;
8  // event handler
```

Script 13.33 Registering the click event for the buttons.

```
17  // register events
18  controlBtn.addEventListener(
    MouseEvent.CLICK, handleClick );
19  moveBtn.addEventListener( MouseEvent.CLICK,
    handleClick );
20  transparentBtn.addEventListener(
    MouseEvent.CLICK, handleClick );
```

7. To register the click event for both buttons, place the cursor at the end of line 18, press Enter, and in lines 19 and 20 type

```
moveBtn.addEventListener(
→ MouseEvent.CLICK, handleClick );
transparentBtn.addEventListener(
→ MouseEvent.CLICK, handleClick );
```

Now both buttons have code hints enabled, and the event handler is registered to receive the click event from both of them (**Script 13.33**)

8. Preview the action.

Save the file, check the syntax, correct any errors, then test the movie (see "Previewing Actions at Work").

You have not yet scripted the event handler to react to clicks from those buttons; this step is intended to make sure you entered everything correctly so far. In the following tasks you will add interactivity for the new buttons.

9. Save the document as a template, name it ClipControlMaster, and close the file.

You can use this master button script as the basis for other buttons that control movie-clip playback in your Flash creations. For instructions on saving documents as templates, see Chapter 1.

To change the x/y position of a movie clip:

1. Open a new document using the ClipControlMaster template you created in the preceding task.

Save the document using the name MoveClip.fla.

2. In the Actions layer, select keyframe 1 and access the Actions panel.

The template's script appears in the Script pane.

continues on next page

3. To create interaction code for the button instance named moveBtn, do the following:

▲ Place the cursor at the end of line 15 (after the closing brace) and press Enter to begin a new code block.

▲ In lines 16–18 type:

```
else if( pEvent.target ==
→ moveBtn )
   {
   }
```

This section of the event handler tells Flash to execute the code in between the braces only when someone clicks the button instance named moveBtn. Lines 16–18 of your script should match **Script 13.34**.

4. To tell Flash to position the movie-clip instance animMc at specific coordinates, do the following:

▲ Place the cursor at the end of line 17 (after the opening brace) and press Enter to create a new line.

▲ In lines 18–20, type

```
// move the clip
animMc.x = 20;
animMc.y = 50;
```

The script tells Flash to modify the *x* and *y* coordinates of the object animMc at run-time. Flash Player positions the object by its registration point, the same way the Property inspector does during authoring.

5. Preview the action.

Save the file, check the syntax (your code should match **Script 13.35**), correct any errors, then test the movie (see "Previewing Actions at Work").

In the Flash Player window, the animMc clip starts out in the middle of the Stage. Once you click the moveBtn button, Flash repositions animMc to the new coordinates (**Figure 13.33**).

Script 13.34 Checking for events triggered by moveBtn.

```
14        this.animMc.stop();
15    }
16    else if( pEvent.target == moveBtn )
17    {
18    }
19 }
```

Script 13.35 The completed script to move a movie clip to a new position

```
 9 function handleClick( pEvent:MouseEvent
   ):void
10 {
11    if( pEvent.target == controlBtn )
12    {
13      // handle event
14      animMc.stop();
15    }
16    else if( pEvent.target == moveBtn )
17    {
18      // move the clip
19      animMc.x = 20;
20      animMc.y = 50;
21    }
22 }
```

Before pressing Move button

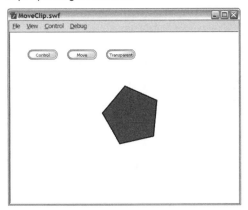

After pressing Move button

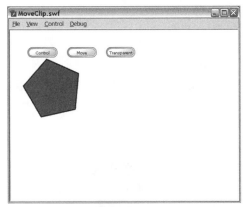

Figure 13.33 The pentagon is a movie clip named animMc (inside the movie clip is a motion tween that spins the shape and shrinks it); the button labeled Move has the instance name moveBtn. Initially, the spinning shape is at the center of the Stage. The script you created moves the movie clip instance animMc to the upper-left corner when someone clicks moveBtn.

Script 13.36 Checking for events triggered by transparentBtn.

```
20      animMc.y = 50;
21  }
22  else if( pEvent.target == transparentBtn
      )
23  {
24  }
25 }
```

To set the transparency of a movie clip:

1. Continuing with the file from the preceding task (MoveClip.fla), save a new copy and name it `TransparentClip.fla`.

2. In the Actions layer, select keyframe 1 and access the Actions panel.

3. To create interaction code for `transparentBtn`, in the Script pane do the following:

   ▲ Place the cursor at the end of line 21 (after the closing brace) and press Enter to begin a new code block.

   ▲ In lines 22–24, type

   ```
   else if( pEvent.target ==
   → transparentBtn )
       {
       }
   ```

   This section of the event handler executes only when `transparentBtn` has been clicked (**Script 13.36**).

4. To modify the transparency of animMc, do the following:

   ▲ Place the cursor at the end of line 23 (after the opening brace) and press Enter to create a new line.

   ▲ In lines 24 and 25 type

   ```
   // make the clip 50% transparent
   animMc.alpha = 0.5;
   ```

   This code sets the alpha property of animMc to 50 percent, making the graphic content of the movie clip translucent.

continues on next page

5. Preview the action.

Save the file, check the syntax (the code should match **Script 13.37**), correct any errors, then test the movie (see "Previewing Actions at Work").

In the Flash Player window, when you click transparentBtn, Flash applies a 50-percent transparency to animMc (**Figure 13.34**). The other button instances continue to perform the tasks you scripted earlier: the button named moveBtn repositions the movie clip named animMc; the button named controlBtn stops playback of animMc.

✔ Tip

■ When the movie clip to which you apply transparency is the only graphic-object on the Stage, it's hard to see the change the script in the preceding task makes. To see the transparency more clearly, add text or draw a shape on a layer below the MovieClips layer in your document. Then test the movie again.

To move a clip across the screen using enterFrame:

1. Continuing with the file from the preceding task (TransparentClip.fla), save a new copy and name it AnimateClip.fla.

2. In the Timeline, in the Actions layer, select keyframe 1 and access the Actions panel.

3. To create a movement variable, in the Script pane do the following:

▲ Place the cursor at the end of line 31 (after the semicolon) and press Enter to begin a new line.

▲ In lines 32–34, type

```
// animate the clip across the
→ screen
// speed in pixels
var moveX:Number = 10;
```

Script 13.37 The new script to make animMc transparent.

```
 9  function handleClick( pEvent:MouseEvent
    ):void
10  {
11    if( pEvent.target == controlBtn )
12    {
13      // handle event
14      animMc.stop();
15    }
16    else if( pEvent.target == moveBtn )
17    {
18      // move the clip
19      animMc.x = 20;
20      animMc.y = 50;
21    }
22    else if( pEvent.target == transparentBtn
      )
23    {
24      // make the clip 50% transparent
25      animMc.alpha = 0.5;
26    }
27  }
```

Before pressing Transparent button

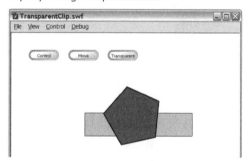

After pressing Transparent button

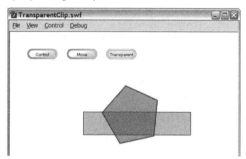

Figure 13.34 The script that controls the button instance named transparentBtn applies a new transparency value to the movie clip named animMc.

Script 13.38 Defining the moveX variable and registering for the enterFrame event.

```
31  transparentBtn.addEventListener(
    MouseEvent.CLICK, handleClick );
32  // animate the clip across the screen
33  // speed in pixels
34  var moveX:Number = 10;
```

Script 13.39 Defining the moveClip event handler.

```
33  // speed in pixels
34  var moveX:Number = 10;
35  // event handler
36  function moveClip( pEvent:Event ):void
37  {
38  }
```

The script should match **Script 13.38**. A *variable* is a scripted container that stores a piece of information. The value 10 here represents 10 pixels on the Stage. The variable moveX stores this value for later use. In the animation script you will create in the following steps, the moveX variable tells Flash how far to reposition the movie clip named animMc.

4. To define the moveClip event handler, do the following:

▲ With the cursor at the end of line 34 (after the semicolon), press Enter to begin a new line.

▲ In lines 35–38, type

```
// event handler
function moveClip(
→ pEvent:Event ):void
{
}
```

The event handler for enterFrame looks very similar to the event handlers for button events. The difference is that the event is now an Event rather than a MouseEvent (**Script 13.39**).

continues on next page

Extra-Credit Scripting Task

You've learned the basics of making buttons that stop playback of movie clips in Flash. Now you're ready to make a button that starts the movie clip playing again. With the skills you have learned so far in this chapter, try this exercise on your own.

Open the TransparentClip.fla you created in the preceding task. Save the file as pausePlay.fla. Add another button to the main Timeline, and give it an instance name. Register for the click event of the button using the same handleClick event handler. In the event handler, add a check for the new button, and trigger animMc to play(); when the new button is clicked.

USING BUTTONS TO CONTROL GRAPHIC-OBJECTS

5. To tell Flash to reposition the movie clip named animMc each time the playhead moves to a new frame, do the following:

▲ Place the cursor in line 37 (after the opening brace) and press Enter to begin a new line.

▲ In lines 38 and 39, type

```
// move the clip by the amount
→ specified
animMc.x = animMc.x + moveX;
```

This line of code redefines the x position of animMc by taking the current value of its x property and adding the value of the moveX variable (10). Since the Flash Player calls the moveClip event handler every time the playhead enters a frame, the script moves animMc 10 pixels to the right each frame (**Script 13.40**).

6. To register for the main Timeline's enterFrame event, do the following:

▲ With the cursor at the end of line 40 (after the closing brace), press Enter to begin a new line.

▲ In lines 41 and 42, type

```
// register event
addEventListener(
→ Event.ENTER_FRAME, moveClip );
```

Anytime the playhead advances in Flash, any object currently on the Stage can receive an enterFrame event. This event is independent of user interaction.

7. Preview the action.

Save the file, check the syntax (the code should match **Script 13.41**), correct any errors, then test the movie.

Your movie opens in a Flash Player window. Without any user interaction, the movie clip named animMc moves across the screen while still playing its animation. Eventually the clip moves off the edge of the screen. You can click the Move button to bring it back to the visible Stage area.

Script 13.40 The complete event-handler code to move animMc by 10 pixels.

```
36 function moveClip( pEvent:Event ):void
37 {
38   // move the clip by the amount specified
39   animMc.x = animMc.x + moveX;
40 }
```

Script 13.41 The complete event-handler code to move animMc across the screen frame by frame.

```
32 // animate the clip across the screen
33 // speed in pixels
34 var moveX:Number = 10;
35 // event handler
36 function moveClip( pEvent:Event ):void
37 {
38   // move the clip by the amount specified
39   animMc.x = animMc.x + moveX;
40 }
41 // register event
42 addEventListener( Event.ENTER_FRAME,
   moveClip );
```

Script 13.42 Checking to see if `animMc` has reached the edge of the Stage.

```
39    animMc.x = animMc.x + moveX;
40    if( animMc.x >= stage.stageWidth )
41    {
42    }
43 }
```

To stop moving the clip when it's off the screen:

1. Continuing with the file from the preceding task (AnimateClip.fla), select keyframe 1 in the Actions layer.

2. To script your Flash creation to check if the movie clip named `animMc` has reached the edge of the Stage, do the following:

   ▲ In the Script pane of the Actions panel, place the cursor at the end of line 39 (after the semicolon) and press Enter to begin a new code block.

   ▲ In lines 40–42, type

   ```
   if( animMc.x >= stage.stageWidth )
   {
   }
   ```

   You can access the Stage you see during authoring using the `stage` property of an interactive object in ActionScript. The code in line 40 checks to see if the horizontal coordinate of `animMc`'s registration point (the *x* property) is greater than or equal to (`>=`) the width of the Stage (`stageWidth`). If that's the case, `animMc` has moved off stage (**Script 13.42**).

3. To unregister the `enterFrame` event, do the following:

   ▲ Place the cursor in line 41 (after the opening brace) and press Enter to begin a new line.

   ▲ In line 42, type

   ```
   removeEventListener(
   → Event.ENTER_FRAME, moveClip );
   ```

   Just as you can register for an event handler to receive an event, you can unregister when you no longer want to receive the event (see the sidebar "The Mystery of the `enterFrame` Event," later in this chapter).

continues on next page

4. Preview the action.

Save the file, check the syntax (the code should match **Script 13.43**), correct any errors, then test the movie (see "Previewing Actions at Work").

The movie clip named animMc moves to the right; when it reaches the right-hand edge of the Flash Player window, animMc stops moving horizontally but continues displaying its spinning animation. When animMc reaches the edge of the Flash Player window, Flash unregisters the enterFrame event that moves animMc 10 pixels for each new frame displayed. If the registration point of your animated clip is not all the way to the left, the animation may still be partially visible.

Once the unregistration takes place, clicking the Move button repositions animMc, but the clip no longer moves to the right.

Script 13.43 The code to stop the clip from moving once it is off the Stage.

```
36  function moveClip( pEvent:Event ):void
37  {
38    // move the clip by the amount specified
39    animMc.x = animMc.x + moveX;
40    if( animMc.x >= stage.stageWidth )
41    {
42      removeEventListener( Event.ENTER_FRAME,
        moveClip );
43    }
44  }
```

The Mystery of the enterFrame Event

This chapter focuses on events triggered by the user—mouse clicks, rollovers, key presses, and so on. There are many other events in ActionScript 3.0 that do not directly depend on user interaction, and enterFrame is one example.

Whenever Flash advances the playhead across all Timelines—whether an individual movie clip is playing or paused—the enterFrame event is triggered. You can take advantage of this fact to make Flash perform actions periodically (as in the task "To move a clip across the screen using enterFrame," earlier in this chapter). To do so, you register an event handler to receive this "heartbeat" event using the following code:

```
addEventListener( Event.ENTER_FRAME, eventHandler );
```

The enterFrame event is very useful for scripted animation.

Keep in mind, however, that the event continues to run as long as your movie runs. When you don't need the event anymore—for example, when an animation has completed—you should *unregister* the event using removeEventListener. The code for unregistering takes the following format:

```
removeEventListener( Event.ENTER_FRAME, eventHandler );
```

You can unregister mouse events in the exact same way.

Using
Non-Flash Graphics

Adobe Flash CS3 Professional's drawing tools are powerful and flexible, but you may prefer the tools offered by another vector graphics program—Adobe Illustrator or Adobe FreeHand, for example. Or you may want to use artwork created in Adobe Photoshop or include scanned photos or other bitmaps in your Flash document. Fortunately, you can import those graphics into Flash, and improvements in Flash CS3's importing features make the import and translation process smoother and more reliable.

Flash can import vector art and bitmapped graphics either through the Clipboard or via the Import command. You can also drag and drop items from Photoshop CS3, Illustrator CS3, and FreeHand versions 7–11 (MX), directly into Flash.

Flash has two import commands: Import to Stage and Import to Library. The two work similarly. Some import dialogs offer slightly different options depending on which command you choose. The tasks in this chapter use Import to Stage.

What Graphics Formats Does Flash Import?

Flash imports a variety of bitmapped and vector-graphic file formats. Flash CS3 can import the following types of files: Adobe Illustrator version 10 or earlier, Adobe Photoshop, AutoCAD DXF, Bitmap (BMP), Enhanced Windows Metafile (EMF, only on Windows), Adobe FreeHand versions 7–11, FutureSplash Player (SPL), GIF and animated GIF, JPEG, PNG, Flash Player 6/7, and Windows Metafile (WMF). If you have QuickTime 4 or later installed on your system together with Flash CS3, you can also import the following file formats: MacPaint (PNTG), PICT (as a bitmap on Windows), QuickTime Image (QTIF), Silicon Graphics Image (SGI), TGA, and TIFF.

Importing Bitmaps

No matter what type of non-Flash artwork you wish to import, the first steps of the import process are the same. For simple bitmaps, the import commands bring the artwork directly into Flash.

To import bitmaps:

1. In a Flash document, choose File > Import > Import to Stage.

   The Import dialog appears (**Figure 14.1**).

   When you choose Import to Stage, Flash imports the file into your document, stores a master bitmap asset in the library, and places an instance of the bitmap on the Stage in the current keyframe of the active layer (**Figure 14.2**).

2. From the Enable (Mac) or Files of Type (Windows) menu, choose the format of the file you want to import.

3. Navigate to the file on your system.

4. Select the file.

5. Click Import (Mac) or Open (Windows).

   The bitmap is now available in the Library and on the Stage.

✔ Tips

■ In step 1 of this task, you could choose File > Import > Import to Library. The Import to Library command places assets in the library but skips placing an instance of the asset on the Stage.

■ You can edit an imported bitmap in any installed bitmap-editing program. Select the bitmap in the Library panel, Control-click (Mac) or right-click (Windows) the bitmap icon, and choose Edit With from the contextual menu. In the window that opens, navigate to an editing program and click Open. Edit and save the bitmap; Flash updates it in the library.

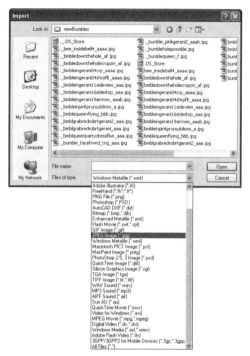

Figure 14.1 Bring graphics created in other applications into your Flash document through the Import dialog.

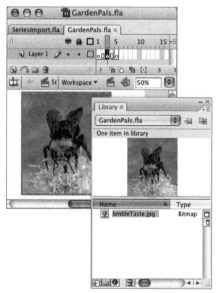

Figure 14.2 When you import a bitmap to the Stage, Flash also stores a master copy of the bitmap in the library.

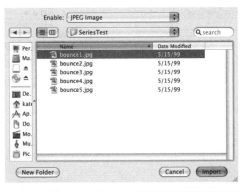

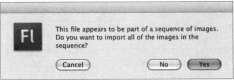

Figure 14.3 When you import one file in a series of numbered files (top), Flash asks whether you want to import the whole series (bottom).

To import a series of graphics files:

1. Follow steps 1–5 of the preceding task. In step 2, choose the appropriate format, and navigate to the first file in the series.

   The series must be in a single folder, and the filenames must differ only by a number at the end—for example, bounce1, bounce2, and bounce3. If these conditions are met, a dialog appears, asking if you want to import a series of sequential images (**Figure 14.3**).

2. In the dialog, click Yes.

   Flash places each image in a separate keyframe in the active layer (**Figure 14.4**).

continues on next page

Preview mode shows images in keyframes

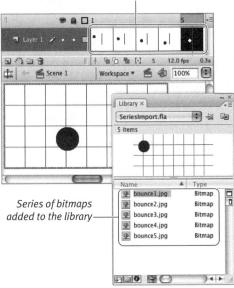

Series of bitmaps added to the library

Figure 14.4 When Flash imports a numbered series of files, it places each one in a separate keyframe in the Timeline of the current document.

IMPORTING BITMAPS

Importing Photoshop Files

When you import content from Photoshop, Flash automatically imports according to your Preferences settings. Using the Import command opens the PSD Import dialog, where you can view and change the settings for individual layers.

To set import preferences for Photoshop (PSD) files:

1. From the Flash (Mac) or Edit (Windows) menu, choose Preferences.

   The Preferences dialog appears.

2. In the Category list, choose PSD File Importer.

   Options for importing PSD files appear on the right side of the dialog (**Figure 14.5**).

3. To set options for importing image layers (**Figure 14.6**), do one of the following:

   ▲ To retain as much of an image layer's opacity and applied blend modes as Flash can handle, select "Bitmap images with editable layer styles."

   ▲ To replicate the look of the image layer most faithfully, select the Flattened Bitmap Images radio button. When this radio button is selected, to have Flash create both a bitmap and a movie clip containing the bitmap, select the Create Movie Clips check box.

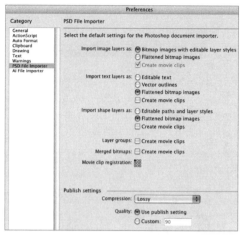

Figure 14.5 Choosing PSD File Importer from the Category list in the Preferences dialog gives you access to options for importing PSD files.

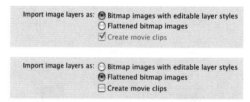

Figure 14.6 You have two choices for importing PSD image layers. If you choose to import them with editable layer styles (top), Flash automatically creates movie-clip symbols to hold the imported layers and applies appropriate Flash blend modes to the symbol instance. If you import image layers as bitmaps (bottom), you can choose to create movie clips to hold them, or import only the bitmaps.

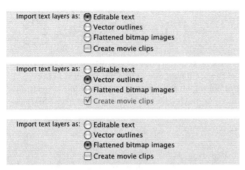

Figure 14.7 You have three options for importing PSD text: as editable text fields (top), as editable shapes (middle), and as bitmaps (bottom). If you choose to import text as editable shapes, Flash automatically creates movie clips to hold them.

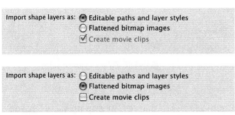

Figure 14.8 When you import PSD shape layers as editable paths (top), Flash automatically places the paths inside a movie-clip symbol. When you import shape layers as bitmaps (bottom), you can choose whether or not to have Flash place them in movie clips by checking the Create Movie Clips check box.

Layer groups: ☐ Create movie clips

Figure 14.9 When you import PSD layer groups, you can have Flash place them inside movie clips.

Merged bitmaps: ☐ Create movie clips

Figure 14.10 If you choose to merge PSD layers for import, you can have Flash place the merged layers inside movie clips.

4. To set options for importing text layers (**Figure 14.7**), do any of the following:

   ▲ To import text in fully editable static text fields, select Editable Text.

   ▲ To import text as editable shapes, select Vector Outlines.

   ▲ To import text as bitmaps, select Flattened Bitmap Images.

   ▲ To have Flash place the editable text or flattened bitmap inside a movie-clip symbol on import, select the Create Movie Clips check box.

5. To set options for importing shape layers (**Figure 14.8**), do one of the following:

   ▲ To import an editable shape that retains as much of its opacity and applied blend modes as Flash can handle, select the "Editable paths and layer styles radio button."

   ▲ To replicate the look of the shape most faithfully, select the Flattened Bitmap Images radio button. When this radio button is selected, to have Flash place the bitmap inside a movie-clip symbol, select the Create Movie Clips check box.

6. To convert grouped layers to movie clips, in the Layer Groups section, select the Create Movie Clips check box (**Figure 14.9**).

7. To convert any merged layers to movie clips, in the Merged Bitmaps section, select the Create Movie Clips check box (**Figure 14.10**). (For more on merging layers, see the next task, "To import content from PSD files.")

   continues on next page

8. To set the registration point for any movie-clip symbols created during the import process, in the Movie Clip Registration section, click one of the nine squares in the Registration model (**Figure 14.11**).

By default, Flash assigns the same registration point to all movie clips created during import. You can override this setting for individual movie clips in the PSD Import dialog. To learn more about the registration point and symbols, see Chapter 7.

9. In the Publish Settings section (**Figure 14.12**), choose one of the following from the Compression pop-up menu:

▲ To retain all image data for imported PSD items when publishing your Flash file, choose Lossless. Flash applies Lossless compression when creating the SWF file for playback. Lossless compression creates the highest-quality images, but also creates larger file sizes. To learn more about publishing, see Chapter 17.

or

▲ To apply JPEG compression to imported PSD items during publishing (Figure 14.12), choose Lossy. Select the Use Publish Setting radio button to apply the JPEG quality currently specified in Publish Settings, or choose the Custom radio button and enter a value between 0 and 100 to override the JPEG quality. Higher values retain more image data, creating better-looking images but larger files.

10. Click OK to confirm the current Preferences settings and close the dialog.

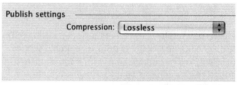

Figure 14.11 In the Preferences dialog's PSD Importer category, clicking one of the nine squares in the symbol registration model sets the default registration point for movie-clip symbols imported from PSD files.

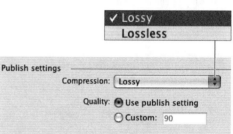

Figure 14.12 The Compression pop-up menu lets you choose which compression method Flash applies during publishing. Lossless compression (top) preserves all the image data. Lossy compression (bottom) lets you determine how much data is lost.

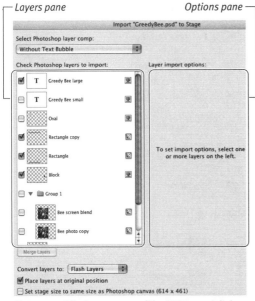

Layers pane   *Options pane*

Figure 14.13 The Layers pane of the PSD Import dialog displays a scrolling list of content available for import. When you select an item in the list, its settings appear in the Options pane of the dialog. General import settings appear in the lower half of the dialog.

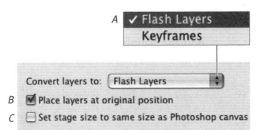

Figure 14.14 The lower portion of the PSD Import dialog offers settings that apply to the entire imported content. You can choose how Flash deals with the PSD file's layer structure (A), how to position the imported objects on the Stage (B), and whether or not to resize the Stage to match the dimensions of the PSD file (C).

To import content from PSD files:

1. Follow steps 1–5 of the first task in the preceding section, "Importing Bitmaps." In step 2, choose Photoshop as the format, and navigate to the file you want to import.

   After you click the Import (Mac) or Open (Windows) button, the PSD Import dialog appears (**Figure 14.13**).

2. To set import options that apply to the whole document, in the lower portion of the PSD Import dialog (**Figure 14.14**), do any of the following:

   ▲ From the Convert Layers To pop-up menu, choose a conversion method. To re-create the PSD file's layer structure as Timeline layers, choose Flash Layers. To convert the PSD layers to keyframes, choose Keyframes.

   ▲ To have Flash place the items on the Stage at their original x and y coordinates, select the "Place layers at original position" check box. Otherwise, Flash centers imported layers on the Stage (the imported items will retain their positions relative to one another).

   ▲ To resize the Stage of your Flash document to match the dimensions of the PSD file, select the "Set Stage size to same size as Photoshop canvas" check box.

continues on next page

A Note About Photoshop Adjustment Layers

Flash has no equivalent to Photoshop's adjustment layers. If a selected layer has an adjustment layer and you want to maintain the visual effect, import the selected layer as a bitmap. Otherwise, Flash ignores the adjustment layer on import.

IMPORTING PHOTOSHOP FILES

429

3. To identify layers for import, in the Layers pane, select the check box to the left of each item you want to import; deselect the check box next to any items you don't want to import (**Figure 14.15**).

If the PSD file contains layer groups, the layers pane displays them hierarchically. Click the triangle to the left of the group name to expand or collapse the set. To select (or deselect) the check boxes of all the layers in a group, select (or deselect) the check box to the left of the group name.

4. To merge layers for import, in the Layers pane, Shift-click the name of each layer you want to combine, then click the Merge Layers button (**Figure 14.16**).

Flash creates a new layer in the Layers pane with a default name of Merged Bitmap. The individual layers are listed hierarchically beneath the Merged Bitmap layer. Flash combines the items on the merged layers and imports them as a bitmap.

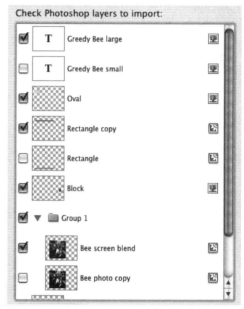

Figure 14.15 in the Layers pane, selected check boxes indicate items you want to import.

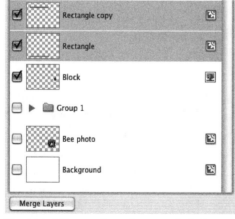
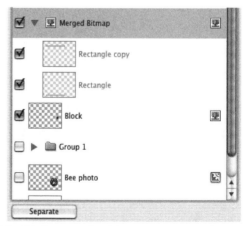

Figure 14.16 To merge layers for import, in the Layers pane, shift-click the name of each layer you want to combine (left), then click the Merge Layers button. Flash combines the layers. Original layers appear hierarchically beneath the merged layer (right).

Enter instance name —

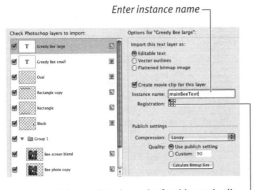

Select registration point for this movie clip —

Figure 14.17 Selecting an item in the Layers pane gives you access to its import settings in the Options pane. Whenever the item can be imported as a movie clip, Flash displays an Instance Name field and a Registration model. Choosing a new registration point for an individual movie clip overrides the default registration-point location currently set in Preferences. The new registration point applies only to the movie clip created from the selected item in the Layers pane.

Figure 14.18 When you use the Import to Style command, Flash imports all the items selected in the Layers pane and places them on the Stage (top). (Here, import options were set to re-create the PSD layers in the Flash Timeline.) Flash adds a folder to the library to hold the assets created by importing the PSD files (bottom).

5. To override PSD Import Preference settings for individual layers, click the layer name to select it in the Layers pane and choose new settings in the Options pane (**Figure 14.17**).

6. After selecting the layers that you want to import and adjusting the import settings as desired, click OK.

   Flash imports all the selected items, places them on the Stage, and places the associated assets in the library (**Figure 14.18**).

✔ Tips

■ If the source PSD file contains *layer comps* (a layer-management feature for quickly viewing various combinations of visible and hidden layers), a Layer Comp pop-up menu appears at the top of the PSD Import dialog. When you select a comp version from the menu, Flash automatically selects the check boxes of the visible layers in that version and deselects the check boxes of layers that are hidden.

■ You can Shift-click to select multiple contiguous PSD layers; the settings you choose in the right-hand pane apply to all the selected items.

■ You can rename the layers during import. In the Layers pane, double-click the name of a layer to activate its text field; enter a new name, and press Enter to confirm the name. When Flash creates the layers and assets, it uses the new name.

Importing Adobe Illustrator Files

When you import graphics from an Adobe Illustrator (AI) file, Flash automatically assigns import settings according to your Preferences settings. One Preferences setting lets you choose whether or not to view the AI Import dialog as part of the import process. When you opt to view the dialog, you can use it to view and change the settings for individual items.

To set preferences for importing AI files:

1. From the Flash (Mac) or Edit menu (Windows), choose Preferences.

   The Preferences dialog appears.

2. In the Category list, choose AI File Importer.

   Options for importing Illustrator files appear on the right side of the dialog (**Figure 14.19**).

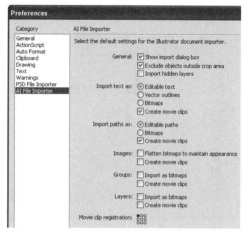

Figure 14.19 Choose AI File Importer in the Category list of the Preferences dialog to create default settings for importing content from Illustrator files.

Import to Library vs. Import to Stage

When you import files, you must choose to import to the Stage or to the library. When you import graphic content to the Stage, Flash places the imported items on the Stage, and, when appropriate, re-creates any layer hierarchy in the main Timeline of the Flash document. Flash also places the imported content in the library of the Flash document.

When you import to the library, the imported content is placed in the library, but for Photoshop, Illustrator, and Fireworks PNG files, Flash also creates a movie-clip or graphic symbol that contains the imported content. Flash places the imported content on the symbol's Stage, and re-creates the layer hierarchy in the symbol's Timeline.

Note that some dialogs present slightly different choices when you choose Import to Library than when you choose Import to Stage. For example, when you import Illustrator and Photoshop files directly to the library, the Import dialog has no option for placing objects at their original position or for setting the Stage size. Imported objects do retain their positions relative to one another, however, and Flash centers the imported artwork as a whole inside the movie-clip symbol.

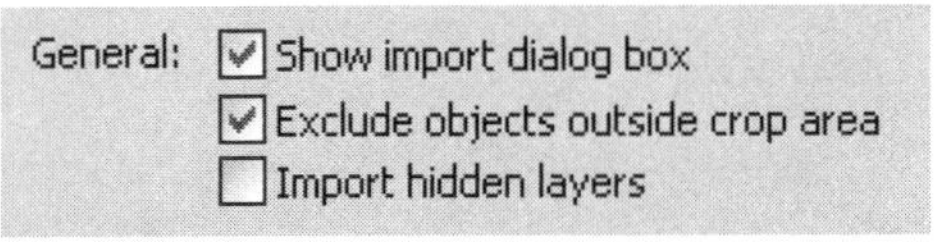

Figure 14.20 The General section of the AI Import dialog lets you decide whether to view the Import dialog box as part of the import procedure. You can also set defaults for importing (or not importing) hidden layers and objects that lie outside the AI file's Artboard.

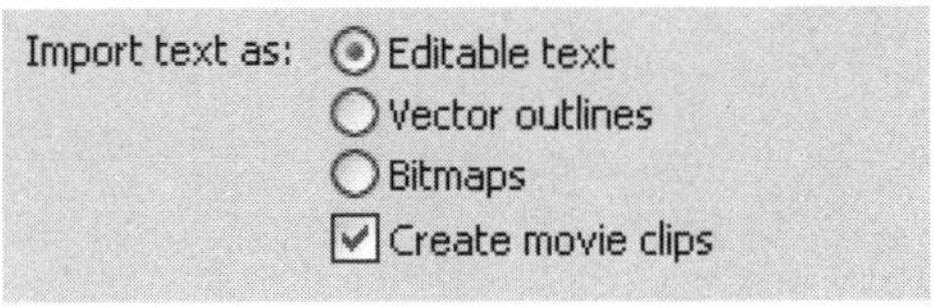

Figure 14.21 Options for importing text include fully editable text fields, editable vector shapes, and bitmaps. You can also choose to have Flash create a movie-clip symbol to contain the imported text.

3. In the General section (**Figure 14.20**) do any of the following:

▲ To have Flash open the AI Import dialog (where you can change import settings) before importing, select the "Show Import dialog box" check box. When this box is deselected, Flash imports the file's content using all the preferences settings without showing you the dialog.

▲ To prevent Flash from importing objects that are not on the Artboard (the Illustrator equivalent to Flash's Stage), select "Exclude objects outside crop area."

▲ To import layers that are currently hidden in the AI file, select Import Hidden Layers.

4. To set options for importing text (**Figure 14.21**), do any of the following:

▲ To import text in fully editable text fields in Flash, select the Editable Text radio button. (If you have designated the text as Static, Input, or Dynamic in Illustrator, Flash re-creates that style of text field in Flash.)

▲ To import text as editable shapes, select the Vector Outlines radio button.

▲ To import text as bitmaps, select the Bitmaps radio button.

▲ To have Flash place the chosen form of imported text inside a movie-clip symbol, select the Create Movie Clips check box.

continues on next page

IMPORTING ADOBE ILLUSTRATOR FILES

5. To set options for importing paths (**Figure 14.22**), do any of the following:

  ▲ To import editable Bézier paths, select the Editable Paths radio button.

  ▲ To import paths as bitmaps, select the Bitmaps radio button.

  ▲ To have Flash place the imported path inside a movie-clip symbol, select the Create Movie Clips check box.

6. To set options for importing images, groups, and layers, in the appropriate sections (**Figure 14.23**), do any of the following:

  ▲ To preserve the look of the images, in the Images section, select the "Flatten bitmaps to maintain appearance" check box.

  ▲ To bring groups or layers in as bitmaps, in the Groups or Layers section, select the Import As Bitmaps check box.

  ▲ To have Flash place each image, group, or layer inside a movie-clip symbol, select the Create Movie Clips check box in the appropriate section.

7. To set the default registration point for the movie-clip symbols created during the import process, in the Movie Clip Registration section, click one of the nine squares in the registration model (**Figure 14.24**).

8. Click OK to confirm the settings and close the dialog.

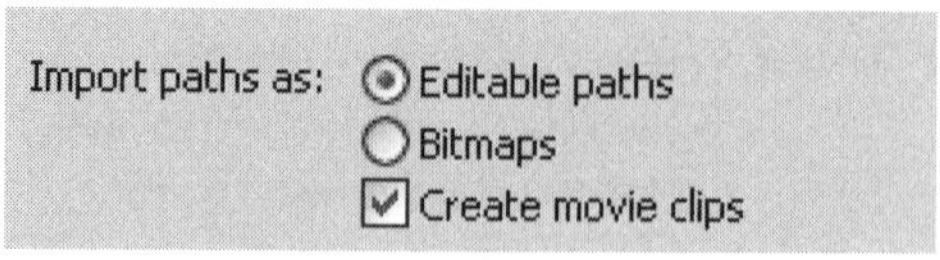

Figure 14.22 You can choose to import Illustrator paths as editable Béziers or as bitmaps.

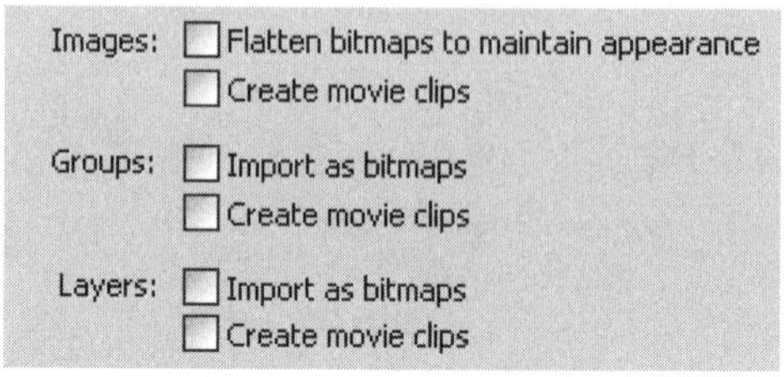

Figure 14.23 When you import images, groups, and/or layers, you can flatten them into a bitmap, or you can import them as movie clips that retain the layer structure.

Figure 14.24 Clicking one of the nine squares in the registration model in the AI Import Preferences dialog sets the default location for the registration point of all movie clips created during the AI import process.

IMPORTING ADOBE ILLUSTRATOR FILES

Layers pane   *Options pane*

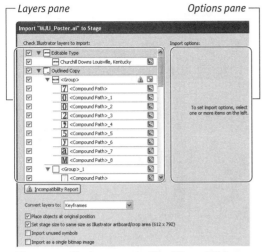

Figure 14.25 The Layers pane of the AI Import dialog displays a scrolling list of content available for import. When you select an item in the list, its settings appear in the Options pane of the dialog. General import settings appear in the lower portion of the dialog.

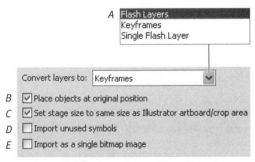

Figure 14.26 The lower portion of the AI Import dialog offers settings that apply to the entire imported content. You can choose how Flash deals with the AI file's layer structure (A), how to position the imported objects on the Stage (B), whether or not to resize the Stage to match the dimensions of the AI file (C), and whether or not to import unused symbols (D). There is also an option to override all settings for individual items and flatten the items selected in the Layers pane into a bitmap (E).

To import content from AI files:

1. Follow steps 1–5 of the first task in the section "Importing Bitmaps," earlier in this chapter. In step 2, choose Adobe Illustrator as the format, and navigate to the file you want to import.

   After you click the Import (Mac) or Open (Windows) button, the Importing External File dialog appears. The dialog contains a progress bar and a Stop (Mac) or Cancel (Windows) button for ending the procedure. If you have set AI Import Preferences to open the AI Import dialog (see the preceding task), when Flash completes the first phase of the import process, the AI Import dialog appears (**Figure 14.25**). If you have chosen not to open the dialog, Flash imports the content of the AI file using the Preferences settings.

2. To set import options that apply to the whole document, in the lower portion of the AI Import dialog (**Figure 14.26**), do any of the following:

   ▲ From the Convert Layers To pop-up menu, choose a conversion method. To re-create the AI file's layer structure in your Flash document, choose Flash Layers. To convert the layers to keyframes, choose Keyframes. To place all imported items on one layer in the Flash Timeline, choose Single Flash Layer.

   ▲ To have Flash place items using their original *x* and *y* coordinates, select the "Place objects at original position" check box. Otherwise, Flash centers imported layers on the Stage (the imported items retain their positions relative to one another).

continues on next page

▲ To resize the Stage of your Flash document to match the dimensions of the AI Artboard, select the "Set Stage size to same size as Illustrator Artboard" check box.

▲ To import symbols that are in the AI file's library but not currently located on the Artboard, select the Import Unused Symbols check box.

▲ To have Flash flatten all selected layers into a bitmap image, select the "Import as a single bitmap image" check box.

3. To identify layers for import, in the Layers pane, select the check box to the left of each item you want to import; deselect the check box next to any items you don't want to import (**Figure 14.27**).

The Layers pane organizes the AI layers (and the sublayers containing the items on each layer) hierarchically. To expand or collapse layers and sublayers, click the triangle to the left of the layer's name.

4. To override AI Import Preference settings for individual items, click the layer name to select it in the Layers pane and choose new settings in the Options pane (**Figure 14.28**).

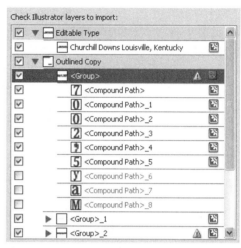

Figure 14.27 The Layers pane identifies which content Flash should import. Items with selected check boxes do import; items with deselected check boxes don't.

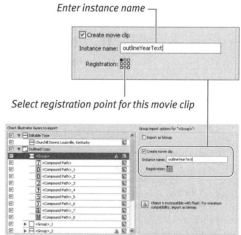

Figure 14.28 Selecting an item in the Layers pane gives you access to its import settings in the Options pane. Whenever the item can be imported as a movie clip, Flash displays an Instance Name field and a Registration model. Choosing a new registration point for an individual movie clip overrides the default registration-point location currently set in Preferences. The new registration point applies only to the movie clip created from the selected item in the Layers pane.

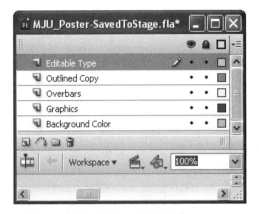

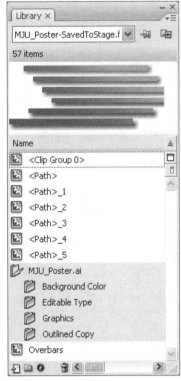

Figure 14.29 Flash imports all the items selected in the Layers pane, places them on the Stage (here import options were set to re-create the AI layers in the Flash Timeline), and places the associated assets in the library. Flash adds a folder to the library to hold the assets created by importing the AI files.

5. After selecting all the items you want to import and adjusting their import settings as desired, click OK.

Flash imports all the selected items, places them on the Stage, and places the associated assets in the library (**Figure 14.29**).

✔ Tips

- You can Shift-click to select multiple contiguous AI layers; the settings you choose in the right-hand pane apply to all the selected items.

- You can rename the layers in the import process. In the Layers pane, double-click the name of a layer to activate its text field, enter a new name, and press Enter to confirm the name. When Flash creates the layers and assets, it uses the new name.

- To select or deselect the check boxes of all the items in one layer, deselect the top-level layer. Flash automatically deselects all the items within that layer. The same technique works for group layers.

Dealing with Incompatibility

Although elements in Adobe Illustrator CS3 and Flash CS3 are more compatible than ever, some items still won't translate or will translate poorly. A major incompatibility—color space—arises from differences between traditional graphic design and Web design. Illustrator artists often work in the CMYK color space used in print publishing. Web designers work in RGB. When you import an AI file, Flash can translate the CMYK colors to RGB for you, but the result may be less than ideal. Incompatibilities can also occur when the source material uses filters and blends that Flash can't handle. The Import dialog has a warning system that flags compatibility problems and advises you of the best import settings to use.

To view a report of incompatibilities for the file as a whole, click the Incompatibility Report button. Flash opens a dialog listing potential problems (**Figure 14.30**). To have Flash change the import settings to make the imported item look as much like the original as possible, select the "Apply recommended import settings" check box, and click Close (If the issue is one of color space, the dialog offers some good advice: to get the best translation of CMYK to RGB, convert your file to RGB in Illustrator.)

An alert symbol (a yellow triangle with an exclamation point) appears in the Layers pane next to each item that presents a problem. When you select that item, an Alert button also appears in the Options pane (**Figure 14.31**). Click the Alert button to open a dialog describing the problem. Another type of incompatibility arises when fonts used in the AI file are not available for Flash to use. The incompatibility report doesn't address font problems, but Flash displays a warning dialog during import, giving you the option to substitute a default font or to choose your own substitute font.

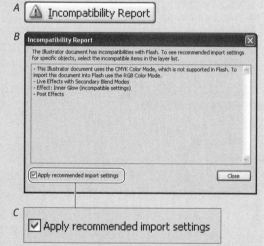

Figure 14.30 To view a list of incompatibilities between the source AI file and Flash, click the Incompatibility Report button (A). Flash opens a dialog listing problem areas (B). To have Flash automatically set problem objects to import as bitmaps to keep their original AI look, select the "Apply recommended import settings" check box in the dialog (C).

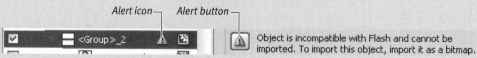

Figure 14.31 Any item that presents a possible problem for translation between Illustrator and Flash displays an alert icon in the Layers pane. Select the item, and a general description of the problem appears in the Options pane. Click the Alert button to view more details.

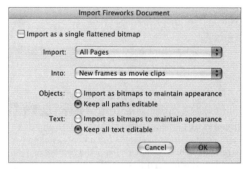

Figure 14.32 The Import Fireworks Document dialog offers options for importing Fireworks files.

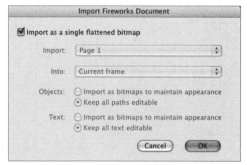

Figure 14.33 Selecting the "Import as a single flattened bitmap" check box in the Import Fireworks Document dialog lets you flatten Fireworks content before bringing it into Flash.

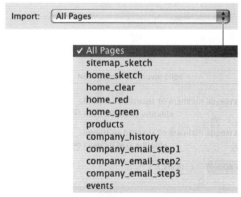

Figure 14.34 The Import pop-up menu in the Import Fireworks Document dialog lets you select one page or all pages of a Fireworks file for import.

Importing Fireworks Files

Flash CS3 offers more options for importing content from Adobe Fireworks files than did previous versions of Flash.

To import Fireworks content as a single bitmap:

1. Follow steps 1–5 of the first task in the section "Importing Bitmaps," earlier in this chapter. In step 2, choose PNG File as the format, and navigate to the file you want to import.

   After you click the Import (Mac) or Open (Windows) button, the Import Fireworks Document dialog appears (**Figure 14.32**).

2. Select the "Import as a single flattened bitmap" check box at the top of the dialog.

   Flash disables all the other import options (**Figure 14.33**).

3. Click OK.

   Flash flattens the Fireworks content and places the bitmap in the currently selected keyframe of the main Timeline and in the library of the Flash document.

To import selected Fireworks content as editable content:

1. Follow step 1 in the preceding task. Make sure that the "Import as a single flattened bitmap" check box is deselected.

2. To select pages to import, do one of the following:

   ▲ To import the content of a single page, from the Import pop-up menu, select the desired page.

   ▲ To import all the content in the document, select All Pages (**Figure 14.34**).

continues on next page

3. To determine how Flash places imported content in the Timeline, from the Into pop-up menu, choose one of the following (**Figure 14.35**):

▲ **New Frames As Movie Clips.** When importing multiple pages, Flash creates separate movie-clip symbols for each Fireworks page and places each instance in a separate keyframe in the main Timeline of the Flash document.

▲ **New Scenes As Movie Clips.** When importing multiple pages, Flash creates separate movie-clip symbols for each Fireworks page and places each instance in the initial keyframe of a separate scene in the main Timeline.

▲ **Current Frame As Movie Clip.** When importing one page, Flash creates a movie-clip symbol and places an instance in the currently selected keyframe of the Flash Timeline.

▲ **New Layer.** When importing one page, Flash adds a new layer to the Timeline and places the imported content in that layer as a flattened bitmap.

4. To determine whether imported items can be edited, in the Objects and Text sections, do one of the following:

▲ To import objects or text as bitmaps, choose the "Import as bitmaps..." radio button in the appropriate section.

▲ To import editable objects or text, choose the "Keep all paths/text editable" radio button in the appropriate section. This setting creates objects and text that you can edit within Flash.

5. Click OK.

Flash imports the content of the Fireworks file according to the selected options, placing bitmaps and/or movie-clip symbol instances on the Stage. Flash also creates a library folder named Fireworks Objects containing the imported assets.

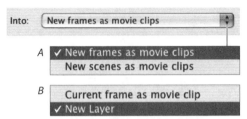

Figure 14.35 Choose a setting from the Into pop-up menu in the Import Fireworks Document dialog to determine how Flash places imported content in the Timeline. This menu presents different options depending on whether you choose to import multiple Fireworks pages (A) or just one page (B).

✔ Tip

■ If you import a Fireworks object as a flattened bitmap, it retains a connection with its original source file. Select the bitmap asset in the library, and from the options menu choose Edit in Fireworks. Flash opens the original file in Fireworks. When you finish your edits, Flash reimports the updated file.

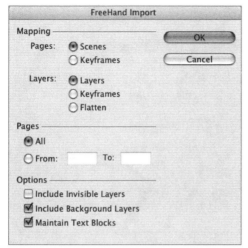

Figure 14.36 When you import files from FreeHand versions 7 through 11 (MX), you have control over how the elements appear in the Flash document.

Importing from FreeHand

To import content from an Adobe FreeHand file, you can use copy and paste, or you can drag content from an open FreeHand file directly onto the Stage in Flash. But with content created in FreeHand version 7 or later, you have the most control when you choose File > Import > Import to Stage (or Import to Library). That opens the FreeHand Import dialog, giving you options for importing.

To import a FreeHand file to the Stage:

1. Open a Flash document.

2. Follow steps 1–5 of the first task in the section "Importing Bitmaps," earlier in this chapter. In step 2, choose FreeHand as the format, and navigate to the file you want to import.

   After you click the Import (Mac) or Open (Windows) button, the FreeHand Import dialog appears (**Figure 14.36**).

3. In the Mapping section, do any of the following:

   ▲ To create a new scene from each FreeHand page, in the Pages subsection, select Scenes.

   ▲ To create a new keyframe from each FreeHand page, in the Pages subsection, select Keyframes.

   ▲ To create a new layer from each FreeHand layer, in the Layers subsection, select Layers.

   ▲ To create a new keyframe from each FreeHand layer, in the Layers subsection, select Keyframes.

   ▲ To combine multiple FreeHand layers into one layer, in the Layers subsection, select Flatten.

   continues on next page

4. In the Pages section, to select the pages to import, do one of the following:

- ▲ To import the entire FreeHand file, select All.

- ▲ To import a range of pages from the FreeHand file, select From/To and then enter the first and last page number.

5. In the Options section, do any of the following:

- ▲ To import any hidden layers from the FreeHand file, select Include Invisible Layers.

- ▲ To import the background layer of the FreeHand file, select Include Background Layers.

- ▲ To have Flash create editable text blocks from any FreeHand text blocks, select Maintain Text Blocks. Otherwise, Flash imports the text characters as grouped shapes.

6. Click OK.

The Importing External File dialog appears, with a Stop (Mac) or Cancel (Windows) button for canceling the operation. Flash imports the FreeHand graphics and places them on the Stage, creating layers and/or keyframes in the main Timeline of your document according to the import options you selected (**Figure 14.37**). Flash adds notes to Flash's Output panel about how many objects were imported or created (**Figure 14.38**). To view this information, access the Output panel, for example, by choosing Window > Output.

Figure 14.37 Flash imports FreeHand files according to the settings in the FreeHand Import dialog. Here, the import options were set to include the background layer.

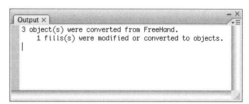

Figure 14.38 When you import FreeHand files, Flash gives you information about how many FreeHand objects the file contained and how many objects Flash had to create in the import process. Flash adds the information for each FreeHand file import to the Flash Output panel.

✔ Tips

- ■ Before Flash 8, if you imported a FreeHand file containing overlapping shapes on a single layer, those shapes segmented one another. Flash CS3 imports the FreeHand shapes as drawing-objects; there's no problem with inadvertent segmenting.

- ■ If you import a FreeHand file containing objects with transparent lens fills, Flash sets the imported objects' transparency to re-create the transparent effect.

ADDING SOUND

It's amazing how much a classic silent film conveys with just moving pictures and text, but that era is history. Audio is a vital feature of today's Web sites. In Adobe Flash CS3 Professional, you can incorporate sound in your projects, either as an ongoing background element or as a synchronized element that matches a particular piece of action—say, a slapping sound that accompanies a pair of hands clapping.

One way to add sound to Flash movies is to import sound clips to the library and then attach instances of the sound clips to keyframes. You can access sounds and control synchronization of sounds via the Frame Properties tab of the Property inspector. You can also use ActionScript to add sounds to Flash movies, but doing so is beyond the scope of this book.

Flash offers a limited form of sound editing. You can clip the ends off a sound and adjust its volume, but you must do other kinds of sound editing outside Flash. When you publish your finished movie, pay attention to the sampling rate and compression of sounds to balance sound quality with the file size of your finished movie. You learn more about these considerations in Chapter 17.

Importing Sounds

The procedure for importing sounds is similar to that for importing bitmaps or other artwork. You use either of these commands: File > Import > Import to Stage or File > Import > Import to Library. Both commands bring the sound file into the library for the current document. Neither actually places the sound, however. You must drag a copy of the sound from the Library panel into a specific keyframe.

To import a sound file:

1. Open the file to which you want to add sounds.

2. Choose File > Import > Import to Stage or press ⌘-R (Mac) or Ctrl-R (Windows) (**Figure 15.1**).

    You can also choose File > Import > Import to Library. The standard file-import dialog appears (**Figure 15.2**).

3. From the Enable pop-up menu (Mac) or the Files of Type pop-up menu (Windows), choose the format of the sound file you want to import.

    Choose All Sound Formats to see files in any sound format.

4. Navigate to the sound file on your system.

5. Select the file.

Figure 15.1 Choose File > Import > Import to Stage (or Import to Library) to bring sounds into your Flash document.

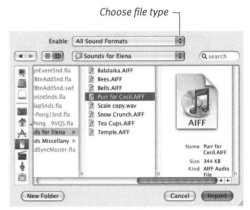

Figure 15.2 The Import dialog lets you import sound files into Flash. Choose a sound-file type that is appropriate for your platform from the pop-up menu of file types. You can also choose to see all sound formats.

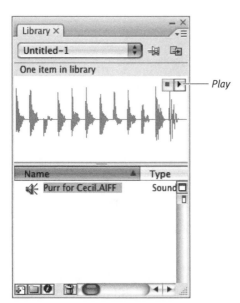

Play

Figure 15.3 Flash keeps sound files in the library. You can see the waveform for a selected sound in the preview window. Click the Play button to hear the sound.

6. Click Import (Mac) or Open (Windows).

Flash imports the sound file you selected, placing it in the library. The waveform of the sound appears in the library's preview window (**Figure 15.3**). Sound files can be quite large; as sounds import, a dialog named Working appears, showing a progress bar. You can stop the import by clicking the Stop (Mac) or Cancel (Windows) button in the dialog.

✔ Tips

■ For imported graphics, the File > Import > Import to Stage command places an instance on the Stage in the selected keyframe. For sounds imported to Flash, that's not true. Imported sounds wind up in the library; you must place them in the keyframe yourself.

■ You can hear a sound without placing it in a movie. Select the sound in the Library panel. Flash displays the waveform in the preview window. To hear the sound, click the Play button in the preview window.

IMPORTING SOUNDS

What Sound Formats Does Flash Import?

Flash deals only with *sampled sounds*—those that have been recorded digitally or converted to digital format. Flash imports AIFF-format files for the Mac OS, WAV-format files for Windows, and MP3-format files for both platforms. In addition, with the combination of Flash CS3 and QuickTime 4 (or later versions), users on both platforms can import QuickTime movies containing just sounds and Sun AU files; Mac users can import WAV, Sound Designer II, and System 7 sounds; and Windows users can import AIFF sounds. Any sounds you import or copy into a Flash document reside in the file's library.

Adding Sounds to Frames

You can assign a sound to a keyframe the same way you place a symbol or bitmap: by selecting the keyframe and then dragging a copy of the sound from an open Library panel (either that document's or another's) to the Stage. You can also assign any sound that resides in a document's library to a selected keyframe in that document by choosing the sound from the Sound pop-up menu in the Frame Properties tab of the Property inspector.

To assign a sound to a keyframe:

1. Open a Flash document to which you want to add sound.

   The Ping-Pong animation you created in Chapter 11 makes a good practice file. The document contains four keyframes in which a ball connects with a paddle. Adding sound can heighten the reality of that contact: You can make the sound realistic (say, a small *thwock*) or make it humorous, if the sound is unexpected (a *boing*, for example).

2. Add a new layer for the sounds in your document, name it Sound, and set its Layer Height Property to 200% (**Figure 15.4**).

   For details on how to set up a sound layer, see the sidebar "Organizing Sounds."

3. In the Timeline, select the Sound layer, and add keyframes at frames 5, 10, 15, and 20.

   These four keyframes match the keyframes in which the ball hits one of the paddles in the animation (**Figure 15.5**).

4. Import the sound you want to hear when the paddle connects with the ball.

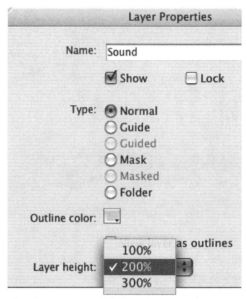

Figure 15.4 It's a good idea to enlarge sound layers to make viewing sound waves easier. Double-click the layer icon in the Timeline to access the Layer Properties dialog, then choose 200% or 300% for Layer height.

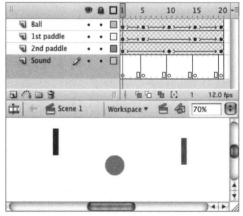

Figure 15.5 Create a separate layer for the sounds in your movie. In that layer, add a keyframe at each place where you want a sound to occur. Here, the keyframes in the Sound layer correspond to the keyframes in other layers where the ball makes contact with a paddle.

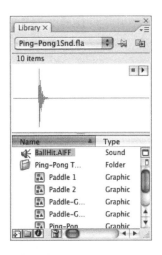

Figure 15.6
After you've imported a sound, it appears in the Library panel. Select the sound, and drag it to a keyframe.

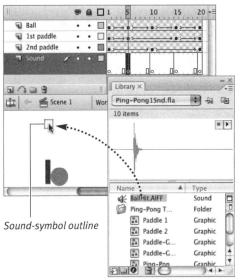

Sound-symbol outline

Waveform of the sound assigned to keyframe 5

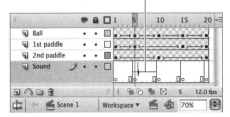

Figure 15.7 When you drag a sound from the Library panel to the Stage, you see the symbol outline (top). A sound has no visible presence on the Stage, but Flash displays the sound's waveform in the Timeline (bottom).

5. In the Timeline, select keyframe 5 of the Sound layer.

This is the first frame in which the ball and paddle connect.

6. Access the Library panel, and select your sound (**Figure 15.6**).

Its waveform appears in the preview window.

7. Drag a copy of the sound from the Library panel to the Stage.

Although sounds have no visible presence on the Stage, you must drag the sound copy to the Stage. As you drag the sound, you see the outline of a box on the Stage. When you release the mouse button, Flash puts the sound in the selected keyframe and displays the waveform in that keyframe and any in-between frames associated with it (**Figure 15.7**).

8. In the Timeline, select keyframe 10 of the Sound layer.

This is the second frame in which the ball and paddle connect.

9. Access the Frame Properties tab of the Property inspector.

continues on next page

ADDING SOUNDS TO FRAMES

10. From the Sound pop-up menu, choose your sound.

All the sounds in the document's library are available from the Frame Properties tab of the Property inspector's Sound pop-up menu (**Figure 15.8**). You don't have to drag a copy of the sound to the Stage each time you want to turn on that sound in a keyframe.

For now, leave the other settings in the Frame Properties tab of the Property inspector alone. You'll learn more about them in later tasks.

11. Repeat steps 6 and 7 (or 8, 9, and 10) for keyframes 15 and 20.

After adding the sound to the four keyframes, you're ready to play the movie and check out the sounds (**Figure 15.9**). As each paddle strikes the ball, Flash plays the assigned sound, adding a level of realism to this simple Ping-Pong animation.

✔ Tip

- If you want to try adding sounds to your Flash projects, but you don't have the equipment to record your own, lots of copyright-free sounds are available. You can purchase CDs of sounds for use in projects; there are also online sites with downloadable sounds. Just make sure the sounds are copyright free before you download them for use in your own project.

Figure 15.8 In the Frame Properties tab of the Property inspector, the Sound pop-up menu lists all the sounds that are in the library of the current document. From this menu, you can choose a sound that you want to assign to the keyframe that's selected in the Timeline.

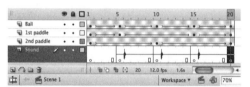

Figure 15.9 For each spot in the movie where a sound should occur, add a sound to a keyframe in the Sound layer. A condensed image of the sound's waveform appears in the keyframe span. Within a single keyframe, you won't see much of the waveform; in keyframe 20, for example, just the initial line is visible.

ADDING SOUNDS TO FRAMES

Organizing Sounds

Nothing prevents you from placing sounds in layers that contain other content, but your document will be easier to handle—and sounds will be easier to find for updating and editing—if you always put sounds in separate layers reserved for a soundtrack. Here are some tips for working with layers for sounds:

◆ Name layers as a reminder of their content. For detailed instructions on working with layers, see Chapter 6.

◆ Place all the sound layers either at the bottom of the Timeline or at the top, so you can find them easily. The position of layers in the stacking order has no effect on the playback of sounds in the movie.

◆ Create a layer folder for sounds. Flash Player 8 and 9 can handle up to 32 sounds playing at one time; earlier Flash Player versions can handle up to 8 simultaneous sounds. (You'll learn about publishing for Flash Player in Chapter 17.) If you put each sound on a separate layer, that's a lot to track. If you'll be working with lots of sound layers, create a layer folder and name it SoundTracks. Placing all the sound layers in the SoundTracks folder makes it easier to work with the sounds (**Figure 15.10**)

◆ Increase the height for sound layers to make it easier to see the waveform (a graphic image of the sound) for that layer. Choose Modify > Timeline > Layer Properties (or double-click the layer icon of the selected layer) to access the Layer Properties dialog. From the Layer Height pop-up menu, choose 200% or 300% to make the layer taller. Click OK.

◆ After you've placed sounds in a layer, lock the layer—to prevent yourself from adding graphics to it accidentally—by clicking the bullet in the Lock column.

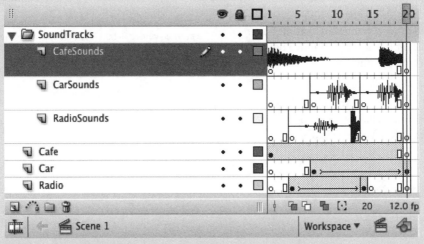

Figure 15.10 It's best to keep sounds in separate layers from the graphics and actions in your movie. To organize multiple sound layers, place them in a separate layer folder. Increase the layer height for sound layers to make more room for the waveforms.

Adding Sounds to Buttons

Auditory feedback helps people who view your Flash creation interact with buttons correctly. For buttons that look like real-world buttons, adding a click sound to the Down frame provides a more realistic feel. For more fanciful buttons or ones disguised as part of the scenery of your movie, adding sound to the Over frame lets users know they've discovered a hot spot.

To enhance buttons with auditory feedback:

1. Open a Flash document containing a button symbol to which you want to add sound.

   (To learn about working with button symbols, see Chapter 12.)

2. Open the file's Library panel (choose Window > Library), and select the button symbol you want to modify.

3. From the Library panel's options menu, choose Edit (**Figure 15.11**).

   Flash opens the button in symbol-editing mode.

4. In the button symbol's Timeline, add a new layer (click the Add Layer button), and name it Sound.

5. In the Sound layer, select the Over and Down frames, Control-click (Mac) or right-click (Windows) and choose Convert to Blank Keyframes (**Figure 15.12**).

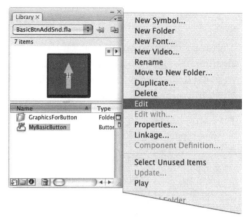

Figure 15.11 To edit a symbol, you can select it in the Library panel and choose Edit from the options menu.

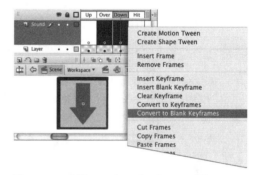

Figure 15.12 Add a new layer for the sounds in a button symbol. In that layer, create keyframes for the button states where you plan to assign sounds.

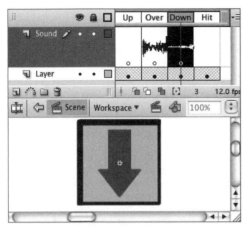

Figure 15.13 Flash displays the waveform of the assigned sound in the keyframe. Unlike movie Timelines, button-symbol Timelines have no in-between frames that can contain part of the waveform. Increasing the layer height for a button symbol's Sound layer enlarges any waveforms in the button's frames, letting you see more detail.

6. Using the techniques described in "Adding Sounds to Frames," earlier in this chapter, assign a sound to the Over frame and a different sound to the Down frame.

Flash displays as much of the waveform as possible in each frame. When you add sounds to buttons, it makes sense to increase the height of the layer that contains sounds (**Figure 15.13**). Make sure that the sound's Sync property is set to Event (the default) in the Property inspector. (You'll learn more about setting the Sync property in the next section.)

7. Return to document-editing mode.

Every instance of the button symbol in the document now has sounds attached.

8. To hear the buttons in action, choose Control > Enable Simple Buttons.

When you move the pointer over the button, Flash plays the sound you assigned to the Over frame. When you click the button, you hear the sound you assigned to the Down frame.

✔ Tip

- The most common frames to use for button feedback are the Over and Down frames, but you can add sounds to any of the button symbol's frames. Sounds added to the Up frame play when the pointer rolls out of the active button area. Sounds added to the Hit frame play when you release the mouse button within the active button area.

ADDING SOUNDS TO BUTTONS

Using Event Sounds

One of the sound settings available in the Frame Properties tab of the Property inspector is Sync. The Sync setting determines the way Flash synchronizes the sounds in your movie. Sync has four settings: Event, Start, Stop, and Stream. The default is Event.

Event sounds play independently of the main Timeline. Flash starts an event sound at a keyframe in a movie; the event sound plays until Flash reaches the end of the sound clip or encounters an instruction to stop playing that sound or all sounds. Long event sounds can continue to play after the playhead reaches the last frame in the movie. If your movie loops, every time the playhead passes a frame with an event sound, Flash starts another instance of that sound playing.

To understand how synchronization works, it's helpful to work in a file that has identifying text in keyframes.

To set up a file for testing sounds:

1. Create a 20-frame, three-layer Flash document.

2. Label the layers Objects, Sound 1, and Sound 2.

3. In all layers, insert keyframes into frames 1, 5, 10, 15, and 20.

4. In the Objects layer, place identifying text on the Stage for each keyframe.

5. Import several sounds of different lengths into the file's library.

    This example uses a 15.8-second sound clip of a musical-scale passage, a water drop sound, a melodic passage, and some rhythm sounds.

6. Save the document as a template for use throughout this chapter, and name it SoundSyncMaster (**Figure 15.14**).

Figure 15.14 After setting up a testing file for use in this chapter, choose File > Save As Template to access the Save As Template dialog. Save the file as SoundSyncMaster. Be sure to close the template document after creating it. For detailed instructions on saving documents as templates, see Chapter 1.

Independent Sounds vs. Synchronized Sounds

Unsynchronized sound clips play independently of the frames in a movie and can even continue playing after the playhead reaches the last frame in the movie. Flash starts these *event sounds* at a specific frame, but thereafter, event sounds play without relation to specific frames. On one viewer's computer, the sound may take ten frames to play; on a slower setup, the sound may finish when only five frames have appeared.

Flash can also synchronize entire sound clips with specific frames. Flash breaks these *stream sounds* or *streaming sounds* into smaller pieces and attaches each piece to a specific frame. For streaming sounds, Flash forces the animation to keep up with the sounds. On slower setups, Flash draws fewer frames so important actions and sounds stay together.

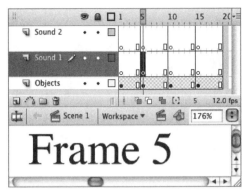

Figure 15.15 Select the keyframe to which you want to assign a sound. Settings that you create in the Frame Properties tab of the Property inspector are applied to the selected keyframe.

Figure 15.16 In the Frame Properties tab of the Property inspector, choose a sound from the Sound pop-up menu.

Figure 15.17 From the Sync pop-up menu, choose Event to make the assigned sound start in the selected keyframe and play to the end of the sound, without synchronizing to any subsequent frames of the movie.

To make an assigned sound an event sound:

1. Open a new document using the SoundSyncMaster template you created in the preceding task.

2. In the Timeline, select keyframe 5 of the Sound 1 layer (**Figure 15.15**).

3. In the Frame Properties tab of the Property inspector, from the Sound pop-up menu, choose a long sound, such as the 15.8-second sound named Scale.AIFF (**Figure 15.16**).

4. From the Sync pop-up menu, choose Event (**Figure 15.17**).

   The Scale.AIFF sound is assigned to keyframe 5 of the Sound 1 layer.

5. Position the playhead in keyframe 1, and play your movie (choose Control > Play).

   In a movie that has a standard frame rate of 12 frames per second (fps), the 15.8-second Scale sound continues to play after the playhead reaches the last frame of the movie.

✔ Tip

- To understand better how Flash handles event sounds, choose Control > Loop Playback. Now play the movie again, and let it loop through a couple of times. Each time the playhead enters keyframe 5, Flash starts another instance of the Scale sound, and you begin to hear not one set of notes going up the scale, but a cacophony of bad harmonies. When you stop the playback, each sound instance plays out until its end—an effect sort of like people singing a round.

USING EVENT SOUNDS

453

To play overlapping instances of the same sound:

1. Using the file you created in the preceding task, to assign a sound to a later point in the movie's Timeline, do either of the following:

   ▲ Select keyframe 15 of the Sound 1 layer.

   ▲ Select keyframe 15 of the Sound 2 layer.

   Because Flash starts a new instance of an event sound even if that sound is already playing, you have the choice of adding a second instance to the same layer as the first or adding it to a different layer.

2. In the Frame Properties tab of the Property inspector, from the Sound pop-up menu, choose the same sound (Scale.AIFF).

3. From the Sync pop-up menu, choose Event. The Scale.AIFF sound is assigned to keyframe 15 of whichever layer you chose (**Figure 15.18**).

4. Position the playhead in keyframe 1, and play your movie one time.

   When the playhead reaches keyframe 5, the Scale.AIFF sound starts. When the playhead reaches keyframe 15, another instance of the Scale.AIFF sound starts, and the two sounds play together (you hear two voices). When the first instance ends, you again hear only one voice. Within a single layer, each frame can contain only one sound. To make Flash begin playing different sounds at the same point in a movie, you must put the sounds in separate layers.

5. Save this file for use in a later task; name it OverlapSnds.fla.

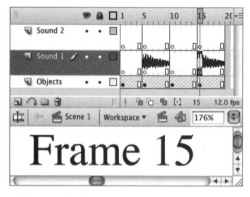

Figure 15.18 You can add a second instance of your sound and make it play on top of the first. Event sounds play independent of the main Timeline, so you're free to add the second sound to the same layer as the first (top). Alternatively, you can add the second sound to its own layer (bottom).

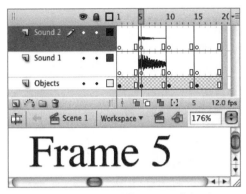

Figure 15.19 To make two different sounds begin playing simultaneously, you must put each sound in a different layer in a keyframe at the same spot in the Timeline—for example, keyframe 5.

✔ Tip

■ All the information required to play an event sound lives in the keyframe to which you assigned that sound. When you play the movie, Flash pauses at that keyframe until all the information has downloaded. It's best to reserve event syncing for short sound clips; otherwise, your movie may be interrupted by long pauses for downloading sounds.

To start different sounds simultaneously:

1. Open a new document using the SoundSyncMaster template you created earlier in this chapter.

2. In the Timeline, select keyframe 5 of the Sound 1 layer.

3. In the Frame Properties tab of the Property inspector, from the Sound pop-up menu, choose the first sound (here, Scale.AIFF).

4. From the Sync pop-up menu, choose Event.

5. In the Timeline, select keyframe 5 of the Sound 2 layer.

6. In the Frame Properties tab of the Property inspector, from the Sound pop-up menu, choose a different sound (here, Melody.AIFF).

You can also import a new sound to your movie's library or open the Library panel of another movie containing the sound you want to use and then drag a copy of the sound to the Stage.

Flash places the waveform for the second sound in keyframe 5 of the Sound 2 layer (**Figure 15.19**).

7. In the Frame Properties tab of the Property inspector, from the Sync pop-up menu, choose Event.

8. Position the playhead in keyframe 1, and play your movie one time.

When the playhead reaches keyframe 5, Flash starts playing the Scale.AIFF and Melody.AIFF sounds simultaneously.

Using Start Sounds

Start sounds behave just like event sounds, with one important difference: Flash doesn't play a new instance of a start sound if that sound is already playing.

To set an assigned sound's Sync parameter to Start:

1. Open OverlapSnds.fla, the file you created in "To play overlapping instances of the same sound," earlier in this chapter.

   You should have one instance of the Scale.AIFF sound in keyframe 5 and another in keyframe 15. The second instance is in the Sound 1 or Sound 2 layer, depending on what you did in the earlier task.

2. In the Timeline, select the keyframe 15 that contains the Scale.AIFF sound (**Figure 15.20**).

3. In the Frame Properties tab of the Property inspector, from the Sync pop-up menu, choose Start (**Figure 15.21**).

4. Position the playhead in keyframe 1, and play your movie one time.

   When the playhead reaches keyframe 5, the Scale.AIFF sound starts. When the playhead reaches keyframe 15, nothing changes; you continue to hear just one voice as the Scale.AIFF sound continues playing. When a sound is playing and Flash encounters another instance of the same sound, the Sync setting determines whether Flash plays that sound. When Sync is set to Start, Flash doesn't play another instance of the sound.

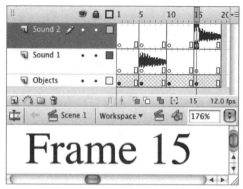

Figure 15.20 To change a sound's Sync setting, first select the keyframe that contains the sound.

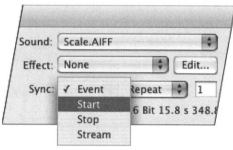

Figure 15.21 To prevent Flash from playing another instance of a sound if that sound is already playing, choose Start from the Sync pop-up menu in the Frame Properties tab of the Property inspector.

✔ Tip

■ To avoid playing multiple instances of a sound when a movie loops, set the sound's Sync property to Start. If the sound is still playing when Flash starts the movie again, Flash lets the sound play, adding nothing new. If the sound has finished, Flash starts the sound again when the playhead enters a keyframe containing the sound.

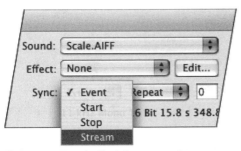

Figure 15.22 To make Flash force a sound to synchronize with a specific frame of your movie, choose Stream from the Sync pop-up menu in the Frame Properties tab of the Property inspector.

The Mystery of Streaming Sound

When you choose Stream as the Sync setting for a sound, Flash divides that sound clip into smaller subclips and embeds them in individual frames. The movie's frame rate determines the subclips' size. In a movie with a frame rate of 10 frames per second (fps), for example, Flash divides streaming sounds into subclips that are a tenth of a second long. For every 10 frames, Flash plays 1 second of the sound.

Flash synchronizes the start of each subclip with a specific frame of the movie. If the sound plays back faster than the computer can draw frames, Flash sacrifices some visuals (skips drawing some frames of the animation) so that sound and images match up as closely as possible. Setting a sound's Sync property to Stream ensures, for example, that you hear the door slam when you see it swing shut—not a few seconds before. If the discrepancy between sound-playback speed and frame-drawing speed is big enough, however, those dropped frames make the movie look jerky, just as it would if you set a low frame rate to begin with.

Using Stream Sounds

Stream sounds are specifically geared for playback over the Web. When Sync is set to Stream, Flash breaks a sound into smaller sound clips. Flash synchronizes these sub-clips with specific frames of the movie—as many frames as are required to play the sound. Flash stops streaming sounds when playback reaches a new keyframe or an instruction to stop playing either that specific sound or all sounds.

Unlike event sounds, which must download fully before they can play, stream sounds can start playing after a few frames have downloaded. This situation makes streaming the best choice for long sounds, especially if you'll be delivering your movie over the Web.

To make an assigned sound a stream sound:

1. Open a new document using the SoundSyncMaster template you created earlier in this chapter.

2. In the Timeline, in the Sound 1 layer, remove keyframe status from keyframe 10 (select it and choose Modify > Timeline > Clear Keyframe).

3. In the Timeline, in the Sound 1 layer, select keyframe 5.

4. In the Frame Properties tab of the Property inspector, from the Sound pop-up menu, choose a long sound (here, Scale.AIFF).

5. From the Sync pop-up menu, choose Stream (**Figure 15.22**).

continues on next page

6. To see how the sound fits into the available time in your movie, in the Sound section of the Frame Properties tab of the Property inspector, click the Edit button.

   The Edit Envelope dialog appears.

   At 15.8 seconds, the Scale.AIFF sound is too long to play completely in the frames between keyframe 5 and keyframe 15. When Sync is set to Stream, Flash plays only as much of the sound as can fit in the frames that are available to it—in this case, slightly less than a second. In the Edit Envelope dialog, a vertical line indicates where Flash truncates this instance of the sound (**Figure 15.23**).

7. To close the Edit Envelope dialog, click OK or Cancel.

   The truncated waveform appears in frames 5–15 (**Figure 15.24**).

8. Position the playhead in keyframe 1, and play your movie to hear the sound in action.

   When the playhead reaches keyframe 5, the Scale.AIFF sound starts. When the playhead reaches keyframe 15, the keyframe span ends, and Flash stops playback of the Scale.AIFF sound.

9. Choose Control > Loop Playback, and then play the movie to hear the sound in looping mode.

   Flash repeats the same snippet of sound, stopping it each time the playhead reaches keyframe 15.

Edit button

Sound will stop playing here

Figure 15.23 When you set a sound's Sync to Stream, you can check how much of the sound will play, given the number of in-between frames there are for the sound to play in. In the Frame Properties tab of the Property inspector, click the Edit button (top) to open the Edit Envelope dialog (bottom). The sound-editing window displays a sound's full waveform in relation to time or to frame numbers.

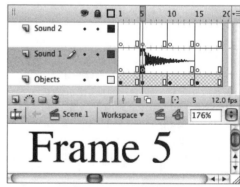

Figure 15.24 There is time enough in the ten-frame span from keyframe 5 to keyframe 15 to play only the first note of the Scale sound. Flash displays just that much of the full 15.8-second waveform in the Timeline.

✔ Tips

- You can hear streaming sounds play as you drag the playhead through the Timeline (a technique called *scrubbing*). As the playhead moves over the waveform, you can see how the images and sounds fit together. You can then add or delete frames to better synchronize the sounds with the images onscreen.

- Try Shift-clicking the Timeline to take the playhead to a particular frame (or Shift-dragging the playhead to that frame). As long as you hold down the Shift key and the mouse button, Flash repeats the portion of sound that synchronizes with the frame where the playhead is.

- If your stream sound is getting cut off too soon, switch the units of measure in the Edit Envelope dialog to see how many frames you need to add to accommodate the sound (**Figure 15.25**).

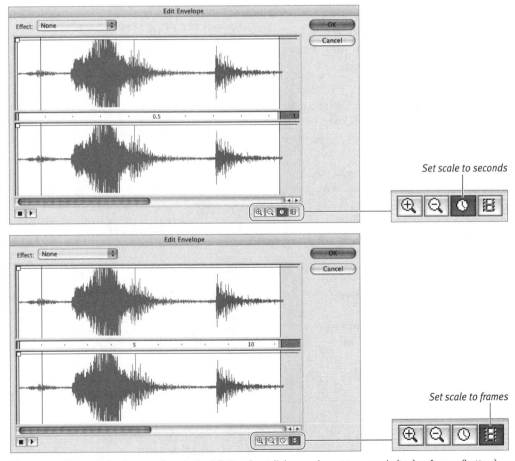

Set scale to seconds

Set scale to frames

Figure 15.25 The scale for the waveform in the Edit Envelope dialog can be set to seconds (top) or frames (bottom). If you set the scale to frames, you can see exactly how many frames you need to provide enough time for the major parts of the sound to finish. (For this sound, you would need 11 frames.) Usually, you want to make room for the segments of the wave that have the greatest amplitude.

USING STREAM SOUNDS

Stopping Sounds

Although event sounds normally play to the end, you can force them to stop at a specific keyframe. To issue an instruction to stop a specific sound, set that sound's Sync parameter to Stop.

To stop playback of a sound:

1. Create a new single-layer 15-frame Flash document with two fairly long event sounds (at least 2 or 3 seconds each); place one sound in keyframe 1 and the other in keyframe 5.

   In this example, keyframe 1 contains the sound Rhythm.AIFF, and keyframe 5 contains the sound Melody.AIFF. Make sure that Sync is set to Event for both sounds.

2. In the Timeline, at frame 8, insert a new blank keyframe (**Figure 15.26**).

   The blank keyframe cuts off the waveform in the Timeline, but on playback, both event sounds continue to play after the playhead reaches keyframe 8.

3. Select keyframe 8.

4. In the Frame Properties tab of the Property inspector, from the Sound pop-up menu, choose Rhythm.AIFF.

5. From the Sync pop-up menu, choose Stop (**Figure 15.27**).

   Flash uses this instruction to stop playback of the Rhythm.AIFF sound at keyframe 8.

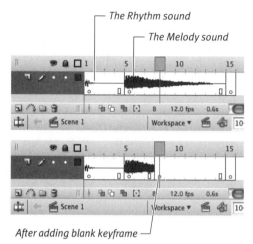

The Rhythm sound

The Melody sound

After adding blank keyframe

Figure 15.26 Inserting a new keyframe cuts off your view of the preceding sound's waveform in the Timeline. If the sound is an event sound, however, it continues playing even when the playhead moves past the keyframe.

Figure 15.27 To stop a sound's playback at a specific point in a movie, create and then select the keyframe where the sound should stop. In the Frame Properties tab of the Property inspector, from the Sound pop-up menu, choose the sound you want to stop. From the Sync pop-up menu, choose Stop. Here, the Stop instruction refers to the Rhythm sound.

Sync is set to Stop for this keyframe —

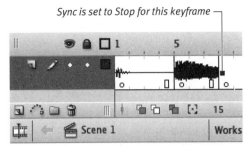

Figure 15.28 In the Timeline, a small square in the middle of a keyframe indicates the presence of the stop-sound instruction.

Flash places a small square in the middle of keyframe 8 in the Timeline to indicate that the frame contains a stop-sound instruction (**Figure 15.28**).

6. Position the playhead in keyframe 1, and play your movie to hear the sounds in action.

The Rhythm.AIFF sound starts immediately; Melody.AIFF kicks in at keyframe 5. When the playhead reaches keyframe 8, Rhythm.AIFF cuts out, but Melody.AIFF plays on even after the playhead reaches the end of the movie.

✔ Tips

■ The Stop setting and the sound that it stops can be in different layers. The Stop setting stops playback of all instances of the specified sound that are currently playing in any layer.

■ To stop only one instance of a sound, set the Sync parameter of that instance to Stream; then, in the layer containing that instance, put a blank keyframe in the frame where you want that instance of the sound to stop.

Repeating Sounds

Flash's sound-repeating parameter allows you to play a sound several times in a row without adding other instances of the sound to a frame. If you type a value in the Repeat field in the sound area (the right side) of the Frame Properties tab of the Property inspector, Flash plays the sound the specified number of times. You can repeat event sounds and streaming sounds. The sound's Sync parameter applies to the whole set of repeated sounds. You can also set sounds to loop until further instruction.

To set a Repeat value:

1. Create a five-frame Flash document with a short event sound in keyframe 1.

   This task uses a sound called Drip.AIFF.

2. In the Timeline, select keyframe 1.

3. In the sound area (the right side) of the Frame Properties tab of the Property inspector, from the Repeat pop-up menu, choose Repeat, the default setting (**Figure 15.29**).

4. Type *3* in the field to the right of the Repeat menu (**Figure 15.30**).

   Flash extends the sound's waveform by stringing together three copies of it. In the Timeline, Flash displays as much of the extended waveform as will fit in the available frames (**Figure 15.31**).

5. Save this document for use in the next task; name it RepeatSnds.fla.

Figure 15.29 The Repeat menu in the Frame Properties tab of the Property inspector has settings for playing a sound a set number of times (Repeat) or replaying a sound until instructed to stop (Loop).

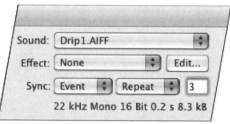

Figure 15.30 Typing a value in the Repeat field tells Flash how many times to play the selected sound.

Figure 15.31 When Repeat is set to 0 or 1, Flash displays just the original waveform in the Timeline (top). When Repeat is set to a number greater than 1, Flash displays as much of the repeated waveform as there is room for (bottom).

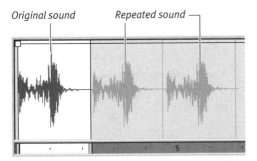

Original sound   *Repeated sound*

Figure 15.32 You can see a precise waveform for the repeated sound graphed against seconds or frames (shown here) of your movie in the Edit Envelope dialog. The grayed-out waveforms are the repeated portion of the sound.

✔ Tips

■ To see the extended waveform graphed against seconds or frames, click the Edit button in the Frame Properties tab of the Property inspector. The full sound appears in the Edit Envelope dialog (**Figure 15.32**).

■ Although you can use the Repeat parameter with sounds whose Sync parameter is Stream, doing so adds to the size of your published file.

Using Buttons to Control Sounds

In this chapter, you learn to use sounds two ways. You create user-friendly buttons with audio feedback by adding sounds to keyframes in button symbols. You create sound tracks or sound effects for animation by adding and removing sound instances directly in the Timeline during authoring. A third way to work with sound is to use ActionScript (AS) to control sounds during playback—loading, playing, and stopping sounds as needed at runtime. For AS 2.0, Flash provides a set of Behaviors for common sound-related tasks. Behaviors attach scripts directly to sound-control objects (button symbols, button components, or movie clips). You can use Behaviors to set up buttons that load and play a specific sound, that replay a loaded sound, or that stop all event sounds that are currently playing whether they were loaded with AS or placed in the Timeline during authoring. For AS 3.0, you must script any sound-control objects yourself. You can create frame scripts that target sound-control objects and carry out the same types of sound-control tasks as the AS 2.0 Behaviors. With either version of ActionScript, when setting up buttons to control sounds you must set the sound's Linkage properties. Scripting sounds is a complex task, beyond the scope of this book. To learn about creating basic frame scripts in ActionScript 3.0, see Chapter 13.

Editing Sounds

Flash lets you make limited changes in each instance of a sound in the Edit Envelope dialog. You can change the start point and end point of the sound (that is, cut a piece off the beginning or end of the waveform) and adjust the sound's volume.

Flash offers six predefined volume edits: Left Channel, Right Channel, Fade Left to Right, Fade Right to Left, Fade In, and Fade Out. These sound-editing templates create common sound effects, such as making a sound grow gradually louder (Fade In) or softer (Fade Out), or (for stereo sounds) making the sound move from one speaker channel to the other.

In addition to changing a sound's volume, you can make a sound shorter by instructing Flash to remove sound data from the beginning of the waveform, the end, or both.

To assign packaged volume effects:

1. Open the document you created in the preceding task (RepeatSnds.fla).

   This is a five-frame movie with an event sound that loops three times within those frames.

2. In the Timeline, select keyframe 1.

   This frame contains the sound Drip.AIFF.

3. In the sound area of the Frame Properties tab of the Property inspector, click the Edit button.

   The Edit Envelope dialog appears, with a sound-editing window showing the waveform of the sound from keyframe 1 (**Figure 15.33**).

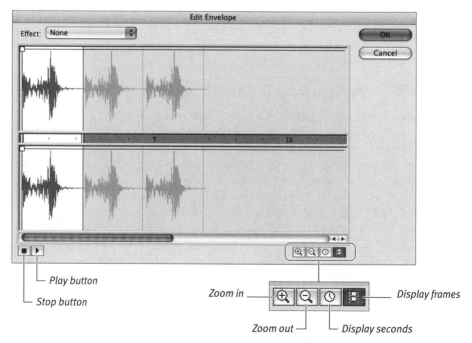

Figure 15.33 Flash lets you perform simple sound editing—for length and volume—in the Edit Envelope dialog.

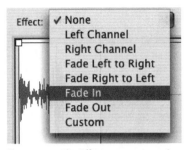

Figure 15.34 The Effect pop-up menu in the Edit Envelope dialog offers six templates for common sound effects that deal with volume. Choose Fade In to make the sound start soft and grow in volume.

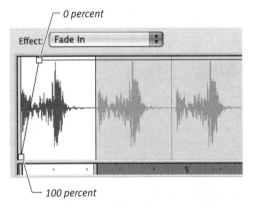

Figure 15.35 The Fade In effect brings the sound's envelope down to 0 percent (the bottom of the sound-editing window) at the start of the sound and quickly raises it to 100 percent (the top of the sound-editing window).

4. In the Edit Envelope dialog, click the Display Frames button.

The sound-editing window can measure the length of the sound in seconds or in frames. Clicking the filmstrip icon in the lower-right corner of the window sets the units to frames; clicking the clock icon sets the units to seconds.

5. From the Effect pop-up menu, choose Fade In (**Figure 15.34**).

Flash adjusts the sound envelope (**Figure 15.35**). When the envelope line is at the top of the sound-editing window, Flash plays 100 percent of the available sound. When the envelope line is at the bottom of the window, Flash plays 0 percent of the available sound.

6. Click the Play button to hear the sound with its fade-in effect.

The first iteration of the sound starts soft and grows louder. The repetitions play at full volume.

7. Click OK.

Flash returns you to document-editing mode.

✔ Tip

■ If you don't need to look at your sound's waveform, you can bypass the Edit Envelope dialog. Just choose an effect from the Effect pop-up menu in the sound area of the Frame Properties tab of the Property inspector.

EDITING SOUNDS

To customize volume effects:

1. Follow steps 1–3 in the preceding task.

2. From the Effect pop-up menu in the Edit Envelope dialog, choose Custom (**Figure 15.36**).

3. In the sound-editing window, drag the square envelope handles that appear at the beginning of the sound in both channels down to 0 percent.

4. In the right channel (the top section of the window), click the waveform at three places to set a different level for each repetition of the sound; for this sound, add handles near the marks for frames 2, 4, and 5.

   Flash adds envelope handles so both channels have four handles.

5. In the right-channel window, drag the second handle up to the 50 percent volume level (**Figure 15.37**).

6. Repeat step 5 for the left channel.

7. In both channels, drag the third handle to the 50 percent level and the fourth handle to the 100 percent level.

   You can use as many as eight handles to create a variety of volume changes within one sound.

8. Click the Play button to hear the sound with its fade-in effect.

   Flash fades in the first iteration of the sound, plays the second iteration at half volume, and plays the third iteration at full volume.

9. Click OK.

✔ Tip

■ To remove unwanted envelope handles, drag them out of the sound-editing window.

Figure 15.36 To edit the volume of a sound yourself, from the Effect pop-up menu in the Edit Envelope dialog, choose Custom.

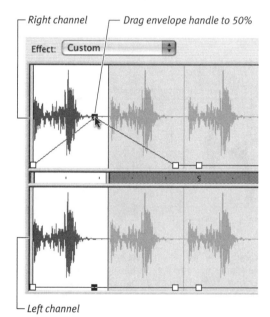

Figure 15.37 Click the waveform in the sound-editing window to add a handle. Drag the handle to adjust the sound envelope. You can make the sound envelope the same or different for both channels. For monaural sounds, both waveforms are identical.

EDITING SOUNDS

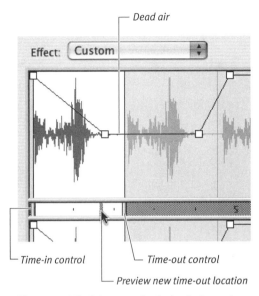

Dead air

Effect: Custom

Time-in control *Time-out control*

Preview new time-out location

Figure 15.38 Flash lets you trim the beginning and end of a sound in the Edit Envelope dialog's sound-editing window. Here, dragging the time-out control clips off the end of the sound where the wave's amplitude is smaller, almost a flat line. (The small amplitude indicates very soft sound or silence).

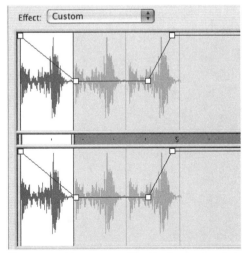

Effect: Custom

Figure 15.39 After you reposition the time-out control, the new, shorter waveform appears in the Edit Envelope dialog's sound-editing window.

To edit sounds for length:

1. Using the movie you created in the preceding task, select keyframe 1.

2. To access the Edit Envelope dialog, in the Frame Properties tab of the Property inspector, click the Edit button.

3. In the sound-editing window, drag the time-out control (the second bar in the "Timeline" between the two channels) to the place where the waveform goes flat (**Figure 15.38**).

   Flash shortens the sound in both channels (**Figure 15.39**).

4. Click OK.

   Flash returns you to document-editing mode. Now all three iterations of the repeating sound are visible in the Timeline (**Figure 15.40**).

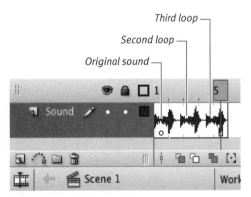

Third loop

Second loop

Original sound

Figure 15.40 After you shorten the sound, all three iterations fit into the five-frame movie.

✔ Tips

- To remove dead air from the beginning of a sound, drag the time-in control. Flash places a light gray background behind the initial portion of the sound's waveform to indicate that it won't play.

- Although you can change the start and end points of a sound in Flash, you still have the whole sound taking up room in the SWF file. If you find yourself trimming many sounds in Flash, consider investing in a sound-editing program that lets you leave the excess on the cutting-room floor rather than behind the curtains in Flash.

- When you choose to repeat sounds, Flash links the repeated sounds and displays them as a single waveform in the Edit Envelope dialog, where you can edit them. You can change the volume so the sound gets louder with each repetition, for example. (See "Repeating Sounds," earlier in this chapter.)

16

ADDING VIDEO

From wildlife Web cams to YouTube postings, video is everywhere on the Web. Adobe Flash CS3 Professional makes it easy to add video content to Flash movies to give your audience a full multimedia experience. You can embed video data into the Flash Timeline, add a special component to the Flash document for displaying external video files that have been translated to Adobe Flash Video (FLV) format, or have Flash link to external QuickTime files. The first two options let end users view the video in Flash Player, while the third option requires you to publish your Flash content as a QuickTime movie. Advanced scripters can also use ActionScript to dynamically display FLV files as streaming-video in their Flash creations.

Flash's built-in Video Import Wizard and the stand-alone Adobe Flash CS3 Video Encoder both let you translate video files into Flash-ready format. (The Video Encoder is automatically installed with the default installation of Flash.) In this chapter, you'll learn to use the Video Import Wizard to prepare files for use in Flash. You'll work with embedded video clips and use the FLVPlayback component to display video from external FLV files in Flash Player.

About the Video Import Wizard

Flash CS3's Video Import Wizard walks you through the process of importing and encoding video clips for use in Flash. The wizard also offers modest video-editing features for adjusting a video clip's image area, frame size, and length.

The biggest decision you have to make when using the wizard is how Flash will deliver the video data to your viewers. You can embed the video data into the Flash document, or keep the data in an external file and display the video via a special Flash element—the FLVPlayback component.

Embedded video adds to the size of a published Flash movie and forces users to wait for all the video data to download before there's anything to watch. Video displayed using the FLVPlayback component doesn't add to the size of the published movie. How long users must wait to see the video depends on whether you use progressive or streaming video and on the particulars of each user's computer setup.

You can have the FLV video download progressively from a Web server. This method divides the video data into small segments. The video can start playing as soon as a few segments have downloaded, which means less waiting for your viewers.

You can have Flash stream the FLV video, either from a Flash Video Streaming Service or from your own server using Flash Media Server. With this method the video can start playing as soon as enough data for the initial frames has downloaded; the server continues to download video data while the end user watches. To use streaming video, you must have access to a Flash Media Server, have a Flash Video Streaming Service account with your ISP, or use a dedicated streaming service, such as LimeLight Networks.

In addition, Flash can deploy video for use with mobile devices and can link to external QuickTime video files. The QuickTime option works only with Flash Player 3–5, however, and requires that you deliver your final content as a QuickTime movie by publishing to a QuickTime (MOV) file. To learn about publishing, see Chapter 17.

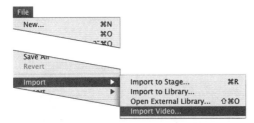

Figure 16.1 Choose File > Import > Import Video to open Flash's Video Import Wizard.

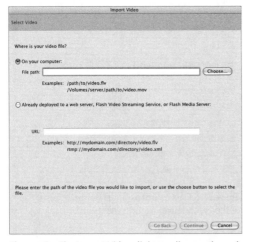

Figure 16.2 The Import Video dialog walks you through the process of setting up video clips for use in your Flash movie. The first step is choosing a video file.

Figure 16.3 To locate video on your computer for import, select the On Your Computer radio button, and either enter the file's path or navigate to the file and select it.

Figure 16.4 To import video that's on an external server, select the "Already deployed to a Web server" radio button and enter the clip's URL.

Importing Video for Progressive Download or Streaming

You begin to import your video by starting the wizard, locating the video file, and choosing how you want to deliver (or deploy) the video. The remaining steps vary depending on the deployment method you choose. Let's look first at deploying video for progressive download or streaming over the Web.

To prepare video for progressive download or streaming in Flash Player:

1. In an open Flash document, choose File > Import > Import Video (**Figure 16.1**).

   The Select Video page of the Import Video dialog appears (**Figure 16.2**).

2. To use a file on your hard drive, select the On Your Computer radio button (**Figure 16.3**) and do either of the following:

   ▲ Enter the location of the file in the File Path field.

   ▲ Click the Choose (Mac) or Browse (Windows) button. When the Open dialog appears, navigate to your file, select it, and click the Open button. The Video Import Wizard returns you to the Select Video page and enters the file's path in the File Path field.

   or

   To use a file that is located on a Web server, select the "Already deployed to a Web server" radio button (**Figure 16.4**) and enter the file's address in the URL field.

   continues on next page

3. Click Continue (Mac) or Next (Windows).

The Deployment page of the Import Video dialog appears, with options for delivering the video content to your audience (**Figure 16.5**).

4. To set a delivery method, select one of the following radio buttons (**Figure 16.6**):

▲ To feed the video data in chunks using HTTP streaming, select "Progressive download from a Web server."

▲ To stream the video from a server using Flash Video Streaming Service, select "Stream from Flash Video Streaming Service." (You must have a Flash Media Server account with your ISP or use another media-streaming service to deliver this type of video to your audience.)

▲ To stream the video from your own Flash Media Server, select "Stream from Flash Media Server."

5. Click Continue (Mac) or Next (Windows).

The Encoding window appears (**Figure 16.7**)

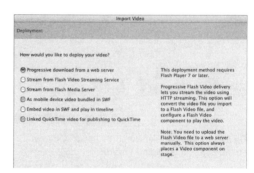

Figure 16.5 The Deployment page of the Import Video dialog presents options for delivering Flash content to your audience.

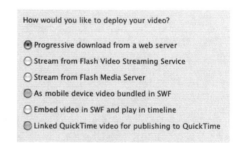

Figure 16.6 Flash's Video Import Wizard offers six methods for delivering video content.

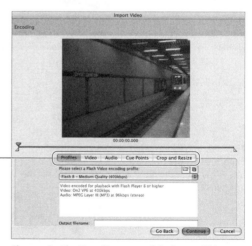

Figure 16.7 The Encoding page of the Import Video dialog has five sections: predefined settings for video and audio compression (A), custom settings for video compression (B), custom settings for audio compression (C), tools for creating cue points, or markers for use with ActionScript (D), and tools for modifying the clip's dimensions and length (E).

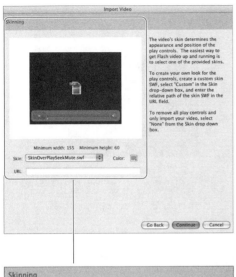

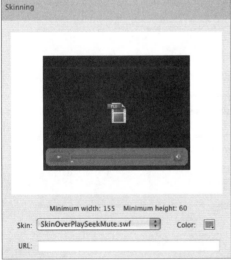

Figure 16.8 In the Skinning page of the Import Video dialog, you can choose a skin that creates user-interface controls for the progressive or streaming video displayed in your Flash movie.

6. Select one of the following sections:

▲ To use built-in video- and audio-encoding settings, click the Profiles button (Mac) or Encoding Profiles tab (Windows) and choose a preset from the pop-up menu.

▲ To use custom video-encoding settings, click the Video button (Mac) or tab (Windows) and choose from the options that appear.

▲ To use custom audio-encoding settings, click the Audio button (Mac) or tab (Windows) and choose from the options that appear.

▲ To mark specific frames of your clip so that you can target them with ActionScript, click the Cue Points button (Mac) or tab (Windows) and use the Add Cue Point and Add Parameters menus to create cue points and set cue-point parameters.

▲ To crop the video image, resize the video-display window, or change the video's length, click the Crop and Resize button (Mac) or tab (Windows) and choose from the options that appear.

You'll learn about specific settings for each section of the Encoding page in subsequent tasks.

7. Click Continue (Mac) or Next (Windows). The Skinning page appears (**Figure 16.8**).

continues on next page

8. To create playback controls for end users, from the Skin pop-up menu, choose either of the following:

▲ To create a controller bar that floats on top of the image in the video-display window, choose a skin whose name starts with the words *SkinOver* (**Figure 16.9**).

▲ To create a controller bar that sits beneath the video-display window, choose a skin whose name starts with the words *SkinUnder*.

9. Click Continue (Mac) or Next (Windows).

The Finish Video Import page appears (**Figure 16.10**), describing the assets created by the wizard and giving a brief overview of how to use them (see the sidebar "Final Steps for Using FLVPlayback," later in this chapter).

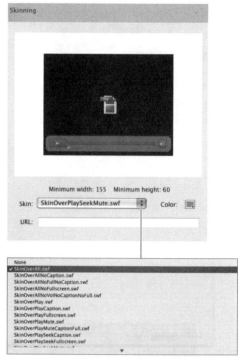

Figure 16.9 Each skin in the pop-up menu uses a different set of elements to create the controller bar. Skins that contain the word *Over* get layered on top of the video image; skins that contain the word *Under* wind up just below the video-display window.

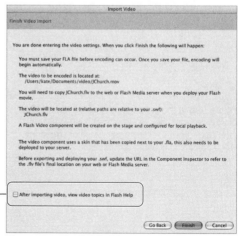

Figure 16.10 The Finish Video Import page of the Import Video dialog provides information about how to work with the video files for publishing. To learn more, select the "After importing video, view video topics in Flash Help" check box.

10. Click Finish.

If you haven't yet saved the file you're working in, Flash opens the Save As (Mac) or Save In (Windows) dialog. Navigate to the place where you want to save the file, enter a name in the Save As (Mac) or Save In (Windows) field, and click Save. The Flash Video Encoding Progress dialog appears. To stop the encoding process, click the Cancel button. Next, a Loading FLV Dimensions dialog appears showing a progress bar. When loading has finished, Flash places an instance of the FLVPlayback component on the Stage. The properties of the instance are already set to point to the source video file and to use the skin you chose in step 8.

✔ Tips

■ In step 8, to create a video clip with no controller bar, choose None from the Skin pop-up menu.

■ To select a color for the controller bar, in the Video Import dialog's Skinning page, click the Color control and choose a new color from the pop-up swatch set.

About Encoding Outside the Wizard

If you need to encode a number of video files using the same settings, you may find it tedious to bring them into Flash individually using the Video Import Wizard. Flash's stand-alone video encoder—Adobe Flash CS3 Video Encoder—lets you encode multiple files in batches.

Using the stand-alone encoder, you create a list of files, then choose encoding options in dialogs. The encoder's dialogs for setting video- and audio-compression, creating cue points, cropping and resizing, and assigning skins are nearly identical to those in the Video Import Wizard (described in this chapter).

You can also create video files for use in Flash with any third-party application that outputs files in FLV format; Adobe's Premier Pro or After Effects, for example, can do so.

Importing Embedded Video

When you choose progressive download or streaming as the deployment method for a video clip, the encoded video data remains in an external file. When you choose embedded as the deployment method, the video data becomes part of the FLA and SWF files. The import process for embedded video differs slightly from that for progressive or streaming video. The Video Import Wizard has an extra page of settings for embedding and offers some additional editing possibilities. There are no options for creating cue points or skins for embedded clips.

To import and embed video clips:

1. Follow steps 1–3 in the preceding task.

    If you want Flash to place the video in the Timeline for you, before starting the import process, in the Flash document's Timeline, select the keyframe where the embedded video should begin playing.

2. In the Deployment page of the Import Video dialog, select the radio button labeled "Embed video in SWF and play in Timeline" (**Figure 16.11**).

3. Click Continue (Mac) or Next (Windows).

    The Embedding page of the Import Video dialog appears, with options for working with embedded video clips (**Figure 16.12**).

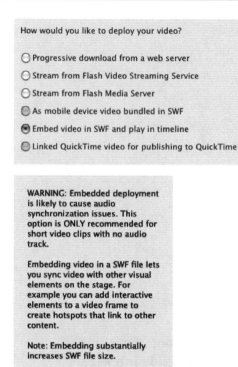

How would you like to deploy your video?

- Progressive download from a web server
- Stream from Flash Video Streaming Service
- Stream from Flash Media Server
- As mobile device video bundled in SWF
- ⦿ Embed video in SWF and play in timeline
- Linked QuickTime video for publishing to QuickTime

WARNING: Embedded deployment is likely to cause audio synchronization issues. This option is ONLY recommended for short video clips with no audio track.

Embedding video in a SWF file lets you sync video with other visual elements on the stage. For example you can add interactive elements to a video frame to create hotspots that link to other content.

Note: Embedding substantially increases SWF file size.

Figure 16.11 When you choose embedding as the deployment method (top), Flash puts all of the video data into the published SWF file. This method has pluses and minuses, as indicated in the warning text that appears in the dialog when you choose to embed (bottom).

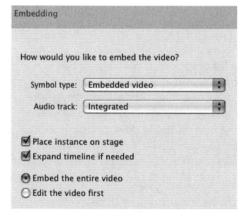

Embedding

How would you like to embed the video?

Symbol type: [Embedded video ⬍]
Audio track: [Integrated ⬍]

☑ Place instance on stage
☑ Expand timeline if needed

⦿ Embed the entire video
◯ Edit the video first

Figure 16.12 Before you get to the encoding options for embedded video clips, you must choose settings for working with the embedded video.

Figure 16.13 The Symbol Type menu in the Embedding page of the Import Video dialog gives you the choice of turning the video clip into an animated graphic symbol or a movie-clip symbol, or placing the frames of the video directly into the main Timeline.

Figure 16.14 With embedded video, you can include the sound track within the video itself, or have the codec extract it into a separate sound file that you can use like any other sound asset in Flash.

4. From the Symbol Type pop-up menu (**Figure 16.13**), choose one of the following:

▲ **Embedded Video** places the video frames directly into the main Timeline of your movie.

▲ **Movie Clip** places the video frames into the Timeline of a movie-clip symbol.

▲ **Graphic** places the video frames into the Timeline of an animated graphic symbol.

5. From the Audio Track pop-up menu (**Figure 16.14**), choose either of the following:

▲ **Separate** creates two assets in the library, one for the clip's sound track, the other for the clip's video. Only the video asset will be placed on the Timeline.

▲ **Integrated** incorporates the sound and video tracks in a single asset.

6. To have Flash automatically place video frames in the Timeline (if you chose Embedded in step 4) or place a symbol instance on the Stage (if you chose Movie Clip or Graphic in step 4), select the "Place instance on Stage" check box.

Upon completing the import process, Flash places the video or symbol instance in the currently selected keyframe.

7. If you chose Embedded or Graphic in step 4, to have Flash add enough frames to the main Timeline to display all the video's frames, select the "Expand Timeline if needed" check box.

continues on next page

8. To import the complete source video, select the "Embed the entire video" radio button (**Figure 16.15**).

If you prefer, you can trim the video and/or create multiple short clips before importing (see the next section, "To edit embedded video clips").

9. Click Continue (Mac) or Next (Windows). The Encoding window appears.

10. Set the desired options in the Profiles (Mac) or Encoding Profiles (Windows), Video, Audio, and Crop and Resize sections (for details, see the next section, "Setting Encoding Options").

11. Follow steps 9 and 10 of the preceding task.

To edit embedded video clips:

1. Follow steps 1–7 in the preceding task.

2. In the Embedding page of the Import Video dialog, select the "Edit the video first" radio button.

3. Click Continue (Mac) or Next (Windows). The Split Video page appears (**Figure 16.16**).

Figure 16.15 To import the full video, select the "Embed the entire video" radio button in the Embedding page of the Import Video dialog. To shorten a video clip before embedding it, or to cut it up into multiple short clips, select the "Edit the video first" radio button.

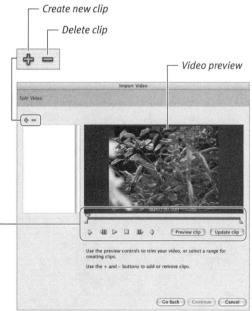

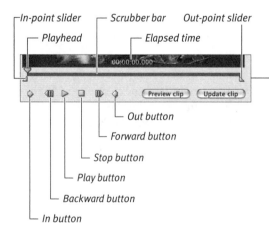

Figure 16.16 When you choose to edit embedded video before importing it, the Video Import Wizard's Split Video page gives you tools for trimming the video and creating multiple short clips from the original video file.

Drag in-point slider

Flash creates new in-point

Position playhead

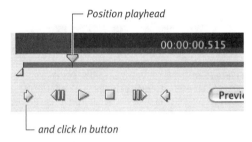

and click In button

Flash creates new in-point

Figure 16.17 To create a new in-point for an embedded video clip, you can drag the in-point slider itself (top) or drag the playhead, then click the In button to set the in-point (bottom).

✔ Tip

■ If you're not sure where you want the clip to begin or end, click the Play button and watch the video. When you see material that's near where you want the clip to start or end, click the Stop button. Now use the Forward and Backward buttons (or drag the playhead) to fine-tune the location of the playhead. Finally, click the In or Out button to set the appropriate point.

4. To choose a new first frame for the embedded video clip, do any of the following (**Figure 16.17**):

▲ Drag the in-point slider (the triangle on the left side of the scrubber bar) to the spot where you want the video to start.

▲ Click the Forward button to move the playhead and in-point slider forward one frame at a time.

▲ Click the Backward button to move the playhead and in-point slider backward one frame at a time.

▲ Drag the playhead to a new location on the scrubber bar, then click the In button (the right-facing arrow) to bring the in-point slider to that location and shorten the scrubber bar.

5. To choose a new last frame for the embedded video clip, repeat step 4, but using the out-point slider (the triangle on the right side of the scrubber bar) and the Out button (the left-facing arrow).

6. To confirm the settings for the clip, click the Create Clip button (the plus sign).

Flash creates a clip using the current in- and out-points and adds it to the list of clips to import, giving it a default name.

7. Click Continue (Mac) or Next (Windows).

The Encoding page appears. Choose the desired encoding settings (see the next section, "Setting Encoding Options").

8. Click Continue (Mac) or Next (Windows).

The Finish Video Import page appears.

9. Click Finish.

Setting Encoding Options

The Encoding page of Flash's Video Import Wizard offers five sections of settings: Profiles (Mac) or Encoding Profiles (Windows), Video, Audio, Cue Points, and Crop and Resize. These sections are identical for clips deployed as progressive download and streaming. For embedded clips, there are no options for cue points; and for clips that you edit before embedding, there are no trimming options. Otherwise the encoding options for embedded clips are the same as for clips deployed as progressive download and streaming.

To use preset encoding settings:

1. In the Encoding page of the Import Video dialog, select the Profile button (Mac) or Encoding Profile tab (Windows).

   Flash displays the profile options (**Figure 16.18**).

2. From the pop-up menu, choose one of the preset profiles (**Figure 16.19**).

   Flash chooses the appropriate settings in the Video and Audio sections of the Encoding page. A description of the current settings appears in the box below the menu.

Figure 16.18 The Profiles (Mac) or Encoding Profiles (Windows) section of the Encoding page offers packaged settings for video and audio compression.

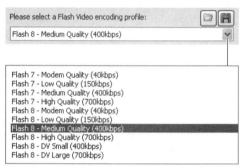

Figure 16.19 The Flash Video Encoding Profile menu offers ten preset encoding settings that optimize the video for playback in different versions of Flash Player using various data rates.

The Mystery of Encoding

In choosing encoding settings, your goal—a constant juggling act for Web developers—is to balance quality and file size. With video, that balance is particularly important because of the large amounts of data involved. Each pixel in a video image contains 24 bits of information; if the video image is a 100-by-100–pixel square, that's already 240,000 bits for each frame, and for video viewed over the Web, you usually want to display at least 10 frames per second to sustain the illusion of motion. Each second of uncompressed video can easily contain millions of bits of data.

To bring those numbers down to a reasonable range for transmission over the Web, you need to eliminate and/or compress some of that data. The Profiles section of the Video Import dialog's Encoding page offers packaged video- and audio-compression settings that strike a good balance for specific situations. To create other trade-offs, you can assign custom settings in the Video and Audio sections of the dialog. Use the Crop and Resize section to eliminate data outright by shortening the video and/or cropping out some of the image area.

SETTING ENCODING OPTIONS

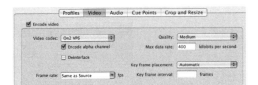

Figure 16.20 The Video section of the Encoding page lets you choose custom settings for encoding the video data.

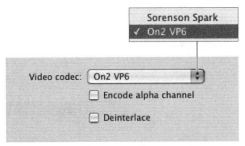

Figure 16.21 From the Video Codec menu, you can choose which codec Flash uses to do the video encoding. Both Sorenson Spark and On VP6 create deinterlaced video. On2 VP6 can also encode any alpha-channel data that exists in the video file.

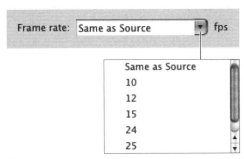

Figure 16.22 The default Frame Rate setting—Same As Source—keeps the source video's original rate and is recommended for anyone who's new to using video.

To use custom video-encoding settings:

1. In the Encoding page of the Import Video dialog, select the Video button (Mac) or tab (Windows).

   The options for encoding video appear (**Figure 16.20**).

2. To have Flash carry out video encoding, select the Encode Video check box.

   If you wish to encode audio only, deselect the check box, and select the Encode Audio check box in the Audio section of the Encoding page.

3. To choose a codec, the program that encodes the video data, in the Video Codec section (**Figure 16.21**), from the pop-up menu, select either of the following:

   ▲ For publishing a SWF file for playback in Flash Player 6 or 7, choose Sorenson Spark. To create deinterlaced video, choose the Deinterlace check box.

   ▲ For publishing a SWF file for playback in Flash Player 8 or 9, choose On2 VP6. To include alpha-channel data (if any exists) in your video, select the Encode Alpha Channel check box; to create deinterlaced video, select the Deinterlace check box.

4. To choose the rate at which Flash displays the frames of your video, select a setting from the Frame Rate pop-up menu (**Figure 16.22**).

continues on next page

SETTING ENCODING OPTIONS

5. To set the maximum data rate (the number of bits required to produce one second of video playback) (**Figure 16.23**), do either of the following:

▲ Choose a preset rate (Low, Medium, or High) from the Quality menu; the corresponding maximum data rate appears in the Max Data Rate field.

▲ Enter a new value in the Max Data Rate field (On the Mac you can choose Custom from the Quality menu before entering a value. In Windows, you must enter the value first, then the menu changes to Custom.) Click outside the field to confirm the setting. (On the Mac pressing Enter when the field is active deletes the values in the field; in Windows pressing Enter moves you to the next page of the dialog, but your custom values are recorded in the field.)

6. To determine how often the codec stores the data needed to redraw a full video frame (a *keyframe*), from the Key Frame Placement menu (**Figure 16.24**), choose either of the following:

▲ **Automatic** saves the data to create a keyframe for every 2 seconds of playback. (If the original video clip played at 30 fps, the Automatic setting would create keyframes every 60 frames.)

▲ **Custom** saves the data to create keyframes at other intervals. In the Key Frame Interval field, enter the number of frames you want between keyframes. Smaller intervals translate to saving more keyframes, resulting in larger file sizes. (On the Mac you can choose Custom from the Quality menu before entering a value. In Windows, you must enter the value first, then the menu changes to Custom.)

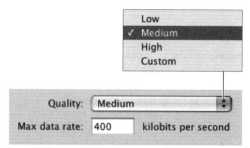

Figure 16.23 The data rate has a direct impact on a published SWF's file size and the quality of the video images your viewers see. Higher rates translate to better-quality images and larger SWFs. Larger files can cause playback to pause as data downloads for viewers with slow connections.

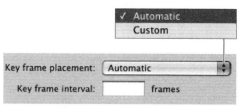

Figure 16.24 The codec can create keyframes for video. For each keyframe, the codec saves all the data required to draw the image; for other frames, the codec saves only the data for areas of the image that changed from the previous frame.

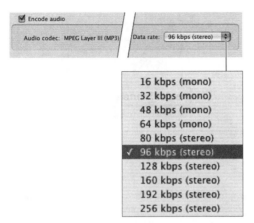

Figure 16.25 Flash's Video Import Wizard uses MP3 as the codec for encoding the audio portion of a video clip. To encode the audio, select the Encode Audio check box. (To eliminate the audio data, deselect the check box.) You can also choose a data rate for encoded audio.

To use custom audio-encoding settings:

1. In the Encoding page of the Import Video dialog, select the Audio button (Mac) or tab (Windows).

The options for encoding audio appear (**Figure 16.25**). Audio encoding in Flash is always done with MP3.

2. To encode the audio portion of your video clip, check the Encode Audio check box.

If the check box is deselected, the imported video clip will have no audio track.

3. From the Data Rate menu, choose one of the six stereo or four mono settings. Higher settings create better-quality sound tracks.

About Profiles

Once you've created custom settings for video and/or audio encoding, you can save them for use with other video clips. Saved settings are called *profiles*. In the Profiles (Mac) or Encoding Profiles (Windows) section of the Import Video dialog's Encoding page, click the Save Encoding Profile button (the diskette icon). The Save Encoding Profile dialog appears. Navigate to the location where you want to save the profile; in the Save As (Mac) or File Name (Windows) field, enter a name for your profile; and click Save. Flash saves the settings from the Video and Audio sections of the Encoding page as an XML file.

To load a saved profile, in the Profiles (Mac) or Encoding Profiles (Windows) section of the Encoding page, click the Load Encoding Profile button (the folder icon). The Load Encoding Profile dialog appears. Navigate to the saved profile, select it, and click Open. Flash applies the custom settings to the Video and/or Audio sections of the Encoding page.

To set cue points for progressive or streaming video:

1. In the Encoding page of the Import Video dialog, select the Cue Points button (Mac) or tab (Windows).

   The options for creating cue points appear (**Figure 16.26**).

2. In the scrubber bar, drag the playhead to the spot you want to mark as a cue point.

3. Click the Add Cue Point button (the plus sign) (**Figure 16.27**).

   Flash adds a cue-point marker to the scrubber bar and adds the cue-point data to the cue-point list, giving the cue point a default name and activating the name field.

4. Type a name for the cue point.

5. In the Type column, click the arrow to activate the pop-up menu, and choose either of the following:

   ▲ **Event** creates cue points that can be used to trigger ActionScript.

   ▲ **Navigation** creates cue points that can be scripted to work like bookmarks for video. Using ActionScript, you can take viewers directly to the cue-point frame. The codec creates a keyframe for these cue points. You can also use navigation cue points to trigger ActionScript.

Figure 16.26 Use the Cue Points section of the Import Video dialog's Encoding page to mark specific frames as cue points. You can then use ActionScript to advance the video to those frames or to synchronize events with specific segments of video.

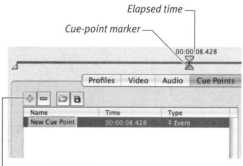

Figure 16.27 Click the Add Cue Point button to add a cue point to the list; a cue-point marker indicates the cue point's location in the scrubber bar. As you drag the playhead in the scrubber bar, you can choose a cue point visually, by what appears in the video-preview window, or by the elapsed time that appears below the video-preview window. The elapsed time appears in the form hour:minute:second:millisecond.

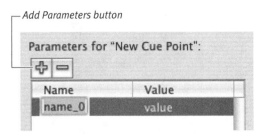

Add Parameters button

Parameters for "New Cue Point":

Name	Value
name_0	value

Figure 16.28 Click the Add Parameters button to create ActionScript parameters for a selected cue point.

6. To set a cue point's parameters (for use with ActionScript), with the cue point selected in the cue-point list, in the Parameters list, click the Add Parameters button (the plus sign).

Flash adds default Name and Value parameters to the list for the selected cue point (**Figure 16.28**). To change either parameter, double-click it in the list to activate a text field, then enter the new parameter.

✔ Tips

■ Click anywhere in the scrubber bar with the pointer to bring the playhead right to that spot.

■ To set a cue point at a precise elapsed time, use the left- and right-arrow keys on the keyboard. Pressing the left-arrow key decreases the elapsed time by one millisecond; pressing the right-arrow key increases it.

■ To modify an existing cue point, select it in the cue-point list, then drag the cue-point marker in the scrubber bar to the spot where you want the cue point to be.

■ You can save your current list of cue points and their parameters as an XML file. You can then load that file to create cue points at the same locations in another video clip. Click the diskette icon to open the Save Cue Points File dialog. To load a saved XML file of cue points, click the folder icon, and in the Load Cue Points File dialog that appears, navigate to the saved file.

The Mystery of Quality and Data Rate

The encoding settings for Quality and Max Data Rate are interrelated. Higher image quality requires more data. The Max Data Rate refers to the amount of data used to create the video image during playback. The smaller the data rate, the less data the codec uses to define each frame of the video. Compare two quality settings: a quality setting of Low creates a data rate of 150 kilobits per second (Kbps); at Medium, the data rate is 400 Kbps. That's more than twice as much data. The medium-quality video image is slower to download than the low-quality video, but more faithful to the original.

To change the video's dimensions and length:

1. In the Encoding page of the Import Video dialog, select the Crop and Resize button (Mac) or tab (Windows).

   Options for editing the video appear (**Figure 16.29**).

2. To crop out unwanted areas of the video image, in the Crop section, enter new values in the fields correlating to the four sides of the image (**Figure 16.30**).

   A dotted line in the video-preview window indicates where the codec will crop the image.

3. To reduce or enlarge the video frame, in the Resize section, select the Resize Video check box (**Figure 16.31**), and do any of the following:

   ▲ To enter specific dimensions, from the pop-up menu, choose Pixels, then enter new values in the Width and/or Height fields.

   ▲ To reduce or enlarge the frame relative to its original size, from the pop-up menu, choose Percent, then enter new values in the Width and/or Height fields.

   ▲ To preserve the original frame's ratio of width to height, select the Maintain Aspect Ratio check box.

Figure 16.29 Use the Crop and Resize section of the Import Video dialog's Encoding page to crop the image area, resize the video frame, and reduce the video's length.

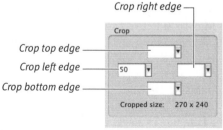

Figure 16.30 To crop the video image, enter new values in the cropping fields. For example, to remove 50 pixels from the left side of the video image, enter 50 in the left-hand field.

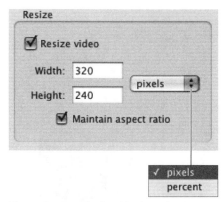

Figure 16.31 To make the video frame larger or smaller, use the Resize controls. You can resize to specific dimensions (choose pixels) or resize relative to the original frame size (choose percent).

4. To change the length of the clip, drag the in-point and out-point sliders (the triangles on either side of the scrubber bar) to position them at the desired new first and last frames.

The elapsed-time counter below the video-preview window updates as you drag each slider. The elapsed time for the in- and out-points and the total time for the video also appear in the Trim section of the dialog.

✔ Tips

■ It's often easiest to crop an image visually. Click the pop-up triangle to the right of any Crop field to activate a slider for that field. Drag the slider to position the dotted-line crop mark interactively in the preview window.

■ You don't have to be in the Crop and Resize view of the Encoding page to trim most video clips. Unless you are embedding your video clip and have chosen to edit it inside the Video Import Wizard, the scrubber bar, playhead, and in- and out-point sliders are present in all of the Encoding sections. Dragging the in- and out-point sliders trims the video clip. The advantage to trimming in the Crop and Resize view is that you can see the precise timing of the in-point and the out-point, plus you can see the duration of the whole clip with its current in- and out-points.

Working with Embedded Video

Depending on the settings you choose when you use the Video Import Wizard to create embedded video clips, Flash places an instance of the clip on the Stage or just places the embedded-video asset in the library. When automatically placing an instance on the Stage, Flash can create enough frames in the Timeline to show the full video, or allow the existing keyframe span to truncate the video. When you place an instance of an embedded clip into the Timeline yourself, you need to create a keyframe span that accommodates as much of the video as you want to show.

To place embedded video clips in the Timeline:

1. Open a Flash document and import the embedded video as described in "Importing Embedded Video," earlier in this chapter.

2. In the Timeline, select the keyframe in which you want the embedded video to start playing.

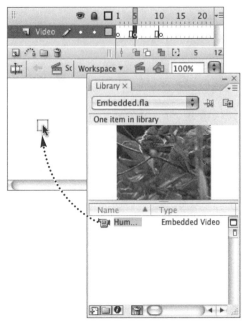

Figure 16.32 To place embedded video in a Flash movie, drag an instance of the embedded-video clip from the library to the Stage.

The Mystery of Embedded Video

Embedded video clips bear similarities to some Flash symbols, yet embedded video is a unique type of element. Like animated graphic symbols, embedded video clips play within—and must synchronize with—frames in the main movie Timeline. Like sound clips, embedded video clips can contain audio, although if you import the audio as an integrated track, you won't see the sound's waveform in the Timeline. As with any symbol, you place an instance of an embedded-video clip by dragging a copy from the library window to the Stage. The Property Inspector gives you information about selected instances of embedded video clips. You can modify a selected instance of an embedded video clip in many of the ways that you modify other objects in Flash: you can use the free-transform tool, for example, to resize, rotate, or skew the video image. To give an embedded video clip an independent Timeline and to gain the same control over the clip's appearance that you have over movie clips (to be able to change the clip's brightness, tint, or alpha, for example), you must place the embedded video clip inside a Flash movie-clip symbol.

Figure 16.33 Flash alerts you when you attempt to add embedded video that has more frames than the current keyframe span where you are placing it.

Before adding embedded-video instance

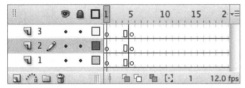

After adding embedded-video instance

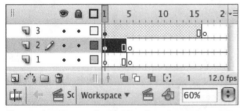

Figure 16.34 Layer 3 in this Timeline shows the result of answering Yes in the dialog that warns that the current keyframe span is too short: Flash adds enough frames to display the full 16-frame clip. Layer 2 shows the result for answering No: the existing keyframe span truncates the video.

3. From the Library panel, drag a copy of the embedded video clip to the Stage (**Figure 16.32**).

Unlike movie clips, which play in their own independent Timeline, embedded video clips need to fit their frames into the Timeline of the movie or movie clip containing them. Each time you drag an instance of an embedded video clip to the Stage, if the span for the selected keyframe contains fewer frames than the clip, a warning dialog asks whether you want to add enough frames to display the entire clip (**Figure 16.33**).

4. To enlarge the keyframe span, click Yes.

Flash adds enough frames to the span to reveal the entire video clip (**Figure 16.34**).

or

To retain the current number of frames in the keyframe span, click No.

Flash places the video clip on the Stage, but the keyframe span cuts off the end of the clip.

Previewing Embedded Video Clips

In Flash's authoring environment, embedded video clips display their images within the keyframe span that contains the clip. You can simply play the movie (choose Control > Play) or move the playhead through the Timeline to view the changing video frames. If the embedded clip has an audio track, however, you must use one of the test modes to preview the sound. (If you import the audio track as a separate sound asset and place an instance in the movie, the audio plays when you drag the playhead through the Timeline or you choose Control > Play). You must also use one of the test modes to see the embedded video in context with interactive elements, such as movie clips or scripted buttons.

Working with the FLVPlayback Component

When you use Flash's Video Import Wizard to import video for progressive download or streaming, the wizard adds a component named FLVPlayback to the library and places an instance of it on the Stage. You can replace the component instance's generic icon with a frame from the video clip, change the source file, and modify the other parameters.

To choose source video for an FLVPlayback instance:

1. Select the FLVPlayback component instance on the Stage.

2. Access the Component Inspector panel.
   If the panel isn't open, choose Window > Component Inspector.

3. Select the Parameters button (Mac) or tab (Windows).
   Parameter settings associated with the component appear in a two-column table (**Figure 16.35**).

4. To choose the video that appears in the video-display window during playback, in the Name column click the Source parameter.
   A search button (a magnifying glass icon) activates in the Value column.

5. Click the search button.
   The Content Path dialog appears.

6. To identify the source video file (it must be in FLV format), do either of the following:

   ▲ Enter a URL for the source video in the Content Path field (**Figure 16.36**).

   ▲ To find the file you want, click the folder icon on the right side of the field. In the Browse for FLV File dialog that appears, navigate to the file you want, and click Open. Flash enters the URL in the Content Path field.

Figure 16.35 The Component Inspector panel's Parameters section contains settings for all of the parameters of a selected instance of the FLVPlayback component.

Enter URL

Browse to locate file

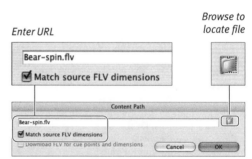

Figure 16.36 The Content Path dialog allows you to identify the video that the FLVPlayback-component instance will display to the end user.

WORKING WITH THE FLVPLAYBACK COMPONENT

Figure 16.37 The filename in the Value column for the Source parameter of the FLVPlayback component is the file that end users see in the finished movie.

7. To determine how Flash sizes the FLVPlayback component instance, do either of the following:

   ▲ To resize the component to fit the source video, select the Match Source FLV Dimensions check box.

   ▲ To resize the video to fit within the default FLVPlayback component (320 by 240 pixels), deselect the Match Source FLV Dimensions check box.

8. Click OK.

   Flash updates the Source parameter with the file name (**Figure 16.37**). Depending on what you chose in step 7, Flash also resizes the FLVPlayback component instance on the Stage. The instance now points to the desired encoded video file.

✔ Tips

■ If the skin you've chosen for the FLVPlayback instance includes a volume-control slider, you can set the starting slider position. Double-click the value for Volume and enter a new number: 1 sets the slider all the way to the right (full volume); values from 0.9 down to 0.1 set the slider farther to the left (lower volumes); a value of 0 sets the slider all the way to the left (no sound).

■ To create a controller bar that appears only when the end user positions the pointer over the video-display window, choose True from the pop-up menu in the Value column for SkinAutoHide.

About the FLVPlayback Component

Flash's Video Import Wizard encodes a video file and imports it for use in your Flash movie. When you set the wizard's deployment options to create video for progressive download or streaming, the word *import* is a bit misleading. In fact, the wizard creates a new external file containing encoded video data (an FLV file). This data remains separate from your FLA and SWF files, but the wizard creates a link between your movie and the FLV file via an element known as the *FLVPlayback component*. During the "import" process, the wizard places the FLVPlayback component in the library of your Flash document, places an instance of the component on the Stage, and sets the instance's source parameter to point to the FLV file with the encoded video data. At runtime, the FLVPlayback component creates a video-display window within your Flash movie, and the video from the source FLV file appears in that window.

Components are a special type of Flash element. (You learned a bit about working with the button component in Chapter 12.) Components contain ActionScript that governs their behavior, but you can modify a component's behavior without actually doing any scripting; you simply change parameters in the Components Inspector panel or in the Parameters tab of the Property inspector. ActionScript 3.0 user-interface components such as the button component are not fully compiled. You can modify the graphic elements that make up their look (their skin) the same way you'd modify any graphic element. Unlike ActionScript 3.0 user-interface components, the FLVPlayback component is fully compiled; you cannot directly access its skin to modify it. The FLVPlayback component comes with a variety of packaged skins that create a controller bar for the video-display window. You can choose a new controller-bar style by setting the skin parameter for an FLVPlayback component instance. (You can create new skins for the FLVPlayback component, but that's beyond the scope of this book.)

Like other assets, the FLVPlayback component is reusable. To place another video-display window in your movie, drag a new instance of the FLVPlayback component to the Stage, then set its source parameter to point to the FLV file you want to display. If you have video files that are already in FLV format, you can even bypass the Video Import Wizard. Access the Components panel (by choosing Window > Components, for example). Expand the panel's Video folder, then drag an instance of FLVPlayback to your document. The instance's source parameter is blank, but you can set it to point to an FLV file as described in the task "To choose source video for an FLVPlayback instance."

Figure 16.38 When you position the pointer over the video preview in the Select Preview Frame dialog, a controller bar appears. Drag the slider to select the frame the FLVPlayback instance displays during authoring.

To create an author-time preview for a video component:

1. Follow steps 1–3 in the preceding task.

2. In the Components Inspector, in the Value column, double-click the current Preview parameter, None.

The Select Preview Frame dialog appears. Depending on the length of the video, you may see the message "Loading…" as Flash reads the FLV file. The preview video plays once through.

3. Position the pointer over the dialog's video-preview window.

A controller bar appears (**Figure 16.38**).

4. Drag the slider triangle to move to a specific frame of the video.

Elapsed time appears beneath the preview window. To play the video again, press the Play button.

continues on next page

Animating FLVPlayback Components

The FLVPlayback component is similar to a movie-clip symbol, in that it's an asset that lives in the library, you can modify it using the free-transform tool, you can mask its content using a mask layer, it appears as a static image on the Stage, and it displays its frames only in Flash Player. But there's an important difference: you can't use an FLVPlayback component instance in a motion tween. You can place an FLVPlayback component instance into two keyframes, modify the instance in the second keyframe, and set the span's Tween property to Motion. But when you test the movie, it becomes clear that the tween doesn't work. The video-display window sits in its original spot, and none of the changes you made to it in the second keyframe take place.

If you want to move the component's video-display window around the Stage (or create other animated effects) with motion tweens, first put the FLVPlayback component instance inside a movie-clip symbol. You can then animate the movie-clip symbol instance to get the motion-tween effects you want. (To review the process of creating movie-clip symbols, see Chapter 11; to review motion tweening, see Chapter 9.)

5. With the desired frame of the video showing in the preview window, click OK.

The selected frame appears in the component instance on the Stage, and the preview parameter in the Components Inspector updates to show the elapsed time for that frame (**Figure 16.39**).

✔ Tips

■ Instead of using the FLVPlayback component's prebuilt controller-bar skins, you can use other ActionScript 3.0 video components to create a user interface for controlling video that runs in the FLVPlayback window. Choose None as the skin for the FLVPlayback component instance on the Stage. Access the Components Inspector and expand the Video folder. You'll see a number of user-interface components: PlayButton, PauseButton, VolumeBar, and so on. Drag an instance of each element you want to use to the Stage. You can position the elements anywhere and modify them as you did with the button component (see Chapter 12).

■ You can change the size of an FLVPlayback component instance on the Stage using the free-transform tool, the Transform or Info panel, or the Properties tab of the Property inspector. But if you've chosen a controller-bar skin for your video, be careful. The controller bar must be wide enough to hold all the user-interface elements that are part of the skin (the Play, Pause, and Mute button; the volume slider; and so on). If you narrow the component instance too much, the controller bar may stick out over the edges of the video-display window.

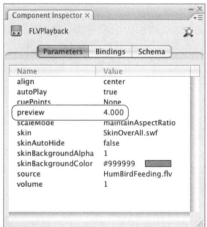

Figure 16.39 By default the FLVPlayback component's Preview parameter is set to None, and it displays a generic icon on the Stage (top). Specifying an elapsed time as the Preview parameter (middle) allows you to see one frame of the video clip during authoring (bottom).

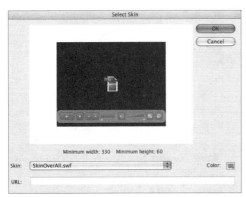

Figure 16.40 Use the Select Skin dialog to change the user controls for video playback.

To change controller-bar skins:

1. Follow steps 1–3 in "To choose source video for an FLVPlayback instance," earlier in this chapter.

2. In the Components Inspector, in the Value column, double-click the current Skin parameter.

   The Select Skin dialog appears, showing the same items as in the Skinning page of the Import Video Wizard (**Figure 16.40**).

3. From the Skin pop-up menu, select a new skin.

   For details, see step 8 of the first task in "Importing Video for Progressive Download or Streaming," earlier in this chapter.

4. If desired, from the Color control, select a new background color for the controller bar.

   continues on next page

Final Steps for Using FLVPlayback

When you publish a Flash movie to make it available to your audience, you must place the resulting SWF file on the Web server that hosts your creation. (You'll learn more about publishing in Chapter 17.) When you use the FLVPlayback component to deliver streaming video or progressive-download video, two other files must go on the server: the FLV file containing the encoded video, and a SWF file containing the controller-bar skin (if you use one for your video). When you use Flash's Video Import Wizard to prepare video for progressive download or streaming, Flash places the encoded FLV file in the same folder as your FLA file. When you publish your movie, Flash places the SWF file of your movie and the SWF file for the controller-bar skin in the folder with your FLA as well.

You may publish your movie many times as you test it during the authoring phase. During that phase, all the required files are in one folder, and the relative pathnames Flash uses to locate these files let you test without problems. Before you publish your movie for final delivery to your audience, make sure that the source parameter for each instance of the FLVPlayback component shows the correct URL for the final location of the source video file on the hosting server (for details about setting the source parameter, see "To choose source video for an FLVPlayback instance," earlier in this section).

5. Click OK.

Flash updates the Skin parameter in the Parameters tab of the Components Inspector and changes the controller bar in the FLVPlayback component instance on the Stage.

✔ Tips

■ To change the color of an FLVPlayback component's controller-bar, select the FLVPlayback component instance on the Stage, access the Component Inspector panel, and select the Parameters button (Mac) or tab (Windows). In the Value column, double-click the hex value or color chip for the SkinBackgroundColor parameter, and choose a new color from the pop-up swatch.

■ You can also create transparency for a controller bar. In the Value column, click the parameter for SkinBackgoundAlpha to activate the parameter's text field. Enter a new value between 1 and 0 (1 equals completely opaque; 0.5 equals 50 percent transparent, and 0 equals fully transparent).

■ You can change the parameters of FLVPlayback component instances in the Parameters tab of the Property inspector. Access the inspector and click the Parameters tab. (If the tab is closed, choose Window > Properties > Parameters). A scrolling list of parameters appears in the tab. As in the tasks above, click the parameter name in the Name column to activate the Value field, then click the field to access the appropriate dialog or tool for selecting a new parameter.

■ Alternatively, double-clicking a parameter in the Value field accesses the dialog or tool for that parameter in one step.

■ With one exception, the changes you make to parameters in the Components Inspector are persistent. Change the skin parameter, and the next time you place an FLVPlayback component instance it will be set to use that skin. The same is true for color, volume, transparency, and other parameters. Only the source parameter changes, to the video you specified in the Video Import Wizard, or to nothing if you place a new component instance yourself.

DELIVERING MOVIES TO YOUR AUDIENCE

17

When you finish creating graphics, animation, and interactivity in Adobe Flash CS3 Professional, it's time to deliver the goods to your audience. You must publish or export the Flash document (FLA) to create a file in a format for playback. You have several formats to choose among. The one that guarantees viewers will see all your animations and take part in all your movie's interactivity is the Flash Player format (SWF). A partially interactive solution is to publish your movie in QuickTime format.

When you install Flash CS3, you can also install version 9 of the Flash Player application. You can view SWF files running directly in Flash Player on your computer. Other programs, such as Web browsers, can also use Flash Player to display Flash content.

You can export movies as a series of images in either bitmap format (GIF or PNG files, for example) or vector format (such as Adobe Illustrator files). You can export a movie in Flash Video format (FLV). Another option for movie delivery is a self-playing file called a *projector*. Users double-click the projector file to open and play the movie. And you can print your entire movie or individual frames, should you want to give someone a hard-copy version of the movie (for storyboarding, for example).

Preparing Your Movie for Optimal Playback

When creating movies to show over the Web, you face the issue of quality versus quantity. Higher quality increases file size, leading to longer download times and slower movies. Things that add to a file's size include bitmaps (especially animated bitmaps), video clips, sounds, multiple areas of simultaneous animation, embedded fonts, gradients, and the use of separate graphic elements instead of symbols and groups. Flash's simulated streaming helps you find out where your movie is bogging down. The Size Report and Bandwidth Profiler reveal which frames may cause download hang-ups. You can then rethink or optimize the problem areas.

To use the Bandwidth Profiler:

1. Open the Flash document that you want to test for playback over the Web.

2. Choose Control > Test Movie (or Test Scene).

   Flash exports the movie and opens it in Flash Player.

3. From Flash Player's View menu, choose Download Settings, and select the download speed you want to test.

   The menu lists eight speeds, all of which are customizable. To change them, choose View > Download Settings > Customize (**Figure 17.1**). By default, Flash lists five common connection speeds—14.4 Kbps, 28.8 Kbps, 56 Kbps, DSL, and T1—with settings that simulate real-world data-transfer rates. You can see the settings in the Custom Download Settings dialog (**Figure 17.2**). To create a custom setting, enter new values, and then click OK.

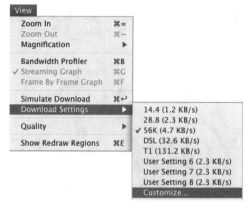

Figure 17.1 To create a custom connection speed for simulating playback over the Web, from the test environment's View menu, choose Download Settings > Customize.

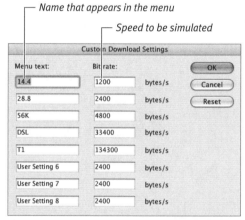

Figure 17.2 At its default setting, Flash offers choices for simulating five standard connection speeds. You can change the names and rates for these speeds in the Custom Download Settings dialog.

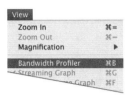

Figure 17.3 To view a graph of the amount of data in each frame, choose View > Bandwidth Profiler when a Flash Player window is open.

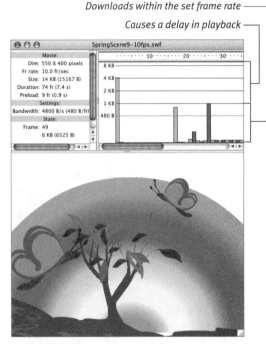

Downloads within the set frame rate
Causes a delay in playback

Figure 17.4 The Bandwidth Profiler graph at the top of the Flash Player window shows how much data each movie frame contains. Each bar in this version of the graph represents a frame of the movie.

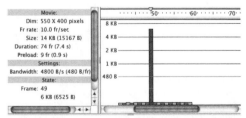

Figure 17.5 In Frame by Frame Graph mode, the height of each bar indicates how much data the frame holds.

4. From Flash Player's View menu, choose Bandwidth Profiler (**Figure 17.3**).

At the top of the Test Movie window, Flash graphs the amount of data that is being transmitted against the movie's Timeline (**Figure 17.4**). The bars represent the number of bytes of data per frame. The bottom line (highlighted in red) represents the amount of data that will safely download fast enough to keep up with the movie's frame rate. Any frame that contains a greater amount of data forces the movie to pause while the data downloads.

To view the contents of each frame separately:

1. From the Flash Player's View menu, choose Frame by Frame Graph, or press ⌘-F (Mac) or Ctrl-F (Windows).

Flash presents a single bar for each frame in the Bandwidth Profiler graph. The numbers along the top of the graph represent frames (**Figure 17.5**). The height of the bar represents the amount of data in that frame.

2. Select a bar.

Specifics about that frame and the movie in general appear in the profile window.

To see how frames stream:

1. From the Flash Player's View menu, choose View > Streaming Graph, or press ⌘-G (Mac) or Ctrl-G (Windows).

   Flash displays the frames as alternating bars of light and dark gray, sized to reflect the time each one takes to download (**Figure 17.6**). The numbers along the top of the streaming graph represent frames as a unit of time based on the frame rate. (In a 10-fps movie, for example, each number represents .1 second.) Where frames contain little data, several bars may appear in a single time unit. Frames that have lots of data may stretch out over several time units.

2. Select a bar.

   Specifics about that frame and the movie in general appear in the profile window (**Figure 17.7**).

To display a download-progress bar:

- With Bandwidth Profiler active, from Flash Player's View menu, choose Simulate Download, or press ⌘-Return (Mac) or Ctrl-Enter (Windows).

   As the animation plays in the test window, Flash highlights the numbers of the Timeline in green to show where you are in the download process.

To exit Bandwidth Profiler:

- From Flash Player's View menu, choose Bandwidth Profiler again to deselect it.

✔ Tip

- To get information about the amount of data in each frame in text form, choose Generate Size Report in the Flash tab of the Publish Settings dialog. During the publishing process, Flash creates an ActionScript file showing the number of bytes of data in each frame of the movie.

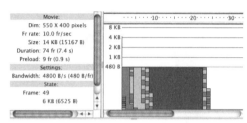

Figure 17.6 In Streaming Graph mode, the width of each bar indicates how long the frame takes to download at the given connection speed and frame rate. In this movie, frame 49 contains 6 KBytes of data and takes about 1.3 seconds to download at a frame rate of 10 fps over a 56-Kbps modem.

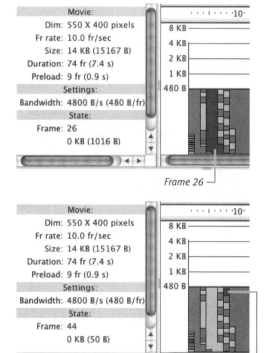

Frame 26

Frame 44

Figure 17.7 The profile window to the left of the graph displays information about the movie. The State section identifies the selected frame (the frame highlighted in red) and lists the amount of data in that frame. You can see that frame 26 (top) has 1016 bytes of information, whereas frame 44 (bottom) contains only 50 bytes.

A Note About Accessibility

As you think about the best ways to deliver Flash movies to your audience, also consider the fact that some members of the audience may have physical conditions that affect the way they interact with your site. As the Web has become more visually interesting, it presents challenges to visually impaired users who want to take advantage of the many resources available.

Our society is becoming more sensitive to the ways in which activities and resources exclude people with disabilities. Web designers need to use Flash to make not only eye-catching Web sites that dazzle with artwork, animation, interactivity, sound, and video, but also sites that convey information to a wide range of people. Remember that some of your users are unable to view or hear a site's content; some may not use a mouse, instead navigating and exploring the site by tabbing to each element in turn.

To address the issue of accessible Web sites, Flash lets you make content available to screen-reading software that uses Microsoft Active Accessibility (MSAA) technology. (At the time Flash CS3 was released, MSAA was available only for Windows and works only with Internet Explorer.) Screen readers provide audio feedback about a variety of elements on a Web site, reading aloud the labels of buttons, for example, or reading the contents of text fields. Through Flash's accessibility features, you can create descriptions of objects for the screen reader; prevent the screen reader from attempting to describe certain objects (such as purely decorative movie clips); and assign keyboard commands that let the user manipulate objects by pressing keys or tabbing through text fields, for example.

The considerations that go into making an effective, accessible site are too numerous and complex to cover in this book. But you can check out the tools for defining accessible objects in the Accessibility panel. Choose Window > Other Panels > Accessibility to open the panel, or click the Accessibility icon near the lower-right corner of the Properties tab of the Property inspector (**Figure 17.8**). The accessibility parameters for selected objects appear in the panel.

Adobe outlines some of the basic concepts of accessible Web design in the Help panel (see the topic Using Flash > Best Practices > Accessibility Guidelines). More information is available from Adobe's Accessibility Resource Center (http://www.adobe.com/resources/accessibility/).

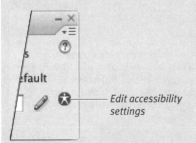

Edit accessibility settings

Figure 17.8 Clicking the Accessibility icon (left) in the Document Properties tab of the Property inspector opens the Accessibility panel (right). Use these settings to make selected objects in your movie available (or unavailable) to screen-reader software.

Publishing

To make your movie available to the public, you must publish or export it. Flash's Publish function is geared toward presenting material on the Web and creating a range of formats for various viewers. The Export feature has similar settings but creates just one format at a time (see the sidebar "Publishing vs. Exporting").

To set the publishing format:

1. Open the Flash document you want to publish.

2. Choose File > Publish Settings, or press Option-Shift-F12 (Mac) or Ctrl-Shift-F12 (Windows) (**Figure 17.9**).

   The Publish Settings dialog appears. The top of the dialog displays a Current Profile and buttons for working with profiles. If you're working in a new document and have never created a profile, Default is your only option. If you open a file made with a previous version of Flash, the profile name reflects that version. A profile is the compilation of settings for the various publishing options. You can save settings in new profiles. Leave the current profile in place.

3. Click the Formats button (Mac) or tab (Windows) (**Figure 17.10**).

4. Choose one of the eight format options.

   The options are Flash (.swf), HTML (.html), GIF Image (.gif), JPEG Image (.jpg), PNG Image (.png), Windows Projector (.exe), Macintosh Projector, and QuickTime with Flash Track (.mov).

5. To set the options for a selected format, select the button (Mac) or tab (Windows) associated with that format (as outlined in separate tasks later in this chapter).

Figure 17.9 To access the settings for publishing a movie, choose File > Publish Settings.

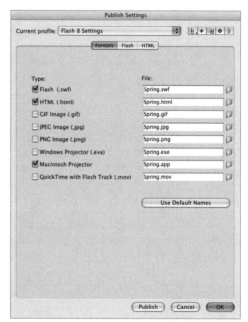

Figure 17.10 The Formats section of the Publish Settings dialog lets you publish your Flash content in as many as seven formats at the same time. An eighth format choice creates an HTML document for displaying the published files in a browser.

6. To save these settings with the current file, click OK.

Flash uses these settings each time you choose the Publish or Publish Preview command for this document. Flash also uses a file's current publish settings when you enter test mode (by choosing Control > Test Movie or Control > Test Scene).

✔ Tip

■ If the Document Properties tab of the Property inspector is open, you can access the Publish Settings dialog quickly. In the Publish section of the tab, click the Settings button.

Publishing vs. Exporting

Flash's Publish command uses a document's Publish Settings to create all the elements needed to display your Flash creation on the Web: a Flash Player (SWF) file, an HTML file, and a JavaScript file. The JavaScript and HTML files work together, creating HTML code that displays the SWF (running in Flash Player) in a browser window. The JavaScript file also performs version detection, ensuring that end users have the right version of Flash Player to view your content. The Publish command can also create alternate file formats—GIF, JPEG, PNG, and QuickTime—and the HTML needed to display them in the browser window. Alternate formats let you make some of the animation and interactivity of your site available even to end users who lack the Flash Player plug-in. Finally, the Publishing command can create stand-alone projector files.

Flash's Export Movie command translates a Flash document directly into a single format. In general, the options for exporting to alternate graphics formats—GIF, JPEG, and PNG—are the same as for publishing to those formats. The arrangement of some options differs between the export and publish dialogs, and some formats have more options in the Publish Settings dialog. In the Publish Settings dialog you have, for example, the choice to remove gradients from GIFs (to keep the file size small), whereas in the Export GIF dialog, you don't have that option. Exporting to QuickTime differs significantly from Publishing to QuickTime. When publishing to QuickTime, you are limited to working with content created for Flash Player version 5 or earlier, but you preserve the interactivity features of your movie, such as buttons and links. When you export to QuickTime, you lose any interactivity features, but you can output animation created for any version of the Flash Player. The dialogs used in exporting to QuickTime offer much more control over output than does the Publish Settings dialog. QuickTime export works by playing back the SFW file in Flash Player, then capturing each frame of the animation (including animation generated by ActionScript) and writing it to a frame in a QuickTime MOV file.

Another difference between publishing and exporting is that Flash stores the publish settings with the FLA file for reuse. You must set export options each time you export a FLA file, even when you re-export the same FLA file to the same format.

PUBLISHING

To publish a movie:

1. Open the Flash file you want to publish.

2. To issue the Publish command, do either of the following:

   ▲ Choose File > Publish Settings.

   The Publish Settings dialog appears. You can follow the steps in the preceding task to set new format options or accept the current settings. Then click the Publish button (**Figure 17.11**).

   ▲ Choose File > Publish, or press Shift-F12.

   The Publishing dialog appears, displaying a progress bar and a button for canceling the procedure (**Figure 17.12**). Flash uses the publish settings stored with your Flash document, creating a new file for each format selected in the Publish Settings dialog.

✔ Tips

■ By default, Flash places the published files in the same location as the original Flash file. You can choose a new location. In the formats section of the Publish Settings dialog, click the folder icon to the right of the filename. The Select Publish Destination dialog appears, allowing you to select a new location for the file.

■ You can open your browser and preview a movie in one step. Choose File > Publish Preview. Flash offers a menu that contains all the formats selected in the Publish Settings dialog (**Figure 17.13**). Choose a format. Flash publishes the file in that format, using the current settings, and opens the movie in a browser window.

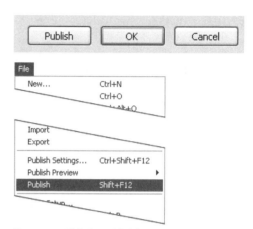

Figure 17.11 Click the Publish button in the Publish Settings dialog (top) or choose File > Publish (bottom) to publish your Flash files.

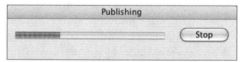

Figure 17.12 To cancel the publishing process, click the Stop (Mac) or Cancel (Windows) button in the Publishing dialog. If you've published the file before, the dialog may appear only briefly, making it difficult to cancel the operation.

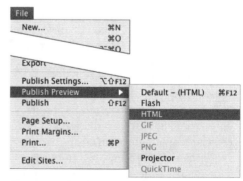

Figure 17.13 The File > Publish Preview submenu displays all the formats selected in the Publish Settings dialog. Flash publishes your movie in the selected format and opens it in your browser.

PUBLISHING

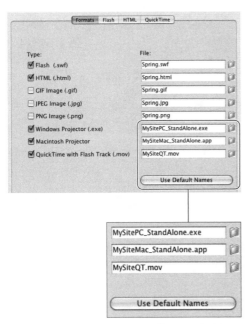

Figure 17.14 You can type your own filenames in the fields of the Publish Settings dialog box. Just be sure to end the name with the proper extension. To return to the default name, click the Use Default Names button.

- You can use Publish Preview to test your Flash creation in a browser window. However, if you're testing SWF files that reside on your local system, and your Flash movie links to a URL on the network, you can run into security issues. For testing purposes, you may need to change the security settings in the Flash section of the Publish Settings dialog (setting the Local Playback Security setting to Access Network Only) or you may need to give special permissions to the file you're testing (see the sidebar "A Note About Flash Player 9's Security Settings," later in this chapter).

- Flash makes one of the formats the default for Publish Preview. To publish in the default format, press ⌘-F12 (Mac) or F12 (Windows). If you want to do lots of testing in a format other than SWF (to test your animated GIF versions, for example), set your publish settings in only that format. Then that format is the default, and you can choose it quickly by using the keyboard shortcut.

- By default, Flash names the published files by adding the appropriate extension to the filename—adding .gif for a GIF file or .png for a PNG file, for example. Change the name by typing a different name in the File field in the Publish Settings dialog. To return to the default name, click the Use Default Names button (**Figure 17.14**).

- The Publish and Publish Preview commands don't give you a chance to name the published files; they take the names directly from the Publish Settings dialog. If you want to publish multiple versions of a movie, each with different settings, you must make sure that you don't overwrite the published file. Rename the published file, move that file to a new location, or type a different name in the Formats section of the Publish Settings dialog.

Working with Flash Player Settings

The stand-alone Flash Player is an application file that installs with Flash. The Player opens when you double-click the icon of a SWF file. (From within Flash Player, you can use the File > Open command to open and play SWF files.) To prepare a Flash movie for playing in the stand-alone Player, choose either the Publish or Export command in the Flash editor. The options are basically the same for both commands.

To publish a Flash Player (SWF) file:

1. From an open Flash document, choose File > Publish Settings.

   The Publish Settings dialog appears; choose a base publishing profile, or leave the current setting.

2. Click the Formats button (Mac) or tab (Windows).

3. In the Type section, select Flash (.swf).

   If you wish, type a new name in the File field for the Flash (SWF) file. Be sure to include the .swf extension.

4. Select the Flash button (Mac) or tab (Windows) (**Figure 17.15**).

5. Set Flash options as described in the following tasks.

6. Click Publish.

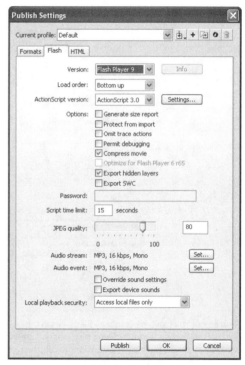

Figure 17.15 The Flash section of the Publish Settings dialog offers options for publishing your Flash movie as a Flash Player (SWF) file.

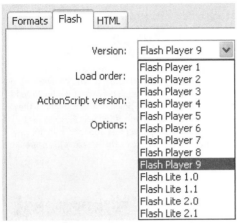

Figure 17.16 Choose a version of Flash Player to publish to. Publishing to earlier versions makes some features of Flash CS3 unavailable but ensures that a wider audience will have the correct player.

To choose a Flash Player version:

◆ In the Flash section of the Publish Settings dialog, from the Version pop-up menu, choose a version of Flash Player (**Figure 17.16**).

Your options are Flash Player 1 (formerly known as FutureSplash Animator) through 9 and Flash Lite 1.0, 1.1, 2.0, and 2.1 (players that work in devices such as mobile phones). If you publish your file to a Flash Player version earlier than 9, you lose some features specific to Flash CS3.

✔ Tips

■ Before you start scripting using ActionScript, in the Flash section of the Publish Settings dialog, select the earliest version of Flash Player you plan to use to deliver content to your audience. The Actions Toolbox in the Actions panel provides feedback about actions that won't work in the selected player version.

■ When you choose Flash Player 6 from the Version pop-up menu, the Optimize for Flash Player 6 r65 check box becomes active. Select the check box to enable Flash to take advantage of performance improvements made to Flash Player 6 (these enhancements appear in Flash Player 6 release 65 and later).

■ When you choose Flash Player 6, 7, 8, or 9, the Compress Movie check box becomes active. Compressing a file that has lots of text or ActionScript helps keep the file size down.

WORKING WITH FLASH PLAYER SETTINGS

To control how Flash draws the movie's frames:

◆ In the Flash section of the Publish Settings dialog, from the Load Order pop-up menu, choose the order in which Flash loads a movie's layers for display (**Figure 17.17**).

To choose the version of ActionScript used (Flash Player 6–9):

◆ In the Flash section of the Publish Settings dialog, from the pop-up menu, choose ActionScript version 1. 0, 2.0, or 3.0 (**Figure 17.18**).

This setting tells Flash which version of the scripting language you've used in your document so the compiler treats the code appropriately. The menu becomes active only when you've chosen Player 6, 7, 8, or 9.

✔ Tips

■ Flash's components rely on ActionScript. It's crucial that the ActionScript version selected in the Publish Settings dialog match the components used in the FLA. If the FLA contains components from one ActionScript version and you publish to another, the components may not work or may not even appear in the published movie.

■ During authoring, the Components panel displays only components that work with the version of ActionScript currently selected in Publish Settings. To have the panel show ActionScript 3.0 components, for example, you must choose ActionScript 3.0 for publishing.

Figure 17.17 In the Load Order pop-up menu, you choose the order in which Flash draws the layers of the frames of your movie. When playback over the Web is slow, Flash starts displaying individual layers as they download. The Top Down setting tells Flash to send (and display) the top layer first and then work its way to the bottom layer. Bottom Up does just the opposite.

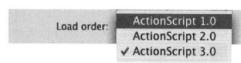

Figure 17.18 ActionScript 1.0, 2.0, and 3.0 present different tasks for the compiler when Flash publishes a SWF file. Be sure to select the version you used (or plan to use) for scripting.

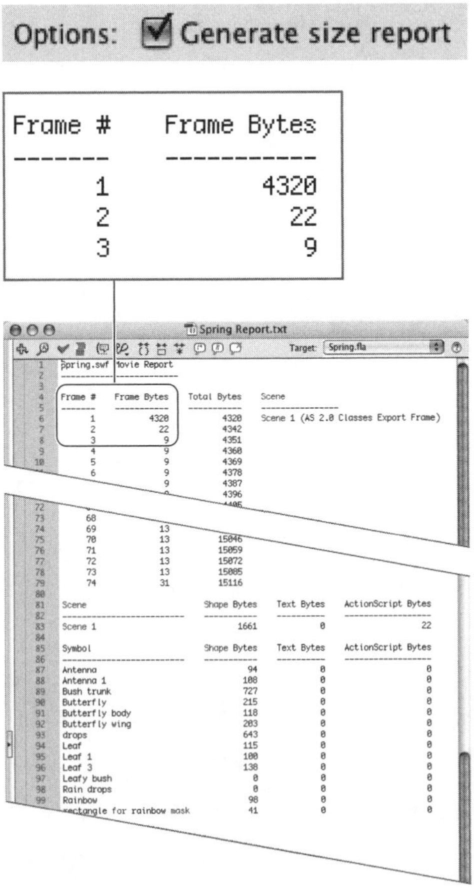

Options: ☑ Generate size report

Frame #	Frame Bytes
1	4320
2	22
3	9

Figure 17.19 Choose Generate Size Report (top) to have Flash create an ActionScript text file that lists the amount of data in your movie (bottom).

Options:
- ☐ Generate size report
- ☑ Protect from import
- ☐ Omit trace actions
- ☐ Permit debugging
- ☑ Compress movie
- ☐ Optimize for Flash Player 6 r65
- ☑ Export hidden layers
- ☐ Export SWC

Figure 17.20 Choose Protect from Import to prevent viewers from converting a SWF file back into a FLA file.

To list the amount of data in the movie by frame:

◆ In the Flash section of the Publish Settings dialog, select the Generate Size Report check box (**Figure 17.19**).

 Flash creates an ActionScript text file listing the frames of the movie and how much data each frame contains. (The Size report text also appears in the Output panel.) This report helps you find frames that bog down the movie's playback. You can then optimize or eliminate some of the content in those frames.

✔ Tips

■ The Size report also details how much data is in each symbol used in the movie. Symbols that aren't used appear in the report, but they contain 0 bytes of data.

■ Depending on how you've sized the output window, and the specific data generated by the Size report, you may see only white space in the Output window. Resize the window or scroll up to view the Size report data.

To protect your work:

◆ In the Flash section of the Publish Settings dialog, under Options, select the Protect from Import check box (**Figure 17.20**).

 This setting prevents viewers from obtaining the SWF file and converting it back to a Flash document (FLA).

✔ Tip

■ You can make the Protect from Import setting selective. Enter a password in the Password field. Only those who enter the correct password can import the SWF file.

To set trace and debug options:

◆ In the Flash section of the Publish Settings dialog, under Options, select either of the following check boxes:

Omit Trace Actions prevents trace actions from appearing in the Output window during debugging (**Figure 17.21**).

Permit Debugging allows remote debugging of ActionScripts (**Figure 17.22**). This option allows you, or other users who are running the debug version of Flash Player, to debug a Flash Player (SWF) file as it plays over the Internet.

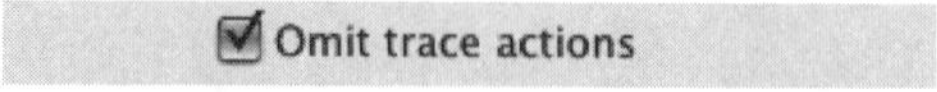

✔ Tip

■ When the Permit Debugging option is selected, you should always enter a password in the Password field (Figure 17.22). This password prohibits unauthorized individuals from accessing your script but allows authorized personnel to debug the file remotely.

To compress the SWF file (Flash Player 6, 7, 8 or 9):

1. In the Flash section of the Publish Settings dialog, choose Flash Player 6, 7, 8, or 9 from the Version pop-up menu.

2. Select the Compress Movie check box in the Options section (**Figure 17.23**).

Compress Movie is an option only when you publish for Flash Player versions 6–9. The setting has no effect on the JPEG-quality and audio-compression settings you choose in the following tasks.

☑ Omit trace actions

Figure 17.21 When you select the Omit Trace Actions option, the Flash compiler strips all trace actions from the SWF file, allowing you to view only non-trace debugging items in the Output window. Omitting trace actions also reduces file size slightly if your scripts contain lots of trace actions.

Figure 17.22 When you select the Permit Debugging option, you should also enter a password to protect movies that are open to remote debugging.

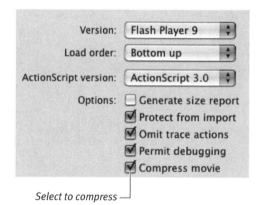

Select to compress

Figure 17.23 When you've chosen to publish to Flash Player versions 6–9, you can also choose to compress the movie. Compression helps to reduce the file size, especially for text-heavy movies or those with lots of ActionScript.

Figure 17.24 To set JPEG compression for any bitmaps in your movie, type a value in the JPEG Quality field or use the slider. A setting of 0 provides the most compression (and the lowest quality, because that compression leads to loss of data); 100 results in the least compression (the highest quality).

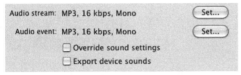

Figure 17.25 You must set the sample rate and compression options for stream sounds and event sounds separately. Click the Set button to access the options for each type of sound.

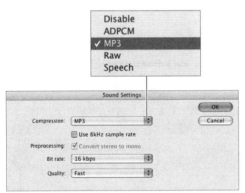

Figure 17.26 Choose a compression method from the Compression pop-up menu. Other options appropriate to the selected method appear. Choose Disable to turn off sound.

Sample-Rate Rule of Thumb

Sample rates are measured in kHz or frequency. Recording for music CDs is done at 44 kHz. For multimedia CD-ROMs, 22 kHz is a standard rate. For music clips in Flash movies played on the Web, 11 kHz is often sufficient. For shorter sounds, including spoken words, you may be able to get away with even lower sampling rates.

To apply JPEG compression to bitmaps:

◆ In the Flash section of the Publish Settings dialog, do either of the following:

▲ Adjust the JPEG Quality slider.

▲ Enter a specific value in the JPEG Quality field (**Figure 17.24**).

This setting controls how Flash applies JPEG compression as it exports the bitmaps in your movie.

✔ Tips

■ Flash doesn't apply JPEG compression to GIF images that you've imported into your movie, because Flash defaults to using lossless compression for GIFs.

■ You can also set compression for individual bitmaps in the library of your Flash document. Select the bitmap in the Library panel. From the panel's options menu, choose Properties to access the Bitmap Properties dialog. A Compression pop-up menu offers two choices: Lossless (PNG/GIF) or Photo (JPEG). (The Photo option creates lossy compression.)

To control compression and sample rate for all movie sounds:

1. In the Flash section of the Publish Settings dialog, for the Audio Stream option (or the Audio Event option), click the Set button (**Figure 17.25**). The Sound Settings dialog appears. Flash divides sounds into two types: stream and event (for more details, see Chapter 15). You must set the compression for each type separately, but the process and options are the same for both.

2. From the Compression pop-up menu (**Figure 17.26**), choose one of the following options:

continues on next page

▲ **Disable** removes sound from the published file.

▲ **ADPCM** compression works best for movies containing mostly short event sounds, such as hand claps or button clicks. (Generally, you'll use this setting in the Audio Event section.) The ADPCM options appear. From the ADPCM Bits pop-up menu, choose one of the four bit rates to determine the degree of compression applied to the sounds (**Figure 17.27**). With the ADPCM setting, you can also set a sample rate and convert stereo sound to mono sound.

▲ **MP3** compression works best for movies containing mostly longer stream sounds. (Generally, you'll use this setting in the Audio Stream section.) The MP3 options appear. From the Bit Rate pop-up menu, choose one of 12 bit rates for the published sounds (**Figure 17.28**). From the Quality pop-up menu, choose Fast when you are testing your movie; choose Medium or Best when you publish for your target audience, as they provide better quality.

▲ **Raw** omits sound compression. Raw does let you control file size by choosing a sample rate and converting stereo sound to mono.

▲ **Speech** sets compression for sounds consisting of spoken words. Choose a sample rate from the pop-up menu that appears.

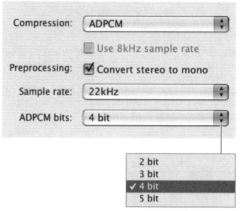

Figure 17.27 The ADPCM Bits pop-up menu lets you control the amount of compression applied to the sounds in your movie. Choose 2-Bit for the greatest degree of compression (resulting in the lowest-quality sound); choose 5-Bit for the least compression (resulting in the highest-quality sound).

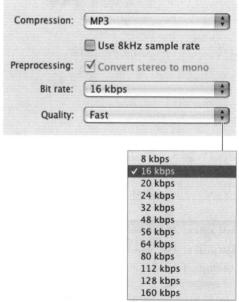

Figure 17.28 With MP3 compression and a bit-rate setting of less than 20 Kbps, Flash converts sounds from stereo to mono. At settings of 20 Kbps and above, you can publish stereo sounds or convert them to mono sounds.

Figure 17.29 Flash CS3 provides security by restricting SWF files from manipulating data on different systems. With Access Local Files Only as the setting, the published SWF file can copy or write data only to files on the local system. With Access Network Only, the SWF file can copy or write data only to files on the network and not on the local system.

To control access to local and network files for security:

◆ To determine which types of files the SWF file can copy data from or write data to, in the Local Playback Security section, in the Flash section of the Publish Settings dialog, from the pop-up menu (**Figure 17.29**), choose either of the following options:

Access Local Files Only. With local-only access, the SWF file can share information with files on the local system where the SWF file resides, but not with files located on the Internet. Local-only access prevents a SWF file from loading XML files from the Internet or posting data from an entry form to the Internet, for example.

Access Network Only. With network-only access, the SWF file can share information only with files located on the Internet, not with local files.

Digitally Recorded Sounds

As motion pictures are to movement, digital recordings are to sound. Both media capture slices of a continuous event. By playing the captured slices back in order, you re-create the event. In a movie, the slices are frames of film; in a digital recording, they're snippets of sound.

You can think of the recording process as capturing a sound wave by laying a grid over it and copying a piece of the wave at each intersection on the grid. The lines across the horizontal axis are the *sample rate*—how often you capture the sound. The lines up and down the vertical axis are the *bit rate*—how much detail you capture about the sound wave's amplitude. The greater the frequency and bit rate (the finer the mesh of your recording grid), the greater the realism of your recording during playback. Unfortunately, greater realism translates into larger files.

The sound options in the Publish Settings dialog give you the flexibility to create different versions of your movie with different sample rates and bit rates without actually changing the sounds embedded in the movie. You might allow yourself larger file sizes and higher-quality sounds for a version being delivered on CD-ROM than for a version being distributed on the Web. As you try different sound options, be sure to listen to your published sounds to determine the best balance between sound quality and file size.

A Note About Flash Player 9's Security Settings

Flash CS3 and Flash Player versions 8 and 9 let you create content that uploads and/or downloads files at runtime; this capability gives Flash more power than it had in earlier versions, but with that power comes the potential to do harm. Flash Player 8 and 9 use a security feature that ensures that SWF files can't perform malicious deeds on the systems of your target audience. Flash's default local-security settings prohibit SWF files running locally (on a single computer) from communicating with files being served on the Internet (and vice versa); to allow such communication, you must give Flash Player specific permissions.

When you choose Flash Player version 8 or 9 in Publish Settings, the security model comes into play. When you publish your Flash creation locally before deploying it to a server and you try out the movie in a browser, clicking a button or link in the movie that connects to the Internet may trigger a warning that Flash Player has stopped an operation that might be unsafe.

If the SWF you're testing doesn't need to communicate with both the local system and the Internet, you can solve the problem by changing your Publish Settings. In the Flash section of the Publish Settings dialog, under Local Playback Security, choose Access Network Only. (Note that if you try out your movie using one of the testing modes, the security alert does not appear. In test mode, Flash automatically trusts all local files being accessed.)

If, after changing the Local Playback Security setting, you still get the warning, you need to give your SWF file special permission to communicate with the Internet. When the Adobe Flash Player Security dialog appears (**Figure 17.30**), click the Settings button. Flash opens a browser window and directs you to a page of the Flash Player documentation on the Adobe site (http:// www.macromedia.com/support/documentation/en/flashplayer/help/settings_manager04a.h tml). This page gives you access to the Adobe Flash Player Settings Manager (**Figure 17.31**).

continues on next page

Figure 17.30 When a SWF file on a local computer attempts to access a file on the Internet, Flash Player 9 won't allow it to, unless you've set the proper security settings. You'll see a warning dialog to alert you to the fact that your settings don't allow this communication.

Global Security Settings tab

Click to add trusted files and/or folders

Figure 17.31 The Global Security Settings tab of the Adobe Flash Player Settings Manager lets you create a list of trusted files and/or folders for Flash Player 9 security. Any SWF files in locations covered by this list can communicate with Internet files.

A Note About Flash Player 9's Security Settings *continued*

Use the Global Security Settings tab of the manager to create a list of trusted items. Flash Player always allows SWF files from the Global Security Settings list to communicate with the Internet, even if they're being run locally. Use the Edit Locations pop-up menu to add individual SWF files or folders to the trusted list or remove them from the list (**Figure 17.32**).

If you'll be doing lots of this type of testing, it makes sense to set up a special Trusted folder where you keep only your own SWF files you need to test. Don't allow Flash Player to trust folders on your system that might include SWF files downloaded from other sources. Such files have the potential to do something dangerous, such as copying information from your system and sending it to an outside location.

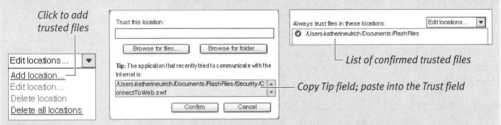

Figure 17.32 Click the Edit Locations pop-up menu to manage a list of trusted files (left). Click Add Location to open a window (middle) where you can add a new file or folder to a trusted list. If you opened the Global Security Settings Manager by clicking the Settings button of the security warning dialog (Figure 17.30), the window's Tip field shows the path name for the file you were working on. Copy and paste that name to the Trusted field (or use one of the Browse buttons to navigate to the file or folder you want to add); click Confirm to add the trusted file to the trusted list (right).

Advanced Sound Handling

Flash automatically applies the sound-compression settings in the Publish Settings dialog to all sound assets that have no specific settings of their own. By selectively assigning higher quality to some sounds, you can keep file size reasonable and still have high-quality sound where you need it.

To set compression options for sounds individually, select a sound asset in the Library panel; then click the Properties button (the *i* icon) at the bottom of the panel or choose Properties from the options menu. The Sound Properties dialog appears. Its Compression pop-up menu gives you access to the same sound-export settings as the Flash section of the Publish Settings dialog.

If you apply individual sound-export settings to some sound assets, Flash uses those settings for those sounds when you publish the movie. For all other sounds in the movie, Flash uses the current sound settings in the Publish Settings dialog.

You can force Flash to ignore the individual sound settings and publish all sounds with the sound-export settings currently selected in the Publish Settings dialog. In the Flash section of the Publish Settings dialog, choose Override Sound Settings. You might use this feature to make a lower-quality Web version of a movie you created for CD-ROM.

Publishing HTML for Flash Player Files

An *HTML document* is a master set of instructions that tells a browser how to display Web content. The Publish function of Flash creates an HTML document that tells the browser how to display the published files for your document (these files can be in SWF, GIF, JPEG, PNG, and/or QuickTime with FlashTracks format—whatever you choose in the Formats section of the Publish Settings dialog). In addition, publishing creates a JavaScript file that works in concert with the HTML document to make your Flash content immediately available to end users (see the sidebar "About Active Content").

The Publish command creates the required HTML by filling in blanks in a template document. Flash comes with 11 templates; you can also create your own.

About Active Content

As the result of a lawsuit about the EOLAS patent, in 2006 Microsoft started changing the way its Internet Explorer browser works. The change affects *active content* that is embedded in HTML documents using the traditional method of `<object>` and `<embed>` tags. (Flash is one type of active content.) The changes require Web-site visitors to activate the content by clicking it. Imagine a site with a Flash animation. If you embed the SWF the traditional way, users first coming to the site through Internet Explorer see a static image. As they move the pointer over the image, a tool tip explains that they must click to activate the content. To get around this barrier to interactive fun, Flash CS3's Publish command creates two files that work together to display content in a browser: an HTML file and a JavaScript file (named AC_RunActiveContent.js). A script in the JavaScript file writes code into the HTML file interactively (the script basically rewrites the code for the `<object>` and `<embed>` tags); this process activates the SWF immediately. End users can see and interact with your Flash content as soon as it appears in the browser window.

For users that don't have JavaScript or have disabled their JavaScript, the HTML file also includes the standard `<object>` and `<embed>` tags within a set of `<noscript>` tags. These tags tell the browser to use this section of code only if the end user lacks JavaScript.

The JavaScript-HTML combination works for all browsers that support the Flash Player. When you use this method, be sure to place the SWF, HTML, and AC_RunActiveContent.js files together in one folder on the server that hosts your site.

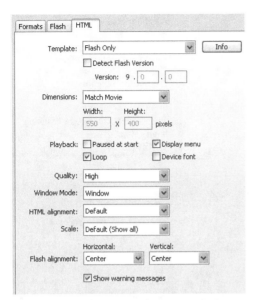

Figure 17.33 The HTML section of the Publish Settings dialog contains options for displaying your Flash movie in the browser window.

To publish HTML for displaying a Flash file:

1. In the Flash document you want to publish for the Web, choose File > Publish Settings.

   The Publish Settings dialog appears; choose a new publishing profile, or leave the current setting.

2. Click the Formats button (Mac) or tab (Windows).

3. In the Type section, choose HTML (.html).

   When you choose HTML, Flash automatically selects Flash (.swf) as well.

4. Select the HTML button (Mac) or tab (Windows) (**Figure 17.33**).

   The options for displaying your Flash movie in the browser window appear in the dialog. When you publish the current file, Flash feeds your choices into the appropriate HTML tags and parameters in the template of your choice.

To create HTML for Flash only:

◆ From the Template pop-up menu, choose Flash Only (**Figure 17.34**).

This template is the simplest one. It uses the HTML-JavaScript method to display your Flash content for viewers who are properly equipped with the Flash Player version that you select in the Flash section of the Publish Settings dialog (see the sidebar "About Active Content," earlier in this chapter). Other viewers will be unable to see your content. (Other template choices create HTML that performs other tasks; for example, the Image Map template creates HTML that displays alternate images or files when the viewer lacks the proper Flash Player plug-in.)

✔ Tip

■ If you can't remember what one of the included HTML templates does, select it from the Template pop-up menu in the HTML tab of the Publish Settings dialog, and then click the Info button next to the menu. Flash displays a brief description, including instructions about choosing alternate formats, if necessary.

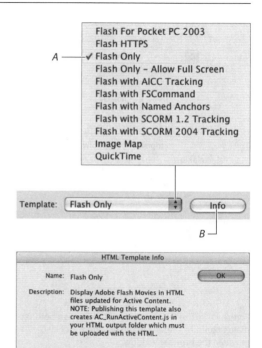

Figure 17.34 Choose Flash Only (A) as the template when you want to create HTML for displaying only a Flash movie with no other options for alternate images. Click the Info button (B) to see a description of what the template does (C).

The Mystery of HTML Templates

The traditional HTML codes (called *tags*) required for displaying a SWF file in a browser window are `<object>` for Internet Explorer (Windows) and `<embed>` for other browsers. (In addition, Flash can use the `<img>` tag to display a file in another format, such as a JPEG image or an animated GIF. If you've created named anchors in your Flash movie and you choose the Flash with Named Anchors template, Flash can create anchor tags for browser navigation, as well.)

Flash's Publish command works hand in hand with HTML templates—which are fill-in-the-blank recipes—and JavaScript to define the parameters of the `<object>` and `<embed>` tags. These parameters include the width and height of the movie window, the quality of the images (the amount of antialiasing to provide), and the way the movie window aligns with the browser window.

Each option and parameter in the HTML section of the Publish Settings dialog has an equivalent template variable. The *template variable* is a code word that starts with the dollar sign (`$`). When you choose an option in the Publish Settings dialog, Flash enters your choice as an HTML tag that replaces the variable in the template document. If you set the width of your movie as 500 pixels in the Publish Settings dialog for HTML, for example, Flash replaces the template variable for width (`$WI`) with the proper coding to display the movie in a window 500 pixels wide. To get a bit more technical, the template variables are actually parameters in a JavaScript function. When you publish a SWF, Flash creates an HTML file that calls the JavaScript function to write out the `<object>` and `<embed>` tags dynamically at runtime (see the sidebar "About Active Content," earlier in this chapter)

Flash's HTML templates contain coding not only for displaying your Flash movie, but also for showing the JPEG, GIF, or PNG version of your movie that you want to make available to viewers who don't have the proper browser player to view Flash.

During the publishing process, Flash saves a copy of the HTML template for your movie, giving it the name of your movie file and adding whatever extension the template file has. (The template files that come with Flash use the extension .html, for example.) You can go into a template file as you would any other text file and modify the HTML coding.

You can extend the Publish command's capacity for creating HTML documents by setting up your own HTML templates. To be available to Flash's template menu, the HTML file must include a title (use the code `$TT`). The HTML file must be inside the HTML folder, which lives in the Configuration Folder. For more details on locating this folder, see the sidebar "The Mystery of the Configuration Folder," in Chapter 1.

To set the dimensions of the movie-display window:

◆ To set the width and height of the rectangle that displays your movie in the browser, from the Dimensions pop-up menu in the HTML section of the Publish Settings dialog (**Figure 17.35**), choose one of the following options:

Match Movie uses the movie's dimensions (specified in the Document Properties dialog).

Pixels lets you specify new dimensions. Type the new values in the Width and Height fields.

Percent lets you specify the dimensions as a percentage of the browser window's dimensions. Type a value between 1 and 100 in the Width and Height fields.

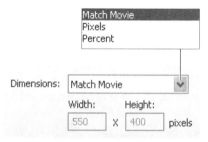

Figure 17.35 Choose a method for sizing the movie-display window (the window in which a browser displays your Flash movie).

Fitting Movies into Browser Windows

When you publish HTML for displaying movies in a Web page, think in terms of three windows:

◆ The *browser window* contains the entire Web page.

◆ Within the browser window is a *movie-display* window (created by the JavaScript script and/or by the HTML <object>, <embed>, and <img> tags) where the Flash Player plug-in displays a Flash movie.

◆ Inside the movie-display window is the actual *movie window*, which corresponds to the Stage of your Flash document.

Each of the three windows has its own dimensions, and you need to tell Flash where to put the windows and how to handle them if, for example, their aspect ratios differ, or if a user resizes the browser window. To instruct browsers on how to deal with these three windows, choose settings in the HTML section of the Publish Settings dialog. When you define a movie-display window with a different width or height from the original Flash document, you must tell Flash how to scale the movie to fit in that window.

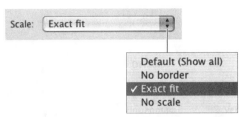

Figure 17.36 The scale method tells Flash how to fit the Flash movie inside the movie-display window that you define. You need to set the scale only if you define a movie-display window with different dimensions from those of the movie itself—as a percentage of the browser width and height, for example.

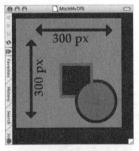

Dimensions:
Match Movie
Scale: No Scale

Dimensions:
100 by 50 pixels
Scale: No Border

Dimensions:
100 by 50 pixels
Scale: Exact Fit

Figure 17.37 This 300-by-300–pixel movie looks quite different in the different dimension-and-scale combinations. The movie-display window's dimensions and the scale setting are identified in the examples above. (Here the browser background has been set to black to make the movie-display window visible.)

To scale the movie to fit a movie-display window:

◆ From the Scale pop-up menu (**Figure 17.36**), choose one of the following options:

Default (Show All) keeps the movie's original aspect ratio (width to height) and resizes the movie so that it fits completely within the newly specified rectangle (**Figure 17.37**). (Be aware that the resized movie may not fill the new rectangle: Gaps may appear on the sides or at the top and bottom.)

No Border keeps the movie's original aspect ratio and resizes the movie so the whole new rectangle is filled with it. (Some of the movie may slop over the edges and be cropped.)

Exact Fit changes the movie's height and width to the new specifications, even if it involves changing the aspect ratio and distorting the image.

No Scale keeps the movie at a constant size. Resizing the browser window can crop the image.

✔ Tip

■ If you define the movie-display window as 100 percent of the width and height of the browser window, in some browser versions, no matter how large your viewer makes the browser window, a scroll bar always appears. Setting the width and height to 95 percent (or lower) ensures that all viewers will be able to enlarge the browser window enough to eliminate the scroll bar.

PUBLISHING HTML FOR FLASH PLAYER FILES

521

To control placement of the movie window in the movie-display window:

◆ To align the movie window within the movie-display window, in the Flash Alignment section of the HTML tab of the Publish Settings dialog, do either of the following:

▲ From the Horizontal pop-up menu, choose Left, Center, or Right.

▲ From the Vertical pop-up menu, choose Top, Center, or Bottom.

Flash positions the movie within the movie-display window (**Figure 17.38**).

To set playback options:

◆ In the Playback area of the HTML section of the Publish Settings dialog (**Figure 17.39**), select any of the following options:

Paused at Start makes users begin the movie manually (by clicking a button or by choosing Play from the contextual menu).

Loop makes the movie start over when it reaches the last frame.

Display Menu creates a contextual menu with playback options available to users.

Device Font speeds playback on Windows systems. The Device Font option allows Windows systems to substitute aliased system fonts for fonts that aren't installed on the user's system. This substitution takes place only in static text blocks where you've enabled device fonts during the authoring phase.

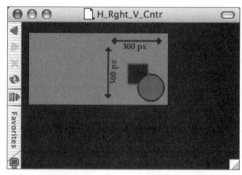

Horizontal: Right; Vertical: Center

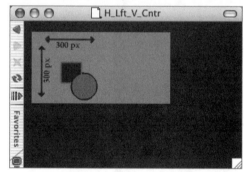

Horizontal: Left; Vertical: Center

Figure 17.38 The Flash Alignment section's Horizontal and Vertical pop-up menus let you position your movie within the movie-display window when the dimensions of that window differ from those of the movie. Compare the results of two different settings for this 300-by-300–pixel movie set inside a 200-by-100–pixel display window (with Scale set to Default). The light gray rectangle is the display window, which automatically fills with the same color as your movie's background.

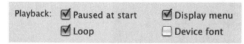

Figure 17.39 The HTML section of the Publish Settings dialog gives you options for controlling playback. You control whether the movie starts playing immediately in the browser window, or if it's in a paused state waiting for user input to start; whether the movie loops, or plays through just once; and whether users can control playback from the contextual menu. For Windows machines, you can improve playback speed by activating device fonts.

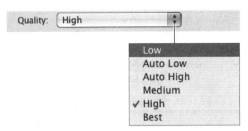

Figure 17.40 The Quality setting for publishing HTML balances image quality against playback speed in a published movie.

Printing from Flash Player

By default, choosing Print from the Flash Player contextual menu prints every frame in the movie. You can restrict printing to certain keyframes by labeling them as printable in the original Flash document. To define a keyframe as printable, select it, and in the Properties tab of the Property inspector, in the Frame Label field enter #p (it must be a lowercase letter *p*). For the contextual menu to be available in Flash Player, you need to set the playback options in the HTML section of the Publish Settings dialog to Display Menu (see "Publishing HTML for Flash Player Files," earlier in this chapter). To disable printing from Flash Player, select any keyframe in your Flash document, and in the Properties tab of the Property inspector, in the Frame Label field enter !#p. When you publish the file, the Print option is disabled in Flash Player's contextual menu.

To control antialiasing and smoothing:

◆ From the Quality pop-up menu in the HTML section of the Publish Settings dialog (**Figure 17.40**), choose one of the following options:

Low. Flash keeps antialiasing off.

Auto Low. Flash starts playback with antialiasing off; but if it finds that the viewer's computer and connection can handle antialiasing while keeping the movie's specified frame rate, Flash turns antialiasing on.

Auto High. Flash turns antialiasing on to start, and turns it off if playback drops below the movie's specified frame rate.

Medium. Taking the middle ground, Flash forgoes bitmap smoothing but does some antialiasing.

High. Flash uses antialiasing on everything but smooths bitmaps only if there is no animation.

Best. Flash keeps antialiasing on and smooths all bitmaps.

To control transparency:

◆ From the Window Mode pop-up menu (**Figure 17.41**), choose one of the following options:

Window plays the Flash movie window in a separate movie-display window within the Web page.

Opaque Windowless plays the Flash movie window directly in the browser window.

Transparent Windowless plays the Flash movie window directly in the browser window.

Figure 17.41 For viewers of your Flash movie who use qualified browsers, you can create a transparency effect that reveals Web-page elements beneath any transparent areas of the movie. In the HTML tab of the Publish Settings dialog, set Window Mode to Transparent Windowless.

More About Window Modes

In Window mode, the movie-display window blocks elements of the Web page on layers below the Flash movie and often blocks (or interferes with) elements above the movie-display window as well. Window mode gives Flash complete control of the window-display area of the screen and therefore results in the best performance. In Opaque Windowless mode, elements of the Web page that lie above the Flash movie do appear. Elements of the Web page that lie below the Flash movie do not appear. The Transparent Windowless setting allows elements of the Web page to show through any areas of your Flash movie that don't contain objects. This setting may slow the playback of your animation. In addition, keyboard commands may behave differently in Opaque Windowless and Transparent Windowless modes, and some browsers may have problems aligning the hit areas of buttons. Be sure to allow more time for testing when you use these modes.

Only certain browsers (and certain versions of Flash Player) support the ability to create transparent backgrounds for published SWF content. The earliest versions of Flash Player that support the Transparent Windowless setting are 6.0.65.0 (Windows) and 6.0.67.0 (Mac). In Mac OS X (browsers in Mac Classic mode don't support the Transparent Windowless setting), Internet Explorer (IE) 5.1 and 5.2 support this setting. In Windows, Internet Explorer 5.0, 5.5, and 6.0 support it. Other browsers that support this setting, on both platforms, include Netscape 7.0 and later, Opera 6 and later, Mozilla 1.0 and later), and AOL/CompuServe.

Title of template for the menu

```
$TTFlash Only
```

```
<body bgcolor="$BG">
```

Background-color variable

New title of template for the menu

```
$TTFlash Only (BlackBackground)
```

```
<body bgcolor="000000">
```

New background-color variable

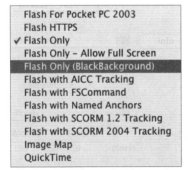

```
Flash For Pocket PC 2003
Flash HTTPS
✓ Flash Only
Flash Only - Allow Full Screen
Flash Only (BlackBackground)
Flash with AICC Tracking
Flash with FSCommand
Flash with Named Anchors
Flash with SCORM 1.2 Tracking
Flash with SCORM 2004 Tracking
Image Map
QuickTime
```

Figure 17.42 The default HTML template picks up the movie's background color as the Web page's background color. You can modify a copy of the template (top). Change the Title tag, and set a specific background color (middle). The new title appears in the Template menu in the HTML tab of the Publish Settings dialog (bottom).

To see warnings about missing alternate content:

◆ At the bottom of the HTML section of the Publish Settings dialog, select the Show Warning Messages check box if you want Flash to notify you if the currently selected template creates tags to display alternate content—a GIF file, for example—but you've neglected to select the appropriate format in the Formats section of the Publish Settings dialog.

✔ Tip

■ The default HTML template automatically sets the background color of your Web page to the background color of your movie. If you want to use a different color, try creating a modified template (**Figure 17.42**). Open the default template, and save a copy with a new name. In the first line of code—$TTFlash Only—change the title to something like $TTFlash Only (BlackBackground), so Flash recognizes and adds the template to the Template menu. In the tag <BODY bgcolor="$BG">, replace $BG with the HTML code for a specific hex color (000000 for a black background, for example). Be sure to place the new template in Flash's HTML folder inside the Configuration folder (for more details about locating this folder, see the sidebar "The Mystery of the Configuration Folder," in Chapter 1). You will see the new template in the Template menu only after you restart Flash.

525

Using Alternate Image Formats

Although most viewers have access to the Flash Player plug-in required to view your Flash content, some may not. You can make at least part of your site available to them by providing alternate image files for their browsers to display. If you're using Flash animation for a simple Web banner, for example, you can use an animated GIF to re-create that banner for viewers who lack the Flash plug-in. Flash can publish alternate GIF, JPEG, PNG, and QuickTime files. Of course, you need a file with the proper HTML coding to direct the viewer's browser to display the alternate file. The HTML Templates named Image Map and QuickTime can assist you in creating the necessary HTML file, as can Flash's version-detection feature (see "Using Version Detection," later in this chapter).

Although each image format has its own set of publishing options, the basic methods for publishing all four alternate formats are the same. This task walks you through the settings for GIF files.

About the Image Map Template

If your Flash file contains button symbols linking to URLs, you can convert that content to an *image map*—a GIF (or PNG or JPEG) file containing hot spots that link to other sites. To have Flash create an image map whose hot spots coincide with your Flash button symbols, choose HTML as well as GIF (or PNG or JPEG) in the Formats section of the Publish Settings dialog. From the Template pop-up menu in the HTML section of the dialog, choose Image Map. Click Publish. Although Flash creates a SWF file whenever you publish HTML format files, the Image Map template creates an HTML file that tells browsers to display the GIF (or PNG or JPG) file and not the SWF. When the browser displays the image map, viewers see your graphic content, and the buttons seem live because they're active links. (Note that the Image Map template creates hot spots only from button symbols, not button components or movie clips acting as buttons. And the button symbol must use the ActionScript 2.0 action getURL. Flash can't create image maps from button symbols targeted by ActionScript 3.0.)

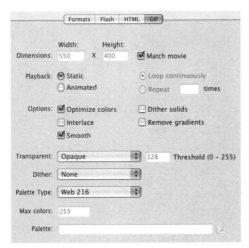

Figure 17.43 Click the GIF button (Mac) or tab (Windows) of the Publish Settings dialog to access the options for creating a static or animated GIF for your alternate image.

Figure 17.44 Deselect Match Movie to enter the dimensions you want the published GIF image to be, or select Match Movie to use the movie's dimensions as the dimensions of your GIF image.

Figure 17.45 To preserve the motion of your Flash movie (though not the sound or interactivity) for viewers who lack the Flash Player plug-in, choose Animated under Playback in the GIF section of the Publish Settings dialog.

To publish GIF files:

1. Open the Flash document, and choose File > Publish Settings.

   The Publish Setting dialog appears; choose a new publishing profile, or leave the current setting.

2. In the Formats section of the dialog, choose GIF Image (.gif).

3. In the GIF section of the dialog (**Figure 17.43**), set GIF options as described in the following tasks.

4. Click Publish.

To set the dimensions of the GIF image:

◆ Under Dimensions in the GIF section of the Publish Settings dialog (**Figure 17.44**), do either of the following:

   ▲ To create a new size for the published GIF image, deselect Match Movie and enter values in the Width and Height fields.

   ▲ To keep the GIF images the same size as the original Flash movie, select Match Movie.

To create static or animated GIFs:

◆ Under Playback in the GIF section of the Publish Settings dialog (**Figure 17.45**), select either of the following options:

   Static creates a static GIF.

   Animated creates an animated GIF. The animation settings become active. To make the animation run repeatedly, select Loop Continuously. To repeat the animation a set number of times, select Repeat and enter a number in the Repeat field. Flash exports all the frames of the movie as an animated GIF.

✔ Tip

- By default, when creating a static GIF, Flash uses the first frame of your movie. To use another frame, create a keyframe at the desired frame number and select it. In the Frame Properties tab of the Property inspector, assign the keyframe the frame label #Static (**Figure 17.46**).

To balance size, download speed, and appearance:

◆ Under Options in the GIF section of the Publish Settings dialog (**Figure 17.47**), select any of the following options:

Optimize Colors removes any unused colors from the GIF file's color table.

Interlace makes the GIF appear quickly at low resolution and come into focus as the download continues. (The Interlace option should be used only for static GIFs.)

Smooth makes Flash use antialiasing to smooth bitmaps for your animated GIF. Deselecting Smooth reduces the size of the file.

Dither Solids applies the dither method selected in the Dither menu to solids as well as gradients and bitmapped images.

Remove Gradients reduces file size by converting gradient fills to solid fills. (Flash uses the first color in the gradient as the solid fill color.)

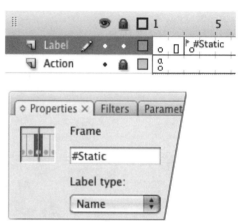

Figure 17.46 Assigning the frame label #Static tells Flash to use that frame for static GIF files.

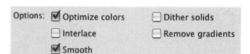

Figure 17.47 The Options settings in the GIF section of the Publish Settings dialog help you limit the amount of time your viewers spend looking at a blank screen, waiting for an image to appear. (The Remove Gradients option is available only in the Publish Settings dialog, not in the Export GIF dialog.)

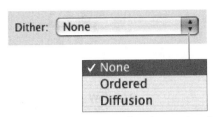

Figure 17.48 The GIF format has three options for dithering colors that aren't included in the current color table.

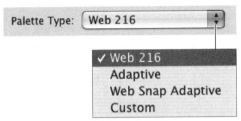

Figure 17.49 Choose a palette that optimizes colors for the published GIF image. You can create custom palettes or use the Web-safe or adaptive palettes provided by Flash.

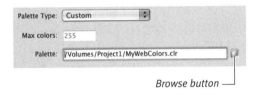

Browse button ⎯

Figure 17.50 When you choose Custom from the Palette Type pop-up menu, you must enter the palette file's path in the Palette field. Click the Browse button (the folder icon) to open a dialog for locating the file.

To control colors that aren't in the current color palette:

1. From the Dither pop-up menu in the GIF section of the Publish Settings dialog (**Figure 17.48**), choose one of the following options:

   None replaces the missing color with the closest match from the current palette.

   Ordered simulates the missing color by applying a regular pattern of colors from the current palette.

   Diffusion simulates the missing color by applying a random pattern of colors from the Web 216 palette. (You must also choose Web 216 as your Palette Type in step 2 for Diffusion to work.)

2. From the Palette Type pop-up menu, choose a color table for use with this GIF (**Figure 17.49**).

   Your choices are Web 216 (the standard 216 Web-safe colors), Adaptive (only colors used in your document; 256 colors maximum), Web Snap Adaptive (a modified Adaptive palette, substituting Web-safe colors for any near matches to colors in the document that aren't Web safe), and Custom (the color table specified in step 4).

3. If you chose Adaptive or Web Snap Adaptive as the Palette Type, in the Max Colors field, type the number of colors you want to use.

   This option lets you further limit the size of the color table available for the GIF and thus reduce file size.

4. If you chose Custom as the Palette Type, load the custom palette (**Figure 17.50**).

   Click the Browse button (the folder icon). The Open dialog appears; navigate to the custom palette file, select it, and click Open.

Using Version Detection

The Flash Player plug-in is widely distributed, but not everyone has the latest player version installed. To make sure your audience has the right player for viewing your Flash content, use either of the two templates that create HTML that performs version detection (see the sidebar "About Version Detection").

To detect the viewer's Flash Player version:

1. In an open Flash document, choose File > Publish Settings.

   The Publish Settings dialog appears; choose a new publishing profile, or leave the current setting.

2. Click the Flash button (Mac) or tab (Windows) in the dialog.

   The settings for Publishing SWF files appear.

3. From the Version pop-up menu, choose Flash Player version 4 or later (**Figure 17.51**).

4. Click the HTML button (Mac) or tab (Windows) in the dialog.

5. From the Template menu, choose Flash Only or Flash HTTPS.

   These are the only included templates that automatically create version-detection code for you.

Figure 17.51 To get automatic version detection when you publish your Flash document, you must select Flash Player 4 or later from the Version pop-up menu in the Flash section of the Publish Settings dialog.

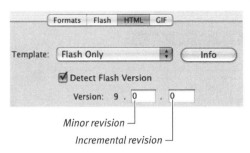

Figure 17.52 When you select the Detect Flash Version check box, the fields for minor and incremental revision numbers become active. Enter the precise version numbers that your end user will need to view your Flash content.

6. Select the Detect Flash Version check box.

If you want to detect specific revisions to the Flash Player, enter them in the fields for minor and incremental revisions (**Figure 17.52**).

7. To confirm your settings, click OK.

When you publish a document using version detection, Flash creates an HTML file that displays the SWF file in a browser window; this HTML file also contains JavaScript coding for detecting the Flash Player version on the end user's system.

About Version Detection

Version detection is the process of verifying what version of Flash Player is running on a viewer's system. Three of the HTML templates that come with Flash CS3—Flash Only, Flash Only – Allow Full Screen and Flash HTTPS—create the coding necessary to carry out one form of version detection. If an end user tries to view your Flash content from a system that has the required player, the browser displays your content. If Flash Player is missing or the version number is too low, the browser displays a Web page containing a link to Adobe's Web site where the correct player can be downloaded. (If you use the Flash HTTPS template, the browser sends the user to an Adobe HTTPS site to download the player.)

Flash's other HTML templates don't carry out version detection. The Image Map and QuickTime templates are specifically designed to create HTML that doesn't require Flash Player; therefore, version detection is unnecessary. The remaining templates use JavaScript that conflicts with the JavaScript used by Flash Only and Flash HTTPS (the script that embeds the SWF file in the HTML). If you want to use one of these templates, you can still get help with version detection from the Publishing command, but you must create an additional short FLA that directs users to your main Flash content. Publish the short FLA using one of the HTML templates that does version detection. If your viewers have the right player version, the short SWF sends them directly to your main content. If they lack the right version, they get directed to the Web site to download the current Flash Player first.

Printing from Flash

When you're editing a Flash document, you can print frames as individual pages or print several frames per page in a storyboard layout. You choose how many frames each row in the storyboard contains. Flash sizes the frames accordingly. Use the Print Margins (Mac) or Page Setup (Windows) command to choose layout options.

To print one frame per page:

1. In an open Flash document, choose File > Print Margins (Mac) or Page Setup (Windows).

The Print Margins or Page Setup dialog appears (**Figure 17.53**).

2. From the Frames pop-up menu, choose All Frames.

3. From the Layout pop-up menu, choose Fit on One Page.

4. Click OK.

5. Choose File > Print.

The Print dialog appears.

6. Enter the desired frame numbers in the From and To fields.

7. Click Print (Mac) or OK (Windows).

✔ Tips

■ If your Macintosh printer isn't capable of printing PostScript, be sure to select the Disable PostScript check box in the Print Margins dialog.

■ To print just the first frame of each scene in a movie, in step 2, choose First Frame Only.

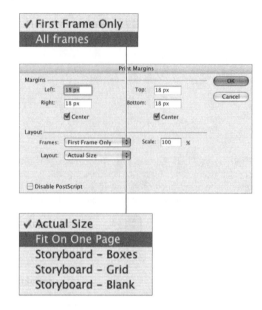

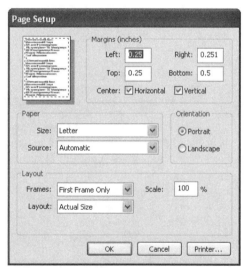

Figure 17.53 The options in the Print Margins (Mac, top) and Page Setup (Windows, bottom) dialogs enable you to print the frames of your movie as single pages or as storyboard layouts during authoring.

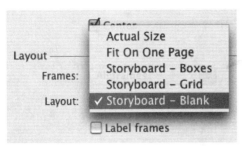

Figure 17.54 The Layout menu of the Print Margins (Mac) or Page Setup (Windows) dialog offers three storyboard options: Boxes, Grid, and Blank.

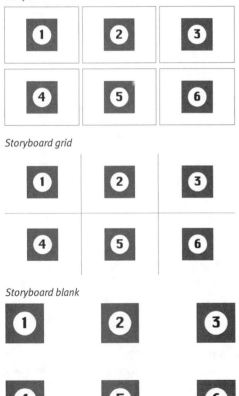

Storyboard boxes

Storyboard grid

Storyboard blank

Figure 17.55 When you print your Flash document in a storyboard layout, each movie frame is either outlined in a box, set inside a grid, or printed as just a frame.

To print storyboard thumbnails:

1. Follow steps 1 and 2 of the preceding task.

2. From the Layout pop-up menu (**Figure 17.54**), choose one of the following options:

   Storyboard—Boxes outlines each movie-frame rectangle.

   Storyboard—Grid prints the frames in a grid.

   Storyboard—Blank prints just the graphic elements of each movie frame. The layout parameters appear.

3. In the Frames field, enter the number of frames you want to print across the page. Flash prints as many as 128 frames in a single storyboard row.

4. In the Frame Margin field, enter the amount of space you want to use between frames in your layout.

5. Click Print (Mac) or OK (Windows).

6. Choose File > Print.
   The Print dialog appears.

7. If you want to print only some pages of your thumbnails, type those page numbers in the From and To fields.

8. Click Print (Mac) or OK (Windows).
   Flash creates the thumbnails, using the options you specified (**Figure 17.55**).

✔ Tip

- To print the scene and frame number below each frame in the layout, select the Label Frames check box in the Page Setup (Windows) dialog. The check box appears in the Print Margins (Mac) dialog as well, but it doesn't actually create labels for your printed thumbnails.

PRINTING FROM FLASH

Exporting Flash to Other Formats

In addition to publishing Flash content to make it available to end users, you can export it. When exporting, you can output the entire movie or just one frame. Flash exports to a variety of formats not available in the Publish Settings dialog. To export content from the currently open Flash document, choose File > Export > Export Image to output one frame, or choose File > Export > Export Movie to output the entire movie. Depending on what export format you choose, different dialog boxes appear with options for output.

On both Mac and Windows, you can export the following file formats: Adobe Illustrator Sequence and Adobe Illustrator Image (.ai); animated GIF, GIF sequence, and GIF image (.gif); DXF Sequence and AutoCAD DXF (.dxf); Encapsulated PostScript 3.0 with Preview (.eps); Flash Document (.swf) and Flash Video (.flv); JPEG Sequence and JPEG Image (.jpg); PNG Sequence and PNG Image (.png); and Exporting QuickTime (.mov). On Windows systems, you can also export to Bitmap Sequence and Bitmap Image (.bmp), Enhanced Metafile Sequence and Image (.emf), WAV audio (.wav), Windows AVI (.avi), and Windows Metafile Sequence and Windows Metafile Image (.wmf). On the Mac, you can also export to PICT Sequence and PICT Image (.pct).

About Projectors

In addition to publishing your movies for playback in a browser, you can publish *projectors*, which are self-sufficient applications that contain an embedded version of Flash Player for displaying Flash content. To play a projector file, the end user double-clicks the file's icon (a round button with a stylized Flash *F*). Projectors are an excellent way to distribute movies directly to people; for example, you can e-mail a Flash-animated greeting card, in the form a projector, to a friend. Projectors are platform-specific, but you can make projectors for both the Mac and Windows platform from either platform.

To create a projector, access the Publish Settings dialog (choose File > Publish Settings). In the Formats section choose which type of projector to produce by selecting the check box for Windows Projector and/or Macintosh Projector. The next time you publish the document, Flash creates projector files for the specified platform(s), along with the files for any other publishing formats you've chosen.

If you are developing your Flash content using the Windows operating system, publishing a Macintosh projector creates a folder with the extension .app. That folder contains all the information needed to create a stand-alone projector for the Mac. Macintosh users never see this folder, but when it's transferred to a Mac, it transforms into a Flash-projector file. You do need to compress the projector-application folder (using WinZip, for example) if you want to send it via e-mail.

INDEX

INDEX

INDEX

M

INDEX

INDEX

find a stable equilibrium between the equality implied by common schooling and the stigma of total exclusion. Segregation embodies the idea that African Americans are an inferior people with whom whites must never have equal social contact. For that reason among others, in 1954 the United States Supreme Court struck down the system of racial segregation in American education. *Brown v. Board of Education* ordered schools to desegregate, clearly as a first step toward ending segregation in all aspects of public life. Towns as far north as Topeka, Kansas; Washington, D.C.; and southern Illinois struggled to comply, while whites in Deep South towns struggled *not* to comply.

Sheridan, Arkansas, coped with *Brown* by getting rid of all its African Americans. Shortly after the 1954 edict came down from the Supreme Court, the all-white Sheridan school board voted to comply, a constructive step taken by only two other towns in Arkansas. Sheridan had been operating an elementary school for African Americans but was busing its black high school students to adjacent counties. The decision to desegregate led to a "firestorm of protest" in the white community, in the words of a Sheridan native, which led to a new meeting the next night at which the school board unanimously reversed itself. Thereafter, as told in Chapter 4, Sheridan's entire black community was induced to leave town, leaving Sheridan all-white on purpose. Thus Sheridan, which would have been one of the most racially progressive towns in Arkansas if its initial school board decision had stood, instead became one of the most backward.[19]

Like Sheridan, Highland Park and University Park, Texas, contiguous "suburbs" entirely surrounded by Dallas, got rid of their black children after 1954. The "Park Cities" already were sundown suburbs allowing no independent African American households, but some of their affluent white families had live-in maids and gardeners. Before the 1954 Supreme Court decision, children of these adults were quietly allowed to attend black schools in Dallas, with tuition paid by Highland Park and University Park. After *Brown,* Park Cities officials realized they would be vulnerable to a desegregation lawsuit. Alderman C. K. Bullard suggested that Park Cities residents who employed African Americans with children be asked to fire them "so that Park Cities would not be confronted with white and Negro children attending classes together." Most African American families moved out by the late 1950s. Dallas didn't actually stop accepting black students from the suburbs until 1961. At least one African American servant with children still lived in Highland Park at that point, so her employer, a rich white family, paid rent on a Dallas address for her so that her children could stay in school in Dallas while living with her at their house in the Park Cities.[20]

Even before *Brown,* whites in many locales were upset with having to pay taxes to support *separate* schools for African American children. Sometimes they responded by driving black families from their communities. In Case Township, north of Norman, Oklahoma, for example, residents grew alarmed because two white landowners hired three or four black families to farm their land. One resident who signed himself "A Hoodlum" wrote to the Norman newspapers: "Farmers of Case township are as just [*sic*] much against mixing up with niggers as the good people of Norman are and what is more they don't intend to have their farms taxed to put up Negro school houses." Eventually the whites burned down one black family's house but may not have succeeded in driving all the African Americans away. I suspect similar reasoning led to anti-black actions in Arkansas, Kentucky, Missouri, and Tennessee.[21]

Around the time of the *Brown* decision, the African American population of at least five counties in Kentucky and Tennessee fell precipitously.[22] Perhaps the black families in these counties moved away voluntarily, but the example of Sheridan raises suspicion. Historian Mary Waalkes has done research on one of the five, Polk County, Tennessee, which abuts North Carolina in the Appalachian Mountains. According to one account, she writes, *Brown* prompted whites there to force black families to sell their farms, "in an effort to rid the county of school children who would have to be integrated into the Polk County system."[23] The number of African Americans in Polk County—which had been 566 in 1890—fell from 75 in 1950 to just 28 ten years later, and only 4 of school age, among 12,160 inhabitants. Across America, many whites in sundown counties felt blessed to have no black children in 1954; as Esther Sanderson put it in 1974, "Scott County [Tennessee] definitely has no segregation problem for there is not a single negro [*sic*] living in the entire county." Some other communities in Arkansas, Kentucky, Missouri, and Tennessee may also have gotten rid of their African Americans after *Brown,* as white families reacted to the possibility that unless the few black families in town could be induced to leave, their children might wind up in "our school."[24]

Other Catalysts

Every sundown town, especially those that expelled their African Americans violently, has its own answer as to why it went all-white. Residents of sundown towns and suburbs rarely refer to the increased racism of the Nadir or to such social and cultural factors as politics, ethnic composition, or labor history. Instead, residents "explain" their town's policy by telling about the incident that triggered it. We must not accept these trigger stories at face value: sometimes there are competing accounts, and often they are after-the-fact rationalizations detailing acts that may or may not have taken place. Even where an account of the beginning of a town's sundown policies is accurate, leaving it as the actual cause of its continuing exclusion is far too simple.

The events that triggered mass expulsions were often instances of black misbehavior. Some African American did something wrong, and whites responded by taking it out on the entire group. Such was the case in Anna, Illinois, in 1909. The convenience store clerk quoted at the beginning of this book who confirmed in 2001 the continuing nickname for Anna, "Ain't No Niggers Allowed," also related Anna's explanation for its policy: "My girlfriend told me how that all got started. A black man raped a white girl, and she's buried up in the cemetery with a memorial stone, and they hung him." Her girlfriend is right: residents of Anna do date its sundown status to 1909. On November 8 of that year, Anna Pelley, a 24-year-old white woman, was murdered in Cairo, some 30 miles south. She was found in an alley near her home the next morning, gagged and strangled, her clothing ripped off. Bloodhounds led police to a black-owned house where they later arrested Will James, a deliveryman for the Cairo Coal & Ice Co. That evening a lynch mob gathered in Cairo, but the police chief quieted them by pointing out that the police weren't sure they had the right man. After all, the evidence against James consisted mostly of the fact that "bloodhounds had sniffed their way to his house," as a contemporary newspaper account put it. The following Friday, November 11, rumors that James had confessed caused whites again to threaten a lynch mob. The sheriff, Frank Davis, decided to get his prisoner out of Cairo. That evening the sheriff, a deputy, and James "boarded the northbound Illinois Central train to escape the lynch mob." But whites in Cairo telephoned news of Davis's flight to Anna, 30 miles north—Anna Pelley's hometown—where another mob assembled to await his arrival.[25]

"It would not do to stay on the train and try to get through Anna with him," the sheriff later explained. "That was the former home of the girl he was accused of killing, and I knew that the news that we were coming would be telephoned and telegraphed to Anna in time for her friends to collect a mob at the depot that would take him from me. So I had the train stopped at Dongola [ten miles south], and we struck out in the darkness across the country eastward." The mob now combed the woods around Dongola. Eventually, walking through the night, the prisoner and his guards reached the little town of Karnak, where Sheriff Davis bought sardines, crackers, and soft drinks for the three of them. They didn't dare stay in Karnak, however, lest they be recognized, so they walked on toward Belknap. There they hoped to catch a 5 PM northbound train on a different railroad and evade Anna and the mob altogether. Unfortunately, a train crew at Karnak had recognized them and relayed their whereabouts back to Cairo. "When we discovered late in the afternoon that a mob was tailing us," in the sheriff's words, "we traveled as fast as we could, in the hope of keeping ahead until dark. . . . But the pursuers closed in on us, and when we found that we were in greater danger of being seen if we kept on than if we hid where we were, we concealed ourselves in the bushes and waited, hoping that they would pass us by, but they found us." [26]

The mob overpowered the prisoner and his guards and forced them onto a southbound train at Karnak. Word of the capture preceded them. When they reached Cairo, thousands of people, many from Anna and other nearby towns, gathered to watch at the main downtown intersection, spanned by a double ornamental steel arch festooned with hundreds of bright lights. (See Portfolio 5.) A reporter described the scene:

> The mob that hanged James was led by women, many of them the wives of influential residents of Cairo. The rope was pulled taut by female relatives of Miss Pelley, aided by several score of their sex. As the Negro was pulled up into the air, these same women sang and screamed in delight.
>
> The men were for the most part spectators until the rope that was strangling the Negro broke and his dying body fell to the ground. Then hundreds of revolvers flashed and 500 bullets crashed into the quivery form of the Negro. The riddled dead man was then dragged through the principal streets of the city to the spot where the Pelley girl was assaulted and slain.
>
> Women applied the torch to the bonfire that had been prepared and into which the body of James was thrown. Ten thousand cheered and danced at the scene.

Interestingly, this became an "equal-opportunity lynching," for the crowd later grabbed another prisoner from the jail, a white photographer accused of killing his wife the previous summer, and hanged him from a telegraph pole at a different downtown location. [27]

When the mob members from Anna returned home on a later Illinois Central train, they decided to drive all African Americans from the town—primarily some 30 or 40 men who worked at a local quarry, along with their families. To the best of my knowledge, Anna has been all-white ever since. So has its twin city, Jonesboro. According to oral tradition, "one old lady who had been a slave" was allowed to stay when the other blacks were driven out. [28]

Few whites displayed any remorse or even embarrassment at the expulsion of African Americans from Anna-Jonesboro. Most residents of Anna felt they had improved their town by the act; some residents of surrounding towns were jealous. For that matter, most whites were not appalled even by the lynchings. Before burning the body of Will James, members of the mob cut out his heart; then they cut it up and carried the pieces away for souvenirs. Afterward, James's half-burned head was displayed on top of a pole in a Cairo park, and photographers sold postcards of his hanging. Ministers justified both lynchings from the pulpit. The *Carbondale Free Press* reprinted with approval an editorial in the *Cairo Bulletin*, "In Memory of Miss Pelley," suggesting

> that on November 10 of each year every Cairo man wear a small knot of rope in the lapel of his coat "as a quiet and dignified manifestation of the end of evil doers of any and all races, who outrage or insult pure womanhood. Every white and colored man of the city can thus place himself on record for law and order for a day each year."

Neither editor saw any irony in using a symbol of a lynching rope as a celebration of "law and order." A public subscription was taken up to purchase an extraordinary tombstone for Pelley (Portfolio 6).[29]

Interracial Rape as Catalyst

Anna is hardly the only community to use rape or murder as an excuse to drive out or keep out all African Americans. Residents of many sundown towns explain their communities' all-white status by invoking incidents that embody the familiar "African American as problem" ideology, but with specific local details about what blacks did wrong *here*. Ever since, to justify the continued vigilance and sometimes brutal actions required to maintain a town or suburb as an all-white community, whites summon up the long-ago alleged misbehavior of the victim class. Interracial rape was the excuse for the 1912 expulsion of African Americans from Forsyth County, Georgia, for example. On September 10 of that year, alleged rapist Edward Collins, an African American, was shot in the Forsyth County jail by a lynch mob. Several other African Americans, allegedly his accomplices, were threatened with lynching, but officers spirited them to Atlanta for safety.[30] The mob then turned upon the African American community. Between September 10 and the end of that year, according to the Forsyth county historian,

notices were given to all the Negro population to leave the county. . . . A few
persisted in staying and were promised protection by their landlords. A few
houses were dynamited and burned and then the whites were notified to get rid
of their Negro tenants or have their houses and barns likewise burned. This accomplished the removal of the rest of the blacks.

The African American population in Forsyth County plummeted from 1,100
in 1910 to 30 in 1920 and 17 in 1930.[31]

Many other expulsions and attempted expulsions followed allegations of
interracial rape. The 1908 riot that swept Springfield, Illinois, for example,
began after Mabel Hallam, a white woman, claimed that George Robinson, a
black man, had raped her. The black community was driven out of Pinckneyville, Illinois, in about 1928; one explanation extant in Pinckneyville today
states that a black man raped a white woman, so the whites got a bus, loaded all
the blacks on it, and took them to East St. Louis. Unconfirmed oral history in
LaSalle-Peru, twin cities in northeastern Illinois, holds that they have been all-
white since the lynching of a black man who raped an Irish American
woman.[32]

Black "Crime Waves" as Catalyst

If not rape, often sundown towns and counties invented black crime waves by
African Americans to "explain" why they drove out their black populations.
When Green Saunders referred to "the second killing of white people by Negroes" as the reason for driving all African Americans from Comanche
County, Texas, he was conflating two very different African American criminals, eight years apart, to create a menace. In about 1878, Mose Jones, an old
ex-slave, had been living with his wife, child, and stepdaughter on the T. J.
Nabers farm. According to Eulalia Wells, "Mose did the morning chores
about the kitchen" and also worked at the stable. "Mose was apparently one of
the most humble of Negroes in town. It was characteristic of him that when he
met white people he at once held his hat against his breast and bowed and
spoke with deep humility." But after his wife died, "Old Mose" snapped. First
he tried to marry his fourteen-year-old stepdaughter. He then killed the stepdaughter, his own daughter, the Nabers' two young boys, "and but for Mrs.
Nabers being a light sleeper would have murdered her and her husband." He
set fire to the house and fled. "By daybreak about 200 men were searching for
Mose," Wells goes on. "He was found about six miles east of town on the other
side of Indian Creek—and was shot." Wells then writes a telling paragraph:

Everyone thought that Old Mose was the only mean Negro in town—so the others were allowed to remain. The Negroes kept coming into the county during the next few years and soon a large settlement of them located in the northeastern part of the county.

To her, writing in 1942, it is natural that whites would have the right to decide whether African Americans as a group will be "allowed to remain" after this one event by an obviously deranged man. And after one more interracial crime—eight years later—Comanche County whites snapped.[33]

To garner support for the 1895 Spring Valley, Illinois, massacre described in the previous chapter, Italian American miners blamed African Americans "for every crime committed in the area," in Felix Armfield's words. "Euramerican whites in the town soon sided with the Italian cause." A Tennessee county historian tells of a similar expulsion based on a wave of thefts and arson but admits that the crimes continued after the African Americans had been driven out. Whites in Wyandotte, Michigan, drove out their African American residents repeatedly, most prominently in 1916. Wyandotte residents treating the 1916 expulsion in the 1940s tried to blame the victims: "Negroes in 1916 era were very low type, ran houses of ill repute, attacked Wyandotte women and children, a real threat to law abiding citizens." But according to Edwina DeWindt, compiler of "Wyandotte History; Negro," African Americans posed no threat; city records from the time show no record of white protests about their behavior. Surely the vaguest crime wave of all took place in Chesterton, Indiana, described by the newspaper editor at the head of this chapter: "All kinds of depredations were going on."[34]

Catalysts Do Not Explain

"Explanations" that blame the origin of sundown policies on criminal characteristics of the excluded group contain two obvious fallacies: collective guilt and circular reasoning. The events described in the Chesterton newspaper neatly exemplify both. When one or more African Americans commit crimes, the entire group is considered responsible and should be punished. And once blacks were gone, since Chesterton subsequently had no major crimes, the paper's editor knows that the town's policy "saved this county many a tragedy," so the townspeople were right to have gotten rid of them. Similarly, once Anna expelled its blacks, it had no more black murderers—even though it never had any to start with, the murder having taken place elsewhere. The "explanation" thus provides continuing justification for a town's continuing policy of excluding African Americans.

I place quotation markes around "explanation" because these crimes or alleged crimes do not really reveal why a town or county drove out its black population, partly because when a European American committed a similar crime, whites as a group faced no similar repercussions. Moreover, often the catalysts do not hold up even as triggers. The attempted rape and murder of Anna Pelley, followed by the lynching of Will James, do not really explain why Anna-Jonesboro went sundown, for example. For one thing, James may have been innocent. Sheriff Davis thought so: "I questioned him a great deal while we were in the woods together and he insisted all the time that he was innocent. I am very much in doubt whether he is the guilty man or not." Moreover, both the murder and the lynching took place 30 miles away, not even in the same county.

In Forsyth County, the mob did apparently get the right person, for the white victim identified three African Americans as the perpetrators, one of whom was lynched, the other two convicted. Even so, interracial rape cannot have been the real cause for the subsequent eviction of the entire black population of the county, because Forsyth was one of six adjacent counties in north Georgia that expelled their African Americans at about this time. Indeed, Forsyth was probably the third to do so, after Towns and Union Counties, and I know no claims of black rape or murder as the catalyst for those expulsions. Whites in Dawson County, between Forsyth and Union, expelled their African Americans about when Forsyth did; all were gone by 1920. Parts of Fannin and Gilmer Counties, just west of Union, also went sundown at this time. No claims of rape were ever made, so far as I know, to justify the expulsions of African Americans from Dawson, Fannin, and Gilmer Counties. Surely contagious rioting in the white communities—"Towns County did it; why haven't we?"—is more likely than any undocumented epidemic of African Americans raping whites in county after contiguous county.[35]

We cannot conclude that interracial rape was really the cause of the attempted expulsion of African Americans from Springfield either, because it turns out there had been no rape. Mabel Hallam dropped all charges against George Robinson; eventually she confessed that she had had sex with her white lover and had invented the black rapist story to escape blame from her husband and friends. The Pinckneyville rape story is thoroughly vague and conflicts with accounts offered by others in town. The alleged rape in LaSalle-Peru is even vaguer, including no date or names, and implies the towns *had* a black population that whites then drove off in the aftermath of a crime. Either the crime took place before the Civil War or the rise and fall of such a population would have to have been rapid and intercensal, since LaSalle and Peru have been all-white in every census from 1860 to the recent past. I suspect both of these sketchy anecdotes are attempts by whites years later to ascribe the sundown policies to origins that seem plausible but in fact did not take place.

Various catalyst stories were reported to explain and justify the 1907 expulsion of Sikhs from Bellingham, Washington. According to one account, the riot may have started "when a gang of young rowdies who were collected on a corner decided to have some fun with the Hindus." Another version held that "the Hindus agreed to pay the landlord of a shack in Old Town $15 a month for the place and as a result a white woman who was living there was forced to move. It is reported that she is the one who incited the trouble." However, underlying conflict between European American and Sikh workers at lumber mills in the city had been festering for some time and was surely more important than any trigger.[36]

Vague or Mislaid Catalyst Stories

If catalysts do not provide satisfying explanations of why towns keep African Americans from living in them, some accounts of the original expulsion or prohibition have grown so vague over time that they can barely function even as catalysts. Tonawanda and North Tonawanda are located at the western end of the Erie Canal. Many African Americans have lived in the area, especially in Buffalo to the south and Niagara Falls to the north, and blacks always worked on the canal boats; such centrally located towns could not have been all-white for decades by accident. As late as 1990, Tonawanda had just 28 African Americans among 17,284 people, while North Tonawanda had 56 among 35,000. It turns out that both were sundown towns. Law professor Bill Kaplin grew up there in the 1940s and '50s and learned only that "some black man allegedly did something bad" long ago; whites then drove out all African Americans and forbade them to live there after that. Kathy Spillman, who grew up in North Tonawanda two decades later, could not recall even that much, although she knew the towns kept out African Americans. Some old-timers in the Tonawandas may remember when and how African Americans were forced out, but it's not a living memory shared by the community as a whole.[37]

Sometimes alternative catalyst stories compete. On Halloween night, 1919, whites in Corbin, Kentucky, a railroad town of about 3,400, forced their African Americans out of town after two white switchmen lost all their money in a poker game with black track layers. To cover their losses, the switchmen said African Americans had robbed them. A mob formed "and searched the city for Negroes," according to the account in the *Lexington Herald*.

> The Negroes who felt the fury of the mob in the greatest degree were a gang of about 200 Negroes working on the Louisville and Nashville grade for ten months at South Corbin, where the railroad company is making big improvements. Crowds went to restaurants and other public places, caught all the Negro employees they could, and drove them singly or in gangs at the point of guns to the depot. Many Negroes were beaten, and 200 were driven out of town.

At gunpoint whites then forced almost the entire African American population onto railroad cars and shipped them to Knoxville, Tennessee. But residents of Corbin haven't found this origin story satisfying over the years, so they make up new ones. One woman volunteered that four black men were lynched for attacking a white woman. One man, interviewed for Robby Heason's gripping 1990 documentary about Corbin as a sundown town, said that he really didn't know what to believe for sure, because "I have heard that story a hundred times since I've been in Corbin, and it's been told to me about a hundred different ways."[38]

Usually even such vague or conflicting accounts still suffice as catalyst stories, because they make reference to black misbehavior. Implicitly, most African Americans are thought to share this characteristic, which is why "we" must exclude them. However, residents of some sundown towns have completely forgotten why they ever expelled African Americans. In 2002, residents of Crossville, Tennessee, knew theirs was a sundown county and had had a black population until about 1905, but they had lost any oral tradition to explain exactly how and why their African Americans were forced out. Other communities have even forgotten that they ever had any African Americans, let alone that they expelled them. Many suburbs display this amnesia, especially those that reopened to blacks more than a decade ago. Chamblee, Georgia, for example, has experienced such international and diverse immigration as a booming suburb of Atlanta that only one-third of its residents in 2000 were born in the United States; still fewer were born in Georgia, and only a handful in Chamblee. The result is that today's residents have no memory that Chamblee became a sundown town after World War II and was all-white in 1970—let alone why. For at least two decades, Chamblee has been thoroughly multiracial and multiethnic, so the town has no reason to maintain an account of why it is or was all-white.

Contagion as Catalyst

Some towns went sundown simply because a neighboring town did so. The neighboring event served as a catalyst of sorts, but actually it shows the absence of a catalyst. The only cause required to set off an expulsion seemed to be envy of a neighboring town that had already driven out its African Americans. In southwestern Missouri, for instance, newspaper editor Murray Bishoff believes that Monett's prosperity after it threw out all its African Americans in 1894 likely contributed to Pierce City's copycat riot seven years later. Bishoff thinks Pierce City in turn became a model for other nearby towns in Missouri and Arkansas. After whites expelled African Americans from Corbin, Kentucky, in 1919, a copycat mob rioted a few months later in Ravenna, 70 miles north, and forced Ravenna's black railroad workers out; Ravenna remained all-white into the 1990s.[39]

As we saw with Anna, a lynching in one town might trigger an expulsion in another. Lynchings typically inflamed white opinion, not against the crime but against the victim class, and often this animus crossed state lines. After the 1931 lynching of Raymond Gunn in Maryville, in northwest Missouri, white passions were inflamed in small towns in northeastern Kansas more than 50 miles distant. In 1920, a huge mob hanged three African American circus workers in Duluth, Minnesota, believing they had raped Irene Tusken, a white woman. In reality, whether she was raped by anyone is doubtful. Nevertheless, in the aftermath, the acting chief of police of neighboring Superior, Wisconsin, declared, "We are going to run all idle Negroes out of Superior and they're going to stay out." His decree was hardly limited to "idle Negroes"; all African Americans employed by a carnival in Superior were fired and told to leave the city, even though they were working, and the overall black population of Superior tumbled from 169 in 1920 to just 51 ten years later. Such edicts again show black communities balanced on a knife edge, for no one even bothered to claim that its members did anything to provoke retribution *here*.[40]

Sometimes epidemics of expulsions or sundown ordinances washed like a wave across entire subregions. In 1886, for example, after whites rioted and drove out African Americans from Comanche County, Texas, nearby residents picked up on the idea, so a broad area of about 3,000 square miles in north-central Texas drove out their African Americans at this time, including all or part of at least four counties. No grievous crime of rape or murder was alleged in those counties to provide a catalyst or excuse; the expulsions were merely copycat actions. We have seen that whites rioted and drove out African Americans from county after county in northern Arkansas and southwestern

Missouri around 1900, and in northern Georgia around 1910. Portfolio 13 tells of an outbreak of expulsions in southern Indiana. I suggest that future investigations may unearth similar epidemics wherever a chain of all-white towns or counties nestles nearby.[41]

If rioting was contagious, so too were quieter methods of achieving sundown status, I believe. These days, municipalities deliberately copy each other's ordinances on many topics, rather than inventing them from scratch. I suspect municipalities copied each other's ordinances in the past as well. If Monticello, the seat of Piatt County, Illinois, passed a sundown ordinance, which an attorney there says it did, then trustees of De Land, a smaller town in Piatt County, would want to keep up with the times, and did, according to its officials—and so on, across the Midwest and the nation. I must admit, however, that while the foregoing seems logical to me,[42] it is entirely speculative.

The contagion of exclusion was even more pronounced in the suburbs. When one suburb, deemed to be prestigious, was all white on purpose, it became the thing to do, and other suburbs hastened to emulate the leader. Soon, almost all of the suburbs around a major city kept out African Americans.

Catalyst Stories as Origin Myths

Although catalysts don't really explain much, they remain important stories nevertheless. Even today, residents of Anna, for instance, cite the story of Anna Pelley's death to explain why their town has no African American residents. Many residents of sundown towns give similar explanations: they admit openly that their town excludes African Americans and proceed to tell why, relying on the catalyzing incident to justify the practice. Thus the story of the initial incident gets elevated into an origin myth.

Origin myths tell us why we are here as a people or why we are the way we are. Often they tell us how to be, how to behave, and that we are right, even "God's chosen people." The Anna myth still functions in these ways, thus helping to keep its sundown policy alive. As late as the 1970s, signs on Route 127 warned, "Nigger, Don't Let the Sun Go Down on You in Anna-Jonesboro," and Anna and Jonesboro still appear to have no black households.

The memory of the rape that triggered the 1912 expulsion from Forsyth County was similarly functioning as an origin myth at least as late as 1987. On January 17 of that year, civil rights leaders from Atlanta marched in the county seat of Forsyth to prove that African Americans had a right to be in the county. They failed: a crowd of more than 500, vastly outnumbering the police officers on hand, pelted the marchers with rocks and bottles. A week later, the civil rights forces numbered 20,000, the counterdemonstrators 1,000, 3,000 police and National Guard members maintained order, and the marchers finished their route. Oprah Winfrey broadcast a live TV show from Forsyth County later in the year. She found the origin myth still very much alive in the minds of some of the residents who attended. One woman said,

> I've been here all my life. I have—my family goes back four generations. . . . And I have a fear of black—I did have a fear of black people. And the only reason was because the girl that got killed back in 1912 is related to me.

The incident was still current, still troubling this woman 75 years later. Another member of the audience brought the fear of African Americans to the present in a more general form: "If niggers come in here, it's going to be like Decatur [Georgia], DeKalb County, Fulton County, Atlanta. It's going to be nothing but a slum area."[43]

In some sundown towns, the origin myth has become coupled with an object or location that keeps it salient today. To this day, adolescents in Anna go in groups to pay their respects to Anna Pelley's tombstone (Portfolio 6)— sort of a rite of passage that keeps vivid and justifies Anna's all-white nature to the next generation. Other towns have "hanging trees" that remind residents what happened to the last African American who wandered within the city limits. Smokey Crabtree, a longtime resident of Fouke, a sundown town in western Arkansas, used a lighthearted tone in 2001 to convey his amusement at Fouke's sundown policy and the symbol that helps to maintain it:

> As far back as the late twenties colored people weren't welcome in Fouke, Arkansas to live, or to work in town. The city put up an almost life sized chalk statue of a colored man at the city limit line, he had an iron bar in one hand and was pointing out of town with the other hand. The city kept the statue painted and dressed, really taking good care of it. Back in those days colored people were run out of Fouke, one was even hung from a large oak tree, and there's a tree that is still referred to as the hanging tree. The man was hung with a necktie and a red handkerchief; a five-dollar bill was sticking out of his pocket for any person wanting to bury the man. The story was that the man had come into Fouke, committed rape among other things, was apprehended and hung. Justice was served. The original "hanging tree" died of natural causes back in the mid sixties. The story has been passed on to another tree that could easily be mistaken for the original tree. My guess is that Fouke will always have a "hang-

ing tree," the name being passed down from one tree to another, keeping the story alive.

Similar stories about hanging trees are in the folklore in Fairfield, Illinois; Crossville, Tennessee; Robbinsville, North Carolina; and other towns. Just as the trees become mythical, so perhaps have the crimes. And just as the trees keep the stories alive, so the stories keep the policy alive.[44]

Towns with strong and extant origin myths seem harder to "crack" than towns that "merely" passed an ordinance or expelled their African Americans as part of a wave of such actions or that have lost their memory of when and why they went sundown. Origin myths that locate a town's anti-black policy in labor conflict seem particularly long-lived. While the punishment—total banning of the race from then on—may be severe, at least a substantial part of the out-group committed the strikebreaking offense, and committed it against "us," the white community, or at least a sizable proportion of it. This may explain why residents of towns with such origin myths seem uncommonly forthcoming about their policy. Origin myths about "black scabs" may also encourage residents to be especially racist toward the next African American who ventures in. Certainly some towns whose origin myths involve black strikebreakers have been particularly vicious toward African Americans for decades afterward. For example, both Pana and Carterville, Illinois, went beyond becoming sundown towns[45] to prohibit blacks from shopping during the daytime as well.

Historical Contingency: The Influence of a Single Individual

Although the underlying factors discussed in the previous chapter—political history, ethnic makeup, and labor relations—helped to explain which communities went sundown, they did not determine the outcome. Neither did the catalysts described in this chapter. Individuals also made a difference. Thus historical contingency inevitably came into play.

Even after an interracial rape, an interracial claim for equality, or another form of catalyst, the actions of one person who tries to start—or sometimes stop—a mob can make all the difference. Sociologists who study mass behavior know that crowds go through a period of indecision while they test their own willingness to go further and become a purposeful mob. Then there is usually a further testing process: members mill about, individuals shout out suggestions, and would-be leaders take tentative steps and gauge the reaction of the rest. Comanche County, Texas, embodied the process in the 1880s. It had 8,600 people, including 79 African Americans. Unfortunately for all of the latter, on July 24, 1886, an African American named Tom McNeal allegedly killed a white farm woman, Sallie Stephens.[46] He was captured the next day, and taken to the farm and hanged by a lynch mob the day after. Comanche County historian Eulalia Wells describes how one man influenced what happened next:

> While he dangled, a certain man climbed upon a large stump and spoke: "Boys, this is the second killing of white people by Negroes and it's more than the people will put up with. I propose we give the Negroes a reasonable time to get out of the county—never allow them to return, and never allow one of color to settle here."

According to Billy Bob Lightfoot, a Comanche County native who wrote a master's thesis on its history, that "certain man" was Green Saunders, who proceeded to denounce African Americans as "by nature evil." Following his suggestion, the mob then rounded up the African American community in nearby De Leon and ordered them "to come out and bury the corpse," in Lightfoot's words. The crowd then gave the blacks who were burying McNeal's body "the warning to pack up and get out within ten days or be killed. Take what they could, leave what could not be sold or carried, but be across the county line by sunset on August 6, 1886." That evening the mob visited every black resident in Comanche County with the same message. Whites posted a sign at the train station in De Leon: "Nigger, Don't Let the Sun Set on Your Head in This Town." Armed white vigilantes then went door-to-door throughout Comanche County. The expulsion was followed by "a lucrative business in souvenirs carried on by an itinerant peddler who sold 'authentic remains of the last Negro buried in Comanche County and pieces of the rope used to hang him with!' through the county as late as 1889," according to Lightfoot. Comanche County then kept out African Americans— and possibly Mexican Americans—for more than a century, but had Saunders not spoken, or had he been a force for tolerance, another outcome might have ensued.[47]

What if just one person had voted differently in Hermann, Missouri? Then Hermann would have admitted black children to its school, which would have put it on a trajectory toward equal rights for African Americans rather than a descent into policies of racial exclusion. Similarly, we have seen that Sheridan, Arkansas, was poised to make the progressive decision to desegregate its schools. Then, owing to the energy, wealth, and racism of one man, it flipflopped and got rid of its entire African American population.

One individual cannot carry the issue without at least some support from a larger public, however. Having it both ways, the same whites in Wyandotte who blamed the bad behavior of African Americans for their 1916 expulsion also condemned the leader of the riot, one Carl Juchartz, "a town character of irresponsible actions and mental capacity unable to even formulate good speaking English." Certainly some individuals are more racist than others, and I'm sure Juchartz led the way. No other whites stopped him, however, and many joined in. The key question is, do those whites willing to keep out African Americans sense that they have at least tacit backing from the police and public? If they do, it only takes a few of them, unfettered by others, to create or maintain a town's racist reputation.[48]

Contingency Again: The Positive Influence of an Individual

Two adjacent articles in the June 17, 1902, *New York Times* show how individuals can cause similar events to lead to very different outcomes, outcomes that then persist for decades. The first is headlined "Bitter Race War Threatened":

> French Lick and West Baden and the valley in which the two famous Indiana health resorts are located bid fair to furnish the next scene of Indiana lawlessness. Both places and the entire length of the valley are threatened with a race war more vicious and more bitter than any that has occurred in the State within the last ten or fifteen years.
>
> Already, reports from the two resorts state, whites have posted notices ordering the Negroes to make a hasty evacuation. The notices, tacked to trees and placed in conspicuous places about the grounds of the two prominent hotels, are adorned with skull and crossbone decorations, underneath which is written the ultimatum. All the waiters at the hostelries have received letters, some signed by the words "White Cap," . . . declaring that if they do not take their departure at once they will be horsewhipped. Some, in fact, were threatened with death. The Negroes are terror-stricken, and many have already obeyed the injunction. Many others, however, having been assured protection, are remaining at their posts.

Immediately below this story, another dispatch, "Race War in Illinois," tells of a similar event 125 miles west, in southeastern Illinois:

> Another attack was made last night on the home of the Rev. Peter Green, pastor of the African Methodist Church at Eldorado. The crowd told Mr. Green to leave town in 24 hours, under penalty of death. He defied the mob and stood at his gate with a shotgun, threatening to shoot the first man who molested him.
>
> The anti-Negro crusade has at last aroused the respectable white element, and an effort will be made to induce the colored people to reopen the Normal and Industrial School.[49]

Eldorado did force out its black preacher and all his congregation, and the school never reopened, "the respectable white element" to the contrary. No governing official, from the town through the county to the state, took any action. According to Robyn Williams, a nearby teacher, Eldorado sported a sundown sign until the 1980s. In about 1990, according to someone who was then a resident, a white couple in Eldorado who adopted a biracial child "had sewage thrown on their lawn" and other problems and left town shortly thereafter.[50]

The next paragraph in the French Lick article, in contrast, tells that the governor has instructed his secretary "to notify him immediately upon receipt of any startling information from the valley." Perhaps for that reason, forced eviction of African Americans from the French Lick area did not take place, and French Lick and West Baden Springs have African American populations to this day.[51]

Another public official who did the right thing was Governor Arthur Weaver of Nebraska. In Lincoln in 1929, a mob of whites drove 200 African Americans from the city after a white policeman was shot. Weaver ordered "that those persons driven out must be permitted to return, and that if any further difficulties ensued, martial law would be instituted." Lincoln stayed interracial.[52]

Business leaders could also make a difference. Bronson, in east Texas, expelled its blacks in 1914; only recently, according to Thad Sitton and James H. Conrad, authors of a fine 1998 study of Texas sawmill towns, were African Americans even allowed to *work* at the Bronson sawmill. In Diboll, on the other hand, 40 miles west, the mill owner, T.L.L. Temple, did not want the word *nigger* spoken, and it wasn't; Diboll remained an interracial town. In Call, Texas, the Ku Klux Klan sent notices to the African American barber and the black dance hall operator in the 1920s telling them to leave town. The management of the local sawmill responded by firing some Klansmen, and Call never drove out its African Americans.[53]

Somewhere between 1870 and 1890, John Hay, Abraham Lincoln's secretary during the Civil War, wrote a poem whose full title is "Banty Tim (Remarks of Sergeant Tilmon Joy to the White Man's Committee of Spunky Point, Illinois)." In it, Hay imagines a meeting of Democrats proposing to expel Spunky Point's sole African American, Banty Tim, to create a sundown town. One white man, Tilmon Joy, faces them down, preventing a mob from forming and preserving Spunky Point as interracial. Excerpts follow:

> I reckon I git your drift, gents—
> You 'low the boy sha'n't stay;
> This is a white man's country;
> You're Dimocrats, you say . . .
>
> Why, blame your hearts, jest hear me!
> You know that ungodly day
> When our left struck Vicksburg Heights, how ripped
> And torn and tattered we lay . . .
>
> Till along toward dusk I seen a thing
> I couldn't believe for a spell:
> That nigger—that Tim—was a crawlin' to me
> Through that fireproof, gild-edged hell!
>
> The Rebels seen him as quick as me,
> And the bullets buzzed like bees;
> But he jumped for me, and shouldered me,
> Though a shot brought him once to his knees;
>
> But he staggered up, and packed me off,
> With a dozen stumbles and falls,
> Till safe in our lines he drapped us both,
> His black hide riddled with balls.
>
> So, my gentle gazelles, that's my answer,
> And here stays Banty Tim:
> He trumped Death's ace for me that day,
> And I'm not goin' back on him!

Hay got several things right, including the white supremacy of the Democrats and the anti-racist idealism stemming from shared experience in the Civil War.[54]

After World War II, a latter-day Tilmon Joy popped up in New York City in the form of ex-GI Leo Miller. On the East Side, Metropolitan Life had just opened Stuyvesant Town, a huge housing project for returning veterans. Miller was outraged that Met Life excluded black veterans. "The courage and sharp shooting of a Negro machine-gunner saved my life with a dozen other white GIs" in the Battle of the Bulge, he pointed out. "Can any one of us who live in Stuyvesant Town say he may not be my neighbor? I can't." Met Life threatened to evict Miller and other white residents who protested its policy, and even after New York City passed a law in 1951 forbidding racial discrimination in "publicly assisted private housing" such as Stuyvesant Town, the company refused to accept applications from blacks, but eventually Miller and his allies won.[55]

One man also stood up to the Roosevelt administration in Boulder City, Nevada, one of the eight sundown towns built by the federal government during the Depression. Clarence Newland, owner of the Green Hut restaurant, hired McKinley Sayles, African American, whose pies were "the best you could buy anywhere in the state of Nevada," in the estimation of Boulder City resident Robert Parker. Townspeople complained to Sims Ely, the czar of the town under the Roosevelt administration, and Ely told Newland to get rid of Sayles.[56] According to Parker, Newland replied, "As long as that Green Hut belongs to me, you're not telling me who to hire and fire around here."[57]

Maybe behind many an interracial town lies a white person—or several—who stopped a threatened eviction, which, because it did not happen, is now lost to history. I know no way to recover the memory of such events and no way to predict where and when such leaders will occur. We have gone about as far as we can in explaining why certain towns across America went sundown, while others did not.

In some towns, whites failed to stop wholesale evictions but did intercede on behalf of an individual person of color. When white residents of Eureka, California, evicted their Chinese population in 1885, eventually only one Chinese American man, Charley Moon, was left in Humboldt County.[58] When a group of Eureka residents came to Tom Bair's Redwood Creek Ranch to take his ranch hand, Bair reportedly stood in the road with a gun and told them that they would have to take him first; the men turned around and left. Moon then worked on the Bair ranch for years and "was well liked and respected"; according to historian Lynwood Carranco, "nobody molested him." James Wilson likewise protected Alecta Smith when whites drove all other African Americans from Harrison, Arkansas, in 1905 and 1909. According to oral history summarized by David Zimmermann, "Wilson met the mob at his door with a shotgun and told them no one in his home was going to be hurt." Another white man in Harrison, George Cotton, didn't go that far, but he did help his black porter escape to safety during the riot, according to Cotton's grandson. Cotton put "Nigger George" in his buggy at midnight and took him to Eureka Springs—a twelve-hour buggy ride.[59]

One man also helped to soften the 1918 expulsion of African Americans from Unicoi County, Tennessee, on the North Carolina line. Like so many other expulsions, this one began with an interracial assault. African American Tom Devert allegedly grabbed a white teenage girl a mile and a half from Erwin, the county seat.[60] Four nearby whites interceded, shooting Devert as he tried to swim across the Nolichucky River with the girl. Whites then tied Devert's body to a locomotive and dragged it back to Erwin. A large mob gathered, and the entire black population, between 60 and 70 people, was forced to watch as his body was burned. A reporter for the *Bristol Herald* paints a dramatic scene:

> Men with pistols, shotguns, and clubs stood before the lined up Negroes to prevent their running away, and as the last cross tie and the last dash of oil was thrown on the heap one of the men is reported to have turned to the cowering crowd and said, "Watch what we are going to do here. If any of you are left in town by tomorrow night, you will meet the same fate."

Whites would have burned down the black part of Erwin that night "but were dissuaded by General Manager L. H. Phettaplace of the C. C. & O. Railway," according to the account published in the nearby *Johnson City Daily*. Erwin and Unicoi County went all-white the next day, but Phettaplace may have saved some lives that riotous night. Jon Voight's character in John Singleton's film *Rosewood,* who helps several African Americans escape from the white riot that destroyed the black community of Rosewood, Florida, is based on a similar person who in fact existed.[61]

"A movie should be made of the experience of the Braden and Wade families in 1954. Carl and Anne Braden bought a house in Shively, a sundown suburb of Louisville, Kentucky, and resold it to Andrew and Charlotte Wade, a black couple. Just past midnight on June 27, a dynamite blast wrecked half of the Wade's house. Although the police had a confession, no one was ever their open racism become the target of legal action or scorn. Either way, residents usually cover up, especially in print. Commemorative histories, in particular, rarely treat embarrassing facts or controversial topics. People don't want to publish anything negative about their own town, especially in the coffee table book that marks its centennial. Consider *One Hundred Years of Progress,* published in 1954 in Anna, Illinois. You will recall that whites in Anna drove out all African Americans in the city in 1909, and the town has been sundown ever since. This 446-page book provides a history of every organization in town, down to the local Dairy Queen. Yet it contains no mention of African Americans, the murder and lynching that led to their banishment, the expulsion itself, their continuing exclusion, or the nickname that confirms Anna's notoriety. These facts are hardly obscure; everyone in town knows them; I confirmed the nickname in my first conversation in the city. Published in the year when the U.S. Supreme Court had just declared segregation illegal, the book can hardly have omitted these facts by accident. The anonymous authors had to have known that to say openly that Anna was now known as "Ain't No Niggers Allowed" would no longer reflect credit on their town.[16]

Only a handful of local histories treat the exclusion of African Americans (or Chinese or Jewish Americans) from their community or county forthrightly. Most—like Anna's—do not. The overt racism that led to sundown suburbs has been especially mystified. In 1961, for example, on the occasion of its 35th anniversary, *Life Newspapers,* serving the west Chicago suburbs, published a 150-page special issue, featuring an article, "Cicero . . . the Best Town in America," that contained not a word about the 1951 race riot that made Cicero nationally notorious. This is all too typical of the publications put out by local newspapers and historical societies. The result is not happy for today's researcher.[17]

One might imagine that priests and preachers might chide their congregations about their un-Christian attitude toward people of color, but clergy, like local historians, avoid controversy by not saying anything bad about their town. In 1960, a Baptist minister in Vandalia, Illinois, told of a nearby town: "When I was pastor in Pinckneyville, they had an unwritten rule that no Negroes should be in town after sundown. No Negro could live in the community." The minister was right about Pinckneyville but ignored the same rule in Vandalia, where he was living. A still more heroic omission comes in the *Proceedings* produced by the annual Valparaiso University Institute on Human Relations from 1950 to 1968, an interracial Lutheran group that often focused on concerns of race relations—but never in Valparaiso. Valparaiso was a sundown town from at least 1890 until the early 1970s. The 1951 conference charged with the crime. Instead, the prosecutor arrested the Bradens and claimed the bombing was Communist plot! Carl Braden was found guilty of sedition, sentenced to fifteen years, and served seven months in jail before his conviction was overturned on appeal."[62]

This chapter and its precedessor, on sociological causation, are first attempts to address why sundown towns came into being. No one has ever tried to answer such questions before. Everything about sundown towns—that the absence of African Americans was involuntary, how widespread they have been, even the origin myths their residents told themselves—has been mystified and left out of history books over the years. The next chapter tells of that mystification. It explains how most Americans came to be ignorant about even the sheer fact of their existence. It also summarizes the methods I used, so you can assess my claims to have proven that these towns do exist and were all-white on purpose.

8

Hidden in Plain View: Knowing and Not Knowing About Sundown Towns

> Local persons giving quotes to the newspaper should be more careful in the wording of such statements to prevent misinterpretation. . . . The Chamber, through this committee, [shall] keep a close watch on future news reporting and take any appropriate action should further detriment to the City of Rogers be detected.
>
> —Report of Rogers, Arkansas, Chamber of Commerce after the Rogers newspaper stated in 1962 that Rogers was a sundown town[1]

BARRING AN OCCASIONAL NEWS STORY about an individual all-white town—typically treated as an anomaly—America's independent sundown towns, numbering in the thousands, have mostly escaped notice until now. Even the origin myths that whites used to explain such towns' racial policies rarely got written down. Sundown suburbs, equally plentiful and concentrated around major cities, could not escape notice, but their whiteness was often dismissed as "natural," resulting from market forces. As I tell audiences how sundown towns and suburbs were created, sometimes they gasp audibly, astonished to learn that there are so many sundown towns and suburbs, that these towns were created intentionally, often by violent means, and sometimes that they themselves live in one.

White residents do know the racial composition of their town, of course; it may even be a reason why they chose to move there. But most haven't thought about *how* it came to be so white; it just seemed natural. Afterward, audience members often come up to tell me that their town or suburb is all-white or was until recently. Now they are curious: could it be that way on purpose? As one person from a sundown town near Champaign, Illinois, put it: "How naive I was growing up! I was in a sundown town and had no clue until now. Sad!"[2]

Knowing and Not Knowing About Sundown Towns

White Americans encounter sundown towns every day but rarely think about them or even realize that they're in one. They look like other towns, especially to most non-black people, who often don't notice the difference between 95% white and 100% white. Motorists driving through Anna, Illinois, might stop to see its famous library, designed in 1913 by Walter Burley Griffith, the Prairie School architect who went on to design Canberra, Australia. Or they might be visiting a mentally ill relative in the Illinois State Hospital. They don't notice that Anna is a sundown town unless they know to ask. Most sundown towns and suburbs are like that: invisible, until a black wayfarer appears and the townspeople do something about it.

At the same time, whites have nicknames for many overwhelmingly white towns: "Colonial Whites" for Colonial Heights, near Richmond, Virginia; "the White Shore" across the Susquehanna River from Harrisburg, Pennsylvania, instead of the West Shore; "Caucasian Falls" for Cuyahoga Falls near Akron, Ohio; "Whiteface Bay" for Whitefish Bay, north of Milwaukee; and so forth across the country to "Lily White Lynwood" outside Los Angeles. Whites make up jokes about the consequences of an African American being found after dark in many sundown towns and suburbs. "Even the squirrels are white in Olney" is a quip about a sundown town in southeastern Illinois known also for its albino squirrels.[3] Such nicknames and jokes show that the whiteness of these towns has registered; whites do understand that the absence of blacks is no accident. Residents of a metropolitan area also know which suburbs are said to be the whitest and which police departments have a reputation for racial profiling. The practice of stopping and questioning African Americans in Darien, Connecticut, for example, was "an open secret in town," according to Gregory Dorr, who grew up there. Nevertheless, when told that many American towns and suburbs kept out African Americans for decades and some still do, often these same individuals claim to be shocked.[4]

Perhaps it is more accurate to say that white Americans know and don't know about sundown towns. This curious combination of knowing and not knowing seems eerily reminiscent of Europe, 1938–45: surely Germans (and Poles, French, Dutch, etc.) knew that Jewish and Romany people were being done away with—their houses and apartments were becoming vacant and available before their very eyes, after all. Yet many professed shock when told about it afterward. I do not claim that America's rash of sundown towns is a Holocaust. The murdered probably total fewer than 2,000 and the refugees fewer than 100,000, nothing like the fury the Nazis unleashed upon Jewish and Rom people. Yet there is a parallel question: why have so few white Americans ever heard of sundown towns, even when they live in one?

"Yvonne Dorset," for example, grew up in Buffalo, Illinois, near Springfield. In 2002 she replied to a discussion at Classmates.com: "I graduated from Tri-City [the high school in Buffalo] in 1963. There weren't any African Americans in my graduating class, but I never thought of it as anything but coincidence. We were brought up to respect all races." As best I can tell, Dorset has lived in Buffalo from 1945 to now. What would we make of a long-term resident of, say, Heidelberg, Germany, who wrote in 2002, "There weren't any Jews in my graduating class, but I never thought of it as anything but coincidence"? Buffalo drove out its African Americans on August 17, 1908. The absence of African Americans from Buffalo today is no more a "coincidence" than the near-absence of Jewish Germans from Heidelberg.[5]

The Unsuspecting Researcher

I don't mean to be hard on Ms. Dorset. It is all too easy to overlook the sundown nature of an all-white town. I know, because I too was oblivious. Until doing the research for this book, I never noticed most sundown towns. Being white myself and having grown up in an all-white neighborhood, I took most all-white neighborhoods, towns, and even counties for granted, assuming that African Americans simply happened not to live in them. Indeed, the biggest mistake I have ever made in print was about sundown towns, and I made it in my most recent book, *Lies Across America*. In an essay comparing three Arkansas counties, I commended Grant County for being "most hospitable of the three for African Americans." *I did not notice that Sheridan, seat of Grant County, was a sundown town!* When I was there (too briefly!) in 1996,[6] about 400 African Americans lived in the county, but whites did not allow them to spend the night in the county seat.[7]

Having learned during *this* research that Sheridan was a sundown town during my previous visit, having confirmed that more than 30 other towns and counties in Arkansas excluded African Americans, having identified 50 more as likely suspects, and having found some 472 probable all-white towns in Illinois alone, I now see how naive *I* was.

American Culture Typically Locates Racism in the South

How could we Americans have been so ignorant of sundown towns for so long? Even if we grew up in a place with few sundown towns nearby—Mississippi, for example—how could we not have known that so many thousands of sundown towns formed elsewhere in the United States? After all, students in New Hampshire know about slavery. Why isn't knowledge of sundown towns part of our living historical tradition?

Our culture teaches us to locate overt racism long ago (in the nineteenth century) or far away (in the South) or to marginalize it as the work of a few crazed deviants who carried out their violent works under cover of darkness. Most high school American history textbooks downplay slavery in the North, so from the start race relations seems to be a sectional rather than national problem. Research shows that white eleventh graders before *and after* taking U.S. history viewed only white southerners as the dominant actors in U.S. racial oppression. American literature likewise puts most overt racism in the South, not the North. In her memoir *I Know Why the Caged Bird Sings,* Maya Angelou characterizes Mississippi with the phrase "Don't Let the Sun Set on You Here, nigger, Mississippi." Tennessee Williams has the sheriff in *Orpheus Descending,* also set in Mississippi, make a similar reference. But Angelou and Williams would have been more accurate had they used the phrase to characterize California or Ohio. William Burroughs makes the same blunder of locating his sundown town in the South in *Naked Lunch.* Malcolm Ross, a member of the Fair Employment Practices Commission during World War II, recognized Calhoun County, Illinois, as a sundown county in his memoir, *All Manner of Men;* astonishingly, Ross then went on to talk about "the white boys from Calhoun County, and a hundred other counties of the South." Calhoun County is just 65 miles southwest of Springfield, the capital; it's not even in southern Illinois. As recently as 2002, Jerrold Packard repeats this stereotype: in *American Nightmare: The History of Jim Crow,* he writes, "Some all-white *Southern* towns" placed sundown signs at their city limits.[8] Actually, among the 184 towns that had sundown signs to my knowledge, only 7 were in the traditional South, along with another 52 in places like the Cumberlands and the Ozarks; 125 were northern and western.

Hollywood perpetuates this stereotype. In *The Fugitive Kind,* the sheriff in a small southern town tells Marlon Brando about a nearby town with a sign saying, "Nigger, Don't Let the Sun Go Down on You in This County." He goes on to say, "Now this ain't that town, and you ain't that nigger, but imagine a sign saying, 'Boy, Don't Let the Sun Rise on You in This County!' "[9] *Sudie and Simpson,* a 1984 film starring Louis Gosset Jr., is set in 1940s Georgia. The local town, Linlow, is shown to have a sign: "Nigger!! Don't Let the Sun Set on You in Linlow." Actually, the sundown syndrome does afflict six counties in Appalachian north Georgia, but otherwise Georgia is almost free of the phenomenon. Danny Glover's 2000 made-for-TV film *Freedom Song,* an otherwise accurate portrayal of the Mississippi Civil Rights Movement, shows a sign saying, "Nigger, Read and Run / If You Can't Read, Run Anyway." Signs with that wording indeed (dis)graced many sundown towns, but none in Mississippi. Meanwhile, in northern locations where black exclusion actually happened, Hollywood covers it up. Take *Grosse Pointe Blank,* for example, a 1997 John Cusack vehicle. This film not only fails to tell that Grosse Pointe was all-white on purpose throughout the era it depicts, it inserts a black alumnus or two into the major character's high school reunion. *Hoosiers,* a 1986 basketball movie starring Gene Hackman, similarly obfuscates the racial reality of 1950s small-town Indiana. As one Indiana resident wrote in 2002, "All southern Hoosiers laughed at the movie called *Hoosiers* because the movie depicts blacks playing basketball and sitting in the stands at games in Jasper. We all agreed no blacks were permitted until probably the '60s and do not feel welcome today." A cheerleader for a predominantly white but interracial Evansville high school tells of having rocks thrown at their school bus as they sped out of Jasper after a basketball game in about 1975, more than twenty years after the events depicted so inaccurately in *Hoosiers.* I know of only one film treatment of residential exclusion[10] and no image of a sundown sign in any movie set in a northern locale.[11]

Placing a sundown sign in fictional Linlow is one of the ways Hollywood connotes southernness, and Tennessee Williams, Danny Glover, and Maya Angelou may have followed the same convention. It's too easy, though, and it's inaccurate. Placing sundown towns in Dixie where they don't occur only encourages Americans to overlook them in the North where they do. In the North, whites don't expect to see such overt racism, so they don't. In her autobiography *My Lord, What a Morning,* Marian Anderson goes along with this convention. She tells of staying in some hotels that made an exception for her, since she was performing in the town's fine-arts series, but would not house any other African Americans. But she speaks only on the South in this regard. This simply does not describe the facts of her accommodations. On many occasions she could not stay the night in white hotels in the North. In northern sundown towns, she could not stay anywhere, even in private homes. Anderson's autobiography never hints at any problem in the North, however. She even tells how Albert Einstein put her up in Princeton without ever mentioning that he volunteered to do so after the only hotel in town said no. Perhaps she didn't want to alienate white northerners who might be potential allies to change southern segregation. The Civil Rights Movement also picked on the "legally" segregated South for the same reason, as Scott Malcomson points out: it made a better target. Ironically, although the NAACP itself was born in the aftermath of the 1908 attempt by white residents to drive all African Americans from Springfield, Illinois, it rarely attacked sundown towns in the North or even acknowledged that they existed.[12]

Even within northern states, whites assume the southern or backward sections have the sundown towns. Literally scores of Illinois residents have said, "Oh, yes, in *southern* Illinois," when they learn what I am studying. "Yes," I reply, "and central Illinois, and northern Illinois, and especially the Chicago and Peoria suburbs." They are shocked. The guidebook to a 1995–97 exhibit at the Indiana State Historical Museum, *Indiana in the Civil War*, came to the same easy conclusion for that state: "Some small towns and rural areas, especially in southern Indiana, developed reputations for hostility and intimidation, causing blacks residing there to leave and discouraging newcomers." Certainly that happened in southern Indiana, but similar intimidation and hostility were also visited upon African Americans in small towns and rural areas around Indianapolis, in the northeast quarter of the state, and just south of Lake Michigan, resulting in sundown towns just about everywhere. Pennsylvania residents aren't surprised to learn that very rural areas such as Warren and Potter Counties are all-white, perhaps on purpose, but are shocked to see the number of all-white towns in the densely settled river valleys of eastern Pennsylvania.[13]

The lack of concern our society pays to racism in the North can also be seen in our culture's stress on lynching as a topic of study, rather than sundown towns, and its particular attention to Southern lynchings. Most studies of lynchings focus solely on the South. The databases themselves show this bias: the principal list, from Tuskegee Institute, includes only nine Southern states (those that seceded, minus Virginia and Texas) plus Kentucky, and Project HAL (Historic American Lynchings), whose list of lynchings some consider the most complete, also includes only the same ten states. Yet controlling for the smaller size of the black population outside the South, lynchings were recorded about as often in Ohio, Kentucky, Indiana, Illinois, and California as in Southern states. Indeed, we simply have no idea how many lynchings occurred in the Midwest or Northeast because of scholars' concentration on the South. Certainly three of the most famous lynching photographs come from the Midwest—Omaha in 1919, the triple hanging in Duluth in 1919, and the twin hangings in Marion, Indiana, in 1930. The result of this overemphasis is an inability of Northern scholars to perceive the racism in their own communities, at least before African Americans moved north in the Great Migration that began around 1915. Even as late as the Civil Rights Movement in the

1960s, the South has simply been viewed as the venue where race relations played out in America.[14]

Inadvertently, I generate this same mistake in conversation: over and over I tell historians and social scientists about my research, and they assume I'm studying the Deep South. Even when I correct them, the correction often fails to register. I tell a sociologist friend that I've just spent months researching sundown towns in the Midwest. Ten minutes later he has forgotten and again assumes I have been traveling through the South.

A Conspiracy of Silence

Deliberate suppression has also played a role in keeping sundown towns hidden. This seems to be true in Myakka City, Florida, a small town twenty miles inland from Sarasota. By 1920, African Americans had built two churches and made up more than a third of the town's population. "But just 20 years later," according to *Tampa Tribune* reporter Roberta Nelson, writing in 2001, "blacks had vanished from Myakka City." Myakka resident Melissa Sue Brewer wrote, "Myakka City 'historians' have erased all mention of African-Americans." Suppressing the memory was hard because the expulsion apparently took place in the late 1930s, recent enough that oral history can still be done. Nelson interviewed one white woman, Marilyn Coker, who moved to Myakka City when she was eight; her late husband, a Myakka native,

> remembered when the Negroes left, and how upset everyone was about it. The [white] people were upset that they were made to leave town. It was a vigilante kind of thing. Most of the people who lived here were not a part of it. But, all of a sudden, one day they were all gone.

Of course, not all white people were upset; some were the "vigilantes." Other Myakka City old-timers remembered specific African American individuals, such as "Preacher Harper, who was ordered to leave on short notice and denied time to sell off his hogs and chickens." Oral history on the disappeared black community may yet bring the full story to light.[15]

"It just breaks my heart to see my town appear in your book," said a librarian in West Frankfort, Illinois, in 2002, a feeling I heard repeated in many other sundown towns. This sentiment causes many residents who are ashamed to be living in all-white communities to hide the nature of their community from outsiders. Residents of sundown towns who are pleased to be living in all-white communities may not want to talk openly about it either, lest passed a resolution about the Cicero, Illinois, riot of that year, condemning Cicero's all-white policy. In later years, the conference printed articles favoring integrated housing, discussed black-white issues in Chicago, Cleveland, and other American cities, and passed resolutions against apartheid in South Africa—but never said a thing about Valparaiso. Even the 1966 conference, "Where You Live," never once mentioned that they were meeting in a sundown town. Yet many speeches and papers were by faculty members and the president of Valparaiso University, who had to know this. For that matter, all participants of color had to be housed on campus because they could not spend the night elsewhere in the city. If the conference and the college had taken a stand *in Valparaiso,* they might have accomplished something. It is not clear that their resolutions had any impact on Cicero, South Africa, or Cleveland. Such studied ignorance has a payoff: one need not do anything. If forced to recognize that they speak in sundown towns, the Pinckneyville minister and Valparaiso professors might feel the need to criticize and try to change their communities. This could be risky: even tenured professors can be let go, and Baptist churches can hire or fire their ministers at any time.[18]

Often residents of sundown towns have gone beyond merely covering up their communities' exclusionary policy to laud their towns as particularly democratic. The centennial history of Pekin, Illinois, published in 1949 by the Pekin Chamber of Commerce, contains this paragraph:

> Pekin has no social divisions. There are no special neighborhoods in Pekin, either social, economic, religious, or racial. It is this Democracy or Near-Equality which frequently first impresses strangers in our city.

Yet Pekin has been notorious as a Klan center ever since the 1920s. It has also long been one of the larger sundown cities in the United States. African Americans across the United States remain in awe of its fearsome reputation even today. In a certain ghoulish sense, the book is accurate, of course. Just as various German cities can boast today that they have no Jewish ghetto, Pekin can brag that it has no black neighborhood. Likewise, in 1942, writing the history of his hometown, Libertyville, an all-white and probably sundown town northwest of Chicago, Lowell Nye said,

> Perhaps the one factor most evident to the newcomer who observes Libertyville's population is its unusually pure American quality. . . . It is an American town that is genuinely American; its basic stock can be identified with no one nationality. Taken as a whole, it is a happy tolerant society.

In her 1938 autobiography, *A Peculiar Treasure,* novelist Edna Ferber made a similar assertion about Appleton, Wisconsin: "a lovely little town of 16,000 people; tree shaded, prosperous, civilized. Creed, color, race, money—these mattered less in this civilized, prosperous community than in any town I've ever encountered." This is an extraordinary claim about a sundown town. Ferber, who was Jewish, may not have encountered anti-Semitism in Appleton, but she could not have failed to notice its complete absence of African Americans, and she had to know that their absence was by design. As historian James Cornelius put it, "When I went to Lawrence University [in 1978], that's one of the first things I learned, that Appleton was a sundown town." "Color, race" made the *key* difference in this "civilized, prosperous community," and in Pekin, and probably in Libertyville. Surely these authors protest too much.[19]

These exuberant proclamations of equalitarianism in sundown towns exemplify not only base hypocrisy but also what sociologists call "herrenvolk democracy"—democracy for the master race. White Americans' verbal commitment to nondiscrimination forms one horn of what Swedish economist Gunnar Myrdal famously called "The American Dilemma." Blatant racism forms the other horn. In elite sundown suburbs, this dilemma underlies what we shall later term the "paradox of exclusivity."

Silence on the Landscape

Having written a book on how America's historic sites and historical markers mostly omit or distort embarrassing facts in our past, I was eager to see what the historical markers in sundown towns say about their racial policies. Most say nothing. From west to east: Tacoma, Washington, expelled its Chinese population on November 5, 1883, but the landscape is silent on the matter. Richland, Washington, created by the U.S. government to house workers producing our atomic bombs, was established as a sundown town and enforced that policy for years, but its landscape is equally silent. Whites drove Chinese Americans from all except a single town in Wyoming, but one cannot learn this on the Wyoming landscape. The extensive state marker for Ste. Genevieve, Missouri, totals more than 300 words, yet never mentions the town's 1930 expulsion of almost all its African Americans. The historical marker for Mariemont, Ohio, a sundown suburb adjoining Cincinnati, states:

> Ground was broken for Mariemont by Mary M. Emery, the village's founder, on
> April 25, 1923. This planned community was designed by eminent town plan-

ner John Nolen and twenty five of America's leading architects. As part of the
"garden city movement," Mariemont was influenced by English models. . . .

but contains not a word on Mariemont's policy of exclusion, started by
Emery. A Pennsylvania state marker tells of the town of Wehrum, now abandoned, but fails to tell how its white residents forced out all African Americans
on a cold February day in 1903; "the Negroes had to find shelter wherever
they could," according to a newspaper account. And so it goes, across the nation to Darien, Connecticut, whose glaring lack of candor I critiqued in *Lies
Across America*.[20]

I know just four exceptions.[21] Nevada City, California, recently erected a
memorial telling of their expulsion of Chinese Americans. An Idaho state historical marker tells of the lynching of five Chinese men in Pierce in 1885 and
the expulsion of all other Chinese from that area. A monument in the cemetery
of Pierce City, Missouri, commemorates the 200 African Americans killed or
driven from that town by white residents in 1901. An indoor exhibit in the
museum in Greenbelt, Maryland, admits that Greenbelt was founded during
the Depression for whites only, although the town's lengthy historical marker
says nothing on the matter.[22] Otherwise, the sundown towns of America, hundreds of which used to boast of their policy with signs and billboards at their
corporate limits, now hide that fact on their landscape.[23]

Local Newspapers Don't Say a Thing and Vanish if They Do

Like centennial histories and historical markers, small-town and suburban
newspapers like to present only the sunny side of their community to outsiders. Early in the sundown town movement, many communities were so
racist that their newspapers happily published full accounts of the actions
their white citizens were taking against their African American neighbors,
sometimes even including editorial exhortations before the events. Later, after
civic leaders realized that these acts might strike outsiders as reprehensible,
the accounts sometimes vanished. Harrison, Arkansas, for example, drove out
its African Americans in 1905 and 1909. This was no trivial event, according
to Jacqueline Froelich and David Zimmermann, whose article is the definitive
treatment of these riots:

> The ethnic cleansing of Harrison . . . is arguably the most important event in
> the town's social history—devastating the lives of those African American citi-
> zens for whom Harrison had been home, encouraging the use of violence to

force social change and protect local interests, and petrifying the town's approach to race for many years to come.

Nevertheless, despite their importance, or rather because of it, the riots were never talked about in Harrison. "Conspicuously missing from the files of the *Harrison Times* newspaper were issues that were printed near the time of the two events," according to David Zimmermann, who had to reconstruct them from other sources. The same thing happened in Tulsa. During that city's now-notorious 1921 race riot, whites attacked Tulsa's African American community on the ground and from the air: six airplanes dropped dynamite bombs to flatten homes and businesses. As Portfolio 10 shows, rioters made a concerted attempt to drive all African Americans out of Tulsa. Although they failed, they did pull off the largest race riot in American history. Later, the newspapers for the period mysteriously (and now famously) disappeared. The riot became, said one resident, "something everybody knew about but nobody wanted to discuss." [24]

Sometimes coverage was stifled from the start. Jim Woodruff, a resident of Springfield, Illinois, and a student of its 1908 race riot, tells how Springfield's newspapers downplayed the riot in anticipation of the celebration of the one hundredth anniversary of Lincoln's birthday the next year. According to historian Arnold Hirsch, major white riots in Chicago after World War II got very little coverage in that city's newspapers, partly at the behest of the Chicago Commission on Human Relations, which was trying to prevent whites in other neighborhoods from engaging in copycat riots of their own. The riot in suburban Cicero, July 10–12, 1951, did get covered, but not for the first two days. Only after the National Guard was called out on July 12 and after the story made the local TV news did the *Tribune* and *Sun-Times* publish anything about that now infamous event. The advent of television did not end the suppression everywhere, however. In 1972, a realtor who wanted to expose the anti-Semitism of La Jolla, California, had to go to Tijuana, Mexico, to be interviewed, because no San Diego television station would touch the story. [25]

Since then, sundown towns have become still more secretive, as most public officials and newspaper editors have come to realize that a town cannot legally keep out would-be residents on account of race. The newspaper editor of Anna, Illinois, said he had considered doing a story or series of stories on Anna's racial makeup and its history several years ago but had been warned off the topic by local businessmen. Not just omission but denial sometimes results. In 2002, I elicited an apparent example of attempted containment by a small-town paper. I spent a day in Villa Grove, Illinois, south of Champaign-

Urbana. As we saw, until recent years Villa Grove had sounded a whistle at 6 PM every evening to warn African Americans to get out of town. My last interview of the day was with the editor of Villa Grove's weekly newspaper. By then, eleven of eleven interviewees had verified that Villa Grove is or at least was a sundown town.[26] Therefore I was blunt:

> "Hello, I'm Jim Loewen. I grew up over in Decatur, and now I'm doing research on all-white towns that are all-white on purpose, including this one."
>
> The editor nodded.
>
> "I understand you have, or used to have until recently, a whistle on your water tower that went off every evening at 6 PM"
>
> "Yes," he agreed.
>
> "Tell me the story about that whistle," I asked.
>
> "I don't know any story about that whistle," he replied.
>
> "OK," I said, and started to make my farewell. Nine of eleven interviewees had already confirmed the story, and I saw no reason to question him further.
>
> As I turned to leave, his secretary asked me, "You mean the story that that was the signal for blacks to be out of town?"
>
> I nodded and replied, "Yes, that story."
>
> "I never heard that story!" she said.[27]

Chambers of Commerce Stifle Coverage

Suppression was general in northern Arkansas. "There is almost a total absence of available written material on the black communities," complained sociologist Gordon Morgan in 1973, trying to write the history of African Americans in the Ozarks. "Some white towns have deliberately destroyed reminders of the blacks who lived there years ago." In Rogers, in northwest Arkansas, the foresighted staff of the Rogers Historical Museum saved evidence of the process of historical repression at work. After the 1962 Fats Domino concerts in Rogers, the *Rogers Daily News* noted this progress in a front-page editorial:

> The city which once had signs posted at the city limits and at the bus and rail terminals boasting "Nigger, You Better Not Let the Sun Set on You in Rogers," was hosting its first top name entertainer—a Negro—at night!

The *Daily News* also ran a front-page news story on the event. The next day, the Rogers Chamber of Commerce called a special meeting of its Publicity and Public Relations Committee. The Chamber called in the reporter and editor of the *Daily News,* the manager of the Victory Theatre, where the concert had taken place, and the chief of police, Hugh Basse, who had been quoted in the news story. The purpose of the meeting was to challenge the newspaper coverage. Singled out for attention was the statement about the signs. The newspaper defended its statement as historically accurate and necessary background for the editorial. The committee contended that the statement was "unnecessary even if a substantiated fact in view of the possible repercussions it might have in the future." [28]

The Rogers Historical Museum obtained and saved the formal two-page "Committee Report" resulting from this meeting. Among its seven conclusions:

- Local persons giving quotes to the newspaper should be more careful in the wording of such statements to prevent misinterpretation.

- The conference with the newspaper representatives was fruitful in that the committee feels a better job of reporting the news will be done.

- A written report [will] be filed with the Board of Directors requesting official Chamber action to bring this matter to the attention of supervisory personnel of the Reynolds chain.

- The Chamber, through this committee, [will] keep a close watch on future news reporting and take any appropriate action should further detriment to the City of Rogers be detected.

The chilling intent is obvious. [29]

Chambers of Commerce still spread disinformation about their towns' sundown policies. A Chamber official in Corbin, Kentucky, a town that drove out its black population in 1919, pretended to be mystified by Corbin's whiteness in the 1991 documentary *Trouble Behind*: "The [African Americans] have chosen to live in either Barbourville, Williamsburg, or north of Clarenton-Corbin . . . but their reasons for that decision—I have no knowledge of that." Certainly Corbin cannot be at fault: "I don't feel there is any more prejudice in Corbin, Kentucky, than you'll find in any other community in the country." This man is intelligent enough to know that other Corbin residents will tell the filmmaker that no African American should move into Corbin, thus exposing the falseness of his statement; in fact, some young white males did just that in other footage in the film. Nevertheless, he thinks it best to dissimulate about Corbin's racism, undoubtedly because it's not good for Corbin's image. [30]

Historical Societies Help to Suppress the Truth

The Rogers Historical Museum is unusual among local historical societies and museums in telling the truth about its community's racist past and saving material that documents that past. The usual response I got when I asked at local libraries, historical societies, and museums if they saved the sundown sign from their community or a photo of it was "Why would we do that?" while they laughed out loud.

Writing historical societies proved particularly useless for most towns. Since I could hardly visit all the probable sundown towns and counties in the United States, I wrote or e-mailed the historical societies in many of them. Unfortunately, like the Chamber of Commerce in Corbin, historical societies don't like to say anything bad about their towns or counties. For example, Shirley De Young, director of the Mower County Historical Society in southern Minnesota, said she had no information confirming Austin and Mower County as sundown communities. Actually, it is common knowledge in Austin that it was sundown from at least 1922 to the 1980s. In 1890, Mower County, of which Austin is the seat, had 36 African Americans, a number surpassed by only six counties in the state. The county then witnessed probably four expulsions of its African Americans: in the late 1890s, shortly before 1920, in 1922 (prompted by a railroad strike, described below), and between 1924 and 1933 (described below). Much later, historian Peter Rachleff studied the famous Hormel strike of 1985–86 in Austin. He wrote:

> It was noticeable that there were exactly two Black workers among the workforce, both of whom were young Africans who had come to the U.S. to attend college and had run out of money. This seemed rather stunning, given the high percentage of African American workers in the meat-packing industry in Omaha, Chicago, KC [Kansas City], etc. When some of us asked about this, union members and retirees recounted a local tale—that in 1922, during the railroad shopmen's strike, a number of African American strikebreakers had been brought in by rail and housed inside the RR roundhouse. A crowd of strikers, family members, and local supporters laid siege to the roundhouse and the strikebreakers fled for their lives, many of them jumping into the Cedar River and swimming to safety . . . or drowning. No African American had lived in Austin since 1922, we were told.[31]

Thanks to historian Roger Horowitz, who did oral history in Austin, we have a detailed account of Austin's last two expulsions. He taped John Winkols, a veteran labor leader, in 1990.

One time Hormel hired 40 niggers . . . and they put 'em all in the plant at one time.

And at that time, you know, they used to scab, you know. Really not their fault, but the companies that hired them scabbed them. Well, first of all, they hired them when the roundhouses were on strike, they hired a boxcar full of 'em . . .

My cousin was up here, and we went to a dance in town. . . . And so my cousin says, "You want to go over to the roundhouse? We're gonna chase the niggers out of town."

I said, "What'd *they* do?" . . .

And he said, "They're scabbing on the workers in the roundhouse, because they're on strike."

"OK, let's go!" [I] had a piece of shovel handle; we went. . . . We surrounded them at the roundhouse and broke it in and went in to the roundhouse. The sheriff or the cops couldn't do nothing because hell, they were the same as the workers. We went in there and run the niggers out. Hit 'em over the head, you know, and tell them to "get goin"! . . . Albert's Creek runs through there, and some of them run that way, and we was after 'em, chased them, and one of them fell in the creek. He got up on his feet and he says, "Lordy mercy, if I ever gets on my feet again, I'll *never* come in this town again!"

Then Hormel hired them forty. We run *them* out of town . . . somewhere between '24 and '33. . . . After supper we got clubs and went down there and we run *them* out. After that they didn't come in no more, because they knew they couldn't hire them.

After the last expulsion, as his last sentence implied, Austin stayed sundown.[32]

De Young's professed ignorance of what was commonly known in Austin is typical of historical society officials. A high school history teacher in northern Indiana wrote that Hobart, Indiana, still had a sundown sign in the 1970s; three other longtime Hobart residents corroborated that Hobart was a sundown town. One Hobart native told of hearing "of a black family attempting to move in and their car being firebombed" in 1980 or 1981. Nevertheless, Elin Christianson, president of the Hobart Historical Society, wrote, "We have received your letter about your research into 'sundown towns.' We have no documentation that Hobart fits the parameters you describe." The careful reader will note that his statement, the native's, and Norwine's may all be correct—but I had asked Christianson about oral history as well as documents. Moira Meltzer-Cohen, then a resident of

Beaver Dam, Wisconsin, did extensive research to confirm Beaver Dam as a sundown town, findings summarized in Chapter 3. She got no help from the historical society: "Unfortunately, when I have approached the historical society and the library about verifying this, they have become defensive and showered me with information about Frederick Douglass" (who once visited Beaver Dam in 1856).[33]

In 2002, Patrick Clark, curator at the Andrew County Museum in northwest Missouri, wrote:

> Fortunately for our county, we should not be listed as a "Sundown Town" for your project. Also, we are not aware of communities in adjacent counties that would be designated as such.

Apparently Clark did not know that Missouri's last spectacle lynching occurred in Maryville, seat of the next county north of Andrew, in 1931. A mob of almost 3,000 whites marched Raymond Gunn, a black man accused of murdering a white schoolteacher, from Maryville to the scene of the crime, 3 miles away. Then they watched as ringleaders chained him "to the ridgepole and burned [him] to death as the schoolhouse itself was consumed," in the words of Arthur Raper's famous book, *The Tragedy of Lynching*. The sheriff permitted the lynching and never arrested anyone. In the aftermath, the huge crowd searched the ashes for teeth and bone fragments and pieces of charred flesh as souvenirs. Then white paranoia set in: rumors swept the town that "a large band of Negroes was moving on Maryville to wreak vengeance for the lynching," in the words of the nearby *St. Joseph Gazette*.[34] This fanciful news "sent Maryville citizens and farmers of the vicinity heavily armed upon the streets . . . late Saturday night." "There was almost a complete exodus of colored people from town following the lynching, and for most of the week they remained away," according to Raper. Whites gave a list of ten African Americans to the black minister "that were branded as undesirable, and he was requested to ask these never to return. This he did." Some whites tried to run all blacks out, but several businessmen refused their demand to fire their janitors, so not all African Americans left immediately. Most did, however, and the black population of Nodaway County, of which Maryville is county seat, fell from 95 in 1930 to 33 ten years later and still fewer thereafter. In 1958, the Maryville Industrial Development Corporation advertised this accomplishment to seek new industries:

This 8,600 population town and surrounding community possesses an abundant number [*sic*] native born, nigger-free, non-union workers who believe in giving an honest day's work for a day's pay.

"We cannot offer any tax inducements," said Joe Jackson Jr., chair of the corporation, but

we can offer them all-white contented labor. We don't have any niggers here in Maryville. There may be three or four left in Nodaway County, but all of them are in their 70s and wouldn't be seeking any jobs in the plants. We had to lynch one nigger back in 1931 . . . and the rest of them just up and left. So we've got an all-white town and all-white labor to offer anybody who brings new industry here.

Many members of the crowd of spectators came from surrounding counties, including Andrew County. Andrew County itself then showed a parallel decline in black population, from 42 in 1930 to 33 in 1940 and 5 by 1960. Moreover, Albany, seat of Gentry County, which adjoins Andrew County to the northeast, "maintained as part of the city code a rule that said blacks couldn't spend the evening in the town," according to a native of Albany. As far as I can ascertain, Gentry County has not had a single black household since at least 1930 and still doesn't. Yet Patrick Clark of the Andrew County Museum is "not aware of communities in adjacent counties" that kept out African Americans. Surely he is in denial.[35]

A recent published example of the problem comes from Chittenden County, Vermont. In 2003, Sylvia Smith wrote an entire article on Mayfair Park, a residential subdivision of South Burlington, Vermont, for the *Chittenden County Historical Society Bulletin*. In it she treats at length "protective covenants, which met required objectives of the Federal Housing Administration for the protection of the subdivision." She tells how they "established strict limits on sizes of lots, buildings, and setbacks." She goes on to quote "covenants pertaining to 'quality of life' concerns," which she believes are "of interest in present times," such as:

No noxious or offensive trade or activity shall be carried on upon any lot nor should anything be done thereon which may become an annoyance or nuisance to the neighborhood. . . . No dwelling costing less than $3,500 shall be permitted on any lot in the tract. These covenants shall run with the land.

The ellipsis in the above quotation indicates a passage left out, of course. That passage was, in substantial part:

> No persons of any race other than the white race shall use or occupy any build-ing or any lot, except that this covenant shall not prevent occupancy by domes-tic servants of a different race domiciled with an owner or tenant.

Precisely this missing sentence makes the covenant "restrictive" rather than merely "protective." Smith later tells that in 1951 a "vote was taken to elimi-nate and revoke the restrictive covenants," but she never mentions what these were. Only those few readers who already know that Mayfair Park was all-white on purpose can possibly understand what was undone in 1951.[36]

Absent from the History Books

Academic historians have long put down what they call "local history," de-ploring its shallow boosterism. But silence about sundown towns is hardly confined to local historians; professional historians and social scientists have also failed to notice them. Most Americans—historians and social scientists included—like to dwell on good things. Speaking to a conference of social studies teachers in Indiana, Tim Long, an Indiana teacher, noted how this characteristic can mislead:

> Today if you ask Hoosiers, "How many of you know of an Underground Rail-road site in Indiana?" everyone raises their hands. "How many of you know of a Ku Klux Klan member in Indiana?" Few raise their hands. Yet Indiana had a million KKK members and few abolitionists.

The same holds for sundown towns: Indiana had many more sundown towns after 1890 than it had towns that helped escaping slaves before 1860. Further-more, Indiana's sundown towns kept out African Americans throughout most of the twentieth century, some of them to this day, while its towns that aided slaves did so for about ten years a century and a half ago. Nevertheless, histori-ans, popular writers, and local historical societies in Indiana have spent far more time researching and writing about Underground Railroad sites than sundown towns. The Underground Railroad shows us at our best. Sundown towns show us at our worst.[37]

Authors have written entire books on sundown towns without ever men-tioning their racial policies.[38] I am reminded of the Hindi scene of the elephant in the living room: everyone in the room is too polite to mention the elephant, but nevertheless, it dominates the living room. Some city planners seem particularly oblivious to race. Karl Lohmann wrote *Cities and Towns of Illinois* in 1951, when most of them were all-white on purpose, but never mentioned a word about race. Instead, he made various uninteresting generalizations, such as that several towns had lakes. Gregory Randall wrote an entire monograph on one sundown suburb of Chicago, Park Forest, which later famously desegregated, but although he grew up in the suburb and also was conversant with research that candidly stated its sundown policy, he claims not to know for sure that Park Forest was all-white by design.[39] Long before he wrote in 2000, Park Forest had desegregated successfully, but Randall cannot tell that story, having never let on that it had been sundown. Randall also treats at length "the Greens"—Greenbelt, Maryland; Greenhills, Ohio; and Greendale, Wisconsin—yet never mentions that all three were founded as sundown towns. In *Toward New Towns for America,* C. S. Stein similarly whitewashes the Greens; Radburn, New Jersey; and several other planned communities.[40]

Two anthropologists, Carl Withers and Art Gallaher, each wrote an entire book on Wheatland, Missouri, a sundown town in a sundown county. Gallaher never mentioned race, and Withers's entire treatment is one sentence in a footnote, "However, no Negroes live now in the county." Penologist James Jacobs wrote "The Politics of Corrections" about the correctional center in Vienna, Illinois, but even though its subtitle focused upon "Town/Prison Relations," he never mentioned that Vienna was a sundown town, while most of the prisoners were black and Latino. This pattern of evasion continues: most entries on sundown suburbs in the *Encyclopedia of Chicago,* for instance, published in 2004, do not mention their striking racial composition, let alone explain how it was achieved. Romeoville, Illinois, for example, went sundown after a deadly battle between black and white workers on June 8, 1893, and stayed that way until the 1970s, but the entry on Romeoville is silent on the matter. Worse yet, the entry on Berwyn blandly says, "While Berwyn's Czech heritage retained its importance, increasing ethnic diversity further tested the city." Considering that Berwyn famously kept African Americans out as recently as 1992, this is another whitewash.[41]

Journalists, too, have dropped the ball. We have seen how business interests sometimes stop local newspapers from saying anything bad about a town. Propensities within journalism also minimize coverage of racial exclusion. Occasionally a race riot or a heinous crime relates to sundown towns and has caused the topic to become newsworthy. The 1908 race riot in Springfield, Illinois, prompted newspapers to note the sundown nature of nearby towns because African Americans driven from Springfield found no refuge in them. A murder brought media attention to Vidor, an east Texas sundown town with a long history of Klan activity and sundown signs. Under court order, Vidor had admitted four black households to its public housing units in 1992, but by 1993, Ku Klux Klan demonstrations and other threats forced out the last African American, William Simpson. When he was gunned down in nearby Beaumont by a young black man on the night after he moved out of Vidor, the irony prompted several news stories about Vidor. But attention waned after the murder; seven years later, Vidor had just a single black household, made up of two persons, among its 11,440 inhabitants in the 2000 census. Reporters for the *New Yorker* and *People* covered the 2002 arrest of the man who killed African American Carol Jenkins for being in Martinsville, Indiana, after dark, but the result was to demonize Martinsville as distinctive. As a result, I could not get an official of the Indiana Historical Bureau to address how general sundown towns might be in Indiana; instead, she repeated, "Martinsville is an entity unto itself—a real redneck town." But Martinsville is not unusual. For the most part, precisely what is so alarming about sundown towns—their astonishing prevalence across the country—is what has made them *not* newsworthy, except on special occasions. Murders sell newspapers. Chronic social pathology does not.[42]

Journalism has been called the "first draft of history," and the lack of coverage of sundown towns in the press, along with the reluctance of local historians to write anything revealing about their towns, has made it easy for professional historians and social scientists to overlook racial exclusion when they write about sundown communities. Most white writers of fiction similarly leave out race. In *White Diaspora,* Catherine Jurca notes that suburban novelists find the racial composition of their communities "so unremarkable" that they never think about it.[43]

So far as I can tell, only a handful of books on individual sundown towns has ever seen print, and this is the first general treatment of the topic.[44] That is an astounding statement, given the number of sundown towns across the United States and across the decades. Social scientists and historians may also have failed to write about sundown towns because they have trouble thinking to include those who aren't there. "People find it very difficult to learn that the absence of a feature is informative," note psychologists Frank Kardes and David Sanbonmatsu. Writers who don't notice the absence of people of color see nothing to explain and pay the topic no attention at all. Where does the subject even fit? Is this book African American history? Assuredly not—most of the towns it describes have not had even one African American resident for decades. It is *white* history . . . but "white history" is not a subject heading in college course lists, the Library of Congress catalog, or most people's minds. Perhaps the new but growing field of "whiteness studies" will provide a home for sundown town research.[45]

I don't mean to excuse these omissions. The absence of prior work on sundown towns is troubling. Omitted events usually signify hidden fault lines in our culture. If a given community has not admitted on its landscape to having been a sundown town in the past, that may be partly because it has not yet developed good race relations in the present. It follows that America may not have admitted to having sundown towns in its history books because it has not yet developed good race relations as a society. Optimistically, ending this cover-up now may be both symptom and cause of better race relations.

To be sure, all-white communities are about much more than race. Tuxedo Park, New York, was noted for its role in the invention of radar. Mariemont, Ohio; Park Forest, Illinois; Highland Park, Texas; and the Greens offer interesting examples of innovative urban design. Edina, Minnesota, boasted the nation's first totally enclosed shopping mall, by the renowned architect Victor Gruen. Arcola, Illinois, is famous for its annual Broom Corn Festival. The Winnetka Plan, named after a Chicago sundown suburb, is a progressive method of teaching taught in most graduate schools of education.

At the same time, however, sundown towns *are* about race. Speaking of the dozen or so race riots that led to all-white towns in Missouri and Arkansas around 1910, historian Patrick Huber calls them "defining events in the history of their communities." Even without a riot—so far as I know, none of the towns listed in the foregoing paragraph experienced such an event—eternal vigilance toward the occasional person of color is the price for maintaining racial purity. Thus to a degree sundown towns are *always* about race.[46]

There is no excuse for being oblivious to that fact. Not to treat the sundown nature of sundown towns—often not even to *see* that nature—points to a weakness in white social science and history. If this seems harsh, well, I too was oblivious for most of my life.

Defining "Sundown Town"

Given that so little historical work existed to be examined and summarized, I was reduced to discovering the facts about sundown towns myself. How should I proceed?

Chapter 1 defined "sundown town" as any organized jurisdiction that for decades kept out African Americans (or others). It also noted that towns could have a black household or two as explicit exceptions. Here we shall see that some additional nuances must be considered. To locate sundown towns, I began with the United States Census, looking for cities with 2,500 or more residents that had no or fewer than 10 African Americans. I usually left towns of fewer than 2,500 residents off my "suspect" list if they had 2–9 blacks in repeated censuses.[47] For cities larger than 10,000, I changed my definition for "all-white town" to "less than 0.1% black," decade after decade.

The census can mislead, however. It includes as part of a town's population African Americans who live in institutions—such as the residents of Anna's mental hospital—in many sundown towns that maintained a taboo against independent black households.[48] Thus only late in my research did I learn that Dwight, in northern Illinois, and Vienna, in southern Illinois, were sundown towns; African Americans in their prisons, included in their census populations, had caused me not to put them on my list of suspected towns. I cannot know how many other sundown towns I have missed by beginning with the census.

The census can also mislead by counting African Americans in white households: live-in maids and gardeners and in later decades black or biracial adopted children. "I cannot account for the 17 and 21 African Americans you list as having lived in Cullman [Alabama] in 1950 and 1960," John Paul Myrick, Cullman County librarian, wrote in 2002. "To my knowledge, there were none that lived here, other than maybe a few domestic workers who lived with their employers and/or perhaps students at the then operating St. Bernard and Sacred Heart colleges." Writing in 1986 about Darien, Connecticut, whose restrictive covenants and "gentleman's agreements" had been the subject of Laura Hobson's bestselling 1947 novel, *Gentleman's Agreement,* Richard Todd noted, "The overwhelming absence in Darien is the absence of black faces. If there was ever a time when a black householder lived here, no one seems to remember it. No black families at all live in Darien now. In the past there were a few black live-in servants, but there appear to be none today." Historian Gregory Dorr, who grew up in Darien, wrote that during his childhood (1968–1990), "no African American families lived in town, and rumor was that only one black family ever attempted (unsuccessfully) to move into town." Yet the census found 58 African Americans in 1990. The solution to this puzzle, as Myrick hints, may be live-in servants who rarely venture out. Certainly that was the case in wealthy Darien.[49]

Inner suburbs present a different census anomaly. These cities typically contain large apartment houses located on major arteries in very urban sectors of the larger metropolitan area—what sociologists call "gesellschaft," the opposite of "gemeinschaft" or community. Since there is little gemeinschaft in such an area, there is no one to feel offended that blacks have moved into "his" or "her" neighborhood—*there is no neighborhood*. With all the shoppers, janitors, deliveries, and other miscellaneous tradespeople of all races, few residents may even realize that a black renter has moved in. Even if they do, being transient themselves, they may not feel a need to protest or realize that their suburb's sundown tradition confers upon them a "right" to protest. The 1990 census showed 54 African Americans in Berwyn, an inner suburb of Chicago, "most, if not all, in apartments," according to Alex Kotlowitz. Two years later, he described how threats, arson, and other bad behavior drove out Clifton and Dolcy Campbell and their three children after they bought a home in a Berwyn neighborhood and moved in. Some neighbors befriended the black family, but city officials did little. As he departed, Clifton Campbell explained, "When we realized that we had no official support for being in Berwyn, we felt like outside intruders." Thus Berwyn still acted as a sundown suburb in 1992.[50]

Sometimes the census "finds" African Americans where they flatly don't exist. It listed 1 African American in Searcy County in the Arkansas Ozarks in 1930, 1940, and 1950, and none in 1960, but found 22 in 1970. Gordon Morgan, who was doing research for his book *Black Hillbillies of the Arkansas Ozarks* around that time, noted, "The later figure is highly questionable and such people cannot be found in the county." Pranksters may be responsible. Jim Clayton wrote that the census for Johnston City, Illinois, showed one African American resident in 1960. This so upset the mayor that he "staged an all-out search to try to find out who that was." The mayor never found out, and Clayton suspects it was a joke by a local. In recent years, when most people fill out their own forms and return them by mail, respondents may also simply check the wrong box by accident.[51]

All-White on Purpose?

Even granted the foregoing issues, the census remains our best starting point, and classifying a community "all-white" based on census data proved doable. In 1970, using the above definition of "all-white town," Illinois had about 424 such towns with more than 1,000 people, as Chapter 3 told. But just because a town or suburb is all-white doesn't make it a place in which African Americans are not *allowed* to live. Were they all white on purpose? What defines "on purpose"?

In a sense, sundown towns self-define: if residents of a town *say* they keep out African Americans, or used to, most likely they do, or did. If African Americans have moved in and quickly out, perhaps reporting unwelcoming behavior, that would be still better evidence. I never assumed that a given town or suburb was all-white on purpose. Only when credible sources, oral or written, confirm that a community expelled its African Americans (or other minority) or took steps to keep them from moving in do I list that community as a sundown town. The rest of this chapter describes the methods and information I used to determine whether a given all-white town was a sundown town and talks about some of the issues involved in making that decision.

Oral History

This chapter has noted the difficulty of relying on written history when doing research on sundown towns. Documents are important to historians and social scientists, of course. Given the widespread suppression of material on *this* topic, however, for historians and social scientists to conclude in their absence that a town did not have sundown policies would be a gross error. Indeed, doing so would allow those community leaders who deliberately left no documentary trail to succeed in bewildering those who would understand their policies. Even in towns where no deliberate suppression was involved, primary written sources are often scarce because small towns often did not keep even such basic records as minutes of city council meetings. Furthermore, the sundown policy in many towns was informal, so nothing was written down in the first place.

Instead, we must talk with longtime residents. Some historians disparage oral history, but about sundown towns, oral history is usually more accurate than written history. The oral histories I have collected typically include revealing details about how and when a town kept out African Americans, details unlikely to have been invented. A key question to put to any historical source is: Is this person in a position to know? One must ask interviewees who say theirs was a sundown town *how* they know what they claim to know. "Where did you learn that?" "Who told you?" "When?" My sources gave persuasive replies, or I didn't rely on them.

I suggest that when it is off the mark, oral history often *understates* the degree to which a town excluded blacks. Although local historians have told me things about their communities that they would never commit to print, what they tell is still often softened by their desire to say only nice things about their hometown. Also, some interviewees may not be in a position to know. Moreover, fear can affect what people will tell. Some African Americans, like some white Americans, fear offending what might be called "the powers that be." Michelle Tate elicited this fear from two of her best interviewees, an elderly African American couple in Mattoon, Illinois: "The saddest part of all was when the woman looked at me and made sure I would not use their names in my paper. I assured her I would not." I elicited the same reluctance from several white interviewees and made the same promises. Fearful interviewees may not divulge all that they know.[52]

Notwithstanding the foregoing cautions, I have found that most respondents are much more open in oral interview than when writing. They do want to help the person who is asking them questions. It is hard not to, after all, when they are in the midst of a conversation, especially when their relative expertise on the history of the locale has been acknowledged. Even pillars of the community, such as officials of the local historical society, are usually much more forthcoming in conversation than in print. A final reason why oral history often works is this: sundown towns were not usually created by far-out racists throwing bombs in the night. Unfortunately, most white residents of sundown towns and suburbs either approved of their policy of exclusion or said nothing to stop its enforcement. The whiteness of all-white towns is therefore the consensual product of entire communities—made tangible in sundown ordinances, in the blanket adoption of restrictive covenants, or by widespread acts of public or private harassment that townspeople commended, participated in, or at least allowed to go unpunished. Therefore knowledge of towns' sundown practices was equally widespread. In town after town, when one asks the right people, one learns how their community went sundown, why, and sometimes when, and who did it.

Of course, it is always best to corroborate white oral history with testimony from African American residents of the nearest interracial town. It is also important to triangulate oral history with census data and written sources.

Ordinances, Written or Oral?

One way that cities and towns went all-white or stayed all-white was by passing an ordinance forbidding African Americans from being within their corporate limits after sundown or prohibiting them from owning or renting property in the town. Or at least they *say* they did. Whether such ordinances ever existed has become controversial. My web site, uvm.edu/~jloewen/, tells of the controversy and lists towns with oral history of an ordinance. I have put considerable effort into finding such ordinances and have found only one, in East Tennessee, reported in Chapter 4. The difficulty in finding ordinances provides a special case of the issues of written versus oral sources when it comes to sundown towns, so it is appropriate to treat those difficulties here.

Diverse written sources tell of sundown ordinances banning African Americans. In Illinois, written references describe sundown ordinances in East Alton, Fairfield, Granite City, Herrin, and Kenilworth. *The Negroes of Nebraska,* a product of the Nebraska Writers' Project during the Depression, tells that Plattsmouth and other cities in Kansas and Nebraska passed sundown ordinances. Documents also tell of other enactments by local governments. The "Inventory of the County Archives" of Pike County, Ohio, for example, prepared by the WPA in 1942, tells how "the Downing family, original proprietors" of Waverly, the county seat, gave to the county its central square, for a courthouse site, in 1861.

> The Downings caused to be written into the agreement accepting the donation of the public square a provision that if any Negroes ever should be permitted to settle within the corporation limits, the square should be sold and the proceeds revert to the down heirs. Present-day Waverly has no Negro residents. The Downings said that the "correct way to treat a Negro was to kill him."[53]

Despite these sources and many other written and oral reports of ordinances, finding such laws has proven difficult. Many—indeed, perhaps most—towns have lost their records. Consider the case of Kenilworth. That affluent Chicago suburb was the creation of its developer, Joseph Sears; widespread oral and written tradition holds that he made it a sundown town in its founding documents. The town's official history, *Joseph Sears and His Kenilworth,* by Colleen Kilner, hired by the Kenilworth Historical Society for the task, begins by designating Kenilworth "Number One on the Suburban Totem Pole" according to "the press," and it is an understatement to call her account of Kenilworth sympathetic. Kilner uses italics to emphasize the four principles that guided Sears:

> These restrictions were incorporated in the village ordinance:
> 1. *Large lots . . .*
> 2. *High standards of construction . . .*
> 3. *No alleys.*
> 4. Sales to *Caucasians only.*

When I visited the Kenilworth Historical Society in 2002, however, my request for Kenilworth's ordinances or incorporation documents baffled them.

Helpful staff members provided boxes of papers, including scattered minutes of meetings of the board Sears created to govern Kenilworth in its early days, but no ordinances. Surely Kenilworth had ordinances—one prohibiting alleys, for example. It cannot be found either, but Kenilworth has no alleys, just as it has no blacks. Moreover, the local acclaim that met Kilner's 1969 book, and its reprinting without change in 1990, suggest that Kenilworth residents had no quarrel with its statement about the restrictive ordinance because it was accurate. Even some recent towns have lost their records. Rolling Hills Estates, for example, founded probably as a sundown suburb of Los Angeles in 1958, can find no ordinances before 1975, according to a municipal clerk there.[54]

Even when records exist, finding these ordinances proves next to impossible because they never got codified—that is, listed in a book, organized by topic or even by year. Attorney Armand Derfner explains, "A lot of ordinances never got codified. They only put in the things they were going to need all the time."[55] And some small towns have never codified their ordinances at all.[56]

Ordinances Are Real, Written or Not

Some white Americans have told me that without a written ordinance, there is little evidence that a town kept out African Americans. This is absurd. Major league baseball, which kept out African Americans from 1890 to 1947, never had a formal prohibition. In fact, Kenesaw Mountain Landis, commissioner of baseball from 1921 through 1944, stated, "There is no rule, formal or informal . . . against the hiring of Negroes in organized baseball." Nevertheless, everyone knew blacks were not allowed, and when the Pittsburgh Pirates sought to hire Josh Gibson from the Negro Leagues in 1943, Landis wouldn't let them. It is the same with sundown towns. Laws about daily practice are rarely read anyway. When newcomers move to a town, they learn the rules from those already there. If people say that it is illegal to park facing south on the east side of a north-south street, newcomers park "correctly," facing north. Oral tradition is crucial because people live in the oral tradition. They don't go to city hall and look up ordinances.[57]

If the written ordinance cannot now be located, so what? If whites have *not* had the power, legally, to keep African Americans out of town since 1917, so what? Tell that to the three African American families in Saline County, Illinois, whose homes whites dynamited in 1923. To Harvey Clark, whose furnishings were destroyed in the 1951 Cicero riot. To the engineers on the Wabash Railroad, who took care to pull their work trains east beyond the Niantic, Illinois, village limits when a black work crew was on board, because it was "against the law" for African Americans to stay in Niantic overnight. Or to black would-be home buyers in Maroa today, who are not shown houses because a realtor doesn't think she should sell to them, because of an ordinance.[58]

Historian Clayton Cramer grasps this point:

> When I lived in La Crescenta, just north of Glendale [California] in the 1970s, locals told me that Glendale had maintained a "no blacks allowed after sundown" ordinance on the books until the end of World War II. I'm not sure that I believe that an actual ordinance to that effect was still on the books that late. Of course, just because it isn't in writing doesn't mean it doesn't get enforced.[59]

Ordinances are passed orally first, after all, by voice vote of the body passing them. Whether they get written down depends on several factors, including the level of record keeping in the town. Here are two examples of ordinances passed orally in rather recent years. New England towns transact some of their important business by town meeting, and in 1973 the annual meeting of Ashby, Massachusetts, voted 148 to 79 *against* inviting people of color into town. Sure enough, the 1980 census showed Ashby with 2,311 people including no African Americans. New Market, in southwestern Iowa, re-passed its sundown ordinance even later, in the 1980s. African American John Baskerville, now a historian at the University of Northern Iowa, tells the story:

> I played in a band called Westwind, from Tarkio, Missouri, in the northwest corner of the state of Missouri. . . . In the summer of 1984 or 1985, we had a chance to play a street dance in New Market for a guy who owned a car dealership and a restaurant . . . [and] was also a member of the New Market city council. We had been playing for a couple of hours and it was starting to get dark, when during one of our breaks between sets, he came over and said exactly, "Hey, we almost had an incident here. The sheriff reminded me that it was against city ordinance for a 'colored' person to be in town after dark and that we were about to break the law. So, since most of the members of the city council are here [it was the only happening party in town that night], we held a special meeting of the council and voted to suspend the law for the night." I mind you, for the NIGHT! He went on to inform me that to his knowledge, all of those little towns in southwest Iowa (Gravity, Bedford, Villisca, most of Taylor county) all had laws prohibiting African-Americans in town after dark and that if we

were going to continue to play in the area, we'd better check first before booking any gigs in the area.

So New Market's sundown ordinance went right back into effect the following night. Twenty years after the 1964 Civil Rights Act made it illegal for a bar owner to keep African Americans out of his or her tavern, the city officials of New Market thought they had the power to keep them out of an entire town, at least after dark. Apparently they still do, for the 2000 census showed no African Americans in New Market, and none in Gravity, Bedford, or Villisca. Indeed, neither Taylor County nor adjoining Adams County had a single black household.[60]

Errors of Inclusion and Exclusion

In the end, I did my damnedest to find the data. But all the deception and omissions, especially in the written record, make sundown towns hard to research. Therefore I cannot be sure of all the claims made about sundown towns in this book. Some towns I list as sundown may not be. Some may merely have happened to have no African Americans, decade after decade. There is also the question of change. A town may have been sundown for decades but may not be sundown today. Chapter 14, "Sundown Towns Today," describes the relaxation of sundown policies in many towns and suburbs since about 1980. I certainly do not claim that all the towns that I describe as confirmed are all-white on purpose to this day.

When deliberating whether to list a town as sundown based on sometimes scanty information, I tried to minimize errors of inclusion and exclusion. An error of inclusion would be falsely classing a town as sundown when it was not. Such a mistake could upset townspeople who might protest that they are *not* racist and the town never had a sundown policy. Uncorrected, the inaccuracy might also deter black families from moving to the town. I don't mean to cause these problems, and I apologize for any such errors. All readers should check out the history of a given town for themselves, rather than taking my word for its policies. Please give me feedback (jloewen@zoo.uvm.edu) if you learn that I have wrongly listed a town as sundown when it was not; I will make a correction on my web site and if possible in future editions of this book. In practical terms, however, I doubt that any notoriety a town mistakenly receives from its listing in my book will make a significant difference to its future. Moreover, if a town protests that it *is* welcoming, such an objection itself ends the harm by countering the notoriety and increasing the likelihood

that African American families will test its waters and experience that welcome[61]—a happy result.

An error of exclusion would be missing a town that kept out African
Americans. Such a mistake might encourage the town to stay sundown and to
continue to cover up its policy. People of goodwill in the community might
imagine no problem exists, while my erroneous omission would hardly
bother those in the town who want to maintain its sundown character. Such
an error might also mislead a black family to move in without fully understanding the risk. Nationally, such errors might convince readers that sundown towns have been less common than is really the case, thus lessening
readers' motivation to eliminate sundown policies and draining our nation's
reservoir of some of the goodwill needed to effect change.

Some towns I have confirmed as sundown through a single specific written source, often by a forthright local historian, or a single oral statement with
convincing details. For example, the following anecdote, told to me by a
Pinckneyville native then in graduate school, would by itself have convinced
me that Pinckneyville, Illinois, was a sundown town and displayed a sign:

> Pinckneyville was indeed a sundown town. I grew up three miles east of town,
> and I can vividly recall—though my mom and aunts vehemently deny it—seeing
> a sign under the city limits sign, saying "No Coloreds After Dark." I don't know
> when they came down; I'd presume late '60s/early '70s, because I don't recall
> them when I was of junior-high age. However, I am sure they did exist, because
> one of my most vivid memories is of being four or five years old and driving to
> town with my dad. I was becoming a voracious reader, and I read the sign and
> said, "But that's wrong, Daddy. They're 'colors' (our local word for 'Crayolas'),
> not 'coloreds.' " He laughed and laughed at me, finally saying, "No, baby,
> not 'colors,' 'coloreds'—you know, darkies. It's just a nicer way of saying
> 'niggers.' "[62]

In fact, many other sources, written and oral, confirm Pinckneyville. For
other towns the evidence is considerably weaker, not always yielding a definite
yes-or-no answer.[63] I believe my responsibility is to state the most likely conclusion based on the preponderance of the evidence I have, even though often
that conclusion may not be proven beyond the shadow of a doubt. To be too
insistent on solid proof before listing a town as sundown risks an error of exclusion. To list a town as sundown with inadequate evidence risks an error of
inclusion. It is a balancing act.

We have seen that evidence of a town's sundown practices can come from oral history, newspapers of the time, local histories, newspaper articles written today based on some of the above, and various other sources, confirmed with census data. Getting such evidence usually requires on-site research, contact with current or former residents, and/or published secondary sources in a library. For most towns, this research is doable and not too difficult: most on-site inquiries quickly reveal whether an all-white town is intentional. My biggest problem was that I soon discovered that most of the thousands of all-white towns in the North had not always been all-white and probably became all-white on purpose. I therefore had far more towns to check out than I could possibly manage.

How have sundown towns managed to stay so white for so long? Their whiteness was enforced, and the next chapter tells how.

PART IV

Sundown Towns in Operation

9

Enforcement

It was well known any black people arriving in town were not to venture beyond
the block the bus stop or train station were in. My father even remembers a
group of three teenage boys bragging that they had seen the "niggers" from the
bus stop walking down the street and stopped them and told them they were not
allowed to leave the bus stop. Another individual who is slightly older than my
parents and lived in Effingham said the police would patrol the train station and
bus stop to ensure black people did not leave them. She stated that she was unsure whether this was due to prejudice on the part of police, or to protect the
black people from the individuals residing in Effingham.

> —Michelle Tate, summarizing oral history collected
> in and around Effingham, Illinois, fall 2002[1]

A STRIKING CHARACTERISTIC of sundown towns is their durability.
Once a town or suburb defines itself "white," it usually stays white for decades. Yet all-white towns are inherently unstable. Americans are always on
the move, going to new places, and so are African Americans. Remaining
white in census after census is not achieved easily. How is this whiteness maintained?

Residents have used a variety of invisible enforcement mechanisms that
become visible whenever an African American comes to town or "threatens"
to come to town. The *Illinois State Register* stated the basic method of enforcement in 1908 in the aftermath of the Springfield riot: "A Negro is an unwelcome visitor and is soon informed he must not remain in the town."[2] But
there are many variations in how this message has been delivered. We shall
begin with the cruder methods relied upon by independent sundown towns,
then "progress" to the more sophisticated and subtler measures that sundown
suburbs have taken to remain overwhelmingly white—but we must note that
even elite sundown suburbs have resorted to violence on occasion.

The Inadvertent Visitor

From time to time, an African American person or family have found themselves in a sundown town completely by accident. Immediately they were suspect, and usually they were in danger. Sundown towns rarely tolerated African
American visitors who happened within their gates when night fell. Even if
they were there inadvertently—even if they had no knowledge of the town's
tradition beforehand—whites viewed them as having no right to be in "our
town" after dark and often replied with behavior that was truly vile, yet in the
service of "good" as defined by the community.

Hiking from town to town was a common mode of travel before the 1920s
and grew common again during the Great Depression. Walking was the most
exposed form of transit through a sundown town. As we saw previously,
whites in Comanche County, Texas, drove out their African Americans in
1886. Local historian Billy Bob Lightfoot tells of an African American who
made a bet some years later that he could walk across the county, but "was
never seen again after he stopped at a farm near De Leon for a drink of water."
He made less than eight miles before whites killed him.[3]

Walking could be just as dangerous in the Midwest. A 1905 article in the
Fairmont, West Virginia, *Free Press* provides a glimpse of the process by
which residents maintained Syracuse, Ohio, as a sundown community:

> In Syracuse, Ohio, on the Ohio river, a town of about 2,000 inhabitants, no
> Negro is permitted to live, not even to stay overnight under any consideration.
> This is an absolute rule in this year 1905, and has existed for several genera-
> tions. The enforcement of this unwritten law is in the hands of the boys from 8
> to 20 years of age . . .
>
> When a Negro is seen in town during the day he is generally told of these
> traditions . . . and is warned to leave before sundown. If he fails to take heed, he
> is surrounded at about the time darkness begins, and is addressed by the leader
> of the gang in about this language: "No nigger is allowed to stay in this town over
> night. Get out of here now, and get out quick."
>
> He sees from 25 to 30 boys around him talking in subdued voices and wait-
> ing to see whether he obeys. If he hesitates, little stones begin to reach him from
> unseen quarters and soon persuade him to begin his hegira. He is not allowed to
> walk, but is told to "Get on his little dog trot." The command is always effective,
> for it is backed by stones in the ready hands of boys none too friendly.
>
> So long as he keeps up a good gait, the crowd, which follows just at his

heels, and which keeps growing until it sometimes numbers 75 to 100 boys, is good-natured and contents itself with yelling, laughing, and hurling gibes at its victim. But let him stop his "trot" for one moment, from any cause whatever, and the stones immediately take effect as their chief persuader. Thus they follow him to the farthest limits of the town, where they send him on, while they return to the city with triumph and tell their fathers all about the function, how fast the victim ran, how scared he was, how he pleaded and promised that he would go and never return if they would only leave him alone.

Then the fathers tell how they used to do the same thing, and thus the heroes of two wars spend the rest of the evening by the old campfire, recounting their several campaigns.[4]

Anywhere that a black man might be unexpected, walking was hazardous. In Sullivan's Hollow, one of the few sundown communities in Mississippi, white farmers caught an African American on foot early in the twentieth century, tied a bundle of barbed wire to his back, and made him crawl a mile on all fours before letting him leave the Hollow. In Ralls County, Missouri, just south of Hannibal, "even the mere sight of a black man at times could throw Ralls County white women into a panic," writes historian Gregg Andrews. "Ilasco judge John Northcutt bound over John Griggsby, an African American, to a grand jury in July, 1906, after Etta Hays accused Griggsby of attempted criminal assault." All Griggsby had done was to step off a train at Salt River and walk in the direction of her house. "Although she admitted that Griggsby never came within fifty yards of her, the judge still held him for the grand jury." Eventually he was released. Griggsby got off easy: I have other stories of black men being convicted or shot on the spot for the same offense.[5]

After a race riot, African American refugees usually faced particular hostility when they fled on foot to other towns, because the rioting was contagious and traveled ahead of them. Roberta Senechal, whose book on the Springfield, Illinois, riot of 1908 is the standard account, writes:

When a lone Springfield refugee appeared on the streets of the village of Spaulding eight miles from the city, he was greeted by a menacing mob of nearly 100 whites. Deputy sheriffs arrived before any harm was done and saw to it that the man moved on. Black refugees sparked hostility outside of Sangamon County, too. . . . When a small band of Springfield blacks appeared in the village of Greenridge in Macoupin County to beg for food, the residents of the place denied them anything and stoned them out of town.[6]

Public Transportation Through Sundown Towns

After 1940, walking from town to town became uncommon, as most Americans had enough money for public transportation or automobiles. But trains and buses posed hazards too when they stopped in sundown towns, and sometimes merely while passing through. Even Pullman porters, just doing their jobs on trains stopped in stations, were threatened in some towns. According to a leader of the Comanche County Historical Museum, "Whites in De Leon would rope black porters and drag 'em through the streets and put them back on the train, just for meanness." Porters took to hiding in the baggage car during the time the train was in Comanche County. Eventually the Houston & Texas Central Rail Road asked De Leon to move the town's sundown sign from the train station, because white residents were using it as a pretext, so De Leon relocated it to the town well. Immediately after the 1899 riot that expelled all African Americans from Pana, Illinois, a traveler passing through observed, "The men have the Afrophobia so badly that the colored porters on the trains crawl under the seats" when they go through Pana. After whites drove African Americans from Pierce City, Missouri, in 1901, according to a reporter,

> citizens declare no Negro porters will be allowed to run through here in trains, and it is probable the 'Frisco line will have to change porters at Springfield hereafter. Today a shot was fired into a train, and it is supposed to have been aimed at the porter.[7]

William Pickens, writing in 1923, told of harassment in the Ozarks: "When trainloads of colored people recently passed through bound from the east to some great convention in Muskogee, Oklahoma, they had to shut the windows and pull down the shades to avoid the murderous missiles that are sometimes hurled especially at 'a nigger in a Pullman' "—by definition "uppity." In Wheeler County, Texas, in the 1920s, according to Arthur Raper, "as one man put it, Negroes were not even permitted 'to stick their heads out of the train coaches.' "[8]

All kinds of dangers might beset the unwary traveler who actually got off at a sundown town. In 1921, an African American had been working in Ballinger, Texas, and took the train home to Teague, in central Texas. "By mistake he took the wrong train and was put off at Comanche in the middle of the night," according to the *Chicago Defender*.

He entered the waiting room of the railroad station, where he was found asleep the next morning by a local police officer. It soon became known that he was in town—the first one to have been seen here for 35 years. Crowds of townspeople gathered around him and among them were many young men and women who never before had seen a man of our Race. For his own safety the man was taken to the county jail and locked up, pending the arrival of the next outgoing train. He was escorted to the station by an armed guard and placed aboard the train.

In Oneida, Tennessee, in about 1940, the police were not so helpful, according to local historian Esther Sanderson, writing in 1958:

> One Negro hobo got off a freight train in Oneida; police and civilians started toward him and he started running. His bullet-riddled body was brought back out of the woods in about an hour. One young pilot from Scott County in World War II who saw the Negro after he was killed remarked on his return from the War, "You know, as I watched the blood flow from the wounds of the dead and dying Negroes on our transport planes, I thought of that old Negro who was killed in Oneida."[9]

Some sundown towns allowed African Americans traveling by train or bus to wait in the stations but venture no farther, even during the day. So far these examples have antedated World War II, but some towns, including Effingham, Illinois, as noted at the head of the chapter, continued to enforce this practice much more recently. David Blair reported that this rule worked a special hardship on black Greyhound bus drivers in Effingham in the mid-1960s. His father worked in the bus station cafeteria.

> He would sometimes give black bus drivers a two block ride to the Brentwood Hotel. . . . White bus drivers could just walk over to it from the station, but black drivers had to call a cab and then wait longer for the cab to show than the walk would have been. My father would offer to give them a lift since he was white. To my knowledge he was never hassled because of it but the black drivers would ask if he was aware that there could be problems just in giving them a two block lift.

Effingham and a few other towns enforced this policy even during the daytime. Many towns did after dark.[10]

Taxis are another form of public transportation, but until recently, taxi drivers in sundown towns simply refused to pick up black would-be fares.

The same refusals still affect taxi service in many urban all-white neighborhoods today. One exception was Ray Pettit, who ran the Liberty Cab Company in Waverly, a sundown town in southern Ohio, until his death in the
1960s. His granddaughter, Jeanne Blackburn, remembers her mother's stories "about how my grandfather would transport blacks out of the city limits,
should they be in town too late to make it on their own, so they would not be
punished." Of course, his assistance, while kind and even possibly lifesaving,
did not challenge the sundown law but enforced it.[11]

Automobile Travel Through Sundown Towns

The advent of private automobiles made life a little safer for African American
travelers, but not much. Often, bad things have happened to motorists of color
whose vehicles broke down. In Memphis, Missouri, near the Iowa line,
around 1960, according to a librarian who grew up there,

> a black family stopped on the edge of town with car trouble. Some local men
> gathered quickly to "stop the agitators from wrecking the town." Even though
> they found an innocent family instead, they saw fit to "scare them out of town."
> It was a "get your car fixed and go" confrontation. I heard that one of the white
> men even shot a "warning shot" over the car just to make his point clear.

She went on to emphasize that many whites in Memphis, including her family,
"found their behavior to be mean, ridiculous and embarrassing," "especially
considering that the black family members did not seek to stop in Memphis
but were there because their car broke down." But no one stood up for the
black family at the side of the road at the time.[12]

Unlike Missouri, whites in Bonneau, South Carolina, didn't miss when
they used a shotgun to warn African Americans to clear out fast. A black
church group had rented a bus and driver from a white-owned company. As
told in the August 17, 1940, *Pittsburgh Courier*, a national African American
newspaper:

> According to the Rev. Mr. [Robert] Mack, the bus developed motor trouble and
> was driven into a filling station at Bonneau and left by the driver with consent of
> the operator while another bus was being secured from North Charleston.
> Leaving Bonneau at 10 o'clock for the second bus, the driver returned at mid-
> night.

As passengers were transferring to the second bus eight white men drove up and ordered the excursioners to "get out here [*sic*] right quick. We don't allow no d——n n————rs 'round here after sundown." The excursioners, the white driver, and the station operator tried to explain the emergency to no avail. A second car drove up with eight more white men who began firing on the group with shotguns. Having no weapons, the excursioners fled into nearby woods. Many were still missing when the bus left at one Monday morning.

Four church members and the white driver were wounded by the shotgun blasts.[13]

In Owosso, Michigan, an ultimatum from an officer of the law terrified a stranded motorist: local historian Helen Harrelson recalls overhearing him frantically phoning relatives in Flint, 25 miles to the east, and saying, " 'The police have given me half an hour to get out of town.' " But sometimes police intervention in sundown towns, while fearful, ironically resulted in better service. Residents of Pinckneyville, Illinois, and Harrison, Arkansas, tell how police helped to get parts or have a car towed to the nearest interracial town. "The blacks were very grateful," my Harrison informants concluded, for the sundown violation was thus avoided. In Arcola, Illinois, according to a then-resident, service was even better: when a black family's bus broke down there on a Sunday, police got a mechanic to open his garage and fix the problem that day, so they could leave Arcola.[14] And in Martinsville, Indiana, located on the highway between Indiana University and Indianapolis, police until recently would carry African American student hitchhikers to the other side of town, thus preserving the racial purity of the town as well as the welfare of the hitch-hiker.[15]

"Keep moving" was the refrain, no matter why African Americans stopped. Local historian Jean Swaim tells of a shameful incident in Cedar County, Missouri: "Even a busload of black choir members who saved the lives of four El Dorado Springs teenagers by pulling them from a burning car were then turned away." In Mena, Arkansas, African Americans did not even have to stop to get in trouble. Shirley Manning, a high school student there in 1960–61, describes the scene:

> The local boys would threaten with words and knives Negroes who would come through town, and follow them to the outskirts of town shouting "better not let the sun set on your black ass in Mena, Arkansas," and they often "bumped" the car with their bumper from behind. I was along in a car which did this, once, and saw it done more than once.

Moving vehicles were also targeted in Benton, in southern Illinois, in the mid-1980s: white teenagers threw eggs and shouted "nigger" at African Americans who drove through town after dark.[16]

Another way to vex African American motorists was to refuse to sell them fuel. Whites in Slocum, Texas, wouldn't sell gas to African Americans until 1929. In Mt. Olive and Gillespie, Illinois, this policy was in effect at least through the 1950s. According to historian John Keiser, who grew up in Mt. Olive, African American motorists routinely carried an extra ten gallon tank in their trunk when traveling from St. Louis to Chicago "because no one would sell them gas en route." A former resident of Pana, Illinois, reported that filling station attendants in that central Illinois town would not pump gas for African American customers as recently as the 1960s. Back then, stations were not self-serve, so "they had to go on to Vandalia or Kinkaid." To this day, many African Americans still take care to drive through Pana without stopping. Gas stations in Martinsville, Indiana, refused to sell to African American motorists as recently as the early 1990s. As racist as Mississippi was during the civil rights struggle, I lived there for eight years and never heard of a town or even an individual gas station that would not sell gasoline to African Americans. It seems irrational to refuse to sell fuel to a person whom you want out of town, when fuel is precisely what they need to *get* out of town. In the case of Pana, moreover, at least fifteen other nearby towns in all directions were also sundown towns, including Vandalia and probably Kinkaid. If they all similarly refused to sell gas to African Americans, central Illinois would wind up with hundreds of stranded black motorists, hardly the outcome whites intended.[17]

"Driving While Black"

Harassment has not stopped; on the contrary, it has become official. In many communities police follow and stop African Americans and search their cars when they drive in or out, making it hard for African Americans to work, shop, or live there. The practice has been going on for decades. Jim Clayton, who grew up in Johnston City, Illinois, writes, "In the late 1940s, the police often followed any car containing blacks that turned off Route 37 into town. And there were many such cars on that route because it was a main line from the South to Chicago." Route 37 is now Interstate 57, but black motorists who stray are still in trouble: 60 miles north, a recent graduate of Salem High School reports that police officers there say on their radio, "Carload of coal coming down X street," to alert other officers to the presence of African Americans. In Dwight, in northern Illinois on the other interstate highway going to Chicago, police used "NCIC" as shorthand for "New Coon In County," whom they then harassed out of town, according to an ambulance volunteer there in the 1980s. Florida resident Melissa Sue Brewer wrote about a related alphabetical expression used by police in that state, "NBD," meaning "Nigger on the Beach after Dark."[18]

Only a few sundown suburbs resorted to the brazen city-limits signs used by some independent sundown towns. Instead, police often provide the first "defense" against African Americans in sundown suburbs. Police harassment, including racial profiling, can be even scarier than private violence, because one can hardly turn to the police for protection. Sundown suburbs near cities with sizable African American populations are especially likely to rely on their police—and the notoriety in the black community they earn—to stay white. Mary Pat Baumgartner pointed this out about "Hampton," her pseudonym for a New York City suburb: "Since [residents] cannot do away with [arterial] streets altogether, however, they turn to the police to scrutinize those who use them." Residents of sundown suburbs expect and applaud police harassment of outsiders. As Gary Kennedy, state representative from Dallas, wrote, "Blacks, Chicanos, and even poor whites with older automobiles avoid Highland Park for fear of being hassled by the police."[19]

Gregory Dorr, now a professor of history at the University of Alabama, spent the first 22 years of his life in Darien, Connecticut, a sundown suburb of New York City. He reports,

> Darien's Explorer Post 53 is one of the only volunteer adult-student run ambulance corps in the nation. Well, the "Posties" (as we called them) all had belt-worn pagers that could also double as police scanners. They (and those of us with them) often monitored the police, for giggles and grins and to give friends a warning if cops were called to break up a party. Whenever an African American was spotted in town, most frequently walking or hitching along Route 1 or I-95, the cops were called to check them out. They often stopped these folks, questioned them, etc. About the only black folk not harassed were those who were obviously domestics waiting at the few bus stops along Route 1.[20]

Recently such racial profiling has become newsworthy, leading to the term "DWB," "Driving While Black." Lawsuits or public protests have been lodged against the practice in suburbs in Maryland, New Jersey, Illinois, California, and several other states. White Americans sometimes get a sense of the adventure DWB entails when they are passengers in black-driven cars in sundown towns. Consider this account from Vandalia, Illinois, in about 1998:

When I was in high school in the late '90s, a (white) friend from my high school and I were back seat passengers in a car driven by a friend from a neighboring town, who was black. One of his friends, who was also black, sat in the passenger seat. We ended up driving on the town's main road, and the two guys got extremely nervous, claiming that every time they drove through Vandalia, they got pulled over by the police for no good reason. One of them said a police officer pulled him over to simply ask, "What's your business here?" Sure enough, an officer pulled us over and forcefully asked for all of our licenses. He claimed that the driver had taken too long to turn on his headlights, which I didn't think was the case. As soon as the officer saw our licenses, he got a very embarrassed look on his face, said he was sorry to bother us, and left. He spoke directly to my girl friend and me. Our parents were fairly prominent figures in the town, and as soon as the officer saw our last names on our licenses, he felt embarrassed for stopping us for no real reason. Who knows how the scenario would have played out had those two guys not had the two of us with them.[21]

In an ironic sense, the police are not to blame, for in a way, they're only doing good police work! As a Glendale, California, police officer explained to resident Lois Johnson, officers stopped any African American person after dark "because they did not live there." The police never could have stopped white motorists because *they* did not live there—the officers would find that out only *after* they stopped them. In sundown towns African Americans by definition "should not be there," hence are suspicious.[22]

Sometimes these practices die hard. A communications company in Carmel, Indiana, a suburb of Indianapolis that had been all-white until the 1980s, employed a number of African Americans in the mid-1990s. By this point, Carmel had about 250 black residents in a total population of some 30,000. After DWB complaints, including a successful lawsuit against the city's police department, Carmel created special tags for black employees of the company, visible to police officers, to identify those black drivers as acceptable. Thus *they*—unlike all other African American motorists—would be safe from unprovoked stops. Carmel was no longer all-white, but apparently its police had not gotten the message.[23]

Sundown During the Daytime

A few towns, including Effingham; Owosso; Buchanan County, Virginia; Burnside, Kentucky, according to oral history; Pollock, Louisiana; Arab, Alabama; Carterville, Gillespie, and East Alton, Illinois; and in some years Syracuse, Ohio, did not allow African Americans within their city limits even during the day. During World War II, historian Herbert Aptheker saw a sign at the edge of Pollock, "Nigger Stay Out of Pollock." Aptheker characterized Pollock as "somewhat unusual for it forbade black people into the town— period." Michelle Tate, who interviewed residents of several Illinois sundown towns, reports that Gillespie, a city of about 4,000 near St. Louis, had a similar sign at the edge of town into the early 1960s. "Even after the sign was removed, it was still an unwritten rule that black people entering this town would not be tolerated, day or night." The signs at the edge of Buchanan County, in western Virginia, said the usual—"Nigger, Don't Let the Sun Set on You in This County"—as remembered by a white man who grew up nearby, but "blacks were afraid to go to Grundy," the county seat, day or night, according to an African American who grew up not far away in West Virginia in the 1940s. He worked for an upholstery shop in Bluefield, and "when we went to Grundy, I had to get out of the cab and get in the back under a tarp with the furniture until we got to the house." Then he got out and helped deliver the furniture. "Then I had to get back in the back under the tarp until we got back to Tazewell [County], and then I could get back in the cab." [24]

Towns such as Martinsville and Pana that would not let African Americans buy gas thus intimidated them from further shopping, even during the day. In sundown suburbs, black shoppers have long been a concern. In 1956, Dearborn resident George Washabaugh wrote his mayor to complain, "More and more niggers are beginning to shop in our shopping centers, and I wish there was some way we could stop this." In 2005, shopping is still an issue in some majority-white suburbs. Mall managers don't want their shopping centers to get identified as "too black," which can prompt whites to shop elsewhere. Malls have died in response to the presence of young African Americans—even in solidly white middle-class areas—because white shoppers flee black youth. Also, a mall can easily lose its cachet; then cutting-edge retailers move to trendier locations. Suburban city officials also know that shopping malls often desegregate first, leading to white uneasiness that can fuel white residential flight. Today some suburbs do what they can to discourage African Americans from visiting their malls: persuading public transportation agencies not to service the malls with bus routes from black neighborhoods, surveiling African American shoppers and making them uneasy, and having police follow black motorists. [25]

Many towns that might tolerate an occasional African American during the day, shopping or buying gas, drew the line at full-time workers. This was especially true if they had to stay the night, even if it was known to be for a short period of time. A white man named J. J. Wallace invited a black carpenter into Norman, Oklahoma, in 1898 to do construction work. The mayor and other whites beat up Wallace because of it and ran the African American out of town. Wallace sued the government, arguing lack of protection, but the court concluded that neither it nor the state could be expected to do anything about local sentiment—even though the mayor helped lead the attack. Unfortunately, this case set an important precedent that shielded sundown town governments from legal consequences when they failed to stop whites who attacked African American workers and their white employers, according to law professor Al Brophy.[26]

The following clipping shows an example of the kind of terror that African American workers often encountered in sundown towns. It is from Rogers, Arkansas, probably between 1910 and 1920.

> A Bentonville contractor was building one of the first brick business houses here and he brought with him a colored man to carry the mortar hod, figuring that no white man would want to do such heavy, menial labor. A group of young men were gathered in the Blue saloon when the Negro entered, probably looking for his employer. The group seized the Negro and began telling what they were going to do with him. A well had been started at the rear of a business house but after going down some feet, the work was halted and the hole covered with planks.
>
> It was suggested they drop the Negro in the old well after they had hanged him but others objected on the ground that the odor from the ones already planted there was becoming objectional to the neighborhood. As some of the men pulled aside the planks to investigate, the ones holding the trembling Negro loosened their grip on their victim.
>
> It was the chance for escape he had been seeking, and in a matter of seconds he was just a blur on the horizon—and he never did return to Rogers. It was just another of the incidents that gave all colored people good excuses for not stopping here.

The incident was meant to be funny, for had the men been serious, they could easily have apprehended the runaway via auto or horse. Yet the prank was not entirely in jest, for it accomplished the disemployment of the man, surely one of its aims.[27]

An attorney not only is a hired worker but is necessary for court to proceed. Nevertheless, in Platte City, Missouri, north of Kansas City, a black attorney defending two clients "was met at the front door [of the courthouse] by a mob of white men" in December 1921, according to a report in the *Chicago Defender*. "The leader of the mob had a handkerchief bound around his mouth. Pointing an automatic revolver at [W. F.] Miles's head, he ordered him to turn around and leave town. Miles, his life in danger, did as he was bid." The sheriff and a deputy overtook him and brought him back to the court. The attorney then

> explained to the judge that he was being threatened in connection with the defense of the McDaniels and asked the court that note of the matter be made in the court record. The judge upbraided him for making any such charge before the jury. . . . Following this the court admonished Miles to have his clients change their pleas from not guilty to guilty. Miles did so and they were immediately sentenced to three years in the penitentiary. Miles persuaded the sheriff to protect him until he should reach Kansas City.[28]

As the attorney's saga implies, even when African Americans were admitted, their daytime position in many sundown towns could be quite tenuous. In 1923, Benton, Illinois, flirted with barring African Americans during the day. Whites threw a threatening note into the Franklin Hotel, "giving the colored help warning to leave town within a certain length of time," according to the *Benton Republican*. "The darkies left at once, with the result that the hotel was helpless and Mr. Ross was forced to close down his dining rooms Monday." The report went on to note, "Benton has never been very friendly to colored people making their homes here, but have never been partial before as to where they would permit them to work and where they would not be permitted to work." Apparently the movement did not become general, however, and African Americans were able to continue working elsewhere in Benton, so long as they did not stay after dark.[29]

During the Depression, the Civilian Conservation Corps (CCC) set up work camps in various locales to house formerly unemployed young men who worked on projects to better the community, such as sewage systems, state parks, and soil erosion barriers. The projects benefited the community, but sundown towns nevertheless often did not want them if it meant putting up with African American workers. In Richmond, California, just north of Berkeley, whites objected continuously to an interracial CCC camp in 1935; finally the company was replaced with one that was all-white. Yet Richmond was not even all-white, although most of its 270 African Americans in 1940 had to live in North Richmond, an unincorporated area outside the Richmond city limits. In Burbank, a suburb of Los Angeles, the CCC tried to locate an African American company in Griffith Park, but park commissioners refused to let them, citing an "old ordinance of the cities of Burbank and Glendale which prohibited Negroes from remaining inside municipal limits after sun down." Portfolio 18 shows how residents of Mt. Vernon, a sundown town in southwestern Missouri, threatened bloodshed to keep out a proposed black CCC camp.[30]

Wyandotte, Michigan, went a step beyond Mt. Vernon: it would not accept African American workers even during the daytime, commuting from Detroit. In December 1935, 55 Works Progress Administration men were sent to Wyandotte to build new sewers; 40 were African American. According to the *Wyandotte Daily News*:

> F. W. Liddle, director of the work projects in this city, refused to allow the men to go to work on the projects and so informed the director in Detroit. He stated as his reason for refusing to allow the men to work, the feeling in Wyandotte on the part of many against Negroes. . . . All projects were halted in the city for today.

The city's other newspaper, the *Herald,* claimed that Liddle's action "was based more on a desire to protect the colored workers than any racial prejudice. Wyandotte has never been a pleasant place for Negroes. In years gone by, colored people who tried to effect a residence here were either compelled or induced to leave town."[31]

During World War II, the War Department grew concerned because a huge defense contractor in East Alton could not hire African Americans. Truman K. Gibson Jr., aide to the secretary of war, reported:

> East Alton does not allow any Negroes to come into town. They can't ride on the public transportation system. The Mayor has said that if they come in, he will not be responsible for their protection. No Negroes live or work in East Alton. I am not entirely unacquainted with the attitude of many downstate cities toward Negroes.[32]

Even after World War II, many sundown towns and counties continued to exclude black workers. In Grundy County, Tennessee, Dr. Oscar Clements hired four African American bricklayers from Chattanooga. Whites drove them off, saying, "We won't even allow Negroes to come into Grundy County, much less work here." A better outcome occurred in Aurora, Indiana, near Cincinnati on the Ohio River. A contractor brought in four African American workers, whereupon "a crowd attacked them and tried to drive them away," according to historian Emma Lou Thornbrough, "while a citizens' committee warned the employer to get rid of them. This he refused to do, and the Negroes finished the job for which they were employed, but under police protection." Unfortunately, this set no precedent: Aurora displayed a sundown sign as recently as the 1960s, and a student at nearby Northern Kentucky University reported that Aurora was still a sundown town as of November 2002.[33]

Also after World War II, residents of Greenbelt, Maryland, a sundown suburb outside Washington built by the FDR administration during the Depression, shunned African Americans doing daytime janitorial work, denying them even customary salutations. Some residents tried to keep the local store from selling them food for lunch, but the Greenbelt council dismissed the objections. Whites in Neoga, in central Illinois, tried to keep out black workers even later. Michelle Tate interviewed an elderly African American couple in Mattoon, Illinois; the husband had worked on railroad tracks in various towns in central Illinois.

> The woman repeatedly spoke of her fear when he was working in Neoga. The railroad crew traveled places on an old school bus. This is where the men slept at night when they had finished working for the day. He talked of people meeting the bus on the way into [Neoga] and yelling to keep the "niggers" out of their town. He even stated that one time, when they were working in Neoga, a group of white men from Neoga came to Mattoon and broke out all the windows in the bus and tore up the inside, including leaving feces inside.

Thus residents expressed their outrage that blacks would be working in Neoga day or night.[34]

Night Work in Sundown Towns

Night work has long posed special problems for African Americans in sundown towns. A former worker at the Oregon Shakespeare Festival in Ashland wrote, "Most think that Ashland was such a town," and noted that theater almost always involves night work. In the 1950s, the Shakespeare Festival "hired their first black actress, and she had to be escorted as she traveled to and from the theatre for safety." Commonwealth Edison in the sundown town of Pekin, Illinois, was employing African Americans by the mid-1980s, but these workers drew unwanted police attention at least until the mid-1990s, according to an African American in nearby Peoria: "Those who worked the third shift, police would follow you in and follow you out, until they got a sense of where you were going." Similar harassment was visited upon African Americans working the third shift in the huge Ford plant in Dearborn.[35]

Two librarians in Oak Lawn, a sundown suburb southwest of Chicago, told me proudly in 1997, "We had a black woman working here in the library for almost two years, on the front desk, and no one was ever prejudiced to her." But they agreed it was not prudent for her to work the evening shift. Similarly, an African American college student from the Cleveland area said, "My mom worked in Parma, and they never encouraged her to stay late to get overtime. It was always, 'Why don't you come in early. . . . ' They didn't want her in Parma after dark." Door-to-door selling is especially problematic. An African American woman hired to sell vacuum cleaners door-to-door in Mahomet, Illinois, a sundown town just west of Champaign-Urbana, told me, "The company warned me not to be there after dark." Many African Americans would never consider taking jobs requiring them to be outdoors alone in sundown towns, even in daylight.[36]

Economic and Social Ostracism

Ford, the Oak Lawn library, and Commonwealth Edison were demonstrating some boldness merely by hiring African Americans to work in sundown towns. After all, one way to keep out African Americans is to refuse to employ them; independent sundown towns have often followed that route. Nick Khan hired an African American to work at his motel in Paragould, in northeast Arkansas, in 1982. He was warned not to do it but defied the warning.[37] The 2000 census showed 31 African Americans in Paragould, among more than 22,000 people, but white residents I spoke with in 2002 knew of no independent black households.[38] I asked Khan why so few black adults lived in Paragould. "They don't get jobs," was his reply. Himself a Pakistani American, he added, "Nobody would hire *us*. We are only here because we own the property." I told Khan about the remarks of a woman who went to her high school reunion at Paragould High School in 1997 after living out of state for four decades. She saw that the town was still all-white in 1997, as it had been 40 years before, and asked how this could be. "Oh, we have a committee that takes care of that," she was told. "They don't *need* a committee," Khan replied. "If black people come in, they will find that they're not welcome here. No one will hire them."[39]

When employers defy community sentiment and do hire African Americans, they then face a form of secondary boycott. During the summer of 1982, for example, the Shell station in Goshen, Indiana, hired a young black woman, the adopted daughter of a white Goshen couple. Within a month, business dropped off so precipitously that she had to be let go. Even owning the property may not suffice: in the 1970s, a black couple bought a gas station in Breese, a sundown town in southwestern Illinois. "I never heard of anyone harrassing or threatening them, people just didn't buy gas there," explained Stephen Crow, a 1976 graduate of Breese High School. So of course they had to leave. Nick Khan survived in Paragould only because his clientele came from outside the town.[40]

In Medford, a sundown town in southwestern Oregon, whites used another ploy, unwillingness to sell. In 1963, they refused to let an African American family buy groceries, according to former Medford resident Elice Swanson. "They moved out of the valley in about 6 months." Dyanna McCarty told of an incident she saw herself, when she was in seventh grade in Arcola, a central Illinois town of 2,700, in 1978. There had been talk in town that a new family was moving in. "They had two small kids (this news excited me, new babysitting opportunities) and the husband worked in Mattoon," she wrote.

> Later in the week I was in the school office . . . when I saw a black woman at the secretary's desk. She looked angry. I overheard that her children could not get registered for school until all their records got transferred. I also overheard lots of conversation regarding not knowing what happened to the records and blaming the mail service, etc. It didn't dawn on me what was happening until a few days later, after school at my grandfather's shop, which was located across the side alley from the Bi-Rite Grocery store. The same woman I had seen in the office at school pulled up to the Bi-Rite and got out of her car with her two kids. She went to the front door and there was a *closed* sign on it and the doors were locked. She looked around, as I did, because the parking lot was full; people inside looked to be shopping. I met her gaze and in a brief instant, I had an epiphany. The light bulb was so bright, I thought I was blinded. I was so angry. I took her across the alley and she met my grandpa; they talked in hushed tones while I played with the kids. I overheard them talking about where she could get some things, he offered her gas, he had his own above ground tank, and he gave her the names and locations of some Amish friends of his that could supply her with milk, eggs, meat, etc.
>
> They were there one day and a couple of weeks later they were gone. I don't blame them for leaving in the middle of the night. . . . Business slowed at my grandfather's shop for awhile, but it picked back up with time; he was the only auto body shop in [town].[41]

It was a good thing her grandfather's position was secure, because whites who befriended black newcomers often found themselves ostracized, socially and economically. In her remarkable memoir, *The Education of a WASP,* Lois Mark Stalvey tells how her white neighbors in suburban Omaha in the early 1960s broke off friendships with her and ultimately got her husband fired, simply because she tried to help a black couple buy a home in their all-white neighborhood. They moved to Philadelphia.[42]

Many white liberals in sundown towns and suburbs worry about social ostracism, so their anti-racism never gets voiced beyond the confines of home. Here is an example from Cullman, a sundown town in northern Alabama. "The first time I remember seeing a Confederate flag (flying on a car in Birmingham), I asked what it was, and Mother told it was waved by troublemakers who believed in being hateful to colored people," wrote a Cullman native about her childhood.

> During the Civil War centennial celebrations when my friends' parents dressed up and went to balls, my parents informed us that the Southern side had nothing to be proud of. In 1963 Mother insisted that we watch the March on Washington on television and kept saying, "This is history. This is history." . . . At the same time, my parents made it clear that my sister and I were not to repeat their most liberal sentiments to just anyone: "There are some things we just don't talk about outside the home."

Virginia Cowan writes of living with her mother-in-law for three months in Barnsdall, Oklahoma, in 1952:

> On the outskirts of town, I saw a big white sign with black letters that said, "Nigger, don't let the sun set on your black ass in this town." I couldn't believe it. . . . I stayed in Barnsdall three months. I never saw a black, ever. When they were talked about, it was always "those niggers" or "those uppity niggers." I cringed every time I heard that word. If someone I knew used it, I just walked away. Mom had asked me please not to make waves. She had to live there, after I left. So, I kept my mouth shut.[43]

Many residents of sundown towns expressed displeasure with their town's anti-black policies when they talked with me. Their disapproval seemed sincere, but they never mentioned voicing such sentiments to their fellow townspeople. They seem to feel they have performed as citizens if they disapprove privately, especially if they move away. One result is that everyone thinks the silent majority in their town favors continued exclusion, since no one speaks up. Edmund Burke famously said, "The only thing necessary for the triumph of evil is for good men to do nothing." Even today, especially in sundown suburbs, many whites are still afraid of being put down by other whites as "nigger lovers" (though elite suburbanites may not use the term itself), so their anti-racist impulses get immobilized. They do nothing. Their quiescence helps explain why sundown towns and suburbs usually stay all-white for decades.

Harassing Invited Guests

Even invited visitors—musicians, athletic teams, or houseguests of private citizens—have been attacked or threatened in sundown towns. African American musicians have often run afoul of sundown rules, partly because their job usually entails working after dark. When students at the University of Oklahoma invited a black band to play for a dance in 1922, residents of Norman left no doubt that the city's sundown rule applied on campus as well. Here is the account in an African American newspaper:

> A gang of ruffians have disgraced this city again in an attempt to maintain the vicious reputation of the city not to let Negroes stay in the municipality after sundown. For many years Norman has had signs and inscriptions stuck around in prominent places which read: "Nigger, don't let the sun go down on you in this berg." Saturday night, when Singie Smith's Orchestra of Fort Worth, Texas, attempted to play in the dance hall where they were employed by the students of the University, a mob of outlaws stormed the hall and practically wrecked it.
>
> A mob of approximately 500 surrounded the dance hall soon after the dance started and began to throw bricks. They were armed with clubs, guns, and some carried ropes. There was talk of lynching the Negroes, and it was said that several automobile loads of persons went to the city park to prepare for the hanging, telling the rest to bring the "niggers." Sheriff W. H. Newblock quickly gathered in all available deputies and deputized nearly 100 students of the U of Oklahoma, in order to protect the musicians.
>
> The orchestra was taken to the interurban station and sent to Oklahoma City when the mob grew in strength and it became evident that there would soon be trouble. Fights occurred between the mob and students who formed a bodyguard while the Negroes were escorted to the station.
>
> Negroes are occasionally seen on the streets of Norman in the daytime, but

the "rule" that they leave at night is strictly enforced. Several other Oklahoma towns have similar customs.

Several prominent businessmen were seen in the mob here Saturday night.[44]

Henry Louis Gates Jr. tells of an incident in about 1960, similar in a way to the "prank" in Rogers, Arkansas. In Oakland, county seat of Garrett, the county at the western tip of Maryland, whites threatened an African American jazz man, Les Clifford:

> Mr. Les was "up Oakland," a town full of crackers and rednecks, if ever there was one, located on Deep Creek Lake, 25 or so miles from Piedmont. They hated niggers up Oakland. . . . NIGGERS READ AND RUN, Daddy claimed a sign there said. AND IF YOU CAN'T READ, RUN ANYWAY.
>
> Anyway, Mr. Les was up at The Barn, a redneck hangout, flirting with all the white women, gyrating and spinning those sinuous tones, making that saxophone into a snake, a long, shiny, golden snake. A keg of beer apiece for these rednecks and a couple of hours of Les's snake working on their minds and their girlfriends' imaginations was all it had taken. Let's lynch that nigger, someone finally shouted. And so they did—or tried to, at least. Somebody called the state cops, and they busted down the door just about the time they were going to kick the table out from under Mr. Les and leave him dangling from the big central rafter. They would have given his horn back afterward, they said. To his family, they said.

As in Rogers, the men may not really have planned to kill Clifford; Gates's father, Henry Louis Gates Sr., thought "they were just scaring him." But as in Rogers, the incident was not entirely in jest. According to Gates Sr., Clifford had been dating a white woman: "That's what it was all about." The mock hanging was meant to frighten Clifford from the community to stop the relationship.[45]

Even when audiences loved their performances, musicians and athletes faced the problem of where to spend the night. This difficulty repeatedly beset barnstorming black baseball teams and the two famous black basketball teams, the Harlem Globetrotters and the Harlem Magicians, whenever they played in sundown towns. The town baseball team of El Dorado Springs, a sundown town in western Missouri, invited a black Kansas City team to play them, but the guests were then denied food and lodging. One man made an accommodation: Dr. L. T. Dunaway locked the team in his second-floor office "and some citizens took food to them," according to local historian Jean Swaim. African American workers paving U.S. 54 through El Dorado Springs in the 1940s "also had to spend their nights locked in that office." Swaim does not say whether they were locked in to prevent them from being at large in the town after sundown or to preclude violence against them by local white residents for that offense. Robinson is a small city in southeast Illinois whose main claim to fame is the invention of the Heath Bar. Mary Jo Hubbard, who grew up in Robinson in the 1950s and '60s, remembers

> an incident that took place in the early to mid '60s that involved a visiting high school basketball team that was not allowed to stay in the hotel and were put up in the local jail overnight while the basketball tournament was going on. I remember my parents being horrified at the time that children spent the night in the jail . . . but it did happen. That should tell you something about the town.[46]

Even the great contralto Marian Anderson repeatedly had trouble finding a place to sleep. When she sang at Princeton University in 1937, Princeton's only hotel refused her, as noted in the previous chapter, so Albert Einstein invited her to stay with him; "the two remained friends for life," according to a 2002 exhibit on Einstein at the American Museum of Natural History. In February 1958, Anderson had the same problem in Goshen, Indiana, when she sang at Goshen College, and had to stay the night in Elkhart, ten miles away, because the Goshen Hotel would not allow a black person to stay there. When Anderson sang in Appleton, Wisconsin, she had to sleep in Neenah or Menasha.[47] Actually, hotels in sundown towns like Goshen and Appleton did not differ from hotels in non-sundown towns like Princeton; between 1890 and about 1960, *most* hotels in America would not let African Americans stay the night.[48] But sundown towns posed additional complications. They had, of course, no African American hotels or other facilities. Hence *no* hotel would have housed Marian Anderson or any other African American. And because there were no African American residents, no black private homes existed to house stranded travelers in an emergency. Finally, Goshen and Appleton would not *allow* an African American to spend the night. That is the difference between Princeton and Goshen: Goshen was a sundown town, while Princeton was not. Hence no Einstein stepped forward in Goshen or Appleton. A professor who might volunteer to host Anderson in Goshen would endanger the singer as well as his or her own family.[49]

Scottsdale, Arizona, illustrated the difference in 1959. Twelve years after Jackie Robinson integrated the major leagues, the Boston Red Sox recruited their first African American player (they were the last team to do so). When Pumpsie Green joined the team for spring training camp in Scottsdale that spring, he was not housed in the hotel with the rest of the team, nor anywhere else in Scottsdale. The Red Sox claimed all the hotels were full with tourists, so there was no room for one more player, who just happened to be Green! The real reason was Scottsdale: "Blacks could not live there after dark, and so he was sent seventeen miles away to live in Phoenix," according to Howard Bryant, author of *Shut Out: A Story of Race and Baseball in Boston*.[50]

When residents of sundown towns did step forward to house African American visitors, they often found the experience unnerving. In 1969, a choir from Southern Baptist College performed in Harrison, Arkansas. "It had a black member," according to the wife of a couple I spoke with in Harrison in 2002. "We put her up, but we worried lest our house get blown up." Grey Gundaker, who now teaches American studies at William and Mary, went to junior high school in Manitowoc, Wisconsin, a sundown town on Lake Michigan, between 1962 and 1964. He remembers one occasion when the policy was violated at a stable where he worked after school. "When an African American man who drove a horse van came through town and needed a place to stay, the owner of the stable, Larry Bowlin, put him up. . . . Larry told us kids not to tell, that it would be very dangerous for his friend if he were caught." Left unsaid: it would also be dangerous for Bowlin and his family.[51]

White residents tried to avoid triggering a town's sundown sensibility. In 1982, a young woman was planning her wedding in Pinckneyville, Illinois, where she had grown up, a sundown town 60 miles southeast of St. Louis. "I asked a dear college friend, who was also a long-time friend of my husband's, to be an usher. When going over lists with my mother, she said, 'Who's this Roy?'" The bride-to-be reminded her mother of a photo of her and Roy, who was African American. "She turned six shades of white and said, 'You don't actually think he'll come, do you?' I dug in my heels and swore that if he wasn't welcomed, I'd elope. . . . I did give in somewhat, though: I agreed to move my 6:30 wedding to 6:00 PM so there'd be plenty of daylight while he was in town."[52]

Occasional acts of violence greeted visitors and hosts in these situations, showing that Bowlin's fear and the bride's rescheduling were justified. In September 1946, for example, a white army officer allowed a black army officer to stay overnight in his home in West Lawn in southwest Chicago, according to reporter Steve Bogira. "The two had served together in the war, and the black officer was visiting from out of town. Word got out in the neighborhood, and soon a mob was stoning the home, smashing windows, and yelling, 'Lynch the nigger lover.' " Chicago was not a sundown town, of course, but West Lawn was a sundown neighborhood.[53]

The Importance of the City Limits

Carnival, circus, and railroad workers—who carry their accommodations with them—make plain the difference between sundown towns and towns with no sundown policy but whose hotels were white-only. Sundown towns told black people not to spend the night even when no hotel was involved. Little towns such as Niantic and Villa Grove in central Illinois forced African American railroad workers to move their work cars beyond the town limits at night. A retired miner who has lived his entire life in Zeigler, in southern Illinois, said in 2002, "Nigra [*sic*] employees would be working with the carnivals, and they had to leave [Zeigler] by sundown." Having spent time in Zeigler, I suspect they didn't leave, because all the surrounding towns are also sundown towns that would have been no better. Probably they simply hid in their carnival vehicles for the night, but they probably moved them beyond the city limits.[54]

To be sure, some rural areas have also been closed to African Americans. In his 1908 classic *Following the Color Line,* Ray Stannard Baker wrote, "A farmer who lives within a few miles north of Indianapolis told me of a meeting held only a short time ago by 35 farmers in his neighborhood, in which an agreement was passed to hire no Negroes, nor to permit Negroes to live anywhere in the region." Later in this chapter we will learn of the lynching of a white farm owner near Lamb, Illinois, who would not dismiss his black farm employee. Much less violent measures were employed at least as recently as 2001 to ensure that rural land is not sold to an African American.[55]

More often, the rules have been looser beyond the city limits. In 1925 in Price, Utah, for example, a white mob twice overpowered the sheriff and hanged Robert Marshall, an African American accused of murdering a white deputy, Marshall being not quite dead after the first hanging. In the aftermath, Price became a sundown town. Four years later, another African American, Howard Browne Sr., was able to settle with his family outside Price, but Price itself, in Browne's words, "was off-limits to blacks." In the 1940s and '50s in Colorado, migrant Mexican beet-field workers were housed in adobe colonies or "colonias" outside of towns, according to a survey of Colorado race relations by the University of Colorado Latino/a Research and Policy Center. After the season, when the colonias closed, some had to winter in Denver slums, unable to live inside the city limits of the towns where they had worked.[56]

For a while in the 1930s, an African American man was allowed to live at the Perry County Fairgrounds at the edge of Pinckneyville, taking care of the horses. Greenup, Illinois, in Cumberland County, some 40 miles west of Terre Haute, Indiana, had a similar policy. Indeed, a longtime resident said that the Cumberland County Fairgrounds was deliberately left out of Greenup's incorporated boundaries because African Americans sometimes stayed there. That way African Americans going to the fair, caring for livestock, or working for the ride operators could stay at the fairgrounds without violating the town's sundown ordinance. An exception was likewise made for two men at the Clark County Fairgrounds in Martinsville, fifteen miles east, in the 1950s. As a former resident wrote, "The rule was, 'Better not catch 'em here after dark—oh, except for Russell and Rabbit.' " Martinsville was nicer than the Chicago suburb Arlington, according to labor historian Mel Dubofsky: "As I recall, Arlington, Illinois was one of your 'sundown towns' into the 1960s. Blacks could work at the track but they could not appear on city streets after dark nor sleep anywhere but at the stables."[57]

In about 1952, the high school band director at LaSalle-Peru was coordinating the visit of the university band of a Big Ten school, probably the University of Michigan. As Chapter 1 told, LaSalle and Peru are adjoining sundown towns on the Illinois River in northern Illinois. To save costs, he planned to have his band members house the visiting university students. Then he got advance publicity for their concert, including a photograph of the band, and realized several of its members were African American. What to do? According to my source, a student at the time, "he feared being in violation of the unwritten but well-acknowledged sundown rule." His prudent solution: he went to a band member who lived outside LaSalle-Peru but in the school district, and asked him to host the African American band members. "This worked out all right, and I don't recall any fracas or community uprising."[58]

Perhaps the most remarkable example of the power of the city line—and yet it was subtle, even invisible until pointed out—was at Elizabethtown College in Pennsylvania in the late 1940s, probably continuing into the '50s. According to a 1950 graduate of the college, to house returning servicemen after World War II, Elizabethtown College put up a barracks-like "dormitory." One end of the long building extended across the city line, so to abide by Elizabethtown's sundown rule, the college required its black students to live in that end of the barracks. The students then crossed over into Elizabethtown within their own dormitory and exited on campus to attend class. In 1948 or 1949, a black gospel quartet performed at the college and had to be put up for the night. As in LaSalle-Peru, a farmer outside the town provided the hospitality.[59]

In sundown counties, the county line plays the role of the city limits. Often, especially in the Cumberlands and Appalachia, it boasted the usual sundown signs. A 1906 report in the *Charlotte Observer* tells what happened when a telephone trunk line was put through Madison County, a sundown county[60] in western North Carolina:

> Negroes were employed on the works and the company building the line was put in some inconvenience by the citizens of Madison refusing to allow the Negroes to stay in the county over night. The Negro laborers were forced to go beyond the Madison county line to spend their nights.[61]

The power of the city limits can be seen still more graphically in suburbia. Often the jurisdictional line between city and suburb is not even visible on the landscape, yet these lines frequently result in an all-white suburb on one side, a majority-black neighborhood just across the street. (Portfolio 30 shows one such line in Maryland.) Driving along Eight Mile Road—the boundary between overwhelming black Detroit and sundown suburb Warren—shows visually that social class is not responsible for suburban segregation, because the houses look the same on both sides.

Something artificial and additional, obviously tied to the invisible line between city and suburb, has kept African Americans on one side in Detroit, whites on the other in Warren. When town boundaries also form racial divides, that shows the extent to which public policies have maintained all-white suburbs.[62]

Zoning

Suburban incorporation gave suburbs power over zoning, which in turn conferred "unprecedented power to control development," according to historian David Freund, which then played a key role in keeping suburbs white. Originally meant to keep out disamenities such as polluting industries, zoning became a tool to keep out the "wrong kind of people." After such decisions as

Lee Sing and *Buchanan v. Warley* (described in Chapter 4) made it more dif-
ficult to exclude blacks openly, suburban town governments soon saw that
"regular" zoning might accomplish the same result, at least on a class basis.
Beginning as early as 1900 and continuing "for many years," sociologist Gary
Orfield notes, "suburban governments used their zoning authority to exclude
African Americans." It was no accident that Edina became the first town in
Minnesota to set in place a comprehensive zoning ordinance, Edina being
the premier sundown suburb of Minneapolis–St. Paul. Cities like Edina
banned mobile homes, public housing, subsidized housing, housing for the
elderly, and apartments—and thus the kind of people who would live in such
housing.[63]

In the New York metropolitan area in the mid-1970s, more than 99% of
all undeveloped land zoned for residential use was restricted to single-family
housing. The next step was to impose minimum acreage requirements for
single-family homes. During the 1960s, more than 150 New Jersey suburbs
increased their minimum lot sizes. In Connecticut, in 1978, more than 70% of
all residentially zoned land carried a one-acre minimum lot size. Greenwich,
an upper-class suburb of New York City, had a four-acre minimum. Much of
St. Louis County surrounding St. Louis has a three-acre minimum. Given the
cost of land in metropolitan areas, such large-lot zoning keeps out inexpensive
homes and the people who might buy them. To make doubly sure, elite suburbs require new houses to be larger than a certain number of square feet or
cost more than a certain amount. These economic measures could not keep
out affluent African Americans, but the reputation they fostered for community elitism did.[64]

Incorporation also let local officials decide if their communities would
participate in subsidized or public housing. "Most suburbs never created
local housing authorities," according to Michael Danielson, so they never
got public housing. Some highly populated suburban counties did create
public housing authorities but neglected to build any, he further points out.
"DuPage County Housing Authority [just west of Chicago] was established
in 1942, but had yet to construct a single unit 30 years later." St. Louis
County, which surrounds St. Louis on three sides, had 50 units of public
housing in 1970 for a population of 956,000, while St. Louis city had
10,000 units for a population of 622,000. Even suburbs that *do* accept public housing often limit it to the elderly or require prior residence in the suburb for at least a year.[65]

Race, not the market, usually underlies suburban vetoes of public housing and subsidized housing. After a developer tried to build subsidized housing in Parma, a sundown suburb of Cleveland, voters in 1971 overwhelmingly endorsed a proposal requiring public approval for any subsidized housing project. Other Cleveland suburbs followed suit. "Racial fears were prominent in the controversy," Danielson reports. In 1970, Parma had just 50 African Americans in a total population of 100,216, and "one official announced that he did 'not want Negroes in the City of Parma.' " From coast to coast, sundown suburbs of all social classes have voted down public housing. And not just public housing—any housing that African Americans might likely inhabit. After Ford opened a huge assembly plant in Mahwah, New Jersey, for example, the town refused to let the United Auto Workers build subsidized housing there, so thousands of workers, many of them African American, had to commute every day from Newark.[66]

Farley and Frey explain how sundown suburbs have used their independent "zoning laws, school system, and police" to maintain racial purity:

> Zoning ordinances were changed and variances granted or denied to prevent construction that might be open to blacks. Public schools hired white teachers, administrators, and coaches. As a result, in most Midwestern and Eastern metropolitan areas, white families who wished to leave a racially changing city could choose from a variety of suburbs knowing their neighbors would be white and that their children would attend segregated schools.

Circularities get built in. Some working-class or multiclass sundown suburbs have passed ordinances requiring teachers, firefighters, police officers, and other city workers to live within their corporate limits. Thus they can be assured that all their employees will be white. Their schools, police departments, and other offices then present all-white facades to any black would-be newcomers. In turn, African Americans are ineligible to be hired for future openings, since they would first have to move in to be considered. This is subtler than an open prohibition: race does not get used as a criterion for hiring or for residence, yet the suburb stays white.[67]

When all else fails and a black family actually manages to acquire a house in a sundown community, incorporation confers the right to take it for the "public good." No matter if the black family doesn't want to sell, even for an above-market price. For many decades, independent towns and sundown suburbs alike have used this power of eminent domain to force the sale, condemning the land for a public purpose such as a park or school playground.

For instance, in Deerfield, a sundown suburb fifteen miles northwest of Chicago, the Progress Development Corporation bought two tracts of land in 1959 and planned to build integrated housing. An Episcopal minister told his congregation about it, which, according to Ian McMahan, "was as if a bomb had exploded in the quiet town of Deerfield." First the city invented trivial building violations to stop the work. Then an organization called the North Shore Residents' Association polled Deerfield residents and found they were eight to one against letting blacks in. Finally, Deerfield decided to keep out the development by designating the tracts as parks; that proposal passed in a referendum in late 1959 but "only" by a two-to-one margin, with an astonishing 95% of all eligible voters casting ballots. Progress Development took Deerfield to court, accusing the city of coming up with the parks as subterfuges to stay all-white, but McMahan says Deerfield prevailed, at least as of 1962, and he must be right, because 40 years later, of 18,420 residents, only 61 were African American.[68]

Defended Neighborhoods

Officials of sundown suburbs also have subtler weapons at their disposal in their fight to keep their communities white. Their jobs have two main components—providing public services and keeping out undesirables—according to research in the 1960s summarized by Danielson. Sometimes the two conflict, and when they do, "residents of upper- and middle-class suburbs in the Philadelphia area ranked maintenance of their community's social characteristics—defined in terms of keeping out 'undesirables' and maintaining the 'quality' of residents—as a more important objective for local government than . . . the provision of public services." At the "behest" of the wealthy, as Rosalyn Baxandall and Elizabeth Ewen put it in their study of suburban Long Island, "officials in Nassau County allowed all public roads to fall into disrepair. Moreover, private estate roads were built like mazes—winding and deliberately confusing. Most of the North and South Shore beaches were marked CLOSED with large private property signs, and were guarded as well." Baumgartner found that residents of "Hampton," her pseudonym for a New York City suburb, "would rather bear the inconvenience of narrow and congested streets on a day-by-day basis than make it easier for the inhabitants of New York City to reach the town." Even street signs are in short supply in Darien, Connecticut, making it hard to find one's way around that elite sundown suburb. Darien doesn't really *want* a lot of visitors, a resident pointed out, and keeping Darien confusing for strangers might deter criminals—perhaps a veiled reference to African Americans. Some Darien residential streets are even posted "Private."[69]

Many sundown suburbs thus exemplify what urban sociologists call "defended neighborhoods." Sidewalks and bike paths are rare and do not connect to those in other communities inhabited by residents of lower social and racial status. Some white suburbs of San Francisco opted out of the Bay Area Rapid Transit system, fearing it might encourage African Americans to move in. Some white suburbs and neighborhoods in and around Washington, D.C., similarly showed no interest in that area's Metro rapid transit. Many sundown suburbs choose not to provide other public amenities that might draw outsiders. If by accident of geography or history they already have such facilities, they usually make access difficult for outsiders. Thus suburbs may admit only residents to beaches. Parks, tennis courts, and playgrounds may be few or located on minor roads where visitors will be unlikely to find them. Rather than set aside large areas for parks, private lawns take on a park-like appearance. Some of these towns come to exemplify what economist John Kenneth Galbraith famously called "public squalor and private affluence." According to Frederique Krupa, writing in 1993, San Marino, an elite suburb of Los Angeles, "closes its parks on weekends to make sure the neighboring Asian and Latin communities are excluded," thus keeping out everyone, even its own residents.[70]

Policies and Ordinances

For years, the public policies and restrictions of suburbs have carried a purposeful racial tinge and have been selectively enforced. Their racial aspect was evident to Bob Johnson and his family in southern California in 1960:

> We lived in Sunland near Glendale. We took the kids to the Verdugo Plunge [swimming pool] in Glendale. There was a sign that said only for residents of Glendale. We are white and did not want to go back home, so we paid our money and they did not ask for our drivers license or identification. I was puzzled how they monitored whether or not I was from Glendale. Then I realized that was a way to keep blacks out since no blacks lived in Glendale.

A Detroit suburbanite had a similar experience in the Dearborn area in about 1985: "Dearborn passed a city ordinance that only city residents could use its parks—*i.e.* whites only. I visited my aunt and uncle who lived there and was never asked for any ID to prove I was a resident, but the local papers had several stories about African Americans who were asked for ID and then re-moved from the parks."[71]

White suburbs still pass all sorts of ordinances to discourage nonwhite visitors and residents. Highland Park, Texas, has been a leader in criminaliz-ing ordinary behavior. It may have more "No" signs per capita than any other city in the nation. The Dallas suburb brags about being a city of parks, but it does not want outsiders to use them. Lakeside Park is its largest park and con-tinues into Dallas; Highland Park has made it illegal to eat lunch in its portion of Lakeside. Too much litter, said city officials, but the *Dallas Morning News* suspected that an aversion to the possibility of African American picnickers underlay the ordinance. Highland Park also prohibits swimming, wading, climbing trees, drinking alcohol, sleeping, "protractedly lounging," and sit-ting on railings or "any other property in a park which . . . is not designated or customarily used for such purposes." Outsiders cannot play tennis; reser-vations are for residents only, and it is illegal to play without one.[72] In 1982, the suburb made headlines for ticketing thirteen joggers, ten of whom were nonresidents, for jogging on city streets; this offense cost a $15 fine or a night in jail. It made fishing without a city permit against the law and charged $5 per year for a fishing permit. Highland Park police have also repeatedly arrested African Americans and Mexican Americans for being "drunk in car." The latter is "a non-existent crime," according to reporter Jane Wolfe. The fishing permit is legal nonsense too, because a Texas fishing license, "which costs $4.50 a year for state residents, entitles the holder to fish free of charge in any body of public water in Texas," as reporter Doug Swanson noted. "And the creeks and lakes of Highland Park, [game warden Billy] Walker said, are public."[73]

Every department of sundown suburbs has been used to enforce these policies and to maintain their communities' desired reputation of being un-friendly to minorities. Police in Cicero, Illinois, told African American would-be residents they could not move their own furniture into Cicero without a permit. The school system played its part too. In 1981, when Christopher Phillips began as a new teacher in the Cicero Public Schools, his introduction to the community came at the district's faculty assembly as the fall semester began. "The superintendent stood at the podium before all the district's teachers and the first words he spoke were, 'There are no blacks in the Cicero Public Schools, and there will be none as long as I am superintendent.' He re-ceived wild applause."[74]

Dearborn's longtime mayor Orville Hubbard used the city's police and fire departments and even its sanitation department to harass black newcomers until they fled the city. African Americans who tried to move in found their gas turned off and their garbage uncollected, by city policy. According to David Good, Hubbard's biographer, Hubbard told a reporter that "as far as he was concerned, it was against the law for Negroes to live in his suburb." In 1956, Hubbard said to an Alabama journalist, "They can't get in here. We watch it. Every time we hear of a Negro moving in—for instance, we had one last year—we respond quicker than you do to a fire." Good tells that Dearborn police officers and firefighters made wake-up visits to the new black family's house every hour or so through the night in response to alleged trouble calls. Recall sociologist Karl Taeuber's finding that whites in the Detroit metropolitan area in 1970 were five times more likely than African Americans, even controlling for differences in income, to live in the suburbs. Certainly these actions by Dearborn's city government help to explain why.[75]

Dearborn was an extraordinary case because its mayor was so outspoken, but Good cautions us not to see Hubbard as unique: "In a sense, Orville Hubbard's view was no different from that in any of a dozen or more other segregated suburbs that ringed the city of Detroit—or in hundreds of other such communities scattered across the country."[76]

Restrictive Covenants

The U.S. Supreme Court found openly anti-black ordinances unconstitutional in 1917 in *Buchanan v. Warley,* but sundown towns and suburbs nevertheless acted as if they had the power to be formally all-white until at least 1960; informally some communities have never given up this idea. The federal government was hardly likely to enforce *Buchanan v. Warley* until after World War II; on the contrary, it was busily creating all-white suburbs itself until then. After 1917, most sundown suburbs resorted to restrictive covenants. Covenants were usually private, part of the deed one signed when buying from the developer. Like the Great Retreat, restrictive covenants first targeted Chinese Americans in the West, originating in California in the 1890s, and then spread to the East, where Jews and blacks were targeted for exclusion. The United States Supreme Court unanimously declined to interfere with restrictive covenants in *Corrigan v. Buckley,* a 1926 case originating in Washington, D.C. The Court reasoned that restrictive covenants were agreements between private citizens, hence were OK, whereas ordinances were passed by governments.[77]

Covenants weren't really private, though, because many suburban governments would not approve new developments without them. Nor would the Federal Housing Administration (FHA) insure loans without them. Many communities proceeded to encumber every square inch of their residential land with restrictive covenants, agreement to which became part of the purchase of the property. Thus covenants worked just as well as ordinances to make entire towns all-white. This practice was particularly common in California. In February 1929, for example, the Palos Verdes Homes Association in Palos Verdes Estates, California, published a booklet, "Palos Verdes Protective Restrictions," including this language: "No person not of the white race (except servants and students) shall use or occupy any part of the property." That phrasing was unusual; almost never were students exempt from the restriction. Here is a more typical covenant, from a suburb in Montgomery County, Maryland, built shortly after World War II:

> No persons of any race other than the Caucasian race shall use or occupy any lot or any building, except that this covenant shall not prevent occupancy by a domestic servant of a different race domiciled with an owner or a tenant.[78]

Across the United States, suburbs and white residential districts in cities now hastened to adopt restrictive covenants. According to sociologist Douglas Massey, the Chicago Real Estate Board started using them in 1919. By 1940, more than 80% of the Chicago area was covered by covenants, according to the NAACP. Actually, the proportion of the Chicago suburbs that were covered by covenants was much higher than 80%, because the remaining 20% included those neighborhoods in the city where African Americans already lived. Across the United States, exclusionary covenants were the rule rather than the exception.[79]

In 1948, in *Shelley v. Kraemer,* the U.S. Supreme Court ruled that no court could *enforce* a racial covenant. Although it didn't make voluntary covenants illegal, *Shelley v. Kraemer* nevertheless began to make a difference. In the late 1940s, civic leaders and realtors in South Pasadena, California, tried to blanket the entire city with restrictive covenants. "When pressed about the status of African Americans, Mexican Americans, and Asian Americans," historian Charlotte Brooks writes, "they announced that such people could work in the town, as long as they left by dusk." According to Brooks, "The covenant campaign eventually failed, due to the publicity it received and the *Shelley v. Kraemer* decision." *Shelley v. Kraemer* implied for the first time (since the neglected 1917 decision) that there might be something wrong or illegal about racial exclusion.[80]

Real Estate Agents as the Front Line of Defense

After the Supreme Court emasculated racial covenants, realtors became the front line of defense, keeping suburbs white. According to James Hecht, realtors had conceived of restrictive covenants and popularized them in the first place. After 1948, despite *Shelley v. Kraemer,* realtors could still simply say with impunity, "We don't sell to blacks." Indeed, in 1948 the Washington, D.C., Real Estate Board Code of Ethics adopted the following statement: "No property in a white section should ever be sold, rented, advertised, or offered to colored people." In St. Louis in that year, realtors zoned the entire metropolitan area into "white" and "black" neighborhoods and forbade any realtor "under pain of expulsion to sell property in the white zone to a Negro," as one realtor explained to Dorothy Newman. Even as late as 1957, a teaching manual for Realtors put out by the National Association of Real Estate Boards counseled against introducing "undesirable influences" into a block. Included among these undesirable influences were bootleggers, gangsters, or "a colored man of means who was giving his children a college education and thought they were entitled to live among whites."[81]

These real estate practices had a long history. In 1913, the National Association of Real Estate Boards (now the National Association of Realtors) instructed its members, according to urban historian Stephen Meyer, "not to contribute to residential race mixing." In 1924, the same year that the United States passed the Immigration Restriction Act, Realtors added to their Code of Ethics Article 34, which stated:

> A Realtor should never be instrumental in introducing into a neighborhood a character of property or occupancy, members of any race or nationality, or any individuals whose presence will clearly be detrimental to property values in that neighborhood.

That African Americans (and sometimes Jews) had this effect was an article of faith. "Through this code," Hecht writes, "America's Realtors became committed to segregated neighborhoods.[82] Even when a homeowner was willing to sell to a Negro, the Realtor was prohibited from being a party to such a transaction."[83]

Usually realtors were surprisingly open about refusing to sell to blacks (see Portfolio 28.) In 1944 in Salt Lake City, Utah, for example, Carlos Kimball chaired a "Non-White Housing Control Committee." According to an article in the *Pittsburgh Courier,* he got "most Salt Lake real estate dealers" to

sign pledges "to restrict non-whites from white communities." Kimball
pointed out that these pledges were "in accordance with the National Association of Real Estate Boards' code of ethics which forbids the sale of property
to anyone who might 'lower community standards.' " Kimball then sent a circular about the policy to "Negro leaders" in the Salt Lake City area.[84]

For two decades after *Shelley v. Kraemer,* African Americans routinely encountered open race-based exclusion and could do nothing about it. Most
whites thought it was proper to exclude blacks, and exclusion was legal. Consequently African Americans had no available remedy. Consider this complaint, sent to the Connecticut Civil Rights Commission in 1955:

> A building firm has been advertising houses for quite some time with a mini-
> mum down payment for veterans. Today, my wife and I went out to see about the
> purchase of one of these houses. When we talked to the man the first thing he
> told us was that an agreement had been made that they would sell only to white
> people. . . . I have tried for months to find some kind of improved living condi-
> tions. I have answered hundreds of ads for apartments but the moment they find
> I am a Negro, the answers given are "Filled," "The neighbors object," or some-
> one else might.

The commission's files reveal its totally ineffective response:

> A representative called at the construction company named in this letter. They
> were building 208 homes. A partner in the business said their only interest was
> in selling the homes as fast as they could be constructed. He felt that if it were
> known that a Negro family had purchased a house it might be more difficult to
> sell to white purchasers.

The commission could do nothing because "the development has received
no subsidy from any public agency and consequently does not come within
the purview of the Public Accommodations Act. The complainant was advised to this effect." Thus seven years after the Supreme Court ruled restrictive covenants unenforceable, this couple had no recourse for housing
segregation even in "liberal" Connecticut.[85]

Since real estate agents depend on other agents to find buyers for their
listings, keeping realtors in line usually proved easy. In 1961 the Greenwich,
Connecticut, Real Estate Board criticized one of its members, Olive Braden,
for selling to Jews. So she sent a memo to her staff: "From this date on, when
anyone telephones us in answer to an ad in any newspaper and their name is,

or appears to be Jewish, do not meet them anywhere!" In a suburb of Houston, according to Benjamin Epstein and Arnold Foster, "a builder and a real estate agent who joined in selling a home to a Jewish family were punished severely. The builder was not permitted to build any more homes in that village; the agent was refused property listings in the area." [86]

Sometimes real estate agents in sundown towns have screened out the "wrong kind" of Gentile *whites.* An interesting incident in Martinsville, Indiana, in about 1995, shows an agent unhappy with her would-be clients. Jonathan Welch had a new job in Franklin; his wife, Amy, worked in Greencastle. Martinsville lies in between, so they shopped there for a home. In Amy Welch's words:

> We spent an evening driving around the village, which seemed very nice, and found a beautiful house that we decided to call on. I made arrangements with the real-estate lady to view the house; Jon unfortunately couldn't come with. The house seemed nice, as was the agent. . . . When the tour was complete, she told me I was more than welcome to call her with any questions or concerns and gave me her business card. When I took out my wallet to put away her card, my picture fold fell out onto the bar and opened up to a portrait of some very good friends—good friends who happen to be engaged and Japanese and African American. She looked at the photo, put her finger on the very corner of the picture and turned it slowly toward her, like it could jump up and bite her if she made any sudden movements! Anyway, she said to me: "Oh, you associate with those kind of people?" . . . I turned her business card around to her in the same manner and said, "Yup." And left.

Obviously, the realtor felt that for Martinsville to stay all-white required not only keeping out blacks, but also vigilance as to the type of whites one allows in. [87]

Other Elements of the "System"

Realtors were only part of the system that kept African Americans out of sundown suburbs. Bankers played key roles. In the mid-1950s, the Detroit Urban League reported conversations with various bankers. One said he would loan to blacks regardless of where they bought, but another wouldn't deal with African Americans, period. A third "would not make the first Negro loan in a white area." Another banker tried "to substantiate this position by contending that it is not good common sense to make one friend and alienate eighteen friends, even though the one is a sound credit risk." The FHA sided with the majority. In most cities, no banker like the first even existed.

FHA approval is often required for a bank loan, and Chapter 5 explained how racist were its national policies. In Detroit, according to Thomas Sugrue, author of *Origins of the Urban Crisis,* federal appraisors working for the Home Owners Loan Corporation, predecessor to the FHA, gave a D to "every Detroit neighborhood with even a tiny African American population" and colored it red on their maps. The FHA inherited these maps and the tradition of redlining, nationally as well as in Detroit. Should a potential buyer somehow surmount the credit hurdle, every subsequent step of the homebuying process requires cooperation with someone—invariably someone white in a sundown suburb. The home has to be inspected or appraised, a title search must be completed and the title insured, and so forth. Each of these steps proved difficult or impossible for black would-be homebuyers.[88]

The Grosse Pointe System

Realtors in Grosse Pointe, Michigan, also screened whites, but in a cruder manner. They developed a "point system" (no pun intended) for keeping out undesirables. When the system became public knowledge in 1960, a furor of publicity erupted, including stories in the *New York Times* and *Time* magazine. Don and Mary Hunt, author of several guides to Michigan, supply a useful summary:

> For years into the 1950s, prospective Grosse Pointe home buyers were excluded by the Grosse Pointe Realtors' infamous point system. Prospective buyers were assigned points to qualify for the privilege of living here. A maximum score was 100, with 50 points the minimum for ethnically inoffensive applicants [WASPs]. But Poles had to score 55 points, Greeks 65, Italians, 75, and Jews 85. The private detectives hired to fill out the reports didn't even bother to rate African Americans or Asian Americans. The questions included:
>
> 1. Is their way of living typically American?
> 2. Appearances—swarthy, slightly swarthy, or not at all?
> 3. Accents—pronounced, medium, slight, not at all?
> 4. Dress—neat, sloppy, flashy, or conservative?

Realtors relied on private investigators who interviewed neighbors of would-be newcomers. Although Jews could allegedly gain entry, they had to be pretty special. Dr. J. B. Rosenbaum was "only half-Jewish" and his wife was a Gentile. Moreover, his mother was a direct descendant of Carter Braxton, a signer of the Declaration of Independence, and Rosenbaum had invented an artificial heart and had received several academic awards in recognition of this achievement. Grosse Pointe rejected him.[89]

The Grosse Pointe Brokers Association threatened to expel any member who didn't use the point system. This was a meaningful threat, because without cooperation from other realtors, representing buyers and sellers, they could no longer do business in the community. And association members backed up the threat with action, expelling at least two members for selling to ineligible buyers under the point system before 1960. One had sold to Italian Americans, the other to a doctor who had remarried and whose new wife had not been screened. No member had dared sell to an African American.[90]

The 1960 furor seemed to lead to action. In May 1960, Michigan's attorney general and the state's commissioner of corporation securities ordered Grosse Pointe to abandon the point system within 30 days. The minister of a Grosse Pointe church stated, "Jesus Christ could never qualify for residence in Grosse Pointe," which was true, of course, he being Jewish and probably swarthy to boot. "It's very unfortunate that the word 'swarthy' ever was used," said the secretary of the Grosse Pointe Brokers Association, still defending the point system. "In our definition, the word 'swarthy' doesn't always mean what it says. Applied to Jews, it would mean how much like a Jew does he look. This relates to his features, rather than just coloring." After hearings on Grosse Pointe, the commissioner of corporation securities, Lawrence Gubow, issued an administrative regulation known as Rule 9, barring realtors from discriminating on the basis of race, religion, or national origin.

Ultimately, however, the publicity resulted in no change. According to Norman C. Thomas, who wrote the standard work on the subject, "Reaction to Rule 9 was swift and vigorous." Officials of the Grosse Pointe Property Owners Association "launched a movement to write into the Michigan constitution an unqualified right of a property owner to refuse to sell or rent 'to any person whatsoever.' " The state legislature then passed a law specifically repealing Rule 9, but the Democratic governor vetoed it. Finally, in 1962 the Michigan Supreme Court unanimously killed Rule 9. It was too much policy making by administrative fiat, the court said, intruding into the powers of the legislature. Grosse Pointe realtors went back to business as usual with fair-skinned whites only.[91]

As implied by the intervention of the Grosse Pointe Property Owners Association, realtors were not the only problem. In 1969, nine years after the scandal over the point system, some residents in Grosse Pointe Farms, one of the five related towns known collectively as Grosse Pointe, tried to get their community to agree with the principle of open housing, which had been endorsed by Congress and the Supreme Court just the year before. Calling themselves the Committee on Open Housing, they proposed an ordinance that levied civil penalties against discrimination in housing on the basis of race, sex, age, or national origin. "It was the showdown for Grosse Pointe on integration," according to Kathy Cosseboom, author of a book on race relations in Grosse Pointe. The Real Estate Board and the Grosse Pointe Property Owners Association opposed it. The ordinance went down to defeat, 2,271 to 1,596, with half of all registered voters going to the polls, high for such a referendum.[92]

Despite these attitudes, in July 1966, the first African American family moved into Grosse Pointe. They had not been able to buy directly through a realtor, and they met with some hostility as well as some welcome from residents. Two months after they moved in, whites placed gravestones on their front lawn. Nevertheless, another black family moved in. The next year, however, both families moved out of the region. In March 1968, shortly before his death, Martin Luther King Jr. spoke at Grosse Pointe High School; he was repeatedly interrupted by hecklers. In 1990, Grosse Pointe had just twelve African American households, most of them live-in domestic couples, according to political scientist Andrew Hacker.[93]

The publicity does allow us to see how exclusion worked in one elite suburb. Otherwise, Grosse Pointe was hardly exceptional. According to Cosseboom, similar crises over sundown policies took place in nearby Birmingham and Bloomfield Hills. Within 10 miles of Detroit lie perhaps 40 more sundown suburbs, including Grosse Ile and Wyandotte—some elite, some middle-class, some working-class, some multiclass.[94]

Picking on Children

An additional factor keeping African American families out of all-white counties and towns was the matter of schooling for their children. Just raising the question would be likely to provoke a hostile response from whites in a sundown jurisdiction. In states that practiced de jure segregation—Delaware, Maryland, West Virginia, Kentucky, Missouri, Arkansas, Texas, Arizona, and parts of Indiana, Illinois, Kansas, Nebraska, New Jersey, New Mexico, Ohio, Pennsylvania, and Oklahoma, as well as the traditional South—white officials in sundown towns sometimes encouraged threats or violence against a black family to avoid the expense of setting up a new black school for them. In Duncan, Arizona, for example, the signs at the edge of town after World War II "included the usual 'Welcome' and 'Goodbye,' but also, 'Nigger, Don't Let The Sun Go Down On You Here,' " according to Betty Toomes, who lived in Duncan at the time. In 1949, "a Mormon farmer who needed a large number of hands on his 100-acre cotton field" hired the Earl and Corinne Randolph family and provided them with a house. They became "the first colored family ever to live there." Toomes accompanied Corinne Randolph to see the principal of the Consolidated Duncan Schools to get their children enrolled. He promised her an answer the next day. The answer came that very night: after midnight the Randolphs were "awakened by shots and the sounds of horses' hoofs very close to their house which was very isolated; it was probably a half mile from the highway and there were no other houses around it." Frightened, the family huddled "until the shooting and the shouting and the galloping stopped. Then they looked out of the window and they saw three crosses burning." They refused to give in, however, and eventually the Greenlea County Public Schools set up a "colored school" just for the Randolph children.[95]

Obviously children are a weak spot; parents cannot be with them at all times to protect them from harm. In northern states where children were not legally segregated by race, white parents and teachers often looked even less kindly on black faces in their previously all-white classrooms. In the early 1960s, Floyd Patterson, heavyweight champion of the world, tried to move into Scarsdale, a suburb of New York City. According to historian James Grossman, his son was beaten up and the family was hounded out of town. A black girl in high school in Oak Lawn, outside Chicago, "got spit upon and lasted just two weeks" in the fall of 1974, according to a woman who lived in Oak Lawn at the time. In about 1975, Dale Leftridge was transferred to Fremont, Nebraska, a sundown town near Omaha, as a manager on the Chicago and North Western Railroad. Within weeks he requested a transfer to Minneapolis, according to historian Eric Arnesen: "What put a 'dagger' in his heart was the cold treatment his young daughter received from other children." In 1982, into Corbin, Kentucky, moved an African American family whose son signed up to play football, according to Robby Heason's documentary *Trouble Behind*. He practiced with the football team, and "most of the kids were pulling for it," but his mother received death threats for her son if he were ever to play in a varsity game, so they left. In Perryville, Arkansas, in about 1987, "in first grade, our teacher told us not to play with the one black child on the playground," according to a woman who grew up in that sundown town near Little Rock. "We didn't. She left."[96]

Nothing physical happened to the only African American student in West Lawn in southwest Chicago. Although legally part of Chicago, West Lawn is almost a sizable suburb unto itself, including Midway Airport and the largest indoor mall in Chicago. In 1986, Steve Bogira wrote an extensive story on West Lawn and environs. Several residents told him that West Lawn wasn't really a sundown part of Chicago. "They referred to 'that colored mailman and his wife'—a reclusive black couple who, they said, had been living there for years. . . . No one knew how they got there or anything else about them." Bogira met with the couple, Fred and Mary Clark, and learned that they had raised their daughter there. She was the only African American student in her elementary school. Bogira then interviewed West Lawn resident Alexis Leslie, who went to school with the Clarks' daughter.

> "I felt bad for her—she seemed so lonely," Leslie says. "And I imagine a lot of other kids felt bad for her too. But it never occurred for us to actually be friends with her or even to talk to her—because to do so would put us in the same position she was in. There was also some apprehension, with the belief system we had, about the kind of person she was—was she someone you actually *wanted* to be friends with? Because she was black. I often felt bad later, because I didn't have the moral stamina to actually talk to her."

Imagine going through elementary school without a single conversation with a fellow student! Still, the greater sorrow today may be Leslie's.[97]

Often teachers have encouraged students to isolate the one or two black children who ventured into a sundown town or suburb. Once in a while, this backfired. A Pinckneyville, Illinois, resident told how a high school gym teacher in the 1980s tried to get his students to shun Quincy, the one black child in the school:

> He asked his class, "Are any of you friends with Quincy?" My son said, "I am." "Take a lap." Then he asked again. My son's friend said, "I am." "Take *two* laps." Eventually every boy in the class volunteered.

She was going to complain to the principal, "but my son asked me not to: 'Mom, we won.' " More often, whites maintained a united front, and the "intruders" left. In the early 1990s, for instance, an African American family tried to move into Berwyn, a sundown suburb just west of Chicago. The *Wall Street Journal* wrote a piece about how Berwyn had changed and how, despite minor aggravations, the family would stay. A week later the family left, James Rosenbaum at nearby Northwestern University wrote, because "they couldn't stand the harassment, especially against the kids." A resident of Ozark, Arkansas, recalled, "We used to have some blacks here, and we got rid of them." As a junior high school student in 1995, she saw two African American children get beaten up by white students as they got off their school bus on the first day of school in the fall. "They didn't even get to school." The family soon moved. A former police officer in Winston County, Alabama, much of which may yet be a sundown county, told me, "In 1996 [whites] held a meeting to try to kick the one black child out of the school in Addison." He believed that the child stayed in school, but imagine the social conditions under which s/he attended.[98]

How One Town Stayed White Down the Years

Wyandotte, Michigan, illustrates the intimidation, violence, and even murder that towns and suburbs have used to enforce their sundown policy. Indeed, because Wyandotte began as an independent town but then became a suburb of Detroit, it shows how the same methods were used in both environments. Its public library has preserved a file of newspaper clippings, letters, and other material collected by Edwina DeWindt in 1945[99] that reveal the history of race relations in that city.

Ironically, Wyandotte's first non-Indian settler may have been John Stewart, "a free man of color and a Methodist" missionary to the Indians, who arrived at Wyandotte, an Indian village, in 1816. Despite this multiracial start, the last Wyandotte Indians were pushed out of Michigan in 1843, and Wyandotte also excluded African Americans some time before the Civil War, much earlier than most sundown towns. According to an October 1898 story in the *Wyandotte Herald*, "So far as *The Herald* remembers, [Wyandotte] has never had any permanent colored population." Table 2 shows Wyandotte's population by race, from the U.S. census. Its numbers look like those from many other towns and suburbs: as Wyandotte grew from 2,731 in 1870 to 41,061 a century later, its African American population stayed minuscule, 0 in 1870 and 18, or 0.04%, in 1970. Along the years, the numbers fluctuated slightly, as the table shows.[100]

Table 2. Population by Race, Wyandotte, Michigan, 1870–2000

Year	Total Pop.	Black Pop.	% Black
1870	2,731	0	0%
1890	3,817	0	0%
1910	8,287	2	0.02%
1930	28,368	9	0.03%
1950	36,846	16	0.04%
1970	41,061	18	0.04%
1990	30,938	73	0.23%
2000	28,006	146	0.52%

"Wyandotte History; Negro" allows us to see the drama beneath those numbers. To maintain such racial "purity," Wyandotte has long resorted to violence and the threat of violence. In 1868, "a colored wood chopper" moved into town:

> He was a quiet, peaceable fellow who on his trips downtown had been reviled by rude boys. . . . One day a boy was foolish enough to strike him, upon which the worm turned and gave his assaulter a trouncing. The old spirit was aroused again; threats were made that the old darky should be driven out of town, and steps were taken to organize for that purpose, but . . . the authorities took a firm stand. . . . Twenty special constables were sworn in . . . and the trouble was over.

This 1868 response by "the authorities" was much better than African Americans would get in Wyandotte later in the century. Nevertheless, by 1870, the woodcutter was gone and Wyandotte had returned to a black population of zero.[101]

In the early 1870s, "a colored barber opened a tonsorial parlor in the block between Kim and Oak streets." A mob riddled the barbershop with bullets and ran the barber out of town. Shortly thereafter, a white mob stormed a little steamer that had landed in Wyandotte with a black deckhand on board and beat him nearly unconscious. In 1881 and again in 1888, whites threatened and expelled black hotel workers from Wyandotte, and in 1890, Wyandotte again had no African Americans among its 3,817 residents. In 1907, four young white men accosted African American William Anderson at the West Wyandotte train station. They "asked him if he was going to work in the shipyard, and although he gave a negative answer," they gave him "a severe beating" and robbed him of $9.25. The authorities did nothing in response to any of these incidents.[102]

Often Wyandotte whites had only to threaten violence. In the words of the Wyandotte file, "the policy popularly pursued to enforce the 'tacit legislation' (no Negroes in Wyandotte) is to approach the 'stray' Negro and abruptly warn him that a welcome mat is not at the gates of the city. This quiet reminder hastens the Negro's footsteps with no further action." But by 1916, mere threats must not have worked, because a few African Americans again lived in Wyandotte. In late August of that year occurred the worst riot in Wyandotte's history. According to a story subheaded "Race Riot Monday Night" in the *Herald,* whites bombarded a black boardinghouse, smashed its doors and windows, drove out all African Americans, and killed one. "Colored People Driven from Town," announced the *Herald.* "Most of the Negroes left town Monday night or Tuesday morning."[103]

A year later, a few African Americans were back in Wyandotte, working at Detroit Brass. This led to another expulsion. DeWindt quotes a newspaper account:

> The Negro flare-up in 1917 developed from a strike at the Detroit Brass Co., the only industry to hire Negroes. Near the factory were boarding houses and there were loose immoral relations between white and black. The city officials did nothing to stop it. The long festering indignation broke out in mob action.

DeWindt then notes that immoral behavior by African Americans was not the real issue, only an excuse. By 1930, 9 African Americans called Wyandotte home, among 28,368 residents, but 7 were female, and all 9 were probably live-in maids and gardeners. As far as I could determine, Wyandotte condoned no independent black households in the 1920s or 1930s.[104]

In the 1940s, police arrested or warned African Americans for "loitering suspiciously in the business district" or being in the park, and white children stoned African American children in front of Roosevelt High School. In about 1952, a black family moved into Wyandotte with tragic results, according to Kristina Baumli, who grew up in Wyandotte in that era and is now a professor at the University of Pennsylvania:

> After several weeks of hazings and warnings and escalating threats, [they] were killed and found floating in the Detroit River. My family couldn't give me more details. I asked if they thought this was true, or just a rumor—and they said that were pretty sure it was true, if not well investigated by the police.

More recently, Baumli reports, Elizabeth Park in Wyandotte has been a racial battleground, "where, I'm told, vigilantes enforced the sundown laws extra-legally. I believe the extent of it was just beating people up if they strayed after dark—my impression is that they beat everyone including women and kids."[105]

Over the years, then, African Americans repeatedly tried to settle in Wyandotte, only to be repulsed repeatedly. In the 1980s, Wyandotte caved in as a rigid sundown town, but its reputation lingers, and in 2000 it still was only 0.5% black.

Violence

Similar series of incidents underlie the zeroes or single digits under "Negro population" in the census, decade after decade, of other all-white towns and suburbs across the United States. Over the years, African Americans have even tried to move into towns with ferocious reputations, such as Syracuse, Ohio: according to a 1905 newspaper report, "two attempts have been made by Negro families to settle in the town, but both families were summarily driven out." When all else fails, after ordinances and covenants were decreed illegal, when steering, discriminatory lending, and the like have not sufficed, when an African American family is not deterred by a community's reputation—when they actually buy and move in—then residents of sundown towns and suburbs have repeatedly fallen back on violence and threat of violence to keep their communities white.[106]

Often the house has been the target. Residents of many sundown towns described incidents involving the destruction of homes newly purchased and occupied by African Americans. Here is a typical account, by a woman who grew up in Brownsburg, Indiana, a few miles west of Indianapolis. She had a conversation with her mother about sundown towns in November 2002 and brought up the topic of sundown signs. Her mother replied, "If you want to know if Brownsburg had them, they did."

> I then asked her about the black family I remembered. My memory was of ru-
> mors spreading around my school that they had been chased out by fire. (I
> thought it was crosses burning or something of that nature.) She said when I
> was around eleven, a black family moved in and their house burned to the
> ground.[107]

Sometimes the person was the target. If sundown towns have often mis-treated transient visitors such as athletic teams and jazz bands, the person of color who comes into a sundown town with the intent to live there has faced more serious consequences. Residents of town after town regaled me with stories of African Americans who had been killed or injured for the offense of moving in or simply setting foot in them. More stories of violence to maintain sundown towns and suburbs have come to my attention than I can possibly recount here; I have posted some at uvm.edu/~jloewen/sundown. In one way, all the stories are alike: whites use bad behavior to drive out black would-be residents. Often these stories become active elements of the reputations in ongoing sundown towns and suburbs. In LaSalle-Peru, there is a story about a black family that "moved into town, and shortly after the father was found drowned in the Illinois [River]," according to a woman whose parents grew up there. An African American family moved into Oneida, Tennessee, in 1925, according to Scott County historian Esther Sanderson, "but dynamite was dropped on their house and they were severely injured. They soon left and no others ever came in." Writing in 1958, she concluded, "There is not a colored family living in Scott County at the present time." Chapter 7 told that many sundown towns have "hanging trees" that they point out to visitors. Residents of Pinckneyville tell stories of African Americans hanged in at least *three* different places. Even if apocryphal, stories such as these intimidate black would-be newcomers.[108]

Residents of sundown towns who hired or befriended African Americans sometimes found that their membership in the white community did not protect them from violent reprisal. In Marlow, Oklahoma, in 1923, a prominent hotel owner was killed because he refused to get rid of his African American employee. "Marlow's 'Unwritten Law' Against Race Causes Two Deaths," headlined the *Pittsburgh Courier*. "Violation of Ban by Owner of Hotel Leads to Shooting." Here is its account:

> Marlow's unwritten law, exemplified by prominent public signs bearing the command: "Negro, don't let the sun go down on you here," caused the death Monday night of A. W. Berch, prominent hotel owner, and the fatal wounding of Robert Jernigan, the first colored man who stayed here more than a day in years.
>
> They were victims of a mob of more than fifteen men, who went to the hotel where Jernigan had been employed three days ago as a porter and shot them down when Berch attempted to persuade them to desist from their threat to lynch the man.
>
> Marlow, one of the several towns in Oklahoma which has not allowed our people to settle in their vicinity for years, has abided by the custom of permitting no members of the race to remain there after nightfall.

Last Saturday Berch brought Robert Jernigan here to serve as a porter in his hotel. A few hours later he received an anonymous communication ordering him to dismiss the porter at once and drive him from the city.

Berch ignored the letter.

The mob went to the hotel early Monday evening, its members calling loudly for the man and announcing their intention of hanging him on the spot.

The hotel proprietor, with Jernigan at his side, hurried into the lobby to intercede, but was shot dead before he could speak. Jernigan also fell, mortally wounded.

Their assailants then fled.

Mrs. Berch, who witnessed the shooting, said she thought she recognized the man who killed her husband, but authorities Tuesday said they had no clews as to the identity of members of the mob. They were not masked.

Berch's daughter Almarion also witnessed the shooting, at the age of two. She confirmed in 2004 what the last paragraph implies: that nothing was done about the crimes.[109]

As far as I have been able to learn, nothing was done about the 1922 lynching of J. T. Douglas in Hardin County in southeastern Illinois, either. Also unlike most victims of lynching in America, Douglas was white, a landowner, and prominent in the community. Unlike most (though not all) victims, he was not accused of a serious crime such as murder or rape. His offense? He broke the sundown "law" of that part of Hardin County by letting an African American live on his farm. According to the nearby Golconda *Herald-Enterprise*:

FARMER SHOT TO DEATH NEAR LAMB, HARDIN CO.
WAS ATTEMPTING TO PROTECT
COLORED MAN WHO LIVED
AS TENANT ON FARM

One of the most brutal murders that was ever committed in Southern Illinois was the shooting to death of J. T. Douglas, a prominent farmer residing near Lamb, in Hardin county, Thursday night shortly after midnight.

J. H. Douglas, this city, reports that his uncle had a colored hired man living on his farm and that some people of the locality had protested against him keeping the fellow and had warned him that trouble would result if he was not sent away. The murdered man did not heed the warning and his hired man stayed on.

Thursday night about midnight, a mob, composed of parties unknown, went to the house of the colored man and began shooting into the house. Mr. Douglas, from his home about a quarter of a mile away, heard the shooting and hastened to the scene. Just as he was about to enter the house, after calling to the Negro, he was shot dead.

The murder has caused great excitement and indignation in Hardin county, and every effort will be made to find out who composed the mob and did the shooting. Several are suspected and arrests no doubt will soon follow.

I could not find news stories of any arrests.[110]

White suburbs have largely avoided being tagged with the reputations for unsavory behavior that plague independent sundown towns. As we have seen, suburbs have used a variety of subtler methods to achieve all-white status, including clauses in their founding documents, unwritten policies of their developers, formal acts by suburban governments, restrictive covenants embedded in deeds, realtor steering, and redlining by lenders or insurers. Many suburbs seem too genteel to resort to violence and intimidation. This aura may be undeserved, however. Some suburbanites who would never attend a Klan meeting contacted their nearest klavern in time of need. As Stetson Kennedy, who famously infiltrated the KKK in the 1940s, put it, "The Klan has long served as an unofficial police force for maintaining racial zoning." When the William and Daisy Myers family moved into Levittown, Pennsylvania, in 1957, crosses burned throughout Levittown. Whites painted "KKK" on a neighbor's house because members of the family who lived there had not joined the mob. Leaders of the "Levittown Betterment Committee" contacted the Klan and other hate groups to get help in driving the Myerses out. Nearly 100 Levittowners signed to form a local klavern.[111]

Most suburbs have not relied on outsiders. When African American families managed to move into formerly all-white neighborhoods despite all the preventive measures taken by the suburbs, residents themselves typically resorted to shunning, threats of violence, and violence itself. In fact, violence in sundown suburbs and neighborhoods has been, if anything, even more widespread than the attacks on blacks in independent sundown towns. The Great Migration of African Americans from the South to northern cities, beginning around 1915 and continuing into the 1960s, struck many white suburbanites as a threatened "invasion" of their neighborhoods and led to, in Meyer's words, "thousands of small acts of terrorism" by whites determined to keep the newcomers out. Between 1917 and 1921, for example, whites firebombed the homes of 58 African American families that tried to move into white neighborhoods on the South Side of Chicago. "Rather than cresting in the

1920s," Meyer concluded, "the most vicious and extensive violence occurring in the North during the two decades following World War II." In Chicago during just the first two years after World War II, whites bombed 167 homes bought or rented by African Americans in white neighborhoods, "killing four persons, permanently crippling eight, and injuring scores of others," Stetson Kennedy summarized.[112]

Some of the most severe and most important violence occurred in the West Lawn neighborhood of Chicago. In 1946, an African American couple, Theodore and Ida Turner, tried to occupy an apartment in Airport Homes, temporary apartments that the Chicago Housing Authority was building for veterans near Midway Airport. A mob of West Lawn residents drove them out, along with two other African American families and a Jewish couple that had befriended them. "No black ever again attempted to move into Airport Homes," wrote Steve Bogira. Indeed, as historian Arnold Hirsch put it, "Chicago Housing Authority policy was made in the streets." Thirty-five years later, West Lawn and adjacent communities were still more than 99.9% white, containing 113,000 whites and 111 blacks in the 1980 census.[113]

Restrictive covenants kept African Americans out of most white suburbs until well after World War II. A new wave of violence struck after their legal demise. "We must refuse to sell to colored people whether the covenants are valid or invalid," shouted a leader of the Woodlawn Property Owners, trying to keep a Chicago neighborhood all-white in October 1953. "If the colored people were convinced that life in Woodlawn would be unbearable, they would not want to come in." That was in a sundown neighborhood in an interracial city. In sundown suburbs, it was often worse. After Oak Park, Illinois, failed to keep out Percy Julian's family, as described in "Sundown Suburbs," his home "suffered both bomb and arson attacks in 1950 and 1951," in the words of Arnold Hirsch. Whites in nearby Cicero have repeatedly used violence to repel African American would-be residents. "The first Negro family to enter the middle-class Chicago suburb of Deerfield," according to housing expert James Hecht, "moved out of their rented apartment after windows were broken and excrement was smeared on the front walls of the house."[114]

By no means have the Chicago suburbs been unique. Meyer tells of the campaign whites in the Los Angeles suburb of Maywood mounted in 1942 to force out two African American families. "Keep Maywood White" was the headline in the *Maywood-Bell Southwest Herald*. In nearby Fontana, where African Americans could only live outside the city limits on a floodplain, whites firebombed the O'Day Short family when they bought a house in town, killing Mr. and Mrs. Short and their young children in December 1945.

No one was ever convicted of the bombing, and Fontana remained all-white into the 1960s. On the opposite coast, whites in Oceanside, Long Island, threw a bomb through the dining room window of one of its few black-owned homes in 1967. This made an impact: the owner put his home up for sale, and as of 2000, Oceanside still had just 184 African Americans among its 33,000 residents.[115]

Violence to keep communities all-white may have peaked in the 1980s. In 1985 and 1986, the Klanwatch Project counted 45 cases of arson or cross burning and "hundreds of acts of vandalism, intimidation, and other incidents" aimed at "members of minority groups who had moved into mostly white areas." In 1989 alone, Klanwatch listed 130 cases, and that was surely an underestimate, since the Chicago Commission on Human Rights recorded an average of 100 racial hate crimes each year between 1985 and 1990 in neighborhoods undergoing "racial transition" just in that city.[116]

Developing a Reputation

The best way to stay all-white, many communities concluded, was to behave with such outrageous hostility to African Americans who happened by or tried to move in that a reputation for vicious white supremacy circulated among African Americans for many miles around. Historian Emma Lou Thornbrough told that sundown towns built anti-black reputations in Indiana during the Nadir. By 1900, for example, Leavenworth, "the county seat of Crawford County, had the reputation of being the most 'anti-Negro' town on the Ohio River. Captains of riverboats were said to discipline African American crewmen by threatening to put them off the boat at Leavenworth. By 1900 there was only one Negro resident in Crawford County." Today, African Americans as far away as Florida and California know and spread the reputation of Pekin, a sundown town in central Illinois. Achieving a similar notoriety is the rationale for the otherwise irrational refusal of gas stations in some sundown towns to sell gasoline to African Americans. After all, most motorists do have enough gas to get to the next town, and they will carry with them the message that Pana, Martinsville, and other towns that had this policy are to be avoided at all costs.[117]

Often the first thing said to an African American in a sundown town was to ask if he knew the reputation of the town. Even "pet Negroes," as local whites sometimes referred to them, were in trouble as soon as they ventured beyond the specific town or part of town where they were known. Aaron "Rock" Van Winkle, "born a slave" and "owned by Peter Van Winkle," whose son-in-law was a state senator from Rogers, Arkansas, was "in Rogers on business," according to an article in the 1904 *Rogers Democrat*. "In a joking way one of our citizens said to him: 'See here, Rock, you know that sundown don't want to find a Negro in Rogers.' " The newspaper went on to relate the quip with which "the old Negro" reproached the white man. Nevertheless, the white man's statement, while perhaps said "in a joking way," was also flatly true. Both he and Van Winkle would have known that it was not to be challenged directly and that saying it was a warning, the first step in enforcement.[118]

Some places have built national reputations as sundown towns. From east to west, these would include Darien, Connecticut; the Levittowns in New York and Pennsylvania; Forsyth County, Georgia; Cuyahoga Falls and Parma, Ohio; Dearborn, Grosse Pointe, Warren, and Wyandotte, Michigan; Elwood, Huntington, and Martinsville, Indiana; Cicero, Pekin, Pana, and Franklin and Williamson counties, Illinois; Cullman, Alabama; the Ozarks as a region; Idaho, statewide; Vidor and Santa Fe, Texas; and several suburbs of Los Angeles.[119] Especially in the African American community, these reputations endure. "This colored person in Florida knew of Pana, Illinois, and its reputation," a woman who grew up in Pana related, "and that astonished me." Virginia Yearwood, a native of Pierce City, Missouri, reported that African Americans with whom she worked in the 1970s in California knew about Pierce City's anti-black policy.[120]

Reputations are even more important within metropolitan areas. A 1992 Detroit area survey showed that 89% of white respondents and 92% of blacks thought that residents of suburban Dearborn "would be upset" if a black family moved in. As a result, only 37% of African Americans rated Dearborn a "desirable" place to live, compared to 66% of white respondents. Of the black respondents who ranked Dearborn "undesirable," 78% cited the racial prejudice of its residents as their reason. Many residents of sundown suburbs such as Dearborn are happy that African Americans consider their town undesirable. Then less enforcement is required to keep it white. Moreover, a reputation as overwhelmingly white is part of a suburb's claim to social status. At the same time, residents of Dearborn don't want their city's reputation to get out of hand. While they are proud to be from an all-white community, at the same time they know enough to be ashamed. To put this another way, many whites want their town or suburb to have a certain notoriety in the African American community for unfriendly police and unwelcoming residents, so long as this can be accomplished without giving the town a black eye, as it were, in the white community.[121]

Sometimes reputations can get out of hand. Tamaroa, a town of about 800 people in southern Illinois, excluded African Americans perhaps around 1900. I did not find anyone who claimed to know how or when. But every person I talked with from Tamaroa or near Tamaroa knew that the town had become infamous as "the rock throwers" some time later. A member of the historical society in nearby Pinckneyville, also a sundown town, told how African Americans from the nearby interracial town of Du Quoin occasionally walked along the railroad tracks to go north. As they passed through Tamaroa, white youths would throw rocks at them. On one occasion the stoning got out of hand and they killed a man. A woman who grew up in Tamaroa, now living in a senior center in Du Quoin, confirmed this account: "They stoned one to death." She was indignant at her town's resulting notoriety: "People all around call us 'rock throwers,' but that was so long ago!" The Pinckneyville historian suggested that Tamaroa's reputation didn't rest on that one incident: another African American tried to run through on the railroad right-of-way but was grabbed and castrated, and a third was hung. Asked how he knew about these incidents,[122] he replied, "Several residents of Tamaroa told me those stories. One man told me he witnessed the hanging. They took him down and burned him on a brush pile."[123]

In a sense Tamaroa's notoriety is unwarranted, however, because the town does not differ from hundreds of other sundown towns. Indeed, the generic nickname for slingshot across the United States in the first half of the twentieth century was "nigger shooter."[124] Moreover, white reactions to this day to an African American in a "white neighborhood" anywhere in America often include fear and hostility. In the 1970 feature film *Watermelon Man,* African American director Melvin Van Peebles depicted a comical example: police in a white suburb respond to phone calls from homeowners frightened by African American actor Godfrey Cambridge, a white suburbanite who has suddenly turned black during the previous night. Cambridge is merely jogging the same route he did the day before, when he was white. As David Harris noted more recently, jogging through white neighborhoods remains problematic, not only in the movies, but also in real suburbia.[125]

The 1964 Civil Rights Act Made Little Difference

Some of these problems might have eased with passage of the 1964 Civil Rights Act, but that legislation was aimed at the South and was not enforced in sundown towns, most of which are not in the South. Thus the 1964 law left all-white towns and suburbs largely untouched. Many towns simply did not obey it for decades. "We were not allowed to serve any colored after sundown," said a woman who had been a waiter in the mid-1970s in Arcola, Illinois. "A white man came in and said, 'I have my buddy in the truck. Will you serve him?' He then served the friend at the booth, getting the stuff from me at the counter." Telling this in 2002, the woman was proud that she let that happen, in violation of the rules.[126]

In 1974, Dale Leftridge, one of the first African Americans allowed to become a railroad engineer in the United States, took trains to South Pekin, Illinois. Ten years after the Civil Rights Act outlawed racial discrimination in public accommodations, the Chicago & North Western Railroad had to post a security guard from the train at the motel, "because the townspeople didn't want blacks in their town," in Leftridge's words. Two years later, a black social worker from the state office in Madison had to stay at a smaller motel outside of Sheboygan, Wisconsin. She couldn't stay at the main hotel within the city, according to June Rosland, then also a social worker in Wisconsin. "And she had an MSW [Master's of Social Work]!"[127]

Nick Khan in Paragould said that when he bought his motel in 1982, no motels in town let African Americans spend the night. Paragould had been a sundown town since 1908, when its 40 black families were ordered to leave at gunpoint. The restaurant across the road locked the door on two black Union Pacific Rail Road workers staying with him in 1983 when they walked over and tried to eat there. Police came and accused the African Americans of trying to break in, according to Khan. "The white boys in the restaurant were cracking up over it. The black guys were so scared." After that, "they never used to go out. If I'm outside, they'll come out, sit in the chairs. But if they go downtown, they'll get arrested!" So they bought takeout fried chicken at Kentucky Fried Chicken and ate it in their rooms.[128]

How are these things possible, so many years after the Civil Rights Act? Enforcement of the law, which should have depended on the federal government, in reality depended on African Americans. Black pioneers tested restaurants and motels across the South, sat wherever they wanted on buses, and sometimes got beaten or killed for their trouble, forcing the government to act. Having no black children, sundown towns had no black students to desegrate their schools after 1954. Having no black populations, these towns had no African Americans to test their public accommodations after 1964. Members of the St. Louis chapter of SNCC, the Student Nonviolent Coordinating Committee, responsible for so many southern sit-ins, did announce to the media that they were going to test restaurants and motels in Williamson County, Illinois, shortly after passage of the act. Almost every community in

Williamson County and adjoining Franklin County was a sundown town then, including Benton, Carterville, Christopher, Herrin, Johnston City, Mulkeytown, Royalton, Sesser, West Frankfort, and Zeigler. The Williamson County sheriff talked with all the motel owners and restaurant owners and told them they had two choices, according to Jim Clayton: "Either they could accommodate them, and they'd all go back to St. Louis, or they could refuse, and all hell would break loose." They complied. Afterward they put their signs back up—"White Only" or "Management Reserves the Right to Refuse Service to Anyone"—and Williamson and Franklin counties disobeyed the law for another two decades.[129]

Today many sundown towns exhibit a pattern exactly opposite to that found in the classic pre-1954 segregated southern city (and many northern ones). Back then, black travelers usually could neither stay in the city's hotels and motels nor eat in its major restaurants, but African Americans were allowed to live in the city, albeit on the "wrong side of the tracks." Today, most motels and restaurants in sundown towns serve African Americans without a second thought, but blacks still cannot live within the city limits.

Throughout the expulsions, the prohibitions, the shunning, and all the other acts that sundown towns have used to stay all-white, all the while an individual "pet" black, such as Aaron Van Winkle in Arkansas—sometimes an entire household—has often been allowed to stay. The next chapter tells of these anomalies—African Americans permitted to live, usually without much difficulty, in towns and counties that nevertheless designated themselves "sundown."

10

Exceptions to the Sundown Rule

During my life I have heard oral history of at least two instances in Missouri where one or a few ex-slaves (or their descendants) were allowed to remain in a county or town, but any visiting blacks were quickly informed that they were "not to let the sun set on them." It is as if there were an unspoken feeling of "these are our blacks and they are okay, but other blacks are unwelcome and dangerous strangers."

—Laurel Boeckman, reference librarian,
State Historical Society of Missouri, 2002[1]

TOWNS THAT TOOK GREAT PAINS to define themselves as sundown towns have nevertheless often allowed an exception or two. Within their otherwise all-white populations, occasionally an African American person or even household was at least tolerated and sometimes celebrated. When Pana, Illinois, for example, forced out its African American population in 1899, whites did not force the black barber and his family to leave. He had an exclusively white clientele and many acquaintances—even friends—in the white community, and no one had a complaint about *him*. Pana did post sundown signs at its corporate limits, signs that remained up at least until 1960, and permitted no other African Americans to move in, so it definitely became a sundown town. Other towns have let in more temporary intruders: flood refugees, soldiers during wartime, college students, and visiting interracial athletic teams and their fans.[2]

What experiences do these exceptions have, in towns that by definition do not allow them to be there? What are their lives like? What difference—if any—do they make?

African American Servants

Many African Americans in sundown towns were or are servants. In a way, they don't violate the sundown rule, because they don't live on their own. Huntington, Indiana, is so anti-black that two residents reported in 2002 that its police still stop any African Americans driving through and warn them "to get out of town—now." Yet a black couple lived in Huntington in the 1920s and 1930s. They were servants in the household of William Schacht, owner of a rubber factory and one of the richest people in town. She was the family's maid and cook, he their handyman. "They lived in the Schacht house, but their movements were circumscribed. They couldn't go downtown—a few blocks away—without problems," according to a man who grew up in the town in those decades. "They spent most of the time indoors." And they had no children, so there were no African American children in the schools. At this same time, after the 1919 riot in which whites drove out the African American population of Marion, Ohio, home of president-to-be Warren G. Harding, "local lore has it that there was one black family left in Marion after the riot," writes Harding scholar Phillip Payne, "and that the woman and her family remained because she had been the Hardings' maid." Also, her husband was the barber, so he knew, serviced, and in a limited sense was friends with upper-class whites.[3]

In the suburbs, these live-in exceptions were common. Laura Hobson's novel about anti-Semitism in Darien, Connecticut, in the 1940s, *Gentleman's Agreement,* pointed out the town's practice of not letting Jews or African Americans live there. Meanwhile, when she wrote, Darien had about 150 African Americans, mostly female—live-in maids, nannies, gardeners, and the like. Similarly, Kenilworth, Illinois, the richest suburb of Chicago, had a population that was 4.3% African American in 1930, all live-in servants. On the West Coast, Beverly Hills, a famed affluent suburb of Los Angeles, had 397 African Americans in 1920. Almost 300 were female; the imbalance implies that at least 200 were live-in maids and nannies. In fact, probably every African American was a maid, gardener, or other live-in servant, because the total of 397 included just four children, all girls who probably assisted their mothers or were older teenagers working on their own. This sexual imbalance then worsened: by 1960, Beverly Hills had 649 African Americans, of whom 554 were females.[4]

Often these exceptions were codified into law. In 1912, Virginia passed a law providing for all-white and all-black neighborhoods or towns: "It shall be unlawful for any colored person, not then residing in a district so defined and designated as a white district, or who is not a member of a family then therein residing, to move into and occupy as a residence any building or portion thereof in such white district," and vice versa. The act immediately went on to make the exception: "Nothing herein contained shall preclude persons of either race employed as servants by persons of the other race from residing upon the premises of which such employer is the owner or occupier." After the Supreme Court invalidated such laws in 1917, suburbs switched to restrictive covenants to keep out African Americans. Typically those covenants similarly exempted servants, as did this succinct example from Chicago suburb Villa Park: "Said premises shall not be conveyed or leased to, or occupied by, any person who is not a Caucasian, except servants." Examples in my collection range from California to Minnesota to Vermont to Florida.[5]

When entire suburbs made it their policy for all neighborhoods to be covered by these covenants, they became sundown towns. After World War II, for example, South Pasadena, California, did so, according to this 1947 newspaper report:

> The city of S. Pasadena, California, provides an example of the extreme to which the trend toward restrictive racial and religious covenants can go. In South Pasadena restrictive covenants, denying persons not of the Caucasian race the right to live within its municipal boundaries, are a matter of official policy. The city administration has been charged with promoting the program under which the entire city will be blanketed with restrictive agreements. South Pasadena is to be completely "white." Of course, persons not of Caucasian ancestry will not be completely barred from residence in South Pasadena. The restrictive covenants specify that non-Caucasians may reside in the city as servants, caretakers, and in similar menial work. Non-Caucasians may work in the city in other capacities, but they must be outside its limits by nightfall.

Again, live-in servants did not and could not constitute real exceptions, because they could not live within the city limits on their own. Often their children could not live there at all; maids and gardeners with children sent them to live with relatives. Sometimes, as in Texas's Park Cities, the suburban school district or the maid's employer paid for her children to attend schools in the central city. Sundown suburbs thus ensured that the only African Americans their white children would meet were servants in positions of inferiority.[6]

Like the Schacht servants in Huntington, live-in servants have often had to practice invisibility. There were African American maids in Johnston City, in southern Illinois, in the 1920s, but "they weren't allowed out of doors after dark," according to Jim Clayton, a *Washington Post* reporter who grew up there. A former resident of nearby Herrin spoke to historian Paul Angle around 1950:

> Some Herrin families do keep hired Negro help in their homes overnight. I had a "Clarissa" who lived with me for four years. The old feeling of "being out of the city limits by dark" was still with her, however. She didn't like to answer my door after the evening meal and usually stayed right in her room. She never appeared on the streets after dark.

Angle's informant seems to locate her maid's "feeling" within the employee, but town policy was to blame. Her acts were prudent and would be appropriate in Herrin for several more decades. A member of the Batesville Historical Society told of "a prominent family" in that southeastern Indiana town "who employed black maids, chefs, chauffeurs for business functions. Those employees were told to never be on the streets at night." Their housekeeper, who worked for them on a more permanent basis, "would only go outdoors to attend the earliest [morning] Mass at the local Catholic church."[7]

As in independent sundown towns, servants in sundown suburbs have also had to watch the sun. In the late 1940s, for example, Lois Johnson, who lived in Glendale, a suburb of Los Angeles, would see maids running to the bus stop "so they would not be caught there after dark." In 1940, among 81,992 residents, Glendale had 68 African Americans, three to one female, surely the ratio of maids to gardeners and chauffeurs; they included just two individuals under 21 years old, both likely maids in their late teens. Probably all 68 were live-in servants, who apparently had no more freedom to poke their heads out of doors after sundown than black servants in Huntington or Herrin. Even more constricted were the lives of servants in Wyandotte, Michigan, the sundown suburb near Detroit, who stayed indoors day and night. Writing in about 1945, Mable Bishop Gilmer told of "a high class type of Negroes, descendants of slaves of George Washington, and so-named Washington." They were the servants she knew as a child in the wealthy Bishop family. "These Negroes sensing the Wyandotte attitude never left the house to enter the streets but sent the Bishop children on errands for their personal needs."[8]

Sometimes African American servants even got in trouble while on their employer's property. In 1948, a graduate student from Panama and his wife came to Norman, Oklahoma, home of the University of Oklahoma, accompanied by their black Panamanian maid. According to a student at the university at the time:

One evening at sundown the maid was hanging clothes out on the line. Apparently someone reported her to the police, because they came and arrested her and took her to the station. She was frightened because she could not speak English and did not know why she was picked up. Her employer . . . got the maid released and, I believe, got the university administration to talk to the police so the maid would be safe from police harassment.[9]

Surely no one in modern America, outside of prison, has lived more restricted or more fearful lives than these lonely live-in African American servants in intentionally all-white communities. Over time, however, live-in maids, gardeners, and other domestic help became less crucial to the lifestyle of even the rich and famous and certainly of the middle class. Gas, oil, and electric heat eliminated the need to stoke the coal furnace, washers and dryers decreased the work on wash day, and gardening and landscaping got redefined as a hobby rather than a chore, at least in the middle class. We see this change in Darien, for example, which showed 161 African Americans in the 1940 census, 112 in 1960, and just 75 in 1990, always three-quarters female because maids and nannies outnumber butlers and gardeners. Similarly, by 1960, the proportion of African American servants in Kenilworth—4.3% in 1930—had fallen to 1.3%, and in 2000, 0.2%—just 4 individuals. Grosse Pointe, Michigan, had 140 African Americans in 1940, 36 in 1960, and just 11 by 1980. These statistics reflect the decline in live-in servants in America, not increased white supremacy in Darien, Kenilworth, or Grosse Pointe.

Hotel Workers

Sundown towns often allowed hotel workers after dark. Such porters, waiters, maids, and others don't exactly violate the sundown rule because they don't live in a residential neighborhood. In the 1930s and '40s and possibly later, an African American lived in the basement of the Pacific House hotel in Effingham, Illinois. He made a living driving a team of horses hitched to a coach, supplying rides from the railroad depot to the Pacific House and elsewhere. A man who lived in Miami Beach in the late 1940s and early '50s, tells that Miami Beach was a sundown town then but made exceptions "for hotel maids and bus boys and Sarah Vaughan!" Like Darien and Beverly Hills, Miami Beach's African American population was more than three-quarters female and included almost no children. Bill Alley of the Southern Oregon Historical Society tells of one African American man in the 1920s, George Washington Maddox, in Medford, which was otherwise a sundown town. Maddox, a dwarf, shined shoes at the Medford Hotel. In southern Pennsylvania, "for decades Ephrata had but a single black resident—George Harris, a barber, who first came to town as a seasonal employee of the grand Mountain Springs Hotel summer resort in or around 1848," according to Cynthia Marquet of the local historical society. "He moved here permanently in 1882 and remained until his death in 1904." Marquet adds, "After Harris died no black persons . . . lived in Ephrata for decades." In 1960, Ephrata had 7,688 people and no African Americans. I must note that Marquet goes on to add, "In my 18 years at the Historical Society, I have never encountered any suggestion that their presence was forbidden." However, three residents of nearby communities tell that the Ku Klux Klan recruits in Ephrata and holds an annual march there and that they hear that African American families usually move out[10] soon after moving into the town.[11]

Like servants, the lives of these hotel workers could be remarkably constricted. Indiana writer William Wilson told of his aunt and uncle who ran The Tavern, a hotel in New Harmony, Indiana, in the 1920s, and of "Aunt Minnie's Lizzie, . . . the only Negro permitted to live in the town. She had a room in the hotel and never went out on the street, day or night. . . . She must have had a great deal of what we used to call 'inner resources.' Certainly she was a finer person than the group of intolerant white people in the town who made it necessary for her to stay indoors."[12]

Some white communities would not abide African Americans even as household servants or hotel workers. When a horse breeder from Kentucky who had bought a farm in Washington County, Indiana, in 1888, brought a black stable hand to care for his horses, there was so much excitement that the stable hand had to be sent back to Kentucky. Five years later, a visitor from Louisville who brought a black cook was forced to send her away because of threats of violence. A wealthy visitor to Utica, Indiana, had a hard time securing permission to bring his carriage driver into the town, because no African Americans were allowed within the city limits. A newspaper in Springdale, Arkansas, itself a sundown town, told of an event in nearby Rogers in 1894: "A hotel in Rogers employs a colored boy to wait on the tables and one night recently some person posted a notice on the gate post warning the proprietor to discharge the boy or steps would be taken to rid the town of his presence. The notice was signed 'citizens.' " Apparently the "boy" left. The River Park Hotel in Wyandotte, Michigan, had African American waiters in 1880 and 1881 "who sang beautifully," according to a newspaper account, but apparently were later expelled. Seven years later, the manager of the hotel arrived with "a retinue of colored servants," but whites in Wyandotte expelled them too. In

1880, three African Americans—two barbers and a cook—came to Bluffton, Indiana, the cook to work in a local hotel. Historian Emma Lou Thornbrough writes that all three "received written notices that they must leave, and the proprietor of the hotel who employed the cook, as well as the sheriff of the county, received warnings to get rid of the Negroes." They did.[13]

Refugees, Soldiers, Students, and Other Transients

Even large numbers of African Americans have sometimes been allowed in sundown towns when they were clearly temporary and when human kindness overrode the sundown rule. Johnston City, Illinois, provided an example during the 1937 flood of the Mississippi River. As its town history recounts:

> On January 20 we received word that some 200 [flood refugees] were to be brought here from around Mounds and Mound City. Eventually this number grew to 287, and these homeless people were housed in the Miner's Hall, the Baptist Tabernacle, [and abandoned stores] . . . About half the refugees brought here were colored, and although the town had the reputation of never permitting a black to remain overnight here, they were welcomed with courtesy and kindness in 1937.

Of course, the gesture was easier because the refugees were never perceived as possible residents; from the start, whites understood their sojourn was to be only temporary. "When the danger of flooding had passed, the black people were transferred to Wolf Lake," the account concludes, "the white refugees to Anna."[14]

During World War II, Camp Ellis in west-central Illinois had some African American troops. According to a local lawyer, "Lewiston—an all-white community—opened its restaurants, taverns, theaters, and other public places to African-American servicemen." Lachlan Crissey, the local state's attorney at the time, wrote, "The attitude adopted by most of the people there was, 'Well, they're soldiers, the same as our boys, and if they are shot they bleed and die the same way.' Therefore, the Negro soldiers are free to enter the restaurants, stores, taverns, picture shows, and other public places." Other sundown towns around Lewistown were not so hospitable; as Crissey went on to say, "This was the exception, and not the rule." Again, everyone in Lewistown knew that the soldiers were never going to stay there permanently.[15]

Many towns that would never let them stay in houses permitted African

American and African college and prep-school students to live on campus. Again, it helped that townspeople knew the students were only temporary. In the 1960s, missionaries of the United Brethren Church in Christ recruited students from Sierra Leone to attend Huntington College in Huntington, Indiana, the college for that denomination. The town let the Africans live on campus; indeed, they could even get haircuts in town, while African American students could not. Pretty much the same thing happened at Bethany College in Lindsborg, Kansas, a sundown town founded by "conservative and lily-white Swedes in 1869," in the words of reporter Matt Moline, except at Bethany the Africans were from Kenya rather than Sierra Leone and were Lutheran rather than Brethren. Similarly, African students attended Chapman College in Orange, California, in the 1960s, according to history professor Harold Forsythe, one of the first African Americans to attend Chapman. They were perhaps among the first blacks allowed to spend the night and told Forsythe, "It was a tough town in which to live." [16]

Darien, Connecticut, has no college, but beginning in the early 1980s, its public high school let a few African American girls, mostly from Harlem, attend under the aegis of A Better Chance (ABC), a program that sends minority teenagers to prep schools and affluent suburban high schools to prepare them to enter elite colleges. To avoid the long commute from New York City, the girls live in a group home in Darien, but again, whites know there is no chance that they might stay after they graduate from high school.

Most sundown towns were not hospitable even to transients. The response of Elco, in southern Illinois, to majority-white but interracial religious meetings was typical. In 1923, William Sowders, founder of the Gospel Assembly Churches, established a camp meeting at Elco. He continued to lead religious revivals there for eighteen years, but Elco residents were upset because Sowders allowed people of all races to attend these meetings. In 1941, World War II and local opposition caused him to abandon the Elco camp meeting. [17]

Having a Protector

Now we move to the "real" exceptions: African Americans who lived on their own in towns that did not allow African Americans to live on their own. Some sundown towns made exceptions not just for live-in domestics, hotel workers, and students, but for an actual independent African American household or two. This pattern was more common in the nontraditional South—Appalachia, Texas, and the like—than in the North or West. In areas where slavery had existed before 1865, elderly black couples made use of the "faithful slave" stereotype, so beloved of whites seeking to defend the "peculiar institution" in their minds, to persist in otherwise all-white communities. Often they became locally famous and were remembered decades later with affection.

When whites drove out African Americans from all or parts of six counties southwest of Fort Worth, Texas, in 1886, for example, they made exceptions for a handful of old ex-slaves in Hamilton County, including "Uncle Alec" Gentry and "Aunt Mourn" Gentry, both about 80 years old. "When released from slavery, they were taken to Hamilton County by their former master and given a patch of ground and log cabin. They have lived there ever since," in the words of the Hamilton's centennial county history, *Parade of Progress*. Portfolio 19 shows "Uncle Alec," bent over obsequiously. Even in northern communities with no tradition of slavery, aged ex-slaves were sometimes the only African Americans allowed to stay when towns went sundown. According to local historian Terry Keller, when Anna, Illinois, drove out its African Americans in 1909, they exempted "one old lady who had been a slave." In the quote at the head of this chapter, Laurel Boeckman makes clear the exceptional position of individuals such as these. Many counties and towns in Appalachia, Arkansas, Texas, and the Midwest show a slowly diminishing number of African Americans between 1890 and 1930 because they did not allow new blacks in, and their "Uncle Alecs" and "Aunt Mourns" gradually died or left.[18]

Even though they lived independently, ex-slaves who remained in sundown towns typically had white protectors—often their ex-owners. Protection was important. "Doc" Pitts, the only African American in Beaver Dam, Wisconsin, was the trusted servant and groom of Judge Silas Lamoreaux, President Cleveland's general land commissioner. When the judge returned home to Beaver Dam, he brought Pitts with him to care for his horses. Initially he existed under the protection of Beaver Dam's leading citizen, but after the death of his employer, Beaver Dam allowed Pitts to remain. A town history published about 1941 referred to Pitts as "the town's black." After Pitts's death, Beaver Dam had no black resident. When whites in Corbin, Kentucky, drove out their African Americans in 1919, they missed "Nigger Dennis," "the Mershons' 'man,' " according to historian Hank Everman, referring to one of the wealthier families in town. During the 1919 riot, "the Mershons and Dr. Siler hid him for several days while other blacks fled Corbin." Dennis stayed on, and so did "the beloved 'Aunt Emma' Woods," in Everman's phrase, "a fine cook, laundress, and cleaning lady," and possibly Dennis's mother. In 1930, whites tried to lynch three African Americans in Ste.

Genevieve, in the Bootheel of Missouri. Frustrated by state troopers, the whites turned their wrath on the entire black population. The only African Americans to stay were the extended family of the custodian of the Catholic Church, who was shielded by the priest.[19]

Even with defenders, some sundown towns were too dangerous. During the 1886 eviction of African Americans from the counties southwest of Fort Worth, Matt Fleming, who owned a butcher shop in Comanche County, "offered the services of his shotgun and himself to protect his two colored employees . . . if they wanted to stay," according to Comanche County historian Billy Bob Lightfoot. They left anyway, " 'to keep you from getting into trouble, Mr. Fleming.' " Of course, the employees may also have mistrusted their chances for survival with only one protector against the wrath of the community. "One of the town's doctors refused to have his Negro maid driven from her home," continues Lightfoot, "but a visit from the mob made the girl [*sic*] insist that she be allowed to go to Dublin. The doctor finally gave in and drove the girl across the line himself."[20]

Other Survival Tactics

Some African Americans managed to survive without a protector. Sometimes maintaining a low profile worked as a survival stratagem for African Americans who lived independently. After the 1908 race riot in Springfield, Illinois, when small towns all around Springfield were expelling their African Americans, residents of Pleasant Plains made an exception, ordering all blacks out, except for one elderly couple who were "old and law abiding." When Ambrose Roan, probably the only African American man in Porter County, Indiana, died in 1911 at the age of 66, the *Chesterton Tribune* called him "a hard working, peaceful man, of quiet, unassuming ways." The tiny town of Hazel Dell, Illinois, a few miles south of Greenup, had an African American blacksmith. According to a Greenup resident. "He simply disappeared at sundown and you never saw him again until morning." The fact that his occupation was simultaneously useful and archaic, thus not a threat to most whites, probably helped ensure his safety.[21]

Living in such nonresidential places as above a downtown business worked for some African American individuals, although not for families. Huntington, Indiana, would never let African Americans live independently in a neighborhood, but it allowed an elderly African American man to live downtown, in an otherwise abandoned upstairs room above a store. He was called "Rags" and made a living by washing windows in the downtown area.

"He, too, was tolerated but watched," according to an elderly Huntington native.[22]

Overt identification with the white community was another survival tactic. Such blacks became "Tonto figures"—taking pains to associate with the "white side," differentiated from the hordes of blacks outside of the city limits. White workers in Austin, Minnesota, repeatedly expelled African Americans, and Austin became a sundown town, but like many others, it allowed one African American to stay—the shoeshine "boy." Union member John Winkols tells about him:

> And I'll tell you a good one: so one time we had Frank—I forget his last name— he was shining shoes in the barbershop and then afterwards he bell-hopped for the bus in town here, and everybody liked him. . . . He'd never go in the packing house because he knew he couldn't, he didn't *want* to go there.
>
> So one day I was walking along . . . and here came a couple of niggers, and they stood there by the bridge facing the packing house, and . . . [Frank] says, "Y'know, John," he says, "when the damn niggers start comin' into this town, I'm gonna get the hell outta here." And he was *black!* He was black! *He* didn't want them to come into town either. . . . But we never had no trouble with Frank at all.

Indeed, they didn't; Frank knew with which side of the color line he had to identify if he was to remain in Austin.[23]

Often the one African American in town becomes a celebrity, in a perverse sort of way. Everyone "knows" that person, including their harmless eccentricities. Piety is good, as is always having cookies ready for neighboring children or going by a nickname—but not voting, wanting to work at jobs where whites also work, or attending civic meetings. African Americans who played this part well became genuinely liked by whites. Kathleen Blee, author of *Women of the Klan,* collected a good example from an Indiana woman in the 1980s: "We didn't hate the niggers. We had the Wills family that lived right here in [this] township. And they were like pet coons to us. I went to school with them." Often they got known by nicknames, such as "Snowball" for the only African American in West Bend, Wisconsin, or "Nigger Slim" for the father of the only black family in Salem, Illinois.[24]

Sometimes whites make a big deal out of the only African American in town. After the person's death, everyone turns out for the funeral. Decades after death, such a person may get warm retrospective articles in the local newspaper. "If there is any one character that everyone hears about sooner or later in connection with West Bend it is 'Snowball,' "wrote Dorothy Williams in a 1980 town history. "Snowball," or Elmer Lynden, was "a young Negro [*sic*] about 25 years old" who was killed by two police officers, allegedly while resisting arrest, in 1924. In 1936 the *Chesterton Tribune* in Chesterton, Indiana, ran a story, "Only Colored Couple," about the death of Ambrose Roan 24 years earlier:

> The story goes that when Ambrose Roan found his eternity the present Congregational church choir showed its respect and love for their "Uncle Tom" by singing a number of his beloved hymns. Mrs. Roan was so much moved by this act of courtesy that she invited the entire group of singers for a good Negro cooked chicken dinner.[25]

Staying out of the File Folder

The exceptions would need all the publicity they could get, because their position was always precarious. To become widely and affectionately known, they usually displayed strong but innocuous personalities, the opposite of the low-profile approach favored by the Hazel Dell blacksmith. Often they dressed exceptionally well or exceptionally badly. Usually they allowed and even encouraged whites to call them "nigger." Sometimes they played a clownish role. Whites in Arab, a sundown town in the hills of north Alabama, let an African American live in a nearby hamlet, according to a local expert who has lived in Arab since 1927. "There was one in the Roof community; they called him 'Rabbit,' 'Nigger Rabbit.' Everybody liked him." He lived there until he died. These lone African Americans had *better* be liked by all, because if one person doesn't, even if one person merely doesn't know who they are, they may be in danger. Indeed, he blamed the anti-black nature of Arab on "one guy, really, a chiropractor," an extreme white supremacist whom no one opposed. All it takes is one white person willing to attack, because it is hard for other whites to come to the defense of the person of color. Whites who do may risk being called "nigger lovers" and accused of the opposite of racial patriotism.[26]

What the exception to the sundown rule tries to achieve is a nonthreatening individuality. Newspaper stories in the 1920s repeatedly featured George Washington Maddox for his full name and for being probably the only dwarf as well as the only African American in Medford, Oregon. Casey, population about 2,500, in eastern Illinois, was a sundown town complete with a sign at its city limits saying something like "Nigger, Don't Let the Sun Shine on Your

Back in Casey," according to nearby resident Carolyn Stephens, but for many years whites exempted their nurse-midwife. Elizabeth Davis was locally famous as "Nigger Liz, the best midwife in Clark County" and the only African American allowed to live in Casey (see Portfolio 20). Eventually she grew old and died there in 1963.[27]

I call this the "file folder phenomenon." Upon first encounter with a person different from ourselves, we all tend to place him or her in a file folder: "woman," "teenager," "lesbian," "black," and so on. Elizabeth Davis needed to be filed as "Nigger Liz, the midwife." She could not afford to be a little-known member of her race, because then she would be filed as "black" first, which would never do, not in a sundown county. George Washington Maddox needed his full name—and his nonthreatening status as a dwarf—in order to live peacefully in Medford. Similarly, the sole African American allowed to remain in Harrison, Arkansas, after its 1909 race riot "insisted that her name was Alecta Caledonia Melvina Smith," which shows her as a strong character, but she also let whites call her "Aunt Vine," which played along with the inferior status connoted by *uncle* and *auntie* as applied to older African Americans.[28]

In a fine book on race relations during the Nadir period in Monroe, Michigan, an interracial city, James DeVries describes the file folder phenomenon:

> In their daily interactions with Negroes, the racist perceptions of Monroe's citizens were brought into play. The framework of the childlike Negro was raised to consciousness whenever African Americans who were not personally known appeared on city streets. Indeed, Negroes who arrived in Monroe in the early 20th century found that their presence was carefully noted.

One of Kathleen Blee's interviewees, a white Indiana woman, provides an example of file folder thinking. She agreed that it might have been all right if a local restaurant served food to a local African American in a back room: "I don't think . . . anybody would have thought anything about it. I certainly wouldn't have of our local Negroes. But, not a strange Negro. You get several of them together and they become niggers. Individually they're fine people." To avoid being pigeonholed into this imperiled outgroup, blacks in sundown towns have struggled to establish themselves as individuals.[29]

The Suburban File Folder

Surviving as the exception in a sundown town is always fraught with peril, because at any point one might be accosted by whites who see one as "a nigger" rather than a specific person. One must then hope that other whites who know one as an individual will come to the rescue. In suburbia this rarely happened: there it is too hard for an African American to create and maintain celebrity as an individual. Suburbs have less community—less "gemeinschaft," as sociologists say. There is less "talk" about neighbors and other townspeople, who aren't known as well, and families move in and out even more rapidly than in independent towns. So it is harder for all the residents to learn that a given African American family is OK, that they are the allowed exception.

Alice Thompson, a longtime resident of Brea, California, a sundown suburb of Los Angeles, told in 1982 of one man who almost made it:

> There were no Negroes in Brea; they were not allowed. We had a shoeshine man who we called Neff, and he always spoke to all the kids and everything. He had a little cigar store in front of the barbershop; another man ran a little cigar counter and he [Neff] had the shoeshine place. But at six o'clock, some people say ten but I believe it was six, the bus came through and he left for Fullerton. Fullerton has always had more colored people. He was an awful nice old man, but Brea just would not allow them to be here and I don't know how they stopped them.
> [Who are they?]
> I don't know, I would say, maybe, the Ku-Klux Klan.[30]

Fred and Mary Clark did succeed in staying in West Lawn, the sundown neighborhood of Chicago where they were the only black household. Indeed, the Clarks were no interlopers. They had lived in West Lawn since 1893, before there *was* a West Lawn. Nevertheless, newcomers to West Lawn had to learn that their existence was tolerated, or the Clarks were in trouble. "Even now that the Clarks are older," wrote reporter Steve Bogira in 1986, "they have to worry about the reaction of whites—especially young ones—to their presence."

> "Walking down the street is not a pleasant ordeal . . . ," Fred says. "School kids will come and throw stones." . . . The Clarks don't even sit on the porch—they mainly stay inside the house, where they're out of the way of white animosity. Mostly out of the way, that is—they still have rocks and bricks tossed through

their windows periodically, still find racist graffiti scribbled on their garage at times. Several years ago, after all of their front windows, upstairs and downstairs, had been smashed with rocks one night, the Clarks put the house up for sale. "When people would come to look at it and they found a black was here they'd move on," Mary says. "So it wasn't no way of selling it."

Many decades ago, when West Lawn had more gemeinschaft, white neighbors helped guard the house when whites attacked African Americans throughout Chicago during the 1919 race riot. Gradually "the old-timers moved out, and the new neighbors seemed less comfortable with the Clarks." As an adult, Fred Clark "has been chased through the neighborhood several times, had rocks thrown at him, but his docile attitude has kept him from serious harm."[31]

Exceptions That Embody the Rule

Even transient African Americans, by the sheer fact of their existence, can prompt some change for the better. Bus passengers might find themselves in Cullman, Alabama, a rest stop on U.S. 31, the main route from Nashville to Birmingham and points south. During the segregation era, according to a woman who grew up in Cullman, African Americans

> would step off in Cullman to look for restrooms only to be turned back, and mothers could be heard explaining to their crying children that they would have to wait until farther down the road. Mother never told us that without a catch in her voice. By the time I can remember, a bus station had been built that had a set of facilities for each race—the only place in Cullman that did, to the best of my knowledge.

Those "colored" restrooms brought Cullman partway into the era of "mere" segregation (although African Americans still could not eat or sleep in the town) and therefore marked an advance compared to total exclusion.[32]

Similarly, the solitary black household allowed as the exception in a sundown town can humanize that community to a degree. At least whites have made a distinction among African Americans, even if only to separate out one or two Tonto figures from the otherwise backward horde. And their presence—and that of their children—does "desegregate" some of the institutions in town, such as the public schools and the library, even if only nominally. But I wouldn't want to claim too much for this process. Allowing one African

American person or household has rarely led to a difference in a sundown town's policy or alleviated the racism that defends and rationalizes that policy.

On the contrary: publicizing the African American as an exception reminds the community that this is the *only* African American allowed in the area, thus ironically reinforcing the sundown rule. Even Greenwood, Indiana, for example, a town whose hostility toward African Americans was legendary, had its one African American household as an exception. In the words of Joycelyn Landrum-Brown, an African American who grew up nearby, "The whites in that town 'just loved' that black family," and "they did not come to any harm."[33]

The Austin, Minnesota, story shows another ideological payoff that allowing one household to stay when all others are driven out can have for whites, as they can claim not to be racist: "We're not against all African Americans, after all—look at Frank!" More accurately, whites can claim to be *appropriately* racist. The problem lies with those *other* African Americans—"the damn niggers." Even Frank—"and he was *black*"—agrees. Thus instead of allowing their positive feelings about George Washington Maddox or Elizabeth Davis to prompt some questioning of their exclusionary policies, whites in Medford, Oregon, and Casey, Illinois, merely emphasized how exceptional these individuals were. In turn, this allowed whites to affirm once more how inferior *other* African Americans were, in their eyes. In about 1950, whites in Marshall, Illinois, a sundown town just east of Casey, even declared their exception, "Squab" Wilson, the barber, to be "an honorary white man." Afraid of losing this honor—and perhaps his white clientele and his permission to live in Marshall—Wilson refused to cut the hair of a black writer living temporarily at the nearby Handy Writers Colony, until novelist James Jones threatened him with a boycott.[34]

Interaction with people such as "Frank" or Wilson provides residents of sundown towns with no meaningful experience with African Americans, because such individuals take care not to reveal opinions or characteristics different from those of the white majority. Unfortunately, unless they enlist in the armed forces, most residents of sundown towns never get to know African Americans, except superficially in athletic contests and from television. The impact of the exclusion of African Americans on the residents of these towns—and on white Americans in general—will be the subject of the next chapter.

PART V

Effects of Sundown Towns

11

The Effect of Sundown Towns on Whites

And I said "nigger," and my mother corrected me: "When we're in *this* town you must call them 'Negroes.' "

—"Susan Penny" of Oblong, Illinois, telling of her childhood trip to Terre Haute, Indiana, c. 1978 [1]

WHAT DIFFERENCE DO SUNDOWN TOWNS and suburbs make? In particular, what effect do they have on their inhabitants? Is growing up in an intentionally all-white town unlike growing up in an integrated town? Sociologist William J. Wilson uses "social isolation" as an explanation (in part) for the social pathology of the black ghetto. Here we explore the social pathology of the *white* ghetto, if you will, caused by its comparable social isolation. We will see that residents of sundown towns do become more racist toward African Americans and also more prejudiced toward gays and other minorities. Sundown towns also collect white racists from the outside world who are attracted by the towns' lack of diversity.

White Seems Right

My research shows that residents of sundown towns and suburbs are much more racist toward African Americans than are residents of interracial towns, and also more prejudiced toward gays and other minorities. But do sundown communities collect white supremacists or create them? The question is important. If sundown towns merely collected racists, they might be doing American society a service by sequestering bigots away from the rest of us. Sundown towns do collect white racists from the outside world who are attracted by their lack of diversity. Unfortunately, they also create racists. Living in an all-white community leads many residents to defend living in an all-white community.

These generalizations do not describe everyone in a sundown town, suburb, or neighborhood.[2] Many young adults leave sundown communities precisely to experience greater diversity and escape the stifling atmosphere of conformity that many of these places foster. Indeed, if they want to be successful, young people almost have to leave independent sundown towns, because these towns impart a worldview that limits their horizons. Children of elite sundown suburbs, on the other hand, are likely to move into positions of corporate and political leadership in years to come. This makes their constricted upbringing a problem for us all, because sundown communities inculcate a distinctive form of obtuse thinking about American society—I have elsewhere called it "soclexia"[3]—that incorporates remarkable ethnocentrism as well as NIMBY (Not In My Back Yard) politics.

The first and mildest effect on one's thinking that results from living in a sundown town is the sense that it is perfectly normal to live in an all-white community. Even towns that went sundown by violently expelling their African Americans quickly come to seem all-white "naturally." Billy Bob Lightfoot, historian of Comanche County, Texas, caught this sense when describing the aftermath of that county's expulsion of its black residents in 1886: "Almost immediately it seemed as though there had never been a Negro in Comanche County, and within a month the only reminder . . . was a sign on the public well in De Leon: 'Nigger, don't let the sun go down on you in this town.' "[4] "Almost immediately," whites do not really notice that the town is *not* normal and that an initial incident, in this case a violent expulsion, and a subsequent series of enforcement measures, some violent, were required to achieve and maintain this abnormal result.[5]

Decades later, it is even easier to take a town's whiteness for granted. Not everyone moves to sundown towns to avoid African Americans, after all. Many whites locate in them without even knowing they are sundown towns. Once they have moved in, residents are still less likely to reflect upon the racial composition of their new community. The sun rises in the east and sets in the west, the children go to school, the adults to work, and all seems as it should be. All-white town governments, churches, choral groups, audiences, and even school athletic teams come to appear perfectly normal. African Americans come to seem unusual—abnormal—except maybe on television.

Children who grow up in sundown towns find it especially easy to develop the sense that it is normal, even proper, to grow up in a place where everyone looks like you, racially, and that blacks are *not* the same and not really proper. But newcomers, too, rarely challenge the whiteness of their newly chosen communities. Instead, they tend to take on the culture, including the political ideology and patterns of race relations, into which they move. Carl Withers studied a small Missouri sundown town, Wheatland, in 1940. "New settlers still come in, a dozen or two a year in the whole county," he wrote. "Those who stay become in remarkably short time 'just like everybody else here,' in speech, dress, mannerisms, attitudes, and general way of life. Most of those who are unable to adjust to the community's mores soon sell out and move away." Jacob Holdt, a Dane whose exposé on race relations in the United States, *American Pictures,* was briefly famous in the 1980s, describes Danes' accommodation to racism in the United States: "I have met Danish Americans who were red-hot Social Democrats back in Denmark, but in the course of just five years had been transformed into the worst reactionaries."[6]

Withers's finding—that newcomers become just like everybody else—holds especially true for new arrivals to sundown suburbs. As *Newsweek* put it in 1957, during the peak rush to suburbia: "When a city dweller packs up and moves his family to the suburbs, he usually acquires a mortgage, a power lawn mower, and a backyard grill. Often although a lifelong Democrat, he also starts voting Republican." Sometimes families even change their party membership before they move, a pattern sociologists call anticipatory socialization. The same adjustment seems to take place regarding race relations, which explains why sundown towns that were quite small before suburbanization usually stay all-white after suburbanization, even though nine-tenths of their populations may now be new arrivals. Sundown acorns produce white oak trees. Socialization to suburbia thus increases the level of racism in metropolitan areas, as people move from multiracial cities to all-white suburbs.[7]

White Privilege

Once living in an all-white town seems normal, residents come to think of it as a *right*. Going against this right seems wrong. As we saw in the "Enforcement" chapter, a person of color who strays into an all-white town looks out of place, even outrageous. A white person who claims that this is not how a town should be can similarly sound out of place, even outrageous.

In 1987, Oprah Winfrey, broadcasting from Forsyth County, Georgia, then a sundown county, explored this mentality:

> Winfrey: You don't believe that people of other races have the right to live here?

> Unidentified Audience Member #2: They have the right to live wherever they want to, but we have the right to choose if we want a white community also. That's why we moved here.

This viewpoint is hardly confined to places as "extreme" as Forsyth County, which expelled its African Americans en masse in 1912. "White people have a right to keep blacks out of their neighborhoods if they want to, and blacks should respect that right" was one of the opinion statements presented to people by the National Opinion Research Center repeatedly in the 1970s, and in 1976, a representative year, 40% of whites across the nation agreed with the item. Of course, many of them lived in all-white suburbs and neighborhoods. Striking is Audience Member #2's "we/they" terminology. White privilege necessarily involves the creation of a black "they"—a racial outgroup. Thus sundown towns increase white racism because they provoke whites to think of a black person not as an individual but as an African American first. The file folder phenomenon rules uncontested.[8]

In 1958, sociologist Herbert Blumer published an important article, "Race Prejudice as a Sense of Group Position," pointing out "that race prejudice exists basically in a sense of group position rather than in a set of feelings." Blumer pointed out that viewing prejudice as feelings "overlooks and obscures the fact that race prejudice is fundamentally a matter of relationship between racial groups." While feelings are definitely involved, prejudice presupposes "that racially prejudiced individuals think of themselves as belonging to a given racial group." It also presupposes that they have an image of the "other" group, against whom they are prejudiced. Blumer went on to identify four feelings that are involved, of which "the third feeling, the sense of proprietary claim, is of crucial importance." "Proprietary claim," of course—the "right" to exclude—is precisely what sundown towns are all about.[9]

This new proprietary claim helps explain why sundown towns usually stayed all-white for so long: once whites have concocted the "privilege" of living in an all-white community, they are then loath to give up this "right." Indeed, what we might call "racial patriotism" keeps them from giving it up. Note the contradiction between the two rights invoked by Winfrey's Audience Member #2: "They" have "the right to live wherever they want," but "we" have "the right to choose if we want a white community." How do "we" exercise that right? Obviously by infringing "their" right to live wherever they want.

A white friend unwittingly displayed this same contradiction upon first learning of my research topic: "I just can't understand why people would *want* to live where they're not wanted!" This statement seems reasonable and I tried to answer it reasonably, but it presumes that African Americans can be expected to assess whether whites want them and should comport themselves accordingly. When "we" (nonblacks) buy a house, we do not assess whether our neighbors will like us. We rarely even meet them before moving in, and if we do, we only meet those right next door. We *presume* we will be accepted or at least tolerated. We also presume the privilege of living wherever we want. My friend's comment does not afford African Americans the same right and instead makes "them" the problem: "they" are wrong to intrude.

Racist Symbols and Mascots

This book is a history of exclusion, yet the excluded are ever-present. They persist in the form of stereotypes and constructions in the minds of those who keep them out. From the Nadir until very recently, sundown town residents have been even more likely than other whites to impersonate African Americans in theatrical productions and revues. After whites in Corbin, Kentucky, drove out all African Americans on Halloween in 1919, May Minstrel Festival with "black-faced comedians" became perhaps its most popular annual event during the 1920s. In Royal Oak, a sundown suburb of Detroit, the Lions Club put on minstrel shows from 1948 to 1968. White residents in blackface performed minstrel shows in all-white towns in Wisconsin, Illinois, and Vermont into the 1970s. Even today, residents of sundown towns are much more likely than in interracial towns to display such atavisms as black "coach boys" or Confederate flags in front of their houses.[10] Students in all-white towns in several states have caused disruptions by wearing Confederate flags, T-shirts, and jackets to school. Such incidents also take place in interracial schools, of course, but much less often, because there they will not go unopposed by other students. Perhaps more worrisome, in some all-white towns, such as Deer Park in eastern Washington, students cause *no* disruption by wearing or displaying Confederate flags, according to recent Deer Park graduates. "You cannot wear all one color—so as to be Goths, etc. But you *can* have Confederate flags on your locker!"[11]

An in-your-face example of white privilege is the use of racial slurs to name athletic teams, a common practice in sundown towns. For several decades Pekin High School in central Illinois called its athletic teams "Chinks" ("Chinklets" for the girls). It was supposed to be funny, referring to the town, named for Peking (Beijing), China; the teams' previous nickname had been "Celestials." When Pekin won the state basketball tournament in 1964 and 1967, the resulting publicity prompted an outcry from outraged Chinese Americans. In 1974, Kung Lee Wang, president of the Organization of Chinese Americans, twice flew to Pekin from his Maryland home. He denounced the name as "a racist slur," met with the mayor, school superintendent, and principals, and addressed the student council. The students then voted 85%

to 15% to stick with "Chinks," and the board of education echoed that decision the following spring. Pekin retained "Chinks" until 1980, when a new school superintendent demanded a change, apparently as a condition of his employment. The change then provoked a student walkout that lasted several days. Unfortunately, the school changed its nickname to "Dragons," which also conjures not only China but also leaders of the Ku Klux Klan.[12] That connotation was not lost in Pekin, which was notorious as a statewide Klan headquarters in the 1920s. Indeed, the Klan owned the *Pekin Times* for a while and ran sections of official Klan philosophy as editorials; today a Klan leader still lives and recruits in Pekin.[13]

"Redskins" is a more common slur used as nickname, chosen by at least three all-white high schools in Illinois and several others in other states. To be sure, naming teams with racial slurs is hardly limited to sundown towns, as the Washington Redskins prove. Nevertheless, without attempting the exhausting task of analyzing the mascots of all U.S. high schools against the racial composition of their student bodies, my impression is that all-white high schools are more likely to adopt racially derogatory nicknames and mascots and less likely to change them when challenged. Many people of color and their allies hate this practice and have protested it, not only to the owners of the Washington NFL team but also in small towns such as Sullivan, Illinois. The typical response from sundown towns—and from supporters of the Washington team—is to deny that they mean anything racist by the nicknames and to say that if people choose to interpret them differently, that's their problem. As Pekin graduate Dianna Adams wrote about the Chinks, "I always thought that it was a compliment to those who chose to take it otherwise."[14]

Names such as "Chinks" and "Redskins" imply that whites are dominant and can use racial slurs anytime they want. Too few Chinese Americans lived in Pekin—and their position was too tenuous—to protest. Similarly, American Indians are less than 1% of the population, and the protesters who appear at every home Redskins football game in D.C. are even fewer, so "we" can do whatever we want.[15] The same sense of privilege holds for displaying a Confederate flag or black coach boy. In interracial towns, whether from fear that such a symbol (or the house behind it) might get vandalized or from a sincere desire not to offend people of color, whites are less likely to flaunt such items.

Athletic Contests in Sundown Towns

In many small towns, high school athletic contests are portentous. Usually a basketball or football game draws more people than any other event of the week; often the game then becomes the main topic of conversation during the next week. The contests are important symbolically as well. Unfortunately, racist mascots are only part of the problem of white misbehavior when players and fans from interracial schools visit sundown towns. Such visits take place under a double cloud of "otherness."

A town already forms an in-group vis-à-vis the next town. In high school athletic contests, this antagonism usually has a lighthearted cast. Cheers like "Smash the Tigers!" aren't meant literally, of course. But when a town is all-white on purpose, the sense of being the racial in-group as well lends a special edge to the contest. A black graduate of Manual, Peoria's most interracial high school, said that when her alma mater plays Pekin, downstate Illinois's largest sundown town, "something racial is definitely going on." A 2001 white graduate of Manual agreed: "There is a special atmosphere when Manual plays Pekin. Lots is at stake. Whole buses of students go, to protect the team." On occasion the team has needed protection; in 1975, for example, according to Randy Whitman, a Manual student at the time, as the team was leaving Pekin "bottles, bricks, and all other kind of debris start pelting the bus." Fans of interracial high school teams near other sundown towns say the same thing: they take a busload of people "to protect their team" in what they surmise is likely to be a hostile environment. Administrators and coaches from interracial schools caution their fans and team members to stay in groups and exhibit extreme decorum when they play schools in sundown towns.[16]

Supporting the cheerleaders become an issue too, especially if they "cheer black." Blacks and whites tend to engage in two quite different styles of cheerleading, each of which can appear laughable to the other. In overwhelmingly white environments, black cheerleaders can face ridicule, even without the racist catcalls that sometimes emanate from fans in a sundown town. When Meadowbrook High School, a majority-white but integrated school southwest of Richmond, Virginia, played Colonial Heights, known informally as "Colonial Whites," the Meadowbrook cheerleading coach recruited extra chaperones to accompany them to help students deal with the racism they routinely experienced there.[17]

Interracial towns and teams need not include a high proportion of African Americans to draw the ire of fans and players in sundown towns. Cleveland, Oklahoma, has a big football rivalry with Hominy, the next town north. According to a 1985 graduate of Hominy High School, that "game was always well attended, even when both teams stank. The story I heard was that the racial difference between Cleveland and Hominy was so great that Cleveland used to call their rivals the 'Hominy Coons.'" In 1990, Hominy had 76

African Americans among 2,342 residents, just 3%, but that looked very black from the vantage point of Cleveland, which had just 8 African Americans—and no black households—among its 3,156 residents, or 0.2%. In a sundown town, emphasizing even the few blacks among an opponent's student body or team can provide a unifying rhetoric for the in-group.[18]

Fans in sundown towns commonly use racial slurs. Across America, coaches and principals from interracial high schools caution their players and fans not to react. They know that racial slurs have often led to more serious altercations. In the 1960s, all-white Cedar Cliff High School in Lemoyne, Pennsylvania, across the river from Harrisburg, played football against Harrisburg's majority-black John Harris High School. According to a high school teacher in the area, "riots occurred every time the game was on the 'White Shore.' " Clearly, more than good-natured rivalries are involved. Fans in some sundown towns seem affronted that African Americans dare to play in their town. Kaye Collins attended Rabun Gap Nacoochee High School, in the northeast corner of Georgia, in 1972–73. "We had a black basketball player on our team, and threats were made against him when we played in Towns County. That was the first time I heard that black people shouldn't be in Towns County after dark." The death threats were made days before the game, but according to Collins, "nothing happened. Our team trounced them!" In the 1990s, whites burned crosses in Dale, Indiana, when a majority-black team from Evansville played there, a high school teacher from the area reported. An African American member of the Danville, Kentucky, football team remembered repeated outrageous fan behavior at Corbin, Kentucky, in the early 1970s. "They would cut the bus tires and the car tires, especially if we were winning." Corbin is the scene of the only film ever made about a sundown town, Robby Heason's documentary *Trouble Behind*. In it, an African American former football player in a nearby town says in 1990,

> We went in there to play; we were scared to death. . . . When we'd come out we'd get "rocked"—they'd throw rocks at your buses, they'd throw big cinderblocks. We had a couple of times where they would throw through the complete windshield. . . . And we had to drive back one night, this is when I was a sophomore, and this is a basketball game, and they crashed the whole front window and we had to drive home without it.

Later in the documentary, Heason films the school superintendent in Corbin saying, "It's a good place to rear our children."[19]

It isn't just fans who misbehave. Often players and even officials act up as well. Cairo, an interracial town at the southern tip of Illinois, played for the regional basketball championship in Anna in 1987. The Cairo Pilots, all black except their coach and one player, led by fifteen points at the half. Thereafter, "every call seemed to favor the hometown Wildcats of Anna-Jonesboro," according to two *Washington Post* reporters at the game. Referees called 24 fouls on Cairo and just 8 on Anna-Jonesboro. Late in the game, a Cairo player struck back after being elbowed by an Anna guard, and a near-riot ensued. "We go through this all the time," said Bill Chumbler, the Cairo coach. "There are no black referees down here, and we know that if it's close near the end, they're going to take it away from us." [20]

Interracial schools have to take measures to shield their black teammates and cheerleaders from harm in some sundown towns. Football and basketball teams in interracial high schools in Evansville—in southwestern Indiana—have a tradition of playing away-games at Jasper, Indiana, "earlier in the day than usual," according to a man who practice-taught in Evansville in 2001. "The reason: it was still commonly understood that for the safety of the student athletes of color and their parents, the team needed to be out of Jasper before dark or as close to it as possible." A 1995 graduate of interracial Carbondale High School in southern Illinois said their wrestling coach warned them to protect their African American players on and off the mat when competing at West Frankfort, a sundown town 20 miles northeast. Athletes in Sullivan, Missouri, were so racist that some coaches chose not to risk letting their African American players play, according to a nearby resident:

> Some local context: It was only about 9 years ago that the sign outside of the town of Sullivan, Missouri, (a stronghold of the KKK in Missouri, and about 30 miles from where I live) was removed. It stated simply "Nigger, don't let the sun set on you in Sullivan." I have friends who live there who have told me of things that they have seen themselves there. My daughter married a man who was born and raised there and has told us that the town fathers, bank president, mayor, and other officials are all known to be members and leaders of the local [KKK] chapter. When my son was in high school and played football, the black kids were always benched when they played in Sullivan. It was not out of discrimination against them, but to protect them from injury. Over the years the coach had too many black players hurt there, and hurt in ways that couldn't be proven were intentional, but appeared to be so. He felt he couldn't risk it any more. The parents went along. [21]

This tradition of racism at athletic contests also besets sundown suburbs, where it has sometimes drawn coverage from major city daily newspapers. The *New York Times* ran a story on Connecticut's 1999 state championship football game between Darien, a sundown suburb, and Weaver High School in north Hartford, where the majority of students are black and Hispanic. "After Game, Aftertaste of Racial Slurs Lingers" was the headline. Weaver won, 69 to 26. "In the hearts of many Weaver players, however, the sweetness of victory mingled with the sting of racism," according to the *Times*. "As the game wore on and the score became more lopsided, members of the Weaver team, all of whom are black or Hispanic, said they heard a number of crude racial epithets hurled at them by Darien's all-white team." Players from Darien, one of the richest suburbs of New York City, also hurled class insults after a Weaver touchdown: "It's O.K. In five years, you'll be working for me." Some Darien players charged that Weaver players had also used racial slurs, and the teams did get together for a constructive session at Weaver later. If the Darien team had included black players, it is unlikely that its white players would have used *nigger,* and if Darien were integrated on social class lines, it would be equally unthinkable that some team members would taunt opposing players for being poor.[22]

Racist language and behavior by athletes and fans begin as early as middle school in some sundown towns.[23] Some situations have grown so tense that interracial middle schools have canceled all future games with sundown schools. Usually this bad behavior takes place at the school in the sundown town. Less often do sundown fans yell racial slurs when they are the visitors, in the minority. Occasionally students in interracial schools engage in belligerent behavior at their home games, aimed at the all-white outsiders. Darla Craft wrote of being a cheerleader of all-white Herrin Junior High School in southern Illinois in 1969–70. "We had a basketball game in Mt. Vernon, where there was racial unrest. As we left the game, we were jumped by a group of African-American girls. I ran, so I wasn't hurt, but a couple of the girls were pretty banged up." Around that time, according to a graduate of Pinckneyville High School, a few miles northwest, "the two or three times we played football or basketball against Sparta or Du Quoin [nearby interracial towns] every year [there] were always melees bordering on race riots. I recall hearing of one game at Sparta at which all of our buses' windows were broken out, and riot police were called in from Carbondale to settle things down." I remember this period of militance in black culture between 1969 and about 1972, but the danger of what might be called "white racial paranoia" also lurks. The Sparta-Pinckneyville fracas may not have been exactly a race riot, considering that Sparta was at the time just 15% black. Surely white Sparta students had to have participated. Perhaps it was primarily an interscholastic melee with racial overtones.[24]

The Talk in Sundown Towns

The foregoing account of bad behavior at athletic contests in sundown towns is not the whole story. Many sundown towns have repeatedly hosted interracial teams and their fans without incident. However, that's partly because the visitors choose to overlook the verbal racism they encounter. Even when on their best behavior, many residents of sundown towns routinely say "nigger." Indeed, another privilege all-white towns confer on their inhabitants is the license to say anything they want about people of color. Perhaps the first thing noticed by visitors to independent sundown towns is their overt verbal racism. During my thirteen years of public schooling in interracial Decatur, Illinois, ending in 1960, I never once heard the word *nigger* in school, on the playground, or said by one of my peers anywhere. But in sundown towns all around Decatur and all across America, the word was in common parlance then and remains the term of choice today. One of the most profound effects of sundown towns is on white rhetoric—on how people in them talk, especially on how they talk about race and about black people.

In 2001, I had a pleasant conversation with a 70-year-old white woman in Sheridan, Arkansas. A year or so earlier, the first African American family to move into Sheridan since blacks were evicted four decades earlier joined her church, Landmark Baptist, the town's most prominent. She favored their membership and said: "Our pastor, I have to hand it to him. He was young, but he knew what to do. He counseled with the nigger family, so then the niggers knew what they were getting into, and it all worked out." This woman did not mean *nigger* maliciously; she seemed happy that the family stayed. She was just thoughtlessly using the term she had heard and used all her life. Her sundown town, fifty years behind the times, encouraged that lack of thought. Many sundown town residents are oblivious to other signs of progress in race relations. In 1993, half the class in Highland High School, a sundown town in Illinois east of St. Louis, thought interracial marriage was still illegal, according to a woman who graduated that year.[25]

One of the chief ways that white Americans have progressed in racial conduct in the fifty years since the 1954 Supreme Court school desegregation decision is in their rhetoric. Words may be shallow, the change may only lie on the surface, but surfaces do matter. People typically relate to each other on the surface, after all. Surface surely matters to African Americans, who take deep offense at whites' use of *nigger*. For that matter, civilized rhetoric is a first step toward civilized behavior. The Civil Rights Movement initiated half a century of conflict and change that has proven difficult but humanizing. Sundown towns have deliberately sidestepped this adventure in healing, through which we are still working our way. Sheridan itself went sundown in 1954, in direct response to *Brown*.

Not just in speech, but also on paper, sundown town residents offend. While they don't write *nigger*, authors typically use *Negro*—often uncapitalized—or the still more ancient *colored people*, even in works intended as serious history and written as late as the 1980s and 1990s. The rest of America left these terms behind decades ago in favor of *black* and *African American*. Writers in independent sundown towns simply haven't bothered to keep up with this progression. When they quote the occasional African American permitted to live in their town as exceptions, often they use dialect. Ralph Rea, for example, historian of Boone County, Arkansas, quotes Alecta Smith, allowed to remain after the expulsions of 1905 and 1909: "Aunt Vine often said that she was 'the best niggah evah bawn, cuz all de rest was run off.' " Of course, just about all Americans pronounce *'cause* "cuz." "Cuz" is correct. But no one writes *cuz* when a white person uses *'cause*. Moreover, whites and blacks from a given part of Arkansas pronounce *ever, born,* and most other words about the same. To put Smith's words in dialect is simply to otherize her, to make her speech different from and inferior to whites' use of language. By even the narrowest definition it is racist, for it treats one group differently and worse than another when they pronounce the same word identically. Such dialect was also antique, even back in 1955.[26]

It is striking when well-meaning whites say *nigger* as a matter of course. More often, whites in sundown towns do not mean well. In 1966, when Gordon Wright and his family moved into Grosse Pointe, Michigan, the first African American family to do so, they endured months of the slur. Adults yelled, "Nigger, go back down South." The Kiwanis Club bus taking children to a park during the summer slowed at the Wright residence so the kids could lean out and yell the epithet. When school started in the fall, the safety patrol boys called the Wright children "niggers" on their way to school.[27]

Kathy Spillman grew up in North Tonawanda, a sundown town near Buffalo, New York, in the 1970s and '80s. "The *nicest* word I learned was *colored. Nigger* was the typical term," she told me. "I learned to hold my breath when blacks walked by, because I was taught they smell bad." Roger Horowitz, now at the Hagley Museum in Delaware, lived in Marquette Park, a sundown neighborhood in Chicago, where "there was and is the casual assumption in bars that you can tell 'nigger jokes.' " Two thousand miles southwest, in Indian Wells, California, Richard Williams and his famous tennis-star daughters Venus and Serena experienced *nigger* at the Pacific Life Open in March, 2001,

MASS MEETING.

A Mass Meeting of the citizens
of this place and vicinity will be
held at Darby's Hall, on Sunday,
Jan. 31, at 2 o'clock P. M., to
devise some lawful means of rid-
ding Crescent City of Chinese.

R. W. Miller, R. G. Knox, L. F. Coburn and
others will address the meeting.

All are invited to attend.

[1] Chinese Americans had lived in Crescent City, California, near the Oregon line, since at least the 1870s. The meeting advertised on this broadside was the first of a series lasting until mid-March, 1886. Eventually "lawful" was dropped and a mob forced the Chinese to depart on three sailing vessels bound for San Francisco. Whites in Humboldt County, the next county south, had already expelled 320 Chinese Americans from Eureka in 1885. In 1886 they drove Chinese from Arcata, Ferndale, Fortuna, Rohnerville, and Trinidad. [2] In 1906 they finished the job, loading these cannery workers onto boxcars, leaving their belongings behind. No Chinese returned to Humboldt Bay until the 1950s. *(Notes for this Portfolio section begin on page 523; photography credits begin on page 525.)*

In an all-night riot in August, 1901, white residents of Pierce City, Missouri, hanged a young black man alleged to have murdered a white woman, killed his grandfather, looted the armory, and used its Springfield rifles to attack the black community. African Americans fired back but were outgunned. [3] The mob then burned several homes including this one, Emma Carter's, incinerating at least two African Americans inside. At 2 A.M., Pierce City's 200 black residents ran for their lives. They found no refuge in the nearest town, Monett, because in 1894 it had expelled its blacks in a similar frenzy and hung a sign, "Nigger, Don't Let The Sun Go Down." [4] The house below stands in the "Black Hills," home to African Americans in Pinckneyville, Illinois, until they were driven out around 1928. A woman born across the street in 1947 recalls being teased in school "for living in niggertown." This house was formerly the black school.

[5] Will James, who had been arrested for the murder of Anna Pelley, has just been hanged under this brilliantly illuminated double arch that was the pride of downtown Cairo, Illinois, on November 11, 1909. Among the thousands of spectators were some from Anna, 30 miles north, where Pelley had grown up. Afterward, they returned home and drove all African Americans out of Anna. [6] Public subscription then paid for this striking granite tombstone commemorating Pelley. Adolescents in Anna still pay their respects at this site, a rite that helps maintain Anna as a sundown town.

Eyewitnesses tell of sundown signs in more than 150 communities in 31 states. Most read, "Nigger, Don't Let The Sun Go Down On You In ___." Some came in series, like the old Burma-Shave signs: "Nigger, If You Can Read," "You'd Better Run," "If You Can't Read," "You'd Better Run Anyway." Despite considerable legwork, I have not located a single photo of such a sign. Local librarians laugh when I ask if they saved theirs or a photo of it: "Why would we do that?" [7] James Allen, who assembled a famous exhibit of lynching postcards, bought this sign around 1985; its only provenance is "from Connecticut." [8] At left is a sign still extant, a black mule, used by residents of sundown towns in Arkansas, Kentucky, Missouri, and Tennessee to warn African Americans to "get their black ass" outside the city limits by sundown. Margaret Alam photographed this example just west of Liberty, Tennessee, in 2003. Other towns used sirens. [9] In 1914, Villa Grove, Illinois, put up this water tower. Sometime thereafter, the town mounted a siren on it that sounded at 6 P.M. to warn African Americans to get beyond the city limits, until about 1998.

[10] On June 1, 1921, whites tried to make Tulsa, Oklahoma, a sundown town. As part of the attack, deputized white men raided a munitions dump, commandeered five airplanes, and dropped dynamite onto the black community, making it the only place in the contiguous United States ever to undergo aerial bombardment. Like efforts to expel blacks from other large cities, the Tulsa mob failed; the job was simply too large.

Earlier, in May, 1911, the teenage son of Laura Nelson, who lived near Boley, Oklahoma, a black town, killed a deputy who was searching their cabin for stolen meat. His mother, trying to protect him, claimed she did it. [11] "Her innocence was determined weeks before the lynching," according to James Allen, who collected this postcard of the lynching. Nevertheless, a white mob from Okemah, a sundown town ten miles east of Boley, hanged Nelson and her son from this bridge spanning the North Canadian River. Residents then stayed up all night to fend off an imagined mob, said to be coming from Boley to sack Okemah. Similar fears prompted similar mobilizations in sundown suburbs during urban ghetto riots in the 1960s.

DON'T LET THE SUN SET ON YOU HERE, UNDERSTAND?

Norman, Okla., Feb. 10.—Agitation involving Race musicians has become quite widespread since the beating up of Howard's orchestra in Miami, Fla., some weeks ago. The latest instance of intimidation occurred in this city.

An orchestra composed of Race men had been sent for to come from Fort Worth, Texas, to play at a dance given for students of the University of Oklahoma. When it was discovered that the musicians were in town a free-for-all fight was only narrowly averted. Like many Southern towns there is a disposition here to make this a lily-white community and keep out from it certain citizens of the republic.

Thus, soon after the dance started a mob gathered outside the hall and began throwing stones and bricks through the windows. An investigation revealed the cause or motive for the mob action. Calls were immediately made for the police, who came in time to save the musicians from further mistreatment. Several score students surrounded the orchestra and escorted it to an interurban station, where it entrained for Fort Worth.

ANTI-NEGRO CRUSADE

Indiana River Towns Are Taking Drastic Measures

TO RID THEMSELVES OF THE OBNOXIOUS

Scores Indicted for Selling Their Votes—In Many Places No Negroes Are Allowed to Live.

Evansville, Ind., Jan. 28.—Cities and towns along the Ohio river have begun a crusade against the negroes. The entire trouble dates back to the lynching of the negroes at Rockport and Boonville for the murder of the white barber, Simmons, at Rockport one night last month. The board of safety of this

University of Oklahoma students invited a black orchestra to play for their dance, but citizens of Norman intervened because the musicians violated Norman's sundown rule. [12] This 1922 story in the *Chicago Defender* uses "Race" where we would use "black." [13] At right, datelined Evansville, a report tells of a wave of anti-black actions in southwestern Indiana in 1901, triggered by "the lynching of the Negroes at Rockport and Boonville for the murder of the white barber." Only contagion can explain how the murder of one barber could prompt three lynchings in Rockport, one in Boonville, and "vigilance committees" to drive African Americans from at least five other towns. [14] The full headline below is "White Men Shoot Up Church Excursioners." Black motorists stranded in sundown towns have always been in danger, no matter their circumstances. In August 1940, a church group in Charleston, South Carolina, hired a bus to attend an event. On their way home, it broke down in the little town of Bonneau. While they were waiting for a replacement bus, sixteen white men came on the scene and ordered them to "get out [of] here right quick. We don't allow no d—n n—rs 'round here after sundown." They then opened fire on the parishioners with shotguns, causing them to flee into nearby woods.

WHITE MEN SHOOT UP CHURCH

EAST AND WEST WAIT AT GATE

GROUP IS TOLD "NO N----RS ALLOWED AFTER SUNDOWN"

MONCKS CORNER, S. C., Aug. 15—(ANP)—Five persons returning from a church excursion at Eutawville Sunday night were wounded by shotgun blasts when they were fired upon at a filling station in Bonneau, near here, by unidentified white men. Frank

Greene was admitted to Dorches-ter County Hospital in Summer-ville suffering from gunshot wounds

5,384 GALL STONES TAKEN FROM WOMAN

WILSON, N. C., Aug 15—The largest number of gall stones ever recorded in the medical history of this section, 5,384, were taken from a 50-year-old woman at Wilson hospital recently. Physicians said, however, that she would recover

—rs 'round here after sundown. The excursioners the white driver and the station operator tried to explain the emergency to no avail. A second car drove up with eight more white men who began firing on the group with shotguns. Having no weapon, the excursioners fled into nearby woods. Many were still missing

and was driven into a filling station at Bonneau and left by the driver with consent of the opera-

Gua In C

CH-AG gested action las ted Univ ate ordinance cials are cons the street cars l ways and the t united city cont ownership. Negr sted against em ployment.

[15] This 1935 linoleum cut by Lin Shi Khan is part of a collection titled *Scottsboro Alabama*. Scottsboro was not a sundown town, but most towns in the nearby Sand Mountains were. [16] For his 1973 novel *Breakfast of Champions*, Kurt Vonnegut drew this Indiana sundown sign. A character relates that when a black family got off a boxcar in "Shepherdstown" during the Depression, perhaps not seeing the sign, and sought shelter in an empty shack for the night, a mob got the man and "sawed him in two on the top strand of a barbed-wire fence." Vonnegut grew up in Indianapolis, surrounded by sundown towns. His is the only visual representation I have found of a sundown sign in the Midwest or West, even though I have evidence of such signs in more than 100 towns in those regions and suspect they stood in more than 1000.

PRESENT:

HIS EXCELLENCY

IN COUNCIL:

His Excellency in Council, in virtue of the provisions of Sub-Section (c) of Section 38 of the Immigration Act, is pleased to Order and it is hereby Ordered as follows:-

For a period of one year from and after the date hereof the landing in Canada shall be and the same is prohibited of any immigrants belonging to the Negro race, which race is deemed unsuitable to the climate and requirements of Canada.

Wilfrid Laurier

To Interior 15 Aug. 1911

The Nadir reached Canada, too. Canada had welcomed fugitive slaves, but by 1910, whites in Canada's western provinces, facing a trickle of African Americans fleeing racism in the Plains states, protested to Ottawa. [17] In 1911, the government replied by prohibiting "any immigrants belonging to the Negro race." The prohibition was repealed two months later, but Canada did send agents to Oklahoma to discourage black immigrants. [18] Some riots that drove African Americans from small towns left documentary hints, such as the telegram below. In Missouri, a black Civilian Conservation Corps unit was scheduled to work in Lawrence County in 1935, prompting this telegram to Gov. Guy Park. I think the "riot and blood shed several years ago" alludes to a riot in Mt. Vernon, Missouri, in 1906, but it may refer to a more recent event. The telegram worked: the camp was moved; and Lawrence County's black population declined to just 21 by 1950.

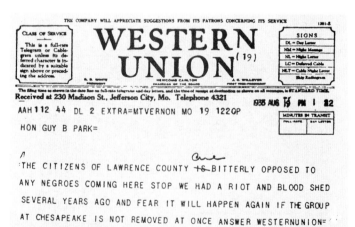

[19] After Comanche and Hamilton counties in Texas drove out their African Americans in 1886, Alec and Mourn Gentry were the only two who "have been permitted to reside in this section," in the words of the 1958 Hamilton County centennial history. " 'Uncle Alec' and 'Aunt Mourn' lived to a ripe old age. . . . They were Gentry Negroes, and former slaves of Capt. F. B. Gentry. . . ." They were no one's uncle or aunt in Hamilton County, of course; these are terms of quasi-respect whites used during the Nadir for older African Americans to avoid "Mr." or "Mrs." (Aunt Jemima Syrup and Uncle Ben's Rice linger as vestiges of this practice.) Gentry's pose shows that he knows his place, essential to his well-being in a sundown county.

"UNCLE ALEC" GENTRY

[20] Elizabeth Davis and her son were the only exceptions allowed in Casey, Illinois, until well after her death in 1963 at 76. She was a nurse-midwife, and this 1952 newspaper photo was accompanied by a poem, "A Tribute to Miss Davis," showing Casey's respect for her. At the same time, Davis was known everywhere as "Nigger Liz," and Casey at one time boasted a sundown sign at the west edge of town.

LOCAL NURSE CARES FOR POLIO PATIENTS
DEC, 1952

Between 1920 and 1928, KKK rallies were so huge that they remain the biggest single meet-ings many towns have ever seen. [21] This lecture in Westfield, Illinois, in 1924 was an exam-ple; a later article told of a "Big Demonstration" planned for "Klan Day" at the Clark County Fair in neighboring Martinsville. Predicted the newspaper, "As we know that a Klan gathering draws spectators like jam draws flies, we can expect that Martinsville on that date will witness the largest gathering of people ever assembled in Clark County." Yet many of these towns— including Martinsville and Westfield—were sundown towns that had already gotten rid of their African Americans and had no Jews and few Catholics, so in a sense there was nothing left for the Klan to do. [22] Similarly, African Americans hardly existed in most of Maine in the 1920s—sometimes owing to sundown policies—yet Milo boasted the "first daylight [Klan] parade in U.S.A." In the 2000 census, Milo finally showed its first African American house-hold. Martinsville and Westfield still have none.

FIRST PARADE IN N.E. STATES
OF KU KLUX KLAN. AND FIRST
DAYLIGHT PARADE IN U.S.A.
AT MILO-MAINE 9/3/23.

PHOTO BY
THE CLEMENT STUDIO
MILO. ME.

[23] Audiences cackle at the last line on this bust of Christopher Columbus. They "know" Italians are not a race. It seems obvious now that there are only three races (Caucasoid, Mongoloid, Negroid), or four (Australoid), or five (American Indian). This was not Hitler's understanding, who "knew" Jews to be a race; nor was it Italian Americans' in 1920 when they erected this bust at the Indiana State Capitol. At that time eugenicists ranked Greeks, Italians, and Slavs *racially* inferior and aimed the 1924 immigration restrictions largely at them. By 1940, however, these races became one—"white." Jews, Armenians, and Turks took just a little longer. Now "white" seems to incorporate Latin and Asian Americans, which most sundown towns have long admitted. In 1960, Dearborn, Michigan, called Arabs "white population born in Asia" and Mexicans "white population born in Mexico" in official documents, thus remaining "all white" as a city. Sundown town policy now seems to be: all groups are fine except blacks.

CHRISTOPHER COLUMBUS
BORN IN GENOA, ITALY 1451. DISCOVERED AMERICA OCTOBER 12, 1492. THIS LAND OF OPPORTUNITY AND FREEDOM WAS THUS PRESERVED FOR HUMANITY BY THE PERENNIAL GENIUS ABIDING IN THE ITALIAN RACE.

REFURBISHED BY KNIGHTS OF COLUMBUS 1956

[24] Although Pekin, Illinois, called its high school athletic teams "Chinks," referencing Peking (now Beijing) China, it insisted this was a compliment and allowed Chinese as residents. The name changed in 1980, but even today many graduates defend the old name. "I can't wait to get Chinks memorabilia, and my kids would love to see it too," stated one alum in 2000. I bought this new T-shirt in Pekin in 2002. It shows visually the bluntly racist rhetoric many residents of sundown towns routinely employ.

Table 32. **General Characteristics for Places of 1,000 to 2,500: 1970**

(For minimum base for derived figures (percent, median, etc.) and meaning of symbols, see text)

Places	Population					
		Sex		Race		
	Total	Male	Female	White	Negro	Other
Rome City	1 354	674	680	1 353	–	1
St. John	1 757	885	872	1 753	–	4
Seelyville	1 195	571	624	1 185	–	10
Shelburn	1 281	623	658	1 280	–	1
Sheridan	2 137	999	1 138	2 133	2	2
Shoals	1 039	489	550	1 039	–	–
Smith Valley (U)	1 679	831	848	1 678	–	1
South Whitley	1 362	639	723	1 360	–	2
Spencer	2 423	1 114	1 309	2 418	3	2
Summitville	1 104	531	573	1 104	–	–
Swayzee	1 073	521	552	1 071	–	2
Sweetser	1 076	520	556	1 075	–	1
Syracuse	1 546	758	788	1 546	–	–
Thorntown	1 399	671	728	1 394	–	5
Town of Pines	1 007	509	498	1 001	–	6
Tri Lakes (U)	1 193	610	583	1 189	1	3
Van Buren	1 057	496	561	1 052	–	5
Veedersburg	1 837	872	965	1 835	1	1
Versailles	1 020	480	540	1 012	–	8
Vevay	1 463	665	798	1 460	–	3
Wakarusa	1 160	558	602	1 153	–	7
Wolkerton	2 006	983	1 023	1 996	2	8
Wolton	1 054	479	575	1 053	–	1
Warren	1 229	562	667	1 229	–	–
Waterloo	1 876	894	982	1 876	–	–
Westfield	1 837	877	960	1 833	3	1
Westport	1 170	552	618	1 170	–	–
Whiteland	1 492	732	760	1 492	–	–
Williamsport	1 661	810	851	1 659	–	2
Winamac	2 341	1 079	1 262	2 335	2	4
Winslow	1 030	469	561	1 029	–	1
Worthington	1 691	788	903	1 688	–	3
Yorktown	1 673	823	850	1 673	–	–
Zionsville	1 857	853	1 004	1 844	1	12

[25] This page from the 1970 census shows how widespread all-white towns—probably sundown towns—have been in Indiana. Twenty-six of these 34 had not a single black resident, and bearing in mind that sundown towns often allowed an exception for one black family, we cannot be sure that *any* of the 34 admitted African Americans. Indiana had twenty times as many African Americans as "Others" in 1970, yet Others lived much more widely. [26] To avoid sundown towns and negotiate travel without danger or embarrassment, African Americans produced guidebooks such as *Travelguide: Vacation and Recreation Without Humiliation* and this *Negro Motorist Green Book.* They listed hotels, restaurants, auto repair shops, etc., that would serve black travelers.

[27] In the mid-1920s, Mena, county seat of Polk County, Arkansas, competed for white residents and tourists by advertising what it had and what it did *not* have. The sentiment hardly died in the 1920s. A 1980 article, "The Real Polk County," began, "It is not an uncommon experience in Polk County to hear a newcomer remark that he chose to move here because of 'low taxes and no niggers.' " [28] Suburbs followed suit. In 1914, developers of Highland Park near Salt Lake City appealed to would-be homebuyers to leave behind the problems of the city, like its smoke. By 1919, the appeal had become racial. Even today, the most prestigious suburbs are often those with the lowest proportions of African Americans.

In 1948, a Federal Housing Administration commissioner boasted that "the FHA has never insured a housing project of mixed occupancy." **[29]** This six-foot concrete block wall was built to separate a white neighborhood from an interracial one in northwestern Detroit so homes on the white side could qualify for FHA loan guarantees. It runs for half a mile, from the city limits to a park. Today African Americans live on both sides, but the wall still divides the neighborhood in two and serves as a reminder on the landscape that federal policies explicitly favored segregated neighborhoods until 1968. **[30]** A street barrier marks the border between North Brentwood, a black community, and Brentwood, Maryland, a sundown suburb into the 1960s. Struck by the absence of any social class difference between homes on both sides of the barrier, I asked Denise Thomas, who grew up in North Brentwood in the 1950s, "What kept people from North Brentwood from crossing that line?" "KKK!" was her heartfelt answer. By that she meant not only the Klan, which burned crosses in North Brentwood, but also many other instances of harassment. "They threw things at us, called us 'nigger,' 'spook,' all kind of things." "The white children?" I asked. "Uh-huh," she affirmed, "and the adults."

"YE OLDE LEVITTOWNE"

No FENCES, EITHER FABRICATED OR GROWING, MAY BE PUT UP WITHOUT THE WRITTEN CONSENT OF COUNTY COMMUNITY CORP."

Only PORTABLE, REVOLVING DRYERS ARE PERMITTED. THEY MUST BE USED ONLY IN THE REAR YARD -- NOT ON SATURDAYS, SUNDAYS OR HOLIDAYS."

Lawns MUST BE CUT AND TALL WEEDS REMOVED AT LEAST ONCE A WEEK BETWEEN APRIL 15TH AND NOVEMBER 15TH."

The TENANT AGREES NOT TO PERMIT THE PREMISES TO BE USED OR OCCUPIED BY ANY PERSON OTHER THAN MEMBERS OF THE **CAUCASIAN RACE**."

COVENANT & RESTRICTIONS, LEVITT & SONS, 1949

www.zippythepinhead.com

[31] In 2002, Bill Griffith's comic strip "Zippy the Pinhead" quoted the regulations set up by Levitt & Sons for the first Levittown. No one made light of them in the 1950s when the three Levittowns were going up. It would not have been cause for amusement or concern then, just everyday life, for Levitt & Sons was by far the largest single homebuilder in post-World War II America. If regulations didn't work, violence usually did. [32] In July, 1951, a mob rioted for three days to keep a black bus driver, Harvey Clark, and his family from occupying an apartment in this building in Cicero, a sundown suburb of Chicago. In this photo, whites have thrown the Clarks' furniture and other possessions into the courtyard of the complex and set it on fire. Eventually a grand jury indicted the owner, Camille DeRose, not the mob! Cicero remained all white until the 1990s.

[33] According to historian Kenneth Jackson, "the most conspicuous city-suburban contrast in the U.S. runs along Detroit's Alter Road" separating Detroit from Grosse Pointe. Just across the line is this park, but Detroit children cannot play on its playground equipment. "It's not fair," observed Reginald Pickins, who grew up less than 50 feet from the border. "Why should we have to have passes to go into their parks? They don't need passes for ours."

[34] Tarzan, the white man who mastered the African jungle, was born in one sundown suburb, Oak Park, Illinois, where his creator, Edgar Rice Burroughs, wrote the first Tarzan books, and gave birth to another sundown town when Burroughs used the proceeds from his novels, movies, and long-running comic strip to create Tarzana, California. In this 1934 strip "the island savages" flee "in terror" from jungle creatures, "believing the beasts were demons conjured up by Tarzan." The strip literally shows white supremacy: Tarzan is more intelligent, courageous, and moral than the black "savages," whom he literally walks all over.

after Venus pulled out of the tournament with knee tendinitis, conceding her match to Serena. "Accusations surfaced that their father, Richard, was fixing his daughters' matches and that the sisters didn't want to play each other," according to an account in *USA Today*. "In Serena's final match two days later against [Kim] Clijsters, the charged-up crowd unleashed its wrath on her, booing Serena's every move." According to Richard Williams, "When Venus and I were walking down the stairs to our seats, people kept calling me 'nigger.' " [28]

Sundown Humor

It isn't just *nigger,* of course. In Pinckneyville, the sundown town in southwestern Illinois, "one of the town's beloved teachers, Doc Thomas, used to openly make racial slurs in the classroom," according to Ron Slater, who graduated from Pinckneyville High School in 1966. "An example of a Doc Thomas comment that sticks in my mind was as follows: 'Well, boys and girls, we have a track meet with Sparta this Friday. Don't think we have to worry though, as it is supposed to be cold, and you know those jungle bunnies don't run so well when it is cold.' " Such a wisecrack, coming casually from the person in charge, can make quite an impact on a classroom. Certainly no defense of African Americans, no opposition to such witticisms, will likely be attempted by a student. [29]

Sundown town rhetoric descends to its lowest point when speakers try to be funny. A recent graduate of Darien High School, the elite Connecticut suburb of New York City, noted that Darien's whiteness "allowed for the kids to joke and to maintain racist stereotypes. A lot of my friends came in with racist jokes, and you never had to worry about it." Many racial jokes considered funny in sundown towns are simply wretched. Consider this quip, told to Ray Elliott when he was teaching in the public schools of Robinson, Illinois, a sundown town near Terre Haute, Indiana, in the mid-1980s. On Martin Luther King Jr. Day, he walked into a restaurant and saw some friends. One said to him, "If they would've killed four more of the sons of bitches, you could've had the whole week off, Elliott!" Real hatred slinks below the surface of that "joke," the same attitude toward King that Linda Dudek remembers from one of her best friends in second grade in Berwyn, Illinois, a sundown suburb just west of Chicago: "That nigger had it coming," the little girl said the day after Martin Luther King Jr. was assassinated, and Dudek continues, "That was pretty much the attitude that prevailed at my grammar school." [30]

Labor historian Ramelle MaCoy remembers this joke, taught by his civics teacher in an all-white high school, about a black hobo who got off a freight train in an Alabama town unaware of the "N——, Don't Let The Sun Set on You Here" signs at the town lines. A gang of whites beat him soundly before asking, "If we let you go will you catch the next train out of here?" "If you let me go I'll catch that one I got off of!"

Telling such a joke in a sundown town classroom lends it a special relevance, an edge. The teller assumes, almost always correctly, that no one will object, and sharing such jokes bonds teller and audience into a racial in-group. Of course, one does not need to be in a sundown town to hear such jokes; almost any all-white environment will do.[31]

On one occasion I found that *I* had told a side-splitting joke in a sundown town. I was telling a volunteer in the Grant County Museum in Sheridan, Arkansas, about sundown towns in other states and mentioned what the name of the sundown town in southern Illinois, Anna, is said to stand for: "Ain't No Niggers Allowed." He laughed uproariously. People from multiracial towns, including white people, don't think it's funny.[32]

"In *This* Town You Must Call Them 'Negroes' "

An incident from New Market, a sundown town in southwestern Iowa, shows that whites do know to behave better in interracial situations. In about 1986, African American John Baskerville went to a high school play there. In Baskerville's words:

> One of the characters was the black maid of the murder victim who found the body, so she had to testify. When the young girl acting as the black maid appeared on stage, we were all shocked. . . . The young white girl appeared in BLACKFACE! She had very black make-up with white lips and bugged-out eyes and dressed like Hattie McDaniel in *Gone With the Wind,* head scarf and all. . . . After the play, the young girl who played the part tried to hide from us. . . . She was so embarrassed because she knew that it was inappropriate and hadn't expected us there.[33]

Sundown town residents also know that *nigger* is an offensive term. I asked "Susan Penny," who grew up in Oblong, a sundown town in southeastern Illinois, in the 1970s and 1980s, "Did you hear the word *nigger* when you were growing up?" "Are you kidding?" she replied.

> I never knew they were called anything *but* "niggers"! I must have been seven years old, and my mother drove us to Terre Haute, my brother and me. And my

brother and I were in awe because there were two things that we had never seen in Oblong: black people and nuns! And I said "nigger," and my mother corrected me, "When we're in *this* town you must call them 'Negroes.' "

The admonition shows that Penny's mother knew full well that African Americans do not appreciate the term; for that matter, she probably knew that some white people in interracial towns don't like it either. So she knew to correct her children's verbal behavior "in *this* town," Terre Haute, where it might earn them disapproval. She also knew that nobody cared in Oblong, so she did not bother to correct their word usage in Oblong. This is a vivid example of a privilege white towns confer on their residents: unlike other Americans, they need not think twice about the terms they use to refer to other groups or the jokes they tell about them. Similarly, the suburbanites in Indian Wells know that *nigger* is offensive. They also know they can get away with it at an almost all-white tennis venue in an almost all-white town.[34] In the 2000 census Indian Wells had just 15 African Americans among its 3,816 residents.[35]

Some high school students from sundown towns imagine somehow that even in interracial situations in the big city, they can behave as they do at home, where they enjoy the privilege of living in a world of white rhetoric. They behave with a paradoxical combination of inappropriate, even dangerous arrogance and inappropriate, even fearful timidity. First they dread going into an interracial restaurant; then they feel they can get away with saying *nigger* in it. Roger Karns, who has taught social studies in several all-white towns in northern Indiana and also coaches swimming, supplied a rich and complex account of the rhetoric that high school students from these towns exhibit when they get to their big city—Fort Wayne, South Bend, Elkhart, or Indianapolis:

Students ask questions like, "Will we get mugged?" "That black (or as frequently, 'colored') guy has on a red t-shirt, is he in a gang?" Or, taking swimmers into a McDonald's, "I saw a black guy, is this neighborhood safe?" "Is that guy a rapper?" And just generalized stupid behavior, fake ghetto accents, caricaturized walks and behavior. I am still surprised that I need to tell these kids that the term "colored" is considered offensive. And several years ago, I had to tell kids specifically that "nigger" was never acceptable. After twenty years of teaching and coaching, I discovered that if I didn't remind them of that before we went to a "big" city, that they would use those kinds of terms and use them loudly. Or they would ask an African-American what gang they were in. Or just point and laugh out the bus window.[36]

Of course, students like these already know *nigger* is offensive. They just imagine such rules don't apply to them because they come from a sundown town. Some of their antics are mainly performed for the benefit of their fellow white students. As they make fun or ask insensitive questions of a member of the black outgroup, the students confirm their membership in their white in-group. Karns explains how the demographic makeup of his students' home-town contributes to their rude and racist behavior:

> I think that growing up in an all white community is detrimental for the white kids. I believe that that kind of upbringing allows people to think of minorities as an "other." It allows you to suspend your normal respect for people. Some of these kids don't see a person walking down the street, they see what amounts to a character. They would never consider being so disrespectful to someone, they just haven't thought about what they are doing as disrespectful because they are seeing a unique "other" and not just the guy down the street.

Here Karns supplies a perfect example and analysis of the "file folder phe-nomenon." His students react to the African Americans they meet not as peo-ple, but as examples of a type. His students are not necessarily bad people, even though they behave badly. In a sense their words and acts are shallow. But their surface racism allows white supremacy to fester and makes it harder for a humane response to come forth the next time race is on the table. As Karns concludes: "Growing up in an all white town has a profound impact on those who grow up there. . . . I believe that the lack of diversity is damag-ing to all." [37]

"We're Not Prejudiced"

These Indiana young people would doubtless deny that they meant anything mean by their comments and antics. Denial is a peculiar characteristic of the talk in sundown towns. When criticized for their racist jokes or use of *nigger,* residents typically deny they are racist. In the early 1990s, football players in Hemet, California, a rapidly growing sundown exurb of Los Angeles, rou-tinely called African Americans on opposing teams "niggers." Scott Bailey, the Hemet quarterback, admitted some of his teammates had aimed the slur at opponents, but "they did not intend it as a racial slur." In Bailey's words, "I don't think anybody who does say it means anything by it." A black football player from Ramona, one of Hemet's opponents, observed, "I just think, you know, there aren't that many black people out there [in the Hemet area], so they think saying that stuff is OK."[38]

Many residents of sundown towns not only deny that their humor is racist, they also deny that their communities' anti-black acts are racist, even as they agree that those acts make it impossible for African Americans to live there safely. A former resident of an Illinois sundown town characterized her former neighbors: "They don't have anything against colored people, they just don't want them to spend the night." Surely there is a certain tension between the two halves of that sentence. "I'm not a racist, but . . . ," a resident of Villa Grove, Illinois, said, prefacing a long story of how in 1990, when he was a senior in Villa Grove High School, he "and 45 or 50 of my buddies" gathered in their pickup trucks at the city limits to head off a carload of African Americans and Latinos from Decatur. They had come intending to date Villa Grove girls, one of whom made the mistake of bragging about it at school. "We beat the shit out of them," he concluded triumphantly, and the episode surely ensured Villa Grove's sundown reputation for another decade or two.[39]

How do residents of sundown towns accomplish the rhetorical feat of admitting they beat up blacks and keep them out while denying they are racist? Only the tiniest proportion of whites are willing to admit to being racist. Typically whites define racism to be almost an empty category, so "we" are not guilty of it. Self-proclaimed white supremacist David Duke saying "I hate niggers" is a case of racism. Almost nothing else passes muster.

This rhetoric of denial is timeless. Here is an example from the *Gentry Journal-Advance,* an Arkansas newspaper, in 1906:

> With a population of 1,000 Gentry has not a solitary Negro inhabitant. We are not prejudiced against the colored man, but we feel that we can get along better without his presence, and are therefore glad to have him remain in some other town or locality. There are plenty of white men here to do the work, ordinarily, and a Negro population under the present conditions, would not only be superfluous, but an annoyance and a nuisance. We are certainly thankful that the dusky denizens have always given our town the go by.

The editor characterizes African Americans as a group as "an annoyance and a nuisance," avoids words such as *people* or *citizens* in favor of "dusky denizens," and clearly favors an indefinite continuation of Gentry's sundown policies. Yet "we are not prejudiced."[40]

A corollary of denial is the curious fact that residents of sundown towns believe they have no problem with racism or race relations. In sharp contrast, people in interracial towns know they do. In Decatur, for example, 33.4% of adults surveyed in about 1985 ranked "racial difficulties" as "the most pressing social problem in Decatur"—well *before* Decatur made national headlines in 1999, when its school system expelled seven African Americans for fighting in the stands during a football game. Few residents of Pana, a sundown town thiry miles south, would rank race relations as their "most pressing social problem." Neither would residents of most sundown suburbs. Nationally, as reported in the 2001 book *Race and Place,* whites living in overwhelmingly white communities perceive the least discrimination against blacks, while whites in majority-black neighborhoods perceived the most. Ironically, then, recognition of "racial difficulties" is a sign of racial progress, and race relations are in fact much more problematic in Pana or sundown suburbs than in Decatur, the latter's moment of notoriety in 1999 notwithstanding. It is true that white children in Pana have no problem getting along with African Americans, since they never encounter them. Nevertheless, as they go through life, these children may encounter some race relations problems that Decatur's white children do not.[41]

The Paradox of Exclusivity

Denial is especially common in suburbia. Residents of elite suburbs are much less likely than residents of independent towns (or working-class suburbs) to admit that their communities keep out African Americans, or did until recently. Their particular need for deniability arises from what we might call the "paradox of exclusivity." We have seen how in metropolitan areas, neighborhoods are ranked more prestigious to the degree that they exclude African Americans, people in the working and lower middle classes, and, in the past, Jews. Such exclusivity connotes social status, even "good breeding." For this reason, white suburbs have usually done little to combat segregation. Instead, they have fostered it. At the same time, exclusivity also suggests prejudice, racism—*"bad* breeding"—even to the elite themselves. As early as 1976, 88% of white Americans agreed with the statement "Black people have a right to live wherever they can afford to," and educated people agreed even more strongly, so residents of sundown suburbs know that they must not admit they live in a place that keeps or kept blacks out.[42]

The ethical paradox is this: on one hand, to live in an exclusive area is good, connoting positive things about oneself and one's family. On the other hand, to exclude is bad, implying negative things about oneself and one's fam-

ily. How do affluent white residents of sundown suburbs deal with this paradox of exclusivity? They don't want to deny that their suburb is exclusive, because exclusivity proves to themselves and others that they are successful and
know how and where to live. But they do want to deny that they are all white
on purpose. So they develop a motivated blindness to the workings of social
structure: soclexia. The talk in sundown suburbs prompts residents to be bad
sociologists and bad historians. Suburban rhetoric has so mystified the exclusion that created sundown suburbs that many suburbanites now sincerely
view residential segregation as nothing but the "natural" outgrowth of countless decisions by individual families.

William H. Whyte Jr. wrote *The Organization Man* in 1956, a study of executives based on fieldwork in Park Forest, a sundown suburb of Chicago. He
noted that several years before he did his research, Park Forest suffered "an
acrid controversy over the possible admission of Negroes."

> For a small group, admission of Negroes would be fulfillment of personal social
> ideals; for another, many of whom had just left Chicago wards which had been
> "taken over," it was the return of a threat left behind.

Most residents, he noted, whom he called "the moderates," were in the middle, and these were "perhaps most sorely vexed." This majority was

> against admission too, but though no Negroes ever did move in, the damage was
> done. The issue had been brought up, and the sheer fact that one had to talk
> about it made it impossible to maintain unblemished the ideal egalitarianism so
> cherished.

In short, most residents of the suburb wanted it to stay sundown[43] but desired
deniability.[44]

In his famous 1944 book about race relations, *An American Dilemma*,
Gunnar Myrdal saw this: "Trying to defend their behavior to others, *people
will twist and mutilate their beliefs of how social reality actually is*" (his italics). Residents deny their town's history of discrimination and its ongoing
sundown apparatus because they want to credit themselves with success, not
blame themselves for prejudice and discrimination. "Yes, we live in an elegant,
affluent, white [but this last goes unstated] area, with lovely amenities and low
crime," people might say. "All of that says good things about us. But anyone
could live here if they wanted to and had the means. It's not our fault; it's to
our credit. America is a meritocracy." That others do not live here merely says

bad things about them, at least implicitly. As Robert Terry put it in *For Whites Only,* commenting on residential segregation in the Detroit area in the 1970s: "Who has ever heard a Northerner admit he did something because he was a racist? Our propensity for moral justification does not permit it. Rather, our racism is couched in quasi-moral terms which command social respectability and accrue social acceptance to us." Just as many white southerners used to believe the legal separation of the races in southern society was natural, many white northerners still seem to believe the geographic separation of the races in northern metropolitan areas is natural.[45]

When the racial composition of their community is so overwhelmingly nonblack that accident cannot plausibly be invoked, residents often blame African Americans for not moving in, saying that blacks "prefer their own." In 2002, I asked a realtor in Kenilworth why no African American family lived in that elite Chicago suburb, to his knowledge. "Birds of a feather flock together," he replied. "People are happier with their own kind." I had noticed his Armenian-sounding last name, so I asked him, "Do you live with other Armenians?" "No," he replied, "but the first generation did. The second generation moved out, lived with other people." I didn't bother to point out that most African Americans are now at least tenth-generation Americans and fourth-generation Chicagoans, much longer than most Armenians.

A resident of an overwhelmingly white neighborhood near a golf club in south Tulsa told me of a black doctor who moved there. He had to move back to north Tulsa, she said, because "his [black] patients rose up in protest." Chapter 8 told how Patrick Clark, curator of the Andrew County (Missouri) Museum, denied that his own county or nearby counties had any history of excluding African Americans. Clark went on to write, "Incidentally, the only community in the state we are familiar with being associated with one racial make-up is/was near St. Louis, Missouri; an all Black community, Kinloch, Missouri"—a small town some 300 miles away. Other whites have echoed Clark's thinking, invoking Boley; Harlem; Mound Bayou, Mississippi; or the South Side ghetto of Chicago.

Some whites go on to hold that the existence of black towns legitimizes the racist policies of white sundown towns. But most black towns and townships never excluded whites.[46] Neither did black neighborhoods. As Myrdal put it in 1944, most mixed residential areas in America "are cases of whites living in 'Negro areas' and not of Negroes living in 'white areas,'" where they would not have been allowed. Even Harlem has never been close to all-black. In 1990, Kinloch had seventeen whites in five white households. Today, although some African Americans do seek majority-black environments, most still prefer diverse neighborhoods with white and black (and other) residents. To a much greater degree, it is *white* Americans who seek "to be with their own kind." To locate the problem in the supposedly free choices of the minority group is soclexic, even though it may be comforting to whites.[47]

Elite suburbanites also avoid responsibility for the racial composition of their community by claiming that African Americans don't have the wherewithal to move there. "It's an economic thing." "They can't afford it here." In America it's considered perfectly all right to exclude on the basis of social class; indeed, an element of the American dream itself is to separate oneself and one's family from the teeming masses. Grouping houses by social class is still a de rigueur principle of real estate. I hope that earlier chapters have laid to rest the claim that income differences explain sundown suburbs. They don't.

It is a small step from blaming African Americans for not having the income to move in to a sundown suburb to blaming them for not having the personal characteristics—IQ, for example—to earn that income. Many residents of elite sundown suburbs take that step. Obviously, to believe that America is a sorting machine based on ability—and African Americans have less ability—eliminates any guilt about living in a community that keeps them out. This explains why *The Bell Curve,* the 1994 book that argued that differences in income by class and race result from differences in intelligence, was so popular in elite sundown suburbs. It located the problem in "them," the outgroups, just as the eugenicists used to do. Precisely because it blames the victim, the resulting ideology is more dangerous than the overt racism of independent sundown towns. Residents of elite sundown suburbs are free to infer that African Americans are inferior, which explains their absence. Residents of such independent sundown towns as Anna or Sheridan can't say that. They *know* their town has kept blacks out.[48]

Claiming that ability results purely from individual achievement rather than one's place in the social structure is also a pleasant way to interpret the high SAT scores earned by one's children and their equally privileged friends in an elite community. Of course, affluent parents really know better. When making decisions about their own children's futures, the rich know that ability is largely socially created, which is why they invest in *Sesame Street Magazine* for their toddler, computer camp for their eight-year-old, and the *Princeton Review* for their eleventh grader facing the SAT. They may get furious when a school principal tries to jettison tracking or their own child does not get into an advanced placement class. They go to great lengths—private schools, hiring "college coaches," and so on—to give their children a leg up in college admission. Thus when it comes to their own children, they are structural sociologists who see positive individual outcomes as the result of expenditures and programs.

However, their awareness of suburban advantages, which they employ to justify why they moved there in the first place, disappears when the time comes to discuss the outcome of the college admission process. Now elite whites no longer brag about or even perceive the benefits of class and racial segregation. Instead, they now "explain" the positive results of these advantages, such as high SAT scores, as stemming from their child's individual intelligence and ability. Suddenly they now assert that aptitude inheres in individuals and the SAT measures aptitude.[49] Again, to believe that America sorts people based on ability—and one's child happens to be among the most able—is more satisfying than to admit that living in a sundown suburb amounts to a deliberate choice to stack the deck. Such Social Darwinism is not only soclexic but dangerous to democracy.

Misled by these rationalizations, rich white segregated children usually do not understand the processes in their own metropolitan areas that conferred advantages upon them, based on their race and social class. They made it, so why can't everyone? In *Privileged Ones,* Robert Coles interviewed a male high school student in a sundown suburb of Boston who exemplified this soclexic thinking: "My father says it'll always be like that; there are people who are prejudiced against anyone who has tried to work hard and make some money, and prejudiced in favor of the people who don't care if they work or not, so long as they collect welfare." In my 63 years in America I have yet to meet a single person "prejudiced in favor of the people who don't care if they work or not," and I suspect neither this boy nor his father have either. But such stereotypes are satisfying, for they imply that as soon as African Americans really apply themselves, our racial problems will be fixed. "We," on the other hand, are not responsible, so there's nothing we can do about it. Knowing no poor people or people of color firsthand, residents of elite sundown suburbs are particularly susceptible to stereotypes to explain the visible differences among neighborhoods.[50]

Racial Stereotypes in Sundown Towns

During the past 25 years, while teaching race relations to thousands of white people and discussing the subject with thousands more, I have found that white Americans expound about the alleged character and characteristics of African Americans in inverse proportion to their contact and experience with them. Isolation and ignorance aren't the only reasons why residents of sundown towns and suburbs are so ready to believe and pass on the worst stereotypes about African Americans, however. They also have a need for denial.

The idea that living in an all-white community leads residents to defend living in an all-white community exemplifies the well-established psychological principle of cognitive dissonance. No one likes to think of himself or herself as a bad person, argued Leon Festinger, who established this principle. People who live in sundown towns believe in the golden rule—or say they do—just like people who live in interracial towns. No one would want to be treated the way sundown towns treat African Americans. On the other hand, it is hard for someone living in an all-white town to define that choice of residence as "wrong" or that policy as "bad for our country." Doing so might entail moving, or taking a risk in trying to change the town's practices. It is much easier to rationalize one's actions by changing one's opinions and beliefs to make what one has done seem right.

What could make living in an all-white town right? The old idea that African Americans constitute the problem, of course. In 1914, Thomas Bailey, a professor in Mississippi, told what is wrong with that line of thinking: "The real problem is not the Negro, but the white man's attitude toward the Negro." Sundown towns only made white attitudes worse. Having driven out or kept out African Americans (or perhaps Chinese Americans or Jewish Americans), their residents then became *more* racist and more likely to believe the worst about the excluded group(s).[51]

That's why the talk in sundown towns brims with amazing stereotypes about African Americans, put forth confidently as reality by European Americans who have never had an honest conversation with an African American in their lives. The ideology intrinsic to sundown towns—that African Americans (or Jews, Chinese Americans, or another group) are the problem—prompts their residents to believe and pass on all kinds of negative generalizations as fact. They are the problem because *they* choose segregation—even though "they" don't, as we have seen. Or they are the problem owing to their criminality—confirmed by the stereotype—misbehavior that "we" avoid by excluding or moving away from them.

Of course, such stereotypes are hardly limited to sundown towns. Summarizing a nationwide 1991 poll, Lynne Duke found that a majority of whites believed that "blacks and Hispanics are likely to prefer welfare to hard work and tend to be lazier than whites, more prone to violence, less intelligent, and less patriotic." Even worse, in sundown towns and suburbs, statements such as these usually evoke no open disagreement at all. Because most listeners in sundown towns have never lived near African Americans, they have no experiential foundation from which to question the negative generalities that they hear voiced. So the stereotypes usually go unchallenged: blacks are less intelligent, lazier, and lack drive, and that's why they haven't built successful careers.[52]

Actually, most African Americans, like most other Americans, are reasonably industrious people who are quietly trying to have a satisfying life and pass on a bit of a start to their children. But many residents of sundown towns and suburbs simply don't believe that. Many also misunderstand basic economics and believe, for example, that African Americans don't pay property taxes when they rent rather than own their homes, not understanding that landlords pay property taxes from the rents they collect. Nor do most whites realize that Social Security acts as a vast transfer program from blacks to whites, because African Americans' life expectancy is so much shorter than that of whites.

Negative generalizations about African Americans are at least as common in sundown suburbs as in independent sundown towns, even though residents of sundown suburbs may have African American friends at work. In a corollary to the "file folder mentality" Chapter 10 described, such individuals are accepted as exceptions, leaving the negative generalizations about the mass of African Americans unscathed. Many residents of these suburbs, especially working- and middle-class suburbs, have fled from city neighborhoods that they believed were about to "turn black." Those who flee such neighborhoods carry white-flight stories with them like a pestilence. Parents think they did the right thing by fleeing the city and its crime and problems, problems they see as inextricably bound up with race. When their children ask them why they moved, they respond with the negative stereotypes, thus passing them on to the next generation. Contact with a nice black co-worker makes no difference. A 1985 study of white voters in Michigan found that residents of blue-collar sundown suburbs of Detroit expressed "a profound distaste for blacks, a sentiment that pervades almost everything they think about government and politics." Many also scapegoated African Americans:

> Blacks constitute the explanation for their vulnerability and for almost everything that has gone wrong in their lives; not being black is what constitutes being middle-class; not living with blacks is what makes a neighborhood a decent place to live.[53]

A librarian in Oak Lawn, a sundown suburb southwest of Chicago, remarked that Oak Lawn residents welcome Hispanics, because "they don't know what they will bring with them. Many know what blacks will bring with them." Many suburbanites left neighborhoods in Chicago when African Americans moved in, she explained, and those areas are now black. They "don't want to have to do that again"; therefore they don't let African Americans in. I asked her, "What would blacks bring with them?" "Crime," she replied immediately. That answer is a textbook example of prejudgment and overgeneralization—in a word, prejudice—from a woman who denied any racial animus herself. We were then joined by a male reference librarian; ironically, both complained about the "Colombian gangs" that now operated in Oak Lawn. Whether African American newcomers would have formed gangs we'll never know, but the fact remains that neither librarian saw any contradiction in justifying excluding African Americans owing to crime while admitting Hispanics despite crime. Since Oak Lawn did not keep out Hispanics, cognitive dissonance did not move them to focus on Hispanic crime. It is *black* crime that really concerned them. At the top end of the status spectrum, residents of Grosse Pointe, Michigan, reacted identically, blocking African Americans while mounting no protest when members of the Mafia, booted out of Canada for criminal behavior, moved in.[54]

Whites often engage in white flight despite evidence right before their eyes that their rationale for leaving makes no sense. Matteson, Illinois, an upper-middle-class suburb south of Chicago, went from 12% black in 1980 to nearly 60% black by 2000. "The blacks moving in are professionals," according to Leonard Steinhorn, co-author of *By the Color of Our Skin*. As a result, the town's median income rose by 73% in the 1980s. "Crime has not increased, schools have maintained the same standards, and home prices continue to rise—if anything, the community is wealthier with its new black residents." Nevertheless, Matteson's whites continue to leave, saying that they "simply want a nice place to raise their kids." As Frederick Douglass put it, back in 1860, such behavior is characteristic of "prejudice, always blind to what it never wishes to see, and quick to perceive all it wishes."[55]

Imagining the "Black Menace"

Sometimes the stereotypes whites form about African Americans create real apprehension in sundown towns. Most residents of these towns see communities outside their city limits as much "blacker" than they are, which frightens them. "Cobden is half black," a local history buff in Dongola, Illinois, a sundown town twelve miles south of Cobden, said in 2003. Actually, Cobden has

16 African Americans among 1,116 residents, or 1.4%. The high school secretary of a sundown town in northeastern Arkansas told me that Oxford, Mississippi, is majority-black, and she worried about it while there; actually, Oxford has 2,463 African Americans among 11,654 residents, about 20%. "We're thinking of going to the Arkansas State Fair this year," she also said, "and a friend told us to take a pistol. It's in a black neighborhood." I told her I'd been to the fairgrounds in Little Rock and never heard of folks having to shoot their way in or out. She didn't laugh. She was considering her friend's advice quite seriously.[56]

In 1994, anthropologist Jane Adams found that a peculiar anxiety gripped residents of Anna, in southern Illinois, about nearby Carbondale, long after student riots at Southern Illinois University and a Black Panther shootout with police there in 1970. "Many people in the area still avoid Carbondale and are afraid to go through the town at night." This fear had no rational basis: student rioters and Black Panthers are long gone, and the campus has been quiet for decades. The fear is partly racial, for African Americans are not gone; Carbondale in 1994 was 20% black, which looks very black from the vantage point of all-white Anna. Thus where one lives affects how one perceives.[57]

When dealing with towns that actually *have* black majorities, fears in sundown towns can become absurd enough to merit the label "paranoia." When West Side High School in Greers Ferry, Arkansas, a sundown town according to a nearby resident, plays Cotton Plant, a majority-black high school to the southeast, the team and buses get escorted by state troopers. When West Side hosts Cotton Plant, according to a recent West Side graduate, administrators warn their students "not to leave jewelry or other valuables in your lockers! Leave them with your parents!" Yet Cotton Plant players are surely already nervous playing in a sundown town and would hardly be likely to wander the halls of an unfamiliar high school scoping out student lockers. A former resident of Herrin, a sundown town in southern Illinois, relates that Herrin natives still warn each other, "Don't go to Colp," a nearby black-majority township, even during the daytime. Residents of independent sundown towns expressed particular anxiety about visiting Atlanta, Detroit, or Washington, D.C., three cities they know have black majorities.[58]

Not just small-town residents, but also some elite white suburbanites seem enfeebled rather than emboldened by their privileged isolated communities and wind up reluctant to go to cultural events or restaurants in central cities. A professor at Western Michigan University reported the reaction of her relatives from Naperville, an elite suburb southwest of Chicago, after going with her to a Jewel Supermarket in Kalamazoo, Michigan: "Oh, how can you go there? Aren't you afraid of being mugged?" The store's interracial clientele made them apprehensive—in broad daylight in Kalamazoo! Imagine their fear of Chicago! Undergraduates at the University of Illinois–Chicago tell that their friends from such suburbs as Naperville went to Iowa or the University of Illinois–Champaign; "they're afraid of Chicago," and not just of those neighborhoods that are in fact dangerous. High school students from sundown suburbs of New York City are similarly wary of Manhattan. "When we rode the subway," said Andy Cavalier about his Darien, Connecticut, school friends, "they would ride wide-eyed, thinking they'd be mugged at any moment." Diane Hershberger, taking high school students from suburban Johnson County to an art exhibit in Kansas City, overheard them saying in worried tones, "I've never been downtown before."[59]

Young people absorb this posture toward the outside world from their parents and other adults in the community, of course. Karns supplied an example:

> My recent Cleveland trip was interesting in that it was two swimmers and their fathers. . ∴. One father was pretty uncomfortable in general. He made several comments about Cleveland being dangerous because of its racial make-up. We were looking for a reasonably priced place to eat . . . and it took awhile. At one stop, he said 'maybe we should find an area with some more white faces,' attached to some comment about safety. I was surprised because this is one of the gentlest, most accepting men I know, and he allowed himself to fall prey to that kind of thinking. I pass this on, not to belittle him but because I think it illustrates the kind of thinking that is created in small all-white communities.[60]

Residents of sundown towns have long feared black-majority towns. According to historian Norman Crockett, author of *The Black Towns,* citizens of Paden and Okemah, sundown towns in eastern Oklahoma, worried they were in danger while in Boley, a neighboring black town. This anxiety escalated to full-blown panic one warm June night in 1911. A month before, a white mob from Okemah had hanged Laura Nelson and her son, African American farmers living near Boley, from the steel bridge that spanned the North Canadian River (see Portfolio 11.) As customary in such matters, the grand jury investigating the lynchings somehow could not determine who was responsible. Now, in the words of Okemah resident W. L. Payne, townspeople "watched movements of the lawless Negro element," fearing retaliation from Boley. On June 23, according to Payne, "a white 'stool pigeon' informed the sheriff of

Okfuskee County that the Negroes were planning to sack and burn Okemah that night. No mercy was to be shown women and children." Terror and confusion reigned within Okemah. Payne tells what happened next:

> Citizens came from every section of the town with firearms. Ammunition dealers soon sold their entire stock of firearms and ammunition. An armed cordon of men was placed around Okemah at the edge of town and all approaches were guarded. Strategic locations within the city limits were soon fortified. Mobilization officers ordered all street lights cut off to prevent the enemy from observing the movements of the town's brave defenders. The light plant engineer was to signal the attack by blowing the whistle. . . . As both young and old scrambled for safety . . . mothers and children often became separated in the mad rush for safety. Hysterical mothers were screaming for their children and pleading for assistance.

The alarm lasted all night, but in the end, Payne concludes, "while Okemah citizens were preparing for war, their colored foes were at home preparing for a good night's rest, which prevented the loss of blood on both sides." But Payne does not draw the obvious lesson: that white fears were silly. Sixty years later, a similar rumor prompted a similar vigil in Anna, Illinois. "Most of the store owners spent the night in their stores with their guns loaded," according to a woman who grew up there. African Americans in Cairo, 30 miles south, were boycotting its stores, and a rumor flew around Anna one weekend "that the blacks (by the way, no one called them blacks—they were always referred to as 'niggers') were going to come up to Anna and cause trouble." All that happened was that "a few blacks came into town to shop—which was not uncommon—and they went home as usual." [61]

Perhaps a bad conscience of sorts (Freud would call it projection) helped motivate the Okemah panic. Similarly, after whites in Maryville, Missouri, lynched Raymond Gunn in 1931 and threatened the rest of Maryville's small black community, a rumor swept through town that 2,000 African Americans from Kansas City, almost 100 miles south, augmented by reinforcements from Omaha, Nebraska, almost 100 miles northwest, were coming to invade Maryville to avenge the lynching. According to a white minister,

> Every [white] man in town was armed, and on the streets. We were sure we were going to have to protect ourselves in blood. The sheriff deputized numerous men to help with the defense. The streets were crowded all night.

The sheriff sought help from other counties, and plans were made to block the oncoming Nebraska horde at the Missouri River bridge. Of course, no attack ever materialized.[62]

Over the years, when African Americans *have* rioted, even if they are miles away, white paranoia in sundown towns has often reached a fever pitch. Karns grew up in Huntington, former vice president Dan Quayle's hometown, a sundown town in northern Indiana:

> My father owned a sporting goods store and among other things he sold guns. During the race riots of the '60s, particularly following King's assassination, he would get phone calls warning him of black "motorcycle gangs" on their way to Huntington from Ft. Wayne to attack the all-white town as well as his business to steal the guns. No attack ever came but it illustrates the paranoia. I remember two or three such incidents.

Huntington is 30 miles from Fort Wayne, hardly a suburb. Glendale, California, is a suburb of Los Angeles, but it lies "about an hour's drive" from Watts, according to a woman who attended high school in Glendale in the mid-1960s. One day, playing tennis after school, she was "shocked to see what appeared to be an incredibly large contingen[t] of National Reserve soldiers! There were tanks, tents, trucks and a lot of soldiers." City officials of this sundown suburb had called out the National Guard to protect Glendale during the Watts riot—from what, they never specified. Officials of Grosse Pointe, Grosse Ile, Dearborn, and other communities took similarly extraordinary precautions in their sundown suburbs during periods of racial unrest in Detroit. Having no African Americans in town, knowing none, having friends who also know no African Americans and live there partly so they cannot—these conditions foster a "we/they" mentality that can escalate to a sense of being besieged, even though no one is at the gates. Even in calm times and notwithstanding their privilege, many residents of elite sundown suburbs seem to feel beleaguered.[63]

Cognitive Dissonance in Martinsville, Indiana

Recent events in Martinsville, Indiana, provide an eerie example of cognitive dissonance at work. Martinsville is a city of 12,000 located 50 miles south of Indianapolis. In 1890, the town had 53 African Americans; by 1930 it had just 4. Martinsville was a Ku Klux Klan hotbed in the 1920s, but so was most of Indiana. In the late 1950s, Martinsville High School played basketball against Crispus Attucks, Indianapolis's de jure segregated black high school, without incident. By 1967, however, when Martinsville played Rushville in football and Rushville's star running back was African American Larry Davis, Martinsville fans were yelling, "Get that nigger!" Then, on September 16, 1968, someone stabbed Carol Jenkins, a 21-year-old African American from Rushville, to death with a screwdriver as she walked along Morgan Street trying to sell encyclopedias door-to-door. It was her first evening in the city, so she knew no one; thus no one had any conceivable personal motive for killing her. At about 7:30 PM, she had gone to a house briefly, seeking refuge from a car with two white men in it who had been shouting at her. So most people (correctly) assumed the motive to be rage at Jenkins as a black person for being in the city after dark.[64]

In the aftermath of the murder, NAACP leaders and reporters from outside the town levied criticism at the city's police department, alleging lack of interest in solving the crime. Martinsville residents responded by appearing to define the situation as "us" against "them," "them" being outsiders and nonwhites. The community seemed to close ranks behind the murderer and refused to turn him in, whoever he was. "The town became a clam," said an Indianapolis newspaper reporter.[65]

Now Martinsville came to see itself not just as a sundown town—it already defined itself as that—but as a community that united in silence to protect the murderer of a black woman who had innocently violated its sundown taboo. To justify this behavior required still more extreme racism, which in turn prompted additional racist behaviors and thus festered further. During the years after Jenkins's murder, gas stations in Martinsville repeatedly refused to sell gasoline to African American customers, at least as late as 1986. Not only the murder but also actions such as these gave Martinsville a particularly scary reputation among African Americans. According to Professor Alan Boehm, who attended Indiana University in the 1970s, Indianapolis's large black middle-class population got the state to build a bypass around Martinsville, "because they did not want their children put in harm's way when they drove between home and the university."[66]

In the 1990s, fans and students in Martinsville intensified their harassment of visiting athletic teams that had black players. In 1998, that tradition won Martinsville an article, "Martinsville's Sad Season," in *Sports Illustrated*: "On January 23, as Bloomington High North's racially mixed team got off the bus upon arriving for a game at Martinsville, about a dozen Martinsville students greeted the visitors with a barrage of racial epithets." Students shouted things like "Here come the darkies." The *Sports Illustrated* account continues:

> During the junior varsity game several Bloomington players were bitten by Martinsville players. During the varsity game a member of Martinsville's all-white team elbowed a black North player in the stomach so fiercely that the player began vomiting. As he was doubled over on the sidelines, a fan yelled, "That nigger's spitting on the floor! Get his ass off the floor." According to a report that Bloomington North filed with the Indiana High School Athletics Association, epithets like "baboon" and threats such as "You're not safe in this town" continued after the game, which Martinsville won 69–66. "It wasn't just nasty," says one Bloomington North fan, an adult who was in attendance, "it was downright scary."

Martinsville was sanctioned: it could not host a conference game in any sport for a year. "This wasn't the first time that charges of racist behavior were leveled against one of Martinsville's teams," the story made clear. "In the last year at least two high schools in central Indiana have dropped the Artesians from their schedules after games were marred by brawls and racial slurs. School administrators in Martinsville . . . were unwilling to discuss the incident or its aftermath."[67]

Ironically, it turned out that no one from Martinsville murdered Carol Jenkins. On May 8, 2002, police arrested Kenneth Richmond, a 70-year-old who had never lived in Martinsville, based on the eyewitness account of his daughter, who sat in his car and watched while he did it when she was seven years old. Although many people inside as well as outside Martinsville believed its residents had been sheltering the murderer these 34 years, in fact no one in the town had known who did it. No matter: cognitive dissonance kicked in anyway. Again, if situations are defined as real, they are real in their consequences. Because everyone *thought* the community had closed ranks in defense of the murderer, additional acts of racism in the aftermath seemed all the more appropriate. Today, having intensified its racism for more than three decades in defense of its imagined refusal to turn over the murderer, Martinsville is finding it hard to reverse course. Recently some residents have tried to move the city toward better race relations, so far with mixed results. They organized meetings on race relations, hold an annual dinner, and hired a consultant to help Martinsville get beyond its past. At the same time, Martinsville's assistant police chief spoke out against gays, Hindus, and Buddhists after the terrorist attacks of September 11, 2001, and won a standing ovation at a subsequent city council meeting. And the Council of Conservative Citizens, descendant of the notorious White Citizens Council, has more members in Martinsville than the diversity organization.[68]

Stereotyping Other Groups

As Martinsville's assistant police chief demonstrated, residents of sundown towns often do not confine their generalizations and stereotypes to African Americans, although blacks have usually been viewed as the most menacing. Sundown towns are more likely than other communities to oppose additional "theys"—other racial groups, gays and lesbians, unusual religious groups, hippies, and Americans who look different or think or act unconventionally. At East High School in Appleton, Wisconsin, for example, formerly a sundown town vis-à-vis African Americans, conflicts between Hmong Americans and whites were a daily occurrence at the school in 1999, according to reporter John Lee.[69] Quoting a student source, Lee wrote, "Usually it begins with a group of white students taunting an Asian student or his friends with epithets, or pushing them into lockers. He said the white youths 'pick on anybody that's different or anybody who hangs around them.' " Meanwhile, at nearby North High School, incidents occurred between white students and Mexican Americans. On the day after white students had defaced a Mexican flag at North, white students came to school "wearing Confederate Battle Flag symbols hanging from pockets on shirts and on car antennas," according to reporter Kathy Nufer. They already owned these symbols, giving the conflict a white supremacy tinge.[70]

Residents of several sundown towns have told me that their towns also harass homosexuals. Springdale, Arkansas, made news in 1998 when every candidate for mayor, speaking before members of the Christian Coalition, attacked the "Human Dignity resolution" passed in nearby interracial Fayetteville. One mayoral candidate even proposed posting "No Fags in Springdale" signs at the city limits, reminiscent of the sundown signs that Springdale used to sport about blacks. Of course, many interracial small towns also manifest hostility toward gays and lesbians.[71] Such hostility shows itself more easily in sundown towns, however, with their heritage of inhospitality toward an entire outgroup. On the other hand, not every sundown town is as anti-gay as Springdale. Gays live safely if semi-closeted in Cullman, a sundown town in northern Alabama, for instance, and some more or less came out in June 2000 via a story in *The Advocate,* "the national gay & lesbian newsmagazine." Conversely, some racially integrated towns and neighborhoods, including New

Hope, Pennsylvania, outside Philadelphia, and Mt. Rainier, Maryland, outside Washington, take quiet pride in welcoming even "out" gays.[72]

Regarding religious "deviants," we might first recall that the Ku Klux Klan in the 1920s was anti-Catholic and anti-Semitic as well as anti-black. And of course most elite sundown suburbs also kept out Jews until well after World War II; some also barred Catholics. In Santa Fe, Texas, a sundown town, Phillip Nevelow, the town's only Jewish student, said in 2000 that schoolmates had subjected him to two years of anti-Semitic harassment, including threats to hang him, and police charged three students with making "terroristic threats." Santa Fe's "reputation for being 'white only,' " in the words of Shelly Kelly, archivist at the University of Houston, surely contributed to the "climate of intolerance" with which his parents charged the school district.[73]

Other sundown towns attacked leftists and labor leaders. A decade after Harrison, Arkansas, expelled its African Americans, its large Ku Klux Klan chapter targeted striking railroad workers and in 1923 hanged one striker from a railroad bridge, herded the rest together, and escorted them to the Missouri line. The result was a sundown town so far as organized labor was concerned. The same thing happened in Bisbee, Arizona, known as a "white man's camp" after it expelled its Chinese miners. On July 12, 1917, Bisbee expelled more than a thousand striking miners, members of the Industrial Workers of the World ("Wobblies"). Across America, working-class whites today complain about getting stopped and harassed by police in elite white suburbs.[74]

Some sundown towns give a hard time even to white heterosexuals if they seem "different." Based on bad experiences in Marlow, Oklahoma, poet Jodey Bateman generalized: "I think the stories of attempts at exclusion of hippies and hitch hikers would make another 'sundown town' book. . . . From this I believe that the 'sundown town' syndrome in very small towns is not just racism but a fear of all outsiders who don't seem respectable enough." A web post makes the same point about another Oklahoma town:

> I am from a small town of 3,500, Stilwell, Oklahoma. I could not wait to get out
> of that place. The grape vine is as brutal as they get. I find in towns with no cul-
> tural diversity there is a cruelty toward folks that are different. . . . For the
> longest time there was a sign outside of town that read "Don't Let The Sun Set
> On Your Black Ass."[75]

When a town goes sundown, the exclusionary mind-set stays for a long time and festers and generalizes. Whites in sundown towns speak authoritatively not only about African Americans, but also about leftists, Muslims, poor whites, union members, or welfare mothers—based on little or no firsthand experience with members of the class. Surely African Americans, Chinese Americans, Jewish Americans, Seventh Day Adventists, gay Americans, lesbian Americans, hippie Americans, poor Americans, and mildly nonconforming Americans cannot all be "the problem." Hence being unwelcoming to every one of those groups obviously cannot fix the problem.

Abraham Lincoln understood the threat to our democracy posed by anti-black prejudice and the likelihood that this sentiment would metastasize to attack other groups. In 1855 he wrote a letter to his lifelong friend Josh Speed, a clause of which has become famous:

> As a nation, we began by declaring that "all men are created equal." We now practically read it "all men are created equal, except Negroes." When the Know-Nothings get control, it will read "all men are created equal, except Negroes, and foreigners, and Catholics." When it comes to this I should prefer emigrating to some country where they make no pretence of loving liberty—to Russia, for instance, where despotism can be taken pure, and without the base alloy of hypocrisy.[76]

Surely Lincoln was right. Surely exclusion itself—not African Americans, not all these other groups—was and remains the problem. Readers might consider if *they* would feel comfortable in a typical sundown town—in Appleton, Wisconsin, say, before it cracked, or Stilwell, Oklahoma. The answer for nonwhites is obvious, but whites too can be at risk if they say the wrong thing, bring home a partner of the opposite sex who is of the wrong race, or *horribile dictu,* bring home a partner of the right race but the same sex. Even if they avoid these transgressions, would whites feel comfortable raising children in a sundown town where the only thing worse than having children who just don't fit in might be having children who *do*?

Inculcating Prejudice in the Next Generation

Cognitive dissonance also helps explain how young whites wind up racist as they mature. Racism is not genetic, of course. Sundown towns help to maintain it. Many sundown towns chose American history textbooks that paid little attention to African Americans and Native Americans for as long as they could. They also preferred the old "Dick and Jane" readers in which all the characters were white. In the early 1970s, when textbooks became more multicultural, the head of the Follette Publishing Company observed, "The day of the all-white textbooks is just about over. The big publishers won't fool with them any more, and all-white towns like Cicero, Illinois, just won't be able to get them in the future." [77]

Despite the efforts of adults, childhood is not a straitjacket, and it is certainly possible for a white child to grow up in a sundown town and not become racist, or to transcend that racism through later life experiences and education. John Wooden, the famous UCLA basketball coach, grew up in notorious Martinsville, yet coached such famous African American basketball players as Kareem Abdul-Jabbar and Sidney Wicks. Presidential candidate Wendell Willkie opposed racism after he left Elwood, his Indiana sundown town (although he never did anything about it while he lived there). Nevertheless, teachers who try to convert white young people in sundown towns to an anti-racist position fight an uphill battle, at best succeeding one student at a time. All the while, when whites do not go to school with blacks and do not live with blacks—and everyone in town knows this results from whites' choices and policies—it is hard for children to conclude that blacks are OK. Logically, they may infer quite the opposite.

Sometimes having been a sundown town can poison the atmosphere even after a school goes majority nonwhite. In 1991, Pam Sturgeon, who is Anglo and was president of the school board in Hawthorne, California, another Los Angeles suburb, said, "When I went to Hawthorne High, Hawthorne was a sundown town. All blacks had to be out of town by sundown or be in jail." By 1991, Hawthorne High was majority black and Hispanic, with considerable conflict between those groups. The teaching staff was still largely Anglo, including many holdovers from its all-white days, and some of them contributed to the problem by refusing to teach works by such authors as Richard Wright and Maya Angelou. Sturgeon referred to the sundown legacy: "A lot of adults in my age group are fighting that bigotry within themselves." [78]

These considerations are perhaps clear for the classic independent sundown town like Martinsville or Sheridan. But if it is unhealthy to bring up children in such obviously racist environments, is it somehow healthier to raise them in sundown suburbs like Hawthorne before it desegregated, or worse yet, in such elite sundown suburbs as San Marino? There the social structure implies that it is correct to distance oneself not only from African Americans, but also from the white lower, working, and middle classes. Can that be good for children to learn? Yet every year thousands of white parents move *to* rather than *from* sundown suburbs, and they do so "for the children."

It would be far better to raise children in towns that do not declare in their very demography that "white is right."

To some white parents, all this is obvious. A new homeowner in a former sundown county outside Atlanta said that many houses in her community were going up for sale "because the community is becoming more racially mixed and the white people are moving further south. The funny part is that I have been wanting to move because I can't stand the thought of my future children growing up around such racism and narrowmindedness. So I suppose their moving is making my life easier." [79]

Independent Sundown Towns Limit the Horizons of Their Children

Independent sundown towns have another effect on their residents that has nothing to do with race, at least not directly: they narrow the horizons of children who come of age within them. It is an axiom of American small-town life that "youth goes elsewhere to become somebody." Young people in independent sundown towns typically hold ambivalent feelings toward the outside world. Some decorate their bedrooms with posters of Michael Jordan (formerly) or Serena Williams (currently) or even a black rapper if they feel rebellious. They are very aware that the outside world differs from their circumscribed little world; indeed, like their parents, high school and college students from all-white towns and suburbs exaggerate the differences and routinely estimate that the population of the United States is 20 to 50% black.[80] So they are wary of the outside world and not sure they want to venture out there.[81]

For the most part, most high school graduates in independent sundown towns don't venture far. One of the first things I noticed in conversations with young people in these towns was their circumscribed aspirations. "Basically, they didn't go anywhere," a woman from Anna, Illinois, said about graduates from Anna-Jonesboro High School. Bill Donahue followed the high school students from Nickerson, a sundown town in central Kansas, when they took their class trip to Washington, D.C., in 2002. "There were a few Nickerson kids who yearned for a broader existence," he reported. "For many students, though, the Washington trip would be . . . a first and last hurrah." He talked with their teacher, Gary McCown, who said "with sad resignation" that he didn't expect much worldly ambitions from students in Nickerson. "They look at what their parents do and what's offered around Nickerson—mostly service jobs—and they think, 'It's not a bad life. It's pleasant. You can walk into the grocery store and be greeted by people you know.' "[82]

When students from Pana High School, in central Illinois, do go on to college, "it's mostly to Eastern or to the community college in Mattoon," according to a former Pana resident. Eastern Illinois University, formerly Eastern Illinois State Teachers College, is located in Charleston, 50 miles east of Pana and almost as white. Mattoon is closer still. Although the University of Illinois, a world-famous institution, is only about an hour from Pana, few students make the drive even to check it out, and fewer still enroll; school personnel cannot recall any who chose the Chicago campus of the university. Students who venture out of state don't venture far either, and afterward, most return to Pana. "They like the small-town life," a recent high school graduate explained. It isn't just preference for the known, however, but also fear of the unknown. "My sister is actually frightened," said a woman who years ago moved to much larger—and interracial—Decatur. "Frightened of cities, frightened of anything she's not familiar with." Such fear marks many small-town residents, but in sundown towns the fear of African Americans looms foremost. Young adults in Pana granted me a certain respect upon learning that I grew up in Decatur: "It's pretty rough over there, isn't it?" Actually, it isn't—they just *think* it is, believing Decatur to be heavily black.[83]

When high school graduates from independent sundown towns do break out, it can be scary for them. Chantel Scherer, a 1988 graduate of Sullivan High School in central Illinois, put it this way:

> I remember growing up in Sullivan where ALL outsiders were made to feel unwelcome. . . . I love where I grew up, but yes, this unrealistic living situation had its implications when those of us who lived there grew up and moved away. I remember being afraid of all the different people when I was 17 and a freshman at college. There were over 30,000 students representing a huge variety of people.[84]

Many people have told how coming from a sundown town made it awkward when they tried to play a role in the larger society. For example, a recent graduate of Granite City High School in southwest Illinois said that his teachers would warn students before field trips to St. Louis, "Don't tell people you're from Granite City, and for God's sake don't tell people you're from an all-white high school!" Of course, such an admonition could only make them *less* at ease in St. Louis, and their resulting parade of emotions—shame, fear, self-consciousness, discomfort—may provide additional reasons not to venture out next time.[85]

The apprehension of residents of independent sundown towns about the outside world often prompts them to inflate their town beyond reason, perhaps to convince themselves they aren't missing much and made the right choice. "They think they're in the middle of the world," my Decatur informant said, characterizing her Pana relatives. "They don't know how small and how backward they are." Deep down, this ethnocentrism is defensive and carries with it an element of soclexia. Deep down, residents of independent sundown towns know they do *not* live at the center of the universe. Their put-downs of the outside world are only a flimsy shield against that knowledge. Here is an obvious example, from someone using the identity Goneaviking, posted to the online discussion site alt.flame.niggers in May 2001:

> Do you want some pictures of niggers hanged in the town square or what, like Fouke, Arkansas, for the "Nigger Don't Let The Sun Set On Your Ass" [sign] in that town? . . . Lots of loggers and farmers down there richer than any nigger in the USA. 80 acres of pine 50 years old = 1,000,000 dollars. 23,000,000 niggers = pure shit.

In fact, Oprah Winfrey by herself probably has more net worth than all 814 residents of Fouke combined. In some part of his or her mind, Goneaviking surely knows that.[86]

Young people who do break out of the cocoon get derided for it by those back home. A student at the University of Illinois, Chicago, told how her friends back in her sundown hometown asked her, "Why would you go there?" She pointed out that Chicago was world-famous for architecture and music, among other things, but that persuaded no one. Friends of another student were more blunt: "Do you know what you're getting yourself into? There's colored people down there!" "Why would you want to live in Washington, D.C.?" inquired hometown friends of Kathy Spillman, from Tonawanda, a sundown town near Buffalo. They seem to have no idea, Spillman noted, that the Smithsonian museums, concerts at the Kennedy Center, theater all over town, and restaurants featuring cuisines from around the world might actually interest someone. Spillman has no patience when these queries cross the line into overt racism. "People from Tonawanda ask me, 'How do you live with all those niggers down there?' I reply, 'I like having sex with them!' "[87]

Many parents in independent sundown towns are content to have their children stay close to home. "They don't seek opportunities to go to cultural events," Susan Penny said about residents of Oblong, Illinois. "They don't leave town except to go to sporting events." They don't expose their children to different milieux on vacations, instead choosing places such as Branson, Missouri, where the entertainment will be familiar and the audiences white. According to Penny, they don't even try ethnic foods.[88]

Elite Sundown Suburbs Limit Their Children in Other Ways

Young people in working-class sundown suburbs behave much like their compatriots in independent sundown towns. They stay close to home, unless service in the armed forces breaks through to enlarge their horizons, racially and occupationally. Young people in elite suburbs such as Beverly Hills, California; Edina, Minnesota; and Darien, Connecticut, display behavior that is both much the same and much different compared to that of their counterparts in independent towns and working-class suburbs. These young people have grown up with a sense of entitlement. The world is their oyster, and they intend to harvest its pearls. Their parents, especially their fathers, mostly don't work in town but in corporate headquarters in the central city or suburban office parks. Their jobs take them across the country or across the world. Their frequent-flier miles take their families for vacations across the country or around the world. Parochial they aren't.

Yet parochial they are. Families like these can go to Bali and never meet a Balinese family, because they stay in the Sanur Beach Hyatt. Like the residents of Pana or Tonawanda, young people from elite sundown suburbs cannot conceive that another place might be superior to their own hometowns; unlike the residents of Pana or Tonawanda, they are not secretly defensive about that. They are truly ethnocentric, which makes it hard for them to learn from other races and cultures. There is also evidence from social psychology that students who discuss issues in multiracial classes "display higher levels of complex thought" and are thus better prepared for college.[89]

The residential segregation by occupation that marks elite sundown suburbs limits their offspring in another way: it enhances social distance. Since most of the people who work in these suburbs cannot afford to live in them— not just the maids and gardeners but also the teachers and police officers— these adults are not really available to children growing up there as any kind of positive role models. Many children in elite suburbs end up not only ignorant of such human activities as carpentry but subtly disdainful of them. They never encounter people in the working class on a plane of social equality. This limits their own occupational horizons and prompts them to feel that they have failed if they don't make it into an elite white-collar occupation.[90]

Sundown Towns Collect Racists

Thus far we have discussed effects sundown towns and suburbs have on people who live in them. Yet these communities not only create racists, but also attract whites who already believe in white supremacy. Ever since they began advertising themselves pridefully as all-white in the early 1900s, sundown towns have attracted people who want to live in all-white communities. Families have moved to Marlow, Oklahoma, "because there were no blacks in the schools there"; to Bishop in southeastern California, from Los Angeles, "because they don't want to deal with 'those people' anymore"; and to Cullman, Alabama, from Birmingham, "to avoid integration." Kelly Burroughs, a 1988 graduate of Havana High School in western Illinois, wrote in 2002:

> I lived in Havana all my life and knew of no [African Americans] that lived there, and yes the rumor that you heard was a wide known fact amongst the community, that niggers were not welcome to purchase or live in our town. As to that holding true today I don't know, I no longer live there, but if you find out please let me know so I can move back.

Burroughs went on to explain, "I would like to see more all white communities. . . . Would I like to live in an all white community, hell yes." [91]

Once racist whites congregate in sundown suburbs or towns, they tend to keep them all-white. Newcomers usually join in happily. As noted previously, a series of violent incidents by whites kept African Americans out of Wyandotte, Michigan, an independent sundown town that was becoming a suburb of Detroit around World War I. The largest single expulsion took place in the late summer of 1916. City assessor F. W. Liddle blamed that riot partly "on the influx of Detroiters who feeling the penetration of Negroes in Detroit sought Wyandotte real estate on the basis of their past knowledge of the [anti] Negro attitude in Wyandotte." [92]

Retirees are free to choose new communities in which to live, unencumbered by the need to commute to work. Often they select towns because they are all-white. One of the selling points for retiring to the Missouri and Arkansas Ozarks has long been their racial composition. A 1972 survey of residents of Mountain Home, Arkansas, found that many were retirees from northern cities, especially Chicago, and chose Mountain Home partly because it was all-white. According to a 1980 article on Polk County, Arkansas, "It is not an uncommon experience in Polk County to hear a newcomer remark that he chose to move here because of 'low taxes and no niggers.' " A store manager in the late 1990s in the Rogers, Arkansas, mall confirmed: "It was not uncommon for folks moving down here from the Chicago area to retire to openly remark that one attraction of the Rogers area was that there were no blacks." A resident of Pana, Illinois, told that white Chicagoans also move there to retire, knowing its anti-black tradition, and have "radically racist ideas."[93]

Florida is of course the nation's premier retirement destination, and northern newcomers—not just retirees—deserve much of the "credit" for that state's extraordinary residential segregation. Carl Fisher, founder of Miami Beach, exemplified those outsiders. According to historian Alan Raucher, Fisher "was appalled by Jim Crow practices in Florida, but he excluded from his developments both blacks and the 'wrong class' of Jews." The influx of northern retirees after World War II hardly opened communities in Florida to African Americans. On the contrary, Florida wound up with the highest levels of residential segregation in America. Recall D, the Index of Dissimilarity, which can vary from 0 (perfect integration) to 100 (complete apartheid). By 1960, Daytona Beach, Fort Lauderdale, Jacksonville, Lakeland, Miami, Orlando, St. Petersburg, and West Palm Beach each had a D greater than 96, close to total apartheid. Scoring 98.1, Fort Lauderdale was the most segregated city in the nation. In contrast, Pensacola and Tampa—Florida cities that were not primarily destinations for northern retirees—scored closer to the southern average of "only" 90.9.[94]

Racist Organizations Favor Sundown Towns

Sundown towns provided fertile recruiting fields for the Ku Klux Klan in the 1920s and still do today. This might seem absurd: why would whites living in places that face no possible "threat" from other races mobilize to protect white supremacy? Again, cognitive dissonance supplies the explanation: living in all-white towns encourages people to support organizations advocating that kind of social structure. Whitley County, Indiana, had about 100 African Americans in 1880 but just 4 by 1920. In 1923, a Ku Klux Klan leader spoke at a large rally in the county seat: "I want to put all the Catholics, Jews, and Negroes on a raft in the middle of the ocean and then sink the raft." According to Kathleen Blee, author of *Women of the Klan*, "the crowd applauded wildly." In overwhelmingly white towns across America in the 1920s, the Klan held parades and rallies that drew the largest single gatherings these towns have had to this day.[95] (Portfolio 22 shows an example.)[96]

Down through the years, Klan leaders have often located in sundown towns. In Indiana in 1923, the Ku Klux Klan attempted to purchase Valparaiso University in Valparaiso, a sundown town, to be its official college. The Klan never came up with the money to complete the deal, however.[97] Edwin DeBarr, leader of the Oklahoma Klan, made his home in Norman, another sundown town, where he headed the School of Pharmacy at the University of Oklahoma and was the university's first vice president. A headquarters of the Illinois KKK was Pekin, also a sundown town. Today's Ku Klux Klan, much less centralized than the 1920s version, has one headquarters in Harrison, Arkansas, "up in the Ozark Mountains," in the words of *The Economist,* "a part of Arkansas from which blacks vanished almost entirely in the early 1900s, and to which few have returned." For a time another Klan center was in Ross, Ohio, a distant suburb of Cincinnati; the first African American family moved into Ross only around 2000. Other KKK groups have set up shop in sundown towns in Pennsylvania, Michigan, Texas, and other states.[98]

Over the years, many other white supremacist organizations and leaders have also sought the supportive environments of sundown towns. In Aurora, Missouri, in 1911, Wilbur Phelps founded *The Menace,* an anti-Catholic newspaper that had a circulation of 1,000,000 by 1914. Father Coughlin, the notorious radio anti-Semite of the 1930s and '40s, broadcast from Royal Oak, a sundown suburb of Detroit. His followers smashed windows of Jewish shops in New York City in the early 1940s, emulating the Nazis' notorious Kristallnacht. Gerald L. K. Smith, a right-wing extremist and radio evangelist in the 1930s and 1940s, devoted his magazine, *The Cross and the Flag,* to exposing the workings of an alleged "international Jewish conspiracy." When he ran for president on the ticket of the Christian Nationalist Party in 1948, his platform included deporting African Americans from the country. After meeting opposition when trying to locate in the Los Angeles area, Smith moved his headquarters to Eureka Springs, Arkansas, partly because it was all-white.[99] Smith died in 1976, but a passion play and the statue "Christ of the Ozarks," both sparked by Smith, live on in Eureka Springs. Robert Welch, founder of the far-right John Birch Society, charged that an international Communist conspiracy was behind the 1954 Supreme Court decision that called for schools to be desegregated. The Birch Society has had headquarters in Belmont, Massachusetts; San Marino, California; and Appleton, Wisconsin. All were sundown towns, I believe,[100] and San Marino also kept out Jews.[101]

Today many right-wing racist groups still find havens in sundown towns and counties. The "Intelligence Report" put out by the Southern Poverty Law Center is the most complete national list of extreme right-wing and racist organizations. Groups on that list are disproportionately headquartered in sundown towns or frequently recruit in them.[102] The Southern Illinois Patriot's

League, for example, is in Benton, Illinois. East Peoria is home to Matt Hale, head of the World Church of the Creator, a white supremacist religion that inspired a follower to go on a 1999 shooting rampage in Illinois and Indiana against people of color that ended with three dead and several others wounded. Even when headquartered in larger interracial cities, such organizations repeatedly meet, march, and recruit in overwhelmingly white towns such as Parma, Ohio; Elwood, Indiana; and Simi Valley, California. Richard Barrett runs his Nationalist Movement from his home in Jackson, Mississippi, but held rallies in Forsyth County, Georgia, on Martin Luther King Jr.'s birthday in 1987 and again in 1997. He noted gleefully, "The Census lists zero point zero zero percent of the population of the all-American county as African," and called it "Fortress Forsyth."[103]

Many residents in all-white or nearly all-white counties and towns disapprove of white supremacist groups. Nevertheless, the style of rhetoric that we have seen is customary in communities with a sundown legacy confers upon these groups a form of legitimacy. As David Zimmermann said, discussing the KKK chapter in Harrison, Arkansas, "Maybe the Klan is here because it's comfortable here." Thom Robb directs the national Knights of the Ku Klux Klan, pastors a Baptist church, and publishes *The Crusader,* a Klan magazine, in Zinc, a tiny suburb of Harrison. He agreed in 2003: "I moved to Boone County in 1972 from Tucson, Arizona, to raise my child in an area that reflects traditional American cultural values." In 2002, a leader of Aryan Nations announced that his organization was moving to Potter County, in north-central Pennsylvania, precisely because it is so white. Even when located in isolated small towns, these hate groups often have considerable influence through music, literature, and word of mouth with white young people, especially prisoners, throughout the United States. Thus not only do sundown towns and suburbs affect how their own residents think and behave, they also affect the larger society.[104]

The impact of sundown towns and suburbs is not limited to whites. The next chapter asks the opposite question: what is their impact on African Americans who *don't* live in them? Sundown towns and suburbs are based on the premise that African Americans must be kept out because they are likely to be problems. When that ideology reaches African Americans—as it inevitably does—the result is not happy.

12

The Effect of Sundown Towns on Blacks

We had realized years ago, to our sorrow, that the housing market, above all else, stands as a symbol of racial inequality.

—Daisy Myers, pioneering black resident of
Levittown, Pennsylvania, writing in 1960 [1]

IN CONVERSATION WITH EACH OTHER, many African Americans believe that when racial privilege is at stake, Caucasians (the term often used) are to be feared. "Whites will stop at nothing," a sociologist friend said to me. I thought he was overstating his case, but the actions whites have taken to maintain sundown towns and suburbs support his position.

We have seen that the deepening racism of the Nadir—exemplified by its progeny, sundown towns and suburbs—not only affected where African Americans might live but also how, by sapping their morale. Through the years, sundown towns and suburbs have influenced the thinking, modified the travel behavior, and limited the opportunities of African Americans who never even set foot in them. The ordinances, restrictive covenants, acts of private violence, police harassment, white flight, NIMBY zoning, and other mechanisms used to maintain sundown towns have also contributed, we will see, to a certain wariness in African American culture, leading to a persistence of caution that in turn helps maintain sundown towns today.

In metropolitan areas, sundown suburbs in turn gave rise to overwhelmingly black inner-city neighborhoods and a handful of majority-black suburbs. This residential segregation continues to take a toll on many African Americans in the present, making it harder for them to achieve the cultural capital and make the social connections that lead to upward mobility. The ideology that drives sundown towns and suburbs—that blacks are problems to be avoided—also hurts African Americans psychologically, especially when they internalize the low expectations that result from it.

Feeling Ill at Ease

Especially during the Nadir, travel was difficult and often unsafe for African Americans, and not just in the South. Older African Americans can still recall how trips had to be meticulously planned to reach places with restrooms or overnight accommodations in a timely manner. A resident of Rochester, Indiana, recalled that a black chauffeur died in his car in about 1940 because he was not allowed to stay in a local hotel. He had rented a room for the little white boy he was chauffeuring but was not allowed in himself, and he either froze or was asphyxiated by exhaust fumes. Much more common was "mere" humiliation. Until well after the passage of the 1964 Civil Rights Act, which outlawed segregation in public accommodations such as restaurants and motels, African Americans coped by compiling guidebooks of places that would not harm or embarrass them (Portfolio 26). Families also assembled their own lists and shared them with friends.[2]

Or they stayed home. Speaking of her childhood in the 1950s, an African American woman said, "We didn't *go* on trips. My father absolutely refused to take a vacation. Part of that was because he worried about being terrorized on the road." "Terrorized" is an appropriate word choice, because segregation and especially sundown towns rest ultimately on the threat of terror. Her family lived in Mattoon in central Illinois, surrounded by sundown towns. Not only do these communities tell African Americans that many white people consider them so despicable that they must be barred en masse, they also serve as a reminder that we do not really live under the rule of law where black people are concerned.[3]

Although any stop for gas, food, or lodging might prove humiliating to the black traveler, sundown towns posed the worst hazards. In other towns, even if hotels and restaurants refused to serve African Americans, they could secure shelter within the black community. Sundown towns had no black community, of course. Worse still, black travelers were acutely aware that they stuck out in these all-white towns, not only as unusual but also as illegitimate and unwanted. Allison Blakely, professor of African American studies at Boston University, recalls that in the mid-1960s, "blacks were afraid to drive through Grants Pass or Medford" in southwestern Oregon. "A black friend of mine put a loaded pistol on the front seat of his car when he drove through those towns." To this day, some African Americans are very aware of sundown towns and their reputations, even in distant states.[4]

Even benign experiences in sundown towns made impacts that lasted for decades. Joycelyn Landrum-Brown, a psychologist at the University of Illinois–Urbana, grew up in Indianapolis. She wrote about a trip she made with her parents to Greenwood, ten miles south of Indianapolis, in about 1960:

> If you will recall, my parents had gone to Greenwood to pick up a puppy from one of my mother's co-workers who lived there. I overheard the grownups talking about how we had to get out of town because black people were not allowed in town after dark. I remember being terrified sitting in the back seat of our car holding my new puppy as we drove from Greenwood to Indianapolis. I believe this memory is behind my fear of driving rural highways and traveling through small rural towns (particularly in Indiana).

Olen Cole interviewed an elderly African American who as a young worker in the Civilian Conservation Corps in the 1930s rode through Taft, California. "As we entered the city a sign read, 'Read nigger and run; if you can't read— run anyway. Nigger don't let the sun go down on you in Taft,' " he told Cole in about 1995. "The importance of this experience is that it remained vivid in [his] memory," Cole notes. "Many years later he is still able to remember the entire wording on the sign." [5]

Sundown town reputations remain vivid and current in African American culture. A 70-year-old black professional woman in an interracial town in central Illinois put it this way in 2002: "You did not stop *anywhere*. There was a lot of fear. There still is. I had to go down to Effingham [a notorious nearby sundown town] recently to observe . . . and I was not happy about it." Many older African Americans are still reluctant even to enter sundown towns. The former CCC worker went on to tell Olen Cole, "Even today when I visit Fresno, I make it a point to bypass Taft." An African American professor at Southern Arkansas University related that as of 2001, "blacks don't stop when they pass through Sheridan," the town 30 miles south of Little Rock that got rid of its African American population in 1954. A resident of Paxton, a sundown town north of Champaign, Illinois, said in 2000, "I invited a black man who wouldn't drive into Paxton for Sunday dinner. He'd come [only] if I drove him." An elderly African American woman living in central Missouri avoids the entire southwestern corner of that state. She is very aware that after whites in Springfield, the prime city of the Ozark Mountains, lynched three African Americans on Easter Sunday, 1906, "all the blacks left out of that area," as she put it. Neosho, Stockton, Warsaw, Bolivar, and other Ozark towns are almost devoid of African Americans, who fled the entire region, she said; even today, those are "not places where *I* would feel comfortable going." [6]

Particularly within their own metropolitan area, African Americans know well which suburbs do not welcome them. Only 9% of African Americans in the Detroit area in the late 1990s said they thought Dearborn, the sundown suburb just west of Detroit, would welcome a black family moving in, while 86% said the family would not be welcome. In a 2002 article in the *Detroit News* titled "Invisible Boundaries Created Dividing Line Between Black, White Suburbs," David Riddle, a Wayne State University history professor, explained that the violent anti-black events of the 1970s in the sundown suburb of Warren still affected that city's image three decades later: "When a municipality acquires a reputation like that, I think it's self-sustaining." A professor of African American studies at Bradley University in Peoria told why he would not consider moving to nearby Morton: "Clearly what I've read about the area influences me. Based on what you know, you don't feel comfortable raising your family there, and exposing your children to those influences." [7]

Writing about "mere" segregation on the fiftieth anniversary of *Brown v. Board of Education,* Colbert King, who is African American, agreed with the decision's language:

> To separate [children] from others of similar age and qualifications solely because of their race generates a feeling of inferiority as to their status in the community that may affect their hearts and minds in a way unlikely ever to be undone.

"It does affect you, as a child, and later as a grown man," King wrote, "in ways 'unlikely ever to be undone.' There is a wariness you can't shake." Historically, the still more hurtful existence of sundown towns and suburbs made many African Americans justifiably fearful, less apt to explore new experiences and locales. Even today, many African Americans do *not* feel that the world is their oyster, ready to be explored and enjoyed. And why should they? It would give anyone pause to realize that merely being in a town after dark can be a life-threatening offense. This worry about acceptance, this feeling ill at ease, is the opposite of "white privilege"—that sense of security felt by upper- and middle-class whites that they will *never* be challenged as out of place. [8]

Black Avoidance Helps Maintain Sundown Towns

Today, residents of all-white towns and suburbs often blame African Americans for being overly cautious. A longtime resident of Arab, Alabama, thinks so. After telling how whites used to keep African Americans out of Arab even during the day, he assured me in 2002, "It'd be different now." Of course, blaming blacks for not moving in serves as a handy excuse for whites who do not want to acknowledge that their town ever had a policy to keep them out. However, sometimes whites have a point. Certainly African American sociologist Orlando Patterson thinks they do: "Persisting segregation is partly—and for most middle-class Afro-Americans, largely—a voluntary phenomenon." In response to the Civil Rights Movement, whites lost some of their sense of privilege, especially in the South. No longer do most whites assume they are entitled to exclude African Americans. On public opinion polls, fewer and fewer whites agree with such items as "Blacks should not push into areas where it is known they are not wanted." Ironically, however, in the black community pessimism about white attitudes has grown. In 1968, 47% of African Americans felt whites wanted to see blacks "get a better break," 31% thought them indifferent, and 22% thought whites wanted to "keep blacks down." By 1992, just 22% of African Americans believed whites wanted to see them get a better break, 52% thought them indifferent, and 26% felt whites wanted to keep them down. Such pessimism is hardly conducive to social action.[9]

Most black families merely follow the line of least resistance. In 2001, reporter David Mendell spoke with 66-year-old Willie Buchanan, who bought a house in "Blackfish Bay," as wags call the majority-black neighborhood near Whitefish Bay, an overwhelmingly white suburb north of Milwaukee. Buchanan "said he moved where he felt most comfortable," according to Mendell. "You like to live around people who you feel want to be your neighbor," said Buchanan. "I don't think prejudice is as bad as it used to be. But it's still around, so I just decided to move here."[10]

Such thinking is understandable. Law professor Sheryll Cashin calls it "integration exhaustion." As actor Sidney Poitier put it, explaining why the Poitier family moved to Mt. Vernon, an interracial suburb of New York City, after having problems trying to buy a house in West Los Angeles: "Our children are established in a multi-racial community in Mount Vernon. They attend multi-racial schools. . . . We don't want to barter that kind of atmosphere for something that is hostile." Ruby Dee, another black actor who with her husband, Ossie Davis, chose an already integrated neighborhood in New Rochelle, New York, offered a similar explanation: "I want to be friends with my neighbors. I don't want to be tolerated, on my best behavior, always seeking my neighbor's approval. . . . I admire the pioneers who risk so much in the process of integration, but I cannot break that ice." Reasonably enough, many African American families want to live near neighbors who will accept them, and the best way to find whites like that is in neighborhoods where they already live near African American families.[11]

Choosing this line of least resistance may not lead to the best results for the family in the long run, however. African Americans moving into those neighborhoods that are known to be open to them often wind up in areas with higher tax rates and lower tax bases than whiter suburbs. Eventually these economic realities take their toll, and families find that their homes did not appreciate as fast as those in whiter suburbs. Cashin points to a host of more serious social problems that arise after suburbs go majority black. Certainly following the line of least resistance does not lead to the best results for the metropolitan area. When black families move to an interracial suburb that everyone knows is open—indeed, that is likely to go all black—they only contribute to the sundown suburb problem.[12]

Nevertheless, calling African American complicity in residential segregation "voluntary" overstates the case. According to sociologist Gary Orfield, speaking in 2000, African Americans do still believe in the integrated American dream: 99% favor desegregation, and 59% favor busing if needed to get there. Worry about sundown reactions deters many. In Detroit, Reynolds Farley and others pointed out, only 31% of African Americans said they would be "willing to be the African American pioneer on an all-white block" in 1992, compared to 38% in 1976. But sociologist John Logan stresses, "Black preferences are strongly affected by beliefs about whites' attitudes and behavior," so "their reluctance to live in a predominantly white neighborhood is due to their belief that whites would react negatively." Reputations are important. In Arab, for instance, the 2000 census showed just a single black household among 7,139 total population. "Why so few?" I asked a longtime resident. He referred to the violent exclusion of the past: "That happened a long time ago, and it's still in their [blacks'] minds."[13]

Before smiling at the old ex-CCC worker who still avoids Taft six decades after he learned it was sundown, we might note that Taft also did not change for decades. According to Ronald McGriff, chair of social sciences at the nearby College of the Sequoias, "as recent as the 1980s, [residents of Taft] trashed a black home (with paint and graffiti) and [the family] was told to 'get out of town.'" Before making light of the black man who would come for Sunday dinner in Paxton only if his white host drove him, whites might remember that one can never be sure when one's car might break down. Before blaming African Americans for not moving into Arab, we must note that Arab boasted a sign, "Nigger, Don't Let The Sun Set On Your Black Ass in Arab, Alabama," until the early 1990s, according to Benjamin Johnson, a former University of

Alabama student—hardly "a long time ago." I must confess that I felt unsafe and uneasy when I first started doing this research in such notorious sundown towns as Alba, Texas, and Cicero, Illinois. I worried lest "they" discover my liberal attitudes, before I fully understood that my white skin made me safely part of the in-group.[14]

David Grann, a *New Republic* journalist visiting Vidor, Texas, in 1998, made light of African Americans' continued concern about that town: "Several blacks in the surrounding area told me they still don't stop there for gas at night, even though the hand-painted sign on Main Street saying 'Nigger, Don't Let the Sun Set on You in Vidor' was taken down some 30 years ago." He obviously thought African Americans were overdoing their prudence. But if one doesn't know for sure, one is putting oneself and one's family at risk. African Americans have a legitimate right to fear violent consequences, as well as such lesser repercussions as shunning, if they move into a sundown community. Moreover, just five years before Grann's visit, racial slurs, shunning, refusals to hire, and death threats drove four black households from Vidor's public housing complex, leaving the town again all-white by design. This book is replete with examples of vicious white retribution visited upon unsuspecting African Americans who didn't know enough to be wary of sundown towns and might have survived had they been more prudent. Today, most sundown towns and suburbs would react more placidly than Vidor back in 1993, but some residents might not be welcoming. As an elderly African American in a neighboring town said in 2002, explaining why there are no African Americans in Nashville, Illinois, "If people are inhospitable to you, you leave."[15]

Still, African Americans can overdo their caution into their own form of racial paranoia. Sometimes African Americans take a certain pleasure in overstating the danger: "look what those white folks have done *now*!" There is a streak of gallows humor in black rhetoric that takes mordant satisfaction in seizing on, retelling, and even exaggerating examples of racist white behavior. Patterson writes that African Americans perceive whites as "technically clever, yes; powerful, well armed, and prolific, to be sure; but without an ounce of basic human decency." Despite all the wretched acts by whites recounted in this book, that is too strong. Such thinking only exaggerates the extent and importance of white racism and invites African Americans to show too much caution. The African American woman who "was not happy about" having to go to Effingham, Illinois, in broad daylight in 2002 showed this paranoia, just like the white suburbanite from Naperville who frets about going to a concert in Chicago's Loop. In both cases, a self-fulfilling prophecy sets in: nothing bad happens to the person who avoids places dominated by the other race, and that happy fact legitimizes the avoidance, leaving intact the belief that the opposite race still poses a threat.[16]

Psychological Costs of Sundown Towns

No other group, not even Native Americans, has been so disparaged by the very structure of American society. No other group has been labeled a pariah people—literally to be kept outside the gates of our sundown towns and suburbs. As Daisy Myers put it in 1960, "The housing market, above all else, stands as a symbol of racial inequality." Just as sundown towns drained the morale of African Americans during the Nadir, so sundown suburbs, especially elite suburbs, still contribute to demoralization in black neighborhoods elsewhere in the metropolitan area.[17]

Arna Bontemps and Jack Conroy observed about Watts, the African American ghetto that exploded into violence in Los Angeles in 1965: "A crushing weight fell on the spirit of the neighborhood when it learned that it was hemmed in, that prejudice and malice had thrown a wall around it." On the other side of the country, Irwin Quintyne moved in 1961 to North Amityville, one of the "black townships" that adjoin sundown suburbs on Long Island. He remembered in 2003 how "other growing Long Island communities, Levittown in particular, made it clear that they didn't want blacks." The message hammered home to black suburbanites by their neighboring all-white community is "We do not care who you are or what you have done; so far as *this* town is concerned, you are a nigger and unfit for human companionship." Partly as a result of this message, North Amityville; Kinloch, Missouri; and several other black townships lost morale and came to house drug markets and problem families.[18]

Successful African Americans may be particularly upset by these slights, because their peers, elite whites, are the least likely of all white Americans to accept African Americans into their neighborhoods and organizations. As Ellis Cose famously raged:

> I have done everything I was supposed to do. I have stayed out of trouble with the law, gone to the right schools, and worked myself nearly to death. *What more do they want?* Why in God's name won't they accept me as a full human being?[19]

It *is* frustrating: even voicing the hurt can hurt, because it can seem as if affluent African Americans are only whining because white people won't be their friends. A similar misinterpretation gets applied to school desegregation: "What is it about black people? Do they *need* white children next to them to learn successfully?" But that was not Cose's point in 1993, nor was it the point of *Brown v. Board of Education* in 1954. As the Supreme Court pointed out in decisions flowing from *Brown,* whites are the lawmaking group in America. When they segregated the schools, it was part of a program of white supremacy that declared blacks inferior. That is why segregated schools were *inherently* unequal, as the *Brown* decision stated: the enforced racial separation itself both presupposed and signified black inferiority.

Every time black ingress into a previously white neighborhood prompts white egress to more distant sundown suburbs, all African Americans in the metropolitan area are invited to remember that they are still so despised by our mainstream culture that whites feel they must flee them en masse. Black poet Langston Hughes mused on this matter in 1949 in "Restrictive Covenants," which said in part:

> When I move
> Into a neighborhood
> Folks fly.
> Even every foreigner
> That can move, moves.
> Why?

Cose goes to the heart of the matter: residential exclusion (and the school segregation it purchases) strikes at blacks' worth *as full human beings.* That's why it festers. That's why black respondents on Long Island were significantly less satisfied with their lives than whites with significantly lower incomes, in a 1990 study reported by Cose.[20]

After experiencing some of Chicago's sundown neighborhoods and sundown suburbs firsthand in 1965, Martin Luther King Jr. observed, "Segregation has wreaked havoc with the Negro. . . . Only a Negro can understand the social leprosy that segregation inflicts upon him. Every confrontation with restriction is another emotional battle in a never-ending war." "Social leprosy" is an evocative term for the pariah status that sundown towns and suburbs enforce upon African Americans, inexact only in that leprosy can now be cured.[21]

Countee Cullen's poem "Incident," written in the 1920s, suggests the sting that African Americans can internalize from racial slights:

Once riding in old Baltimore,
Heart-filled, head-filled with glee,
I saw a Baltimorean
Keep looking straight at me.

Now I was eight and very small,
And he was no whit bigger,
And so I smiled, but he poked out
His tongue, and called me, "Nigger."

I saw the whole of Baltimore
From May until December;
Of all the things that happened there
That's all that I remember.

Such behavior wasn't limited to an eight-year-old white boy in Baltimore in 1911. As we have seen, residents of sundown towns persist in expressing racial slights and taunts. Young black adults have supplied many examples of being called "nigger" and worse in these towns in the last ten years, such as this experience by a high school athlete in Pekin, in central Illinois, in 1999:

In track, I was the Conference Champion in the 3200 meters and in cross-country I was Conference and Sectional Champion. One occurrence that I would never forget about running cross-country is when I had a meet in Pekin, Illinois. While running along the course, someone riding alone in a car shouted out the word "Nigger." This was my first time experiencing racism. Throughout my years of living [in Peoria], I had never been in the act of racism. Till this day I can remember this occurrence very visually. This event made me aware that racism does still exist in the '90s.

And till this day the memory sears.[22]

Internalizing Low Expectations

Since the 1970s, the research literature in social science and education has stressed that the expectations teachers and others have of children—and ultimately the expectations children have of themselves—make a key difference to their performance in school (and later life), and expectations vary by race (and class and sometimes gender). If teachers think of African American children as less intelligent, they will expect less from them. Soon they get less from them. After a while African American children may start expecting less from themselves. The generalizations that are intrinsic to sundown towns and suburbs—that African Americans must be kept out because they are problematic people who are likely to be intellectually inferior, if not criminal—pervade our general culture. Sociologists Dale Harvey and Gerald Slatin demonstrated how teachers have internalized these expectations. They showed photographs of children to teachers and found them all too willing to predict different levels of school performance based solely on snapshots. "White children were more often expected to succeed and black children more often expected to fail," they summarized.[23]

Unfortunately, these lower expectations can become self-fulfilling prophecies for some members of the oppressed group. African Americans in segregated environments can find it hard to break out of this cycle of lower expectations and inferior self-worth. De facto segregation is no kinder to the excluded minority than the old de jure segregation that the Supreme Court threw out as unconstitutional in 1954; besides, as this book has shown, sundown towns are all-white by policy and official actions, not just de facto. All-black schools often do not and sometimes cannot convince black children they are fully equipped, genetically and intellectually, to challenge the white world. Since the raison d'être for segregated schooling was (and is) to keep an allegedly inferior group from "contaminating" and slowing the progress of white students, it can be hard for teachers in black schools to convince their charges that they are fully equal and ready to take on all comers. "Segregation promotes the devaluation of black life even among blacks, and can lead to self-hatred," wrote psychiatrist Alvin Poussaint in 2002. In this respect teachers in segregated black schools face the same uphill battle faced by teachers in segregated white schools in sundown suburbs who are trying to convince their charges that blacks are fully equal.[24]

All the while, the act of living in sundown neighborhoods and attending all-white schools communicates to everyone in the society that whites are superior. So does the higher prestige accorded to whiter suburbs. The ideology underlying sundown communities relies on stereotypes about African Americans, stereotypes that unfortunately reach African Americans. Claude Steele and his associates at Stanford show that these stereotypes can then "dramatically depress" the performance of African American students on the SAT and similar tests, a phenomenon Steele calls "stereotype threat." In subtle experiments, Steele has created stereotype threats for white students that depress their performance, and the same for women as a group, and so forth. Thus books such as The Bell Curve, which claims African Americans have lower intelligence genetically, in turn help to maintain precisely the lower test scores that they claim to "explain," by maintaining the stereotype that African Americans are inferior.[25]

All this is why Malcolm X famously said, "A segregated school system produces children who, when they graduate, graduate with crippled minds." Black parents try to convince their children that they are valuable human beings, but it's not easy when society devalues them. It's also hard to answer such logical questions as "Why are we in the ghetto?" "Why do whites move away?" As an eight-year-old black child said to Jacob Holdt, commenting on this white antagonism: "We must have done *something* wrong!" And lo, the old "blacks as problem" ideology, expressed so clearly in the origin myths of sundown towns, surfaces miles away in the minds and mouths of the victims.[26]

Excluding African Americans from Cultural Capital

Residential segregation makes it easier to give African Americans inferior educations, health care, and other public services. Study after study has shown how expenditures per pupil are higher in suburban schools than in inner cities, even though everyone knows that suburban pupils have many advantages—from their own computers to a higher proportion of two-parent households—that make them easier to teach. Kati Haycock of the Education Trust notes the incongruity: "We take the kids who are most dependent on their teachers for academic learning and assign them teachers with the weakest academic base." Residential segregation not only makes this systematic disadvantaging possible, it makes it desirable, even prestigious, in the eyes of white suburbanites.[27]

Confining most African Americans to the opposite of sundown suburbs—majority-black, inner-city neighborhoods—also restricts their access to what Patterson calls cultural capital: "those learned patterns of mutual trust, insider knowledge about how things really work, encounter rituals, and social sensibilities that constitute the language of power and success." Sundown suburbs shut blacks out from coming into contact with these patterns of the dominant culture,[28] at least before college. This cultural segregation shows up even in something as basic as patterns of speech: many African Americans sound identifiably "black" on the telephone. Their accent and voice timbre are "different." The difference is not racial; Chinese Americans I knew in Mississippi in the 1960s either spoke "Southern white English" (more than half), "Southern black English" (a few), or Chinese-accented English (many persons older than 40). Historian Barbara J. Fields points out that there is no such thing as "black English" in England, where West Indian immigrants' children learn the English of their class and region. But in America, as a consequence of the Great Retreat, "black English" intensified.[29]

In turn, not coming into contact with patterns of the dominant culture is one reason why African Americans (and to a degree Hispanics and Native Americans) average much lower scores than European Americans on college entrance exams such as the SAT. The SAT and related tests suffer from racial and class (and some gender) bias. This unfairness is in addition to such problems as the far greater access white students have to coaching classes and personal tutors. It derives from the statistical methods the Educational Testing Service, the administrator of the SAT, uses to select items to be included on the tests.[30] Until this bias is eliminated, African Americans need exposure to the vocabulary and thoughtways of white suburbanites to do well on standardized tests. Sundown suburbs prevent that by keeping black children away from high-scoring white children, as well as from the amenities that help them score high.

Research in Chicago by James Rosenbaum and others confirms Patterson's general point. The Chicago Housing Authority (CHA), burned by the white resistance to African Americans who tried to live in Airport Homes after World War II, changed its policies to comply with sundown suburbs and neighborhoods. It built public housing for blacks in black neighborhoods and public housing for whites in white neighborhoods. As a result, CHA was sued for racial segregation in what became known as the Gautreaux litigation. In 1969, federal judge Richard Austin ordered CHA to locate public housing for blacks in predominantly white neighborhoods scattered throughout the city. Eventually, the relief was ordered to extend to the white suburbs as well.[31] The result, getting under way in 1976, located more than 5,000 families in more than 100 predominantly white communities in Cook County and five suburban counties.

Rosenbaum took advantage of the marvelous natural experiment provided by this order. He compared families that happened to get selected for housing in white neighborhoods with families that applied but were not selected. He found that being exposed to new surroundings had transforming effects on the families placed in white neighborhoods: 95% of their children graduated from high school and 54% went on to college. (Both of these rates were higher than for European Americans nationally.) Black parents in suburbia were also much more likely than parents in inner cities to find work in the suburbs. Rosenbaum concluded that residential segregation was itself the problem, promoting hopelessness and keeping poor black families from connecting with the larger society.[32]

Even apparently unrelated social problems such as crime and school dropout rates turn out to be related to residential segregation, according to research by Wayne State University professor George Galster. He analyzed the segregation level and various quality of life indicators across U.S. cities, based on the 1990 census. Looking at Detroit, America's most segregated metropolitan area, he concluded that if its segregation level were cut in half, "the median income of black families would rise 24%; the black homicide rate would fall 30%; the black high school dropout rate would fall 75%; and the black poverty rate would fall 17%." The Galster and Gautreaux research shows that blaming the pathological conditions of ghetto neighborhoods on their inhabitants gets causation at least partly backward.[33]

Excluding African Americans from Social Connections

Gautreaux also worked for an additional reason: social connections. Following a 1973 article by Mark Granovetter, "The Strength of Weak Ties," sociologists have come to see that Americans connect with the larger society in important ways through casual and seemingly unimportant relations. A whole new career might result from a tip from a friend's older sister's boyfriend. "Again and again," wrote sociologist Deirdre Royster in 2003, "the white men I spoke with described opportunities that had landed in their laps, not as the result of outstanding achievements or personal characteristics, but rather as the result of the assistance of older white neighbors, brothers, family friends." The trouble is, these networks are segregated, so important information never reaches black America.[34]

Sundown suburbanites know only whites, by definition, except perhaps a few work contacts. Thus sundown suburbs contribute to economic inequality by race. In the Milwaukee metropolitan area, for instance, often listed as America's second most segregated, African Americans "earn just 49 cents for every dollar that whites earn, far below the national average of 64 cents to the dollar," according to reporter Stephanie Simon. Overwhelmingly white suburbs, with which Milwaukee abounds, play a large role in maintaining this inequality. Similarly, urban studies professor Carolyn Adams found that occupational segregation is worse in the Philadelphia suburbs than in the city itself and blames residential segregation, because networks in inner-city neighborhoods stay within the " 'hood." Even affluent African Americans who live in majority-black suburbs face this limitation.[35]

Darien, Connecticut, nicely illustrates the concentration of opportunity in the casual networks of elite sundown suburbs. Teenagers there have so many summer job offers, as well as other prospects, that they have no interest in working at Darien's McDonald's. Nearby suburbs are almost as elite. So the restaurant hires a private bus from East Harlem, an hour away, filled with teenagers and adults who feel fortunate to work at McDonald's. There they have no meaningful interaction with Darien residents at the take-out window, so they make no connections that might lead to upward mobility.[36]

Because suburbs have become increasingly important economically and culturally, excluding African Americans from suburbs increasingly keeps them out of the centers of American corporate, civic, and cultural life. Many manufacturing jobs have long been located in sundown suburbs such as Dearborn, Michigan, and Brea, California. As whites left the city, they took still more of America's jobs to the suburbs with them. Geographer Charles Christian studied this process in the Chicago metropolitan area, where many jobs moved to the suburbs. Generally, the jobs went to the suburbs with the smallest black populations; in the two suburbs that gained the most jobs, Franklin Park and Des Plaines, "there appears to be no black population." This trend accelerated in the last two decades, during which not only factories but also corporate headquarters have been moving to the suburbs.[37]

Reviewing *Urban Inequality,* a recent comparative urban research study, Anne Shlay summarized, "It is better to be black in Atlanta than in Detroit." Atlanta does not have many of the sundown suburbs, like Grosse Pointe and Wyandotte, that have long cursed Detroit. This makes it easier for African Americans to amass cultural capital and make social connections in Atlanta. Atlanta attaches less stigma to blackness, and upward and geographic mobility is easier there.[38]

William J. Wilson sees this exodus of jobs to the suburbs as the biggest single cause of inner-city hopelessness, which in turn leads to drugs, gangs, and the breakdown of the black family. It also removes from inner-city neighborhoods connections with people who have jobs. Remaining residents face yet another burden: unequal commuting. Most commutes are now suburb to suburb rather than suburb to inner city, and African Americans have the longest commutes to work of any racial/ethnic group.[39]

Our society then stigmatizes the entire racial group identified with the resulting concentration of hopelessness, not only those members of it who live in the ghetto. Meanwhile, the racial group that forced the concentrating—whites—does not get stigmatized as a group. Instead, whiteness gets valorized owing to its identification with elegant elite sundown suburbs. This unequal burden of stigma versus honor is one more social cost blacks bear, derived from sundown towns.

We know how to end these social costs. The Gautreaux families, simply by dint of living in white suburbia, were able to make connections that led to educational and occupational opportunity. That they did so well, even though mostly headed by single mothers on welfare, shows the power of racial and economic integration. Conversely, the much worse educational and occupational outcomes of those *not* selected to participate shows the debilitating influence of segregation, hence ultimately of sundown suburbs, on African Americans in the inner city. The achievements of the Gautreaux families augur that the quick eradication of sundown towns would foster the development not only of whites who are less racist, but also of blacks who are more successful.

The next chapter shows that sundown towns also have bad effects on America as a whole and especially on our metropolitan areas. The more sundown suburbs a metropolitan area has, the lower the vitality of its inner city and perhaps of the entire area.

13

The Effect of Sundown Towns
on the Social System

Our standard of decency in expenditure, as in other ends of emulation, is set by
the usage of those next above us in reputability; until, in this way, especially in
any community where class distinctions are somewhat vague, all canons of reputability and decency, and all standards of consumption, are traced back by in-
sensible gradations to the usages and habits of thought of the highest social and
pecuniary class—the wealthy leisure class.
                    —Thorstein Veblen, *The Theory of the Leisure Class,* 1899 [1]

NOT ONLY DO SUNDOWN TOWNS and suburbs hurt African Americans
and warp white Americans, they also have negative consequences for the social system as a whole. Metropolitan areas in particular are social systems,
complexly interlinked. Just as a power surge can cascade through an electrical
grid, an overconcentration of whites in one neighborhood can cause difficulties elsewhere in the social system.

Sundown Suburbs Can Hurt Entire Metropolitan Areas

Racial exclusion can decrease opportunity for everyone in a metropolitan area
if it makes that area less attractive to newcomers. Detroit was the nation's most
segregated metropolitan area in 2000.[2] Historically Detroit has been bur-
dened with some of the nation's most notorious sundown suburbs. Without a
doubt, this hypersegregation has hurt the city of Detroit itself. Housing prices
within the city reflect Detroit's dismal economic position: its median home
cost just $25,600 in 1990, dead last among America's 77 cities with 200,000
or more people. In comparison, the median home in Boston cost $161,400, in
Los Angeles $244,500. Detroit also ranked 73rd of 77 in median income.[3]

Homes in Detroit are also worth much less than suburban homes: in 1999, the median Detroit home was valued at $63,400, less than half the median value elsewhere in the metropolitan area. Homes in Boston, in contrast, were worth only slightly less than homes outside Boston, while the median home in Los Angeles was worth more than homes outside Los Angeles. Since the 1950s, Detroit has lost half its population. George Lin, who styles himself an "urban explorer," calls it "the most tragic case of urban abandonment in the United States." Famous for abandoned homes, Detroit also boasts abandoned office buildings, factories, warehouses, and hotels, including several skyscrapers.[4]

While there is no doubt that sundown suburbs have hurt the city of Detroit, they may not have hurt the outlying parts of its metropolitan area. Taken as a whole, the Detroit metropolitan area is among the nation's most prosperous; in 1997, metropolitan Detroit families averaged $56,000 in income, well above New York City ($49,500) or Los Angeles ($47,600). Moreover, a metropolitan area's growth or decline rests on many causes, from the rise and fall of specific industries and even companies to the historic location of hospitals or universities. Still, there is evidence that Detroit's hypersegregation, with sundown suburbs clustered around a central city that in 2000 was 82% black, hurts its prospects as a metropolitan area. Certainly many people in Detroit think so. "Segregation Keeps Businesses, Professionals from Locating to Detroit Area," headlined the *Detroit News* in 2002. The article cited "business officials" as saying, "For a firm evenly split between Detroit and another city as the possible home of its new headquarters, the distasteful aroma of segregation could be a deciding factor." Metropolitan Detroit, not just the city, shrank in population between 1970 and 1998 by 3%, while the United States grew by 32%. Corporate leaders in St. Louis, Cleveland, and other hypersegregated metropolitan areas have voiced similar worries. The three cities that continued to lose the most population in the first three years of the new millennium were Detroit, Cincinnati, and St. Louis, all among our most segregated.[5]

Many whites in hypersegregated cities like Detroit have thrown in the towel on their central city. As Leah Samuel put it, describing the debate in the Detroit Theater Organ Society (DTOS) over whether to move their huge Wurlitzer pipe organ from the Senate Theater in downtown Detroit, "relocating Detroit institutions to the suburbs is a well-established tradition." Dick Leichtamer, president of the society, blames declining attendance on "the part of town that it's in." Former president George Orbits agreed: "The people just do not want to come to Detroit." But Samuel points out, "Despite the fears of crime that they cite as a reason for the move, DTOS board members admit that they don't recall any serious negative incidents involving concertgoers."

It isn't specific fear of crime that drives the exodus so much as a sense that leaving is the right thing to do. But whether a metropolitan area can draw conventions and tourists with nothing to do in its core city remains to be seen.[6]

Sundown Towns Stifle Creativity

In addition to discouraging new people, hypersegregation may also discourage new ideas. Urban theorist Jane Jacobs has long held that the mix of peoples and cultures found in successful cities prompts creativity. An interesting study by sociologist William Whyte shows that sundown suburbs may discourage out-of-the-box thinking. By the 1970s, some executives had grown weary of the long commutes with which they had saddled themselves so they could raise their families in elite sundown suburbs. Rather than move their families back to the city, they moved their corporate headquarters out to the suburbs. Whyte studied 38 companies that left New York City in the 1970s and '80s, allegedly "to better [the] quality-of-life needs of their employees." Actually, they moved close to the homes of their CEOs, cutting their average commute to eight miles; 31 moved to the Greenwich-Stamford, Connecticut, area. These are not sundown towns, but adjacent Darien was, and Greenwich and Stamford have extensive formerly sundown neighborhoods that are also highly segregated on the basis of social class. Whyte then compared those 38 companies to 36 randomly chosen comparable companies that stayed in New York City. Judged by stock price, the standard way to measure how well a company is doing, the suburbanized companies showed less than half the stock appreciation of the companies that chose to remain in the city.[7]

Evidence from Tacoma, Washington, suggests that cities with a racial mix may be more hospitable to new ideas. Today Tacoma has an enormous inferiority complex compared to the metropolitan juggernaut to its north, Seattle. Some commentators, including journalist Charles Mudede, tie Tacoma's relative lack of progress to its sundown policies vis-à-vis Chinese Americans in 1885:

> Tacoma's officials . . . helped force most of the city's Chinese community onto a train headed for Portland. Tacoma faced national embarrassment because of the incident, and its backward way of settling racial disputes became known as "The Tacoma Method." It has yet to recover from this humiliating recognition: recently, the *Tacoma News Tribune* published an article titled "Tacoma faces up to its darkest hour," which posits that Tacoma might have turned out differently had it not booted out its Chinese population.

The *News Tribune* laments the missing Chinese Americans and their ideas, pointing out that to this day Tacoma remains the only city on the West Coast with no large Chinese American population. In addition, the restrictive mindset established when Tacoma's expulsion of Chinese immigrants was allowed to stand was not conducive to new ideas and new peoples.[8]

Independent sundown towns also hurt their own futures by being closed to new ideas. Nick Khan of Paragould, Arkansas, said nearby interracial Jonesboro is growing much more than Paragould. "If this thing [racism] goes out of here, Paragould will grow rapidly." "To this day, it's a very stuck-in-the-past town," said a 1983 high school graduate of Red Bud, Illinois, a sundown town near St. Louis. "Any time the community is presented with opportunities to provide tax incentives or otherwise bring something new in, the council votes it down." There are exceptions. Some sundown towns do better than others. Murray Bishoff, who lives in Pierce City, Missouri, and works in nearby Monett, thinks Pierce City, which drove out its African Americans in 1901 and has been sundown ever since, has been hurt by its sundown policy. Meanwhile, Monett, which drove out its blacks in 1894 and has been equally white since, is doing better. In 1999, Monett's per capita income was nearly 40% higher than Pierce City's, although still below average for the state. Effingham, an important rail and interstate highway junction in central Illinois, is a printing center and boasts a big new Krispy Kreme doughnut factory, although its per capita income remains below average for Illinois. Effingham and Monett may be exceptions, but on the whole, I think Khan is right. Some industries are reluctant to move to all-white communities because their nonwhite managers cannot easily find places to live. Even the white managers of these firms increasingly consider such towns backward and unappealing.[9]

Some residents feel that a limited future is not too high a price to pay for the joys of living in an all-white town. While doing a community study of a southern Illinois sundown town in 1958, Herman Lantz and J. S. McCrary elicited this comment from a white barber:

> I don't think that they would let any Negroes live here today, even if a new industry came in and said they would settle here if they could hire Negroes. I don't think that we would let them. That is, as bad as we need industry, if it meant bringing in Negroes, we would not want it. We don't allow any Negroes here now.

In 2002, a genealogist reported the same sentiment from a neighbor in nearby West Frankfort: "Some folks say we've got to let the blacks in, if we want to have progress. Well, we're *not* going to do it!" Such insular people are unlikely to seek new ideas or recruit new companies. They understand that racism interferes with their ability to enjoy the outside world, but given their fears about that world and especially about its African Americans, they do not want to invite that world into their sundown sanctuary.[10]

Research suggests that gay men are also important members of what Richard Florida calls "the creative class"—those who come up with or welcome new ideas and help drive an area economically.[11] Metropolitan areas with the most sundown suburbs also show the lowest tolerance for homosexuality and have the lowest concentrations of "out" gays and lesbians, according to Gary Gates of the Urban Institute. He lists Buffalo, Cleveland, Detroit, Milwaukee, and Pittsburgh as examples. Recently, some cities—including Detroit—have recognized the important role that gay residents can play in helping to revive problematic inner-city neighborhoods, and now welcome them.[12]

The distancing from African Americans embodied by all-white suburbs intensifies another urban problem: sprawl, the tendency for cities to become more spread out and less dense. Sprawl can decrease creativity and quality of life throughout the metropolitan area by making it harder for people to get together for all the human activities—from think tanks to complex commercial transactions to opera—that cities make possible in the first place. Asked in 2000, "What is the most important problem facing the community where you live?" 18% of Americans replied sprawl and traffic, tied for first with crime and violence. Moreover, unlike crime, sprawl is increasing. Some hypersegregated metropolitan areas like Detroit and Cleveland are growing larger geographically while actually losing population.[13]

Sundown Suburbs Make Integrated Neighborhoods Hard to Achieve

In most northern metropolitan areas, the key race relations issue, generating the most anguish and the most headlines, has long been the black ghetto and its expanding edge. Conflict at this "frontier" provoked the great Chicago race riot back in 1919 and hundreds of clashes since, in Chicago and elsewhere. This boundary is still where white resistance is most apparent, where blockbusting and white flight take place, where whites sometimes riot. News stories from the inner city are also usually full of conflict: gang or school violence, disputes between black residents and Asian or Jewish store owners, or charges of police brutality. Our media naturally go where the action is. Like journalists, most social scientists have directed their attention to the inner city, trying to figure out what to do about its indisputable social pathologies, and to the line of demarcation between the ghetto and the adjacent frontline suburb, refining such concepts as "tipping point theory" to predict when whites will flee and blockbusting will succeed.

All this seems reasonable enough, on the surface. Many—not all—inner-city neighborhoods do manifest social problems, and white flight from working-class sundown suburbs closer to the expanding black ghetto does confirm white racism. But there is more to it. The engine that drives "frontline" suburbs to go overwhelmingly black lies neither in those suburbs nor in the expanding black ghetto, but across town—in the elite sundown suburb. Concentrating on where the problems appear can cause journalists and social scientists alike to overlook the seat of the problem. It is hard for interracial suburbs to retain whites when overwhelmingly white suburbs offer more prestige. Indeed, residents of elite sundown suburbs often put down interracial suburbs precisely because they are interracial. Like residents of independent sundown towns, sundown suburbanites also exaggerate how black an interracial suburb is. Carole Goodwin found that as soon as a few blacks moved into Oak Park, an interracial frontline suburb just west of Chicago, people in more distant sundown suburbs perceived it to be half-black. They further "knew" it would go all-black.[14] Believing this prediction legitimized their own decision to locate in sundown suburbs nowhere near a black or interracial neighborhood.[15]

The resistance to integration in these placid all-white elite suburbs, often miles away from the frontline suburb, drives the entire blockbusting process. Interviewed by a Detroit newspaper in 1955, a working-class homeowner in an interracial suburb understood this all too well: "It gets so tiresome being asked all the time to sell your house. I bet they don't call out in Grosse Pointe or Bloomfield Hills or Palmer Park all the time asking those people if they want to sell." She was complaining about real estate agents who solicited whites to sell and then steered black would-be buyers into these "changing neighborhoods," rather than to all-white suburbs.[16]

Even without steering, African Americans know they may not be welcome and will not feel welcome in places such as Grosse Pointe. Understandably, they therefore prefer interracial suburbs to all-white ones, so they move to recently desegregated towns. Meanwhile, European Americans know they will be welcome and feel welcome in sundown suburbs; indeed, some choose them precisely because they are so white. Others move there to get real amenities—fine schools, nice parks, good city services, safety, and aesthetic values—but the biggest single draw of sundown suburbs is status. Housing segregated along race and class lines still signifies social power and success. As families prosper, they both display and purchase their status by moving to a more prestigious and exclusive neighborhood, and the whiter the suburb, the higher its status. In that sense, *most* families move to elite sundown suburbs because they are so white. We have seen that upper-class suburbs such as Darien, Connecticut; Tuxedo Park, New York; Kenilworth, Illinois; Edina, Minnesota; and Beverly Hills, California, were founded as white (and usually WASP) enclaves. Each is the richest and most prestigious suburb of its metropolitan area, or close to it. Kenilworth, for example, was Chicago's wealthiest suburb in 1990 and the sixth richest town in the United States, according to historian Michael Ebner. Other towns ultimately compare themselves to these elite white suburbs. The value of living in all-white suburbs thus filters down from the upper class to all other (white) classes.[17]

In the quote at the head of this chapter, Thorstein Veblen famously explained how the upper class typically influences all Americans' values. Tuxedo Park offers literal confirmation of Veblen's analysis, for it was the epitome of taste, as defined by resident Emily Post and yes, the source of the dinner jacket that bears its name. Post was the daughter of architect Bruce Price, who designed the town. From 1920 to at least 1975, she set the standard of good behavior for the entire United States, with her book *Etiquette,* daily newspaper column on good taste, and weekly radio show.[18] So long as towns such as Tuxedo Park bestow the highest status and are so very WASP, neighborhoods that are less WASP and less affluent cannot afford to welcome African Americans—or sometimes even Jews or Hispanics—without further reducing their own social status. Thus the existence and prestige of these places in turn makes it harder for interracial suburbs to stay interracial. Even many families who don't want to avoid African Americans do want to move to "better" suburbs, which means whiter suburbs.[19]

Sundown Suburbs Cause White Flight

Why would white home buyers flee an interracial area, especially one where African Americans made up only 1% of the population? Careful research by Ingrid Gould Ellen shows how sundown suburbs cause white flight elsewhere in the metropolitan area. She points out that it isn't merely racism that fuels this flight, but also three predictions by white suburbanites. First, whites "know" that when African Americans move in, property values go down. And in fact, they have a point: the same home in an elite sundown suburb is usually worth more than in the inner city. But there is more to it. Excluding African Americans from sundown suburbs creates pent-up housing demand in black neighborhoods, so blacks will likely outbid whites when one former sundown suburb opens up. Back in 1917 in *Buchanan v. Warley,* the Supreme Court saw that white property owners would be damaged if they could not sell to all, rather than only to whites. This is another reason—on the demand side, having nothing to do with white flight—why a former sundown suburb may quickly go majority-black.[20]

Ellen invites us to answer this question: when African Americans move into a formerly sundown suburb, who is more likely to move first—renters or owners? The obvious answer would be renters; it is much easier for renters to move, being more transient and usually less wedded to their communities. If avoidance of African Americans were the primary motivation for white flight, renters would leave first. In fact, owners usually move first. Ellen suggests that renters, having no investment at stake, feel less need to leave.[21] So it isn't just living near African Americans that bothers many white suburbanites; it is also concern for property values.

In the past, a fleeing family, "knowing" that property values are going down because blacks are moving in, often sold to a real estate speculator for less than market value, the agent having said, "It's all you can hope for now." Speculators had two advantages over regular buyers: they often offered cash, and they were white. Cash was important, because the selling family needed it for the down payment on their new house in the sundown suburb to which they were moving. Also, until recently many lending institutions would not grant mortgages to black families in still-white areas, so the middleman's role was essential. Second, the sellers saved face with their former neighbors by selling to a white. In one study in Chicago, 24 of 29 parcels that were sold between 1953 and 1961 were sold through speculators and purchased by black families on installment contracts.[22] Property values did not go down, especially not at first. On the contrary, usually the speculator *raised* the price substantially and then sold the home to a black family willing to pay more for a residence in one of the few "white" neighborhoods where blacks could buy. The average markup among the 24 Chicago parcels was 73%! Luigi Laurenti compared twenty interracial neighborhoods and nineteen all-white neighborhoods in seven cities from 1943 to 1955. He concluded, "The entry of nonwhites was much more often associated with price improvement or stability than with price weakening." Thus even though the first of Ellen's three predictions—that when African Americans move in, property values go down—isn't accurate, the fleeing white family never learned that part of the story. Instead, it "knew" that black newcomers lower property values and carried that prediction to its new community.[23]

Ellen's second prediction is that whites "know" that communities go all-black once a few African Americans enter. So they flee. It is the prophecy, not the actual racial composition of a town or neighborhood in the present—nor simple avoidance of African Americans—that prompts the exodus. Of course, it becomes a self-fulfilling prophecy because whites who believe it leave. Sundown suburbs are particularly likely to go overwhelmingly black once they crack and admit their first African American family. In the Cleveland metropolitan area in the 1980s, for instance, George Galster found that among census tracts starting with the same black percentage back in 1970, those predicted to have stronger "segregationist sentiments" lost much more of their white populations. Their own ideology supplies the reason. To those European American residents of sundown suburbs who believe it is correct to live in all-white towns, when even a handful of African American families move in, their town no longer seems defensible.[24]

Bellwood, Illinois, illustrates the process. Until 1968, Bellwood had been a sundown suburb west of Chicago. Then its first African American family moved in. By 1970, 1.1% of Bellwood's total population of 22,096 was black. At this point, the dam burst: by 1980 Bellwood was more than one-third black. Bellwood tried to stop the flood, restricting realtor solicitation and banning "For Sale" signs. Bellwood tried to end realtor steering by sending black and white would-be home buyers to see if African Americans got shown homes in "changing neighborhoods" while European Americans got shown homes in securely white suburbs. The suburb tried to market its homes to white home buyers and counsel blacks about available homes in nearby all-white suburbs. Bellwood even took its case before the United States Supreme Court and won the ability to sue realtors who steer, but it did no good—in fact, the case only further publicized to African Americans throughout the Chicago metropolitan area that Bellwood was now open to them. By 2000, Bellwood was 82% African American.[25]

Sometimes whites start to flee a town or neighborhood before the percentage of African Americans reaches even 1%. "Lily White Lynwood," for instance, as it was called, a sundown suburb of Los Angeles, had just 9 African Americans in 1960, and 89 "others," among 31,614 residents. All 9 were female; surely all were maids in white households. By 1970, 160 African Americans lived in Lynwood among 42,387 whites and 806 others, less than 0.4%, a tiny crack in the dike, but enough: ten years later, almost 15,000 blacks lived in Lynwood.[26] Now Mexicans and Mexican Americans also flooded in, and by 2000, fewer than 1,500 non-Hispanic whites still lived in Lynwood.

Sundown Suburbs Put Their Problems Elsewhere

We have seen that sundown suburbs behave as defended neighborhoods. Once they get into the NIMBY mind-set, they try to keep out *any* problem or "problem group," pawning off their own social problems on central cities and multiracial, multiclass inner suburbs. Consider those members of society who are dramatically downwardly mobile—some alcoholics and drug addicts; some Down syndrome children; most criminals; people unhinged and impoverished by divorce; many schizophrenics; elderly people whose illness and incapacity have exhausted their resources and their relatives; employees fired when an industry downsizes and no one wants their skills. Every social class—even the most affluent—generates some of these people. Elite sundown suburbs offer no facilities to house, treat, or comfort such people—no halfway houses for the mentally ill or ex-criminals, no residential drug treatment facilities, no public housing, often not even assisted-living complexes for the elderly or persons with disabilities. This is no accident. Elite white suburbanites don't want such facilities in their neighborhoods and have the prestige, money, and knowledge to make their objections count. "Without such homes, people with mental illnesses often wind up homeless, especially in wealthy areas," according to an AP article telling how an elite white neighborhood in Greenwich, Connecticut, blocked a halfway house for years.[27]

When sundown suburbanites do become homeless, they simply have to leave. Most sundown suburbs do not allow homeless people to spend the night on their streets, and of course they provide no shelters for them. "In suburban jurisdictions," said Nan Roman, of the National Alliance to End Homelessness, in 2000, "there is no sense that these are our people." Community leaders worry that if their suburb provides services, that will only bring more homeless people to their town because no other suburb does. The result, nationally, is that cities provide 49% of all homeless assistance programs, suburbs 19%, and rural areas 32%. Yet suburbs have more people than cities and rural areas combined. Less affluent inner suburbs and central cities must cope with the downwardly mobile people that more affluent sundown suburbs produce, as well as with their own. These social problems burden cities twice. First, cities provide some of the halfway houses, shelters, and other social services. Second, cities can tax neither their own agencies nor the nonprofit institutions that provide those services, even though they use police, fire protection, streets, and other city services.[28]

Black and interracial neighborhoods end up with most of the other "disamenities" in metropolitan areas, too, such as trash "transfer stations" (in former times these were "dumps"); impound lots for abandoned and illegally parked cars; storage lots for street cleaners, buses, and other city vehicles; public housing projects; and maintenance yards for street repair supplies. Zoning protects affluent white neighborhoods from these problems, which generate truck traffic, odors, and noise. Private disamenities, such as polluting industries, can make black and interracial areas still worse, while most sundown suburbs have the clout to keep them out. One result, according to survey data, is that African Americans are almost twice as likely as whites to rate their neighborhood "poor." Probably they're right! Foretelling that interracial neighborhoods will go downhill, compared to sundown neighborhoods, is the third prediction by whites that Ellen believes accounts for white flight. Again, whites don't have to be racist to want to avoid such neighborhoods.[29]

Suburban Hitchhikers

Not only disamenities but also amenities can burden cities and older multiracial suburbs. Such amenities as universities, museums, cathedrals, churches, parks, arts organizations, concert halls, and nonprofit hospitals are located in central cities but are used by people from the suburbs, including the sundown suburbs. Indeed, some amenities, such as private colleges and universities, are used *mostly* by suburbanites. These institutions do not pay property taxes.[30] Their users, too, pay no taxes to the city, except sales tax on incidental purchases. Yet cities provide services—police, streets, fire protection—to these amenities and their users. In some cities, as much as a third of the potential tax base is exempt from taxes, compared to as little as 3% in many suburbs. In some metropolitan areas, this has been an issue for a long time. In 1943, for example, Dallas Mayor J. W. Rodgers pointed out that "well-heeled" residents of the Park Cities, the two sundown "suburbs" entirely surrounded by Dallas, relied more than most Dallas residents on Love Field, the Dallas airport. They "needed to assume their rightful burden in its upkeep and administration," in the words of Dallas historian Darwin Payne. The *Dallas News* called the Park Cities " 'suburban hitchhikers' using Dallas's facilities free of charge."[31]

The use of city services by suburban visitors wouldn't be so bad if it were a two-way street, but it's not. City residents do not use suburban facilities equally and often are not allowed to. We have seen how sundown suburbs often barricade their amenities against outsiders or make them hard to find. No sign points to the beach in Darien, for example, and a visitor who does manage to find it encounters signs marking it "Private." A sentry checks even cyclists and pedestrians for beach stickers that only Darien residents can get.

Even basketball courts are amenities worth keeping African Americans away from in Ohio, according to a man who grew up in the sundown suburbs of Cincinnati: "Saint Bernard and Elmwood Place were two of a number of all-white towns in the Millcreek Valley area of Cincinnati when I was growing up. Just a few years ago, the parks and basketball hoops still bore signs saying that the facilities were for the use of St. Bernard residents only." [32]

One response might be, "What's wrong with that? Don't Darien taxpayers pay to keep that beach clean? Doesn't St. Bernard maintain those basketball courts?" But Darien residents would be furious if New York City kept them out of Central Park. Ohio suburbanites would protest if Cincinnati kept them away from its beautiful new Riverfront Park. Residents of sundown suburbs consider it their right to make use of the facilities of the central city. They do not reciprocate.

In yet another way, elite sundown suburbs fail to pay their way: their zoning, lot requirements, and other restrictions force their maids, supermarket clerks, police officers, and even teachers to live elsewhere. These people simply cannot afford to live in the affluent suburbs where they work. These suburbs have never allowed public housing, and they impose minimum lot and zoning restrictions that make private housing too costly. Thus the property taxes paid by affluent whites in elite sundown suburbs do not help pay for the city services their employees use. Instead, less affluent and less white towns house them and try to educate their children, without the benefit of the tax base their employers' homes and businesses would provide.

A few suburbs have done better in providing public housing, including Summit, New Jersey; Palo Alto, California; and Prince Georges County, Maryland. But again, it's hard for a suburb to do this as long as it's the only one; it may wind up majority-black and labeled a social problem. In the Washington metropolitan area, Prince Georges County was one of the few suburbs that allowed FHA-subsidized apartments; as a result, it wound up with nearly all of them, as of the mid-1970s. By 2000, the county was about 64% African American. [33]

Better Services, Lower Taxes

In his famous book *An American Dilemma,* written as World War II wound down, Gunnar Myrdal noted that residential segregation has been a key factor accounting for the subordinate status of African Americans. Separating people geographically makes it much easier to provide better city services to some than to others, to give some children better schooling than others, and indeed to label some people better than others. In Roosevelt, the black township on Long Island, "as tax money dried up, the schools withered," as *Washington Post* reporter Michael Powell put it. Across the United States, Jianping Shen concluded in 2003, schools with 50% or more minority enrollment had the highest rate of teachers teaching outside their field, the highest rate of inexperienced teachers and teachers with temporary certification, and the highest teacher attrition. Money is not the only issue. Professors in some schools of education routinely try to place their best graduates in elite suburban school districts, partly because they boast better working conditions and higher salaries, but also because they are more prestigious; hence the placements reflect credit back upon the graduate school. "The best teachers should be in the best schools"—this attitude permeates the field. "Most teachers consider it a promotion to move from poor to middle-class schools," Kahlenberg notes, "and the best teachers usually transfer out of low-income schools at the first opportunity." Again, the whites in Ingrid Ellen's research are often right to associate predominantly black neighborhoods with poor schools—even if it's not African Americans' fault.[34]

Often, the better schools and nicer amenities that suburbs offer come bundled with *lower* taxes. The reason is simple: elite suburbs often have "five times as much taxable property per capita as the poorest suburbs," according to social scientist Michael Danielson. In 1990, Philadelphia had the highest tax burden in its metropolitan area, yet brought in less money per pupil than elite suburbs with much lower tax rates. Black townships suffer from this problem even worse than cities. Roosevelt, for example, has a student population that was "99.7% black and Latino in 2002," according to Powell. "They attend decrepit schools and read tattered textbooks." Yet, "to support these failing schools, homeowners here pay the highest property tax rates on Long Island, as their 1½-square-mile town has no commercial tax base to speak of. Far wealthier and far whiter towns border Roosevelt to the north and east."[35]

Companies frequently leave interracial areas to get lower taxes. Often, sundown suburbs wind up with an area's best taxable draws. In 1956, for example, Edina, Minnesota, got Southdale shopping center, still a potent commercial site. On Long Island, what Powell calls "the massive and successful Roosevelt Field shopping malls" were built just five miles north of Roosevelt, "with the help of county subsidies and zoning regulations. From the point of view of Roosevelt, however, the malls might as well have been in Des Moines, because tax revenue is not shared across town lines." The result was catastrophic for the black township. "As Roosevelt Field thrived, stores died in Roosevelt itself," further shrinking Roosevelt's taxable property base.[36]

Sundown Communities and the Political System

Finally, sundown towns influence their residents' politics. With this discussion we return to the effects of these towns on whites with which the chapter began, but now in the context of their impact on our political system as a whole. The racial exclusiveness of sundown suburbs helped move the Republican Party away from the equal-rights creed of Lincoln, which had lingered in vestigial form as late as 1960. Most independent sundown towns started out Democratic, but beginning in 1964, voters defected for racial reasons—first to Alabama governor George Wallace and then to Richard Nixon and subsequent Republicans. Anecdotal evidence and some statistical analyses suggest that in 1964, in his first presidential campaign, Wallace carried most sundown towns in the Indiana Democratic primary, for example, while winning 35% of the white vote statewide. He did even better in the Wisconsin primary, winning more than 40% of the white vote. His only issue—and he was clear about it—was President Lyndon Johnson's use of the federal bureaucracy to improve race relations. For Wallace to do so well as an awkward, angry southern white in his first try for national office made a striking comment about midwestern white voters and their desire for continued white supremacy.[37]

In the 1964 general election, the two parties again began to articulate consistently different racial programs, for the first time since 1890. Democrats after Johnson would be identified with civil rights, and Republicans after Goldwater would be identified with resistance to civil rights. In 1968, Richard Nixon followed an explicit "southern strategy," appealing to white southerners upset about black claims to equality and dismissing black voters. Nixon called for "law and order," condemned civil rights (and student) protests, and said he favored neither integrationists nor segregationists. He appointed four Supreme Court justices thought to be soft on desegregation, ordered the Justice Department to oppose immediate desegregation in 1969 in *Alexander v. Holmes,* and sent a bill to Congress to outlaw busing for desegregation.

Nixon's southern strategy also turned out to be a winning strategy in sundown suburbs and independent sundown towns. After 1964, most sundown towns and suburbs voted Republican or, in 1968 and 1972, for Wallace. Before 1964, Owosso, a sundown town between Lansing and Flint, Michigan, had usually voted Republican, but not for racial reasons, the two parties not being clearly different in racial policies. That year, however, it went for Democrat Lyndon Johnson, "an exception and a mistake, according to everyone interviewed here" by a *New York Times* reporter in 1968. In 1968, Owosso switched to George Wallace. "A lot of people like what he has to say about handling riots and aggressive law enforcement," said a local Republican leader. The reporter saw through this rhetoric, noting, "Such talk seems ironic in a town where the most pressing law-and-order problem is teen-agers' hot-rodding past the pizza house on Friday and Saturday nights." The real issue was that "Owosso has no Negroes, has never had any, and, according to many private opinions, does not want any." After 1968, Owosso voted Republican.[38]

Owosso was hardly alone. Bill Outis grew up in Sandoval, Illinois, which he thinks was a sundown town, moved to Ramsey in 1962, another sundown town, and now lives in Pana, a third. In 1968, he recalled, Sandoval and Ramsey high school students held straw votes for president. About half voted for Nixon, the Republican and eventual winner, half for Wallace, and *one student* in each high school chose Hubert Humphrey, the Democrat nominee. Dearborn, Michigan, held a huge rally for Wallace in May 1972, and Wallace went on to win a stunning victory in Michigan's 1972 Democratic primary. Across the North, Wallace frequently spoke in sundown towns, where he knew he could count on positive crowds. Kathy Spillman reports on her hometown in upstate New York: "George Wallace was so popular in North Tonawanda. And this was a Democratic union town!"[39]

With his "southern strategy," Richard Nixon headed off Wallace in 1968. Once in office, Nixon stated that denying housing to people because of their race was wrong, but it was equally wrong for towns to have integrated housing "imposed from Washington by bureaucratic fiat." The next successful Republican candidate, Ronald Reagan, deliberately chose a citadel of white supremacy—the Neshoba County Fair in Mississippi—as the kickoff site for his presidential campaign, where he declared his support for "states' rights," code words signaling that the federal government should leave local jurisdictions alone to handle the "race problem" as they see fit. George W. Bush understands the rhetoric in sundown suburbs, having chosen one (Highland Park, Texas) as home for his family. As a result of such leadership, Republicans have carried most sundown towns since 1968, sometimes achieving startling unanimity. For example, Donahue noted that every single student from Nickerson, Kansas, that he met during their field trip to Washington in 2002 was sympathetic to the Republican Party. Of course, those groups that usually vote most Democratic—African Americans and Jewish Americans—simply aren't represented in sundown towns. So the "southern strategy" turned out to be a "southern and sundown town strategy," especially effective in sundown suburbs. Macomb County, for example, the next county north of Detroit, voted overwhelmingly for Wallace in the 1972 Democratic primary. Wooed by Nixon, many of these voters then became "Reagan Democrats" and now are plain Republicans. The biggest single reason, according to housing attorney Alexander Polikoff, was anxiety about "blacks trapped in ghettos trying to penetrate white neighborhoods." [40]

Republicans do especially well in sundown suburbs owing not only to their racial ideology, but also to their NIMBY principles and small-government philosophy. [41] But these principles too have a racial tinge and tie in with the soclexia that results from living in sundown towns and suburbs. In *Chain Reaction,* their analysis of the GOP's appeal to racism from 1964 to 1990, Thomas and Mary Edsall pointed to Republicans' use of the stereotype that whites work and succeed, while blacks don't work, hence don't succeed. As former Nixon aide John Ehrlichman put it, Republicans win in the suburbs partly because they present positions on crime, education, and housing in such a way that a voter could "avoid admitting to himself that he was attracted by a racist appeal." [42]

Sundown suburbs are politically independent and usually quash efforts at metropolitan government. Their school systems are separate and usually oppose metro-wide desegregation. They resist mightily what they view as intrusions by people or governments from the larger metropolitan area or the state. In New Jersey, trying to comply with a New Jersey supreme court decision mandating equal educational opportunity, the legislature passed the Quality Education Act, and Governor Jim Florio proposed higher taxes on families earning more than $100,000 to pay for it. Suburbanites responded by voting out of office many of the politicians who supported the equalization bill, including Florio, whom they replaced with Republican Christine Todd Whitman. [43]

The Edsalls point out that the principle of self-interest explains what otherwise might seem to be an ideological contradiction: sundown suburbanites usually try to minimize expenditures by the state and federal governments, but locally they favor "increased suburban and county expenditures, guaranteeing the highest possible return to themselves on their tax dollars." The Edsalls cite Gwinnett County, Georgia, as an example. Gwinnett, east of Atlanta, is "one of the fastest growing suburban jurisdictions in the nation, heavily Republican (75.5% for Bush [senior]), affluent, and white (96.6%)." Its residents "have been willing to tax and spend on their own behalf as liberally as any Democrats." Such within-county expenditures increase the inequality between white suburbs and interracial cities. They also do nothing to redress or pay for the ways that Gwinnett residents use and rely upon Atlanta and its public services.[44]

Meanwhile, white suburbs favor "policies of fiscal conservatism at the federal level." Interestingly, despite enjoying more than half a century of federal intervention on behalf of whites in suburbia—FHA and Veterans Administration (VA) loan guarantees, FHA and VA policies that shut out blacks, highway subsidies, and all the rest—residents feel they achieved home ownership in their all-white suburb entirely on their own. Since 1968, whenever African Americans have mobilized to try to get the federal government to act on *their* behalf, suburban Republicans have rejected the idea: "We've done so much for them already." Many white suburbanites identified attempts of the federal government to be fair about housing, such as the 1968 housing act, with the Democratic Party, and considered them outrageous examples of "special interests" and "federal intervention in local affairs."

Today the most important national impact of sundown towns and suburbs is through their influence on the Republican Party. The Edsalls conclude, "The suburban vote is becoming the core of the Republican base." Since elected officials from safe districts develop seniority, suburban Republicans dominate committees in the House of Representatives and in state legislatures when Republicans control those bodies. They also wield much power over their party in most states.[45]

Where Is "the Problem"?

Most people, looking around their metropolitan area, perceive inner-city African American neighborhoods as "the problem." It then follows all too easily that African Americans themselves can get perceived as the source of the problem. Residents of affluent sundown suburbs rarely see such newly black elite suburbs as Country Club Hills, south of Chicago, or Mitchellville, east of Washington, D.C., but problematic inner-city and inner-suburban neighborhoods are on their commute to the city's center. So whites generalize: blacks can't do anything right, can't even keep up their own neighborhoods. All African Americans get tarred by the obvious social problems of the inner city. For that matter, some ghetto residents themselves buy into the notion that they are the problem and behave accordingly.

Focusing on African Americans and overlooking the impact of sundown suburbs on the social system as "the problem" is understandable. When I visit central cities and sundown suburbs, the former look problematic to me too.

As I drove with friends in the late 1990s through an overwhelmingly white elite section of Lower Merion, just outside Philadelphia, for example, no problems seemed evident. The streets were in good repair, the houses were in perfect condition, the landscaping was gorgeous. White racism was nowhere visible. A few miles west, in the Ardmore part of Lower Merion, problems struck our eyes, sometimes our noses, or even our buttocks, transmitted by the suspension of our car. Ardmore is an interracial neighborhood; most of the people visible walking on the streets, playing on the sidewalks, or washing their cars are African Americans. Ardmore has been saddled with most of Lower Merion's disamenities, such as halfway houses and maintenance yards, perhaps because its residents are not as politically connected or socially powerful as families in the rich white neighborhood.

The affluent white and interracial working-class parts of Lower Merion are part of the same political jurisdiction, so the unfairness in clumping most of Lower Merion's disamenities in one area is clear. It is not quite so obvious how the pleasures of a lovely spring day in Kenilworth, say, are the flip side of the problems in distressed neighborhoods just eight miles away in Chicago. Since affluent sundown suburbs are not politically connected to nearby inner-city neighborhoods, the system of white supremacy that makes them so much nicer is not obvious. Most people automatically problematize the ghetto. The problems in black neighborhoods look like black problems.

It takes an exercise of the sociological imagination to problematize the sundown suburb. As one drives west from downtown on Chicago Avenue toward Oak Park, the adjacent suburb, the problems of the Near Northwest neighborhood in Chicago are plain. Oak Park then presents its own problem: can it stay interracial, having gone from 0.2% African American in 1970 to 22.4% in 2000? The source of both problems lies not on Chicago Avenue in either city, however, but elsewhere—in neighborhoods miles away that look great, such as Kenilworth, which in 2000 had not one black household among its 2,494 total population. Once one knows its manifestations, white supremacy is visible in Kenilworth, the sundown suburb, and in Near Northwest Chicago, and it is inferable in Oak Park as well. Lovely white enclaves such as Kenilworth withdraw resources disproportionately from the city. They encourage the people who run our corporations, many of whom live in them, not to see race as their problem. The prestige of these suburbs invites governmental officials to respond more rapidly to concerns of their residents, who are likely to be viewed as more important people than black inner-city inhabitants. And they make interracial suburbs such as Oak Park difficult to keep as interracial oases.

Are these problems of metropolitan areas getting worse or better? Is our nation getting over sundown towns, or do they continue unabated into the 21st century? What effect is America's increasing racial and ethnic complexity having on sundown towns and suburbs? These are the questions the next chapter will address.

PART VI

The Present and Future
of Sundown Towns

14

Sundown Towns Today

In 1968, the Kerner Commission . . . warned that the United States was in danger of splitting into "two societies, one black, one white—separate and unequal." Over thirty years later, that danger seems to have been realized. The dream of a residentially integrated society has been laid to rest by the phenomenon of white flight from the cities and a marked unwillingness of whites to live in neighborhoods with significant numbers of those of another race.
—Donald Deskins Jr. and Christopher Bettinger,
"Black and White Spaces in Selected Metropolitan Areas," 2002[1]

DURING THE LAST FEW YEARS while I have been doing the research for this book, many people have asked, after learning that hundreds or thousands of sundown towns and suburbs dot the map of the United States, "Still? Surely it's not like that today?" It is a good question—so good that it's hard to answer, because it is hard to know for sure whether a town remains sundown as of the present moment. But those who ask the question usually mean it rhetorically and assume the answer to be "Of course not."

Unfortunately, many towns are still locked into the exclusionary policies of the past, and this chapter will begin by looking at a few of them. We will then see that some social scientists conclude that America as a social system is moving toward more intense residential segregation; such innovations as neighborhood associations and gated communities support that judgment.

Discouraging as those trends are, I take a more optimistic view. Sundown towns have been on the defensive since the start of the Civil Rights Movement, which prompted the zeitgeist to move back toward what it had been before the Nadir of race relations set in. We will see that 1968 may be as important a date in changing the spirit of race relations in America in a positive direction as 1890 was in a negative direction. Since 1968, residential prohibitions against Jews, Asians, Native Americans, and Hispanics have mostly disappeared.

Even regarding African Americans, the sundown signs and formal policies have come down everywhere. Many towns and suburbs relaxed their exclusionary policies in the 1980s and 1990s, and we will probe why. In the end, whether we are moving toward more or less racial exclusion will be left for you to assess.

The Persistence of Sundown Towns

It's easy to empathize with those who assume that sundown towns cannot still be "like that today." That they still might be interferes with our sense of progress and our claim to live under law. And progress has been made. As recently as the 1990s, some sundown towns still flaunted their condition with signs saying "Don't Let The Sun Go Down On You in __," according to credible reports from Arab, Alabama; Marlowe, Oklahoma; and Sullivan, Missouri; in 1998, a related text was posted in White County, Indiana. By 2005, I knew of no town so reckless, although two small towns in Tennessee still displayed black mules painted near their city limits (see Portfolio 8)[2]

But was this apparent progress real? Are sundown policies no longer enforced? Consider the experience of Clarence Moore, a pioneering archaeologist in the Lower Mississippi Valley. In 1910, mostly using black workers, he excavated American Indian sites on Little River, which parallels the Mississippi a few miles northwest of Memphis. Dan and Phyllis Morse, who reissued Moore's classic work in 1998, state in their preface that Moore "dared not proceed beyond Lepanto, Arkansas, on Little River because blacks were not tolerated there. Race relations remain strained in that region." That's a polite way of saying what my research in the area confirms: almost a century later, African Americans *still* do not and probably cannot live in much of the northeastern corner of Arkansas or the western half of the Bootheel of Missouri. Nor is this area unique.[3]

Many decades ago, some Americans were shocked that towns and counties openly kept out people of color. During World War II, Malcolm Ross of the federal Fair Employment Practices Commission learned about Calhoun County, the sundown county 65 miles southwest of Springfield, Illinois. He was outraged, calling the county "an earthly paradise for those who hate Negro Americans. But can the rest of America remain indifferent to their 'self-determination?' " Ross obviously meant the question rhetorically. Surely he would have been dismayed to learn that sixty years later, the 2000 census would record not one black household in Calhoun County.[4]

Similarly, in 1952 Paul Angle wrote in *Bloody Williamson,* his famous history of Ku Klux Klan and other violence in southern Illinois, "Even today, in several Williamson County towns . . . no Negro is permitted to remain overnight." More than half a century later, in several towns in Williamson County and adjacent Franklin County, no African American is yet permitted to live.[5] Zeigler, for example, had no black householder in 2000, and when I asked the town librarian in 2002 if she thought Zeigler had stopped being a sundown town, she replied, "I wish it would change, but I don't see it changing here." According to Deidre Meadows, who graduated from Johnston City High School in 1990, "When I was a sophomore in high school, we had a black family move in town for about a month. They were driven out by hate crimes." The 2000 census showed not one African American family among 3,557 residents in Johnston City. Speaking in 2002 of a third sundown town, Sesser, which also had no black household in the 2000 census, an African American in nearby Du Quoin said, "You would have some problems if you went there, right now." Angle's phrase "even today" connotes his sense that sundown towns were an anachronistic relic from our past in 1952. I wonder what he would think to learn that such practices were still allowed in 2005.[6]

Corbin, a sundown town in the Kentucky Cumberlands, had not relented as of 1990. In his 1991 movie on the community, *Trouble Behind,* Robby Heason asked a young white man if it would be a good thing for blacks to move into Corbin. "Black people should not live here," he replied. "They never have, and they shouldn't." He did not know that African Americans *had* lived in Corbin until whites drove them out at gunpoint in 1919, and his attitude surely boded ill should a black family try to move in. As of 2000, almost none had; Corbin's 7,742 people included just 6 African Americans; adjacent North Corbin had just 1 African American among 1,662 inhabitants. Around 1990, McDonald's brought in an African American to manage a new restaurant, but he and his family left before it even opened, reportedly after a cross was burned in his yard.[7]

Although the public accommodations section of the 1964 Civil Rights Act did not get enforced in most sundown towns for at least ten years after its passage, since the 1980s, most restaurants and hotels in sundown towns have complied with the law and do now provide food and lodging to transients. Now African Americans can eat in restaurants and sleep in motels in otherwise all-white towns. Buying or renting residential property in neighborhoods is quite another matter.

Even public accommodations can still be a problem in out-of-the-way sundown towns. Speaking of the western half of the Bootheel, in rural southeastern Missouri, Frank Nickell, director of the Center for Regional History, wrote in 2002, "Many restaurants, motels, cemeteries, etc., remain off-limits to African-Americans." In some sundown towns, African Americans may get served successfully but must endure glares from white customers while they eat. Whites in Erwin, Tennessee, drove African Americans from Unicoi County in 1918. Rebecca Tolley-Stokes, archivist at East Tennessee State University, wrote about a recent incident involving Erwin:

> Several years ago I was friends with a woman who worked at a convenience store just off the interstate [in Johnston City, twelve miles north of Erwin]. I was visiting with her one evening when a black couple stopped there for gas and to inquire about a hotel room for the night in the next town, Erwin. Jennifer told them that they would have trouble getting a room if they just showed up. Additionally, she told them that she would call and make the reservation for them because if the owner spoke to someone who she/he thought was black, the owner would tell the caller that their rooms were all booked up.

In Erwin, motel operators apparently still wanted to discriminate, but not enough to cause an altercation. Erwin still had no black households as of 2000, and according to Tolley-Stokes, "all the blacks in the area have been warned within their own communities to steer clear of Erwin." In a few other towns, an altercation seems likely if an African American tries to stay after dark. In 1995, Christy Thompson of Cedar Key, Florida, said about African American tourists, "I saw a couple of 'em not long ago, a black man and woman riding bicycles down by the pier, but I guarantee they didn't spend the night. They've *all* been told there's only one way in and one way out and you better be out before dark." That was 1995. What about 2004? Cedar Key had no black households in the 2000 census.[8]

Even after the turn of the millennium, there were also still towns that African Americans believed were not safe simply to pass through. "Never walk in Greenwood [Arkansas] or you will die," an African American college student said, dead seriously, to a group of other students and me at the University of the Ozarks in 2002. The 2000 census listed 17 African Americans in Greenwood, however, including two households, so perhaps his information was out of date. A black undergraduate at the University of Illinois–Chicago told in September 2001 of Beecher, a white suburb of Chicago, "Blacks need to have enough gas to get through." Certainly they would not want to have to purchase fuel from the Beecher gas station called Knute's Kountry Korner, whose three *K*'s are no accident, according to the student.

Beecher's reputation in the black community may be warranted; in the 2000 census, the town had 1,993 people, including not one African American.[9]

Oral history in and around New Palestine, Indiana, suggests that African Americans do well to be wary of it. If they can help it, African Americans "don't drive through New Palestine," according to a former New Palestine resident, who has friends in the community. A black woman moved to New Palestine "somewhere between 1992 and 1995 and lasted two days." A former teacher tells that there is oral history still current in the school system that the KKK donated land for the New Palestine High School, "with the stipulation the mascot was to be a dragon." A professor at DePauw University confirmed that New Palestine's athletic teams had been the Redbirds; "in the 1920s, when the KKK craze hit, they became the Dragons." School officials contest this and claim "Dragons" is a coincidence. Still, the 2000 census lists New Palestine with no African Americans at all, and to be the first African American family to move into New Palestine would require courage. And what do we make of the comment that the manager of a gas station in Mt. Sterling, Ohio, made in 1991 to an African American woman, then 30 years old, when she stopped for directions: "Girl, you don't know what danger you're in"? Was he being helpful? Trying to steer her away from trouble? Or himself trying to intimidate her? Or just being "funny"? Prudently, she did not do the research required to find out, but Mt. Sterling had no black family in it at the time.[10]

The Present Moment

I cannot know if every town I describe as sundown in the past is still sundown as of 2005. Indeed, I do not think that every town I describe as sundown even in the recent past is still sundown today. The foregoing anecdotes don't prove that African Americans *cannot* live in Zeigler, Erwin, Cedar Key, Beecher, New Palestine, Mt. Sterling, and other such places, even though the 2000 census does not show a single black family in any of those towns. Proving continuing exclusion to the present moment is difficult,[11] and by its nature the proof must be anecdotal.

We shall consider several examples, beginning with Anna, Illinois. The 2000 census listed 89 blacks among Anna's 5,136 total population. Anna also had 14 Asians, 49 Mexican Americans, 24 other Latinos, 13 American Indians, and a few persons listing more than one race. At first glance, Anna seems no longer to be a sundown town. But Anna's 89 African Americans may all reside at the state mental hospital. The 2000 census lists just one family with a black householder in Anna, with just two people, and we cannot be sure they are both black.[12] In 2002, neither the Anna newspaper editor nor the reference librarian could think of a single black family in Anna or in adjacent Jonesboro. "Oh no, there are no black people in Anna today," a farmer near Anna said in 2004. Is Anna still sundown? A prudent answer would be yes, at least until there is evidence to the contrary, given that the phrase "Ain't No Niggers Allowed" is still current in and around the town. But I do not know for sure.[13]

Has Villa Grove changed—the town in central Illinois that sounded a siren at 6 PM every evening to tell African Americans to be gone? In about 1999, Villa Grove stopped sounding its siren. I had hoped it stopped the practice because residents became ashamed of why it was first put in place, no longer cared to explain its origin to their children or guests, and had reconsidered their sundown policy. No, I learned, it stopped owing to complaints about the noise from residents living near the water tower, on which the siren was located (see Portfolio 9). On the other hand, in 2000 Villa Grove had 8 African Americans among its 2,553 residents, in two households. Perhaps Villa Grove now accepts black families, perhaps not. Certainly many African Americans in nearby Champaign-Urbana still avoid driving through or stopping in the town.

It isn't always clear, even to a town's own residents, whether African Americans can live there in peace. A state trooper told of his hometown, Chandler, Indiana, near Evansville. It had been a sundown town complete with sign. Around 1971, a black family moved in, to be greeted by a burning cross in their front yard; "they were run off." Two years later, a second family tried, and they were not molested; years later their children graduated successfully from the high school. So Chandler seemed to have opened up. But Ronald Willis, who pastored the Methodist Church in Chandler from 2001 to 2004, painted a gloomier portrait. In the fall of 2001, a black family moved into a house across the street from the church, and Willis heard "words of hatred, violence, and intolerance" from members of his own congregation as they dropped off their children for preschool. "Within a few days the family moved." Willis went on to tell of inhumane acts that he witnessed as late as 2003. The 2000 census credited Chandler with three black households, but their situation seems precarious.[14]

What about Martinsville, Illinois, a sundown town near Terre Haute, Indiana? In 2002, I asked an attorney who grew up in Martinsville, "What would happen if a black family moved into Martinsville today?" "I really don't know," he replied. "It's hard to imagine that there'd be a violent reaction, and yet, it wouldn't surprise me." As of 2002, none had tried, although two black men had worked for Marathon Oil Company in Martinsville around 1990 and had not been run out.[15]

Consider this claim about Fouke, in southwest Arkansas, made by "goneaviking" at the discussion site alt.flame.niggers: "As of 2 PM May 23 2001, it is still nigger free, no niggers bus in, and urine head would piss in his pants if he stopped in that town." I don't think "goneaviking" lives in Fouke, but some citizens of Fouke may share this attitude toward African Americans. Smokey Crabtree, who does live in Fouke, confirmed in 2001, "As of this date there are no colored people living within miles of Fouke, so the attention getter, the means to shake the little town up isn't 'the Russians are coming,' it's 'someone is importing colored people into town.' " The census found two elderly African Americans among Fouke's 814 residents in 2000, but no household, and I believe "goneaviking" and Crabtree. At the least, they show that considerable animus exists in and about Fouke toward the idea of black residents.[16]

It's pretty clear that North Judson, in northern Indiana, has not given in. A history teacher from that area said in 2001 that a black family moved there in the late 1990s but left within a week, owing to harassment. The 2000 census showed just 1 African American—a child—in the town of 1,675 people. And Elwood, in central Indiana, definitely has not. "Elwood is by reputation still off-limits," a black former police officer in nearby Marion reported in 2002, and the 2000 census confirmed his judgment, finding no African Americans in Elwood's 9,455 population. There is no way such a large town could show such a complete absence without continuing enforcement. According to a teacher in a nearby town, in recent years Elwood has hosted[17] a Ku Klux Klan headquarters and an annual KKK parade.[18]

The 2000 census

In the 2000 census, Scott County, west of Springfield, Illinois, had not one black household. Stark County, northwest of Peoria, had just one. Mason County, between Peoria and Springfield, where oral history says the sheriff used to tell black newcomers to move on, had not a single black family. It is unlikely that entire counties, located near sizable interracial cities, could show such a dearth of African Americans without continuing enforcement. On the other hand, sometimes the census can falsely indicate that a town or county is still sundown, if African Americans have moved in since it was taken. Steeleville, Illinois, 60 miles southeast of St. Louis, had 2,077 people in 2000, with no African Americans. But according to a librarian at the Steeleville Library, since 2001 "about a dozen Mexicans and three or four colored" moved to Steeleville to work at a new plant. So Steeleville may no longer be a sundown town.[19]

When the census shows an influx of African Americans, it can also be inaccurate to conclude that a former sundown town now admits blacks. As we saw in earlier chapters, the 2000 census includes African Americans in institutions, live-in servants, and plain errors, and is already five years out of date. For Pinckneyville, Illinois, near Steeleville, the 2000 census shows 1,331 blacks among 5,464 residents, but that includes the inmates, mostly African American, of a large state prison. The census lists five households with a black householder, but two longtime residents I talked with agreed that only one African American couple lived in the town. That couple had lived in town for some 25 years and raised children there. One of my conversation partners asked the other his view of them. "They're harmless," he replied. After he left, she said that his comment shocked her. "You see what an insult that is? Would you like that to be said about you? This man is intelligent, he's very well-spoken, he sat behind me at a funeral and so I know he has a beautiful singing voice. 'Harmless!' " She was disappointed in her friend. I pointed out that his comment was typical sundown town rhetoric—if whites judge a given African American harmless, then she or he can stay—and she agreed. Such a judgment exempts *that* family, while implying that whites still reserve the right to bar blacks who have *not* proven themselves "harmless." A black resident of nearby Du Quoin said that Pinckneyville's one black couple was joined by another in 2000 (just in time for the census), but the landlord wouldn't renew their lease, probably owing to pressure from his white neighbors, so the couple moved to Du Quoin. Thus we cannot simply list Pinckneyville as no longer sundown owing to the 2000 census. Research today is required. In August 2004, a woman who grew up in Pinckneyville wrote: "I was just home this past weekend for a funeral, and while the 'official' anti-black rules may no longer be in effect, the talk and the attitudes sure are."[20]

There is no substitute for firsthand research. Such information, up-to-date at least as of 2002, suggests that Windsor, a small town of 1,100 people in central Illinois, has not changed its anti-black policy. The 2000 census found no African Americans in Windsor, and a businessman who runs a bookstore in nearby Mattoon told a story that explains why:

> Just this past summer [2002] a customer came in [from Windsor] and related to me that she was babysitting for a friend's half-black grandchild. Within a few days of beginning to watch the child she was threatened, a cross was burnt in

her yard, and her own children were threatened. She said she had filed a police report but didn't know if that even made it to a public record. She didn't seem to think that the officer taking the report cared. One of the gentlemen attending our church grew up in Windsor, and as we reminisced one evening he shared that blacks were definitely not welcome.[21]

It seems reasonable to use the present tense as of this writing: African Americans *cannot* live in Windsor, as well as most of the other towns described above. But again, that was 2002. Before coming to a conclusion about a specific town as of *this* moment, do your own research.

Sundown Exurbs

Not only do many sundown towns remain all-white, but whites are still forming new ones and converting independent sundown towns to sundown suburbs by fleeing to them from newly desegregating inner suburbs. One way to find these new sundown places is by studying what the census calls CDPs—census designated places. These are unincorporated areas that nevertheless contain substantial residential populations, often more than 2,500. Many are new developments that have not yet incorporated and probably will do so by the next census. Many are distant suburbs—"exurbs"—that exemplify urban sprawl. Other CDPs have remained unincorporated for decades because residents are content to have counties supply their schooling, policing, and other services.

CDPs vary from census to census, so I mostly omitted them from my analysis, having my hands more than full with my already impossible effort to learn something about the past of every all-white incorporated town larger than 1,000. I couldn't help notice, however, that CDPs seemed much more likely to be all-white in 1990 and 2000 than did incorporated places. This trend is discouraging, because it means we are growing new sundown exurbs just as many of our older sundown suburbs are finally giving up their restrictive policies.

Sundown exurbs often breathe new vitality into independent sundown towns that otherwise might become smaller and more obsolete. I anticipated finding such exurbs in metropolitan areas, and I was not disappointed. Independent sundown towns in northwestern Indiana, for example, are filling with whites fleeing sundown suburbs of Chicago as they become interracial. But I had not anticipated finding sundown exurbs around smaller cities with much smaller black populations. In central Illinois, whites depart Peoria for

Morton and Metamora. They leave Springfield for Sherman and Ashland. Little sundown towns such as Farmer City, Mahomet, St. Joseph, and Villa Grove have become havens for whites who commute to work in Champaign-Urbana.

White flight from majority-black large cities such as Birmingham or Detroit to sundown suburbs is not news, but flight from smaller cities such as Champaign-Urbana is a new phenomenon, partly because such cities are not very black. Nevertheless, race is definitely a factor in many people's decision to subject themselves to such commutes. A Champaign-Urbana resident emphasized, "People leave Champaign-Urbana and move out to Farmer City, St. Joe, and so forth, *to* live in an all-white town." In 2000, Champaign was just 15.6% black and Urbana 14.3%, so five-sixths of their residents were non-black. Surprised that whites would find living in such a majority uncomfortable, I asked, *"In order* to live in an all-white town?" "Yes," she replied, and several residents of Mahomet and Monticello agreed. In 2000, Mahomet had 7 African Americans among 4,877 people (0.1%), Monticello 4 among 5,138 (0.1%), St. Joseph 3 among 2,912 (0.1%), and for the purists, Farmer City had 0 among 2,055.[22]

Similarly, whites fleeing the African American population of Decatur (19.5%) move to places such as Maroa (0.2%), Niantic (0.0%), and Pana (0.1%), 30 miles south. Consider this conversation I had in 2001 with a spokeswoman for Pana:

> [Why do you like Pana?]
>> Because it's quiet. We don't have any—[Breaks off]
>> We don't have—[Breaks off]
>> Well, it's quiet.
> [You say the schools are good. Are they better than Decatur's?]
>> Yes . . . We don't have much of a racial mix here. So we don't have some of the problems they have. Our kids feel real safe here. There's no police in the schools. Well, there's one, but he comes in and goes out. It's just real quiet here.

Her satisfaction with Pana partly owes to its "racial mix": 4 blacks among 4,514 people, including no black household and no children of school age. Even though Decatur is just one-fifth black, Pana residents are very aware and wary of its African American population. When Jesse Jackson came to Decatur in 1999 to garner publicity for several African Americans expelled from high school for fighting in the stands during a football game, residents of Pana expressed intense satisfaction about their isolation from that kind of fray. As one resident said, "If Jesse Jackson did stuff again in Decatur, you'd hear 'nigger' all over McDonald's in Pana."[23]

The lengths some whites go to avoid African Americans is surprising. The seat of Forsyth County is 40 miles from Atlanta. In 2002, a newcomer relayed that when her family moved to the Atlanta area, "our realtor told us that if we did not like 'blacks' then Forsyth was the perfect place for us." Despite the distance, Forsyth County evolved from independent sundown county to sundown suburb before finally desegregating in the late 1990s. Oak Grove, Missouri, has become a bedroom community for people working in Independence and even Kansas City who seek an all-white environment, even though it lies more than 40 miles east of Kansas City. Whites commute to Birmingham, Alabama, from all-white Cullman, 50 miles away. Whites leave Los Angeles for Bishop, California, 300 miles away, because Los Angeles is "too black," although this is a relocation, not a commute. In their search for stable white neighborhoods, some white families have moved across the country, leaving the suburbs of large multiracial metropolitan areas for smaller and less multiracial areas.[24]

Surely the white-flight prize goes to those who flee Joplin, Missouri. A librarian in the Joplin Public Library told of her neighbor who moved from Joplin to Webb City around 1985, because "his daughter was about to enter the seventh grade and he didn't want her to go to school with blacks at that age." The librarian stayed in touch during the relocation process and reported:

> At one point [the mother] told me she had found the perfect house for their family, only it was on the wrong side of the street. The line between Joplin and Webb City was that street, and the house she liked was on the Joplin side, so she couldn't consider it. Eventually they found a house in Webb City.

Webb City adjoins Joplin, as the story implies, but the move amazes because Joplin itself was just 2% black. Webb City, on the other hand, had just 1 African American among its 7,500 residents, and that person was not of school age.[25]

White flight to sundown exurbs is a national problem. Forsyth County more than doubled in the 1990s, making it the second fastest-growing county in the country. While Forsyth is no longer flatly closed to African Americans, for every new black resident 100 new whites move in. Many of the other fast-growing counties share similar demographics, including Delaware County,

2.6% black, outside Columbus, Ohio; Pike County, Pennsylvania, 3.3% black, outside New York City; and Douglas County, 0.7% black, near Denver. The racial motivation behind this sprawl is clear, at least to Atlanta sociologist Robert Bullard: "That's not where people of color are."[26]

Neighborhood Associations

In addition to sundown exurbs, another innovation threatens to maintain sundown suburbs, morphed into a new form: suburbs hypersegregated by social class. I first noticed this alarming development in 1999, driving past large subdivisions north of Dallas. On one side, for as far as I could see, were "Exclusive Homes from $279,000 to $299,000." On the other, again stretching to the horizon, were "Exclusive Homes from $299,000 to $339,000," or thereabouts. The authors of *Suburban Nation* decry this trend: "For the first time we are now experiencing ruthless segregation by minute gradations of income." If a lot owner tries to build a $200,000 house in a $350,000 development, "the homeowners' association will immediately sue."[27]

As they did with separation from African Americans, realtors and developers tout class-based segregation as prudent investment strategy. In a 2001 syndicated article, Ellen Martin advised home buyers not to ignore the "financial advantages" of "a prestigious address and a fancy ZIP code." She quoted Leo Berard, "charter president" of the National Association of Exclusive Buyer Agents: "You're almost always better off trading down on the amenities of a home if the payoff is getting into a classy neighborhood." Then the home is more likely to appreciate in value.[28]

Such thinking may be prudent for the individual investor, but the result on the societal level is a dramatic increase in the separation of the rich from the poor, and even from the only slightly less rich. In 1970, as this new economic segregation got under way based on these minute differences in house price, Kenneth Jackson noted that the median household income in cities was 80% of that in suburbs. Just thirteen years later, it had sunk to 72%. According to economist Richard Muth, writing around 1980, the median income in American cities rose at about 8% per mile as one moved away from the central business district. By ten miles away, income doubled. The United States already has more economic inequality than any other industrialized nation; now we are winding up with greater geographic separation between the classes.

Homeowners associations maintain the barriers once residents have moved in. The resulting isolation has unfortunate consequences for the rich, the poor, and the country, just as the previous chapters showed the unfortunate repercussions of sundown towns upon whites, blacks, and the social system. Children of the rich don't learn working-class skills or develop respect for working-class people, because every nearby family inhabits the same occupational niche as their parents. Poor children, meanwhile, end up with little knowledge of the occupations of the affluent and how to enter them. Separating everyone by class also has negative effects for continuity, because over time families need different kinds of housing. They may begin with an apartment, relocate to a starter home, move up to a three-bedroom ranch, then require a larger house to accommodate the birth of twins or the decline of a parent. Reduced economic circumstances or an empty nest may dictate a smaller home, followed by a condominium when they become senior citizens. If each move requires relocation to another area because each neighborhood—or even the entire suburb—is limited to a given income level and house size, towns may find it difficult to maintain a sense of community.[29]

Homeowners associations are multiplying nationwide. By 2000, 42,000,000 Americans lived in neighborhoods governed by these associations. Especially in the fast-growing suburbs of the South and West, almost all new homes now come with a homeowners association attached. Above all else, these associations aim to protect property values. One result is a plethora of rules.[30] Sometimes these rules are eerily reminiscent of an earlier time, such as the common requirement that "all pickup trucks must be out by sundown." These days, neighborhood associations never mention race, but in earlier times they were quite frank about it. One of the first neighborhood associations, the University District Property Owners' Association near Los Angeles, was established in 1922 as the Anti-African Housing Association.[31]

Gated Communities

A related development is the gated community, all of whose units are usually priced within a narrow range. According to author Robert Kaplan, gated communities came to the United States from South America, particularly Brazil. In 1985, gated communities were rare, but by 1997, more than 3,000,000 American households lived behind walls. Mary Snyder, a city planning professor, estimates that eight out of ten new developments in the United States are gated. Gated communities are particularly prevalent on Long Island and in California. Entire towns have gone gated in Florida, Illinois, and California.[32]

Gated communities epitomize defended neighborhoods, providing *no* amenities, not even streets, that are open to the public. Their walls and fences keep the public away from streets, sidewalks, playgrounds, parks, beaches, and even rivers and trails—resources that normally would be shared by all the citizens of a metropolitan area. The rationale for all this exclusion is allegedly relief from crime, and some communities do offer that. But often the security is largely illusory:[33] the gatehouses in many gated communities are never staffed.[34]

In fact, status and marketability, rather than security, usually drive gating. Often the gating is only symbolic and the gates never close. A development in an elite suburb northeast of Columbus, Ohio, went gated more than a decade after its initial opening. According to a student who had spent most of his life in the community, it had five unsold houses; after it went gated, they sold quickly. Before the gates, no crime had bedeviled the area; the increased security served no real purpose other than increased status and salability. According to a real estate salesman in suburban Maryland. "Any upscale community now would have to be gated. That's what makes it upscale."[35]

We have seen how whites have often used the occasion of retirement to relocate to sundown towns. Today the tradition of retiring to white enclaves continues, often gated and built around private beaches, golf courses, marinas, or all three. They may provide community, because purchase of a house or town house includes use of a clubhouse, restaurant, sports facilities, and other amenities. Whether residents also connect to any larger, more diverse community is dubious. Certainly such old-fashioned aspects of community as Girl Scout cookie sellers, trick-or-treaters, and political canvassers are forbidden. While not quite racially segregated, these new towns and developments advertise themselves as "exclusive" and are often overwhelmingly white, although race goes unmentioned. A friend who stayed in a gated community in Sarasota, Florida, in 2002 reported that she saw no black residents. Conversely, all the workers were people of color, "but they had to be out by nightfall, along with their pickups." Blakely and Snyder likewise encountered almost no nonwhites while interviewing in gated communities.[36]

End of the Nadir

Offsetting such negative developments has been a massive shift in the zeitgeist, the spirit of the times, achieved by the Civil Rights Movement, beginning in 1954. The Civil Rights Movement did not take place in a vacuum, of course. Just as race relations worsened after 1890 in the context of national and even international ideological developments, so did the improvements in race relations after World War II. We identified the three *i*'s—Indian wars, immigrants, and imperialism—as underlying causes of the worsening of race relations during the Nadir. Three factors also help explain why the racism of the Nadir began to erode after 1940.

First came the Great Migration. While the move of African Americans from the South to northern cities further inflamed the racism of some white northerners, it also created black voting blocs in northern cities. The Great Retreat further concentrated African Americans from scattered towns across the North into a few large cities. Soon a few African Americans were back in Congress, elected from those cities. African Americans also won seats in state legislatures and on city councils. Although whites continued to dominate the powerful positions of mayor and governor, they now took care not to alienate urban black voters with overtly racist rhetoric. Moreover, this moderation in rhetoric affected both parties, because from 1912 through 1962, neither party could take black votes for granted.

A second crack in the wall of white supremacy came from abroad: the imperialist sun began to set. Emboldened by the erosion of certainty in the European vision prompted by World Wars I and II, conquered nations—India, the Philippines, Indonesia, and later most of Africa—won their independence. Now the United States faced a new international environment: we had to relate to self-governing countries of color around the world. After World War II, engaged in a struggle with the USSR for world supremacy, the United States had no desire to antagonize these newly independent nonwhite nations by behaving badly toward our own citizens of color. On the positive side, seeing African leaders such as Haile Selassie of Ethiopia and Kwame Nkrumah of Ghana on the world stage made it easier for white Americans to understand that African Americans had done and could achieve important things.

Third and most important was the role played by World War II. Germany gave white supremacy a bad name. It is always in victors' interests to demonize the vanquished, but the Nazis made this task easy. Americans saw in the German death camps the logical end result of eugenics and apartheid, and it appalled us. As we sought to differentiate ourselves from Hitler's discredited racial policies, our own overt racism now made us uneasy. Swedish social scientist Gunnar Myrdal called this conflict our "American dilemma" and predicted in 1944, "Equality is slowly winning." [37]

World War II made a new rhetoric available to those who wanted to treat nonwhites as equal citizens. In Redwood City, 22 miles south of San Francisco, the newly built home of John J. Walker, black war veteran, was burned in December 1946, "after he had received threats to move out," according to a news story in *Pacific Citizen*. The couple planned to rebuild. Perhaps in reaction, some realtors suggested making the entire San Mateo peninsula, perhaps even including San Francisco itself, a sundown area. On July 11, 1947, Harry Carskadon, an agent in nearby Atherton, proposed that the peninsula was "not a proper place" for "Negroes, Chinese, and other racial minorities" and urged exclusive "white occupancy in the region." Other realtors were only slightly more tolerant: "Several members of the realty board felt the only way to handle the minority problem was to set aside acreage and subdivide it for minority groups with schools, business districts, etc.," according to the *Pacific Citizen*. But Emmit Dollarhyde, president of the Santa Clara County NAACP, called this "native fascist racism." He maintained that "Negro and other minority war veterans" who "risked their lives to protect our country from foreign fascism" deserved better. Carskadon's proposal was shelved, and by 1950 Redwood City had 410 African Americans among its 25,544 residents.[38]

The anti-Nazi ideology opened more sundown suburbs to Jews than to African Americans. Probably *Gentleman's Agreement*, Elia Kazan's 1948 Academy Award–winning movie exposing Darien, Connecticut, as an anti-Jewish sundown town, would not have been made except in the postwar anti-Nazi era.[39] To be sure, Darien did not immediately open to Jews. Four decades later, a realtor still cautioned that if a Jewish client asked him about Darien, "Would I be comfortable there?" he would caution her, "No. Don't even look. The brokers will be nice and you can buy a house. But can you enjoy the amenities? Can you join the club?" I suspect he would answer the same in 2005. Many other sundown suburbs did welcome Jews, however.[40]

The Civil Rights Movement

Those three factors underlay the legal challenge to segregation and the ensuing Civil Rights Movement. In turn, the Civil Rights Movement, coupled with the legal campaigns that civil rights lawyers waged against segregated schools and other institutions, began to open sundown towns and suburbs to African Americans. Of course, the movement and the lawsuits mostly took place in the South, where independent sundown towns were few, but they did lead to the quick desegregation of most southern sundown suburbs.

The Civil Rights Movement rarely addressed northern sundown towns and suburbs directly, and when it did, such as Martin Luther King Jr.'s 1966 march for open housing in Cicero, Illinois, it usually failed. Still, the movement's success in the South did help to undercut the rationale for sundown towns in the North. White northerners were jolted by the televised images of black young people peacefully picketing and sitting in and getting beaten or jailed in the process. These images made clear that white misbehavior—not alleged black inferiority—was the source of America's racial problem. Now that African Americans were no longer seen as the problem, white students and faculty pressured their colleges and universities to participate in the solution by recruiting and admitting black students. Now welcoming African Americans was the thing to do in college, while just the opposite still held in the sundown suburbs and neighborhoods from which so many college students had come.

The Civil Rights Movement took actions that exposed some of America's racial contradictions, which helped President Lyndon Johnson, leaders of Congress, and Earl Warren and other Supreme Court justices mobilize the power of the federal government to oppose racial segregation. However, the government did little about housing, because whites were most opposed to residential desegregation. A 1961 poll by the Connecticut Civil Rights Commission shows this in an allegedly liberal New England state. The commission's survey of Connecticut residents, "Attitudes Toward Specific Areas of Racial Integration," found that 95% of whites "favored" or "would accept" racial integration in public schools, 86% in parks and recreational areas, and 76% in hotels. But only 28% favored integration in "private residential neighborhoods," while another 29% would accept it; a plurality, 37%, opposed such integration. Opposition to residential integration was higher than to any other form of integration except "[private] parties." Ironically, Connecticut, like many northern states, had supposedly outlawed racial discrimination in housing decades earlier, although its open-housing law was not enforced. The commission concluded drily, "Opposition to integration in both public and private housing is greater than might be expected in view of the fact that such discrimination has been illegal for years."[41]

1968 as Turning Point

While the foregoing factors and the Civil Rights Movement did begin to erode the ideological foundation of sundown towns, such communities kept forming, especially in the suburbs, probably reaching their peak number in 1968. Three critical events took place in that year that began to weaken sundown towns directly. First, Dr. Martin Luther King Jr. was assassinated by a white racist in Memphis.[42] As some Democrats embraced President Lincoln in his martyrdom, so some formerly recalcitrant whites now mourned King and, to a degree, accepted his cause. Second, and in reaction to King's murder, Congress passed Title VIII of the Civil Rights Act of 1968, the Fair Housing Act. Even though enforcement has been spotty, by its very existence this law clearly put the federal government on the side of prohibiting rather than promoting racial discrimination in housing. Third, the Supreme Court held in *Jones v. Mayer* that an 1866 civil rights law bars discrimination in the rental and sale of property.

Sociologist Karl Taeuber summarized the positive results of these changes:

> Most federal housing programs did strengthen their anti-discrimination poli-
> cies and practices during the 1970s. The Department of Justice filed and won
> court cases and settlements against state and local housing agencies and private
> real estate companies. Many state and municipal fair housing agencies were
> provided some tools for effective enforcement. There was a proliferation of pri-
> vate fair housing groups and neighborhood efforts to foster and preserve
> racially mixed neighborhoods.[43]

Then, as commonly happens, public opinion shifted in the wake of public policy. The National Opinion Research Center (NORC) asked Americans to agree or disagree with the statement "White people have a right to keep blacks out of their neighborhoods if they want to, and blacks should respect that right." In 1968, only 43% disagreed, but four years later, 63% did. Even in the Detroit metropolitan area—the most segregated in America—the proportion of whites agreeing with the NORC statement fell from 60% in 1964 to 20% in 1990. Thus, since 1968, whites who argue for sundown towns and suburbs have been on the defensive. Indeed, the proportion of whites openly in favor of racial segregation of neighborhoods declined nationally to just 15% by 1994.[44]

These responses must be taken with a large grain of salt. There is a huge gap between what people say when asked by strangers and what they do.[45] Depending on the situation, the proportion of whites who discriminate against people of color is often much higher than the proportion who admit they do. Still, it is an important first step that many closet white supremacists are now unwilling to be white supremacist when asked.

After 1968, Sundown Towns Began to Desegregate

The Civil Rights Movement wound down around 1970, leaving sundown towns and suburbs largely untouched in the North. But wheels had been set in motion. Developments in American popular culture comprised another force for change. Beginning with Elvis Presley in the 1950s, American popular music grew increasingly interracial. So have most sports, many television shows, and some movies, beginning with 1961's *A Raisin in the Sun,* which specifically treated sundown neighborhoods. In the 1970s, white teenagers put up posters of such African Americans as Diana Ross and Jimi Hendrix in their bedrooms. In the 1980s, it was Bill Cosby and Alice Walker, among others. In the 1990s, Michael Jackson, Michael Jordan, and Denzel Washington were popular, and in the new millennium, Venus and Serena Williams, Tiger Woods, and an endless succession of hip-hop stars were in fashion.[46] Nor can the influence of Oprah Winfrey be discounted: it is harder to keep African Americans out of your town when you keep inviting them into your living room via television.

In 1972, the National Association of Realtors finally adopted a pro-fair-housing position. The federal Home Mortgage Disclosure Act of 1975 required banks to release data on their lending patterns, making it possible to see if they were redlining. In 1977, redlining was officially outlawed by the Community Reinvestment Act, which requires banks to lend money throughout the regions they serve, including poor neighborhoods (without taking undue risks). Although the federal government showed less concern about segregated housing in the Reagan-Bush years (1981–93), the 1988 Fair Housing Amendments Act strengthened the enforcement of open housing laws and increased the punitive damages that plaintiffs could win for proving housing discrimination. White residents still resorted to violence to keep out blacks, but increasingly in the 1980s and '90s, the perpetrators got arrested. All this made a difference: in the 1990s, the number of African Americans concentrated in all-black census tracts declined dramatically.[47]

Proponents of integration have also won additional legal victories striking down some of the ordinances that suburbs have used to keep out undesirables. Brenden Leydon sued Greenwich, Connecticut, after a guard kept him from jogging on Greenwich Point, a 147-acre park with a beach on Long Island Sound. Greenwich allowed nonresidents to walk on its beaches only if they paid a $6 fee and were accompanied by a Greenwich resident. In 2000, the Connecticut Appellate Court said the ordinance "violates a public trust doctrine that says municipalities hold parks on behalf of all citizens." In the late 1990s, a similar challenge invalidated Dearborn's ordinance that only residents could use its parks. In 2003, nearby Grosse Pointe lost the tax exempt status of its parks when a judge ruled that they were not "open to the public generally." Several other sundown suburbs faced comparable legal challenges as of 2004.[48]

Hispanics and Asians Prompt Change

Today, Hispanics and Asians live throughout the United States, not just in the West. In the 2000 census, Hispanics and "Others" outnumbered African Americans by 20% in America's 100 largest metropolitan areas, and while the West has America's most diverse population, other sections have become surprisingly multicultural as well. Hispanics will soon outnumber African Americans in the Midwest. Asians now are the largest nonwhite group in many towns in the upper Midwest.

Even during the depths of the Nadir, most sundown towns did not keep out Mexican Americans. Except in the West, most did not bar Asian Americans. As a result, nationally, Hispanics or Asians with third-grade educations are more likely to live among whites than is an African American with a Ph.D. today. Historically, even sundown suburbs such as Cicero and Berwyn, Illinois, long notorious for their hostility to African Americans, allowed Mexican Americans as residents. By the 2000 census, Cicero's 85,616 population was almost 80% Hispanic, and Berwyn's was almost 40% and rising.

Today, not only Mexican Americans but Mexican nationals, right off the truck that brought them to work for a chicken processing factory in a little Arkansas Ozarks town or a broom corn factory in Arcola, Illinois, are immediately allowed to live in those sundown towns and have their children attend school. Most can speak no English and may also have had little schooling in Spanish in Mexico. Some are unfamiliar with such basics of modern life as a supermarket, laundromat, or library. Asian Americans—even Hmongs and Khmers with little English and very different cultural backgrounds—have found even readier acceptance. As Ricardo Herrera put it, speaking of California in 2000, "For the purposes of suburban migration 'out and up' from Los Angeles, in certain complex ways Asian Americans and Latinos have been treated as 'non-black' in contradistinction to being treated as 'non-white.' " Although they have much less in common with white Americans than do black Americans, these immigrants are admitted by towns and suburbs that continue to keep out African American families who have lived in this country, worshiped Jesus Christ, and spoken English for ten generations.[49]

However, once sundown towns admit Hispanics and Asian Americans, to admit African Americans may seem tolerable, rather than a catastrophe to be mobilized against.[50] The rush of Latino and Asian Americans into Cicero and Berwyn finally loosened the prohibitions against African Americans, and both suburbs now have black householders, including homeowners. In 2000, Cicero had 956 African Americans in 275 households; 54 own their homes; Berwyn had 588 African Americans in 221 black households; 81 own. This is a transformation: such numbers would have been inconceivable in 1981, when the school superintendent bragged that there would be no blacks in the Cicero Public Schools "as long as I am superintendent" and was wildly applauded.[51]

Ironically, some of the more racist whites have been leaving Cicero and Berwyn because the suburbs have grown "too Mexican" for them. For decades, Cicero had required firefighters and police officers to live within the city, partly to avoid hiring African Americans. Since African Americans were kept out of town, they couldn't be hired, and since no African Americans worked in the police and fire departments, it was easy to mobilize those departments to keep blacks out of town. Now Cicero's firefighters are trying to eliminate the residency requirement, supposedly to encourage African Americans living elsewhere to apply. "But critics suspect another motive," according to reporter Danielle Gordon: "White workers want the freedom to escape . . . [Cicero's] fast-growing Latino population." The irony that racist whites are arguing for a rule change that may lead to the hiring of nonwhites is not lost on African Americans, who have suffered decades of humiliation in Cicero and Berwyn.[52]

In Dearborn, Michigan, thousands of Arab Americans moved in while African Americans were kept out. The statue of Orville Hubbard, mayor of Dearborn from 1942 to 1978, was one of the 100 historic sites treated in my last book, *Lies Across America.* I poked fun at its accompanying historical marker—"He made Dearborn known for punctual trash collection"—and pointed out that Hubbard actually made Dearborn notorious for being a sundown suburb. In 2000, Dearborn's director of public information wrote me to complain about the entry: "We are proud to be home to more than 70 nationalities, including African-Americans, Arab-Americans, and Hispanics in addition to people from Western and Eastern Europe." Dearborn also makes this point on its web site. In the 2000 census, Dearborn had 1,275 African Americans, more than 1% of its nearly 100,000 total population, a sea change from twenty years earlier. Surely Dearborn's Arab Americans and Hispanics helped make this possible, if only by contributing to a new rhetoric. To brag about Dearborn's diversity is not compatible with keeping out African Americans.[53]

Recent research by Nancy Denton suggests that this complexity helps to desegregate formerly all-white neighborhoods across the nation. Whites do not often flee neighborhoods that become 50% nonwhite *if* those nonwhites include substantial numbers of Asian Americans and Hispanics as well as African Americans, and the number of census tracts with all four groups has soared. Nationally, residential segregation against African Americans decreased most in metropolitan areas where Asians and Latinos were most prevalent.[54]

Even in small independent towns across the Midwest, including sundown towns, Mexicans and Mexican Americans now do much of the work. In 2000, Arcola, Illinois, for example, was 20% Mexican, mostly employed by its broom corn factories. Beardstown, Illinois, west of Springfield, also had about 20% Mexicans, mostly employed by Excel, a meatpacker. Both were sundown towns, and Arcola may still be, but Beardstown has changed. Wyatt Sager, a lifelong resident, welcomes the change: "We would never have heard Mexican music 10 years ago. Now it is commonplace to hear different ethnic music. Beardstown has a much greater world scope now than it did 10 years ago." Immigrants from Senegal followed the Mexicans to Excel, and Beardstown now has eleven black households among its 5,766 residents. But Arcola shows that it is too early to tell: perhaps Mexican Americans and Asian Americans will become "honorary whites," leaving African Americans again shut out.[55] A realtor in Barry County, a sundown county in the Missouri Ozarks, leaned in this direction in remarks made in 1994:

> Blacks are so different that I just can't stand them. I can't help it, I hate them. My Doberman pinscher, Lady, used to terrorize Blacks. I really enjoyed that. I can tolerate Mexicans—I even have some Mexicans working for me—but I just can't tolerate Blacks.[56]

The Process of Change

In the last decade of the twentieth century and the first decade of the new millennium, even in the absence of Asians or Hispanics, many formerly sundown communities caved in peacefully and no longer keep out African Americans. A composite depiction of the process goes something like this: a white couple or two with adopted biracial children moved to town and enrolled their school-age children, thus desegregating the school system. Then a young white woman, daughter of longtime residents, left for the big city, had an affair with a young African American man, and returned home with her biracial child to live in the town. Eventually the child's father joined them. White residents did nothing to him, partly because he wasn't exactly an outsider, with his family connections. An African American couple moved in perhaps a year later . . . and lo, the town was no longer sundown.

Even towns that have not yet accepted a black household often do include adopted biracial children of white parents or children of interracial couples. "We see more and more interracial families," said a librarian in Cullman, Alabama. Most are young white women with interracial children, divorced, with no father living in town. This pattern is so common that I came to believe it happens on purpose. It may be too strong to suggest that some white teenage girls, disgusted at the hypocrisy shown by their parents and sundown community on race relations, deliberately set out to get pregnant by an African American male. Certainly they do set out to experience what their narrow-minded towns have told them is forbidden fruit.[57]

The children have mixed experiences. "I hope it will get better and I think it has some," reported a resident of Piggott, Arkansas, a sundown town near the Missouri Bootheel. "We have two black children in our church now with a white mother, who grew up in this community. She married while in college. They were accepted pretty well up until teen age. I know it has been hard on them." Often the dating age poses a problem. In 1992, the one African American student in Benton High School in Illinois, a girl in the junior class, accepted an invitation from a white football player to the junior/senior prom. "And that was it," in the words of a teacher in the school. "She was ostracized by the students from then on." She stuck it out for the rest of the school year and her family then moved. In these cases, the students never achieved full individuality in white eyes but remained merely representatives of a problematic race.[58]

Things were a little better in Comanche, Texas. In 2000, after an absence of more than a century, Comanche again had African American children in school: Talila Harlmon and her brother. "I do things by myself a lot," said Talila.

I feel like I have to try harder to fit in. That's why I keep my hair braided and long, to look like the other girls. . . . The other girls, they go out to get their hair done—but I can't go, because the hairstylists here can't do my hair. I wish there were more black kids. I'd have someone to relate to in history class, when they're talking about the slaves or Martin Luther King. If I were at a school with black kids, I could go to their house, they could come to mine. With a bunch of kids' parents here, the white girls can't date Hispanics or blacks. It bothers me. Some people aren't like that. I went to the prom with a white boy whose parents didn't mind. But sometimes kids in our school will be having a party, and if I find out and say why wasn't I invited, you could tell that they really want to invite me but they can't.

Thus Talila went to her prom and was not ostracized for it. Still, she gets lonely. "But my mom takes me places, and we go do stuff. My mom tells me it's just life, you just have to deal with it." [59]

Students Can Make a Difference

Whites in several sundown towns in Arkansas, Illinois, and Wisconsin report that even one or two African American high school students can help to humanize a community. Some residents use their existence as grounds to stop defining their towns as sundown towns. When this is done as a first step toward welcoming African American families, it is a positive step. Interaction with the one or two African American or mixed-race children can help white students learn to treat nonwhites with respect. Maybe Talila Harlmon had that effect in Texas.

In the 1990s in Sheridan, Arkansas, not long after white football fans were screaming, "Get the nigger," as told in Chapter 4, Sheridan High School got its first African American student. He lived outside Sheridan; for several more years, Sheridan still did not allow African Americans to be in town after dark. Regardless, "they made a mascot of him, loved him to death," my source reported. "Of course, *some* didn't." Being "a mascot" in Sheridan continues the pattern of the "pet Negro" who often played an ultra-humble or clown role in previous decades. But sometimes whites accept the lone African Americans as people, not mascots or Tontos or other "representatives of their race." They get known as individuals and beat the file folder phenomenon. Often they find themselves particularly well liked, partly because some white students are consciously doing what they can to break through their cocoon of isolation and prejudice and join the larger interracial world. [60]

Students have sometimes prompted the collapse of a town's racist policies. ABC students, mostly African American, came into Appleton in the early 1970s. Hayden Knight, born in Trinidad and raised in Brooklyn, remembers when he arrived in Appleton as a high school student in 1973: "Appleton knew about the Green Bay Packers and that was it." [61] He went on to add, "It

was quite a shock. Appleton was small-minded at that time. We ABC kids
helped them get through that." In 1960, exactly one African American lived in
Appleton, a sundown city of almost 50,000 people. Twenty years later, 47
did, but most were students at Lawrence University or the ABC program. But
in the 1980s, Appleton finally relented: the 1990 census found 163 African
Americans among 65,695 residents, and by no means were they all students.
Knight ended up returning to Cedarburg, Wisconsin, where he coaches soc-
cer in the high school and helps to diversify another formerly all-white town.[62]

On the other hand, sometimes lone black students have made little difference. In 1974 James Lockhart spent his senior year in Highland Park High
School, a Dallas sundown suburb, the first African American student. Whites
called him "nigger," ripped his pants, and stole his books. Afterward, Lockhart recalled, "At first a lot of people rejected me. But later, as they got to know
me better, they accepted me. They said I'd scared them because they'd never
been around blacks." His parents viewed the harassment as the work of "no
more than five students." Nevertheless, Highland Park, former home to both
President George W. Bush and Vice President Richard Cheney, did not really
desegregate until May 2003. In that month, the first African American family
bought a house in the suburb. James Ragland, columnist for the *Dallas Morning News,* commented:

> I find it hard to believe that no black person ever has owned a home in Highland
> Park, an exclusive suburb often referred to as "the bubble."
>
> No black CEO. No black athlete. No black entertainer. No black entrepre-
> neur. No black lawyer or doctor.
>
> No one?
>
> "As far as we know, that's true," said Tom Boone, editor of *Park Cities
> People.*

Thus so far as Highland Park knows, it was a sundown suburb until 2003.[63]
Unless the new black family gets driven out by hateful incidents, which I
doubt will happen, and if additional African American households join them,
then Highland Park has finally cracked.[64]

Athletics Can Prompt Change

Athletics can provide a bridge. In town after sundown town, principals and
teachers say that their lone black student fits in if s/he could play ball. In Duncan, Arizona, in 1950, athletics even provided a bridge across racially separate

schools. Earl Randolph Jr. was kept out of Duncan High School and confined to a "school" devised just for himself and his siblings, but he was allowed to play on Duncan's athletic teams. Partly owing to his prowess, according to Duncan resident Betty Toomes, "they were unbeatable." The next year, the family moved to nearby Clifton, Duncan's traditional rival, and "Duncan was very sorry to see them go." Earl Randolph Jr. went on to become a multisport varsity athlete at Arizona State University.[65]

Not only does the individual black student find acceptance through athletics, but the high school and even the town modifies its definition of the ingroup. When all-white athletic teams become interracial, even if they remain mostly white, gradually the rhetoric changes: no longer do team members or fans indulge in the racial slurs of their sundown past. No longer do they throw rocks at the team buses of visiting interracial squads. Overtly racist comments and behaviors cannot be performed by interracial teams, because the African Americans on the team would not allow it. Indeed, white students on an interracial team would never yell "nigger" at an opposing player in the first place. It would never occur to them to "otherize" their opponents on *racial* grounds, since doing so would otherize some of their own players. Of course, interracial teams and fans can still otherize opponents in other ways: parody their fight songs, disrupt their cheers, call opposing linemen "sissies," and so forth. But they don't use racial slurs or think in racial terms. Such rhetoric would create an ingroup—whites—that would be divisive and inappropriate on an interracial team in an interracial town.

Within interracial schools, athletics are a unifier, say principals across the land. Cairo, Illinois, has had a difficult racial history, verging on open warfare in the early 1970s.[66] Even in that milieu, Cairo's athletic teams brought some students together. According to Bruce Brinkmeyer, the white quarterback at the time, "We were just trying to play ball, and when you see a black teammate out there sweating and working just like you, you don't see him as different." By 1987, thanks to racial bias from a neighboring sundown town, athletics was bringing some racial harmony to the entire city. After unfair officiating at a basketball game in Anna that year, whites and blacks in Cairo were outraged together.[67] As Cairo's white school superintendent, Ed Armstrong, put it:

This time it was obvious even to some people who might not be as objective in their racial attitudes as they should be, that the team was mistreated. It was obvious why. There's an awful lot of racial hatred involved. The whites in Cairo see that, and they know it's not fair. Their team, a black team, was suffering unfairly.[68]

Hate rhetoric directed toward Mexican American basketball players performed the same unifying service in Beardstown in 2003. About 20 fans of nearby Brown County High School, a sundown county, showed up wearing sombreros and yelling "We want tacos" at the Beardstown team. According to Beardstown senior Tomas Alvarez, "People were mad. They really care about the image of Beardstown. That wasn't just against an ethnic group. It was against the whole town."[69]

Letting in a mere handful of African Americans may not always do the trick, as shown by Hemet, southeast of Los Angeles. As reporter Bill Jennings put it in 1992, "Hemet was pretty well a sundown town, meaning blacks could work over here during the day but they had better head for Perris or wherever at dusk." In 1989, Hemet had about 23 African Americans among its 25,000 residents, less than 0.1%. Three were on the Hemet High School football team, 6% of its 50-man roster. Still, Hemet's white players continued their long tradition of taunting African Americans on opposing teams as "niggers." Having three black teammates did not suffice to humanize Hemet's rhetoric, and the three apparently said little about the matter. By 2000, 1,500 African Americans lived in Hemet, 2.6% of the total population. No more reports of race-baiting at its athletic contests made the press.[70]

Colleges Can Prompt Change

African American college students have usually made less impact on sundown towns. They stay on campus and are seen as transients, so they don't challenge or ameliorate the sundown rule. All too often, neither do their institutions, which have more often been a captive of their town rather than a point of leverage to change it. The University of Oklahoma was a large state university in the relatively small sundown town of Norman, but the university itself kept out African American students until after a court order in 1949. According to George Callcott, university historian, the University of Maryland made no attempt to change the exclusionary policy of University Park, Maryland, which prohibited Jews as well as African Americans: "The University administration was very conservative and wouldn't have *wanted* to touch it." Likewise, to the best of my knowledge, throughout the years down to 1968, Lawrence University made no attempt to change Appleton, Wisconsin; North Central College made no impact in Naperville, Illinois; Eastern New Mexico University made none in Portales, New Mexico; and several colleges never tried to desegregate their sundown suburbs of Los Angeles.[71]

In a few towns colleges did promote tolerance. Regarding Jews, the University of California made a difference in La Jolla, in southern California. La Jolla had a "gentleman's agreement" to keep out Jews and African Americans from the 1920s through about 1959. Most and probably all residential areas were covered by covenants limiting owners and tenants to "the Caucasian race," interpreted to exclude Jews. After *Shelley v. Kraemer* made covenants unenforceable, La Jolla relied on realtors to discourage Jewish would-be buyers. "Every Jewish person I know was given the runaround," explained the wife of a Jewish scientist hired by the Scripps Institution of Oceanography, part of the University of California system, regarding their failed attempt to buy a house in La Jolla in 1947. In the 1950s, the California university system wanted to locate a major new campus in La Jolla. The man in charge of the process, Roger Revelle, felt, "You can't have a university without having Jewish professors." Clark Kerr, president of the University of California system, agreed. In 1958, Revelle made "a more or less famous speech," as he put it later, to the Real Estate Brokers Association in which he said, "You've got to make up your mind. You're either going to have a university or you're going to have an anti-Semitic covenant. You can't have both." Even faced with this ultimatum, most realtors still wouldn't comply, but their unanimity was broken: two agents—Jim Becker and Joseph Klatt—refused to exclude Jews in the 1960s, and the University of California at San Diego came into being. Becker died in 1981; at least as late as 1996, Jews in La Jolla still "remember[ed] his stand against the La Jolla real estate brokers," according to historian Mary Ellen Stratthaus. In the late 1960s, when many colleges began to recruit African American students, they—along with progressive white students and professors—pushed their institutions to make a difference in their communities. For example, the next chapter tells how faculty members at Valparaiso University led a private campaign in 1969 that desegregated their sundown town in northwestern Indiana.[72]

The South

Responding to all of these factors, some sundown towns across the United States have given up their exclusionary policies. We shall begin our quick tour in the South, which has progressed furthest in doing away with sundown towns, owing to the influence of the Civil Rights Movement. The traditional South had the fewest sundown towns to begin with; there, sundown towns were mostly limited to newer suburbs that developed mostly after World War II. These suburbs stayed all-white only for two to three decades and began to desegregate as early as the 1970s. Most suburbs of Southern cities desegregated before the 1990s.

Chamblee, Georgia, is an example. By 1970 it had become a sundown suburb; its 9,127 residents included just 1 black woman, probably a maid. Then, during the 1980s, Chamblee not only desegregated, it became cosmopolitan, even international. By 1990, among 7,668 residents were 1,482 African Americans and 1,108 others, mostly Asians and Asian Americans. By the 2000 census, two-thirds of Chamblee's 9,838 residents were born outside the United States.[73]

International immigrants were not required to achieve the integration of southern suburbs. Pearl, a suburb of Jackson, Mississippi, exemplifies the more usual process. Like Chamblee and many other formerly rural southern towns, as Pearl suburbanized, it got rid of its African American residents. By 1970, Pearl had 9,623 residents, including just 10 African Americans, disproportionately female, probably live-in servants. But Pearl's life span as a sundown suburb was brief, because in January 1970, public schools throughout Mississippi were fully desegregated by federal court order. Now most white neighborhoods and suburbs in the state, including Pearl, opened rather suddenly to African American residents.

It wasn't that thousands of white Mississippians suddenly realized they should let African Americans live next door to them, although some did come to that conclusion. Rather, the policy of racism and resistance that the state and city had followed from 1890 to 1970 had failed, at least so far as the schools were concerned. The whites who ran the public schools had done everything they knew to do to keep them segregated; the result was they were now fully desegregated. This unanticipated outcome removed the wind from the sails of those whites who had previously been determined to avoid residential desegregation. Gordon Morgan's survey of white attitudes in Mountain Home, a sundown town in the Arkansas Ozarks, caught this sense of inevitability. Most of his respondents expected that African Americans "*will* move in, in about five years."[74] To be sure, whites could still flee a neighborhood when a black family entered, just as they could enroll their own children in a private school. But they had lost faith in their ability to keep blacks out of their neighborhood, having failed to keep them out of their white public schools. By 1980, Pearl had 2,341 African Americans among its now nearly 21,000 residents. The same thing happened in other sundown suburbs across Mississippi[75] and the South.[76]

Some progress also took place a little later in the nontraditional South, where sundown towns and counties abounded. At least half of the independent sundown towns in the nontraditional South stopped excluding African Americans in the 1990s or since the 2000 census. Consider Arkansas. During the Nadir, whites expelled African Americans from many places in the Ozarks, as well as from other towns and counties in the northwestern half of Arkansas, most recently from Sheridan in 1954. By 1960, six Arkansas counties had no African Americans at all (Baxter, Fulton, Polk, Searcy, Sharp, and Stone), seven more had one to three, and another county had just six. I suspect all fourteen were sundown counties and have confirmed eight.

By 1990, census figures showed little change, but in the 1990s, many of these counties seem to have relaxed their restrictions. The 2000 census showed that every Arkansas county had at least ten African Americans except Searcy, with three, and Stone, with nine. Some counties showed considerable change. Benton County, which grew from 97,499 people in 1990 to 153,406 in 2000—fueled by growth at Wal-Mart's corporate headquarters—included 629 African Americans in that new larger population. African Americans were only 0.4% of the total in 2000, and the black increase amounted to fewer than one person in every 100 newcomers. Nevertheless, African Americans have reasserted their right to live in Benton County. The same holds for Sharp County, farther east in the Ozarks: 84 African Americans lived there in 2000, in 24 households.

Six Arkansas counties still teetered on the verge of being all-white, with only one or two black households in 2000. All lay in the Ozarks: Searcy and Stone, of course, and Fulton, Izard, Marion, and Newton.[77] Otherwise, counties in the rest of Arkansas—although not every town—seem willing to tolerate African American residents. The public schools of Sheridan, Arkansas, for example, desegregated around 1992, when students from two small nearby interracial communities were included in the new consolidated high school. In about 1995, the first black family moved back into Sheridan, and in the late 1990s they were joined by three more families—slow progress, but progress nevertheless. A few Appalachian counties in Virginia, North Carolina, Tennessee, and Kentucky may still keep out African Americans—including Erwin, as we have seen—but some of these places also cracked in the 1990s.[78]

The West

Most sundown towns and suburbs in the Far West cracked before 2000. These communities did not have residents who experienced and lost the battle for formal school segregation, but they shared with southern suburbs continued growth in the period 1970–2000. In addition, the West became increasingly multiracial, with continuing immigration of Hispanics and Asians. The West boasted most of the towns noted in earlier chapters as closed to Mexicans and Mexican Americans, Asians and Asian Americans, and Native Americans. But by 1970, most of these communities were open to nonblack minorities. Then they opened to African Americans as well.

The West's new multiethnic suburbs are very different from its old sundown suburbs. Journalist William Booth summed up research by Hans Johnson and others at the Public Policy Institute of California:

> The fastest-growing suburbs, with lots of new, relatively affordable tract housing—the kind of places whites used to fly to—became some of the most ethnically and racially diverse neighborhoods in the state during the 1990s. Ozzie and Harriet now live beside Soon Yoo and Mercedes Guerrero.

Asian and Latin Americans have been much less likely than European Americans to bar African Americans from their neighborhoods.[79]

With upward mobility, however, the anti-racist idealism of these groups may decrease over time, like that of white ethnic groups. Research by Camille Zubrinsky Charles suggests this is happening. She found that when asked to draw their "ideal multi-ethnic neighborhood," Latinos, especially those from Central America, and Asian Americans were *more* likely than whites to draw them containing *no* African Americans.[80]

Nevertheless, William Clark found much less segregation against African Americans in southern California in 2002, especially against rich African Americans:

> The change in the status of blacks is particularly striking. As late as 1970, rich and poor blacks were equally likely to be segregated from white households, but today in Southern California, high-income black households live in highly integrated neighborhoods. Families with incomes less than $10,000 had an Index of Dissimilarity close to 90—highly segregated[81]—while D for those with earnings above $60,000 = 40, reasonably integrated.

Some rich suburbs were still overwhelmingly white. Elite Indian Wells had only five black households. But most suburbs of San Francisco and Los Angeles had at least 150 African Americans and may be moving toward "postracial" identities. Statewide, using the term *segregated* for census tracts that are

> 80% monoracial, only 25% of California neighborhoods were segregated in 2000, down from 43% in 1990.[82]

Most independent sundown towns in the West are also giving up their policy of racial exclusion. A swath of towns in southwestern Oregon were sundown towns, according to oral history and other sources, including Eugene, Umpqua, Grants Pass, Klamath Falls, Medford, and others. In 2000, Grants Pass had 76 African Americans, Klamath Falls, 96, and Medford, 313, leaving their restrictive pasts behind. Eugene had 1,729, and most were not students at the University of Oregon. Another sundown town, Tillamook, on the coast due west of Portland, had just 7 blacks among its 4,352 residents and no households, so we cannot be sure it has given in.[83] But most towns in the Far West have. Kennewick, Washington, which had a sundown sign in the 1940s, had 579 African Americans in 2000. Oregon City, where the KKK drove out the only black citizen in 1923, had no African Americans at all as late as 1980; ten years later it boasted eight families. Taft, California, which like Kennewick formerly had a sundown sign, showed five black households in the 2000 census, at least a beginning.[84]

The Midwest

News from the Midwest is not so encouraging. I estimate that about half of Illinois's sundown towns have changed. To calculate this estimate, I examined 2000 census data for the 167 Illinois communities that I had confirmed as sundown towns as of mid-2004.[85] Of these, 59, or almost 40%, were no longer "all white." To that total, I added a few towns that had no black households as of 2000 but have opened up since then, such as Steeleville, based on the information that at least two African American families recently moved in without opposition.

I tried to be positive, so I included Vandalia, for example, the state capital for a time in the nineteenth century. In 1960, it had 5,537 residents, of whom not one was African American. In 1962, when Joseph Lyford wrote *The Talk in Vandalia,* the town was openly sundown. He quotes one minister saying ruefully,

> We call our town the land of Lincoln, but the hotels won't rent a room to a Negro, and no Negro can buy property or rent a home in Vandalia. There is an old saying that people in Vandalia are glad to help a Negro as long as he keeps on going right out of town.

Vandalia was still sundown as of the late 1990s. A college professor who grew up there wrote:

> Sometime in the mid-90s, a black couple moved to Vandalia. . . . The neighbors of this black couple at first were outraged. I heard the couple referred to as "those people," as in "What are those people doing in our town?" As the neighbors got to know the couple, though, they learned they were really nice people, and then everyone quieted down. After a year or so, the couple moved away. I'm not sure why, but I heard that the wife never felt comfortable in Vandalia. I certainly can't blame her.

By 2000 Vandalia's numbers had swelled to 6,975, including 1,047 African Americans. Had Vandalia had a change of heart or policy? Not exactly; the 2000 census counted inmates at the nearby Vandalia Correctional Center as part of the population of the city. But also around 1995, ironically, the Ku Klux Klan brought about some improvement. My source continues:

> Vandalia was the site of a big KKK rally also sometime in the mid-90s. . . . The rally did have a positive effect on the town in a way, as several churches and groups banded together to hold candlelight vigils to protest the KKK. Many people in Vandalia came forward arguing that racism is not acceptable. Things have gotten better in Vandalia since then. We now have a handful of black families who seem to live and work in the town with no trouble. I don't hear as many racist comments.

Despite Vandalia's amelioration, however, the professor wanted to remain anonymous, and the 2000 census showed only five African Americans in just two households, not counting its huge prison population. Thus Vandalia may still be a sundown town, but I think it has given up that distinction, since the professor indicated "a handful" of families moved in since 2000.[86]

As elsewhere, suburbs showed the most improvement. A disproportionate share of the 59 Illinois towns that opened by 2000 were suburbs. Granite City, a suburb of St. Louis, is an example. According to a man who grew up in Granite City and whose father lived there from 1919 to 1997:

> Blacks who worked in Granite City (mainly in the steel mills) had to walk directly to the streetcar line to catch the first streetcar out of the city. There was one exception: a janitor who worked for Ratz Drug Store on 19th and State

Street. He was known as "Peg" because of his peg leg and was allowed to sleep in the basement of the building.

Around 1980 Granite City relented; by 1990 69 African Americans lived among its 32,862 residents, and the 2000 census showed 622. An administrator at Manchester College in Indiana said in 1997 that students from Granite City "are very racist" and have to be worked with closely if they become dormitory counselors. Maybe ten years from now, that will no longer be necessary, for in 2002 as I drove around the town, I saw interracial groups of children walking home from school and using the library together.[87]

Other Illinois towns, from Anna through Zeigler alphabetically, do not allow as much optimism. Of course, still other Illinois towns may now welcome African Americans, but none has recently knocked at their gates. So I would estimate that more than 40%—and probably at least half—of Illinois's former sundown towns no longer keep out African Americans. If at least 50% of Illinois's sundown communities had abandoned their sundown policies, then across the Midwest, my impression is that at least two-thirds have caved in, because some other states seem more progressive than Illinois. In Wisconsin, for example, a higher proportion of sundown towns seem to have lowered their barriers during the 1980s and especially the '90s. Some places even welcomed them. Fond du Lac, which had had 178 African Americans in the nineteenth century before the Great Retreat, had just 12 in 1970, but 112 in 1990 and 767 by 2000. West Bend had only 31 in 1990, but that included a deputy sheriff, showing considerable acceptance. To be sure, not every Wisconsin sundown town now accepts African Americans. In 1990, eleven Milwaukee suburbs were "violating agreements that they take steps to promote fair housing," according to the Milwaukee County public works director. Milwaukee's suburbs averaged just 2% black in 2000, while Milwaukee was 37% black. The Milwaukee metropolitan area remains the second most segregated in the United States, after Detroit, owing mostly to suburban exclusion.[88]

Many Indiana communities dropped their sundown policies in the 1990s. Portfolio 25 shows the 1970 census for 34 Indiana towns of 1,000 to 2,500 population. Of the eight communities I confirmed as sundown towns in 1970, only one has broken for sure, Zionsville, with 29 African Americans among its now 8,775 residents. Nevertheless, where there had been 26 communities with no African Americans at all, by 2000 there were just 3. There had been no towns with more than one black household, so all 34 might have had sundown policies, with one household or individual—like Granite City's "Peg"—allowed as an exception.[89] Now ten had two or more households.

Among larger towns, Chesterton, in northern Indiana, had only 9 African Americans out of 9,124 people in 1990 and a long history of keeping blacks out. But by 2000, it had thirteen black households, including that of its postmaster, who retired and continues to live there. Clearly Chesterton stopped excluding African Americans around 1990. Valparaiso, a few miles south, admitted them earlier. Merrillville, a suburb of Gary, is now 23% African American. The Northwest Indiana Quality of Life Council recently gave the region a poor rating for its race relations, but at least Chesterton, Valparaiso, and Merrillville have moved beyond exclusion.[90]

Many towns elsewhere in the Midwest have also begun to let in African American residents. Is Warren, Michigan, just north of Detroit, open? As early as 1990, it appeared to have cracked, having 1,047 African Americans among 144,864 total population. That was the year that John and Cynthia Newell and their young son moved to Warren. Because they were African American, they had a rough time. Skinheads burned a cross on the lawn of their rented home. According to "The Cost of Segregation," a 2002 *Detroit News* story:

> In the two years the Newells lived on Campbell near Nine Mile, they were accosted by teen-agers who told them to "go back to Africa" and stuffed their mailbox with "White Power" stickers. "I had a white friend that I lost my friendship with because they kept calling her 'nigger lover' whenever we walked to the store," Cynthia Newell said. "They threw eggs at her when she was with me. All of the neighbors weren't racist. Some of them wanted to socialize. But they couldn't because they were afraid for their safety."

Warren was touch-and-go for a while, but by 2000, Warren had 3,697 African Americans, less than 3% but clearly a black presence.[91]

Whether Owosso, Michigan, is still a sundown town is less clear. In 2000, Owosso had 27 black residents, but that included "kids from Africa in the Bible College," in the words of local historian Helen Harrelson. In 1942 Owosso had allowed African Americans traveling by bus to be in the bus station but no farther. In 2002, when a member of the Owosso High School class of '42 asked a hotel clerk at his sixtieth reunion, "Are Negroes allowed to leave the bus station?" she considered the question absurd. However, the same year, asked if Owosso was still a sundown town, Harrelson replied, "It hasn't really changed yet. Sure, they let in one or two, if they behave themselves. I doubt if there are any black kids in the [public] schools." The 2000 census did show children of school age, among eight households with black house-holders; I think Harrelson was overly pessimistic.[92]

Ohio seems to have made more progress. It had no county in 2000 with fewer than about 40 African Americans. Waverly, which stoned and drove out its sole African American resident decades ago, had 51; nearby Piketon, which likewise drove out its lone black resident, had 21. The cities of Parma and Cuyahoga Falls, which had achieved national notoriety for keeping out African Americans, had almost 1,000 each.

Sundown Suburbs and Neighborhoods

Because social scientists have computed the Index of Dissimilarity for metro-politan areas throughout the period studied by this book, D is useful to assess change in sundown neighborhoods and suburbs over time.[93] From 1860 to 1960, the index increased until the average northern city had a D of 85.6; southern cities averaged 91.9—close to the total apartheid denoted by D = 100. After about 1968, D finally started to decline. Black suburbanization then grew during the 1970s and 1980s, although much of the increase went to a few black suburbs. The average D for all metropolitan areas with large black populations was 69 in 1980 and 64 in 1990. The number of hypersegregated cities (D > 85) decreased from 14 to 4 during the '80s, while the number showing only moderate segregation (D < 55) increased from 29 to 55.[94]

Residential segregation declined further in the 1990s. By 2000, some midsize cities in the South and West boasted D's as low as 40 to 45—low enough to suggest that residential segregation was drawing to a close there. The largest changes took place in the South, owing partly to desegregated countywide school systems. In such metropolitan areas, moving to whiter suburbs does not secure a whiter school district, eliminating one reason for such moves.

Older cities in the Midwest and Northeast—exactly the areas most plagued by sundown suburbs—showed the smallest decreases. Between 1968 and 1980, when the proportion of black students in overwhelmingly minority schools (90–100%) was falling in the rest of the nation, in the Northeast it actually rose 6% to almost half, higher than any other region. In Milwaukee, jeers and flying bricks met black marchers in the 1960s when they crossed the bridge over the Menomonee River to the white neighborhoods on the other side. In 2000, an astonishing 96% of all African Americans in the Milwaukee metropolitan area still lived within Milwaukee itself. David Mendell pointed to the role sundown suburbs played in contributing to this statistic:

In Milwaukee, many middle-class blacks have settled in mostly black city neighborhoods on the north side. That trend follows a history of racial inequity in the Milwaukee area. Until the civil rights era, some suburbs enforced laws that forbade blacks to buy homes in their communities or to walk the streets after 10 PM

For the Milwaukee metropolitan area, D was 83 in 1990 and 82 in 2000. This means 82% of all African Americans in the Milwaukee area would have to move to white neighborhoods for Milwaukee to achieve a uniform racial mix. Moreover, at its current rate of improvement, it will take four hundred years for the level of segregation in Milwaukee to resemble such southern metropolitan areas as Greenville, South Carolina, or Raleigh-Durham, North Carolina, today. Detroit, Philadelphia, and some other "rustbelt" metropolitan areas showed equally minuscule declines.[95]

Even around Detroit, however, most suburbs have admitted a few African Americans. Patti Becker, who has mapped Detroit for decades, calls this "honest integration" to distinguish it from the expanding black ghetto of Detroit, now spilling over into suburbs. Despite this progress, segregated neighborhoods remain the rule, especially in the East and Midwest. In 1995, Maggie Jorgensen, a longtime advocate of integration in Shaker Heights, Ohio, one of the few integrated suburbs in the Midwest, said, "It's still a battle to convince [white] people that it's OK to live in an integrated community." Ingrid Ellen, taking an optimistic view, began her 2000 book, *Sharing America's Neighborhoods,* with the claim "Racially mixed neighborhoods are no longer as rare or as unstable as people tend to think. Nearly one-fifth of all neighborhoods in the United States were racially mixed in 1990."[96] But this is hardly an impressive rebuttal of what "people tend to think," since more than 80% of all neighborhoods were *not* racially mixed, according to her.[97]

Some elite suburbs have given in, if at all, only barely. Kenilworth, for example, the elite Chicago suburb, admitted an African American family in the mid-1960s, but that didn't go so well. A woman who graduated from high school in Kenilworth in 1971 wrote,

I clearly remember when the first black family moved in around 1964. They were very nice and both parents were professionals. I was in seventh grade. Some boys from my class actually stuck a large wooden cross in the family's lawn and burned it. Even during those times I was shocked at the prejudice.

That family stayed for more than a decade but eventually left, and by 2002, no African American households existed in Kenilworth. Tuxedo Park, New York, America's first gated community, had at most one black or interracial family in the 2000 census. The four municipalities that made up Chevy Chase, Maryland, next to Washington, D.C., had just six families with at least one African American householder; their 19 people comprised 0.3% of Chevy Chase's population.[98] On the other hand, Edina, the upper-class sundown suburb west of Minneapolis, had 546 African Americans among 47,425 total population, more than 1%. Beverly Hills and Palos Verdes Estates, elite suburbs of Los Angeles, were also open: Beverly Hills had about 500 African Americans, almost 2% of its population, while Palos Verdes Estates had 132, almost 1%.[99]

Perhaps the best summary is to say that progress has been real but uneven.[100] Metropolitan areas in the Midwest and Northeast have maintained "almost an iron curtain," in sociologist John Logan's phrase, dividing black neighborhoods from white. Most suburbs in the South and West have torn this curtain down.[101]

One Step Forward, One Back?

It would be wrong to end our analysis of the present on this optimistic note. Clouds loom. Despite the symbolic importance of the 1968 law, in 1993 law professor John Boger gave a pessimistic summary of its impact: "By most accounts, the Fair Housing Act has been a disappointing failure." Nancy Denton agrees, finding that "hypersegregation persists and often is worsening" in most metropolitan areas.[102]

If the positive zeitgeist of the Reconstruction and post-Reconstruction years in the North was undone by the view of African Americans as "the problem" during the Nadir, then the changes wrought by the Civil Rights Movement are endangered by the fact that many whites see African Americans as "the problem" today. Even if many white Americans no longer think that sundown towns and suburbs are appropriate ways to deal with that "problem," most people still do not turn first to history and social structure to explain why African Americans have less wealth, lower test scores, and are concentrated in inner cities and a few suburbs. Refurbished as "the ghetto as problem," this rhetoric remains alive and well and is both the result of unequal race relations in America and the cause of further inequality.[103] The solution still seems to be flight to outlying communities that are, if not quite sundown, preponderantly white and affluent. Thus "the ghetto as problem" continues to legitimize overwhelmingly white suburbs and neighborhoods in the eyes of many non-black residents.[104]

To be sure, many former sundown towns and suburbs now include a handful of African American families. Although this marks an important first step toward real integration, the danger of soclexia lurks close behind. Just as living in an all-white community once seemed "natural," now token desegregation quickly comes to seem natural. To paraphrase Billy Bob Lightfoot, quoted about Comanche County, Texas, as a sundown county, almost immediately it seems as though there had always been a few African Americans in Grosse Pointe, Edina, or Beverly Hills. Now these elite suburbs may develop an ideology that endangers further progress. Their new demography now allows their white residents to claim they never were racist—"it's class." In other words, token residential desegregation can prompt whites to forget that their town or suburb flatly kept out African Americans for decades. Without this memory, how can whites understand why there are so few African Americans there now?

I can explain this best by analogy. In the 1990s, many former "segregation academies," founded in the South around 1970 when public schools massively desegregated, relaxed their whites-only policies. Jackson Preparatory Academy in Mississippi now proclaims this goal on its web site: "To achieve the broader educational goal of preparing students to participate in the world community, Prep is committed to diversity in race, color, and national origin in the student body, faculty, and programs." Its student body looks integrated to whites, now that African Americans are no longer shut out entirely. White students may not remember that "Prep" was founded for whites only, to avoid contact with African Americans, but the black community remembers, making many black students reluctant to apply. White students can infer that it is "natural" for a school to be less than 5% black, but it isn't, not in central Mississippi. Even worse, they may conclude that the shortage of black students results from differences in merit, with African Americans being less able on standardized tests.[105]

We have seen how residents often interpret the continued overwhelmingly white population of sundown suburbs as the result of economic differences and individual housing decisions, including those made by black families. Even worse, suburban whiteness can get laid at the eugenics doorstep: whites can blame African Americans for being too stupid or lazy to be successful enough to live in their elite all-white town. Token desegregation makes these interpretations easier to believe, because now nonblacks can point to a handful of black families to "prove" that "we have nothing to do with the overwhelming whiteness of our suburb." Such "explanations" only compound the problem, because whites can infer that racism is over, the metropolitan area and the nation are fair regarding race, and African Americans are responsible for whatever racial inequalities remain. Between 2000 and 2005, arguments such as these have intensified in America, not just in discussions about residential segregation but about affirmative action and many other policy areas. That is why it is so important to know the history of sundown towns and suburbs—to give this cheery optimism the lie.

Perhaps the most prestigious suburban mix at present is 1% African American—just enough to avoid the charge of sundown policies but not enough "to be a problem," not enough to pull down school test scores or perpetrate much crime. That old "African Americans as the problem" line of thought comes through once again. Thus in the 1990s, Forsyth County was the fastest-growing county in Georgia and the second-fastest in the United States, according to the census, partly because it was so white, yet no longer sundown.[106]

Unfortunately, 1% is not black enough to prompt a town or county to face that its schools and other institutions are still white in culture, rather than American in culture. Maybe elite suburbs will go just this black and no further, since elite suburbs seem to get what they want. I doubt it, however, because when a town is only 99% nonblack, rather than 100% nonblack, it is harder to mobilize the white violence, police harassment, and other tools required to keep out additional black newcomers.

One Future: Increasing Exclusion

Keeping out people who do not live the way "we" live is an increasingly common response to America's increasing gap between the affluent and the working class, not to mention the poor. Some analysts consider São Paulo, Brazil, a city of 18,000,000, an augury of future urban life in our country. São Paulo is "populated by the fantastically wealthy and the severely poor with little in between," to quote *Washington Post* reporter Anthony Faiola, writing in 2002. And São Paulo illustrates where gated communities and microscopic economic segregation may be taking us. Faiola told of life in Alphaville, "a walled city where the privileged live behind electrified fences patrolled by a private army of 1,100." Affluent residents "whisk to and from their well-guarded homes to work, business meetings, afternoons of shopping, even church," via helicopter. The city boasts 240 helipads, compared to 10 in New York City. "Brazil has one of the most marked disparities of wealth in the world," continued Faiola, "with the richest 10 percent of the population controlling more than 50 percent of the wealth." While this sentence may be correct,[107] it is embarrassing that Faiola did not seem to know that in the United States, the richest 10 percent of the population controls more than 66 percent of the wealth.[108]

Certainly, residential exclusion is still the norm within the United States. The census took what it calls the American Housing Survey (AHS) in 1993 (and earlier years), including 680 subsamples called kernel clusters. Within these clusters, the AHS begins with one respondent and then asks the same questions of up to fifteen others in residences nearest the respondent. According to sociologist Samantha Friedman, in 1993 about 80% of all whites lived in all-white clusters.[109] The only reason this book doesn't treat 80% of American cities and towns is that larger municipalities escape getting listed because they have black neighborhoods as well as white neighborhoods. Especially in the East and Midwest, most white neighborhoods remain overwhelmingly white, but overwhelmingly black neighborhoods elsewhere in these cities deflect them from being classed as sundown. Sundown neighborhoods persist today partly because our social system, a captive of its history, still builds in residential segregation in many ways. Business principles in the three key industries related to where Americans live—development, banking, and real estate—continue to encourage the new forms of residential exclusion described above.[110]

Another Future: Decreasing Exclusion

As I took my leave of John Peters, the black retiree with whom I talked in Du Quoin in 2002, a biracial town in southern Illinois, a retired white neighbor dropped in unannounced, to chat and maybe go somewhere with Peters. After spending so many days in towns and suburbs where casual interaction simply could not take place across racial lines, I'm afraid I stared at the two of them. Racially integrated towns and neighborhoods are becoming more common and more stable, however. Soon, I believe, they will no longer be viewed as unusual. At least, I believe it when I'm in my "glass half full" frame of mind.

At the same time, many sundown towns and suburbs have not caved in. In one sundown town, the reference librarian, sympathetic to my research, warned me twice in 2002 to "be careful who you talk with." She wasn't kidding; she was concerned for me, and I am white. I also recall my last conversation in Arcola, Illinois, also in the library. I was talking with the librarian and her mother about Arcola's remarkable history of exclusion and asked if it was still a sundown town. In the 2000 census, Arcola had one household with an African American householder, a family of three, but neither woman knew of such a household. One said, and the other concurred, "There was a black family here ten or fifteen years ago, but they moved on." They didn't know if the family was forced out, but they agreed Arcola was a sundown town. Just then a young man, maybe eighteen years old, walked in. His ears perked up as soon as he heard "black family," and he stopped, shocked. "Blacks in Arcola?" he asked intently. "Where? Who?" We hastened to assure him that we were just talking about things in the past. Was he just curious? Or fixing to act? I could not tell.

Nationally, research popularized around the 50th anniversary of *Brown v. Board* in 2004 shows that many African American students attend class in metropolitan areas whose schools are now more segregated by race than they were ten or twenty years ago. Perhaps the most accurate assessment of the state of sundown towns at present would be to leave it up in the air. Everywhere I went in sundown towns and suburbs, I met some people who would like their community to move beyond its restrictive policy. On the other hand, a gap between attitudes and behavior remains. Many whites endorse the principle of desegregation while living in white areas and are privately uncomfortable with the thought of African Americans moving in. Therefore they do not act on their principles, which allows those who do—the excluders—to carry the day.[111]

Living in a place where not everyone looks alike and not everyone votes alike is surely good for the mind as well as the children. Also, since people usually defend their choice of place to live, living where not everyone looks alike pushes residents to defend living where not everyone looks alike, thus making them less racist in their attitudes. Scenes like the interracial friendship I witnessed in Du Quoin do take place all across the country, and if they don't in your neighborhood, the next chapter suggests possible steps to take. Indeed, the question before us now is: What can we do to end sundown towns and suburbs in our lifetime? What can we get our institutions to do, and what can we do ourselves?

15

The Remedy:
Integrated Neighborhoods and Towns

> And now a child
> Can understand,
> This is the law
> Of all the land,
> All the land.
> —Three Dog Night, "Black and White,"
> 1972 song about school integration

WE HAVE SEEN that sundown towns and neighborhoods have bad effects on whites, blacks, and our social system as a whole. Surely we want to stop all this. So how do we get there? How do we desegregate sundown towns and suburbs, racially and maybe even economically?

This final chapter is a call to action on four fronts: investigation, litigation, institutional policy changes, and personal choice. At the end, I add my plea for a Residents' Rights Act that could be passed by state or federal governments to make it in the interest of sundown towns to change their policies immediately. I must add that I submit these remedies humbly.[1] I am sure that lawyers, community activists, and other experts will find them wanting.

Bringing the History of Sundown Towns into the Open Is a First Step

To end our segregated neighborhoods and towns requires a leap of the imagination: Americans have to understand that white racism is still a problem in the United States. This isn't always easy. Most white Americans do not see racism as a problem in their neighborhood. We need to know about sundown towns to know what to *do* about them.

During the Nadir, and even to the 1960s in most places, sundown towns were not at all shy about their policies. Nothing could be more blatant, after all, than a sign stating "Nigger, Don't Let the Sun Go Down on You in __," or a brochure advertising "No Negroes" as a selling point of a suburban neighborhood. So it is encouraging that few sundown towns and suburbs today, even those whose sundown policies remain in force, admit that they keep out African Americans. Hypocrisy is to be encouraged as a first step toward humane behavior. When residents claim that their community is all-white by accident or blame African Americans for not moving in, at least they no longer openly brag that the town is anti-black. No longer do whites feel it is OK to advertise their racism. Since 1968, when overt discrimination became illegal, they know to keep it hidden.

On the other hand, this secrecy helps racism endure. "The truth will make us free," goes an important verse of the anthem of the Civil Rights Movement, "We Shall Overcome." Surely it is right: surely one reason we are not free of sundown towns is that the causes of residential segregation have been obscured. In 2002, the Pew Research Center surveyed attitudes about housing and race. Surprisingly, they found that only 50% of Americans "had heard that 'neighborhoods are still mostly racially segregated.' "[2] And as late as November of that year, a professor could routinely e-mail a web discussion list in history, in an attempt to begin a discussion of what he called "the problems of mandating desegregation," this assumption: "Residential segregation is the result of individual, rather than government actions." Had he known about the violent expulsions that gave rise to so many independent sundown towns, condoned by local governments, or the blatant acts of public policy (and also violent resistance) that led to sundown suburbs, he simply could not have written such a sentence.[3]

Awareness of unfairness undercuts unfairness. People who perceive that the social system discriminates against racial minorities are more likely to support policies to reduce that discrimination. Racists know this. That's why denial of racism is a time-honored tactic. During the lawsuit to integrate the University of Mississippi, the State of Mississippi actually claimed in 1962 that Ole Miss was not segregated; no African Americans "happened" to go there. Therefore the school had not rejected African American James Meredith owing to race! Amazingly, the trial judge bought this claim, but John Minor Wisdom, speaking for the Federal Court of Appeals, held it to be "nevernever land" and proclaimed, "What everybody knows the court must know." Similarly, if we wish to mobilize lawyers, judges, local institutions, and families to do something about sundown towns, we must make them realize what the residents of these towns already understand. If everyone in Anna knows that the letters of the town's name stand for "Ain't No Niggers Allowed," then "the court must know," and so must we all. These policies need to be exposed, "hidden in plain view" no longer.[4]

Concealment has been especially vital in the suburbs. The system of racial status that sundown suburbs embody needs mystification to work. Remember the paradox of exclusivity: living in an exclusive area is good, connoting positive things about one's family, but participating in exclusion is bad, connoting "lower-class" prejudices. Therefore white families achieve status by living in elite sundown suburbs only so long as the racial policy of those suburbs remains hidden. Exposing the unsavory historical roots of sundown towns and suburbs can help to decrease the status that most Americans confer upon elite white communities and undercut the policies that still keep them that way. Elite suburban racism is particularly vulnerable, because no one can defend a suburb's all-white racial composition as right without appearing "lower-class." Thus the paradox of exclusivity provides a point of leverage for opening suburban communities to African American residents.

In many communities, then, more research is the first order of the day. Indeed, in some towns, time is running out. Doing oral history on the period 1890 to 1940, the peak years for creating sundown towns, is becoming difficult, because people who came of age even toward the end of it are now nearing their 90s. Children may not learn the local history that their parents and grandparents know. At my web site are suggestions as to how to proceed. Professional historians and sociologists can do much of this research, but so can local historians, "mere" residents, even middle-school students.[5] My hope is that this beginning will inspire researchers in each state to identify more of these towns, tell how they came to be sundown, how they preserved their racial exclusivity, and hopefully how they are changing.[6] The race relations history of any neighborhood or town deserves to be investigated if its population has long been overwhelmingly white. Of course it is possible that no African Americans ever happened to go there, but it is more likely that formal or informal policies of exclusion maintained the whiteness of the place.

Most states have historical marker programs that now incorporate advisory committees, including professional historians, that must approve the text of any new marker for accuracy before it goes up. After completing the research required to convince such a panel, the next step, with the assistance of church groups, civic organizations, or the local historical society, is to propose an accurate marker telling your town's history of exclusion and offering to fund and erect it.[7] Even if opposition mobilizes to block the marker, the result-ing uproar itself will end the secrecy.

Truth and Reconciliation

Once we know what happened, we can start to reconcile. Publicizing a town's racist actions can bring shame upon the community, but recalling and ad-mitting them is the first step in redressing them. In every sundown town live potential allies—people who care about justice and welcome the truth. As a white man said in Corbin, Kentucky, on camera in 1990, "Forgetting just continues the wrong." "Recovering sundown towns" (or wider metro-politan areas or states) might set up truth and reconciliation commissions modeled after South Africa's to reveal the important historical facts that underlie their continuing whiteness, reconcile with African Americans in nearby communities, and thus set in motion a new more welcoming atmo-sphere.[8]

The next step after learning and publicizing the truth is an apology, preferably by an official of the sundown town itself. In 2003, Bob Reynolds, mayor of Harrison, Arkansas, which has been all-white ever since it drove out its African Americans in race riots in 1905 and 1909, met with other commu-nity leaders to draw up a collective statement addressing the problem. It says in part, "The perception that hangs over our city is the result of two factors: one, unique evils resulting from past events, and two, the silence of the general population toward those events of 1905 and 1909." The group, "United Christian Leaders," is trying to change Harrison, and it knows that truth is the starting place. "98 years is long enough to be silent," said Wayne Kelly, one of the group's members. George Holcomb, a retiree who is also a reporter for the *Harrison Daily Times,* supports a grand jury investigation into the race riots: "Get the records, study them, give the people an account of what happened. Who lost property, what they owned, who had it stolen from them and who ended up with it."[9]

In some towns, as Holcomb's comment implies, truth and reconciliation logically leads to reparations. This book has mentioned many towns and counties whose African American residents were driven out at gunpoint between 1890 and 1954. I spent a morning walking around the former black neighborhood in Pinckneyville, Illinois, for instance. It was a haunt-ing experience. I photographed houses, including one that formerly was the black school (Portfolio 4), and talked with residents, all of them white, of course. Today whites call the area "the Black Hills," by which they do *not* imply a similarity to a Sioux sacred site in South Dakota. In about 1928, whites drove African Americans from Pinckneyville. "They strung one black up, at the square," a cemetery worker told me as he showed me around the black section of the town cemetery, which has only two stones but perhaps twenty graves, he said.[10]

What about the home pictured in Portfolio 3, burned by whites as they drove African Americans from Pierce City, Missouri? All 200 African Americans in Pierce City ran for their lives at 2 a.m. on August 19, 1901. Almost certainly the family that owned this house got no compensation for its destruction and probably never even felt safe enough to return to try to sell the burned-out hulk and the land. Do their heirs have a claim? Virginia Yearwood grew up in one of the houses that was not destroyed. She wrote, "As a result [of the riot], a number of very nice homes with views had been standing empty for a very long time. My Uncle Emil bought one of these nice homes (nice for that time) which had been formerly occupied by blacks. . . . It must have been really tragic as all the houses were abandoned for a long time, some with belongings still in them." Did Uncle Emil pay for the home? Surely he did not pay the owners.[11]

What of the owners of the black private school in Eldorado, Illinois—Eldorado Normal and Industrial Institute—who were stoned in 1902, "and the principal, Jefferson D. Alston, his wife, and pupils were compelled to leave for fear of mob violence," in the words of the *Indianapolis Freeman?* Governor Richard Yates of Illinois said they would get protection, but that never happened, and all African Americans in Eldorado fled to nearby Metropolis to save their lives. Did they get a fair price for their property? Certainly it was a distress sale. As Gordon Morgan, whose monograph *Black Hillbillies of the Arkansas Ozarks* is the pioneering treatment of the disappearance of African Americans from that region, asked in 1973, "To what extent are those counties legally liable for allowing the forcing of blacks out, under duress, without assuring that they or their descendants were adequately compensated for loss of life, property, or opportunities?"[12]

We are not talking ancient history. In 2004, I talked with Almarion Hollingsworth, whose father, A. W. Birch, owned the hotel in Marlow, Oklahoma, a sundown town, refused to fire his black porter, and was shot by a mob that then killed the porter. She has lived 81 of her 83 years without a father. Does she have a claim? What of the porter's children? What about Cleveland Bowen, who was 3 years old when whites in Forsyth County, Georgia, "told us we had to be out by sundown," according to testimony taken in 1987, when he was 78?

We left that same night. It was kind of rainy. I slept. I was only about three years old, but everybody was so scared and everything, I remember it. We came off and left cotton and corn in the field and two mules and two cows standing in the yard. My daddy said he picked just two bales of cotton and sold 'em and the rest was left in the field. I heard my Daddy say he was just one payment from having paid for the farm. We had 40 acres. My daddy—it hurt him so bad, he cried like a whupped child. We rented a farm out here, and my daddy never did get it together to buy another farm.[13]

And what about the black children of Vienna, Illinois, driven from their homes in a firestorm in 1954 and now in their fifties? What about the lost opportunities of all the people driven out in all the expulsions described in this book—opportunities to make a living in the towns from which they were "cleansed"? Most of them were employed, after all. What about the possibilities African Americans lose out on today, growing up in central city neighborhoods surrounded by poor people and rusting factories, while whites in sundown suburbs grow up surrounded by resources and opportunities?

Legal Remedies

There are precedents for reparations. After the 1885 murder and expulsion of Chinese coal miners in Rock Springs, Wyoming, the United States paid survivors and heirs $150,000. Springfield, Illinois, did pay damages to black citizens whose property was destroyed in the 1908 riot; indeed, the city had to issue bonds to pay all the claims. More famously, the United States paid $20,000 to every Japanese American who had been placed in a concentration camp during World War II. More recently, North Carolina made modest reparations to people its Eugenics Board ordered sterilized between 1929 and 1974. On one occasion, a state paid monetary reparations to African Americans to compensate them for losing their homes and employment as the result of violent expulsion. In 1994, Florida paid nine survivors of the 1923 Rosewood massacre—in which whites destroyed an entire black town, leaving a sundown town nearby—$150,000 each. A state commission recommended that Oklahoma follow suit in 2001, to compensate survivors and heirs of blacks attacked in the 1921 riot when whites tried to make Tulsa a sundown city, killing somewhere between 30 and 300 African Americans in the process. But Oklahoma and Tulsa seem to lack the political and moral backbone to emulate Florida, even though a similar breakdown of the state and city function of maintaining order made the riot possible. Having failed to get Oklahoma to pass a reparations bill, attorneys have launched a lawsuit in federal court.[14]

Nevertheless, Rosewood remains a useful precedent for reparations, particularly since it resulted in at least one sundown town, Cedar Key. So does what happened in West Frankfort, Illinois. Whites drove Sicilians and African Americans from that southern Illinois city on August 5 and 6, 1920. Many of the Sicilians returned to live in West Frankfort within the week, but African Americans have not returned in any number to this day. Some Sicilians then brought suit for damages, and a U.S. federal court eventually awarded them more than $11,000 (the equivalent of more than $100,000 in 2005). African Americans won nothing, having no chance to obtain justice from a town that had just expelled them. According to a newspaper account, "They have sent back a representative to settle their bills and wind up all affairs of the colored race in this city."[15]

The case for reparations resulting from the many violent expulsions that led to sundown towns avoids most of the issues that are brought up by opponents of reparations for slavery. We do know or can learn who specifically was injured in each expulsion. Some victims and many heirs are still alive. Also, slavery was not illegal, while the expulsions of the Nadir were, yet federal, state, and city governments refused to provide African Americans with the equal protection of the laws guaranteed them under the Fourteenth Amendment to the Constitution. In 1863, the federal government punished the whites from Anna, Illinois, who had expelled African Americans from Union County—and that was *before* passage of the Fourteenth Amendment. But from 1890 to 1968, the federal government rarely if ever interfered with a sundown town. It showed no interest in prosecuting the whites who expelled African Americans from Anna in 1909, for example. State and local governments were often equally lax. As David Zimmermann put it, writing about the 1905 and 1909 race riots that drove African Americans from Harrison, "Diligent research has failed to reveal any records of actions taken by law enforcement officers or any other local officials to protect Harrison's African American community at any time preceding, during, or after the attacks." Thus not only the perpetrators but also local and state governments share responsibility for repairing the damages caused by the expulsions and the sundown towns that resulted.[16]

Legal actions can remedy other governmental actions and inactions that have helped sundown towns last so long. As we have seen, beginning in the 1930s, the federal government *required* neighborhoods to be all-white for participation in mortgage and housing programs, and it even built several sundown towns itself. State governments were also complicit bystanders that ignored or facilitated actions that created sundown towns and counties. Most local governments of sundown towns and counties worked actively to keep their jurisdictions all-white; some still do. Governmental complicity yesterday can provide openings for judicial intervention today. The previous chapter gave examples of lawsuits that have succeeded against sundown towns and their exclusive ways. The 1977 Seventh Circuit decision known as "Arlington Heights II" held that plaintiffs do not have to prove that town officials had a conscious intent to keep out minorities; it is enough to show that their policies had that effect. Of course, since sundown towns and suburbs have oral traditions of intent as well as effect, sound historical research can make lawsuits against them very winnable.[17]

State courts hold promise, too, because many states already have useful open housing laws on their books, some dating to the Reconstruction era.[18] The Mount Laurel judgment in New Jersey and the New Castle case in New York, as summarized by historian Kenneth Jackson, require suburbs "to accept a 'fair share' of the disadvantaged populations in their areas and to make 'an affirmative effort to provide housing for lower-income groups.' " In 1999, "an affordable housing developer" sued Bluffdale, "an all-white suburb of 4,500 people south of Salt Lake City, Utah, for what they contend is a discriminatory zoning scheme that will continue to exclude racial and ethnic minorities and people with disabilities," according to the National Low Income Housing Coalition. Apparently the plaintiff succeeded in winning new policies from Bluffdale. And in 2000, a federal district court found that Sunnyvale, Texas, a suburb of Dallas, had long engaged in what the court concluded was "discriminatory zoning."[19] The judge's opinion includes a careful and useful review of federal law in these cases and notes that "the Fair Housing Act prohibits not only direct discrimination but practices with racially discouraging effects."[20]

These decisions offer important precedents, because many sundown suburbs have used zoning, minimum lot size, and related polices to keep out African Americans. If such cases as Sunnyvale can be won without specific evidence of exclusionary practices, then testimony about these practices should make successful legal actions against sundown towns and suburbs still easier. That these practices originated decades ago does not render them moot, for once a policy is in effect, the burden shifts to the community to show that its policy has changed. Many sundown towns have done nothing to publicize or implement a new policy, which is why they continue to be all-white. Now that suburbs have become more populous and more important economically than inner cities or small towns and rural areas, it is critical that they shake off their sundown origins.

Undoing *Milliken v. Bradley*

Unfortunately, one legal decision constitutes a dangerous precedent. The previous chapter told how school desegregation decisions in southern states helped lead communities there toward residential desegregation. This same process had begun to desegregate northern metropolitan areas too, until halted by the U.S. Supreme Court in 1974. In *Milliken v. Bradley,* the Court "largely freed white suburban districts from any legal obligation to participate in metropolitan desegregation efforts," as Jack Balkin put it, writing in 2001. African Americans in Detroit had recognized that the Detroit public schools were going overwhelmingly black, so they sought desegregation with white populations in the suburbs. Of course, the white schools of Dearborn, Warren, and other suburbs did not admit to being white as a matter of law or public policy—de jure. They merely served the children who lived within their district boundaries, and those children just "happened" to be all white—de facto.[21]

The *Milliken* opinion awarded primacy to suburban school district boundaries. Supreme Court Justice Potter Stewart cast the deciding vote, denying African American students' request for integration with suburban schools. We have seen how most white Americans came to view residential segregation as natural, rather than resulting from governmental policies. Like them, Stewart claimed to be baffled about the causes of residential and school segregation:

> It is this essential fact of a predominantly Negro school population in Detroit—caused by unknown and perhaps unknowable factors such as immigration, birth rates, economic changes, or cumulative acts of private racial fears—that accounts for the "growing core of Negro schools," a "core" that has grown to include virtually the entire city.[22]

The factors behind all-white suburbs *are* knowable, of course. "Immigration, birth rates, and economic changes" do *not* explain why thousands of workers built cars in Dearborn and Warren, but the black ones all lived in Detroit or Inkster while the white ones lived where they worked. "Private racial fears" do play a role, but not merely because they motivate thousands of private decisions by individual white and black families. These private racial fears result in part from a panoply of private *and public* policies that have been responsible for making and keeping suburbs white. Indeed, sundown towns show that no clear distinction can be maintained between de jure and de facto segregation. For decades, as we have seen, government officials were decisively involved in keeping Dearborn white, for example. Previous chapters told of the repeated attempts by African Americans to live in Wyandotte and the repeated private acts of violence by Wyandotte residents and formal acts by its city government to keep them out. A similar list of violent and nonviolent actions performed or condoned by city governments has interfered with the free choices of African Americans to live in Grosse Ile, Grosse Pointe, and other suburbs in the Detroit area. When the perpetrators of violence go unpunished, the government is again involved, albeit one step removed from the actual acts against black would-be residents.

Evidently little of this information about Detroit's sundown suburbs—including the explicit actions over the years taken by their governments to stay all-white—was considered by the Supreme Court.[23] In the absence of this information, five of the nine justices held, as Potter Stewart put it, "the mere fact of different racial compositions in contiguous districts does not itself imply or constitute a violation." Therefore they said that residential segregation was not open to remedy by litigation. In turn, school segregation resulting from residential segregation was also not open to remedy. Absurdly, so long as a sundown suburb avoided segregating its handful of black students into a majority-black school, the judges held that it was operating lawfully. Thus because Dearborn, Grosse Ile, the Grosse Pointes, Warren, Wyandotte, and others had been so racist as to exclude African Americans almost totally, in 1974 their school systems were declared not racially segregated.

Looking back three decades later, the importance of *Milliken* is obvious. This ruling largely ended the efforts of federal courts to desegregate school systems in the North, following the promise of *Brown*. Today we can see that not only was this decision bad sociology, it also amounted to a tragedy for Detroit and the nation. In effect, it told whites that if they didn't want to live in a majority-black neighborhood, have their children attend an overwhelmingly black school, and suffer the lower prestige and other disadvantages that such schools and neighborhoods entail, they had better move to a sundown suburb. At the same time, the decision signaled suburbs that they could continue to be all-white, so long as they did not openly say they were. The consequences were further white abandonment of Detroit (and some other central cities), continued resistance to African American newcomers in the suburbs, and further mystification of the sundown process.[24]

In *Milliken,* the majority stated, "It must first be shown that there has been a constitutional violation within one district that produces a significant segregative effect in another district."[25] Perhaps a new case can be brought against those Detroit suburbs that remain overwhelmingly white today, fully revealing the links between past public policies in sundown suburbs and residential segregation, and then making the obvious connection between that residential segregation and today's overwhelmingly black schools in Detroit.[26]

Local Institutions Can End Sundown Towns

Litigation is not the only avenue to change racist policies. People connected with institutions—governments, corporations, school systems—can get them to act to undo sundown towns. Here are some specific steps, starting with the gentlest and moving to the harshest. Every sundown town or county should announce officially that it intends to become more diverse and should set up a human relations commission to accomplish that end. The town should then send a letter to every real estate agent in its area informing them that housing in the town is open without regard to race, requiring them to state their intent to show, rent, and sell property to all, and inviting them to contact the human relations commission in case of any problem. Schools and city departments should also state their intent to welcome and hire nonwhite employees to overcome their town's history of exclusion and should drop any requirement that prospective employees must live within their boundaries before employment.[27] As with historical markers, if a jurisdiction refused a request from citizens to do or say these things, the resulting publicity would be valuable in itself.

Of course, talk is cheap. Many sundown towns have already subscribed to anti-discrimination statements and keep on discriminating.[28] Nevertheless, such statements are a first step. Moreover, the presence of a human relations commission counterbalances the "bad apples" that otherwise can seem to speak for a sundown town while the majority does nothing. It sends a signal that some whites, at least, will oppose acts of hostility toward a black would-be resident, and it provides people of color with a place to report threats or other problems.[29]

Fayetteville and Jacksonville, North Carolina, which are among the least segregated cities in the United States, show what leaders of local institutions can do—in this case the local commanders of the United States armed forces. Fayetteville is near Fort Bragg. After the 1964 Civil Rights Act pointed the way, Army leadership helped open Fayetteville's golf courses, bars, and other public facilities. Camp Lejeune, a Marine Corps base, made a similar difference in Jacksonville.[30] Because the armed forces realizes that its men and women live or spend time in nearby communities, for decades it has made relationships with nearby communities, including race relations, part of the evaluation process for base commanders. To be sure, some commanders treat this requirement merely as a bureaucratic nuisance. Nevertheless, it helps, and every government agency—state and federal—needs to make these concerns part of the job definitions of those who run its local offices. After all, government offices and agencies exist in almost every sundown town. Imagine what might happen if each of them tried seriously to end their town's exclusionary policies![31]

Governments in metropolitan areas or state governments can also equalize the amount of money spent on students in different school districts, so students enjoy something approaching equal educational opportunity. In most states, the way we pay for public K–12 education, as well as other local public services, pits suburb against suburb across a metropolitan area. This competition makes it in no suburb's interest to provide or even allow affordable housing. Equalizing tax dollars across the state or across municipalities in a metropolitan area solves this problem.[32] Although elite sundown suburbs often oppose such tax equity, courts have found unequal property-tax-based school finance systems unconstitutional in twenty-one states, and other states have taken steps toward more equality without the spur of lawsuits. Whites move to sundown suburbs for four main reasons: to achieve status, avoid African Americans, enjoy amenities such as better parks and nicer neighborhoods, and provide better schools for their children—and not necessarily in that order. Fiscal equalizing can remove the last two as incentives luring whites to move to white suburbs.[33]

Schools can adopt other policies that promote school and neighborhood integration. In some districts—Denver and Louisville, for example—previously all-white or all-black neighborhoods can get neighborhood schools back, with no busing, if they desegregate residentially. This provides an incentive for residents of sundown neighborhoods to let African Americans move in, so their own children won't have to be bused out. Some school systems, including Wake County, North Carolina (Raleigh), and LaCrosse, Wisconsin, take care to make each of their schools diverse in social class, as well as race.[34]

School districts can also take steps to end "test flight." In today's metropolitan real estate markets, lofty school test scores have become a sought-after commodity. One reason why parents move to the suburbs is to get good schools, and an easy—if shallow—way to compare schools is by standardized test scores. In Massachusetts, for example, according to a 2000 report, "school districts that score badly on the MCAS [that state's standardized test] are likely to have houses for sale as parents try to move their kids to schools with better scores." The trouble is, high scores on standardized tests correlate with race (white and Asian) and class (affluent) at least as well as with good teaching. Elsewhere I have presented some of the reasons why African Americans, Native Americans, and Hispanics score lower on these tests.[35] Given these gaps, it is in suburbs' interest to keep out these groups so their schools will look better as measured by the test scores, so their homes will be worth more.[36]

School districts should disaggregate scores by race, income category, and academic program. Disaggregating allows everyone to face the statistics openly. Many white parents will not move into a school district that they think will disadvantage their children. Yet white students in an interracial district may score as well as white students in an elite sundown suburb, so they are *not* being disadvantaged—but that fact cannot be inferred from overall school means that include black students.[37] Similarly, college-oriented parents will not move into a school district if they think its students are likely to score poorly on college entrance exams. Yet some economically diverse high schools prepare their college-bound students at least as well as elite sundown high schools, where almost everyone is college-bound, but their success cannot be inferred from overall school averages that include non-college-bound students.[38]

Institutions of higher learning can also help to desegregate sundown towns and suburbs by admitting students without giving so much credit to the stacked deck that elite suburbs provide. This means jettisoning standardized tests such as the SAT and ACT or factoring into account their built-in racial and class biases, as well as the various aids that elite suburban children use to score higher on them.[39] It also means returning to straight high school grade-point averages rather than something called "uncapped GPAs," which artificially raise the grades students get when they take advanced placement (AP) courses. Enhancing grades in AP courses results in striking geographic unfairness: the *average* uncapped GPA for suburban students admitted to the University of California at Berkeley in 1999 was at least 4.33, for example, when an A equals 4.0. Meanwhile, the valedictorian of an inner-city high school with a straight A average but no AP courses earned "only" a 4.0 and was not even competitive—and all because of where the student lived.[40]

Corporations can also do much to undo sundown towns and suburbs. Many companies are already becoming good citizens regarding race relations. Some got the message the hard way, after bad racial practices brought them notoriety. Once a company has been doing a good job hiring and promoting people of color, it naturally becomes more concerned about the race relations of the communities where it is located. Now it has African American managers who want to live in hospitable and pleasant towns, and white executives who want to keep those managers happy. The Quaker Oats Company required Danville, in central Illinois, to pass an open-housing ordinance as a condition of locating a plant there, for example, and Danville isn't even a sundown town; we can infer that Quaker Oats would never locate in a town that it knew excluded blacks. And not just Quaker; Earl Woodard, executive director of the Chamber of Commerce in Martinsville, Indiana, notorious for its sundown policy, complained in 1989 that owing to "its bad image," Martinsville "hasn't nabbed a single one" of the industrial facilities that "rained down on central Indiana" in the 1980s.[41]

White Families Can Dismantle Sundown Towns

Those of us not a part of any large corporation or other institution and without much governmental influence—what can we do? Surely every American has a stake in remedying sundown towns and suburbs. White people created sundown towns, and whites—and "others"—can dismantle them.

People who live in an overwhelmingly white community can move. After they realize that choices by white families to live in white neighborhoods aggregate to form a social problem that then affects an entire metropolitan area, some whites refuse to live in a place that is part of the problem rather than part of the solution.[42] When they move to an interracial neighborhood, often they help it get better schools, parks, and all the other accoutrements that make a successful community.

Moving into an interracial or majority-black community can seem intimidating for whites from sundown towns who have never known African American friends and neighbors. It needn't be. Sociologist Karyn Lucy found the best race relations in majority-black suburbs. Whites who moved into these suburbs after they were already substantially black "get along [particularly] well with their neighbors and are involved in neighborhood activities." My experience confirms her findings.[43] Whites do not have to be so bold as to move to predominantly black neighborhoods, however. Almost every metropolitan area contains at least one majority-white suburb that is struggling to stay interracial against the pressures deriving from sundown suburbs. Moving there not only provides such suburbs with incoming white families that help them stay integrated, it can also deter white flight by families who already live there.[44]

People who don't live in sundown neighborhoods can challenge the "paradox of exclusivity" described in Chapter 11. Asking "Why?" with quiet astonishment when acquaintances announce that they are thinking of moving to a town or suburb known to be overwhelmingly white invites people to explain their decision—suddenly no longer obvious—to live in such places and may make them think. So do questions such as "But don't you hate to send your children to such an overwhelmingly white school system?" put to residents of such towns. Such conversations begin to reverse the status hierarchy that confers prestige on residents of all-white or overwhelmingly white communities, in turn, decreasing their hold on the popular definition of "the nice part of town." This challenging of racial exclusion is beginning to happen: as early as 1992, the authors of *Detroit Divided* noticed that some whites in the Detroit area rated Dearborn—renowned for its sundown policies—undesirable because they did not want racist neighbors. Suddenly where one is "supposed to" live isn't so clear. Decreasing the prestige of all-white neighborhoods and towns helps all parts of the metropolitan area become more open and attractive to all races and social classes.[45]

Whites who don't want to move from their overwhelmingly white communities can instead move their towns toward diversity and justice. White residents can persuade their school system that it cannot be competent without a seriously interracial faculty. Nor can a police department be fair—or perceived as fair—while being all-white. They can persuade their zoning board that these new teachers, police officers, etc., need to be able to live in the community where they teach, so affordable housing must become a priority. They can represent the excluded, who by definition cannot represent themselves because they have been kept out. They can even bring them in: in 1969, residents of Valparaiso, in northern Indiana, brought families from Chicago public housing projects to new homes in Valparaiso. The residents made the mistake of revealing their plan before finalizing their first home purchase, and a white supremacist stepped in to buy the house at a higher price. Eventually, however, they relocated Barbara Frazier-Cotton and her children, and later another family, to Valparaiso. At first, telephoned threats and cars slowly driving by were terrifying. Frazier-Cotton tells of "sleeping with the lights and

television on to dissuade would-be intruders." Valparaiso University students
set up patrols outside the house at night, and white couples sometimes slept in
the home to provide support. Despite the opposition, Frazier-Cotton stuck it
out for ten years, during which she earned a bachelor's degree from Valparaiso and her six children got a start that helped each of them build middle-
class careers. Valparaiso was a tough case. If a few white liberals could crack it
in the 1970s, surely most sundown towns and suburbs can be overcome
today.[46]

Sometimes old-fashioned protests help. Demonstrators, mostly from Atlanta and mostly African American, marched in Forsyth County, Georgia, in
early 1987, continuing into the 1990s. Five residents of Forsyth County
marched with the group on the first day, and more thereafter. Racist groups
such as Richard Barrett's Nationalist Movement held counterdemonstra-
tions, not understanding that *all* publicity about sundown behavior helps
bring about change. Oprah Winfrey gave coverage to the issue on two occasions. By the late 1990s, Forsyth County had several hundred black residents,
while sundown counties to its north,[47] such as Towns County, without the
benefit of demonstrations or publicity, did not.[48]

White families have standing to bring cases on their own behalf against realtors, city officials, and others responsible for their town's all-white makeup.
Quoting Justice William O. Douglas for a unanimous Supreme Court in *Trafficante v. Met Life et al.,* tenants in a California apartment house whose manager kept out African Americans "had lost the social benefits of living in an
integrated community; . . . [and] had suffered embarrassment and economic
damage in social, business, and professional activities from being 'stigmatized' as residents of a 'white ghetto.' " This 1972 case and others decided
more recently provide useful precedents for white families to act to force sundown towns to reverse course and announce that they have done so.[49]

African American Challenges to Sundown Towns

Even well-meaning whites cannot desegregate a sundown town without the
help of black households. This book hopes to spur action to end sundown
towns, suburbs, and neighborhoods, and some of that action can be taken
only by African Americans. I believe a black family, backed by an alert civil
rights attorney if necessary, can now buy a home in most of America's persisting sundown towns. Some towns would still meet them with a freeze-out or violence, but black families have increasingly found welcoming neighbors.

Admittedly, moving into a sundown town differs from any other civil rights action. Unlike the marcher or sit-in participant of years past, the black family moving into a sundown town eats and sleeps on the picket line, and risks all its members, including babies, toddlers, and elderly. "There is a terrible isolation that surrounds the lone black family in a hostile white neighborhood," pointed out Dorothy Newman, an expert on segregated housing, in the 1970s. Even today, for African Americans to move into a town that has not had any African Americans for decades violates the norm, and sociologists know that norm violators usually get sanctioned. So blacks are right to be cautious. Families do not seek to be pioneers in civil rights; they simply want a nice place to live. Even absent any hostility from whites, there are logistical problems in moving to a sundown town: "Where can we go to get our hair styled? Where will we go to church? Will we find friends?" An African American who lives in Peoria suggested a major reason why black families don't desegregate the many sundown towns and suburbs around that city: "Black kids raise a fit about being the only black kids in the high school."[50]

African Americans have a legacy of heroes who have gone before to inspire them. One I knew personally: Medgar Evers, selfless leader of the Mississippi Civil Rights Movement. Evers's vision of the America of the future did not encompass allowing sundown suburbs to remain all-white. In her memoir of him, his widow, Myrlie, makes this clear:

> One of Medgar's greatest pleasures during those summers in Chicago was the chance to explore the suburbs. Whenever he could, he would borrow a car and drive out of the city to wander up one street and down another looking at houses. He had a dream of the sort of house he hoped someday to live in, the kind of street and neighborhood and town where he might raise a family, and the white suburbs of Chicago seemed to him right out of that dream. He would spend whole days just driving slowly through the suburbs of Chicago's North Shore, looking at the beautiful houses and wishing. Years later, when we were in Chicago together, he took me on these drives and by that time he had picked out specific houses that came closest to his dream.

One of the suburbs Evers drove through four decades ago was Kenilworth. Although one black family did live there in the 1960s and '70s, today Kenilworth still awaits its pioneer. So do many others.[51]

Black efforts *have* changed sundown towns. In town after town, African Americans have braved appalling conditions, sometimes bringing along friends and family members for backup, usually persevering in the long run and winning the right to live in the former sundown town in peace. Sociologist

George Henderson became the first black homeowner in Norman, Oklahoma, when he joined the faculty of the University of Oklahoma in 1967. In his memoirs, Henderson wrote, "Garbage was thrown on our lawn, a couple of car windows were broken, and we received obscene phone calls." In an interview with the student newspaper 35 years later, he recalled, "I feared for my family, but I was willing to die trying to make a difference. I had to come to terms with the fact I might be killed, but I believe that anything worth living for should be worth dying for." Henderson's fears were not exaggerated, for residents of Norman had engaged in repeated acts of real or threatened violence toward African Americans over the years. Indeed, historian Bill Savage, who came to the University of Oklahoma the year before Henderson, was shown a big tree on a hill in Norman by a man who said his father took him there just ten years earlier, in 1957 or '58, and pointed to a black man hanging from it, "the last black man to violate the sundown rule in Norman." [52]

Sundown suburbs can be equally threatening. In 1957, William and Daisy Myers were the first African Americans to move into Levittown, Pennsylvania, built as a sundown suburb after World War II. They faced telephoned death threats, a mob milling across the street, and burning crosses on neighboring lawns. Daisy Myers, wife and mother of the family, kept a journal during the ordeal. She makes vivid the possible costs they anticipated:

> We thought we should take the three children to York, Pennsylvania [to stay with their grandparents], but because Lynda was so young we decided to keep her with us. I felt that she would be too much of a burden on Bill's family, with a formula to prepare and the other attention an infant requires. I remember saying to Bill that if we were killed in the house, Lynda would be too young to know. At least we would have the boys to carry on. [53]

Despite the initial tension, usually the enterprise ends happily. A lawyer who left the black ghetto of San Francisco for a white neighborhood was struck "that for the first time I was friendly with my immediate neighbors. They have the same interests we do." In his 1970 book about housing desegregation, James Hecht summarized, "When a Negro family moves into a white area there are problems which few whites appreciate, but these problems usually are far less than the blacks anticipated." He traced records of some 500 black families who had moved into previously all-white neighborhoods in the Buffalo, New York, area since 1964. "None are known to have moved back to the ghetto," he reported. "About fifty of these families, including most of those who experienced unpleasant incidents, were interviewed in

some depth. All were glad they had made the move. All would do it again."
Hecht was able to generalize these results beyond Buffalo:

> Most of the families who moved found something else they had not anticipated,
> a warm welcome by some of their new neighbors. Fair housing groups through-
> out the nation report that black families moving into white neighborhoods usu-
> ally had more friendly calls of welcome than did white families who moved into
> the same neighborhoods.

The Gautreaux program in Chicago likewise proves that whites *do* accept
African American neighbors, even low-income ones.[54]

Victor Ward started the process of change in Cherokee, Oklahoma, during the summer of 1977. A young petroleum engineer newly minted by Mari-
etta College in Ohio, Ward landed a job with Conoco, and they assigned him
to Cherokee. "I arrived at the beginning of the summer and started to look for
a place to live. I started with my work associates, and then asked around. And
they sent me from one person to the next and I got 'No, that's not available,'
and 'Sorry, that's been rented.' " Ward ended up "in a shack, really, at the edge
of town, didn't even have electricity." Then he got a breakthrough: a woman
who had earlier turned him down phoned him at the Conoco office. She said
she had talked with her pastor about it. Ward repeated her words to him: "I'm
thinking, if I'd sent my son to some other town, I would hope they wouldn't
treat him the way the people of Cherokee have treated you." So she rented to
Ward, who became the first African American to live in previously sundown
Cherokee, at least the first in decades. His co-workers socialized with him
after work and invited him to their homes, and he had a fine summer. That he
came in under the aegis of Conoco surely helped, but so did Ward's positive
outlook. "I think at the end of the day, I kind of won the town." The census
showed Cherokee with no African Americans in 1950, 1960, and 1970, but
five in 1980, after Ward's breakthrough. Cherokee may need another Ward,
however, because in 1990 it was back to its former all-white status, and in
2000 it had but two African Americans, and no black households.[55]

Often blacks do "win the town." Henderson is now a treasured senior
member of the faculty and community in Norman. Although it took decades,
Levittown now honors the Myerses: in December 1999, Bristol Township
mayor Sam Fenton invited Daisy Myers to Levittown (her husband had died
in 1987) and offered her a public apology. Levittown named a blue spruce tree
in front of the municipal building "Miss Daisy" and uses it as the township

Christmas tree. There can be no doubt that white residents now fully accept the right of African Americans to live in both Norman and Levittown.[56]

Sometimes it takes two attempts. After the first family is forced out from a town, the racists who rebuffed them may be surprised to receive mixed messages, even condemnation, from other residents, so they don't mount another attack when another family tries, a year or so later.

Passing a Residents' Rights Act

All the solutions suggested thus far may not suffice to remedy the tougher cases, whether these turn out to be independent towns like Anna or elite suburbs like Kenilworth. Indeed, the remedies America has tried thus far are reminiscent of the "freedom of choice" phase of school desegregation (1955–69). Just as policies in that discredited era placed the burden of desegregating our nation's schools on individual black children, so our attempts at desegregating our nation's neighborhoods have placed the burden on individual black families. But our nation has a *national interest* in desegregating white communities.

What is needed is a law—a Residents' Rights Act—that makes it in an entire town's interest to welcome African Americans. This proposed remedy embodies the conclusion reached by Zane Miller, who wrote a history of Forest Park, Ohio, established as a sundown suburb of Cincinnati in the 1950s. He noted that African Americans first began to move into Forest Park during 1967, and by 1970, 470 lived in "larger Forest Park." This was more than enough to make Forest Park a frontline suburb, and by 2000 its population was 56% black. Miller understood the key role played by Cincinnati's all-white suburbs in Forest Park's transformation and realized that the only way to achieve stable racial desegregation in metropolitan areas is by attacking sundown suburbs.

> What Forest Park . . . needed was a national and metropolitan policy which would . . . open up the wedges of overwhelmingly white suburbs on the metropolitan area's western and eastern flanks. . . . Until that happened, the pattern of metropolitan ghettoization within scattered political jurisdictions would persist.[57]

Sociologist Herbert Gans, who studied New Jersey's Levittown (now called Willingboro), came up with a similar recommendation: "If all communities must integrate, no one can expect to live in all-white communities." So did William Levitt himself, whose company built more sundown suburbs than any other. Levitt knew that sundown suburbs were bad for America. Nevertheless, he continued to build them. "Only when all builders are forced to sell on a fair basis, he reasoned, would any of them be able to 'afford' an end to discrimination," according to housing expert Dorothy Newman. Otherwise, if Levitt didn't keep African Americans out, he'd be the only developer that didn't, so all the blacks would flood into his towns. When members of CORE demonstrated at his sundown development in Belair, Maryland, Levitt called on President John F. Kennedy to put some real teeth into his ineffectual order opposing discrimination in housing, to force all suburbs to end discrimination. Kennedy did not respond, and Levitt took no steps on his own to desegregate the communities he built.[58]

Ironically, the evolution of Levitt's development in New Jersey shows that Levitt had a point. The three Levittowns developed very differently. The first black family moved into Levittown, Pennsylvania, in 1957; the town wasn't very welcoming and by 2000 was still only 2.4% black. "Not a single one of the Long Island Levittown's 82,000 residents was black" in 1960, according to Kenneth Jackson, and by 2000 only 266 were, just 0.5% of 53,067 residents, a clear reflection of its racist heritage. The third Levittown, now Willingboro, New Jersey, had a very different history. In 1958, William Levitt announced that he would not sell any of its homes to African Americans. New Jersey's governor ordered an investigation; U.S. Senator Clifford Case requested that the FHA refuse to insure mortgages in Levittown; and two African Americans who were turned away from the development sued Levitt in state court. Levitt took the case to the New Jersey Supreme Court, claiming his houses were a private matter, but the court held that the involvement of the FHA and other agencies made them publicly assisted, and Levitt was forced to desegregate Willingboro. Eventually, agents began to steer African Americans *toward* Willingboro, which by 1980 was 38% black. Willingboro residents struggled to stay interracial in the midst of overwhelmingly white competitors; one step was to ban "For Sale" signs, to slow white flight. But the U.S. Supreme Court struck down the ban, finding that the town failed to establish that it was necessary to maintain integration. In 2000, Willingboro does remain integrated, being 61% black, but some commentators dismiss it as "black" or "80% black," which may be a self-fulfilling description. Thus Willingboro may wind up proving Levitt's (and Gans's and Miller's) larger contention: that it is hard for one suburb to stay interracial while others stay all-white. Willingboro also shows that government action—in this case by a governor, senator, and court—is the surest way to cause change.[59]

To be effective, a law must be written to preclude a town from merely *claiming* that it welcomes all newcomers without regard to race. After all, since 1968, towns don't admit they are all-white on purpose, realtors don't admit they steer, bankers don't admit they redline, police deny racial profiling, and in many places, neighbors deny they threaten or shun. Proving that officials of a town or suburb keep out African American residents today can thus be difficult, just as in the early 1960s no southern registrar would admit that would-be voters had to be white to register, even though their majority-black county might have thousands of white and only a handful of black registered voters. Therefore I suggest a Residents' Rights Act parallel to the registration clause of the Voting Rights Act of 1965 (extended and strengthened in 1982). This law provides that in counties with an unusual disparity between the percentage of the black and white electorates registered to vote, the Department of Justice can send in federal examiners, once complaints have been received from ten individuals who were rebuffed when trying to register. Similarly, a blatant disparity between the percentage of a town's population that is African American compared to the proportion in the metropolitan area (the entire state for independent sundown towns) will trigger sanctions under the Residents' Rights Act[60]—*when coupled with at least two valid complaints from families who were rebuffed when trying to buy or rent a home in the community and a careful showing that it was a sundown town.*[61] Proving that a community was a sundown town is doable if it was one, even if gathering candid admissions of continuing discriminatory behavior in the present is not. Because sundown policies are typically self-maintaining, it is appropriate to shift the burden to the community to show that it has changed them.

The Residents' Rights Act in Operation

Congress or a state could pass a Residents' Rights Act.[62] If Congress acted, the required complaints would go to the Department of Housing and Urban Development, which would have the power to hear complaints of recent discrimination and collect evidence on whether the town has a sundown past. The first consequence for towns that trigger the Residents' Rights Act will be federal housing examiners, parallel to the elections examiners of the Voting Rights Act. These examiners will investigate complaints, provide community relations services to the town, and meet with town officials, real estate agents, schools, and representatives of churches and other organizations to try to create an atmosphere more hospitable to African Americans or others claiming to have been excluded. The examiners can require local officials to proclaim that their town is open to all, set up a human relations commission, and order all real estate agents licensed to sell property in the town to state their intent to show, rent, and sell property without regard to race. The examiners will also be empowered to sit in on meetings between agents and African American would-be renters or purchasers.

Real estate agents may not be the problem, or at least not the whole problem, so housing examiners may not lead to real progress. In that event, the examiners will have the power to penalize the town. What sanctions are appropriate? Everyone from city officials to bankers to police to nearby neighbors may play a role in making it hard for African Americans to move to sundown towns and suburbs. So sanctions must make it in all these actors' interest to open up. The Clean Air Act offers a useful parallel. Under its provisions, if a city's air quality falls below a certain minimum, no more tax dollars can be spent on highways and development until it cleans up its air. Similarly, under the Residents' Rights Act, no more tax dollars can be spent on discretionary programs in a sundown town or suburb until it cleans up its segregation. Tax money that assists innocent people, such as for disaster relief, aid to disabled children, and the like, will still flow. Ongoing expenditures will not be affected. But the town will be shut out from seeking new funds for sewage facilities, police training, and 1,001 other programs. After all, every dollar of federal or state tax money spent in a sundown community is a dollar spent only on white Americans, yet collected from all Americans.

There are precedents for this. In 1947, under the auspices of the American Heritage Foundation, the United States government and America's railroads sent a "Freedom Train" around the country, carrying original copies of the Declaration of Independence and other important documents. This joint public-private venture proved very successful, drawing some 3,500,000 visitors in 322 cities. Columnist Drew Pearson helped instigate the effort. When Pearson learned that the train was scheduled to stop at Glendale, California, knowing that Glendale was a sundown town, "on his national radio broadcast he stated that the train would not stop in Glendale because Negroes could not stay there after dark," according to Bob Johnson, who remembers the broadcast.[63] The train also bypassed Birmingham, Alabama, after city officials there refused to let African Americans visit it except during hours specifically set aside for them. Langston Hughes wrote a poem about the Freedom Train, including the line "Everybody's got a right to board the Freedom Train." In its refusal to visit segregated Birmingham and sundown Glendale, the Freedom Train indeed lived up to its name.[64]

The chief federal judge for southern Illinois wants to deny Benton federal tax dollars today because it is a sundown town. His district, the Southern District of Illinois, epitomizes the sundown problem in America. The United States District Court holds court in two cities there: East St. Louis, 97.7% black, and Benton, 99.5% white. Judge G. Patrick Murphy is trying to keep a new $70,000,000 federal courthouse from being built in Benton. "I think it is fundamentally wrong to send the resources of the federal government, particularly in regard to the court system, to a community that is not diverse and is not enthusiastic about letting our employees participate fully in community life," said Murphy in October 2002. The mayor of Benton, Patricia Bauer, made her position clear: "We are a very small community, and I don't apologize[65] for Benton's racial makeup." [66]

Murphy is not the only official concerned about sundown towns. An attorney in Monticello, Illinois, said that his central Illinois sundown town had similar "trouble getting federal funding" for a county courthouse project, because they had no nonwhite workers. In 1982, a class action lawsuit filed on behalf of African Americans alleged widespread deliberate housing discrimination throughout East Texas. In response to the complaint, U.S. District Court judge William Wayne Justice ordered desegregation of public housing in towns throughout East Texas. Several, including Vidor and Alba, were sundown towns, so of course their public housing projects were all-white; *every* public expenditure in those towns was reserved for whites. In 1992, Vidor gained national notoriety when several black households moved into a public housing project, became the town's first African American residents, and were all driven out by Ku Klux Klan demonstrations, racial slurs, and threats.[67]

Making sundown towns ineligible for federal or state funds may not suffice, especially in affluent communities. Some school districts and institutions of higher education similarly turned their back on funds for education, loans for dormitories, and the like, choosing to stay segregated. If needed, a simpler sanction will come into play, making use of the income tax code: denial of the federal home mortgage interest deduction. This deduction has long been one of the important ways our tax code favors middle- and higher-income Americans, allowing homeowners to deduct the largest single component of their housing outlay, while renters get no such break. The rationale for this deduction is our national interest in encouraging home ownership. Surely America has no national interest in encouraging home ownership in sundown towns, however. So it should grant no exemption for mortgage interest payments by homeowners who choose to live in such communities.[68]

Denial of the mortgage interest exemption has additional benefits that should make it attractive to lawmakers. It costs nothing and commits the federal government to no massive new program of housing construction; on the contrary, it brings in revenue. Second, we have seen that because all-white suburbs have more prestige, typically they enjoy higher housing values.[69] Removal of the interest exemption will make such property less valuable, offsetting this gain from sundown policies.[70] Third, it allows for local control. A sundown town or suburb can opt to stay all-white. Alternatively, it can desegregate any way it wants, from developing low-cost housing to recruiting African American families to buy existing homes. Best of all, eliminating the mortgage interest exemption avoids problematizing "the poor black family," for whom perpetual government assistance seems required. Instead, the Residents' Rights Act recognizes segregated white communities as the problem and makes it in their residents' interest to stop their problematic behavior.

Indeed, all a town has to do to end or avoid these sanctions is to publicize that it is now open to all, take the steps suggested by federal housing examiners, and admit a few African American residents. As soon as its population no longer displays the blatant racial disparity that triggered suspicion in the first place, it will be off the list. For example, Grosse Pointe will need to become about 2.3% black, 1.5% higher than its 2000 proportion, 0.8%. Since it had 5,670 people in 2000, this requires it to welcome 85 more African Americans—an easy task, since neighboring Detroit has 775,000 African Americans and is more than 82% black. Independent sundown towns such as Arcola might find it harder. Arcola would need about 38 more African Americans to reach 1.54% black, one-tenth as black as Illinois statewide. It could (and should) recruit them, perhaps from larger nearby towns such as Decatur and Champaign—after all, it now draws white flight from those towns. If it finds this problematic, then after recruiting two or three families, thus moving beyond the sundown town threshold, it could ask the examiners to be removed from the sanction list, so long as they concur that the town has ended its discriminatory practices. The Residents' Rights Act requires not integration but an end to exclusion. It merely uses demography as evidence that exclusion has ceased. Recovering sundown towns can submit other evidence showing they have ended their restrictive policies and thus avoid any penalty.

At present, instead of penalizing sundown towns, governments reward them. For the last quarter of the twentieth century, sundown towns in southern Illinois, for example, got *more* than their share of federal expenditures. During that era, Kenneth Gray, representative in Congress for the region, earned the nickname "Prince of Pork" for all the federal money he brought to his hometown, West Frankfort, all-white since it drove out its African Americans in 1920, and to nearby sundown towns. Independent sundown towns often languish economically: their leaders don't seek new ideas or new companies, so employment plummets. Instead of withdrawing state and federal aid from these towns, governments award them prisons and juvenile detention centers to give their economies a boost. To penologists, places such as Chehalis, Washington; Clarinda, Iowa; Izard County, Arkansas; Pollock, Louisiana; Brown County, Dwight, Pinckneyville, Vandalia, Vienna, and other locations in Illinois; Perry County, Indiana; Wayne County and various other white valleys in Pennsylvania; the Adirondack counties of New York; Garrett County, Maryland; and other places with overwhelmingly white populations[71] seem to be ideal. In a circular process, prisons then put more people into sparsely settled, overwhelmingly white districts—people who cannot vote—magnifying the clout of their representatives in state legislatures.[72]

Governments also often honor sundown towns. At their city limits, sometimes right where the infamous sundown signs used to be, now stand congratulatory signs toasting the towns with such designations as "Governor's Hometown Award," "Illinois Main Street Community," "Illinois Certified City," "Michigan Educational Excellence Award," "U.S. Dept. of Education Exemplary School," and the like. Surely no sundown town deserves these awards. The Illinois Main Street program, for example, run by the lieutenant governor's office, has to do mostly with revitalizing downtowns. Among its guidelines are "Demonstrate broad-based private- and public-sector support for downtown revitalization" and "Develop vision and mission statements." Surely "broad-based support" should include support from people other than whites. Surely a town should have a vision of itself as a multiracial community, moved beyond its petty prejudices. Surely Main Streets that a state recognizes as exemplary should be streets that people of color can feel comfortable strolling down. Owosso, Michigan, won the 2000 Michigan Educational Excellence Award, but Owosso High School cannot help but impart racism, along with chemistry, algebra, and its other subjects, owing to its historically intentional racial makeup. Mariemont, Ohio, boasts a plaque saying "U.S. Dept. of Education Exemplary School," but an all-white school can hardly be exemplary. Surely citizens should demand that civic and educational competitions like these establish standards of racial tolerance that communities must meet before they can receive these awards.

Integrated Neighborhoods and Towns Are Possible

The Residents' Rights Act would have aided integration in Southfield, Michigan, which, according to *Detroit Divided,* had "the distinction of being the only prosperous Detroit suburb with a large and growing black population: 29% in 1990." Precisely because it had this "distinction," by 2000 Southfield was 56% black. In the absence of policies that would open up overwhelmingly white suburbs, towns such as Southfield are likely to become overwhelmingly nonwhite.[73]

The recent past offers hope for an end to racial exclusion, however. The previous chapter showed that at least half of our sundown towns and suburbs have probably given way. Surely we can desegregate the last half. Some tough towns have cracked. Residents of Valley Stream on Long Island intimidated realtors and black clients in the 1980s. Nevertheless, by 1990, it had 149 African Americans among its 33,946 residents, and in 2000, 2,714 African Americans called Valley Stream home. Even Martinsville, Indiana, whose sundown notoriety was confirmed by new episodes of hateful behavior in the 1990s, may have given in. The 2000 census showed two African American households, and reports indicate that one or two other families have since moved in.

Entire suburbs have resisted "tipping point" theory, which predicts that once African Americans reach a certain proportion—often said to be 15%— whites will flee. Park Forest, Illinois, shows how. Its leaders made a conscious decision to stop being a sundown town in 1961. Ted Hipple, who lived in Park Forest at the time, described the process:

> Blacks were moving from Chicago to the suburbs, and some looked at housing in Park Forest. Leo [Jacobson] and others in the government, to avoid any possible clustering of the black families and any resulting blockbusting consequences, were instrumental in allocating them to various parts of town, well separated from each other, with prior notification of the neighbors that a black family would be moving in.

As of 2000, Park Forest was still stably integrated, with 9,247 African Americans in a total population of 23,462. Another Chicago suburb, Oak Park, employed a similar strategy. In the early 1970s, Oak Park "began to experience substantial black in-migration," according to Carole Goodwin, who wrote *The Oak Park Strategy* about its methods for staying interracial. Oak Park garnered national renown as an integrated suburb after giving up its sundown status. "In 1977," Goodwin wrote, "Oak Park could not confidently be called a racially stable, integrated community." But by 2000, Oak Park could be, having 11,788 African American residents among more than 52,000 total population, about 22%. White demand for houses continues to be strong; Oak Park led all suburban zip codes in housing appreciation over the period 1998–2003.[74]

In the last twenty years, whites have sometimes moved *into* majority-black neighborhoods.[75] When this happens, liberals often cry gentrification, but the resulting class and racial mix usually lasts for many years, to the betterment of municipal services and the city's tax base. Tipping point theory cannot explain gentrification. Nor can it explain Mt. Rainier, Maryland, a working-class suburb of Washington, D.C., that was 56% black in 1990, 62% in 2000, and probably 59% in 2005. "The experiment of living together," said one white newcomer in 2003, "as opposed to being polarized as black or white or Latino, makes those labels break down and leaves a whole lot more room for finding common ground."[76]

Once a town eases its restrictive policies, all kinds of interesting people may move in. Among the families that seek to live in multiracial towns are multiracial families. D'Vera Cohn visited meetings of the Interracial Family Circle, a Washington, D.C., area group, in 2002. "The pros and cons of different neighborhoods are constant topics of conversation," she wrote. She quoted the group's president, Nancy Leigh Knox: "People want to be where it's diverse. Everyone talks about it as being the primary criterion." Knox and her husband are white but have two black adopted sons. "We want our children to live where there are lots of different kinds of people," Knox said. It turns out lots of people are like Knox, and not just members of interracial families. A librarian in Decatur, my central Illinois hometown, spoke with pride of his interracial neighborhood in the West End, which had been a sundown neighborhood when I grew up in it. "And there's a gay couple on the block, and no one thinks anything about it!" Because of whites who want to live in tolerant places, towns such as Mt. Rainier and Oak Park and interracial neighborhoods within cities not only survive but develop cachet. Other towns and neighborhoods may not be as well known for being integrated, especially those that are working- and lower-middle-class, but they endure, decade after decade, providing African Americans and European Americans (and Asian Americans, Hispanics, and Native Americans) with unheralded places to live that are stably 10% to 80% black.[77]

The goal is worth pursuing, partly because living in an integrated environment causes each racial group to define "we" nonracially. Interracial contact itself thus usually becomes a humanizing process. Here is an example from Baltimore, back in about 1947, in the words of a white housewife, 37 years old, the mother of three children:

> When a colored family moved next door to us I was horrified. I just couldn't see why they wanted to live where white people lived. I wanted my husband to move right away. We have lived here for fifteen years and we own our home. I would never let our children play with the children next door, or even talk with them. But in spite of all I told them about colored people, they still talked with them. One day my youngest boy came in the house with a ball that he said the little colored boy next door had given him. I was mad and made him give it back. My child was hurt, and it seemed that I was both cruel and unfair to him. After several weeks it suddenly occurred to me that those people weren't bothering me at all. They were polite and always spoke to us. Their children were—well—just children. My husband and Mr. W __ soon began to talk to each other over the back fence, and Mrs. W __ and I also began to exchange greetings. The children run back and forth to both houses. We do favors for each other just as other neighbors do. They're no different now from any of my other neighbors.

That is only one woman's opinion, of course, but other researchers made a systematic comparison of the attitudes of white residents of two integrated public housing projects and two white-only projects. Attitudes in the integrated projects were much more favorable toward people of different races.[78]

In suburbs like Oak Park and Mt. Rainier, whose residents made a decision to stay integrated, white residents have perforce made black friends. As Emilie Barnett of Shaker Heights, Ohio, put it, "Because there was a need to do this, we came to know people intimately. It was the only way we could get past race."[79]

Desegregating independent sundown towns benefits their residents, especially their children, by lessening their unease about the interracial outside world, thus expanding their options for college, vacations, and places to live and work. Children in elite sundown suburbs already have lots of options, but desegregation can likewise help them decrease their stereotypes about other races and be more comfortable in interracial milieux. Research by Orfield shows that most students in desegregated schools hold positive views about their experience. More than 90% of a sample of high school juniors in Louisville, Kentucky, for example, say they are comfortable working with stu-

dents of another race. Whites and blacks also feel they can discuss racial issues across racial lines. Adults benefit too. In her Philadelphia-area research,
Carolyn Adams found that "the most liberal racial attitudes were observed
among whites living in neighborhoods that were racially integrated—defined
as those in which at least 5% of the local population was black." [80] Merely en-
countering African Americans as neighbors, PTA members, and so on can
improve white rhetoric, because social and political discussions are impoverished by the absence of African Americans. We have seen that sundown towns
both collect and create racists, while integrated towns both collect and create
anti-racists. Just as cognitive dissonance makes whites more racist when they
live in a sundown town, which they must justify, so it makes whites less racist,
even anti-racist, when they live in a multiracial town, which they must justify.
Ideology and attitudes thus flow from social structure, with profound consequences for the next generation. For readers wanting a personal rationale for
living an integrated lifestyle, this is one. [81]

Moving Toward an Integrated America

America should not *have* white neighborhoods or black neighborhoods. It
should have just neighborhoods. People who live in interracial neighborhoods and towns have taken an important stand in favor of better race relations. Integration is no panacea, but there is no substitute. There seems to be
no stable resting point between slavery—which, though stable in a way, required constant vigilance—and fully equal democracy. Since we have not yet
attained fully equal democracy, race relations remains unstable, fluid, a source
of continuing contention in our society. In this situation, those who act for
racial justice are also helping to build social stability—maybe even the
"beloved community" yearned for in the Civil Rights Movement. Integrated
towns and suburbs are a necessary first step to integrated hearts and minds.
Until we solve the problem of sundown neighborhoods and towns, we do not
have a chance of solving America's race problem.

It all seems to be taking a very long time. As the last chapter noted, "Ain't
No Niggers Allowed" Anna—the town with which this book began—still may
not allow African Americans to live within its city limits. Surely its continued
existence as a sundown town—and that of all the other sundown towns and
suburbs that still have not changed—tells us it is taking far too long.

The remedies suggested here—especially the Residents' Rights Act—remove the all-important badge of governmental approval or at least government neutrality from sundown towns and suburbs. In "Black and White,"

their 1972 hit song about school integration, the rock group Three Dog Night showed that they understood the importance of government action. After the federal government finally enforced school desegregation in the South, they sang, "Now a child can understand / This is the law of all the land / *All* the land." But was it? School desegregation was the law only in the South. In the North, after *Milliken,* sundown suburbs maintained school segregation by excluding African Americans from their neighborhoods.

> So now the child remains confused.
> Blacks passing through may be abused.
> What is the law of all the land?
> Do sundown policies still stand?

Or might we yet, as Three Dog Night put it, "learn together to read and write"? Then indeed, as they go on to sing, "The whole world looks upon the sight / A beautiful sight." [82]

Appendix
Methodological Notes on Table 1

General notes

Several states, including Minnesota, the Dakotas, and notably Texas, had counties with as few as 3 to 999 residents, especially in 1890. Table 1 excludes them; such tiny populations should not be given equal weight as datapoints compared to counties with 5,000 or 50,000 people. Moreover, there is little reason to believe that African Americans were shut out if none appear in a county with a mere handful of inhabitants. Leaving out such counties also accords with my general omission of hamlets smaller than 1,000.

The second column under each date, counties with "<10 bl.," includes counties listed in the first column, counties with "0 bl." This is appropriate: any county with no African Americans obviously also has fewer than ten. Thus the columns "<10 bl." convey correct information without requiring addition from another column.

Why does Table 1 omit Alaska and Hawaii?

I omitted Alaska and Hawaii because they were not states during the Nadir and have had quite different racial histories since. Both are complexly multiracial, with Native American and Inuit populations in Alaska, and Native Hawaiian, Japanese, Chinese, and Filipino Americans, and others in Hawaii. Perhaps enterprising readers can investigate whether whites created sundown neighborhoods, suburbs, or towns in those states.

Minnesota's mixed pattern

Minnesota showed more counties in 1890 with no blacks, but more in 1930 with just a few blacks; however, in 1890 its counties had much lower total populations. Nine had fewer than 5,000, compared to just one in 1930. Their average population, excluding the counties containing Minnesota's three major cities—Duluth, Minneapolis, and St. Paul—was 18,502 in 1930, 50% more than the 1890 average of 12,102. Since their total populations were up, Minnesota counties should have had more African Americans in 1930. Instead, by 1930, seven of every eight black Minnesotans lived in Minneapolis–St. Paul, compared to less than one-third of whites, thus confirming a retreat to the city.

States with no counties in either year with fewer than ten blacks

Having only three counties, Delaware could not show any trend using county analysis. Neither could Rhode Island with five, although blacks did lose ground in three of Rhode Island's five counties and showed a sizable population increase only in Providence. In Connecticut, only three counties showed increases in African American population, comparing 1930 to 1890: Fairfield County near New York City, Hartford, and New Haven. These are Connecticut's most urban counties, and whites moved to them too, but whites also moved to other counties such as Middlesex, Windham, Litchfield, and New London. Blacks did not. The same pattern held in Massachusetts, New Jersey, and New York. By 1930, New York held many sundown towns and suburbs but at most one sundown county.

As a former slave state, every Maryland county had at least 1,000 African Americans in 1890, except one, Garrett, the farthest west, which had 185. By 1930, Garrett had gone overwhelmingly white, with only 24 African Americans (and just 4 by 1940). Although Garrett thus didn't quite make the cut by 1930, I have confirmed that it became and remained a sundown county. Moreover, although Maryland has no other sundown counties, it has many sundown suburbs that developed after 1890. So Maryland is no exception either.

States with only slightly greater numbers of counties with zero or fewer than ten blacks in 1930

Some of the trends in Table 1 seem inconsequential, but they are not when the huge increases in black population in Northern states are considered. Between 1890 and 1930 the black population of Pennsylvania, for example, increased almost fourfold, so for the state to show "only" a slight increase in the number of counties with few or no African Americans actually offers spectacular corroboration of the Great Retreat. The same point holds for West Virginia. Kansas had the same number of counties with no African Americans in 1930 that it had in 1890, but by the latter year its overall black population had increased by 72%. Meanwhile, the number of its counties with fewer than ten blacks actually increased. Similarly, no county in Ohio was all-white in 1890, compared to just one in 1930; one county had fewer than ten blacks in 1890, compared to just two 40 years later. Underlying this modest trend, however, are statistics like these: 13.6% of Ohio's black population lived in small cities (2,400 to 10,000) in 1860, a proportion that rose to 18.7% by 1890. Then by 1930, that proportion fell to a mere 5.0%—dramatic evidence of the Great Retreat, verified by numerous examples of confirmed sundown towns. Nevada's retreat was modest, but the state had only 242 African Americans in 1890 and possessed no large city to retreat to by 1930, Las Vegas being still in swaddling clothes.[1]

Confirmation by Jack Blocker

Historian Jack Blocker showed the Great Retreat in the Midwest with a different statistical method. Studying communities in Ohio, Indiana, and Illinois, he found an inverse correlation or no correlation between the black population in 1860 and its growth by 1890. In other words, African Americans dispersed in those decades; they did not move primarily to places where blacks already lived. But after 1890 the correlations turned positive in Indiana and Ohio, and after 1910 in Illinois, as African Americans concentrated in fewer locations. As Blocker put it, after about 1890, "dispersion, the pattern of the previous 30 years, was replaced by concentration."[2]

Do more counties introduce a bias?

Some states, mostly in the West, had considerably more counties by 1930, which might seem to make it easier to have more counties with no or few African Americans. Actually, the increased number of counties did not introduce a bias, because the populations of these states increased proportionately much more than their number of counties.

Consider Idaho, for example, which had only 18 counties in 1890 and had 44 by 1930. In 1890 its counties averaged fewer than 5,000 in total population. In 1930, its counties average more than 10,000. Based on total population, the average county had more than twice as great a chance to attract African Americans in 1930. Yet they did not. Only one Idaho county in 1890 had no African Americans; in 1930, fourteen counties had none. Only eight counties in 1890 had 1–9 African Americans; by 1930, nineteen counties had 1–9. Again, bear in mind that the 1930 counties averaged more than twice as many people, even though most were now smaller in area. Each is therefore a legitimate datapoint. Population, not geographic area, is the important variable. We are not testing whether a given array of square miles would draw black residents; rather, the assumption is that African Americans, unencumbered by prohibitions, would go where other populations go.

Notes

CHAPTER 1: THE IMPORTANCE OF SUNDOWN TOWNS

1. "All-white" will be defined below.
2. Mere neighborhoods won't do, although occasionally I do briefly discuss sundown neighborhoods, especially when they are very large.
3. Such communities forced me to ease my definition of "all-white town" to include places with as many as nine African Americans, since a single household might easily include six or seven. Nonhousehold blacks, such as prison inmates, live-in servants, and interracial children adopted by white parents, also do not violate sundown town rules that forbid African American households, so they should be excluded from census totals. See the longer discussion in Chapter 8. From here on I will stop using quotation marks around "all-white" or "white town," but they are implied.
4. I give 1970 populations because in that year, most sundown towns and suburbs had not changed and definitely still maintained sundown policies.
5. John M. Goering, "Introduction," in John M. Goering, ed., *Housing Desegregation and Federal Policy* (Chapel Hill: University of North Carolina Press, 1986), 10; Michael N. Danielson, *The Politics of Exclusion* (NY: Columbia University Press, 1976), 223.
6. The total includes 50 towns smaller than 1,000 whose racial histories I learned.
7. I would like to thank the Newberry Library for an Arthur Weinberg fellowship early in my research. Their staff proved very helpful even though their extensive collection of local histories, for reasons discussed in Chapter 8, did not. I also want to thank the University of Illinois, Chicago, especially Anthony Martin and his student advisors, and the University of Illinois, Urbana, especially Unit One/Allen Hall, for extending month-long residences, access to students and colleagues, and use of their libraries. The Library of Congress, the Catholic University library, and the census at the University of Maryland were also helpful, as was David Andrew Timko when he was at the Census Bureau library. David Cline was a fun and helpful intern.
8. My web site, uvm.edu/~jloewen/sundown, contains a bibliography on sundown towns. The topic is at least mentioned in Ray Stannard Baker, *Following the Color Line* (New York: Harper Torchbook, 1964 [1908]); V. Jacque Voegeli, *Free But Not Equal* (Chicago: University of Chicago Press, 1967); Frank U. Quillen, *The Color Line in Ohio* (Ann Arbor: Wahr, 1913); David Gerber, *Black Ohio and the Color Line* (Urbana: University of Illinois Press, 1976); Emma Thornbrough, *The Negro in Indiana* (Indianapolis: IN Hist. Bureau, 1957); Howard Chudacoff, *Mobile Americans: Residential and Social Mobility in Omaha* (New York: Oxford University Press, 1971); James DeVries, *Race and Kinship in a Midwestern*

Town (Urbana: University of Illinois Press, 1984); Roberta Senechal, *The Sociogenesis of a Race Riot* (Urbana: University of Illinois Press, 1990); and unpublished papers by Jack Blocker Jr. on Illinois, Indiana, and Ohio. A few sources treat individual sundown towns; they are footnoted in later chapters and listed at my web site.

9. Malcolm Brown and John Webb (WPA), *Seven Stranded Coal Towns* (Washington, D.C.: GPO, 1941); John Coggeshall, "Carbon-Copy Towns? The Regionalization of Ethnic Folklife in Southern Illinois's Egypt," in Barbara Allen and Thomas J. Schlereth, eds., *Sense of Place* (Lexington: University Press of Kentucky, 1990), 103–19; C. S. Stein, *Toward New Towns for America* (Boston: MIT Press, 1966); Lewis Atherton, *Main Street on the Middle Border* (Bloomington: Indiana University Press, 1954).

10. James Danky, e-mail, 6/2002.

11. To be sure, whites still occasionally kill African Americans because they are black, the most notorious recent incident being the 1998 murder of James Byrd Jr. in Jasper, Texas, who was dragged to death behind a pickup truck, but these incidents are not lynchings. A lynching is a public murder, and the dominant forces in the community are usually in league with the perpetrators. Byrd's death was "merely" a hate crime and a homicide.

12. Historians debated Woodward's thesis and persuaded him to recognize that he had overstated it, but 1890–1920 or so is now recognized as a crucial formative period for the "new South."

13. C. Vann Woodward, *The Strange Career of Jim Crow* (New York: Oxford University Press 1975 [1955]); Edwin Yoder Jr., "The People, Yes," *Washington Post Book World,* 6/15/2003, 6.

14. The most important national treatment of this backlash is Rayford W. Logan's *The Negro in American Life and Thought: The Nadir,* reprinted as *The Betrayal of the Negro* (New York: Macmillan Collier, 1965 [1954]), although it too focused on the South. George Sinkler's *The Racial Attitudes of American Presidents* (Garden City, NJ: Doubleday, 1971) includes some treatment of the North. Leon Litwack's pioneering work *North of Slavery* (Chicago: University of Chicago Press, 1961) treats the antebellum North, while his later books, *Been in the Storm So Long* (New York: Knopf, 1979) and *Trouble in Mind: Black Southerners in the Age of Jim Crow* (New York: Knopf, 1998), as the subtitle of the latter suggests, concentrate on the traditional South. Local works are cited in note 8 above and in later chapters.

15. Woodward, ibid., xiii.

16. Du Quoin resident, 9/2002; Tim Wise, *White Like Me* (New York: Soft Skull Press, 2005), 17.

17. Edwina M. DeWindt, "Wyandotte History; Negro" (Wyandotte, MI: typescript, 1945, in Bacon Library, Wyandotte), 12, citing *Wyandotte Herald,* 10/7/1898.

18. DeWindt, "Wyandotte History; Negro," 4.

19. Vienna city employee, 2/2004, confirmed by two other residents; —, "Three Negro Homes Burned Here Monday," *Vienna Times,* 9/9/1954.

20. William Gremley, "Social Control in Cicero," in Allen Grimshaw, *Racial Violence in the U.S.* (Chicago: Aldine, 1969), 170–83; Stephen G. Meyer, *As Long as They Don't Move Next Door* (Lanham, MD: Rowman & Littlefield, 2000), 118.

21. Peter M. Bergman and Mort N. Bergman, *The Chronological History of the Negro in America* (New York: Mentor, 1969), 527; David Lewis, *King* (Urbana: University of Illinois Press, 1978), 321; Norbert Blei, *Neighborhood* (Peoria: Ellis Press, 1987), 29.

22. The term "ethnic cleansing" grew popular in the 1990s to describe what happened as Yugoslavia broke apart. From areas under Serb control, Muslims and Croatians fled, were ex-

pelled, sometimes even murdered; pretty much the same happened to Serbs and Muslims in areas under Croatian control; and so forth. The term does not mean "mass murder"; most victims fled but did not perish.

23. My web site, uvm.edu/~jloewen/sundown, lists some of these riots.

24. Since sundown towns are rare in the traditional South, I excluded Wilson, Carter, Clinton, and Gore.

25. Cedar County had 37 African American residents in 1890; just 2 remained by 1930. West Branch has a substantial Quaker population, however, and initial research unearthed no oral tradition of sundown practices in the town.

26. Even in 2000, Johnson City, Texas, had not 1 black resident among its 1,191 total population; in *Master of the Senate* (New York: Knopf, 2002), Robert A. Caro implies but does not quite state that they were not allowed.

27. Cheney traveled to Wyoming to register to vote shortly before the 2000 nominating convention to avoid conflict with the Twelfth Amendment, which prohibits electing a president and vice president from the same state.

28. McKinley, Bryan, Teddy Roosevelt, Harding, Willkie, Dewey, Truman, LBJ, and George W. Bush grew up or lived in confirmed or probable sundown towns (TR and LBJ are "probable"). Parker, Taft, Hughes, Davis, Cox, Smith, FDR, Landon, Eisenhower, Stevenson, JFK, Goldwater, McGovern, Ford, Reagan, Bush I, Dukakis, and Dole grew up in towns that probably did allow African Americans. I haven't confirmed or disconfirmed the towns identified with Coolidge, Hoover, Nixon, Humphrey, and Mondale.

29. William D. Jenkins, *Steel Valley Klan* (Kent: Kent State University Press, 1990), 65; Ed Hayes, e-mail to Salem High School bulletin board, Classmates.com, 11/2002; Phillip Payne, e-mail, 10/2002; Morris Milgram, "South Has Little to Fear from Truman of Missouri, *Pittsburgh Courier,* 10/2/1944; David Mark, "Carpetbagging's Greatest Hits," *Washington Post,* 8/15/2004.

30. Since 2002, most Krispy Kreme mix has been made in a new factory in Effingham.

31. Catherine Jurca, *White Diaspora* (Princeton: Princeton University Press, 2001), 42.

32. For a discussion of race in *Gone with the Wind* see Loewen, "Teaching Race Relations Through Feature Films," *Teaching Sociology* 19 (1/91): 82–83, reprinted in Diana Papademas, *Visual Sociology* (Washington, D.C.: ASA, 1994).

33. Chapter 8 discusses three Hollywood films that set sundown towns in the traditional South, where they rarely existed in real life.

34. Kathy Orr, "West Lawn: From Marsh to Thriving Neighborhood," West Lawn Chamber of Commerce, westlawncc.org, 1/2004; Steve Bogira, "Hate, Chicago Style" *Chicago Reader,* 12/5/86.

35. Colp resident, 9/2002.

36. Pennsylvania teacher, e-mail, 8/2002.

37. In 2000, Naperville was 3.0% African American, Edina 1.2%, and Darien 0.4%. Thus all three may have passed beyond being sundown suburbs, although since the totals include nonhousehold blacks, Darien may not have. Please note my repeated cautions against concluding that a sundown town or suburb remains sundown as of the date you read about it.

38. Meyer, *As Long as They Don't Move Next Door,* 1.

39. Doing otherwise would have entangled my prose in a mass of adjectives like "formerly," "continuing," or perhaps "recovering" sundown towns. In turn, such judgments would have led to countless errors, because I could not know if a practice confirmed in the past continues in the present.

40. James Pool, *Hitler and His Secret Partners* (New York: Pocket Books, 1997), 117; Jewish Virtual Library, us-israel.org/jsource/Holocaust/kristallnacht.html, 11/2003.

41. Anna editor, 10/2002; Anna librarian, 10/2002; Union County farmer, 1/2004.

42. Newman, ibid; Robert Park, *Human Communities: The City and Human Ecology* (New York: Free Press, 1952), 14.

43. Untitled story about Anna, *Carbondale (Ill.) Free Press,* 11/13/1909; John Baker, post at his web site at cougartown.com, 3/2001; Deborah Morse-Kahn, *Edina: Chapters in the City History* (Edina: City of Edina, 1998), 94–95; Edina resident, 1963; Don Cox, "Linguistic Expert Says Ancient Indian Languages Are Dying," *Reno Gazette-Journal,* 1/2/2002, sfgate.com/cgi-bin/article.cgi?file=/news/archive/2002/01/02/state1722EST7955. DTL; William H. Jacobsen Jr., 8/23/2003.

CHAPTER 2: THE NADIR

1. Leola Bergmann, "The Negro in Iowa," *Iowa Journal of History and Politics,* 1969 [1948], 44–45.

2. Robert Green, Laura L. Becker, and Robert E. Coviello, *The American Tradition* (Columbus: Merrill, 1984), 754.

3. Rayford W. Logan, who first employed "Nadir of race relations" as a term (so far as I know), used "1877–1901" in the subtitle of his 1954 book, *The Negro in American Life and Thought: The Nadir,* but his book actually treats 1877–1921, to the end of the Wilson administration. Although I use (and defend) somewhat different dates (1890–1930s), my thinking has been greatly influenced by Logan's fine work, reprinted as *The Betrayal of the Negro* (New York: Macmillan Collier, 1965 [1954]).

4. In 1859, Arkansas passed a law requiring all free Negroes to leave the state by January 1, 1860. Any free blacks who remained after the deadline could be sold into slavery. But this law never applied to slaves and was more a reaction to fear of slave revolts, said to be instigated by free blacks, than an attempt to create an all-white state.

5. Quoted in James M. McPherson, *Battle Cry of Freedom* (New York: Oxford University Press, 1988), vi.

6. Shepherd W. McKinley, reviewing Heather Cox Richardson's *The Death of Reconstruction* on H-South, h-net.org/~south/, 5/16/2002, citing xiii–xiv.

7. See Robert Dykstra, *Bright Radical Star* (Ames: Iowa State University Press, 1997).

8. In reality, Native Americans would not be included until 1924.

9. Sally Albertz, "Fond du Lac's Black Community and Their Church, 1865–1943," in Clarence B. Davis, *Source of the Lake* (Fond du Lac, WI: Action Printing, 2002), 34–35.

10. During the Civil War and Reconstruction, expulsions happened in other states too, of course, again mostly in Democratic areas. For example, 187 African Americans lived in Washington County, Indiana, 20 miles northwest of Louisville, Kentucky, before the Civil War. By 1870, just 18 remained, and a county history published in 1916 stated, "Washington County has for several decades boasted that no colored man or woman lived within her borders." Willie Harlen, president of the Washington County Historical Society, credits the expulsion to the Knights of the Golden Circle, a secret organization of Copperhead Democrats in northern states that also provided something of a model for the Ku Klux Klan. Cf. Emma Lou Thornbrough, *The Negro in Indiana* (Indianapolis: Indiana Historical Bureau, 1957), 225; Harlen, e-mail, 10/2002.

11. *Chesterton Tribune,* 7/24/1903; Darrel Dexter, *A House Divided: Union County, Illinois*

(Anna: Reppert, 1994), 75; V. Jacque Voegeli, *Free but Not Equal* (Chicago: University of Chicago Press, 1967), 89.

12. Many soldiers had *not* died for this purpose, to be sure, but solely to hold the nation together. I know that, and Lincoln knew it. See Chapter 6 of James Loewen, *Lies My Teacher Told Me* (New York: New Press, 1995) for a more nuanced treatment of this issue. But increasingly as the war went on, that *is* why they died, and Lincoln's saying so helped make it true.

13. Lerone Bennett, *Black Power U.S.A.: The Human Side of Reconstruction* (Baltimore: Penguin, 1969), 11.

14. I intend "Ku Klux Klan" as a synecdoche for all the groups—Red Shirts, Knights of the White Carnelia, and plain Democrats—who used violence and intimidation to end interracial governments in the South.

15. *History of Lower Scioto Valley* (Chicago: Interstate, 1884), 737; Jeanne Blackburn, e-mail, 11/2003.

16. James Loewen, *Lies Across America* (New York: New Press, 1999), 394–404, summarizes the collapse of Republican anti-racism after 1890.

17. The proportion also takes immigration into account.

18. See Carey McWilliams, *A Mask for Privilege* (New Brunswick: Transaction Books, 1999 [1948]), 14.

19. Philip A. Klinkner and R. M. Smith, *The Unsteady March* (Chicago: University of Chicago Press, 1999), 96.

20. Of course, one did not have to be Republican to dream of wealth. But tycoons such as J. P. Morgan and John D. Rockefeller were Republican, almost without exception. Democrats were more likely to deride such wealth as excessive and at base crooked, rather than a sign of merit.

21. Arkansas librarian, 9/2002; Douglas opinion, *Jones v. Alfred H. Mayer Co,* 392 U.S. 409, 445–47 (1968), also quoted in Joe R. Feagin, *Racist America* (New York: Routledge, 2000), 25.

22. After 1896, if not before, schools became segregated statewide in Delaware, Maryland, West Virginia, Kentucky, Missouri, Arkansas, Oklahoma, Texas, and Arizona, as well as much of Ohio, Indiana, Illinois, Kansas, and California. Of course, the South already had segregated schools.

23. Donald Grant, *The Anti-Lynching Movement* (San Francisco: R & E, 1975), 66–67.

24. Ray Stannard Baker, "The Color Line in the North," *American Magazine* 65 (1908), in Otto Olsen, ed., *The Negro Question: From Slavery to Caste, 1863–1910* (New York: Pitman, 1971), 268; Quillen, *The Color Line in Ohio,* 120; Loewen, *Lies Across America,* 400.

25. Historian John Weaver, e-mail to H-Net Ohio History list, 1/2003.

26. Bergmann, "The Negro in Iowa," 44–45.

27. Michael L. Cooper, *Playing America's Game* (New York: Lodestar, 1993), 10; Gordon Morgan, "Emancipation Bowl," Department of Sociology, University of Arkansas, Fayetteville, n.d.

28. "The Passing of Colored Firemen in Chicago," Chicago *Defender,* 3/11/1911; Lester C. Lamon, *Black Tennesseans, 1900–1930* (Knoxville: University of Tennessee Press, 1977), 141.

29. Ralph R. Rea, *Boone County and Its People* (Van Buren, AR: Press-Argus, 1955), 121; Fon Louise Gordon, *Caste and Class: The Black Experience in Arkansas, 1880–1920* (Athens: University of Georgia Press, 1995), 45.

30. Jacqueline Froelich and David Zimmermann, "Total Eclipse: The Destruction of the African American Community of Harrison, Arkansas, in 1905 and 1909," *Arkansas Historical Quarterly* 58, 2 (1999): 141–42; Zimmermann quoted in Laurinda Joenks, "Roughness of Citizens Blamed on Lean Times," *The Morning News,* 5/7/2000.

31. Joenks, "Roughness of Citizens."

32. Frederick Douglass pointed this out at the time, in 1895: "The American people have fallen in with the bad idea that this is a Negro problem, a question of the character of the Negro, and not a question of the nation." Quoted in Kevin Gaines, *Uplifting the Race* (Chapel Hill: University of North Carolina Press, 1996), 67.

33. See Baker, "The Color Line in the North," 266.

34. Heather Cox Richardson, *The Death of Reconstruction* (Cambridge: Harvard University Press, 2001), xiii–xiv, 119, 224; McKinley, review of same on H-South, h-net.org/~south/, 5/16/2002.

35. Morgan, "Emancipation Bowl."

36. Actually, only South Carolina's ever had a black majority.

37. Since some textbook authors still made such claims as late as the 1970s, many readers may have encountered this biased interpretation of Reconstruction in high school as fact. For correction, refer to any modern treatment of the period, such as Bennett, *Black Power, U.S.A.,* or Eric Foner, *Reconstruction* (New York: Harper & Row, 1988).

38. Albert Bushnell Hart, *Essentials of American History* (New York: American Book Co., 1905), 504; W. E. B. DuBois, *Black Reconstruction* (Cleveland: World Meridian, 1964 [1935]), 722; Loewen, *Lies Across America,* 39, 164–93.

39. Carl Wittke, *Tambo and Bones* (Westport, CT: Greenwood, 1968 [1930]), 93; Joseph Boskin, *Sambo* (New York: Oxford University Press, 1986), 85; James Weldon Johnson, *Black Manhattan* (New York: Knopf, 1930), 93; James DeVries, *Race and Kinship in a Midwestern Town* (Urbana: University of Illinois Press, 1984), 51.

40. Loewen, "Teaching Race Relations Through Feature Films," *Teaching Sociology* 19 (1991): 82; Adrian Turner, *A Celebration of* Gone with the Wind (New York: W. H. Smith, 1992), 166, citing *Variety*.

41. Richard Weiss, "Racism in the Era of Industrialization," in Gary Nash and Richard Weiss, eds., *The Great Fear* (New York: Holt, Rinehart, & Winston, 1970), 136; Andrew R. Heinze, "Jews and American Popular Psychology," *Journal of American History* 88, 3 (2001): 959–60; Dinesh D'Souza, *The End of Racism* (New York: Free Press, 1995), 118.

42. John Higham, *Strangers in the Land* (New Brunswick: Rutgers University Press, 1955), 265; Gordon A. Craig, "The X-Files," *New York Review of Books,* 4/12/2001, 57.

43. The last of the latter was Carleton Coon, whose *The Origin of Races,* published in 1962 (New York: Knopf), claimed that *Homo sapiens* evolved five different times, blacks last. Its poor reception by anthropologists, followed by evidence from archaeology and paelontology that mankind evolved once, and in Africa, finally put an end to such pseudoscience.

44. Logan, *The Betrayal of the Negro,* 360–70; Nancy J. Weiss, "Wilson Draws the Color Line," in Arthur Mann, ed., *The Progressive Era* (Hinsdale, IL: Dryden, 1975), 144; Harvey Wasserman, *America Born and Reborn* (New York: Macmillan, 1983), 131.

45. W. E. B. DuBois, *The Seventh Son* (New York: Random House, 1971), 2:594.

46. Richard Delgado and Jean Stefancic, *Home-Grown Racism* (Boulder: University of Colorado Latino/a Research & Policy Center, 1999), 30, 44, 74.

47. Willis D. Weatherford and Charles S. Johnson, *Race Relations* (Boston: D. C. Heath, 1934), 314; Lorenzo J. Greene, Gary Kremer, and Antonio Holland, *Missouri's Black Heritage* (Co-

lumbia: University of Missouri Press, 1993), 151; Bergman and Bergman, *The Chronological History of the Negro in America,* 458.

48. Greene, Kremer, and Holland, *Missouri's Black Heritage,* 151; Walter E. Williams, *The State Against Blacks* (New York: McGraw-Hill, 1982), Chapter 8.

49. The First Lady and Interior Secretary Harold Ickes made some important symbolic gestures, such as allowing Marian Anderson to sing at the Lincoln Memorial in 1939.

CHAPTER 3: THE GREAT RETREAT

1. Emma Lou Thornbrough, *The Negro in Indiana* (Indianapolis: Indiana Historical Bureau, 1957), 224.

2. I define the "traditional South" as Virginia, North Carolina, South Carolina, Georgia, Florida, Alabama, Tennessee, Mississippi, and Louisiana—states historically dominated by slavery. Note 63 in this chapter defends this definition.

3. Admittedly, some towns in the Midwest went sundown vis-à-vis African Americans earlier, during the Civil War, and some even before it, but most towns in that region and elsewhere did so later.

4. Unlike most southern Illinois towns, Cairo never tried to get rid of its black population. It simply had too many blacks. Also, some whites in and around Cairo adhered to traditional southern race relations, using African Americans as cotton pickers, maids, janitors, railroad labor, etc., and would have opposed any expulsion. Map 1 shows this area of traditional southern race relations in Illinois.

5. *Cairo Bulletin* quoted in *Marion Daily Republican,* 8/12/1920.

6. Historian Jeri L. Reed, e-mail, 6/2002; *Guide and Directory for the City of Rogers* (Benton County, 1907), 4; "Siloam Springs, Arkansas," brochure in collection of Siloam Springs Museum; Michael Birdwell, e-mail, 5/2002; *Terry County Herald,* 3/27/1908; Betty Dawn Hamilton, e-mail, 7/2002; Eulalia N. Wells, *Blazing the Way* (Blanket, TX: author, 1942), 77.

7. *Owosso and Shiawassee County Directory, 1936* (Owosso: Owosso Chamber of Commerce, 1936); David M. Chalmers, *Hooded Americanism* (New York: Franklin Watts, 1976 [1965]), 165; David M. P. Freund, "Making It Home," Ph.D. dissertation, University of Michigan, 1999, 225.

8. "Come see Woodson" ad from Dale Steiner.

9. There was a wave of anti-Chinese activity just before the Civil War, including expulsions from many mining camps and small towns in 1858–59. See Stanford Lyman, *Chinese Americans* (New York: Random House, 1974), 60.

10. Craig Storti, *Incident at Bitter Creek* (Ames: Iowa State University Press, 1991), 112–15, 118, 125, 159–60; Bill Bryson, *Made in America* (New York: Morrow, 1994), 127; Grant K. Anderson, "Deadwood's Chinatown," in Arif Dirlik, ed., *Chinese on the American Frontier* (Lanham, MD: Rowman & Littlefield, 2001), 423; Ed Marston, "Truth-telling Needs a Home in the West," *High Country News,* 9/25/2000; "Files Found in Oregon Detail Massacre of Chinese," *New York Times,* 8/20/1995; Brigham Madsen, *Corinne: The Gentile Capital of Utah* (Salt Lake City: Utah State Historical Society, 1980), 252.

11. Florence C. Lister and Robert H. Lister, "Chinese Sojourners in Territorial Prescott," in Dirlik, ed., *Chinese on the American Frontier,* 55; Kathy Hodges, e-mail, 6/2002; Li-hua Yu, "Chinese Immigrants in Idaho," Ph.D. dissertation, Bowling Green State University, 1991, Chapter 7; Priscilla Wegars, e-mail, 8/2003, summarizing her "The History and Archaeol-

ogy of the Chinese in Northern Idaho, 1880 Through 1910," Ph.D. dissertation, University of Idaho, 1991.

12. Jean Pfaelzer, paper presented to the American Studies Association, Washington, DC, 2001; Pfaelzer, "A Proposal for *Driven Out: Ethnic Cleansing and Resistance*," n.d., 4, 10; Visalia oral history via Gilbert Gia, e-mail, 9/2002; Keith Easthouse, "The Chinese Expulsion— Looking Back on a Dark Episode," *North Coast Journal Weekly*, 2/27/2003, northcoast journal.com/022703/cover0227.html, 2/2004; Kevin Hearle, e-mails, 9/2002, 5/2004, quoting Diann Marsh, *Santa Ana: An Illustrated History* (San Diego: Heritage, 1994), 95–96; cf. Pfaelzer, *Driven Out* (New York: Random House, forthcoming).

13. Lynwood Carranco, "Chinese Expulsion from Humboldt County," in Roger Daniels, ed., *Anti-Chinese Violence in North America* (New York: Arno Press, 1978), 332–39.

14. The *Humboldt Times* overstated its case: several other towns kept out Chinese Americans in 1937. Also, apparently not all Chinese Americans were expelled from Orleans, an inland mining hamlet barely in Humboldt County.

15. Easthouse, "The Chinese Expulsion"; Carranco, "Chinese Expulsion from Humboldt County."

16. Joseph A. Dacus, *Annals of the Great Strike* (New York: Arno Press, 1969 [1877]; Online Encyclopedia of Seattle and King County History, historylink.org, 3/2003.

17. A few places drove out their blacks well before 1890.

18. Cf. Jack S. Blocker Jr., "Choice and Circumstance," Organization of American Historians, Toronto, 4/1999, 2–3.

19. Ibid.; Loewen, *The Mississippi Chinese* (Prospect Heights, IL: Waveland, 1988).

20. I did not study Alaska or Hawaii and did very little research on Montana and the Dakotas.

21. I used 1930 statistics in Table 1 to avoid contamination from the Great Depression. I didn't want readers to imagine that African Americans may have retreated to the cities for economic reasons. Using 1930 avoids this issue, because the Crash happened on October 24, 1929, only months before enumerators fanned out to take the 1930 census, and it had prompted little population movement by that time. (For the record, the Great Depression actually prompted some migration *from* big cities back to subsistence farming in the South.)

22. Columns with < 10 African Americans include those with none.

23. I define the "traditional" South as Virginia, North Carolina, South Carolina, Georgia, Florida, Alabama, Tennessee, Mississippi, and Louisiana. A later section in this chapter explains why the table includes Arkansas and Texas. The Appendix tells why Table 1 omits Alaska and Hawaii, describes idiosyncracies in some states, and discusses other methodological issues underlying the table. Arizona, New Mexico, and Oklahoma were not states in 1890; I substituted data from 1910, the first census after statehood.

24. Minnesota had more counties in 1890 with no blacks, but more in 1930 with just a few blacks.

25. The Appendix also comments on other states whose counties showed only slight trends. It also summarizes recent work by historian Jack Blocker Jr. that reinforces the conclusions presented here.

26. Additional causes included a farm depression in the South, harm done to cotton by the boll weevil in 1915–16, and the South's continuing denial of civil rights to African Americans.

27. Beloit (WI) *News*, 8/25/1916, quoted in C. K. Doreski, *Writing America Black: Race Rhetoric in the Public Sphere* (New York: Cambridge University Press, 1998), 31–32.

28. T. J. Woofter Jr., *Negro Problems in Cities* (New York: Harper & Row, 1969 [1928]), 28–31, quotes from 31.

29. My web site lists confirmed counties in all states.

30. I don't believe the detail that he literally met them at the line, but I do believe that the sheriff enforced the sundown policy.

31. Malcolm Ross, *All Manner of Men* (New York: Reynal & Hitchcock, 1948), 66; 83-year-old Mason County resident, 4/2000; Carol Speakman, 9/2002.

32. This figure is approximate. I may have overlooked a town or two that exceeded 1,000 in 1970 but not in adjoining censuses; I omitted some usually unincorporated places the census tags as CDPs, or "census designated places."

33. All suspected and confirmed sundown towns are listed at uvm.edu/~jloewen/sundown. Another researcher might come up with slightly different numbers, because I included smaller towns that people brought to my attention as sundown towns and did not include a few small towns that reached 1,000 people only in recent censuses. Other reasons to exclude an occasional town were judgment calls and my own exhaustion. I also excluded CDPs unless I knew them to be considered towns by residents of the area.

34. These communities are listed at uvm.edu/~jloewen/sundown. The exception was Newton. Confirmed towns form a scattered subset of all suspect towns, clustered near locations where I had speaking engagements, knew someone, or otherwise had connections. In addition, I contacted all 56 suspected sundown towns on Map 1. The proportion of confirmed sundown towns among those 56 was very similar to that among my scattered subset, so I don't believe any important error resulted from my nonrandom sampling.

35. I often use 1970 figures because most sundown towns were still all-white on purpose in that year. To be sure, some still are, but many relaxed their policy in the 1970s or thereafter, especially towns that grew rapidly. Using 1970 figures is conservative in that it underestimates the size of the cities today.

36. My process of information gathering was not perfectly random: when I invited audience members to share with me information about sundown towns, for example, people from overwhelmingly white towns that were *not* sundown towns would not be likely to speak, having nothing to impart. But I also made efforts to learn about *all* towns on Map 1, for example, and the proportion of confirmed sundown towns that I uncovered from that quest was no different than that obtained from volunteered sources.

37. Actually, we shall compute confidence limits for our estimate of 99.5% of 278 unknown towns, or 277 probable towns.

38. To find the standard error of the difference of two percentages, first we calculate each standard error separately. Beginning with the 194 towns on which we have information, the formula is $s_{p1} = \sqrt{pq/n}$, where n = the number of towns for which we have data (194), p = the proportion that were sundown (.995), and q = (1 - p) or .005. This standard error = .005 or 0.5%.

    We also need to compute the standard error of the percentage of sundown towns among the 228 towns for which we have no information. Since we don't know this percentage, we can assume just 90% will be, lower than the most likely estimate; such a conservative assumption provides a larger-than-likely standard error, which results in a more conservative overall estimate. Using the same formula, we substitute: n = 228, p = .9, and q = .1. This standard error = .020 or about 2%.

    We then combine these two standard errors, using the formula $s_{(p1-p2)} = \sqrt{s^2_{p1} + s^2_{p2}}$, to find the standard error of the difference of two percentages, which = .0205 or 2.05%.

39. Statistical tables tell us that 99 times out of 100, a range that is ÷2.58 standard errors from our best estimate will include the actual percentage. 2.58 x .0205 = .053 or 5.3%.

40. This correction is not normally computed, is unlikely to drop the lower limit as low as 90%, and is at least partly offset by the conservatively calculated standard error described in note 38.

41. Three previous authors have estimated the extent of sundown towns in Illinois. Their estimates are in basic accord with mine. "Illinois: Mecca of the Migrant Mob," originally published in 1923 by the well-known black sociologist Charles S. Johnson, tells of "Granite City, where [Negroes] by ordinance may not live within the city limits . . . and 200 other towns where they may not live at all." Johnson's short essay does not list these towns. My number of likely suspects, 474, is larger than Johnson's, perhaps because when he wrote in 1923, some towns were still in the process of expelling their African Americans or resolving that none were to be admitted. Also, he may not have included towns smaller than 2,500, and he did not try to research the entire state. Sociologist Roberta Senechal quotes Johnson's sentence with approval in her fine study of the 1908 race riot in Springfield, Illinois. Writing of towns "that forbade blacks to cross the city limits or remain after dark," historian John Keiser compiled "a list of some 52 Illinois cities in which such unwritten 'ordinances' were said to exist by the local citizens," and he did not claim to have researched the subject exhaustively. One other book, *Land Between the Rivers*, a 1973 coffee-table book by three professors at Southern Illinois University, briefly acknowledges that sundown towns were widespread in that section of the state: "Many Southern Illinois towns solved the problem simply by refusing to allow blacks within the town boundaries between sunset and sunup." Such candor is rare; also worth noting is these authors' nonchalant use—well after the Civil Rights Movement—of the rhetoric that African Americans are "the problem" and keeping them out "solved the problem." See Charles S. Johnson, "Illinois: Mecca of the Migrant Mob," reprinted in Tom Lutz and Susanna Ashton, eds., *These "Colored" United States: African American Essays from the 1920s* (New Brunswick: Rutgers University Press, 1996), 109; Roberta Senechal, *The Sociogenesis of a Race Riot* (Urbana: University of Illinois Press, 1990), 129; John Keiser, "Black Strikebreakers and Racism in Illinois, 1865–1900" (*Journal of the Illinois State Historical Society* 65 (1972), 314; and C. William Horrell, Henry D. Piper, and John Voigt, *Land Between the Rivers* (Carbondale: Southern Illinois University Press, 1973), 163.

42. Of course, the smaller the community, the more likely that the absence of African Americans is not due to a policy of exclusion.

43. I know I missed sundown towns in this way, because two—Dwight and Vienna—came to my attention during my research.

44. Copperheads were pro-South Democrats, so called by pro-Union Republicans.

45. *Magnificent Whistle Stop: The 100-Year Story of Mendota, Illinois* (Mendota: Mendota Centennial Committee, 1953), 332; *Tribune* quoted in Ronald L. Lewis, *Black Coal Miners in America* (Lexington: University Press of Kentucky, 1987), 85; Tom Trengove, e-mail, 9/2002; male undergraduate, University of Illinois–Chicago, 9/2001.

46. Administrative secretary, University of Illinois, 2/2001.

47. Paul M. Angle, *Bloody Williamson* (New York: Knopf, 1952), 98, 110–15; Carl Planinc, 9/2002.

48. Senechal, *The Sociogenesis of a Race Riot,* 129.

49. Two other writers estimated impressionistically the extent of sundown towns in Indiana. Emma Lou Thornbrough's 1957 comment is reproduced at the head of the chapter. Kathleen Blee, author of the 1991 book *Women of the Klan* (Berkeley: University of California

Press, 1991), 78, cited Leibowitz as the authority for this sentence: "Sundown laws that prohibited blacks from remaining in town after sunset were enforced, though often unwritten, in nearly every small town in Indiana."

50. Irving Leibowitz, *My Indiana* (Englewood Cliffs: Prentice-Hall, 1964), 208.

51. Frances L. Peacock, "The Opposite of Fear Is Love: An Interview with George Sawyer," *Quaker Life*, 3/2002, fum.org/QL/issues/0203/index.htm, 6/2002.

52. These 229 include 212 towns larger than 1,000 in population that were overwhelmingly white in census after census, as well as 17 hamlets with fewer than 1,000 residents that oral and/or written historical sources confirmed as having sundown policies. This number is smaller than in Illinois because Indiana has fewer towns, being a smaller state with a smaller population.

53. These communities are listed at uvm.edu/~jloewen/sundown. The number of confirmed sundown towns in Indiana is smaller than in Illinois because I spent less time researching Indiana.

54. The 1970 census is the next after Leibowitz's 1964 claim. It also allows thirteen years for possible desegregation after Thornbrough's 1957 statement and follows the 1954 *Brown v. Board of Education* school desegregation decision by sixteen years.

55. See uvm.edu/~jloewen/sundown for a list of confirmed Indiana sundown towns with evidence.

56. Leibowitz, *My Indiana,* 208; Mike Haas, "You Betcha," post to alt.discrimination, 2/18/2002.

57. The 126 towns, 9 confirmed, and 10 suspects are listed at uvm.edu/~jloewen/sundown. I omitted towns smaller than 2,500 for two reasons: out of respect for Wisconsin's small statewide black population—just under 3% in 1970, less than half Indiana's—and because I knew I would not have time to investigate any of Wisconsin's smaller towns on site.

There is some circularity in allowing a state's small overall black population, which is depressed partly by its towns' sundown policies, to "excuse" the overwhelming whiteness of its towns. If *all* Wisconsin towns kept out African Americans, then the statewide proportion would be 0%, and I would have to infer that *no* towns were sundown! This may be a larger problem in Idaho and Oregon, the latter owing in part to its law flatly excluding blacks, passed in 1849.

58. These populations are approximate, rounded for the period 1970–2000.

59. Former Sheboygan resident, 10/2002; Grey Gundaker, e-mail, 7/2002.

60. The exception was Doc Pitts, whose story Chapter 10 will tell.

61. Moira Meltzer-Cohen, e-mail, 9/2002.

62. Priscilla Wegars, "Entrepreneurs and 'Wage Slaves': Their Relationship to Anti-Chinese Racism in Northern Idaho's Mining Labor Market, 1880–1910," in Marcel van der Linden and Jan Lucassen, eds., *Racism and the Labour Market* (Bern: Peter Lang, 1995), 471–72; Jim Kershner, "Segregation in Spokane," *Columbia* 14, 4 (2000–01), wshs.org/columbia/0400-a2.htm, 3/2003.

63. Those nine states, along with Arkansas and Texas, seceded to form the Confederacy, of course. Table 1 includes Arkansas and Texas because they had large areas that, like West Virginia, opposed both secession and slavery. The northwestern half of Arkansas supplied many recruits for the United States Army after U.S. forces broke the Confederacy's hold on it. The Confederacy had to occupy much of north Texas, owing to Unionist sentiments there. Early in the twentieth century, Texas became more western than southern. Arkansas

and Texas were also the only former Confederate states to desegregate their state universities in the immediate aftermath of *Brown*.

Table 1 also includes three other states—Maryland, Kentucky, and Missouri—that had substantial areas that were traditionally southern. These states did not secede and, on balance, included more areas that were not traditionally southern.

64. Thornbrough, *The Negro in Indiana,* 225.

65. I have not confirmed Belmont as a sundown town but think it was. In 1980, it had 1,420 people including 1 African American. By 2000 it had 11. Burnsville barely reached 1,000 population in 2000. A handful of even smaller Mississippi communities may be sundown hamlets, listed at uvm.edu/~jloewen/sundown. I have confirmed one, Mize, population about 300, southeast of Jackson. Mize is the "capital" of Sullivan's Hollow, a rural area known for past outlawry, including intimidation of African Americans. The fact that Mize is widely known as "No-Nigger Mize" and Sullivan's Hollow is notorious for the practice implies that sundown towns are unusual enough in the traditional South that even such a small one is remarked about.

66. Putting a practice in the past—"Alabama *had* two sundown counties"—might imply that both counties now admit African Americans, which I don't know to be true. At the same time, putting the practice in the present might imply that they still keep blacks out today—which I also don't know for sure. Here as elsewhere (unless context implies otherwise), using *has* means that a town or county kept African Americans (or other groups) out for decades and not that it necessarily does so now. Chapter 14 treats this problem of verb tense at greater length.

67. These counties and towns are listed at uvm.edu/~jloewen/sundown.

68. "Threat Against W. Va. Families Is Laid to Klan," *Pittsburgh Courier,* 10/27/1923.

69. I deliberately echo the title of Harry Caudill's well-known 1963 book about the region's depressed economic conditions, which unfortunately contains no mention that the region expelled most of its African Americans four or five decades earlier and kept them from returning.

70. This was the school where Martin Luther King Jr. was photographed and the result enlarged and plastered on billboards across the South with the caption "Martin Luther King at Communist Training School." Neither Horton nor Highlander was Communist.

71. George Brosi, 6/1999; Esther S. Sanderson, *County Scott and Its Mountain Folk* (Nashville: Williams Printing, 1958), 186; John Egerton, *Shades of Gray* (Baton Rouge: Louisiana State University Press, 1991), 69; Charles Martin, e-mail, 6/2000; cf. "Scottsboro Trial Moved Fifty Miles," *New York Times,* 3/8/1933, 14.

72. William Pickens, "Arkansas—A Study in Suppression," *The Messenger* 5 (1923), reprinted in Tom Lutz and Susanna Ashton, eds., *These "Colored" United States: African American Essays from the 1920s* (New Brunswick: Rutgers University Press, 1996), 35; Milton Rafferty, *The Ozarks* (Fayetteville: University of Arkansas Press, 2001), 60; use of *Negro* in 2001 is antiquated.

73. Gordan D. Morgan, *Black Hillbillies of the Arkansas Ozarks* (Fayetteville: University of Arizona Department of Sociology, 1973 typescript), 60.

74. William H. Jacobsen Jr., 8/2003; Don Cox, "Linguistic Expert Says Ancient Indian Languages Are Dying," *Reno Gazette-Journal,* 1/2/2002, sfgate.com/cgi-bin/article.cgi?file=/news/archive/2002/01/02/state1722EST7955.DTL, 8/2003; Loren B. Chan, "The Chinese in Nevada," in Arif Dirlik, ed., *Chinese on the American Frontier* (Lanham, MD:

Rowman & Littlefield, 2001), 96–97. Elmer Rusco, *"Good Time Coming?" Black Nevadans in the 19th Century* (Westport, CT: Greenwood, 1975), 207.

75. "Tale of Two Cities," *Pacific Citizen,* 1/4/1947; Fred S. Rolater, e-mail, 6/2002.

76. MariaElena Raymond, e-mail, 9/02; Margaret Marsh, *Suburban Lives* (New Brunswick: Rutgers University Press, 1990), 172; Richard Delgado and Jean Stefancic, *Home-Grown Racism* (Boulder: University of Colorado Latino/a Research & Policy Center, 1999), 30, 44, 74.

77. *Bellingham Souvenir Police Album,* photocopy, no date, 11; —, "The Hindus Have Left Us," *Bellingham Herald,* 9/6?/1907; cf. —, "Hindus Hounded from City," *Bellingham Herald,* 9/5/1907.

78. These include North Fond du Lac, Neenah, Menasha, Kimberly, Little Chute, Kaukauna, and Green Bay.

79. Michael Dougan, *Arkansas Odyssey* (Little Rock: Rose Publishing, 1994), 317; "An Elco Man Says Feeling Is Strong Against Negroes," *Cairo Bulletin,* 2/19/1924; "Attempt Is Made to Dynamite Cauble Home," *Cairo Bulletin,* 3/4/1924; "No Reason for Sending Troops to Elco, Opinion," *Cairo Bulletin,* 3/7/1924; Scott Peeples, "Building Diversity Awareness Day," Appleton, WI, 4/8/2003, 2, paraphrasing Bob Lowe; Andrew Kirchmeier, 4/2002; Jack Tichenor, 2/2004.

80. Carey McWilliams, *A Mask for Privilege* (New Brunswick: Transaction, 1999 [1948]), 6–7; Michael Powell, "Separate and Unequal in Roosevelt, Long Island," *Washington Post,* 4/21/2002.

81. William Stock, "Nigger Sam," *Urban Hiker,* 37, urbanhiker.net/archive/febstories/UH-02_03(stock).pdf, 6/2003; Elizabeth C. Baxter, 5/2003, and e-mail, 5/2003.

82. When capitalized, *Realtor* is a trademark of the National Association of Realtors (formerly the National Association of Real Estate Boards). The NAR has long tried unsuccessfully to get journalists to capitalize *realtor* when referring to an NAR member and use *real estate agent* otherwise. Currently the NAR campaigns to get its own members to use *REALTOR* in all capital letters with a trademark symbol attached. This book uses *realtor* as synonymous with the unwieldy *real estate agent.* Often, as here, I do not know whether the agent was a member of the NAR or NAREB. I use *Realtor* only when membership in the national or local association is part of the story.

83. "Housing: How High the Barriers," *ADL Bulletin* 16, 1 (1959), 2; former Delray Beach resident, 8/2000; Mary Ellen Stratthaus, "Flaw in the Jewel: Housing Discrimination Against Jews in La Jolla, California," *American Jewish History* 84, 3 (1996): 194; Leonard Valdez, e-mail, 4/2003.

84. Charles T. Clotfelter concurs: "The 1970 census marked a high-water mark for the residential segregation of blacks." See his *After Brown* (Princeton: Princeton University Press, 2004), 80.

85. Portfolio 25 and Map 1 (page 63) demonstrate this point for Indiana and Southern Illinois.

86. As noted in Chapters 1 and 14, "can be confirmed" does not imply that the discrimination necessarily continues to the present.

87. The exact number depends on the size of what is referred to as a "town."

88. Baker meant not that African Americans were excluding others, but that ghettoes were becoming exclusively black as "other classes of people" left.

89. Howard Chudacoff, *Mobile Americans: Residential and Social Mobility in Omaha* (New York: Oxford University Press, 1971), 127; Ray Stannard Baker, "The Color Line in the

North," *American Magazine* 65 (1908), in Otto Olsen, ed., *The Negro Question: From Slavery to Caste, 1863–1910* (New York: Pitman, 1971), 268.

90. D is particularly useful because it is not affected by the overall proportion of African Americans in the metropolitan area, and because it has intuitive clarity. D works for two groups at a time, here blacks and nonblacks.

91. Reynolds Farley and William H. Frey, "Changes in the Segregation of Whites from Blacks During the 1980s," *American Sociological Review* 59, 1 (1994): 24.

92. In fact, segregation was even worse than that, especially in the North. At any given moment, northern metropolitan areas looked more integrated than they really were, owing to the Great Migration, which continued at least to 1968. This influx of African Americans from the South led to blockbusting, in turn creating "transitional" or "changing" neighborhoods. Such neighborhoods are temporarily desegregated and artificially reduce D. After factoring out changing neighborhoods, Ds in both regions would rise, but especially in the North. Perhaps 94 would be a reasonable estimate for the average D in both regions, controlling for transitional neighborhoods.

93. James Loewen and Charles Sallis, eds., *Mississippi: Conflict and Change* (New York: Pantheon, 1980), 177, 186–87; Art T. Burton, "Gunfight at Boley, Oklahoma," on Bennie J. McRae Jr.'s "Lest We Forget" web site, coax.net/people/lwf/gunfight.htm, 5/2003; William E. Bittle and Gilbert Geis, *The Longest Way Home* (Detroit: Wayne State University Press, 1964), 37.

94. These were not the first black homes to be blown up in Okemah. The nearby *Paden Press* observed on 3/16/1905, "Once the darkey was not allowed to have his habitat in the town [Okemah] and he was discouraged by high explosives."

95. Norman Crockett, *The Black Towns* (Lawrence: Regents Press of Kansas, 1979), 92; W. L. Payne, "Okemah's Night of Terror," in Hazel Ruby McMahan, ed., *Stories of Early Oklahoma,* on Rootsweb, rootsweb.com/pub/usgenweb/ok/okfuskee/history/town/oknite01 .txt; "Terrific Blast Rocks Town From Slumber Saturday," *Okemah Daily Leader* 4/23/ 1908, on Rootsweb, rootsweb.com/~okokfusk/cities.htm, 5/2003.

96. Okmulgee Historical Society, *History of Okmulgee County, Oklahoma* (Tulsa: History Enterprises, 1985), 166–68.

97. Bittle and Geis, *The Longest Way Home,* 37.

98. William E. Bittle and Gilbert Geis, "Racial Self Fulfillment and the Rise of an All-Negro Community in Oklahoma," in August Meier and Elliott Rudwick, eds., *The Making of Black America II* (New York: Atheneum, 1969), 116–21.

99. Sometimes whites—especially "river rats" in floodplains—live in similar settlements, but with a key difference: residents of black townships outside sundown towns are not *allowed* to live elsewhere.

100. Oakley V. Glenn, untitled manuscript (summary of events leading to a Eugene Human Rights Commission), (Eugene: Commission on Human Rights Office, n.d.), 3.

101. Clarence D. Stephenson, "Indiana Area Blacks Battle for Civil Rights," *Indiana Gazette,* 6/8/1985, and *175th Anniversary History of Indiana County* (Indiana: A.D. Halldin, 1979), 2:770–74, citing Dorothy Lydic et al., "Negro Progress in Indiana County," WPA manuscript, 1938, and Ralph Stone, "A Social Picture of Chevy Chase," Indiana (PA) State College (now Indiana University of Pennsylvania), 1960, 2–5.

102. Cullman librarian, e-mail, 3/2002; former Cullman resident, e-mail, 5/2002; Helen Bass Williams, manuscript fragment, "History of Negroes in Southern Illinois," n.d., in possession of Mary O'Hara; Noel Hall, 9/2002; untitled clipping in J. A. Gordon, comp.,

"Days Beyond Recall," vol. 2, reprints from *Warsaw Bulletin,* in Carthage (IL) Museum collection.

103. Brentwood, Central Islip, Flanders, Freeport, Gordon Heights, Hempstead, New Cassel, North Amityville, North Bay Shore, North Bellport, Roosevelt, and Uniondale.

104. Examples include North Brentwood, Maryland, outside Washington, D.C., and Kinloch, Missouri, outside of St. Louis. Unlike townships, North Brentwood incorporated in 1924 and is proud today to claim the title of "oldest incorporated black town in Maryland."

105. Vivian S. Toy, "Stuck in Last Place," *New York Times,* 5/4/2003; Leonard Blumberg and Michael Lalli, "Little Ghettoes: A Study of Negroes in the Suburbs," *Phylon* 27 (1966): 125; Andrew Wiese, *Places of Their Own* (Chicago: University of Chicago Press, 2004), 6, 17, 21; Harold M. Rose, *Black Suburbanization* (Cambridge: Ballinger, 1976), 29.

106. According to historian Lee Buchsbaum (e-mail, 3/2003), its prostitutes, all of whom were black, "could only be patronized by white customers. Black men were not even allowed in the building, day or night." The sheriff never challenged the arrangement, so long as he was paid off.

107. After the 1933 repeal of Prohibition nationally, it continued for many decades in some counties and the entire state of Oklahoma. So did white purchases of alcohol in black townships in those places.

108. Buchsbaum, e-mail, 3/2003; Jane Adams, e-mail, 6/2003; Stone, "A Social Picture of Chevy Chase," 7; Dean E. Murphy, "This Land Is Made, Finally, for Chinese Settlers," *New York Times,* 6/29/2003.

109. "Denver Closing Door of Hope Against Americans," Chicago *Defender,* 4/9/1910.

110. Chudacoff, *Mobile Americans,* 156.

111. Ibid.; original has "ethic group" in error.

CHAPTER 4: HOW SUNDOWN TOWNS WERE CREATED

1. Cf. "Decatur, Indiana, Is Suffering from a Bad Attack of 'Negrophobia,' " *Indianapolis Freeman,* 6/14/1902.

2. Jean Nipps Swaim, "Black History in Cedar County, Missouri," in *Black Families of the Ozarks,* Bulletin 45 (Springfield, MO: Greene County Archives, n.d.), 2:534.

3. Swaim doubts that any specific event took place, but I think it did, because the black population decline was so precipitous and the ensuing sundown ideology so strong.

4. Swaim, "Black History in Cedar County," 535; Cedar County historian, 10/2002. Swaim, 10/2002, does not know why blacks evacuated the county and thinks some merely relocated to Humansville, across the line in Polk County. Possibly, but Polk County also showed a drastic decline in black population shortly thereafter.

5. In most of the riots Horowitz describes, mass murder competed with forced relocation as an outcome; in almost all of the riots I have uncovered, forced relocation was the preferred outcome and killings were few and in the service of that goal. Exceptions include Rock Springs, Wyoming (1885); Rosewood, Florida (1923); and possibly Zeigler, Illinois (1905), and Mindenmines, Missouri (unknown date).

6. Donald Horowitz, *The Deadly Ethnic Riot* (Berkeley: University of California Press, 2001), 1–2.

7. Patrick Huber, "Race Riots and Black Exodus in the Missouri Ozarks, 1894–1905," Ozark Cultural Celebration, Harrison, AR, 9/2002, 7.

8. Straight-line 1908 projection based on 1900 and 1910 total populations; 1908 total percentage increase then applied to 1900 African American population.

9. Roberta Senechal, *The Sociogenesis of a Race Riot* (Urbana: University of Illinois Press, 1990), 135.

10. National outrage over this riot helped spark the formation of the NAACP the next year.

11. Nancy C. Curtis, *Black Heritage Sites: The North* (New York: New Press, 1996), 59; officer quoted in Allen C. Guelzo, *Abraham Lincoln, Redeemer President* (Grand Rapids: Eerdmans, 1999), 452; Philip A. Klinkner and R. M. Smith, *The Unsteady March* (Chicago: University of Chicago Press, 1999), 106–7.

12. Cf. ustrek.org/odyssey/semester2/013101/013101beckyriot1.html, 11/3/2002, based on Senechal, *The Sociogenesis of a Race Riot*; Klinkner and Smith, *The Unsteady March*.

13. Taylorville had a small African American population and did not go sundown, although new African Americans, especially refugees from Springfield, may have been kept out.

14. *Illinois State Register* quoted in Senechal, *The Sociogenesis of a Race Riot*, 129, 191; William English Walling, "The Race War in the North," *Independent*, 9/3/1908, 529–34, reprinted in Jonathan Birnbaum and Clarence Taylor, eds., *Civil Rights Since 1787* (New York: New York University Press, 2000), 187; Lester C. Lamon, *Black Tennesseans, 1900–1930* (Knoxville: University of Tennessee Press, 1977), 134.

15. See Chapter 6 for a fuller account of Spring Valley.

16. Carterville had already been sundown when this expulsion of strikebreakers took place.

17. Otto H. Olsen, *The Negro Question: From Slavery to Caste, 1863–1910* (New York: Pitman, 1971), xxi; "Negroes Have Always Avoided Beardstown," unidentified Beardstown newspaper clipping, 1929, via S. Lynn Walter; Malcolm Ross, *All Manner of Men* (New York: Reynal & Hitchcock, 1948), 51; Felix Armfield, "Fire on the Prairies," *Journal of Illinois History 3*, 3 (2000): 191; Victor Hicken, "The Virden and Pana Mine Wars of 1898," *Illinois State Historical Society Journal* 52, 2 (1959): 265–78; Millie Meyerholtz, *When Hatred and Fear Ruled* (Pana, IL: Pana News, 2001); Paul M. Angle, *Bloody Williamson* (New York: Knopf, 1952), 99–109; "Race War in Illinois," *New York Times*, 6/17/1902; "The Eldorado, Illinois Affair," *Indianapolis Freeman*, 7/19/1902; Senechal, *The Sociogenesis of a Race Riot*, 129–30; untitled article datelined "Anna, Ill., Nov. 13," *Carbondale Free Press*, 11/13/1909; Winifred M. Henson, "History of Franklin County, Illinois," M.A. thesis, Colorado State College of Education, 1942, 143; Pinckneyville native and homeowner, 9/2002, Pinckneyville motel owner, 9/2002, and warranty deed record, Edwards Addition Block 5 Lot 11, sale by Colored Free Will Baptist Church to Riley J. Boyd, 8/29/1928; "Lynch Law in Lacon," *Lacon Journal*, 11/10/1898; for Zeigler controversy see Ruby B. Goodwin, *It's Good To Be Black* (Garden City, NY: Doubleday, 1953), 174–75, Angle, *Bloody Williamson*, 128–31, Allan Patton, *In the Shadow of the Tipple: Zeigler, Illinois* (Zeigler: author, 1994), 34–38, Bob Proctor, 9/2002, and Noel Hall, 9/2002.

18. Again, according to Murray Bishoff, they got the wrong man.

19. Murray Bishoff, "Monett's Darkest Hour: The Lynching of June 28, 1894," *Monett Times*, 6/27–28/1994; Connie Farrow, " 'The Anger and the Hatred Ends,' " *News-Leader*, 8/18/2001.

20. Bishoff, "Monett's Darkest Hour"; Huber, "Race Riots and Black Exodus in the Missouri Ozarks, 1894–1905," 10.

21. Tom W. Dillard, "Madness with a Past: An Overview of Race Violence in Arkansas History," Arkansas Black History Online, cals.lib.ar.us/butlercenter/abho/bib/MADNESS.pdf,

2003, 7; Gordon D. Morgan, "Black Hillbillies of the Arkansas Ozarks," Department of Sociology, University of Arkansas, Fayetteville, 1973, 60.

22. My web site has a page collecting information on expulsion riots across the nation.

23. The departure of a major employer, such as a railroad, might affect most African American families at once. In that event, however, *some* blacks who worked for other employers—in domestic service, etc.—would remain, and whites would not develop a tradition that they prohibited African Americans from staying the night.

24. Frank U. Quillen, *The Color Line in Ohio* (Ann Arbor, MI: Wahr, 1913), 166.

25. James Allen et al., *Without Sanctuary* (Santa Fe: Twin Palms, 2000), shows lynching postcards and other souvenir photos.

26. "The Lynching of 'Nigger Pete,' " *Mena Star,* 2/16/1986; "The Real Polk County," *The Looking Glass* (Hatfield, AR), 1/1980, 16; Inez Lane, "Down Back Roads," *The Looking Glass,* 5/1977, 24; "Those Warning Notices," *Mena Star* 7/21/1897; "The Mayor Gives Good Advice," *Mena Star,* 8/17/1898; Shirley Manning, e-mail, 9/2002.

27. James B. Jones Jr., "A Chronological List of Lynchings in Tennessee, 1866–1946," Southern History Net, southernhistory.net, 3/2002; Stewart E. Tolnay and E. M. Beck, *A Festival of Violence* (Urbana: University of Illinois Press, 1995), 219; "Lynch Law in Lacon," *Lacon Journal,* 11/10/1898; Jack S. Blocker Jr., "Choice and Circumstance," Organization of American Historians, Toronto, 4/1999, Table 5.

28. *Burlington* (VT) *Free Press,* 6/1/1925.

29. Henson, *History of Franklin County, Illinois,* 151; Sally Albertz, e-mail, 5/2002.

30. Howard Goodman, "Bigotry: Oregon's Sad History," *Salem Statesman Journal, Oregon Territory* magazine, 2/8/1981, G3-5.

31. Lynwood Carranco, "The Chinese in Humboldt County, California: A Study in Prejudice," *Journal of the West,* January 1973, 334.

32. All sundown towns with evidence of ordinances are listed at my web site, uvm.edu/~jloewen/sundown. Information from readers confirming or disconfirming these towns can be e-mailed to me through that site.

33. Donald M. Royer, "Indiana's 'Sundown Ordinances' in Nineteen Indiana Towns and Cities" (Indianapolis: Indiana Civil Rights Commission, 1965), photocopy in the Indiana University Library, Bloomington; Olen Cole Jr., *The African-American Experience in the Civilian Conservation Corps* (Gainesville: University Press of Florida, 1999), 57.

34. Chapter 8 tells why I think these towns probably did pass such ordinances and describes the difficulty of locating them today.

35. Monticello lawyer, 10/2002; former De Land trustee, 10/2002; De Land official, 10/2002.

36. Jon L. Craig et al., eds., *Ordinance Law Annotations* (Colorado Springs: Shepard's/McGraw-Hill, 1990 [1969]), 433; cf. John T. Noonan, opinion in *Ho v. SFUSD,* 9715926, 6/4/1998, at Findlaw, laws.lp.findlaw.com/9th/9715926.html.

37. This was the amendment, you will recall, that was passed to guarantee equal rights to all Americans without regard to race. By 1917, the Court had effectively gutted it so far as its utility for improving the rights of African Americans.

38. Charles S. Johnson, *Negro Housing* (New York: Negro Universities Press, 1969 [1932]), 36–40; Susan D. Carle, "Race, Class, and Legal Ethics in the Early NAACP (1910–1920)," *Law and History Review* 20, 1 (2002), historycooperative.org/journals/lhr/20.1/carle.html, 8/2004; T. J. Woofter Jr., *Negro Problems in Cities* (New York: Harper & Row, 1969 [1928]), 71; Peter M. Bergman and Mort N. Bergman, *The Chronological History of the Negro in America* (New York: Mentor, 1969), 367, 380; *Buchanan v. Warley,* 245 U.S. 60.

39. Actually, scores of "exclusively white" towns dotted the North and West by 1915, some much larger than North Chattanooga, but people in North Chattanooga were oriented toward southern cities and towns, where sundown policies were rare.

40. J. Voigt, "Segregation for Suburb," *Chattanooga Daily Times,* 11/10/1915; "North Chattanooga Is Exclusively White Now," 12/22/1915, on Southern History web site, southern history.net/index.cfm?FuseAction=DisplayArticleContent&Art_ID=8933, 5/2003.

41. Indianapolis, for example, passed a residential zoning ordinance in 1926.

42. W. A. Low and V. A. Clift, eds., *Encyclopedia of Black America* (New York: McGraw-Hill, 1981), 446.

43. Vincent Jaster, "Education in Brea," interviewed by Cynthia Churney, California State University–Fullerton, Oral History #1720, 4/10–24/1982, 40.

44. Although Arthurdale had no African Americans until at least 1990, I do not know for sure that it was set up on a white-only basis.

45. Decatur, IL, resident, 20/2001; Martinsville native, 10/2002.

46. Emma Lou Thornbrough, edited and with final chapter by Lana Ruegamer, *Indiana Blacks in the Twentieth Century* (Bloomington: Indiana University Press, 2000), 2–3; Thornbrough, *The Negro in Indiana* (Indianapolis: Indiana Historical Bureau, 1957), 225–26; former resident of Crawford County, e-mail, 9/2002.

47. Hank Roth, "Who Is Hank Roth?" pnews.org/bio/5bio.shtml, 6/2003.

48. My web site lists these towns, along with others to be added as information comes in.

49. Willie Harlen, letter, 10/18/2002; David Roediger, e-mail, 8/2003.

50. Jim Clayton, e-mail, 11/2002; Judy Tonges, e-mail, 9/2002.

51. Niles resident, e-mail, 11/2002.

52. Lorenzo J. Greene, Gary Kremer, and Antonio Holland, *Missouri's Black Heritage* (Columbia: University of Missouri Press, 1993), 107, 147.

53. Stephen Vincent studied two small African American communities in east-central Indiana that went into a similar decline, and for the same reasons. He concluded, "The special bond shared by these [black] families and their surrounding white neighbors was loosened if not altogether undone in the late nineteenth century." Stephen A. Vincent, *Southern Seed, Northern Soil* (Bloomington: Indiana University Press, 1999), 127.

54. Robert Azug and Stephen Maizlish, eds., *New Perspectives on Race and Slavery in America* (Lexington: University Press of Kentucky, 1986), 118–21, 125; Robert C. Nesbit, *History of Wisconsin,* vol. III: *Urbanization and Industrialization, 1873–1893* (Madison: Wisconsin Historical Society, 1985), 437–38. Nesbit dates the community to 1848, but in 1860 only 10 blacks lived in the whole of Grant County, compared to 98 by 1870.

55. Edwina M. DeWindt, "Wyandotte History; Negro," typescript, 1945, in Bacon Library, Wyandotte, MI, 20–21; southern Illinois woman, 10/2002.

56. "Mass Meeting, Bell City, Mo. Resolutions," from Frank Nickell, Center for Regional History, Southestern Missouri State University.

57. DeWindt, "Wyandotte History; Negro," 2.

58. *Chesterton Tribune,* 1/26/1922; Edward H. Sebesta, e-mail, 7/2002.

59. Dorothy K. Newman et al., *Protest, Politics, and Prosperity* (New York: Pantheon, 1978), 144.

60. Deborah Morse-Kahn, *Edina: Chapters in the City History* (Edina: City of Edina, 1998), iii, 56–59.

61. Ibid., 56–59, 61, 94–95; Joyce Repya, 9/1999.

62. Chamblee native, 3/2003; former mayor, 3/2003.

63. Kathryn P. Nelson, *Recent Suburbanization of Blacks* (Washington, DC: HUD Office of Economic Affairs, 1979), 13.

64. Thomas L. Philpott, *The Slum and the Ghetto* (New York: Oxford University Press, 1978), 154.

65. Patrick M. McMullen, "Gated Communities," entry for *Encyclopedia of Chicago,* draft, 10/17/2000; Albert F. Winslow, *Tuxedo Park* (Tuxedo Park: Tuxedo Park Historical Society, 1992), 64–66.

66. Richland and Norris were not exactly suburbs but new communities near huge new military-industrial entities. The developers of Park Forest felt pressured by the FHA to set up their city for whites only. The original plan for Boulder City, Nevada, was also influenced by Howard's ideas, but that plan was never carried out. Also, one restauranteur defied the federal czar of Boulder City and hired a black cook.

67. Edward J. Blakely and Mary Gail Snyder, *Fortress America* (Washington, DC: Brookings, 1997), 19; Cynthia Mills Richter, "Integrating the Suburban Dream: Shaker Heights, Ohio," Ph.D. dissertation, University of Minnesota, 1999, 19; Allan Hepburn, review of Catherine Jurca's *White Diaspora, Journal of American History* 89, 4 (2003), 1572; "Blacks in Greenbelt," otal.umd.edu/~vg/mssp96/ms12/expla.html, 10/2002; Zane Miller, *Suburb* (Knoxville: University of Tennessee Press, 1981), 128; campus.murraystate.edu/academic/faculty/Bill.Mulligan/Kyv.htm, 9/2003; Mike Davis, *City of Quartz* (London: Verso, 1990), 161–67; Robert Parker, "Robert Parker Discusses Afro-Americans in Boulder City," interview with Dennis McBride, 11/9/1986, Banyan Library web site, banyan.library.unlv.edu/cgi-bin/htmldesc.exe?CISOROOT=/Hoover_Dam&CISOPTR=56&CISOMODE=1, 11/2004; Dennis McBride, "The Boulder City Dictator," *Las Vegas Review-Journal,* lst100.com/part1/ely.html, 11/2004.

68. John H. Denton quoted by Michael N. Danielson, *The Politics of Exclusion* (New York: Columbia University Press, 1976), 31; Frank Harold Wilson, *Footsteps from North Brentwood* (North Brentwood, MD: Historical Society, 1997), 8; Darwin Payne, *Big D* (Dallas: Three Forks Press, 1994), 216–17.

69. Larry McClellan, "Phoenix," entry for *Encyclopedia of Chicago,* draft, 10/1/1999.

70. Sheridan natives, about 65 and 75 years old, in Grant County Museum, 10/2001; Jean Bancroft, post to AAPS Online Forum, aaps.forums.practicenotes.com/forums/Thread.cfm?CFID=946732&CFTOKEN=65413367&&Thread_ID6881&mc=4, 10/15/2003. Note that Searcy the town is quite different from Searcy County, a sundown county in the Ozarks, and is not in Searcy County.

71. De Land official, 10/2002.

CHAPTER 5: SUNDOWN SUBURBS

1. Supplied by Joyce Repya, associate planner for Edina, 9/1999.

2. "A Northern City 'Sitting on Lid' of Racial Trouble," *US News & World Report,* 5/11/1956, 38–40; David L. Good, *Orvie: The Dictator of Dearborn* (Detroit: Wayne State University Press, 1989), 40–41, 264, 386–87; Reynolds Farley, Sheldon Danziger, and Harry Holzer, *Detroit Divided* (New York: Russell Sage, 2000), 154–55; August Meier and Elliott Rudwick, *Black Detroit and the Rise of the UAW* (New York: Oxford University Press, 1979), 12.

3. Andrew Wiese, *Places of Their Own* (Chicago: University of Chicago Press, 2004), 49.

4. Kenneth T. Jackson, *Crabgrass Frontier* (New York: Oxford University Press, 1985),

283–84; M. P. Baumgartner, *The Moral Order of a Suburb* (New York: Oxford University Press, 1988), 6; Thomas Byrne Edsall and Mary D. Edsall, *Chain Reaction* (New York: Norton, 1992), 229, 231.

5. John Palen, *The Suburbs* (New York: McGraw-Hill, 1995), xiii, 3–7; Lizabeth Cohen, *A Consumers' Republic* (New York: Knopf, 2003), 255.

6. Moving to the suburbs was hardly the obvious path to "the good life." From Johannesburg to Lima to Jakarta, suburbs are inconvenient places where poor people live who must travel miles to the central city to work or attend cultural events. In nineteenth-century America, elegant rowhouse districts such as Boston's Beacon Hill were what American families wanted as they grew more affluent.

7. Larry Peterson, e-mail, 3/2004.

8. Ford quoted in Jackson, *Crabgrass Frontier,* 75.

9. Jackson, *Crabgrass Frontier,* 149–50, 272–73.

10. Ellen James Martin, "Set Some Priorities When Buying in a Classy Community," Universal Press Syndicate, in *Chicago Tribune,* 9/14/2001.

11. Thomas Pettigrew, "Attitudes on Race and Housing," in Amos Hawley and Vincent Rock, eds., *Segregation in Residential Areas* (Washington, DC: National Academy of Sciences, 1973), 38; Andrew Hacker, "Sociology and Ideology," in Max Black, ed., *The Social Theories of Talcott Parsons* (Englewood Cliffs, NJ: Prentice-Hall, 1961), 289; Stephen G. Meyer, *As Long as They Don't Move Next Door* (Lanham, MD: Rowman & Littlefield, 2000), 1.

12. Other similar suburbs include Stamford, Connecticut; Montclair and Orange, New Jersey; New Rochelle and Mt. Vernon, New York; Coral Gables, Florida; Webster Groves, Missouri, and Pasadena, California.

13. Jackson, *Crabgrass Frontier,* 100–1, 241.

14. Bernard Nelson, *The Fourteenth Amendment and the Negro Since 1920* (New York: Russell & Russell, 1946), 23–24; Colleen Kilner, *Joseph Sears and His Kenilworth* (Kenilworth: Kenilworth Historical Society, 1990), 138, 143, her italics.

15. Newlands, senator from Nevada, honed his racism as a leader of anti-Chinese sentiment there. In 1909, he wrote "Race tolerance . . . means race amalgamation, and this is undesirable" and argued that the United States "should prevent the immigration of all people other than those of the white race." Quoted in Loren B. Chan, "The Chinese in Nevada," in Arif Dirlik, ed., *Chinese on the American Frontier* (Lanham, MD: Rowman & Littlefield, 2001), 88–89.

16. Not all of those 18 may have been black; some may be nonblacks in an interracial family. In all, Chevy Chase had 42 African Americans, but that total includes live-in maids and gardeners. The census also showed 20 mixed-race persons who listed "black" or "African American" among their component identities, hard to classify, since the census does not reveal how they identified. Some may be mixed-race children adopted by white couples. I summed the four entities that collectively make up Chevy Chase: Chevy Chase (town), Chevy Chase Section Three, Chevy Chase Section Five, and Chevy Chase Village.

17. Marc Fisher, "Chevy Chase, 1916: For Everyman, a New Lot in Life," *Washington Post,* 2/15/1999; washingtonpost.com/wp-srv/local/2000/chevychase0215.htm, 1/2003.

18. Fisher, "Chevy Chase, 1916."

19. Mt. Auburn Cemetery web site, mountauburn.org/history.htm, 8, 2004.

20. Unlike sundown suburbs, sundown cemeteries rarely forced out existing black "residents."

21. "Denial by Cemetery Company of Burial Space for Colored Person, Held Not to Be Violation of a Civil Right," 258 IL 36, in Illinois State Archives.

22. David Charles Sloane, *The Last Great Necessity* (Baltimore: Johns Hopkins University Press, 1995), 188, 268.

23. Kilner, *Joseph Sears and His Kenilworth;* Michael Ebner, *Creating Chicago's North Shore* (Chicago: University of Chicago Press, 1988), 230, 314; Harry Rubenstein, 9/2000; "Housing: How High the Barriers," *ADL Bulletin* 16, 1 (1959): 2.

24. The Ku Klux Klan did target Jews and Catholics verbally in independent sundown towns in the mid-1920s, but rarely did they actually drive them out or keep them out.

25. Grosse Pointe did not completely bar Jews but required them to amass more points on Grosse Pointe's notorious "point system" than any other permitted group. See pages 262–64.

26. I don't think many whites really believed Jews were genetically less intelligent. The attacks on Jews, whether by Nazis in Europe or by real estate developers in the United States, were more subtle than those on African Americans. Jews were considered "crafty" rather than intelligent—a distinction wholly in the mind of the beholder.

27. Some are listed at uvm.edu/~jloewen/sundown.

28. We shall see in the next chapter that this perception has some validity.

29. Laura Z. Hobson, *Gentleman's Agreement* (New York: Simon & Schuster, 1947); "Housing Discrimination Against Jews," *ADL Reports* 2, 5 (1959), 41; Graham Hutton, *Midwest at Noon* (Chicago: University of Chicago Press, 1946), 48; Mary Ellen Stratthaus, "Flaw in the Jewel: Housing Discrimination Against Jews in La Jolla, California," *American Jewish History* 84, 3 (1996): 190.

30. *Memorandum on Specific Methods for Promoting Good Will Among Racial Groups in Illinois* (Illinois Interracial Commission, 1943), #4, 2; Jackson, *Crabgrass Frontier,* 241; Levitt & Sons, ad taken out after murder of Martin Luther King Jr., 4/1968, in exhibit, "Levittown," Pennsylvania State Museum, Harrisburg, 11/2002; Geoffrey Mohan writing in *Newsday,* quoted by Kevin Schultz, e-mail, 6/2002.

31. Donald Cunnigen, "Myrdal, Park, and Second Generation African American Sociologists," in Bruce Hare, ed., *2001 Race Odyssey* (Syracuse: Syracuse University Press, 2002), 42; Arnold Hirsch, *Making the Second Ghetto* (Cambridge: Cambridge University Press, 1983), 63; James Hecht, *Because It Is Right* (Boston: Little, Brown, 1970), 8.

32. Thomas Sugrue, *Origins of the Urban Crisis* (Princeton: Princeton University Press, 1996), 43; Jack Star, "Negro in the Suburbs," *Look,* 5/16/1967; Brian Berry et al., *Chicago* (Cambridge: Ballinger, 1976), 30; Troy Duster, "The 'Morphing' Properties of Whiteness," in Birgit Rasmussen et al., eds., *The Making and Unmaking of Whiteness* (Durham: Duke University Press, 2001), 119; Mike Davis, *City of Quartz* (London: Verso, 1990), 167.

33. Abrams quoted by Jackson, *Crabgrass Frontier,* 214, cf. 208, 213, 229–43; Lawrence J. Vale, *From the Puritans to the Projects* (Cambridge: Harvard University Press, 2000), 169–70; Lockwood quoted in Newman, *Protest, Politics, and Prosperity,* 163.

34. W. A. Low and V. A. Clift, eds., *Encyclopedia of Black America* (New York: McGraw-Hill, 1981), 449; "Outline of Protective Covenants for Mayfair Park," supplied by Elise Guyette, 4/2003.

35. Palen, *The Suburbs,* 58; Cohen, *A Consumers' Republic,* 196; Nancy A. Denton, "Segregation and Discrimination in Housing," in Rachel Bratt, Chester Hartman, and Michael E. Stone, eds., reader on housing (Philadelphia: Temple University Press, forthcoming), ms. pp. 23–24; cf. Thomas W. Hanchett, "The Other 'Subsidized Housing,' " in John Bauman

et al., *From Tenements to the Taylor Homes* (University Park, PA: Penn State University Press, 2000), 166.

36. Low and Clift, eds., *Encyclopedia of Black America*, 451–52.

37. The first and fourth chapters of *Because It Is Right* by James Hecht bring to life the process by which white suburbs ignored 1968 and stayed overwhelmingly white through the 1970s (and some to this day), with examples of African Americans who could not buy even though they were doctors, lawyers, or famous professional athletes.

38. Douglas Massey, talk at the Fund for an Open Society (OPEN), Philadelphia, 12/2000; Michael N. Danielson, *The Politics of Exclusion* (New York: Columbia University Press, 1976), 12; David M. P. Freund, *Colored Property*, 15, typescript, 2001; cf. Hecht, *Because It Is Right*, chapters 1 and 4.

39. Western shore native, e-mail, 11/2002; state worker, 9/2002.

40. Margery Turner et al., *All Other Things Being Equal* (Washington, DC: Urban Institute, 2002), executive summary, i-v; Shanna Smith, in panel discussion, "A Foot in the Door? New Evidence on Housing Discrimination," Urban Institute, Washington, DC, 2/4/2003.

41. Jackson, *Crabgrass Frontier*, 283. By 1990, most of Baltimore's sundown suburbs had relented, and the proportion of African Americans in Baltimore and Baltimore County (not quite the same as the metropolitan area) who lived in Baltimore County was 16.4%; by 2000, it was 26.6%.

42. For a list, see uvm.edu/~jloewen/sundown/.

43. Harold M. Rose, *Black Suburbanization* (Cambridge: Ballinger, 1976), 5, 7, 9, 29, 31, 47–48, 84, 158.

44. Michael Powell, "Separate and Unequal in Roosevelt, Long Island," *Washington Post*, 4/21/2002; Joe T. Darden, "African American Residential Segregation," in Robert D. Bullard et al., *Residential Apartheid* (Los Angeles: UCLA Center for Afro-American Studies, 1994), 88–89.

45. Camilo Jose Vergara, *American Ruins* (New York: Monacelli, 1999), 92; Danielson, *The Politics of Exclusion*, 8–9; Arthur Hayes, "Managed Integration," *Black Enterprise*, 7/1982, 44; Meyer, *As Long as They Don't Move Next Door*, 217.

46. Jeff R. Crump, "Producing and Enforcing the Geography of Hate," in Colin Flint, ed., *Spaces of Hate* (New York: Routledge, 2003), 227.

CHAPTER 6: UNDERLYING CAUSES

1. John C. Boger, "Toward Ending Residential Segregation: A Fair Share Proposal for the Next Reconstruction," *North Carolina Law Review* 71 (1993): 1576.

2. My web site, uvm.edu/~jloewen/sundown, lists these towns.

3. Therefore I use "all-white" to refer to towns that admit Asian, Native, and Mexican Americans, while barring African Americans.

4. John Ogbu, *Minority Education and Caste* (New York: Academic Press, 1978).

5. Jews and Mexicans *are* "white," of course, by the definitions of 2005. Jews weren't exactly, between 1900 and about 1950, and Mexicans weren't exactly, between 1930 and about 1970. Later chapters comment on this issue.

6. "His Flight to Save Prisoner," *Carbondale Daily Free Press*, 11/13/1909; Darrel Dexter, *A House Divided: Union County, Illinois* (Anna: Reppert, 1994), 73–75.

7. Dexter, *House Divided*, 75.

8. Jerry Poling, *A Summer Up North* (Madison: University of Wisconsin Press, 2002), 10.

9. Forrest C. Pogue Public History Institute web site, campus.murraystate.edu/academic/ faculty/Bill.Mulligan/Kyv.htm, 10/2004; Robert Parker, "Robert Parker Discusses Afro-Americans in Boulder City," interview with Dennis McBride, 11/9/1986, Banyan Library web site, banyan.library.unlv.edu/cgi-bin/htmldesc.exe?CISOROOT=/Hoover_Dam& CISOPTR=56&CISOMODE=1, 11/2004; "A Northern City 'Sitting on Lid' of Racial Trouble," *US News & World Report,* 5/11/1956, 38–40; Michigan Advisory Committee on Civil Rights, *Civil Rights and the Housing and Community Development Act of 1974, v. I: Livonia* (Washington, D.C.: U.S. Commission on Civil Rights, 1975), 6; George Hunter, "Booming City Has Home to Fit Every Need, Price Range," *Detroit News,* 2/2/97.

10. Chairman, Illinois Inter-Racial Commission, 11/19/1943, minutes in Illinois State Archives.

11. Sociologist Gordon Morgan suggests that African Americans left some Ozark counties in the early decades of the twentieth century because they lacked the critical mass necessary to maintain community. This is an aspect of social isolation and at first blush seems reasonable. In *The Mississippi Chinese* (Cambridge, MA: Harvard University Press, 1971), I myself wrote, "There will come a time of 'critical mass,' when a Chinese community in any sense of the word will prove unmaintainable," and went on to predict a rapid drop in the population of Chinese Americans in the Mississippi Delta. The prediction came true after 1975. But the Chinese case was different: economic and educational upward mobility led to geographic mobility for their children, while at the same time, the end of racial segregation in Mississippi eliminated the peculiar niche for Chinese Americans as a middleman minority, leaving no particular reason for new immigrants to enter the Delta.

  To be sure, when the African American population falls below a minimum, it becomes difficult to date or marry another African American or support a black church. Until Missouri's schools desegregated (well after 1954), fifteen African American children were required before a school district had to provide a "colored school," and eight of high-school age before it had to provide a high school. In the absence of a school for their children, some parents will certainly move. Morgan's hypothesis doubtless explains why some African Americans left, especially families with children seeking marriage mates. He believes it explains Huntsville, Arkansas, which had 15 blacks in 1940 and just 1 in 1950, and it may.

  Critical mass also helps explain the departure of most of the remaining African Americans from Maryville, Missouri, after the 1931 lynching described in Chapter 7. Most blacks fled immediately, and enrollment at the "colored school" fell from sixteen students to six. Two years later it closed entirely, causing the black population of Nodaway County to decline still further. But the root cause of Nodaway as a sundown county remains the lynching and subsequent threats to the black community, not critical mass. (See Patrick Huber and Gary Kremer, "A Death in the Heartland," presented at Missouri Conference on History, St. Louis, 3/1994, 10.) Similarly, critical mass theory does not explain why black newcomers no longer entered counties across America after 1890, as they had earlier. If numbers alone could explain why a group leaves an area, then no new group would ever enter unless they could do so en masse.

12. Andrew Wiese, *Places of Their Own* (Chicago: University of Chicago Press, 2004), 19, 145.

13. Boger, "Toward Ending Residential Segregation," 1576.

14. I simplify. Affluent whites also choose elite suburbs for other reasons, such as better schooling, as later chapters acknowledge, but again "better" often implicitly involves separation from people seen as problems—usually those of lower caste and class position.

15. Michael N. Danielson, *The Politics of Exclusion* (NY: Columbia University Press, 1976), 9–10; Frederick M. Wirt et. al., *On the City's Rim* (Lexington, MA: D.C. Heath, 1972), 43, citing research by John Kain and Joseph Persky.

16. Karl Taeuber, "Racial Segregation: The Persisting Dilemma," *The Annals* 422 (11/1975), 91.

17. "A Northern City 'Sitting on Lid' of Racial Trouble," 38–40; Michigan Advisory Committee on Civil Rights, *Civil Rights and the Housing and Community Development Act of 1974, v. I: Livonia* (Washington, D.C.: U.S. Commission on Civil Rights, 1975), 6; George Hunter, "Booming City Has Home to Fit Every Need, Price Range," *Detroit News,* 2/2/97.

18. Albert Hermalin and Reynolds Farley quoted in Dorothy K. Newman et. al., *Protest, Politics, and Prosperity* (New York: Pantheon, 1978), 143; Farley, Sheldon Danziger, and Harry J. Holzer, *Detroit Divided* (New York: Russell Sage, 2000), 165.

19. *Worth* supplied four other lists of 50 towns each, covering the richest 250 towns in all.

20. Bobbie Gossage, "The Best Address," *Worth* 11, 4 (5/2002), 59; Ellen Revelle Eckis, interviewed 2/1996 by Mary Ellen Stratthaus, "Flaw in the Jewel: Housing Discrimination against Jews in La Jolla, California," *American Jewish History,* 84, 3 (1996), 219, n.1.

21. Garrett County historian, 5/2002.

22. Texas A&M professor, 9/99; woman from Buffalo, 7/2002.

23. Inadvertently, this argument assumes that African Americans are much better at economic prognostication than whites, who seem not to have the common sense to avoid these backwaters. It also implies that their all-white status is not worth correcting: either it results from blacks' rational choice or, if white residents do forbid their entrance, African Americans do well to avoid these towns anyway.

24. Stephan Thernstrom and Abigail Thernstrom, *America in Black and White* (New York: Simon & Schuster, 1997).

25. Nicole Etcheson, *The Emerging Midwest* (Indianapolis: Indiana University Press, 1996), 97.

26. Contrast Robert Gerling: *Highland: An Illinois Swiss Community in the American Civil War* (Highland, IL: Highland Historical Society, 1978), 21, for example, with *The History of Peoria County* (Chicago: Johnson & Co., 1880), 360, 409, 418.

27. Princeton, another Republican town, is near but not on the Illinois River or it would also be an exception.

28. Dexter, *House Divided,* 73–75; *Combined History of Shelby and Moultrie Counties, Illinois* (Philadelphia: Brink, McDonough, 1881), 31; I. J. Martin, *Notes on the History of Moultrie County and Sullivan, Illinois* (Sullivan: R. Eden Martin, 1990), 29; Jacque Neal, e-mail, 10/2001; Moultrie County teacher at Illinois Council for the Social Studies, 9/2002.

29. S. M. Lipset, *Political Man* (Garden City, NY: Doubleday Anchor, 1963 [1960]), 374–83.

30. Western Virginia, of course, succeeded.

31. Esther S. Sanderson, *County Scott and Its Mountain Folk* (Nashville: Williams Printing, 1958), 187.

32. Michael W. Fitzgerald, *The Union League Movement in the Deep South* (Baton Rouge: Louisiana State University Press, 1989), 17–18; David K. Shipler, *A Country of Strangers* (New York: Knopf, 1997), 108; Cullman librarian, e-mail, 7/2002; Steve Hicks, 6/2002; Haleyville librarian, 6/2002.

33. Melissa Sue Brewer, "Historical Context: Sundowning in Myakka City," typescript, Myakka

City, 2002, 1; Ralph R. Rea, *Boone County and Its People* (Van Buren, AR: Press-Argus, 1955), 53; several other county histories.

34. Mark Lause, e-mails, 6/2002, citing *History of Franklin, Jefferson, Washington, Crawford, and Gasconade Counties, Missouri* (Chicago, 1888); Art Draper, e-mail, 7/2002.

35. Bob Neymeyer, e-mail, 5/2002.

36. Lancaster resident, 8/2004.

37. Political scientist Larry Peterson suggests that Italian Americans also lacked social power to keep blacks out. He further notes that Jews fled "racially changing neighborhoods as fast as, if not faster than, other whites" (Peterson, e-mail, 3/2004).

38. Jan Reiff, 9/2001; T. J. Woofter Jr., *Negro Problems in Cities* (New York: Harper & Row, 1969 [1928]), 39; Hillel Levine and Lawrence Harmon, *The Death of an American Jewish Community* (New York: Free Press, 1992), 6; Thomas Sugrue, *Origins of the Urban Crisis* (Princeton: Princeton University Press, 1996), 243–44; Charles Bright, e-mail, 4/2004.

39. Noel Ignatiev, *How the Irish Became White* (New York: Routledge, 1995), 112, and quoting John Finch, "an English Owenite who traveled the United States in 1843," 97.

40. Carl Weinberg tells of the beginning of this white ethnic solidarity, vis-à-vis blacks, in the aftermath of the successful United Mine Workers strike at Virden, Illinois, in 1898. See "The Battle of Virden, the UMWA, and the Challenge of Solidarity," in Rosemary Feurer, ed., *Remember Virden, 1898* (Chicago: Illinois Humanities Council, n.d.), 7–8.

41. Yes, I know *Norwegians* dominate Lake Wobegone, which is precisely why they tell Swedish jokes on occasion.

42. Granite City Public Library, *75th Year Celebration of the City of Granite City, Illinois* (Granite City: n.p., 1971), 24; Matthew Jacobson, *Whiteness of a Different Color* (Cambridge: Harvard University Press, 1998).

43. Peter Baldwin, "Italians in Middletown, 1893–1932," B.A. thesis, Wesleyan University, 1984, 18–19; David Roediger, 8/2003.

44. Ronald L. Lewis, *Black Coal Miners in America* (Lexington: University Press of Kentucky, 1987), 81.

45. Some Greek Americans never returned to Zeigler, however, and the town still has fewer than it did before the expulsion.

46. John Higham, *Strangers in the Land* (New Brunswick: Rutgers University Press, 1955), 264; *Marion Daily Republican*, 8/13/1920, 1; Williamson County genealogist, 9/2002; Winifred M. Henson, "History of Franklin County, Illinois," M.A. thesis, Colorado State College of Education, 1942, 143; retired Zeigler miner, 9/2002.

47. Sometimes they played this role wittingly, having no loyalty to a labor union that had kept them out, and sometimes unwittingly, having been lied to by company recruiters, lured in from hundreds of miles away, and now unable to leave owing to company coercion and lack of funds.

48. See conflicting reports in Caroline Waldron, " 'Lynch-law Must Go!' " *Journal of American Ethnic History*, Fall 2000, 50–74; Felix Armfield, "Fire on the Prairies," *Journal of Illinois History* 3, 3 (2000): 188–97; Arna Bontemps and Jack Conroy, *Anyplace but Here* (New York: Hill & Wang, 1966 [1945]), 143; and various newspaper articles.

49. Millie Meyerholtz, *When Hatred and Fear Ruled . . . Pana, Illinois* (Pana, IL: Pana News, 2001), 1; citing Eleanor Burhorn, *Strike of Coal Miners at Pana, Illinois—1898–99*, 7, 12–13; Victor Hicken, "The Virden and Pana Mine Wars of 1898," *Illinois State Historical Society Journal* 52, 2 (1959), 274.

50. Meyerholtz, *When Hatred and Fear Ruled,* 8, 17, 21, 25–26, 33; Lewis, *Black Coal Miners in America,* 92–93.

51. Marvin L. Van Gilder, *The Story of Barton County* (Lamar, MO: Reiley, 1972), 20; staff member, Missouri Southern State College, 4/2001.

52. Paul M. Angle, *Bloody Williamson* (New York: Knopf, 1952), 120–25; Patton, *In the Shadow of the Tipple,* 30–32.

53. Angle wrote contemporaneously with Goodwin but should have known of her as a source because of her prominence in the black community.

54. It isn't always clear, especially in the oral tradition, which disaster was which, or who—by race and ethnicity—was blown up when. Historian Paul Angle claims most of the dead were Hungarians; others think most of the casualties were African Americans. Historians also disagree with each other and with the oral tradition as to the causes of the disasters, without explaining adequately the basis for their positions. At the time, the mine management thought the strikers blew up the strikebreakers, and a coroner's jury agreed. On the other hand, an inquiry by the state called it an accident and blamed it on gas buildup, and Angle and Patton agree.

55. Angle, *Bloody Williamson,* 126–30; Patton, *In the Shadow of the Tipple,* 34–36; Ruby B. Goodwin, *It's Good to Be Black* (Garden City, NY: Doubleday, 1953), 174–75.

56. Of course, it has always been easier for the white industrialist or mine operator to be more tolerant on race than for white workers. It's in the capitalist's immediate interest to hire anyone who will work for lower wages. African Americans have long constituted a reserve army of unemployed and underemployed labor, often willing to work at lower pay than whites. Sometimes capitalists hired African Americans for this reason and worked them alongside whites in the same jobs for lower pay, which of course had a chilling effect on white workers' efforts to win higher wages. It's also in owners' interests to hire people who will work when others won't, during a strike. Capitalists often found it easy to engage African Americans as strikebreakers. Blacks had little solidarity with white workers and their unions, since those same unions had shut them out of skilled jobs and restricted union membership to whites only. Hiring the best person for the job regardless of color also fits with the capitalist ethos and with the shards of anti-racist idealism that sometimes remained from the broken vessel of Republican abolitionism. Most important, after African Americans have been hired, the capitalist remains above his black employees—as well as his white employees—in social status, whereas the white worker is not above a black co-worker. Thus when the workplace integrates, the white worker is asked to give up white supremacy, while the capitalist is not.

57. Since these industries were among the few that employed African Americans, such occupational exclusion may have helped to cause the Great Retreat to the cities. But African Americans were no more likely to find jobs in these occupations in cities. I am also not persuaded that the rise of unions suffices to explain all-white towns and counties, because African Americans in such nonunion fields as domestics, barbers, janitors, haulers, and farmworkers also left.

58. Peterson, e-mail, 3/2004; Marc Karson and Ronald Radosh, "The AFL and the Negro Worker, 1894–1949," in Julius Jacobson, ed., *The Negro and the American Labor Movement* (Garden City, NY: Doubleday Anchor, 1968), 157–58.

CHAPTER 7: CATALYSTS AND ORIGIN MYTHS

1. *Chesterton Tribune,* 7/24/1903.
2. The census did find five individual African Americans, but black householders are the more important test of sundown policies.
3. Emma Lou Thornbrough, *The Negro in Indiana* (Indianapolis: Indiana Historical Bureau, 1957), 226–27; Steve Byers, e-mail, 6/2002; history teacher, 4/2002.
4. *The Worker,* 7/26/1903, quoted in Philip Foner and Ronald Lewis, eds., *The Black Worker from 1900 to 1919* (Philadelphia: Temple University Press, 1980), 198; Andrew Kirchmeier, 4/2002.
5. Ruby B. Goodwin, *It's Good to Be Black* (Garden City, NY: Doubleday, 1953); "Gentleman of Color Elected Alderman," *Herrin News,* 4/25/1918, 4.
6. Paul M. Angle, *Bloody Williamson* (New York: Knopf, 1952), 97–109; Herbert Gutman, "The Negro and the UMW," in Julius Jacobson, *The Negro and the American Labor Movement* (Garden City, NY: Doubleday Anchor, 1968), 49.
7. Nebraska Writers' Project, *The Negroes of Nebraska* (Omaha: Urban League, 1940), 10; Philip Jenkins, e-mail, 8/2002; Gutman, "The Negro and the UMW," 99.
8. This "local legend" was still extant in 2002, when I interviewed residents of Zeigler.
9. Allan Patton, *In the Shadow of the Tipple: Zeigler, Illinois* (Zeigler: author, 1994), 28.
10. Cf. Willis D. Weatherford and Charles S. Johnson, *Race Relations* (Boston: D. C. Heath, 1934), 59; Ralph E. Luker, *The Social Gospel in Black and White* (Chapel Hill: University of North Carolina Press, 1991), 237; Mark Odintz, "Slocum, Texas," in *Handbook of Texas Online,* tsha.utexas.edu/handbook/online/articles/view/SS/hls57.html, 2003; Sitton and Conrad, *Nameless Towns,* 108–9.
11. Thornbrough, *The Negro in Indiana,* 225.
12. Ferguson quoted in Roberta Senechal, *The Sociogenesis of a Race Riot* (Urbana: University of Illinois Press, 1990), 136; Deepak Madala, Jennifer Jordan, and August Appleton, "Prominent Resident Killed," library.thinkquest.org/2986/Killed.html, 8/2002.
13. Perhaps they were only trying to get a key. Accounts differ.
14. One black barber, Alex Johnson, was allowed back, a pattern we shall encounter frequently.
15. "KKK in Owosso," *Owosso Press,* 10/11/1871; Helen Harrelson, 10/15/2002.
16. John Womack, "Blacks, The First Year[s] in Oklahoma," typescript, Norman, 1982, 4–7.
17. Bianca White, "The History/Ocoee: Legacy of the Election Day Massacre," iml.jou.ufl .edu/projects/Fall01/white/2ocoee1.html, 12/2002; Evan Bennett, e-mail, 2/1998; Edwin Reuter, *The American Race Problem* (New York: Crowell, 1927), 418; cf. Maxine Jones, "The African-American Experience in Twentieth-Century Florida," in Michael Gannon, ed., *The New History of Florida* (Gainesville: University Press of Florida, 1996).
18. "Drive Out Race After Bloody Tilt," *Chicago Defender,* 9/24/1921; Afi O. Scruggs, e-mail, 9/2002.
19. Male Sheridan native, about 65 years of age, and female native, about 75, 10/2001; professor, Southern Arkansas University, 10/2001.
20. C. K. Bullard quoted in Dorothy Brown, "The Encircled Schools: Park Cities and Wilmington," *Dallas Times Herald,* 11/30/1975; Charles Martin, e-mail, 7/2002.
21. Womack, "Blacks, The First Year[s] in Oklahoma," 22–24.
22. My web site, uvm.edu/~jloewen/sundown, lists these counties.
23. Waalkes goes on to note, "I have also heard that Polk County simply pressured black families to send their children to school in Bradley County."

24. Mary Waalkes, e-mail, 7/2002; Esther S. Sanderson, *Scott County, Gem of the Cumberlands* (Huntsville, TN: author, 1974), 72.

25. Judith Joy, "Memorial to a Slain Girl Recalls a Violent Episode in Cairo's History," *Centralia Sentinel,* 1/3/1982, based on 1909 accounts in the *Sentinel.*

26. "His Flight to Save Prisoner," *Carbondale Daily Free Press,* 11/13/1909; Judith Joy, "Memorial to a Slain Girl."

27. "Hang and Burn Negro—White Man Also Lynched," *Carbondale Daily Press,* 11/12/1909.

28. Untitled article datelined "Anna, Ill., Nov. 13," *Carbondale Daily Free Press,* 11/13/1909; Dexter, *House Divided,* 73–75; local historian, 6/10/2003.

29. Donald F. Tingley, *The Structuring of a State: The History of Illinois, 1899 to 1928* (Urbana: University of Illinois Press, 1980), 291–92; James Allen et al., *Without Sanctuary* (Santa Fe: Twin Palms, 2000), #46, 181–84; "In Memory Of Miss Pelley," *Carbondale Free Press,* 11/17/1909.

30. Two were tried and hanged in Cummins, the county seat.

31. Garland C. Bagley, *History of Forsyth County, Georgia, II* (Greenville, SC: Southern Historical Press, 1985), 614.

32. Philip A. Klinkner and R. M. Smith, *The Unsteady March* (Chicago: University of Chicago Press, 1999), 106–7; Pinckneyville motel owner, 9/2002; LaSalle native, 6/2000.

33. Eulalia N. Wells, *Blazing the Way* (Blanket, TX: author, 1942), 159–61.

34. Felix Armfield, "Fire on the Prairies," *Journal of Illinois History* 3, 3 (2000); Arna Bontemps and Jack Conroy, *Anyplace but Here* (New York: Hill & Wang, 1966 [1945]); Edwina M. DeWindt, "Wyandotte History; Negro," typescript, 1945, in Bacon Library, Wyandotte, MI; *Chesterton Tribune,* 7/24/1903.

35. "His Flight to Save Prisoner"; Senechal, *The Sociogenesis of a Race Riot,* 158; Roadside Georgia, Forsyth County, roadsidegeorgia.com/county/forsyth.html, 1/2004; and Dawson County, roadsidegeorgia.com/county/dawson.html, 1/2004.

36. "Hindus Hounded from City," *Bellingham Herald,* 9/5/1907.

37. Bill Kaplin, 4/2002; Kathy Spillman, 12/2000.

38. *Lexington Herald,* 11/1/1919, and Corbin resident, quoted in Robby Heason, *Trouble Behind* (Cicada Films, 1990); Hank Everman, "Corbin, Kentucky: A Socioeconomic Anomaly," Department of History, Eastern Kentucky University, 2002, unpaginated.

39. George C. Wright, *A History of Blacks in Kentucky* 2 (Lexington: Kentucky Historical Society, 1992), 15; Murray Bishoff, 9/2002.

40. Patrick Huber and Gary Kremer, "A Death in the Heartland," paper presented at Missouri Conference on History, St. Louis, 3/1994, 12–13; "The Lynchings," Minnesota Historical Society, collections.mnhs.org/duluthlynchings/web_assets/icon_arrowback.gif, 12/2003.

41. Wells, *Blazing the Way,* 162; Billy Bob Lightfoot, "The Negro Exodus from Comanche County, Texas," *Southwestern Historical Quarterly* 56 (1953): 410–13; John Leffler, "Comanche County," *The Handbook of Texas Online,* 6/2002.

42. I have not found any midwestern ordinances, let alone a chain of dated ordinances that would demonstrate their diffusion. Chapter 8 discusses this problem.

43. "June 12, 1992," Nationalist web site, nationalist.org/docs/law/supreme.html#Top, 1/2004; Andrew H. Myers, "Winter Day in Georgia," typescript, 1997; Oprah Winfrey, "Vintage Oprah: Racial Tension in Georgia," Harpo Productions, Chicago, 2001 (1987), 7.

44. Smokey Crabtree, *Too Close to the Mirror* (Fouke: Days Creek Production, 2001), 186.

45. But then, some towns whose origin myths do not include black strikebreakers also refused to let African Americans work or shop in them during the day.

46. Apparently he did; I use "allegedly" because there was no trial, hence no proof beyond a reasonable doubt.

47. Wells, *Blazing the Way,* 162; Lightfoot, "The Negro Exodus from Comanche County, Texas," 410–13; Leffler, "Comanche County."

48. DeWindt, "Wyandotte History; Negro," 16.

49. "Race War In Illinois" and "Bitter Race War Threatened," *New York Times,* 6/17/1902.

50. Robyn Williams, e-mail, 9/2002; employee of Southern Illinois University who lived in Eldorado for several years in the early 1990s.

51. "Bitter Race War Threatened."

52. Peter M. Bergman and Mort N. Bergman, *The Chronological History of the Negro in America* (New York: Mentor, 1969), 444.

53. Thad Sitton and James H. Conrad, *Nameless Towns: Texas Sawmill Communities, 1880–1942* (Austin: University of Texas Press, 1998), 71–73, 112.

54. John Hay, *The Pike County Ballots* (Boston: Houghton Mifflin, 1912 [1871]), 21–24.

55. Miller is quoted in Martha Biondi, *To Stand and Fight* (Cambridge: Harvard University Press, 2003), 128; cf. 124–32.

56. I believe that Sayles did not live in Boulder City but commuted from Las Vegas, so he did not violate Boulder City as a sundown town.

57. "Robert Parker discusses Afro-Americans in Boulder City," transcript of 11/9/1986 interview, Banyan Library, UNLV, banyan.library.unlv.edu/cgi-bin/htmldesc.exe?CISOROOT= /Hoover_Dam&C ISOPTR=56&CISOMODE=1, 10/2004.

58. Although most Humboldt County sources state—some even brag—that all other Chinese Americans were expelled from the county, apparently some Chinese miners survived in Orleans, a mining hamlet in the remote northeastern corner of the county, sheltered by whites and perhaps using European names. See Philip Sanders and Laura Sanders, "The Quiet Rebellion," *Humboldt Historian,* 1998, cited by Keith Easthouse, "The Chinese Expulsion," *North Coast Journal Weekly,* northcoastjournal.com/022703/cover0227.html, 2/2004.

59. Easthouse, "The Chinese Expulsion"; Lynwood Carranco, "Chinese Expulsion from Humboldt County," in Roger Daniels, ed., *Anti-Chinese Violence in North America* (New York: Arno Press, 1978), 336–37; Laurinda Joenks, "Roughness of Citizens Blamed on Lean Times," *The Morning News,* 5/7/2000.

60. Again, I use "allegedly" because there was no trial.

61. Audree Webb Pratt, "Unicoi County Court: 1876–1918," M.A. thesis, East Tennessee State University, 1960, 27–29; "Erwin Mob Shoots and Burns Body of Negro Who Attacked Girl," *Bristol Herald,* 5/21/1918; "Triple Tragedy at Erwin on Sunday When Negro Runs Wild," *Johnson City Daily,* 5/20/1918; cf. Charles Edward Price Papers, Box 1, Folder 6, "Blacks in Unicoi County, Tennessee," undated, "Blacks: Tom Devert," Hoskins Library, University of Tennessee.

62. Anne Braden, *The Wall Between* (Knoxville: University of Tennessee Press, 1999 [1958]), 137-38, 253, 286.

CHAPTER 8: HIDDEN IN PLAIN VIEW

1. Rogers Chamber of Commerce Publicity and Public Relations Committee, "Committee Report," 1/29/1962, in Rogers Historical Museum files.

2. Comment on presentation, 1/2003, via James Onderdonk Jr., e-mail, 2/2003.

3. The squirrels may not be true albinos.

4. Ray Elliott, e-mail, 7/2002, citing conversation with Olney resident; Gregory Dorr, e-mail, 7/2002.

5. "Yvonne Dorset," e-mail via Classmates.com, 12/2002; a 1952 graduate of the high school in Buffalo writes that some African Americans did live just north of Buffalo, outside the village limits.

6. About a year later, an African American family moved into Sheridan.

7. James Loewen, *Lies Across America* (New York: New Press, 1999), 198–99.

8. Terrie Epstein, "History and Racial Identity in an Urban High School," *AHA Perspectives,* 12/2001, 26; Maya Angelou, *I Know Why the Caged Bird Sings* (New York: Random House, 1969), 47; Tennessee Williams, *Orpheus Descending* (Peter Hall, dir., 1990); William Burroughs, *Naked Lunch* (New York: Grove, 1962 [1959]); Malcolm Ross, *All Manner of Men* (New York: Reynal & Hitchcock, 1948), 66; Jerrold Packard, *American Nightmare, The History of Jim Crow* (New York: St. Martin's, 2002), 108, my italics.

9. *The Fugitive Kind* derives from Tennessee Williams's play *Orpheus Descending,* from which it takes these lines.

10. This would be *Gentleman's Agreement,* Elia Kazan's 1948 movie adaptation of Laura Hobson's novel, a sensitive portrayal of anti-Semitism in Darien, Connecticut, although it makes no mention of Darien's exclusion of African Americans. Also, Lorraine Hansberry's play *A Raisin in the Sun*—about a black family that encounters opposition, rejects a buyout offer, and finally moves into a sundown neighborhood—was filmed.

11. Longtime southern Indiana resident, 10/2002; Evansville cheerleader, 12/2004. Jasper was the site of the 1954 regional tournament fictionally depicted in the movie. Milan, the town on which Hollywood's fictional Hickory was based, was also an all-white town, probably sundown.

12. Marian Anderson, *My Lord, What a Morning* (Madison: University of Wisconsin Press, 1992 [1956]), 239–40, 267–68; "Einstein" exhibit label, American Museum of Natural History, 12/2002; Scott L. Malcomson, *One Drop of Blood* (New York: Farrar, Straus, and Giroux, 2000), 383. Of course, the Civil Rights Movement also targeted the South because conditions were worse there than in much of the North (sundown towns excepted). Most important, the movement was largely born in southern black churches and colleges.

13. *Comprehensive Handbook* to *Indiana in the Civil War: Away from the Battle,* exhibit at Indiana State Museum, 1995–1997, 17.

14. Jack Blocker Jr., "Channeling the Flow," unpublished ms., Ch. 5, "Violence."

15. Roberta Nelson, "Myakka City's Black History a 'Mystery,' " *Tampa Tribune,* 2/26/2001; Melissa Sue Brewer, e-mail, 8/2002. Brewer has confirmed these details with the 1930 manuscript census and other records.

16. Librarian, West Frankfort, IL, 9/2002; *One Hundred Years of Progress: The Centennial History of Anna, Illinois* (Cape Girardeau: Missourian Printing, 1954).

17. *Life Newspapers 35th Anniversary Issue* (Northbrook, IL: Liberty Group, 12/1961), "Cicero . . . the Best Town in America," 139.

18. Baptist minister quoted in Joseph Lyford, *The Talk in Vandalia* (Santa Barbara: Center for the Study of Democratic Institutions, 1962), 93.

19. *The Pekin Centenary 1849–1949* (Pekin: Pekin Chamber of Commerce, 1949), 93–95; Lowell Nye, *Our Town* (Libertyville: Lions Club, 1942), 11; Edna Ferber, *A Peculiar Treasure* (New York: Doubleday, 1939), 57; James Cornelius, 7/2002.

20. Clarence D. Stephenson, *175th Anniversary History of Indiana County* (Indiana, PA: A. D.

Halldin, 1978–80), 354, quoting *Indiana County Gazette,* 2/25/1903; cf. Denise Dusza Weber, *Delano's Domain: A History of Warren Delano's Mining Towns of Vintondale, Wehrum and Claghorn,* vol. I, *1789–1930* (Indiana, PA: A. G. Halldin, 1991); Loewen, *Lies Across America,* 408–13.

21. Please tell me of more: jloewen@zoo.uvm.edu.

22. Three cities that tried but failed to expel their African Americans have recently marked those events. Springfield, Missouri, put up a historical marker about its Easter lynchings of 1906. Springfield, Illinois, set up a walking tour denoted by eight historical markers telling of its 1908 race riot. Tulsa, Oklahoma, erected a black granite memorial in its Greenwood section detailing whites' 1921 attempts to drive all African Americans from Tulsa. Because these cities remained interracial, African American citizens existed to help spur the memorials, and European Americans had not joined hands for decades in support of a sundown policy, so they were more open to telling the truth. Similarly, a state historical marker in Detroit tells accurately of the 1948 court case won by the Orsel McGhee family when their white Detroit neighbors tried to keep them from moving in by invoking "a restrictive covenant forbidding non-white residents," to quote the marker. (The case was merged with *Shelley v. Kraemer,* and the U.S. Supreme Court declared racial covenants unenforceable, as Chapter 9 tells.) Another Michigan marker, erected in 2004, tells of the riot that greeted Dr. Ossian Sweet when he moved into a sundown neighborhood in Detroit in 1925.

23. Pinky Zalkin, e-mail, 11/2002; *Idaho Highway Historical Marker Guide* (Boise: Idaho Transportation Department, 1990), 10; Connie Farrow, " 'The Anger and the Hatred Ends,' " Springfield (MO) *News-Leader,* 8/18/2001.

24. Jacqueline Froelich and David Zimmermann, "Total Eclipse: The Destruction of the African American Community of Harrison, Arkansas, in 1905 and 1909," *Arkansas Historical Quarterly* 58, 2 (1999): 159; Laurinda Joenks, "Roughness of Citizens Blamed on Lean Times," *Springdale* (AR) *Morning News,* 5/7/2000, paraphrasing Zimmermann; Randy Krehbiel, "Answers the Facts Cannot Provide," *Tulsa World,* 6/5/2000.

25. Arnold Hirsch, *Making the Second Ghetto* (Cambridge: Cambridge University Press, 1983), 60–63; Mary Ellen Stratthaus, "Flaw in the Jewel: Housing Discrimination Against Jews in La Jolla, California," *American Jewish History* 84, 3 (1996): 199.

26. The 2000 census showed 8 African Americans among 2,553 people, including two households.

27. Anna editor, 10/2002; Villa Grove editor and secretary, 10/2002.

28. Gordon D. Morgan, "Black Hillbillies of the Arkansas Ozarks," Department of Sociology, University of Arkansas, Fayetteville, 1973, 21; "A Really Good Show," *Rogers Daily News,* 1/25/1962.

29. Rogers Chamber of Commerce Publicity and Public Relations Committee, "Committee Report," 1/29/1962, in Rogers Historical Museum files.

30. Robby Heason, *Trouble Behind* (Cicada Films, 1990).

31. Peter Rachleff, e-mail, 6/2002.

32. John Winkols, interview by Roger Horowitz c. 1990, tape 37 side 2.

33. History teacher, e-mail, c. 6/2002; Hobart native, e-mail, 8/2004; Elin Christianson, e-mail, 9/2002; Moria Meltzer-Cohen, e-mail, 9/2002.

34. No "large band of Negroes" could have existed. The nearest black population was St. Joseph, just 4% black, and two counties away.

35. Patrick Clark, e-mail, 7/2002; Arthur F. Raper, *The Tragedy of Lynching* (New York: Dover, 1970 [1933]), 407, 427–28; cf. MacKinlay Kantor, *Missouri Bittersweet* (New York: Dou-

bleday, 1969), 140-69; Patrick Huber and Gary Kremer, "A Death in the Heartland," presented at Missouri Conference on History, St. Louis, 3/1994, 7; "Maryville Alarmed Over Riot Rumors," *St. Joseph Gazette,* 1/18/1931; cf. John Rachal, "An Oral History with Jan Handke," University of Southern Mississippi Oral History Program, 5/8/1996, lib.usm.edu/~spcol/crda/oh/handketrans.htm, 8/2003; Howard B. Woods, "Lynching Spectre Still in Mo. Town; Maryville Group Cites 'N . . . Free' Community," *St. Louis Argus,* 10/10/1958; Albany native, e-mail, 10/2002.

36. Sylvia J. Smith, "The Island on Williston Road Otherwise Known as Mayfair Park," *Chittenden County Historical Society Bulletin* 36, 4 (2003): 8–9; "Outline of Protective Covenants for Mayfair Park," supplied by Elise Guyette, 4/2003.

37. Tim Long, Great Lakes Regional Conference, National Council for the Social Studies, Indianapolis, 4/2002.

38. My web site, uvm.edu/~jloewen/sundown/, provides an "anti-bibliography" that critiques studies whose authors should have noted that the communities they described were all-white on purpose.

39. William H. Whyte Jr. based *The Organization Man,* his famous 1956 interpretation of suburbia, on fieldwork in Park Forest, and the next chapter quotes from Whyte's account of a controversy over the possible admission of "Negroes," resolved by renewing the community's decision to keep them out. Randall knew Whyte's work. See Whyte, *The Organization Man* (New York: Simon & Schuster, 1956), 311.

40. Karl B. Lohmann, *Cities and Towns of Illinois* (Urbana: University of Illinois Press, 1951); Gregory Randall, *America's Original GI Town: Park Forest, Illinois* (Baltimore: Johns Hopkins University Press, 2000); C. S. Stein, *Toward New Towns for America* (Boston: MIT Press, 1966).

41. Carl Withers, *Plainville, USA* (Westport: Greenwood, 1971 [1945]), 4, n.; Art Gallaher, *Plainville Fifteen Years Later* (NY: Columbia University Press, 1961); Gallaher, "Plainville: The Twice-Studied Town," 285–303 of Arthur Vidich, Joseph Bensman, and Maurice Stein, *Reflections on Community Studies* (New York: Wiley, 1964); James Jacobs, "The Politics of Corrections; Town/Prison Relations as a Determinant of Reform," *Social Service Review 50,* 4 (1976), 623–63; Otto H. Olsen, *The Negro Question: From Slavery to Caste, 1863–1910* (New York: Pitman, 1971), xxi; James R. Grossman, Ann D. Keating, and Janice L. Reiff, eds., *Encyclopedia of Chicago* (Chicago: University of Chicago Press, 2004); Alex Kotlowitz, "How Regular Folks in Berwyn, Ill., Tried to Fight Prejudice," *Wall St. Journal,* 6/3/1992.

42. Merrill Matthews, Jr., "Human Experimentation," *Texas Republic,* 3/1994, 28; Richard Stewart, "Desegregation at Public Housing Ripped by Audit," *Houston Chronicle,* 7/11/1997; Indiana Historical Bureau official, 10/2004.

43. Catherine Jurca, *White Diaspora* (Princeton: Princeton University Press, 2001), 8.

44. At uvm.edu/~jloewen/sundown/, a bibliography lists all books and articles that treat sundown towns significantly. It includes several novels, including three for younger readers. Undoubtedly my literature review has been incomplete, and readers can post suggestions.

45. Frank Kardes and David Sanbonmatsu, "Omission Neglect," *Skeptical Inquirer* 27, 2 (2003): 45.

46. Patrick Huber, "Race Riots and Black Exodus in the Missouri Ozarks, 1894–1905" (Harrison, AR: Ozark Cultural Celebration, 9/2002).

47. I began with the census definition of "city"—larger than 2,500 in total population. Then I

discovered towns far smaller than 2,500 that posted signs, passed ordinances, spread the word informally, burned houses, or took other steps to keep out African Americans (and sometimes other groups). So I enlarged my definition of "town" to include places from 1,000 to 2,500. When jurisdictions even smaller than 1,000 came to my attention for excluding African Americans, I included them as well, although I did not try to study these hamlets systematically. (In many states, I have not been able to study towns smaller than 2,500 systematically and have merely taken note of information on them when I obtain it in the course of my research.)

Such small towns can be important, partly because when they do expand, usually they remain sundown. Malcolm Ross investigated East Alton, Illinois, for example, for the Fair Employment Practices Commission during World War II. The town's industrial patriarch, F. W. Olin, told him that East Alton had an ordinance dating back to 1895, when a "Negro boy" committed some crime, and men had gone hunting for him with shotguns. He got away, but his angry pursuers reportedly swore that no Negro would ever again set foot in East Alton. Ross noted that during the next fifty years, East Alton had grown from a few families to a sizable town without any Negro ever having stayed the night. During World War II, Olin's munitions plant employed more than 13,000 workers—not one of them African American or Native American. In 1940, shortly before Ross wrote, its population had increased to 4,680, with 1 stray African American. By 1960, East Alton had 7,309 residents but only 4 African Americans, probably none of whom lived in an independent household. It finally cracked in the 1990s.

Larger cities tested my operational definition in a different way. A cutoff of ten proved too low to do justice to large cities widely known to keep out African Americans, such as Cicero. In 1951, as we have seen, the governor had to call out the Illinois National Guard to stop a riot against one African American who had tried (and failed) to move into Cicero. "Of primary significance in understanding the violence," sociologist William Gremley points out, "is the fact that it was widely believed by the residents of the community that no Negroes lived in Cicero." Actually, the U.S. Census in 1950 showed 31 African Americans in the city, but they were apparently live-in servants, biracial adopted children, or individuals living unobtrusively in rental property. Cicero clearly defined itself as a sundown town, no matter what the census said. Indeed, according to a report issued after the 1951 riot, "It is said that no Negroes now live within the limits of Cicero, although one or two families have done so in the past." But "fewer than ten African Americans" would have missed Cicero. So for cities larger than 10,000, I changed my definition for "all-white town" to "less than 0.1% black," decade after decade. For towns smaller than 10,000, "fewer than ten blacks" remained in force.

48. Live-in institutions include prisons, hospitals and long-term care facilities, armed forces bases, and residential colleges and prep schools. Other groups understood to be nonhousehold include railroad track-laying crews, CCC work camps, Job Corps trainees, and construction personnel.
49. John Paul Myrick, e-mail, 3/2002; Richard Todd, "Darien, Connecticut," *New England Monthly*, 3/1986, 43; Gregory Dorr, e-mail, 7/2002.
50. Kotlowitz, "How Regular Folks in Berwyn, Illinois, Tried to Right Prejudice."
51. Morgan, "Black Hillbillies of the Arkansas Ozarks," 152; Jim Clayton, e-mail, 11/2002.
52. Michelle Tate, typescript, 10/2002.
53. Nebraska Writers' Project, *The Negroes of Nebraska* (Omaha: Urban League, 1940), 10; "In-

ventory of the County Archives," WPA Federal Writers Project, Waverly, 1942, supplied by James L. Murphy, 3/2004; James Emmitt, *Life and Reminiscences* (Chillicothe, OH: Peerless, 1888), 287–89.

54. Colleen Kilner, *Joseph Sears and His Kenilworth* (Kenilworth: Kenilworth Historical Society, 1990), viii, 143, her italics; Paul Wong, e-mail, 8/2003.

55. Derfner successfully sued a small town to change an ordinance that he was able to find in its records, but neither the original ordinance nor the new version ever got into the file of codified ordinances.

    It is possible that knowledge of *Buchanan v. Warley* prompted city councils to avoid putting any ordinance in writing, thus making legal attack more difficult, but I doubt it. Not only does no oral history or other evidence support this hypothesis, I have uncovered no concern about such a challenge outside the South. Moreover, southern and border cities continued to enact *Buchanan*-like segregation ordinances for decades, despite their unconstitutionality.

56. Armand Derfner, 11/2003.

57. Landis quoted in Ken Burns, *Baseball* (PBS, 1994).

58. Harrisburg (IL) *Daily Register,* 4/5/1923.

59. Clayton Cramer, e-mail, 6/2000.

60. Letter to *New York Times* citing 3/15/1973 story, my italics; John D. Baskerville, e-mail, 7/2003; I eliminated the name of the city councilor because Baskerville was not certain of it.

61. Nationally it is also possible, I suppose, that a plethora of errors of inclusion might convince readers that sundown towns have been more common than in reality they have. Such errors might unnecessarily increase readers' motivation to eliminate sundown policies, sending some readers charging off to fix something that isn't broken. Since so many towns and suburbs *have* been unwelcoming to African Americans, however, increasing the cross-racial hospitality of all-white communities, even some that were all-white only by accident, will hardly harm our nation.

62. Pinckneyville native, e-mail, 6/2001.

63. My web site, uvm.edu/~jloewen/sundown, contains a longer discussion of my methods, including my assessment of sources on three additional towns, and can help you decide if you should trust my judgment.

CHAPTER 9: ENFORCEMENT

1. Michelle Tate, typescript, 10/2002.

2. *Illinois State Register,* 8/17 or 8/18/1908, quoted in Roberta Senechal, *The Sociogenesis of a Race Riot* (Urbana: University of Illinois Press, 1990), 129.

3. Billy Bob Lightfoot, "The Negro Exodus from Comanche County, Texas," *Southwestern Historical Quarterly* 56 (January 1953): 415.

4. "For White Men Only," Fairmont (WV) *Free Press,* 12/7/1905.

5. Ann Hammons, *Wild Bill Sullivan* (Jackson: University Press of Mississippi, 1980), 52; Gregg Andrews, *City of Dust* (Columbia: University of Missouri Press, 1996), 11; probably notes from an interview by Van Ravenswaay, Missouri state supervisor of the WPA Federal Writers Project, with Judge Williams, 11/20/1937, now in folder 1089, Western Historical Manuscript Collection, University of Missouri.

6. Senechal, *The Sociogenesis of a Race Riot,* 130.

7. Comanche County historical society spokesman, 8/2003; Lightfoot, "The Negro Exodus

from Comanche County, Texas," 415; Bud Kennedy, "Signs of a Racist Past in the Small Towns of Texas," *Ft. Worth Star Telegram*, 2/17/2002, realcities.com/mld/startelegram/mon/news/columnists/bud_kennedy/archive.htm; Ronald L. Lewis, *Black Coal Miners in America* (Lexington: University Press of Kentucky, 1987), 83–84; "Negroes Killed or Driven Away," *Chicago Tribune,* 8/21/1901.

8. William Pickens, "Arkansas—A Study in Suppression," originally published in *The Messenger 5* (January 1923), reprinted in Tom Lutz and Susanna Ashton, eds., *These "Colored" United States* (New Brunswick: Rutgers University Press, 1996), 35; Arthur F. Raper, *The Tragedy of Lynching* (New York: Dover, 1970 [1933]), 452.

9. "See First Dark Face in County in Many Years," *Chicago Defender,* 4/2/1921; Esther Sanderson, *County Scott and Its Mountain Folk* (Nashville: Williams Printing, 1958), 186.

10. Tate, typescript, 10/2002; David Blair, e-mail via Classmates.com, 3/5/2003; motel clerk, Owosso, 10/2002.

11. Jeanne Blackburn, e-mail, 11/2003.

12. Scotland native, e-mail, 6/2002.

13. "White Men Shoot Up Church Excursioners," *Pittsburgh Courier,* 8/17/1940.

14. Barbara Elliott Carpenter fictionalizes this incident in *Starlight, Starbright . . . ,* a novel for teenagers (Bloomington, IL: 1st Books, 2003), 185–200, including the antipathy that underlay the helpful gesture.

15. Helen Harrelson, 10/2002; former Pinckneyville resident, e-mail, 6/2002; elderly white Harrison couple, 9/2002; Arcola native, e-mail, 1/2003; cf. Barbara Elliott Carpenter, e-mail, 9/2002; several African Americans at Crispus Attucks Museum, Indianapolis, 8/2001.

16. Jean Nipps Swaim, "Black History in Cedar County, Missouri," in *Black Families of the Ozarks,* Bulletin 45 (Springfield, MO: Greene County Archives, n.d.), 2:535; Shirley Manning, e-mail, 9/2002; Carl Jackson, 1/2004.

17. John Keiser, 1/2005; woman at Richland Community College, 10/2001; Thad Sitton and James H. Conrad, *Nameless Towns: Texas Sawmill Communities, 1880–1942* (Austin: University of Texas Press, 1998), 108–9; Millie Meyerholtz, *When Hatred and Fear Ruled . . . Pana, Illinois: The 1898–99 Mine War* (Pana, IL: Pana News, 2001), 34; 1986 Resident Assistant at Indiana University, e-mail, 11/5/2002.

18. James Clayton, e-mail, 11/2002; student from Salem, University of Illinois–Chicago, 10/2002; Melissa Sue Brewer, e-mail, 8/2002; Dwight ambulance volunteer, e-mail, 10/2003; cf. Kenneth Meeks, *Driving While Black* (New York: Broadway, 2000); David A. Harris, *Profiles in Injustice* (New York: New Press, 2002).

19. Mary Pat Baumgartner, *The Moral Order of a Suburb* (New York: Oxford University Press, 1988), 119–20; Gary Kennedy, e-mail, 6/2002.

20. Gregory Dorr, e-mail, 7/2002.

21. Bob Johnson, e-mail, 1/2003; name withheld by request, e-mail, 10/2002.

22. Ibid.

23. Harris, *Profiles in Injustice,* 105.

24. Frank U. Quillen, *The Color Line in Ohio* (Ann Arbor: Wahr, 1913), 161; Wali R. Kharif, e-mail, 9/2002, citing William Hiram Parrish, interview, 12/23/1975, and Walter Maxey, interview, 12/29/1975, in the Folklife Collection, Western Kentucky University; Elvin Light, 6/2002; Herbert Aptheker, remarks at the graveside of Mary Brown, Saratoga, CA, 5/6/2000, and letter, 7/7/2000; Tate, typescript, 10/2002; Wise County, Virginia, native, e-mail, 8/2002; African American Bluefield native, b. 1932, 3/2004.

25. Washabaugh quoted in David M. P. Freund, "Making It Home," Ph.D. dissertation, University of Michigan, 1999, 548; Carole Goodwin, *The Oak Park Strategy* (Chicago: University of Chicago Press, 1979), 98; Baumgartner, *The Moral Order of a Suburb*, 119–20; Diane Hershberger, 11/2000.

26. Al Brophy, 4/2002.

27. "Tricksters Discourage Black Settlers," undated, unidentified newspaper clipping in files of Rogers Historical Museum.

28. "Attorney Is Driven from Court," *Chicago Defender*, 12/24/1921.

29. "Negroes Are Threatened," *Benton Republican*, 7/26/1923.

30. Olen Cole Jr., *The African-American Experience in the Civilian Conservation Corps* (Gainesville: University Press of Florida, 1999), 19, 30, 57; Shirley Ann Moore, "Getting There, Being There," in Joe W. Trotter Jr., ed., *The Great Migration in Historical Perspective* (Bloomington: Indiana University Press, 1991), 57, 107–11.

31. DeWindt, "Wyandotte History; Negro," 24–26, quoting *Wyandotte Daily News*, 12/4/1935, and *Wyandotte Herald*, 12/6/1935.

32. Truman K. Gibson, Jr., civilian aide to the secretary of war, remarks to Illinois Inter-Racial Commission, 12/19/1943, minutes in Illinois State Archives, 7.

33. Stetson Kennedy, *Jim Crow Guide* (Boca Raton: Florida Atlantic University Press, 1990 [1959]), 80; Emma Lou Thornbrough, *The Negro in Indiana* (Indianapolis: Indiana Historical Bureau, 1957), 226.

34. "Blacks in Greenbelt," summarizing research by W. H. Form, otal.umd.edu/~vg/mssp96/ms12/expla.html, 10/2002; Tate, typescript, 10/2002.

35. Former theater worker, e-mail, 10/2002; Peoria resident, 2/2001.

36. Oak Lawn librarians, 4/1997; University of Illinois–Chicago student, 9/2001; person at Mattoon, 10/2002.

37. Khan let the man live in the motel; after a few months he went back to his hometown.

38. The 2000 census lists nine households with at least one black householder, so Paragould may be moving beyond its sundown status.

39. Jim Clayton, 11/2002; Nick Khan, 9/2002.

40. Female 1983 Goshen College graduate, relayed by Kathryn Reimer, e-mail, 9/2004; Stephen Crow, e-mail via Classmates.com, 11/2004.

41. Elice Swanson, e-mail, 1/2003; Dyanna McCarty, e-mail, 10/2002 (her italics).

42. Lois Mark Stalvey, *The Education of a WASP* (New York: William Morrow, 1970).

43. Cullman native, e-mail, 5/2002; Virginia Cowan, "An Essay," robandjen.net/jen/mom.html, 10/2002.

44. "Norman Mob After Singie Smith Jazz," Norman, OK, 2/5/1922, in *Oklahoma City Black Dispatch*, 2/9/1922, 1, thanks to Al Brophy; "Don't Let the Sun Set on You Here, Understand?" *Chicago Defender*, 2/11/1922.

45. Henry Louis Gates Jr., *Colored People* (New York: Knopf, 1994), 119–20; Henry Louis Gates Sr., 7/2002.

46. Swaim, "Black History in Cedar County, Missouri," 535; Mary Jo Hubbard, e-mail to Classmates.com bulletin board, 12/2002, her ellipses.

47. Ironically, Neenah and Menasha may also have been sundown towns, but at least someone or some hotel in one of them was willing to let her spend the night.

48. In her autobiography, Anderson tells how hotels occasionally housed black celebrities such as herself, even though she could sense they admitted no other African Americans.

49. Marian Anderson, *My Lord, What a Morning* (Madison: University of Wisconsin Press, 1992 [1956]), 239–40, 267–68; "Einstein" exhibit label, American Museum of Natural History, 12/2002; Judy Zimmerman Herr, e-mail, 3/2002; librarian, Appleton, 4/2002.

50. Howard Bryant, *Talk of the Nation,* NPR, 9/26/2002.

51. Elderly couple, Harrison, AR, 9/2002; Grey Gundaker, e-mails, 7/2002.

52. Pinckneyville native, e-mail, 6/2001.

53. Steve Bogira, "Hate, Chicago Style," *Chicago Reader,* 12/5/1986.

54. Zeigler miner, 9/2002.

55. Ray Stannard Baker, *Following the Color Line* (New York: Harper Torchbook, 1964 [1908]), 126.

56. Browne quoted in Shane Johnson, "Read No Evil," *Salt Lake City Weekly,* 9/25/2003, slweekly.com/editorial/2003/feat_2003-09-25.cfm, 10/2003; Richard Delgado and Jean Stefancic, *Home-Grown Racism* (Boulder: University of Colorado Latino/a Research & Policy Center, 1999), 30, 44, 74.

57. Pinckneyville resident, Greenup resident at Mattoon, 10/2002; Martinsville native, 10/2002; Mel Dubofsky, e-mail, 6/2002.

58. Former resident, LaSalle-Peru, e-mail, 10/2001.

59. Elizabethtown graduate, 8/2004.

60. Actually, although considered a sundown county, Madison County does contain Mars Hill, a small college town that allowed African Americans to live in it.

61. "Where Negroes are Barred," *Charlotte Daily Observer,* 8/18/1906.

62. Dante Chinni, "Along Detroit's Eight Mile Road, a Stark Racial Split," *Christian Science Monitor,* csmonitor.com/2002/1115/p01s02-ussc.html, 11/15/2002.

63. Freund, "Making It Home," 93–95, 120; Orfield quoted in Dennis R. Judd, "The Role of Governmental Policies in Promoting Residential Segregation in the St. Louis Metropolitan Area," *Journal of Negro Education* 66, 3 (1997): 233; Deborah Morse-Kahn, *Edina: Chapters in the City History* (Edina: City of Edina, 1998), 94.

64. Michael N. Danielson, *The Politics of Exclusion* (New York: Columbia University Press, 1976), 53, 59–61; Dorothy K. Newman et al., *Protest, Politics, and Prosperity* (New York: Pantheon, 1978), 159.

65. Danielson, *The Politics of Exclusion,* 93, 102.

66. Kenneth T. Jackson, *Crabgrass Frontier* (New York: Oxford University Press, 1985), 224–25; Danielson, *The Politics of Exclusion,* 40, 100–1.

67. Farley and Frey, "Changes in the Segregation of Whites from Blacks During the 1980s," 26.

68. Ian D. McMahan, *The Negro in White Suburbia* (New York: Freedom of Residence Funds, 1962), 22–24; James Hecht, *Because It Is Right* (Boston: Little, Brown, 1970), 27.

69. Danielson, *The Politics of Exclusion,* 28, citing Oliver P. Williams et al., *Suburban Differences and Metropolitan Policies* (Philadelphia: University of Pennsylvania Press, 1965), 217–19; Rosalyn Baxandall and Elizabeth Ewen, *Picture Windows: How the Suburbs Happened* (New York: Basic Books, 2000), 23–24; Baumgartner, *The Moral Order of a Suburb,* 119–20; former Darien resident, 7/98.

70. Herbert Gans, 1/2001; Frederique Krupa, "Los Angeles: Buying the Concept of Security," Chapter 3 of "Privatization of Public Space," unpaginated, translucency.com/frede/pps.html, 1/2004.

71. Detroit suburbanite, e-mail, 6/2002; Bob Johnson, e-mail, 1/2003.

72. In 1975, two young white students, one law, one medical, committed the crime of "playing

tennis without a reservation." Violation carries a $25 fine, but "the court clerk lowered each of their fines to $5," according to reporter Alice Love. Nevertheless, the students "stuck with their decision to pay their debt behind bars." After some publicity, an anonymous source from Southern Methodist University paid their fines, which was a relief to the students because Highland Park also does not let prisoners have books in their cells. See Alice Love, "Students Prefer Jail Stay to $5 Fines," *Dallas Times Herald,* 10/16/1975.

73. Edward H. Sebesta, e-mail, 7/2002; "Picnicking Banned at Highland Park Park," *Dallas Morning News,* 7/2/1989; Debbie K. Solomon, "Jogging to Court," *Dallas Times Herald* 2/25/1982; Doug J. Swanson, "Official Calls HP's Fishing Permit Illegal," *Dallas Times Herald,* 2/23/1980.

74. Camille DeRose, *The Camille DeRose Story* (Chicago: Erle Press, 1953), 169; Christopher Phillips, e-mail, 6/2000.

75. "A Northern City 'Sitting on Lid' of Racial Trouble," 38–40; David L. Good, *Orvie: The Dictator of Dearborn* (Detroit: Wayne State University Press, 1989), 40–41, 264, 386–87.

76. Ibid.; Good, "Orville Hubbard—The Ghost Who Still Haunts Dearborn," *Detroit News,* 1/3/1997, detnews.com/history/hubbard/hu2/98.

77. Reynolds Farley, Sheldon Danziger, and Harry J. Holzer, *Detroit Divided* (New York: Russell Sage, 2000), 148; Nelson, *The Fourteenth Amendment and the Negro Since 1920,* 31; *Corrigan v. Buckley,* 299 Fed 898 (1924) and 271 U.S. 328.

78. Palos Verdes Homes Association: "Palos Verdes Protective Restrictions" (Palos Verdes Estates: n.p., 1929), sent by Paul Wong, e-mail, 7/2003; Maryland restrictive covenant sent by Christopher Lewis, 12/2002.

79. Massey, talk at OPEN, Philadelphia, 12/2000; NAACP estimate in Gunnar Myrdal, *An American Dilemma* (New York: McGraw-Hill, 1964 [1944]), 624; Margaret Marsh, *Suburban Lives* (New Brunswick: Rutgers University Press, 1990), 201.

80. *Shelley v. Kraemer,* 334 U.S. 1, 1948; Charlotte Brooks, e-mail, 9/2002.

81. Hecht, *Because It Is Right,* 51; Kennedy, *Jim Crow Guide,* 75; St. Louis realtor quoted in Newman et al., *Protest, Politics, and Prosperity,* 151; manual quoted in Stephen G. Meyer, *As Long as They Don't Move Next Door* (Lanham, MD: Rowman & Littlefield, 2000), 7; cf. Lorenzo J. Greene, Gary Kremer, and Antonio Holland, *Missouri's Black Heritage* (Columbia: University of Missouri Press, 1993), 164.

82. Hecht capitalizes "Realtor" to refer to members of the National Association of Real Estate Boards, later the National Association of Realtors. Most of my sources, oral or written, were not so precise, and neither is the public at large, so I use the generic *realtor* (uncapitalized) to mean any licensed seller of real estate.

83. Hecht, *Because It Is Right,* 51; Realtors Code of Ethics quoted in Newman, *Protest, Politics, and Prosperity,* 149.

84. "Barred: Non-Whites Restricted from Urban Areas by Salt Lake Realtors," *Pittsburgh Courier,* 5/20/1944.

85. "Typical Cases: Private Housing—Commercial Development," *Connecticut Civil Rights Bulletin* 1, 4 (1955): 3.

86. Benjamin R. Epstein and Arnold Foster, *"Some of My Best Friends . . ."* (New York: Farrar, Straus, and Cudahy, 1962), 117–18, 120.

87. Amy Karelus Welch, e-mail, 10/2001, relayed by Andrew B. Raker.

88. William L. Price, *Factors Influencing and Restraining the Housing Mobility of Negroes in Metropolitan Detroit* (Detroit: Urban League, c. 1955), 10, 14; Thomas Sugrue, *Origins of the Urban Crisis* (Princeton: Princeton University Press, 1996), 44.

89. Don and Mary Hunt, *Hunts' Guide to Southeast Michigan* (Waterloo, MI: Midwestern Guides, 1990), 122; Norman C. Thomas, *Rule 9: Politics, Administration, and Civil Rights* (New York: Random House, 1966), 35–36.

90. Thomas, *Rule 9*, 44–45.

91. "G.P. Gets 30 Days to Ban Point System," *Detroit News*, 5/14/1960; "Klan Standards Prevail in G.P., Rabbi Charges," *Detroit News*, 5/14/1960; Joseph Wolff and Bob Popa, "Special Jewish 'Point' Form Described at G.P. Inquiry," *Detroit News*, 5/3/1960; Thomas, *Rule 9*, 5, 61, 63, 68.

92. Kathy Cosseboom, *Grosse Pointe, Michigan* (East Lansing: Michigan State University Press, 1972), 12–13.

93. Ibid., 9, 11; Andrew Hacker, "Grand Illusion," *New York Review of Books*, 6/11/1998, 28.

94. Cosseboom, *Grosse Pointe, Michigan*, 55.

95. Charles T. Clotfelter, *After Brown* (Princeton: Princeton University Press, 2004), 18–19; Betty Toomes, transcript of interview (Yuma, AZ, 1963: Robert B. Powers, interviewer), sunsite.berkeley.edu:2020/dynaweb/teiproj/oh/warren/powers/@Generic_BookTextView/4030, 1/2003.

96. Former Oak Lawn resident, e-mail, 10/2002; Eric Arnesen, *Brotherhoods of Color* (Cambridge: Harvard University Press, 2001), 246; James Grossman, 9/2001; Robby Heason, *Trouble Behind;* female undergraduate, University of the Ozarks, 9/2002.

97. West Lawn Chamber of Commerce, Westlawnncc.org, 1/2003; Steve Bogira, "Hate, Chicago Style."

98. Pinckneyville woman, 9/2002; James Rosenbaum, letter, 11/1996; female undergraduate, University of the Ozarks, 9/2002; Winston County law enforcement officer, 6/02.

99. Apparently material was added to this file as late as the late 1950s.

100. Thelma Marsh, *Moccasin Trails to the Cross,* excerpts, and Squire Grey Eyes, "Farewell to A Beloved Land," Wyandot Nation of Kansas web site, ku.edu/kansas/wn/8/2003; Edwina M. DeWindt, "Wyandotte History; Negro," typescript, 1945, in Bacon Library, Wyandotte, MI, 4.

101. DeWindt, "Wyandotte History; Negro," 12, citing *Wyandotte, Past, Present, and Future 1854–1917*, 17.

102. Ibid., 6, 13, 17.

103. Ibid., 2, 15, citing *Wyandotte Herald*, 8/25/1916.

104. Ibid., 16–17.

105. Ibid., 24–30, quoting *Wyandotte Herald*, 12/6/1935, and *Wyandotte Daily News*, 12/4/1935; Kristina Baumli, e-mail, 6/2000.

106. "For White Men Only," Fairmont, WV, *Free Press*, 12/7/1905.

107. Brownsburg source wishes to remain anonymous, e-mail, 11/2002.

108. LaSalle-Peru native, e-mail, 1/2004; Sanderson, *County Scott and Its Mountain Folk*, 186.

109. "Marlow's 'Unwritten Law' Against Race Causes Two Deaths," *Pittsburgh Courier*, 12/29/1923; Almarion Hollingsworth, 2/2004. The *Courier* misspelled Berch's name, which I corrected. Berch had also organized and circulated a petition requesting an anti-Klan law prohibiting masks, requiring secret organizations to file membership lists, etc., that may have contributed to the enmity against him. See Berch, "Initiative Petition #83," supplied by Hollingsworth, and "Klan Murder Says Wife," in the political tabloid *Jack Walton's Paper*, 1/6/1924.

110. "Farmer Shot to Death Near Lamb, Hardin Co.," *Golconda* (IL) *Herald-Enterprise*, 11/2/1922.

111. Kennedy, *Jim Crow Guide,* 82; J.D. Mullane, "Still a Long Way to Go," *Bucks County Courier Times,* phillyburbs.com/millmag/race.shtml, 7/2002; Daisy Myers, "Breaking Down Barriers," *Pennsylvania Heritage* 28, 3 (2002): 11.

112. Reynolds Farley and William H. Frey, "Changes in the Segregation of Whites from Blacks During the 1980s," *American Sociological Review* 59, 1 (1994): 24–25; Jodi Becker, "Chicago Matters," on Chicago Public Radio, c. 2002; Meyer, *As Long as They Don't Move Next Door,* 6; Kennedy, *Jim Crow Guide,* 82.

113. "For White Men Only," Fairmont (WV) *Free Press,* 12/7/1905; Sanderson, *County Scott and Its Mountain Folk,* 186; Bogira, "Hate, Chicago Style"; Arnold Hirsch, *Making the Second Ghetto* (Cambridge: Cambridge University Press, 1093), 41.

114. Hirsch, *Making the Second Ghetto,* 63; Hecht, *Because It Is Right,* 201, 204–5.

115. Meyer, *As Long as They Don't Move Next Door,* 76–77; Kristina Baumli, e-mail, 8/2001; Baxandall and Ewen, *Picture Windows,* 30.

116. Meyer, *As Long as They Don't Move Next Door,* 219; Kennedy, *Jim Crow Guide,* 82.

117. Thornbrough, *The Negro in Indiana,* 224; Emma Lou Thornbrough, *Indiana Blacks in the Twentieth Century,* edited and with final chapter by Lana Ruegamer (Bloomington: Indiana University Press, 2000), 2–3.

118. Reprinted as "County Press Pays High Tribute to a Former Slave," *Rogers Daily News* (?), 7/1/1950. In a 2001 brochure on "Cultural Diversity in Benton County" the Rogers Historical Museum agrees that the statement was a warning, not just a joke.

119. Idaho statewide may not be more racist than, say, Montana or Oregon, but it has collected several extremist white power groups that have given it that reputation, deserved or not.

120. White woman at Richland Community College, 10/2001; Clayton Cramer, e-mail, 6/2000.

121. Farley, Danziger, and Holzer, *Detroit Divided,* 186–87, 193.

122. I do not have independent confirmation of the local historian's stories, but he seems a thoughtful source to me. Even if exaggerated, the stories show that Tamaroa's reputation for violence toward African Americans is well known.

123. Pinckneyville historian, 9/2002; Du Quoin woman, 9/2002.

124. In the Ozarks, it was "nigger flipper"—yet many Ozarks youth never saw a black person until after they were grown, since most of the region had driven out its African American population.

125. Harris, *Profiles in Injustice,* 102.

126. Woman at Mattoon, 10/2002.

127. Leftridge quoted in Arnesen, *Brotherhoods of Color,* 245; June Rosland, 4/2002.

128. Michael Dougan, *Arkansas Odyssey* (Little Rock: Rose Publishing, 1994), 318; Nick Khan, 9/2002.

129. Jim Clayton, 11/2002.

CHAPTER 10: EXCEPTIONS TO THE SUNDOWN RULE

1. Laurel Boeckman, e-mail, 6/2002.

2. See Millie Meyerholtz, *When Hatred and Fear Ruled* (Pana: Pana News, 2001).

3. Elderly Huntington resident as interviewed and reported by his son and by me, 6/2002; Phillip Payne, e-mail, 11/2002.

4. Michael Ebner, *Creating Chicago's North Shore* (Chicago: University of Chicago Press, 1988), 234; Kenilworth realtor, 10/2002.

5. *Virginia Acts of Assembly*, 330–31; 1947 Villa Park deed, extant in 1963, sent by Donna Marquart, 8/2002.

6. "Tale of Two Cities," *Pacific Citizen*, 1/4/1947.

7. Jim Clayton, 11/2002; Paul M. Angle, *Bloody Williamson* (New York: Knopf, 1952), 98; Batesville Historical Society member, e-mail, 9/2002.

8. Bob Johnson, e-mail, 1/2003; Mable Bishop Gilmer, paragraph in Edwina M. DeWindt, "Wyandotte History; Negro," typescript, 1945, in Bacon Library, Wyandotte, MI, 14.

9. Jodey Bateman, e-mail, 7/2002.

10. Some have not moved out; by 1990 Ephrata had 27 African Americans, including four households, among 12,133 residents.

11. Hilda Feldhake, ed., *Effingham County Illinois, Past and Present* (Effingham: n.p., 1968), 338; former Miami Beach resident, e-mail, 7/2002; "Since You Asked," Medford, OR, *Mail Tribune*, 1998, mailtribune.com/news/dailynws.htm, 2001; Cynthia Marquet, 9/2002; Judy Zimmerman Herr, e-mail, 3/2002; Millersville University student, 3/2002; longtime Pennsylvania resident, e-mail, 4/2002.

12. William E. Wilson, *On the Sunny Side of a One-Way Street* (New York: Norton, 1958), 91, thanks to Wanda L. Griess, letter, 9/2002.

13. Emma Lou Thornbrough, *The Negro in Indiana* (Indianapolis: Indiana Historical Bureau, 1957), 225–27; untitled clipping, *Springdale News*, 7/13/1894, in files of Rogers Historical Museum; DeWindt, "Wyandotte History; Negro," 8, 11.

14. Pearl Roberts, *Glimpses of the Past in Johnston City, Illinois, 1894–1945* (Johnston City: Business & Professional Women's Club, 1977), 123.

15. "Local attorney" quoted in exhibit on Camp Ellis at Dickson Mounds Museum, 2001; Lachlan Crissey, "Racial Minorities in the Operation of County Government," in Illinois Inter-racial Commission, *First Annual Report* (Springfield: State of Illinois, 1945), 32.

16. Roger Karns, e-mail, 9/2002; Matt Moline, e-mail, 6/2002; Harold S. Forsythe, e-mail, 7/2002.

17. Gospel Assembly web site, dmgospelassembly.org/church/aboutus2.html, 12/2003.

18. *Parade of Progress: Hamilton County, 1858–1958* (Hamilton: Hamilton Herald-News, 1958), unpaginated; Terry Keller, 6/10/2003.

19. Moira Meltzer-Cohen, e-mail, 9/2002; Jean Messinger, *A Closer Look at Beaver Dam* (Colorado Springs: Cottonwood Press, 1981); Hank Everman, "Corbin, Kentucky: A Socioeconomic Anomaly," Department of History, Eastern Kentucky University, 2002, unpaginated; Lorenzo J. Greene, Gary Kremer, and Antonio Holland, *Missouri's Black Heritage* (Columbia: University of Missouri Press, 1993), 153; Patrick J. Huber, e-mail, 9/2002.

20. Billy Bob Lightfoot, "The Negro Exodus from Comanche County, Texas," *Southwestern Historical Quarterly* 56 (January 1953): 414.

21. Woman from Greenup at Mattoon, 10/2002; Roberta Senechal, *The Sociogenesis of a Race Riot* (Urbana: University of Illinois Press, 1990), 130; "Death of Ambrose Roan," *Chesterton Tribune*, 11/30/1911.

22. Elderly Huntington native interviewed by his son, e-mail, 6/2002.

23. John Winkols, interview by Roger Horowitz c.1990, in "Pete Winkols Interview," tape 37 side 2, UPWA Oral History Project, State Historical Society of Wisconsin, Madison.

24. Dorothy E. Williams, *The Spirit of West Bend* (Madison: Straus Printing, 1980), 318; Barbara Carpenter, e-mail, 10/2002; Kathleen M. Blee, *Women of the Klan* (Berkeley: University of California Press, 1991), 156, based on oral history, c.1987.

25. Carolyn Stephens, e-mail, 11/2001, recounting conversation with George Hendrick;

George Hendrick, Helen Howe, and Don Sackrider, *James Jones and the Handy Writers' Colony* (Carbondale: Southern Illinois University Press, 2001), 121; Williams, *The Spirit of West Bend,* 318; "Only Colored Couple," *Chesterton Tribune,* 8/20/1936, referring to 1/4/1912 story. The 1936 story uses markedly more stereotypical language than the 1912 story quoted earlier, perhaps indicating that Porter County's attitudes toward African Americans had hardened in the decades since the deaths of its only black couple.

26. Long-term Arab resident, 6/2002.
27. Carolyn Stephens, e-mail, 1/2001.
28. Ralph R. Rea, *Boone County and Its People* (Van Buren, AR: Press-Argus, 1955), 141–42.
29. James DeVries, *Race and Kinship in a Midwestern Town* (Urbana: University of Illinois Press, 1984), 58; Blee, *Women of the Klan,* 156. Bear in mind that this interview took place around 1987, 23 years after the public accommodations section of the 1964 Civil Rights Act became law.
30. Alice J. Thompson, "Changing Social Values in Brea," interviewed by Ann Towner, California State University–Fullerton, Oral History #1726, 4/17/1982, 22.
31. Steve Bogira, "Hate, Chicago Style," *Chicago Reader,* 12/5/1986.
32. Cullman native, e-mail, 5/2002.
33. Joycelyn Landrum-Brown quoting her mother, e-mail, 8/2002.
34. Greenup, Illinois, resident, 6/2000; Martinsville, Illinois, resident, 10/2002; Hendrick, Howe, and Sackrider, *James Jones and the Handy Writers' Colony* 115, 121, 133; Carolyn Stephens, e-mail, 2/2001; Stephens, 9/2002.

CHAPTER 11: THE EFFECT OF SUNDOWN TOWNS ON WHITES

1. Oblong native, 4/2000.
2. Like all-white towns, all-white neighborhoods are usually no accident, and residents of sundown neighborhoods show most of the characteristics of residents of sundown towns and suburbs, especially if the neighborhood is large enough to have its own high school.
3. Loewen, "Soclexia," New England Sociological Society keynote address, 4/1997.
4. Actually, at this time the sign stood at the train station.
5. Lightfoot, "The Negro Exodus from Comanche County, Texas," 415.
6. Carl Withers, *Plainville, USA* (Westport, CT: Greenwood, 1971 [1945]), 6; Jacob Holdt, *American Pictures* (Copenhagen: American Pictures Foundation, 1987?), 16.
7. *Newsweek,* 4/1/1957, 42, quoted in J. John Palen, *The Suburbs* (New York: McGraw-Hill, 1995), 81.
8. Oprah Winfrey, "Vintage Oprah: Racial Tension in Georgia," Harpo Productions, Chicago, 2001 (1987), 4; Howard Schuman, Charlotte Steeh, and Lawrence Bobo, *Racial Attitudes in America* (Cambridge: Harvard University Press, 1985), 60.
9. Herbert Blumer, "Race Prejudice as a Sense of Group Position," *Pacific Sociological Review* 1, 1 (1958): 3–4.
10. Also called "lawn jockeys," these figures stopped being painted black several decades ago, except in sundown towns. Most manufacturers never bothered to change their molds, however, so the now "Caucasian" coach boys still have thick lips and a broad nose but are painted "white." Residents of Beaver Dam, a southern Wisconsin sundown town, invented a new form, "black boys in Green Bay Packers garb," according to former resident Moira Meltzer-Cohen, who sent photos.
11. Hank Everman, "Corbin, Kentucky: A Socioeconomic Anomaly," Department of History,

Eastern Kentucky University, 2002, unpaginated; David M. P. Freund, "Making It Home," Ph.D. thesis, University of Michigan, 1999, 409; Moira Meltzer-Cohen, e-mail, 9/2002; University of Washington undergraduates, 2/2002.

12. Teams from New Palestine High School in Indiana had been "Redbirds." In the 1920s, when the KKK craze hit, they too became "Dragons," according to a professor at DePauw University, 10/2001. According to Chris Meno (e-mail, 10/2002), who has family connections in the town, oral tradition in New Palestine and at the high school holds that the Klan donated land for the high school with the stipulation the mascot was to be a dragon. Although New Palestine is less than 10 miles from Indianapolis, it was still all-white in 2000. Meno tells that a black woman moved to New Palestine somewhere between 1992 and 1995 and "lasted two days. Blacks don't even drive through."

13. Rick Baker, "Pekin Students Veto 'Chinks' Name Change," 11/28/1974, clipping in Pekin library, name of newspaper omitted; Rose M. Hasler, *Pekin, Illinois: A Pictorial History* (St. Louis: Bradley, 1998), 42; "KKK Holds Local Recruiting Session," *Pekin Times,* 11/29/1999; Karen McDonald, "KKK Recruiting Local Teen-agers," *Peoria Journal Star,* 11/29/1999.

14. Ted Boyer, letter, *Decatur Herald and Review,* 11/13/2001; Dianna Adams, 10/2000 e-mail to Classmates.com bulletin board.

15. This "we" includes African Americans as well as European Americans, because many Redskin players and fans are black. Native Americans and their supporters launched a legal challenge to the Washington Redskins logo, since it is illegal for the government to grant trademarks for racial slurs. They won initially, were reversed, and are now appealing. If the suit succeeds, the team might change its nickname rather than face competition for T-shirt and souvenir sales.

16. Peoria resident, 2/2001; male undergraduate, University of Illinois–Chicago, 9/2001; Randy Whitman, e-mail via Classmates.com, 6/2004.

17. Circa 1993 Meadowbrook graduate, 12/2002.

18. Hominy, Oklahoma, native, e-mail, 11/2001.

19. Western Shore teacher, e-mail, 11/2002; Kaye Collins, e-mail, 6/2002; social studies teacher, Great Lakes National Council for the Social Sciences (NCSS), 4/2001; Robby Heason, *Trouble Behind* (Cicada Films, 1990).

20. David Marniss and Neil Henry, "Race 'War' in Cairo," *Washington Post,* 3/22/1987.

21. Indiana teacher, e-mail, 10/2004; undergraduate, University of Illinois–Urbana, 4/2000; Missouri resident, e-mail, 6/2000.

22. Paul Zielbauer, "After Game, Aftertaste of Racial Slurs Lingers," *New York Times,* 12/14/1999.

23. My web site, uvm.edu/~jloewen/sundown, provides examples.

24. Darla Craft, email via Classmates.com, 10/2002; Pinckneyville native, e-mail, 6/2001.

25. Longtime Sheridan resident, Grant County Musuem, Sheridan, AR, 10/2001; University of Illinois–Urbana undergraduate from Highland, 10/2002.

26. Ralph R. Rea, *Boone County and Its People* (Van Buren, AR: Press-Argus, 1955), 141–42.

27. Kathy Cosseboom, *Grosse Pointe, Michigan: Race Against Race* (East Lansing: Michigan State University Press, 1972), 52.

28. Kathy Spillman, 12/2000; Roger Horowitz, 9/2000; "Williams Sisters Will Skip Indian Wells Again," *USA Today,* 3/6/2003; "Williams Recounts Racist Taunts," *International Herald Tribune,* 3/27/2001.

29. Ron Slater, e-mail via classmates.com, 10/2002.

30. Ray Elliott, 9/2002; Linda Dudek, e-mail via classmates.com, 8/2002.

31. Ramelle MaCoy, e-mail to Ken Lawrence, 3/2003.

32. Grant County Museum volunteer, 10/2001.

33. John D. Baskerville, e-mail, 7/2003.

34. Actually the Williams family, unlike the usual African American in such a situation, had some resources, notably their own eminence. They have boycotted the Pacific Life Open since 2001. In 2003 the tournament director called the incident "unfortunate" and said "he understands why the Williamses are staying away" but went on to claim "the event will do just fine without them."

35. Oblong native, 4/2000.

36. Roger Karns, e-mail, 5/2002.

37. Ibid.

38. Pete Danko, "Hemet Team Uses Racial Slurs, Rivals Say," *Riverside County Press Enterprise,* 11/19/1989.

39. Villa Grove native, 9/2002.

40. *Gentry Journal-Advance,* reprinted in *Rogers Democrat,* 10/17/1906.

41. Maren A. Stein, "The Agricommercial Tradition," in Daniel J. Elazar, ed., *Cities of the Prairie Revisited* (Lincoln: University of Nebraska Press, 1986), 229; Susan Welch et al., *Race and Place* (Cambridge: Cambridge University Press, 2001), 85–92.

42. Joe T. Darden, "African American Residential Segregation," in Robert D. Bullard et al., *Residential Apartheid* (Los Angeles: UCLA Center for Afro-American Studies, 1994), 82.

43. Five years later, Park Forest stopped excluding blacks.

44. William H. Whyte Jr., *The Organization Man* (New York: Simon & Schuster, 1956), 311.

45. Gunnar Myrdal, *An American Dilemma* (New York: Harper & Row, 1944), lxxiii; Robert Terry, *For Whites Only* (Grand Rapids: Eerdmans, 1970), 41.

46. Colony, Alabama, has long been about one-eighth white, according to a librarian in nearby Cullman. In 1960 whites made up about half of the population in Chevy Chase Heights, Pennsylvania. Of course, to white residents in the nearly all-white neighboring town of Indiana, African Americans seemed in the overwhelming majority. In 1930 Colp, Illinois, had 1,250 residents, including 397 whites. Today it has a white mayor. Nevertheless, a white woman who lived and taught school in Herrin in the 1980s assured me in 2001 that Colp was all-black. Again, believing such a fallacy helped her to rationalize the fact that for decades Herrin was all-white, except for live-in maids. Over the years, whites have made up one-tenth to one-quarter of North Amityville's population, on Long Island, and Hispanics are now about one-eighth. When residents of the sundown towns near Boley charged that Boley made whites leave at sundown, "O. H. Bradley, editor of the *Boley Progress,* insisted that many whites lived near Boley, several shopped there both day and night, and most used it as their P.O.," according to historian Norman Crockett. Crockett does admit that whites were discouraged from buying real estate in Boley and Mound Bayou. Poet Jodey Bateman "was told by a black man from Tatum that up until 1972, whites could not stay overnight there." Tatum is a tiny hamlet of fewer than 200 people in southern Oklahoma; Bateman notes drily, "I don't know if whites ever tried to visit Tatum at night." Certainly neither I nor other whites had any difficulty living in Mound Bayou around 1970. Moreover, when a black community *has* kept out whites, sometimes it did so to avoid white retaliation. Leaders knew that one reason whites allowed their town to exist was because its all-black nature legitimized segregation in white eyes. Hence some "black" towns and townships maintained a low profile about their openness to all. See Patrick Clark, e-mail, 7/2002; Myrdal, *An Amer-*

ican Dilemma, 619; Norman Crockett, *The Black Towns* (Lawrence: Regents Press of Kansas, 1979), 74–75; Jodey Bateman, e-mail, 7/2002.

47. Kenilworth realtor, 10/2002; Tulsa resident, 9/2000.

48. Richard J. Hermstein and Charles Murray, *The Bell Curve* (New York: Free Press, 1994), Chapters 2–16.

49. Some years ago the Educational Testing Service, which once called the SAT the Scholastic Aptitude Test, dropped "Aptitude"; they could not defend the claim that the test measured "aptitude for college work." ETS renamed it the Scholastic Assessment Test, but perhaps due to the obvious redundancy, more recently ETS simply calls it the SAT. This has the added advantage of not drawing attention to the name change; most people still think the acronym means "Scholastic Aptitude Test."

50. Robert Coles, *Privileged Ones* (Boston: Little, Brown, 1977), 259; cf. 296–97.

51. Thomas P. Bailey, *Race Orthodoxy in the South* (New York: Neale, 1914), 41.

52. Lynne Duke, "But Some of My Best Friends Are . . . ," *Washington Post* National Weekly Edition, 1/14/1991.

53. Douglas S. Massey and Nancy A. Denton, *American Apartheid* (Cambridge: Harvard University Press, 1993), 94, citing Stanley B. Greenberg, *Report on Democratic Defection* (Washington, DC: Analysis Group, 1985), 13–18, 28.

54. Oak Lawn librarian, 1997; Cosseboom, *Grosse Pointe,* 56.

55. Leonard Steinhorn, "Is America Integrated?" History News Network, 12/23/2002, hnn.us/articles/1174.html, 5/2004; Frederick Douglass, *Douglass Monthly* 3 (10/1860): 337.

56. Dongola genealogist, 6/2003; Arkansas secretary, 9/2002.

57. Jane Adams, *The Transformation of Rural Life, 1890–1990* (Chapel Hill: University of North Carolina Press, 1994), 227.

58. Darla Craft, e-mail via Classmates.com, 10/2002; undergraduate at University of the Ozarks, 9/2002; Herrin native in Decatur, 9/2001; Donahue, "Wrestling with Democracy," 26.

59. Professor, Western Michigan University, 11/2000; undergraduates, University of Illinois–Chicago, 9/2001; André Cavalier, 7/1998; Diane Hershberger, 11/2000.

60. Karns, e-mail, 5/2002.

61. Norman Crockett, *The Black Towns* (Lawrence: Regents Press of Kansas, 1979), 74; W. L. Payne, "Okemah's Night of Terror," in Hazel Ruby McMahan, ed., *Stories of Early Oklahoma,* on Rootsweb, rootsweb.com/~okokfusk/cities.htm, 5/2003; Anna native, e-mail, 1/2003.

62. Arthur F. Raper, *The Tragedy of Lynching* (New York: Dover, 1970 [1933]), 426.

63. Karns, e-mail, 5/2002; Glendale native, e-mail, 11/2003.

64. Mark Singer, "Who Killed Carol Jenkins?" *New Yorker,* 1/7/2002, 25.

65. Ibid., 26.

66. Ibid.; 1987 Indiana University residence advisor, e-mail, 11/2002; Alan Boehm, e-mail, 6/2002.

67. "Martinsville's Sad Season," *Sports Illustrated,* 2/23/1998, 24.

68. Singer, "Who Killed Carol Jenkins?"; Bill Hewitt, "Slow Justice," *People Weekly* 58, 3, July 15, 2002: 89ff., web3.infotrac.galegroup.com/ . . . , #A88718549, 11/2002; Jeff Herlig, "Dateline Diversity" radio program, 11/1/2002, words-at-work.com/dateline.htm, 1/2003; Stephen Stuebner, "Extremists Undermine a Small Town's Efforts to Overcome a Legacy of Racism," *Intelligence Report* 107 (2002), indianacofcc.org, 12/2003.

69. Hmongs are refugees from highland Laos, many of whom had enlisted to fight on our side during the Vietnam War in both Vietnam and Laos.

70. John Lee, "Three Incidents at HS Connected," *Appleton Post-Crescent,* 10/7/1999; Kathy W. Nufer, "Racial Tensions Mount at North," *Post-Crescent,* 9/24/1999.

71. Matthew Shepard was killed for being gay in Laramie, Wyoming, and Laramie was never a sundown town. African Americans, too, have showed intolerance toward gays.

72. "Anti-Gay Extremism," posted at Yahoo.com News Community Headlines, 7/18/1998, and followup by CWBarton, 7/23/1998; New Hope resident, 4/2001; Mt. Rainier gay/lesbian page, hometown.aol.com/glmr20712/page2.html, 10/2002.

73. Shelly H. Kelly, e-mail, 7/2002; Claudia Kolker, "Santa Fe, Texas: Town Struggles to Outgrow Hate," *San Francisco Chronicle,* 9/11/2000.

74. Brooks Blevins, "The Strike and the Still," *Arkansas Historical Quarterly* 52, 4 (1993): 405-20; Charles C. Alexander, *The Ku Klux Klan in the Southwest* (Lexington: University of Kentucky Press, 1965), 62; Katie Benton-Cohen, e-mail, 8/2003.

75. Jodey Bateman, e-mail, 7/2002; post by cyberella5 at virtualtourist.com/f/p/1489/?r=ae52, 5/2002.

76. Abraham Lincoln, letter to Joshua Speed, 8/24/1855, Abraham Lincoln Online, showcase. netins.net/web/creative/lincoln/speeches/speed.htm, 5/2003.

77. Paul Delaney, "Use of 'Multi-Ethnic Textbooks' Grows," *New York Times,* 6/7/1971.

78. Elaine Woo and Kim Kowsky, "Schools' Racial Mix Boils Over," *Los Angeles Times,* 6/14/1991, via LexisNexis.

79. Forsyth County resident, e-mail, 5/2002.

80. The correct figure is less than 13%.

81. Joseph Amato, review of Richard Davies, *Main Street Blues* (Columbus: Ohio State University Press), in *American Historical Review,* 2/2000, 236-37; student estimates from University of Vermont undergraduates, introductory sociology, 1990-96.

82. Longtime resident of Anna now at Northern Illinois University, 10/2002; Donahue, "Wrestling with Democracy," 27.

83. Native of Pana in Decatur, 10/2001; Pana fast-food workers and other residents, 10/2001.

84. Chantel Scherer, e-mail via Classmates.com, 12/2002.

85. Granite City High School graduate (c.1995) at Ripon College, 4/2002.

86. Oblong native, 4/2000; post by goneaviking to uncensored-news.com/alt.flame.niggers, 5/23/2001.

87. Pana native in Decatur, 10/2001; undergraduates, University of Illinois–Chicago, 9/2001; Kathy Spillman, 12/2000.

88. Oblong native, 4/2000.

89. Anthony L. Antonio et al., "Effects of Racial Diversity on Complex Thinking in College Students," ingenta.com/journals/browse/bpl/psci, summarized in "How Racial Diversity Helps Students to Think," *Chronicle of Higher Education,* e-mail, 8/4/2004.

90. Coles, *Privileged Ones,* 416-18.

91. Oklahoma informant, e-mail, 5/2003; former Bishop resident, e-mail, 8/2002; Cullman native, e-mail, 5/2002; Kelly Burroughs, e-mail via Classmates.com, 11/2002.

92. Edwina M. DeWindt, "Wyandotte History; Negro," typescript, 1945, in Bacon Library, Wyandotte, MI, 22.

93. "The Real Polk County," 1/9(?)/1980; Gordon D. Morgan, "Black Hillbillies of the

Arkansas Ozarks," Department of Sociology, University of Arkansas, Fayetteville, 1973, 155–59; wife of store manager, e-mail, 8/2002; Pana resident, 10/2001.

94. Alan Raucher, review of Mark S. Foster, *Castles in the Sand,* in *Journal of American History,* 3/2002, 1574; Mark S. Foster, *Castles in the Sand* (Gainesville: University Press of Florida, 2000), 159–60, 209–10; Karl Taeuber, *Negroes in Cities* (Chicago: Aldine, 1965), 32–37.

95. Among the many overwhelmingly white towns that hosted huge KKK rallies were Milo, Maine; Montpelier, Vermont; Fond du Lac, Wisconsin; Brookston and Valparaiso, Indiana; Fisher and Palestine, Illinois; Grand Saline, Texas; Grants Pass, Oregon; and several suburbs of Los Angeles.

96. Kathleen M. Blee, *Women of the Klan* (Berkeley: University of California Press, 1991), 172.

97. Blee, *Women of the Klan,* 213, believes some clause in the original charter of the university may have prevented the sale. Others hold that the growing split between the national Klan headquarters in Georgia and the Indiana leadership may have prompted the national organization to withhold the funds.

98. Lance Trusty, "All Talk and No 'Kash,' " *Indiana Magazine of History* 82, 1 (1986): 19, 21; James Loewen, *Lies Across America* (New York: New Press, 1999), 238; "Still Riding, with a Bigger Banner," *The Economist,* 4/8/2000, 29–30; Transylvania University student, 10/2001; Central Michigan University student, 10/2002; Texas A&M staffer, e-mail, 6/2000.

99. There is debate about whether Eureka Springs was a sundown town or whether its African Americans departed voluntarily. However, according to a man who lived in Eureka Springs in the mid-1970s, the town has some oral tradition that after the last African American man "died or left town, his house was burned to the ground and that no blacks had lived in the county since that incident" (former Eureka resident, e-mail, 6/2002).

100. I have not confirmed Belmont, but its demographics were stark. In 1930, for example, among 21,748 people in the suburb lived 16 African Americans, 15 of whom were female. None was younger than the age bracket 15–19; surely the fifteen women were live-in maids and the other one was a live-in butler or gardener.

101. John Higham, *Strangers in the Land* (New Brunswick: Rutgers University Press, 1988), 180; Aviva Kempner, *The Life and Times of Hank Greenberg,* PBS-TV documentary, 4/4004; Michael Tomasky, "New York's Finest," *New York Review of Books,* 2/12/2004, 28; Michael Dougan, *Arkansas Odyssey* (Little Rock: Rose, 1994), 608; former Eureka resident, e-mail, 6/2002; Robert Welch, "A Letter to the South," John Birch Society, jbs.org/visitor/focus/refute/letter_south.htm, 5/2003; Tony Platt, e-mail, 9/2002; Stephen Kercher, review of *Joseph McCarthy: A Modern Tragedy,* exhibit at Outagamie Museum, *Journal of American History,* 12/2002, 1004.

102. Many organizations on the list, like most other organizations, are headquartered in cities that are too large to be uniracial. A disproportionate share are headquartered in the South, which still has many racists but few sundown towns.

103. Southern Poverty Law Center Intelligence Report, splcenter.org/intelligenceproject/ip-index.html, 5/2003; re Simi Valley, see the John Birch Society web site, jbs.org, 4/2003; Nationalist web site, nationalist.org/ATW/1997/feb.html, 10/1998.

104. Zimmermann quoted in Laurinda Joenks, "Roughness of Citizens Blamed on Lean Times," *The Morning News,* 5/7/2000; Robb quoted in Jacqueline Froelich, "A City Confronts Its Ghosts," *Arkansas Democrat-Gazette,* 4/27/2003; Potter County discussed on *All Things Considered,* National Public Radio, 2/15/2002.

CHAPTER 12: THE EFFECT OF SUNDOWN TOWNS ON BLACKS

1. Daisy Myers, "Breaking Down Barriers," *Pennsylvania Heritage* 28, 3 (2002): 12.
2. Shirley Willard, "Black History in Fulton County Since 1920s," Fulton County Historical Society, Rochester, n.d., unpaginated.
3. Middle-aged Mattoon woman, 2/2004.
4. Allison Blakely, e-mail, 9/2002.
5. Joycelyn Landrum-Brown, e-mail, 8/2002; Olen Cole Jr., *The African-American Experience in the Civilian Conservation Corps* (Gainesville: University Press of Florida, 1999), 25.
6. Mattoon woman, 10/2002; Cole, *The African-American Experience;* Paxton resident, 10/2000; Southern Arkansas University professor, 10/2001; Missouri resident, 7/2002.
7. Reynolds Farley, Sheldon Danziger, and Harry Holzer, *Detroit Divided* (New York: Russell Sage, 2000), 154–55; Gordon Trowbridge and Oralandar Brand-Williams, "Invisible Boundaries Created Dividing Line Between Black, White Suburbs," *Detroit News,* 1/14/2002, detnews.com/2002/homepage/0201/14/index.htm, 1/2002; Bradley professor, 2/2001.
8. Colbert King, "The Kings of Foggy Bottom," *Washington Post Magazine,* 2/1/2004, 20.
9. Elderly Arab resident, 6/2002; Orlando Patterson, *The Ordeal of Integration* (Washington, DC: Civitas/Counterpoint, 1997), 46; Susan Welch et al., *Race and Place* (Cambridge: Cambridge University Press, 2001), 38.
10. David Mendell, "Midwest Housing Divide Is Still Race," *Chicago Tribune,* 6/21/2001, mumford1.dyndns.org/cen2000/newspdf/chicagotribune0621.html, 7/2003.
11. Sheryll Cashin, *The Failures of Integration* (New York: Public Affairs, 2004), 9; Sidney Poitier and Ruby Dee quoted in Andrew Wiese, *Places of Their Own* (Chicago: University of Chicago Press, 2004), 154, 157.
12. Cashin, *The Failures of Integration,* 137–60, 171–75.
13. Gary Orfield, talk at OPEN meeting, Philadelphia, 12/2000; Farley, Danziger, and Holzer, *Detroit Divided,* 204; John R. Logan, review of same in *Contemporary Sociology* 31, 5 (2002), 519; Light, 6/2002.
14. Cole, *The African-American Experience in the Civilian Conservation Corps,* 25; Ronald McGriff, e-mail, 6/2002; Benjamin Johnson, post 8/6/2001, umb.edu/forum/1/AMST203/member/Forums/s-484415211-.html#47101 6211, 12/18/2002.
15. David Grann, "Firestarters," *New Republic,* 7/20/1998, 17; Richard Stewart, "Desegregation at Public Housing Ripped by Audit," *Houston Chronicle,* East Texas Bureau, 7/11/1997; Mimi Swartz, "Vidor in Black and White," *Texas Monthly,* 12/1991, 161; Du Quoin resident, 9/2002.
16. Patterson, *Ordeal of Integration,* 65.
17. Myers, "Breaking Down Barriers," 12.
18. Arna Bontemps and Jack Conroy, *Anyplace but Here* (New York: Hill & Wang, 1966), 9, quoted in Quintard Taylor, *In Search of the Racial Frontier* (New York: Norton, 1998), 301; Vivian S. Toy, "Stuck in Last Place," *New York Times,* 5/4/2003.
19. Ellis Cose, *The Rage of a Privileged Class* (New York: HarperCollins, 1993), 1.
20. Ibid., 39; Langston Hughes, "Restrictive Covenants," in Arnold Rampersad, ed., *The Collected Poems of Langston Hughes* (New York: Vintage, 1994), 361.
21. Martin Luther King Jr., remarks at Palmer House, Chicago, summer 1965, quoted in *How Long? Not Long* (Chicago: Leadership Council for Metropolitan Open Communities, 1986).

22. Student of Joseph Braun's at Illinois State University, 9/1999, e-mailed by Braun, 11/2001.

23. Dale Harvey and Gerald Slatin, "The Relationship Between Child's SES and Teacher Expectations," *Social Forces* 54, 1 (1975): 141. James Loewen, "The Difference Race Makes," in Howard Ball et al., eds., *Multicultural Education* (Hillsdale, NJ: Erlbaum, 1998), 53–55, summarizes some of the expectation literature about race.

24. Poussaint quoted in Gordon Trowbridge and Oralandar Brand-Williams, "The Past: A policy of exclusion," *Detroit News,* 1/14/2002, at mumford1.dyndns.org/cen2000/othersay/ detroitnews/Stories/Blacks . . . , 7/2003.

25. See Claude Steele, in Steele, Teresa Perry, and Asa Hilliard III, *Young, Gifted, and Black* (Boston: Beacon, 2004); Steele and Joshua Aronson, "Stereotype Threat and the Intellectual Test Performance of African Americans," *Journal of Personality and Social Psychology* 69 (1995): 797–811; and J. Aronson et al., "When White Men Can't Do Math," *Journal of Experimental Social Psychology* 35 (1999): 29–46.

26. Malcolm X, *Malcolm X Speaks,* quoted in Joseph R. Conlin, *Morrow Book of Quotations in American History* (New York: Morrow, 1984), 327.

27. Kati Haycock, "Passing Grades," *Trust,* summer 2000, 13.

28. Only affirmative action allows an appreciable number of African Americans into America's elite colleges, where this capital is most readily acquired. One reason why affirmative action is necessary leads right back to sundown suburbs: African Americans average much lower than European Americans on standardized tests. The reasons are several, but excluding African Americans residentially is one factor, coupled with test bias on the SAT (and ACT). See James Loewen, "Presentation," "Discussion," and "A Sociological View of Aptitude Tests," in Eileen Rudert, ed., *The Validity of Testing in Education and Employment* (Washington, DC: U.S. Commission on Civil Rights, 1993), 41–45, 58–62, 73–91, and James Loewen, Phyllis Rosser, and John Katzman, "Gender Bias on SAT Items," American Educational Research Association, 4/1988, ERIC ED294915.

29. Patterson, *The Ordeal of Integration,* 9, 20; Barbara J. Fields, "Of Rogues and Geldings," *American Historical Review,* 108 #5 (12/2002), 1401.

30. See Loewen, "Presentation," "Discussion," and "A Sociological View of Aptitude Tests," 41–45, 58–62, 73–91; Loewen, Rosser, and Katzman, "Gender Bias on SAT Items."

31. This relief, placing Section 8 families in white suburbs, resulted from a related lawsuit against HUD.

32. I relied on several articles by Rosenbaum, but the most accessible compilation of these results is in Leonard S. Rubinowitz and James E. Rosenbaum, *Crossing the Class and Color Lines: From Public Housing to White Suburbia* (Chicago: University of Chicago Press, 2000).

33. Galster summarized in Trowbridge and Brand-Williams, "The Past: A Policy of Exclusion."

34. Mark Granovetter, "The Strength of Weak Ties," *American Journal of Sociology* 78 (1973): 1360–80; Deirdre A. Royster, *Race and the Invisible Hand: How White Networks Exclude Black Men from Blue-Collar Jobs* (Berkeley: University of California Press, 2003), 182.

35. Stephanie Simon, "Segregation Still Strong in North," *Los Angeles Times,* 1/19/2003, reprinted in *Holland* (MI) *Sentinel,* 3/30/2003, hollandsentinel.com, 4/2003; Carolyn Adams et al., *Philadelphia: Neighborhoods, Division, and Conflict* (Temple University Press, 1991), 53.

36. Former Darien resident, 8/1999.

37. Charles Christian, "Emerging Patterns of Industrial Activity Within Large Metropolitan

Areas," in Gary Gappert and Harold M. Rose, eds., *The Social Economy of Cities* (Beverly Hills: Sage, 1975), 241.

38. Anne B. Shlay, review of Alice O'Connor, Chris Tilly, and Lawrence Bobo, eds., *Urban Inequality,* in *Contemporary Sociology* 31, 5 (2002): 511.

39. William J. Wilson, *When Work Disappears* (New York: Vintage, 1996).

CHAPTER 13: THE EFFECT OF SUNDOWN TOWNS ON THE SOCIAL SYSTEM

1. Thorstein Veblen, *The Theory of the Leisure Class* (New York: NAL/Mentor, 1953 [1899]), 81.

2. This statement is based on its Index of Dissimilarity, D = 85, meaning that 85% of its African Americans would have to move to nonblack areas to achieve a completely neutral distribution of both races.

3. More recent figures, which may not reflect identical methodology, show some narrowing of this gap. According to the *American Housing Survey, 1999,* median owner-occupied housing units in 1999 were valued at $63,400 in the city of Detroit, $168,200 in Boston, and $215,600 in Los Angeles (Census web site, census.gov/prod/2001pubs, 5/2004).

4. John Logan et al., "Ethnic Diversity Grows, Neighborhood Integration Lags Behind," Mumford Center, 12/18/2001, 7, mumford1.dyndns.org/cen2000/WholePop/WPreport/page1.html, 1/2003; Reynolds Farley, Sheldon Danziger, and Harry Holzer, *Detroit Divided* (New York: Russell Sage, 2000), 1–2; *American Housing Survey, 1999,* at U.S. Census, census.gov/prod/2001pubs, 5/2004; Carolyn Crowley, "Urban Explorers, Crawling and Climbing into the Past," *Washington Post,* 12/30/2001.

5. Farley, Danziger, and Holzer, *Detroit Divided;* Francis X. Donnelly, "Region Pays Price for Reputation," *Detroit News,* 1/21/2002, detroitnews/2002/homepage/0201/21/index.htm, 2/2002.

6. Leah Samuel, "Organ Transplant," *Detroit Metro Times,* 9/10/2003.

7. Jane Jacobs, *The Death and Life of Great American Cities* (New York: Vintage, 1961), Chapter 11, and *Cities and the Wealth of Nations* (New York: Vintage, 1985); William Whyte, *City* (New York: Doubleday, 1988), 288; cf. discussion in Andres Duany, Elizabeth Plater-Zyberk, and Jeff Speck, *Suburban Nation* (New York: Farrar, Straus, and Giroux, 2000), 9.

8. Charles Mudede, "How Tacoma Fought Seattle for the Future and Lost," *The Stranger* 9, 47 (2000), thestranger.com/2000-08-10/feature-2.html, 6/2003.

9. Nick Khan, 9/2002; Red Bud native, 2/2004.

10. Herman Lantz and J. S. McCrary, *People of Coal Town* (Carbondale: Southern Illinois University Press, 1971 [1958]), 42; West Frankfort genealogist reported to me, 9/2002.

11. Lesbians more often locate in suburbs, although they do seem to prefer multiracial suburbs, according to Gates. I do not know of research on the relationship of lesbians to creativity and economic development.

12. Gary Gates, "The Demographics of Diversity," Urban Institute, 6/3/2003, also summarizing Richard Florida's findings; Tatsha Robertson, "Finding Hope in Gay Enclaves," *Boston Globe,* 1/15/2003.

13. Pew Center for Civic Journalism, *Straight Talk From Americans—2000,* pewcenter.org/doingcj/research/r_ST2000nat1.html#nation, 6/2003; Haya El Nasser and Paul Overberg, "What You Don't Know About Sprawl," *USA Today,* 2/22/2001.

14. Actually, as of 2000 Oak Park was still just 22% black.

15. Carole Goodwin, *The Oak Park Strategy* (Chicago: University of Chicago Press, 1979), 108–9.

16. Quoted in Thomas Sugrue, *Origins of the Urban Crisis* (Princeton: Princeton University Press, 1996), 196.

17. Michael Ebner, *Creating Chicago's North Shore* (Chicago: University of Chicago Press, 1988), 230, 314.

18. Post died in 1960, but her granddaughter-in-law, Elizabeth Post, brought out the 12th edition of *Etiquette* in 1969.

19. Patrick M. McMullen, "Gated Communities," entry for *Encyclopedia of Chicago*, draft, 10/17/2000; Albert F. Winslow, *Tuxedo Park* (Tuxedo Park: Tuxedo Park Historical Society, 1992).

20. Ingrid Gould Ellen, *Sharing America's Neighborhoods* (Cambridge: Harvard University Press, 2000), 71.

21. Larry Peterson, who has studied housing and race in the Chicago suburbs for four decades, points out that another reason owners move first is the behavior of realtors. Since they make far more money from sales than rentals, it is in their interest to encourage turnover, so they focus on persuading white homeowners to sell.

22. Installment contracts differ from mortgages in that the buyer builds no legal equity until payments are complete. Missing a single payment can put the buyer in default, leading to the loss of the entire investment and leaving the speculator free to sell the house again.

23. Arnold Hirsch, *Making the Second Ghetto* (Cambridge: Cambridge University Press, 1983), 32; Luigi Laurenti, "Property Values and Neighborhood Integration," in Raymond Mack, ed., *Race, Class, and Power* (New York: American Book Co., 1968), 435.

24. George Galster, "Neighborhood Racial Change, Segregationist Sentiments, and Affirmative Marketing Policies," *Journal of Urban Economics* 27 (1990): 334–61, summarized in Ellen, *Sharing America's Neighborhoods*, 63.

25. Arthur Hayes, "Managed Integration," *Black Enterprise*, 7/1982, 43; Goodwin, *The Oak Park Strategy*, 157–58; cf. Ellen, *Sharing America's Neighborhoods*, 162–63.

26. White flight is not inevitable. Whites are not fleeing Mt. Rainier, Maryland, for example, which was 56% black in 1990 and just 62% black in 2000. In the last twenty years, whites have sometimes moved *into* majority-black neighborhoods, such as parts of Capitol Hill in Washington, D.C., and made them majority-white. Between 1960 and 1970, Kirkwood, a neighborhood in Atlanta, went from being 91% white to 97% black. Then in the 1990s, some whites returned, making Kirkwood 14% white by 2000. Tipping point theory, which holds that whites will not flee until a neighborhood reaches a certain percentage and then will leave, cannot explain gentrification. Nor can it explain Lynwood.

27. Richard Morin, "The Odds of Being Poor," *Washington Post*, 3/23/1999; "Proposed Group Home Sparks Long Legal Battle," Associated Press, 3/16/2002, on Advocacy and Protection for People with Mental Illness web site, geocities.com/ahobbit.geo/group_home .html, 6/2003; "Local Judge Rejects Effort to Stop Group Home in Greenwich," Associated Press, in *Hartford Courant*, 9/9/2002, on Homeless News web site, groups.yahoo .com/group/HomelessNews/message/2094, 6/2003.

28. Mary Otto, "Suburbs Struggle to Help Homeless," *Washington Post*, 12/18/2000.

29. Jonathan Kozol, *Savage Inequalities* (New York: Crown, 1991), 7–9; Ellen, *Sharing America's Neighborhoods*, 4, 118.

30. Some do pay a lesser amount that reimburses a city for some of the services—police, streets, fire protection, etc.

31. Kozol, *Savage Inequalities*, 55; Darwin Payne, *Big D: Triumphs and Troubles* (Dallas: Three Forks Press, 1994), 214.

32. Longtime Cincinnati suburbanite, e-mail, 11/2002.

33. Michael N. Danielson, *The Politics of Exclusion* (New York: Columbia University Press, 1976), 88, 110.

34. Gunnar Myrdal, *An American Dilemma* (New York: McGraw-Hill, 1964 [1944]), 618–22; Jianping Shen, "Have Minority Students Had a Fair Share of Quality Teachers?" *Poverty & Race* 12, 4 (7/2003), 7; Michael Powell, "Separate and Unequal in Roosevelt, Long Island," *Washington Post*, 4/21/2002.

35. Danielson, *The Politics of Exclusion*, 21; Carolyn Adams et al., *Philadelphia: Neighborhoods, Division, and Conflict* (Philadelphia: Temple University Press, 1991), 163; Powell, "Separate and Unequal in Roosevelt, Long Island."

36. Witold Rybczynski, *City Life* (New York: Harper Collins, 1995), 206–7; Powell, "Separate and Unequal."

37. Dan T. Carter, *The Politics of Rage* (New York: Simon & Schuster, 1995), 433; John Gehm, *Bringing it Home* (Chicago: Chicago Review Press, 1984), 193; Janet L. McCoy, "AU Prof: Remember Wallace for Changing U.S. Political Ideology," at auburn.edu/administration/univrel/news/archive/9_98news/9_98wal lace.html, 8/2003; Ken Rudin, "Flunking Out of the Electoral College," *Washington Post*, 10/15/1999, washingtonpost.com/wp-srv/politics/campaigns/junkie/archive/jun kie101599.htm, 8/2003.

38. "Quiet Town in Michigan Has 'a Feeling for Wallace,' " *New York Times*, 9/12/1968.

39. Bill Outis, 10/2001; Reynolds Farley, Sheldon Danziger, and Harry Holzer, *Detroit Divided* (New York: Russell Sage, 2000), 11; Dan T. Carter, *The Politics of Rage* (New York: Simon & Schuster, 1995), 434; Kathy Spillman, 12/2000.

40. Nixon quoted in George Lipsitz, "The Possessive Investment in Whiteness," in Jonathan Birnbaum and Clarence Taylor, eds., *Civil Rights Since 1787* (New York: New York University Press, 2000), 674; Donahue, "Wrestling with Democracy," 18; Sugrue, *Origins of the Urban Crisis*, 266; Alexander Polikoff, "Racial Inequality and the Black Ghetto," *Poverty & Race* 13, 6 (11/2004), 1.

41. To be sure, the Republican administration in 2001–05 hardly shrank the federal government.

42. Thomas Edsall and Mary Edsall, *Chain Reaction* (New York: Norton, 1992), 226, 229; Dan T. Carter, "The Southern Strategy," in Birnbaum and Taylor, eds., *Civil Rights Since 1787*, 738; cf. David M. P. Freund, "Making It Home," Ph.D. dissertation, University of Michigan, 1999.

43. Sheryll Cashin, *The Failures of Integration* (New York: Public Affairs, 2004), 270.

44. Edsall and Edsall, *Chain Reaction*, 228.

45. Ibid., 226, 229.

CHAPTER 14: SUNDOWN TOWNS TODAY

1. Donald Deskins Jr. and Christopher Bettinger, "Black and White Spaces in Selected Metropolitan Areas," in Kate A. Berry and Martha L. Henderson, eds., *Geographical Identities of Ethnic America* (Reno: University of Nevada Press, 2002), 38.

2. Benjamin Johnson, post to umb.edu/forum/1/AMST203/member/Forums/s-484415211-.html#471016211, 8/2001; former Marlowe resident, e-mail, 11/2004; Missouri resident,

e-mail, 6/2000; Roger Karns, e-mail, 5/2002; Margaret Alexander Alam, e-mails and photo, 9/2003.

3. Dan F. Morse and Phyllis A. Morse, "Introduction," *The Lower Mississippi Valley Expeditions of Clarence Bloomfield Moore* (Tuscaloosa: University of Alabama Press, 1998), 2.

4. Malcolm Ross, *All Manner of Men* (New York: Reynal & Hitchcock, 1948), 66.

5. Herrin, which was sundown when Angle was there, had 104 African Americans, almost 1% of its population, in 2000.

6. Paul M. Angle, *Bloody Williamson* (New York: Knopf, 1952), 98; Zeigler librarian, 9/2002; Deidre Meadows, e-mail via Classmates.com, 9/2002; Du Quoin resident, 9/2002.

7. Robby Heason, *Trouble Behind* (Cicada Films, 1990).

8. Frank Nickell, e-mail, 6/2002; professor, Taylor University, 6/2004; Rebecca Tolley-Stokes, e-mail, 8/2002; Michael D'Orso, *Like Judgment Day* (New York: Putnam's, 1996), 329.

9. Undergraduate, University of the Ozarks, 9/2002; undergraduate, University of Illinois–Chicago, 9/2001.

10. Chris Meno, e-mail, 10/2002; professor, DePauw University, 10/2001; clerk, National Afro-American Museum at Central State University, 10/2000.

11. If the census shows no black families, that does not prove that African Americans *cannot* live there. Only continuing incidents prove that, and I cannot be up to the moment for every town I've studied. For most communities my information is current only as of 2001–04 or even earlier. Checking each town anew would take years, at the end of which we would be in a new present, no longer up to the moment. Also, in many sundown towns the question simply cannot be resolved, even with up-to-date information, owing to no recent trials. Until another black family (or better, two or three) tests a town by trying to move in, we cannot know for sure if it still keeps out African Americans. We know it did, but we do not know that it does.

12. Listing more than one race was allowed on the 2000 census for the first time. Few (<5%) chose such categories, and usually I omitted them, being unsure how they classed themselves. Neither I nor the census achieved consistency, however. Sometimes I included individuals of both African and European ancestry as "black," and the census apparently includes nonblack family members, as it should, in its table of population in households with one or more black householder. I use the term "black household" to mean "household with one or more black householders." Like the IRS, I required "households" to include more than one person; otherwise I could not distinguish them from unattached individuals.

13. Anna editor and reference librarian, 9/2002; Anna farmer, 1/2004.

14. Illinois state trooper, 1/2004; Ronald Alan Willis, e-mail, 9/2004.

15. Martinsville native, 10/2002.

16. Post by "goneaviking" to uncensored-news.com/alt.flame.niggers, 5/23/2001; Smokey Crabtree, *Too Close to the Mirror* (Fouke: Days Creek Production, 2001), 186.

17. Of course, many residents of Elwood want no part of such events, the KKK marches in many multiracial towns, and "hosting" KKK events costs Elwood money for police overtime. See "The High Price of Policing Hate," 10/28/2002, Anti-Defamation League, adl.org/learn/news/cost_of_hate.asp, 6/2003.

18. North Judson teacher, 4/2001; former Marion, Indiana, policeman, 6/2002; Indiana teacher, e-mail, 6/2000.

19. David Cline, e-mail, 6/2003, confirming conversation with Steeleville librarian, 6/2003.

20. Two Pinckneyville residents, 9/2002; Du Quoin resident, 9/2002; Pinckneyville native, e-mail, 8/2004.

21. Mattoon businessman, e-mail, 10/2002.

22. Champaign-Urbana resident, 2000.

23. Pana spokeswoman, 10/2001; Pana resident, 10/2001.

24. Forsyth County, GA, resident, e-mail, 5/2002; native of Oak Grove, 3/2004; D'Vera Cohn, "1990s Further Reshape Suburbs," *Washington Post,* 5/25/2001.

25. Librarian, Joplin Public Library, 9/2002.

26. Robert Bullard quoted in Jonathan Tilove, "2000 Census Finds America's New Mayberry Is Exurban, and Overwhelmingly White," Newhouse News Service, 2001, newhouse.com/archive/story1a051001.html, 8/2004.

27. Andres Duany, Elizabeth Plater-Zyberk, and Jeff Speck, *Suburban Nation* (New York: Farrar, Straus, and Giroux, 2000), 43.

28. Ellen James Martin, "Set Some Priorities When Buying in a Classy Community," *Chicago Tribune,* 9/14/2001.

29. Kenneth T. Jackson, *Crabgrass Frontier* (New York: Oxford University Press, 1985), 8; Duany, Plater-Zyberk, and Speck, *Suburban Nation,* 44.

30. Common rules include no JetSkis or boats in driveway; no fence, no gazebo, no unapproved lawn furniture; any doghouse must resemble your house and must be hidden from the street by a six-foot fence or greenery. Diane Hershberger of Kansas City told of subdivisions in suburban Johnson County where "you can't leave your garage doors open, you can't work on your cars in your own driveway, you can't hang laundry outside at any time." These restrictions need not be racial. Sociologist Karyn Lacy described a suburb that has gone majority black and has similar rules: "Residents must not allow their grass to grow more than 4 inches tall. (At the same time, they are also precluded from not maintaining grass at all.) Detractors are hit with heavy penalties." Diane Hershberger, 11/2000; Karyn Lacy, "A Part of the Neighborhood," *International Journal of Sociology and Social Policy* 22 (2002): 62.

31. Elizabeth Razzi, "House Rules," *Kiplinger's Magazine,* 9/2000, 87–88; Frederique Krupa, "Los Angeles: Buying the Concept of Security," Chapter 3 of "Privatization of Public Space," unpaginated, translucency.com/frede/pps.html, 1/2004.

32. Kaplan quoted in Anthony Faiola, "Brazil's Elites Fly Above Their Fears: Rich Try to Wall Off Urban Violence," *Washington Post* Foreign Service, 6/1/2002; Edward J. Blakely and Mary Gail Snyder, *Fortress America* (Washington, DC: Brookings, 1997), 2–3, 7, 17, 26.

33. The entry gates at Country Club Estates in New Albany, Ohio, where houses sold in 2000 for $800,000 to $1,200,000, open automatically when a car drives close to them. No sign tells this, so I suppose some would-be thieves might be deterred. Exit gates in most gated communities open automatically.

34. Blakely and Snyder, *Fortress America,* 69.

35. Ibid., 17, 83; Columbus Academy student, 10/2000.

36. Lacy, "A Part of the Neighborhood"; Annemei Curlin, 8/2002; Blakely and Snyder, *Fortress America,* 153–54.

37. Gunnar Myrdal, *An American Dilemma* (New York: Harper & Row, 1944), 9.

38. "Real Estate Operator's Plan for Exclusion of Minorities Condemned by Civic Leaders," *Pacific Citizen,* 7/5/1947.

39. In the late 1940s, most Jewish American leaders chose to downplay the Holocaust, "with an eye to an internal assimilationist goal and an external Cold War agenda," according to Tim Cole, "Representing the Holocaust in America" [reviewing Peter Novick's *The Holocaust in*

American Life], *Public Historian* 24, 4 (2002): 128. In the 1960s, according to Novick and Cole, American Jewish leaders made "a U-turn," and by 1990 the Holocaust had become "the iconic event of the twentieth century, for American Jews in particular and Americans more generally." This increased emphasis on the Holocaust, exemplified by the very popular Holocaust Museum near the Mall in Washington, D.C., includes modest attention to our reluctance to accept Jewish refugees during and before World War II, but almost none to the rise of anti-Semitism in America during the Nadir.

40. Richard Todd, "Darien, Connecticut," *New England Monthly,* 3/1986, 43.

41. "Attitudes Toward Specific Areas of Racial Integration," *Connecticut Civil Rights Bulletin* 3, 4 (1961): 2.

42. Yes, the event is disputed. I do think James Earl Ray did it, but I don't believe he acted alone; see James Loewen, *Lies My Teacher Told Me* (New York: New Press, 1995), 224.

43. Karl Taeuber, "Research Issues Concerning Trends in Residential Segregation," University of Wisconsin Center for Demography and Ecology, Madison, Working Paper 83-13, 11/1982, 5.

44. Howard Schuman, Charlotte Steeh, and Lawrence Bobo, *Racial Attitudes in America* (Cambridge: Harvard University Press, 1985), 59–60; Reynolds Farley and William H. Frey, "Changes in the Segregation of Whites from Blacks During the 1980s," *American Sociological Review* 59, 1 (1994), 27; Orlando Patterson, *The Ordeal of Integration* (Washington, DC: Civitas/Counterpoint, 1997), 61.

45. Commenting on the NORC item, Howard Schuman, Charlotte Steeh, and Lawrence Bobo concur. Evidence indicates that some of the 63% agreed more in the abstract than in the concrete. In 1972, NORC also asked respondents to choose "between two possible laws to vote on. One law says that a homeowner can decide for himself who to sell his house to, even if he prefers not to sell to blacks. The second law says that a homeowner cannot refuse to sell to someone because of their race or color. Which law would you vote for?" Only 34% supported the second alternative. See Schuman, Steeh, and Bobo, *Racial Attitudes in America,* 97.

46. To be sure, much popular culture is youth culture, which makes it partly a matter of the life cycle. One cannot project the life cycle onto society as a whole. When today's white teenagers become parents and reach thirty or forty, they may choose to live in white suburbia. After all, some white parents who moved to sundown towns in the 1980s had venerated African Americans such as Muhammad Ali or Ray Charles in the 1960s.

47. Dorothy K. Newman et al., *Protest, Politics, and Prosperity* (New York: Pantheon, 1978), 141, 152; Stephen G. Meyer, *As Long as They Don't Move Next Door* (Lanham, MD: Rowman & Littlefield, 2000), 220; Paul Jargowsky, "Concentration of Poverty Declines in the 1990s," *Poverty & Race* 12, 4 (7/2003), 1; David Mendell, "Midwest Housing Divide Is Still Race," *Chicago Tribune,* 6/21/2001, at mumford1.dyndns.org/cen2000/newspdf/chicago tribune0621.html, 7/2003.

48. Associated Press, "Ruling Opens Connecticut Beaches," *Washington Post,* 5/11/2000; Deborah Pollard, professor, University of Michigan–Dearborn, e-mail, 7/2002; *Michigan State Tax Commission v. Grosse Pointe,* Michigan Tax Tribunal #284,585, Opinion, 7/16/2003.

49. Ricardo A. Herrera, e-mail, 6/2000.

50. This is reminiscent of the finding that multiethnic towns were less likely than monoethnic towns to exclude blacks between 1890 and 1940.

51. Mendell, "Midwest Housing Divide Is Still Race"; Christopher Phillips, e-mail, 6/2000.

52. Danielle Gordon, "Residency Rules Ignite Race Debate," *Chicago Reporter,* 12/1998, chicagoreporter.com/1999/01-99/tear400.gif, 4/2003.

53. James Loewen, *Lies Across America* (New York: New Press, 1999), 170–72; Michael Bsharah, letter, 7/20/2000; Dearborn Online, dearborn-mi.com, c.10/2002.

54. Leonard Steinhorn, "Is America Integrated?" History News Network, 12/23/2002, hnn.us/articles/1174.html, 5/2004; Nancy A. Denton, "Segregation and Discrimination in Housing" in Rachel Bratt, Chester Hartman, and Michael E. Stone, eds., reader on housing (Philadelphia: Temple University Press, forthcoming), ms. pp. 23–28; Susan Welch et al., *Race and Place* (Cambridge: Cambridge University Press, 2001), 168.

55. This would not be the first time. Between 1920 and 1950 or so, as we have seen, "white" came to incorporate Jews, Italians, and other groups that had been considered separate races. Irish became "white" earlier; Arabs, Pakistanis, and Asian Indians later. Chinese Americans were admitted to "white" public schools in the Mississippi Delta in the 1930s and '40s. Today, "white" may be incorporating most Asian, Pacific, Mexican, and affluent Native Americans. Certainly their acceptance in sundown towns implies as much.

   This process offers payoffs for "real" whites. For one, the oft-repeated claim that whites will be a minority by 2040 or 2050 may not come to pass: "white" may simply morph into a broader category by then. Also, whites have often used their acceptance of "honorary whites" to avoid the charge of racism. Sundown town residents are quick to cite their Mexican and Asian Americans to prove that they are not prejudiced, even though they still do exclude African Americans. Admitting Hispanics and Asian Americans may help make these groups more racist over time, as it did Chinese Americans in Mississippi (see Loewen, *The Mississippi Chinese: Between Black and White* [Prospect Heights, IL: Waveland Press, 1988], 93, 195–200).

56. Arcola official, 9/2002; Darrin Burnett, "Cross Burning Fans Flames in Beardstown," Jacksonville (IL) *Journal-Courier,* 8/13/1996; Sager quoted in S. Lynne Walker, "Dealing with Change," *Springfield State Journal-Register,* 11/12/2003; comment by real estate broker at Ozarkopathy web site, ozarkopathy.org, 8/2003 and e-mail, 9/2003.

57. Lisa Coleman, e-mail, 7/2002.

58. Piggott, AR, resident, e-mail, 8/2002; Benton, IL, teacher, 9/2002.

59. "Alone in the Crowd," *New York Times Magazine,* 7/16/2000, 56.

60. Sheridan native at Grant County Museum, 10/2001.

61. Actually, the Green Bay Packers were the next-to-last team in the National Football League to accept a black player, doing so only in 1950, three years after Jackie Robinson. See Larry Names, *The History of the Green Bay Packers,* vol. IV: *The Shameful Years* (Wautoma: Angel Press, 1995), 44.

62. Dan Benson, "Despite Rocky Start, Minorities Call Cedarburg Home," *Milwaukee Journal Sentinel,* 3/14/2001.

63. Ragland noted, "The latest census data in 2000 showed 34 blacks residing in Highland Park, but as far as anyone knows, they're renting." This is another case where the census counts people who are not known to local residents. Perhaps they are live-in servants, adopted children, inmates of penal, educational, or other institutions, or mistakes by census respondents.

64. Dorothy Brown, "The Encircled Schools: Park Cities and Wilmington," *Dallas Times Herald,* 11/30/1975; James Ragland, "New HP Couple Spurs Media Tizzy," *Dallas Morning News,* 6/9/2003; cf. Mark Miller, "At Last," MSNBC News, 6/4/2003, msnbc.com/news/922226, 6/2003.

65. Betty Toomes, transcript of interview (Yuma, AZ, 1963: Robert B. Powers, interviewer), sunsite.berkeley.edu:2020/dynaweb/teiproj/oh/warren/powers/@Generic_BookTextView/4030, 1/2003.

66. White snipers repeatedly shot at the black housing project, forcing residents to douse their lights; blacks in turn fired at the police station and at firemen answering calls. All public officials were white, elected at-large by voters polarized along racial lines; blacks took the city to court, demanding single-member districts so they could win some representation on the city council. See James Loewen, "Report for Land of Lincoln Legal Assistance Foundation in *Kendrick et al. v. Moss et al.,*" typescript, Burlington, VT, 1979.

67. Mexican American basketball players played the same unifying role in Beardstown in 2003. About 20 fans of nearby Brown County High School, a sundown county, showed up wearing sombreros and yelling "We want tacos" at the Beardstown team. According to Beardstown senior Tomas Alvarez, "People were mad. They really care about the image of Beardstown. That wasn't just against an ethnic group. It was against the whole town." Quoted in Walker, "Dealing with Change."

68. David Marniss and Neil Henry, "Race 'War' in Cairo," *Washington Post,* 3/22/1987.

69. Alvarez quoted in Walker, "Dealing with Change."

70. Bill Jennings, "Left-hander Finds Many Who Impress," *Riverside Press Enterprise,* 12/11/1992, via LexisNexis; Pete Danko, "Hemet Team Uses Racial Slurs, Rivals Say," *Riverside County Press Enterprise,* 11/19/1989.

71. George Callcott, 5/2004.

72. San Diego Online, sandiego-online.com/retro/janretr1.stm, 3/2003; Mary Ellen Stratthaus, "Flaw in the Jewel: Housing Discrimination Against Jews in La Jolla, California," *American Jewish History* 84, 3 (1996): 189, 193–95, 198, 201–2, 210, 215–16.

73. John Palen, *The Suburbs* (New York: McGraw-Hill, 1995), xiv, 3.

74. Actually, while Mountain Home's population ballooned from 3,936 in 1970 to 9,027 by 1990, its black population decreased from 1 to 0. Not until 2000, when three African American families finally ventured in, did Mountain Home cease being a sundown town. Long before that, the sense that integration was unavoidable played a major role in desegregating sundown suburbs across most of the South.

75. For a brief period after World War II, three other suburbs in Mississippi tried to emulate northern sundown suburbs and became almost all-white: Southaven, a suburb of Memphis, East Tupelo, a former suburb of Tupelo, and D'Iberville, on the Gulf Coast. Each went through a brief period—no more than twenty years—as a sundown suburb, but none is sundown any longer.

76. Gordon D. Morgan, "Black Hillbillies of the Arkansas Ozarks," Department of Sociology, University of Arkansas, Fayetteville, 1973, 155–59.

77. Izard County had actually grown whiter. In 1960, it had 54 African Americans, about evenly divided between males and females, while in 2000 it had 191—but the increase was illusory. The 191 African Americans included just 12 females and 179 males; a state prison accounts for almost all of them.

78. White male resident, Sheridan, about 65 years of age, Grant County Museum, 10/2001.

79. William Booth, "Booming California Suburbs Highly Diverse, Data Show," *Washington Post,* 8/18/2002; cf. Juan O. Sandoval, Hans P. Johnson, and Sonya M. Tafoya, "Who's Your Neighbor," *California Counts* 4, 1 (2002): 5.

80. Camille Zubrinsky Charles, talk, OPEN meeting, Philadelphia, 12/2000.

81. Remember, the higher the D, the greater the segregation, with 100 being complete apartheid.

82. William A. V. Clark, "Residential Segregation Trends," in Abigail Thernstrom and Stephan Thernstrom, eds., *Beyond the Color Line* (Stanford: Hoover Institution, 2002), 86, hoover.stanford.edu/publications/books/fulltext/colorline/83.pdf, 2/2003.

83. Tillamook did have 28 African American residents in 1970, however. I have not studied race relations in Tillamook after 1970.

84. Eric Wetterling, "An Interview with Ernie de la Bretonne," 5/4/1997, "The Tri-Cities," users.owt.com/rpeto/wet/tri-cities.html, 10/2002.

85. The number of confirmed sundown towns later rose to nearly 200.

86. Joseph Lyford, *The Talk in Vandalia* (Santa Barbara: Center for the Study of Democratic Institutions, 1962), 34; professor from Vandalia, 10/2002.

87. Former Granite City resident, e-mail, 10/1999; Manchester College administrator, 11/1997.

88. Stephanie Simon, "Segregation Still Strong in North," *Los Angeles Times,* 1/19/2003, reprinted in *Holland* (MI) *Sentinel,* 3/30/2003, hollandsentinel.com, 4/2003; Daniel P. Henley Jr., "Study Says Suburbs Violate Agreement on Fair Housing," *Milwaukee Journal,* 7/11/1990.

89. One of the 34, Smith Valley, listed as unincorporated in 1970, was no longer a census town.

90. Betty Canright, e-mail, 1/2003; John Gehm, *Bringing It Home* (Chicago: Chicago Review Press, 1984); David Mitchell, "A Struggled Balance of Hope and Fear," *Valparaiso Times,* 6/29/2003.

91. Gordon Trowbridge and Oralandar Brand-Williams, "The Past: A Policy of Exclusion," *Detroit News,* 1/14/2002, at mumford1.dyndns.org/cen2000/othersay/detroitnews/Stories/Blacks . . . , 7/2003.

92. Helen Harrelson, 10/2002.

93. D has no utility *within* a sundown town or suburb, because such towns are monoracial.

94. Taeuber, "Research Issues Concerning Trends in Residential Segregation," 6; Farley and Frey, "Changes in the Segregation of Whites from Blacks During the 1980s," 30.

95. Gary Orfield, *Public School Desegregation in the U.S., 1968–1980* (Washington, DC: Joint Center for Political Studies, 1983), 4; Simon, "Segregation Still Strong in North"; Mendell, "Midwest Housing Divide Is Still Race"; Kathryn P. Nelson, *Recent Suburbanization of Blacks* (Washington, DC: HUD Office of Economic Affairs, 1979), 13; John Logan, "Ethnic Diversity Grows, Neighborhood Integration Lags Behind," Lewis Mumford Center, 12/18/2001, 7, mumford1.dyndns.org/cen2000/WholePop/WPreport/page1.html, 1/2003.

96. Ellen defines "integrated"—which I think she uses as a synonym for "racially mixed"—as 10 to 50% black. This can be problematic for cities such as Washington, D.C., or Jackson, Mississippi, both more than 60% black, or Willingboro, New Jersey, two-thirds black, for in such jurisdictions, neighborhoods that mimic the city appear "segregated." Ironically, only if some neighborhoods are overwhelmingly black will others be white enough to appear "integrated." To be sure, these cities' metropolitan areas are much less than 50% black, and that is the appropriate overall area to analyze. Nevertheless, since I live in a stably integrated 80% black neighborhood, I would be happier if Ellen had widened her definition to include it.

97. Patti Becker, 7/2004; Cynthia Mills Richter, "Integrating the Suburban Dream: Shaker Heights, Ohio," Ph.D. dissertation, University of Minnesota, 1999, 110; Ingrid Gould Ellen, *Sharing America's Neighborhoods* (Cambridge: Harvard University Press, 2000), 1.

98. Chevy Chase, Chevy Chase Village, Section Three, and Section Five. Note that not all nineteen were necessarily black.

99. Kenilworth native, e-mail, 12/2002; Ellen, *Sharing America's Neighborhoods,* 21; Kenilworth realtor, 10/2002.

100. America's seven FDR towns, all sundown from the start, exemplify this unevenness. Greenbelt, Maryland, is now 41% black, while Greenhills, Ohio, is 2.6% black. Richland, Washington, the atomic town, allowed African Americans to live within its city limits in the 1950s; in 1971 it hired a black assistant city manager; and by 2000 it was 1.4% black. Greendale, Wisconsin, is just 0.3% black but does have fifteen different African American households. Boulder City, Nevada (the Hoover Dam town) had eight black households by 1998, but Norris, Tennessee (the TVA town) may still be sundown: in 2000 it had exactly one black couple and a black child. Arthurdale, West Virginia, is very small; in 2000 it had at most two male African American individuals. On Richland, see Bob Carlson, post to The Sandbox #102 (11/1/2000), the.sandbox.tripod.com/BOXarchives/BOX2000-05.htm, 7/2003.

101. Logan quoted in Simon, "Segregation Still Strong in North."

102. John C. Boger, "Toward Ending Residential Segregation: A Fair Share Proposal for the Next Reconstruction," *North Carolina Law Review* 71 (1993): 1583; Nancy Denton, "Are African Americans Still Hypersegregated?" in Robert D. Bullard, et al., eds., *Residential Apartheid* (Los Angeles: UCLA Center for Afro-American Studies, 1994), 62

103. In this sense, our thinking has not yet returned to the understanding that Republicans had reached when they passed the Civil Rights Amendments around 1868: that slavery and postslavery discrimination, not "the Negro," was the problem.

104. Jargowsky, "Concentration of Poverty Declines in the 1990s," 1.

105. Jackson Preparatory Academy, jacksonprep.edu, 5/2003.

106. Census Bureau statement on Forsyth County at Chamber of Commerce web site, forsythchamber.org/800/community/history.php, 1/2004.

107. Estimates of the proportion of the wealth owned by given proportions of the population differ notoriously from country to country, depending on who did them, using what methodology.

108. Anthony Faiola, "Brazil's Elites Fly Above Their Fears." For U.S. figure, see, inter alia, Donald L. Barlett and James B. Steele, *America: Who Stole the Dream?* (Kansas City: Andrews and McMeel, 1996), 4–5, 8; Foundation for the Mid South, "The Mid South IDA Initiative, Request for Proposals," fndmidsouth.org/PDFs/Grant_Guidelines.pdf, 7/2003, 2; Social Security Network, "Social Security Testimony: Balanced Capitalism," socsec.org/opinions/testimony/leone_capitalism.htm, 7/2003; Institute for Washington's Future, "Precarious Prosperity: Washington's Economy in 1999," forwashington.org/pub/reports/pp-2.php, 2, 7/2003. Interestingly, income is distributed more equally in the United States, where the highest 10% of earners gets 30.5% of the income; in Brazil they get 46.7%. Jon Jeter, "New Generations Face Old Struggles in Brazil," *Washington Post,* 11/13/2003.

109. This is similar to the 80% that Ingrid Ellen calculated.

110. Samantha Friedman, 5/2002.

111. See John Logan, "Choosing Segregation," Lewis Mumford Center, 3/2002, mumford1.dyndns.org/cen2000/SchoolPop/SPReport/page1.html, 1/2003.

CHAPTER 15: THE REMEDY

1. Ending sundown towns and suburbs will not cure all our nation's racial problems; other approaches, such as working to improve minority neighborhoods and schools, make sense too. See, inter alia, Sheryll Cashin's suggestions in the last chapter of *The Failures of Integration* (New York: Public Affairs, 2004).

2. Moreover, almost 30% of their respondents, having been told that neighborhoods are segregated, did *not* agree that this was "a bad thing."

3. Pew Research Center for the People and the Press, people-press.org/cen01rpt.htm, 4/2003; David Herr, e-mail to H-South, 11/2002.

4. Anne B. Shlay, review of Alice O'Connor, Chris Tilly, and Lawrence Bobo, eds., *Urban Inequality,* in *Contemporary Sociology* 31, 5 (2002): 510; *Meredith v. Fair,* 305 F.2d, 344–45.

5. For an example of work on race relations produced by middle-school students, see Bernadette Anand et al., *Keeping the Struggle Alive: Studying Desegregation in Our Town* (New York: Teachers College Press, 2002).

6. I hope this book spawns a genre of "sundown studies," because much remains to be investigated. My web site, uvm.edu/~jloewen/sundown, has a page for posting your findings. It also suggests topics for further research, including studies of the moment-by-moment process by which a town went sundown, the contagion by which many did at once, why white supremacists locate in sundown towns and whether their expectations of support are met, communities that refused to go all-white, what prompted towns to relent, and how they desegregated successfully.

7. States might usefully require an honest historical marker in every sundown town within its borders, telling the origin of its policy, summarizing its population by race over time, and relating incidents that kept it all-white. States might also require towns to include a unit in a middle- or high school history course about their history, including their racial history. Since no black citizens exist to prompt such steps in sundown towns, such a nudge from outside might be in order.

8. Robby Heason, *Trouble Behind* (Cicada Films, 1990).

9. Jacqueline Froelich, "A City Confronts Its Ghosts," *Arkansas Democrat-Gazette,* 4/27/2003.

10. Pinckneyville resident and cemetery worker, 9/2002.

11. Virginia Yarwood with Clayton E. Cramer, *Depression Life: A Memoir of Growing Up in Texas* (manuscript in possession of Cramer, 2002), 6.

12. Murray Bishoff, 9/2002; Bishoff, "The Lynching That Changed Southwest Missouri," part 2, *Monett* (MO) *Times,* 8/15/1991; "The Eldorado, Illinois Affair," *Indianapolis Freeman,* 7/19/1902; "Race War in Illinois," *New York Times,* 6/17/1902; Gordon D. Morgan, "Black Hillbillies of the Arkansas Ozarks," Department of Sociology, University of Arkansas, Fayetteville, 1973, ii, 10.

13. Cleveland Bowen quoted in Morris S. Thompson, "Marchers Descend on County that Progress Forgot," *Washington Post,* 1/24/1987.

14. Roberta Senechal, *The Sociogenesis of a Race Riot* (Urbana: University of Illinois Press, 1990), 182; Sucheng Chan, *Asian Americans* (New York: Simon & Schuster/Twayne, 1991), 50; "N.C. to Aid Sterilization Victims," *Washington Post,* 9/29/2003; Donald E. Skinner, "UUs Lead as Riot Survivors Receive Payments in Tulsa," *UUWorld,* 5/2002, 45; cf. Alfred L. Brophy, *Resurrecting the Dreamland* (New York: Oxford University Press,

2002); Scott Gold, "Judge Weighs Suit on Tulsa's '21 Riot," *L.A. Times,* 2/14/2004, latimes.com/news/nationworld/nation/la-na-riot14feb14,1,3332317.sto ry, 2/2004.

15. Winifred M. Henson, "History of Franklin County, Illinois," M.A. thesis, Colorado State College of Education, 1942, 144; *Marion Daily Republican,* 8/13/1920, 1.

16. Zimmermann quoted in Laurinda Joenks, "Roughness of Citizens Blamed on Lean Times," *Springdale* (AR) *Morning News,* 5/7/2000.

17. *Metro. Hous. Dev. Corp. v. Arlington Hts.,* 558 F.2d 1283 (7th Cir. 1977), *cert. denied,* 434 U.S. 1025 (1978). Cf. *Huntington NAACP v. Huntington,* 844 F.2d 926, 938 (2d Cir.), *aff'd,* 488 U.S. 15 (1988) (per curiam).

18. State courts are also important because the present makeup of the Supreme Court discourages some lawyers from seeking redress there. Ironically, the Fourteenth Amendment to our national constitution, guaranteeing "equal protection" without regard to race, is now used by whites to blunt attempts to redress past discrimination against nonwhites, so state courts may be more hospitable than the Supreme Court to anti-discrimination cases.

19. Of course, Sunnyvale did not zone its residential areas whites-only. But it did engage in a pattern of acts—requiring one-acre (or more) lots throughout the entire town, banning apartments, and refusing to cooperate with nearby towns in accepting government-assisted Section 8 renters—that the court found had "a discriminatory effect on African Americans *and* are motivated by a discriminatory purpose." In the 1990 census, the most recent when the case was decided, Sunnyvale had 16 African Americans among its 2,228 residents, including four households with black householders, so it did not quite qualify as a sundown suburb by my definition, but the court found that "the statistics speak for themselves." 109 F.Supp.2d 533–34.

20. Kenneth T. Jackson, *Crabgrass Frontier* (New York: Oxford University Press, 1985), 301; *South Burlington County NAACP v. Township of Mount Laurel,* 336 A.2d 713 (NJ 1975), "Mount Laurel I"; same, 92 NJ 158, 456 A.2d 390 (1983), "Mount Laurel II"; cf. Osborne Reynolds Jr., *Handbook of Local Government Law* (St. Paul: West, 1982), 371–74, David Kirp, John Dwyer, and Larry Rosenthal, *Our Town* (New Brunswick: Rutgers University Press, 1995), 9, and Lizabeth Cohen, *A Consumers' Republic* (New York: Knopf, 2003), 236–37; *Dews v Bluffdale,* 109 F. Supp. 2d 526; cf. "Litigation and Grassroots Advocacy to Promote Affordable Housing," National Low Income Housing Coalition: The NIMBY Report, 11/2000; nlihc.org, 2/2003; 109 F.Supp.2d 526; cf. "Fiscal Zoning Struck Down in Texas," NIMBY Report, 12/2000, nlihc.org, 2/2003, and Westlaw KeyCite History.

21. Jack Balkin, "Is the 'Brown' Decision Fading to Irrelevance?" *Chronicle of Higher Education,* 11/9/2001, B12.

22. Potter Stewart, concurring opinion, *Milliken I,* 1974, 756, 418 U.S. 717, 94 S.Ct. 3112, 41 L.Ed.2d 1069, n.2.

23. Evidence of racial residential exclusion committed or condoned by suburban governments was in the trial transcript, but the appeals court didn't consider it because the court found that evidence of school segregation policies sufficient to decide the case in favor of the plaintiffs. The Supreme Court reversed that finding but then failed to consider the trial court's evidence on residential exclusion!

24. Reynolds Farley, Sheldon Danziger, and Harry J. Holzer, *Detroit Divided* (New York: Russell Sage, 2000), 40–41.

25. The next sentence continues, "Specifically, it must be shown that racially discriminatory acts of the state or local school districts . . . have been a substantial cause of interdistrict seg-

regation." Surely showing racially discriminatory acts by city governments—facilitated by state laws empowering exclusionary zoning and the like—should suffice. Furthermore, school districts probably participated in keeping out minorities by refusing to hire black teachers and other actions.

26. *Milliken v. Bradley,* 418 U.S. 717, 745 (1974).

27. Requiring such residence afterward is perfectly acceptable.

28. In 1990, for example, Villa Grove, IL, still sounded its siren at 6 PM every evening to warn African Americans to get out of town before dark and had not a single African American resident. Nevertheless, Villa Grove passed an elaborate series of ordinances mandating "Fair Housing": "It is hereby declared to be the policy of the city . . . to assure equal opportunity to all persons to live in decent housing facilities regardless of race, color . . ." These ordinances hardly represented a sea change of public policy; they turn out to be boilerplate paragraphs outlawing discrimination, identical to language passed by Oakland, Illinois—another confirmed sundown town that in 1990 had no African American residents—and probably many other Illinois towns seeking continued federal subsidies for their housing programs.

29. Villa Grove City Council, Ordinance 092490, Section 97.01, Declaration of Policy.

30. Fayetteville also teaches that the United States should pursue policies that decrease the income inequalities and narrow the wealth gap between blacks and whites. Black family income there is higher as a percentage of white family income than in any other North Carolina city, owing to the military. I write as President George W. Bush is asking Congress to repeal the inheritance tax. I do not understand how we can make any pretense to equal opportunity when children of the rich can inherit, untaxed, thousands of times as much as children of the middle class, let alone children of the poor. Since about 1980, the federal government has taken many steps to increase the wealth gap between poor and rich and between blacks and whites. They have worked; the gap has grown. We need to shrink it.

31. Catherine Lutz, *Homefront* (Boston: Beacon Press, 2001), 110, 125, 129; C. M. Waynick et al., *North Carolina and the Negro* (Raleigh: North Carolina Mayors' Cooperating Commission, 1964), 114–15; Andrew H. Myers, "Black, White, and Olive Drab," Ph.D. dissertation, University of Virginia, Charlottesville, 1998, 424–25; Darrell Fears and Claudia Deane, "Biracial Couples Report Tolerance," *Washington Post,* 7/5/2001.

32. The Minneapolis–St. Paul metropolitan area did this, and not just for school finances but for overall tax dollars. According to Myron Orfield, author of *American Metropolitics,* it then realized an unanticipated benefit: instead of pitting city legislators against suburban legislators against those from outer suburbs, delegates to the state from the metropolitan area now found themselves more unified, even across parties, and were able to develop clout to get assistance for their area from state government. Fiscal equalizing also mitigates some of the shockingly unequal ways we treat children based upon where they happen to live. See Myron Orfield, talk at OPEN meeting, Philadelphia, 12/2000, and his web site, metroresearch.org; cf. Jonathan Kozol, *Savage Inequalities* (New York: Crown, 1991).

33. Lizabeth Cohen, *A Consumers' Republic* (New York: Knopf, 2003), 249.

34. Gary Orfield, OPEN, 12/2000; Orfield, "Residential Segregation: What Are the Causes?" *Journal of Negro Education* 66, 3 (1997): 208; Brigid Schulte and Dan Keating, "Choosing Route to Ending Gap Rife with Risk," *Washington Post,* 9/3/2001.

35. See James Loewen, "Presentation," "Discussion," and "A Sociological View of Aptitude Tests," in Eileen Rudert, ed., *The Validity of Testing in Education and Employment*

(Washington, DC: U.S. Commission on Civil Rights, 1993), 41–45, 58–62, 73–91; cf. "Analysis" in the same volume, 161; Loewen, Phyllis Rosser, and John Katzman, "Gender Bias on SAT Items," American Educational Research Association, 4/1988, ERIC ED294915.

36. Associated Press story, 12/1/2000, reprinted in "Worldview," *Stay Free!* 18 (n.d.), 8.

37. According to a South Orange/Maplewood, New Jersey, school administrator, disaggregating scores by race persuaded some of his white parents that their kids would not suffer from attending a diverse high school. Only then would they move in.

　　　Disaggregating scores by race and perhaps class is consistent with the No Child Left Behind Act. The disparities may lead some parents to pressure the school system to develop more effective educational programs for their children. Educators may analyze the tests to see if they accurately measure what students are learning. If some racists or elitists use the results to demean children of color or children of poverty, well, probably they were already doing so.

38. Gary Orfield, OPEN, 12/2000; Orfield, "Residential Segregation," 208; Schulte and Keating, "Choosing Route to Ending Gap Rife with Risk"; Associated Press story, 12/1/2000, reprinted in "Worldview," *Stay Free!* 18 (n.d.), 8.

39. The statistical process used to vet SAT items makes it unlikely that any item disproportionately favorable to African Americans or poor Americans will ever appear on an SAT; it follows that the more students know about suburban white culture, the higher their SAT score is likely to be. Coaching and test-wiseness also favor those in elite sundown suburbs compared to students in multiclass interracial cities.

40. See Loewen, "Preliminary Conclusions on Admissions of Racial/Ethnic Groups at the University of California Berkeley," typescript, Washington, DC, 2000.

41. Michael Danielson, *The Politics of Exclusion* (New York: Columbia University Press, 1976), 146; Earl Woodard as paraphrased by Jeff Swiatek, "Martinsville Tired of Living with Image of Racism, Bigotry," *Indianapolis Star,* 6/25/1989.

42. On their way out of town, nonblacks might sell or rent their home to a black family, thus fixing sundown towns all by themselves. As they leave, they might arm that family with introductions to their best friends, a church, and other organizations that will provide sources of strength as they perform the lonely, even risky work of opening a sundown town for use by all. Organizational allies include the Fund for an Open Society in Philadelphia (opensoc .org, 215–482-OPEN) and the National Fair Housing Alliance, in Washington, DC (nation alfairhousing.org, 202-898-1661).

43. Since 1996, I have lived in a neighborhood in Washington, D.C., that is more than 80% African American. For seven years I lived in majority-black neighborhoods in Tougaloo and Jackson, Mississippi. In all three places I have enjoyed my neighbors and have never been made to feel out of place.

44. Karyn Lacy, "A Part of the Neighborhood," *International Journal of Sociology and Social Policy* 22 (2002): 59–60.

45. Farley, Danziger, and Holzer, *Detroit Divided,* 194.

46. John Gehm, *Bringing It Home* (Chicago: Chicago Review Press, 1984); David Mitchell, "A Struggled Balance of Hope and Fear," *Valparaiso Times,* 6/29/2003.

47. Admittedly, these counties are also farther from Atlanta.

48. Oprah Winfrey, "Vintage Oprah: Racial Tension in Georgia," Harpo Productions, Chicago, 2001 (1987), 13.

49. *Trafficante v. Met Life et al.*, 409 U.S. 205 (1972).

50. Dorothy K. Newman et al., *Protest, Politics, and Prosperity* (New York: Pantheon, 1978), 139; Peoria native, 2/2001.

51. Myrlie B. Evers with William Peters, *For Us, the Living* (Garden City, NY: Doubleday, 1967), 30–31.

52. I think this hanging was apocryphal, at least at so late a date, but the story intimidates anyway. Bill Savage notes via Robert Griswold, e-mail, 6/2002; George Henderson, *Our Souls to Keep* (Yarmouth, ME: Intercultural Press, 1999), 210; Melissa Merideth, "Henderson Sparked Civil Rights Movement at OU," *Oklahoma Daily Online*, 2/18/2002, oudaily .com/vnews/display.v/ART/2002/02/18/3d3c2e102b065?in_archive=1, 6/2003; Bill Savage, 2/26/2004.

53. Daisy Myers, 1957 journal rewritten in 1960 as manuscript, "Sticks and Stones," excerpted as sign in exhibit on Levittown, Pennsylvania State Museum, Harrisburg, 9/2002.

54. Attorney quoted in Andrew Wiese, *Places of Their Own* (Chicago: University of Chicago Press, 2004), 160; James Hecht, *Because It Is Right* (Boston: Little, Brown, 1970), 199, 209–10.

55. Victor Ward, 6/2002.

56. J. D. Mullane, "Exhibit Recalls Clashes in Summer of 1957," *Bucks County Courier Times*, 7/9/2002, phillyburbs.com/couriertimes/levittown50th/0103daisy.htm, 7/2002.

57. Zane Miller, *Suburb* (Knoxville: University of Tennessee Press, 1981), 145, 219.

58. Herbert Gans, *The Levittowners* (New York: Pantheon, 1967), 428; Newman, *Protest, Politics, and Prosperity,* 140; cf. Cynthia Mills Richter, "Integrating the Suburban Dream: Shaker Heights, Ohio," Ph.D. dissertation, University of Minnesota, 1999, 102.

59. Jackson, *Crabgrass Frontier,* 241; Ingrid Gould Ellen, *Sharing America's Neighborhoods* (Cambridge: Harvard University Press, 2000), 162–63; Karen Beck Pooley, "The Other Levittown: Race and Place in Willingboro, New Jersey," The Next American City web site, americancity.org/Archives/Issue2/pooley_issue2.html, 3/2004; *Linmark Associates v. Willingboro,* 431 U.S. 85 (1977).

60. What defines a blatant disparity under the Residents' Rights Act? I suggest that any town less than one-tenth as black as its state—or any suburb less than one-tenth as black as its metropolitan area—falls under suspicion. (To a degree, this rewards widespread sundown areas. The Ozark Plateau, for example, is so large that it makes up a considerable part of the total populations of Missouri and Arkansas. Thus its whiteness pulls down the statewide proportion of African Americans, especially in Arkansas, making the trigger—one-tenth of that proportion—artificially low. This may be a serious problem in Idaho if it is true, as some claim, that the entire state has been inhospitable to African Americans.) Of course, only blacks in households with an African American householder will count, to avoid including prisoners, maids, live-in caregivers, etc. (The appropriate adjustment would also be made to total population: number in households.) In 2000, Illinois was 15.4% black, so to avoid qualifying, towns must be 1.54% black. In Indiana, the benchmark is 0.87% black.

    Obviously all towns having no African Americans at all will immediately qualify, such as Elwood, Indiana, still reportedly off-limits to blacks as of 2002. So will our old favorite Anna, having no more than two people in families with a black householder in 2000. Since their histories immediately confirm them as sundown towns, after two complaints Elwood and Anna will immediately face sanctions. In 2000, Arcola, Illinois, had one qualifying household with 3 people in it among 2,652 residents, or 0.1%. That was far less than the required 1.54%, so Arcola qualifies. Former sundown town Valparaiso, Indiana, on the other hand, now being about 1.6% black, is exempt.

    The calculation is similar within metropolitan areas. The Detroit primary metropolitan area was 23.4% black in 2000. Any jurisdiction within that area that was less than one-tenth as black, or less than 2.34% black, will trigger sanctions—if it has been confirmed as having a sundown past—once two complaints have been received. Grosse Pointe's point system and other details of its past confirm the five Grosse Pointe jurisdictions as sundown towns. Statistically, Grosse Pointe itself, 0.8% black in 2000, qualifies, as does Grosse Pointe Farms, 0.6%, Grosse Pointe Shores, 0.6%, and Grosse Pointe Woods, 0.6% black; Grosse Pointe Park, a whopping 2.95% black, is exempt. Many other Detroit suburbs also qualify, such as Grosse Ile at less than 0.4% black, Dearborn at 1.3%, and our old friend Wyandotte, 0.5%, each of which "boasts" a sundown past.

61. I suggest two complaints, rather than the ten required under the Voting Rights Act, because to seek housing with enough tenacity to be rebuffed requires more time and energy than to try to register to vote. Moreover, the reputation set in place by sundown towns' past policies is their first line of defense, chilling many black would-be newcomers before they even try. Finally, the main trigger for the Residents' Rights Act, unlike the Voting Rights Act—in addition to the statistical disparities required by both acts—is the finding of a sundown past.

62. Congress can act under the authority granted by Section 5 of the Fourteenth Amendment. To ensure that the Supreme Court will find it constitutional, Congress needs to show a widespread pattern of intentional past actions by local governments across the United States to keep out African Americans. This book makes such a showing; readers can contribute additional evidence of sundown towns at my web site, uvm.edu/~jloewen/sundown. States can (and should) pass their own versions, tailored to their local conditions, without having to worry quite so much about a judicial challenge.

63. An official at the Museum of America's Freedom Trains said, "I don't know that there was ever any talk of the Freedom Train stopping in Glendale," but the museum staff hasn't researched the matter, so far as I can tell. Museum official, e-mail, 7/2003.

64. Richard Sommer and Glenn Forley, "The Democratic Monument," paper given at "Commemoration and the City," Savannah, GA, 2/2002; Bob Johnson, e-mail, 1/2003.

65. She should apologize, because she knows full well how Benton has maintained its "racial makeup." Long notorious for not letting African Americans stay after dark, Benton flirted in 1923 with the idea of barring them even during the day. Its citizens have never stopped their tradition of racist behavior. In the mid-1980s, teenage boys hurled eggs and epithets at African Americans driving through Benton after dark. In 1992, students ostracized the only African American girl in Benton High School after she accepted a social invitation from a white boy. In the late 1990s, Benton students put graffiti on the bus from visiting Carbondale High School, a nearby interracial school, according to a 2000 Carbondale graduate, and some Benton basketball players shouted "nigger" at Carbondale's African American players. Residents throughout Franklin and Williamson counties report repeated KKK rallies and cross burnings in Benton within the last five years. In about 1998, according to a Benton High School history teacher, whites burned a cross on the lawn of an elderly Benton resident merely because he had a black physical therapist from another town work on him in his home. Among Benton's 6,880 residents in 2000, the census found only 2 African Americans in a household with a black householder. (It did find 20 blacks, 17 of whom were males, mostly 18–44, undoubtedly temporary residents connected with some institution. Another 13 people listed two races, white and black. Indeed, all of Franklin County, of which Benton

is the seat, had just 59 African Americans among nearly 40,000 residents, about 0.1%, and half of those did not live in households with an African American householder.) In 2001 and 2002, several Benton residents said they thought Benton had no black families. Benton shows no indication—including its mayor's posture—that it is over being a sundown town. African American from Colp, 1/2004; undergraduate from Carbondale, University of Illinois, 10/2000; Benton teacher, 9/2002.

66. "Judge Wants Courthouse Built in More Diverse Community," *Coles County Daily Times Courier,* 10/11/2002.

67. Monticello attorney, 2002; Richard Stewart, "Desegregation at Public Housing Ripped by Audit," *Houston Chronicle,* 7/11/1997; Janet Heimlich and Bob Edwards, "Housing Discrimination in Texas," *Federal Document Clearing House,* 7/10/1997, morning edition.

68. Florence Roisman suggested this remedy to me, based on John C. Boger, "Toward Ending Residential Segregation: A Fair Share Proposal for the Next Reconstruction," *North Carolina Law Review* 71 (1993): 1608–14. Boger's proposal is detailed and nuanced; he also suggests taxing the interest on municipal bonds issued by governments found in violation.

69. This is already changing, however, as noted below regarding such suburbs as Oak Park, Illinois.

70. The sanction ignores renters, but renters own no housing, so they have not participated in refusing to sell or rent to African Americans. It also seems to omit families who have no mortgages, hence pay no mortgage interest, but it does actually sanction them by making their homes less attractive to would-be buyers, thus decreasing their resale value.

71. Perhaps penologists may have in mind a "social Alcatraz" theory—like the frigid waters and archetypal sharks around Alcatraz (the sharks are not man-eating, it turns out), the area surrounding these prisons is presumably hostile to black escapees. More likely, the political clout of sundown legislators explains the placement of these prisons in their districts. Such locations may amount to cruel and unusual punishment. In sundown towns, African American prisoners and juveniles have few role models who look like them among guards and administrators. They have little chance to see a black psychologist or medical doctor, learn from a black teacher, meet with a black prison volunteer, or talk with a black college student intern, because there are no African Americans in the community. Family members and friends live miles away, making it hard for prisoners to maintain ties to the outside world. Visitors who do make the trip usually take care to be out of town by nightfall. In sum, locating prisons in sundown towns ensures that prisoners, many of whom are people of color, will be guarded, cared for when ill, counseled, and "rehabilitated" by people who live in towns that prevent African Americans from living within their corporate limits. This is hardly good penology. It also invites sundown town residents to grow more racist. A resident of Vienna described the discourse in that southern Illinois town after Vienna got its prison around 1970: "Since that time, you get constant remarks about black people and how bad they are. Of course, [prisoners] are the only black people they know" (Vienna resident, 2/2004).

72. Susan Luke, "Barbie and Ken, and All Things Presidential," *Washington Post,* 8/10/2003; Mary Otto, "Grasping for a Thread of Hope," *Washington Post,* 9/7/2004.

73. Farley, Danziger, and Holzer, *Detroit Divided,* 180.

74. Don DeMarco, talk at OPEN Conference, Philadelphia, 11/2000; Ted Hipple, e-mail, 10/24/2001; Carole Goodwin, *The Oak Park Strategy* (Chicago: University of Chicago Press, 1979), 1, 53; CNN/*Money* Fiserv CSW report, money.cnn.com, 7/2003.

75. Whites moved into majority-black census tracts on Capitol Hill, in Washington, D.C., and

made them majority-white. Between 1960 and 1970, Kirkwood, a neighborhood in Atlanta, went from being 91% white to 97% black. Then in the 1990s, some whites returned, making Kirkwood 14% white by 2000.

76. Lesley Reid and Robert Adelman, "The Double-Edged Sword of Gentrification in Atlanta," *ASA Footnotes* 31, 4 (2003): 8; Mark Knight quoted in Nurith C. Aizenman, "Diversity Puts Vitality into Aging Mt. Rainier," *Washington Post,* 12/30/2003, washingtonpost.com, 1/2004.

77. D'Vera Cohn, "Integrated People, Integrated Places," *Washington Post* 7/29/2002; librarian, Decatur, 10/2002.

78. Baltimore woman quoted in J. W. Dees Jr. and J. S. Hadley, *Jim Crow* (Westport, CT: Negro Universities Press, 1970 [1951]), 159; Eunice and George Grier, "Discrimination in Housing" (New York: Anti-Defamation League of B'nai B'rith, 1960), 34, citing generally Morton Deutsch and Mary Evans Collins, *Interracial Housing* (Minneapolis: University of Minnesota Press, 1951).

79. Barnett quoted in Richter, "Integrating the Suburban Dream: Shaker Heights, Ohio," 48.

80. I must admit that this racial liberalism may also result from the flight of more racist whites from these neighborhoods.

81. Gary Orfield, talk at OPEN, Philadelphia, 12/2000; Carolyn Adams et al., *Philadelphia: Neighborhoods, Division, and Conflict* (Philadelphia: Temple University Press, 1991), 24.

82. Three Dog Night, "Black and White," 1972; the "sundown policies" quatrain is mine, with apologies.

APPENDIX

1. Jack Blocker Jr., "Contours of African-American Migration in Ohio, 1850–1930" (Cambridge: British Society for Population Studies, 1998), tables 3, 9.

2. Jack Blocker Jr., "Choice and Circumstance," paper presented at Organization of American Historians meeting 4/1999, 29, 34–35. He did not use the term "Great Retreat." Cf. his "Contours of African-American Migration in Ohio, 1850–1930," 7; "Patterns of African-American Migration in Illinois, 1860–1920" (Edwardsville, IL: Conference on African Americans in Illinois History, 1998), and "Opportunity, Community, and Violence in the Shaping of Indiana's African-American Migration, 1860–1930" (Minneapolis: Conference on Race, Ethnicity, and Migration, 2000).

PORTFOLIO

All notes for this section refer to image numbers.

2. Lynwood Carranco, "Chinese Expulsion from Humboldt County," in Roger Daniels, ed., *Anti-Chinese Violence in North America* (New York: Arno Press, 1978), 336; Joseph F. Endert, "Chinese," *Bulletin of the Del Norte County Historical Society* (3/1978 [1965]), 5–6; "DN Pioneers Load Sons of Flowery Kingdom on Boats," *Del Norte Triplicate* Bicentennial Edition, 1976; Jean Pfaelzer, talk (Washington, D.C.: American Studies Association., 2001); Keith Easthouse, "The Chinese Expulsion: Looking Back on a Dark Episode," *North Coast Journal Weekly,* 2/27/2003, northcoastjournal.com/022703/cover0227.html, 2/2004.

4. "Negroes Killed or Driven Away, *Chicago Tribune,* 8/21/1901; Murray Bishoff, 9/2002.

6. Donald F. Tingley, *The Structuring of a State: The History of Illinois, 1899 to 1928* (Urbana: University of Illinois Press, 1980), 291–92.

7. These towns and counties are listed on my website, uvm.edu/~jloewen/sundown.

9. Jimmy Allen, e-mail, 10/2002; Margaret Alexander Alam, e-mail, 11/04/2003; *Villa Grove News,* 7/4/1976; seven Villa Grove residents.

11. Scott Ellsworth, *Death in a Promised Land* (Baton Rouge: Louisiana University Press, 1982); Alfred L. Brophy, *Reconstructing the Dreamland: The Tulsa Race Riot of 1921* (New York: Oxford University Press, 2002); cf. William F. Pinar, *The Gender of Racial Politics and Violence in America* (New York: Peter Lang, 2001), 1174; Kelly Kurt, "After 75 Years, Tulsa Heals," Burlington *Free Press,* 6/2/96; James Allen, et al., *Without Sanctuary* (Santa Fe: Twin Palms, 2000), #38, 179–80; W. L. Payne, "Okemah's Night of Terror," in Hazel Ruby McMahan, ed., *Stories of Early Oklahoma,* on Rootsweb, rootsweb.com/~okokfusk/cities.htm, 5/2003.

13. "Don't Let The Sun Set On You Here, Understand?" *Chicago Defender,* 2/11/1922; "Norman Mob After Singie Smith Jazz," Norman, OK, 2/5/1922, in *Oklahoma City Black Dispatch,* 2/9/1922; "White Men Shoot Up Church Excursioners," *Pittsburgh Courier,* 8/17/1940.

15. Lin Shi Khan and Tony Perez, *Scottsboro, Alabama: A Story in Linoleum Cuts* (New York: New York University Press, 2001 [1935]), 49; "Scottsboro Trial Moved Fifty Miles," *New York Times,* 3/8/1933.

16. Kurt Vonnegut Jr., *Breakfast of Champions,* (New York: Delacorte, 1973), 245–46; Vonnegut, 3/2005.

18. R. Bruce Shepard, *Deemed Unsuitable* (Toronto: Umbrella Press, 1997), 3.

20. *Parade of Progress: Hamilton County, 1858–1958* (Hamilton: *Hamilton Herald-News,* 1958), unpaginated; Charles Titus, 6/2000; Carolyn Stephens, e-mail, 2/2001.

24. David M. P. Freund, *Making It Home* (Ann Arbor: Univeristy of Michigan Ph.D., 1999), 515; Rick Baker, "Pekin Students Veto 'Chinks' Name Change," 11/28/1974 clipping in Pekin library, name of newspaper omitted; Jane White, Pekin High School, 1950, post at Classmates.com, 6/1/2000.

28. "The Real Polk County" (Mena: no publication indicated, 1/9?/1980), 16.

30. "A Northern City 'Sitting on Lid' of Racial Trouble," *US News & World Report,* 5/11/1956, 38–40; Denise Thomas, 10/2003.

31. Bill Griffith, "Zippy the Pinhead," *Washington Post,* 6/24/2002

32. Camille DeRose, *The Camille DeRose Story* (Chicago: Erle Press, 1953), 171.

33. Kenneth T. Jackson, *Crabgrass Frontier* (New York: Oxford University Press, 1985), 278; Reginald Pickins quoted in Kurth, "Exclusivity Tax," *Detroit News,* 2/21/2001, detnews.com/2001/homepage/0102/21/index.htm.

34. Edgar Rice Burroughs, "Tarzan," 12/2/1934, in Robert C. Harvey, *Children of the Yellow Kid* (Seattle: University of Washington Press, 1998), 77.

Photography Credits and Permissions

Index

gay and lesbian residents, 86–87, 362,
   506n11
gentrification, 448, 507n21, 522–23n75
the Great Migration, 58, 393, 470n92
the Great Retreat, 53, 75, 142
housing projects, 130
Index of Dissimilarity, 80–81, 144, 339,
   414, 470n90, 470n92
lifestyle issues, 120–21
overcrowding, 127
present status, 398–400, 414–16, 513n96
school segregation, 420
segregated neighborhoods, 14, 17, 80–81,
   101, 133, 317–18, 358–60, 473n37
sprawl, 362
tax base, 368, 369–70, 507n30
white flight, 363–66, 379, 388–90, 400,
   416–17, 435, 447, 507n21, 523n80
See also suburbs, sundown
Metropolitan Life project, 189
Mexican Americans, 75–76, **P23**
   caste minorities, 138, 478n5
   migrant workers in Colorado, 249–50
   official racial classification, 42, 512n55
   sports, 405, 512n67
   in urban neighborhoods, 155–56
Meyer, Stephen, 16–17, 121, 259, 273–74
Meyerholtz, Millie, 160
Miami, Florida, 339
Miami Beach, Florida, 284, 339
Michigan, 9
   county demographics, 56t, 57
   Grosse Pointe system, 263
   Ku Klux Klan, 340
   prohibition of African Americans, 25, 27
   Upper Peninsula, 146, 155
   voting patterns, 372
Midwest
   the Great Retreat, 59–67, 455
   present status, 410–16, 513n85
Miles, W. F., 238–39
Milgram, Morris, 13
Military Intelligence Department, 40
Miller, Leo, 189
Miller, Zane, 440
Milliken v. Bradley, 429–31, 451, 517n23,
   517n25
Mills County, Texas, 77
Milo, Maine, 503n95, **P22**
Milwaukee, Wisconsin, 68, 140–41
   present status, 355, 412, 414–15
   tolerance of homosexual residents, 362
Minden, Nevada, 23, 75
Mindenmines, Missouri, 161
miners' strikes, 158–62, 165, 482nn53–54

Minneapolis-St. Paul area, 454, 518n32
Minnesota, 56t, 57, 69, 453–54, 464n24
   county demographics, 56t
Minority Education and Caste (Ogbu), 138
minority groups, 15, 23, 471n106
   caste minorities, 138
   gay and lesbian groups, 86–87, 362,
      502n71, 506n11
   official racial classifications, 42, 512n55
   present status, 398–400
   See also white ethnic groups
minstrelsy, 39–40, 303, 312
miscegenation, 28, 34, 150
Mississippi, 5, 194–96, 234, 464n23
   Civil Rights Movement, 437
   the Great Retreat, 70
   sundown towns, 70, 468n65
   University of Mississippi integration,
      422–23
   voting rights, 33
The Mississippi Chinese (Loewen), 479n11
Mississippi County, Arkansas, 76–77
Missouri, 67, 77, 213, 264, 520n60
   black mule signs, **P8**
   county demographics, 56t, 57
   enforcement of sundown rules, **P18**
   the Great Retreat, 71, 74
   organized labor's exclusion of blacks, 43
   present status, 380, 381–82
   school segregation, 461n22
Missouri and North Arkansas Railroad, 36–37
Mitchellville, Maryland, 374
Mize, Mississippi, 468n65
mob violence. *See* expulsions of black
   Americans; Chinese Retreat, lynchings
Mohan, Geoffrey, 127
Moline, Matt, 287
Monett, Missouri, 95–96, 181, 361, **P3**
Monroe, Michigan, 292
Montana, 9, 56t, 57, 75, 464n20
   county demographics, 56t
Montclair, New Jersey, 133, 476n12
Montgomery County, Maryland, 258
Monticello, Illinois, 100, 182, 388, 444
Montlake, Tennessee, 170
Montpelier, Vermont, 99, 503n95
Moon, Charley, 189–90
Moore, Clarence, 380
Morgan, Gordon, 74, 96, 204–5, 215, 407,
   425, 479n11
Morgan, J. P., 461n20
Morgan County, Tennessee, 72
Morse, Dan and Phyllis, 380
Morse-Kahn, Deborah, 109–10
Morton, Illinois, 345, 388

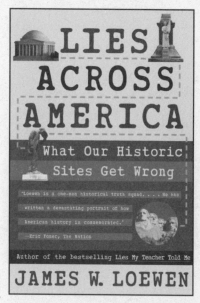